The Conscious Reader

The Conscious Reader *third edition*

◆◆◆

Caroline Shrodes
San Francisco State University

Harry Finestone
California State University, Northridge

Michael Shugrue
*The College of Staten Island
of The City University of New York*

Macmillan Publishing Company
New York

Collier Macmillan Publishers
London

Acknowledgments

Copyright works, listed in the order of appearance, are printed by permission of the following.

Joan Didion, "On Keeping a Notebook." Reprinted with the permission of Farrar, Straus & Giroux Inc., from *Slouching Towards Bethlehem* by Joan Didion, copyright © 1966 by Joan Didion.

Vladimir Nabokov, "The Beginning of Consciousness," from *Speak, Memory*. Published by permission of Mrs. Vladimir Nabokov. Copyright 1950 by Vladimir Nabokov, © 1960, 1966 by Vladimir Nabokov. All rights reserved. This material was first published in *The New Yorker*.

Peter Werner, "Both Sides Now," excerpted from the book *Stories Parents Seldom Hear: College Students Write About Their Lives and Families* by Harriet Harvey. Copyright © 1983 by Harriet Harvey. Reprinted by permission of Delacorte Press/Seymour Lawrence. A Merloyd Lawrence Book.

(Continued on page 797)

Macmillan Publishing Company
866 Third Avenue, New York, New York 10022

Collier Macmillan Canada, Inc.

Library of Congress Cataloging in Publication Data
Main entry under title:

The conscious reader.

Includes index.
1. College readers.   I. Shrodes, Caroline.
II. Finestone, Harry.   III. Shugrue, Michael.
PE1122.C586   1985   808'.0427   84-3856
ISBN 0-02-410350-0

Printing: 4   5   6   7   8   Year: 5   6   7   8   9   0   1   2

ISBN 0-02-410350-0

Preface

—◆◆◆—

. . . the unexamined life is not worth living.
—**Plato,** *The Apology*

Some years ago, Alvin Toffler deplored the fact that students can finish twelve years of schooling without once asking themselves such basic questions as "What's life about? What am I here for? What's better than something else? What's worth dying for?"

Believing that the development of writing skills depends on the heightening of consciousness, the editors of *The Conscious Reader* invite students to examine and to respond to the basic questions that writers since Plato have posed. The selections included engage our interests by their style and by their focus on issues of universal concern. They reflect the continuity between past and present, serve as a catalyst to self-expression, sharpen our perceptions, and widen our sympathies. Consciousness heightened through reading develops effective writing, and the act of writing fosters self-definition. As we extend awareness by reading, we become increasingly conscious of the reservoir of memories and experiences from which to draw and the variety of forms and techniques that give shape to our writing.

Over two-thirds of the readings in this book are nonfiction prose, primarily exposition or argument. Some of the essays are personal and readily comprehensible and provide models for early writing assignments. Others, more complex, should help students develop the ability to reason abstractly. Although most of the authors included are accomplished literary stylists, others are primarily distinguished for their contributions to popular culture, science, philosophy, and psychology.

We have also included twenty-three stories and thirty-five poems. The inclusion of imaginative literature in a composition course needs no special justification. It serves a number of important goals: to enhance the pleasure of reading, to educate the emotions as well as the mind, to stimulate original creative efforts, and to provide vicarious experience with which to test the ideas expressed in essays. The dramatic situations, vivid character portrayals, and the verbal compression of fiction and poetry also suggest techniques to enliven student writing. We are more than ever convinced that the most stimulating as well as most economical means of helping students to develop conceptual literacy is to expose them to literate essays and imaginative literature, both of which will arrest their interest and challenge their thinking.

In this third edition of *The Conscious Reader*, we have responded to colleagues who have asked for essays with a greater range of length. Approximately one third of the selections are new. We have overhauled the section on popular culture to replace readings of strictly contemporary appeal with enduring examples. A few new works are neither brief nor simple. However, their excellence and significance override possible objections to sophistication. Finally, there are new sections on science and technology and on education.

We have added a head note for each selection and have designed suggestions for discussion and writing to help students explore multiple levels of understanding. The suggestions invite students to pay careful attention to thought and structure and to compare their experience with the vision of life expressed in the selections. Exploring cultural patterns both similar and alien to one's own should encourage a continuing dialectic in classroom discussion as well as in writing. Also to encourage discussion we have included selections that represent a wide range of academic disciplines and interests—from psychology to biology and computer science.

The thematic groupings represent a convenient division of the book. The readings begin with the search for self and move to consideration of the self in relation to others—parents, friends, and lovers. The next section focuses on art and society, including discussions of both popular culture and the cultural tradition. The readings continue with a variety of statements about our aspirations and failures to ensure a sense of freedom and human dignity for all. The fifth section explores many facets of the world of science and technology. The book concludes with the examined life. The selections mediate between problems of education and human concerns and then return full cycle to the individual's search for meaning and value.

If there is a dominant theme in these readings, it is that neither understanding of the past nor projections of the future can eliminate conflict from our lives and that opposing forces in the self and society are a part of the human condition. Indeed, it is vital that they contend. For it is primarily through conscious recognition and expression of these conflicting forces that we may find our way to a tolerance of ambiguity and to an increased freedom of choice.

Acknowledgments

We wish to acknowledge and thank the following reviewers of the second edition of *The Conscious Reader:* Rick Eden, University of New Mexico; Lester Fisher, University of New Hampshire; Alan Gribbon, University of Texas at Austin; Angela Ingram, Southwest Texas State University; Kathleen Bell, University of Miami; Jeff Schonberg, Hardin-Simmons University; Peter Page, University of New Mexico; Michael Hogan, University of New Mexico; Pauline Adams, Michigan State University; Harry Silverman, Michigan State University; Sophia Blaydes, West Virginia University; Lynn Beene, University of New Mexico; Scott Wiggerman, Southwest Texas State University; Dick Heaberlin, Southwest Texas State University; Phyllis Stowell, St. Mary's

College; Mary McCord, University of Texas at San Antonio; Durthy Washington, University of Texas at San Antonio; and Samuel Chell, Carthage College.

We also want to thank the following individuals for their continued commitment and concern: Mary Catherine Farley, Robert E. Jackson, Elizabeth Berry, John Hartog, David Kay, Gale Larson, Jerome Richfield, Anne Finestone, and Eve Finestone. Finally, for his valuable help, we wish to thank our editor at Macmillan, Eben W. Ludlow.

C. S.
H. F.
M. S.

Contents

◆◆◆

The Search for Self

Fiction

Poetry

Personal Relationships: Parents and Children

Letters and Personal Reminiscence

Essays

Fiction

Poetry

Personal Relationships: Men and Women

Essays

Fiction

The Cultural Tradition: Popular Culture

The Cultural Tradition: Art and Society

Science, Technology, and the Future

Freedom and Human Dignity

Essays

Fiction

Poetry

The Examined Life: Education

The Examined Life: Personal Values

Essays

Fiction

Poetry

Selected Rhetorical Contents

The following arrangement of expository essays will suggest ways in which readers can approach the selections. The classifications are not, of course, rigid, and many selections might fit as easily into one category as another.

Identification

Comparison/Contrast

Definition

Analysis

Illustration

Argument and Persuasion

The Search for Self

◆◆◆

As I dance, whirling and joyous, happier than I've ever been in my life, another bright faced dancer joins me. . . . The other dancer has obviously come through all right, as I have done. She is beautiful, whole, and free. And she is also me.

> —**Alice Walker,** "When the Other Dancer Is the Self"

I think we are well advised to keep on nodding terms with the people we used to be, whether we find them attractive company or not. Otherwise they turn up unannounced and surprise us, come hammering on the mind's door at 4 A.M. of a bad night and demand to know who deserted them, who betrayed them, who is going to make amends. . . . We forget the loves and the betrayals alike, forget what we whispered and what we screamed, forget who we were.

> —**Joan Didion,** "On Keeping a Notebook"

Personal life, no longer a refuge from deprivations suffered at work, has become as anarchical, as warlike, and as full of stress as the marketplace itself. The cocktail party reduces sociability to social combat.

> —**Christopher Lasch,** "Changing Modes of Making It: From Horatio Alger to the Happy Hooker"

Whether in the pastoral joys of country life or in the labyrinthine city, we Americans are always seeking. We wander, question. But the answer waits in each separate heart—the answer of our own identity and the way by which we can master loneliness and feel that at last we belong.

> —**Carson McCullers,** "Loneliness . . . An American Malady"

For writing *is* discovery. The language that never leaves our head is like colorful yarn, endlessly spun out multicolored threads dropping into a void, momentarily compacted, entangled, fascinating, elusive . . . writing that is discovery forces the capturing, the retrieving, the bringing into focus these stray and random thoughts. Sifting through them, we make decisions that are as much about the self as about language.

—**James E. Miller,** "Discovering the Self"

All of our lives we are accompanied vaguely by the selves we might be. Man is the only creature that can imagine being someone else. The fantasy of being someone else is the basis of sympathy, of humanity. . . . The past 20 years have stimulated the anti-self. They have encouraged the notion of continuous self-renewal. . . .

—**Lance Morrow,** "Daydreams of What You'd Rather Be"

Personal Reminiscence
◆◆◆

Jack London
What Life Means to Me

Jack London (1876–1916), American novelist and short-story writer, drew upon his extensive travels in such works as *The Call of the Wild* (1903) and his South Sea tales and developed social themes in such works as *The Iron Heel* (1907). Although London experienced the loss of many illusions about man's goodness and integrity, he retained his belief in human nobility and excellence.

I was born in the working-class. Early I discovered enthusiasm, ambition, and ideals; and to satisfy these became the problem of my child-life. My environment was crude and rough and raw. I had no outlook, but an uplook rather. My place in society was at the bottom. Here life offered nothing but sordidness and wretchedness, both of the flesh and the spirit; for here flesh and spirit were alike starved and tormented.

Above me towered the colossal edifice of society, and to my mind the only way out was up. Into this edifice I early resolved to climb. Up above, men wore black clothes and boiled shirts, and women dressed in beautiful gowns. Also, there were good things to eat, and there was plenty to eat. This much for the flesh. Then there were the things of the spirit. Up above me, I knew, were unselfishnesses of the spirit, clean and noble thinking, keen intellectual living. I knew all this because I read "Seaside Library" novels, in which, with the exception of the villains and adventuresses, all men and women thought beautiful thoughts, spoke a beautiful tongue, and performed glorious deeds. In short, as I accepted the rising of the sun, I accepted that up above me was all that was fine and noble and gracious, all that gave decency and dignity to life, all that made life worth living and that remunerated one for his travail and misery.

But it is not particularly easy for one to climb up out of the working-class—especially if he is handicapped by the possession of ideals and illusions. I lived on a ranch in California, and I was hard put to find the ladder whereby to climb. I early inquired the rate of interest on invested money, and worried my child's brain into an understanding of the virtues and excellencies of that remarkable invention of man, compound interest. Further, I ascertained the current rates of wages for workers of all ages, and the cost of living. From all this data I concluded that if I began immediately and worked and saved until I was fifty years of age, I could then stop working and enter into participation in a fair portion of the delights and goodnesses that would then be open to me higher up in society. Of course, I resolutely determined not to marry, while I quite forgot to consider at all that great rock of disaster in the working-class world—sickness.

But the life that was in me demanded more than a meagre existence of scraping and scrimping. Also, at ten years of age, I became a newsboy on the streets of a city, and found myself with a changed uplook. All about me were still the same sordidness and wretchedness, and up above me was still the same paradise waiting to be gained; but the ladder whereby to climb was a different one. It was now the ladder of business. Why save my earnings and invest in government bonds, when, by buying two newspapers for five cents, with a turn of the wrist I could sell them for ten cents and double my capital? The business ladder was the ladder for me, and I had a vision of myself becoming a baldheaded and successful merchant prince.

Alas for visions! When I was sixteen I had already earned the title of "prince." But this title was given me by a gang of cut-throats and thieves, by whom I was called "The Prince of the Oyster Pirates." And at that time I had climbed the first rung of the business ladder. I was a capitalist. I owned a boat and a complete oyster-pirating outfit. I had begun to exploit my fellow-creatures. I had a crew of one man. As captain and owner I took two-thirds of the spoils, and gave the crew one-third, though the crew worked just as hard as I did and risked just as much his life and liberty.

This one rung was the height I climbed up the business ladder. One night I went on a raid amongst the Chinese fishermen. Ropes and nets were worth dollars and cents. It was robbery, I grant, but it was precisely the spirit of capitalism. The capitalist takes away the possessions of his fellow-creatures by means of a rebate, or of a betrayal of trust, or by the purchase of senators and supreme-court judges. I was merely crude. That was the only difference. I used a gun.

But my crew that night was one of those inefficients against whom the capitalist is wont to fulminate, because, forsooth, such inefficients increase expenses and reduce dividends. My crew did both. What of his carelessness: he set fire to the big mainsail and totally destroyed it. There weren't any dividends that night, and the Chinese fishermen were richer by the nets and ropes we did not get. I was bankrupt, unable just then to pay sixty-five dollars for a new mainsail. I left my boat at anchor and went off on a bay-pirate boat on a raid up the Sacramento River. While away on this trip, another gang of bay pirates raided my boat. They stole everything, even the anchors; and later on, when I recovered the drifting hulk, I sold it for twenty dollars. I had slipped back the one rung I had climbed, and never again did I attempt the business ladder.

From then on I was mercilessly exploited by other capitalists. I had the muscle, and they made money out of it while I made but a very indifferent living out of it. I was a sailor before the mast, a longshoreman, a roustabout;

I worked in canneries, and factories, and laundries; I mowed lawns, and cleaned carpets, and washed windows. And I never got the full product of my toil. I looked at the daughter of the cannery owner, in her carriage, and knew that it was my muscle, in part, that helped drag along that carriage on its rubber tires. I looked at the son of the factory owner, going to college, and knew that it was my muscle that helped, in part, to pay for the wine and good fellowship he enjoyed.

But I did not resent this. It was all in the game. They were the strong. Very well, I was strong. I would carve my way to a place amongst them and make money out of the muscles of other men. I was not afraid of work. I loved hard work. I would pitch in and work harder than ever and eventually become a pillar of society.

And just then, as luck would have it, I found an employer that was of the same mind. I was willing to work, and he was more than willing that I should work. I thought I was learning a trade. In reality, I had displaced two men. I thought he was making an electrician out of me; as a matter of fact, he was making fifty dollars per month out of me. The two men I had displaced had received forty dollars each per month; I was doing the work of both for thirty dollars per month.

This employer worked me nearly to death. A man may love oysters, but too many oysters will disincline him toward that particular diet. And so with me. Too much work sickened me. I did not wish ever to see work again. I fled from work. I became a tramp, begging my way from door to door, wandering over the United States and sweating bloody sweats in slums and prisons.

I had been born in the working-class, and I was now, at the age of eighteen, beneath the point at which I had started. I was down in the cellar of society, down in the subterranean depths of misery about which it is neither nice nor proper to speak. I was in the pit, the abyss, the human cesspool, the shambles and charnel-house of our civilization. This is the part of the edifice of society that society chooses to ignore. Lack of space compels me here to ignore it, and I shall say only that the things I there saw gave me a terrible scare.

I was scared into thinking. I saw the naked simplicities of the complicated civilization in which I lived. Life was a matter of food and shelter. In order to get food and shelter men sold things. The merchant sold shoes, the politician sold his manhood, and the representative of the people, with exceptions, of course, sold his trust; while nearly all sold their honor. Women, too, whether on the street or in the holy bond of wedlock, were prone to sell their flesh. All things were commodities, all people bought and sold. The one commodity that labor had to sell was muscle. The honor of labor had no price in the market-place. Labor had muscle, and muscle alone, to sell.

But there was a difference, a vital difference. Shoes and trust and honor had a way of renewing themselves. They were imperishable stocks. Muscle, on the other hand, did not renew. As the shoe merchant sold shoes, he continued to replenish his stock. But there was no way of replenishing the laborer's stock of muscle. The more he sold of his muscle, the less of it remained to him. It was his one commodity, and each day his stock of it diminished. In the end, if he did not die before, he sold out and put up his shutters. He was a muscle bankrupt, and nothing remained to him but to go down into the cellar of society and perish miserably.

I learned, further, that brain was likewise a commodity. It, too, was different from muscle. A brain seller was only at his prime when he was fifty or sixty years old, and his wares were fetching higher prices than ever. But a laborer was worked out or broken down at forty-five or fifty. I had been in the cellar of society, and I did not like the place as a habitation. The pipes and drains were unsanitary, and the air was bad to breathe. If I could not live on the parlor floor of society, I could, at any rate, have a try at the attic. It was true, the diet there was slim, but the air at least was pure. So I resolved to sell no more muscle, and to become a vender of brains.

Then began a frantic pursuit of knowledge. I returned to California and opened the books. While thus equipping myself to become a brain merchant, it was inevitable that I should delve into sociology. There I found, in a certain class of books, scientifically formulated, the simple sociological concepts I had already worked out for myself. Other and greater minds, before I was born, had worked out all that I had thought and a vast deal more. I discovered that I was a socialist.

The socialists were revolutionists, inasmuch as they struggled to overthrow the society of the present, and out of the material to build the society of the future. I, too, was a socialist and a revolutionist. I joined the groups of working-class and intellectual revolutionists, and for the first time came into intellectual living. Here I found keen-flashing intellects and brilliant wits; for here I met strong and alert-brained, withal horny-handed, members of the working-class; unfrocked preachers too wide in their Christianity for any congregation of Mammon-worshippers; professors broken on the wheel of university subservience to the ruling class and flung out because they were quick with knowledge which they strove to apply to the affairs of mankind.

Here I found, also, warm faith in the human, glowing idealism, sweetnesses of unselfishness, renunciation, and martyrdom—all the splendid, stinging things of the spirit. Here life was clean, noble, and alive. Here life rehabilitated itself, became wonderful and glorious; and I was glad to be alive. I was in touch with great souls who exalted flesh and spirit over dollars and cents, and to whom the thin wail of the starved slum child meant more than all the pomp and circumstance of commerical expansion and world empire. All about me were nobleness of purpose and heroism of effort, and my days and nights were sunshine and starshine, all fire and dew, with before my eyes, ever burning and blazing, the Holy Grail, Christ's own Grail, the warm human, long-suffering and maltreated, but to be rescued and saved at the last.

And I, poor foolish I, deemed all this to be a mere foretaste of the delights of living I should find higher above me in society. I had lost many illusions since the day I read "Seaside Library" novels on the California ranch. I was destined to lose many of the illusions I still retained.

As a brain merchant I was a success. Society opened its portals to me. I entered right in on the parlor floor, and my disillusionment proceeded rapidly. I sat down to dinner with the masters of society, and with the wives and daughters of the masters of society. The women were gowned beautifully, I admit; but to my naïve surprise I discovered that they were of the same clay as all the rest of the women I had known down below in the cellar. "The colonel's lady and Judy O'Grady were sisters under their skins"—and gowns.

It was not this, however, so much as their materialism, that shocked me. It is true, these beautifully gowned, beautiful women prattled sweet little ideals and dear little moralities; but in spite of their prattle the dominant key of the life they lived was materialistic. And they were so sentimentally selfish! They assisted in all kinds of sweet little charities, and informed one of the fact, while all the time the food they ate and the beautiful clothes they wore were bought out of dividends stained with the blood of child labor, and sweated labor, and of prostitution itself. When I mentioned such facts, expecting in my innocence that these sisters of Judy O'Grady would at once strip off their blood-dyed silks and jewels, they became excited and angry, and read me preachments about the lack of thrift, the drink, and the innate depravity that caused all the misery in society's cellar. When I mentioned that I couldn't quite see that it was the lack of thrift, the intemperance, and the depravity of a half-starved child of six that made it work twelve hours every night in a Southern cotton mill, these sisters of Judy O'Grady attacked my private life and called me an "agitator"—as though that, forsooth, settled the argument.

Nor did I fare better with the masters themselves. I had expected to find men who were clean, noble, and alive, whose ideals were clean, noble, and alive. I went about amongst the men who sat in the high places—the preachers, the politicians, the business men, the professors, and the editors. I ate meat with them, drank wine with them, automobiled with them, and studied them. It is true, I found many that were clean and noble; but with rare exceptions, they were not *alive*. I do verily believe I could count the exceptions on the fingers of my two hands. Where they were not alive with rottenness, quick with unclean life, they were merely the unburied dead—clean and noble, like well-preserved mummies, but not alive. In this connection I may especially mention the professors I met, the men who live up to that decadent university ideal, "the passionless pursuit of passionless intelligence."

I met men who invoked the name of the Prince of Peace in their diatribes against war, and who put rifles in the hands of Pinkertons with which to shoot down strikers in their own factories. I met men incoherent with indignation at the brutality of prize-fighting, and who, at the same time, were parties to the adulteration of food that killed each year more babies than even red-handed Herod had killed.

I talked in hotels and clubs and homes and Pullmans and steamer-chairs with captains of industry, and marvelled at how little travelled they were in the realm of intellect. On the other hand, I discovered that their intellect, in the business sense, was abnormally developed. Also, I discovered that their morality, where business was concerned, was nil.

This delicate, aristocratic-featured gentleman, was a dummy director and a tool of corporations that secretly robbed widows and orphans. This gentleman, who collected fine editions and was an especial patron of literature, paid blackmail to a heavy-jowled, black-browed boss of a municipal machine. This editor, who published patent medicine advertisements and did not dare print the truth in his paper about said patent medicines for fear of losing the advertising, called me a scoundrelly demagogue because I told him that his political economy was antiquated and that his biology was contemporaneous with Pliny.

This senator was the tool and the slave, the little puppet of a gross, uneducated machine boss; so was this governor and this supreme court judge; and all three rode on railroad passes. This man, talking soberly and earnestly about the beauties of idealism and the goodness of God, had just betrayed his comrades in a business deal. This man, a pillar of the church and heavy contributor to foreign missions, worked his shop girls ten hours a day on a starvation wage and thereby directly encourage prostitution. This man, who endowed chairs in universities, perjured himself in courts of law over a matter of dollars and cents. And this railroad magnate broke his word as a gentleman and a Christian when he granted a secret rebate to one of two captains of industry locked together in a struggle to the death.

It was the same everywhere, crime and betrayal, betrayal and crime—men who were alive, but who were neither clean nor noble, men who were clean and noble but who were not alive. Then there was a great, hopeless mass, neither noble nor alive, but merely clean. It did not sin positively nor deliberately; but it did sin passively and ignorantly by acquiescing in the current immorality and profiting by it. Had it been noble and alive it would not have been ignorant, and it would have refused to share in the profits of betrayal and crime.

I discovered that I did not like to live on the parlor floor of society. Intellectually I was bored. Morally and spiritually I was sickened. I remembered my intellectuals and idealists, my unfrocked preachers, broken professors, and clean-minded, class-conscious workingmen. I remembered my days and nights of sunshine and starshine, where life was all a wild sweet wonder, a spiritual paradise of unselfish adventure and ethical romance. And I saw before me, ever blazing and burning the Holy Grail.

So I went back to the working-class, in which I had been born and where I belonged. I care no longer to climb. The imposing edifice of society above my head holds no delights for me. It is the foundation of the edifice that interests me. There I am content to labor, crowbar in hand, shoulder to shoulder with intellectuals, idealists, and class-conscious workingmen, getting a solid pry now and again and setting the whole edifice rocking. Some day, when we get a few more hands and crowbars to work, we'll topple it over, along with all its rotten life and unburied dead, its monstrous selfishness and sodden materialism. Then we'll cleanse the cellar and build a new habitation for mankind, in which there will be no parlor floor, in which all the rooms will be bright and airy, and where the air that is breathed will be clean, noble, and alive.

Such is my outlook. I look forward to a time when man shall progress upon something worthier and higher than his stomach, when there will be a finer incentive to impel men to action than the incentive of today, which is the incentive of the stomach. I retain my belief in the nobility and excellence of the human. I believe that spiritual sweetness and unselfishness will conquer the gross gluttony of today. And last of all, my faith is in the working-class. As some Frenchman has said, "The stairway of time is ever echoing with the wooden shoe going up, the polished boot descending."

Suggestions for Discussion

1. Discuss the adequacy of London's metaphor of "the colossal edifice of society" in present-day America.

2. Describe the several ways in which London attempted to attain "all that gave decency and dignity to life."

3. Compare eighteen-year-old London's perception of "the naked simplicities of the complicated civilization" in which he lived with that of your classmates.

Suggestions for Writing

1. London has called this piece "What Life Means to Me." Describe in you own words what that is.

2. In a short paper recall an illusion you formerly had and describe the events which destroyed that illusion.

Joan Didion

On Keeping a Notebook

Joan Didion (b. 1934), California-born, began her career when she won Vogue's Prix de Paris award in her senior year of college. She later became an associate editor of *Vogue* and has written columns for *The Saturday Evening Post* and *Life.* Her novels *Run River* (1963) and *Play It as It Lays* (1971) and her collection of essays *Slouching Towards Bethlehem* (1969) have established her as an important American writer. She and her husband, writer John Gregory Dunne, have collaborated on several screenplays. In keeping her notebook, as recounted in *Slouching Towards Bethlehem,* the author recounts not facts but feelings, "an indiscriminate and erratic assemblage with meaning only for its maker" and sometimes not for her.

" 'That woman Estelle,' " the note reads, " 'is partly the reason why George Sharp and I are separated today.' *Dirty crepe-de-Chine wrapper, hotel bar, Wilmington RR, 9:45 a.m. August Monday morning.*"

Since the note is in my notebook, it presumably has some meaning to me. I study it for a long while. At first I have only the most general notion of what I was doing on an August Monday morning in the bar of the hotel across from the Pennsylvania Railroad station in Wilmington, Delaware (waiting for a train? missing one? 1960? 1961? why Wilmington?), but I do remember being there. The woman in the dirty crepe-de-Chine wrapper had come down from her room for a beer, and the bartender had heard before the reason why George Sharp and she were separated today. "Sure," he said, and went on mopping the floor. "You told me." At the other end of the bar is a girl. She is talking, pointedly, not to the man beside her but to a cat lying in the triangle of sunlight cast through the open door. She is wearing a plaid silk dress from Peck & Peck, and the hem is coming down.

Here is what it is: the girl has been on the Eastern Shore, and now she is going back to the city, leaving the man beside her, and all she can see ahead are the viscous summer sidewalks and the 3 A.M. long-distance calls that will make her lie awake and then sleep drugged through all the steaming mornings left in August (1960? 1961?). Because she must go directly from the train to lunch in New York, she wishes that she had a safety pin for the hem of the plaid silk dress, and she also wishes that she could forget about the hem and the lunch and stay in the cool bar that smells of disinfectant and malt and make friends with the woman in the crepe-de-Chine wrapper. She is afflicted by a little self-pity, and she wants to compare Estelles. That is what that was all about.

Why did I write it down? In order to remember, of course, but exactly what was it I wanted to remember? How much of it actually happened? Did any of it? Why do I keep a notebook at all? It is easy to deceive oneself on all those scores. The impulse to write things down is a peculiarly compulsive one, inexplicable to those who do not share it, useful only accidentally, only secondarily, in the way that any compulsion tries to justify itself. I suppose that it begins or does not begin in the cradle. Although I have felt compelled to write things down since I was five years old, I doubt that my daughter ever will, for she is a singularly blessed and accepting child, delighted with life exactly as life presents itself to her, unafraid to go to sleep and unafraid to wake up. Keepers of private notebooks are a different breed altogether, lonely and resistant rearrangers of things, anxious malcontents, children afflicted apparently at birth with some presentiment of loss.

My first notebook was a Big Five tablet, given to me by my mother with the sensible suggestion that I stop whining and learn to amuse myself by writing down my thoughts. She returned the tablet to me a few years ago; the first entry is an account of a woman who believed herself to be freezing to death in the Arctic night, only to find, when day broke, that she had stumbled onto the Sahara Desert, where she would die of the heat before lunch. I have no idea what turn of a five-year-old's mind could have prompted so insistently "ironic" and exotic a story, but it does reveal a certain predilection for the extreme which has dogged me into adult life; perhaps if I were analytically inclined I would find it a truer story than any I might have told about Donald Johnson's birthday party or the day my cousin Brenda put Kitty Litter in the aquarium.

So the point of my keeping a notebook has never been, nor is it now, to have an accurate factual record of what I have been doing or thinking. That would be a different impulse entirely, an instinct for reality which I sometimes envy but do not possess. At no point have I ever been able successfully to keep a diary; my approach to daily life ranges from the grossly negligent to the merely absent, and on those few occasions when I have tried dutifully to record a day's events, boredom has so overcome me that the results are mysterious at best. What is this business about "shopping, typing piece, dinner with E, depressed"? Shopping for what? Typing what piece? Who is E? Was this "E" depressed, or was I depressed? Who cares?

In fact I have abandoned altogether that kind of pointless entry; instead I tell what some would call lies. "That's simply not true," the members of my family frequently tell me when they come up against my memory of a shared event. "The party was *not* for you, the spider was *not* a black widow, *it wasn't that way at all.*" Very likely they are right, for not only have I always had trouble distinguishing between what happened and what merely might have happened, but I remain unconvinced that the distinction, for my purposes, matters. The cracked crab that I recall having for lunch the day my father came home from Detroit in 1945 must certainly be embroidery, worked into the day's pattern to lend verisimilitude; I was ten years old and would not now remember the cracked crab. The day's events did not turn on cracked crab. And yet it is precisely that fictitious crab that makes me see the after-noon all over again, a home movie run all too often, the father bearing gifts, the child weeping, an exercise in family love and guilt. Or that is what it was to me. Similarly, perhaps it never did snow that August in Vermont; perhaps there never were flurries in the night wind, and maybe no one else felt the ground hardening and summer already dead even as we pretended to bask in it, but that was how it felt to me, and it might as well have snowed, could have snowed, did snow.

How it felt to me: that is getting closer to the truth about a notebook. I sometimes delude myself about why I keep a notebook, imagine that some thrifty virtue derives from preserving everything observed. See enough and write it down, I tell myself, and then some morning when the world seems drained of wonder, some day when I am only going through the motions of doing what I am supposed to do, which is write—on that bankrupt morning I will simply open my notebook and there it will all be, a forgotten account with accumulated interest, paid passage back to the world out there: dialogue overheard in hotels and elevators and at the hat-check counter in Pavillon (one middle-aged man shows his hat-check to another and says, "That's my old football number"); impressions of Bettina Aptheker and Benjamin Sonnen-berg and Teddy ("Mr. Acapulco") Stauffer; careful *aperçus* about tennis bums and failed fashion models and Greek shipping heiresses, one of whom taught me a significant lesson (a lesson I could have learned from F. Scott Fitzgerald, but perhaps we all must meet the very rich for ourselves) by asking, when I arrived to interview her in her orchid-filled sitting room on the second day of a paralyzing New York blizzard, whether it was snowing outside.

I imagine, in other words, that the notebook is about other people. But of course it is not. I have no real business with what one stranger said to another at the hat-check counter in Pavillon; in fact I suspect that the line "That's my old football number" touched not my own imagination at all, but merely some memory of something once read, probably "The Eighty-Yard Run." Nor is my concern with a woman in a dirty crepe-de-Chine wrapper in a Wilmington bar. My stake is always, of course, in the unmentioned girl in the plaid silk dress. *Remember what it was to be me:* that is always the point.

It is a difficult point to admit. We are brought up in the ethic that others, any others, all others, are by definition more interesting than ourselves; taught to be diffident, just this side of self-effacing. ("You're the least impor-tant person in the room and don't forget it," Jessica Mitford's governess would hiss in her ear on the advent of any social occasion; I copied that into my notebook because it is only recently that I have been able to enter a room without hearing some such phrase in my inner ear.) Only the very young and the very old may recount their dreams at breakfast, dwell upon self, interrupt with memories of beach picnics and favorite Liberty lawn dresses and the rainbow trout in a creek near Colorado Springs. The rest of us are expected, rightly, to affect absorption in other people's favorite dresses, other people's trout.

And so we do. But our notebooks give us away, for however dutifully we record what we see around us, the common denominator of all we see is always, transparently, shamelessly, the implacable "I." We are not talking here about the kind of notebook that is patently for public consumption, a structural conceit for binding together a series of graceful *pensées;* we are talking about something private, about bits of the mind's string too short to use, an indiscriminate and erratic assemblage with meaning only for its maker.

And sometimes even the maker has difficulty with the meaning. There does not seem to be, for example, any point in my knowing for the rest of my life that, during 1964, 720 tons of soot fell on every square mile of New York City, yet there it is in my notebook, labeled "FACT." Nor do I really need to remember that Ambrose Bierce liked to spell Leland Stanford's name "£eland $tanford" or that "smart women almost always wear black in Cuba," a fashion hint without much potential for practical application. And does not the relevance of these notes seem marginal at best?:

> In the basement museum of the Inyo County Courthouse in Independence, California, sign pinned to a mandarin coat: "This MANDARIN COAT was often worn by Mrs. Minnie S. Brooks when giving lectures on her TEAPOT COLLECTION."

> Redhead getting out of car in front of Beverly Wilshire Hotel, chinchilla stole, Vuitton bags with tags reading:
>
> MRS LOU FOX
> HOTEL SAHARA
> VEGAS

Well, perhaps not entirely marginal. As a matter of fact, Mrs. Minnie S. Brooks and her MANDARIN COAT pull me back into my own childhood, for although I never knew Mrs. Brooks and did not visit Inyo County until I was thirty, I grew up in just such a world, in houses cluttered with Indian relics and bits of gold ore and ambergris and the souvenirs my Aunt Mercy Farnsworth brought back from the Orient. It is a long way from that world to Mrs. Lou Fox's world, where we all live now, and is it not just as well to remember that? Might not Mrs. Minnie S. Brooks help me to remember what I am? Might not Mrs. Lou Fox help me to remember what I am not?

But sometimes the point is harder to discern. What exactly did I have in mind when I noted down that it cost the father of someone I know $650 a month to light the place on the Hudson in which he lived before the Crash? What use was I planning to make of this line by Jimmy Hoffa: "I may have my faults, but being wrong ain't one of them"? And although I think it interesting to know where the girls who travel with the Syndicate have their hair done when they find themselves on the West Coast, will I ever make suitable use of it? Might I not be better off just passing it on to John O'Hara? What is a recipe for sauerkraut doing in my notebook? What kind of magpie keeps this notebook? *"He was born the night the Titanic went down."* That seems a nice enough line, and I even recall who said it, but is it not really a better line in life than it could ever be in fiction?

But of course that is exactly it: not that I should ever use the line, but that I should remember the woman who said it and the afternoon I heard it. We were on her terrace by the sea, and we were finishing the wine left from lunch, trying to get what sun there was, a California winter sun. The woman whose husband was born the night the *Titanic* went down wanted to rent her house, wanted to go back to her children in Paris. I remember wishing that I could afford the house, which cost $1,000 a month. "Someday you will," she said lazily. "Someday it all comes." There in the sun on her terrace it seemed easy to believe in someday, but later I had a low-grade afternoon hangover and ran over a black snake on the way to the supermarket and was flooded with inexplicable fear when I heard the checkout clerk explaining to the man ahead of me why she was finally divorcing her husband. "He left me no choice," she said over and over as she punched the register. "He has a little seven-month-old baby by her, he left me no choice." I would like to believe that my dread then was for the human condition, but of course it was for me, because I wanted a baby and did not then have one and because I wanted to own the house that cost $1,000 a month to rent and because I had a hangover.

It all comes back. Perhaps it is difficult to see the value in having one's self back in that kind of mood, but I do see it; I think we are well advised to keep on nodding terms with the people we used to be, whether we find them attractive company or not. Otherwise they turn up unannounced and surprise us, come hammering on the mind's door at 4 A.M. of a bad night and demand to know who deserted them, who betrayed them, who is going to make amends. We forget all too soon the things we thought we could never forget. We forget the loves and the betrayals alike, forget what we whispered and what we screamed, forget who we were. I have already lost touch with a couple of people I used to be; one of them, a seventeen-year-old, presents little threat, although it would be of some interest to me to know again what it feels like to sit on a river levee drinking vodka-and-orange-juice and listening to Les Paul and Mary Ford and their echoes sing "How High the Moon" on the car radio. (You see I still have the scenes, but I no longer perceive myself among those present, no longer could even improvise the dialogue.) The other one, a twenty-three-year-old, bothers me more. She was always a good deal of trouble, and I suspect she will reappear when I least want to see her, skirts too long, shy to the point of aggravation, always the injured party, full of recriminations and little hurts and stories I do not want to hear again, at once saddening me and angering me with her vulnerability and ignorance, an apparition all the more insistent for being so long banished.

It is a good idea, then, to keep in touch, and I suppose that keeping in touch is what notebooks are all about. And we are all on our own when it comes to keeping those lines open to ourselves: your notebook will never help me, nor mine you. "*So what's new in the whiskey business?*" What could that possibly mean to you? To me it means a blonde in a Pucci bathing suit sitting with a couple of fat men by the pool at the Beverly Hills Hotel. Another man approaches, and they all regard one another in silence for a while. "So what's new in the whiskey business?" one of the fat men finally says by way of welcome, and the blonde stands up, arches one foot and dips it in the pool, looking all the while at the cabaña where Baby Pignatari is talking on the telephone. That is all there is to that, except that several years later I saw the blonde coming out of Saks Fifth Avenue in New York with her California complexion and a voluminous mink coat. In the harsh wind that day she looked old and irrevocably tired to me, and even the skins in the mink coat were not worked the way they were doing them that year, not the way she would have wanted them done, and there is the point of the story. For a while after that I did not like to look in the mirror, and my eyes would skim the newspapers and pick out only the deaths, the cancer victims, the premature coronaries, the suicides, and I stopped riding the Lexington Avenue IRT because I noticed for the first time that all the strangers I had seen for years— the man with the seeing-eye dog, the spinster who read the classified pages every day, the fat girl who always got off with me at Grand Central—looked older than they once had.

It all comes back. Even that recipe for sauerkraut: even that brings it back. I was on Fire Island when I first made that sauerkraut, and it was raining, and we drank a lot of bourbon and ate the sauerkraut and went to bed at ten, and I listened to the rain and the Atlantic and felt safe. I made the sauerkraut again last night and it did not make me feel any safer, but that is, as they say, another story.

Suggestions for Discussion

1. What rhetorical devices does the author use to bring her subject into focus? For example, she compares and contrasts two women in the bar and her daughter and herself.

2. What kinds of details are employed to explain the varied purposes of keeping a notebook?

3. How does the author explain the paradox "I imagine . . . that the notebook is about other people. But of course it is not."

4. Account for the adverbs and adjectives used in the statement "the common denominator of all we see is always, transparently, shamelessly, the implacable 'I.' "

5. How do the citations in the notebook contribute to the central thesis? to the tone? to the author's sense of self? to her writing?

6. Explain: "I have already lost touch with a couple of people I used to be. . . ."

7. T. S. Eliot uses the term *objective correlative* to describe the artist's faculty of achieving emotional impact "by finding a set of objects, a situation, a chain of events, which shall be the formula of that particular emotion such that when the external facts are given, the emotion is immediately evoked." How do the items in the notebook illustrate this theory?

Suggestions for Writing

1. Keep a journal in which you record the events or thoughts of each day. What does it tell you about other people? about yourself?

2. Write an essay on question 4 or 6 above.

3. Write an essay in which you interweave excerpts from your journal with commentary on them.

Vladimir Nabokov
The Beginning of Consciousness

Vladimir Nabokov (1899–1977) was born in Russia and educated at Trinity College, Cambridge. He was a professor at Cornell University and a regular contributor to popular magazines. Among his works written in English are *The Real Life of Sebastian Knight* (1941); *Pnin* (1957); *Lolita* (1958); *Pale Fire* (1962); two collections of short stories, *Nabokov's Dozen* (1958) and *Nabokov's Quartet* (1966); *King, Queen, Knave* (1968); *Ada* (1969); and an autobiography, *Speak, Memory* (1951). Nabokov describes the awakening of his consciousness as a series of "spaced flashes with intervals between them gradually diminishing until bright blocks of perception are formed, affording memory a slippery hold." His sense of self and his awareness that his parents were his parents came after he had learned numbers and speech.

The cradle rocks above an abyss, and common sense tells us that our existence is but a brief crack of light between two eternities of darkness. Although the two are identical twins, man, as a rule, views the prenatal abyss with more calm than the one he is heading for (at some forty-five hundred heartbeats an hour). I know, however, of a young chronophobiac who experienced something like panic when looking for the first time at homemade movies that had been taken a few weeks before his birth. He saw a world that was practically unchanged—the same house, the same people—and then realized that he did not exist there at all and that nobody mourned his absence. He caught a glimpse of his mother waving from an upstairs window, and that unfamiliar gesture disturbed him, as if it were some mysterious farewell. But what particularly frightened him was the sight of a brand new baby carriage standing there on the porch, with the smug, encroaching air of a coffin; even that was empty, as if, in the reverse course of events, his very bones had disintegrated.

Such fancies are not foreign to young lives. Or, to put it otherwise, first and last things often tend to have an adolescent note—unless, possibly, they are directed by some venerable and rigid religion. Nature expects a full-grown man to accept the two black voids, fore and aft, as stolidly as he accepts the extraordinary visions in between. Imagination, the supreme delight of the immortal and the immature, should be limited. In order to enjoy life, we should not enjoy it too much.

I rebel against this state of affairs. I feel the urge to take my rebellion outside and picket nature. Over and over again, my mind has made colossal efforts to distinguish the faintest of personal glimmers in the impersonal darkness on both sides of my life. That this darkness is caused merely by the walls of time separating me and by bruised fists from the free world of timelessness is a belief I gladly share with the most gaudily painted savage. I have journeyed back in thought—with thought hopelessly tapering off as I went—to remote regions where I groped for some secret outlet only to discover that the prison of time is spherical and without exits. Short of suicide, I have tried everything. I have doffed my identity in order to pass for a conventional spook and steal into realms that existed before I was conceived. I have mentally endured the degrading company of Victorian lady novelists and retired colonels who remembered having, in former lives, been slave messengers on a Roman road or sages under the willows of Lhasa. I have ransacked my oldest dreams for keys and clues—and let me say at once that I reject completely the vulgar, shabby, fundamentally medieval world of Freud, with its crankish quest for sexual symbols (something like searching for Baconian acrostics in Shakespeare's works) and its bitter little embryos spying, from their natural nooks, upon the love life of their parents.

Initially, I was unaware that time, so boundless at first blush, was a prison. In probing my childhood (which is the next best to probing one's eternity) I see the awakening of consciousness as a series of spaced flashes, with the intervals between them gradually diminishing until bright blocks of perception are formed, affording memory a slippery hold. I had learned numbers and speech more or less simultaneously at a very early date, but the inner knowledge that I was I and that my parents were my parents seems to have been established only later, when it was directly associated with my discovering their age in relation to mine. Judging by the strong sunlight that, when I think of that revelation, immediately invades my memory with lobed sun flecks through overlapping patterns of greenery, the occasion may have been my mother's birthday, in late summer, in the country, and I had asked questions and had assessed the answers I received. All this is as it should be according to the theory of recapitulation; the beginning of reflexive consciousness in the brain of our remotest ancestor must surely have coincided with the dawning of the sense of time.

Thus, when the newly disclosed, fresh and trim formula of my own age, four, was confronted with the parental formulas, thirty-three and twenty-seven, something happened to me. I was given a tremendously invigorating shock. As if subjected to a second baptism, on more divine lines than the Greek Catholic ducking undergone fifty months earlier by a howling, half-drowned half-Victor (my mother, through the half-closed door, behind which an old custom bade parents retreat, managed to correct the bungling archpresbyter, Father Konstantin Vetvenitski), I felt myself plunged abruptly into a radiant and mobile medium that was none other than the pure element of time. One shared it—just as excited bathers share shining seawater—with creatures that were not oneself but that were joined to one by time's common flow, an environment quite different from the spatial world, which not only man but apes and butterflies can perceive. At that instant, I became acutely aware that the twenty-seven-year-old being, in soft white and pink, holding my left hand, was my mother, and that the thirty-three-year-old being, in hard white and gold, holding my right hand, was my father. Between them, as they evenly progressed, I strutted, and trotted, and strutted again, from sun fleck to sun fleck, along the middle of a path, which I easily identify today with an alley of ornamental oaklings in the park of our country estate, Vyra, in the former Province of St. Petersburg, Russia. Indeed, from my present ridge or remote, isolated, almost uninhabited time, I see my diminutive self as celebrating, on that August day 1903, the birth of sentient life. If my left-hand-holder and my right-hand-holder had both been present before in my vague infant world, they had been so under the mask of a tender incognito; but now my father's attire, the resplendent uniform of the Horse Guards, with that smooth golden swell of cuirass burning upon his chest and back, came out like the sun, and for several years afterward I remained keenly interested in the age of my parents and kept myself informed about it, like a nervous passenger asking the time in order to check a new watch.

My father, let it be noted, had served his term of military training long before I was born, so I suppose he had that day put on the trappings of his old regiment as a festive joke. To a joke, then, I owe my first gleam of complete consciousness—which again has recapitulatory implications, since the first creatures on earth to become aware of time were also the first creatures to smile.

Suggestions for Discussion

1. How does the author convey the tone of the panic that can be aroused by contemplating the "prenatal abyss"?

2. By specific reference to the text, explain the author's statement that "first and last things often tend to have an adolescent note."

3. Identify all the phrases in this selection that grow out of the image of existence as a "brief crack of light between two eternities of darkness." How literal is this image intended to be? What overtones of experience and myth are there in the image?

4. At the end of the fourth paragraph Nabokov writes, "the beginning of reflexive consciousness in the brain of our remotest ancestor must surely have coincided with the dawning of the sense of time." By what logical process does he arrive at this conclusion? Is the process defensible? Is the conclusion trustworthy?

Suggestions for Writing

1. Recall an incident in your childhood that marked a dramatic change in your concept of yourself or your parents, or your concept of the passage of time.

2. Discuss this paradox in relation to its context: "In order to enjoy life, we should not enjoy it too much."

◇◇◇◇

Peter Werner

Both Sides Now

Peter Werner (pseudonym) as a Yale freshman was one of a small number permitted to enroll in a writing course in the seventies. He grew up in a large, devout Roman Catholic family in East Meadow, Long Island. After receiving his degree at Yale he studied playwriting in graduate school, and after working in a bank he took a job teaching English in the New York public schools. Werner portrays some of the conflicts and ironies in his experience with "both sides" of the economic structure.

When I was in high school, I don't know how many afternoons I spent upstairs in my bedroom, listening to the neighborhood kids playing roller hockey in the street while I struggled to play the guitar. I was trying to teach myself, and from a huge book of music titled something like *Greatest Hits of the Sixties with Simplified Chords*, I had chosen Joni Mitchell's "Both Sides Now."

The chords were simple, and the song seemed to demand a voice that wasn't too good. As with so many of the folk songs of that era, the lyrics seemed so much more earnest when sung poorly, as if the words demanded to be heard no matter what the quality of the singer's voice. I finally managed to learn the song, and a few more after that, before deciding that as bad as my voice was, it would never sound as earnest as Bob Dylan's, so there was not much point in going on.

And yet to this day I still remember the chords and lyrics to "Both Sides Now," for over the years the song took on an ironic significance as circumstances in my own life changed. What I should have learned from the song was how multifaceted and deeply layered these two sides can be.

When I was living at home, I thought I already had seen both sides. I grew up rather comfortably on suburban Long Island in a family that gradually grew to include eight children. My father supported us all with his job as a space engineer under government contract to NASA.

Then the United States landed a man on the moon, and my father was laid off along with thousands of other space engineers on Long Island. Suddenly we had no money and I saw the "other side." According to government statistics, we were living in poverty, but things weren't much different than before. They were just a bit more strained. For me, the two sides then were simply "richer" and "poorer."

Since coming to Yale I have had a chance to see more of these two sides. Here I learned that in many cases "richer" and "poorer" also define the distinction between "superior" and "inferior." Money, education, and family background all play their part in determining human value. Some people are meant to serve others; others to be served.

As a bursary student, I find myself in a strange position. One minute I'll be on one side, sipping sherry at a reception, while men and women in starched white uniforms offer me hors d'oeuvres from silver platters. The next minute I'll be on the other side, washing dishes in a hot kitchen of one of Yale's dining halls, or wearing a red jacket and serving my fellow classmates a French dinner. I meet students whose fathers are millionaires, then talk to dining hall workers who try to support a family on seven thousand dollars a year. When I joined the Duke's Men, an informal singing group at Yale, our spring concert tour took us through a series of posh resorts and hotels, a world of servants and masters, another world with two sides.

Here are some glimpses of the two sides:

A Phone Call Home

Tom is one of my three roommates, a blond surfer from a Los Angeles suburb. Although our relationship was rather cool early in the year, as the months have progressed we've become close friends. When we're drunk, we call each other by the names of characters taken from a Lawrence novel on our freshman reading list.

I can tell that Tom's family is well off, not by any of Tom's possessions but by his general demeanor and the fact that he's well traveled. I know that Tom thinks my family is comfortable enough, if not abundantly wealthy, and God knows I haven't done anything to make him think otherwise. We're among the last to be able to take advantage of an already slipping fashion dictate that demands that rich and poor alike wear nothing but jeans and cotton T-shirts, and so it's been difficult for me to guess just how much money Tom is used to, and impossible for Tom to realize how poor my own family has become.

We weren't always poor, but we were never wealthy. When my father still had his job as a space engineer, our family of ten lived in a barn-red colonial home in a suburban neighborhood and had a beige Chrysler Town and Country station wagon parked in the driveway. After my father lost his job, he couldn't find other work as an engineer. He tried his hand at real estate and lost money. There were no savings to draw from, and the family had a desperate struggle hanging on to the house and the car. When relatives had no more money to lend us, government assistance became a necessity, and my mother started training as a nurse in order to bring money into the household.

Tonight I find myself chiding Tom for his upper-class prejudices and social naïveté. This always confuses Tom, because he has no way of knowing where I'm coming from and no reason to suspect the personal vindictiveness that creeps into these "consciousness raising" sessions. Tom is trying to convice me that the reason he didn't have any friends among the Chicanos who attended his high school is not because they were poor but because they lived so far away. In fact he does, he insists, have white friends who are really quite poor.

"Listen to this," he says. "I have this friend. There are four kids in his family, and his father makes twenty thousand dollars a year."

I can't quite figure out the moral to this story, although I'm afraid of what's coming. In the best days, my father supported ten people on twenty-three thousand a year.

"Well . . . ?" I say, waiting for a conclusion.

Tom says nothing.

"Is that poor? Is twenty thousand dollars a year poor?" I ask, and my voice is angry and condescending.

Tom is annoyed that his humanitarianism in unappreciated. His head cocks back and his eyes go cold.

"Well . . . my old man makes a hundred grand a year."

Those words, that number, affect me as if I had just been drenched with a bucket of ice water. I want to shout back, "Well, my 'old man' is unemployed and we get six thousand dollars a year from welfare. So how do you like that?" Instead I say nothing.

Tom tries to press his point. He thinks I don't understand.

"Well, how much does your father make?"

"Fuck you," I reply.

Tom shakes his head in disgust and goes into his room to study. He's learned that there's no point in talking to me when I get into one of my moods. And like I've said, he's seen no sign of my family's financial state. When my parents visited on parents' day, the Chrysler was in good condition. My father still had his fine cashmere coat, and my mother's "simple black dress" did not betray its age. So he can't understand my anger.

I think about that number and I realize that there are some who would consider it pocket money, but still it's more than four times what my father ever made, and I resent it. I resent the way Tom takes the money for granted and I resent the way he takes it for granted that my own family is well off. I wish I had the courage to tell him the truth.

How much easier it would be if I were black or Puerto Rican. Then I would be expected to be poor. They could look at me and marvel at how I was advancing. "Look! He goes to Yale!" But to be white and poor. The white rich really don't want to know about it. It upsets them; they think it's disgusting. You're upsetting the order of things. Blacks are poor. Puerto Ricans are poor. They can't help it. They're not smart enough to handle money. But whites aren't handicapped. If they're not rich, it's their own fault. They're not living up to their race. They're a disgrace.

The noise from the stereo is beginning to annoy me. That weirdo David Bowie. It is Tom's record, not mine (which makes it all the more annoying). But the stereo is mine. None of us brought a stereo in September, so the kid who's on welfare had to go home to bring one back. The same thing with the typewriter. The kid whose dad earns a hundred grand a year shows up at Yale without a typewriter. I spend half my summer earnings to buy a decent machine, half that summer slaving in a department store. And Tom just uses it whenever he wants.

Typical, I think. That's why his people are rich and my people aren't.

Bowie keeps whining. It is the same record that was playing when my brother Michael visited in December. Hearing the record, the first thing he said when he came in the door was, "What's going on here? Have you gone gay?"

Michael sat down without taking off his coat, and we tried to catch up with each other on the past few months. After about ten minutes he stood up to remove his coat.

"Boy, it's hot in here."

"Well, you should have taken your coat off."

"I just got sort of used to wearing it around the house. We haven't had any heat this past week."

"What?" I shouted, and broke into laughter. I pictured my family seated around the big oak table in the dining room, eating dinner in their winter coats, my sister Ann trying to avoid dipping her fur cuffs into her food.

"Dad wasn't able to pay the oil bill, so they stopped delivering." Michael was laughing too. He fell back onto the couch and the two of us sat there laughing until tears came to our eyes.

Remembering the laughter, I realize that it would take a great effort to make myself upset about the incident. My family isn't miserable in their predicament; they are able to laugh about it. They're as happy as ever. Then my anger returns when I realize that Tom is happy too.

It's easy not to mind being poor if you think the wealthy are miserable. It's easy to go to see a play or a movie or read a book where the rich are at each other's throats and they're lonely and unhappy and their lives are empty and half of them end up committing suicide. The rich are different and they get their just desserts in the end.

But Tom is really not so different from me. That is one of the reasons we're so close. I can easily see myself in Tom's position through a simple quirk of fate called parentage. I might not have been happier but things would have been much more . . . convenient. Tom is no different, and yet he has so much more. Not only has he money, but he has the ability to enjoy it.

But now it's easy to let the heating incident upset me, and tears of anger burn in my eyes. I remember going home two weeks later for Christmas vacation to discover that, for financial reasons, my family had learned to make do without lunch. My stomach, conditioned to Yale's twenty-one meal plan, was not pleased with this. In the afternoon I would rummage around the kitchen, looking for a quick snack to tide me over until dinner. But there was nothing that could be called "quick." There were no convenience foods that could be taken from a package. They were too expensive. Everything had to be washed or peeled and cooked, and a simple snack would entail a major production. There wasn't even a loaf of bread. My father made fresh rolls before each meal. It was cheaper.

On New Year's Eve, I was particularly hungry. My stomach nagged me all day and I looked forward to supper. But when supper came there was nothing but soup. Soup and the fresh hot rolls I had grown sick of—three to a person. I wanted to cry, but I held back the tears.

I don't now. I pick up my books and go into my room so that no one will see me. I'd like to hate Tom. I'd like so much to hate him but I cannot, and that makes me feel guilty. I am consorting with the enemy.

I try to hate, but the closest I can come to hate is jealousy. I want to have money also. Realizing this, the guilt presses against my lungs like stones. I want to travel. I want to have a swimming pool. I might enjoy a boat. Someday I might be able to have these things, but how could I enjoy them while others were miserable? How do the wealthy do it?

I try to escape to my books. I pick up my Religious Studies assignment. *The Documents of Vatican II*. The words become blurred as I read, the tears swelling in my eyes.

> In His goodness and wisdom, God chose to reveal Himself and to make known to us the hidden purpose of His will by which through Christ, the Word made Flesh, man has access to the Father in the Holy Spirit and comes to share in His divine nature. Through His revelation, therefore, the invisible God, out of

the abundance of His love, speaks to men as friends and lives among them so that He may invite them and take them into fellowship with Himself.

The book lands in a pile of dust underneath the bed, for in my present state it seems more than likely that Christ was sent forth by Herod. Something had to be done to keep the starving masses from revolting.

My thoughts return to my family at home. My father has taken to going to our church each weekday morning and praying for guidance.

"Just trust in God," he always said. "Don't worry about tomorrow. Everything will work out according to God's will."

I had stopped worrying about tomorrow, but I'd never really trusted in God. And yet things had worked out. For me. But the rest of the family were still at home.

My mother had joined the charismatic movement of our church. She was going to be rebaptized in the Holy Spirit. Born again. But still she was able to say to my father, "Why don't you spend less time in church and more time looking for a job?"

My father laughed and called her a Holy Roller.

My sadness increases, and I want to talk to my parents. I want to call home and hear the voices of my family. They always sound happy. Mary will talk about her school play, *Oklahoma!* And in the background I might hear Paul practicing his French horn. That will cheer me up.

I wait until I've calmed down enough so that my voice will sound normal over the phone. I check my face in the mirror so that my roommates won't see I've been crying.

I go to the phone in the living room and dial my number. It takes a while for the connection to go through. The phone starts ringing, and then there is a click followed by a white fuzzy sound.

A nasal tape-recorded voice speaks.

"The number you have reached, five-five-five, four-eight-nine-five, has been disconnected. Please check the number you are calling to make sure that you have dialed correctly."

I let the receiver fall and the voice starts to repeat itself from the floor. I have dialed correctly. My parents haven't paid the phone bill again. Tears come, and then sobs, and there is nothing I can do to stop them.

In the next room, I can see Tom at his desk, concentrating on his chemistry.

Kevin

Kevin is a full-time dishwasher at Timothy Dwight College. I work with him five days a week. He is twenty-five years old and mentally retarded.

"Peter, are you going home for Thanksgiving?"

"Yes."

"Where do you live?"

"Long Island."

"Are you taking a plane?"

"Kevin, I live on Long Island."

"I know. Are you taking a plane?"

I tell him where Long Island is. I tell him that it's two hours away by car. The next day, Kevin starts again.

"Peter, are you going home for Thanksgiving?"

"Yes."

"Are you taking a plane . . .?"

This goes on every day for two weeks until Thanksgiving arrives.

His affliction is not severe. His speech is normal and he is physically healthy and coordinated, though he is barely five feet tall. He wears the same brown corduroy jeans and tan shoes to work every day, topped by a blue work shirt and a black rubber apron. I remember the pants and shoes when they were new.

"Peter, look what I got for my birthday."

Kevin has a thing about his birthday. He keeps track of it as if it might become lost if he didn't.

"In eight months and ten days I'll be twenty-six years old. Last year the students surprised me on my birthday. They came in and decorated the whole dish machine. The whole place. They didn't do it this year though. Maybe they'll do it again next year. I don't know. Maybe they will. . . .

"In four years I'll be thirty . . . In five years I'll be thirty-one . . . In six years I'll be . . . I'll be . . . How old will I be?"

He's obsessed with rules and instructions. They must not be transgressed. Everything must follow a certain order. There is no room for change.

"Peter, take some trays over there. They need trays. . . .No, not those trays, those are for the coffee cups. Did you hear me? Hey! Where are you going? Bring those back! Those are for the coffee cups!"

Kevin might have the mind of a child, but physically he is a man, and his mind doesn't quite know how to handle this:

"I know about sex. I read those magazines. *Playboy. Playgirl.* I go to the movies. The filthiest movie I every saw, *Superfly.* Oh, boy, you should have seen it. . . .

"If I had a girl in bed you know what I'd do? You know what I'd do? I'd suck her titties. That's what I'd do. . . .

"I got my back pay today. Almost a hundred dollars. Maybe I won't give it to my mother. Maybe I'll get a girlfriend with it. Put on my fancy clothes and get a girlfriend. Go dancing. Maybe she'll let me play sex with her. . . .

"Is that your girlfriend, Peter? Ahhhh. I know you. I bet you're a big lady's man. I bet you've even kissed her. You'll see. I'm gonna kiss a girl some day. . . .

"I'm twenty-five years old and I've never even kissed a girl. Really. Never. I ain't lyin'. Never."

He's proud of his job. He's proud of his salary. Thursday comes and it's payday.

"Whad'ja get, Peter? Lemmee see. I made a hundred and sixty-four dollars this week. Sunday I worked overtime. I'm a good worker. Juan's a good worker too. I make more than he does."

His parents are separated.

"My father's down in Milford. He's married again. I make more than he does."

Thinking about him, I realize now that I've never once seen Kevin do anything to hurt anyone. He's never been selfish, never cruel. His virtues are rather amazing considering the home life that he tells me about.

"My mother takes all my money. She gives me ten dollars a week. I can't do nothin'. If I don't give it to her she'll throw me out of the house. . . .

"My brother's in trouble with the police. He's been stealin' cars and pushin' dope. He got in an accident and the doctor found out they were carryin' drugs in their underwear. The car was stolen. He's sixteen years old. He has to go to a special school now. . . .

"I saw my mother playing sex with one of her boyfriends. I did. I went in her room to get something and there they were, playin' sex. Boy, she was mad. She said, 'Get the hell out of this room!' That was last year."

Due to the recent decision to lay off forty-three dining hall employees, Kevin faces the prospect of losing his job.

"Why does Yale want to do this to me? They have work. I'm a good worker. I never take a break. I'm workin' all day. Who's gonna load the machine if I'm gone? You? You, Peter? You don't know how. You're not fast. You'll be here all night. . . .

"I don't even know how to collect unemployment. I never did it before. I don't want to. They don't mail it to you. You have to go and pick it up. . . .

"They need me here. Who's gonna do all these things? . . . What's gonna happen when I'm gone?"

The Bank Collector

During our spring break, the Duke's Men made a concert tour to Washington and some of the southern states. We spent one night late in our tour at the summer estate of one of the Dukes' girlfriends in Baltimore. Her father is a lung surgeon in Washington.

The estate was on a river leading into Chesapeake Bay. Bolstered by four white pillars, the house stood on a hill about two hundred yards from the private docks, where two sailboats and a motor boat were moored. Inside the house, the floors were covered with Persian rugs and the rooms were filled with antiques.

On one side of the house was a closed-in porch that had a lovely view of the river. It was pleasantly furnished with a green rug and white wicker furniture set against green walls. The large plants that hung from the ceiling thrived in the sun that poured in through the glass windows and doors.

Against one wall was a long shelf holding a collection of antique small mechanical banks. Little metal clowns, acrobats, hunters, and Uncle Sams stood poised, ready to spring into action upon being fed a coin. The amusing figures, painted in bright but now aging colors, created a carnival atmosphere that contrasted with the formality of the rest of the house.

What is it that is so alluring about a carnival? Is it that seductively evil force that always seems to be running through a noisy, crowded, rundown fairground on a hot summer night? Is it the false and deceptive smile of the Kewpie doll?

I looked down at the shelf of antique banks and that same force seemed to be present. The metal figures all wore unchanging smiles that seemed to say they had a secret. They were doing something wrong and getting away with it.

"I see you've found my banks," a voice behind me spoke.

I turned to face the doctor.

"Yes. They're very interesting."

"It's not a big collection," he said, sitting down, "but several of them are fine specimens. Quite rare."

I sat down in a chair across from him.

"It's a great hobby," he continued, "but it's expensive. That's why I've only got twenty-three."

I sympathized with him. I bet myself that some of his banks could have cost more than two hundred dollars.

"It used to be you could buy a whole collection for the same amount that just one bank costs today," he said nostalgically. "But now it seems like everybody's got their own collection. The banks are just about all bought up now. You won't find one just sitting around in an antique shop anymore.

"Every now and then someone will put an ad in the classified section of a magazine that he has one for sale, and he'll get offers from all over the country. I had a friend who answered one of them. He recognized that the bank in question was a very rare one, but the guy selling it didn't know it. It turned out there were only two of them left in the whole country. Well, he bought it from this guy for only two thousand dollars.

"The next thing he did was take it to a well-known collector, who was going to give him ten thousand dollars for it. But this guy got a better offer from the Shorelys—you know, the banking Shorelys. Oh, well. Anyway, he sold it to them for twenty-two thousand dollars.

"The collector thought he had it all wrapped up for ten thousand, and it was swept from right under his feet," the doctor chuckled. "Twenty-two thousand dollars. That's a twenty-thousand-dollar profit in just a few days. Not bad."

I was too dumbfounded to say anything. The doctor continued his monologue.

"Here, let me show you one of mine." He went over to the shelf, took down one of the banks, and set it on the table in front of us. The base of the bank was a blue circus pedestal, one of those round structures that trainers train elephants to stand on. In the top of the base was a slot for coins. At the back of the base stood a vertical bar that became a curved fork above the pedestal. A cast-iron acrobat balanced between the sides of the fork on a metal bar which he held on to.

The figure was dressed in a white clown's suit that had been painted on and had now turned creamy with age. He had red buttons and trim, a pair of red pointed slippers, and a red stocking cap. His black face was frozen in a leering grin.

"This one's a prize," the doctor said, giving it a pat. "Look at him. Not a scratch on him. That's all the original paint and there's not a scratch on him. He cost me seven thousand dollars just a few years back. I don't know how much he's worth now. At least twelve. Watch this," he said, reaching into his pocket. He pulled out a nickel and fitted it into the clown's cap. The metal figure bent slowly forward until his head was quite close to the base. The coin fell into the slot in the blue drum, and the figure swung back up again, grinning proudly.

The doctor's face fell. "He's supposed to do a flip, but he needs adjusting. Maybe with something heavier . . . ."

He reached into his pocket for a quarter. This time he gave the clown a little push as he fitted the coin into the cap. The clown performed a full flip and he resurfaced with that same evil grin.

"There!" the doctor said proudly. "With something heavier, like a half-dollar, he'll do two flips."

The little metal acrobat swung back and forth on his stand, basking in glory with his huge, gloating grin. I began to understand what evil secret that hunk of metal possessed. He held the power to keep a person fed and alive for several years. That was the power that ran through those atoms of iron. That was the force that give the metal man life.

The doctor was still speaking.

"You know, if you get your hands on some money these days and you want to invest it, you've got a problem. Look at the stock market. This country's ecomony is a mess." He smiled at his shelves of banks. "That's what's so great about these things. They're good investments. They're safe. People are taking an interest in these things again. Anything from the early days of America. That's where you should put your money these days, in anything American."

Anything American.

Breakfast at Timothy's

In my job as a dishwasher at Timothy Dwight College I usually worked dinners, but one of the workers had asked me to fill in for him at breakfast one day when he would be away. I needed the money so I agreed, expecting to wash dishes. When I reported to work, though, it turned out that I was expected to work on the serving line.

At all of Yale's dining halls, a hot breakfast is served until nine o'clock. After nine, only continental breakfast is available; students serve themselves cold cereal, toast, or Danish. When nine o'clock rolled around, I still had some scrambled eggs, one piece of French toast, and one piece of regular toast. I decided to finish serving them, rather than bring them back to the kitchen, where they would just be thrown out.

At about ten after nine, a resident fellow of Timothy Dwight showed up for breakfast. He was a tall man, about forty-five years old, with stumpy gray hair and a pair of wire-rimmed glasses. He mumbled something and pointed in the direction of the French toast. I put the toast on a plate and served it to him.

"Okay," he growled, "would you like to give me some eggs? I asked for eggs."

I took another plate and gave him some eggs. He was angry.

"Now would you like to give me some toast to eat with the eggs?" I reached for the last piece of toast and put it on his plate.

"Now," he exploded, "would you like to give me two pieces of toast instead of one piece of toast?"

"That was the last piece," I told him as I put two more pieces of bread in the toaster. Then I remembered that it was after nine o'clock and that I didn't have to be making more toast.

"If you want breakfast," I said, "you should get down here before nine o'clock."

He looked at me, his eyes filled with contempt. He spoke through clenched teeth and the words fell from his lips like bird droppings.

"Tomorrow," he snarled, "you can come and serve me breakfast in my room before nine o'clock."

"Don't count on it," I said. I reached behind me to the toaster and pushed up the slices of bread, half toasted. If he wanted toast, he could make it himself. He stalked out of the kitchen.

When he left, I realized I was shaking. My eyes were burning and it was hard for me to swallow. If I had been alone in my room, I probably would have cried. It hurt to be treated as if I were inferior. I felt a hate for that man stronger than any hate I had ever felt before, and the strength of that hate scared me. I would have liked to see him dead.

In Our Nation's Capital

I sat at a table in the Crystal Room of the Sheraton Carlton Hotel in Washington, D.C. The Duke's Men had been hired to sing at a Saint Patrick's Day luncheon in honor of the Irish ambassador to the United States and of the hotel's manager, who was retiring.

People had gathered an hour earlier to sip cocktails in the Mount Vernon Room, and the Duke's Men hadn't passed up the opportunity either. We were among the first ones there, and we watched the room fill around us with Washington VIPs. The only one that most of us could recognize was J. W. Fulbright. Danny, one of the Duke's Men, whose father is a Washington lawyer, was able to point out important congressmen, aides, consultants, etc. They didn't look like much to me.

More interesting than these stale Washington politicians were the wives they brought with them. Their identities were concealed behind layers of face powder, and most of them were dressed all in green for the occasion. Each of them was responsible for maintaining and advancing the social status of her family, and they were all trying to engage in friendly conversation with women a step ahead of them on the social ladder, in hope that room might be made for them on that step. Their behavior reminded me of the tigers in "Little Black Sambo" who chased each other's tails around a tree in a continuous circle until they turned to butter. Lunch was called, and the women were saved from a similar fate.

I vowed not to sit with any Duke's Men, to force myself to eat and talk with some of these people. I saw it as an educational experience. I sat alone at a table and chased away any of the Duke's Men that tried to join me. Two unassuming men in clerical collars sat down and introduced themselves as monsignors with Irish-sounding names, and that was as far as our conversation went. I began to despair and was unconsoled by the chlorine smell of the hot tuna crepes on my plate. Then a woman who introduced herself as "Grosvenor" sat down and announced that the rest of the seats at the table were reserved for an important congressman, his wife, and an admiral. She greeted the two monsignors, whom she didn't seem very interested in, and started a conversation with me.

She asked me what I was studying, and I told her I was interested in writing. Her eyes lit up, and she told me that she, too, was a writer. She had been an editor for *Business Week,* and a Washington columnist. She was retired, and was now writing a book of amusing anecdotes about "all the famous people" in Washington. I listened intently as she rattled off a story about Prince Charles's visit to Washington.

". . . Well, he was standing on the reception line, and everybody had been carefully screened, you know, and there was a man there and nobody knew who he was or how he got in. . . ."

She was quite tickled by the tale she was telling, and her breath came in short little pants, like that of an overexcited toy poodle.

"Well, finally he reached up to the prince, and he shook his hand and the prince asked, 'And what is your connection?' And do you know what he said?" she gasped. "Do you know what he said? . . . 'Western Union'!"

She repeated "Western Union!" and I realized that I was supposed to laugh. So I laughed politely, trying to figure out the punchline.

The congressman, his wife, and the admiral arrived, and a waiter appeared and filled our wineglasses. Danny later informed me that the congressman was one of the five most powerful men in Washington, along with Ford and Kissinger. His wife was a huge woman with a beaked nose, an elaborate hairdo, and a double chin that danced when she turned her head. She was dressed in pink. The congressman was also fat, and both he and the admiral were bald, roundheaded men whose faces were distorted by thick lenses set in jet-black frames. All of them appeared to be well into their seventies.

Mrs. Grosvenor introduced us, and I remembered to stand up as I shook their hands.

"This young man," Mrs. Grosvenor informed them, "has been most delightful to talk to. He's interested in becoming a writer."

"Awhh," the admiral guffawed, "you'd better tell him to find another field. There's no money in writing. He won't make a cent." He turned to me and looked at me as a father would. "Really, you'd better study something else. Why, you'd be better off in the army!"

"Listen to him," the congressman's wife advised me. "He knows what he's talking about. Why, since the admiral retired, he's simply been raking it in!" The table burst into laughter, and even the two monsignors, who had been totally uninvolved in the conversation, smiled sheepishly.

"He's been . . . He's been . . ." the woman tried to speak through her uncontrollable laughter. "He's been . . . working as a . . . 'consultant'!" And the table was overcome by renewed fits of laughter.

The admiral sat with a huge grin on his face, quite proud of himself.

"You've got to have money, son," he continued, suddenly turning quite somber, "because without money, you're nothing. You don't go anywhere without money."

"He's right, you know." Mrs. Grosvenor frowned. "Money talks."

I waited for more laughter. I waited for them to acknowledge their joke. But there was no laughter, no acknowledgment. These people were serious.

Special People

Mary is a full-time worker at the dining hall where I work part-time as a dishwasher. She's one of those women who can be big and fat but somehow you never notice their size. Although she must be close to sixty, she has a spirited personality that might belong to a sixteen-year-old girl. There is something dry and clean about her; she is the definition of "baby powder fresh." Her hair is dyed dark black; her skin is white with a thin dusting of powder, and her lips bright red with lipstick. She always has a kind word for everyone, and all of the students love her.

One Saturday night, just as we were ready to close the serving line, a busload of Yale alumni appeared with their wives, ready to be served dinner. They were members of the Yale Club of Hartford and had been expected two hours earlier in the evening. But they hadn't arrived, and nobody was ready for them now. General havoc took place in the kitchen as the workers tried to whip up a last-minute meal for the Old Blues and their wives.

I became increasingly annoyed. It especially pained me to see Mary running around excitedly as the Yale Club sat there coolly, waiting to be served. She ran by me in a huff and shouted.

"Quick, Peter! Get some coffee cups! They need coffee cups!"

I walked up to the stack of clean cups with deliberate slowness and started counting them out onto a tray, one by one.

"Hurry up, for Christ's sake," Mary whined. "These people are waiting."

"All right! Don't worry about it. They'll get their goddamn coffee cups," I shouted at her, loud enough for the Yale Club to hear. They looked on in disapproval and Mary walked by them shaking her head.

"Boy, these student workers," she said. "They're so slow!"

I felt terrible.

I had taken my anger out on Mary when she was the one I was angry *for*. I hated to see her so subservient, and yet it was I who put her down further, and in front of them. So much so that she'd had to defend herself. I couldn't understand how everything had gotten so twisted.

She approached me afterward, when we were cleaning up.

"You know, Peter, You'd better watch it. You were wrong to wise off in front of those people."

"I know, Mary." I tried to apologize. "I'm sorry."

"Those were special people," she said, her face set in earnest, "and you had to go and get wise. They don't like that, you know."

"Oh, Mary," I said, exasperated, "those were not special people."

"Yes they were. The manager made a special trip down here to tell us to make sure that they were well taken care of. You'd better be careful, you know. They might report you. You might lose your job."

She turned to the counter and started shoving cottage cheese into a container.

I almost cried for her. I wanted to take her in my arms and try to convince her that there weren't any "special people," that she was as special as anyone else in the world.

I put my arm on her shoulder.

"Mary, there's no such thing as special people. People are people. That's all."

She stood there, shaking her head and shoveling the cottage cheese.

"Peter, you're wrong. Those were special people and you had to open your big mouth."

"Mary, look at them," I said, pointing toward the dining room. "What's so special about them?"

"Peter. Shush. They'll hear you."

"Mary," I pleaded, "can't you see that you're more special to me than any of those people? That's why I got so mad. I hated seeing you run around for them."

Her eyes suddenly glazed with tears and she hurried to the refrigerator with the cottage cheese.

"Peter, what am I going to do with you?" she called back. "You're gonna give me gray hairs. You're gonna get yourself in trouble too. You don't know your place. Those were special people."

Suggestions for Discussion

1. With what details does Werner describe the ironic significance of the song, "Both Sides Now"? How does he portray the multifaceted and deep-layered character of the two sides?

2. Account for the tone of the section "A Phone Call Home."

3. How can the heating incident both amuse and upset him?

4. How is irony expressed in the juxtaposition of the sketches of Kevin and the bank collector?

5. What does the narrative of "The Nation's Capital" tell you about the author's, the admiral's, and Mrs. Grosvenor's values?

6. Compare Mary's and Peter's implicit definition of "special people."

7. What do you infer is Peter's sense of self at the stage of life he portrays in "Both Sides Now"?

Suggestions for Writing

1. Describe one or more of your experiences with "both sides" of the economic structure.

2. On the basis of his descriptions of the people he encountered at Yale and his reactions to them, write a character study of Peter.

Jorge Luís Borges

Borges and Myself

Translated by Norman Thomas di Giovanni

Jorge Luís Borges (b. 1899), Argentine poet, short-story writer, essayist, critic, and university professor, is regarded as the greatest living man of letters writing in Spanish. Best known for his esoteric short fiction, Borges received little recognition in America until the publication in 1968 of English translations of *Ficciónes, Labyrinths,* and *The Aleph.* In this very short piece the writer speaks of his dual nature, the self who surrenders everything to the creative Borges so that he can weave his tales and poems.

It's to the other man, to Borges, that things happen. I walk along the streets of Buenos Aires, stopping now and then—perhaps out of habit—to look at the arch of an old entranceway or a grillwork gate; of Borges I get news through the mail and glimpse his name among a committee of professors or in a dictionary of biography. I have a taste for hourglasses, maps, eighteenth-century typography, the roots of words, the smell of coffee, and Stevenson's prose; the other man shares these likes, but in a showy way that turns them into stagy mannerisms. It would be an exaggeration to say that we are on bad terms; I live, I let myself live, so that Borges can weave his tales and poems, and those tales and poems are my justification. It is not hard for me to admit that he has managed to write a few worthwhile pages, but these pages cannot save me, perhaps because what is good no longer belongs to anyone—not even the other man—but rather to speech or tradition. In any case, I am fated to become lost once and for all, and only some moment of myself will survive in the other man. Little by little, I have been surrendering everything to him, even though I have evidence of his stubborn habit of falsification and exaggerating. Spinoza held that all things try to keep on being themselves; a stone wants to be a stone and the tiger, a tiger. I shall remain in Borges, not in myself (if it is so that I am someone), but I recognize myself less in his books than in those of others or than in the laborious tuning of a guitar. Years ago, I tried ridding myself of him and I went from myths of the outlying slums of the city to games with time and infinity, but those games are now part of Borges and I will have to turn to other things. And so, my life is a running away, and I lose everything and everything is left to oblivion or to the other man.

Which of us is writing this page I don't know.

Suggestions for Discussion

1. Who is the speaker?

2. What is his relationship to and attitude toward Borges, the writer?

3. With what details are the dual aspects of his personality made clear? Define them.

4. How does he substantiate his belief that he is "fated to become lost once and for all"?

5. On the basis of this brief sketch, what conclusions are you invited to draw about the creative process and about the sources and subject matter of Borges' art?

Suggestions for Writing

1. Read a number of Borges's short stories and analyze the basis of their appeal.

2. The concept of the double appears frequently in literature. Write a sketch of a character in literature (Conrad's "The Secret Sharer," Melville's "Bartleby the Scrivener," Dostoevsky's "The Double," Poe's "William Wilson") who might be described as having a double.

3. Record your daily activities and thoughts for a week, paying no attention to mechanics or organization. Then select one of the journal items for full and logical development.

A. Alvarez
Sylvia Plath: A Memoir

Alfred Alvarez (b. 1929), English critic and teacher, has been the poetry editor and poetry critic for *The Observer* since 1956. He is the author of *Stewards of Excellence* and *The School of Donne* and is a regular contributor to *The Spectator*. His memoir of Sylvia Plath, which appeared first in *New American Review*, was later included in his book *The Savage God* (1971), a study of suicide. Although Plath was often able to turn her "anger, implacability, and her roused, needle-sharp sense of trouble" into her creativity, even into a kind of celebration, she succumbed to depression and everything, according to Alvarez who knew her well, finally conspired to destroy her.

They were living in a tiny flat not far from the Regent's Park Zoo. Their windows faced onto a run-down square: peeling houses around a scrappy wilderness of garden. Closer to the Hill, gentility was advancing fast: smart Sunday newspaper house-agents had their boards up, the front doors were all fashionable colors—"Cantaloupe," "Tangerine," "Blueberry," "Thames Green"—and everywhere was a sense of gleaming white interiors, the old houses writ large and rich with new conversions.

Their square, however, had not yet been taken over. It was dirty, cracked, and racketty with children. The rows of houses that led off it were still occupied by the same kind of working-class families they had been built for eighty years before. No one, as yet, had made them chic and quadrupled their price—though that was to come soon enough. The Hughes' flat was one floor up a bedraggled staircase, past a pram in the hall and a bicycle. It was so small that everything seemed sideways on. You inserted yourself into a hallway so narrow and jammed that you could scarcely take off your coat. The kitchen seemed to fit one person at a time, who could span it with arms outstretched. In the living room you sat side by side, longways on, between a wall of books and a wall of pictures. The bedroom off it, with its flowered wallpaper, seemed to have room for nothing except a double bed. But the colors were cheerful, the bits and pieces pretty, and the whole place had a sense of liveliness about it, of things being done. A typewriter stood on a little table by the window, and they took turns at it, each working shifts while the other minded the baby. At night they cleared it away to make room for the child's cot. Later, they borrowed a room from another American poet, W. S. Merwin, where Sylvia worked the morning shift, Ted the afternoon.

This was Ted's time. He was on the edge of a considerable reputation. His first book had been well received and won all sorts of prizes in the States, which usually means that the second book will be an anticlimax. Instead, *Lupercal* effortlessly fulfilled and surpassed all the promises of *The Hawk in the Rain*. A figure had emerged on the drab scene of British poetry, powerful and undeniable. Whatever his natural hesitations and distrust of his own work, he must have had some sense of his own strength and achievement. God alone knew how far he was eventually going, but in one essential way he had already arrived. He was a tall, strong-looking man in a black corduroy jacket, black trousers, black shoes; his dark hair hung untidily forward; he had a long, witty mouth. He was in command.

In those days Sylvia seemed effaced; the poet taking a back seat to the young mother and housewife. She had a long, rather flat body, a longish face, not pretty but alert and full of feeling, with a lively mouth and fine brown eyes. Her brownish hair was scraped severely into a bun. She wore jeans and a neat shirt, briskly American: bright, clean, competent, like a young woman in a cookery advertisement, friendly and yet rather distant.

Her background, of which I knew nothing then, belied her housewifely air: she had been a child prodigy—her first poem was published when she was eight—and then a brilliant student, winning every prize to be had, first at Wellesley High School, then at Smith College: scholarships all the way, straight A's, Phi Beta Kappa, president of this and that college society, and prizes for everything. A New York glossy magazine, *Mademoiselle,* had picked her as an outstanding possibility and wined her, dined her, and photographed her all over Manhattan. Then, almost inevitably, she had won a Fulbright to Cambridge, where she met Ted Hughes. They were married in 1956, on Bloomsday. Behind Sylvia was a self-sacrificing, widowed mother, a schoolteacher who had worked herself into the ground so that her two children might flourish. Sylvia's father—ornithologist, entomologist, ichthyologist, international authority on bumblebees, and professor of biology at Boston University—had died when she was nine. Both parents were of German stock and were German-speaking, academic, and intellectual. When she and Ted went to the States after Cambridge, a glittering university career seemed both natural and assured.

On the surface it was a typical success story: the brilliant examination-passer driving forward so fast and relentlessly that nothing could ever catch up with her. And it can last a lifetime, provided nothing checks the momentum, and the vehicle of all those triumphs doesn't disintegrate into sharp fragments from sheer speed and pressure. But already her progress had twice lurched to a halt. Between her month on *Mademoiselle* and her last year in college she had had the nervous breakdown and suicide attempt which became the theme of her novel, *The Bell Jar*. Then, once reestablished at Smith—"an outstanding teacher," said her colleagues—the academic prizes no longer seemed worth the effort. So in 1958 she had thrown over university life—Ted had never seriously contemplated it—and gone free-lance, trusting her luck and talent as a poet. All this I learned much later. Now Sylvia had simply slowed down; she was subdued, absorbed in her new baby daughter, and friendly only in that rather formal, shallow, transatlantic way that keeps you at your distance.

Ted went downstairs to get the pram ready while she dressed the baby. I stayed behind a minute, zipping up my son's coat. Sylvia turned to me, suddenly without gush:

"I'm so glad you picked *that* poem," she said. "It's one of my favorites but no one else seemed to like it."

For a moment I went completely blank; I didn't know what she was talking about. She noticed and helped me out.

"The one you put in *The Observer* a year ago. About the factory at night."

"For Christ's sake, Sylvia *Plath*." It was my turn to gush. "I'm sorry. It was a lovely poem."

"Lovely" wasn't the right word, but what else do you say to a bright young housewife? I had picked it from a sheaf of poems which had arrived from America, immaculately typed, with self-addressed envelope and international reply coupon efficiently supplied. All of them were stylish and talented but that in itself was not rare in those days. The late fifties was a period of particularly high style in American verse, when every campus worth its name had its own "brilliant" poetic technician in residence. But at least one of these poems had more going for it than rhetorical elegance. It had no title, though later, in *The Colossus*, she called it "Night Shift." It was one of those poems which starts by saying what it is *not* about so strongly that you don't believe the explanations that follow:

> It was not a heart, beating,
> That muted boom, that clangor
> Far off, not blood in the ears
> Drumming up any fever
>
> To impose on the evening.
> The noise came from outside:
> A metal detonating
> Native, evidently, to
>
> These stilled suburbs: nobody
> Startled at it, though the sound
> Shook the ground with its pounding.
> It took root at my coming . . .

It seemed to me more than a piece of good description, to be used and moralized upon as the fashion of that decade dictated. The note was aroused and all the details of the scene seemed continually to be turning inward. It is a poem, I suppose, about fear, and although in the course of it the fear is rationalized and explained (that pounding in the night is caused by machines turning), it ends by reasserting precisely the threatening masculine forces there were to be afraid of. It had its moments of awkwardness—for example, the prissy, pausing flourish in the manner of Wallace Stevens: "Native, evidently, to . . ." But compared with most of the stuff that thudded unsolicited through my letterbox every morning, it was that rare thing: the always unexpected, wholly genuine article.

I was embarrassed not to have known who she was. She seemed embarrassed to have reminded me, and also depressed.

After that I saw Ted occasionally, Sylvia more rarely. He and I would meet for a beer in one of the pubs near Primrose Hill or the Heath, and sometimes we would walk our children together. We almost never talked shop; without mentioning it, we wanted to keep things unprofessional. At some point during the summer Ted and I did a broadcast together. Afterward we collected Sylvia from the flat and went across to their local. The recording had been a success and we stood outside the pub, around the baby's pram, drinking our beers and pleased with ourselves. Sylvia, too, seemed easier, wittier, less constrained than I had seen her before. For the first time I understood something of the real charm and speed of the girl.

About that time my wife and I moved from our flat near Swiss Cottage to a house higher up in Hampstead, near the Heath. A couple of days before we were due to move I broke my leg in a climbing accident, and that put out everything and everyone, since the house had to be decorated, broken leg or not. I remember sticking black and white tiles to floor after endless floor, a filthy dark brown glue coating my fingers and clothes and gumming up my hair, the great, inert plaster cast dragging behind me like a coffin as I crawled. There wasn't much time for friends. Ted occasionally dropped in and I would hobble with him briefly to the pub. But I saw Sylvia not at all. In the autumn I went to teach for a term in the States.

While I was there *The Observer* sent me her first book of poems to review. It seemed to fit the image I had of her: serious, gifted, withheld, and still partly under the massive shadow of her husband. There were poems that had been influenced by him, others which echoed Theodore Roethke or Wallace Stevens; clearly, she was still casting about for her own style. Yet the technical ability was great, and beneath most of the poems was a sense of resources and disturbances not yet tapped. "Her poems," I wrote, "rest secure in a mass of experience that is never quite brought out into the daylight. . . . It is this sense of threat, as though she were continually menaced by something she could see only out of the corners of her eyes, that gives her work its distinction."

Throughout this time the evidence of the poems and the evidence of the person were utterly different. There was no trace of the poetry's despair and unforgiving destructiveness in her social manner. She remained remorselessly bright and energetic: busy with her children and her beekeeping in Devon, busy flat-hunting in London, busy seeing *The Bell Jar* through the press, busy typing and sending off her poems to largely unreceptive editors (just before she died she sent a sheaf of her best poems, most of them now classics, to one of the national British weeklies; none was accepted). She had also taken up horse-riding again, teaching herself to ride on a powerful stallion called Ariel, and was elated by this new excitement.

Cross-legged on the red floor, after reading her poems, she would talk about her riding in her twanging New England voice. And perhaps because I was also a member of the club, she talked, too, about suicide in much the same way: about her attempt ten years before which, I suppose, must have been very much on her mind as she corrected the proofs of her novel, and about her recent car crash. It had been no accident; she had gone off the road deliberately, seriously, wanting to die. But she hadn't, and all that was now in the past. For this reason I am convinced that at this time she was not contemplating suicide. On the contrary, she was able to write about the act so freely because it was already behind her. The car crash was a death she had survived, the death she sardonically felt herself fated to undergo once every decade:

> I have done it again.
> One year in every ten
> I manage it—
>
> A sort of walking miracle . . .
> I am only thirty.
> And like the cat I have nine times to die.
>
> This is Number Three . . .

In life, as in the poem, there was neither hysteria in her voice, nor any appeal for sympathy. She talked about suicide in much the same tone as she talked about any other risky, testing activity: urgently, even fiercely, but altogether without self-pity. She seemed to view death as a physical challenge she had, once again, overcome. It was an experience of much the same quality as riding Ariel or mastering a bolting horse—which she had done as a Cambridge undergraduate—or careening down a dangerous snow slope without properly knowing how to ski—an incident, also from life, which is one of the best things in *The Bell Jar*. Suicide, in short, was not a swoon into death, an attempt "to cease upon the midnight with no pain"; it was something to be felt in the nerve-ends and fought against, an initiation rite qualifying her for a *life* of her own.

God knows what wound the death of her father had inflicted on her in her childhood, but over the years this had been transformed into the conviction that to be an adult meant to be a survivor. So, for her, death was a debt to be met once every decade: in order to stay alive as a grown woman, a mother, and a poet, she had to pay—in some partial, magical way—with her life. But because this impossible payment involved also the fantasy of joining or regaining her beloved dead father, it was a passionate act, instinct as much with love as with hatred and despair. Thus in that strange, upsetting poem "The Bee Meeting," the detailed, doubtless accurate description of a gathering of local beekeepers in her Devon village gradually becomes an invocation of some deadly ritual in which she is sacrificial virgin whose coffin, finally, waits in the sacred grove. Why this should happen becomes, perhaps, slightly less mysterious when you remember that her father was an authority on bees; so her beekeeping becomes a way of symbolically allying herself to him, and reclaiming him from the dead.

The tone of all these late poems is hard, factual and, despite the intensity, understated. In some strange way, I suspect she thought of herself as a realist: the deaths and resurrections of "Lady Lazarus," the nightmares of "Daddy," and the rest had all been proved on her pulses. That she brought to them an extraordinary inner wealth of imagery and associations was almost beside the point, however essential it is for the poetry itself. Because she felt she was simply describing the facts as they had happened, she was able to tap in the coolest possible way all her large reserves of skill: those subtle rhymes and half-rhymes, the flexible, echoing rhythms and offhand colloquialism by which she preserved, even in her most anguished probing, complete artistic control. Her internal horrors were as factual and precisely sensed as the barely controllable stallion on which she was learning to ride or the car she had smashed up.

So she spoke of suicide with a wry detachment, and without any mention of the suffering or drama of the act. It was obviously a matter of self-respect that her first attempt had been serious and nearly successful, instead of a mere hysterical gesture. That seemed to entitle her to speak of suicide as a subject, not as an obsession. It was an act she felt she had a right to as a grown woman and a free agent, in the same way as she felt it to be necessary to her development, given her queer conception of the adult as a survivor, an imaginary Jew from the concentration camps of the mind. Because of this there was never any question of motives: you do it because you do it, just as an artist always knows what he knows.

Perhaps this is why she scarcely mentioned her father, however clearly and deeply her fantasies of death were involved with him. The autobiographical heroine of *The Bell Jar* goes to weep at her father's grave immediately before she holes up in a cellar and swallows fifty sleeping pills. In "Daddy," describing the same episode, she hammers home her reasons with repetitions:

> At twenty I tried to die
> And get back, back, back to you.
> I thought even the bones would do.

I suspect that finding herself alone again now, however temporarily and voluntarily, all the anguish she had experienced at her father's death was reactivated: despite herself, she felt abandoned, injured, enraged, and bereaved as purely and defenselessly as she had as a child twenty years before. As a result, the pain that had built up steadily inside her all that time came flooding out. There was no need to discuss motives because the poems did that for her.

These months were an amazingly creative period, comparable, I think, to the "marvellous year" in which Keats produced nearly all the poetry on which his reputation finally rests. Earlier she had written carefully, more or less painfully, with much rewriting and, according to her husband, with constant recourse to *Roget's Thesaurus*. Now, although she abandoned none of her hard-earned skills and discipline, and still rewrote and rewrote, the poems flowed effortlessly, until, at the end, she occasionally produced as many as three a day. She also told me that she was deep into a new novel. *The Bell*

Jar was finished, proofread and with her publishers; she spoke of it with some embarrassment as an autobiographical apprentice-work which she had to write in order to free herself from the past. But this new book, she implied, was the genuine article.

Considering the conditions in which she worked, her productivity was phenomenal. She was a full-time mother with a two-year-old daughter, a baby of ten months, and a house to look after. By the time the children were in bed at night she was too tired for anything more strenuous than "music and brandy and water." So she got up very early each morning and worked until the children woke. "These new poems of mine have one thing in common," she wrote in a note for a reading she prepared, but never broadcast, for the BBC, "they were all written at about four in the morning—that still blue, almost eternal hour before the baby's cry, before the glassy music of the milkman, settling his bottles." In those dead hours between night and day, she was able to gather herself into herself in silence and isolation, almost as though she were reclaiming some past innocence and freedom before life got a grip on her. Then she could write. For the rest of the day she was shared among the children, the housework, the shopping, efficient, bustling, harassed, like every other housewife.

Yet lonely she was, touchingly and without much disguise, despite her buoyant manner. Despite, too, the energy of her poems, which are, by any standards, subtly ambiguous performances. In them she faced her private horrors steadily and without looking aside, but the effort and risk involved in doing so acted on her like a stimulant; the worse things got and the more directly she wrote about them, the more fertile her imagination became. Just as disaster, when it finally arrives, is never as bad as it seems in expectation, so she now wrote almost with relief, swiftly as though to forestall further horrors. In a way, this is what she had been waiting for all her life, and now it had come she knew she must use it. "The passion for destruction is also a creative passion," said Michael Bakunin, and for Sylvia also this was true. She turned anger, implacability, and her roused, needle-sharp sense of trouble into a kind of celebration.

I have suggested that her cool tone depends a great deal on her realism, her sense of fact. As the months went by and her poetry became progressively more extreme, this gift of transforming every detail grew steadily until, in the last weeks, each trivial event became the occasion for poetry: a cut finger, a fever, a bruise. Her drab domestic life fused with her imagination richly and without hesitation. Around this time, for example, her husband produced a strange radio play in which the hero, driving to town, runs over a hare, sells the dead animal for five shillings, and with the blood money buys two roses. Sylvia pounced on this, isolating its core, interpreting and adjusting it according to her own needs. The result was the poem "Kindness," which ends:

> The blood jet is poetry,
> There is no stopping it.
> You hand me two children, two roses.

There was, indeed, no stopping it. Her poetry acted as a strange, powerful lens through which her ordinary life was filtered and refigured with extraordinary intensity. Perhaps the elation that comes of writing well and often helped her to preserve that bright American façade she unfailingly presented to the world. In common with her other friends of that period, I chose to believe in this cheerfulness against all the evidence of the poems. Or rather, I believed in it, and I didn't believe. But what could one do? I felt sorry for her but she clearly didn't want that. Her jauntiness forestalled all sympathy, and, if only by her blank refusal to discuss them otherwise, she insisted that her poems were purely poems, autonomous. If attempted suicide is, as some psychiatrists believe, a cry for help, then Sylvia at this time was not suicidal. What she wanted was not help but confirmation: she needed someone to acknowledge that she was coping exceptionally well with her difficult routine life of children, nappies, shopping, and writing. She needed, even more, to know that the poems worked and were good, for although she had gone through a gate Lowell had opened, she was now far along a peculiarly solitary road on which not many would risk following her. So it was important for her to know that her messages were coming back clear and strong. Yet not even her determinedly bright self-reliance could disguise the loneliness that came from her almost palpably, like a heat haze. She asked for neither sympathy nor help but, like a bereaved widow at a wake, she simply wanted company in her mourning. I suppose it provided confirmation that, despite the odds and the internal evidence, she still existed.

It was an unspeakable winter, the worst, they said, in a hundred and fifty years. The snow began just after Christmas and would not let up. By New Year the whole country had ground to a halt. The trains froze on the tracks, the abandoned trucks froze on the roads. The power stations, overloaded by million upon pathetic million of hopeless electric fires, broke down continually; not that the fires mattered, since the electricians were mostly out on strike. Water pipes froze solid; for a bath you had to scheme and cajole those rare friends with centrally heated houses, who became rarer and less friendly as the weeks dragged on. Doing the dishes became a major operation. The gastric rumble of water in outdated plumbing was sweeter than the sound of mandolins. Weight for weight, plumbers were as expensive as smoked salmon, and harder to find. The gas failed and Sunday joints went raw. The lights failed and candles, of course, were unobtainable. Nerves failed and marriages crumbled. Finally, the heart failed. It seemed the cold would never end. Nag, nag, nag.

In December *The Observer* had published a still uncollected poem by Sylvia called "Event"; in mid-January they published another, "Winter Trees." Sylvia wrote me a note about it, adding that maybe we should take our children to the zoo and she would show me "the nude verdigris of the condor." But she no longer dropped into my studio with poems. Later that month I met the literary editor of one of the big weeklies. He asked me if I had seen Sylvia recently.

"No. Why?"

"I was just wondering. She sent us some poems. Very strange."

"Did you like them?"

"No," he replied. "Too extreme for my taste. I sent them all back. But she sounds in a bad state. I think she needs help."

Her doctor, a sensitive, overworked man, thought the same. He prescribed sedatives and arranged for her to see a psychotherapist. Having been bitten once by American psychiatry, she hesitated for some time before writing for an appointment. But her depression did not lift, and finally the letter was sent. It did no good. Either her letter or that of the therapist arranging a consultation went astray; apparently the postman delivered it to the wrong address. The therapist's reply arrived a day or two after she died. This was one of several links in the chain of accidents, coincidences, and mistakes that ended in her death.

I am convinced by what I know of the facts that this time she did not intend to die. Her suicide attempt ten years before had been, in every sense, deadly serious. She had carefully disguised the theft of the sleeping pills, left a misleading note to cover her tracks, and hidden herself in the darkest, most unused corner of a cellar, rearranging behind her the old firelogs she had disturbed, burying herself away like a skeleton in the nethermost family closet. Then she had swallowed a bottle of fifty sleeping pills. She was found late and by accident, and survived only by a miracle. The flow of life in her was too strong even for the violence she had done it. This, anyway, is her description of the act in *The Bell Jar;* there is no reason to believe it false. So she had learned the hard way the odds against successful suicide; she had learned that despair must be counterpoised by an almost obsessional attention to detail and disguise.

By these lights she seemed, in her last attempt, to be taking care not to succeed. But this time everything conspired to destroy her. An employment agency had found her an *au pair* girl to help with the children and housework while Sylvia got on with her writing. The girl, an Australian, was due to arrive at nine o'clock on the morning of Monday, February 11th. Meanwhile, a re-current trouble, Sylvia's sinuses were bad; the pipes in her newly converted flat froze solid; there was still no telephone, and no word from the psycho-therapist; the weather continued monstrous. Illness, loneliness, depression, and cold, combined with the demands of two small children, were too much for her. So when the weekend came she went off with the babies to stay with friends in another part of London. The plan was, I think, that she would leave early enough on Monday morning to be back in time to welcome the Austra-lian girl. Instead, she decided to go back on the Sunday. The friends were against it but she was insistent, made a great show of her old competence and seemed more cheerful than she had been for some time. So they let her go. About eleven o'clock that night she knocked on the door of the elderly painter who lived below her, asking to borrow some stamps. But she lingered in the doorway, drawing out the conversation until he told her that he got up well before nine in the morning. Then she said goodnight and went back upstairs.

Around six A.M. she went up to the children's room and left a plate of bread and butter and two mugs of milk, in case they should wake hungry before the *au pair* girl arrived. Then she went back down to the kitchen, sealed the door and window as best she could with towels, opened the oven, laid her head in it, and turned on the gas.

The Australian girl arrived punctually at nine A.M. She rang and knocked a long time but could get no answer. So she went off to search for a telephone kiosk in order to phone the agency and make sure she had the right address. Sylvia's name, incidentally, was not on either of the doorbells. Had every-thing been normal, the neighbor below would have been up by then; even if he had overslept, the girl's knocking should have aroused him. But as it happened, the neighbor was very deaf and slept without his hearing aid. More important, his bedroom was immediately below Sylvia's kitchen. The gas seeped down and knocked him out cold. So he slept on through all the noise. The girl returned and tried again, still without success. Again she went off to telephone the agency and ask what to do; they told her to go back. It was now about eleven o'clock. This time she was lucky: some builders had arrived to work in the frozen-up house, and they let her in. When she knocked on Sylvia's door there was no answer and the smell of gas was overpowering. The builders forced the lock and found Sylvia sprawled in the kitchen. She was still warm. She had left a note saying, "Please call Dr.——" and giving his telephone number. But it was too late.

Had everything worked out as it should—had the gas not drugged the man downstairs, preventing him from opening the front door to the *au pair* girl— there is no doubt she would have been saved. I think she wanted to be; why else leave her doctor's telephone number? This time, unlike the occasion ten years before, there was too much holding her to life. Above all, there were the children: she was too passionate a mother to want to lose them or them to lose her. There were also the extraordinary creative powers she now unequivocally knew she possessed: the poems came daily, unbidden and unstoppable, and she was again working on a novel about which, at last, she had no reservations.

Why, then, did she kill herself? In part, I suppose, it was "a cry for help" which fatally misfired. But it was also a last, desperate attempt to exorcise the death she had summoned up in her poems. I have already suggested that perhaps she had begun to write obsessively about death for two reasons. First, when she and her husband separated, however mutual the arrangement, she went through again the same piercing grief and bereavement she had felt as a child when her father, by his death, seemed to abandon her. Second, I believe she thought her car crash the previous summer had set her free; she had paid her dues, qualified as a survivor, and could now write about it. But, as I have written elsewhere, for the artist himself art is not necessarily therapeutic; he is not automatically relieved of his fantasies by expressing them. Instead, by some perverse logic of creation, the act of formal expression may simply make the dredged-up material more readily available to him. The result of handling it in his work may well be that he finds himself living it out. For the artist, in short, nature often imitates art. Or, to restate the cliché, when an artist holds a mirror up to nature he finds out who and what he is; but the knowledge may change him irredeemably so that he becomes that image.

I think Sylvia, in one way or another, sensed this. In an introductory note she wrote to "Daddy" for the BBC, she said of the poem's narrator, "she has to act out the awful little allegory once over before she is free of it." The allegory in question was, as she saw it, the struggle in her between a fantasy Nazi father and a Jewish mother. But perhaps it was also a fantasy of containing in herself her own dead father, like a woman possessed by a demon (in the poem she actually calls him a vampire). In order for her to be free of him, he has to be released like a genie from a bottle. And this is precisely what the poems did: they bodied forth the death within her. But they also did so in an intensely living and creative way. The more she wrote about death, the stronger and more fertile her imaginative world became. And this gave her everything to live for.

I suspect that in the end she wanted to have done with the theme once and for all. But the only way she could find was "to act out the awful little allegory once over." She had always been a bit of a gambler, used to taking risks. The authority of her poetry was in part due to her brave persistence in following the thread of her inspiration right down to the Minotaur's lair. And this psychic courage had its parallel in her physical arrogance and carelessness. Risks didn't frighten her; on the contrary, she found them stimulating. Freud has written, "Life loses in interest, when the highest stake in the game of living, life itself, may not be risked." Finally, Sylvia took that risk. She gambled for the last time, having worked out that the odds were in her favor, but perhaps, in her depression, not much caring whether she won or lost. Her calculations went wrong and she lost.

It was a mistake, then, and out of it a whole myth has grown. I don't think she would have found it much to her taste, since it is a myth of the poet as a sacrificial victim, offering herself up for the sake of her art, having been dragged by the Muses to that final altar through every kind of distress. In these terms, her suicide becomes the whole point of the story, the act which validates her poems, gives them their interest, and proves her seriousness. So people are drawn to her work in much the same spirit as *Time* featured her at length: not for the poetry but for the gossipy, extra-literary "human interest." Yet just as the suicide adds nothing at all to the poetry, so the myth of Sylvia as a passive victim is a total perversion of the woman she was. It misses altogether her liveliness, her intellectual appetite and harsh wit, her great imaginative resourcefulness and vehemence of feeling, her control. Above all, it misses the courage with which she was able to turn disaster into art. The pity is not that there is a myth of Sylvia Plath but that the myth is not simply that of an enormously gifted poet whose death came recklessly, by mistake, and too soon.

I used to think of her brightness as a façade, as though she were able, in a rather schizoid way, to turn her back on her suffering for the sake of appearances, and pretend it didn't exist. But maybe she was also able to keep her unhappiness in check because she could write about it, because she knew she was salvaging from all those horrors something rather marvelous. The end came when she felt she could stand the subject no longer. She had written it out and was ready for something new.

> The blood-jet is poetry,
> There is no stopping it.

The only method of stopping it she could see, her vision by then blinkered by depression and illness, was that last gamble. So having, as she thought, arranged to be saved, she lay down in front of the gas oven almost hopefully, almost with relief, as though she were saying, "Perhaps this will set me free."

On Friday, February 15th, there was an inquest in the drab, damp coroner's court behind Camden Town: muttered evidence, long silences, the Australian girl in tears. Earlier that morning I had gone with Ted to the undertakers in Mornington Crescent. The coffin was at the far end of a bare, draped room. She lay stiffly, a ludicrous ruff at her neck. Only her face showed. It was gray and slightly transparent, like wax. I had never before seen a dead person and I hardly recognized her; her features seemed too thin and sharp. The room smelled of apples, faint, sweet but somehow unclean, as though the apples were beginning to rot. I was glad to get out into the cold and noise of the dingy streets. It seemed impossible that she was dead.

Even now I find it hard to believe. There was too much life in her long, flat, strongly boned body, and her longish face with its fine brown eyes, shrewd and full of feeling. She was practical and candid, passionate and compassionate. I believe she was a genius. I sometimes catch myself childishly thinking I'll run into her walking on Primrose Hill or the Heath, and we'll pick up the conversation where we left off. But perhaps that is because her poems still speak so distinctly in her accents: quick, sardonic, unpredictable, effortlessly inventive, a bit angry, and always utterly her own.

Suggestions for Discussion

1. What complications do you discern in the author's picture of Sylvia Plath's earlier background, her parents, her domestic life, and her early successes?

2. How does the author relate Sylvia Plath's poetry to her experience, especially in the case of "Daddy"?

3. What details and theories give support to Alvarez's views about the meaning of suicide for Sylvia Plath, the precipitating events leading to her last attempt, and her lack of intention to succeed in it?

4. Explain the statement in context, "For the artist, in short, nature often imitates art."

5. Study the organization of the memoir. How are earlier events in Plath's life related to the chronologically narrated incidents of the author's association with her? How does the author use his narrative to illuminate the poems he quotes?

6. Toward the end of the memoir, Alvarez objects to readers' being "drawn to her work . . . not for the poetry but for the gossipy, extraliterary 'human interest.' Yet the suicide adds nothing at all to the poetry. . . ." How can this statement be reconciled with his clarification of the poetry noted in question 5?

Suggestion for Writing

Read the poetry of Sylvia Plath or her early novel *The Bell Jar.* Attempt to account for the enormous impact her writing has on college students.

Maxine Hong Kingston
No Name Woman

Maxine Hong Kingston (b. 1940) was born in Stockton, California, and graduated from the University of California. Her two books, *The Woman Warrior*
(1976) from which this excerpt has been taken and *China Men* (1980), both
focus on her experiences as a Chinese American. "No Name Woman" graphically portrays the complex problems of cultural identity and implicitly suggests
the author's sense of self.

"You must not tell anyone," my mother said, "what I am about to tell you.
In China your father had a sister who killed herself. She jumped into the
family well. We say that your father has all brothers because it is as if she had
never been born.

"In 1924 just a few days after our village celebrated seventeen hurry-up
weddings—to make sure that every young man who went 'out on the road'
would responsibly come home—your father and his brothers and your grandfather and his brothers and your aunt's new husband sailed for America, the
Gold Mountain. It was your grandfather's last trip. Those lucky enough to get
contracts waved good-bye from the decks. They fed and guarded the stowa-
ways and helped them off in Cuba, New York, Bali, Hawaii. 'We'll meet in
California next year,' they said. All of them sent money home.

"I remember looking at your aunt one day when she and I were dressing;
I had not noticed before that she had such a protruding melon of a stomach.
But I did not think, 'She's pregnant,' until she began to look like other pregnant women, her shirt pulling and the white tops of her black pants showing.
She could not have been pregnant, you see, because her husband had been
gone for years. No one said anything. We did not discuss it. In early summer
she was ready to have the child, long after the time when it could have been
possible.

"The village had also been counting. On the night the baby was to be born
the villagers raided our house. Some were crying. Like a great saw, teeth
strung with lights, files of people walked zigzag across our land, tearing the
rice. Their lanterns doubled in the disturbed black water, which drained away
through the broken bunds. As the villagers closed in, we could see that some
of them, probably men and women we knew well, wore white masks. The
people with long hair hung it over their faces. Women with short hair made
it stand up on end. Some had tied white bands around their foreheads, arms,
and legs.

"At first they threw mud and rocks at the house. Then they threw eggs
and began slaughtering our stock. We could hear the animals scream their
deaths—the roosters, the pigs, a last great roar from the ox. Familiar wild
heads flared in our night windows; the villagers encircled us. Some of the
faces stopped to peer at us, their eyes rushing like searchlights. The hands
flattened against the panes, framed heads, and left red prints.

"The villagers broke in the front and the back doors at the same time, even though we had not locked the doors against them. Their knives dripped with the blood of our animals. They smeared blood on the doors and walls. One woman swung a chicken, whose throat she had slit, splattering blood in red arcs about her. We stood together in the middle of our house, in the family hall with the pictures and tables of the ancestors around us, and looked straight ahead.

"At that time the house had only two wings. When the men came back, we would build two more to enclose our courtyard and a third one to begin a second courtyard. The villagers rushed through both wings, even your grandparents' rooms, to find your aunt's, which was also mine until the men returned. From this room a new wing for one of the younger families would grow. They ripped up her clothes and shoes and broke her combs, grinding them underfoot. They tore her work from the loom. They scattered the cooking fire and rolled the new weaving in it. We could hear them in the kitchen breaking our bowls and banging the pots. They overturned the great waist-high earthenware jugs; duck eggs, pickled fruits, vegetables burst out and mixed in acrid torrents. The old woman from the next field swept a broom through the air and loosed the spirits-of-the-broom over our heads. 'Pig.' 'Ghost.' 'Pig,' they sobbed and scolded while they ruined our house.

"When they left, they took sugar and oranges to bless themselves. They cut pieces from the dead animals. Some of them took bowls that were not broken and clothes that were not torn. Afterward we swept up the rice and sewed it back up into sacks. But the smells from the spilled preserves lasted. Your aunt gave birth in the pigsty that night. The next morning when I went for the water, I found her and the baby plugging up the family well.

"Don't let your father know that I told you. He denies her. Now that you have started to menstruate, what happened to her could happen to you. Don't humiliate us. You wouldn't like to be forgotten as if you had never been born. The villagers are watchful."

Whenever she had to warn us about life, my mother told stories that ran like this one, a story to grow up on. She tested our strength to establish realities. Those in the emigrant generations who could not reassert brute survival died young and far from home. Those of us in the first American generations have had to figure out how the invisible world the emigrants built around our childhoods fit in solid America.

The emigrants confused the gods by diverting their curses, misleading them with crooked streets and false names. They must try to confuse their offspring as well, who, I suppose, threaten them in similar ways—always trying to get things straight, always trying to name the unspeakable. The Chinese I know hide their names; sojourners take new names when their lives change and guard their real names with silence.

Chinese-Americans, when you try to understand what things in you are Chinese, how do you separate what is peculiar to childhood, to poverty, insanities, one family, your mother who marked your growing with stories, from what is Chinese? What is Chinese tradition and what is the movies?

If I want to learn what clothes my aunt wore, whether flashy or ordinary, I would have to begin, "Remember Father's drowned-in-the-well sister?" I cannot ask that. My mother has told me once and for all the useful parts. She will add nothing unless powered by Necessity, a riverbank that guides her life. She plants vegetable gardens rather than lawns; she carries the odd-shaped tomatoes home from the fields and eats food left for the gods.

Whenever we did frivolous things, we used up energy; we flew high kites. We children came up off the ground over the melting cones our parents brought home from work and the American movie on New Year's Day—*Oh, You Beautiful Doll* with Betty Grable one year, and *She Wore a Yellow Ribbon* with John Wayne another year. After the one carnival ride each, we paid in guilt; our tired father counted his change on the dark walk home.

Adultery is extravagance. Could people who hatch their own chicks and eat the embryos and the heads for delicacies and boil the feet in vinegar for party food, leaving only the gravel, eating even the gizzard lining—could such people engender a prodigal aunt? To be a woman, to have a daughter in starvation time was a waste enough. My aunt could not have been the lone romantic who gave up everything for sex. Women in the old China did not choose. Some man had commanded her to lie with him and be his secret evil. I wonder whether he masked himself when he joined the raid on her family.

Perhaps she encountered him in the fields or on the mountain where the daughters-in-law collected fuel. Or perhaps he first noticed her in the market-place. He was not a stranger because the village housed no strangers. She had to have dealings with him other than sex. Perhaps he worked an adjoining field, or he sold her the cloth for the dress she sewed and wore. His demand must have surprised, then terrified her. She obeyed him; she always did as she was told.

When the family found a young man in the next village to be her husband, she stood tractably beside the best rooster, his proxy, and promised before they met that she would be his forever. She was lucky that he was her age and she would be the first wife, an advantage secure now. The night she first saw him, he had sex with her. Then he left for America. She had almost forgotten what he looked like. When she tried to envision him, she only saw the black and white face in the group photograph the men had had taken before leaving.

The other man was not, after all, much different from her husband. They both gave orders: she followed. "If you tell your family, I'll beat you. I'll kill you. Be here again next week." No one talked sex, ever. And she might have separated the rapes from the rest of living if only she did not have to buy her oil from him or gather wood in the same forest. I want her fear to have lasted just as long as rape lasted so that the fear could have been contained. No drawn-out fear. But women at sex hazarded birth and hence lifetimes. The fear did not stop but permeated everywhere. She told the man, "I think I'm pregnant." He organized the raid against her.

On nights when my mother and father talked about their life back home, sometimes they mentioned an "outcast table" whose business they still seemed to be settling, their voices tight. In a commensal tradition, where food is precious, the powerful older people made wrongdoers eat alone. Instead of letting them start separate new lives like the Japanese, who could become samurais and geishas, the Chinese family, faces averted but eyes glowering sideways, hung on to the offenders and fed them leftovers. My aunt must have lived in the same house as my parents and eaten at an outcast table. My mother spoke about the raid as if she had seen it, when she and my aunt, a daughter-in-law to a different household, should not have been living together at all. Daughters-in-law lived with their husbands' parents, not their own; a synonym for marriage in Chinese is "taking a daughter-in-law." Her husband's parents could have sold her, mortgaged her, stoned her. But they had sent her back to her own mother and father, a mysterious act hinting at disgraces not told me. Perhaps they had thrown her out to deflect the avengers.

She was the only daughter; her four brothers went with her father, husband, and uncles "out on the road" and for some years became western men. When the goods were divided among the family, three of the brothers took land, and the youngest, my father, chose an education. After my grandparents gave their daughter away to her husband's family, they had dispensed all the adventure and all the property. They expected her alone to keep the traditional ways, which her brothers, now among the barbarians, could fumble without detection. The heavy, deep-rooted women were to maintain the past against the flood, safe for returning. But the rare urge west had fixed upon our family, and so my aunt crossed boundaries not delineated in space.

The work of preservation demands that the feelings playing about in one's guts not be turned into action. Just watch their passing like cherry blossoms. But perhaps my aunt, my forerunner, caught in a slow life, let dreams grow and fade and after some months or years went toward what persisted. Fear at the enormities of the forbidden kept her desires delicate, wire and bone. She looked at a man because she liked the way the hair was tucked behind his ears, or she liked the question-mark line of a long torso curving at the shoulder and straight at the hip. For warm eyes or a soft voice or a slow walk—that's all—a few hairs, a line, a brightness, a sound, a pace, she gave up family. She offered us up for a charm that vanished with tiredness, a pigtail that didn't toss when the wind died. Why, the wrong lighting could erase the dearest thing about him.

It could very well have been, however, that my aunt did not take subtle enjoyment of her friend, but, a wild woman, kept rollicking company. Imagining her free with sex doesn't fit, though. I don't know any women like that, or men either. Unless I see her life branching into mine, she gives me no ancestral help.

To sustain her being in love, she often worked at herself in the mirror, guessing at the colors and shapes that would interest him, changing them frequently in order to hit on the right combination. She wanted him to look back.

On a farm near the sea, a woman who tended her appearance reaped a reputation for eccentricity. All the married women blunt-cut their hair in flaps about their ears or pulled it back in tight buns. No nonsense. Neither style blew easily into heart-catching tangles. And at their weddings they displayed themselves in their long hair for the last time. "It brushed the backs of my knees," my mother tells me. "It was braided, and even so, it brushed the backs of my knees."

At the mirror my aunt combed individuality into her bob. A bun could have been contrived to escape into black streamers blowing in the wind or in quiet wisps about her face, but only the older women in our picture album wear buns. She brushed her hair back from her forehead, tucking the flaps behind her ears. She looped a piece of thread, knotted into a circle between her index fingers and thumbs, and ran the double strand across her forehead.

When she closed her fingers as if she were making a pair of shadow geese bite, the string twisted together catching the little hairs. Then she pulled the thread away from her skin, ripping the hairs out neatly, her eyes watering from the needles of pain. Opening her fingers, she cleaned the thread, then rolled it along her hairline and the tops of her eyebrows. My mother did the same to me and my sisters and herself. I used to believe that the expression "caught by the short hairs" meant a captive held with a depilatory string. It especially hurt at the temples, but my mother said we were lucky we didn't have to have our feet bound when we were seven. Sisters used to sit on their beds and cry together, she said, as their mothers or their slave removed the bandages for a few minutes each night and let the blood gush back into their veins. I hope that the man my aunt loved appreciated a smooth brow, that he wasn't just a tits-and-ass man.

Once my aunt found a freckle on her chin, at a spot that the almanac said predestined her for unhappiness. She dug it out with a hot needle and washed the wound with peroxide.

More attention to her looks than these pullings of hairs and pickings at spots would have caused gossip among the villagers. They owned work clothes and good clothes, and they wore good clothes for feasting the new seasons. But since a woman combing her hair hexes beginnings, my aunt rarely found an occasion to look her best. Women looked like great sea snails—the corded wood, babies, and laundry they carried were the whorls on their backs. The Chinese did not admire a bent back; goddesses and warriors stood straight. Still there must have been a marvelous freeing of beauty when a worker laid down her burden and stretched and arched.

Such commonplace loveliness, however, was not enough for my aunt. She dreamed of a lover for the fifteen days of New Year's, the time for families to exchange visits, money, and food. She plied her secret comb. And sure enough she cursed the year, the family, the village, and herself.

Even as her hair lured her imminent lover, many other men looked at her. Uncles, cousins, nephews, brothers would have looked, too, had they been home between journeys. Perhaps they had already been restraining their curiosity, and they left, fearful that their glances, like a field of nesting birds, might be startled and caught. Poverty hurt, and that was their first reason for leaving. But another, final reason for leaving the crowded house was the never-said.

She may have been unusually beloved, the precious only daughter, spoiled and mirror gazing because of the affection the family lavished on her. When her husband left, they welcomed the chance to take her back from the in-laws; she could live like the little daughter for just a while longer. There are stories that my grandfather was different from other people, "crazy ever since the little Jap bayoneted him in the head." He used to put his naked penis on the dinner table, laughing. And one day he brought home a baby girl, wrapped up inside his brown western-style greatcoat. He had traded one of his sons, probably my father, the youngest, for her. My grandmother made him trade back. When he finally got a daughter of his own, he doted on her. They must have all loved her, except perhaps my father, the only brother who never went back to China, having once been traded for a girl.

Brothers and sisters, newly men and women, had to efface their sexual color and present plain miens. Disturbing hair and eyes, a smile like no other, threatened the ideal of five generations living under one roof. To focus blurs, people shouted face to face and yelled from room to room. The immigrants I know have loud voices, unmodulated to American tones even after years away from the village where they called their friendships out across the fields. I have not been able to stop my mother's screams in public libraries or over telephones. Walking erect (knees straight, toes pointed forward, not pigeon-toed, which is Chinese-feminine) and speaking in an inaudible voice, I have tired to turn myself American-feminine. Chinese communication was loud, public. Only sick people had to whisper. But at the dinner table, where the family members came nearest one another, no one could talk, not the outcasts nor any eaters. Every word that falls from the mouth is a coin lost. Silently they gave and accepted food with both hands. A preoccupied child who took his bowl with one hand got a sideways glare. A complete moment of total attention is due everyone alike. Children and lovers have no singularity here, but my aunt used a secret voice, a separate attentiveness.

She kept the man's name to herself throughout her labor and dying; she did not accuse him that he be punished with her. To save her inseminator's name she gave silent birth.

He may have been somebody in her own household, but intercourse with a man outside the family would have been no less abhorrent. All the village were kinsmen, and the titles shouted in loud country voices never let kinship be forgotten. Any man within visiting distance would have been neutralized as a lover—"brother," "younger brother," "older brother"—one hundred and fifteen relationship titles. Parents researched birth charts probably not so much to assure good fortune as to circumvent incest in a population that has but one hundred surnames. Everybody has eight million relatives. How useless then sexual mannerisms, how dangerous.

As if it came from an atavism deeper than fear, I used to add "brother" silently to boys' names. It hexed the boys, who would or would not ask me to dance, and made them less scary and as familiar and deserving of benevolence as girls.

But, of course, I hexed myself also—no dates. I should have stood up, both arms waving, and shouted out across libraries, "Hey, you! Love me back." I had no idea, though, how to make attraction selective, how to control its direction and magnitude. If I made myself American-pretty so that the five or six Chinese boys in the class fell in love with me, everyone else—the Caucasian, Negro, and Japanese boys—would too. Sisterliness, dignified and honorable, made much more sense.

Attraction eludes control so stubbornly that whole societies designed to organize relationships among people cannot keep order, not even when they bind people to one another from childhood and raise them together. Among the very poor and the wealthy, brothers married their adopted sisters, like doves. Our family allowed some romance, paying adult brides' prices and providing dowries so that their sons and daughters could marry strangers. Marriage promises to turn strangers into friendly relatives—a nation of siblings.

In the village structure, spirits shimmered among the live creatures, balanced and held in equilibrium by time and land. But one human being flaring up into violence could open up a black hole, a maelstrom that pulled in the sky. The frightened villagers, who depended on one another to maintain the real, went to my aunt to show her a personal, physical representation of the break she had made in the "roundness." Misallying couples snapped off the future, which was to be embodied in true offspring. The villagers punished her for acting as if she could have a private life, secret and apart from them.

If my aunt had betrayed the family at a time of large grain yields and peace, when many boys were born, and wings were being built on many houses, perhaps she might have escaped such severe punishment. But the men—hungry, greedy, tired of planting in dry soil, cuckolded—had had to leave the village in order to send food-money home. There were ghost plagues, bandit plagues, wars with the Japanese, floods. My Chinese brother and sister had died of an unknown sickness. Adultery, perhaps only a mistake during good times, became a crime when the village needed food.

The round moon cakes and round doorways, the round tables of graduated size that fit one roundness inside another, round windows and rice bowls— these talismans had lost their power to warn this family of the law: a family must be whole, faithfully keeping the descent line by having sons to feed the old and the dead, who in turn look after the family. The villagers came to show my aunt and her lover-in-hiding a broken house. The villagers were speeding up the circling of events because she was too shortsighted to see that her infidelity had already harmed the village, that waves of consequences would return unpredictably, sometimes in disguise, as now, to hurt her. This roundness had to be made coin-sized so that she would see its circumference: punish her at the birth of her baby. Awaken her to the inexorable. People who refused fatalism because they could invent small resources insisted on culpability. Deny accidents and wrest fault from the stars.

After the villagers left, their lanterns now scattering in various directions toward home, the family broke their silence and cursed her. "Aiaa, we're going to die. Death is coming. Death is coming. Look what you've done. You've killed us. Ghost! Dead ghost! Ghost! You've never been born." She ran out into the fields, far enough from the house so that she could no longer hear their voices, and pressed herself against the earth, her own land no more. When she felt the birth coming, she thought that she had been hurt. Her body seized together. "They've hurt me too much," she thought. "This is gall, and it will kill me." With forehead and knees against the earth, her body convulsed and then relaxed. She turned on her back, lay on the ground. The black well of sky and stars went out and out and out forever; her body and her complexity seemed to disappear, without home, without a companion, in eternal cold and silence. An agoraphobia rose in her, speeding higher and higher, bigger and bigger; she would not be able to contain it; there would be no end to fear.

Flayed, unprotected against space, she felt pain return, focusing her body. This pain chilled her—a cold, steady kind of surface pain. Inside, spasmodically, the other pain, the pain of the child, heated her. For hours she lay on the ground, alternately body and space. Sometimes a vision of normal comfort obliterated reality: she saw the family in the evening gambling at the dinner table, the young people massaging their elders' backs. She saw them congratulating one another, high joy on the mornings the rice shoots came up. When these pictures burst, the stars drew yet further apart. Black space opened.

She got to her feet to fight better and remembered that old-fashioned women gave birth in their pigsties to fool the jealous, pain-dealing gods, who do not snatch piglets. Before the next spasms could stop her, she ran to the pigsty, each step a rushing out into emptiness. She climbed over the fence and knelt in the dirt. It was good to have a fence enclosing her, a tribal person alone.

Laboring, this woman who had carried her child as a foreign growth that sickened her every day, expelled it at last. She reached down to touch the hot, wet, moving mass, surely smaller than anything human, and could feel that it was human after all—fingers, toes, nails, nose. She pulled it up on to her belly, and it lay curled there, butt in the air, feet precisely tucked one under the other. She opened her loose shirt and buttoned the child inside. After resting, it squirmed and thrashed and she pushed it up to her breast. It turned its head this way and that until it found her nipple. There, it made little snuffling noises. She clenched her teeth at its preciousness, lovely as a young calf, a piglet, a little dog.

She may have gone to the pigsty as a last act of responsibility: she would protect this child as she had protected its father. It would look after her soul, leaving supplies on her grave. But how would this tiny child without family find her grave when there would be no marker for her anywhere, neither in the earth nor the family hall? No one would give her a family hall name. She had taken the child with her into the wastes. At its birth the two of them had felt the same raw pain of separation, a wound that only the family pressing tight could close. A child with no descent line would not soften her life but only trail after her, ghost-like, begging her to give it purpose. At dawn the villagers on their way to the fields would stand around the fence and look.

Full of milk, the little ghost slept. When it awoke, she hardened her breasts against the milk that crying loosens. Toward morning she picked up the baby and walked to the well.

Carrying the baby to the well shows loving. Otherwise abandon it. Turn its face into the mud. Mothers who love their children take them along. It was probably a girl; there is some hope of forgiveness for boys.

"Don't tell anyone you had an aunt. Your father does not want to hear her name. She has never been born." I have believed that sex was unspeakable and words so strong and fathers so frail that "aunt" would do my father mysterious harm. I have thought that my family, having settled among immigrants who had also been their neighbors in the ancestral land, needed to clean their name, and a wrong word would incite the kinspeople even here. But there is more to this silence: they want me to participate in her punishment. And I have.

In the twenty years since I heard this story I have not asked for details nor said my aunt's name; I do not know it. People who can comfort the dead can also chase after them to hurt them further—a reverse ancestor worship. The real punishment was not the raid swiftly inflicted by the villagers, but the family's deliberately forgetting her. Her betrayal so maddened them, they saw to it that she would suffer forever, even after death. Always hungry, always needing, she would have to beg food from other ghosts, snatch and steal it from those whose living descendants give them gifts. She would have to fight the ghosts massed at crossroads for the buns a few thoughtful citizens leave to decoy her away from village and home so that the ancestral spirits could feast unharassed. At peace, they could act like gods, not ghosts, their descent lines providing them with paper suits and dresses, spirit money, paper houses, paper automobiles, chicken, meat, and rice into eternity—essences delivered up in smoke and flames, steam and incense rising from each rice bowl. In an attempt to make the Chinese care for people outside the family, Chairman Mao encourages us now to give our paper replicas to the spirits of outstanding soldiers and workers, no matter whose ancestors they may be. My aunt remains forever hungry. Goods are not distributed evenly among the dead.

My aunt haunts me—her ghost drawn to me because now, after fifty years of neglect, I alone devote pages of paper to her, though not origamied into houses and clothes. I do not think she always means me well. I am telling on her, and she was a spite suicide, drowning herself in the drinking water. The Chinese are always very frightened of the drowned one, whose weeping ghost, wet hair hanging and skin bloated, waits silently by the water to pull down a substitute.

Suggestions for Discussion

1. What is the tone of the author's address to Chinese Americans? In what sense does this paragraph logically follow her mother's story?

2. Why must Chinese emigrants try to confuse their offspring as well as "the gods"?

3. How did the author piece together the reasons for her aunt's adultery?

4. With what details does the reader get a picture of the lives of daughters in old China?

5. What does the phrase "taking a daughter-in-law" as a synonym for marriage tell the reader about men–women relationships in old China?

6. With what details do you learn about differing attitudes toward boys and girls?

7. Compare the conjectured and real behavior of the aunt's lover with hers after her ostracism.

8. How did the economy, plagues, floods, and wars affect attitudes toward adultery?

9. Trace the organization of the aunt's story. Compare the way in which it is narrated in the mother's words and in those of the author? What purpose is served by the author's intervening introspections?

10. How does the author account for the aunt's suicide?

11. How does Kingston convey that the story of her aunt was a story "to grow up on"? Kingston speaks of being haunted by the ghost of her aunt. What do her introspections tell you implicitly of her sense of self?

Suggestions for Writing

1. Narrate a story "to grow up on" which tested your "strength to establish realities."

2. The critic, John Leonard, called the book, in which this is the first chapter, "a poem turned into a sword." Justify this assessment by analyzing the writer's diction and tone.

◇◇◇◇

Maya Angelou
Finishing School

Maya Angelou (b. 1928) has had careers as dancer, poet, television writer and producer, actress, and writer. She has served as coordinator of the Martin Luther King Southern Christian Leadership Conference. Her books include *I Know Why the Caged Bird Sings* (1970), from which this selection is taken, and a recent memoir, *The Heart of a Woman* (1981). The irony of the title is immediately apparent to the reader of this graphic portrait of Angelou's racist employer.

Recently a white woman from Texas, who would quickly describe herself as a liberal, asked me about my hometown. When I told her that in Stamps my grandmother had owned the only Negro general merchandise store since the turn of the century, she exclaimed, "Why, you were a debutante." Ridiculous and even ludicrous. But Negro girls in small Southern towns, whether poverty-stricken or just munching along on a few of life's necessities, were given as extensive and irrelevant preparations for adulthood as rich white girls shown in magazines. Admittedly the training was not the same. While white girls learned to waltz and sit gracefully with a tea cup balanced on their knees, we were lagging behind, learning the mid-Victorian values with very little money to indulge them. . . .

We were required to embroider and I had trunkfuls of colorful dishtowels, pillowcases, runners and handkerchiefs to my credit. I mastered the art of crocheting and tatting, and there was a life-time's supply of dainty doilies that would never be used in sacheted dresser drawers. It went without saying that all girls could iron and wash, but the finer touches around the home, like setting a table with real silver, baking roasts, and cooking vegetables without meat, had to be learned elsewhere. Usually at the source of those habits. During my tenth year, a white woman's kitchen became my finishing school.

Mrs. Viola Cullinan was a plump woman who lived in a three-bedroom house somewhere behind the post office. She was singularly unattractive until she smiled, and then the lines around her eyes and mouth which made her look perpetually dirty disappeared, and her face looked like the mask of an impish elf. She usually rested her smile until late afternoon when her women friends dropped in and Miss Glory, the cook, served them cold drinks on the closed-in porch.

The exactness of her house was inhuman. This glass went here and only here. That cup had its place and it was an act of impudent rebellion to place it anywhere else. At twelve-o'clock the table was set. At 12:15 Mrs. Cullinan sat down to dinner (whether her husband had arrived or not). At 12:16 Miss Glory brought out the food.

It took me a week to learn the difference between a salad plate, a bread plate, and a dessert plate.

Mrs. Cullinan kept up the tradition of her wealthy parents. She was from Virginia. Miss Glory, who was a descendant of slaves that had worked for the

Cullinans, told me her history. She had married beneath her (according to Miss Glory). Her husband's family hadn't had their money very long and what they had "didn't 'mount to much."

As ugly as she was, I thought privately, she was lucky to get a husband above or beneath her station. But Miss Glory wouldn't let me say a thing against her mistress. She was very patient with me, however, over the housework. She explained the dishware, silverware, and servants' bells. The large round bowl in which soup was served wasn't a soup bowl, it was a tureen. There were goblets, sherbet glasses, ice-cream glasses, wine glasses, green glass coffee cups with matching saucers, and water glasses. I had a glass to drink from, and it sat with Miss Glory's on a separate shelf from the others. Soup spoons, gravy boat, butter knives, salad forks, and carving platter were additions to my vocabulary and in fact almost represented a new language. I was fascinated with the novelty, with the fluttering Mrs. Cullinan and her Alice-in-Wonderland house.

Her husband remains, in my memory, undefined. I lumped him with all the other white men that I had ever seen and tried not to see.

On our way home one evening, Miss Glory told me that Mrs. Cullinan couldn't have children. She said that she was too delicate-boned. It was hard to imagine bones at all under those layers of fat. Miss Glory went on to say that the doctor had taken out all her lady organs. I reasoned that a pig's organs included the lungs, heart and liver, so if Mrs. Cullinan was walking around without those essentials, it explained why she drank alcohol out of unmarked bottles. She was keeping herself embalmed.

When I spoke to Bailey about it, he agreed that I was right, but he also informed me that Mr. Cullinan had two daughters by a colored lady and that I knew them very well. He added that the girls were the spitting image of their father. I was unable to remember what he looked like, although I had just left him a few hours before, but I thought of the Coleman girls. They were very light-skinned and certainly didn't look very much like their mother (no one ever mentioned Mr. Coleman).

My pity for Mrs. Cullinan preceded me the next morning like the Cheshire cat's smile. Those girls, who could have been her daughters, were beautiful. They didn't have to straighten their hair. Even when they were caught in the rain, their braids still hung down straight like tamed snakes. Their mouths were pouty little cupid's bows. Mrs. Cullinan didn't know what she missed. Or maybe she did. Poor Mrs. Cullinan.

For weeks after, I arrived early, left late and tried very hard to make up for her barrenness. If she had had her own children, she wouldn't have had to ask me to run a thousand errands from her back door to the back door of her friends. Poor old Mrs. Cullinan.

Then one evening Miss Glory told me to serve the ladies on the porch. After I set the tray down and turned toward the kitchen, one of the women asked, "What's your name, girl?" It was the speckled-face one. Mrs. Cullinan said, "She doesn't talk much. Her name's Margaret."

"Is she dumb?"

"No. As I understand it, she can talk when she wants to but she's usually quiet as a little mouse. Aren't you, Margaret?"

I smiled at her. Poor thing. No organs and couldn't even pronounce my name correctly.

"She's a sweet little thing, though."

"Well, that may be, but the name's too long. I'd never bother myself. I'd call her Mary if I was you."

I fumed into the kitchen. That horrible woman would never have the chance to call me Mary because if I was starving I'd never work for her. . . .

That evening I decided to write a poem on being white, fat, old and without children. It was going to be a tragic ballad. I would have to watch her carefully to capture the essence of her loneliness and pain.

The very next day, she called my by the wrong name. Miss Glory and I were washing up the lunch dishes when Mrs. Cullinan came to the doorway. "Mary?"

Miss Glory asked, "Who?"

Mrs. Cullinan, sagging a little, knew and I knew. "I want Mary to go down to Mrs. Randall's and take her some soup. She's not been feeling well for a few days."

Miss Glory's face was a wonder to see. "You mean Margaret, ma'am. Her name's Margaret."

"That's too long. She's Mary from now on. Heat that soup from last night and put it in the china tureen and, Mary, I want you to carry it carefully."

Every person I knew had a hellish horror of being "called out of his name." It was a dangerous practice to call a Negro anything that could be loosely construed as insulting because of the centuries of their having been called niggers, jigs, dinges, blackbirds, crows, boots and spooks.

Miss Glory had a fleeting second of feeling sorry for me. Then as she handed me the hot tureen she said, "Don't mind, don't pay that no mind. Sticks and stones may break your bones, but words . . . You know, I been working for her for twenty years."

She held the back door open for me. "Twenty years. I wasn't much older than you. My name used to be Hallelujah. That's what Ma named me, but my mistress give me 'Glory,' and it stuck. I likes it better too."

I was in the little path that ran behind the houses when Miss Glory shouted. "It's shorter too."

For a few seconds it was a tossup over whether I would laugh (imagine being named Hallelujah) or cry (imagine letting some white woman rename you for her convenience). My anger saved me from either outburst. I had to quit the job, but the problem was going to be how to do it. Momma wouldn't allow me to quit for just any reason.

"She's a peach. That woman is a real peach." Mrs. Randall's maid was talking as she took the soup from me, and I wondered what her name used to be and what she answered to now.

For a week I looked into Mrs. Cullinan's face as she called me Mary. She ignored my coming late and leaving early. Miss Glory was a little annoyed because I had begun to leave egg yolk on the dishes and wasn't putting much heart in polishing the silver. I hoped that she would complain to our boss, but she didn't.

Then Bailey solved my dilemma. He had me describe the contents of the cupboard and the particular plates she liked best. Her favorite piece was a casserole shaped like a fish and the green glass coffee cups. I kept his instructions in mind, so on the next day when Miss Glory was hanging out clothes and I had again been told to serve the old biddies on the porch, I dropped the empty serving tray. When I heard Mrs. Cullinan scream, "Mary!" I picked up the casserole and two of the green glass cups in readiness. As she rounded the kitchen door I let them fall on the tiled floor.

I could never absolutely describe to Bailey what happened next, because each time I got to the part where she fell on the floor and screwed up her ugly face to cry, we burst out laughing. She actually wobbled around on the floor and picked up shards of the cups and cried, "Oh, Momma. Oh, dear Gawd. It's Momma's china from Virginia. Oh, Momma, I sorry."

Miss Glory came running in from the yard and the women from the porch crowded around. Miss Glory was almost as broken up as her mistress. "You mean to say she broke our Virginia dishes? What we gone do?"

Mrs. Cullinan cried louder, "That clumsy nigger. Clumsy little black nigger."

Old speckled-face leaned down and asked, "Who did it, Viola? Was it Mary? Who did it?"

Everything was happening so fast I can't remember whether her action preceded her words, but I know that Mrs. Cullinan said, "Her name's Margaret, goddamn it, her name's Margaret." And she threw a wedge of the broken plate at me. It could have been the hysteria which put her aim off, but the flying crockery caught Miss Glory right over her ear and she started screaming.

I left the front door wide open so all the neighbors could hear.

Mrs. Cullinan was right about one thing. My name wasn't Mary.

Suggestions for Discussion

1. With what details does Angelou bring the Cullinan household to life?

2. Angelou's changed views of Mrs. Cullinan are very marked. Characterize the contrasting portraits and suggest the means by which each is made graphic.

3. What is the significance of the name changes? How do they contribute to Angelou's view of Mrs. Cullinan?

4. Angelou uses fresh and surprising language on occasion; how does the phrase (par. 1) "munching along on a few of life's necessities" contribute to her reminiscence? She states that Mrs. Viola Cullinan usually "rested her smile until late afternoon." What does that description tell you about her employer?

5. What does the enumeration of each type of glass and silverware contribute to Angelou's thesis?

6. What is Angelou's central thesis? Relate the title to her experiences? To whom does it appear to be addressed?

7. How would you describe the tone of the piece? Cite examples in which the diction contributes to the tone. Cite examples of irony.

Suggestions for Writing

1. Describe a person or situation in which your initial impressions were reversed or changed. By means of setting, characterization, dialogue, figurative language, and simple narrative account for your shifts in attitude.

2. Write a narrative in which you or a person you know are the victim of discrimination or injustice.

Lillian Hellman

An Unfinished Woman

Lillian Hellman (b. 1905) is an American playright who has focused on psychological and social themes in such works as *The Children's Hour* (1934), *The Little Foxes* (1939), *Watch on the Rhine* (1941), *Another Part of the Forest* (1946), and *The Autumn Garden* (1951). She also worked as a professional play reader and a book reviewer for the *New York Herald Tribune,* and in 1966 she edited *The Short Novels of Dashiell Hammett.* She has published two memoirs, *An Unfinished Woman* (1969) and *Pentimento* (1973). In this memoir the adolescent Hellman makes some significant and rather terrifying discoveries about herself.

I was, they told me, turning into a handful. Mrs. Stillman said I was wild, Mr. Stillman said that I would, of course, bring pain to my mother and father, and Fizzy said I was just plain disgusting mean. It had been a bad month for me. I had, one night, fallen asleep in the fig tree and, coming down in the morning, refused to tell my mother where I had been. James Denery the Third had hit me very hard in a tug-of-war and I had waited until the next day to hit him over the head with a porcelain coffee pot and then his mother complained to my mother. I had also refused to go back to dancing class.

And I was now spending most of my time with a group from an orphanage down the block. I guess the orphan group was no more attractive than any other, but to be an orphan seemed to me desirable and a self-made piece of independence. In any case, the orphans were more interesting to me than my schoolmates, and if they played rougher they complained less. Frances, a dark beauty of my age, queened it over the others because her father had been killed by the Mafia. Miriam, small and wiry, regularly stole my allowance from the red purse my aunt had given me, and the one time I protested she beat me up. Louis Calda was religious and spoke to me about it. Pancho was dark, sad, and to me, a poet, because once he said, "*Yo te amo.*" I could not sleep a full night after this declaration, and it set up in me forever after both sympathy and irritability with the first sexual stirrings of little girls, so masked, so complex, so foolish as compared with the sex of little boys. It was Louis Calda who took Pancho and me to a Catholic Mass that could have made me a fourteen-year-old convert. But Louis explained that he did not think me worthy, and Pancho, to stop my tears, cut off a piece of his hair with a knife, gave it to me as a gift from royalty, and then shoved me into the gutter. I don't know why I thought this an act of affection, but I did, and went home to open the back of a new wristwatch my father had given me for my birthday and to put the lock of hair in the back. A day later when the watched stopped, my father insisted I give it to him immediately, declaring that the jeweler was unreliable.

It was that night that I disappeared, and that night that Fizzy said I was disgusting mean, and Mr. Stillman said I would forever pain my mother and father, and my father turned on both of them and said he would handle his family affairs himself without comments from strangers. But he said it too late. He had come home very angry with me: the jeweler, after my father's complaints about his unreliability, had found the lock of hair in the back of the watch. What started out to be a mild reproof on my father's part soon turned angry when I wouldn't explain about the hair. (My father was often angry when I was most like him.) He was so angry that he forgot that he was attacking me in front of the Stillmans, my old rival Fizzy, and the delighted Mrs. Dreyfus, a new, rich boarder who only that afternoon had complained about my bad manners. My mother left the room when my father grew angry with me. Hannah, passing through, put up her hand as if to stop my father and then, frightened of the look he gave her, went out to the porch. I sat on the couch, astonished at the pain in my head. I tried to get up from the couch, but one ankle turned and I sat down again, knowing for the first time the rampage that could be caused in me by anger. The room began to have other forms, the people were no longer men and women, my head was not my own. I told myself that my head had gone somewhere and I have little memory of anything after my Aunt Jenny came into the room and said to my father, "Don't you remember?" I have never known what she meant, but I knew that soon after I was moving up the staircase, that I slipped and fell a few steps, that when I woke up hours later in my bed, I found a piece of angel cake—an old love, an old custom—left by my mother on my pillow. The headache was worse and I vomited out of the window. Then I dressed, took my red purse, and walked a long way down St. Charles Avenue. A St. Charles Avenue mansion had on its back lawn a famous doll's-house, an elaborate copy of the mansion itself, built years before for the small daughter of the house. As I passed this showpiece, I saw a policeman and moved swiftly back to the doll palace and crawled inside. If I had known about the fantasies of the frightened, that ridiculous small house would not have been so terrible for me. I was surrounded by ornate, carved reproductions of the mansion furniture, scaled for children, bisque figurines in miniature, a working toilet seat of gold leaf in suitable size, small draperies of damask with a sign that said "From the damask of Marie Antoinette," a miniature samovar with small bronze cups, and a tiny Madame Récamier couch on which I spent the night, my legs on the floor. I must have slept, because I woke from a nightmare and knocked over a bisque figurine. The noise frightened me, and since it was now almost light, in one of those lovely mist mornings of late spring when every flower in New Orleans seems to melt and mix with the air, I crawled out. Most of that day I spent walking, although I had a long session in the ladies' room of the railroad station. I had four dollars and two bits, but that wasn't much when you meant it to last forever and when you knew it would not be easy for a fourteen-year-old girl to find work in a city where too many people knew her. Three times I stood in line at the railroad ticket windows to ask where I could go for four dollars, but each time the question seemed too dangerous and I knew no other way of asking it.

Toward evening, I moved to the French Quarter, feeling sad and envious as people went home to dinner. I bought a few Tootsie Rolls and a half loaf of bread and went to the St. Louis Cathedral in Jackson Square. (It was that night that I composed the prayer that was to become, in the next five years, an obsession, mumbled over and over through the days and nights: "God forgive me, Papa forgive me, Mama forgive me, Sophronia, Jenny, Hannah, and all others, through this time and that time, in life and in death." When I was nineteen, my father, who had made several attempts through the years to find out what my lip movements meant as I repeated the prayer, said, "How much would you take to stop that? Name it and you've got it." I suppose I was sick of the nonsense by that time because I said, "A leather coat and a feather fan," and the next day he bought them for me.) After my loaf of bread, I went looking for a bottle of soda pop and discovered, for the first time, the whorehouse section around Bourbon Street. The women were ranged in the doorways of the cribs, making the first early evening offers to sailors, who were the only men in the streets. I wanted to stick around and see how things like that worked, but the second or third time I circled the block, one of the girls called out to me. I couldn't understand the words, but the voice was angry enough to make me run toward the French Market.

The Market was empty except for two old men. One of them called to me as I went past, and I turned to see that he had opened his pants and was shaking what my circle called "his thing." I flew across the street into the coffee stand, forgetting that the owner had known me since I was a small child when my Aunt Jenny would rest from her marketing tour with a cup of fine, strong coffee.

He said, in the patois, *"Que faites, ma 'fant? Je suis fermé."*

I said, *"Rien. Ma tante attend*—Could I have a doughnut?"

He brought me two doughnuts, saying one was *lagniappe,* but I took my doughnuts outside when he said *"Mais où est vo' tante à c'heure?"*

I fell asleep with my doughnuts behind a shrub in Jackson Square. The night was damp and hot and through the sleep there were many voices and, much later, there was music from somewhere near the river. When all sounds had ended, I woke, turned my head, and knew I was being watched. Two rats were sitting a few feet from me. I urinated on my dress, crawled backwards to stand up, screamed as I ran up the steps of St. Louis Cathedral and pounded on the doors. I don't know when I stopped screaming or how I got to the railroad station, but I stood against the wall trying to tear off my dress and only knew I was doing it when two women stopped to stare at me. I began to have cramps in my stomach of a kind I had never known before. I went into the ladies' room and sat bent in a chair, whimpering with pain. After a while the cramps stopped, but I had an intimation, when I looked into the mirror, of something happening to me: my face was blotched, and there seemed to be circles and twirls I had never seen before, the straight blonde hair was damp with sweat, and a paste of green from the shrub had made lines on my jaw. I had gotten older.

Sometime during that early morning I half washed my dress, threw away my pants, put cold water on my hair. Later in the morning a cleaning woman appeared, and after a while began to ask questions that frightened me. When she put down her mop and went out of the room, I ran out of the station. I walked, I guess, for many hours, but when I saw a man on Canal Street who worked in Hannah's office, I realized that the sections of New Orleans that were known to me were dangerous for me.

Years before, when I was a small child, Sophronia and I would go to pick up, or try on, pretty embroidered dresses that were made for me by a colored dressmaker called Bibettera. A block up from Bibettera's there had been a large ruin of a house with a sign, ROOMS—CLEAN—CHEAP, and cheerful people seemed always to be moving in and out of the house. The door of the house was painted a bright pink. I liked that and would discuss with Sophronia why we didn't live in a house with a pink door.

Bibettera was long since dead, so I knew I was safe in this Negro neighborhood. I went up and down the block several times, praying that things would work and I could take my cramps to bed. I knocked on the pink door. It was answered immediately by a small young man.

I said, "Hello." He said nothing.

I said, "I would like to rent a room, please."

He closed the door but I waited, thinking he had gone to get the lady of the house. After a long time, a middle-aged woman put her head out of a second-floor-window and said, "What you at?"

I said, "I would like to rent a room, please. My mama is a widow and has gone to work across the river. She gave me money and said to come here until she called for me."

"Who your mama?"

"Er. My mama."

"What you at? Speak out."

"I told you. I have money . . ." But as I tried to open my purse, the voice grew angry.

"This is a nigger house. Get you off. *Vite.*"

I said, in a whisper, "I know. I'm part nigger."

The small young man opened the front door. He was laughing. "You part mischief. Get the hell out of here."

I said, "Please"—and then, "I'm related to Sophronia Mason. She told me to come. Ask her."

Sophronia and her family were respected figures in New Orleans Negro circles, and because I had some vague memory of her stately bow to somebody as she passed this house, I believed they knew her. If they told her about me I would be in trouble, but phones were not usual then in poor neighborhoods, and I had no other place to go.

The woman opened the door. Slowly I went into the hall.

I said, "I won't stay long. I have four dollars and Sophronia will give more if . . ."

The woman pointed up the stairs. She opened the door of a small room. "Washbasin place down the hall. Toilet place behind the kitchen. Two-fifty and no fuss, no bother."

I said, "Yes ma'am, yes ma'am," but as she started to close the door, the young man appeared.

"Where your bag?"

"Bag?"

"Nobody put up here without no bag."

"Oh. You mean the bag with my clothes? It's at the station. I'll go and get it later . . ." I stopped because I knew I was about to say I'm sick, I'm in pain, I'm frightened.

He said, "I say you lie. I say you trouble. I say you get out."

I said, "And I say you shut up."

Years later, I was to understand why the command worked, and to be sorry that it did, but that day I was very happy when he turned and closed the door. I was asleep within minutes.

Toward evening, I went down the stairs, saw nobody, walked a few blocks and bought myself an oyster loaf. But the first bite made me feel sick, so I took my loaf back to the house. This time, as I climbed the steps, there were three women in the parlor, and they stopped talking when they saw me. I went back to sleep immediately, dizzy and nauseated.

I woke to a high, hot sun and my father standing at the foot of the bed staring at the oyster loaf.

He said, "Get up now and get dressed."

I was crying as I said, "Thank you, Papa, but I can't."

From the hall, Sophronia said, "Get along up now. *Vite.* The morning is late."

My father left the room. I dressed and came into the hall carrying my oyster loaf. Sophronia was standing at the head of the stairs. She pointed out, meaning my father was on the street.

I said, "He humiliated me. He did. I won't . . ."

She said, "Get you going or I will never see you whenever again."

I ran past her to the street. I stood with my father until Sophronia joined us, and then we walked slowly, without speaking, to the streetcar line. Sophronia bowed to us, but she refused my father's hand when he attempted to help her into the car. I ran to the car meaning to ask her to take me with her, but the car moved and she raised her hand as if to stop me. My father and I walked again for a long time.

He pointed to a trash can sitting in front of a house. "Please put that oyster loaf in the can."

At Vanalli's restaurant, he took my arm. "Hungry?"

I said, "No, thank you, Papa."

But we went through the door. It was, in those days, a New Orleans custom to have an early black coffee, go to the office, and after a few hours have a large breakfast at a restaurant. Vanalli's was crowded, the headwaiter was so sorry, but after my father took him aside, a very small table was put up for us—too small for my large father, who was accommodating himself to it in a manner most unlike him.

He said, "Jack, my rumpled daughter would like cold crayfish, a nice piece of pompano, a separate bowl of Béarnaise sauce, don't ask me why, French fried potatoes . . ."

I said, "Thank you, Papa, but I am not hungry. I don't want to be here."

My father waved the waiter away and we sat in silence until the crayfish came. My hand reached out instinctively and then drew back.

My father said, "Your mother and I have had an awful time."

I said, "I'm sorry about that. But I don't want to go home, Papa."

He said, angrily, "Yes, you do. But you want me to apologize first. I do apologize but you should not have made me say it."

After a while I mumbled, "God forgive me, Papa forgive me, Mama forgive me, Sophronia, Jenny, Hannah . . ."

"Eat your crayfish."

I ate everything he had ordered and then a small steak. I suppose I had been mumbling throughout my breakfast.

My father said, "You're talking to yourself. I can't hear you. What are you saying?"

"God forgive me, Papa forgive me, Mama forgive me, Sophronia, Jenny . . ."

My father said, "Where do we start your training as the first Jewish nun on Prytania Street?"

When I finished laughing, I liked him again. I said, "Papa, I'll tell you a secret. I've had very bad cramps and I am beginning to bleed. I'm changing life."

He stared at me for a while. Then he said, "Well, it's not the way it's usually described, but it's accurate, I guess. Let's go home now to your mother."

We were never, as long as my mother and father lived, to mention that time again. But it was of great importance to them and I've thought about it all my life. From that day on I knew my power over my parents. That was not to be too important: I was ashamed of it and did not abuse it too much. But I found out something more useful and more dangerous: if you are willing to take the punishment, you are halfway through the battle. That the issue may be trivial, the battle ugly, is another point.

Suggestions for Discussion

1. What do the details describing Hellman's "bad month" tell you about her personality? How are you led to account for her behavior?

2. What is conveyed about Hellman's relationship to Sophronia? What is Sophronia's attitude toward Hellman's escapade? What is the attitude toward Hellman of the people in the household with the pink door?

3. In what sense is this a narrative of initiation?

4. How are Hellman's feelings about her mother and father conveyed?

5. What did the author's running away from home tell her about herself?

6. What is the significance of Hellman's prayer? Account for her father's attitude toward it.

7. In the last paragraph the author makes a distinction between the two lessons she learned. What is it?

Suggestions for Writing

1. Write a narrative in which you recall an episode in your early adolescence and suggest its significance to your life.

2. Did you ever exercise your "power" over your parents? Describe an episode in which you took advantage of their concern and caring for you.

◇◇◇◇

Alice Walker
When the Other Dancer is the Self

Alice Walker (b. 1944) has received numerous awards for her fiction: *The Color Purple* (1982), a best-selling novel, was nominated for the Book Critics' Circle Award and received the American Book Award, the Candace Award of the National Coalition of 100 Black Women, and a Pulitzer Prize. She has also published two collections of short stories, *You Can't Keep a Good Woman Down* (1981) and *In Love and Trouble.* Her most recent book, *In Search of Our Mothers' Gardens: Womanist Prose* (1983), includes this reminiscence of the effect of a traumatic injury to her eye on her self image.

It is a bright summer day in 1947. My father, a fat, funny man with beautiful eyes and a subversive wit, is trying to decide which of his eight children he will take with him to the county fair. My mother, of course, will not go. She is knocked out from getting most of us ready: I hold my neck stiff against the pressure of her knuckles as she hastily completes the braiding and then be-ribboning of my hair.

My father is the driver for the rich old white lady up the road. Her name is Miss Mey. She owns all the land for miles around, as well as the house in which we live. All I remember about her is that she once offered to pay my mother thirty-five cents for cleaning her house, raking up piles of her magnolia leaves, and washing her family's clothes, and that my mother—she of no money, eight children, and a chronic earache—refused it. But I do not think of this in 1947. I am two and a half years old. I want to go everywhere my daddy goes. I am excited at the prospect of riding in a car. Someone has told me fairs are fun. That there is room in the car for only three of us doesn't faze me at all. Whirling happily in my starchy frock, showing off my biscuit-polished patent-leather shoes and lavender socks, tossing my head in a way that makes my ribbons bounce, I stand, hands on hips, before my father. "Take me, Daddy," I say with assurance; "I'm the prettiest!"

Later, it does not surprise me to find myself in Miss Mey's shiny black car, sharing the back seat with the other lucky ones. Does not surprise me that I thoroughly enjoy the fair. At home that night I tell the unlucky ones all I can remember about the merry-go-round, the man who eats live chickens, and the teddy bears, until they say: that's enough, baby Alice. Shut up now, and go to sleep.

It is Easter Sunday, 1950. I am dressed in a green, flocked, scalloped-hem dress (handmade by my adoring sister, Ruth) that has its own smooth satin petticoat and tiny hot-pink roses tucked into each scallop. My shoes, new T-strap patent leather, again highly biscuit-polished. I am six years old and have learned one of the longest Easter speeches to be heard that day, totally unlike the speech I said when I was two: "Easter lilies/pure and white/blossom in/ the morning light." When I rise to give my speech I do so on a great wave of love and pride and expectation. People in the church stop rustling their new crinolines. They seem to hold their breath. I can tell they admire my dress, but it is my spirit, bordering on sassiness (womanishness), they secretly applaud.

"That girl's a little *mess*," they whisper to each other, pleased.

Naturally I say my speech without stammer or pause, unlike those who stutter, stammer, or, worst of all, forget. This is before the word "beautiful" exists in people's vocabulary, but "Oh, isn't she the *cutest* thing!" frequently floats my way. "And got so much sense!" they gratefully add . . . for which thoughtful addition I thank them to this day.

It was great fun being cute. But then, one day, it ended.

I am eight years old and a tomboy. I have a cowboy hat, cowboy boots, checkered shirt and pants, all red. My playmates are my brothers, two and four years older than I. Their colors are black and green, the only difference in the way we are dressed. On Saturday nights we all go the picture show, even my mother; Westerns are her favorite kind of movie. Back home, "on the ranch," we pretend we are Tom Mix, Hopalong Cassidy, Lash LaRue (we've even named one of our dogs Lash LaRue); we chase each other for hours rustling cattle, being outlaws, delivering damsels from distress. Then my parents decide to buy my brothers guns. These are not "real" guns. They shoot "BBs," copper pellets my brothers say will kill birds. Because I am a girl, I do not get a gun. Instantly I am relegated to the position of Indian. Now there appears a great distance between us. They shoot and shoot at everything with their new guns. I try to keep up with my bow and arrows.

One day while I am standing on top of our makeshift "garage"—pieces of tin nailed across some poles—holding my bow and arrow and looking out toward the fields, I feel an incredible blow in my right eye. I look down just in time to see my brother lower his gun.

Both brothers rush to my side. My eye stings, and I cover it with my hand. "If you tell," they say, "we will get a whipping. You don't want that to happen, do you?" I do not. "Here is a piece of wire," says the older brother, picking it up from the roof; "say you stepped on one end of it and the other flew up and hit you." The pain is beginning to start. "Yes," I say. "Yes, I will say that is what happened." If I do not say this is what happened, I know my brothers will find ways to make me wish I had. But now I will say anything that gets me to my mother.

Confronted by our parents we stick to the lie agreed upon. They place me on a bench on the porch and I close my left eye while they examine the right. There is a tree growing from underneath the porch that climbs past the railing to the roof. It is the last thing my right eye sees. I watch as its trunk, its branches, and then its leaves are blotted out by the rising blood.

I am in shock. First there is intense fever, which my father tries to break using lily leaves bound around my head. Then there are chills: my mother tries to get me to eat soup. Eventually, I do not know how, my parents learn what has happened. A week after the "accident" they take me to see a doctor. "Why did you wait so long to come?" he asks, looking into my eye and shaking his head. "Eyes are sympathetic," he says. "If one is blind, the other will likely become blind too."

This comment of the doctor's terrifies me. But it is really how I look that bothers me most. Where the BB pellet struck there is a glob of whitish scar tissue, a hideous cataract, on my eye. Now when I stare at people—a favorite pastime, up to now—they will stare back. Not at the "cute" little girl, but at her scar. For six years I do not stare at anyone, because I do not raise my head.

Years later, in the throes of a mid-life crisis, I ask my mother and sister whether I changed after the "accident." "No," they say, puzzled. "What do you mean?"

What do I mean?

I am eight, and, for the first time, doing poorly in school, where I have been something of a whiz since I was four. We have just moved to the place where the "accident" occurred. We do not know any of the people around us because this is a different county. The only time I see the friends I knew is when we go back to our old church. The new school is the former state penitentiary. It is a large stone building, cold and drafty, crammed to overflowing with boisterous, ill-disciplined children. On the third floor there is a huge circular imprint of some partition that has been torn out.

"What used to be here?" I ask a sullen girl next to me on our way past it to lunch.

"The electric chair," says she.

At night I have nightmares about the electric chair, and about all the people reputedly "fried" in it. I am afraid of the school, where all the students seem to be budding criminals.

"What's the matter with your eye?" they ask, critically.

When I don't answer (I cannot decide whether it was an "accident" or not), they shove me, insist on a fight.

My brother, the one who created the story about the wire, comes to my rescue. But then brags so much about "protecting" me, I become sick.

After months of torture at the school, my parents decide to send me back to our old community, to my old school. I live with my grandparents and the teacher they board. But there is no room for Phoebe, my cat. By the time my grandparents decide there *is* room, and I ask for my cat, she cannot be found. Miss Yarborough, the boarding teacher, takes me under her wing, and begins to teach me to play the piano. But soon she marries an African—a "prince," she says—and is whisked away to his continent.

At my old school there is at least one teacher who loves me. She is the teacher who "knew me before I was born" and bought my first baby clothes. It is she who makes life bearable. It is her presence that finally helps me turn on the one child at the school who continually calls me "one-eyed bitch." One day I simply grab him by his coat and beat him until I am satisfied. It is my teacher who tells me my mother is ill.

My mother is lying in bed in the middle of the day, something I have never seen. She is in too much pain to speak. She has an abscess in her ear. I stand looking down on her, knowing that if she dies, I cannot live. She is being treated with warm oils and hot bricks held against her cheek. Finally a doctor comes. But I must go back to my grandparents' house. The weeks pass but I am hardly aware of it. All I know is that my mother might die, my father is not so jolly, my brothers still have their guns, and I am the one sent away from home.

"You did not change," they say.
Did I imagine the anguish of never looking up?

I am twelve. When relatives come to visit I hide in my room. My cousin Brenda, just my age, whose father works in the post office and whose mother is a nurse, comes to find me. "Hello," she says. And then she asks, looking at my recent school picture, which I did not want taken, and on which the "glob," as I think of it, is clearly visible, "You still can't see out of that eye?"

"No," I say, and flop back on the bed over my book.

That night, as I do almost every night, I abuse my eye. I rant and rave at it, in front of the mirror. I plead with it to clear up before morning. I tell it I hate and despise it. I do not pray for sight. I pray for beauty.

"You did not change," they say.

I am fourteen and baby-sitting for my brother Bill, who lives in Boston. He is my favorite brother and there is a strong bond between us. Understanding my feelings of shame and ugliness he and his wife take me to a local hospital, where the "glob" is removed by a doctor named O. Henry. There is still a small bluish crater where the scar tissue was, but the ugly white stuff is gone. Almost immediately I become a different person from the girl who does not raise her head. Or so I think. Now that I've raised my head I win the boy-friend of my dreams. Now that I've raised my head I have plenty of friends. Now that I've raised my head classwork comes from my lips as faultlessly as Easter speeches did, and I leave high school as valedictorian, most popular student, and *queen*, hardly believing my luck. Ironically, the girl who was voted most beautiful in our class (and was) was later shot twice through the chest by a male companion, using a "real" gun, while she was pregnant. But that's another story in itself. Or is it?

"You did not change," they say.

It is now thirty years since the "accident." A beautiful journalist comes to visit and to interview me. She is going to write a cover story for her magazine that focuses on my latest book. "Decide how you want to look on the cover," she says. "Glamorous, or whatever."

Never mind "glamorous," it is the "whatever" that I hear. Suddenly all I can think of is whether I will get enough sleep the night before the photography session: if I don't, my eye will be tired and wander, as blind eyes will.

At night in bed with my lover I think up reasons why I should not appear on the cover of a magazine. "My meanest critics will say I've sold out," I say. "My family will now realize I write scandalous books."

"But what's the real reason you don't want to do this?" he asks.

"Because in all probability," I say in a rush, "my eye won't be straight."

"It will be straight enough," he says. Then, "Besides, I thought you'd made your peace with that."

And I suddenly remember that I have.

I remember:

I am talking to my brother Jimmy, asking if he remembers anything unusual about the day I was shot. He does not know I consider that day the last time my father, with his sweet home remedy of cool lily leaves, chose me, and that I suffered and raged inside because of this. "Well," he says, "all I remember is standing by the side of the highway with Daddy, trying to flag down a car. A white man stopped, but when Daddy said he needed somebody to take his little girl to the doctor, he drove off."

I remember:

I am in the desert for the first time. I fall totally in love with it. I am so overwhelmed by its beauty, I confront for the first time, consciously, the meaning of the doctor's words years ago: "Eyes are sympathetic. If one is blind, the other will likely become blind too." I realize I have dashed about the world madly, looking at this, looking at that, storing up images against the fading of the light. *But I might have missed seeing the desert!* The shock of that possibility—and gratitude for over twenty-five years of sight—sends me literally to my knees. Poem after poem comes—which is perhaps how poets pray.

On Sight

> I am so thankful I have seen
> The Desert
> And the creatures in the desert
> And the desert Itself.
>
> The desert has its own moon
> Which I have seen
> With my own eye.
>
> There is no flag on it.
>
> Trees of the desert have arms
> All of which are always up
> That is because the moon is up
> The sun is up
> Also the sky
> The stars
> Clouds
> None with flags.
>
> If there *were* flags, I doubt
> the trees would point.
> Would you?

But mostly, I remember this:

I am twenty-seven, and my baby daughter is almost three. Since her birth I have worried about her discovery that her mother's eyes are different from other people's. Will she be embarrassed? I think. What will she say? Every day she watches a television program called "Big Blue Marble." It begins with a picture of the earth as it appears from the moon. It is bluish, a little battered-looking, but full of light, with whitish clouds swirling around it. Every time I see it I weep with love, as if it is a picture of Grandma's house. One day when I am putting Rebecca down for her nap, she suddenly focuses on my eye. Something inside me cringes, gets ready to try to protect myself. All children are cruel about physical differences, I know from experience, and that they don't always mean to be is another matter. I assume Rebecca will be the same.

But no-o-o-o. She studies my face intently as we stand, her inside and me outside her crib. She even holds my face maternally between her dimpled little hands. Then, looking every bit as serious and lawyerlike as her father, she says, as if it may just possibly have slipped my attention: "Mommy, there's a *world* in your eye." (As in, "Don't be alarmed, or do anything crazy.") And then, gently, but with great interest: "Mommy, where did you *get* that world in your eye?"

For the most part, the pain left then. (So what, if my brothers grew up to buy even more powerful pellet guns for their sons and to carry real guns themselves. So what, if a young "Morehouse man" once nearly fell off the steps of Trevor Arnett Library because he thought my eyes were blue.) Crying and laughing I ran to the bathroom, while Rebecca mumbled and sang herself off to sleep. Yes indeed, I realized, looking into the mirror. There *was* a world in my eye. And I saw that it was possible to love it: that in fact, for all it had taught me of shame and anger and inner vision, I *did* love it. Even to see it drifting out of orbit in boredom, or rolling up out of fatigue, not to mention floating back at attention in excitement (bearing witness, a friend has called it), deeply suitable to my personality, and even characteristic of me.

That night I dream I am dancing to Stevie Wonder's song "Always" (the name of the song is really "As," but I hear it as "Always"). As I dance, whirling and joyous, happier than I've ever been in my life, another bright-faced dancer joins me. We dance and kiss each other and hold each other through the night. The other dancer has obviously come through all right, as I have done. She is beautiful, whole and free. And she is also me.

Suggestions for Discussion

1. How does the author use detail to portray herself at various ages? To portray her mother?

2. What changes in her personality and view of herself take place in the several age periods that Walker describes?

3. The line "you did not change" recurs. What is its relation to the narrative in the several scenes?

4. What is the significance of the repeated reference to raising her head at various stages of the author's development?

5. How does Walker equate prayer with poetry?

6. How does her daughter's comment on her eye affect her attitude?

7. What does the title signify?

Suggestions for Writing

1. Write a series of short vignettes illustrating how you viewed yourself and/or others viewed you at various stages of your development.

2. Describe the ways in which a traumatic episode in your childhood or that of a person close to you has affected your attitudes or behavior.

◇◇◇◇

Essays

—◆◆◆◆—

James E. Miller, Jr.

Discovering the Self

James E. Miller (b. 1920), American educator and author, has served as a professor of English at the University of Chicago since 1962. The editor of *College English* from 1960 to 1966, he is the author of several scholarly works on Fitzgerald, Whitman, and Melville. In this excerpt from his book *Word, Self, Reality* (1972) Miller develops his thesis that by means of language we "proclaim our identities, shape our lives, and leave our impress on the world."

"I speak; therefore I am."

Though this declaration may seem a little strange at first, it can be supported by considerable evidence. The individual establishes his individuality, his distinction as a human being, through language. He *becomes*—through language. Not only does he proclaim his existence, his being, through speech, but also his identity—the special and particular nature that makes him *him*. The declaration may then be rewritten: "I speak; *thus,* I am."

The creation of the self must, by its very nature, be a cooperative affair. The potentiality for language acquisition and language-use appears to be granted as a birthright. But the accident of birth will determine whether the language acquired will be Chinese, Swahili, Spanish, or English. And the

> . . . the mentality of mankind and the language of mankind created each other. If we like to assume the rise of language as a given fact, then it is not going too far to say that the souls of men are the gift from language to mankind.
>
> The account of the sixth day should be written, He gave them speech, and they became souls.
>
> —Alfred North Whitehead, *Modes of Thought,* 1938

the accident will determine the nature of the dialect acquired within the language. These "accidents" assume the presence of people and a culture that together bring the language to the individual.

If, then, the individual creates himself through language, it is only with the help provided by a sympathetic environment; a mother who encourages him to babble, to distinguish sounds and consequences, and then to utter sentences; and a host of other people who act and react linguistically around him. Gradually as the individual develops, he acquires not only language but what might be called a "linguistic personality," a set of language behavior patterns that make up a substantial part of his identity as a person different from other persons.

This *creation of the self*—in the sense of the self's development into a distinctive person with distinctions that are in large part linguistic (or asserted or fulfilled through language)—is a creation of the self in a kind of gross or obvious sense. Few would quarrel with the rough outline sketched above, though some might want to express it in a different set of terms. But there is another, more subtle sense in which we can speak of the creation of the self implied in "I speak; therefore I am." This profounder sense is implied in Alfred North Whitehead's assertion that "it is not going too far to say that the souls of men are the gift from language to mankind." Where a nineteenth-century divine, or a twentieth-century philosopher, might refer to "souls," the modern psychologist might refer to the sense of an enduring self. This sense is generated, sustained, and preserved in language.

One way through which the sense of self is generated appears in the basic human impulse to sort through one's thoughts, or to think through the day's (or a lifetime's) experiences. To follow this impulse throws the individual back on his language resources. The experiences and thoughts that make up one's life are, in some sense, the essence of the individual, the things that are uniquely his and that make him what he is. In the process of sorting through his thoughts, or of disentangling and examining his tangled experiences, he is in effect defining himself, outlining himself, asserting and proclaiming himself. There can be no more vital activity for the individual: the results and the actions (new thoughts and new experiences) proceeding from it will further

---

. . . the fundamental human capacity is the capacity and the need for creative self-expression, for free control of all aspects of one's life and thought. One particularly crucial realization of this capacity is the creative use of language as a free instrument of thought and expression. Now having this view of human nature and human needs, one tries to think about the modes of social organization that would permit the freest and fullest development of the individual, of each individual's potentialities in whatever direction they might take, that would permit him to be fully human in the sense of having the greatest possible scope for his freedom and initiative.

—**Noam Chomsky**, "Linguistics and Politics—Interview," 1969.

> It is language . . . that really reveals to man that world which is closer to him than any world of natural objects and touches his weal and woe more directly than physical nature. For it is language that makes his existence in a community possible; and only in society, in relation to a "Thee," can his subjectivity assert itself as a "Me."
>
> —Ernst Cassirer, *Language and Myth*, 1946.

define his identity, not only for him but for the world he inhabits. In the old vocabulary, he is in this process revitalizing, reconstituting, refreshing, renewing his soul.

To live an aware life, the individual must begin with an awareness of self. He must conduct a running examination and periodic reexaminations of the self—in language, the medium of furthest reaches, deepest diving, most labyrinthine windings. The sorting through might well begin with the ordinary, everyday experiences of life. A diary or journal enables one to sift through and evaluate experiences, as well as to come to understand them and their significance—or insignificance. Most of us do this sifting and evaluation in moments of reverie or in that state of mental vagabondage just before sleep. There is some (even great) advantage, however, in subjecting ourselves to the discipline of written language, in which the vague and the mushy and the muddled must give way to the specific, the firm, the clearly formulated.

For writing *is* discovery. The language that never leaves our head is like colorful yarn, endlessly spun out multicolored threads dropping into a void, momentarily compacted, entangled, fascinating, elusive. We have glimpses that seem brilliant but quickly fade; we catch sight of images that tease us with connections and patterns that too-soon flow on; we hold in momentary view a comprehensive arrangement (insight) that dissolves rapidly and disappears.

Writing that is discovery forces the capturing, the retrieving, the bringing into focus these stray and random thoughts. Sifting through them, we make decisions that are as much about the self as about language. Indeed, writing

> I did not exist to write poems, to preach or to paint, neither I nor anyone else. All of that was incidental. Each man had only one genuine vocation—to find the way to himself. He might end up as poet or madman, as prophet or criminal—that was not his affair, ultimately it was of no concern. His task was to discover his own destiny—not an arbitrary one—and live it out wholly and resolutely within himself. Everything else was only a would-be existence, an attempt at evasion, a flight back to the ideas of the masses, conformity and fear of one's own inwardness.
>
> —Hermann Hesse, *Demian*, 1925.

is largely a process of choosing among alternatives from the images and thoughts of the endless flow, and this choosing is a matter of making up one's mind, and this making up one's mind becomes in effect the making up of one's self. In this way writing that is honest and genuine and serious (though not necessarily without humor or wit) constitutes the discovery of the self. It is not uncommon, before the choices are made, before the words are fixed on paper, to be quite unsure of which way the choices will go. Most people have experienced the phenomenon of their opinions or feelings changing, some-times markedly, in the process of writing a paper which forces confrontations with language and choices among expressions. All people have experienced the clarification of their views and perspectives as they have worked through the process of placing them on paper. It is not at all unusual to find an indi-vidual who is uncertain and unclear about his feelings on a subject or an issue, but who, on discovering his attitude in the process of writing, becomes com-mitted, often dedicated, and sometimes even fanatical: he has come to know himself. When this happens the individual is not being insincere, but is sim-ply experiencing the discoveries of writing—discoveries that are often surpris-ing and frequently exhilarating.

As suggested earlier, in setting forth on this voyage of self-discovery, it is best to begin, not with the problems of the universe, but with what appear to be the trivia of everyday events. Indeed, it might turn out ultimately that the big is somehow indirectly connected with the little. The self-examination which requires simply the writing of an account of one's life for a single day might bring unexpected illumination. Such an account would necessitate re-viewing in detail and reliving imaginatively moments of pain and fun, joy and sobriety. A list of the events of that day (or week, month) would require consideration as to what, for an individual, constitutes events. Presumably they left some kind of mark—intellectual, emotional, imaginative. What kind of mark, how deep, how long-lasting? There might be public events and pri-vate events—events for which there were some, perhaps many, witnesses, and events that had no witnesses at all.

The list of a day's events in an individual's life might be posed against a list of the general public events and happenings—in the community, town, state, country, or world. Where do the two lists intersect, if at all? Did any of the world's events leave any mark on the individual, or did they reach him re-motely or impersonally through the mass media, newspapers, radio-TV, and then fade into the distance? A third list might be composed of a close friend's perspective on the personal events on the first list, some of which he will have witnessed (but only externally), and others of which he will be totally

---

YEE-AH! I feel like part of the shadows that make company for me in this warm *amigo* darkness.
I am "My Majesty Piri Thomas," with a high on anything and like a stoned king, I gotta survive my kingdom.
I'm a skinny, dark-face, curly-haired, intense Porty-Ree-can—Unsatisfied, hoping, and always reaching.
—Piri Thomas, *Down These Mean Streets*, 1967.

Interviewer: Is there anything else you can say to beginning writers?

Simenon: Writing is considered a profession, and I don't think it is a profession. I think that everyone who does not *need* to be a writer, who thinks he can do something else, ought to do something else. Writing is not a profession but a vocation of unhappiness. I don't think an artist can ever be happy.

Interviewer: Why?

Simenon: Because, first, I think that if a man has the urge to be an artist, it is because he needs to find himself. Every writer tries to find himself through his characters, through all his writing.

Interviewer: He is writing for himself?

Simenon: Yes. Certainly.

—**Georges Simenon,** *Writers at Work: The Paris Review Interviews,* 1958.

unaware. Compilation of these lists, either in fact or imagination, may enable the individual to see the narrative of his life as marking a circle around him, with him—absolutely alone—at the center.

This circle marks the individual's personal turf, material for his intellectual and imaginative use or growth that is his and his alone, impossible to share totally with anyone, no matter how close. One who begins to feel a sense of the preciousness of this material, this segment of life that is his and no one else's, is in fact feeling a sense of the self. If he begins to discover sequence and sense—a kind of unified narrative—in the events of his life for a day, he is making the discovery of self that the process of writing brings about: the unification must come from the indivdual's unique sensibility and identity.

Henry James had something of all this in mind in some advice he gave to young writers: "Oh, do something from your point of view; an ounce of example is worth a ton of generalities . . . do something with life. Any point of view is interesting that is a direct impression of life. You each have an impression colored by your individual conditions; make that into a picture, a picture framed by your own personal wisdom, your glimpse of the American world. The field is vast for freedom, for study, for observation, for satire, for truth."

Suggestions for Discussion

1. In earlier sections of his book *Word, Self, Reality,* Miller defines language as a form of creation whereby we create both our world and ourselves. With what details does Miller support his belief that it is through language that we create ourselves and our world?

2. What role does environment play in enabling the individual to create himself or herself through language?

3. How does sorting through one's thoughts or thinking through one's experiences relate to self-definition? What role does choice play in this process?

4. How do the quotations from Whitehead, Chomsky, Cassirer, Hesse, Thomas, and Simenon relate to the author's central thesis?

5. Miller maintains the continuity of his thought by careful linking of his paragraphs. Identify the transitional devices that bind each of the paragraphs to the preceding and the following one. Identify the logic that justifies the division of the essay into its constituent paragraphs.

6. Examine the ninth paragraph ("Writing that is discovery . . .") to determine (a) what subject matter is in it, (b) what transitional devices give it internal coherence, (c) what stages of development the discussion undergoes.

7. The eighth paragraph ("For writing *is* discovery.") includes an ingenious simile: language is like yarn. Test whether this simile is merely ornamental, useful in conveying the thought, or essential to the thought by rewriting the paragraph in abstract, nonfigurative language and comparing your version with Miller's original.

Suggestions for Writing

1. Keep a journal recording your fleeting impressions, daydreams, night dreams, feelings, and random thoughts as well as your more considered reflections over a period of two weeks. Include your thoughts about your own immediate activities, memories evoked of past events, and reflections on what is going on in the world. Be concerned with getting down on paper as much as possible of what you are feeling and what has gone through your mind and don't concern yourself with the usual mechanics of writing or with the possibly repetitive nature of some of your feelings. At the end of this two-week period, reread your journal and attempt to discover what recurrent patterns of feeling and thought have emerged. Write a brief analysis of the nature of your own thoughts, what experiences seem to precipitate them, what patterns seem to repeat themselves. What do you make of such repetitions?

2. Select one of the journal entries that most interests you and elaborate on it in the form of a short essay or narrative in which you attempt to give shape and unity to the earlier expression.

3. Make the lists suggested in Miller's essay and write a commentary on your discoveries.

Theodore Roethke
Some Self-analysis

Theodore Roethke (1908–1963), American poet, taught during the last years of his life at the University of Washington. *The Waking: Poems, 1933–1953* was the winner of the Pulitzer Prize for Poetry in 1953. He received the Bollingen Award for Poetry in 1958. A collected volume, *Words for the Wind,* appeared in 1958, and *The Far Field* was published posthumously in 1964. In this statement, written when he was an undergraduate, Roethke recounts his hopes for the writing course he is taking, assesses his strengths and limitations as a writer, and expresses his faith in himself.

I expect this course to open my eyes to story material, to unleash my too dormant imagination, to develop that quality utterly lacking in my nature—a sense of form. I do not expect to acquire much technique. I expect to be able to seize upon the significant, reject the trivial. I hope to acquire a greater love for humanity in all its forms.

I have long wondered just what my strength was as a writer. I am often filled with tremendous enthusiasm for a subject, yet my writing about it will seem a sorry attempt. Above all, I possess a driving sincerity,—that prime virtue of any creative worker. I write only what I believe to be the absolute truth,—even if I must ruin the theme in so doing. In this respect I feel far superior to those glib people in my classes who often garner better grades than I do. They are so often pitiful frauds,—artificial—insincere. They have a line that works. They do not write from the depths of their hearts. Nothing of their was ever born of pain. Many an incoherent yet sincere piece of writing has outlived the polished product.

I write only about people and things that I know thoroughly. Perhaps I have become a mere reporter, not a writer. Yet I feel that this is all my present abilities permit. I will open my eyes in my youth and store this raw, living material. Age may bring the fire that molds experience into artistry.

I have a genuine love of nature. It is not the least bit affected, but an integral and powerful part of my life. I know that Cooper is a fraud—that he doesn't give a true sense of the sublimity of American scenery. I know that Muir and Thoreau and Burroughs speak the truth.

I can sense the moods of nature almost instinctively. Ever since I could walk, I have spent as much time as I could in the open. A perception of nature—no matter how delicate, how subtle, how evanescent,—remains with me forever.

I am influenced too much, perhaps, by natural objects. I seem bound by the very room I'm in. I've associated so long with prosaic people that I've dwarfed myself spiritually. When I get alone under an open sky where man isn't too evident—then I'm tremendously exalted and a thousand vivid ideas and sweet visions flood my consciousness.

I think that I possess story material in abundance. I have had an unusual upbringing. I was let alone, thank God! My mother insisted upon two things,—that I strive for perfection in whatever I did and that I always try to be a gentleman. I played with Italians, with Russians, Poles, and the "sissies" on Michigan Avenue. I was carefully watched, yet allowed to follow my own inclinations. I have seen a good deal of life that would never have been revealed to an older person. Up to the time I came to college then I had seen humanity in diverse forms. Now I'm cramped and unhappy. I don't feel that these idiotic adolescents are worth writing about. In the summer, I turn animal and work for a few weeks in a factory. Then I'm happy.

My literary achievements have been insignificant. At fourteen, I made a speech which was translated into twenty-six languages and used as Red Cross propaganda. When I was younger, it seemed that everything I wrote was eminently successful. I always won a prize when I entered an essay contest. In college, I've been able to get only one "A" in four rhetoric courses. I feel this keenly. If I can't write, what can I do? I wonder.

When I was a freshman, I told Carleton Wells that I knew I could write whether he thought so or not. On my next theme he wrote "You can Write!" How I have cherished that praise!

It is bad form to talk about grades, I know. If I don't get an "A" in this course, it wouldn't be because I haven't tried. I've made a slow start. I'm going to spend Christmas vacation writing. A "B" symbolizes defeat to me. I've been beaten too often.

I do wish that we were allowed to keep our stories until we felt that we had worked them into the best possible form.

I do not have the divine urge to write. There seems to be something surging within,—a profound undercurrent of emotion. Yet there is none of that fertility of creation which distinguishes the real writer.

Nevertheless, I have faith in myself. I'm either going to be a good writer or a poor fool.

Suggestions for Discussion

1. There are a number of paradoxical statements in Roethke's self-analysis, written when he was an undergraduate. Identify and explain.

2. Contrast Roethke's image of himself with what you imagine would be the view of this parents, his instructors, his contemporaries.

Suggestions for Writing

1. Write a statement of your expectations in a course in composition following the format of Roethke's statement. Include an analysis of your strengths and weaknesses, formative influences, sense of present accomplishment, and hopes for the future.

2. In the light of his self-analysis, comment on a selection of Roethke's published poems.

◇◇◇◇

Carson McCullers
Loneliness . . . An American Malady

Carson McCullers (1917–1967), a Southern writer, was awarded Guggenheim Fellowships in 1942 and in 1946. Her published works include *The Heart Is a Lonely Hunter* (1940), *Reflections in a Golden Eye* (1941), *The Member of the Wedding* (1946), *The Ballad of the Sad Cafe* (1951), and *Clock Without Hands* (1961). This excerpt from *The Mortgaged Heart* (1971) suggests that the way by which we master loneliness is "to belong to something larger and more powerful than the weak, lonely self".

This city, New York—consider the people in it, the eight million of us. An English friend of mine, when asked why he lived in New York City, said that he liked it here because he could be so alone. While it was my friend's desire to be alone, the aloneness of many Americans who live in cities is an involuntary and fearful thing. It has been said that loneliness is the great American malady. What is the nature of this loneliness? It would seem essentially to be a quest for identity.

To the spectator, the amateur philosopher, no motive among the complex ricochets of our desires and rejections seems stronger or more enduring than the will of the individual to claim his identity and belong. From infancy to death, the human being is obsessed by these dual motives. During our first weeks of life, the question of identity shares urgency with the need for milk. The baby reaches for his toes, then explores the bars of his crib; again and again he compares the difference between his own body and the objects around him, and in the wavering, infant eyes there comes a pristine wonder.

Consciousness of self is the first abstract problem that the human being solves. Indeed, it is this self-consciousness that removes us from lower animals. This primitive grasp of identity develops with constantly shifting emphasis through all our years. Perhaps maturity is simply the history of those mutations that reveal to the individual the relation between himself and the world in which he finds himself.

After the first establishment of identity there comes the imperative need to lose this new-found sense of separateness and to belong to something larger and more powerful than the weak, lonely self. The sense of moral isolation is intolerable to us.

In *The Member of the Wedding* the lovely 12-year-old girl, Frankie Addams, articulates this universal need: "The trouble with me is that for a long time I have just been an *I* person. All people belong to a *We* except me. Not to belong to a *We* makes you too lonesome."

Love is the bridge that leads from the *I* sense to the *We*, and there is a paradox about personal love. Love of another individual opens a new relation between the personality and the world. The lover responds in a new way to nature and may even write poetry. Love is affirmation; it motivates the *yes* responses and the sense of wider communication. Love casts out fear, and in the security of this togetherness we find contentment, courage. We no longer fear the age-old haunting questions: "Who am I?" "Why am I?" "Where am I going?"—and having cast out fear, we can be honest and charitable.

For fear is a primary source of evil. And when the question "Who am I?" recurs and is unanswered, then fear and frustration project a negative attitude. The bewildered soul can answer only: "Since I do not understand 'Who I am,' I only know what I am *not*." The corollary of this emotional incertitude is snobbism, intolerance, and racial hate. The xenophobic individual can only reject and destroy, as the xenophobic nation inevitably makes war.

The loneliness of Americans does not have its source in xenophobia; as a nation we are an outgoing people, reaching always for immediate contacts, further experience. But we tend to seek out things as individuals, alone. The European, secure in his family ties and rigid class loyalties, knows little of the moral loneliness that is native to us Americans. While the European artists tend to form groups or aesthetic schools, the American artist is the eternal maverick—not only from society in the way of all creative minds, but within the orbit of his own art.

Thoreau took to the woods to seek the ultimate meaning of his life. His creed was simplicity and his *modus vivendi* the deliberate stripping of external life to the Spartan necessities in order that his inward life could freely flourish. His objective, as he put it, was to back the world into a corner. And in that way did he discover "What a man thinks of himself, that it is which determines, or rather indicates, his fate."

On the other hand, Thomas Wolfe turned to the city, and in his wanderings around New York he continued his frenetic and lifelong search for the lost brother, the magic door. He too backed the world into a corner, and as he passed among the city's millions, returning their stares, he experienced "That silent meeting [that] is the summary of all the meetings of men's lives."

Whether in the pastoral joys of country life or in the labyrinthine city, we Americans are always seeking. We wander, question. But the answer waits in each separate heart—the answer of our own identity and the way by which we can master loneliness and feel that at last we belong.

Suggestion for Discussion

How does the author establish the connections between loneliness and identity? between *I* and *We?* between lack of a sense of identity and fear? between fear and hatred or destruction? between Thoreau's search and that of Thomas Wolfe?

Suggestions for Writing

1. Develop or challenge Thoreau's belief, "What a man thinks of himself, that it is which determines, or rather indicates, his fate."

2. Develop an essay in which you argue that country life is or is not more conducive to the development of a sense of self than city life.

◇◇◇◇

Bruno Bettelheim
The Child's Need for Magic

Bruno Bettelheim (b. 1903) was born in Vienna and educated at the University of Vienna. Having survived the Nazi holocaust, he became an American psychoanalyst and educator and was director of the remarkable University of Chicago Sonia Shankman Orthogenic School from 1944 to 1973. He has written many penetrating works on parents and children and the significance of the holocaust. In this excerpt from *The Uses of Enchantment* (1976) the author believes that fairy tales provide answers to the child's pressing questions about his identity and his world.

Myths and fairy stories both answer the eternal questions: What is the world really like? How am I to live my life in it? How can I truly be myself? The answers given by myths are definite, while the fairy tale is suggestive; its messages may imply solutions, but it never spells them out. Fairy tales leave to the child's fantasizing whether and how to apply to himself what the story reveals about life and human nature.

The fairy tale proceeds in a manner which conforms to the way a child thinks and experiences the world; this is why the fairy tale is so convincing to him. He can gain much better solace from a fairy tale than he can from an effort to comfort him based on adult reasoning and viewpoints. A child trusts what the fairy story tells, because its world view accords with his own.

Whatever our age, only a story conforming to the principles underlying our thought processes carries conviction for us. If this is so for adults, who have learned to accept that there is more than one frame of reference for comprehending the world—although we find it difficult if not impossible truly to think in any but our own—it is exclusively true for the child. His thinking is animistic.

Like all preliterate and many literate people, "the child assumes that his relations to the inanimate world are of one pattern with those to the animate world of people: he fondles as he would his mother the pretty thing that pleased him; he strikes the door that has slammed on him." It should be added that he does the first because he is convinced that this pretty thing loves to be petted as much as he does; and he punishes the door because he is certain that the door slammed deliberately, out of evil intention.

As Piaget has shown, the child's thinking remains animistic until the age of puberty. His parents and teachers tell him that things cannot feel and act; and as much as he may pretend to believe this to please these adults, or not to be ridiculed, deep down the child knows better. Subjected to the rational teachings of others, the child only buries his "true knowledge" deeper in his soul and it remains untouched by rationality; but it can be formed and informed by what fairy tales have to say.

To the eight-year-old (to quote Piaget's examples), the sun is alive because it gives light (and, one may add, it does that because it wants to). To the child's animistic mind, the stone is alive because it can move, as it rolls down a hill. Even a twelve-and-a-half-year-old is convinced that a stream is alive and has a will, because its water is flowing. The sun, the stone, and the water are believed to be inhabited by spirits very much like people, so they feel and act like people.

To the child, there is no clear line separating objects from living things; and whatever has life has life very much like our own. If we do not understand what rocks and trees and animals have to tell us, the reason is that we are not sufficiently attuned to them. To the child trying to understand the world, it seems reasonable to expect answers from those objects which arouse his curiosity. And since the child is self-centered, he expects the animal to talk about the things which are really significant to him, as animals do in fairy tales, and as the child himself talks to his real or toy animals. A child is convinced that the animal understands and feels with him, even though it does not show it openly.

Since animals roam freely and widely in the world, how natural that in fairy tales these animals are able to guide the hero in his search which takes him into distant places. Since all that moves is alive, the child can believe that the wind can talk and carry the hero to where he needs to go, as in "East of the Sun and West of the Moon." In animistic thinking, not only animals feel and think as we do, but even stones are alive; so to be turned into stone simply means that the being has to remain silent and unmoving for a time. By the same reasoning, it is entirely believable when previously silent objects begin to talk, give advice, and join the hero on his wanderings. And since everything is inhabited by a spirit similar to all other spirits (namely, that of the child who has projected his spirit into all these things), because of this inherent sameness it is believable that man can change into animal, or the other way around, as in "Beauty and the Beast" or "The Frog King." Since there is no sharp line drawn between living and dead things, the latter, too, can come to life.

When, like the great philosophers, children are searching for the solutions to the first and last questions—"Who am I? How ought I to deal with life's problems? What must I become?"—they do so on the basis of their animistic thinking. But since the child is so uncertain of what his existence consists, first and foremost comes the question "Who am I?"

As soon as a child begins to move about and explore, he begins to ponder the problem of his identity. When he spies his mirror image, he wonders whether what he sees is really he, or a child just like him standing behind this glassy wall. He tries to find out by exploring whether this other child is really, in all ways, like him. He makes faces, turns this way or that, walks away from the mirror and jumps back in front of it to ascertain whether this other one has moved away or is still there. Though only three years old, the child is already up against the difficult problem of personal identity.

The child asks himself: "Who am I? Where did I come from? How did the world come into being? Who created man and all the animals? What is the purpose of life?" True, he ponders these vital questions not in the abstract, but mainly as they pertain to him. He worries not whether there is justice for individual man, but whether *he* will be treated justly. He wonders who or what projects him into adversity, and what can prevent this from happening to him. Are there benevolent powers in addition to his parents? Are his parents benevolent powers? How should he form himself, and why? Is there hope for him, though he may have done wrong? Why has all this happened to him? What will it mean for his future? Fairy tales provide answers to these pressing questions, many of which the child becomes aware of only as he follows the stories.

From an adult point of view and in terms of modern science, the answers which fairy stories offer are fantastic rather than true. As a matter of fact, these solutions seem so incorrect to many adults—who have become estranged from the ways in which young people experience the world—that they object to exposing children to such "false" information. However, realistic explanations are usually incomprehensible to children, because they lack the abstract understanding required to make sense of them. While giving a scientifically correct answer makes adults think they have clarified things for the child, such explanations leave the young child confused, over powered, and intellectually defeated. A child can derive security only from the conviction that he understands now what baffled him before—never from being given facts which create *new* uncertainties. Even as the child accepts such an answer, he comes to doubt that he has asked the right question. Since the explanation fails to make sense to him, it must apply to some unknown problem—not the one he asked about.

It is therefore important to remember that only statements which are intelligible in terms of the child's existing knowledge and emotional preoccupations carry conviction for him. To tell a child that the earth floats in space, attracted by gravity into circling around the sun, but that the earth doesn't fall to the sun as the child falls to the ground, seems very confusing to him. The child knows from his experience that everything has to rest on something, or be held up by something. Only an explanation based on that knowledge can make him feel he understand better about the earth in space. More important, to feel secure on earth, the child needs to believe that this world is held firmly in place. Therefore he finds a better explanation in a myth that tells him that the earth rests on a turtle, or is held up by a giant.

If a child accepts as true what his parents tell him—that the earth is a planet held securely on its path by gravity—then the child can only imagine that gravity is a string. Thus the parents' explanation has led to no better understanding or feeling of security. It requires considerable intellectual maturity to believe that there can be stability to one's life when the ground on which one walks (the firmest thing around, on which everything rests) spins with incredible speed on an invisible axis; that in addition it rotates around the sun; and furthermore hurtles through space with the entire solar system. I have never yet encountered a prepubertal youngster who could comprehend all these combined movements, although I have known many who could repeat this information. Such children parrot explanations which according to their own experience of the world are lies, but which they must believe to be true because some adult has said so. The consequence is that children come to distrust their own experience, and therefore themselves and what their minds can do for them.

In the fall of 1973, the comet Kohoutek was in the news. At that time a competent science teacher explained the comet to a small group of highly intelligent second- and third-graders. Each child had carefully cut out a paper circle and had drawn on it the course of the planets around the sun; a paper ellipse, attached by a slit to the paper circle, represented the course of the comet. The children showed me the comet moving along at an angle to the planets. When I asked them, the children told me that they were holding the comet in their hands, showing me the ellipse. When I asked how the comet which they were holding in their hands could also be in the sky, they were all nonplussed.

In their confusion, they turned to their teacher, who carefully explained to them that what they were holding in their hands, and had so diligently created, was only a model of the planets and the comet. The children all agreed that they understood this, and would have repeated it if questioned further. But whereas before they had regarded proudly this circle-cum-ellipse in their hands, they now lost all interest. Some crumpled the paper up, others dropped the model in the wastepaper basket. When the pieces of paper had been the comet to them, they had all planned to take the model home to show their parents, but now it no longer had meaning for them.

In trying to get a child to accept scientifically correct explanations, parents all too frequently discount scientific findings of how a child's mind works. Research on the child's mental processes, especially Piaget's, convincingly demonstrates that the young child is not able to comprehend the two vital abstract concepts of the permanence of quantity, and of reversibility—for instance, that the same quantity of water rises high in a narrow receptacle and remains low in a wide one; and that subtraction reverses the process of addition. Until he can understand abstract concepts such as these, the child can experience the world only subjectively.

Scientific explanations require objective thinking. Both theoretical research and experimental exploration have shown that no child below school age is truly able to grasp these two concepts, without which abstract understanding is impossible. In his early years, until age eight or ten, the child can develop only highly personalized concepts about what he experiences. Therefore it seems natural to him, since the plants which grow on this earth nourish him as his mother did from her breast, to see the earth as a mother or a female god, or at least as her abode.

Even a young child somehow knows that he was created by his parents; so it makes good sense to him that, like himself, all men and where they live were created by a superhuman figure not very different from his parents— some male or female god. Since his parents watch over the child and provide him with his needs in his home, then naturally he also believes that something like them, only much more powerful, intelligent, and reliable—a guardian angel—will do so out in the world.

A child thus experiences the world order in the image of his parents and of what goes on within the family. The ancient Egyptians, as a child does, saw heaven and the sky as a motherly figure (Nut) who protectively bent over the earth, enveloping it and them serenely. Far from preventing man from later developing a more rational explanation of the world, such a view offers security where and when it is most needed—a security which, when the time is ripe, allows for a truly rational world view. Life on a small planet surrounded by limitless space seems awfully lonely and cold to a child—just the opposite of what he knows life ought to be. This is why the ancients needed to feel sheltered and warmed by an enveloping mother figure. To depreciate protective imagery like this as mere childish projections of an immature mind is to rob the young child of one aspect of the prolonged safety and comfort he needs.

True, the notion of a sheltering sky-mother can be limiting to the mind if clung to for too long. Neither infantile projections nor dependence on imaginary protectors—such as a guardian angel who watches out for one when one is asleep, or during Mother's absence—offers true security; but as long as one cannot provide complete security for oneself, imaginings and projections are far preferable to no security. It is such (partly imagined) security which, when experienced for a sufficient length of time, permits the child to develop that feeling of confidence in life which he needs in order to trust himself—a trust necessary for his learning to solve life's problems through his own growing rational abilities. Eventually the child recognizes that what he has taken as literally true—the earth as a mother—is only a symbol.

A child, for example, who has learned from fairy stories to believe that what at first seemed a repulsive, threatening figure can magically change into a most helpful friend is ready to believe that a strange child whom he meets and fears may also be changed from a menace into a desirable companion. Belief in the "truth" of the fairy tale gives him courage not to withdraw because of the way this stranger appears to him at first. Recalling how the hero of many a fairy tale succeeded in life because he dared to befriend a seemingly unpleasant figure, the child believes he may work the same magic.

I have known many examples where, particularly in late adolescence, years of belief in magic are called upon to compensate for the person's having been deprived of it prematurely in childhood, through stark reality having been forced on him. It is as if these young people feel that now is their last chance to make up for a severe deficiency in their life experience; or that without having had a period of belief in magic, they will be unable to meet the rigors of adult life. Many young people who today suddenly seek escape in drug-induced dreams, apprentice themselves to some guru, believe in astrology, engage in practicing "black magic," or who in some other fashion escape from reality into daydreams about magic experiences which are to change their life for the better, were prematurely pressed to view reality in an adult way. Trying to evade reality in such ways has its deeper cause in early formative experiences which prevented the development of the conviction that life can be mastered in realistic ways.

What seems desirable for the individual is to repeat in his life span the process involved historically in the genesis of scientific thought. For a long time in his history man used emotional projections—such as gods—born of his immature hopes and anxieties to explain man, his society, and the universe; these explanations gave him a feeling of security. Then slowly, by his own social, scientific, and technological progress, man freed himself of the constant fear for his very existence. Feeling more secure in the world, and also within himself, man could now begin to question the validity of the images he had used in the past as explanatory tools. From there man's "childish" projections dissolved and more rational explanations took their place. This process, however, is by no means without vagaries. In intervening periods of stress and scarcity, man seeks for comfort again in the "childish" notion that he and his place of abode are the center of the universe.

Translated in terms of human behavior, the more secure a person feels within the world, the less he will need to hold on to "infantile" projections—mythical explanations or fairy-tale solutions to life's eternal problems—and the more he can afford to seek rational explanations. The more secure a man is within himself, the more he can afford to accept an explanation which says his world is of minor significance in the cosmos. Once man feels truly significant in his human environment, he cares little about the importance of his planet within the universe. On the other hand, the more insecure a man is in himself and his place in the immediate world, the more he withdraws into himself because of fear, or else moves outward to conquer for conquest's sake. This is the opposite of exploring out of a security which frees our curiosity.

For these same reasons a child, as long as he is not sure his immediate human environment will protect him, needs to believe that superior powers, such as a guardian angel, watch over him, and that the world and his place within it are of paramount importance. Here is one connection between a family's ability to provide basic security and the child's readiness to engage in rational investigations as he grows up.

As long as parents fully believed that Biblical stories solved the riddle of our existence and its purpose, it was easy to make a child feel secure. The Bible was felt to contain the answers to all pressing questions: the Bible told man all he needed to know to understand the world, how it came into being, and how to behave in it. In the Western world the Bible also provided prototypes for man's imagination. But rich as the Bible is in stories, not even during the most religious of times were these stories sufficient for meeting all the psychic needs of man.

Part of the reason for this is that while the Old and New Testaments and the histories of the saints provided answers to the crucial questions of how to live the good life, they did not offer solutions for the problems posed by the dark sides of our personalities. The Biblical stories suggest essentially only one solution for the asocial aspects of the unconscious: repression of these (unacceptable) strivings. But children, not having their ids in conscious control, need stories which permit at least fantasy satisfaction of these "bad" tendencies, and specific models for their sublimation.

Explicitly and implicitly, the Bible tells of God's demands on man. While we are told that there is greater rejoicing about a sinner who reformed than about the man who never erred, the message is still that we ought to live the good life, and not, for example, take cruel revenge on those whom we hate. As the story of Cain and Abel shows, there is no sympathy in the Bible for the agonies of sibling rivalry—only a warning that acting upon it has devastating consequences.

But what a child needs most, when beset by jealousy of his sibling, is the permission to feel that what he experiences is justified by the situation he is in. To bear up under the pangs of his envy, the child needs to be encouraged to engage in fantasies of getting even someday; then he will be able to manage at the moment, because of the conviction that the future will set things aright. Most of all, the child wants support for his still very tenuous belief that through growing up, working hard, and maturing he will one day be the victorious one. If his present sufferings will be rewarded in the future, he need not act on his jealousy of the moment, the way Cain did.

Like Biblical stories and myths, fairy tales were the literature which edified everybody—children and adults alike—for nearly all of man's existence. Except that God is central, many Bible stories can be recognized as very similar to fairy tales. In the story of Jonah and the whale, for example, Jonah is trying to run away from his superego's (conscience's) demand that he fight against the wickedness of the people of Nineveh. The ordeal which tests his moral fiber is, as in so many fairy tales, a perilous voyage in which he has to prove himself.

Jonah's trip across the sea lands him in the belly of a great fish. There, in great danger, Jonah discovers his higher morality, his higher self, and is wondrously reborn, now ready to meet the rigorous demands of his superego. But the rebirth alone does not achieve true humanity for him: to be a slave neither to the id and the pleasure principle (avoiding arduous tasks by trying to escape from them) nor to the superego (wishing destruction upon the wicked city) means true freedom and higher selfhood. Jonah attains his full humanity only when he is no longer subservient to either institution of his mind, but relinquishes blind obedience to both id and superego and is able to recognize God's wisdom in judging the people of Nineveh not according to the rigid structures of Jonah's superego, but in terms of their human frailty.

Suggestions for Discussion

1. How does Bettelheim distinguish myths from fairy tales? the Bible from fairy tales?

2. Who is Piaget? How has he influenced current thought regarding the way children think and learn?

3. Explain Bettelheim's reference to children as "animistic thinkers." How does this description of them relate to their need for fairy tales?

4. What similarities does the author see between the child and the philosopher? How do they differ?

5. Explain why Bettelheim believes it mistaken to deprive children of fairy tales. How does he relate their need for fairy tales to the difficulties they have in comprehending scientific ideas?

Suggestions for Writing

1. Using one or more fairy tales with which you are familiar, write an essay explaining how magical elements might serve to explain the universe to a child.

2. Write a comparison between a fairy tale and one of the popular children's stories about ordinary life.

 ◇◇◇◇

Lance Morrow

Daydreams of What You'd Rather Be

Lance Morrow (b. 1939), who was educated at Harvard, has been a contributor to *Time* since 1976. The author speculates on the relationship between the self and the antiself, which may sometimes be a monster and at others the basis of our humanity.

Kierkegaard once confided to his journal that he would have been much happier if he had become a police spy rather than a philosopher. Richard Nixon always wanted to be a sportswriter. If one considers these fantasies together, they seem to have got weirdly crossed. It is Nixon who should have been the police spy. On the other hand, Kierkegaard would probably have made an extraordinarily depressing sportswriter *(Fear and Trembling: The Angst of Bucky Dent).*

We have these half-secret old ambitions—to be something else, to be someone else, to leap out of the interminable self and into another skin, another life. It is usually a brief out-of-body phenomenon, the sort of thing that we think when our gaze drifts away in the middle of a conversation. Goodbye. The imagination floats through a window into the conjectural and finds there a kind of bright blue antiself. The spirit stars itself in a brief hypothesis, an alternative, a private myth. What we imagine at such moments can suggest peculiar truths of character.

One rummages in closets for these revelations. Kierkegaard's fancy about being a police spy is a dark, shiny little item: a melancholic's impulse toward sneaking omnipotence, the intellectual furtively collaborating with state power, committing sins of betrayal in police stations in the middle of the night. It is not far from another intellectual's fantasy: Norman Mailer once proposed that Eugene McCarthy, the dreamboat of the late '60s moderate left, might have made an ideal director of the FBI. McCarthy agreed. But of course, McCarthy had a sardonic genius for doubling back upon his public self and making it vanish. He did magic tricks of self-annihilation. Nixon's imaginary career—wholesome, all-American, unimpeachable—may suggest both a yearning for blamelessness (what could possibly be tainted in his writing about baseball?) and an oblique, pre-emptive identification with an old enemy: the press.

The daydream of an alternative self is a strange, flitting thing. This wistful speculation often occurs in summer, when a vacation loosens the knot of one's vocational identity. Why, dammit, says the refugee from middle management on his 13th day on the lake, why not just stay here all year? Set up as a fishing guide. Open a lodge. We'll take the savings and . . . The soul at odd moments (the third trout, the fourth beer) will make woozy rushes at the pipe dream. Like a gangster who has cooperated with the district attorney, we want a new name and a new career and a new house in a different city—and maybe a new nose from the D.A.'s cosmetic surgeon.

Usually, the impulse passes. The car gets packed and pointed back toward the old reality. The moment dissolves, like one of those instants when one falls irrevocably in love with the face of a stranger through the window as the bus pulls away.

Sometimes, the urge does not vanish. The results are alarming. This month Ferdinand Waldo Demara Jr. died. That was his final career change. His obituary listed nearly as many metamorphoses as Ovid did. Demara, "the Great Imposter," spent years of his life being successfully and utterly some-one else: a Trappist monk, a doctor of psychology, a dean of philosophy at a small Pennsylvania college, a law student, a surgeon in the Royal Canadian Navy, a deputy warden at a prison in Texas. Demara took the protean itch and amateur's gusto, old American traits, to new frontiers of pathology and fraud.

Usually, it is only from the safety of retrospect and an established self that we entertain ourselves with visions of an alternative life. The daydreams are an amusement, a release from the monotony of what we are, from the life sentence of the mirror. The imagination's pageant of an alternative self is a kind of vacation from one's fate. Kierkegaard did not really mean he should have been a police spy, or Nixon that he should have been a sportswriter. The whole mechanism of daydreams of the antiself usually depends upon the fantasy remaining fantasy. Hell is answered prayers. God help us if we had actually married that girl when we were 21.

In weak, incoherent minds, the yearning antiself rises up and breaks through a wall into actuality. That seems to have happened with John W. Hinckley Jr., the young man who shot Ronald Reagan last year. Since no strong self disciplined his vagrant aches and needs, it was his antiself that pulled the trigger. It was his nonentity. The antiself is a monster sometimes, a cancer, a gnawing hypothesis.

All of our lives we are accompanied vaguely by the selves we might be. Man is the only creature that can imagine being someone else. The fantasy of being someone else is the basis of sympathy, of humanity. Daydreams of pos-sibility enlarge the mind. They are also haunting. Around every active mind there always hovers an aura of hypothesis and the subjunctive: almost every conscious intellect is continuously wandering elsewhere in time and space.

The past 20 years have stimulated the antiself. They have encouraged the notion of continuous self-renewal—as if the self were destined to be an end-less series of selves. Each one would be better than the last, or at least differ-ent, which was the point: a miracle of transformations, dreams popping into reality on fast-forward, life as a hectic multiple exposure.

For some reason, the more frivolous agitations of the collective antiself seem to have calmed down a little. Still, we walk around enveloped in it, like figures in the nimbus of their own ghosts on a television screen. Everything that we are not has a kind of evanescent being within us. We dream, and the dream is much of the definition of the true self. Last week Lena Horne said that she has always imagined herself being a teacher. Norman Vincent Peale says fervently that he wanted to be a salesman—and of course that is, in a sense, what he has always been. Opera singer Grace Bumbry wants to be a professional race-car driver. Bill Veeck, former owner of the Chicago White Sox, confides the alternate Veeck: a newspaperman. In a "nonfiction short story," Truman Capote wrote that he wanted to be a girl. Andy Warhol con-fesses without hesitation: "I've always wanted to be an airplane. Nothing more, nothing less. Even when I found out that they could crash, I still wanted to be an airplane."

The antiself has a shadowy, ideal life of its own. It is always blessed (the antiself is the Grecian Urn of our personality) and yet it subtly matures as it runs a course parallel to our actual aging. The Hindu might think that the antiself is a premonition of the soul's next life. Perhaps. But in the last moment of this life, self and antiself may coalesce. It should be their parting duet to mutter together: "On the whole, I'd rather be in Philadelphia."

Suggestions for Discussion

1. Why does Morrow think the Kierkegaard-Nixon fantasies seem to have got weirdly crossed? In his third paragraph he suggests the validity of the fantasies. How?

2. What are the symptoms, dangers, and values of dreaming of an alternative self?

3. What is the significance of the last sentence?

Suggestions for Writing

1. Describe the alternative self or selves which you have aspired to be.

2. Select one of the following statements and develop it in several paragraphs: A vacation loosens the knot of one's vocational identity; the daydreams are an amusement, a release . . . from the life sentence of the mirror; hell is answered prayers; the antiself is a monster sometimes, a cancer, a gnawing hypothesis; all of our lives we are accompanied vaguely by the selves we might be; the fantasy of being someone else is the basis of sympathy, of humanity; the past 20 years have stimulated the antiself; we dream, and the dream is much of the definition of the true self.

Ellen Goodman

The Company Man

Ellen Goodman (b. 1942) was educated at Radcliffe College and pursued a career as a journalist. She was a researcher and reporter for *Newsweek*, a feature writer for the *Boston Globe*, and a syndicated columnist with Washington Post Writers Group. She has been a Nieman fellow at Harvard University and named columnist of the year by the New England Women's Press Association. In 1980 she won a Pulitzer Prize for distinguished commentary. Her books include *Turning Points* (1979) and *At Large* (1981), a collection of newspaper columns. In this essay she portrays a workaholic whose sense of self is totally based upon his identification with his company.

He worked himself to death, finally and precisely, at 3:00 A.M. Sunday morning.

The obituary didn't say that, of course. It said that he died of a coronary thrombosis—I think that was it—but everyone among his friends and acquaintances knew it instantly. He was a perfect Type A, a workaholic, a classic, they said to each other and shook their heads—and thought for five or ten minutes about the way they lived.

This man who worked himself to death finally and precisely at 3:00 A.M. Sunday morning—on his day off—was fifty-one years old and a vice-president. He was, however, one of six vice-presidents, and one of three who might conceivably—if the president died or retired soon enough—have moved to the top spot. Phil knew that.

He worked six days a week, five of them until eight or nine at night, during a time when his own company had begun the four-day week for everyone but the executives. He worked like the Important People. He had no outside "extracurricular interests," unless, of course, you think about a monthly golf game that way. To Phil, it was work. He always ate egg salad sandwiches at his desk. He was, of course, overweight, by 20 or 25 pounds. He thought it was okay, though, because he didn't smoke.

On Saturdays, Phil wore a sports jacket to the office instead of a suit, because it was the weekend.

He had a lot of people working for him, maybe sixty, and most of them liked him most of the time. Three of them will be seriously considered for his job. The obituary didn't mention that.

But it did list his "survivors" quite accurately. He is survived by his wife, Helen, forty-eight years old, a good woman of no particular marketable skills, who worked in an office before marrying and mothering. She had, according to her daughter, given up trying to compete with his work years ago, when the children were small. A company friend said, "I know how much you will miss him." And she answered, "I already have."

"Missing him all these years," she must have given up part of herself which had cared too much for the man. She would be "well taken care of."

His "dearly beloved" eldest of the "dearly beloved" children is a hard-working executive in a manufacturing firm down South. In the day and a half before the funeral, he went around the neighborhood researching his father, asking the neighbors what he was like. They were embarrassed.

His second child is a girl, who is twenty-four and newly married. She lives near her mother and they are close, but whenever she was along with her father, in a car driving somewhere, they had nothing to say to each other.

The youngest is twenty, a boy, a high-school graduate who has spent the last couple of years, like a lot of his friends, doing enough odd jobs to stay in grass and food. He was the one who tried to grab at his father, and tried to mean enough to him to keep the man at home. He was his father's favorite. Over the last two years, Phil stayed up nights worrying about the boy.

The boy once said, "My father and I only board here."

At the funeral, the sixty-year-old company president told the forty-eight-year old widow that the fifty-one-year-old deceased had meant much to the company and would be missed and would be hard to replace. The widow didn't look him in the eye. She was afraid he would read her bitterness and, after all, she would need him to straighten out the finances—the stock options and all that.

Phil was overweight and nervous and worked too hard. If he wasn't at the office, he was worried about it. Phil was a Type A, a heart-attack natural. You could have picked him out in a minute from a lineup.

So when he finally worked himself to death, at precisely 3:00 A.M. Sunday morning, no one was really surprised.

By 5:00 P.M. the afternoon of the funeral, the company president had begun, discreetly of course, with care and taste, to make inquiries about his replacement. One of three men. He asked around: "Who's been working the hardest?"

Suggestions for Discussion

1. What does the clause "and thought for five or ten minutes about the way they lived" tell the reader about the author's point of view? About her tone?

2. What is the significance of the statement that the man who died was one of six vice-presidents and one of three who might . . . have moved to the top spot?

3. Why doesn't the author identify the man by name until the end of the third paragraph?

4. Goodman makes statements about Phil, then qualifies them. Cite instances. What is the nature of the qualification? How does this technique add to the characterization? To the tone?

5. What does the brief item on each family member and the company president tell readers about Phil? About themselves?

6. Account for the repetition of Phil's age and the hour of his death.

7. What is the significance of the president's question after the funeral?

8. What is the implicit statement that Goodman makes about workaholics? About large companies?

9. Speculate upon Phil's sense of self.

Suggestions for Writing

1. Make a study of a person you know whose sense of self is based on his or her identification with an institution, a business, a school, or a character in fiction.

2. If you know a workaholic, write a description using incidents and dialogue that illuminate his or her character.

Christopher Lasch

Changing Modes of Making It: From Horatio Alger to the Happy Hooker

Christopher Lasch (b. 1932) is an American historian and writer. He has taught at the University of Rochester since 1970. His publications include *The New Radicalism in America* (1965), *The Agony of the American Left* (1969), *The World of Nations* (1973), *Haven in a Heartless World: The Family Beseiged* (1977), and *The Culture of Narcissism* (1978) from which this excerpt was selected. In it Lasch traces the changing views of success in our culture.

> *American society is marked by a central stress upon personal achievement, especially secular occupational achievement. The "success story" and the respect accorded to the self-made man are distinctly American if anything is. . . . [American society] has endorsed Horatio Alger and has glorified the rail splitter who became president.*
>
> —*Robin Williams*

> *The man of ambition is still with us, as in all times, but now he needs a more subtle initiative, a deeper capacity to manipulate the democracy of emotions, if he is to maintain his separate identity and significantly augment it with success. . . . The sexual problems of the neurotic competing for some ephemeral kudos in mid-century Manhattan are very different from the problems of the neurotic in turn-of-the-century Vienna. History changes the expression of neurosis even if it does not change the underlying mechanisms.*
>
> —*Philip Rieff*

. . . *The Eclipse of Achievement*   In a society in which the dream of success has been drained of any meaning beyond itself, men have nothing against which to measure their achievements except the achievements of others. Self-approval depends on public recognition and acclaim, and the quality of this approval has undergone important changes in its own right. The good opinion of friends and neighbors, which formerly informed a man that he had lived a useful life, rested on appreciation of his accomplishments. Today men seek the kind of approval that applauds not their actions but their personal attributes. They wish to be not so much esteemed as admired. They crave not fame but the glamour and excitement of celebrity. They want to be envied rather than respected. Pride and acquisitiveness, the sins of an ascendant capitalism, have given way to vanity. Most Americans would still define success as riches, fame, and power, but their actions show that they have little interest in the substance of these attainments. What a man does matters less than the fact that he has "made it." Whereas fame depends on the performance of notable deeds acclaimed in biography and works of history, celebrity—the reward of those who project a vivid or pleasing exterior or have otherwise attracted attention to themselves—is acclaimed in the news media, in gossip columns, on talk shows, in magazines devoted to "personalities." Accordingly it is evanescent, like news itself, which loses its interest when it loses its novelty. Worldly success has always carried with it a certain poignancy, an awareness that "you can't take it with you"; but in our time, when success is so largely a function of youth, glamour, and novelty, glory is more fleeting than ever, and those who win the attention of the public worry incessantly about losing it.

Success in our society has to be ratified by publicity. The tycoon who lives in personal obscurity, the empire builder who controls the destinies of nations from behind the scenes, are vanishing types. Even nonelective officials, ostensibly preoccupied with questions of high policy, have to keep themselves constantly on view; all politics becomes a form of spectacle. It is well known that Madison Avenue packages politicians and markets them as if they were cereals or deodorants; but the art of public relations penetrates even more deeply into political life, transforming policy making itself. The modern prince does not much care that "there's a job to be done"—the slogan of American capitalism at an earlier and more enterprising stage of its development; what interests him is that "relevant audiences," in the language of the Pentagon Papers, have to be cajoled, won over, seduced. He confuses successful completion of the task at hand with the impression he makes or hopes to make on others. Thus American officials blundered into the war in Vietnam because they could not distinguish the country's military and strategic interests from "our reputation as a guarantor," as one of them put it. More concerned with the trappings that with the reality of power, they convinced themselves that failure to intervene would damage American "credibility." They borrowed the rhetoric of games theory to dignify their obsession with appearances, arguing that American policy in Vietnam had to address itself to "the relevant 'audiences' of U.S. actions"—the communists, the South Vietnamese, "our allies (who must trust us as 'underwriters')," and the American public.

When policy making, the search for power, and the pursuit of wealth have no other objects than to excite admiration or envy, men lose the sense of objectivity, always precarious under the best of circumstances. Impressions overshadow achievements. Public men fret about their ability to rise to crisis, to project an image of decisiveness, to give a convincing performance of executive power. Their critics resort to the same standards: when doubts began to be raised about the leadership of the Johnson administration, they focused on the "credibility gap." Public relations and propaganda have exalted the image and the pseudoevent. People "talk constantly," Daniel Boorstin has written, "not of things themselves, but of their images."

In the corporate structure as in government, the rhetoric of achievement, of singe-minded devotion to the task at hand—the rhetoric of performance, efficiency, and productivity—no longer provides an accurate description of the struggle for personal survival. "Hard work," according to Eugene Emerson Jennings, ". . . constitutes a necessary but not sufficient cause of upward mobility. It is not a route to the top." A newspaper man with experience both in journalism and in the Southern Regional Council has reported that "in neither, I realized, did it matter to the people in charge how well or how badly I performed. . . . Not the goals, but keeping the organization going, became the important thing." Even the welfare of the organization, however, no longer excites the enthusiasm it generated in the fifties. The "self-sacrificing company man," writes Jennings, has become "an obvious anachronism."* The upwardly mobile corporate executive "does not view himself as an organization man." His "anti-organizational posture," in fact, has emerged as his "chief characteristic." He advances through the corporate ranks not by serving the organization but by convincing his associates that he possesses the attributes of a "winner."

As the object of the corporate career shifts "from task-orientation and task-mastery to the control of the other player's moves," in the words of Thomas Szasz, success depends on "information about the personality of the other players." The better the corporate executive or bureaucrat understands the personal characteristics of his subordinates, the better he can exploit their mistakes in order to control them and to reassert his own supremacy. If he knows that his subordinates lie to him, the lie communicates the important information that they fear and wish to please him. "By accepting the bribe, as it were, of flattery, cajolery, or sheer subservience implicit in being lied to, the recipient of the lie states, in effect, that he is willing to barter these items for the truth." On the other hand, acceptance of the lie reassures the liar that he will not be punished, while reminding him of his dependence and subordination. "In this way, both parties gain a measure . . . of security." In Joseph Heller's novel *Something Happened,* the protagonist's boss makes it clear that he wants from his subordinates not "good work" but "spastic colitis and nervous exhaustion."

> God dammit, I want the people working for me to be worse off than I am, not better. That's the reason I pay you so well. I want to see you right on the verge. I want it right out in the open. I want to be able to hear it in a stuttering, flustered, tongue-tied voice. . . . Don't trust me. I don't trust flattery, loyalty, and sociability. I don't trust deference, respect, and cooperation. I trust fear.

According to Jennings, the "loyalty ethic" has declined in American business among other reasons because loyalty can "be too easily simulated or feigned by those most desirous of winning."

The argument that bureaucratic organizations devote more energy to the maintenance of hierarchical relations than to industrial efficiency gains strength from the consideration that modern capitalist production arose in the first place not because it was necessarily more efficient that other methods of organizing work but because it provided capitalists with greater profits and power. The case for the factory system, according to Stephen Marglin, rested

---

*In the 1950s, the organization man thought of an attractive, socially gifted wife as an important asset to his career. Today executives are warned of the "apparent serious conflict between marriage and a management career." A recent report compares the "elite corps of professional managers" to the Janissaries, elite soldiers of the Ottoman empire who were taken from their parents as children, raised by the state, and never allowed to marry. "A young man considering [a managerial] career might well think of himself as a modern-day Janissary—and consider very, very carefully whether marriage in any way conforms to his chosen life."

not on its technological superiority over handicraft production but on the more effective control of the labor force it allowed the employer. In the words of Andrew Ure, the philosopher of manufactures, introduction of the factory system enabled the capitalist to "subdue the refractory tempers of work people." As the hierarchical organization of work invades the managerial function itself, the office takes on the characteristics of the factory, and the enforcement of clearly demarcated lines of dominance and subordination within management takes on as much importance as the subordination of labor to management as a whole. In the "era of corporate mobility," however, the lines of superiority and subordination constantly fluctuate, and the successful bureaucrat survives not by appealing to the authority of his office but by establishing a pattern of upward movement, cultivating upwardly mobile superiors, and administering "homeopathic doses of humiliation" to those he leaves behind in his ascent to the top.

The Art of Social Survival   The transformation of the myth of success—of the definition of success and of the qualities believed to promote it—is a long-term development arising not from particular historical events but from general changes in the structure of society: the shifting emphasis from capitalist production to consumption; the growth of large organizations and bureaucracies; the increasingly dangerous and warlike conditions of social life. More than twenty-five years have passed since David Riesman argued that the transition from the "invisible hand" to the "glad hand" marked a fundamental change in the organization of personality, from the inner-directed type dominant in the nineteenth century to the other-directed type of today. Other scholars at that time, when interest in culture and personality studies was stronger than it is now, proposed similar descriptions of the changing character structure of advanced capitalist society. William H. Whyte's "organization man," Erich Fromm's "market-oriented personality," Karen Horney's "neurotic personality of our time," and the studies of American national character by Margaret Mead and Geoffrey Gorer all captured essential aspects of the new man: his eagerness to get along well with others; his need to organize even his private life in accordance with the requirements of large organizations; his attempt to sell himself as if his own personality were a commodity with an assignable market value; his neurotic need for affection, reassurance, and oral gratification; the corruptibility of his values. In one respect, however, these studies of American culture and personality created a misleading impression of the changes that were taking place beneath what Riesman called the "bland surface of American sociability." The critics of the forties and fifties mistook this surface for the deeper reality.

According to Erich Fromm, Americans had lost the capacity for spontaneous feeling, even for anger. One of "the essential aims of the educational process" was to eliminate antagonism, to cultivate a "commercialized friendliness." "If you do not smile you are judged lacking in a 'pleasing personality'—and you need a pleasing personality if you want to sell your services, whether as a waitress, a salesman, or a physician." Like many social scientists, Fromm exaggerated the degree to which aggressive impulses can be socialized; he saw man as entirely a product of socialization, not as a creature of instinct whose partially repressed or sublimated drives always threaten to break out in all their original ferocity. The American cult of friendliness conceals but does not eradicate a murderous competition for goods and position;

indeed this competition has grown more savage in an age of diminishing expectations.

In the fifties, affluence, leisure, and the "quality of life" loomed as major issues. The welfare state had allegedly eradicated poverty, gross economic inequalities, and the conflicts to which they formerly gave rise. The seeming triumphs of American capitalism left social critics little to worry about except the decline of individualism and the menace of conformity. Arthur Miller's Willy Loman, the salesman who wants no more out of life than to be "well liked," symbolized the issues that troubled the postwar period. In the seventies, a harsher time, it appears that the prostitute, not the salesman, best exemplifies the qualities indispensable to success in American society. She too sells herself for a living, but her seductiveness hardly signifies a wish to be well liked. She craves admiration but scorns those who provide it and thus derives little gratification from her social successes. She attempts to move others while remaining unmoved herself. The fact that she lives in a milieu of interpersonal relations does not make her a conformist or an "other-directed" type. She remains a loner, dependent on others only as a hawk depends on chickens. She exploits the ethic of pleasure that has replaced the ethic of achievement, but her career more than any other reminds us that contemporary hedonism, of which she is the supreme symbol, originates not in the pursuit of pleasure but in a war of all against all, in which even the most intimate encounters become a form of mutual exploitation.

It is not merely that pleasure, once it is defined as an end in itself, takes on the qualities of work, as Martha Wolfenstein observed in her essay on "fun morality"—that play is now "measured by standards of achievement previously applicable only to work." The measurement of sexual "performance," the insistence that sexual satisfaction depends on proper "technique," and the widespread belief that it can be "achieved" only after coordinated effort, practice, and study all testify to the invasion of play by the rhetoric of achievement. But those who deplore the transformation of play into performance confine their attention to the surface of play, in this case to the surface of sexual encounters. Beneath the concern for performance lies a deeper determination to manipulate the feelings of others to your own advantage. The search for competitive advantage through emotional manipulation increasingly shapes not only personal relations but relations at work as well; it is for this reason that sociability can now function as an extension of work by other means. Personal life, no longer a refuge from deprivations suffered at work, has become as anarchical, as warlike, and as full of stress as the marketplace itself. The cocktail party reduces sociability to social combat. Experts write tactical manuals in the art of social survival, advising the status-seeking partygoer to take up a commanding position in the room, surround himself with a loyal band of retainers, and avoid turning his back on the field of battle.

The recent vogue of "assertiveness therapy," a counter-program designed to equip the patient with defenses against manipulation, appeals to the growing recognition that agility in interpersonal relations determines what looks on the surface like achievement. Assertiveness training seeks to rid the patient of "feelings of anxiety, ignorance, and guilt that . . . are used efficiently by other people to get us to do what they want." Other forms of game therapy alert patients to the "games people play" and thus attempt to promote "game-free intimacy." The importance of such programs, however, lies not so much in their objectives as in the anxiety to which they appeal and the vision of reality that informs them—the perception that success depends on psychological manipulation and that all of life, even the ostensibly achievement-oriented realm of work, centers on the struggle for interpersonal advantage, the deadly game of intimidating friends and seducing people.

The Apotheosis of Individualism   The fear that haunted the social critics and theorists of the fifties—that rugged individualism had succumbed to conformity and "low-pressure sociability"—appears in retrospect to have been premature. In 1960, David Riesman complained that young people no longer had much social "presence," their education having provided them not with "a polished personality but [with] an affable, casual, adaptable one, suitable to the loose-jointed articulation and heavy job turnover in the expanding organizations of an affluent society." It is true that "a present-oriented hedonism," as Riesman went on to argue, has replaced the work ethic "among the very classes which in the earlier stages of industrialization were oriented toward the future, toward distant goals and delayed gratification." But this hedonism is a fraud; the pursuit of pleasure disguises a struggle for power. Americans have not really become more sociable and cooperative, as the theorists of other-direction and conformity would like us to believe; they have merely become more adept at exploiting the conventions of interpersonal relations for their own benefit. Activities ostensibly undertaken purely for enjoyment often have the real object of doing others in. It is symptomatic of the underlying tenor of American life that vulgar terms for sexual intercourse also convey the sense of getting the better of someone, working him over, taking him in, imposing your will through guile, deception, or superior force. Verbs associated with sexual pleasure have acquired more than the usual overtones of violence and psychic exploitation. In the violent world of the ghetto, the language of which now pervades American society as a whole, the violence associated with sexual intercourse is directed with special intensity by men against women, specifically against their mothers. The language of ritualized aggression and abuse reminds those who use it that exploitation is the general rule and some form of dependence the common fate; that "the individual," in Lee Rainwater's words, "is not strong enough or adult enough to achieve his goal in a legitimate way, but is rather like a child, dependent on others who tolerate his childish maneuvers"; accordingly males, even adult males, often depend on women for support and nurture. Many of them have to pimp for a living, ingratiating themselves with a woman in order to pry money from her; sexual relations thus become manipulative and predatory. Satisfaction depends on taking what you want instead of waiting for what is rightfully yours to receive. All this enters everyday speech in language that connects sex with aggression and sexual aggression with highly ambivalent feelings about mothers.*

*In the late sixties, white radicals enthusiastically adopted the slogan, "Up against the Wall, Motherfucker!" But the term has long since lost its revolutionary associations, like other black idioms first popularized among whites by political radicals and spokesmen for the counterculture, and in slightly expurgated form has become so acceptable that the term "mother" has everywhere become, even among tenny-boppers, a term of easygoing familiarity or contempt. Similarly the Rolling Stones and other exponents of hard or acid rock, who used the obscenity of the ghetto to convey a posture of militant alienation, have given way to groups that sing more sweetly, but still in ghetto accents, of a world where you get only what you're prepared to take. The pretense of revolutionary solidarity having evaporated, as the zonked-out lovefest of the "Woodstock Nation" deteriorated into the murderous chaos of Altamont, the underlying cynicism surfaces more clearly than ever. Every mother for himself!

In some ways middle-class society has become a pale copy of the black ghetto, as the appropriation of its language would lead us to believe. We do not need to minimize the poverty of the ghetto or the suffering inflicted by whites on blacks in order to see that the increasingly dangerous and unpredictable conditions of middle-class life have given rise to similar strategies for survival. Indeed the attraction of black culture for disaffected whites suggests that black culture now speaks to a general condition, the most important feature of which is a widespread loss of confidence in the future. The poor have always had to live for the present, but now a desperate concern for personal survival, sometimes disguised as hedonism, engulfs the middle class as well. Today almost everyone lives in a dangerous world from which there is little escape. International terrorism and blackmail, bombings, and hijackings arbitrarily affect the rich and poor alike. Crime, violence, and gang wars make cities unsafe and threaten to spread to the suburbs. Racial violence on the streets and in the schools creates an atmosphere of chronic tension and threatens to erupt at any time into full-scale racial conflict. Unemployment spreads from the poor to the white-collar class, while inflation eats away the savings of those who hoped to retire in comfort. Much of what is euphemistically known as the middle class, merely because it dresses up to go to work, is now reduced to proletarian conditions of existence. Many white-collar jobs require no more skill and pay even less than blue-collar jobs, conferring little status or security. The propaganda of death and destruction, emanating ceaselessly from the mass media, adds to the prevailing atmosphere of insecurity. Far-flung famines, earthquakes in remote regions, distant wars and uprisings attract the same attention as events closer to home. The impression of arbitrariness in the reporting of disaster reinforces the arbitrary quality of experience itself, and the absence of continuity in the coverage of events, as today's crisis yields to a new and unrelated crisis tomorrow, adds to the sense of historical discontinuity—the sense of living in a world in which the past holds out no guidance to the present and the future has become completely unpredictable.

Older conceptions of success presupposed a world in rapid motion, in which fortunes were rapidly won and lost and new opportunities unfolded every day. Yet they also presupposed a certain stability, a future that bore some recognizable resemblance to the present and the past. The growth of bureaucracy, the cult of consumption with its immediate gratifications, but above all the severance of the sense of historical continuity have transformed the Protestant ethic while carrying the underlying principles of capitalist society to their logical conclusion. The pursuit of self-interest, formerly identified with the rational pursuit of gain and the accumulation of wealth, has become a search for pleasure and psychic survival. Social conditions now approximate the vision of republican society conceived by the Marquis de Sade at the very outset of the republican epoch. In many ways the most farsighted and certainly the most disturbing of the prophets of revolutionary individualism, Sade defended unlimited self-indulgence as the logical culmination of the revolution in property relations—the only way to attain revolutionary brotherhood in its purest form. By regressing in his writings to the most primitive level of fantasy, Sade uncannily glimpsed the whole subsequent development of personal life under capitalism, ending not in revolutionary brotherhood but in a society of siblings that has outlived and repudiated its revolutionary origins.

Sade imagined a sexual utopia in which everyone has the right to everyone else, where human beings, reduced to their sexual organs, become absolutely anonymous and interchangeable. His ideal society thus reaffirmed the capitalist principle that human beings are ultimately reducible to interchangeable objects. It also incorporated and carried to a surprising new conclusion Hobbes's discovery that the destruction of paternalism and the subordination of all social relations to the market had stripped away the remaining restraints and the mitigating illusions from the war of all against all. In the resulting state of organized anarchy, as Sade was the first to realize, pleasure becomes life's only business—pleasure, however, that is indistinguishable from rape, murder, unbridled aggression. In a society that has reduced reason to mere calculation, reason can impose no limits on the pursuit of pleasure—on the immediate gratification of every desire no matter how perverse, insane, criminal, or merely immoral. For the standards that would condemn crime or cruelty derive from religion, compassion, or the kind of reason that rejects purely instrumental applications; and none of these outmoded forms of thought or feeling has any logical place in a society based on commodity production. In his misogyny, Sade perceived that bourgeois enlightenment, carried to its logical conclusions, condemned even the sentimental cult of womanhood and the family, which the bourgeoisie itself had carried to unprecedented extremes.

At the same time, he saw that condemnation of "woman-worship" had to go hand in hand with a defense of woman's sexual rights—their right to dispose of their own bodies, as feminists would put it today. If the exercise of that right in Sade's utopia boils down to the duty to become an instrument of someone else's pleasure, it was not so much because Sade hated women as because he hated humanity. He perceived, more clearly than the feminists, that all freedoms under capitalism come in the end to the same thing, the same universal obligation to enjoy and be enjoyed. In the same breath, and without violating his own logic, Sade demanded for women the right "fully to satisfy all their desires" and "all parts of their bodies" and categorically stated that "all women must submit to our pleasure." Pure individualism thus issued in the most radical repudiation of individuality. "All men, all women resemble each other," according to Sade; and to those of his countrymen who would become republicans he adds the ominous warning: "Do not think you can make good republicans so long as you isolate in their families the children who should belong to the republic alone." The bourgeois defense of privacy culminates—not just in Sade's thought but in the history to come, so accurately foreshadowed in the very excess, madness, infantilism of his ideas—in the most thoroughgoing attack on privacy; the glorification of the individual, in his annihilation.

Suggestions for Discussion

1. Explain Rieff's statement that "The man of ambition is still with us, as in all times, but now he needs a more subtle initiative, a deeper capacity to manipulate the democracy of emotions, if he is to maintain his separate identity and significantly augment it with success." How is this statement illustrated in Lasch's essay?

2. What does the tone of the first paragraph in the section "The Eclipse of Achievement" tell the reader about Lasch's view of current attitudes toward success?

3. How does the author describe the changes in corporate life and mobility?

4. How does Lasch support his view that Fromm "exaggerated the degree to which aggressive impulses can be socialized"? How do the views of Sade support Fromm's statement?

5. Why does Lasch regard the prostitute as a symbol of success in American society?

6. How does the author support his view that "the pursuit of pleasure disguises a struggle for power"?

7. What is meant by "the arbitrary quality of experience"?

8. What view of the self do you think Lasch espouses in his analysis?

Suggestions for Writing

1. Develop an essay on question 1 above.

2. Describe a "self-made man" you know or have observed by placing him in a work setting or in his home and recording the kind of dialogue you would expect him to have with a member of his family.

3. Select one of Lasch's value judgments and on the basis of your experience support or refute it.

4. Write an essay in which you analyze cultural attitudes that are expressed in rock music.

Fiction

—◆◆◆—

William Faulkner

The Bear

William Faulkner (1897–1962) lived most of his life in Oxford, Mississippi. After a year at the University of Mississippi, he joined the Royal Canadian Air Force, out of eagerness to fight in World War I. His novels, set in his imaginary Yoknapatawpha County, include *The Sound and the Fury* (1929), *Light in August* (1932), *Absalom, Absalom!* (1936), and *The Hamlet* (1940). In 1949 he won the Nobel Prize for Literature. In this story of initiation the boy learns that "what the heart holds to becomes truth, as far as we know the truth."

He was ten. But it had already begun, long before that day when at last he wrote his age in two figures and he saw for the first time the camp where his father and Major de Spain and old General Compson and the others spent two weeks each November and two weeks again each June. He had already inherited then, without ever having seen it, the tremendous bear with one trap-ruined foot which, in an area almost a hundred miles deep, had earned itself a name, a definite designation like a living man.

He had listened to it for years: the long legend of corncribs rifled, of shotes and grown pigs and even calves carried boldly into the woods and devoured, of traps and deadfalls overthrown and dogs mangled and slain, and shotgun and even rifle charges delivered at point-blank range and with no more effect than so many peas blown through a tube by a boy—a corridor of wreckage and destruction beginning back before he was born, through which sped, not fast but rather with the ruthless and irresistible deliberation of a locomotive, the shaggy tremendous shape.

It ran in his knowledge before he ever saw it. It looked and towered in his dreams before he even saw the unaxed woods where it left its crooked print, shaggy, huge red-eyed, not malevolent but just big—too big for the dogs which tried to bay it, for the horses which tried to ride it down, for the men and bullets they fired into it, too big for the very country which was its constricting scope. He seemed to see it entire with a child's complete divination before he ever laid eyes on either—the doomed wilderness whose edges were being constantly and punily gnawed at by men with axes and plows who feared it because it was wilderness, men myriad and nameless even to one another in the land where the old bear had earned a name, through which ran not even a mortal animal but an anachronism, indomitable and invincible, out of an old dead time, a phantom, epitome and apotheosis of the old wild life at which the puny humans swarmed and hacked in a fury of abhorrence and fear, like pygmies about the ankles of a drowsing elephant: the old bear solitary, indomitable and alone, widowered, childless, and absolved of mortality—old Priam reft of his old wife and having outlived all his sons.

Until he was ten, each November he would watch the wagon containing the dogs and the bedding and food and guns and his father and Tennie's Jim, the Negro, and Sam Fathers, the Indian, son of a slave woman and a Chickasaw chief, depart on the road to town, to Jefferson, where Major de Spain and the others would join them. To the boy, at seven, eight, and nine, they were not going into the Big Bottom to hunt bear and deer, but to keep yearly rendezvous with the bear which they did not even intend to kill. Two weeks later they would return, with no trophy, no head and skin. He had not expected it. He had not even been afraid it would be in the wagon. He believed that even after he was ten and his father would let him go too, for those two weeks in November, he would merely make another one, along with his father and Major de Spain and General Compson and the others, the dogs which feared to bay at it and the rifles and shotguns which failed even to bleed it, in the yearly pageant of the old bear's furious immortality.

Then he heard the dogs. It was in the second week of his first time in the camp. He stood with Sam Fathers against a big oak beside the faint crossing where they had stood each dawn for nine days now, hearing the dogs. He had heard them once before, one morning last week—a murmur, sourceless, echoing through the wet woods, swelling presently into separate voices which he could recognize and call by name. He had raised and cocked the gun as Sam told him and stood motionless again while the uproar, the invisible course, swept up and past and faded; it seemed to him that he could actually see the deer, the buck, blond, smoke-colored, elongated with speed, fleeing, vanishing, the woods, the gray solitude, still ringing even when the cries of the dogs had died away.

"Now let the hammers down," Sam said.

"You knew they were not coming here too," he said.

"Yes," Sam said. "I want you to learn how to do when you didn't shoot. It's after the chance for the bear or the deer has done already come and gone that men and dogs get killed."

"Anyway," he said, "it was just a deer."

Then on the tenth morning he heard the dogs again. And he readied the too-long, too-heavy gun as Sam had taught him, before Sam even spoke. But this time it was no deer, no ringing chorus of dogs running strong on a free scent, but a moiling yapping an octave too high, with something more than indecision and even abjectness in it, not even moving very fast, taking a long time to pass completely out of hearing, leaving then somewhere in the air that echo, thin, slightly hysterical, abject, almost grieving, with no sense of a fleeing, unseen, smoke-colored, grass-eating shape ahead of it, and Sam, who had taught him first of all to cock the gun and take position where he could see everywhere and then never move again, had himself moved up beside him; he could hear Sam breathing at his shoulder, and he could see the arched curve of the old man's inhaling nostrils.

"Hah," Sam said. "Not even running. Walking."

"Old Ben!" the boy said. "But up here!" he cried. "Way up here!"

"He do it every year," Sam said. "Once. Maybe to see who in camp this time, if he can shoot or not. Whether we got the dog yet that can bay and hold him. He'll take them to the river, and then he'll send them back home. We may as well go back too; see how they look when they come back to camp."

When they reached the camp the hounds were already there, ten of them crouching back under the kitchen, the boy and Sam squatting to peer back into the obscurity where they had huddled, quiet, the eyes luminous glowing at them and vanishing, and no sound, only that effluvium of something more than dog, stronger than dog and not just animal, just beast, because still there had been nothing in front of that abject and almost painful yapping save the solitude, the wilderness, so that when the eleventh hound came in at noon and with all the others watching—even old Uncle Ash, who called himself first a cook—Sam daubed the tattered ear and the raked shoulder with turpentine and axle grease, to the boy it was still no living creature, but the wilderness which, leaning for the moment down, had patted lightly once the hound's temerity.

"Just like a man," Sam said. "Just like folks. Put off as long as she could having to be brave, knowing all the time that sooner or later she would have to be brave to keep on living with herself, and knowing all the time before hand what was going to happen to her when she done it."

That afternoon, himself on the one-eyed wagon mule which did not mind the smell of blood nor, as they told him, of bear, and with Sam on the other one, they rode for more than three hours through the rapid, shortening winter day. They followed no path, no trail even that he could see; almost at once they were in a country which he had never seen before. Then he knew why Sam had made him ride the mule which would not spook. The sound one stopped short and tried to whirl and bolt even as Sam got down, blowing its breath, jerking and wrenching at the rein, while Sam held it, coaxing it forward with his voice, since he could not risk tying it, drawing it forward while the boy got down from the marred one.

Then, standing beside Sam in the gloom of the dying afternoon, he looked down at the routed over-turned log, gutted and scored with claw marks and, in the wet earth beside it, the print of the enormous warped two-toed foot. He knew now what he had smelled when he peered under the kitchen where the dogs huddled. He realized for the first time that the bear which had run in his listening and loomed in his dreams since before he could remember to the contrary, and which, therefore, must have existed in the listening and dreams of his father and Major de Spain and even old General Compson, too, before they began to remember in their turn, was a mortal animal, and that if they had departed for the camp each November without any actual hope of bringing its trophy back, it was not because it could not be slain, but because so far they had had no actual hope to.

"Tomorrow," he said.

"We'll try tomorrow," Sam said. "We ain't got the dog yet."

"We've got eleven. They ran him this morning."

"It won't need but one," Sam said. "He ain't here. Maybe he ain't nowhere. The only other way will be for him to run by accident over somebody that has a gun."

"That wouldn't be me," the boy said. "It will be Walter or Major or—"

"It might," Sam said. "You watch close in the morning. Because he's smart. That's how come he has lived this long. If he gets hemmed up and has to pick out somebody to run over, he will pick out you."

"How?" the boy said. "How will he know—" He ceased. "You mean he already knows me, that I ain't never been here before, ain't had time to find out yet whether I—" He ceased again, looking at Sam, the old man whose face revealed nothing until it smiled. He said humbly, not even amazed, "It was me he was watching. I don't reckon he did need to come but once."

The next morning they left the camp three hours before daylight. They rode this time because it was too far to walk, even the dogs in the wagon; again the first gray light found him in a place which he had never seen before, where Sam had placed him and told him to stay and then departed. With the gun which was too big for him, which did not even belong to him, but to Major de Spain, and which he had fired only once—at a stump on the first day, to learn the recoil and how to reload it—he stood against a gun tree beside a little bayou whose black still water crept without movement out of a canebrake and crossed a small clearing and into cane again, where, invisible, a bird—the big woodpecker called Lord-to-God by Negroes—clattered at a dead limb.

It was a stand like any other, dissimilar only in incidentals to the one where he had stood each morning for ten days; a territory new to him, yet no less familiar than that other one which, after almost two weeks, he had come to believe he knew a little—the same solitude, the same loneliness through which human beings had merely passed without altering it, leaving no mark, no scar, which looked exactly as it must have looked when the first ancestor of Sam Father's Chickasaw predecessors crept into it and looked about, club or stone ax or bone arrow drawn and poised; different only because, squatting at the edge of the kitchen, he smelled the hounds huddled and cringing beneath it and saw the raked ear and shoulder of the one who, Sam said, had had to be brave once in order to live with herself, and saw yesterday in the earth beside the gutted log the print of the living foot.

He heard no dogs at all. He never did hear them. He only heard the drumming of the woodpecker stop short off and knew that the bear was looking at him. He never saw it. He did not know whether it was in front of him or behind him. He did not move, holding the useless gun, which he had not even had warning to cock and which even now he did not cock, tasting in his saliva that taint as of brass which he knew now because he had smelled it when he peered under the kitchen at the huddled dogs.

Then it was gone. As abruptly as it had ceased, the woodpecker's dry, monotonous clatter set up again, and after a while he even believed he could hear the dogs—a murmur, scarce a sound even, which he had probably been hearing for some time before he even remarked it, drifting into hearing and then out again, dying away. They came nowhere near him. If it was a bear they ran, it was another bear. It was Sam himself who came out of the cane and crossed the bayou, followed by the injured bitch of yesterday. She was almost at heel, like a bird dog, making no sound. She came and crouched against his leg, trembling, staring off into the cane.

"I didn't see him," he said. "I didn't, Sam!"

"I know it," Sam said. "He done the looking. You didn't hear him neither, did you?"

"No," the boy said. "I—"

"He's smart," Sam said. "Too smart." He looked down at the hound, trembling faintly and steadily against the boy's knee. From the raked shoulder a few drops of fresh blood oozed and clung. "Too big. We ain't got the dog yet. But maybe someday. Maybe not next time. But someday."

So I must see him, he thought. *I must look at him.* Otherwise, it seemed to him that it would go on like this forever, as it had gone on with his father and Major de Spain, who was older than his father, and even with old General Compson, who had been old enough to be a brigade commander in 1865. Otherwise, it would go on forever, next time and next time, after and after and after. It seemed to him that he could never see the two of them, himself and the bear, shadowy in the limbo from which time emerged, becoming time; the old bear absolved of mortality and himself partaking, sharing a little of it, enough of it. And he knew now what he had smelled in the huddled dogs and tasted in his saliva. He recognized fear. *So I will have to see him,* he thought, without dread or even hope. *I will have to look at him.*

It was June of the next year. He was eleven. They were in camp again, celebrating Major de Spain's and General Compson's birthdays. Although the one had been born in September and the other in the depth of winter and in another decade, they had met for two weeks to fish and shoot squirrels and turkey and run coons and wildcats with the dogs at night. That is, he and Boon Hoggenbeck and the Negroes fished and shot squirrels and ran the coons and cats, because the proved hunters, not only Major de Spain and old General Compson, who spent those two weeks sitting in a rocking chair before a tremendous iron pot of Brunswick stew, stirring and tasting, with old Ash to quarrel with about how he was making it and Tennie's Jim to pour whiskey from the demijohn into the tin dipper from which he drank it, but even the boy's father and Walter Ewell, who were still young enough, scorned such, other than shooting the wild gobblers with pistols for wagers on their marksmanship.

Or, that is, his father and the others believed he was hunting squirrels. Until the third day, he thought that Sam Fathers believed that too. Each morning he would leave the camp right after breakfast. He had his own gun now, a Christmas present. He went back to the tree beside the bayou where he had stood that morning. Using the compass which old General Compson had given him, he ranged from that point; he was teaching himself to be a better-than-fair woodsman without knowing he was doing it. On the second day he found the gutted log where he had first seen the crooked print. It was almost completely crumbled now, healing with unbelievable speed, a passionate and almost visible relinquishment, back into the earth from which the tree had grown.

He ranged the summer woods now, green with gloom; if anything, actually dimmer than in November's gray dissolution, where, even at noon, the sun fell only in intermittent dappling upon the earth, which never completely dried out and which crawled with snakes—moccasins and water snakes and rattlers, themselves the color of the dappling gloom, so that he would not always see them until they moved, returning later and later, first day, second day, passing in the twilight of the third evening the little log pen enclosing the log stable where Sam was putting up the horses for the night.

"You ain't looked right yet," Sam said.

He stopped. For a moment he didn't answer. Then he said peacefully, in a peaceful rushing burst as when a boy's miniature dam in a little brook gives way, "All right. But how? I went to the bayou. I even found that log again. I—"

"I reckon that was all right. Likely he's been watching you. You never saw his foot?"

"I," the boy said—"I didn't—I never thought—"

"It's the gun," Sam said. He stood beside the fence motionless—the old man, the Indian, in the battered faded overalls and the five-cent straw hat which in the Negro's race had been the badge of its enslavement and was now the regalia of his freedom. The camp—the clearing, the house, the barn and its tiny lot with which Major de Spain in his turn had scratched punily and evanescently at the wilderness—faded in the dusk, back into the immemorial darkness of the woods. *The gun,* the boy thought. *The gun.*

"Be scared," Sam said. "You can't help that. But don't be afraid. Ain't nothing in the woods going to hurt you unless you corner it, or it smells that you are afraid. A bear or a deer, too, has got to be scared of a coward the same as a brave man has got to be."

The gun, the boy thought.

"You will have to choose," Sam said.

He left the camp before daylight, long before Uncle Ash would wake in his quilts on the kitchen floor and start the fire for breakfast. He had only the compass and a stick for snakes. He could go almost a mile before he would begin to need the compass. He sat on a log, the invisible compass in his invisible hand, while the secret night sounds, fallen still at his movements, scurried again and then ceased for good, and the owls ceased and gave over to the waking of day birds, and he could see the compass. Then he went fast yet still quietly; he was becoming better and better as a woodsman, still without having yet realized it.

He jumped a doe and a fawn at sunrise, walked them out of the bed, close enough to see them—the crash of undergrowth, the white scut, the fawn scudding behind her faster than he had believed it could run. He was hunting right, upwind, as Sam had taught him; not that it mattered now. He had left the gun; of his own will and relinquishment he had accepted not a gambit, not a choice, but a condition in which not only the bear's heretofore inviolable anonymity but all the old rules and balances of hunter and hunted had been abrogated. He would not even be afraid, not even in the moment when the fear would take him completely—blood, skin, bowels, bones, memory from the long time before it became his memory—all save that thin, clear, immortal lucidity which alone differed him from this bear and from all the other bear and deer he would ever kill in the humility and pride of his skill and endurance, to which Sam had spoken when he leaned in the twilight on the lot fence yesterday.

By noon he was far beyond the little bayou, farther into the new and alien country than he had ever been. He was traveling now not only by the old, heavy, biscuit-thick silver watch which had belonged to his grandfather. When he stopped at last, it was for the first time since he had risen from the log at dawn when he could see the compass. It was far enough. He had left the camp nine hours ago; nine hours from now, dark would have already been an hour old. But he didn't think that. He thought, *All right. Yes. But what?* and stood for a moment, alien and small in the green and topless solitude, answering his own question before it had formed and ceased. It was the watch, the compass, the stick—the three lifeless mechanicals with which for nine hours he had fended the wilderness off; he hung the watch and compass carefully on a bush and leaned the stick beside them and relinquished completely to it.

He had not been going very fast for the last two or three hours. He went no faster now, since distance would not matter even if he could have gone fast. And he was trying to keep a bearing on the tree where he had left the compass, trying to complete a circle which would bring him back to it or at least intersect itself, since direction would not matter now either. But the tree was not there, and he did as Sam had schooled him—made the next circle in the opposite direction, so that the two patterns would bisect somewhere, but crossing no print of his own feet, finding the tree at last, but in the wrong place—no bush, no compass, no watch—and the tree not even the tree, because there was a down log beside it and he did what Sam Fathers had told him was the next thing and the last.

As he sat down on the log he saw the crooked print—the warped, tremendous, two-toed indentation which, even as he watched it, filled with water. As he looked up, the wilderness coalesced, solidified—the glade, the tree he sought, the bush, the watch and the compass glinting where a ray of sunshine touched them. Then he saw the bear. It did not emerge, appear; it was just there, immobile, solid, fixed in the hot dappling of the green and windless noon, not as big as he had dreamed it, but as big as he had expected it, bigger, dimensionless, against the dappled obscurity, looking at him where he sat quietly on the log and looked back at it.

Then it moved. It made no sound. It did not hurry. It crossed the glade, walking for an instant into the full glare of the sun; when it reached the other side it stopped again and looked back at him across one shoulder while his quiet breathing inhaled and exhaled three times.

Then it was gone. It didn't walk into the woods, the under-growth. It faded, sank back into the wilderness as he had watched a fish, a huge old bass, sink and vanish into the dark depths of its pool without even any movements of its fins.

He thought, *It will be next fall.* But it was not next fall, nor the next nor the next. He was fourteen then. He had killed his buck, and Sam Fathers had marked his face with the hot blood, and in the next year he killed a bear. But even before that accolade he had become as competent in the woods as many grown men with the same experience; by his fourteenth year he was a better woodsman than most grown men with more. There was no territory within thirty miles of the camp that he did not know—bayou, ridge, brake, landmark, tree and path. He could have led anyone to any point in it without deviation, and brought them out again. He knew the game trails that even Sam Fathers did not know; in his thirteenth year he found a buck's bedding place, and unbeknown to his father he borrowed Walter Ewell's rifle and lay in wait at dawn and killed the buck when it walked back to the bed, as Sam had told him how the old Chickasaw fathers did.

But not the old bear, although by now he knew its footprints better than he did his own, and not only the crooked one. He could see any one of the three sound ones and distinguish it from any other, and not only by its size. There were other bears within these thirty miles which left tracks almost as large, but this was more than that. If Sam Fathers had been his mentor and the back-yard rabbits and squirrels at home his kindergarten, then the wilderness the old bear ran was his college, the old male bear itself, so long unwifed and childless as to have become its own ungendered progenitor, was his alma mater. But he never saw it.

He could find the crooked print now almost whenever he liked, fifteen or ten or five miles, or sometimes nearer the camp than that. Twice while on stand during the three years he heard the dogs strike its trail by accident; on the second time they jumped it seemingly, the voices high, abject, almost human in hysteria, as on that first morning two years ago. But not the bear itself. He would remember that noon three years ago, the glade, himself and the bear fixed during that moment in the windless and dappled blaze, and it would seem to him that it had never happened, that he had dreamed that too. But it had happened. They had looked at each other, they had emerged from the wilderness old as earth, synchronized to the instant by something more than the blood that moved the flesh and bones which bore them, and touched, pledged something, affirmed something more lasting than the frail web of bones and flesh which any accident could obliterate.

Then he saw it again. Because of the very fact that he thought of nothing else, he had forgotten to look for it. He was still hunting with Walter Ewell's rifle. He saw it cross the end of a long blow-down, a corridor where a tornado had swept, rushing through rather than over the tangle of trunks and branches as a locomotive would have, faster than he had ever believed it could move, almost as fast as a deer even, because a deer would have spent most of that time in the air, faster than he could bring the rifle sights up with it. And now he knew what had been wrong during all the three years. He sat on a log, shaking and trembling as if he had never seen the woods before nor anything that ran them, wondering with incredulous amazement how he could have forgotten the very thing which Sam Fathers had told him and which the bear itself had proved the next day and had now returned after three years to reaffirm.

And now he knew what Sam Fathers had meant about the right dog, a dog in which size would mean less than nothing. So when he returned alone in April—school was out then, so that the sons of farmers could help with the land's planting, and at last his father had granted him permission, on his promise to be back in four days—he had the dog. It was his own, a mongrel of the sort called by Negroes a fyce, a ratter, itself not much bigger than a rat and possessing that bravery which had long since stopped being courage and had become foolhardiness.

It did not take four days. Alone again, he found the trail on the first morning. It was not a stalk; it was an ambush. He timed the meeting almost as if it were an appointment with a human being. Himself holding the fyce muffled in a feed sack and Sam Fathers with two of the hounds on a piece of a plow-line rope, they lay down wind of the trail at dawn of the second morning. They were so close that the bear turned without even running, as if in surprised amazement at the shrill and frantic uproar of the released fyce, turning at bay against the trunk of a tree, on its hind feet; it seemed to the boy that it would never stop rising, taller and taller, and even the two hounds seemed to take a desperate and despairing courage from the fyce, following it as it went in.

Then he realized that the fyce was actually not going to stop. He flung, threw the gun away, and ran; when he overtook and grasped the frantically pin-wheeling little dog, it seemed to him that he was directly under the bear.

He could smell it, strong and hot and rank. Sprawling, he looked up to where it loomed and towered over him like a cloudburst and colored like a thunderclap, quite familiar, peacefully and even lucidly familiar, until he remembered: This was the way he had used to dream about it. Then it was gone. He didn't see it go. He knelt, holding the frantic fyce with both hands, hearing the abashed wailing of the hounds drawing farther and farther away, until Sam came up. He carried the gun. He laid it down quietly beside the boy and stood looking down at him.

"You've done seed him twice now with a gun in your hands," he said. "This time you couldn't have missed him."

The boy rose. He still held the fyce. Even in his arms and clear of the ground, it yapped frantically, straining and surging after the fading uproar of the two hounds like a tangle of wire springs. He was panting a little, but he was neither shaking nor trembling now.

"Neither could you!" he said. "You had the gun! Neither did you!"

"And you didn't shoot," his father said. "How close were you?"

"I don't know, sir," he said. "There was a big wood tick inside his right hind leg. But I didn't have the gun then."

"But you didn't shoot when you had the gun," his father said. "Why?"

But he didn't answer, and his father didn't wait for him to, rising and crossing the room, across the pelt of the bear which the boy had killed two years ago and the larger one which his father had killed before he was born, to the bookcase beneath the mounted head of the boy's first buck. It was the room which his father called the office, from which all the plantation business was transacted; in it for the fourteen years of his life he had heard the best of all talking. Major de Spain would be there and sometimes old General Compson, and Walter Ewell and Boon Hoggenbeck and Sam Fathers and Tennie's Jim, too, were hunters, knew the woods and what ran them.

He would hear it, not talking himself but listening—the wilderness, the big woods, bigger and older than any recorded document of white man fatuous enough to believe he had bought any fragment of it or Indian ruthless enough to pretend that any fragment of it had been his to convey. It was of the men, not white nor black nor red, but men, hunters with the will and hardihood to endure and the humility and skill to survive, and the dogs and the bear and deer juxtaposed and reliefed against it, ordered and compelled by and within the wilderness in the ancient and unremitting contest by the ancient and immitigable rules which voided all regrets and brooked no quarter, the voices quiet and weighty and deliberate for retrospection and recollection and exact remembering, while he squatted in the blazing firelight as Tennie's Jim squatted, who stirred only to put more wood on the fire and to pass the bottle from one glass to another. Because the bottle was always present, so that after a while it seemed to him that those fierce instants of heart and brain and courage and wiliness and speed were concentrated and distilled into that brown liquor which not women, not boys and children, but only hunters drank, drinking not of the blood they had spilled but some condensation of the wild immortal spirit, drinking it moderately, humbly even, not with the pagan's base hope of acquiring the virtues of cunning and strength and speed, but in salute to them.

His father returned with the book and sat down again and opened it: "Listen," he said. He read the five stanzas aloud, his voice quiet and deliberate in the room where there was no fire now because it was already spring. Then he looked up. The boy watched him. "All right," his father said. "Listen." He read again, but only the second stanza this time, to the end of it, the last two lines, and closed the book and put it on the table beside him. "She cannot fade, though thou hast not thy bliss, forever wilt thou love, and she be fair," he said.

"He's talking about a girl," the boy said.

"He had to talk about something," his father said. Then he said, "He was talking about truth. Truth doesn't change. Truth is one thing. It covers all things which touch the heart—honor and pride and pity and justice and courage and love. Do you see now?"

He didn't know. Somehow it was simpler than that. There was an old bear, fierce and ruthless, not merely just to stay alive, but with the fierce pride of liberty and freedom, proud enough of the liberty and freedom to see it threatened without fear or even alarm; nay, who at times even seemed deliberately to put that freedom and liberty in jeopardy in order to savor them, to remind his old strong bones and flesh to keep supple and quick to defend and preserve them. There was an old man, son of a Negro slave and an Indian king, inheritor on the one side of the long chronicle of a people who had learned humility through suffering, and pride through the endurance which survived the suffering and injustice, and on the other side, the chronicle of a people even longer in the land than the first, yet who no longer existed in the land at all save in the solitary brotherhood of an old Negro's alien blood and the wild and invincible spirit of an old bear. There was a boy who wished to learn humility and pride in order to become skillful and worthy in the woods, who suddenly found himself becoming so skillful so rapidly that he feared he would never become worthy because he had not learned humility and pride, although he had tried to, until one day and as suddenly he discovered that an old man who could not have defined either had led him, as though by the hand, to that point where an old bear and a little mongrel of a dog showed him that, by possessing one thing other, he would possess them both.

And a little dog, nameless and mongrel and many-fathered, grown, yet weighing less than six pounds, saying as if to itself, "I can't be dangerous, because there's nothing much smaller than I am; I can't be fierce, because they would call it just a noise; I can't be humble, because I'm already too close to the ground to genuflect; I can't be proud, because I wouldn't be near enough to it for anyone to know who was casting the shadow, and I don't even know that I'm not going to heaven, because they have already decided that I don't possess an immortal soul. So all I can be is brave. But it's all right. I can be that, even if they still call it just noise."

That was all. It was simple, much simpler than somebody talking in a book about youth and a girl he would never need to grieve over, because he could never approach any nearer her and would never have to get any farther away. He had heard about a bear, and finally got big enough to trail it, he trailed it four years and at last met it with a gun in his hands and he didn't shoot. Because a little dog—But he could have shot long before the little dog covered the twenty yards to where the bear waited, and Sam Fathers could have shot at any time during that interminable minute while Old Ben stood on his hind feet over them. He stopped. His father was watching him gravely across the spring-rife twilight of the room; when he spoke, his words were as quiet as the twilight, too, not loud, because they did not need to be because they would last. "Courage, and honor, and pride," his father said, "and pity, and love of justice and of liberty. They all touch the heart, and what the heart holds to becomes truth, as far as we know the truth. Do you see now?"

Sam, and Old Ben, and Nip, he thought. And himself too. He had been all right too. His father had said so. "Yes, sir," he said.

Suggestions for Discussion

1. What do the details in the first three paragraphs contribute to the meaning and tone of the story?

2. By what means are you made aware that the bear has a symbolic and mystical meaning?

3. Trace the steps by which the boy conquers his fear. What role does Sam Fathers play? the mongrel dog? the boy's father? How does his father's reading of Keats' "Ode on a Grecian Urn" help the boy to interpret his experience? What do his father's concluding words enable him to see?

4. From what point of view is the story told? How does the use of interior monologue and dialogue contribute to the reader's sense of immediacy?

Suggestions for Writing

1. Compare the manner in which Faulkner develops his narrative with that of Hemingway in the next selection. What do these two stories have in common? In what respects do they differ? Compare the point of view, diction and tone, and characterization. Compare them as stories of initiation. Compare the nature of the protagonist's anxiety or fear in each story. How is it manifested and how resolved?

2. Relate the boy's fears and resolution of them to the concept of identity.

3. Record an experience in which you describe an early fear and the ways in which you overcame it.

Ernest Hemingway
Indian Camp

Ernest Hemingway (1898–1961), novelist and short-story writer, began his ca-
reer as a reporter and during World War I served with an ambulance unit in
France and Italy. After the war he lived in Paris as a correspondent for the
Hearst papers. During the Spanish Civil War he went to Spain as a war correspondent. His works include the collections of short stories *In Our Time* (1925),
Men Without Women (1927), *The Fifth Column and the First 49 Stories* (1938);
and the novels *The Sun Also Rises* (1926), *A Farewell to Arms* (1929), *For Whom
The Bell Tolls* (1940), and *The Old Man and the Sea* (1952), which was awarded
a Pulitzer Prize. In 1954 he received the Nobel Prize for Literature. This is a story
of initiation, from the collection *In Our Time,* in which the boy is exposed to a
violent birth and death.

At the lake shore there was another rowboat drawn up. The two Indians
stood waiting.

Nick and his father got in the stern of the boat and the Indians shoved it
off and one of them got in to row. Uncle George sat in the stern of the camp
rowboat. The young Indian shoved the camp boat off and got in to row Uncle
George.

The two boats started off in the dark. Nick heard the oarlocks of the other
boat quite a way ahead of them in the mist. The Indians rowed with quick
choppy strokes. Nick lay back with his father's arm around him. It was cold
on the water. The Indian who was rowing them was working very hard, but
the other boat moved further ahead in the mist all the time.

"Where are we going, Dad?" Nick asked.

"Over to the Indian camp. There is an Indian lady very sick."

"Oh," said Nick.

Across the bay they found the other boat beached. Uncle George was
smoking a cigar in the dark. The young Indian pulled the boat way up on the
beach. Uncle George gave both the Indians cigars.

They walked up from the beach through a meadow that was soaking wet
with dew, following the young Indian who carried a lantern. Then they went
into the woods and followed a trail that led to the logging road that ran back
into the hills. It was much lighter on the logging road as the timber was cut
away on both sides. The young Indian stopped and blew out his lantern and
they all walked on along the road.

They came around a bend and a dog came out barking. Ahead were the
lights of the shanties where the Indian bark-peelers lived. More dogs rushed
out at them. The two Indians sent them back to the shanties. In the shanty
nearest the road there was a light in the window. An old woman stood in the
doorway holding a lamp.

Inside on a wooden bunk lay a young Indian woman. She had been trying
to have her baby for two days. All the old women in the camp had been
helping her. The men had moved off up the road to sit in the dark and smoke
out of range of the noise she made. She screamed just as Nick and the two

Indians followed his father and Uncle George into the shanty. She lay in the lower bunk, very big under a quilt. Her head was turned to one side. In the upper bunk was her husband. He had cut his foot very badly with an ax three days before. He was smoking a pipe. The room smelled very bad.

Nick's father ordered some water to be put on the stove, and while it was heating he spoke to Nick.

"This lady is going to have a baby, Nick," he said.

"I know," said Nick.

"You don't know," said his father. "Listen to me. What she is going through is called being in labor. The baby wants to be born and she wants it to be born. All her muscles are trying to get the baby born. That is what is happening when she screams."

"I see," Nick said.

Just then the woman cried out.

"Oh, Daddy, can't you give her something to make her stop screaming?" asked Nick.

"No. I haven't any anaesthetic," his father said. "But her screams are not important. I don't hear them because they are not important."

The husband in the upper bunk rolled over against the wall.

The woman in the kitchen motioned to the doctor that the water was hot. Nick's father went into the kitchen and poured about half of the water out of the big kettle into a basin. Into the water left in the kettle he put several things he unwrapped from a handkerchief.

"Those must boil," he said, and began to scrub his hands in the basin of hot water with a cake of soap he had brought from the camp. Nick watched his father's hands scrubbing each other with the soap. While his father washed his hands very carefully and thoroughly, he talked.

"You see, Nick, babies are supposed to be born head first but sometimes they're not. When they're not they make a lot of trouble for everybody. Maybe I'll have to operate on this lady. We'll know in a little while."

When he was satisfied with his hands he went in and went to work.

"Pull back that quilt, will you, George?" he said. "I'd rather not touch it."

Later when he started to operate Uncle George and three Indian men held the woman still. She bit Uncle George on the arm and Uncle George said, "Damn squaw bitch!" and the young Indian who had rowed Uncle George over laughed at him. Nick held the basin for his father. It all took a long time.

His father picked the baby up and slapped it to make it breathe and handed it to the old woman.

"See, it's a boy, Nick," he said. "How do you like being an interne?"

Nick said, "All right." He was looking away so as not to see what his father was doing.

"There. That gets it," said his father and put something into the basin.

Nick didn't look at it.

"Now," his father said, "there's some stitches to put in. You can watch this or not, Nick, just as you like. I'm going to sew up the incision I made."

Nick did not watch. His curiosity had been gone for a long time.

His father finished and stood up. Uncle George and the three Indian men stood up. Nick put the basin out in the kitchen.

Uncle George looked at his arm. The young Indian smiled reminiscently.

"I'll put some peroxide on that, George," the doctor said.

He bent over the Indian woman. She was quiet now and her eyes were closed. She looked very pale. She did not know what had become of the baby or anything.

"I'll be back in the morning," the doctor said, standing up. "The nurse should be here from St. Ignace by noon and she'll bring everything we need."

He was feeling exalted and talkative as football players are in the dressing room after a game.

"That's one for the medical journal, George," he said. "Doing a Caesarean with a jack-knife and sewing it up with nine-foot, tapered gut leaders."

Uncle George was standing against the wall, looking at his arm.

"Oh, you're a great man, all right," he said.

"Ought to have a look at the proud father. They're usually the worst sufferers in these little affairs," the doctor said. "I must say he took it all pretty quietly."

He pulled back the blanket from the Indian's head. His hand came away wet. He mounted on the edge of the lower bunk with the lamp in one hand and looked in. The Indian lay with his face toward the wall. His throat had been cut from ear to ear. The blood had flowed down into a pool where his body sagged the bunk. His head rested on his left arm. The open razor lay, edge up, in the blankets.

"Take Nick out of the shanty, George," the doctor said.

There was no need of that. Nick, standing in the door of the kitchen, had a good view of the upper bunk when his father, the lamp in one hand, tipped the Indian's head back.

It was just beginning to be daylight when they walked along the logging road back toward the lake.

"I'm terribly sorry I brought you along, Nickie," said his father, all his post-operative exhilaration gone. "It was an awful mess to put you through."

"Do ladies always have such a hard time having babies?" Nick asked.

"No, that was very, very exceptional."

"Why did he kill himself, Daddy?"

"I don't know, Nick. He couldn't stand things, I guess."

"Do many men kill themselves, Daddy?"

"Not very many, Nick."

"Do many women?"

"Hardly ever."

"Don't they ever?"

"Oh, yes. They do sometimes."

"Daddy?"

"Yes."

"Where did Uncle George go?"

"He'll turn up all right."

"Is dying hard, Daddy?"

"No, I think it's pretty easy, Nick. It all depends."

They were seated in the boat, Nick in the stern, his father rowing. The sun was coming up over the hills. A bass jumped, making a circle in the water. Nick trailed his hand in the water. It felt warm in the sharp chill of the morning.

In the early morning on the lake sitting in the stern of the boat with his father rowing, he felt quite sure that he would never die.

Suggestions for Discussion

1. How is the emotional tension of the story built up by the descriptive details of the journey to the Indian camp and the arrival at the shanties?

2. Inside the hut, what images of slight, sound, and smell take you into the heart of the scene?

3. What is the effect of the rather cold, scientific attitude of the doctor-father? of his laconic explanations to his son interspersed with details of action? Note the verbs he uses.

4. What do Uncle George and the young Indian observers contribute to the reader's rising sense of horror?

5. How are you prepared for the suicide of the husband?

6. Comment on the irony of the concluding conversation and the significance of the experience in Nick's emotional growth and awareness of life and death.

7. Explain the final sentence.

8. By specific reference to the text, support the view that this is primarily a story of Nick's initiation.

Suggestions for Writing

1. Discuss the story as a commentary on the condition of Indians in rural areas or on reservations today.

2. Write about an early experience in which you learned about birth or death, death or violence.

3. Compare and contrast "Indian Camp" and "The Bear" as stories of initiation. Consider the boys' fears, their fathers' attitudes, and the resolution of the action.

Elizabeth Taylor

Girl Reading

Elizabeth Taylor (1912–1975) was born in England and is distinguished for her short stories. Among her publications are *In a Summer Season* (1961), *The Wedding Group* (1968), and *The Devastating Boys and Other Stories* (1972). She was a frequent contributor to *The New Yorker*. "Girl Reading", from *A Dedicated Man and Other Stories* (1965), is a story of Ettas's evolving experience from initial insecurity to a sense of power.

Etta's desire was to belong. Sometimes she felt on the fringe of the family, at other times drawn headily into its very center. At mealtimes—those occasions of argument and hilarity, of thrust and counterstroke, bewildering to her at first—she was especially on her mettle, turning her head alertly from one to another as if watching a fast tennis match. She hoped soon to learn the art of riposte and already used, sometimes unthinkingly, family words and phrases; and had one or two privately treasured memories of even having made them laugh. They delighted in laughing and often did so scoffingly—"at the expense of those less fortunate" as Etta's mother would senteniously have put it.

Etta and Sarah were school friends. It was not the first time that Etta had stayed with the Lippmanns in the holidays. Everyone understood that the hospitality would not be returned, for Etta's mother, who was widowed, went out to work each day. Sarah had seen only the outside of the drab terrace house where her friend lived. She had persuaded her elder brother, David, to take her spying there one evening. They drove fifteen miles to Market Swanford and Sarah, with great curiosity, studied the street names until at last she discovered the house itself. No one was about. The street was quite deserted and the two rows of houses facing one another were blank and silent as if waiting for a hearse to appear. "Do hurry!" Sarah urged her brother. It had been a most dangerous outing and she was thoroughly depressed by it. Curiosity now seemed a trivial sensation compared with the pity she was feeling for her friend's drab life and her shame at having confirmed her own suspicions of it. She was threatened by tears. "Aren't you going in?" her brother asked in great surprise. "Hurry, hurry," she begged him. There had never been any question of her calling at that house.

"She must be very lonely there all through the holidays, poor Etta," she thought, and could imagine hour after hour in the dark house. Bickerings with the daily help she had already heard of and—Etta trying to put on a brave face and make much of nothing—trips to the public library the highlight of the day, it seemed. No wonder that her holiday reading was always so carefully done, thought Sarah, whereas she herself could never snatch a moment for it except at night in bed.

Sarah had a lively conscience about the seriousness of her friend's private world. Having led her more than once into trouble, at school, she had always afterwards felt a disturbing sense of shame; for Etta's work was more important than her own could ever be, too important to be interrupted by escapades. Sacrifices had been made and scholarships must be won. Once—it was a year ago when they were fifteen and had less sense—Sarah had thought up some rough tomfoolery and Etta's blazer had been torn. She was still haunted by her friend's look of consternation. She had remembered too late, as always—the sacrifices that had been made, the widowed mother sitting year after year at her office desk, the holidays that were never taken and the contriving that had to be done.

Her own mother was so warm and worldly. If she had anxieties she kept them to herself, setting the pace of gaiety, up to date and party-loving. She was popular with her friends' husbands who, in their English way, thought of her comfortably as nearly as good company as a man and full of bright ways as well. Etta felt safer with her than with Mr. Lippmann, whose enquiries were often too probing; he touched nerves, his jocularity could be an embarrassment. The boys—Sarah's elder brothers—had their own means of communication which their mother unflaggingly strove to interpret and, on Etta's first visit, she had tried to do so for her, too.

She *was* motherly, although she looked otherwise, the girl decided. Lying in bed at night, in the room she shared with Sarah, Etta would listen to guests driving noisily away or to the Lippmanns returning, full of laughter, from some neighbor's house. Late night door-slamming in the country disturbed only the house's occupants, who all contributed to it. Etta imagined them pottering about downstairs—husband and wife—would hear bottles clinking, laughter, voices raised from room to room, goodnight endearments to cats and dogs and at last Mrs. Lippmann's running footsteps on the stairs and the sound of her jingling bracelets coming nearer. Outside their door she would pause, listening, wondering if they were asleep already. They never were. "Come in!" Sarah would shout, hoisting herself up out of the bed clothes on one elbow, her face turned expectantly towards the door, ready for laughter—for something amusing would surely have happened. Mrs. Lippmann, sitting on one of the beds, never failed them. When they were children, Sarah said, she brought back *petits fours* from parties; now she brought back *faux pas*. She specialised in little stories against herself—Mummy's Humiliations, Sarah named them—tactless things she had said, never-to-be-remedied remarks which sprang fatally from her lips. Mistakes in identity was her particular line, for she never remembered a face, she declared. Having kissed Sarah, she would bend over Etta to do the same. She smelt of scent and gin and cigarette smoke. After this they would go to sleep. The house would be completely quiet for several hours.

Etta's mother had always had doubts about the suitability of this *ménage*. She knew it only at second hand from her daughter, and Etta said very little about her visits and that little was only in reply to obviously resented questions. But she had a way of looking about her with boredom when she returned, as if she had made the transition unwillingly and incompletely. She hurt her mother—who wished only to do everything in the world for her, having no one else to please or protect.

"I should feel differently if we were able to return the hospitality," she told Etta. The Lippmanns' generosity depressed her. She knew that it was despicable to feel jealous, left out, kept in the dark, but she tried to rationalize her feelings before Etta. "I could take a few days off and invite Sarah here," she suggested.

Etta was unable to hide her consternation and her expression deeply wounded her mother. "I shouldn't know what to do with her," she said.

"Couldn't you go for walks? There are the Public Gardens. And take her to the cinema one evening. What do you do at *her* home?"

"Oh, just fool about. Nothing much." Some afternoons they just lay on their beds and ate sweets, keeping all the windows shut and the wireless on loud, and no one ever disturbed them or told them they ought to be out in the fresh air. Then they had to plan parties and make walnut fudge and deflea the dogs. Making fudge was the only one of these things she could imagine them doing in her own home and they could not do it all the time. As for the dreary Public Gardens, she could not herself endure the asphalt paths and the bandstand and the beds of salvias. She could imagine vividly how dejected Sarah would feel.

Early in these summer holidays, the usual letter had come from Mrs. Lippmann. Etta, returning from the library, found that the charwoman had gone early and locked her out. She rang the bell, but the sound died away and left an ever more forbidding silence. All the street, where elderly people dozed in stuffy rooms, was quiet. She lifted the flap of the letter-box and called through it. No one stirred or came. She could just glimpse an envelope, lying face up on the doormat, addressed in Mrs. Lippmann's large, loopy, confident handwriting. The house-stuffiness wafted through the letter-box. She imagined the kitchen floor slowly drying, for there was a smell of soapy water. A tap was steadily dripping.

She leaned against the door, waiting for her mother's return, in a sickness of impatience at the thought of the letter lying there inside. Once or twice, she lifted the flap and had another look at it.

Her mother came home at last, very tired. With an anxious air, she set about cooking supper, which Etta had promised to have ready. The letter was left among her parcels on the kitchen table, and not until they had finished their stewed rhubarb did she send Etta to fetch it. She opened it carefully with the bread knife and deepened the frown on her forehead in preparation for reading it. When she had, she gave Etta a summary of its contents and put forward her objections, her unnerving proposal.

"She wouldn't come," Etta said. "She wouldn't leave her dog."

"But, my dear, she has to leave him when she goes back to school."

"I know. That's the trouble. In the holidays she likes to be with him as much as possible, to make up for it."

Mrs. Salkeld, who had similar wishes about her daughter, looked sad. "It is too one-sided," she gently explained. "You must try to understand how I feel about it."

"They're only too glad to have me. I keep Sarah company when they go out."

They obviously went out a great deal and Mrs. Salkeld suspected that they were frivolous. She did not condemn them for that—they must lead their own lives, but those were in a world which Etta would never be able to afford the time or money to inhabit. "Very well, Musetta," she said, removing the girl further from her by using her full name—used only on formal and usually menacing occasions.

That night she wept a little from tiredness and depression—from disappointment, too, at the thought of returning in the evenings to the dark and empty house, just as she usually did, but when she had hoped for company. They were not healing tears she shed and they did nothing but add self-contempt to her other distresses.

A week later, Etta went the short distance by train to stay with the Lippmanns. Her happiness soon lost its edge of guilt, and once the train had rattled over the iron bridge that spanned the broad river, she felt safe in a different country. There seemed to be even a different weather, coming from a wider sky, and a riverside glare—for the curves of the railway line brought it close to the even more winding course of the river, whose silver loops could be glimpsed through the trees. There were islands and backwaters and a pale heron standing on a patch of mud.

Sarah was waiting at the little station and Etta stepped down onto the platform as if taking a footing into promised land. Over the station and the gravelly lane outside hung a noonday quiet. On one side were grazing meadows, on the other side the drive gateways of expensive houses. The Gables was indeed gabled and so was its boathouse. It was also turreted and balconied. There was a great deal of woodwork painted glossy white, and a huge-leaved Virginia creeper covered much of the red brick walls—in the front beds were the salvias and lobelias Etta had thought she hated. Towels and swim-suits hung over balcony rails and a pair of tennis shoes had been put out on a window-sill to dry. Even though Mr. Lippmann and his son, David, went to London every day, the house always had—for Etta—a holiday atmosphere.

The hall door stood open and on the big round table were the stacks of new magazines which seemed to her the symbol of extravagance and luxury. At the back of the house, on the terrace overlooking the river, Mrs. Lippmann, wearing tight, lavender pants and a purple shirt, was drinking vodka with a neighbour who had called for a subscription to some charity. Etta was briefly enfolded in scented silk and tinkling bracelets and then released and introduced. Sarah gave her a red, syrupy drink and they sat down on the warm steps among the faded clumps of aubretia and rocked the ice cubes to and fro in their glasses, keeping their eyes narrowed to the sun.

Mrs. Lippmann gossiped, leaning back under a fringed chair-umbrella. She enjoyed exposing the frailties of her friends and family, although she would have been the first to hurry to their aid in trouble. Roger, who was seventeen, had been worse for drink the previous evening, she was saying. Faced with breakfast, his face had been a study of disgust which she now tried to mimic. And David could not eat, either; but from being in love. She raised her eyes to heaven most dramatically, to convey that great patience was demanded to her.

"He eats like a horse," said Sarah. "Etta, let's go upstairs." She took Etta's empty glass and led her back across the lawn, seeming not to care that her mother would without doubt begin to talk about her the moment she had gone.

Rich and vinegary smells of food came from the kitchen as they crossed the hall. (There was a Hungarian cook to whom Mrs. Lippmann spoke in German and a Portuguese "temporary" to whom she spoke in Spanish.) The food was an important part of the holiday to Etta, who had nowhere else eaten *Sauerkraut* or *Apfelstrudel* or cold fried fish, and she went into the dining-room each day with a sense of adventure and anticipation.

On this visit she was also looking forward to the opportunity of making a study of people in love—an opportunity she had not had before. While she unpacked, she questioned Sarah about David's Nora, as she thought of her; but Sarah would only say that she was quite a good sort with dark eyes and an enormous bust, and that as she was coming to dinner that evening, as she nearly always did, Etta would be able to judge for herself.

While they were out on the river all the afternoon—Sarah rowing her in a dinghy along the reedy backwater—Etta's head was full of love in books, even in those holiday set books Sarah never had time for—*Sense and Sensibility* this summer. She felt that she knew what to expect, and her perceptions were sharpened by the change of air and scene, and the disturbing smell of the river, which she snuffed up deeply as if she might be able to store it up in her lungs. "Mother thinks it is polluted," Sarah said when Etta lifted a streaming hand from trailing in the water and brought up some slippery weeds and held them to her nose. They laughed at the idea.

Etta, for dinner, put on the liberty silk they wore on Sunday evenings at school and Sarah at once brought out her own hated garment from the back of the cupboard where she had pushed it out of sight on the first day of the holidays. When they appeared downstairs, they looked unbelievably dowdy, Mrs. Lippmann thought, turning away for a moment because her eyes had suddenly pricked with tears at the sight of her kind daughter.

Mr. Lippmann and David returned from Lloyd's at half-past six and with them brought Nora—a large, calm girl with an air of brittle indifference towards her fiancé which disappointed but did not deceive Etta, who knew enough to remain undeceived by banter. To interpret from it the private tendernesses it hid was part of the mental exercise she was to be engaged in. After all, David would know better than to have his heart on his sleeve, especially in this *dégagé* family where nothing seemed half so funny as falling in love.

After dinner, Etta telephoned her mother, who had perhaps been waiting for the call, as the receiver was lifted immediately. Etta imagined her standing in the dark and narrow hall with its smell of umbrellas and furniture polish.

"I thought you would like to know I arrived safely."

"What have you been doing?"

"Sarah and I went to the river. We have just finished dinner." Spicy smells still hung about the house. Etta guessed that her mother would have had half a tin of sardines and put the other half by for her breakfast. She felt sad for her and guilty herself. Most of her thoughts about her mother were deformed by guilt.

"What have you been doing?" she asked.

"Oh, the usual," her mother said brightly. "I am just turning the collars and cuffs of your winter blouses. By the way, don't forget to pay Mrs. Lippmann for the telephone call."

"No. I shall have to go now. I just thought . . ."

"Yes, of course, dear. Well, have a lovely time."

"We are going for a swim when our dinner has gone down."

"Be careful of cramp, won't you? But I mustn't fuss from this distance. I know you are in good hands. Give my kind regards to Mrs. Lippmann and Sarah, will you, please. I must get back to your blouses."

"I wish you wouldn't bother. You must be tired."

"I am perfectly happy doing it," Mrs. Salkeld said. But if that were so, it was unnecessary, Etta thought, for her to add, as she did: "And someone has to do it."

She went dully back to the others. Roger was strumming on a guitar, but he blushed and put it away when Etta came into the room.

As the days went quickly by, Etta thought that she was belonging more this time than ever before. Mr. Lippmann, a genial patriarch, often patted her head when passing, in confirmation of her existence, and Mrs. Lippmann let her run errands. Roger almost wistfully sought her company, while Sarah disdainfully discouraged him; for they had their own employments, she implied; her friend—"my best friend," as she introduced Etta to lesser ones or adults—could hardly be expected to want the society of schoolboys. Although he was a year older than themselves, being a boy he was less sophisticated, she explained. She and Etta considered themselves to be rather worldly-wise—Etta having learnt from literature and Sarah from putting two and two together, her favourite pastime. Her parents seemed to her to behave with the innocence of children, unconscious of their motives, so continually betraying themselves to her experienced eye, when knowing more would have made them guarded. She had similarly put two and two together about Roger's behaviour to Etta, but she kept these conclusions to herself—partly from not wanting to make her friend feel self-conscious and partly—for she scorned self-deception—from what she recognised to be jealousy. She and Etta were very well as they were, she thought.

Etta herself was too much absorbed by the idea of love to ever think of being loved. In this house, she had her first chance of seeing it at first hand and she studied David and Nora with such passionate speculation that their loving seemed less their own than hers. At first, she admitted to herself that she was disappointed. Their behaviour fell short of what she required of them; they lacked a romantic attitude to one another and Nora was neither touching nor glorious—neither Viola nor Rosalind. In Etta's mind to be either was satisfactory; to be boisterous and complacent was not. Nora was simply a plump and genial girl with a large bust and a faint moustache. She could not be expected to inspire David with much gallantry and, in spite of all the red roses he brought her from London, he was not above telling her that she was getting fat. Gaily retaliatory, she would threaten him with the bouquet, waving it about his head, her huge engagement ring catching the light, flashing with different colours, her eyes flashing too.

Sometimes, there was what Etta's mother would have called "horseplay," and Etta herself deplored the noise, the dishevelled romping. "We know quite well what it's instead of," said Sarah. "But I sometimes wonder if *they* do. They would surely cut it out if they did."

As intent as a bird-watcher, Etta observed them, but was puzzled that they behaved like birds, making such a display of their courtship, an absurd-looking frolic out of a serious matter. She waited in vain for a sigh or secret glance. At night, in the room she shared with Sarah, she wanted to talk about them more than Sarah, who felt that her own family was the last possible source of glamour or enlightenment. Discussing her bridesmaid's dress was the most she would be drawn into and that subject Etta felt was devoid of romance. She was not much interested in mere weddings and thought them rather banal and public celebrations. "With an overskirt of embroidered net," said Sarah in her decisive voice. "How nice if you could be a bridesmaid, too; but she has all those awful Greenbaum cousins. As ugly as sin, but not to be left out." Etta was inattentive to her. With all her studious nature she had set herself to study love and study it she would. She made the most of what the holiday offered and when the exponents were absent she fell back on the textbooks—*Tess of the D'Urbervilles* and *Wuthering Heights* at that time.

To Roger she seemed to fall constantly into the same pose, as she sat on the river bank, bare feet tucked sideways, one arm cradling a book, the other outstretched to pluck—as if to aid her concentration—at blades of grass. Her face remained pale, for it was always in shadow, bent over her book. Beside her, glistening with oil, Sarah spread out her body to the sun. She was content to lie for hour after hour with no object but to change the colour of her skin and with thoughts crossing her mind as seldom as clouds passed overhead—and in as desultory a way when they did so. Sometimes, she took a book out with her, but nothing happened to it except that it became smothered with oil. Etta, who found sunbathing boring and enervating, read steadily on—her straight, pale hair hanging forward as if to seclude her, to screen her from the curious eyes of passers-by—shaken by passions of the imagination as she was. Voices from boats came clearly across the water, but she did not heed them. People going languidly by in punts shaded their eyes and admired the scarlet geraniums and the greenness of the grass. When motor-cruisers passed, their wash jogged against the mooring stage and swayed into the boathouse, whose lacy fretwork trimmings had just been repainted glossy white.

Sitting there, alone by the boathouse at the end of the grass bank, Roger read, too; but less diligently than Etta. Each time a boat went by, he looked up and watched it out of sight. A swan borne towards him on a wake, sitting neatly on top of its reflection, held his attention. Then his place on the page was lost. Anyhow, the sun fell too blindingly upon it. He would glance again at Etta and briefly, with distaste, at his indolent, spread-eagled sister, who had rolled over on to her stomach to give her shiny back, crisscrossed from the grass, its share of sunlight. So the afternoons passed, and they would never have such long ones in their lives again.

Evenings were more social. The terrace with its fringed umbrellas—symbols of gaiety to Etta—became the gathering place. Etta, listening intently, continued her study of love and as intently Roger studied her and the very emotion which in those others so engrossed her.

"You look still too pale," Mr.Lippmann told her one evening. He put his hands to her face and tilted it to the sun.

"You shan't leave us until there are roses in those cheeks." He implied that only in his garden did sun and air give their full benefit. The thought was there and Etta shared it. "Too much of a bookworm, I'm afraid," he added and took one of her textbooks which she carried everywhere for safety, lest she should be left on her own for a few moments. *"Tess of the D'Urbervilles,"* read out Mr. Lippmann. "Isn't it deep? Isn't it on the morbid side?" Roger was kicking rhythmically at a table leg in glum embarrassment. "This won't do you any good at all, my dear little girl. This won't put the roses in your cheeks."

You are doing that," his daughter told him—for Etta was blushing as she always did when Mr. Lippmann spoke to her.

"What's a nice book, Babs?" he asked his wife, as she came out on to the terrace. "Can't you find a nice story for this child?" The house must be full, he was sure, of wonderfully therapeutic novels if only he knew where to lay hands on them. "Roger, you're our bookworm. Look out a nice storybook for your guest. This one won't do her eyes any good." Buying books with small print was a false economy, he thought, and bound to land one in large bills from an eye specialist before long. "A very short-sighted policy," he explained genially when he had given them a little lecture to which no one listened.

His wife was trying to separate some slippery cubes of ice and Sarah sprawled in a cane chair with her eyes shut. She was making the most of the setting sun, as Etta was making the most of romance.

"We like the same books," Roger said to his father. "So she can choose as well as I could."

Etta was just beginning to feel a sense of surprised gratitude, had half turned to look in his direction when the betrothed came through the french windows and claimed her attention.

"In time for a lovely drink," Mrs. Lippmann said to Nora.

"She is too fat already," said David.

Nora swung round and caught his wrists and held them threateningly. "If you say that once more, I'll . . . I'll just . . ." He freed himself and pulled her close. She gasped and panted, but leant heavily against him. "Promise!" she said again.

"Promise what?"

"You won't ever say it again?"

He laughed at her mockingly.

They were less the centre of attention than they thought—Mr. Lippmann was smiling, but rather at the lovely evening and that the day in London was over; Mrs. Lippmann, impeded by the cardigan hanging over her shoulders, was mixing something in a glass jug and Sarah had her eyes closed against the evening sun. Only Etta, in some bewilderment, heeded them. Roger who had his own ideas about love, turned his head scornfully.

Sarah opened her eyes for a moment and stared at Nora, in her mind measuring against her the wedding dress she had been designing. She is too fat for satin, she decided, shutting her eyes again and disregarding the bridal gown for the time being. She returned to thoughts of her own dress, adding a little of what she called "back interest" (though lesser bridesmaids would no doubt obscure it from the congregation—or audience) in the form of long velvet ribbons in turquoise. . . or rose? She drew her brows together and with her eyes still shut said, "All the colours of the rainbow aren't very many, are they?"

"Now, Etta dear, what will you have to drink?" asked Mrs. Lippmann.

Just as she was beginning to ask for some tomato juice, Mr. Lippmann interrupted. He interrupted a great deal, for there were a great many things to be put right, it seemed to him. "Now, Mommy, you should give her a glass of sherry with an egg beaten up in it. Roger, run and fetch a nice egg and a whisk, too . . . all right Babsie dear, I shall do it myself . . . don't worry child," he said, turning to Etta and seeing her look of alarm. "It is no trouble to me. I shall do this for you every evening that you are here. We shall watch the roses growing in your cheeks, shan't we, Mommy?"

He prepared the drink with a great deal of clumsy fuss and sat back to watch her drinking it, smiling to himself, as if the roses were already blossoming. "Good, good!" he murmured, nodding at her as she drained the glass. Every evening, she thought, hoping that he would forget; but horrible though the drink had been, it was also reassuring; their concern for her was reassuring. She preferred it to the cold anxiety of her mother hovering with pills and thermometer.

"Yes," said Mr. Lippmann, "we shall see. We shall see. I think your parents won't know you." He puffed out his cheeks and sketched with a curving gesture the bosom she would soon have. He always forgot that her father was dead. It was quite fixed in his mind that he was simply a fellow who had obviously not made the grade; not everybody could. Roger bit his tongue hard, as if by doing so he could curb his father's. I must remind him again, Sarah and her mother were both thinking.

The last day of the visit had an unexpected hazard as well as its own sadness, for Mrs. Salkeld had written to say that her employer would lend her his car for the afternoon. When she had made a business call for him in the neighbourhood she would arrive to fetch Etta at about four o'clock.

"She is really to leave us, Mommy? asked Mr. Lippmann at breakfast, folding his newspaper and turning his attention on his family before hurrying to the station. He examined Etta's face and nodded. "Next time you stay longer and we make rosy apples of these." He patted her cheeks and ruffled her hair. "You tell your Mommy and Dadda next time you stay a whole week."

"She *has* stayed a whole week," said Sarah.

"Then a fortnight, a month."

He kissed his wife, made a gesture as if blessing them all, with his newspaper raised above his head, and went from the room at a trot. "Thank goodness," thought Sarah, "that he won't be here this afternoon to make kind enquiries about *her* husband."

When she was alone with Etta, she said, "I'm sorry about that mistake he keeps making."

"I don't mind," Etta said truthfully, "I am only embarrassed because I know that you are." That's *nothing*, she thought; but the day ahead was a different matter.

As time passed, Mrs. Lippmann also appeared to be suffering from tension. She went upstairs and changed her matador pants for a linen skirt. She tidied up the terrace and told Roger to take his bathing things off his window-sill. As soon as she had stubbed out a cigarette, she emptied and dusted the ashtray. She was conscious that Sarah was trying to see her with another's eyes.

"Oh, do stop taking photographs," Sarah said tetchily to Roger, who had been clicking away with his camera all morning. He obeyed her only because he feared to draw attention to his activities. He had just taken what he hoped would be a very beautiful study of Etta in a typical pose—sitting on the river bank with a book in her lap. She had lifted her eyes and was gazing across the water as if she were pondering whatever she had been reading. In fact, she had been arrested by thoughts of David and Nora and, although her eyes followed the print, the scene she saw did not correspond with the lines she read. She turned her head and looked at the willow trees on the far bank, the clumps of borage from which moorhens launched themselves. "Perhaps next time that I see them, they'll be married and it will all be over," she thought. The evening before, there had been a great deal of high-spirited sparring about between them. Offence meant and offence taken they assured one another. "If you do that once more . . . I am absolutely serious," cried Nora. "You are trying not to laugh," David said. "I'm not. I am absolutely serious." "It will end in tears," Roger had muttered contemptuously. Even good-tempered Mrs. Lippmann had looked down her long nose disapprovingly. And that was the last, Etta supposed, that she would see of love for a long time. She was left once again with books. She returned to the one she was reading.

Roger had flung himself on to the grass near by, appearing to trip over a tussock of grass and collapse. He tried to think of some opening remark which might lead to a discussion of the book. In the end, he asked abruptly, "Do you like that?" She sat brooding over it, chewing the side of her finger. She nodded without looking up and, with a similar automatic gesture, she waved away a persistent wasp. He leaned forward and clapped his hands together smartly and was relieved to see the wasp drop dead into the grass, although he would rather it had stung him first. Etta, however, had not noticed this brave deed.

The day passed wretchedly for him; each hour was more filled with the doom of her departure than the last. He worked hard to conceal his feelings, in which no one took an interest. He knew that it was all he could do, although no good could come from his succeeding. He took a few more secret photographs from his bedroom window, and then he sat down and wrote a short letter to her, explaining his love.

At four o'clock, her mother came. He saw at once that Etta was nervous and he guessed that she tried to conceal her nervousness behind a much jauntier manner to her mother than was customary. It would be a bad hour, Roger decided.

His own mother, in spite of her linen skirt, was gaudy and exotic beside Mrs. Salkeld, who wore a navy-blue suit which looked as if it had been sponged and pressed a hundred times—a depressing process unknown to Mrs. Lippmann. The pink-rimmed spectacles that Mrs. Salkeld wore seemed to reflect a little colour on to her cheekbones, with the result that she looked slightly indignant about something or other. However, she smiled a great deal, and only Etta guessed what an effort it was to her to do so. Mrs. Lippmann gave her a chair where she might have a view of the river and she sat down, making a point of not looking round the room, and smoothed her gloves. Her jewellery was real but very small.

"If we have tea in the garden, the wasps get into Anna's rose-petal jam," said Mrs. Lippmann. Etta was not at her best, she felt—not helping at all. She was aligning herself too staunchly with the Lippmanns, so that her mother seemed a stranger to her, as well. "You see, I am at home here," she implied, as she jumped up to fetch things or hand things round. She was a little daring in her familiarity.

Mrs. Salkeld had contrived the visit because she wanted to understand and hoped to approve of her daughter's friends. Seeing the lawns, the light reflected from the water, later this large, bright room, and the beautiful poppy-seed cake the Hungarian cook had made for tea, she understood completely and felt pained. She could see then, with Etta's eyes, their own dark, narrow house, and she thought of the lonely hours she spent there reading on days of imprisoning rain. The Lippmanns would even have better weather, she thought bitterly. The bitterness affected her enjoyment of the poppy-seed cake. She had, as puritanical people often have, a sweet tooth. She ate the cake with a casual air, determined not to praise.

"You are so kind to spare Etta to us," said Mrs. Lippmann.

"*You* are kind to invite her," Mrs. Salkeld replied, and then for Etta's sake, added: "She loves to come to you."

Etta looked self-consciously down at her feet.

"No, I don't smoke," her mother said primly. "Thank you."

Mrs. Lippmann seemed to decide not to, either, but very soon her hand stole out and took a cigarette—while she was not looking, thought Roger, who was having some amusement from watching his mother on her best behavior.

Wherever she was, the shagreen cigarette case and the gold lighter were near by. Ashtrays never were. He got up and fetched one before Etta could do so.

The girls' school was being discussed—one of the few topics the two mothers had in common. Mrs. Lippmann had never taken it seriously. She laughed at the uniform and despised the staff—an attitude she might at least have hidden from her daughter, Mrs. Salkeld felt. The tea-trolley was being wheeled away and her eyes followed the remains of the poppy-seed cake. She had planned a special supper for Etta to return to, but she felt now that it was no use. The things of the mind had left room for an echo. It sounded with every footstep or spoken word in that house where not enough was going on. She began to wonder if there were things of the heart and not the mind that Etta fastened upon so desperately when she was reading. Or was her desire to be in a different place? Lowood was a worse one—she could raise her eyes and look round her own room in relief; Pemberley was better and she would benefit from the change. But how can I help her? she asked herself in anguish. What possible change—and radical it must be—can I ever find the strength to effect? People had thought her wonderful to have made her own life and brought up her child alone. She had kept their heads above water and it had taken all her resources to do so.

Her lips began to refuse the sherry Mrs. Lippmann suggested and then, to her surprise and Etta's astonishment, she said "yes" instead.

It was very early to have suggested it, Mrs. Lippmann thought, but it would seem to put an end to the afternoon. Conversation had been as hard work as she had anticipated and she longed for a dry martini to stop her from yawning, as she was sure it would; but something about Mrs. Salkeld seemed to discourage gin drinking.

"Mother, it isn't half-past five yet," said Sarah.

"Darling, don't be rude to your Mummy. I know perfectly well what the time is." (Who better? she wondered.) "And this isn't a public house, you know."

She had flushed a little and was lighting another cigarette. Her bracelets jangled against the decanter as she handled Mrs. Salkeld her glass of sherry, saying, "Young people are so stuffy," with an air of complicity.

Etta, who had never seen her mother drinking sherry before, watched nervously, as if she might not know how to do it. Mrs. Salkeld—remembering the flavor from Christmas mornings many years ago and—more faintly—from her mother's party trifle—sipped cautiously. In an obscure way she was doing this for Etta's sake. "It may speed her on her way," thought Mrs. Lippmann, playing idly with her charm bracelet, having run out of conversation.

When Mrs. Salkeld rose to go, she looked round the room once more as if to fix it in her memory—the setting where she would imagine her daughter on future occasions.

"And come again soon, there's a darling girl," said Mrs. Lippmann, putting her arm round Etta's shoulder as they walked towards the car. Etta, unused to but not ungrateful for embraces, leaned awkwardly against her. Roger, staring at the gravel, came behind carrying the suitcase.

"I have wasted my return ticket," Etta said.

"Well, that's not the end of the world," her mother said briskly. She thought, but did not say, that perhaps they could claim the amount if they wrote to British Railways and explained.

Mrs. Lippmann's easy affection meant so much less than her own stiff endearments, but she resented it all the same and when she was begged, with enormous warmth, to visit them all again soon her smile was a prim twisting of her lips.

The air was bright with summer sounds, voices across the water and rooks up in the elm trees. Roger stood back listening in a dream to the good-byes and thank-yous. Nor was *this* the end of the world, he told himself. Etta would come again and, better than that, they would also grow older and so be less at the mercy of circumstances. He would be in a position to command his life and turn occasions to his own advantage. Meanwhile, he had done what he could. None the less, he felt such dejection, such an overwhelming conviction that it *was* the end of the world after all, that he could not watch the car go down the drive, and he turned and walked quickly—rudely, offhandedly, his mother thought—back to the house.

Mrs. Salkeld, driving homewards in the lowering sun, knew that Etta had tears in her eyes. "I'm glad you enjoyed yourself," she said. Without waiting for an answer, she added: "They are very charming people." She had always suspected charm and rarely spoke of it, but in this case the adjective seemed called for.

Mr. Lippmann would be coming back from London about now, Etta was thinking. And David will bring Nora. They will all be on the terrace having drinks—dry martinis, not sherry.

She was grateful to her mother about the sherry and understood that it had been an effort towards meeting Mrs. Lippmann's world half-way, and on the way back, she had not murmured one word of criticism—for their worldliness or extravagance or the vulgar opulence of their furnishings. She had even made a kind remark about them.

I might buy her a new dress, Mrs. Salkeld thought—something like the one Sarah was wearing. Though it does seem a criminal waste when she has all her good school clothes to wear out.

They had come onto the main road, and evening traffic streamed by. In the distance the gas holder looked pearl grey and the smoke from factories was pink in the sunset. They were nearly home. Etta, who had blinked her tears back from her eyes, took a sharp breath, almost a sigh.

Their own street with its tall houses was in shadow. "I wish we had a cat," said Etta, as she got out of the car and saw the next door tabby looking through the garden railings. She imagined burying her face in its warm fur, it loving only her. To her surprise, her mother said: "Why not?" Briskly, she went up the steps and turned the key with its familiar grating sound in the lock. The house with its smell—familiar, too—of floor polish and stuffiness, looked secretive. Mrs. Salkeld, hardly noticing this, hurried to the kitchen to put the casserole of chicken in the oven.

Etta carried her suitcase upstairs. On the dressing-table was a jar of marigolds. She was touched by this—just when she did not want to be touched. She turned her back on them and opened her case. On the top was the book she had left on the terrace. Roger had brought it to her at the last moment. Taking it now, she found a letter inside. Simply "Etta" was written on the envelope.

Roger had felt that he had done all he was capable of and that was to write in the letter those things he could not have brought himself to say, even if he had had an opportunity. No love letter could have been less anticipated and Etta read it twice before she could realise that it was neither a joke nor a mistake. It was the most extraordinary happening of her life, the most incredible.

Her breathing grew slower and deeper as she sat staring before her, pondering her mounting sense of power. It was as if the whole Lippmann family—Nora as well—had proposed to her. To marry Roger—a long, long time ahead though she must wait to do so—would be the best possible way of belonging.

She got up stiffly—for her limbs now seemed too clumsy a part of her body with its fly-away heart and giddy head—she went over to the dressing-table and stared at herself in the glass. "I am I," she thought, but she could not believe it. She stared and stared, but could not take in the tantalising idea.

After a while, she began to unpack. The room was a place of transit, her temporary residence. When she had made it tidy, she went downstairs to thank her mother for the marigolds.

Suggestions for Discussion

1. What does the metaphor of Etta watching a tennis match tell you about Sarah's family?

2. With what details does the reader learn about Sarah and her relationship to Etta? By what means does one learn about Sarah's mother and other members of the family?

3. Why did Etta resent questions from her mother about her visits to the Lippmanns? Why are "Etta's thoughts about her mother deformed by guilt"? How is the guilt conveyed?

4. What do the activities and conversations of Mrs. Lippmann tell you about her attitudes and values?

5. The story is written from the omniscient author point of view, and the focus shifts back and forth from Sarah and Etta to both mothers and to members of Sarah's family. How does the story achieve a singleness of purpose?

6. "Etta's desire was to belong" we are told in the first sentence. With what incidents and commentary is her concern validated? How successful is she in achieving her desire? How is her success communicated?

7. On what are Etta's reflections on love based? How do you account for her disappointment in her observations of David and Nora?

8. Relate the contrasting phrases "things of the mind" and "things of the heart" to Etta's evolving experience.

9. Account for Etta's awareness of a "mounting sense of power." What is the significance of the disbelief that "I am I"?

10. Relate the title to the theme of the story.

Suggestions for Writing

1. Describe a friend, relative, or yourself in a state of being in love.

2. Compare and contrast your family with that of a friend.

3. Develop your own definition and comparison of "things of the mind" and "things of the heart."

4. Drawing upon specific incidents in the story, write a character study of Etta.

Poetry

T.S. Eliot
The Love Song of J. Alfred Prufrock

Thomas Stearns Eliot (1888–1965) was born in St. Louis, was educated at Harvard University, and studied in Paris and Oxford. He settled in England in 1914 and became a British subject in 1927. His most influential poem, *The Waste Land*, was published in 1922, followed by *The Hollow Men* (1925), *Poems: 1909–1925* (1925), and *Poems: 1909–1935* (1936). His criticism includes *The Use of Poetry and the Use of Criticism* (1933), *Essays Ancient and Modern* (1936), *Notes Toward the Definition of Culture* (1948), and *To Criticize the Critic* (1965). His best-known poetic dramas are *Murder in the Cathedral* (1935), *The Family Reunion* (1939), and *The Cocktail Party* (1950). Prufrock's opposed selves in this dramatic monologue are separated from each other, the one exploring the idea of human involvement and the other observing it in comfortable isolation.

> *S'io credesse che mia risposta fosse*
> *A persona che mai tornasse al mondo,*
> *Questa fiamma staria senza piu scosse.*
> *Ma perciocche giammai di questo fondo*
> *Non torno vivo alcun, s'i'odo il vero,*
> *Senza tema d'infamia ti rispondo.*

> ["If I believed that my answer would be to one who
> would ever return to the world, this flame would
> shake no more; but since no one ever returns alive
> from this depth, if what I hear is true, I answer you
> without fear of infamy."—Dante's *Inferno*, XXVII, 61-66]

Let us go then, you and I,
When the evening is spread out against the sky
Like a patient etherised upon a table;

Let us go, through certain half-deserted streets,
The muttering retreats
Of restless nights in one-night cheap hotels
And sawdust restaurants with oyster-shells:
Streets that follow like a tedious argument
Of insidious intent
To lead you to an overwhelming question . . .
Oh, do not ask, "What is it?"
Let us go and make our visit.

In the room the women come and go
Talking of Michelangelo.

The yellow fog that rubs its back upon the window-panes,
The yellow smoke that rubs its muzzle on the window-panes
Licked its tongue into the corners of the evening,
Lingered upon the pools that stand in drains,
Let fall upon its back the soot that falls from chimneys,
Slipped by the terrace, made a sudden leap,
And seeing that it was a soft October night,
Curled once about the house, and fell asleep.

And indeed there will be time
For the yellow smoke that slides along the street,
Rubbing its back upon the window-panes;
There will be time, there will be time
To prepare a face to meet the faces that you meet;
There will be time to murder and create,
And time for all the works and days of hands
That lift and drop a question on your plate;
Time for you and time for me,
And time yet for a hundred indecisions,
And for a hundred visions and revisions,
Before the taking of a toast and tea.

In the room the women come and go
Talking of Michelangelo.

And indeed there will be time
To wonder, "Do I dare?" and, "Do I dare?"
Time to turn back and descend the stair,
With a bald spot in the middle of my hair—
[They will say: "How his hair is growing thin!"]
My morning coat, my collar mounting firmly to the chin,
My necktie rich and modest, but asserted by a simple pin—
[They will say: "But how his arms and legs are thin!"]
Do I dare
Disturb the universe?
In a minute there is time
For decisions and revisions which a minute will reverse.

For I have known them all already, known them all:—
Have known the evenings, mornings, afternoons,

I have measured out my life with coffee spoons;
I know the voices dying with a dying fall
Beneath the music from a farther room.
   So how should I presume?

   And I have known the eyes already, known them all—
The eyes that fix you in a formulated phrase,
And when I am formulated, sprawling on a pin,
When I am pinned and wriggling on the wall,
Then how should I begin
To spit out all the butt-ends of my days and ways?
   And how should I presume?

   And I have known the arms already, known them all—
Arms that are braceleted and white and bare
[But in the lamplight, downed with light brown hair!]
Is it perfume from a dress
That makes me so digress?
Arms that lie along a table, or wrap about a shawl.
   And should I then presume?
   And how should I begin?

Shall I say, I have gone at dusk through narrow streets
And watched the smoke that rises from the pipes
Of lonely men in shirt-sleeves, leaning out of windows? . . .
   I should have been a pair of ragged claws
Scuttling across the floors of silent seas.

And the afternoon, the evening, sleeps so peacefully!
Smoothed by long fingers,
Asleep . . . tired . . . or it malingers,
Stretched on the floor, here beside you and me.
Should I, after tea and cakes and ices,
Have the strength to force the moment to its crisis?
But though I have wept and fasted, wept and prayed,
Though I have seen my head [grown slightly bald] brought in upon a platter,
I am no prophet—and here's no great matter;
I have seen the moment of my greatness flicker,
And I have seen the eternal Footman hold my coat, and snicker,
And in short, I was afraid.

And would it have been worth it, after all,
After the cups, the marmalade, the tea,
Among the porcelain, among some talk of you and me,
Would it have been worth while,
To have bitten off the matter with a smile,
To have squeezed the universe into a ball
To roll it toward some overwhelming question,
To say: "I am Lazarus, come from the dead.
Come back to tell you all, I shall tell you all"—

If one, settling a pillow by her head,
    Should say: "That is not what I meant at all.
    That is not it, at all."

And would it have been worth it, after all,
Would it have been worth while,
After the sunsets and the dooryards and the sprinkled streets,
After the novels, after the teacups, after the skirts that trail along the floor—
And this, and so much more?—
It is impossible to say just what I mean!
But as if a magic lantern threw the nerves in patterns on a screen:
Would it have been worth while
If one, settling a pillow or throwing off a shawl,
And turning toward the window, should say:
    "That is not it at all,
    That is not what I meant, at all."

No! I am not Prince Hamlet, nor was meant to be;
Am an attendant lord, one that will do
To swell a progress, start a scene or two,
Advise the prince; no doubt, an easy tool,
Deferential, glad to be of use,
Politic, cautious, and meticulous;
Full of high sentence, but a bit obtuse;
At times, indeed, almost ridiculous—
Almost, at times, the Fool.

    I grow old . . . I grow old . . .
I shall wear the bottoms of my trousers rolled.

    Shall I part my hair behind? Do I dare to eat a peach?
I shall wear white flannel trousers, and walk upon the beach.
I have heard the mermaids singing, each to each.

    I do not think that they will sing to me.

    I have seen them riding seaward on the waves
Combing the white hair of the waves blown back
When the wind blows the water white and black.

    We have lingered in the chambers of the sea
By sea-girls wreathed with seaweed red and brown
Till human voices wake us, and we drown.

Suggestions for Discussion

1. Who are "you and I"?

2. What evidence can you find in the structural development of the poem to support
   the view that one self in the dramatic monologue acts out the conflict and the other
   assumes the role of observer? Cite lines from the poem in which shifts in mood and
   tone occur. How does the poem achieve dramatic unity?

3. Contrast the images of Prufrock's interior world with those of the external world.

How does their recurring juxtaposition illuminate the doubleness of the speaker and contribute to tone? How is sensory experience used to convey the circularity of the dialogue with self? Why are the images of the etherized patient, the staircase, winding streets, cat, and fog especially appropriate dramatic symbols of the speaker's state of mind? Trace the use of sea imagery. How does it function differently in the metaphor of the crab and the vision of the mermaids? How do both relate to theme and tone? What do the allusions to John the Baptist, Lazarus, and Hamlet have in common?

4. Distinguish between the dramatic and the lyric elements. How is the mock heroic used to satirize both speaker and society? Study the effects of repetition on rhythm, tone, and meaning. How do the stanzas and the typographical breaks mark the shifts in tone? Discuss the relationship of tone to syntax, refrain, internal rhyme, diction, tempo, and melody. Comment on the irony in the title.

5. How does time function in the poem? How does the shift in tense from present to present perfect and future provide a key to the poem's resolution? What form does the speaker's recognition take? By what means does the poet evoke sympathy for Prufrock, who is psychically impotent to establish an intimate human relationship? To what do you attribute Prufrock's rejection of human encounter? What part does his self-mockery play in our response to him? Does the poem move beyond pathos and self-mockery?

6. In what respect may the poem be viewed as an expression of a search for self?

Suggestions for Writing

1. Write a character study of Prufrock in which you refer directly to the poem.

2. Write a dialogue in which your interior self is counterpointed against your social self or *persona*.

Dylan Thomas

The Force That Through the Green Fuse Drives the Flower

Dylan Thomas (1914–1953) was born in Wales. He was a newspaper reporter for a time and worked for the BBC during World War II. He gained recognition as a lyric poet in his twenties and grew in popularity until his death while on a lecture tour in the United States. His *Collected Poems* appeared in 1953. A collection of his stories, sketches, and essays, *Quite Early One Morning,* was published in 1954; a group of stories and and essays, *A Prospect of the Sea,* in 1955; and a verse play, *Under Milk Wood,* in 1954. The poet views natural forces as both destructive and life giving; the poem is an expression of his sense of the energy, both creative and destructive, that runs through all things.

The force that through the green fuse drives the flower
Drives my green age; that blasts the roots of trees
Is my destroyer.
And I am dumb to tell the crooked rose
My youth is bent by the same wintry fever.

The force that drives the water through the rocks
Drives my red blood; that dries the mouthing streams
Turns mine to wax.
And I am dumb to mouth unto my veins
How at the mountain spring the same mouth sucks.

The hand that whirls the water in the pool
Stirs the quicksand; that ropes the blowing wind
Hauls my shroud sail.
And I am dumb to tell the hanging man
How of my clay is made the hangman's lime.

The lips of time leech to the fountain head;
Love drips and gathers, but the fallen blood
Shall calm her sores.
And I am dumb to tell a weather's wind
How time has ticked a heaven round the stars.

And I am dumb to tell the lover's tomb
How at my sheet goes the same crooked worm.

Suggestions for Discussion

1. What images suggest the relationship the poet sees between the world of nature and that of human passions?

2. How does the poet express the sense that the energy that runs through all things is both creator and destroyer? How does the two-line refrain at the end of each stanza relate this theme to the voice of the poet?

3. What images depict contrasting forces of life and death? How does the diction convey the sense of sexual energy?

Personal Relationships: Parents and Children

◆◆◆◆

A boy wants something very special from his father. You hear it said that fathers want their sons to be what they feel they cannot themselves be, but I tell you it also works the other way. I know that as a small boy I wanted my father to be a certain thing he was not. I wanted him to be a proud, silent, dignified father. When I was with other boys and he passed along the street, I wanted to feel a glow of pride: "There he is. That is my father."

—**Sherwood Anderson,** "Discovery of a Father"

My father . . . believed that he (or rather, his wife) could raise children according to his unique moral and intellectual plan, thus proving to the world the values of enlightened, unorthodox child-rearing. I believe that my mother . . . at first genuinely and enthusiastically embraced the experiment, and only later found that in carrying out my father's intense, perfectionist program, she was in conflict with her deep instincts as a mother.

—**Adrienne Rich,** "The Anger of a Child"

. . . I am more than a little sensitive to the way the literature presents adoptive parents. We are usually shown as frozen in the pastures of radio drama, untouched by the changes in attitudes of the last several generations. In point of fact we accept that our children might seek out their roots, even encourage it; we accept it as an adventure like life itself—perhaps painful, one hopes enriching.

—**John Gregory Dunne,** "Quintana"

I am writing about those very things my mother has asked me not to reveal. Shortly after I published my first autobiographical essay seven years ago, my mother wrote me a letter pleading with me never again to write about our family life. . . . "Why do you need to tell the *gringos* about how 'divided' you feel from the family?"

I sit at my desk now, surrounded by versions of paragraphs and pages of this book, considering that question.

. . . I stay away from late-night parties. (To be clear-headed in the morning.) I disconnect my phone for much of the day. I must avoid complex relationships—a troublesome love or a troubled friend. The person who knows me best scolds me for escaping from life. (*Am* I evading adulthood?)

. . . 'Why?" My mother's question hangs in the still air of memory.

    —Richard Rodriguez, "Mr. Secrets"

Behind the newspaper Julian was withdrawing into the inner compartment of his mind where he spent most of his time. This was a kind of mental bubble in which he established himself when he could not bear to be a part of what was going on around him. From it he could see out and judge but in it he was safe from any kind of penetration from without. It was the only place where he felt free of the general idiocy of his fellows. His mother had never entered it but from it he could see her with absolute clarity.

. . . She might as well be made to understand what had happened to her. "Don't think that was just an uppity Negro woman," he said. "That was the whole colored race which will no longer take your condescending pennies. That was your black double. She can wear the same hat as you, and to be sure," he added gratuitously (because he thought it was funny), "it looked better on her than it did on you. What all this means," he said, "is that the old world is gone. The old manners are obsolete. . . . You aren't who you think you are." . . .

    —Flannery O'Connor, "Everything That Rises Must Converge"

Letters and Personal Reminiscences

◆◆◆

Sherwood Anderson

Discovery of a Father

Sherwood Anderson (1876–1941) was an American short-story writer, essayist, and novelist whose writing often reflects his own confusions about man in the modern world of the machine, but whose keen insights into human beings continue to illuminate life for readers of his collection of short stories, *Winesburg, Ohio* 1919, his novels, *Many Marriages* (1922) and *Dark Laughter* (1925), and his semiautobiographical *A Story Teller's Story* (1924). In "Discovery of a Father", from Anderson's *Memoirs* (1939), the boy's negative, even contemptuous, attitude toward his father undergoes a radical change: his earlier wish that his father would be someone else gives way to the secure knowledge that he would never again want another father.

One of the strangest relationships in the world is that between father and son. I know it now from having sons of my own.

A boy wants something very special from his father. You hear it said that fathers want their sons to be what they feel they cannot themselves be, but I tell you it also works the other way. I know that as a small boy I wanted my father to be a certain thing he was not. I wanted him to be a proud, silent, dignified father. When I was with other boys and he passed along the street, I wanted to feel a glow of pride: "There he is. That is my father."

But he wasn't such a one. He couldn't be. It seemed to me then that he was always showing off. Let's say someone in our town had got up a show. They were always doing it. The druggist would be in it, the shoe-store clerk, the horse doctor, and a lot of women and girls. My father would manage to get the chief comedy part. It was, let's say, a Civil War play and he was a comic Irish soldier. He had to do the most absurd things. They thought he was funny, but I didn't.

I thought he was terrible. I didn't see how Mother could stand it. She even laughed with the others. Maybe I would have laughed if it hadn't been my father.

Or there was a parade, the Fourth of July or Decoration Day. He'd be in that, too, right at the front of it, as Grand Marshal or something, on a white horse hired from a livery stable.

He couldn't ride for shucks. He fell off the horse and everyone hooted with laughter, but he didn't care. He even seemed to like it. I remember once when he had done something ridiculous, and right out on Main Street, too. I was with some other boys and they were laughing and shouting at him and he was shouting back and having as good a time as they were. I ran down an alley back of some stores and there in the Presbyterian Church sheds I had a good long cry.

Or I would be in bed at night and Father would come home a little lit up and bring some men with him. He was a man who was never alone. Before he went broke, running a harness shop, there were always a lot of men loafing in the shop. He went broke, of course, because he gave too much credit. He couldn't refuse it and I thought he was a fool. I had got to hating him.

There'd be men I didn't think would want to be fooling around with him. There might even be the superintendent of our schools and a quiet man who ran the hardware store. Once, I remember, there was a white-haired man who was a cashier of the bank. It was a wonder to me they'd want to be seen with such a windbag. That's what I thought he was. I know now what it was that attracted them. It was because life in our town, as in all small towns, was at times pretty dull and he livened it up. He made them laugh. He could tell stories. He'd even get them to singing.

If they didn't come to our house they'd go off, say at night, to where there was a grassy place by a creek. They'd cook food there and drink beer and sit about listening to his stories.

He was always telling stories about himself. He'd say this or that wonderful thing happened to him. It might be something that made him look like a fool. He didn't care.

If an Irishman came to our house, right away father would say he was Irish. He'd tell what county in Ireland he was born in. He'd tell things that happened there when he was a boy. He'd make it seem so real that, if I hadn't known he was born in southern Ohio, I'd have believed him myself.

If it was a Scotchman, the same thing happened. He'd get a burr into his speech. Or he was a German or a Swede. He'd be anything the other man was. I think they all knew he was lying, but they seemed to like him just the same. As a boy that was what I couldn't understand.

And there was Mother. How could she stand it? I wanted to ask but never did. She was not the kind you asked such questions.

I'd be upstairs in my bed, in my room above the porch, and Father would be telling some of his tales. A lot of Father's stories were about the Civil War. To hear him tell it he'd been in about every battle. He'd known Grant, Sherman, Sheridan, and I don't know how many others. He'd been particularly intimate with General Grant so that when Grant went East, to take charge of all the armies, he took Father along.

"I was an orderly at headquarters and Sam Grant said to me, 'Irve,' he said, 'I'm going to take you along with me.'"

It seems he and Grant used to slip off sometimes and have a quiet drink together. That's what my father said. He'd tell about the day Lee surrendered and how, when the great moment came, they couldn't find Grant.

"You know," my father said, "about General Grant's book, his memoirs. You've read of how he said he had a headache and how, when he got word that Lee was ready to call it quits, he was suddenly and miraculously cured.

"Huh," said Father. "He was in the woods with me.

"I was in there with my back against a tree. I was pretty well corned. I had got hold of a bottle of pretty good stuff.

"They were looking for Grant. He had got off his horse and come into the woods. He found me. He was covered with mud.

"I had the bottle in my hand. What'd I care? The war was over. I knew we had them licked."

My father said that he was the one who told Grant about Lee. An orderly riding by had told him, because the orderly knew how thick he was with Grant. Grant was embarrassed.

"But, Irve, look at me. I'm all covered with mud," he said to Father.

And then, my father said, he and Grant decided to have a drink together. They took a couple of shots and then, because he didn't want Grant to show up potted before the immaculate Lee, he smashed the bottle against the tree.

"Sam Grant's dead now and I wouldn't want it to get out on him," my father said.

That's just one of the kind of things he'd tell. Of course, the men knew he was lying, but they seemed to like it just the same.

When we got broke, down and out, do you think he ever brought anything home? Not he. If there wasn't anything to eat in the house, he'd go off visiting around at farm houses. They all wanted him. Sometimes he'd stay away for weeks, Mother working to keep us fed, and then home he'd come bringing, let's say, a ham. He'd got it from some farmer friend. He'd slap it on the table in the kitchen. "You bet I'm going to see that my kids have something to eat," he'd say, and Mother would just stand smiling at him. She'd never say a word about all the weeks and months he'd been away, not leaving us a cent for food. Once I heard her speaking to a woman in our street. Maybe the woman had dared to sympathize with her. "Oh," she said "it's all right. He isn't ever dull like most of the men in this street. Life is never dull when my man is about."

But often I was filled with bitterness, and sometimes I wished he wasn't my father. I'd even invent another man as my father. To protect my mother I'd make up stories of a secret marriage that for some strange reason never got known. As though some man, say the president of a railroad company or maybe a Congressman, had married my mother, thinking his wife was dead and then it turned out she wasn't.

So they had to hush it up but I got born just the same. I wasn't really the son of my father. Somewhere in the world there was a very dignified, quite wonderful man who was really my father. I even made myself half believe these fancies.

And then there came a certain night. Mother was away from home. Maybe there was church that night. Father came in. He'd been off somewhere for two or three weeks. He found me alone in the house, reading by the kitchen table.

It had been raining and he was very wet. He sat and looked at me for a long time, not saying a word. I was startled, for there was on his face the saddest look I had ever seen. He sat for a time, his clothes dripping. Then he got up.

"Come on with me," he said.

I got up and went with him out of the house. I was filled with wonder but I wasn't afraid. We went along a dirt road that led down into a valley, about a mile out of town, where there was a pond. We walked in silence. The man who was always talking had stopped his talking.

I didn't know what was up and had the queer feeling that I was with a stranger. I didn't know whether my father intended it so. I don't think he did.

The pond was quite large. It was still raining hard and there were flashes of lightning followed by thunder. We were on a grassy bank at the pond's edge when my father spoke, and in the darkness and rain his voice sounded strange.

"Take off your clothes," he said. Still filled with wonder, I began to undress. There was a flash of lightning and I saw that he was already naked.

Naked, we went into the pond. Taking my hand, he pulled me in. It may be that I was too frightened, too full of a feeling of strangeness, to speak. Before that night my father had never seemed to pay any attention to me.

"And what is he up to now?" I kept asking myself. I did not swim very well, but he put my hand on his shoulder and struck out into the darkness.

He was a man with big shoulders, a powerful swimmer. In the darkness I could feel the movements of his muscles. We swam to the far edge of the pond and then back to where we had left our clothes. The rain continued and the wind blew. Sometimes my father swam on his back, and when he did he took my hand in his large powerful one and moved it over so that it rested always on his shoulder. Sometimes there would be a flash of lightning and I could see his face quite clearly.

It was as it was earlier, in the kitchen, a face filled with sadness. There would be the momentary glimpse of his face, and then again the darkness, the wind and the rain. In me there was a feeling I had never known before.

It was a feeling of closeness. It was something strange. It was as though there were only we two in the world. It was as though I had been jerked suddenly out of myself, out of my world of the schoolboy, out of a world in which I was ashamed of my father.

He had become blood of my blood; he the strong swimmer and I the boy clinging to him in the darkness. We swam in silence, and in silence we dressed in our wet clothes and went home.

There was a lamp lighted in the kitchen, and when we came in, the water dripping from us, there was my mother. She smiled at us. I remember that she called us "boys." "What have you boys been up to?" she asked, but my father did not answer. As he had begun the evening's experience with me in silence, so he ended it. He turned and looked at me. Then he went, I thought, with a new and strange dignity, out of the room.

I climbed the stairs to my room, undressed in darkness and got into bed. I couldn't sleep and did not want to sleep. For the first time I knew that I was the son of my father. He was a storyteller as I was to be. It may be that I even laughed a little softly there in the darkness. If I did, I laughed knowing that I would never again be wanting another father.

Suggestions for Discussion

1. How does the author bring the subject into focus?

2. Account for the feelings the narrator had toward his father's public behavior.

3. How do the sentence structure and diction contribute to purpose and tone?

4. How do you explain the father's action in taking the boy swimming? How do you account for the boy's changed view of his father?

Suggestions for Writing

1. Write on one of these topics: a portrait of my father; imaginary parents.

2. Write a narrative in which a seemingly simple event effects a change in attitude.

Frank Kafka

Letter to His Father

Translated by Ernest Kaiser and Eithene Wilkins.

Franz Kafka (1883–1924), the German novelist who portrays alienated characters in an absurd world, made little mark during his life but is now considered a major modern writer. Many of his novels have been published posthumously, including *The Trial, The Castle,* and *Amerika.* In the letter, also published posthumously, the author in a legalistic manner indicts himself as well as his father in assessing responsibility for his, Kakfa's, insecurity as a person.

Dearest Father:

You asked me recently why I maintain that I am afraid of you. As usual, I was unable to think of any answer to your question, partly for the very reason that I am afraid of you, and partly because an explanation of the grounds for this fear would mean going into far more details than I could even approximately keep in mind while talking. And if I now try to give you an answer in writing, it will still be very incomplete, because even in writing this fear and its consequences hamper me in relation to you and because [anyway] the magnitude of the subject goes far beyond the scope of my memory and power of reasoning. . . .

Compare the two of us: I, to put it in a very much abbreviated form, a Löwy with a certain basis of Kafka, which, however, is not set in motion by the Kafka will to life, business, and conquest, but by a Löwyish spur that urges more secretly, more diffidently, and in another direction, and which often fails to work entirely. You, on the other hand, a true Kafka in strength, health, appetite, loudness of voice, eloquence, self-satisfaction, worldly dominance, endurance, presence of mind, knowledge of human nature, a certain way of doing things on a grand scale, of course with all the defects and weaknesses that go with all these advantages and into which your temperament and sometimes your hot temper drive you. . . .

However it was, we were so different and in our difference so dangerous to each other that, if anyone had tried to calculate in advance how I, the slowly developing child, and you, the full-grown man, would stand to each other, he could have assumed that you would simply trample me underfoot so that nothing was left of me. Well, that didn't happen. Nothing alive can be calculated. But perhaps something worse happened. And in saying this I would all the time beg of you not to forget that I never, and not even for a single moment, believe any guilt to be on your side. The effect you had on me was the effect you could not help having. But you should stop considering it some particular malice on my part that I succumbed to that effect.

I was a timid child. For all that, I am sure I was also obstinate, as children are. I am sure that Mother spoilt me too, but I cannot believe I was particularly difficult to manage; I cannot believe that a kindly word, a quiet taking of me by the hand, a friendly look, could not have got me to do anything that was wanted of me. Now you are after all at bottom a kindly and softhearted person (what follows will not be in contradiction to this, I am speaking only of the impression you made on the child), but not every child has the endurance and fearlessness to go on searching until it comes to the kindliness that lies beneath the surface. You can only treat a child in the way you yourself are constituted, with vigor, noise, and hot temper, and in this case this seemed to you, into the bargain, extremely suitable, because you wanted to bring me up to be a strong brave boy. . . .

There is only one episode in the early years of which I have a direct memory. You may remember it, too. Once in the night I kept on whimpering for water, not, I am certain, because I was thirsty, but probably partly to be annoying, partly to amuse myself. After several vigorous threats had failed to have any effect, you took me out of bed, carried me out onto the *pavlatche* and left me there alone for a while in my nightshirt, outside the shut door. I am not going to say that this was wrong—perhaps at that time there was really no other way of getting peace and quiet that night–but I mention it as typical of your methods of bringing up a child and their effect on me. I dare say I was quite obedient afterwards at that period, but it did me inner harm. What was for me a matter of course, that senseless asking for water, and the extraordinary terror of being carried outside were two things that I, my nature being what it was, could never properly connect with each other. Even years afterwards I suffered from the tormenting fancy that the huge man, my father, the ultimate authority, would come almost for no reason at all and take me out of bed in the night and carry me out onto the *pavlatche*, and that therefore I was such a mere nothing for him.

That then was only a small beginning, but this sense of nothingness that often dominates me (a feeling that is in another respect, admittedly, also a noble and fruitful one) comes largely from your influence. What I would have needed was a little encouragement, a little friendliness, a little keeping open of my road, instead of which you blocked it for me, though of course with the good intention of making me go another road. But I was not fit for that. You encouraged me, for instance, when I saluted and marched smartly, but I was no future soldier, or you encouraged me when I was able to eat heartily or even drink beer with my meals, or when I was able to repeat songs, singing what I had not understood, or prattle to you using your own favorite expressions, imitating you, but nothing of this had anything to do with my future. And it is characteristic that even today you really only encourage me in anything when you yourself are involved in it, when what is at stake is your sense of self-importance.

At that time, and at that time everywhere, I would have needed encouragement. I was, after all, depressed even by your mere physical presence. I remember, for instance, how we often undressed together in the same bathing hut. There was I, skinny, weakly, slight; you strong, tall, broad. Even inside the hut I felt myself a miserable specimen, and what's more, not only in your eyes but in the eyes of the whole world, for you were for me the measure of all things. But then when we went out of the bathing hut before the people, I with you holding my hand, a little skeleton, unsteady, barefoot on the boards, frightened of the water, incapable of copying your swimming strokes, which you, with the best of intentions, but actually to my profound humiliation, always kept on showing me, then I was frantic with desperation and all my bad experiences in all spheres at such moments fitted magnificently together. . . .

In keeping with that, furthermore, was your intellectual domination. You had worked your way up so far alone, by your own energies, and as a result you had unbounded confidence in your opinion. For me as a child that was not yet so dazzling as later for the boy growing up. From your armchair you ruled the world. Your opinion was correct, every other was mad, wild, *meshugge*, not normal. With all this your self-confidence was so great that you had no need to be consistent at all and yet never ceased to be in the right. It did sometimes happen that you had no opinion whatsoever about a matter and as a result all opinions that were at all possible with respect to the matter were necessarily wrong, without exception. You were capable, for instance, of running down the Czechs, and then the Germans, and then the Jews, and what is more, not only selectively but in every respect, and finally nobody was left except yourself. For me you took on the enigmatic quality that all tyrants have whose rights are based on their person and not on reason. At least so it seemed to me.

Now where I was concerned you were in fact astonishingly often in the right, which was a matter of course in talk, for there was hardly ever any talk between us, but also in reality. Yet this too was nothing particularly incomprehensible; in all my thinking I was, after all, under the heavy pressure of your personality, even in that part of it—and particularly in that—which was not in accord with yours. All these thoughts, seemingly independent of you, were from the beginning loaded with the burden of your harsh and dogmatic judgments; it was almost impossible to endure this, and yet to work out one's thoughts with any measure of completeness and permanence. I am not here speaking of any sublime thoughts, but of every little enterprise in childhood. It was only necessary to be happy about something or other, to be filled with the thought of it, to come home and speak of it, and the answer was an ironical sigh, a shaking of the head, a tapping of the table with one finger: "Is that all you're so worked up about?" or "I wish I had your worries!" or "The things some people have time to think about!" or "What can you buy yourself with that?" or "What a song and dance about nothing!" Of course, you couldn't be expected to be enthusiastic about every childish triviality, toiling and moiling as you used to. But that wasn't the point. The point was, rather, that you could not help always and on principle causing the child such disappointments, by virtue of your antagonistic nature, and further that this antagonism was ceaselessly intensified through accumulation of its material, that it finally became a matter of established habit even when for once you were of the same opinion as myself, and that finally these disappointments of the child's were not disappointments in ordinary life but, since what it concerned was your person, which was the measure of all things, struck to the very core. Courage, resolution, confidence, delight in this and that, did not endure to the end when you were against whatever it was or even if your opposition was merely to be assumed; and it was to be assumed in almost everything I did. . . .

You have, I think, a gift for bringing up children: you could, I am sure, have been of use to a human being of your own kind with your methods; such a person would have seen the reasonableness of what you told him, would not have troubled about anything else, and would quietly have done things the way he was told. But for me a child everything you shouted at me was positively a heavenly commandment, I never forgot it, it remained for me the most important means of forming a judgment of the world, above all of forming a judgment of you yourself, and there you failed entirely. Since as a child I was together with you chiefly at meals, your teaching was to a large extent teaching about proper behavior at table. What was brought to the table had to be eaten up, there could be no discussion of the goodness of the food—but you yourself often found the food uneatable, called it "this swill," said "that brute" (the cook) had ruined it. Because in accordance with your strong appetite and your particular habit you ate everything fast, hot and in big mouthfuls, the child had to hurry, there was a somber silence at table, interrupted by admonitions: "Eat first, talk afterwards," or "faster, faster, faster," or "there you are, you see, I finished ages ago." Bones mustn't be cracked with the teeth, but you could. Vinegar must not be sipped noisily, but you could. The main thing was that the bread should be cut straight. But it didn't matter that you did it with a knife dripping with gravy. One had to take care that no scraps fell on the floor. In the end it was under your chair that there were most scraps. At table one wasn't allowed to do anything but eat, but you cleaned and cut your fingernails, sharpened pencils, cleaned your ears with the toothpick. Please, Father, understand me rightly: these would in themselves have been utterly insignificant details, they only became depressing for me because you, the man who was so tremendously the measure of all things for me, yourself did not keep the commandments you imposed on me. Hence the world was for me divided into three parts: into one in which I, the slave, lived under laws that had been invented only for me and which I could, I did not know why, never completely comply with; then into a second world, which was infinitely remote from mine, in which you lived, concerned with government, with the issuing of orders and with annoyance about their not being obeyed; and finally into a third world where everybody else lived happily and free from orders and from having to obey. I was continually in disgrace, either I obeyed your orders, and that was a disgrace, for they applied, after all, only to me, or I was defiant, and that was a disgrace too, for how could I presume to defy you, or I could not obey because, for instance, I had not your strength, your appetite, your skill, in spite of which you expected it of me as a matter of course; this was the greatest disgrace of all. What moved in this way was not the child's reflections, but his feelings. . . .

It was true that Mother was illimitably good to me, but all that was for me in relation to you, that is to say, is no good relation. Mother unconsciously played the part of a beater during a hunt. Even if your method of upbringing might in some unlikely case have set me on my own feet by means of producing defiance, dislike, or even hate in me, Mother canceled that out again by kindness, by talking sensibly (in the maze and chaos of my childhood she was the very pattern of good sense and reasonableness), by pleading for me, and I was again driven back into your orbit, which I might perhaps otherwise have broken out of, to your advantage and to my own. Or it was so that no real reconciliation ever came about, that Mother merely shielded me from you in secret, secretly gave me something, or allowed me to do something, and then where you were concerned I was again the furtive creature, the cheat, the guilty one, who in his worthlessness could only pursue backstairs methods even to get the things he regarded as his right. Of course, I then became used to taking such courses also in quest of things to which, even in my own view, I had no right. This again meant an increase in the sense of guilt.

It is also true that you hardly ever really gave me a whipping. But the shouting, the way your face got red, the hasty undoing of the braces and the laying of them ready over the back of the chair, all that was almost worse for me. It is like when someone is going to be hanged. If he is really hanged, then he's dead and it's all over. But if he has to go through all the preliminaries to being hanged and only when the noose is dangling before his face is told of his reprieve, then he may suffer from it all his life long. Besides, from so many occasions when I had, as you clearly showed you thought, deserved to be beaten, when you were however gracious enough to let me off at the last moment, here again what accumulated was only a huge sense of guilt. On every side I was to blame, I was in debt to you.

You have always reproached me (and what is more either alone or in front of others, you having no feeling for the humiliation of this latter, your children's affairs always being public affairs) for living in peace and quiet, warmth, and abundance, lack for nothing, thanks to your hard work. I think here of remarks that must positively have worn grooves in my brain, like: "When I was only seven I had to push the barrow from village to village." "We all had to sleep in one room." "We were glad when we got potatoes." "For years I had open sores on my legs from not having enough clothes to wear in winter." "I was only a little boy when I was sent away to Pisek to go into business." "I got nothing from home, not even when I was in the army, even then I was sending money home." "But for all that, for all that—Father was always Father to me. Ah, nobody knows what that means these days! What do these children know of things? Nobody's been through that! Is there any child that understands such things today?" Under other conditions such stories might have been very educational, they might have been a way of encouraging one and strengthening one to endure similar torments and deprivations to those one's father had undergone. But that wasn't what you wanted at all; the situation had, after all, become quite different as a result of all your efforts, and there was no opportunity to distinguish oneself in the world as you had done. Such an opportunity would first of all have had to be created by violence and revolution, it would have meant breaking away from home (assuming one had had the resolution and strength to do so and that Mother wouldn't have worked against it, for her part, with other means). But all that was not what you wanted at all, that you termed ingratitude, extravagance, disobedience, treachery, madness. And so, while on the one hand you tempted me to it by means of example, story, and humiliation, on the other hand you forbade it with the utmost severity. . . .

(Up to this point there is in this letter relatively little I have intentionally passed over in silence, but now and later I shall have to be silent on certain matters that it is still too hard for me to confess—to you and to myself. I say this in order that, if the picture as a whole should be somewhat blurred here and there, you should not believe that what is to blame is any lack of evidence; on the contrary, there is evidence that might well make the picture unbearably stark. It is not easy to strike a median position.) Here, it is enough to remind you of early days. I had lost my self-confidence where you were concerned, and in its place had developed a boundless sense of guilt. (In recollection of this boundlessness I once wrote of someone, accurately: "He is afraid the shame will outlive him, even.") I could not suddenly undergo a transformation when I came into the company of other people; on the contrary, with them I came to feel an even deeper sense of guilt, for, as I have already said, in their case I had to make good the wrongs done them by you in the business, wrongs in which I too had my share of responsibility. Besides, you always, of course, had some objection to make, frankly or covertly, to everyone I associated with, and for this too I had to beg his pardon. The mistrust that you tried to instill into me, at business and at home, towards most people (tell me of any single person who was of importance to me in my childhood whom you didn't at least once tear to shreds with your criticism), this mistrust, which oddly enough was no particular burden to you (the fact was that you were strong enough to bear it, and besides, it was in reality perhaps only a token of the autocrat), this mistrust, which for me as a little boy was nowhere confirmed in my own eyes, since I everywhere saw only people excellent beyond all hope of emulation, in me turned into mistrust of myself and into perpetual anxiety in relation to everything else. There, then, I was in general certain of not being able to escape from you.

Suggestions for Discussion

Kafka gave this letter (from which you have only excerpts) to his mother, asking her to give it to his father. Understandably she never did so, but it was found among Kafka's unpublished manuscripts after his death. Although Kafka had asked his friend Max Brod to destroy all unpublished material, Brod did not comply with this request.

1. Study the legalistic manner in which Kafka indicts himself as well as his father. Assuming you were on a jury, evaluate the points for prosecution and defense of both father and son. What would be your final judgment as to responsibility for the boy's insecurity as a person?

2. Study the scenes through which Kafka dramatizes certain moments of special significance in his childhood. In spite of his attempt to be fair, by what means does he enlist sympathy with the child?

3. What seems to be the role of the mother? Why does the boy more closely identify with her and her family than with his father?

Suggestions for Writing

1. Write about a significant moment in your childhood relationship with your parents. What effect may it have had on your self-image?

2. Write on the parents' image vs. the child's.

3. Contrast this father with the one portrayed in E.E. Cummings's poem "My Father Moved Through Dooms of Love."

◇◇◇◇

Adrienne Rich
The Anger of a Child

Adrienne Rich (b.1929) has been an activist in the women's movement, and her attitudes are reflected in her poetry, literary criticism, and essays on patriarchy in our culture. Her publications include *A Change of World* (1951), *Snapshots of a Daughter-in-Law* (1963), and *The Will to Change* (1971). The following excerpt appears in her book *Of Woman Born* (1976). It reflects her ambivalence toward her parents and "old, smoldering patches of deep-burning anger."

It is hard to write about my mother. Whatever I do write, it is my story I am telling, my version of the past. If she were to tell her own story other landscapes would be revealed. But in my landscape or hers, there would be old, smoldering patches of deep-burning anger. Before her marriage, she had trained seriously for years both as a concert pianist and a composer. Born in a southern town, mothered by a strong, frustrated woman, she had won a scholarship to study with the director at the Peabody Conservatory in Baltimore, and by teaching at girls' schools had earned her way to further study in New York, Paris, and Vienna. From the age of sixteen, she had been a young belle, who could have married at any time, but she also possessed unusual talent, determination, and independence for her time and place. She read—and reads—widely and wrote—as her journals from my childhood and her letters of today reveal—with grace and pungency.

She married my father after a ten years' engagement during which he finished his medical training and began to establish himself in academic medicine. Once married, she gave up the possibility of a concert career, though for some years she went on composing, and she is still a skilled and dedicated pianist. My father, brilliant, ambitious, possessed by his own drive, assumed that she would give her life over to the enhancement of his. She would manage his household with the formality and grace becoming to a medical professor's wife, though on a limited budget; she would "keep up" her music, though there was no question of letting her composing and practice conflict with her duties as a wife and mother. She was supposed to bear him two children, a boy and a girl. She had to keep her household books to the last penny—I still can see the big blue-gray ledgers, inscribed in her clear, strong hand; she marketed by streetcar, and later, when they could afford a car, she drove my father to and from his laboratory or lectures, often awaiting him for hours. She raised two children, and taught us all our lessons, including music. (Neither of us was sent to school until the fourth grade.) I am sure that she was made to feel responsible for all our imperfections.

My father, like the transcendentalist Bronson Alcott, believed that he (or rather, his wife) could raise children according to his unique moral and intellectual plan, thus proving to the world the values of enlightened, unorthodox child-rearing. I believe that my mother, like Abigail Alcott, at first genuinely and enthusiastically embraced the experiment, and only later found that in carrying out my father's intense, perfectionist program, she was in conflict with her deep instincts as a mother. Like Abigail Alcott, too, she must have found that while ideas might be unfolded by her husband, their daily, hourly practice was going to be up to her. ("'Mr. A. aids me in general principles, but nobody can aid me in the detail,' she mourned. . . . Moreover her husband's views kept her constantly wondering if she were doing a good job. 'Am I doing what is right? Am I doing enough? Am I doing too much?'" The appearance of "temper" and "will" in Louisa, the second Alcott daughter, was blamed by her father on her inheritance from her mother.) Under the institution of motherhood, the mother is the first to blame if theory proves unworkable in practice, or if anything whatsoever goes wrong. But even earlier, my mother had failed at one part of the plan: she had not produced a son.

For years, I felt my mother had chosen my father over me, had sacrificed me to his needs and theories. When my first child was born, I was barely in communication with my parents. I had been fighting my father for my right to an emotional life and a selfhood beyond his needs and theories. We were all at a draw. Emerging from the fear, exhaustion, and alienation of my first childbirth, I could not admit even to myself that I wanted my mother, let alone tell her how much I wanted her. When she visited me in the hospital neither of us could uncoil the obscure lashings of feeling that darkened the room, the tangled thread running backward to where she had labored for three days to give birth to me, and I was not a son. Now, twenty-six years later, I lay in a contagious hospital with my allergy, my skin covered with a mysterious rash, my lips and eyelids swollen, my body bruised and sutured, and, in a cot beside my bed, slept the perfect, golden, male child I had brought forth. How could I have interpreted her feelings when I could not begin to decipher my own? My body had spoken all too eloquently, but it was, medically, just my body. I wanted her to mother me again, to hold my baby in her arms as she had once held me; but that baby was also a gauntlet flung down: *my son*. Part of me longed to offer him for her blessing; part of me wanted to hold him up as a badge of victory in our tragic, unnecessary rivalry as women.

But I was only at the beginning. I know now as I could not possibly know then, that among the tangle of feelings between us, in that crucial yet unreal meeting, was her guilt. Soon I would begin to understand the full weight and burden of maternal guilt, that daily, nightly, hourly, *Am I doing what is right? Am I doing enough? Am I doing too much?* The institution of motherhood finds all mothers more or less guilty of having failed their children; and my mother, in particular, had been expected to help create, according to my father's plan, a perfect daughter. This "perfect" daughter, though gratifyingly precocious, had early been given to tics and tantrums, had become permanently lame from arthritis at twenty-two; she had finally resisted her father's Victorian paternalism, his seductive charm and controlling cruelty, had married a divorced graduate student, had begun to write "modern," "obscure," "pessimistic" poetry, lacking the fluent sweetness of Tennyson, had had the final temerity to get pregnant and bring a living baby into the world. She had ceased to be the demure and precocious child or the poetic, seducible adolescent. Something, in my father's view, had gone terribly wrong. I can imagine that whatever else my mother felt (and I know that part of her *was* mutely on my side) she also was made to feel blame. Beneath the "numbness" that she has since told me she experienced at that time, I can imagine the guilt of Everymother, because I have known it myself.

But I did not know it yet. And it is difficult for me to write of my mother now, because I have known it too well. I struggle to describe what it felt like to be her daughter, but I find myself divided, slipping under her skin; a part of me identified too much with her. I know deep reservoirs of anger toward her still exist: the anger of a four-year-old locked in the closet (my father's orders, but my mother carried them out) for childish misbehavior; the anger of a six-year-old kept too long at piano practice (again, at his insistence, but it was she who gave the lessons) till I developed a series of facial tics. (As a mother I know what a child's facial tic is—a lancet of guilt and pain running through one's own body.) And I still feel the anger of a daughter, pregnant, wanting my mother desperately and feeling she had gone over to the enemy.

And I know there must be deep reservoirs of anger in her; every mother has known overwhelming, unacceptable anger at her children. When I think of the conditions under which my mother became a mother, the impossible expectations, my father's distaste for pregnant women, his hatred of all that he could not control, my anger at her dissolves into grief and anger *for* her, and then dissolves back again into anger at her: the ancient, unpurged anger of the child.

My mother lives today as an independent woman, which she was always meant to be. She is a much-loved, much-admired grandmother, an explorer in new realms; she lives in the present and future, not the past. I no longer have fantasies—they are the unhealed child's fantasies, I think—of some infinitely healing conversation with her, in which we could show all our wounds, transcend the pain we have shared as mother and daughter, say everything at last. But in writing these pages, I am admitting, at least, how important her existence is and has been for me.

Suggestions for Discussion

1. What is the tone of Rich's portrait of her father? With what details does it become apparent?

2. With what details does the author convey her anger at her mother?

3. How does the author feel about the relationship of her father and mother?

4. How did Rich recognize her mother's guilt?

5. Account for the author's ambivalence toward her mother.

6. The author concedes that she is writing her "version of the past" and that her mother might tell her story differently. Provide some of the details in the mother's story if told by her.

Suggestions for Writing

1. Write on your views of enlightened child rearing.

2. Recall an episode in your childhood in which you felt anger at your parents.

3. Develop your version of the mother's story.

◇◇◇◇

Essays
— ◆◆◆ —

John Gregory Dunne
Quintana

John Gregory Dunne (b. 1932) was educated at Princeton University. He has written a number of film scripts with his wife, Joan Didion: *The Panic in Needle Park* (1971), *Play It As It Lays* (1972), and *True Confessions* (1982). His publications include *Delano: The Story of the California Grape Strike* (1967), *The Studio* (1969), and *Vegas: A Memoir of a Dark Season* (1974). In this excerpt from *Quintana and Friends* (1978) Dunne acknowledges that if it is important for Quintana to know her parentage, she is free to make the decision and her adoptive parents will respect it.

Quintana will be eleven this week. She approaches adolescence with what I can only describe as panache, but then watching her journey from infancy has always been like watching Sandy Koufax pitch or Bill Russell play basketball. There is the same casual arrogance, the implicit sense that no one has ever done it any better. And yet it is difficult for a father to watch a daughter grow up. With each birthday she becomes more like us, an adult, and what we cling to is the memory of the child. I remember the first time I saw her in the nursery at Saint John's Hospital. It was after visiting hours and my wife and I stood staring through the soundproof glass partition at the infants in their cribs, wondering which was ours. Then a nurse in a surgical mask appeared from a back room carrying a fierce, black-haired baby with a bow in her hair. She was just seventeen hours old and her face was still wrinkled and red and the identification beads on her wrist had not our name but only the letters "NI." "NI" stood for "No Information," the hospital's code for an infant to be placed for adoption. Quintana is adopted.

It has never been an effort to say those three words, even when they occasion the well-meaning but insensitive compliment, "You couldn't love her more if she were your own." At moments like that, my wife and I say nothing and smile through gritted teeth. And yet we are not unaware that sometime in the not too distant future we face a moment that only those of us who are adoptive parents will ever have to face—our daughter's decision to search or not to search for her natural parents.

I remember that when I was growing up a staple of radio drama was the show built around adoption. Usually the dilemma involved a child who had just learned by accident that it was adopted. This information could only come accidentally, because in those days it was considered a radical departure from the norm to inform your son or daughter that he or she was not your own flesh and blood. If such information had to be revealed, it was often followed by the specious addendum that the natural parents had died when the child was an infant. An automobile accident was viewed as the most expeditious and efficient way to get rid of both parents at once. One of my contemporaries, then a young actress, was not told that she was adopted until she was twenty-two and the beneficiary of a small inheritance from her natural father's will. Her adoptive mother could not bring herself to tell her daughter the reason behind the bequest and entrusted the task to an agent from the William Morris office.

Today we are more enlightened, aware of the psychological evidence that such barbaric secrecy can only inflict hurt. When Quintana was born, she was offered to us privately by the gynecologist who delivered her. In California, such private adoptions are not only legal but in the mid-sixties, before legalized abortion and before the sexual revolution made it acceptable for an unwed mother to keep her child, were quite common. The night we went to see Quintana for the first time at Saint John's, there was a tacit agreement between us that "No Information" was only a bracelet. It was quite easy to congratulate ourselves for agreeing to be so open when the only information we had about her mother was her age, where she was from and a certified record of her good health. What we did not realize was that through one bureaucratic slipup we would learn her mother's name and that through another she would learn ours, and Quintana's.

From the day we brought Quintana home from the hospital, we tried never to equivocate. When she was little, we always had Spanish-speaking help and one of the first words she learned, long before she understood its import, was *adoptada*. As she grew older, she never tired of asking us how we happened to adopt her. We told her that we went to the hospital and were given our choice of any baby in the nursery. "No, not that baby," we had said, "not that baby, not that baby . . ." All this with full gestures of inspection, until finally: "That baby!" Her face would always light up and she would say: "Quintana." When she asked a question about her adoption, we answered, never volunteering more than she requested, convinced that as she grew her questions would become more searching and complicated. In terms I hoped she would understand, I tried to explain that adoption offered to a parent the possibility of escaping the prison of genes, that no matter how perfect the natural child, the parent could not help acknowledging in black moments that some of his or her bad blood was bubbling around in the offspring; with an *adoptada*, we were innocent of any knowledge of bad blood.

In time Quintana began to intuit that our simple parable of free choice in the hospital nursery was somewhat more complex than we had indicated. She now knew that being adopted meant being born of another mother, and that person she began referring to as "my other mommy." How old, she asked, was my other mommy when I was born? Eighteen, we answered, and on her stubby little fingers she added on her own age, and with each birthday her other mommy became twenty-three, then twenty-five and twenty-eight. There was no obsessive interest, just occasional queries, some more difficult to answer than others. Why had her other mother given her up? We said that we did not know—which was true—and could only assume that it was because she was little more than a child herself, alone and without the resources to bring up a baby. The answer seemed to satisfy, at least until we became close friends with a young woman, unmarried, with a small child of her own. The contradiction was, of course, apparent to Quintana, and yet she seemed to understand, in the way that children do, that there had been a millennium's worth of social change in the years since her birth, that the pressures on a young unmarried mother were far more in 1966 than they were in 1973. (She did, after all, invariably refer to the man in the White House as President Nixon Vietnam Watergate, almost as if he had a three-tiered name like John Quincy Adams.) We were sure that she viewed her status with equanimity, but how much so we did not realize until her eighth birthday party. There were twenty little girls at the party, and as little girls do, they were discussing things gynecological, specifically the orifice in their mothers' bodies from which they had emerged at birth. "I didn't," Quintana said matter-of-factly. She was sitting in a large wicker fan chair and her pronouncement impelled the other children to silence. "I was adopted." We had often wondered how she would handle this moment with her peers, and we froze, but she pulled it off with such élan and aplomb that in moments the other children were bemoaning their own misfortune in not being adopted, one even claiming, "Well, I was almost adopted."

Because my wife and I both work at home, Quintana has never had any confusion about how we make our living. Our mindless staring at our respective typewriters means food on the table in a way the mysterious phrase "going to the office" never can. From the time she could walk, we have taken her to meetings whenever we were without help, and she has been a quick study on the nuances of our life. "She's remarkably well adjusted," my brother once said about her. "Considering that every time I see her she's in a different city." I think she could pick an agent out of a police lineup, and out of the blue one night at dinner she offered that all young movie directors were short and had frizzy hair and wore Ditto pants and wire glasses and shirts with three buttons opened. (As far as I know, she had never laid eyes on Bodganovich, Spielberg or Scorsese.) Not long ago an actress received an award for a picture we had written for her. The actress's acceptance speech at the televised award ceremony drove Quintana into an absolute fury. "She never," Quintana reported, "thanked *us.*" Since she not only identifies with our work but at times even considers herself an equal partner, I of course discussed this piece with her before I began working on it. I told her what it was about and said I would drop it if she would be embarrassed or if she thought that subject was too private. She gave it some thought and finally said she wanted me to write it.

I must, however, try to explain and perhaps even try to justify my own motives. The week after *Roots* was televised, each child in Quintana's fifth-grade class was asked to trace a family tree. On my side Quintana went back to her great-grandfather Burns, who arrived from Ireland shortly after the

Civil War, a ten-year-old refugee from the potato famine, and on her mother's side to her great-great-great-great-grandmother Cornwall, who came west in a wagon train in 1846. As it happens, I have little interest in family beyond my immediate living relatives. (I can never remember the given names of my paternal grandparents and have never known my paternal grandmother's maiden name. This lack of interest mystifies my wife.) Yet I wanted Quintana to understand that if she wished, there were blood choices other than Dominick Burns and Nancy Hardin Cornwall. Over the past few years, there has been a growing body of literature about adoptees seeking their own roots. I am in general sympathetic to this quest, although not always to the dogged absolutism of the more militant seekers. But I would be remiss if I did not say that I am more than a little sensitive to the way the literature presents adoptive parents. We are usually shown as frozen in the postures of radio drama, untouched by the changes in attitudes of the last several generations. In point of fact we accept that our children might seek out their roots, even encourage it; we accept it as an adventure like life itself—perhaps painful, one hopes enriching. I know not one adoptive parent who does not feel this way. Yet in the literature there is the implicit assumption that we are threatened by the possibility of search, that we would consider it an act of disloyalty on the part of our children. The patronizing nature of this assumption is never noted in the literature. It is as if we were Hudson and Mrs. Bridges, belowstairs surrogates taking care of the wee one, and I don't like it one damn bit.

Often these days I find myself thinking of Quintana's natural mother. Both my wife and I admit more than a passing interest in the woman who produced this extraordinary child. (As far as we know, she never named the father, and even more interesting, Quintana has never asked about him.) When Quintana was small, and before the legalities of adoption were complete, we imagined her mother everywhere, a wraith-like presence staring through the chain-link fence at the blond infant sunbathing in the crib. Occasionally today we see a photograph of a young woman in a magazine—the mother as we imagine her to look—and we pass it to each other without comment. Once we even checked the name of a model in *Vogue* through her modeling agency; she turned out to be a Finn. I often wonder if she thinks of Quintana, or of us. (Remember, we know each other's names.) There is the possibility that having endured the twin traumas of birth and the giving up of a child, she blocked out the names the caseworker gave her, but I don't really believe it. I consider it more likely that she has followed the fairly well-documented passage of Quintana through childhood into adolescence. Writers are at least semipublic figures, and in the interest of commerce or selling a book or a movie, or even out of simple vanity, we allow interviews and photo layouts and look into television cameras; we even write about ourselves, and our children. I recall wondering how this sentient young woman of our imagination had reacted to four pages in *People*. It is possible, even likely, that she will read this piece. I know that it is an almost intolerable invasion of her privacy. I think it probable, however, that in the dark reaches of night she has considered the possibility of a further incursion, of opening a door one day and seeing a young woman who says, "Hello, Mother, I am your daughter."

Perhaps this is romantic fantasy. We know none of the circumstances of the woman's life, or even if she is still alive. We once suggested to our lawyer that we make a discreet inquiry and he quite firmly said that this was a quest that belonged only to Quintana, if she wished to make it, and not to us. What is not fantasy is that for the past year, Quintana has known the name of her natural mother. It was at dinner and she said that she would like to meet her one day, but that it would be hard, not knowing her name. There finally was the moment: we had never equivocated; did we begin now? We took a deep breath and told Quintana, then age ten, her mother's name. We also said that if she decided to search her out, we would help her in any way we could. (I must allow, however, that we would prefer she wait to make this decision until the Sturm and Drang of adolescence is past.) We then considered the possibility that her mother, for whatever good or circumstantial reasons of her own, might prefer not to see her. I am personally troubled by the militant contention that the natural mother has no right of choice in this matter. "I did not ask to be born," an adoptee once was quoted in a news story I read. "She has to see me." If only life were so simple, if only pain did not hurt. Yet we would never try to influence Quintana on this point. How important it is to know her parentage is a question only she can answer; it is her decision to make.

All parents realize, or should realize, that children are not possessions, but are only lent to us, angel boarders, as it were. Adoptive parents realize this earlier and perhaps more poignantly than others. I do not know the end of this story. It is possible that Quintana will find more reality in family commitment and cousins across the continent and heirloom orange spoons and pictures in an album and faded letters from Dominick Burns and diary entries from Nancy Hardin Cornwall than in the uncertainties of blood. It is equally possible that she will venture into the unknown. I once asked her what she would do if she met her natural mother. "I'd put one arm around Mom," she said, "and one arm around my other mommy, and I'd say, 'Hello, Mommies.'"

If that's the way it turns out, that is what she will do.

Suggestions for Discussion

1. Justify the use of the word *panache* in the description of Quintana.

2. How have attitudes toward adoption changed?

3. How did Quintana's parents learn that she viewed her adoption with equanimity?

4. How does the author feel about the possibility of Quintana's meeting her natural mother?

5. What does the reader learn about the character of Quintana's adoptive father?

Suggestions for Writing

1. Characterize a parent or parents who regard children as possessions.

2. Defend the point of view that adopted children should be aided in seeking their natural parents.

Richard Rodriguez

Mr. Secrets

Richard Rodriguez (b. 1944) was born in San Francisco and attended Stanford University, Columbia University, and the University of California at Berkeley. He has written about his experiences as a scholarship and minority student in Col-lege English and American Scholar. This excerpt from his autobiography, Hun-ger of Memory (1982), reflects his loneliness as a writer and his sensitivity to his parents' reluctance to have their privacy violated.

I am writing about those very things my mother has asked me not to re-veal. Shortly after I published my first autobiographical essay seven years ago, my mother wrote me a letter pleading with me never again to write about our family life. "Write about something else in the future. Our family life is pri-vate." And besides: "Why do you need to tell the *gringos* about how 'divided' you feel from the family?"

I sit at my desk now, surrounded by versions of paragraphs and pages of this book, considering that question.

When I decided to compose this intellectual autobiography, a New York editor told me that I would embark on a lonely journey. Over the noise of voices and dishes in an East Side restaurant, he said. "There will be times when you will think the entire world has forgotten you. Some mornings you will yearn for a phone call or a letter to assure you that you still are connected to the world." There *have* been mornings when I've dreaded the isolation this writing requires. Mornings spent listless in silence and in fear of confronting the blank sheet of paper. There have been times I've rushed away from my papers to answer the phone; gladly gotten up from my chair, hearing the mailman outside. Times I have been frustrated by the slowness of words, the way even a single paragraph never seemed done.

I had known a writer's loneliness before, working on my dissertation in the British Museum. But that experience did not prepare me for the task of writ-ing these pages where my own life is the subject. Many days I feared I had stopped living by committing myself to remember the past. I feared that my absorption with events in the past amounted to an immature refusal to live in the present. Adulthood seemed consumed by memory. I would tell myself otherwise. I would tell myself that the act of remembering is an act of the present. (In writing this autobiography, I am actually describing the man I have become—the man in the present.)

Times when the money ran out, I left writing for temporary jobs. Once I had a job for over six months. I resumed something like a conventional social life. But then I have turned away, come back to my San Francisco apartment to closet myself in the silence I both need and fear.

I stay away from late-night parties. (To be clearheaded in the morning.) I disconnect my phone for much of the day. I must avoid complex relationships—a troublesome lover or a troubled friend. The person who knows me best scolds me for escaping from life. (*Am* I evading adulthood?) People I know get promotions at jobs. Friends move away. Friends get married. Friends divorce. One friend tells me she is pregnant. Then she has a baby. Then the baby has the formed face of a child. Can walk. Talk. And still I sit at this desk laying my words like jigsaw pieces, a fellow with ladies in house-coats and old men in slippers who watch TV. Neighbors in my apartment house rush off to work about nine. I hear their steps on the stairs. (They will be back at six o'clock.) Somewhere planes are flying. The door slams behind them.

"Why?" My mother's question hangs in the still air of memory.

The loneliness I have felt many mornings, however, has not made me forget that I am engaged in a highly public activity. I sit here in silence writing this small volume of words, and it seems to me the most public thing I ever have done. My mother's letter has served to remind me: I am making my personal life public. Probably I will never try to explain my motives to my mother and father. My mother's question will go unanswered to her face. Like everything else on these pages, my reasons for writing will be revealed instead to public readers I expect never to meet.

It is to those whom my mother refers to as the *gringos* that I write. The *gringos*. The expression reminds me that she and my father have not followed their children all the way down the path to full Americanization. They were changed—became more easy in public, less withdrawn and uncertain—by the public success of their children. But something remained unchanged in their lives. With excessive care they continue today to note the difference between private and public life. And their private society remains only their family. No matter how friendly they are in public, no matter how firm their smiles, my parents never forget when they are in public. My mother must use a high-pitched tone of voice when she addresses people who are not relatives. It is a tone of voice I have all my live heard her use away from the house. Coming home from grammar school with new friends, I would hear it, its reminder: My new intimates were strangers to her. Like my sisters and brother, over the years, I've grown used to hearing that voice. Expected to hear it. Though I suspect that voice has played deep in my soul, sounding a lyre, to recall my "betrayal," my movement away from our family's intimate past. It is the voice I hear even now when my mother addresses her son- or daughter-in-law. (They remain public people to her.) She speaks to them, sounding the way she does when talking over the fence to a neighbor.

It was, in fact, the lady next door to my parents—a librarian—who first mentioned seeing my essay seven years ago. My mother was embarrassed because she hadn't any idea what the lady was talking about. But she had heard enough to go to a library with my father to find the article. They read what I wrote. And then she wrote her letter.

It is addressed to me in Spanish, but the body of the letter is in English. Almost mechanically she speaks of her pride at the start. ("Your dad and I are very proud of the brilliant manner you have to express yourself.") Then the matter of most concern comes to the fore. "Your dad and I have only one objection to what you write. You say too much about the family . . . Why do you have to do that? . . . Why do you need to tell the *gringos*? . . . Why do you think we're so separated as a family? Do you really think this, Richard?"

A new paragraph changes the tone. Soft, maternal. Worried for me she adds, "Do not punish yourself for having to give up our culture in order to 'make it' as you say. Think of all the wonderful achievements you have obtained. You should be proud. Learn Spanish better. Practice it with your dad and me. Don't worry so much. Don't get the idea that I am mad at you either.

"Just keep one thing in mind. Writing is one thing, the family is another. I don't want *tus hermanos* hurt by your writings. And what do you think the cousins will say when they read where you talk about how the aunts were maids? Especially I don't want the *gringos* knowing about our private affairs. Why should they? Please give this some thought. Please write about something else in the future. Do me this favor."

Please.

To the adult I am today, my mother needs to say what she would never have needed to say to her child: the boy who faithfully kept family secrets. When my fourth-grade teacher made our class write a paper about a typical evening at home, it never occurred to me actually to do so. "Describe what you do with your family," she told us. And automatically I produced a fictionalized account. I wrote that I had six brothers and sisters; I described watching my mother get dressed up in a red-sequined dress before she went with my father to a party; I even related how the imaginary baby sitter ("a high school student") taught my brother and sisters and me to make popcorn and how, later, I fell asleep before my parents returned. The nun who read what I wrote would have known that what I had written was completely imagined. But she never said anything about my contrivance. And I never expected her to either. I never thought she *really* wanted me to write about my family life. In any case, I would have been unable to do so.

I was very much the son of parents who regarded the most innocuous piece of information about the family to be secret. Although I had, by that time, grown easy in public, I felt that my family life was strictly private, not to be revealed to unfamiliar ears or eyes. Around the age of ten, I was held by surprise listening to my best friend tell me one day that he "hated" his father. In a furious whisper he said that when he attempted to kiss his father before going to bed, his father had laughed: "Don't you think you're getting too old for that sort of thing, son?" I was intrigued not so much by the incident as by the fact that the boy would relate it to *me*.

In those years I was exposed to the sliding-glass-door informality of middle-class California family life. Ringing the doorbell of a friend's house, I would hear someone inside yell out, "Come on in, Richie; door's not locked." And in I would go to discover my friend's family undisturbed by my presence. The father was in the kitchen in his underwear. The mother was in her bathrobe. Voices gathered in familiarity. A parent scolded a child in front of me; voices quarreled, then laughed; the mother told me something about her son after he had stepped out of the room and she was sure he couldn't overhear; the father would speak to his children and to me in the same tone of voice. I was one of the family, the parents of several good friends would assure me. (Richie.)

My mother sometimes invited my grammar school friends to stay for dinner or even to stay overnight. But my parents never treated such visitors as part of the family, never told them they were. When a school friend ate at our table, my father spoke less than usual. (Stray, distant words.) My mother was careful to use her "visitor's voice." Sometimes, listening to her, I would feel annoyed because she wouldn't be more herself. Sometimes I'd feel embarrassed that I couldn't give to a friend at my house what I freely accepted at his.

I remained, nevertheless, my parents' child. At school, in sixth grade, my teacher suggested that I start keeping a diary. ("You should write down your personal experiences and reflections.") But I shied away from the idea. It was the one suggestion that the scholarship boy couldn't follow. I would not have wanted to write about the minor daily events of my life; I would never have been able to write about what most deeply, daily, concerned me during those years: I was growing away from my parents. Even if I could have been certain that no one would find my diary, even if I could have destroyed each page after I had written it, I would have felt uncomfortable writing about my home life. There seemed to me something intrinsically public about written words.

Writing, at any rate, was a skill I didn't regard highly. It was a grammar school skill I acquired with comparative ease. I do not remember struggling to write the way I struggled to learn how to read. The nuns would praise student papers for being neat—the handwritten letters easy for others to read; they promised that my writing style would improve as I read more and more. But that wasn't the reason I became a reader. Reading was for me the key to "knowledge"; I swallowed facts and dates and names and themes. Writing, by contrast, was an activity I thought of as a kind of report, evidence of learning. I wrote down what I heard teachers say. I wrote down things from my books. I wrote down all I knew when I was examined at the end of the school year. Writing was performed after the fact; it was not the exciting experience of learning itself. In eighth grade I read several hundred books, the titles of which I still can recall. But I cannot remember a single essay I wrote. I only remember that the most frequent kind of essay I wrote was the book report.

In high school there were more "creative" writing assignments. English teachers assigned the composition of short stories and poems. One sophomore story I wrote was a romance set in the Civil War South. I remember that it earned me a good enough grade, but my teacher suggested with quiet tact that next time I try writing about "something you know more about—something closer to home." Home? I wrote a short story about an old man who lived all by himself in a house down the block. That was as close as my writing ever got to my house. Still, I won prizes. When teachers suggested I contribute articles to the school literary magazine, I did so. And when I was asked to join the school newspaper, I said yes. I did not feel any great pride in my writings, however. (My mother was the one who collected my prize-winning essays in a box she kept in her closet.) Though I remember seeing my by-line in print for the first time, and dwelling on the printing press letters with fascination: RICHARD RODRIGUEZ. The letters furnished evidence of a vast public identity writing made possible.

When I was a freshman in college, I began typing all my assignments. My writing speed decreased. Writing became a struggle. In high school I had been able to handwrite ten- and twenty-page papers in little more than an hour—and I never revised what I wrote. A college essay took me several nights to prepare. Suddenly everything I wrote seemed in need of revision. I became a self-conscious writer. A stylist. The change, I suspect, was the result of seeing my words ordered by the even, impersonal, anonymous type-writer print. As arranged by a machine, the words that I typed no longer seemed mine. I was able to see them with a new appreciation for how my reader would see them.

From grammar school to graduate school I could always name my reader. I wrote for my teacher. I could consult him or her before writing, and after. I suppose that I knew other readers could make sense of what I wrote—that, therefore, I addressed a general reader. But I didn't think very much about it. Only toward the end of my schooling and only because political issues pressed upon me did I write, and have published in magazines, essays intended for readers I never expected to meet. Now I am struck by the opportunity. I write today for a reader who exists in my mind only phantasmagorically. Someone with a face erased; someone of no particular race or sex or age or weather. A gray presence. Unknown, unfamiliar. All that I know about him is that he has had a long education and that his society, like mine, is often public *(un gringo)*.

Suggestions for Discussion

1. With what details does Rodriguez convey his sense of the isolation and frustration of the writer?

2. What are the nagging concerns and questions that afflict the author?

3. In what sense is Rodriguez's autobiography both private and public?

4. Account for the differences in his parents' public and private lives. How does the mother's letter illuminate them?

5. How does the author clarify his childhood and youthful attitudes toward his family life and that of his friends?

6. Why couldn't the young Rodriguez write about his early life in a diary?

7. Account for his differing view of reading and writing when he was in the eighth grade.

8. How does Rodriguez account for his changed view of writing when he was a college freshman and subsequently? How does his sense of audience shift?

Suggestions for Writing

1. Compare and contrast your childhood views of your family with those you currently have.

2. Describe an episode in which the setting is the family dining room and the characters are you and your parents.

Fiction

—◆◆◆—

William Carlos Williams

The Use of Force

William Carlos Williams (1883–1963) practiced medicine in Rutherford, New Jersey, the factory town in which he was born. *Selected Poems* appeared in 1949, *Collected Later Poetry* (1950), and *Collected Poems* (1951). His long epic poem, *Paterson,* won the National Book Award for Poetry in 1950. *Desert Music* appeared in 1954, *Journey to Love* in 1955. He has also written novels, *White Mule* (1937) and *In the Money* (1940); short stories, *Life Along the Passaic* (1938), *Selected Essays* (1954); and an *Autobiography* (1951). He received the Bollingen Award for poetry in 1953. The simple and direct language in this short story heightens the intensity of the feelings of the doctor, parents, and child.

They were new patients to me, all I had was the name, Olson.

Please come down as soon as you can, my daughter is very sick.

When I arrived I was met by the mother, a big startled looking woman, very clean and apologetic who merely said, Is this the doctor? and let me in. In the back, she added. You must excuse us, doctor, we have her in the kitchen where it is warm. It is very damp here sometimes.

The child was fully dressed and sitting on her father's lap near the kitchen table. He tried to get up, but I motioned for him not to bother, took off my overcoat and started to look things over. I could see that they were all very nervous, eyeing me up and down distrustfully. As often, in such cases, they weren't telling me more than they had to, it was up to me to tell them; that's why they were spending three dollars on me.

The child was fairly eating me up with her cold, steady eyes, and no expression to her face whatever. She did not move and seemed, inwardly, quiet; an unusually attractive little thing, and as strong as a heifer in appearance. But her face was flushed, she was breathing rapidly, and I realized that she had a high fever. She had magnificent blonde hair, in profusion. One of

160

those picture children often reproduced in advertising leaflets and the pho-
togravure sections of the Sunday papers.

She's had a fever for three days, began the father and we don't know what
it comes from. My wife has given her things, you know, like people do, but
it don't do no good. And there's been a lot of sickness around. So we tho't
you'd better look her over and tell us what is the matter.

As doctors often do I took a trial shot at it as a point of departure. Has she
had a sore throat?

Both parents answered me together, No. . . No, she says her throat don't
hurt her.

Does your throat hurt you? added the mother to the child. But the little
girl's expression didn't change nor did she move her eyes from my face.

Have you looked?

I tried to, said the mother, but I couldn't see.

As it happens we had been having a number of cases of diphtheria in the
school to which this child went during that month and we were all, quite
apparently, thinking of that, though no one had as yet spoken of the thing.

Well, I said, suppose we take a look at the throat first. I smiled in my best
professional manner and asking for the child's first name I said, come on,
Mathilda, open your mouth and let's take a look at your throat.

Nothing doing.

Aw, come on, I coaxed, just open your mouth wide and let me take a look.
Look, I said opening both hands wide, I haven't anything in my hands. Just
open up and let me see.

Such a nice man, put in the mother. Look how kind he is to you. Come
on, do what he tells you to. He won't hurt you.

At that I ground my teeth in disgust. If only they wouldn't use the word
"hurt" I might be able to get somewhere. But I did not allow myself to be
hurried or disturbed but speaking quietly and slowly I approached the child
again.

As I moved my chair a little nearer suddenly with one catlike movement
both her hands clawed instinctively for my eyes and she almost reached them
too. In fact she knocked my glasses flying and they fell, though unbroken,
several feet away from me on the kitchen floor.

Both the mother and father almost turned themselves inside out in embarrassment and apology. You bad girl, said the mother, taking her and shaking
her by one arm. Look what you've done. The nice man . . .

For heaven's sake, I broke in. Don't call me a nice man to her. I'm here
to look at her throat on the chance that she might have diphtheria and possibly die of it. But that's nothing to her. Look here, I said to the child, we're
going to look at your throat. You're old enough to understand what I'm saying. Will you open it now by yourself or shall we have to open it for you?

Not a move. Even her expression hadn't changed. Her breaths however
were coming faster and faster. Then the battle began. I had to do it. I had to
have a throat culture for her own protection. But first I told the parents that
it was entirely up to them. I explained the danger but said that I would not
insist on a throat examination so long as they would take the responsibility.

If you don't do what the doctor says you'll have to go to the hospital, the
mother admonished her severely.

Oh yeah? I had to smile to myself. After all, I had already fallen in love with the savage brat, the parents were contemptible to me. In the ensuing struggle they grew more and more abject, crushed, exhausted while she surely rose to magnificent heights of insane fury of effort bred of her terror of me.

The father tried his best, and he was a big man but the fact that she was his daughter, his shame at her behavior, and his dread of hurting her made him release her just at the critical times when I had almost achieved success, till I wanted to kill him. But his dread also that she might have diphtheria made him tell me to go on, go on though he himself was almost fainting, while the mother moved back and forth behind us raising and lowering her hands in an agony of apprehension.

Put her in front of you on your lap, I ordered, and hold both her wrists.

But as soon as he did the child let out a scream. Don't, you're hurting me. Let go of my hands. Let them go I tell you. Then she shrieked terrifyingly, hysterically. Stop it! Stop it! You're killing me!

Do you think she can stand it, doctor! said the mother.

You get out, said the husband to his wife. Do you want her to die of diphtheria?

Come on now, hold her, I said.

Then I grasped the child's head with my left hand and tried to get the wooden tongue depressor between her teeth. She fought, with clenched teeth, desperately! But now I also had grown furious—at a child. I tried to hold myself down but I couldn't. I know how to expose a throat for inspection. And I did my best. When finally I got the wooden spatula behind the last teeth and just the point of it into the mouth cavity, she opened up for an instant but before I could see anything she came down again and gripped the wooden blade between her molars she reduced it to splinters before I could get it out again.

Aren't you ashamed, the mother yelled at her. Aren't you ashamed to act like that in front of the doctor?

Get me a smooth-handled spoon of some sort, I told the mother. We're going through with this. The child's mouth was already bleeding. Her tongue was cut and she was screaming in wild hysterical shrieks. Perhaps I should have desisted and come back in an hour or more. No doubt it would have been better. But I have seen at least two children lying dead in bed of neglect in such cases, and feeling that I must get a diagnosis now or never I went at it again. But the worst of it was that I too had got beyond reason. I could have torn the child apart in my own fury and enjoyed it. It was a pleasure to attack her. My face was burning with it.

The damned little brat must be protected against her own idiocy, one says to one's self at such times. Others must be protected against her. It is a social necessity. And all these things are true. But a blind fury, a feeling of adult shame, bred of a longing for muscular release are the operatives. One goes on to the end.

In the final unreasoning assault I overpowered the child's neck and jaws. I forced the heavy silver spoon back of her teeth and down her throat till she gagged. And there it was—both tonsils covered with membrane. She had fought valiantly to keep me from knowing her secret. She had been hiding that sore throat for three days at least and lying to her parents in order to escape just such an outcome as this.

Now truly she was furious. She had been on the defensive before but now she attacked. Tried to get off her father's lap and fly at me while tears of defeat blinded her eyes.

Suggestions for Discussion

1. How do you explain the child's resistance to the doctor?

2. Account for the doctor's statement: "I had already fallen in love with the savage brat; the parents were contemptible to me."

3. How are the doctor's feelings reflected during the struggle? How does he rationalize them?

4. Attempt to recreate the child's relationship with each of her parents.

5. Comment on the use of force. What alternatives did the doctor have?

Suggestions for Writing

Create a scene in which there is interaction between the child and her parents.

Flannery O'Connor
Everything That Rises Must Converge

Flannery O'Connor (1925–1965), born in Georgia, was educated in Georgia schools and the University of Iowa. She received the O. Henry Award in 1957 and a Ford Foundation grant in 1959. Her books include the novels *Wise Blood* (1952) and *The Violent Bear It Away* (1960). Her collection of short stories, *Everything That Rises Must Converge*, was published posthumously in 1965. The tension between mother and son is aggravated by the racial conflict and leads to a tragic resolution in which the internal conflict merges with the climax of the racial incident.

Her doctor had told Julian's mother that she must lose twenty pounds on account of her blood pressure, so on Wednesday nights Julian had to take her downtown on the bus for a reducing class at the Y. The reducing class was designed for working girls over fifty, who weighed from 165 to 200 pounds. His mother was one of the slimmer ones, but she said ladies did not tell their age or weight. She would not ride the buses by herself at night since they had been integrated, and because the reducing class was one of her few pleasures, necessary for her health, and *free*, she said Julian could at least put himself out to take her, considering all she did for him. Julian did not like to consider all she did for him, but every Wednesday night he braced himself and took her.

She was almost ready to go, standing before the hall mirror, putting on her hat, while he, his hands behind him, appeared pinned to the door frame, waiting like Saint Sebastian for the arrows to begin piercing him. The hat was new and had cost her seven dollars and a half. She kept saying, "Maybe I shouldn't have paid that for it. No, I shouldn't have. I'll take it off and return it tomorrow. I shouldn't have bought it."

Julian raised his eyes to heaven. "Yes, you should have bought it," he said. "Put it on and let's go." It was a hideous hat. A purple velvet flap came down on one side of it and stood up on the other; the rest of it was green and looked like a cushion with the stuffing out. He decided it was less comical than jaunty and pathetic. Everything that gave her pleasure was small and depressed him.

She lifted the hat one more time and set it down slowly on top of her head. Two wings of gray hair protruded on either side of her florid face, but her eyes, sky-blue, were as innocent and untouched by experience as they must have been when she was ten. Were it not that she was a widow who had struggled fiercely to feed and clothe and put him through school and who was supporting him still, "until he got on his feet," she might have been a little girl that he had to take to town.

"It's all right, it's all right," he said. "Let's go." He opened the door himself and started down the walk to get her going. The sky was a dying violet and the houses stood out darkly against it, bulbous liver-colored monstrosities of a uniform ugliness though no two were alike. Since this had been a fashionable neighborhood forty years ago, his mother persisted in thinking they did well to have an apartment in it. Each house had a narrow collar of dirt around it in which sat, usually, a grubby child. Julian walked with his hands in his pockets, his head down and thrust forward and his eyes glazed with the determination to make himself completely numb during the time he would be sacrificed to her pleasure.

The door closed and he turned to find the dumpy figure, surmounted by the atrocious hat, coming toward him. "Well," she said, "you only live once and paying a little more for it, I at least won't meet myself coming and going."

"Some day I'll start making money," Julian said gloomily—he knew he never would—"and you can have one of those jokes whenever you take the fit." But first they would move. He visualized a place where the nearest neighbors would be three miles away on either side.

"I think you're doing fine," she said, drawing on her gloves. "You've only been out of school a year. Rome wasn't built in a day."

She was one of the few members of the Y reducing class who arrived in hat and gloves and who had a son who had been to college. "It takes time," she said, "and the world is in such a mess. This hat looked better on me than any of the others, though when she brought it out I said, 'Take that thing back. I wouldn't have it on my head,' and she said, 'Now wait till you see it on,' and when she put it on me, I said, 'We-ull,' and she said, 'If you ask me, that hat does something for you and you do something for the hat, and besides,' she said 'with that hat, you won't meet yourself coming and going.'"

Julian thought he could have stood his lot better if she had been selfish, if she had been an old hag who drank and screamed at him. He walked along, saturated in depression, as if in the midst of his martyrdom he had lost his faith. Catching sight of his long, hopeless, irritated face, she stopped suddenly with a grief-stricken look, and pulled back on his arm. "Wait on me," she said. "I'm going back to the house and take this thing off and tomorrow I'm going to return it. I was out of my head. I can pay the gas bill with that seven-fifty."

He caught her arm in a vicious grip. "You are not going to take it back," he said. "I like it."

"Well," she said, "I don't think I ought . . ."

"Shut up and enjoy it," he muttered, more depressed than ever.

"With the world in the mess it's in," she said, "it's a wonder we can enjoy anything. I tell you, the bottom rail is on the top."

Julian sighed.

"Of course," she said, "if you know who you are, you can go anywhere." She said this every time he took her to the reducing class. "Most of them in it are not our kind of people," she said, "but I can be gracious to anybody. I know who I am."

"They don't give a damn for your graciousness," Julian said savagely. "Knowing who you are is good for one generation only. You haven't the fog-giest idea where you stand now or who you are."

She stopped and allowed her eyes to flash at him. "I most certainly do know who I am," she said, "and if you don't know who you are, I'm ashamed of you."

"Oh hell," Julian said.

"Your great-grandfather was a former governor of this state," she said. "Your grandfather was a prosperous landowner. Your grandmother was a God-high."

"Will you look around you," he said tensely, "and see where you are now?" and he swept his arm jerkily out to indicate the neighborhood, which the growing darkness at least made less dingy.

"You remain what you are," she said. "Your great-grandfather had a plantation and two hundred slaves."

"There are no more slaves," he said irritably.

"They were better off when they were," she said. He groaned to see that she was off on that topic. She rolled onto it every few days like a train on an open track. He knew every stop, every junction, every swamp along the way, and knew the exact point at which her conclusion would roll majestically into the station: "It's ridiculous. It's simply not realistic. They should rise, yes, but on their own side of the fence."

"Let's skip it," Julian said.

"The ones I feel sorry for," she said, "are the ones that are half white. They're tragic."

"Will you skip it?"

"Suppose we were half white. We would certainly have mixed feelings."

"I have mixed feelings now," he groaned.

"Well let's talk about something pleasant," she said. "I remember going to Grandpa's when I was a little girl. Then the house had double stairways that went up to what was really the second floor—all the cooking was done on the first. I used to like to stay down in the kitchen on account of the way the walls smelled. I would sit with my nose pressed against the plaster and take deep breaths. Actually the place belonged to the Godhighs but your grandfather Chestny paid the mortgage and saved it for them. They were in reduced circumstances," she said, "but reduced or not, they never forgot who they were."

"Doubtless that decayed mansion reminded them," Julian muttered. He never spoke of it without contempt or thought of it without longing. He had seen it once when he was a child before it had been sold. The double stairways had rotted and been torn down. Negroes were living in it. But it remained in his mind as his mother had known it. It appeared in his dreams regularly. He would stand on the wide porch, listening to the rustle of oak leaves, then wander through the high-ceilinged hall into the parlor that opened onto it and gaze at the worn rugs and faded draperies. It occurred to him that it was he, not she, who could have appreciated it. He preferred its threadbare elegance to anything he could name and it was because of it that all the neighborhoods they had lived in had been a torment to him—whereas she had hardly known the difference. She called her insensitivity "being adjustable."

"And I remember the old darky who was my nurse, Caroline. There was no better person in the world. I've always had a great respect for my colored friends," she said. "I'd do anything in the world for them and they'd . . ."

"Will you for God's sake get off that subject?" Julian said. When he got on a bus by himself, he made it a point to sit down beside a Negro, in reparation as it were for his mother's sins.

"You're mighty touchy tonight," she said. "Do you feel all right?"

"Yes I feel all right," he said. "Now lay off."

She pursed her lips. "Well, you certainly are in a vile humor," she observed. "I just won't speak to you at all."

They had reached the bus stop. There was no bus in sight and Julian, his hands still jammed in his pockets and his head thrust forward, scowled down the empty street. The frustration of having to wait on the bus as well as ride on it began to creep up his neck like a hot hand. The presence of his mother was borne in upon him as she gave a pained sigh. He looked at her bleakly. She was holding herself very erect under the preposterous hat, wearing it like a banner of her imaginary dignity. There was in him an evil urge to break her spirit. He suddenly unloosened his tie and pulled it off and put it in his pocket.

She stiffened. "Why must you look like *that* when you take me to town?" she said. "Why must you deliberately embarrass me?"

"If you'll never learn where you are," he said, "you can at least learn where I am."

"You look like a—thug," she said.

"Then I must be one," he murmured.

"I'll just go home," she said. "I will not bother you. If you can't do a little thing like that for me . . ."

Rolling his eyes upward, he put his tie back on. "Restored to my class," he muttered. He thrust his face toward her and hissed, "True culture is in the mind, the *mind*," he said, and tapped his head, "the mind."

"It's in the heart," she said, "and in how you do things and how you do things is because of who you *are*."

"Nobody in the damn bus cares who you are."

"I care who I am," she said icily.

The lighted bus appeared on top of the next hill and as it approached, they moved out into the street to meet it. He put his hand under her elbow and hoisted her up on the creaking step. She entered with a little smile, as if she were going into a drawing room where everyone had been waiting for her. While he put in the tokens, she sat down on one of the broad front seats for three which faced the aisle. A thin woman with protruding teeth and long yellow hair was sitting on the end of it. His mother moved up beside her and left room for Julian beside herself. He sat down and looked at the floor across the aisle where a pair of thin feet in red and white canvas sandals were planted.

His mother immediately began a general conversation meant to attract anyone who felt like talking. "Can it get any hotter?" she said and removed from her purse a folding fan, black with a Japanese scene on it, which she began to flutter before her.

"I reckon it might could," the woman with the protruding teeth said, "but I know for a fact my apartment couldn't get no hotter."

"It must get the afternoon sun," his mother said. She sat forward and looked up and down the bus. It was half filled. Everybody was white. "I see we have the bus to ourselves," she said. Julian cringed.

"For a change," said the woman across the aisle, the owner of the red and white canvas sandals. "I come on one the other day and they were thick as fleas—up front and all through."

"The world is in a mess everywhere," his mother said. "I don't know how we've let it get in this fix."

"What gets my goat is all those boys from good families stealing automobile tires," the woman with the protruding teeth said. "I told my boy, I said you may not be rich but you been raised right and if I ever catch you in any such mess, they can send you on to the reformatory. Be exactly where you belong."

"Training tells," his mother said. "Is your boy in high school?"

"Ninth grade," the woman said.

"My son just finished college last year. He wants to write but he's selling typewriters until he gets started," his mother said.

The woman leaned forward and peered at Julian. He threw her such a malevolent look that she subsided against the seat. On the floor across the aisle there was an abandoned newspaper. He got up and got it and opened it out in front of him. His mother discreetly continued the conversation in a lower tone but the woman across the aisle said in a loud voice, "Well that's nice. Selling typewriters is close to writing. He can go right from one to the other."

"I tell him," his mother said, "that Rome wasn't built in a day."

Behind the newspaper Julian was withdrawing into the inner compartment of his mind where he spent most of his time. This was a kind of mental bubble in which he established himself when he could not bear to be a part of what was going on around him. From it he could see out and judge but in it he was safe from any kind of penetration from without. It was the only place where he felt free of the general idiocy of his fellows. His mother had never entered it but from it he could see her with absolute clarity.

The old lady was clever enough and he thought that if she had started from any of the right premises, more might have been expected of her. She lived according to the laws of her own fantasy world, outside of which he had never seen her set foot. The law of it was to sacrifice herself for him after she had first created the necessity to do so by making a mess of things. If he had permitted her sacrifices, it was only because her lack of foresight had made them necessary. All of her life had been a struggle to act like a Chestny without the Chestny goods, and to give him everything she thought a Chestny ought to have; but since, said she, it was fun to struggle, why complain? And when you had won, as she had won, what fun to look back on the hard times! He could not forgive her that she had enjoyed the struggle and that she thought *she* had won.

What she meant when she said she had won was that she had brought him up successfully and had sent him to college and that he had turned out so well—good looking (her teeth had gone unfilled so that his could be straightened), intelligent (he realized he was too intelligent to be a success), and with a future ahead of him (there was of course no future ahead of him). She excused his gloominess on the grounds that he was still growing up and his radical ideas on his lack of practical experience. She said he didn't yet know a thing about "life," that he hadn't even entered the real world—when already he was as disenchanted with it as a man of fifty.

The further irony of all this was that in spite of her, he had turned out so well. In spite of going to only a third-rate college, he had, on his own initiative, come out with a first-rate education; in spite of growing up dominated by a small mind, he had ended up with a large one; in spite of all her foolish views, he was free of prejudice and unafraid to face facts. Most miraculous of all, instead of being blinded by love for her as she was for him, he had cut himself emotionally free of her and could see her with complete objectivity. He was not dominated by his mother.

The bus stopped with a sudden jerk and shook him from his meditation. A woman from the back lurched forward with little steps and barely escaped falling in his newspaper as she righted herself. She got off and a large Negro got on. Julian kept his paper lowered to watch. It gave him a certain satisfaction to see injustice in daily operation. It confirmed his view that with a few exceptions there was no one worth knowing within a radius of three hundred miles. The Negro was well dressed and carried a briefcase. He looked around and then sat down on the other end of the seat where the woman with the red and white canvas sandals was sitting. He immediately unfolded a newspaper and obscured himself behind it. Julian's mother's elbow at once prodded insistently into his rib. "Now you see why I won't ride on these buses by myself," she whispered.

The woman with the red and white canvas sandals had risen at the same time the Negro sat down and had gone further back in the bus and taken the seat of the woman who had got off. His mother leaned forward and cast her an approving look.

Julian rose, crossed the aisle, and sat down in the place of the woman with the canvas sandals. From this position, he looked serenely across at his mother. Her face had turned an angry red. He stared at her, making his eyes the eyes of a stranger. He felt his tension suddenly lift as if he had openly declared war on her.

He would have liked to get in conversation with the Negro and to talk with him about art or politics or any subject that would be above the comprehension of those around them, but the man remained entrenched behind his paper. He was either ignoring the change of seating or had never noticed it. There was no way for Julian to convey his sympathy.

His mother kept her eyes fixed reproachfully on his face. The woman with the protruding teeth was looking at him avidly as if he were a type of monster new to her.

"Do you have a light?" he asked the Negro.

Without looking away from his paper, the man reached in his pocket and handed him a packet of matches.

"Thanks," Julian said. For a moment he held the matches foolishly. A NO SMOKING sign looked down upon him from over the door. This alone would not have deterred him; he had no cigarettes. He had quit smoking some months before because he could not afford it. "Sorry," he muttered and handed back the matches. The Negro lowered the paper and gave him an annoyed look. He took the matches and raised the paper again.

His mother continued to gaze at him but she did not take advantage of his momentary discomfort. Her eyes retained their battered look. Her face seemed to be unnaturally red, as if her blood pressure had risen. Julian allowed no glimmer of sympathy to show on his face. Having got the advantage, he wanted desperately to keep it and carry it through. He would have liked to teach her a lesson that would last her a while, but there seemed no way to continue the point. The Negro refused to come out from behind his paper.

Julian folded his arms and looked stolidly before him, facing her but as if he did not see her, as if he had ceased to recognize her existence. He visualized a scene in which, the bus having reached their stop, he would remain in his seat and when she said, "Aren't you going to get off?" he would look at her as at a stranger who had rashly addressed him. The corner they got off on was usually deserted, but it was well lighted and it would not hurt her to walk by herself the four blocks to the Y. He decided to wait until the time came and then decide whether or not he would let her get off by herself. He would have to be at the Y at ten to bring her back, but he could leave her wondering if he was going to show up. There was no reason for her to think she could always depend on him.

He retired again into the high-ceilinged room sparsely settled with large pieces of antique furniture. His soul expanded momentarily but then he became aware of his mother across from him and the vision shriveled. He studied her coldly. Her feet in little pumps dangled like a child's and did not quite reach the floor. She was training on him an exaggerated look of reproach. He felt completely detached from her. At that moment he could with pleasure have slapped her as he would have slapped a particularly obnoxious child in his charge.

He began to imagine various unlikely ways by which he could teach her a lesson. He might make friends with some distinguished Negro professor or lawyer and bring him home to spend the evening. He would be entirely justified but her blood pressure would rise to 300. He could not push her to the extent of making her have a stroke, and moreover, he had never been successful at making any Negro friends. He had tried to strike up an acquaintance on the bus with some of the better types, with ones that looked like professors or ministers or lawyers. One morning he had sat down next to a distinguished-looking dark brown man who had answered his questions with a sonorous solemnity but who had turned out to be an undertaker. Another day he had sat down beside a cigar-smoking Negro with a diamond ring on his finger, but after a few stilted pleasantries, the Negro had rung the buzzer and risen, slipping two lottery tickets into Julian's hand as he climbed over him to leave.

He imagined his mother lying desperately ill and his being able to secure only a Negro doctor for her. He toyed with that idea for a few minutes and then dropped it for a momentary vision of himself participating as a sympathizer in a sit-in demonstration. This was possible but he did not linger with it. Instead, he approached the ultimate horror. He brought home a beautiful suspiciously Negroid woman. Prepare yourself, he said. There is nothing you can do about it. This is the woman I've chosen. She's intelligent, dignified, even good, and she's suffered and she hasn't thought it *fun*. Now persecute us, go ahead and persecute us. Drive her out of here, but remember, you're driving me too. His eyes were narrowed and through the indignation he had generated, he saw his mother across the aisle, purple-faced, shrunken to the dwarf-like proportions of her moral nature, sitting like a mummy beneath the ridiculous banner of her hat.

He was tilted out of his fantasy again as the bus stopped. The door opened with a sucking hiss and out of the dark a large, gaily dressed, sullenlooking colored woman got on with a little boy. The child, who might have been four, had on a short plaid suit and a Tyrolean hat with a blue feather in it. Julian hoped that he would sit down beside him and that the woman would push in beside his mother. He could think of no better arrangement.

As she waited for her tokens, the woman was surveying the seating possibilities—he hoped with the idea of sitting where she was least wanted. There was something familiar-looking about her but Julian could not place what it was. She was a giant of a woman. Her face was set not only to meet opposition but to seek it out. The downward tilt of her large lower lip was like a warning sign: DON'T TAMPER WITH ME. Her bulging figure was encased in a green crepe dress and her feet overflowed in red shoes. She had on a hideous hat. A purple velvet flap came down on one side of it and stood up on the other; the rest of it was green and looked like a cushion with the stuffing out. She carried a mammoth red pocketbook that bulged throughout as if it were stuffed with rocks.

To Julian's disappointment, the little boy climbed up on the empty seat beside his mother. His mother lumped all children, black and white, into the common category, "cute," and she thought little Negroes were on the whole cuter than little white children. She smiled at the little boy as he climbed on the seat.

Meanwhile the woman was bearing down upon the empty seat beside Julian. To his annoyance, she squeezed herself into it. He saw his mother's face change as the woman settled herself next to him and he realized with satisfaction that this was more objectionable to her than it was to him. Her face seemed almost gray and there was a look of dull recognition in her eyes, as if suddenly she had sickened at some awful confrontation. Julian saw that it was because she and the woman had, in a sense, swapped sons. Though his mother would not realize the symbolic significance of this, she would feel it. His amusement showed plainly on his face.

The woman next to him muttered something unintelligible to herself. He was conscious of a kind of bristling next to him, a muted growling like that of an angry cat. He could not see anything but the red pocketbook upright on the bulging green thighs. He visualized the woman as she had stood waiting for her tokens—the ponderous figure, rising from the red shoes upward over the solid hips, the mammoth bosom, the haughty face, to the green and purple hat.

His eyes widened.

The vision of the two hats, identical, broke upon him with the radiance of a brilliant sunrise. His face was suddenly lit with joy. He could not believe that Fate had thrust upon his mother such a lesson. He gave a loud chuckle so that she would look at him and see that he saw. She turned her eyes on him slowly. The blue in them seemed to have turned a bruised purple. For a moment he had an uncomfortable sense of her innocence, but it lasted only a second before principle rescued him. Justice entitled him to laugh. His grin hardened until it said to her as plainly as if he were saying aloud: Your punishment exactly fits your pettiness. This should teach you a permanent lesson.

Her eyes shifted to the woman. She seemed unable to bear looking at him and to find the woman preferable. He became conscious again of the bristling presence at his side. The woman was rumbling like a volcano about to become active. His mother's mouth began to twitch slightly at one corner. With a sinking heart, he saw incipient signs of recovery on her face and realized that this was going to strike her suddenly as funny and was going to be no lesson at all. She kept her eyes on the woman and an amused smile came over her face as if the woman were a monkey that had stolen her hat. The little Negro was looking up at her with large fascinated eyes. He had been trying to attract her attention for some time.

"Carver!" the woman said suddenly. "Come heah!"

When he saw that the spotlight was on him at last, Carver drew his feet up and turned himself toward Julian's mother and giggled.

"Carver!" the woman said. "You heah me? Come heah!"

Carver slid down from the seat but remained squatting with his back against the base of it, his head turned slyly around toward Julian's mother, who was smiling at him. The woman reached a hand across the aisle and snatched him to her. He righted himself and hung backwards on her knees, grinning at Julian's mother. "Isn't he cute?" Julian's mother said to the woman with the protruding teeth.

"I reckon he is," the woman said without conviction.

The Negress yanked him upright but he eased out of her grip and shot across the aisle and scrambled, giggling wildly, onto the seat beside his love.

"I think he likes me," Julian's mother said, and smiled at the woman. It was the smile she used when she was being particularly gracious to an inferior. Julian saw everything lost. The lesson had rolled off her like rain on a roof.

The woman stood up and yanked the little boy off the seat as if she were snatching him from contagion. Julian could feel the rage in her at having no weapon like his mother's smile. She gave the child a sharp slap across his leg. He howled once and then thrust his head into her stomach and kicked his feet against her shins. "Be-have," she said vehemently.

The bus stopped and the Negro who had been reading the newspaper got off. The woman moved over and set the little boy down with a thump between herself and Julian. She held him firmly by the knee. In a moment he put his hands in front of his face and peeped at Julian's mother through his fingers.

"I see yoooooooo!" she said and put her hand in front of her face and peeped at him.

The woman slapped his hand down. "Quit yo' foolishness," she said, "before I knock the living Jesus out of you!"

Julian was thankful that the next stop was theirs. He reached up and pulled the cord. The woman reached up and pulled it at the same time. Oh my God, he thought. He had the terrible intuition that when they got off the bus together, his mother would open her purse and give the little boy a nickel. The gesture would be as natural to her as breathing. The bus stopped and the woman got up and lunged to the front, dragging the child, who wished to stay on, after her. Julian and his mother got up and followed. As they neared the door, Julian tried to relieve her of her pocketbook.

"No," she murmured, "I want to give the little boy a nickel."

"No!" Julian hissed. "No!"

She smiled down at the child and opened her bag. The bus door opened and the woman picked him up by the arm and descended with him, hanging at her hip. Once in the street she set him down and shook him.

Julian's mother had to close her purse while she got down the bus step but as soon as her feet were on the ground, she opened it again and began to rummage inside. "I can't find but a penny," she whispered, "but it looks like a new one."

"Don't do it!" Julian said fiercely between his teeth. There was a streetlight on the corner and she hurried to get under it so that she could better see into her pocketbook. The woman was heading off rapidly down the street with the child still hanging backward on her hand.

"Oh little boy!" Julian's mother called and took a few quick steps and caught up with them just beyond the lamppost. "Here's a bright new penny for you," and she held out the coin, which shone bronze in the dim light.

The huge woman turned and for a moment stood, her shoulders lifted and her face frozen with frustrated rage, and stared at Julian's mother. Then all at once she seemed to explode like a piece of machinery that had been given one ounce of pressure too much. Julian saw the black fist swing out with the red pocketbook. He shut his eyes and cringed as he heard the woman shout, "He don't take nobody's pennies!" When he opened his eyes, the woman was disappearing down the street with the little boy staring wide-eyed over her shoulder. Julian's mother was sitting on the sidewalk.

"I told you not to do that," Julian said angrily. "I told you not to do that!"

He stood over her for a minute, gritting his teeth. Her legs were stretched out in front of her and her hat was on her lap. He squatted down and looked her in the face. It was totally expressionless. "You got exactly what you deserved," he said. "Now get up."

He picked up her pocketbook and put what had fallen out back in it. He picked the hat up off her lap. The penny caught his eye on the sidewalk and he picked that up and let it drop before her eyes into the purse. Then he stood up and leaned over and held his hands out to pull her up. She remained immobile. He sighed. Rising above them on either side were black apartment buildings, marked with irregular rectangles of light. At the end of the block a man came out of a door and walked off in the opposite direction. "All right," he said, "suppose somebody happens by and wants to know why you're sitting on the sidewalk?"

She took the hand and, breathing hard, pulled heavily up on it and then stood for a moment, swaying slightly as if the spots of light in the darkness were circling around her. Her eyes, shadowed and confused, finally settled on his face. He did not try to conceal his irritation. "I hope this teaches you a lesson," he said. She leaned forward and her eyes raked his face. She seemed trying to determine his identity. Then, as if she found nothing familiar about him, she started off with a headlong movement in the wrong direction.

"Aren't you going on to the Y?" he asked.

"Home," she muttered.

"Well, are we walking?"

For answer she kept going. Julian followed along, his hands behind him. He saw no reason to let the lesson she had had go without backing it up with an explanation of its meaning. She might as well be made to understand what had happened to her. "Don't think that was just an uppity Negro woman," he said. "That was the whole colored race which will no longer take your condescending pennies. That was your black double. She can wear the same hat as you, and to be sure," he added gratuitously (because he thought it was funny), "it looked better on her than it did on you. What all this means," he said, "is that the old world is gone. The old manners are obsolete and your graciousness is not worth a damn." He thought bitterly of the house that had been lost for him. "You aren't who you think you are," he said.

She continued to plow ahead, paying no attention to him. Her hair had come undone on one side. She dropped her pocketbook and took no notice. He stooped and picked it up and handed it to her but she did not take it.

"You needn't act as if the world had come to an end," he said, "because it hasn't. From now on you've got to live in a new world and face a few realities for a change. Buck up," he said, "it won't kill you."

She was breathing fast.

"Let's wait on the bus," he said.

"Home," she said thickly.

"I hate to see you behave like this," he said. "Just like a child. I should be able to expect more of you." He decided to stop where he was and make her stop and wait for a bus. "I'm not going any farther," he said, stopping. "We're going on the bus."

She continued to go on as if she had not heard him. He took a few steps and caught her arm and stopped her. He looked into her face and caught his breath. He was looking into a face he had never seen before. "Tell Grandpa to come get me," she said.

He stared, stricken.

"Tell Caroline to come get me," she said.

Stunned, he let her go and she lurched forward again, walking as if one leg were shorter than the other. A tide of darkness seemed to be sweeping her from him. "Mother!" he cried. "Darling, sweetheart, wait!" Crumpling, she fell to the pavement. He dashed forward and fell at her side, crying, "Mamma, Mamma!" He turned her over. Her face was fiercely distorted. One eye, large and staring, moved slightly to the left as if it had become unmoored. The other remained fixed on him, raked his face again, found nothing and closed.

"Wait here, wait here!" he cried and jumped up and began to run for help toward a cluster of lights he saw in the distance ahead of him. "Help, help!" he shouted, but his voice was thin, scarcely a thread of sound. The lights drifted farther away the faster he ran and his feet moved numbly as if they carried him nowhere. The tide of darkness seemed to sweep him back to her, postponing from moment to moment his entry into the world of guilt and sorrow.

Suggestions for Discussion

1. Trace the steps in the rising action of the story, noting shifts between internal and external action. Study the transitions from one narrative mode to another. How are they effected? What point of view is adopted? What is gained or lost by this device?

2. Characterize the son, distinguishing between his apparent self-image and the individual as you see him.

3. What is the central conflict? What details of setting define the conflict? How is it extended into a larger social area? Comment on the way in which each scene heightens the tension and prepares for the climax.

4. How is your impression of the mother's character created? What is your reaction to the Negro woman's striking of the mother, the son's behavior, and the resulting amnesia? Do you assume that the mother will die? Has the author prepared you for acceptance of the climax, or does it seem contrived? If so, why?

5. What is the central symbol of identity and status in the story? What symbolic elements are used in the description of scene?

6. Find examples of irony and relate them to the controlling purpose of the story.

7. Relate the title to the central theme(s) of the story.

Suggestions for Writing

1. Select one of the above questions for development.

2. The relationship between experience and insight is a central theme of the story. Support this statement by specific references.

3. Compare your view of personal identity with that of your mother and/or father.

Delmore Schwartz
In Dreams Begin Responsibilities

Delmore Schwartz (1913–1966), American poet and critic, was a teacher of English at Harvard University from 1940 to 1947. He is best known for *In Dreams Begin Responsibilities* (1938), which consists of a story, poems, and verse-drama, and for a collection of poems, *Summer Knowledge: New and Selected Poems 1938–1958* (1959). He was an editor of *Partisan Review* and poetry editor of *The New Republic.* The six sections of the narrative "In Dreams Begin Responsibilities" follow a logical time sequence determined by the movie framework of the son's dream. This convention permits the narrator-son to imagine events in the premarital lives of his parents and enter into their emotional states in scenes filtered through his own perceptions and feelings.

I

I think it is the year 1909. I feel as if I were in a moving-picture theater, the long arm of light crossing the darkness and spinning, my eyes fixed upon the screen. It is a silent picture, as if an old Biograph one, in which the actors are dressed in ridiculously old-fashioned clothes, and one flash succeeds another with sudden jumps, and the actors, too, seem to jump about, walking too fast. The shots are full of rays and dots, as if it had been raining when the picture was photographed. The light is bad.

It is Sunday afternoon, June 12th, 1909, and my father is walking down the quiet streets of Brooklyn on his way to visit my mother. His clothes are newly pressed, and his tie is too tight in his high collar. He jingles the coins in his pocket, thinking of the witty things he will say. I feel as if I had by now relaxed entirely in the soft darkness of the theater; the organist peals out the obvious approximate emotions on which the audience rocks unknowingly. I am anonymous. I have forgotten myself: it is always so when one goes to a movie, it is, as they say, a drug.

My father walks from street to street of trees, lawns and houses, once in a while coming to an avenue on which a street-car skates and gnaws, progressing slowly. The motorman, who has a handle-bar mustache, helps a young lady wearing a hat like a feathered bowl onto the car. He leisurely makes change and rings his bell as the passengers mount the car. It is obviously Sunday, for everyone is wearing Sunday clothes and the street-car's noises emphasize the quiet of the holiday (Brooklyn is said to be the city of churches). The shops are closed and their shades drawn but for an occasional stationery store or drugstore with great green balls in the window.

My father has chosen to take this long walk because he likes to walk and think. He thinks about himself in the future and so arrives at the place he is to visit in a mild state of exaltation. He pays no attention to the houses he is passing, in which the Sunday dinner is being eaten, nor to the many trees which line each street, now coming to their full green and the time when they will enclose the whole street in leafy shadow. An occasional carriage passes, the horses' hooves falling like stones in the quiet afternoon, and once in a while an automobile, looking like an enormous upholstered sofa, puffs and passes.

My father thinks of my mother, of how lady-like she is, and of the pride which will be his when he introduces her to his family. They are not yet engaged and he is not yet sure that he loves my mother, so that, once in a while, he becomes panicky about the bond already established. But then he reassures himself by thinking of the big men he admires who are married: William Randolph Hearst and William Howard Taft, who has just become the President of the United States.

My father arrives at my mother's house. He has come too early and so is suddenly embarrassed. My aunt, my mother's younger sister, answers the loud bell with her napkin in her hand, for the family is still at dinner. As my father enters, my grandfather rises from the table and shakes hands with him. My mother has run upstairs to tidy herself. My grandmother asks my father if he has had his dinner and tells him that my mother will be down soon. My grandfather opens the conversation by remarking about the mild June weather. My father sits uncomfortably near the table, holding his hat in his hand. My grandmother tells my aunt to take my father's hat. My uncle, twelve years old, runs into the house, his hair tousled. He shouts a greeting to my father, who has often given him nickels, and then runs upstairs, as my grandmother shouts after him. It is evident that the respect in which my father is held in this house is tempered by a good deal of mirth. He is impressive, but also very awkward.

II

Finally my mother comes downstairs and my father, being at the moment engaged in conversation with my grandfather, is made uneasy by her entrance, for he does not know whether to greet my mother or to continue the conversation. He gets up from his chair clumsily and says "Hello" gruffly. My grandfather watches this, examining their congruence, such as it is, with a critical eye, and meanwhile rubbing his bearded cheek roughly, as he always does when he reasons. He is worried; he is afraid that my father will not make a good husband for his oldest daughter. At this point something happens to the film, just as my father says something funny to my mother: I am awakened to myself and my unhappiness just as my interest has become most intense. The audience begins to clap impatiently. Then the trouble is attended to, but the film has been returned to a portion just shown, and once more I see my grandfather rubbing his bearded cheek, pondering my father's character. It is difficult to get back into the picture once more and forget myself, but as my mother giggles at my father's words, the darkness drowns me.

My father and mother depart from the house, my father shaking hands with my grandfather once more, out of some unknown uneasiness. I stir uneasily also, slouched in the hard chair of the theater. Where is the older uncle, my mother's older brother? He is studying in his bedroom upstairs, studying for his final examinations at the College of the City of New York, having been dead of double pneumonia for the last twenty-one years. My mother and father walk down the same quiet streets once more. My mother is holding my father's arm and telling him of the novel she has been reading and my father utters judgments of the characters as the plot is made clear to him. This is a habit which he very much enjoys, for he feels the utmost superiority and confidence when he is approving or condemning the behavior of other people. At times he feels moved to utter a brief "Ugh" whenever the story becomes what he would call sugary. This tribute is the assertion of his manliness. My mother feels satisfied by the interest she has awakened; and she is showing my father how intelligent she is and how interesting.

They reach the avenue, and the street-car leisurely arrives. They are going to Coney Island this afternoon, although my mother really considers such pleasures inferior. She has made up her mind to indulge only in a walk on the boardwalk and a pleasant dinner, avoiding the riotous amusements as being beneath the dignity of so dignified a couple.

My father tells my mother how much money he has made in the week just past, exaggerating an amount which need not have been exaggerated. But my father has always felt that actualities somehow fall short, no matter how fine they are. Suddenly I begin to weep. The determined old lady who sits next to me in the theater is annoyed and looks at me with an angry face, and being intimidated, I stop. I drag out my handkerchief and dry my face, licking the drop which has fallen near my lips. Meanwhile I have missed something, for here are my father and mother alighting from the street-car at the last stop, Coney Island.

III

They walk toward the boardwalk and my mother commands my father to inhale the pungent air from the sea. They both breathe in deeply, both of them laughing as they do so. They have in common a great interest in health, although my father is strong and husky, and my mother is frail. They are both full of theories about what is good to eat and not good to eat, and sometimes have heated discussions about it, the whole matter ending in my father's announcement, made with a scornful bluster, that you have to die sooner or later anyway. On the boardwalk's flagpole, the American flag is pulsing in an intermittent wind from the sea.

My father and mother go to the rail of the boardwalk and look down on the beach where a good many bathers are casually walking about. A few are in the surf. A peanut whistle pierces the air with its pleasant and active whine, and my father goes to buy peanuts. My mother remains at the rail and stares at the ocean. The ocean seems merry to her; it pointedly sparkles and again and again the pony waves are released. She notices the children digging in the wet sand, and the bathing costumes of the girls who are her own age. My father returns with the peanuts. Overhead the sun's lightning strikes and strikes, but neither of them are at all aware of it. The boardwalk is full of people dressed in their Sunday clothes and casually strolling. The tide does not reach as far as the boardwalk, and the strollers would feel no danger if it did. My father and mother lean on the rail of the boardwalk and absently stare at the ocean. The ocean is becoming rough; the waves come in slowly, tugging strength from far back. The moment before they somersault, the moment when they arch their backs so beautifully, showing white veins in the green and black, that moment is intolerable. They finally crack, dashing fiercely upon the sand, actually driving, full force downward, against it, bouncing upward and forward, and at last petering out into a small stream of bubbles which slides up the beach and then is recalled. The sun overhead does not disturb my father and my mother. They gaze idly at the ocean, scarcely interested in its harshness. But I stare at the terrible sun which breaks up sight, and the fatal merciless passionate ocean. I forget my parents. I stare fascinated, and finally, shocked by their indifference, I burst out weeping once more. The old lady next to me pats my shoulder and says: "There, there, young man, all of this is only a movie, only a movie," but I look up once more at the terrifying sun and the terrifying ocean, and being unable to control my tears I get up and go to the men's room, stumbling over the feet of the other people seated in my row.

IV

When I return, feeling as if I had just awakened in the morning sick for lack of sleep, several hours have apparently passed and my parents are riding on the merry-go-round. My father is on a black horse, my mother on a white one, and they seem to be making an eternal circuit for the single purpose of snatching the nickel rings which are attached to an arm of one of the posts. A hand organ is playing: it is inseparable from the ceaseless circling of the merry-go-round.

For a moment it seems that they will never stop, and I feel as if I were looking down from the fiftieth story of a building. But at length they do get off; even the hand organ has ceased for a moment. There is a sudden and sweet stillness, as if the achievement of so much motion. My mother has acquired only two rings, my father, however, ten of them, although it was my mother who really wanted them.

They walk on along the boardwalk as the afternoon descends by imperceptible degrees into the incredible violet of dusk. Everything fades into a relaxed glow, even the ceaseless murmuring from the beach. They look for a place to have dinner. My father suggests the best restaurant on the boardwalk and my mother demurs, according to her principles of economy and housewifeliness.

However they do go to the best place, asking for a table near the window so that they can look out upon the boardwalk and the mobile ocean. My father feels omnipotent as he places a quarter in the waiter's hand in asking for a table. The place is crowded and here too there is music, this time from a kind of string trio. My father orders with a fine confidence.

As their dinner goes on, my father tells of his plans for the future and my mother shows with expressive face how interested she is, and how impressed. My father becomes exultant, lifted up by the waltz that is being played and his own future begins to intoxicate him. My father tells my mother that he is going to expand his business, for there is a great deal of money to be made. He wants to settle down. After all, he is twenty-nine, he has lived by himself since his thirteenth year, he is making more and more money, and he is envious of his friends when he visits them in the security of their homes, surrounded, it seems, by the calm domestic pleasures, and by delightful children, and then as the waltz reaches the moment when the dancers all swing madly, then, then with awful daring, then he asks my mother to marry him, although awkwardly enough and puzzled as to how he had arrived at the question, and she, to make the whole business worse, begins to cry, and my father looks nervously about, not knowing at all what to do now, and my mother says: "It's all I've wanted from the first moment I saw you," sobbing, and he finds all of this very difficult, scarcely to his taste, scarcely as he thought it would be, on his long walks over Brooklyn Bridge in the revery of a fine cigar, and it was then, at that point, that I stood up in the theater and shouted: "Don't do it! It's not too late to change your minds, both of you. Nothing good will come of it, only remorse, hatred, scandal, and two children whose characters are monstrous." The whole audience turned to look at me, annoyed, the usher came hurrying down the aisle flashing his searchlight, and the old lady next to me tugged me down into my seat, saying: "Be quiet. You'll be put out, and you paid thirty-five cents to come in." And so I shut my eyes because I could not bear to see what was happening. I sat there quietly.

V

But after a while I begin to take brief glimpses and at length I watch again with thirsty interest, like a child who tries to maintain his sulk when he is offered the bribe of candy. My parents are now having their picture taken in a photographer's booth along the boardwalk. The place is shadowed in the mauve light which is apparently necessary. The camera is set to the side on its tripod and looks like a Martian man. The photographer is instructing my parents in how to pose. My father has his arm over my mother's shoulder, and both of them smile emphatically. The photographer brings my mother a bouquet of flowers to hold in her hand, but she holds it at the wrong angle. Then the photographer covers himself with the black cloth which drapes the camera and all that one sees of him is one protruding arm and his hand with which he holds tightly to the rubber ball which he squeezes when the picture is taken. But he is not satisfied with their appearance. He feels that somehow there is something wrong in their pose. Again and again he comes out from his hiding place with new directions. Each suggestion merely makes matters worse. My father is becoming impatient. They try a seated pose. The photographer explains that he has his pride, he wants to make beautiful pictures, he is not merely interested in all of this for the money. My father says: "Hurry up, will you? We haven't got all night." But the photographer only scurries about apologetically, issuing new directions. The photographer charms me, and I approve of him with all my heart, for I know exactly how he feels, and as he criticizes each revised pose according to some obscure idea of rightness, I become quite hopeful. But then my father says angrily: "Come on, you've had enough time, we're not going to wait any longer." And the photographer, sighing unhappily, goes back into the black covering, and holds out his hand, saying: "One, two, three, Now!", and the picture is taken, with my father's smile turned to a grimace and my mother's bright and false. It takes a few minutes for the picture to be developed and as my parents sit in the curious light they become depressed.

VI

They have passed a fortune-teller's booth and my mother wishes to go in, but my father does not. They begin to argue about it. My mother becomes stubborn, my father once more impatient. What my father would like to do now is walk off and leave my mother there, but he knows that that would never do. My mother refuses to budge. She is near tears, but she feels an uncontrollable desire to hear what the palm-reader will say. My father consents angrily and they both go into the booth which is, in a way, like the photographer's, since it is draped in black cloth and its light is colored and shadowed. The place is too warm, and my father keeps saying that this is all nonsense, pointing to the crystal ball on the table. The fortune-teller, a short, fat woman garbed in robes supposedly exotic, comes into the room and greets them, speaking with an accent, but suddenly my father feels that the whole thing is intolerable; he tugs at my mother's arm but my mother refuses to budge. And then, in terrible anger, my father lets go of my mother's arm and strides out, leaving my mother stunned. She makes a movement as if to go after him, but the fortune-teller holds her and begs her not to do so, and I in my seat in the darkness am shocked and horrified. I feel as if I were walking a tight-rope one hundred feet over a circus audience and suddenly the rope is showing signs of breaking, and I get up from my seat and begin to shout once more the first words I can think of to communicate my terrible fear, and once more the usher comes hurrying down the aisle flashing his searchlight, and the old lady pleads with me, and the shocked audience has turned to stare at me, and I keep shouting: "What are they doing? Don't they know what they are doing? Why doesn't my mother go after my father and beg him not to be angry? If she does not do that, what will she do? Doesn't my father know what he is doing?" But the usher has seized my arm, and is dragging me away, and as he does so, he says: "What are *you* doing? Don't you know you can't do things like this, you can't do whatever you want to do, even if other people aren't about? You will be sorry if you do not do what you should do. You can't carry on like this, it is not right, you will find that out soon enough, everything you do matters too much," and as he said that, dragging me through the lobby of the theater, into the cold light, I woke up into the bleak winter morning of my twenty-first birthday, the window-sill shining with its lip of snow, and the morning already begun.

Suggestions for Discussion

1. Trace the development of the narrative in the six sections that follow the time sequence of the movie framework of the son's dream. How does the use of the son as narrator provide a double vision?

2. Relate the title to the action and theme of the story.

3. Describe the son's emotional state. How does it relate to the events of each episode?

4. Analyze the relationship of the parents to each other and that of the son to the parents.

5. Is there a resolution to the conflict? What do you assume will be the son's future?

6. Relate the following images to the theme of the story: the movie audience, the

usher, the old lady, the Coney Island scene, the turbulent ocean, the photographer, the fortune teller.

Suggestion for Writing

Draw a portrait of your parents by means of an imaginary dialogue or a narrative.

Poetry

E. E. Cummings

My Father Moved Through Dooms of Love

Edward Estlin Cummings (1894–1963) was an American whose novel *The Enormous Room* (1922) and whose books of poetry *&* and *XLI Poems* (1925) established his reputation as an avant-garde writer interested in experimenting with stylistic techniques. Awarded several important prizes for poetry, he was also Charles Eliot Norton Lecturer at Harvard University in 1952 and published *i: six nonlectures* (1953). The theme of wholeness and reconciliation of opposites in the father's character is implictly expressed in this poem in which images of death, hate, and decay are counterpointed against images that celebrate life and growth.

my father moved through dooms of love
through sames of am through haves of give,
singing each morning out of each night
my father moved through depths of height

this motionless forgetful where
turned at his glance to shining here;
that if (so timid air is firm)
under his eyes would stir and squirm

newly as from unburied which
floats the first who, his april touch
drove sleeping selves to swarm their fates
woke dreamers to their ghostly roots

and should some why completely weep
my father's fingers brought her sleep:
vainly no smallest voice might cry
for he could feel the mountains grow.

Lifting the valleys of the sea
my father moved through griefs of joy;
praising a forehead called the moon
singing desire into begin

joy was his song and joy so pure
a heart of star by him could steer
and pure so now and now so yes
the wrists of twilight would rejoice

keen as midsummer's keen beyond
conceiving mind of sun will stand,
so strictly (over utmost him
so hugely) stood my father's dream

his flesh was flesh his blood was blood:
no hungry man but wished him food;
no cripple wouldn't creep one mile
uphill to only see him smile.

Scorning the pomp of must and shall
my father moved through dooms of feel;
his anger was as right as rain
his pity was as green as grain

septembering arms of year extend
less humbly wealth to foe and friend
than he to foolish and to wise
offered immeasurable is

proudly and (by octobering flame
beckoned) as earth will downward climb,
so naked for immortal work
his shoulders marched against the dark

his sorrow was as true as bread:
no liar looked him in the head;
if every friend became his foe
he'd laugh and build a world with snow.

My father moved through theys of we,
singing each new leaf out of each tree
(and every child was sure that spring
danced when she heard my father sing)

then let men kill which cannot share,
let blood and flesh be mud and mire,
scheming imagine, passion willed,
freedom a drug that's bought and sold

giving to steal and cruel kind,
a heart to fear, to doubt a mind,
to differ a disease of same,
conform the pinnacle of am

though dull were all we taste as bright,
bitter all utterly things sweet,
maggoty minus and dumb death
all we inherit, all bequeath

and nothing quite so least as truth
—i say though hate were why men breathe—
because my father lived his soul
love is the whole and more than all

Suggestions for Discussion

1. Study the verbal juxtapositions that seem antithetical: "dooms of love"; "depths of height"; "griefs of joy." How is the theme of wholeness and reconciliation of opposites in the character of the father implicitly expressed?

2. Cite passages in which the natural imagery of life, love, birth, and rebirth is counterpointed against images of death, hate, and decay.

3. Compare the images of celebration of life and growth with the imagery in Whitman's "Out of the Cradle Endlessly Rocking." Contrast this father with Kafka's in "Letter to His Father."

Sylvia Plath

Daddy

Sylvia Plath (1932–1963) began her career while still a college student by serving as guest editor of *Mademoiselle*. She studied in both the United States and England, taught at Smith College, and then settled in England, where she lived until her suicide. Her poetry is collected in *The Colossus* (1960), *Ariel* (1965), *Crossing the Water* (1971), and *Winter Trees* (1972), and she contributed to such magazines as *Seventeen*, *Atlantic*, and *The Nation*. *The Bell Jar*, her only novel, was written about her late-adolescent attempt at suicide and was published posthumously in 1963 under the pseudonym Victoria Lucas. In "Daddy," the poet as child recalls the past and reinvokes her brutal image of her father.

You do not do, you do not do
Any more, black shoe
In which I have lived like a foot
For thirty years, poor and white,
Barely daring to breath or Achoo.

Daddy, I have had to kill you.
You died before I had time—
Marble-heavy, a bag full of God,
Ghastly statue with one grey toe
Big as a Frisco seal

And a head in the freakish Atlantic
Where it pours bean green over blue
In the waters off beautiful Nauset.
I used to pray to recover you.
Ach, du.

In the German tongue, in the Polish town
Scraped flat by the roller
Of wars, wars, wars.
But the name of the town is common.
My Polack friend

Says there are a dozen or two.
So I never could tell where you
Put your foot, your root,
I never could talk to you.
The tongue stuck in my jaw.

It stuck in a barb wire snare.
Ich, ich, ich, ich
I could hardly speak.
I thought every German was you.
And the language obscene

An engine, an engine
Chuffing me off like a Jew.
A Jew to Dachau, Auschwitz, Belsen.
I began to talk like a Jew.
I think I may well be a Jew.

The snows of the Tyrol, the clear beer of Vienna
Are not very pure or true.
With my gypsy ancestress and my weird luck
And my Taroc pack and my Taroc pack
I may be a bit of a Jew.

I have always been scared of *you*,
With your Luftwaffe, your gobbledygoo.
And your neat moustache
And your Aryan eye, bright blue.
Panzer-man, panzer-man, O You—

Not God but a swastika
So black no sky could squeak through.
Every woman adores a Fascist,
The boot in the face, the brute
Brute heart of a brute like you.

You stand at the blackboard, daddy,
In the picture I have of you,
A cleft in your chin instead of your foot
But no less a devil for that, no not
Any less the black man who

Bit my pretty red heart in two.
I was ten when they buried you.
At twenty I tried to die
And get back, back, back to you.
I thought even the bones would do.

But they pulled me out of the sack,
And they stuck me together with glue.
And then I knew what to do.
I made a model of you,
A man in black with a Meinkampf look

And a love of the rack and the screw.
And I said I do, I do.
So daddy, I'm finally through.
The black telephone's off at the root,
The voice just can't worm through.

If I've killed one man, I've killed two—
The vampire who said he was you
And drank my blood for a year,
Seven years, if you want to know.
Daddy, you can lie back now.

There's a stake in your fat black heart
And the villagers never liked you.
They are dancing and stamping on you.
They always *knew* it was you.
Daddy, daddy, you bastard, I'm through.

Suggestions for Discussion

1. Discuss the theme and mood of the poem. Comment on the relative maturity or insight the narrator has achieved through the distance of time.

2. What may Sylvia Plath's father have had in common with Kafka's father?

3. To what extent does your reading of A. Alvarez's "Sylvia Plath: A Memoir" illuminate your reading of the poem?

Theodore Roethke
My Papa's Waltz

Theodore Roethke (1908–1963), American poet, taught during the last years of his life at the University of Washington. *The Waking: Poems, 1933–1953* was the winner of the Pulitzer Prize for Poetry in 1953. He received the Bollingen Award for Poetry in 1958. A collected volume, *Words for the Wind,* appeared in 1958, and *The Far Field* was published posthumously in 1964. The poet remembers his antic father and his own difficult childhood.

The whiskey on your breath
Could make a small boy dizzy;
But I hung on like death:
Such waltzing was not easy.

We romped until the pans
Slid from the kitchen shelf;
My mother's countenance
Could not unfrown itself.

The hand that held my wrist
Was battered on one knuckle;
At every step I missed
My right ear scraped a buckle.

You beat time on my head
With a palm caked hard by dirt,
Then waltzed me off to bed
Still clinging to your shirt.

Suggestion for Discussion

Compare the relationship of father and son in this poem with that in Anderson's "Discovery of a Father." Contrast the two mothers.

William Butler Yeats
A Prayer for My Daughter

William Butler Yeats (1865–1939), the leading poet of the Irish literary revival and a playwright, was born near Dublin and educated in London and Dublin. He wrote plays for the Irish National Theatre Society (later called the Abbey Theatre). For a number of years he served as a senator of the Irish Free State. His volumes of poetry range from *The Wanderings of Oisin* (1889) to *The Last Poems* (1939). *The Collected Poems of W. B. Yeats* appeared in 1933, 1950, and 1956; *The Collected Plays of W. B. Yeats* were published in 1934 and 1952. From his view of a chaotic, threatening world, the poet prays for the harmony and order he considers requisite to the growth of his daughter.

Once more the storm is howling, and half hid
Under this cradle-hood and coverlid
My child sleeps on. There is no obstacle
But Gregory's wood and one bare hill
Whereby the haystack- and roof-levelling wind,
Bred on the Atlantic, can be stayed;
And for an hour I have walked and prayed
Because of the great gloom that is in my mind.

I have walked and prayed for this young child an hour
And heard the sea-wind scream upon the tower,
And under the arches of the bridge, and scream
In the elms above the flooded stream;
Imagining in excited reverie
That the future years had come,
Dancing to a frenzied drum,
Out of the murderous innocence of the sea.

May she be granted beauty and yet not
Beauty to make a stranger's eye distraught,
Or hers before a looking-glass, for such,
Being made beautiful overmuch,
Consider beauty a sufficient end,
Lose natural kindness and maybe
The heart-revealing intimacy
That chooses right, and never find a friend.

Helen, being chosen, found life flat and dull
And later had much trouble from a fool,
While that great Queen, that rose out of the spray,
Being fatherless, could have her way
Yet chose a bandy-leggèd smith for man.
It's certain that fine women eat
A crazy salad with their meat
Whereby the Horn of Plenty is undone.

In courtesy I'd have her chiefly learned;
Hearts are not had as a gift but hearts are earned
By those that are not entirely beautiful;
Yet many, that have played the fool
For beauty's very self, has charm made wise,
And many a poor man that has roved,
Loved and thought himself beloved,
From a glad kindness cannot take his eyes.

May she become a flourishing hidden tree
That all her thoughts may like the linnet be,
And have no business but dispensing round
Their magnanimities of sound.
Nor but in merriment began a chase,
Nor but in merriment a quarrel.
O may she live like some green laurel
Rooted in one dear perpetual place.

My mind, because the minds that I have loved,
The sort of beauty that I have approved,
Prosper but little, has dried up of late,
Yet knows that to be choked with hate
May well be of all evil chances chief.
If there's no hatred in a mind
Assault and battery of the wind
Can never tear the linnet from the leaf.

An intellectual hatred is the worst,
So let her think opinions are accursed.
Have I not seen the loveliest woman born
Out of the mouth of Plenty's horn,
Because of her opinionated mind
Barter that horn and every good
By quiet natures understood
For an old bellows full of angry wind?

Considering that, all hatred driven hence,
The soul recovers radical innocence
And learns at last that it is self-delighting,
Self-appeasing, self-affrighting,
And that its own sweet will is Heaven's will;
She can, though every face should scowl
And every windy quarter howl
Or every bellows burst, be happy still.

And may her bridegroom bring her to a house
Where all's accustomed, ceremonious;
For arrogance and hatred are the wares
Peddled in the thoroughfares.
How but in custom and in ceremony
Are innocence and beauty born?
Ceremony's a name for the rich horn,
And custom for the spreading laurel tree.

Suggestions for Discussion

1. Is he imposing on her a conservative ideal of womanhood?

2. What words or images suggest that he might quarrel with the ideas of feminists today?

3. Discuss: "How but in custom and in ceremony/Are innocence and beauty born?"

4. What seems to be the poet's concept of happiness for a woman?

Gwendolyn Brooks

Life for My Child Is Simple, and Is Good

Gwendolyn Brooks (b.1917) is an American poet who grew up in Chicago's slums. Her works, which focus on contemporary Black life in the United States, include *A Street in Bronzeville* (1949); *Annie Allen* (1949), which won a Pulitzer Prize; and *The Bean Eaters* (1960). She also has written a novel and a book for children. In this brief poem the writer sets forth her hopes for her son's joy and growth.

Life for my child is simple, and is good.
He knows his wish. Yes, but that is not all.
Because I know mine too.
And we both want joy of undeep and unabiding things,
Like kicking over a chair or throwing blocks out of a window
Or tipping over an icebox pan
Or snatching down curtains or fingering an electric outlet
Or a journey or a friend or an illegal kiss.
No. There is more to it than that.
It is that he has never been afraid.
Rather, he reaches out and lo the chair falls with a beautiful crash,
And the blocks fall, down on the people's heads,
And the water comes slooshing sloopily out across the floor.
And so forth.
Not that success, for him, is sure, infallible.
But never has he been afraid to reach.
His lesions are legion.
But reaching is his rule.

Suggestions for Discussion

1. Compare Brooks's hopes for her child with those of Yeats for his daughter.

2. What do the joys of "unabiding things" have in common?

3. What oppositions are posed in the poem, and how are they resolved?

Randall Jarrell

The Player Piano

Born in Nashville, Tennessee, and educated at Vanderbilt University, Randall Jarrell (1914–1965) taught for most of his life. A poet and critic, he won two Guggenheim Fellowships and served as Poetry Consultant at the Library of Congress. He was a careful craftsman who drew often on his imagination rather than his personal experience as the source for his poems.

I ate pancakes one night in a Pancake House
Run by a lady my age. She was gay.
When I told her that I came from Pasadena
She laughed and said, "I lived in Pasadena
When Fatty Arbuckle drove the El Mólino bus."

I felt that I had met someone from home.
No, not Pasadena, Fatty Arbuckle.
Who's that? Oh, something that we had in common
Like—like—the false armistice. Piano rolls.
She told me her house was the first Pancake House

East of the Mississippi, and I showed her
A picture of my grandson. Going home—
Home to the hotel—I began to hum,
"Smile a while, I bid you sad adieu,
When the clouds roll back I'll come to you."

Let's brush our hair before we go to bed,
I say to the old friend who lives in my mirror.
I remember how I'd brush my mother's hair
Before she bobbed it. How long has it been
Since I hit my funnybone? had a scab on my knee?

Here are Mother and Father in a photograph,
Father's holding me. . . . They both look so *young*.

I'm so much older than they are. Look at them,
Two babies with their baby. I don't blame you,
You weren't old enough to know any better;

If I could I'd go back, sit down by you both,
And sign our true armistice: you weren't to blame.
I shut my eyes and there's our living room.
The piano's playing something by Chopin,
And Mother and Father and their little girl

Listen. Look, the keys go down by themselves!
I go over, hold my hands out, play I play—
If only, somehow, I had learned to live!
The three of us sit watching, as my waltz
Plays itself out a half-inch from my fingers.

Suggestions for Discussion

1. What is the significance of the title of the poem?

2. Characterize the speaker in the poem.

3. Describe the occurrence which leads the speaker to reminisce about her childhood.

4. What regrets does the speaker express?

Suggestions for Writing

Describe a scene from your childhood that evokes poignant memories.

James Wright

Mutterings over the Crib of a Deaf Child

James Wright (1927–1980) was educated at Kenyon College and the University of Washington. He taught at Hunter College, served as a Fulbright fellow, and won the Yale Series of Younger Poets award (1957). In 1972 he won the Pulitzer Prize for *Collected Poems*. Other books are *Two Citizens* (1973), *Moments of the Italian Summer* (1976), and *To a Blossoming Pear Tree* (1978). The poet laments the fact that his deaf child will be denied both commonplace pleasures and special delights of natural sounds.

"How will he hear the bell at school
Arrange the broken afternoon,
And know to run across the cool
Grasses where the starlings cry,
Or understand the day is gone?"

Well, someone lifting curious brows
Will take the measure of the clock.
And he will see the birchen boughs
Outside sagging dark from the sky,
And the shade crawling upon the rock.

"And how will he know to rise at morning?
His mother has other sons to waken,
She has the stove she must build to burning
Before the coals of the nighttime die;
And he never stirs when he is shaken."

I take it the air affects the skin,
And you remember, when you were young,
Sometimes you could feel the dawn begin,
And the fire would call you, by and by,
Out of the bed and bring you along.

"Well, good enough. To serve his needs
All kinds of arrangements can be made.
But what will you do if his finger bleeds?
Or a bobwhite whistles invisibly
And flutes like an angel off in the shade?"

He will learn pain. And, as for the bird,
It is always darkening when that comes out.
I will putter as though I had not heard,
And lift him into my arms and sing
Whether he hears my song or not.

Suggestions for Discussion

1. Who is the speaker? What are his feelings about the child?

2. What compensations does the deaf child have? How are they conveyed?

3. Justify the use of the word *mutterings* in the title.

Nancy Willard

Questions My Son Asked Me, Answers I Never Gave Him

Nancy Willard (b. 1936) received her Ph.D. from the University of Michigan. She has won the Hopwood Award, a Woodrow Wilson Fellowship, and an O. Henry Award for the best short story in 1970. Her publications include *In His Country: Poems* (1966), *Skin of Grace* (1967), and *The Carpenter of the Sun: Poems* (1974). In this poem Willard responds to her child's questions concerning the nature of his universe with tenderness and whimsy.

1. Do gorillas have birthdays?
   Yes. Like the rainbow they happen,
   like the air they are not observed.

2. Do butterflies make a noise?
   The wire in the butterfly's tongue
   hums gold.
   Some men hear butterflies
   even in winter.

3. Are they part of our family?
   They forgot us, who forgot how to fly.

4. Who tied my navel? Did God tie it?
   God made the thread: O man, live forever!
   Man made the knot: enough is enough.

5. If I drop my tooth in the telephone
   will it go through the wires and bite someone's ear?
   I have seen earlobes pierced by a tooth of steel.
   It loves what lasts.
   It does not love flesh.
   It leaves a ring of gold in the wound.

6. If I stand on my head
   will the sleep in my eye roll up into my head?
   Does the dream know its own father?
   Can bread go back to the field of its birth?

7. Can I eat a star?
   Yes, with the mouth of time
   that enjoys everything.

8. Could we xerox the moon?
   This is the first commandment:
   I am the moon, thy moon.
   Thou shalt have no other moons before thee.

9. Who invented water?
   The hands of the air, that wanted to wash each other.

10. What happens at the end of numbers?
    I see three men running toward a field.
    At the edge of the tall grass, they turn into light.

11. Do the years ever run out?
    God said, I will break time's heart.
    Time ran down like an old phonograph.
    It lay flat as a carpet.
    At rest on its threads I am learning to fly.

Suggestions for Discussion

1. Since each question is answered, why does the author suggest in her title that she did not answer it?

2. What do the son's questions tell you about him? Note the range of his questions.

3. What do the writer's answers tell you about her? How would you characterize the answers?

4. How does figurative language affect the tone? Describe the tone of the answers. In No. 3 Willard says we "forget how to fly." What does she mean? The figure of flying is repeated in the last stanza. What is its significance? How does it relate to the question?

5. On the basis of the questions and answers, how would you describe the relationship of mother and son?

Suggestion for Writing

Write your own answer(s) to a hypothetical question you are either asking yourself or someone is asking you.

Personal Relationships: Men and Women

◆◆◆◆

How can the trade-offs within marriage be measured? He makes more than she does, but he feels less strain now because he's no longer carrying it all. She feels bitter if he is laid off and she has to carry the whole breadwinning burden, as well as take care of the house and kids. He certainly doesn't spend as much time on housework and the kids as she does. But how much of that power does she really want to give up?

Now that we've broken through those rigidly polarized male and female sex roles, will we settle for a diversity of patterns of sharing among women and men?

—**Betty Friedan,** "Why Feminism Must Keep Moving"

Feminism in its third stage would seem to be pushing toward a full demystification of both the feminine and the feminist mystiques in favor of a realistic appreciation of sexual differences, the constraints they place upon us, and the plural virtues they make possible. . . .

The special relationship that femininity affords women to generativity, nurturing, and affection endows them with a unique appreciation of (and responsibility for) the ethics of caring and of affiliation indispensable to the preservation of civilization.

—**Benjamin R. Barber,** "Beyond the Feminist Mystique"

Love and work—these, said Sigmund Freud long ago, are the major arenas of adult life that require resolution if we are to live it satisfactorily. It's still true. Only the problems are different today . . . precisely because we no longer see these two parts of life as so distinctly separated, because work is no longer only the province of men, love only the domain of women.

—**Lillian Rubin,** "Love, Work, and Identity"

Her mind only vaguely grasped what he was saying. Her physical being was for the moment predominant. She was not thinking of his words, only drinking in the tones of his voice. She wanted to reach out her hand in the darkness and touch him with the sensitive tips of her fingers upon the face or the lips. She wanted to draw close to him and whisper against his cheek—she did not care what—as she might have done if she had not been a respectable woman.

—**Kate Chopin,** "A Respectable Woman"

"If you weren't such a drab, ordinary little man," she said, "I'd think you'd planned it all. Sticking your tongue out, saying you were sitting in the catbird seat, because you thought no one would believe me when I told it! My God, it's really too perfect!" She brayed loudly and hysterically, and the fury was on her again. She glared at Mr. Fitweiler. "Can't you see how he has tricked us, you old fool? Can't you see his little game?"

—**James Thurber,** "The Catbird Seat"

Essays

Mary Wollstonecraft
The Rights of Women

Mary Wollstonecraft (1759–1797), whose husband was the radical William Godwin and whose daughter became Mrs. Percy Bysshe Shelley, was a schoolteacher, governess, and a member of a publishing firm. Her *Vindication of the
Rights of Woman* (1792) was an extraordinary defense of the rights of eighteenth-century women. This eighteenth-century diatribe against those who
would keep women enslaved was written with the wish to persuade women to
acquire strength of mind and body.

My own sex, I hope, will excuse me, if I treat them like rational creatures,
instead of flattering their *fascinating* graces, and viewing them as if they were
in a state of perpetual childhood, unable to stand alone. I earnestly wish to
point out in what true dignity and human happiness consists—I wish to persuade women to endeavor to acquire strength, both of mind and body, and to
convince them that the soft phrases, susceptibility of heart, delicacy of sentiment, and refinement of taste, are almost synonymous with epithets of weakness, and that those beings who are only the objects of pity and that kind of
love, which has been termed its sister, will soon become objects of contempt.

Dismissing, then, those pretty feminine phrases, which the men conde-
scendingly use to soften our slavish dependence, and despising that weak
elegancy of mind, exquisite sensibility, and sweet docility of manners, supposed to be the sexual characteristics of the weaker vessel, I wish to show
that elegance is inferior to virtue, that the first object of laudable ambition is
to obtain a character as a human being, regardless of the distinction of sex;
and that secondary views should be brought to this simple touchstone.

This is a rough sketch of my plan; and should I express my conviction with
the energetic emotions that I feel whenever I think of the subject, the dictates
of experience and reflection will be felt by some of my readers. Animated by
this important object, I shall disdain to cull my phrases or polish my style; I

199

aim at being useful, and sincerity will render me unaffected; for, wishing rather to persuade by the force of my arguments, than dazzle by the elegance of my language, I shall not waste my time in rounding periods, or in fabricating the turgid bombast of artificial feelings, which, coming from the head, never reach the heart. I shall be employed about things, not words! and, anxious to render my sex more respectable members of society, I shall try to avoid that flowery diction which has slided from essays into novels, and from novels into familiar letters and conversation.

These pretty superlatives, dropping glibly from the tongue, vitiate the taste, and create a kind of sickly delicacy that runs away from simple unadorned truth; and a deluge of false sentiments and overstretched feelings, stifling the natural emotions of the heart, render the domestic pleasures insipid, that ought to sweeten the exercise of those severe duties, which educate a rational and immortal being for a nobler field of action.

The education of women has, of late, been more attended to than formerly; yet they are still reckoned a frivolous sex, and ridiculed or pitied by the writers who endeavor by satire or instruction to improve them. It is acknowledged that they spend many of the first years of their lives in acquiring a smattering of accomplishments; meanwhile strength of body and mind are sacrificed to libertine notions of beauty, to the desire of establishing themselves—the only way women can rise in the world—by marriage. And this desire making mere animals of them, when they marry they act as such children may be expected to act—they dress; they paint, and nickname God's creatures. Surely these weak beings are only fit for a seraglio!—Can they be expected to govern a family with judgment, or take care of the poor babes whom they bring into the world?

If then it can be fairly deduced from the present conduct of the sex, from the prevalent fondness for pleasure which takes place of ambition, and those nobler passions that open and enlarge the soul; that the instruction which women have hitherto received has only tended, with the constitution of civil society, to render them insignificant objects of desire—mere propagators of fools!—if it can be proved that in aiming to accomplish them, without cultivating their understandings, they are taken out of their sphere of duties, and made ridiculous and useless when the short-lived bloom of beauty is over,[1] I presume that *rational* men will excuse me for endeavoring to persuade them to become more masculine and respectable.

Indeed the word masculine is only a bugbear: there is little reason to fear that women will acquire too much courage or fortitude; for their apparent inferiority with respect to bodily strength, must render them, in some degree, dependent on men in the various relations of life; but why should it be increased by prejudices that give a sex to virtue, and confound simple truths with sensual reveries?

Women are, in fact, so much degraded by mistaken notions of female excellence, that I do not mean to add a paradox when I assert, that this artificial weakness produces a propensity to tyrannize, and gives birth to cunning, the natural opponent of strength, which leads them to play off those contemptible infantine airs that undermine esteem even whilst they excite desire. Let men

---

[1] A lively writer, I cannot recollect his name, asks what business women turned of forty have to do in the world?

become more chaste and modest, and if women do not grow wiser in the same ratio, it will be clear that they have weaker understandings. It seems scarcely necessary to say, that I now speak of the sex in general. Many individuals have more sense than their male relatives; and, as nothing preponderates where there is a constant struggle for an equilibrium, without it has naturally more gravity, some women govern their husbands without degrading themselves, because intellect will always govern.

Suggestions for Discussion

1. Why does the author urge women to reject their conventional image of weakness?

2. How does she relate diction and style to the cause of women's rights? The author acknowledges that her feelings are "energetic." How are you made aware of the strength of her conviction? Why is *fascinating* italicized?

3. How does her own use of language affect her purpose and tone?

4. With what details does she convey her view of marriage? How would you characterize her attitude toward members of her own sex?

5. What evidence is there in this brief excerpt that the author is detached from her subject? deeply involved?

6. According to Wollstonecraft, how does the education of women both reflect and foster the concept of their frivolity and weakness? What does she see as its effect on the family?

7. What causal relationship is established in the last paragraph?

8. How does the concept of self function in the author's argument?

9. What rhetorical devices are used to persuade the reader?

Suggestions for Writing

1. Imagine a dialogue between Mary Wollstonecraft and D. H. Lawrence, whose essay follows. Focus on points of agreement and disagreement.

2. ". . . the first object of laudable ambition is to obtain a character as a human being, regardless of the distinction of sex. . . ." Discuss this statement in the light of your reading on the search for self.

3. Defend or refute the comment that the word *masculine*, as applied to women, is "only a bugbear."

D. H. Lawrence

Give Her a Pattern

D. H. Lawrence (1885–1930) was a schoolteacher before he turned to writing and became one of the great English novelists of the twentieth century. His best-known novels, which focus on relationships between men and women, include *Sons and Lovers* (1913), *Women in Love* (1920), and *Lady Chatterley's Lover* (1928). He also wrote short stories, essays, poetry, and literary criticism. In "Give Her a Pattern," Lawrence castigates men for not accepting women as real human beings of the feminine sex.

The real trouble about women is that they must always go on trying to adapt themselves to men's theories of women, as they always have done. When a woman is thoroughly herself, she is being what her type of man wants her to be. When a woman is hysterical it's because she doesn't quite know what to be, which pattern to follow, which man's picture of woman to live up to.

For, of course, just as there are many men in the world, there are many masculine theories of what women should be. But men run to type, and it is the type, not the individual, that produces the theory, or "ideal" of woman. Those very grasping gentry, the Romans, produced a theory or ideal of the matron, which fitted in very nicely with the Roman property lust. "Caesar's wife should be above suspicion."—So Caesar's wife kindly proceeded to be above it, no matter how far below it the Caesar fell. Later gentlemen like Nero produced the "fast" theory of woman, and later ladies were fast enough for everybody. Dante arrived with a chaste and untouched Beatrice, and chaste and untouched Beatrices began to march self-importantly through the centuries. The Renaissances discovered the learned woman, and learned women buzzed mildly into verse and prose. Dickens invented the child-wife, so child-wives have swarmed ever since. He also fished out his version of the chaste Beatrice, a chaste but marriageable Agnes. George Eliot imitated this pattern, and it became confirmed. The noble woman, the pure spouse, the devoted mother took the field, and was simply worked to death. Our own poor mothers were this sort. So we younger men, having been a bit frightened of our noble mothers, tended to revert to the child-wife. We weren't very inventive. Only the child-wife must be a boyish little thing—that was the new touch we added. Because young men are definitely frightened of the real female. She's too risky a quantity. She is too untidy, like David's Dora. No, let her be a boyish little thing, it's safer. So a boyish little thing she is.

There are, of course, other types. Capable men produce the capable woman ideal. Doctors produce the capable nurse. Business men produce the capable secretary. And so you get all sorts. You can produce the masculine sense of honor (whatever that highly mysterious quantity may be) in women, if you want to.

There is, also, the eternal secret ideal of men—the prostitute. Lots of women live up to this idea: just because men want them to.

And so, poor woman, destiny makes away with her. It isn't that she hasn't got a mind—she has. She's got everything that man has. The only difference is that she asks for a pattern. Give me a pattern to follow! That will always be woman's cry. Unless of course she has already chosen her pattern quite young, then she will declare she is herself absolutely, and no man's idea of women has any influence over her.

Now the real tragedy is not that women ask and must ask for a pattern of womanhood. The tragedy is not, even, that men give them such abominable patterns, child-wives, little-boy-baby-face girls, perfect secretaries, noble spouses, self-sacrificing mothers, pure women who bring forth children in virgin coldness, prostitutes who just make themselves low, to please the men; all the atrocious patterns of womanhood that men have supplied to woman; patterns all perverted from any real natural fullness of a human being. Man is willing to accept woman as an equal, as man in skirts, as an angel, a devil, a baby-face, a machine, an instrument, a bosom, a womb, a pair of legs, a servant, an encyclopaedia, an ideal, or an obscenity; the one thing he won't accept her as, is a human being, a real human being of the feminine sex.

And, of course, women love living up to strange patterns, weird patterns—the more uncanny the better. What could be more uncanny than the present pattern of the Eton-boy girl with flower-like artificial complexion? It is just weird. And for its very weirdness women like living up to it. What can be more gruesome than the little-boy-baby-face pattern? Yet the girls take it on with avidity.

But even that isn't the real root of the tragedy. The absurdity, and often, as in the Dante-Beatrice business, the inhuman nastiness of the pattern—for Beatrice had to go on being chaste and untouched all her life, according to Dante's pattern, while Dante had a cozy wife and kids at home—even that isn't the worst of it. The worst of it is, as soon as a woman has really lived up to the man's pattern, the man dislikes her for it. There is intense secret dislike for the Eton-young-man girl, among the boys, now that she is actually produced. Of course, she's very nice to show in public, absolutely the thing. But the very young men who have brought about her production detest her in private and in their private hearts are appalled by her.

When it comes to marrying, the pattern goes all to pieces. The boy marries the Eton-boy girl, and instantly he hates the *type*. Instantly his mind begins to play hysterically with all the other types, noble Agneses, chaste Beatrices, clinging Doras, and lurid *filles de joie*. He is in a wild welter of confusion. Whatever pattern the poor woman tries to live up to, he'll want another. And that's the condition of modern marriage.

Modern woman isn't really a fool. But modern man is. That seems to me the only plain way of putting it. The modern man is a fool, and the modern young man a prize fool. He makes a greater mess of his women than men have ever made. Because he absolutely doesn't know *what* he wants her to be. We shall see the changes in the woman-pattern follow one another fast and furious now, because the young men hysterically don't know what they want. Two years hence women may be in crinolines—there was a pattern for you!—or a bead flap, like naked negresses in mid-Africa—or they may be wearing brass armor, or the uniform of the Horse Guards. They may be anything. Because the young men are off their heads, and don't know what they want.

The women aren't fools, but they *must* live up to some pattern or other. They *know* the men are fools. They don't really respect the pattern. Yet a pattern they must have, or they can't exist.

Women are not fools. They have their own logic, even if it's not the masculine sort. Women have the logic of emotion, men have the logic of reason. The two are complementary and mostly in opposition. But the woman's logic of emotion is no less real and inexorable than the man's logic of reason. It only works differently.

And the woman never really loses it. She may spend years living up to a masculine pattern. But in the end, the strange and terrible logic of emotion will work out the smashing of that pattern, if it has not been emotionally satisfactory. This is the partial explanation of the astonishing changes in women. For years they go on being chaste Beatrices or child-wives. Then on a sudden—bash! The chaste Beatrice becomes something quite different, the child-wife becomes a roaring lioness! The pattern didn't suffice, emotionally.

Whereas men are fools. They are based on a logic of reason, or are supposed to be. And then they go and behave, especially with regard to women, in a more-than-feminine unreasonableness. They spend years training up the little-boy-baby-face type, till they've got her perfect. Then the moment they marry her, they want something else. Oh, beware, young women, of the young men who adore you! The moment they've got you they'll want something utterly different. The moment they marry the little-boy-baby-face, instantly they begin to pine for the noble Agnes, pure and majestic, or the infinite mother with deep bosom of consolation, or the perfect business woman, or the lurid prostitute on black silk sheets; or, most idiotic of all, a combination of all the lot of them at once. And that is the logic of reason! When it comes to women, modern men are idiots. They don't know what they want, and so they never want, permanently, what they get. They want a cream cake that is at the same time ham and eggs and at the same time porridge. They are fools. If only women weren't bound by fate to play up to them!

For the fact of life is that women *must* play up to man's pattern. And she only gives her best to a man when he gives her a satisfactory pattern to play up to. But today, with a stock of ready-made, worn-out idiotic patterns to live up to, what can women give to men but the trashy side of their emotions? What could a woman possibly give to a man who wanted her to be a boy-baby-face? What could she possibly give him but the dribblings of an idiot?— And, because women aren't fools, and aren't fooled even for very long at a time, she gives him some nasty cruel digs with her claws, and makes him cry for mother dear!—abruptly changing his pattern.

Bah! men are fools. If they want anything from women, let them give women a decent, satisfying idea of womanhood—not these trick patterns of washed-out idiots.

Suggestions for Discussion

1. Consider the title "Give Her a Pattern" in the light of Lawrence's attitude toward women. As he sketches some of the patterns imposed on women by men through the ages, whom does he regard as villain? Is there any evidence that he regards both men and women as victims of their culture?

2. What details provide the basis for the statement that the one thing man "won't accept her as, is a human being, a real human being of the feminine sex"?

3. Observe the repetition of the charge that modern men are fools. What does Lawrence mean by the statement that women are bound by fate to play up to men? How does he suggest that women are not as great "fools" as men?

4. What is the basis for his fatalistic attitude toward the possibility of real change in relationships between men and women?

5. What relationship does he make between art and nature?

6. How does he lead up to a definition of woman's tragedy?

7. How are comparison and contrast employed to develop his thesis?

8. How do structure, diction, exclamatory sentences, and metaphor contribute to tone and purpose?

9. What rhetorical devices are used to persuade the reader?

Suggestions for Writing

1. Write on modern female stereotypes and the mass media.

2. ". . . women love living up to strange patterns. . . ." What are some of these patterns today?

3. "When it comes to marrying, the pattern goes all to pieces." Can you illustrate?

4. Discuss and illustrate the "terrible logic of emotion" from your own experience.

Virginia Woolf

The Angel in the House

Virginia Woolf (1882–1941) was an English novelist and critic known for her experimentation with the form of the novel. Her works include *The Voyage Out* (1915), *Night and Day* (1919), *Jacob's Room* (1922), *Mrs. Dalloway* (1925), *To the Lighthouse* (1927), *Orlando: A Biography* (1928), *The Waves* (1931), *The Years* (1937), *Between the Acts* (1941), and several collections of essays. With her husband, Leonard Woolf, she founded the Hogarth Press. Although Mrs. Woolf was able to overcome certain obstacles to honest writing, she states that women still have "many ghosts to fight, many prejudices to overcome."

When your secretary invited me to come here, she told me that your Society is concerned with the employment of women and she suggested that I might tell you something about my own professional experiences. It is true I am a woman; it is true I am employed; but what professional experiences have I had? It is difficult to say. My profession is literature; and in that profession there are fewer experiences for women than in any other, with the exception of the stage—fewer, I mean, that are peculiar to women. For the road was cut many years ago—by Fanny Burney, by Aphra Behn, by Harriet Martineau, by Jane Austen, by George Eliot—many famous women, and many more unknown and forgotten, have been before me, making the path smooth, and regulating my steps. Thus, when I came to write, there were very few material obstacles in my way. Writing was a reputable and harmless occupation. The family peace was not broken by the scratching of a pen. No demand was made upon the family purse. For ten and sixpence one can buy paper enough to write all the plays of Shakespeare—if one has a mind that way. Pianos and models, Paris, Vienna, and Berlin, masters and mistresses, are not needed by a writer. The cheapness of writing paper is, of course, the reason why women have succeeded as writers before they have succeeded in the other professions.

But to tell you my story—it is a simple one. You have only got to figure to yourselves a girl in a bedroom with a pen in her hand. She had only to move that pen from left to right—from ten o'clock to one. Then it occurred to her to do what is simple and cheap enough after all—to slip a few of those pages into an envelope, fix a penny stamp in the corner, and drop the envelope into the red box at the corner. It was thus that I became a journalist; and my effort was rewarded on the first day of the following month—a very glorious day it was for me—by a letter from an editor containing a cheque for one pound ten shillings and sixpence. But to show you how little I deserve to be called a professional woman, how little I know of the struggles and difficulties of such lives, I have to admit that instead of spending that sum upon bread and butter, rent, shoes and stockings, or butcher's bills, I went out and bought a cat—a beautiful cat, a Persian cat, which very soon involved me in bitter disputes with my neighbours.

What could be easier than to write articles and to buy Persian cats with the profits? But wait a moment. Articles have to be about something. Mine, I seem to remember, was about a novel by a famous man. And while I was writing this review, I discovered that if I were going to review books I should need to do battle with a certain phantom. And the phantom was a woman, and when I came to know her better I called her after the heroine of a famous poem. The Angel in the House. It was she who used to come between me and my paper when I was writing reviews. It was she who bothered me and wasted my time and so tormented me that at last I killed her. You who come of a younger and happier generation may not have heard of her—you may not know what I mean by the Angel in the House. I will describe her as shortly as I can. She was intensely sympathetic. She was immensely charming. She was utterly unselfish. She excelled in the difficult arts of family life. She sacrificed herself daily. If there was chicken, she took the leg; if there was a draught she sat in it—in short she was so constituted that she never had a mind or a wish of her own, but preferred to sympathize always with the minds and wishes of others. Above all—I need not say it—she was pure. Her purity was supposed to be her chief beauty—her blushes, her great grace. In those days—the last of Queen Victoria—every house had its Angel. And when I came to write I encountered her with the very first words. The shadow of her wings fell on my page; I heard the rustling of her skirts in the room. Directly, that is to say, I took my pen in hand to review that novel by a famous man, she slipped behind me and whispered: "My dear, you are a young woman. You are writing about a book that has been written by a man. Be sympathetic; be tender; flatter; deceive; use all the arts and wiles of our sex. Never let anybody guess that you have a mind of your own. Above all, be pure." And she made as if to guide my pen. I now record the one act for which I take some credit to myself, though the credit rightly belongs to some excellent ancestors of mine who left me a certain sum of money—shall we say five hundred pounds a year?—so that it was not necessary for me to depend solely on charm for my living. I turned upon her and caught her by the throat. I did my best to kill her. My excuse, if I were to be had up in a court of law, would be that I acted in self-defense. Had I not killed her she would have killed me. She would have plucked the heart out of my writing. For, as I found, directly I put pen to paper, you cannot review even a novel without having a mind of your own, without expressing what you think to be the truth about human relations, morality, sex. And all these questions, according to the Angel in the House, cannot be dealt with freely and openly by women; they must charm, they must conciliate, they must—to put it bluntly—tell lies if they are to succeed. Thus, whenever I felt the shadow of her wing or the radiance of her halo upon my page, I took up the inkpot and flung it at her. She died hard. Her fictitious nature was of great assistance to her. It is far harder to kill a phantom than a reality. She was always creeping back when I thought I had despatched her. Though I flatter myself that I killed her in the end, the struggle was severe; it took much time that had better have been spent upon learning Greek grammar; or in roaming the world in search of adventures. But it was a real experience; it was an experience that was bound to befall all women writers at that time. Killing the Angel in the House was part of the occupation of a woman writer.

But to continue my story. The Angel was dead; what then remained? You may say that what remained was a simple and common object—a young woman in a bedroom with an inkpot. In other words, now that she had rid herself of falsehood, that young woman had only to be herself. Ah, but what is "herself"? I mean, what is a woman? I assure you, I do not know. I do not believe that you know. I do not believe that anybody can know until she has expressed herself in all the arts and professions open to human skill. That indeed is one of the reasons why I have come here—out of respect for you, who are in process of showing us by your experiments what a woman is, who are in process of providing us, by your failures and successes, with that extremely important piece of information.

But to continue the story of my professional experiences. I made one pound ten and six by my first review; and I bought a Persian cat with the proceeds. Then I grew ambitious. A Persian cat is all very well, I said; but a Persian cat is not enough. I must have a motor car. And it was thus that I became a novelist—for it is a very strange thing that people will give you a motor car if you will tell them a story. It is a still stranger thing that there is nothing so delightful in the world as telling stories. It is far pleasanter than writing reviews of famous novels. And yet, if I am to obey your secretary and tell you my professional experiences as a novelist, I must tell you about a very strange experience that befell me as a novelist. And to understand it you must try first to imagine a novelist's state of mind. I hope I am not giving away professional secrets if I say that a novelist's chief desire is to be as unconscious as possible. He has to induce in himself a state of perpetual lethargy. He wants life to proceed with the utmost quiet and regularity. He wants to see the same faces, to read the same books, to do the same things day after day, month after month, while he is writing, so that nothing may break the illusion in which he is living—so that nothing may disturb or disquiet the mysterious nosings about, feelings round, darts, dashes and sudden discoveries of that very shy and illusive spirit, the imagination. I suspect that this state is the same both for men and women. Be that as it may, I want you to imagine me writing a novel in a state of trance. I want you to figure to yourselves a girl sitting with a pen in her hand, which for minutes, and indeed for hours, she never dips into the inkpot. The image that comes to my mind when I think of this girl is the image of a fisherman lying sunk in dreams on the verge of a deep lake with a rod held out over the water. She was letting her imagination sweep unchecked round every rock and cranny of the world that lies submerged in the depths of our unconscious being. Now came the experience, the experience that I believe to be far commoner with women writers than with men. The line raced through the girl's fingers. Her imagination had rushed away. It had sought the pools, the depths, the dark places where the largest fish slumber. And then there was a smash. There was an explosion. There was foam and confusion. The imagination had dashed itself against something hard. The girl was roused from her dream. She was indeed in a state of the most acute and difficult distress. To speak without figure she had thought of something, something about the body, about the passions which it was unfitting for her as a woman to say. Men, her reason told her, would be shocked. The consciousness of what men will say of a woman who speaks the truth about her passions had roused her from her artist's state of unconsciousness. She could write no more. The trance was over. Her imagination could work no longer. This I believe to be a very common experience with women writers—they are impeded by the extreme conventionality of the other sex. For though men sensibly allow themselves great freedom in these respects, I doubt that they realize or can control the extreme severity with which they condemn such freedom in women.

These then were two very genuine experiences of my own. These were two of the adventures of my professional life. The first—killing the Angel in the House—I think I solved. She died. But the second, telling the truth about my own experiences as a body, I do not think I solved. I doubt that any woman has solved it yet. The obstacles against her are still immensely powerful—and yet they are very difficult to define. Outwardly, what is simpler than to write books? Outwardly, what obstacles are there for a woman rather than for a man? Inwardly, I think, the case is very different; she has still many ghosts to fight, many prejudices to overcome. Indeed it will be a long time still, I think, before a woman can sit down to write a book without finding a phantom to be slain, a rock to be dashed against. And if this is so in literature, the freest of all professions for women, how is it in the new professions which you are now for the first time entering?

Those are the questions that I should like, had I time, to ask you. And indeed, if I have laid stress upon these professional experiences of mine, it is because I believe that they are, though in different forms, yours also. Even when the path is nominally open—when there is nothing to prevent a woman from being a doctor, a lawyer, a civil servant—there are many phantoms and obstacles, as I believe, looming in her way. To discuss and define them is I think of great value and importance; for thus only can the labor be shared, the difficulties be solved. But besides this, it is necessary also to discuss the ends and the aims for which we are fighting, for which we are doing battle with these formidable obstacles. Those aims cannot be taken for granted; they must be perpetually questioned and examined. The whole position, as I see it—here in this hall surrounded by women practising for the first time in history I know not how many different professions—is one of extraordinary interest and importance. You have won rooms of your own in the house hitherto exclusively owned by men. You are able, though not without great labor and effort, to pay the rent. You are earning your five hundred pounds a year. But this freedom is only a beginning; the room is your own, but it is still bare. It has to be furnished; it has to be decorated; it has to be shared. How are you going to furnish it, how are you going to decorate it? With whom are you going to share it, and upon what terms? These, I think are questions of the utmost importance and interest. For the first time in history you are able to ask them; for the first time you are able to decide for yourselves what the answers should be. Willingly would I stay and discuss those questions and answers—but not tonight. My time is up; and I must cease.

Suggestions for Discussion

1. What are the characteristics of this phantom, the Angel in the House? Do they persist today?

2. Why does the author say she had to kill the Angel?

3. What remaining obstacles to truth did she find? In what ways may women still encounter these obstacles?

4. What are the implications in the concluding paragraph concerning relationships with men?

5. "Ah, but what is 'herself'? I mean, what is a woman?" Discuss these rhetorical questions in relation to purpose and tone.

6. What points of agreement or disagreement might Woolf have with Lawrence?

7. What rhetorical devices are employed to persuade the reader?

Suggestions for Writing

1. Describe an Angel in the House you know.

2. Does this phantom of the Angel still haunt contemporary drama, movies, fiction, advertising?

3. Apply one or more of Woolf's generalizations to a woman poet or writer of fiction.

Germaine Greer

The Stereotype

Germaine Greer (b. 1939) is an Australian-born writer and educator, best known as a standard bearer of the women's liberation movement and as the author of the best-selling *The Female Eunuch* (1971), from which this selection is taken, and of *Sex and Destiny: The Politics of Human Fertility* (1984). The stereotype—the Eternal Feminine—sought by women as well as by men, reduces a woman to a cipher and castrates her.

In that mysterious dimension where the body meets the soul the stereotype is born and has her being. She is more body than soul, more soul than mind. To her belongs all that is beautiful, even the very word beauty itself. All that exists, exists to beautify her. The sun shines only to burnish her skin and gild her hair; the wind blows only to whip up the color in her cheeks; the sea strives to bathe her; flowers die gladly so that her skin may luxuriate in their essence. She is the crown of creation, the masterpiece. The depths of the sea are ransacked for pearl and coral to deck her; the bowels of the earth are laid open that she might wear gold, sapphires, diamonds, and rubies. Baby seals are battered with staves, unborn lambs ripped from their mothers' wombs, millions of moles, muskrats, squirrels, minks, ermines, foxes, beavers, chinchillas, ocelots, lynxes, and other small and lovely creatures die untimely deaths that she might have furs. Egrets, ostriches, and peacocks, butterflies and beetles yield her their plumage. Men risk their lives hunting leopards for her coats, and crocodiles for her handbags and shoes. Millions of silkworms offer her their yellow labors; even the seamstresses roll seams and whip lace by hand, so that she might be clad in the best that money can buy.

The men of our civilization have stripped themselves of the fineries of the earth so that they might work more freely to plunder the universe for treasures to deck my lady in. New raw materials, new processes, new machines are all brought into her service. My lady must therefore be the chief spender as well as the chief symbol of spending ability and monetary success. While her mate toils in his factory, she totters about the smartest streets and plushiest hotels with his fortune upon her back and bosom, fingers, and wrists, continuing that essential expenditure in his house which is her frame and her setting, enjoying that silken idleness which is the necessary condition of maintaining her mate's prestige and her qualification to demonstrate it. Once upon a time only the aristocratic lady could lay claim to the title of crown of crea-

> Taught from infancy that beauty is woman's scepter, the mind shapes itself to the body, and roaming round its gilt cage, only seeks to adorn its prison.
>
> —Mary Wollstonecraft, *A Vindication of the Rights of Woman*, 1792, p. 90.

tion: only her hands were white enough, her feet tiny enough, her waist narrow enough, her hair long and golden enough; but every well-to-do burgher's wife set herself up to ape my lady and to follow fashion, until my lady was forced to set herself out like a gilded doll overlaid with monstrous rubies and pearls like pigeon's eggs. Nowadays the Queen of England still considers it part of her royal female role to sport as much of the family jewelry as she can manage at any one time on all public occasions, although the male monarchs have escaped such showcase duty, which develops exclusively upon their wives.

At the same time as woman was becoming the showcase for wealth and caste, while men were slipping into relative anonymity and "handsome is as handsome does," she was emerging as the central emblem of western art. For the Greeks the male and female body had beauty of a human, not necessarily a sexual, kind; indeed they may have marginally favored the young male form as the most powerful and perfectly proportioned. Likewise the Romans showed no bias towards the depiction of femininity in their predominantly monumental art. In the Renaissance the female form began to predominate, not only as the mother in the predominant emblem of *madonna col bambino*, but as an aesthetic study in herself. At first naked female forms took their chances in crowd scenes or diptychs of Adam and Eve, but gradually Venus claims ascendancy, Mary Magdalene ceases to be wizened and emaciated, and becomes nubile and ecstatic, portraits of anonymous young women, chosen only for their prettiness, begin to appear, are gradually disrobed, and renamed Flora or Primavera. Painters begin to paint their own wives and mistresses and royal consorts as voluptuous beauties, divesting them of their clothes if desirable, but not of their jewelry. Susanna keeps her bracelets on in the bath, and Hélène Fourment keeps ahold of her fur as well!

What happened to women in painting happened to her in poetry as well. Her beauty was celebrated in terms of the riches which clustered around her: her hair was gold wires, her brow ivory, her lips ruby, her teeth gates of pearl, her breasts alabaster veined with lapis lazuli, her eyes as black as jet. The fragility of her loveliness was emphasized by the inevitable comparisons with the rose, and she was urged to employ her beauty in love-making before it withered on the stem. She was for consumption; other sorts of imagery spoke of her in terms of cherries and cream, lips as sweet as honey and skin white as milk, breasts like cream uncurdled, hard as apples. Some celebrations yearned over her finery as well, her lawn more transparent than morning mist, her lace as delicate as gossamer, the baubles that she toyed with and the favors that she gave. Even now we find the thriller hero describing his classy dames' elegant suits, cheeky hats, well-chosen accessories and footwear; the imagery no longer dwells on jewels and flowers but the consumer emphasis is the same. The mousy secretary blossoms into the feminine stereotype when she reddens her lips, lets down her hair, and puts on something frilly.

Nowadays women are not expected, unless they are Paola di Liegi or Jackie Onassis, and then only on gala occasions, to appear with a king's ransom deployed upon their bodies, but they are required to look expensive, fashionable, well-groomed, and not to be seen in the same dress twice. If the duty of the few may have become less onerous, it has also become the duty of the many. The stereotype marshals an army of servants. She is supplied with cosmetics, underwear, foundation garments, stockings, wigs, postiches, and hairdressing as well as her outer garments, her jewels, and furs. The effect is to be built up layer by layer, and it is expensive. Splendor has given way to fit, line, and cut. The spirit of competition must be kept up, as more and more women struggle toward the top drawer, so that the fashion industry can rely upon an expanding market. Poorer women fake it, ape it, pick up on the fashions a season too late, use crude effects, mistaking the line, the sheen, the gloss of the high-class article for a garish simulacrum. The business is so complex that it must be handled by an expert. The paragons of the stereotype must be dressed, coifed, and painted by the experts and the style-setters, although they may be encouraged to give heart to the housewives studying their lives in pulp magazines by claiming a lifelong fidelity to their own hair and soap and water. The boast is more usually discouraging than otherwise, unfortunately.

As long as she is young and personable, every woman may cherish the dream that she may leap up the social ladder and dim the sheen of luxury by sheer natural loveliness; the few examples of such a feat are kept before the eye of the public. Fired with hope, optimism, and ambition, young women study the latest forms of the stereotype, set out in *Vogue, Nova, Queen,* and other glossies, where the mannequins stare from among the advertisements for fabulous real estate, furs, and jewels. Nowadays the uniformity of the year's fashions is severely affected by the emergence of the pert female designers who direct their appeal to the working girl, emphasizing variety, comfort, and simple, striking effects. There is no longer a single face of the year: even Twiggy has had to withdraw into marketing and rationed personal appearances, while the Shrimp works mostly in New York. Nevertheless the stereotype is still supreme. She has simply allowed herself a little more variation.

The stereotype is the Eternal Feminine. She is the Sexual Object sought by all men, and by all women. She is of neither sex, for she has herself no sex at all. Her value is solely attested by the demand she excites in others. All she must contribute is her existence. She need achieve nothing, for she is the reward of achievement. She need never give positive evidence of her moral character because virtue is assumed from her loveliness, and her passivity. If any man who has no right to her be found with her she will not be punished, for she is morally neuter. The matter is solely one of male rivalry. Innocently she may drive men to madness and war. The more trouble she

> The myth of the strong black woman is the other side of the coin of the myth of the beautiful dumb blonde. The white man turned the white woman into a weak-minded, weak-bodied, delicate freak, a sex pot, and placed her on a pedestal; he turned the black woman into a strong self-reliant Amazon and deposited her in his kitchen. . . . The white man turned himself into the Omnipotent Administrator and established himself in the Front Office.
> —Eldridge Cleaver, "The Allegory of the Black Eunuchs," *Soul on Ice,* 1968, p. 162

can cause, the more her stocks go up, for possession of her means more the more demand she excites. Nobody wants a girl whose beauty is imperceptible to all but him; and so men welcome the stereotype because it directs their taste into the most commonly recognized areas of value, although they may protest because some aspects of it do not tally with their fetishes. There is scope in the stereotype's variety for most fetishes. The leg man may follow miniskirts, the tit man can encourage see-through blouses and plunging neck-lines, although the man who likes fat women may feel constrained to enjoy them in secret. There are stringent limits to the variations on the stereotype, for nothing must interfere with her function as sex object. She may wear leather, as long as she cannot actually handle a motorbike: she may wear rubber, but it ought not to indicate that she is an expert diver or waterskier. If she wears athletic clothes the purpose is to underline her unathleticism. She may sit astride a horse, looking soft and curvy, but she must not crouch over its neck with her rump in the air.

Because she is the emblem of spending ability and the chief spender, she is also the most effective seller of this world's goods. Every survey ever held has shown that the image of an attractive woman is the most effective adver-tising gimmick. She may sit astride the mudguard of a new car, or step into it ablaze with jewels; she may lie at a man's feet stroking his new socks; she may hold the petrol pump in a challenging pose, or dance through woodland glades in slow motion in all the glory of a new shampoo; whatever she does her image sells. The gynolatry of our civilization is written large upon its face, upon hoardings, cinema screens, television, newspapers, magazines, tins, packets, cartons, bottles, all consecrated to the reigning deity, the female fetish. Her dominion must not be thought to entail the rule of women, for she is not a woman. Her glossy lips and mat complexion, her unfocused eyes and flawless fingers, her extraordinary hair all floating and shining, curling, and gleaming, reveal the inhuman triumph of cosmetics, lighting, focusing, and printing, cropping and composition. She sleeps unruffled, her lips red and juicy and closed, her eyes as crisp and black as if new painted, and her false lashes immaculately curled. Even when she washes her face with a new and creamier toilet soap her expression is as tranquil and vacant and her paint as flawless as ever. If ever she should appear tousled and troubled, her fea-tures are miraculously smoothed to their proper veneer by a new washing powder or a bouillon cube. For she is a doll: weeping, pouting, or smiling, running or reclining, she is a doll. She is an idol, formed of the concatenation of lines and masses, signifying the lineaments of satisfied impotence.

Her essential quality is castratedness. She absolutely must be young, her body hairless, her flesh buoyant, and *she must not have a sexual organ.* No musculature must distort the smoothness of the lines of her body, although she may be painfully slender or warmly cuddly. Her expression must betray no hint of humor, curiosity, or intelligence, although it may signify hauteur to an extent that is actually absurd, or smoldering lust, very feebly signified by drooping eyes and a sullen mouth (for the stereotype's lust equals irrational submission), or, most commonly, vivacity and idiot happiness. Seeing that the world despoils itself for this creature's benefit, she must be happy; the entire structure would topple if she were not. So the image of woman appears plas-tered on every surface imaginable, smiling interminably. An apple pie evokes a glance of tender beatitude, a washing machine causes hilarity, a cheap box

> She was created to be the toy of man, his rattle, and it must jingle in his ears whenever, dismissing reason, he chooses to be amused.
>
> —**Mary Wollstonecraft,** *A Vindication of the Rights of Woman,* 1792, p. 66

of chocolates brings forth meltingly joyous gratitude, a Coke is the cause of a rictus of unutterable brilliance, even a new stick-on bandage is saluted by a smirk of satisfaction. A real woman licks her lips and opens her mouth and flashes her teeth when photographers appear: *she* must arrive at the premiere of her husband's film in a paroxysm of delight, or his success might be murmured about. The occupational hazard of being a Playboy Bunny is the aching facial muscles brought on by the obligatory smiles.

So what is the beef? Maybe I couldn't make it. Maybe I don't have a pretty smile, good teeth, nice tits, long legs, a cheeky ass, a sexy voice. Maybe I don't know how to handle men and increase my market value, so that the rewards due to the feminine will accrue to me. Then again, maybe I'm sick of the masquerade. I'm sick of pretending eternal youth. I'm sick of belying my own intelligence, my own will, my own sex. I'm sick of peering at the world through false eyelashes, so everything I see is mixed with a shadow of bought hairs; I'm sick of weighting my head with a dead mane, unable to move my neck freely, terrified of rain, of wind, of dancing too vigorously in case I sweat into my lacquered curls. I'm sick of the Powder Room. I'm sick of pretending that some fatuous male's self-important pronouncements are the objects of my undivided attention, I'm sick of going to films and plays when someone else wants to, and sick of having no opinions of my own about either. I'm sick of being a transvestite. I refuse to be a female impersonator. I am a woman, not a castrate.

April Ashley was born male. All the information supplied by genes, chromosomes, internal and external sexual organs added up to the same thing. April was a man. But he longed to be a woman. He longed for the stereotype, not to embrace, but to be. He wanted soft fabrics, jewels, furs, makeup, the love and protection of men. So he was impotent. He couldn't fancy women at all, although he did not particularly welcome homosexual addresses. He did not think of himself as a pervert, or even as a transvestite, but as a woman

> Discretion is the better part of Valerie
> though all of her is nice
> lips as warm as strawberries
> eyes as cold as ice
> the very best of everything
> only will suffice
> not for her potatoes
> and puddings made of rice
>
> —**Roger McGough,** *Discretion*

> To what end is the laying out of the embroidered Hair, em-
> bared Breasts; vermilion Cheeks, alluring looks, Fashion gates,
> and artful Countenances, effeminate intangling and insnaring
> Gestures, their Curls and Purls of proclaiming Petulancies,
> boulstered and laid out with such example and authority in
> these our days, as with Allowance and beseeming Conven-
> iency?
>
> Doth the world wax barren through decrease of Genera-
> tions, and become, like the Earth, less fruitful heretofore?
> Doth the Blood lose his Heat or do the Sunbeams become
> waterish and less fervent, than formerly they have been, that
> men should be thus inflamed and persuaded on to lust?
>
> —**Alex. Niccholes,** *A Discourse of Marriage and Wiving,*
> 1615, pp. 143–52

cruelly transmogrified into manhood. He tried to die, became a female impersonator, but eventually found a doctor in Casablanca who came up with a
more acceptable alternative. He was to be castrated, and his penis used as
the lining of a surgically constructed cleft, which would be a vagina. He would
be infertile, but that has never affected the attribution of femininity. April
returned to England, resplendent. Massive hormone treatment had eradicated his beard, and formed tiny breasts: he had grown his hair and bought
feminine clothes during the time he had worked as an impersonator. He became a model, and began to illustrate the feminine stereotype as he was perfectly qualified to do, for he was elegant, voluptuous, beautifully groomed,
and in love with his own image. On an ill-fated day he married the heir to a
peerage, the Hon. Arthur Corbett, acting out the highest achievement of the
feminine dream, and went to live with him in a villa in Marbella. The marriage was never consummated. April's incompetence as a woman is what we
must expect from a castrate, but it is not so very different after all from the
impotence of feminine women, who submit to sex without desire, with only
the infantile pleasure of cuddling and affection, which is their favorite reward.
As long as the feminine stereotype remains the definition of the female sex,
April Ashley is a woman, regardless of the legal decision ensuing from her
divorce. She is as much a casualty of the polarity of the sexes as we all are.
Disgraced, unsexed April Ashley is our sister and our symbol.

Suggestions for Discussion

1. How does the author develop the concept that "beauty is woman's scepter"? How
   does the long series of examples in the first paragraph contribute to purpose and
   tone?

2. What does the author mean by the stereotype? How does she develop and support
   her extended definition?

3. In what context does the author invoke the first person? How does its intrusion
   affect purpose and tone?

4. What purpose is served by the introduction of April Ashley? Do the last two sentences constitute an appropriate summation of what has gone before? Explain.

Suggestion for Writing

1. Drawing on your own experience and observation, write an essay on stereotypes.

Norman Mailer

Who Would Finally Do the Dishes?

Norman Mailer (b. 1923) grew up in Brooklyn and was educated at Harvard University, where he wrote many short stories. He has written *The Naked and the Dead* (1948), *Barbary Shore* (1951), and *An American Dream* (1965). From 1953 to 1963 he edited *Dissent,* and in 1956 he cofounded *The Village Voice.* He is a public personality and columnist and a contributor to many major periodicals, such as the *New York Post, Partisan Review,* and *Esquire.* He received the National Institute of Arts and Letters Grant in literature in 1960. More recent books are *Armies of the Night* (1968), *Of a Fire on the Moon* (1971), *The Prisoner of Sex,* (1971) *The Fight* (1975), and *Ancient Evenings* (1983). This excerpt from *The Prisoner of Sex* (1971), in which the author refers to himself as "he" and "the prisoner," moves from the question of who finally would do the dishes to the issue of the ultimate responsibility of women to select the fathers of their children.

Still he had not answered the question with which he began. Who finally would do the dishes? And in his reading through an Agreement drawn between husband and wife where every piece of housework was divided, and duty-shifts to baby-sit were divided, and weekends where the man worked to compensate the wife for chores of weekday transportation. Shopping was balanced, cooking was split, so was the transportation of children. It was a crystal of a contract bound to serve as model for many another, and began on this high and fundamental premise:

> We reject the notion that the work which brings in more money is more valuable. The ability to earn more money is already a privilege which must not be compounded by enabling the larger earner to buy out his/her duties and put the burden on the one who earns less, or on someone hired from outside.
> We believe that each member of the family has an equal right to his/her own time, work, value, choices. As long as all duties are performed, each person may

use his/her extra time any way he/she chooses. If he/she wants to use it making money, fine. If he/she wants to spend it with spouse, fine. If not, fine.

As parents we believe we must share all responsibility for taking care of our children and home—not only the work, but the responsibility. At least during the first year of this agreement, *sharing responsibility* shall mean:

1. Dividing the *jobs* (see "Job Breakdown" below); and
2. Dividing the *time* (see "Schedule" below) for which each parent is responsible.

There were details which stung:

10. Cleaning: Husband does all the house-cleaning, in exchange for wife's extra childcare (3:00 to 6:30 daily) and sick care.
11. Laundry: Wife does most home laundry. Husband does all dry cleaning delivery and pick up. Wife strips beds, husband remakes them.

No, he would not be married to such a woman. If he were obliged to have a roommate, he would pick a man. The question had been answered. He could love a woman and she might even sprain her back before a hundred sinks of dishes in a month, but he would not be happy to help her if his work should suffer, no, not unless her work was as valuable as his own. But he was complacent with the importance of respecting his work—what an agony for a man if work were meaningless: then all such rights were lost before a woman. So it was another corollary of Liberation that as technique reduced labor to activities which were often absurd, like punching the buttons on an automatic machine, so did the housework of women take on magnitude, for their work was directed at least to a basic end. And thinking of that Marriage Agreement which was nearly the equal of a legal code, he was reminded of his old campaign for mayor when Breslin and himself had called for New York City to become the fifty-first state and had preached Power to the Neighborhoods and offered the idea that a modern man would do well to live in a small society of his own choosing, in a legally constituted village within the city, or a corporate zone, in a traditional religious park or a revolutionary commune—the value would be to discover which of one's social ideas were able to work. For nothing was more difficult to learn in the modern world. Of course, it had been a scheme with all the profound naïveté of assuming that people voted as an expression of their desire when he had yet to learn the electorate obtained satisfaction by venting their hate. Still he wondered if it was not likely that the politics of government and property would yet begin to alter into the politics of sex. Perhaps he had been living with the subject too closely, but he saw no major reason why one could not await a world—assuming there would be a world—where people would found their politics on the fundamental demands they would make of sex. So might there yet be towns within the city which were homosexual, and whole blocks legally organized for married couples who thought the orgy was ground for the progressive action of the day. And there would be mournful areas of the city deserted on Sunday, all suitable for the mood of masturbators who liked the open air and the street, perhaps even pseudo-Victorian quarters where brothels could again be found. There could be city turfs steaming with the nuances of bisexuals living on top of bisexuals, and funky tracts for old-fashioned lovers where the man was the rock of the home; there would always be horizons blocked by housing projects vast as the legislation which had gone into the division of household duties between women and men. There would be every kind of world in the city, but their laws would be founded on sex. It was, he supposed, the rationalized end of that violence which had once existed between men and women as the crossed potential of their love, violence which was part perhaps of the force to achieve and the force to scourge, it had been that violence which entered into all the irrationality of love, "the rooting out of the old bodily shame" of which Lawrence had spoke, and the rooting out of the fear in women that they were more violent than their men, and would betray them, or destroy them in the transcendence of sex; yes, the play of violence had been the drama of love between a man and a woman, for too little, and they were friends never to be gripped by any attraction which could send them far; too much, and they were ruined, or love was ruined, or they must degenerate to bully and victim, become no better than a transmission belt to bring in the violence and injustice of the world outside, bring it in to poison the cowardice of their home. But the violence of lovers was on its way to disappear in all the other deaths of the primitive which one could anticipate as the human became the human unit—human violence would go to some place outside (like the smog) where it could return to kill them by slow degree—and equally. But he had made his determination on beginning his piece that he would not write of sex and violence too long, for that would oblige him to end in the unnatural position of explaining what he had attempted in other work. So he would step aide by remarking that a look at sex and violence was the proper ground of a novel and he would rather try it there. And content himself now with one last look at his remark that "the prime responsibility of a woman probably is to be on earth long enough to find the best mate for herself, and conceive children who will improve the species." Was it too late now to suggest that in the search for the best mate was concealed the bravery of a woman, and to find the best mate, whatever ugly or brutal or tyrannical or unbalanced or heart-searing son of misery he might appear, his values nonetheless, mysterious fellow of values, would inevitably present themselves in those twenty-three chromsomes able to cut through fashion, tradition, and class.

There is a famous study of neurotics which shows that patients who received psychoanalysis had an improvement rate of 44 percent; psychotherapy was more effective—a rate of 64 percent; and 72 percent was the unhappiest improvement, for that was the rate of cure of patients who had never been treated at all. The Eysenck study it is called, and later studies confirm its results. It was, the prisoner decided, a way of telling us that the taste in the mouth of explaining too much is the seating of the next disease. One cannot improve the human condition through comfort and security, or through generalized sympathy and support—it is possible the untreated patients got better because the violence of their neurosis was not drained. The cure of the human was in his leap.

But now he could comprehend why woman bridled at the thought she must "find the best mate for herself and . . . improve the species." How full of death was the idea if one looked at any scheme which brought people who were fundamentally unattracted to each other down marriage aisles, their qualifications superb, their qualities neuter. So he was grateful to a writer who wrote a book. *The Lady,* published in 1910, Emily James Putnam, first dean of Barnard. She was a writer with a whip of the loveliest wit. He would give the last quotation to her for she had given the hint of a way.

Apart from the crude economic question, the things that most women mean when they speak of "happiness," that is, love and children and the little republic of the home, depend upon the favour of men, and the qualities that win this favour are not in general those that are most useful for other purposes. A girl should not be too intelligent or too good or too highly differentiated in any direction. Like a ready-made garment she should be designed to fit the average man. She should have "just about as much religion as my William likes." The age-long operation of this rule, by which the least strongly individualised women are the most likely to have a chance to transmit their qualities, has given it the air of a natural law.

It was finally obvious. Women must have their rights to a life which would allow them to look for a mate. And there would be no free search until they were liberated. So let woman be what she would, and what she could. Let her cohabit on elephants if she had to, and fuck with Borzoi hounds, let her bed with eight pricks and a whistle, yes, give her freedom and let her burn it, or blow it, or build it to triumph, or collapse. Let her conceive her children, and kill them in the womb if she thought they did not have it, let her travel to the moon, write the great American novel, and allow her husband to send her off to work with her lunch pail and a cigar; she could kiss the cooze of forty-one Rockettes in Macy's store window; she could legislate, incarcerate, and wear a uniform; she could die of every male disease, and years of burden was the first, for she might learn that women worked at onerous duties and men worked for egos which were worse than onerous and often insane. So women could have the right to die of men's diseases, yes, and might try to live with men's egos in their own skull case and he would cheer them on their way—would he? Yes, he thought that perhaps they may as well do what they desired if the anger of the centuries was having its say. Finally, he would agree with everything they asked but to quit the womb, for finally a day had to come when women shattered the pearl of their love for pristine and feminine will and found the man, yes that man in the million who could become the point of the seed which would give an egg back to nature, and let the woman return with a babe who came from the root of God's desire to go all the way, wherever was that way. And who was there to know that God was not the greatest lover of them all? The idiocy was to assume the oyster and the clam knew more than the trees and the grass. (Unless dear God was black and half-Jewish and a woman, and small and mean as mother-wit. We will never know until we take the trip. And so saying realized he had been able to end a portentous piece in the soft sweet flesh of parentheses.)

Suggestions for Discussion

1. How does the author finally resolve the question he poses in the opening lines of this excerpt? How does the question serve both a rhetorical and substantive function in the development of Mailer's ideas?

2. Describe the change in tone between the first paragraph and the paragraphs following item 11 of the contract.

3. How does Mailer relate his mayoral campaign to women's liberation?

4. What is Mailer's view of the prime responsibility of women? Of men? What does it tell you about Mailer? What is your reaction?

5. How does the Eysenck study relate to the status of women? What is the meaning of the statement: "The cure of the human was in his leap."

6. Explain the last paragraph in this selection. What concessions has Mailer made, if any?

Suggestions for Writing

1. Write a marriage contract with which you could happily live and introduce it with the premises on which it is based.

2. Discuss your views of the prime responsibility of women or of men.

3. Write a description of a truly liberated woman; of a truly liberated man.

Calvin Trillin

Incompatible, with One L

Calvin Trillin (b.1935) writes regularly for *The Nation* and *The New Yorker*. In addition he is the author of the following books: *U.S. Journal* (1971), *An Education in Georgia* (1971), *American Fried* (1974), *Runestruck* (1977), *Alice, Let's Eat* (1978), and *Killings* (1984). The essay that follows was published in a collection, *Uncivil Liberties* (1982). With wit and understatement he portrays a relationship in which the partners appear to be both compatible and committed.

September 16, 1978

I married Alice under the assumption that she could spell "occurred." She now insists that nothing specific was mentioned about "occurred" in prenuptial discussions. It seems to me, though, that implicit in someone's making a living as a college English teacher is the representation that she is a speller with a repertoire adequate to any occasion. She must have known that the only person in her line of work I had any experience being related to, my Cousin Keith from Salina, once reached the finals of the Kansas State Spelling Bee. She now says Cousin Keith's spelling triumph was never spoken of between us. I distinctly remember, though, that I listed for Alice the highlights of our family's history, as any prospective bridegroom might for his future wife, and Cousin Keith has always been part of my standard Family History recitation—along with my Cousin Neil, who was once the head drum major of the University of Nebraska marching band, and my Uncle Benny Daynofsky, who in his early eighties was knocked down by a car while planting tomatoes in his own backyard in St. Jo. It is significant that she does not deny knowing about Uncle Benny.

Is spelling the sort of thing that modern young couples get straightened out beforehand in marriage contracts? I wouldn't bring it up after all of these years, except that, as it happens, I can't spell "occurred" either. I was forced to look it up twice in order to write the first paragraph, and once more to get this far in the second. Somehow, I had expected to marry someone whose spelling would be, if not perfect, at least complementary to mine. We would face the future with heads held high, and maybe a short song on our lips— confident that together we could spell anything they dished out. Before we had been married a month, the real world started to eat away at that fantasy: It turned out that Alice was not very good on "commitment." I don't mean she didn't have any; she couldn't spell it. I have never been able to spell "commitment" myself.

I know how to spell "embarrass"—usually considered by double-letter specialists to be a much more difficult word. I have been able to spell it for years. I planted "embarrass" in my mind at an early age through a rather brilliant mnemonic device having to do with barstools. In fact, not to make a lot out of it, I had always thought of my ability to spell "embarrass" as a nice little facility to bring to a marriage—the sort of minor bonus that is sometimes found in a husband's ability to rewire lamps. (I don't mean it was the only facility I was able to contribute: Although I can't rewire a lamp, I can bark like a dog and I can blow a hard-boiled egg out of its shell seven times out of ten.) We have now been married thirteen years, and Alice still has not asked me how to spell "embarrass." Apparently, she has a mnemonic device of her own. I have never inquired. That sort of thing doesn't interest me.

For a while, our reformist friends used to urge us to make a list of the words that troubled both of us—their theory being that some wretched consistency in the American educational system would be further documented by the fact that a husband and wife who went to public schools 1,300 miles apart were left without the ability to spell precisely the same words. Not long ago, an analytically inclined Easterner who came over for a drink when Alice happened to be out of town tried to establish some psychological significance in which words Alice and I were able to spell and which ones we weren't. "Is it really an accident that neither of you can spell 'commitment' but both of you can spell 'embarrass'?" he said. It has been my experience that when analytically inclined Easterners ask a question that begins "Is it really an accident . . ." the answer is always yes. I wanted to write Alice to describe the psychological analysis of our spelling problem, but, as it happens, the one word she can spell and I can't is "cockamamie."

Converts to the new politics of lowered expectations have told me that I should simply accept Alice's spelling limitations and comfort myself with thoughts of the many splendid qualities she does have—the way Americans are now supposed to settle for only two gigantic automobiles, reminding themselves that some people in Chad have none at all. I have tried that. I have reminded myself that Alice can explain foreign movies and decipher road maps. I suspect that in a pinch she might be able to rewire a lamp. But, having come of drinking age in the 1950s, I may be culturally immune to the politics of lowered expectations. I can't get over the suspicion that a politician who preaches that doctrine is really arguing that we ought to settle for him. I still find myself thinking back on the old-fashioned scenes I had envisioned for our marriage: We are sitting peacefully in the parlor—after having kissed the little ones goodnight—and I glance up from the desk, where I have been polishing off a letter to the *Times* on our policy in the Far East, and say, "Alice, how do you spell 'referred'?" Alice tells me. Or, on another evening, Alice looks over from her side of the desk (in this version of our marriage, the custodian of an abandoned courthouse in Pennsylvania had sold us an 18th-century double-desk for $85 including delivery to New York in his brother's pickup), where she has been composing a letter to her parents saying how sublimely happy she is. She asks me how to spell "embarrass." I tell her.

Suggestions for Discussion

1. What is the source of Trillin's humor? What does the spelling of *occurred* or *embarrass* have to do with this description of a marriage?

2. Relate the title to the theme of this sketch.

3. Are the author and Alice compatible? How do you know?

4. How serious is Trillin about his immunity to "the politics of lowered expectations"?

Suggestions for Writing

1. Discuss the values of, and obstacles to, marriage contracts or write a marriage contract which reflects your feelings about a satisfying relationship.

2. Discuss your diminished expectations in a relationship.

3. What is the meaning and significance of commitment in a relationship?

 ◇◇◇◇

Carolyn Heilbrun
Androgyny

Carolyn Heilbrun is a professor of English literature at Columbia University. She has published *Toward a Recognition of Androgyny* (1973), from which the following selection is taken; a number of articles and reviews; a history of the Garnetts (a literary family); and a study of Christopher Isherwood. Androgyny defines a condition in which there are no assigned roles for men and women but rather a full range of experience open to both sexes.

"When a subject is highly controversial," Virginia Woolf observed to an audience forty-five years ago, "and any question about sex is that, one cannot hope to tell the truth. One can only show how one came to hold whatever opinion one does hold." My opinion is easily enough expressed: I believe that our future salvation lies in a movement away from sexual polarization and the prison of gender toward a world in which individual roles and the modes of personal behavior can be freely chosen. The ideal toward which I believe we should move is best described by the term "androgyny." This ancient Greek word—from *andro* (male) and *gyn* (female)—defines a condition under which the characteristics of the sexes, and the human impulses expressed by men and women, are not rigidly assigned. Androgyny seeks to liberate the individual from the confines of the appropriate.

There will always be those to whom a clear demarcation between proper behavior for one sex and the other will seem fundamental, as though it had been laid down at the creation. Probably both the traditionalist and the revolutionary are to some extent deluded in this, as in other matters. Thinking about profound social change, conservatives always expect disaster, while revolutionaries confidently anticipate utopia. Both are wrong. But in the end, I am convinced, the future lies with those who believe salvation likelier to spring from the imagination of possibility than from the delineation of the historical.

Yet recognition, not revolution, is the object of this essay. My method is to use the vast world of myth and literature as a universe in which to seek out the sometimes obscure signs of androgyny. My hope is that the occasional interpretation I bring to the literature of the past will suggest new ways of responding to the circumstances of our own lives and the literature of our own times. Once the name of androgyny has been spoken and some of its past appearances identified, the reader to whom the idea is not viscerally unbearable will begin to see this largely undefined phenomenon in many places. The idea of androgyny, at first startling, rapidly becomes less so. If this essay succeeds in its purpose, the reader returning to it later will be struck by the familiarity and simplicity of its central idea. . . .

Androgyny suggests a spirit of reconciliation between the sexes; it suggests, further, a full range of experience open to individuals who may, as women, be aggressive, as men, tender; it suggests a spectrum upon which human beings choose their places without regard to propriety or custom. The unbounded and hence fundamentally indefinable nature of androgyny is best evoked by borrowing a description of Dionysus from the critic Thomas Rosenmeyer's discussion of the *Bacchae* of Euripides: "Dionysus, who is Euripides' embodiment of universal vitality, is described variously by chorus, herdsman, commoners, and princes. The descriptions do not tally, for the god cannot be defined. He can perhaps be totaled but the sum is never definitive; further inspection adds new features to the old. If a definition is at all possible it is a definition by negation or cancelation. For one thing, Dionysus appears to be neither woman nor man; or, better, he presents himself as woman-in-man, or man-in-woman, the unlimited personality. . . . In the person of the god strength mingles with softness, majestic terror with coquettish glances. To follow him or to comprehend him we must ourselves give up our precariously controlled, socially desirable sexual limitations." A better description of the difficulties of defining androgyny could not be hoped for, although we have perhaps reached the stage where the social desirability of sexual limitations is in question. Such, at least, is my hope.

Unfortunately, it is easier to know what we fear from androgyny than what we may hope from it. The question of who will go through doorways first, or who will care for young children, is immediate and practical; the rewards to men from sharing their professional haunts with highly trained women are at best unclear. Change which threatens our established institutions and habits threatens our individual security, regardless of whether those institutions serve us individually well or ill. When Simone de Beauvoir remarked that men have found in women more complicity than the oppressor usually finds in the oppressed, she expressed an understanding of this fear of lost security, palpable to women as to men.

Androgyny appears to threaten men and women even more profoundly in their sexual than in their social roles. There has been a fear, not only of homosexuality or the appearance of homosexuality, but of impotence and frigidity as the consequence of less rigid patterns of sexual behavior. That we already have more than enough impotence and frigidity is apparently blamed more comfortably on the changing of roles than on strict adherence to them. If the man does not pursue, assuming aggressive attitudes, if the woman does not limit her response to consent or refusal, assuming passive attitudes, may we not lose altogether our skill at sexual performance? Women, terrified of "unmanning" men or making themselves less "feminine" and compliant, have failed to explore with men the possibilities inherent in heterosexual love freed from ritualized attitudes. Yet the complicity of women and the insistence of men on maintaining the old sexual order is daily less to be relied on. More and more women, many men, are coming to realize that the delight inherent in male-female relationships, whether in conversation or passion, is capable only of enhancement as the androgynous ideal is approached.

Those youths so often seen almost anywhere in the world today—their long hair and costumes making uneasy, in both senses of the word, the immediate identification of gender—suggest a new homage to androgyny. Indeed, the androgynous ideal is gaining acceptance faster than I had dared hope when I began this book. Then the danger I felt in suggesting so startling an idea was palpable. In the first introduction that I wrote my remarks were hedged about with protestations, defenses, caveats, for I much feared that I would be misunderstood. But ideas move rapidly when their time comes. Today one may speak of androgyny without assuming a defensive tone. One danger perhaps remains: that androgyny, an ideal, might be confused with hermaphroditism, an anomalous physical condition.

Homosexuality and bisexuality have seemed to occur very often in those societies and among those artists who have produced androgynous works. Readers of my own generation may find themselves at first uncomfortable, as I did, in the recognition of widespread homosexuality. Yet I have come to realize that today's youth are less threatened than were we by this subject and, in all likelihood, future generations will be still less concerned.

I made, in this connection, an interesting discovery when I returned in the *Symposium* to Plato's actual story of the circular beings who existed before the split of humans into male and female halves. As Aristophanes, the character in the *Symposium* who presents this myth of sexuality tells the tale; there were originally three wholes: all male, all female, male and female; each person seeking his other, original half might be in search with equal likelihood for someone of the same or of the other sex. I did one of those instant surveys among my friends and acquaintances which are the delight of the pedagogical profession, to discover that I was not alone in having blocked out the homosexual wholes of Plato's parable. Perhaps we all need to be reminded of the necessity of remaining open to new, or newly recovered, ways of being.

In a certain sense this book* is a tribute to the persistence of Victorianism. Most of us nowadays regard the Victorian age as part of the very remote past. Its major ideas, no longer thought to be the imprisoning conventions of our youth, are now consigned to the museum of antique beliefs, where we study them with a certain condescension and amusement. How quaint and implausible they were; how remote their power now seems. Or so we believe. Yet in the matter of sexual polarization and the rejection of androgyny we still accept the convictions of Victorianism; we view everything, from our study of animal habits to our reading of literature, through the paternalistic eyes of the Victorian era.

Masculine domination of life accompanied by extreme sexual polarization was not, of course, unique to the nineteenth century. Patriarchy reached its apotheosis in the years of Victoria's reign, but it is a habit thousands of years old, its roots deep in the Judaeo-Christian tradition. Whether or not patriarchy arose as a reaction to matriarchy is not readily established, and has not easily been accepted at any time by those considered the proper authorities. The opinions of J. J. Bachofen, for example, the chief expounder in the nineteenth century of the belief in an early matriarchy, are not now in academic fashion. For any purposes, however, the verification of theories of prehistoric matriarchy, even were that possible, is not important. Nor is it particularly important to decide whether the male principle at one time ruled the world well. Indeed, one might sensibly argue that the patriarchy, whether or not it supplanted a matriarchy, was necessary to human development and has brought many blessings. Yet I believe that it has also brought many curses to our almost dying earth. What is important now is that we free ourselves from the prison of gender and, before it is too late, deliver the world from the almost exclusive control of the masculine impulse.

If we are still, in our definition of sexual roles, the heirs of the Victorian

*This essay is an introduction to a book of critical pieces on Victorian writers.

age, we must also recognize that our definitions of the terms "masculine" and "feminine" are themselves little more than unexamined, received ideas. According to the conventional view, "masculine" equals forceful, competent, competitive, controlling, vigorous, unsentimental, and occasionally violent; "feminine" equals tender, genteel, intuitive rather than rational, passive, unaggressive, readily given to submission. The "masculine" individual is popularly seen as a maker, the "feminine" as a nourisher. Qualities which the Victorians considered admirable in men they thought perverted in women, an attitude which Freud did much to sanctify. The confident assurance that directing traffic or driving trucks somehow disqualifies women for their "feminine" roles, that the care of young children or the working of crewels disqualifies men for their masculine roles, is indicative of the rigidity with which human beings have been divided, not by talent, inclination, or attribute, but by gender. Recently, for example, *The New York Times* related the story of a young girl who, for lack of enough good boy players, had been drafted onto a Little League baseball team. The ensuing ruckus might have been justified had someone been caught practicing medicine without training or license, though the response where this does happen is less hysterical. The girl was thrown off the team together with the manager who had been unpolitical enough to let her play. There followed long discussions about the weakness and physical vulnerability of girls, the wisdom of their partaking in sports, and so forth. But the obvious points were nowhere mentioned: she had qualified for the team by being able to play better than any available boy, and whatever physical disabilities her sex may be thought to have endowed her with, so wide is the extent of individual variation that she was clearly better able to cope with the rigors of competitive contact sports than many boys. What she had outraged were preconceived ideas of the "feminine" role and the "masculine" rights to certain activities. If in fact a graph showing the frequency distribution of athletic ability in girls is superimposed upon one for boys, the upper end of the graph, signifying highest ability, will perhaps be all male, the lower end perhaps all female, but a wide intermediate range will comprise both sexes. This pattern (or its reverse, with females at the upper end) recurs for almost every human attribute that is thought to be associated with sex, apart from primary sex characteristics.

Yet so wedded are we to the conventional definitions of "masculine" and "feminine" that it is impossible to write about androgyny without using these terms in their accepted, received sense. I have done so throughout this essay, and have placed the terms in quotation marks to make my usage clear. What is more, the term "masculine" is often used pejoratively in what follows. My reason for so using it must be carefully explained.

Because "masculine" traits are now and have for so many years been the dominant ones, we have ample evidence of the danger the free play of such traits brings in its wake. By developing in men the ideal "masculine" characteristics of competitiveness, aggressiveness, and defensiveness, and by placing in power those men who most embody these traits, we have, I believe, gravely endangered our own survival. Unless we can effectively check the power of manly men and the women who willingly support them, we will experience new Vietnams, My Lais, Kent States. Even the animal world is now threatened by the aggression of man, the hunter. So long as we continue to believe the "feminine" qualities of gentleness, lovingness, and the counting of cost in human rather than national or property terms are out of place among rulers, we can look forward to continued self-brutalization and perhaps even to self-destruction.

In appearing to exalt feminine traits, I mean to suggest that these, since they have been so drastically undervalued, must now gain respect, so that a sort of balance is achieved among those in power, and within individuals. Obviously, not all women embody "feminine" characteristics: the parent who said that the National Guard at Kent State should have shot all the students was a mother. Such women are described by Simone de Beauvoir as "the poetesses of the bourgeoisie since they represent the most conservative element in this threatened class. . . . they orchestrate the grand mystification intended to persuade women to 'stay womanly.' " But for the most part, and especially for literary artists, the "feminine" impulses are most frequently embodied in women. The cry within literary works for more balanced human experience, from *The Trojan Women* to *Saint Joan*, has largely been the cry of women.

If the argument on behalf of androgyny sounds, more often than not, like a feminist or "women's lib" cry, that is because of the power men now hold, and because of the political weakness of women. If "feminine" resounds throughout this essay with the echoes of lost virtue, while "masculine" thuds with the accusation of misused power, this is a reflection on our current values, not on the intrinsic virtues of either "masculine" or "feminine" impulses. Humanity requires both.

So typical a Victorian as Leslie Stephen may, in his opinions on androgyny, be seen as equally typical of our own day. Creator of the *Dictionary of National Biography* and father, in a certain sense, of the Bloomsbury group, Leslie Stephen found the condition of androgyny to be evil. He used the words "masculine" and "manly" to indicate the highest praise; for purposes of denigration, "effeminate" and "morbid" were synonymous. His biographer Noel Annan summed up Stephen's views on the sexes in the statement that "men must be manly and women womanly; and the slightest androgynous taint must be condemned."

Yet the androgynous ideal, as Norman O. Brown has shown, persists in all the dreams of mysticism even through the nineteenth century:

> In the West, cabalistic mysticism has interpreted Genesis 1:27—"God created man in his own image . . . male and female created he them"—as implying the androgynous nature of God and of human perfection before the Fall. From cabalism this notion passed into the Christian mysticism of Boehme, where it is fused with the Pauline mysticism of Galatians 3:28—"There can be no male and female; for ye are all one man in Christ Jesus." In neglecting Boehme, or this side of Boehme, later Protestantism only keeps its head in the sand; for, as Berdyaev writes: "The great anthropological myth which alone can be the basis of an anthropological metaphysic is the myth about the androgyne. . . . According to his Idea, to God's conception of him, man is a complete, masculinely feminine being, solar and telluric, logoic and cosmic at the same time. . . . Original sin is connected in the first instance with division into two sexes and the Fall of the androgyne, i.e., of man as a complete being."

In the East, Taoist mysticism, as Needham shows, seeks to recover the androgynous self: one of the famous texts of the Tao Te Ching says:

> He who knows the male, yet cleaves to what is female,
> Becomes like a ravine, receiving all things under heaven.

[Thence] the eternal virtue never leaks away.
This is returning to the state of infancy.

And since poetry, as well as psychoanalysis, is the modern heir of the mystical tradition, the hermaphroditic ideal is central, for example, in the message of Rilke. In *Letters to a Young Poet* he writes: "And perhaps the sexes are more related than we think, and the great renewal of the world will perhaps consist in this, that man and maid, freed from all false feeling and aversion, will seek each other not as opposites, but as brother and sister, as neighbors, and will come together as *human beings.*" But deeper than the problem of the relation between the sexes is the problem of the reunification of the sexes in the self. In Rilke as artist, according to his friend Lou Andreas Salome, "both sexes unite into an entity." And Rilke, in his call to God to perfect him as an artist, calls on God to make him a hermaphrodite.

What poets understood, psychologists discovered. Donald W. MacKinnon, director of the Institute of Personality Assessment and Research at the University of California in Berkeley, wrote in 1962: "[Openness to experience] may be observed, for example, in the realm of sexual identifications and interests, where creative males give more expression to the feminine side of their nature than do less creative men. On a number of tests of masculinity-femininity, creative men score relatively high on femininity, and this despite the fact that, as a group, they do not present an effeminate appearance or give evidence of increased homosexual interests or experiences. Their elevated scores on femininity indicate rather an openness to their feelings and emotions, a sensitive intellect and understanding self-awareness and wide ranging interests including many which in the American culture are thought of as more feminine, and these traits are observed and confirmed by other techniques of assessment. If one were to use the language of the Swiss psychiatrist C. G. Jung, it might be said that creative persons are not so completely identified with their masculine *persona* roles as to blind themselves to or deny expression to the more feminine traits of the *anima.*"

Joseph Campbell in *The Masks of God*, his comprehensive and incisive account of world mythology, tells us that the patriarchal, anti-androgynous view is distinguished "by its setting apart of all pairs of opposites—male and female, life and death, true and false, good and evil." Though Campbell identifies the androgynous ideal as the "archaic view," which predated the patriarchal, we must not therefore suppose that his ideal is to be encountered only "in the dark backward and abysm of time. . . ."

Suggestions for Discussion

1. To what extent is androgyny, as defined by Heilbrun, a liberating mode of personal behavior? To what extent do you feel that human impulses expressed by men and women are rigidly assigned?

2. How valid is the concern that androgyny is a threat to the sexual roles of men and women?

3. How valid is the author's view that the androgynous ideal is rapidly gaining acceptance? If true, to what do you attribute such a shift in attitude?

4. Defend or challenge the author's statement that we ought to free ourselves from the "prison of gender" and, before it is too late, deliver the world from the almost exclusive control of the masculine impulse.

5. In what sense do the author's views transcend the personal and embrace political and societal concerns?

Suggestions for Writing

1. Discuss your sense of the possibilities inherent in heterosexual love freed from ritualized attitudes.

2. Write on any of the above questions for discussion.

3. Discuss the author's statement: "deeper than the problem of the relation between the sexes is the problem of the reunification of the sexes in the self."

4. Write on one of the following topics: the prison of gender; sexual polarization; a spirit of reconciliation between the sexes; the unlimited personality; the imprisoning conventions of youth; the patriarchy as a bringer of blessings or of curses.

Betty Friedan

Why Feminism Must Keep Moving

Betty Friedan (b. 1921) graduated from Smith College and has studied at the University of Colorado, Berkeley, and the University of Iowa. She has served as a consultant to the President's Commission on the Status of Women 1964–1965 and the Rockefeller Foundation Project on the education of women, and has been a visiting professor at Temple University, Yale University, and Queens College of the City University of New York. She is a member of the National Organization for Women and its founding president. She has written the *Feminine Mystique* (1963, revised 1974), *It Changed My Life* (1966), and *The Second Stage* (1981). She has contributed articles to *Saturday Review, The New York Times Magazine, Harper's, New York, Newsday,* and other periodicals. Although the author (in an article published in 1983) believes we have broken through "rigidly polarized male and female sex roles," she feels there are a number of significant questions that must be resolved in the women's movement.

It's been 20 years since "The Feminine Mystique" was published. I keep being surprised as the changes the women's movement set in motion continue to play themselves out in our lives: firewomen, chairpersons, housespouses, the gender gap, Ms, palimony, takeout food, women priests, women rabbis, women prime ministers, women's studies, women's history, double burden, dress for success, assertiveness training, male consciousness raising, role strain, role reversal, networking, sexism, displaced homemakers, equal pay for work of comparable value, marriage contracts, child custody for men, first babies at 40, the twopaycheck family, the single-parent family, "Victor/Victoria," "Tootsie". . . Who could have predicted some of these changes? Not I, certainly.

Early this year, I fled to Harvard as a fellow at the Institute of Politics of the Kennedy School of Government, disheartened, less by the attacks of our acknowledged enemies than by the fury of some of my sister feminists over the position I took in my book, "The Second Stage."

I said the women's movement had to move anew, that the feminine mystique, which defined women only as husband's wife, children's mother, server of the family's physical needs, and never as person, had been transcended. I said that we had come about as far as we could with the male model of equity and that now we needed a model encompassing female experience and female values, which men are beginning to share. Some didn't like my saying that.

Well, we are in the second stage now, whether or not anyone wants to admit it. And I am still a feminist. But I am sick and tired of the new spate of pronouncements claiming that the women's movement is finished and the revolution is lost because the "postfeminist generation" is moving from a different place.

Of course the postfeminist generation is in a different place. This new generation simply takes the personhood of women for granted. If they take women's rights and the opportunities we fought for too much for granted, it's a mark of how far our revolution has come.

Emily, my own daughter the doctor, went from taking it all for granted in college ("I'm not a feminist; I'm a person. It's not necessary to fight for women anymore.") to fervent feminism after one year in medical school ("There are so many of us now, they don't dare do it openly the way they used to. It's worse now that it's so subtle."). But it's not worse that women are 30 percent of the medical school class, rather than 3 percent.

After organizing the women in her medical school on the unfinished business of sex discrimination, my daughter began to concern herself with fundamental issues as to the practice of medicine itself and her own life. She has decided to go into family practice, dealing with the patient as a whole person.

My daughter-in-law Helen is, at the moment, a housewife. The baby was not exactly planned. There were difficult choices to be made, since both she and Jonathan, my younger son, had just finished college, after having dropped out for some years.

I relish their mutual joy, their new confident maturity and sense of themselves in their chosen parenthood — which Jonathan truly shares. Watching him skillfully maneuver Rafael into his snowsuit and throw him over his shoulder into the backpack, I sense he gets at least as much of his male identity from being a father as from being an engineer.

But Helen is unmistakably the mother. She does not let any male doctor-as-God tell her what to do with her baby. She does not apologize for sometimes being "bored out of my gourd" in this "hiatus" during which she concentrates on mothering. The choices in themselves seem to create a new sense of values and of self.

This year, a number of my family of friends had their first babies at 35, at 40, some undergoing rather scary, unexpected complications. Other friends suddenly became obsessed, in their mid-40s, after 20 years of brilliant careers, with the wish to have a child.

But the power of this desire to have a child — when women no longer need to have a child to define themselves as women — seems to be as great as or even greater than ever. Choice has liberated an exultant mother; choice has also liberated women to be generative in other ways.

But there is unfinished business here for many women. Imaginative thinking should be done about maternity leave, paternity leave, time off for parents when their children are sick, parental sabbaticals, reduced schedules, flextime, job sharing, and child-care supports that don't now exist.

It is crucial for feminists to understand the power of the choice to have children and to keep fighting for the right to abortion. But they must give new priority to child-care and to restructuring work. If these issues are not addressed soon, we can fear a new feminine mystique invoked to send women home again to have babies instead of competing for jobs.

During this time of recession-depression, President Ronald Reagan, who has declared a new campaign against abortion, has also suggested that there wouldn't be as much unemployment if women would stop looking for jobs.

After the elections in 1982, political analysts finally began to take seriously the "gender gap," though it had been building for some years, a reaction, in part, to the administration's attitudes toward the Equal Rights Amendment and abortion. The latest Gallup poll found that just 36 percent of women approved of Reagan's job performance, compared with 47 percent of men.

I'm worried now about the new polarizations hinted at by recent polls, cutting across the gender gap, as sharp differences emerge between the married and the unmarried, those with children and with none, the young and the old, the ones with jobs and the unemployed.

The need, or the choice, to marry, or to remain married, takes on new existential and economic importance, for women as for men. For families in poverty today tend primarily to be those headed by women, followed by those headed by men where there is no second income. But the fact that women earn only 59 cents for every dollar men earn still cuts through the illusion of equality.

Will the married be the new elite and those living alone the underclass? Will men and women who make that cherished, costly choice to have children become the permanent second class, while the single-minded take power?

How can the trade-offs within marriage be measured? He makes more than she does, but he feels less strain now because he's no longer carrying it all. She feels bitter if he is laid off and she has to carry the whole breadwinning burden, as well as take care of the house and kids. He certainly doesn't spend as much time on housework and the kids as she does. But how much of that power does she really want to give up?

Now that we've broken through those rigidly polarized male and female sex roles, will we settle for a diversity of patterns of sharing among women and men?

My friends now in their 50s and 60s who fought the battles — the first woman to have a seat on the stock exchange; the first female network vice president; the first executive vice president of a major advertising agency; the nun who became a college president; the housewives who survived their own divorces and became labor arbitrators; the women, passed over for university tenure or union leadership, who brought and won class-action suits — are now facing the frontiers of age.

There are new questions to be asked beyond success, beyond marriage and divorce, as we face husbands' strokes and retirement, and our years to come, living alone. Those are the questions that are now my personal and professional concern.

Are men changing? Those young men, like my son, who carry their little babies so proudly in their backpacks to the supermarket? Those men now suffering the mid-life crises? Men must change. They must develop the flexibility and sensitivity to their own feelings and the feelings of others that have been considered up to now feminine characteristics.

Crazy? Well, who would have thought that the biggest movie hit of 1983 would be a picture called "Tootsie," in which a male actor impersonates a woman so he can get a part in a soap opera and becomes a better man as a woman? We have clearly broken through and beyond the masculine mystique for man and woman to find such hilarious, joyous adventure in being a woman. Which is not the same thing at all as going back to the feminine mystique. It is the next clue in the human mystery.

Suggestions for Discussion

1. What is the effect on tone and substance of the long series of phenomena which reflect changes in the women's movement?

2. How would you answer the questions posed by Friedan? What are the new questions that concern her?

3. What does the author regard as the "next clue in the human mystery"?

Suggestions for Writing

1. Select one of the series in the first paragraph for a fully developed essay.

2. Read Friedan's *The Second Stage* and write your evaluation of it.

3. Support or challenge Friedan's statement that "we've broken through those rigidly polarized male and female sex roles."

Benjamin R. Barber
Beyond the Feminist Mystique

Benjamin R. Barber (b. 1939) is a professor of political science at Rutgers University, editor of the quarterly *Political Theory*, and author of the forthcoming book *Strong Democracy*. Although this essay, published in *The New Republic* in 1983, constitutes a review of five new books by women, it also reflects the author's strong feelings about the women's movement.

Twenty years after the publication of Betty Friedan's *The Feminine Mystique*, radical feminism as a coherent and compelling political ideology is all but dead. As staunch a movement figure as Eleanor Smeal, past president of the National Organization for Women, has wondered aloud whether the term feminism is not inflammatory; perhaps it should be dropped, she has suggested, and concrete reforms emphasized instead. Women continue to confront the biases of the marketplace and the tension between work and family, but nevertheless conservative and even liberal women vote in large numbers against the constitutional instrument feminists have fashioned to liberate them. The feminine mystique is vanquished, but the feminism that did the deed is now itself denounced as a new and nefarious mystique—and not only by reactionary "total women" like Marabel Morgan and Phyllis Schlafly—but by Betty Friedan, the original oracle on mystiques.

How did feminism become a mystique? How has an ideology—and the ideology, not the movement, is my subject—which enjoyed such currency only a few years ago, been so quickly discredited? Why, as Susan Jacoby asked in a recent *New York Times* "Hers" column, are "too many women misconstruing feminism's nature"? False consciousness? Male backlash? Continued patriarchal socialization? None of these answers will do. Men are not that smart, women not that stupid; this is an age in which liberation rhetoric is in vogue, and ideologies of emancipation, even where they fail to win real power, are widely acknowledged as legitimate. The pendulum is indeed on a conservative swing, yet combatants in other struggles have not retreated the way radical feminists have, in disarray, confessing earnest apostasies as they go.

Feminism in what Friedan calls its "second stage" has about it a mood of recantation. In fact, dispassionate observers could see that something was amiss merely by looking at the titles and slogans that lept off the jackets of feminist books ten years ago: Jill Johnston's *Lesbian Nation*, which seemed to suggest that heterosexuality was the female form of treason; Germaine Greer's *The Female Eunuch*, which found an explanation for impotence in being female; Kate Millet's *Sexual Politics*, where the personal became the political and sex was redefined as purely a power relation; Kathrin Perutz's *Marriage is Hell*, which argued marriage was, and Ellen Peck's *The Baby Trap*, which revealed why. The slogans were extraordinary: marriage was hell, sex was political, coitus was killing, married women were prostitutes, babies were traps, intercourse was rape, love was slavery, families were prisons, and men were enemies. But the ideological premises to which the slogans pointed were even more extraordinary: sexual differentiation inevitably led to sexual inequality, reproductivity was a form of bondage, femininity was a rationalization of slavery, and the family was society's chief institution of oppression.

What these premises suggest is that when feminists called for androgyny—the eradication of sexual differences as the condition for political equality between the sexes—they were engaged not in caricature or polemics, but were merely extending the logic of the original attack on the feminine mystique. The feminine mystique had spawned the maternity mystique, the family mystique, the baby mystique, and the reproduction mystique, all of which needed equally to be demystified.

Despite its overt preoccupation with men, this logic ultimately identified the chief obstacle to women's liberation as women themselves: women as they conceived themselves in the false consciousness of their traditional roles and virtues. To be loving, nurturing, empathetic mothers; to be self-effacing, helpful wives; to be civilizing, domesticating, conserving homemakers—these were so many signs of weakness and inadequacy. Radical feminism was to be a revolution carried out in the name of Women against women. To abolish the hold of nature over women might mean to abolish woman's nature. In this climate of hostility to nature, to sexual differentiation, and to the forms of femininity, the new feminist mystique flourished.

The problem was not simply one of rhetorical extravagance. Every revolution required its polemics—oppressors are usually deaf to reasoned whispers. Even man-hating on the model of S.C.U.M. (Society for Cutting Up Men) had a political utility. The difficulty with the new mystique was not that it often challenged or detested men, but that it often challenged and detested women. Women with families, Juliet Mitchell announced in *Women's Estate*, were inclined to "small-mindedness, petty jealousy, irrational emotionality and random violence, dependency, competitive selfishness and possessiveness, passivity, a lack of vision and conservatism." This, we must remind ourselves, is a portrait drawn not by a misogynist but by a feminist. If women in families were despicable, the family itself was in Mitchell's description "by its very nature, there to prevent the future." Betty Friedan had herself denigrated housework as "tasks for feeble-minded girls and eight-year-olds," and likened the home to a "comfortable concentration camp."

The feminine mystique had celebrated the insufficiencies of being female as palpable strengths; the feminist mystique denigrated the strengths of being female as palpable insufficiencies. The problem with being a women was neither misogyny nor external oppression; it was simply *being a woman*. To liberate women could only be to extirpate the woman, leaving behind an androgynous shell of abstract personhood.

Under these circumstances, it is hardly surprising that at the very moment of radical feminism's media triumph, the forces of reaction were gathering. There were hoots of derision from misogynists, paeans to the mysteries of female sexuality from neoromantics like Norman Mailer, and dark warnings from neo-Victorians like George Gilder who announced that if women gave up their aprons, men would revert to barbarism.

But the crucial reaction came from women. And the voice of that protest was meant to address the struggle against women, not the struggle for liberation. With equality itself, there was no intrinsic quarrel—but at what cost?

Freedom was, in the abstract, an attractive goal—but achieved by what means? Women might wish to be free, but not of their womanhood. If accepting sisterhood meant abjuring womanhood—husbands, generativity, love, babies, nurturing—then they would do without sisters.

If the Phyllis Schlaflys and Marabel Morgans were feminine cartoons, their adversaries were feminist cartoons, and as between the two mystiques—if that was to be the choice—a great many women preferred the caricature of femininity. Besides, among the half-deceptions and exaggerations that critics of feminism like Schlafly deployed to distort the feminist position, there were half-truths to which some feminists refused to pay heed, much to their own peril. Abortion was not merely a matter of preference; life was in the scales on both sides, as only a flagrant narcissist could fail to see. Homemaking could be denigrated as an occupation only by belittling millions of women; and in attaching to it only a market value, feminists cheapened rather than enhanced the value many women believed it had. Marriage might produce new forms of bondage, but it also produced new forms of freedom, while the vaunted independence of the liberated and divorced often turned out to mean loneliness and penury. Children were demanding, but they were their own reward and often extended rather than narrowed the boundaries of a woman's life. And work, though it could bestow status in the marketplace, was—for all but the mobile upper-middle class—drudgery, and often narrowed rather than extended a woman's opportunities.

Over and over again, what women seemed to reject was not liberation but the price radical feminists insisted on attaching to it. The Equal Rights Amendment was not defeated by women who despised equality, but by women who liked women and liked being women. Not that the E.R.A. entailed androgyny. That was the pity. The E.R.A. was a relatively innocuous, wholly desirable application of traditional liberal principles to problems of gender discrimination, which, however, appeared to be advanced in the name of an ideology rooted in the feminist mystique. Women were in effect talked out of the amendment by its most vociferous advocates.

It is these disastrous consequences of the feminist mystique that have finally given pause to many feminists, who have recognized that an ideology that repels its own constituents is incoherent. Though not the first, Betty Friedan's recantation signaled the official demise of the feminist mystique she had helped create. Her change of heart, she admits, grew out of disappointment and fatigue: "I am tired of the pragmatic, earthbound battles of the woman's movement," she confesses in *The Second Stage*, "tired of the rhetoric. I want to live the rest of my lif. . . ." To do so, she continues, confession giving way to apostasy, "we must admit and begin openly to discuss feminist denial of the importance of the family, of women's own needs to give and get love and nurture, tenderloving care." *Ad feminem* critics of the movement once used to charge it with covering up internal "woman troubles"; Friedan is now admitting as much: "My own brave words in the early days of the women's movement hid a certain abject terror of making it on my own, in the last days of my self-destructive marriage."

About the same time Friedan's *The Second Stage* was published, another confession-cum-recantation appeared: *The Cinderella Complex*, by Colette Dowling. Dowling was everyone's—certainly her own—ideal of the new, emancipated everywoman, pursuing an independent career with the zeal of an acolyte. Then, to her horror, she fell in love and found herself collapsing back into grateful dependency, all too happy to be "rescued" from the world, all too ready to return to the nest she had just fled. When Dowling finally confronted her oppressor, it was herself she faced. As long as feminists failed to understand this, she concluded, they would struggle with the wrong enemies and win pyrrhic victories.

The queasiness about "freedom" had been around for a number of years before emancipated career women found themselves being distracted by biological time clocks and discovered that a baby or a man could set their personal quest for liberation back a decade overnight. "There is no more radical nor desperately nihilistic statement," Midge Decter had warned in *The New Chastity* (1972),

> to issue forth from the lips of humans than that there are no necessary differences between the sexes. For such differences both issue in' and do in themselves constitute the most fundamental principle of the continuation of life on earth.

It took nine years for Betty Friedan to give a liberal rendering to Decter's neoconservative warning. In *The Second Stage*, she can finally acknowledge that "to deny the part of one's being that has, through the ages, been expressed in motherhood—nurturing loving softness, and tiger strength—is to deny part of one's personhood as a woman." But Friedan seems unaware of how much she is granting. "Nurturing loving softness" is a phrase drawn from the lexicon of the feminine mystique Friedan had set out to discredit twenty years earlier. And personhood is a denial of the concrete specificity of womanhood: the person is a legal abstraction defined by formal rights and is precisely not a woman or a man, a Christian or a Jew, a black or a Caucasian. It is just this dilemma that makes woman's liberation so much more problematic that proponents of either the feminine or the feminist mystique have been willing to allow.

Revisionist feminism is thus feminism in disarray. Dowling's book outraged feminists without pleasing conservatives. The work of another ambivalent feminist, Jean Bethke Elshtain, has drawn much the same ambivalent response. In a provocative essay in the fall 1982 issue of *Dissent* called "Feminism, Family, and Community," Elshtain argued for the importance of traditional familial ties and communal virtues without abjuring her feminism. The *Dissent* piece drew heavy fire, however: first from Barbara Ehrenreich, who in the winter issue defended feminism against second stage revisionism: and then from Marshall Berman, who in the spring issue defended democratic socialism against what he saw as Elshtain's neoauthoritarianism. Yet Elshtain insists in her replies that she remains on the left, and wishes only to argue that "certain radicals and feminists, on certain issues, have lost touch with some of the deepest aspirations among their own (putative) constituencies," and that "the animating ethos of women's familial and communal identities may serve as the nucleus of an alternative to atomistic and technocratic politics."

This is more than the internecine bickering of ideological purists. It issues out of a basic disenchantment—a revisionism that is ready to rewrite the history of the past without yet being ready to revise its blueprint for the future. Barbara Ehrenreich, who is a loyal and unswerving feminist in the face of

Elshtain's revisionism, nonetheless perpetrates an even more startling revisionism of her own in her book, *The Hearts of Men: American Dreams and the Flight From Commitment.* In her fresh if highly selective rewriting of American social history since World War II, Ehrenreich argues that well before the feminist revolt, men were being led into rebellion against their traditional male roles as breadwinners and mortgageholders by a most unlikely configuration of social movements. These included Hugh Hefner's *Playboy* philosophy (the magazine made its debut in 1953), which urged men to prefer an irresponsible bachelorhood where women figured only as particularly delectable consumables, to the responsibilities of marriage and the family; the medical discovery of stress as a major factor in heart disease for the hardworking overachievers who, it now turned out, were literally risking their lives to keep "spoiled" wives and children in the suburban comfort to which they had become accustomed; and finally the Beat Generation, which in its apotheosizing of irresponsibility, sexual promiscuity, male bonding, and "on the road" mobility, had redefined marriage as bondage and achievers as squares.

These three strains of postwar irresponsibility, Ehrenreich argues, infected the newly fashioned suburban family and undermined its foundations in the social culture well before Friedan got around to calling it a comfortable concentration camp.

> The promise of feminism—that there might be a future in which no adult person was either a "dependent creature" or an overburdened breadwinner—came at a time when the ideological supports for male conformity were already crumbling. Physicians had found men the weaker sex; psychologists were finding them perilously "rigid." The War [in Vietnam] reinforced the medical dictum that male aggressiveness was a lethal force; and the counterculture reinforced the promise, from the new psychology, of a richer life for those who could overcome their masculine hang-up.

This is fascinating if debatable social history. Skeptics will point out that Ehrenreich picks and chooses among a plethora of possible sources, and that her actual themes come from the fringe rather than the heart of the 1950s social environment. A quite different moral emerges if one looks not at *Playboy,* cardiological stress, and the Beats (lesson: men were being tempted to abandon the family long before women were being tempted by feminism to imitate them), but at *The Saturday Evening Post,* Salk's polio vaccine, and the growth of television (lesson: marriage was great, kids were getting healthier, and everyone was staying home more—i.e., the family was flourishing as never before), or at *The Bulletin of Atomic Scientists,* the elevation of cancer into a number-one killer, and serial music (lesson: anxiety and alienation were undermining individuals and families).

There are as many lessons to be drawn from social history as there are permutations and combinations of social movements, subgroups, trends, fashions, novelties, and revolutions. To be sure, men were anxious about stress, but they also worried about communism *and* McCarthy, cancer and the Bomb, and on the whole they mostly stayed on the corporate ladder and limited their rebellion to Sunday football on television or chronic insomnia. Men were doubtless resentful of the pressures associated with playing breadwinner, but they did not dream of permitting their wives to work or otherwise share their "man-size" burdens. They were fascinated by the Beats and titillated by the *Playboy* life style, but wore button-down shirts and chinos and restricted their yen for bunnies to Easter with the kids.

Nonetheless, for the purposes of this discussion, what is interesting is not Ehrenreich's selective reading of social history but the conclusions she draws from it—or, rather, fails to draw from it. Are her 1950s dropouts heroes to be welcomed as allies in the feminist struggle against the constraints of the bourgeois family? Or cowards and narcissists to be despised for their immaturity, their materialism, and their mistrust of women? Does portraying Hugh Hefner as a weird predecessor of Betty Friedan exonerate him of sexism or indict her of narcissism? If Jack Kerouac is a harbinger of liberation, then are not feminists so many latter-day hippies in search of missing selves and in flight from the responsibilities of maturity? Ehrenreich does not and apparently cannot answer these questions. She notes that the male revolt of the 1950s was "a blow against the system of social control," which flatters her socialist instincts, but she also recognized that it was self-indulgent, materialistic, and woman-hating, which offends her feminist instincts.

In the end, Ehrenreich can neither avoid nor resolve the central dilemma of feminism: how to be free without mimicking men—how to nurture femininity without relinquishing equality. Those like Elshtain and Friedan who remind women of the joys and responsibilities of loving and generativity (the new acceptable term for "reproductivity"), end up being viewed as traitors using liberal credentials to make arguments no less reactionary than those of a Midge Decter or a Rita Kramer. (Kramer's new book *In Defense of the Family,* [see "What Are Families Really For?" by Peter Steinfels and Margaret O'Brien Steinfel, TNR, May 16], is a neoconservative attack on feminism that does simply celebrate the traditional woman and the traditional family.)

From the point of view of practical politics, feminism's second stage is thus an unmitigated disaster. Its honorable ambivalence, if it does not actually encourage backlash, can produce political paralysis. Its welcome confusions yield factionalism, recantation, and apostasy. Dilemmas and conundrums may occasion great literature and subtle theory, but they do little to rid the world of gender discrimination and sexual inequality.

Happily, there are signs that feminism may be moving into a third stage that rejects both androgyny and inequality, both sexlessness and sexism. The strength of the third stage derives from its return to the tradition of political philosophy within which the problems of gender, reproduction, and the family were given their first and richest conceptualization by philosophers from Plato and Aristotle to Rousseau and Mill. Susan Okin's excellent survey *Women in Western Political Thought* (see my review, TNR, March 1, 1980) was thus distinguished by its willingness to take seriously (though hardly to accept) classical formulations of the relationship between family and society that had been simply dismissed as ideologically noxious by revolutionary first stage feminists.

Third stage feminism is marked not by a concern with the history of ideas, however, but by a new willingness to engage in political theory on the model of the historical tradition. Two recent books, unremarkable and in certain ways even deficient, nonetheless signal a new assertiveness in feminist perspectives: Carol Gilligan's *In a Different Voice,* and Carol McMillan's *Women, Reason and Nature.* Not all feminists will like Gilligan and McMillan, because both are unrelenting in their criticism of the feminist mystique and what they take to be its surrender to masculine paradigms. But their intention is to show that crucial terms in political and moral discourse have been effectively preempted by men to ensure that putatively generic and gender-blind concepts will in fact be patterned on male models.

Gilligan argues that moral development theorists from Freud and Piaget to Erickson and Kohlberg have equated typically male forms of maturation with generic *human* maturity, and labeled female forms of development as early, truncated stages of their male counterparts—that is to say, as atrophied and defined by immaturity. McMillan likewise suggests that the paradigms of reason have traditionally been defined by masculine modes of abstract cognition and analytic logic, thereby leaving women to associate their rather different thought processes with intuition or instinct or other modes of irrationality. In short, if to be grown up is to be a man, then to be a woman is necessarily to be a child; if to be rational is to think like a man, then to think like a woman is to be irrational.

To simplify, feminism in its first stage responded to this domination by male archetypes by in effect demanding that women think like, mature like, and be like men—by insisting that women could do what men do and be what men are. Second stage feminism reacted by accepting the distinctions imposed by the male models, but by saying it's all right to think like a woman; irrationality has its virtues; the male mode of development has its costs.

New feminists like Gilligan and McMillan accept the validity of differences, but insist on the need to reformulate the very categories by which differences are identified and accounted for. Thus, rather than simply acknowledging that women are irrational and demonstrating that irrationality has its uses, McMillan assails an exclusively male analytic-abstract conception of reason. "Emotion has its cognitive and rational aspects," she writes, "and 'feminine' activities are subject to criticism and appraisal no less than masculine ones." Gilligan is equally anxious to expose the conceptual biases built into the literature of moral development, and to suggest that there are female forms of moral development and moral judgment different from but equal in philosophical merit and moral status to the male forms.

This style of argument, which is patently radical, indisputably feminist, yet completely at odds with the feminist mystique, finds an ample resonance in second stage feminism. For example, Betty Friedan is much impressed by a 1980 project of the Stanford Research Institute that distinguished male and female forms of leadership—the male or "Alpha" form being characterized by "analytic, rational, quantitative thinking . . . hierarchical relationships of authority . . . deterministic engineered solutions to specific problems . . . ," the female or "Beta" form being characterized by "synthesizing, intuitive, qualitative thinking . . . a contextual, relational power style . . . tuned to more complex, more open, and less defined aspects of reality." But what are merely intriguing clues in Friedan become careful yet aggressive arguments in Gilligan and McMillan.

Gilligan not only suggests that there are female forms of moral judgment of a very high order to be found in what male standards deprecate as other-directed or dependency-inspired or wishy-washy female responses to moral questions; she also asserts that the "reluctance to judge" which men interpret as moral immaturity evinces a feminine "reluctance to hurt" and a concern for mutually satisfying solutions suggestive of a fully developed and "mature moral understanding." As Gilligan writes:

> The blind willingess to sacrifice people to truth [typical of male moral judgment] . . . has always been the danger of an ethics abstracted from life. This willingness links Gandhi to the biblical Abraham, who prepared to sacrifice the life of his son in order to demonstrate the integrity and supremacy of his faith. Both men, in the limitations of their fatherhood, stand in implicit contrast to the woman who comes before Solomon and verifies her motherhood by relinquishing truth in order to save the life of her child.

Men are inclined to idealize autonomy in their moral systems while condemning the female sensitivity to interdependency as heteronomy. Yet women, as Gilligan perceives, "portray autonomy rather than attachment as the illusory and dangerous quest," and so attempt constantly to reformulate moral dilemmas posed in the formal language of either/or truth, in the concrete relational terms of a web of affection and responsibility. One can wish Gilligan paid more attention to traditional distinctions in "male" ethics (the traditional contrast between intentionalist and consequentialist ethics is pertinent to her discussion) and that she was more willing than she is to examine the moral limitations of what used to be called situational ethics. Nevertheless, by teasing out of preponderantly female kinds of judgment (which she extrapolates from actual female responses to moral questions) a mode of moral reasoning that is clearly ethical yet quite unlike the standard models, Gilligan goes a long way toward "restoring the missing text of women's development" and thereby enlarging "developmental understanding by including the perspective of both sexes." In learning to listen to the different voice she lets us hear, we come to understand "why a morality of rights and noninterference may appear frightening to women in its potential justification of indifference"; just as we can see why "from a male perspective, a morality of responsibility" may appear "inconclusive and diffuse, given its insistent contextual relativism."

Carol McMillan does for reason what Carol Gilligan does for moral judgment:

> . . . even if the contention that women are emotional or more susceptible to compassion than men is actually true, it does not prove that they do not reason but live on an animal-like level of subjective intuitions. And the corollary to this is that the desire to make loving kindness a cardinal virtue of morality, as Schopenhauer wishes to, need not mean that one is asking for a return to savagery. What it does mean is that the rationalist attempt to construe morality as a peculiarly masculine achievement, as one that depends upon the subject-object dyad and on the suppression of feelings, is tantamount to the assertion that what we normally call goodness is something of which men must be logically incapable.

Feminism in its third stage would seem to be pushing toward a full demystification of both the feminine and the feminist mystiques, in favor of a realistic appreciation of sexual differences, the constraints they place upon us, and the plural virtues they make possible. A catalogue of its striking new premises would include the following:

— Women and men are biologically distinct in a way which, although not strictly causal or deterministic, powerfully conditions moral development and

social institutions, and which cannot be theorized or wished away in the name
of an abstract androgyny.

— Sexual differences, neither wholly inevitable nor wholly eradicable, are
in themselves beneficent and life-enriching; liberation can be better won
through their cultivation than their negation.

— Androgyny is not only undesirable in its homogenous uniformity, but
also turns out to be a rationalization for dominant male paradigms disguised
as neutral or generic or human archetypes.

— The special relationship that femininity affords women to generativity,
nurturing, and affection endows them with a unique appreciation of (and responsibility for) the ethics of caring and of affiliation indispensable to the preservation of civilization. Far from oppressing them, these feminine traits are
what distinguish them and the species from animals and gives it its talent
(such as it is) for virtue.

— Given that sexual differences are valuable (rather than indelible), the
quest for justice in social relations cannot be a search for perfect symmetry.
Instead, ways must be found to preserve (or create) political and economic
equality in the face of differing social roles, distinctive gender needs, and
contrasting, if (ideally) complementary approaches to moral development and
reasoning.

These premises, startling by the measure of first-stage feminism, constitute
a fundamental rejection of single standard or unitarian perspectives on the
politics of sex. Third-stage feminism champions the double standard. For the
double standard is objectionable only when it is the concealed reality behind
a single standard hypocritically applied. What was wrong with "separate but
equal" was that separate was not and could not be equal in the context of
segregated education. The challenge of third-stage feminism is how to make
"different but equal" a reality, not because differences are ineluctable, but
because equality is valuable only where it encompasses rather than destroys
them.

Suggestions for Discussion

1. What evidence does Barber provide that some of the original tenets of feminist
   ideology are now discredited?

2. How is each of the three stages of feminism documented?

3. Although this essay constitutes a review of five new books, it is also a statement of
   point of view by Barber. Cite any evidence of bias in substance or tone. What is
   his central thesis? How does he support it?

4. Compare Barber's apparent view of androgyny with that of Carolyn Heilbrun.

5. According to the author what aspects of the feminist mystique led to the second
   stage of feminism?

6. What evidences of ambivalence does Barber find among the feminists who have
   revised their views?

7. What were Ehrenreich's explanations for the undermining of the suburban family?
   What alternatives are suggested by the author? What questions does he feel she
   fails to answer?

8. How do Gilligan and McMillan, as representatives of the third stage of feminism, expose conceptual biases in prevailing views of moral development?

9. In what sense does third stage feminism champion a double standard? How does Barber justify it?

Suggestions for Writing

1. Barber catalogues five new premises of feminism. Select one of them and support or challenge its validity.

2. Read and evaluate any one of the books mentioned in this essay.

3. Defend or challenge the author's view that the E.R.A. was defeated "by women who liked women and liked being women."

◇◇◇◇

Lillian Rubin

Love, Work, and Identity

Lillian B. Rubin (b.1924) is a social scientist who received her Ph.D. at the University of California at Berkeley. She is a practicing psychotherapist and Senior Research Associate at the Institute for the Study of Social Change at the University of California. Her books include *Busing and Backlash: White against White in an Urban School District, Life in the Working-class Family,* and *Women of a Certain Age: The Mid-life Search for Self.* The essay that follows, a chapter in her latest book, *Intimate Strangers* (1983), focuses on the serious problem that emerges because a man's sense of identity is almost invariably related to his work whereas a woman's is more complex, concerned with relationships even when work is important in her life.

> *Life is not a spectacle or a feast; it is a predicament.*
> —George Santayana

Love and work—these, said Sigmund Freud long ago, are the major arenas of adult life that require resolution if we are to live it satisfactorily. It's still true. Only the problems are different today than they were then, precisely because we are trying out new roles and new rules, because we no longer see these two parts of life as so distinctly separated, because work is no longer only the province of men, love only the domain of women.

"The best you can say about love and work is that they coexist," says a man. "Trying to make it all come together is hard as hell because you're always balancing things," complains his wife. "Competing urgencies," a friend once called them, as she tried to explain the inner sense of a woman who is worker, mother, wife.

"My best friend and I have this not so funny joke about keeping the home fires smoldering, not burning," wisecracks a woman. "There's never enough time for anything, least of all sex," her husband complains. "I know it's awful, but by nighttime I have no room left for one more demand on my person," explains his wife.

"Competing urgencies"—an evocative phrase whose meaning is immediately clear to all who live in families where the roles of women and men are no longer so firmly fixed. It's a struggle for both of them, but the "urgencies" are weighted differently for a woman and a man, therefore, the priorities are different for each of them as well—as these words, spoken by a forty-two-year-old college professor, show so clearly.

> I break my ass to spend more time with the kids these days, but it's a killer. Carole can step back the hours she puts in at work, but it's hard as hell for me to do that. I've worked damned hard to get where I am and I can't put it in jeopardy. I know I'm missing out with the kids; it's not just because she tells me, I *know* it. But that pull to my work . . . well, it's irresistible in a way. It's not the same for Carole, which makes me wonder sometimes if that's not just the way it is with men and women.

"But what would you be jeopardizing?" I asked. "You already have tenure and a rather impressive reputation in your field."

> Sure, sure. But you have to keep up if you want to stay up there; you can't live on past accomplishments. [Pausing to think for a while, then continuing more slowly] It's not just that old competitive stuff, that's not all. It's something about the work itself. [Throwing his hands up in a gesture of helplessness] I don't know; it's so much a part of me it feels like I'd have to violate my nature. [Laughing] You're the shrink; what do you think; genes or something?

It's a common story even among those men who now talk about wishing it were different, who now seem to understand the deprivation they have suffered in not being more actively involved in raising their children. And why is it that way? At the most manifest level, we see that, despite all the talk abroad about the importance of family life, despite national conferences on the future of the family, neither government nor industry makes any serious move toward the kinds of institutional changes in the work world that are necessary to permit men to take a more active role inside the family. Still, that's not enough to explain why so many men, who believe they want to, have such difficulty in moderating their commitment to work in favor of love.

Over the last several years, I have asked hundreds of people of all ages and from all walks of life to identify themselves for me, to answer the question "Who are you?" Almost invariably, a man will respond by saying what kind of work he does. "I'm a lawyer," "I'm a carpenter," "I'm a writer," "I'm a teacher," "I'm an electrician"—this is the first thing a man will say about himself. Having located himself in the world of work, having said who he is in the social world, he *may* then have something to say about himself in his private world. Only then, if at all, will he speak about being a husband, a father, a son, a lover. So pronounced is this tendency that, even where a husband and wife are actually sharing roles, it's almost always his work that he turns to first when offering a definition of himself.

It's just this that makes unemployment so difficult for a man—this sense that he has lost himself, that he can't say who he is. An unemployed factory worker said haltingly, "When you've got work, you know you're a somebody. It's been a long time since I had regular work, so . . . well, I don't know. I guess you forget who you are after a while, don't you?" And an architect, unable to find work in his chosen profession, replied to my question angrily, "I can't say I'm an architect because I haven't been 'architecting' for a long time. So what the hell am I?"

Both men are husbands, both are fathers. Because their wives work full time and they do not, both men are heavily involved in family-related activities—child care, cooking, cleaning, laundry, even taking the weekly turn at a child's nursery school. Yet not one of these activities is defining of self, not one really counts in the important task of placing oneself in the world, of being able to say confidently, "I am . . ."

For a woman, it's a different story. For her, even a deeply integrated professional commitment doesn't displace family concerns and relationships from the center of her life and thought. No matter what else she may be or do, she's also a wife and a mother—identities that are central to her definition of self, that she'll own as hers whether you meet her in the office, in the market, or in the kitchen. A working doctor answered my questions by saying, "That's easy! I'm a mother, a physician, and a wife—and I juggle all three all the time." And an unemployed lawyer had no trouble in drawing a word picture of herself: "I'm a wife and mother and a sometimes attorney."

We see it over and over again—the different balance between love and work making itself evident in both their private life and their public one, in how they define themselves and how they are given definition in the world outside the family.

Look, for example, at the jacket of a book written by a man. Almost never does it tell us anything about whether he is married, has children, or how many. And the occupation of his wife is surely of scant moment. Yet all those facts usually are part of the biography of a woman author. It seems to most of us like important information about a woman—enabling us to understand something about her as a person, telling us much about how she lives her life. But it's not so about a man. There, the assumption is that those facts of his life will explain little about who he is, how he lives, what engages him. There, we tend to assume we have as much knowledge of him as we need when we know what work he does and where he does it.

"Do we work to live or live to work?"—the question asked by the great German sociologist Max Weber still concerns us today. Love and work—a difficult balance for most of us, but a predictable one. Historically, men have fallen on one side of the scale, women on the other. If we think for a moment about the qualities inherent in the two, we can understand why. Work is rational and cognitive; love is emotional and experiential. Work is mastery, achievement, competition, separateness; love is sensory, feeling, sharing, union. In work, we manipulate the environment, seek to change one thing into another. A blank page becomes a printed one; a pile of wood and a sack of nails are fashioned into the framework for a house. In love, we're concerned with people not with things—with the inner life not with the outer one.

Put that way, it sounds as if we are not just discussing the ways in which love is separate from work, but the ways also in which women and men differ in their orientation to the world. It's not that men see no value in love and the qualities it calls forth or that women see none in work and the attributes that characterize it. But the balance between the two is different for men and for women—a difference that has profound consequences for the ways in which love and work are integrated for each of them, therefore, for their relations inside the family.

We have, for example, all witnessed the chaos that can go on inside a family; most of us have lived with it. And we probably have all observed that mother usually will be at the center of it, father on the periphery. Children get into a fight, and mother mediates. The sound of breaking glass is heard, and mother rushes to see if someone is hurt. And so it goes until, in angry desperation, she calls for his help. "Damnit, can't you hear what's going on?" she screams at him. "What?" he asks as if just coming awake. "Oh, sorry, I wasn't paying attention." "How can you not hear?" she demands uncomprehendingly. "I just didn't," he answers somewhat defensively.

She can't understand his mode. "How can he just sit there without hearing the kids or me or anything?" He's baffled by hers. "Why does she pay attention? Why can't she let them take care of things themselves? Besides," he complains, "she doesn't have to yell. All she has to do is tell me and I'll do it." And she, exasperated almost to tears, replies angrily, "Why do I have to be the one always to see and tell?" Listen to both sides of the story as this couple, married six years with two children, tell it. He's a thirty-three-year-old computer programmer; she's thirty-one, a systems analyst in a bank. The husband:

> I try, I swear I do. But I don't know what she wants half the time. It's like it's never enough.

The wife:

> He tunes out; I just can't believe how he can do that, but he does it. He's not really insensitive, at least I don't think so, but he has this amazing capacity to just stop being there. I mean, he's there, but he's not *there*.

The husband:

> She accuses me of doing some kind of disappearing act, and I'm never sure what she means. I'm sitting right there.

The wife:

> He can be sitting in the same room, but he doesn't know what's going on around him. There's a wall around him that you can't get past. The whole place can be up in arms, I can be like a screaming banshee, and he won't even pick his head up out of the magazine he's reading. Or sometimes it'll finally get to him, so he looks up and says in that quiet voice of his, "Hey, what's the matter?" And I feel like I'm crazy.

The husband:

> I suppose I do have this ability to shut things out. But what's wrong with that? Why do I have to be involved all the time? Maybe all our lives would be easier if she could do a little more of it.

The wife:

> I try sometimes, I really try to do what he does, but it's absolutely impossible to pull it off. It's like there's a radar inside me that always knows what's going on around me all the time, and you can't just switch it off. It's the same thing in the office; I think it's why I'm good at my job, because I know what's going on with people; it's like I keep watch or something.

Another woman, granting her husband's participation in certain of the tasks of housekeeping and parenting, summed up her tale with the common complaint about how she remains responsible for arranging, organizing, planning, administering.

> Keeping it together is my job; if I waited for him to take that kind of responsibility around here, well . . .

Her husband, uncomprehending, wonders why she's so busy all the time, why she makes so much work for herself.

> She doesn't have to do all that stuff; we'd get along just fine without all that perfection. I don't need her fine meal every night and neither do the kids. I don't know why she does all that, but she must have to do it because she won't listen to me.

She does "all that stuff" partly because she's been trained to worry about such things, to make them her concern, to judge herself as wife, mother, woman by how her children grow, whether she cooks a "fine meal." And she does it also because, in many families, it's still the way she's judged by others, still what's expected of her if she's to meet the requirements of her role.

But, even where "keeping it together" is not all her job, one hears at least some of the same complaints. "I can't tune out, and he has trouble tuning in," says a woman. "She's every vigilant, especially about what's going on with the kids, and it's not my style," says her husband. For her, it's hard to close off even an innocent squabble, while he can hardly make himself hear a war.

It's not planned behavior for either of them, not something they think about, then do. It just seems to happen automatically, as if it were natural. And, given their lifetime of training—he, to attend to matters outside the home; she, inside—they are, by now, doing what comes naturally. But the difficulty in reversing the patterns—the effort it takes to make relatively small changes—suggests that their early experiences with separation and boundary development are involved here as well. For it's not just his investment in the world outside that's at issue in such conflicts but his very separateness itself— the ways in which he can separate and isolate himself even while being physically present.

There are no rights and wrongs here, no one to blame. His relatively rigid boundaries enable him to shut out the world, to turn himself off; her more permeable ones permit no such easy escape. So she hears; he doesn't. The early constriction of his inner psychic life makes it difficult for him to attend to a variety of emotional demands all at once. Her more expansive inner experience leaves her forever vulnerable to competing relational claims, forever trying to mediate, sort, mend, soothe.

One woman, living in a marriage in which she and her husband have made substantial progress in sharing household and child care, read these words before publication and commented:

> It's really important to say that men don't ever seem to think about the things that preoccupy women—I mean, all the baggage we carry around in our heads. I'm always making lists about birthdays and anniversaries and which friends we haven't seen lately and all those millions of things that have to do with the kids. I'm always juggling something. Even when I'm not actually doing it, I'm thinking about it and figuring out how to get it done.

Her husband, who knew nothing about his wife's remarks to me, had his own concerns:

> One thing you should be sure to write about is that women carry a lot of stuff around that's plain unnecessary. That's a big issue between us. She doesn't complain that I don't do my share, but she's always mad because I don't worry about it like she does. She calls it "baggage" and says it gets very heavy. But why the hell can't she put it down? There's a time and place—but not for my Suzanne. It's always all there for her. I sometimes feel sorry for her because I know she lives with more pressure than I do just because she can't seem to separate things out. But I'll be damned if I want to learn to do it her way, even if I could.

Still they struggle—with each other and with themselves. But it's particularly hard when the issues are so obscure, seem so out of their control. For the arguments are not just over a particular chore but over who takes responsibility for the tone, the temper, and the quality of life inside the home.

For the men, the difficulties are compounded by the fact that the initiative for change usually comes from the woman in the family. It's she who has been more discontented with the roles, who wants to change at least some of the rules, who has a vision, inchoate though it may be, of new ways of being in the family. A man, therefore, even one who believes in the change his wife is asking for, usually has less understanding about what has been wrong and how to correct it than she does, feels the internal pressure to change less keenly, and most likely is more ambivalent about it all. So, for example, a thirty-two-year-old husband, married six years and with two small children, says sighing:

> Sometimes I wish I was born forty years earlier; my father and mother had it easier. Mom was there taking care of everything, and he worked without worrying about anything else. She didn't complain because he wasn't doing his share (boy, I get so's I hate that word "share") or he wasn't paying attention to us kids. When we needed a hand taken to us, she'd tell him and he'd do it and make sure we got in line.

"So you sometimes have fantasies about living in a more traditional marriage," I commented. He sat thoughtful for a few minutes, then laughed:

> No, not really—well, fantasies maybe, but nothing I really mean. I don't really believe in master-slave relationships. Nobody likes being a servant, no matter how much they try to pretend it isn't happening. And that's what my mother was to my father in a way—like one of those Stepford wives, you know, almost chronically pleasant. But, if you look for it, you see the cracks here and there. No, it's not what I want; I'm proud of her and what she's able to do, and I don't want to change it. It's just hard sometimes.

Because it's "hard sometimes," they dream about another time when life was easier or better in the family. But then they remember the reality of their own childhood homes. The younger women look at their mothers, now at midlife and beyond, who lived their lives according to the old ways, and say, "Not for me."

> I don't know who's got it harder anymore. I sometimes look at the women who spend the afternoon in the park with their kids, and I get jealous. Their life seems so leisurely compared to mine. Then I look at my mother and my aunts and see that their lives seem so empty, and I know that didn't work, and I don't ever want to live like that either.

Their husbands look at their fathers, suffering the regrets of a lifetime dedicated to work at the expense of love, and say, "There's got to be another way."

> My father did his job just like he was supposed to, and what did he get? No friends, nothing much going for him with his kids, and a heart attack. This experiment we're living is hard as hell, but it's got to be better than how our parents did it, and our kids are going to have a lot better shot at it because they already see possibilities we never even knew about.

The older women, suffering the difficulties of finding an identity at midlife, say to their daughters, "Never again."

> I come from the wrong generation, and I hope there'll never be another one like us. We were taught—no, we weren't taught, we were brainwashed into believing that his work was the most important thing. I hated taking care of the kids by myself all the time. I wanted him to be involved. But I didn't even dare ask for it because I thought there was something the matter with me.

Their husbands, pained at the departure of the children they never got to know, warn their sons, "The cost is too high."

> I was always so involved in my work. Then as I got older, and especially as the kids were getting older and my boy was getting into some trouble, it began to look different to me. I began to wonder what the hell I was doing with my life. I realized I was missing something then, but it was too late; you can never make up those years.

"It was too late"—words that fill us with fear, that harden our determination never to say them about our own lives. So the balance is changing—perhaps too slowly to suit those with a radical temperament, perhaps too quickly for those on the more conservative side. But, whichever their position, most people agree that there have been significant changes in the last two decades. The magnitude of the change may be uncertain yet, but the breadth with which the ideology, at least, has spread across all classes in the society is undeniable. It's there to be seen in the widespread popularity of the new birthing movements which have given fathers a role in the delivery room. And it's there also in the fact that only the smallest proportion of the hundreds of husbands and wives I have spoken with don't give at least a nod to the importance of bringing fathers more actively into the daily care and nurturance of infants and young children.

Men from all walks of life speak unashamedly now of wanting a more intimate connection with their children than they had with their own fathers. A thirty-year-old floor finisher, who has fathered three children in his ten-year marriage, says with feeling:

> It's going to be different between me and my kids, I'll make sure of that. I could never talk to my father, and my kids are never going to say that about me, I

promise. It wasn't just because my father wasn't there physically either; he worked a regular eight-to-five stint, or something like that. It was like he always had something on his mind that was more important than anything I ever had to say to him.

And women speak with equal certainty about the advantages for the whole family when they don't have to do it all alone, as these words from a twenty-nine-year-old woman who works the swing shift at a refinery tell:

Maybe I'm still more involved with the kids in some ways than Art is, but he's a real parent, not just an ordinary father. So our kids know we both can love them and punish them and take care of them in all kinds of ways. He can cook their meals and wipe their noses just like I can.

I've been working swing for the last year. We worried at first about how it would work, but we're doing fine now. He's home by three-thirty, so he's the one who gets to fix their dinner, and watches over the school work of the older two, and sees they all get to the doctor and the dentist or the Little League, or wherever they have to go.

Before I went back to work, he hardly knew what was going on in the house; now he's a real part of it. And, you know, when the older kids were real little, he didn't have much going on with them, but with the baby, he's real involved with her, and she's just as leave to want him as me. [The flow of words stopped for a moment as she looked at me somewhat abashed] I know it's kind of funny to say this, but sometimes I don't like that so much, you know. I mean, I feel a little left out. But mostly it's okay.

Actually, the truth is we're both surprised that it's been good for all of us. [Stopping to think] I'm not telling you it's easy now; don't get me wrong. We still have our differences, and working separate shifts is hard—real hard. But— how am I going to tell you—well, it's a lot better than we figured it to be, that's all.

It's better, yes. But it's a delicate balance such couples are trying to maintain—and a difficult one as they struggle both against the obstacles the world places in their path and against their own inner resistances to change.

At the social level, the world in which they both work puts formidable blocks in the path of change inside the family. Indeed, the organization of work itself makes any major reordering of parenting relationships almost impossible for most people.

Half-time work in any but the low-level office jobs women generally hold is very far from an acceptable alternative in any sector of the work world— whether blue-collar, white-collar, or professional. Paternity leave for men is almost nonexistent except in a few relatively enlightened settings, as this man, a high school teacher, found out with difficulty just before the birth of his son.

When I told my principal I wanted to take a six-month leave when Jonathan was born, he said they couldn't guarantee my job. We took it all the way to the school board, but couldn't get anywhere with them either. So that plan went down the tubes; we couldn't afford to risk my being out of a job—especially these days when teaching jobs are so damned scarce.

Even where company policy permits such leave, there often are unspoken, informal rules that let a man know his opportunities for advancement will be at risk if he takes advantage of it. Speaking of his dilemma when his daughter was born two years earlier, an ambitious twenty-nine-year-old man said:

> I work for one of the few companies that allow a guy to take paternity leave—unpaid, of course. So first of all you have to be able to afford it. If you get past that hurdle—and most people can't—you get the distinct message from your superiors that it's not what they're looking for in a guy on the fast track. So, if that's where you want to be, better beware.

And, once there are children, the problems of finding adequate care for them can be debilitating. In families where a woman is either the main support of the household or married to a man whose salary simply will not cover basic family needs, there is no choice. Then, children often are left in situations which also leave parents torn with concern. Where choice exists, the problems often are enough to overwhelm even those most committed to changing the roles and the rules. One woman, married at twenty-eight after having launched her career, told it this way:

> We agreed before we were married that we would share it all. I was already on my way up in the agency. I was in advertising, you know, and about to be a big success; I'd just landed my first account a couple of months before we got married. Whew, who would have thought [her words trailing off] . . . We had it all figured—we'd both work, have our careers, and at home . . . well, we'd both take care of things there, too. We didn't know; God, we were dumb. People tell you, but I swear you don't know, you just think, "Well, that won't happen to me." Christ, we can be so blind and so . . . so . . . arrogant.
>
> Well, let me tell you. It's easy, all right, until the kids come. Then watch out. Our biggest problem was child care. It was hard with one kid, but with two it got to be such a constant pain and strain that I finally decided I had no choice but to leave work for the next few years. I thought I'd be able to manage it if I could work half time, but that's no go in advertising. Now I piddle around with some freelance stuff at home—nothing much.

Add to all this the fact that discrimination against women in the workplace means that men consistently earn more than women. So long as that's the case, most women will continue to carry the greater responsibility for raising the children and keeping the household going regardless of anyone's good intentions. Similarly, so long as the work men do and the money earned from it are the central sources of their prestige, status, power—even their identity—fatherhood, for most of them, will remain more a biological and economic role than a loving and nurturing one.

Consequently, in most families, it's still mother who takes leave from work at the arrival of a child, not father; still mother who does the primary parenting, especially in the early stages of infancy. As with household tasks, father's child-care activities still all too often come under the heading of helping mother; he still "babysits" his own children. A thirty-one-year-old mother of two small children drew a graphic word picture of a woman who tries to do it all.

> It's not just working hard that makes me crazed. It's wearing so many different hats each day so that I feel fragmented and . . . well, not whole, like there's pieces of me all over the place. He does his share, too, but it's different. He goes off to his job and does whatever he does and then he comes home. He's been to one place and has everything in one basket. And I've gone to twenty places and I'm torn in fifteen different directions.

"Why does it have to be that way?" I asked. "Why can't he be the one to take the children across town to child care, for example?"

Because we work in different directions, and the child-care place is closer to my work than his.

"Why is that?" I wanted to know.

I guess we thought the kids should be closer to me so that I should be able to get to them in a hurry if something goes wrong and they need me.

"Why do you need them closer to you? Couldn't he take care of any emergency that might come up?"

I'm not sure we ever thought about it that way, but anyway, I'm more flexible about my work schedule than he is. Anyhow it's all complicated now because I work at Melissa's child care two mornings a week in exchange for her tuition, otherwise we couldn't afford to send her there. So on those days I'm there from seven-thirty until ten-thirty, then I go to work until four. Then I pick the kids up at their different schools and take them for whatever appointments they have that day—you know, to the doctor or to swimming or whatever. [Sighing wearily] Some days I'm lucky; I can come right home with them, and then I feel practically like I'm having a vacation.

"It certainly sounds like a very tough schedule," I agreed. "You said you and your husband are trying to share these responsibilities, yet you haven't mentioned what he does."

Well, he doesn't ever do any of this kind of stuff because he never takes any time off work unless he's dying or something. [Throwing her hands up in a gesture that suggests she's caught between resignation and understanding] When I'm not mad at him, I suppose I can understand that. People complain about a woman taking time off because of a sick kid, but they kind of expect it. Nobody expects a man to do it.

There are powerful social forces at work here—forces that not only reinforce the decisions people make, but that are, in some important ways, responsible for them. Whatever the changes in recent years, the message is still: Fathers work, mothers "mother" even when they also work. Fathers and mothers may both worry about a sick child, but father generally goes to work. "I just can't take time off," he says. "People are depending on me." Mother stays home. "I just can't leave," she says. "My child needs me."

In her fine article on the joys and problems of shared parenting, psychologist Diane Ehrensaft points out that, while we're thoroughly familiar with the term *working mother*, there's no analog that refers to fathers.* Indeed, the phrase *working father* would strike most of us as redundant. Of course fathers work! Similarly, government statistics tell us how many women in the labor force have children under six years old at home, how many have older children, how many have none. Has anyone ever seen a Bureau of Labor Statistics table that gives matching information about men?

Such indicators of social values are not to be dismissed lightly. Still, there's something more—something that lies in the internal psychological structure of men and women. For, although that psychology is born in and nurtured by the structure of social relations, it ultimately has a life and force of its own.

---

*For this and many other ideas about the issues that confront couples who are sharing parenting, I am indebted to Diane Ehrensaft's excellent article entitled "When Women and Men Mother," *Socialist Review*, Vol. 10 (1980), pp. 37-73, and to hours of fruitful conversation with her.

Therefore, despite the dissatisfactions the old ways produce, there are also what psychologists call *secondary gains*. These gains are embedded in the existing system of relationships, and, however neurotic they may sometimes seem to be when viewed from the outside, they offer comfort and solace on the inside. Thus, for example, if illness is the route to the attention of a preoccupied parent, there's a gain for a child in being ill.

So it is with the traditional relations inside the family. Some men now know in their heads that the power, status, and prestige that accrue to them from their activities in the world outside are secondary gains—rewards for what they have given up inside the family, indeed, in all the relationships of personal life. Yet change comes slowly and with great difficulty since those are the compensations they have experienced for so long, the only ones they really understand emotionally. And women, for whom close personal connections are so important, only reluctantly give up their primacy in relation to the children. For, whatever the difficulties of mothering a child, there are important gains—the intimate connection, the sure knowledge that, whatever else happens, this bond is a permanent one, the sense of power that comes with knowing she has indelibly marked another's life.

In all these ways, the differences in their internal world come together with the external world to make things difficult for those who are trying to find new ways to live—whether out of ideological commitment or economic necessity—as the struggle of this couple shows.

She's a thirty-two-year-old graduate student in public health; he's a thirty-three-year-old doctor who works at a health-maintenance organization in the Midwest—a choice he made for both personal and professional reasons. At the personal level, such work for a doctor means a steady income and regular working hours—time for family life that a physician in private practice generally doesn't have. At the professional level, it seemed to him then to promise the possibility of practicing preventive medicine with a patient population who could not afford such services in the private sector. The wife explains:

> One of the things we're grappling with right now is whether he should leave his job at the clinic and go into private practice. I know we could use the money, but I'm still adamantly against it, because all it means is that for this more money the kids will get less father.

The husband adds:

> It's a big difference being a private doc as opposed to a clinic one. There's a lot more money in private practice, and we really need it the way things are going these days.

The wife:

> He says it's only the money that makes him talk about private practice, but I don't know that I believe it. He looks at the guys he went to med school with who are in private practice, and something tugs at him; he wants to be that successful, too. He was a lot smarter in school than most of them, and it bothers him now to compare himself to them and feel like they're more successful.

The husband:

> I don't know if it's the prestige that worries me like Sue Ellen says. But I work my ass off and I'm not experiencing the rewards I should, so it feels lousy and I get depressed and wonder why I became a doc anyhow.

The wife:

> I know what I want and what I don't want, but I'm kind of torn about it
> because I worry, "What good will it be if he doesn't do what he has to do?
> What'll it cost us?" He's trying to change and not be an ordinary man, and he's
> made a lot of changes, too. But there's that bottom line for a man where they
> have to feel like a success out there in the world, and if he doesn't . . . well,
> then what?

The husband:

> It's a rotten bind for all of us. I like the predictability of the clinic schedule. I
> know when I have to be at the hospital overnight, and except for those times, I
> work a regular work week like everybody else. When we sit down to dinner, I
> don't have to worry I'll be interrupted with phone calls every fifteen minutes.
> It lets me be a real part of my kids' life and that's very important to me. As it
> is, Sue Ellen and I don't get much time together; in private practice . . . forget
> it. I know all that, but it all costs something, too. But then I guess everything
> does, doesn't it?

There's no real disagreement between them. They both know what would
be best for the children, for their own relationship. And they're both willing
to struggle to attain that ideal. But they're torn because they know also that
the costs to the marriage are potentially high no matter which course they
take.

She knows that she wants and needs his involvement in the family in ways
that would not be possible if he were in a private medical practice. And she
asserts that forcefully. But she worries about the price to his self-esteem, to
his sense of himself—and, therefore, to their relationship—when he compares
his success unfavorably to colleagues all around him who still live much more
traditional lives.

He worries too—about how he can continue to participate in raising his
children if he leaves his present job, about the cost to his marriage if he
doesn't earn more money and the financial crunch continues to squeeze them
without relief. Ideology to the contrary, this, he feels, is his singular responsibility. If they can't live as comfortably as they would like, he experiences
that as his failure, not hers. And, despite his denials, like his wife, he's also
aware that a battle is shaping up inside him. He insists it's only money he
worries about, but he finds himself thinking too much about the success of
others, comparing himself to them too often, adding up degrees of status and
prestige, angered because he feels so unrewarded—not just in dollars but in
all the rewards of medicine that were surely a part of the fantasies that led
him into medical training.

It's not only in professional families that such issues arise. A thirty-three-
year-old appliance repair mechanic, married thirteen years with three children, who wants to try it on his own speaks of the same conflicts, both within
himself and with his wife:

> We're talking about my going into business, Kerri and me. I've been in the
> business around here long enough to have a good reputation; people trust me,
> so I wouldn't have trouble getting work. But I'd have to work a lot harder than
> I do now—put in longer hours, probably night work, and I'd never get to see
> Kerri and the kids.

His wife tells her side:

> I don't want him to go into business because whatever money he might make will come out of our hides—me and the kids'. What good is it if we have more money and we don't have much family life left? [With a sigh] But I worry about him and whether he really needs to do it. I mean, what'll we have to pay if he doesn't get to do what he wants? It's one of those things where you can't win, no matter what you do.

Even before marriage, when love is likely to be felt most intensely, the conflict around love, work, and identity is experienced differently for a man and a woman, the balance between love and work, therefore, weighted differently as well—as is epitomized in this story of a young professional couple who are deeply in love and planning to marry.

They came into my office looking for help in resolving a conflict about where they would live. She has an established career on the West Coast; he has just been offered a job in the East. He started the meeting by saying:

> I know Laura's career is as important to her as mine is, and I respect that. Her ability to make that kind of commitment is part of what I value about her.

"Then what's the problem?" I asked. He replied:

> It's simple; I have a job offer in Philadelphia that I simply can't turn down, and I love her very much and want her to come with me, of course.

Laura told her side this way.

> I feel torn in two by this dilemma. I've never been happier in my life than I have been since I came here. I love my work; my career here is assured—just the kind of work life I dreamed about. I have good friends and a whole support network I can count on. When I think about giving it all up, it's so wrenching I can hardly stand it. But I love Michael, too—very much—and I want to be able to go with him. How do I resolve it?

"Is this the only job Michael can get?" I asked. He answered:

> No, but it's the best one. It's the one that will be the most advantageous for the future of my career. It's a career I've dreamed about all my life and worked very hard for. I just don't see how I can pass up an opportunity like this when it comes my way.

"What if Laura can't make this change? Will that make a difference in your plans?" His body tensed, his voice became anxious:

> I don't see how it could. I don't have a choice; I have to take this job.

"It seems to me," I said, "that's not quite accurate. If you decide to take the job even if she can't or won't go with you, then you *have* made a choice—perhaps one you regret or one you wish you didn't have to make, but a choice nevertheless. And it's important that both of you be clear about that." Looking surprised, he responded thoughtfully:

> I suppose that's true; I hadn't thought about it that way. But it doesn't *feel* like a choice. If I don't take this opportunity, I'll never know what I could have done and how far I could go. I can't pass it up; I can't. I love her desperately, and I need her, but I have to go.

"And what about you, Laura? What does it feel like to hear Michael say he has to go whether you join him or not?" She listened to my words with her head in her hands, then, lifting her tear-stained face, she spoke in anguish:

> I don't know, I just don't know. I understand how he feels and I know he does have to take the job. I keep telling myself I can stake out a place for myself in Philadelphia just like I've done here.

"Have you asked Michael to take a compromise job here so that you wouldn't have to make this move?"

> Of course we've talked about it, but it's not a serious consideration. I know he can't do it without feeling abused and deprived. And what good would that be for our relationship?

"And you? How will you feel if you give up what you have here for him knowing that he couldn't do it for you?"

> That's what I'm trying so hard to decide. But, you know, it makes me very angry with myself that I can't do it with good grace. Then I get angry that I even think that way because it's so typical of what women do. But the truth is I know it would be easier for me to do it than for him. That's just the way it still is, I guess.
>
> Damnit, won't it ever change? Will it always be like this—men doing their damn number and we women doing ours? He says he loves me, and I know he does; I haven't any doubt about his devotion. But, if it interferes with his career plans, he knows what he has to do. And look at me, ready to throw up my life and follow him. Do I love him any more than he loves me? I don't think so. It's only that when a man puts love and work on the scale you know what loses. [Sighing deeply] I sometimes think we're doomed.

There's no denying that things have changed. Many more men than ever before are now genuinely involved in family life, just as many more women are committed to work in ways that are new. And there's no denying either that the conflicts they suffer over how their time is divided, the decisions they make when they must choose, the inner experience about what defines them and what places them in the world are still very much related to their gender. Generally, men still are best at the cognitive, rational mode that work requires, so it's where they turn for validation. Usually, women still are more comfortable in the emotional and experiential mode that interpersonal connections require, so that's where they look for fulfillment. For men, therefore, it's still work that gets their first allegiance, if not in word, then in deed; for women, it's still love.

But the struggle doesn't end there. Certainly, all too often, the difference between what we *want* and what we *do* is a striking one. But the very fact of wanting to change our lives is a step forward—a statement of a new level of consciousness that is also a harbinger of change. For the wanting itself impels us to continue to seek new ways to change our relations with each other and, equally important, new ways to raise our children so that they need not suffer the conflicts as we do.

Suggestions for Discussion

1. How does the author explain that a man's sense of identity is almost invariably related to his work whereas a woman's is not?

2. How does she distinguish between love and work?

3. With what details does Rubin suggest that the different balance between love and work for men and women leads to serious gaps in communication and understanding between them?

4. What relationship does the author establish between basic differences in their respective psychic lives and their differing marital attitudes?

5. How have the significant changes in family life in the last two decades affected men and women?

6. How do social forces reinforce the internal differences that affect family life?

7. Evaluate the case of Laura and Michael. How does its probable resolution bear out the prior statements of the author on the differences between men and women regarding work and love?

Suggestions for Writing

1. Discuss Freud's conviction that love and work are the major areas of adult life that require resolution if we are to live satisfactorily.

2. If you were asked by the author to answer the question, who are You? how would you respond?

3. Develop some tentative answers to Max Weber's question: "Do we work to live or live to work?"

4. What are some of the inner resistances to change by either men or women in contemporary households?

Fiction

—◆◆◆◆—

Nathaniel Hawthorne

The Birthmark

Nathaniel Hawthorne (1804–1864) was born of New England Puritan stock in Salem, Massachusetts. His first publication, *Twice-Told Tales* (1837), was followed by the novels *The Scarlet Letter* (1850), *The House of the Seven Gables* (1851), and *The Marble Faun* (1860). Other short fiction includes a second series of *Twice-Told Tales* (1842), *Mosses from an Old Manse* (1846), and *The Snow Image and Other Twice-Told Tales* (1851). In "The Birthmark," Aylmer's love for Georgiana deteriorates into self-love and an obsessive sense of his own omnipotence; his faith in science is reduced to an unconscious belief in the possibility of magical exorcism. The opposed forces in his personality become completely separated, and when they cease to contend there is no possibility of a reconciliation between them.

In the latter part of the last century there lived a man of science, an eminent proficient in every branch of natural philosophy, who not long before our story opens had made experience of a spiritual affinity more attractive than any chemical one. He had left his laboratory to the care of an assistant, cleared his fine countenance from the furnace smoke, washed the stain of acids from his fingers, and persuaded a beautiful woman to become his wife. In those days, when the comparatively recent discovery of electricity and other kindred mysteries of Nature seemed to open paths into the region of miracle, it was not unusual for the love of science to rival the love of woman in its depth and absorbing energy. The higher intellect, the imagination, the spirit, and even the heart might all find their congenial aliment in pursuits which, as some of their ardent votaries believed, would ascend from one step of powerful intelligence to another, until the philosopher should lay his hand on the secret of creative force and perhaps make new worlds for himself. We know not whether Aylmer possessed this degree of faith in man's ultimate control over Nature. He had devoted himself, however, too unreservedly to

257

scientific studies ever to be weaned from them by any second passion. His love for his young wife might prove the stronger of the two; but it could only be by intertwining itself with his love of science and uniting the strength of the latter to his own.

Such a union accordingly took place, and was attended with truly remarkable consequences and a deeply impressive moral. One day, very soon after their marriage, Aylmer sat gazing at his wife with a trouble in his countenance that grew stronger until he spoke.

"Georgiana," said he, "has it never occurred to you that the mark upon your cheek might be removed?"

"No, indeed," said she, smiling; but, perceiving the seriousness of his manner, she blushed deeply. "To tell you the truth, it has been so often called a charm that I was simple enough to imagine it might be so."

"Ah, upon another face perhaps it might," replied her husband; "but never on yours. No, dearest Georgiana, you came so nearly perfect from the hand of Nature that this slightest possible defect, which we hesitate whether to term a defect or a beauty, shocks me, as being the visible mark of earthly imperfection."

"Shocks you, my husband!" cried Georgiana, deeply hurt; at first reddening with momentary anger, but then bursting into tears. "Then why did you take me from my mother's side? You cannot love what shocks you!"

To explain this conversation, it must be mentioned that in the centre of Georgiana's left cheek there was a singular mark, deeply interwoven, as it were, with the texture and substance of her face. In the usual state of her complexion—a healthy though delicate bloom—the mark wore a tint of deeper crimson, which imperfectly defined its shape amid the surrounding rosiness. When she blushed it gradually became more indistinct, and finally vanished amid the triumphant rush of blood that bathed the whole cheek with its brilliant glow. But if any shifting motion caused her to turn pale there was the mark again, a crimson stain upon the snow, in what Aylmer sometimes deemed an almost fearful distinctness. Its shape bore not a little similarity to the human hand, though of the smallest pygmy size. Georgiana's lovers were wont to say that some fairy at her birth hour had laid her tiny hand upon the infant's cheek, and left this impress there in token of the magic endowments that were to give her such sway over all hearts. Many a desperate swain would have risked life for the privilege of pressing his lips to the mysterious hand. It must not be concealed, however, that the impression wrought by this fairy sign manual varied exceedingly according to the difference of temperament in the beholders. Some fastidious persons—but they were exclusively of her own sex—affirmed that the bloody hand, as they chose to call it, quite destroyed the effect of Georgiana's beauty and rendered her countenance even hideous. But it would be as reasonable to say that one of those small blue stains which sometimes occur in the purest statuary marble would convert the Eve of Powers to a monster. Masculine observers, if the birthmark did not heighten their admiration, contented themselves with wishing it away, that the world might possess one living specimen of ideal loveliness without the semblance of a flaw. After his marriage,—for he thought little or nothing of the matter before,—Aylmer discovered that this was the case with himself.

Had she been less beautiful,—if Envy's self could have found aught else to sneer at,—he might have felt his affection heightened by the prettiness of this mimic hand, now vaguely portrayed, now lost, now stealing forth again and glimmering to and fro with every pulse of emotion that throbbed within her heart; but, seeing her otherwise so perfect, he found this one defect grow more and more intolerable with every moment of their united lives. It was the fatal flaw of humanity which Nature, in one shape or another, stamps ineffaceably on all her productions, either to imply that they are temporary and finite, or that their perfection must be wrought by toil and pain. The crimson hand expressed the ineludible gripe in which mortality clutches the highest and purest of earthly mould, degrading them into kindred with the lowest, and even with the very brutes, like whom their visible frames return to dust. In this manner, selecting it as the symbol of his wife's liability to sin, sorrow, decay, and death, Aylmer's sombre imagination was not long in rendering the birthmark a frightful object, causing him more trouble and horror than ever Georgiana's beauty, whether of soul or sense, had given him delight.

At all the seasons which should have been their happiest he invariably, and without intending it, nay, in spite of a purpose to the contrary, reverted to this one disastrous topic. Trifling as it at first appeared, it so connected itself with innumerable trains of thought and modes of feeling that it became the central point of all. With the morning twilight Aylmer opened his eyes upon his wife's face and recognized the symbol of imperfection; and when they sat together at the evening hearth his eyes wandered stealthily to her cheek, and beheld, flickering with the blaze of the wood fire, the spectral hand that wrote mortality where he would fain have worshipped. Georgiana soon learned to shudder at his gaze. It needed but a glance with the peculiar expression that his face often wore to change the roses of her cheek into a deathlike paleness, amid which the crimson hand was brought strongly out, like a bas relief of ruby on the whitest marble.

Late one night, when the lights were growing dim so as hardly to betray the stain on the poor wife's cheek, she herself, for the first time, voluntarily took up the subject.

"Do you remember, my dear Aylmer," said she, with a feeble attempt at a smile, "have you any recollection, of a dream last night about this odious hand?"

"None! none whatever!" replied Aylmer, starting; but then he added, in a dry, cold tone, affected for the sake of concealing the real depth of his emotion, "I might well dream of it; for, before I fell asleep, it had taken a pretty firm hold of my fancy."

"And you did dream of it?" continued Georgiana, hastily; for she dreaded lest a gush of tears should interrupt what she had to say. "A terrible dream! I wonder that you can forget it. Is it possible to forget this one expression?—'It is in her heart now; we must have it out!' Reflect, my husband; for by all means I would have you recall that dream."

The mind is in a sad state when Sleep, the all-involving, cannot confine her spectres within the dim region of her sway, but suffers them to break forth, affrighting this actual life with secrets that perchance belong to a deeper one. Aylmer now remembered his dream. He had fancied himself with his servant Aminadab, attempting an operation for the removal of the birthmark; but the deeper went the knife, the deeper sank the hand, until at length its tiny grasp appeared to have caught hold of Georgiana's heart; whence, however, her husband was inexorably resolved to cut or wrench it away.

When the dream had shaped itself perfectly in his memory Aylmer sat in his wife's presence with a guilty feeling. Truth often finds its way to the mind close muffled in robes of sleep, and then speaks with uncompromising directness of matters in regard to which we practise an unconscious self-deception during our waking moments. Until now he had not been aware of the tyrannizing influence acquired by one idea over his mind, and of the lengths which he might find in his heart to go for the sake of giving himself peace.

"Aylmer," resumed Georgiana, solemnly, "I know not what may be the cost to both of us to rid me of this fatal birthmark. Perhaps its removal may cause cureless deformity; or it may be the stain goes as deep as life itself. Again: do we know that there is a possibility, on any terms, of unclasping the firm gripe of this little hand which was laid upon me before I came into the world?"

"Dearest Georgiana, I have spent much thought upon the subject," hastily interrupted Aylmer. "I am convinced of the perfect practicability of its removal."

"If there be the remotest possibility of it," continued Georgiana, "let the attempt be made, at whatever risk. Danger is nothing to me; for life, while this hateful mark makes me the object of your horror and disgust—life is a burden which I would fling down with joy. Either remove this dreadful hand, or take my wretched life! You have deep science. All the world bears witness of it. You have achieved great wonders. Cannot you remove this little, little mark, which I cover with the tips of two small fingers? Is this beyond your power, for the sake of your own peace, and to save your poor wife from madness?"

"Noblest, dearest, tenderest wife," cried Aylmer, rapturously, "doubt not my power. I have already given this matter the deepest thought—thought which might almost have enlightened me to create a being less perfect than yourself. Georgiana, you have led me deeper than ever into the heart of science. I feel myself fully competent to render this dear cheek as faultless as its fellow; and then, most beloved, what will be my triumph when I shall have corrected what Nature left imperfect in her fairest work! Even Pygmalion, when his sculptured woman assumed life, felt not greater ecstasy than mine will be."

"It is resolved, then," said Georgiana, faintly smiling. "And, Aylmer, spare me not, though you should find the birthmark take refuge in my heart at last."

Her husband tenderly kissed her cheek—her right cheek—not that which bore the impress of the crimson hand.

The next day Aylmer apprised his wife of a plan that he had formed whereby he might have opportunity for the intense thought and constant watchfulness which the proposed operation would require; while Georgiana, likewise, would enjoy the perfect repose essential to its success. They were to seclude themselves in the extensive apartments occupied by Aylmer as a laboratory, and where, during his toilsome youth, he had made discoveries in the elemental powers of Nature that had roused the admiration of all the learned societies in Europe. Seated calmly in this laboratory, the pale philosopher had investigated the secrets of the highest cloud region and of the profoundest mines; he had satisfied himself of the causes that kindled and kept alive the fires of the volcano; and had explained the mystery of fountains, and how it is that they gush forth, some so bright and pure, and others with such rich medicinal virtues, from the dark bosom of the earth. Here, too, at an earlier period, he had studied the wonders of the human frame, and attempted to fathom the very process by which Nature assimilates all her precious influences from earth and air, and from the spiritual world, to create and foster man, her masterpiece. The latter pursuit, however, Aylmer had long laid aside in unwilling recognition of the truth—against which all seekers sooner or later stumble—that our great creative Mother, while she amuses us with apparently working in the broadest sunshine, is yet severely careful to keep her own secrets, and, in spite of her pretended openness, shows us nothing but results. She permits us, indeed, to mar, but seldom to mend, and, like a jealous patentee, on no account to make. Now, however, Aylmer resumed these half-forgotten investigations; not, of course, with such hopes or wishes as first suggested them; but because they involved much physiological truth and lay in the path of his proposed scheme for the treatment of Georgiana.

As he led her over the threshold of the laboratory, Georgiana was cold and tremulous. Aylmer looked cheerfully into her face, with intent to reassure her, but was so startled with the intense glow of the birthmark upon the whiteness of her cheek that he could not restrain a strong convulsive shudder. His wife fainted.

"Aminadab! Aminadab!" shouted Aylmer, stamping violently on the floor.

Forthwith there issued from an inner apartment a man of low stature, but bulky frame, with shaggy hair hanging about his visage, which was grimed with the vapors of the furnace. This personage had been Aylmer's underworker during his whole scientific career, and was admirably fitted for that office by his great mechanical readiness, and the skill with which, while incapable of comprehending a single principle, he executed all the details of his master's experiments. With his vast strength, his shaggy hair, his smoky aspect, and the indescribable earthiness that incrusted him, he seemed to represent man's physical nature; while Aylmer's slender figure, and pale, intellectual face, were no less apt a type of the spiritual element.

"Throw open the door of the boudoir, Aminadab," said Aylmer, "and burn a pastil."

"Yes, master," answered Aminadab, looking intently at the lifeless form of Georgiana; and then he muttered to himself, "If she were my wife, I'd never part with that birthmark."

When Georgiana recovered consciousness she found herself breathing an atmosphere of penetrating fragrance, the gentle potency of which had recalled her from her deathlike faintness. The scene around her looked like enchantment. Aylmer had converted those smoky, dingy, sombre rooms, where he had spent his brightest years in recondite pursuits, into a series of beautiful apartments not unfit to be the secluded abode of a lovely woman. The walls were hung with gorgeous curtains, which imparted the combination of grandeur and grace that no other species of adornment can achieve; and, as they fell from the ceiling to the floor, their rich and ponderous folds, concealing all angles and straight lines, appeared to shut in the scene from infinite space. For aught Georgiana knew, it might be a pavilion among the clouds. And

Aylmer, excluding the sunshine, which would have interfered with his chemical processes, had supplied its place with perfumed lamps, emitting flames of various hue, but all uniting in a soft, impurpled radiance. He now knelt by his wife's side, watching her earnestly, but without alarm; for he was confident in his science, and felt that he could draw a magic circle round her within which no evil might intrude.

"Where am I? Ah, I remember," said Georgiana, faintly; and she placed her hand over her cheek to hide the terrible mark from her husband's eyes.

"Fear not, dearest!" exclaimed he. "Do not shrink from me! Believe me, Georgiana, I even rejoice in this single imperfection, since it will be such a rapture to remove it."

"O, spare me!" sadly replied his wife. "Pray do not look at it again. I never can forget that convulsive shudder."

In order to soothe Georgiana, and, as it were, to release her mind from the burden of actual things, Aylmer now put in practice some of the light and playful secrets which science had taught him among its profounder lore. Airy figures, absolutely bodiless ideas, and forms of unsubstantial beauty came and danced before her, imprinting their momentary footsteps on beams of light. Though she had some indistinct idea of the method of these optical phenomena, still the illusion was almost perfect enough to warrant the belief that her husband possessed sway over the spiritual world. Then again, when she felt a wish to look forth from her seclusion, immediately, as if her thoughts were answered, the procession of external existence flitted across a screen. The scenery and the figures of actual life were perfectly represented, but with that bewitching yet indescribable difference which always makes a picture, an image, or a shadow so much more attractive than the original. When wearied of this, Aylmer bade her cast her eyes upon a vessel containing a quantity of earth. She did so, with little interest at first; but was soon startled to perceive the germ of a plant shooting upward from the soil. Then came the slender stalk; the leaves gradually unfolded themselves; and amid them was a perfect and lovely flower.

"It is magical!" cried Georgiana. "I dare not touch it."

"Nay, pluck it," answered Aylmer,—"pluck it, and inhale its brief perfume while you may. The flower will wither in a few moments and leave nothing save its brown seed vessels; but thence may be perpetuated a race as ephemeral as itself."

But Georgiana had no sooner touched the flower than the whole plant suffered a blight, its leaves turning coal-black as if by the agency of fire.

"There was too powerful a stimulus," said Aylmer, thoughtfully.

To make up for this abortive experiment, he proposed to take her portrait by a scientific process of his own invention. It was to be effected by rays of light striking upon a polished plate of metal. Georgiana assented; but, on looking at the result, was affrighted to find the features of the portrait blurred and indefinable; while the minute figure of a hand appeared where the cheek should have been. Aylmer snatched the metallic plate and threw it into a jar of corrosive acid.

Soon, however, he forgot these mortifying failures. In the intervals of study and chemical experiment he came to her flushed and exhausted, but seemed invigorated by her presence, and spoke in glowing language of the resources of his art. He gave a history of the long dynasty of the alchemists, who spent so many ages in quest of the universal solvent by which the golden principle might be elicited from all things vile and base. Aylmer appeared to believe that, by the plainest scientific logic, it was altogether within the limits of possibility to discover this long-sought medium; "but," he added, "a philosopher who should go deep enough to acquire the power would attain too lofty a wisdom to stoop to the exercise of it." Not less singular were his opinions in regard to the elixir vitae. He more than intimated that it was at his option to concoct a liquid that should prolong life for years, perhaps interminably; but that it would produce a discord in Nature which all the world, and chiefly the quaffer of the immortal nostrum, would find cause to curse.

"Aylmer, are you in earnest?" asked Georgiana, looking at him with amazement and fear. "It is terrible to possess such power, or even to dream of possessing it."

"O, do not tremble, my love," said her husband. "I would not wrong either you or myself by working such inharmonious effects upon our lives; but I would have you consider how trifling, in comparison, is the skill requisite to remove this little hand."

At the mention of the birthmark, Georgiana, as usual, shrank as if a red-hot iron had touched her cheek.

Again Aylmer applied himself to his labors. She could hear his voice in the distant furnace room giving directions to Aminadab, whose harsh, uncouth, misshapen tones were audible in response, more like the grunt or growl of a brute than human speech. After hours of absence, Aylmer reappeared and proposed that she should now examine his cabinet of chemical products and natural treasures of the earth. Among the former he showed her a small vial, in which, he remarked, was contained a gentle yet most powerful fragrance, capable of impregnating all the breezes that blow across a kingdom. They were of inestimable value, the contents of that little vial; and, as he said so, he threw some of the perfume into the air and filled the room with piercing and invigorating delight.

"And what is this?" asked Georgiana, pointing to a small crystal globe containing a gold-colored liquid. "It is so beautiful to the eye that I could imagine it the elixir of life."

"In one sense it is," replied Aylmer; "or rather, the elixir of immortality. It is the most precious poison that ever was concocted in this world. By its aid I could apportion the lifetime of any mortal at whom you might point your finger. The strength of the dose would determine whether he were to linger out years, or drop dead in the midst of a breath. No king on his guarded throne could keep his life if I, in my private station, should deem that the welfare of millions justified me in depriving him of it."

"Why do you keep such a terrific drug?" inquired Georgiana in horror.

"Do not mistrust me, dearest," said her husband, smiling; "its virtuous potency is yet greater than its harmful one. But see! here is a powerful cosmetic. With a few drops of this in a vase of water, freckles may be washed away as easily as the hands are cleansed. A stronger infusion would take the blood out of the cheek, and leave the rosiest beauty a pale ghost."

"Is it with this lotion that you intend to bathe my cheek?" asked Georgiana, anxiously.

"O, no," hastily replied her husband; "this is merely superficial. Your case demands a remedy that shall go deeper."

In his interviews with Georgiana, Aylmer generally made minute inquiries as to her sensations, and whether the confinement of the rooms and the temperature of the atmosphere agreed with her. These questions had such a particular drift that Georgiana began to conjecture that she was already subjected to certain physical influences, either breathed in with the fragrant air or taken with her food. She fancied likewise, but it might be altogether fancy, that there was a stirring up of her system—a strange, indefinite sensation creeping through her veins, and tingling, half painfully, half pleasurably, at her heart. Still, whenever she dared to look into the mirror, there she beheld herself pale as a white rose and with the crimson birthmark stamped upon her cheek. Not even Aylmer now hated it so much as she.

To dispel the tedium of the hours which her husband found it necessary to devote to the processes of combination and analysis, Georgiana turned over the volumes of his scientific library. In many dark old tomes she met with chapters full of romance and poetry. They were the works of the philosophers of the middle ages, such as Albertus Magnus, Cornelius Agrippa, Paracelsus, and the famous friar who created the prophetic Brazen Head. All these antique naturalists stood in advance of their centuries, yet were imbued with some of their credulity, and therefore were believed, and perhaps imagined themselves to have acquired from the investigation of Nature a power above Nature, and from physics a sway over the spiritual world. Hardly less curious and imaginative were the early volumes of the Transactions of the Royal Society, in which the members, knowing little of the limits of natural possibility, were continually recording wonders or proposing methods whereby wonders might be wrought.

But to Georgiana, the most engrossing volume was a large folio from her husband's own hand, in which he had recorded every experiment of his scientific career, its original aim, the methods adopted for its development, and its final success or failure, with the circumstances to which either event was attributable. The book, in truth, was both the history and emblem of his ardent, ambitious, imaginative, yet practical and laborious life. He handled physical details as if there were nothing beyond them; yet spiritualized them all and redeemed himself from materialism by his strong and eager aspiration towards the infinite. In his grasp the veriest clod of earth assumed a soul. Georgiana, as she read, reverenced Aylmer and loved him more profoundly than ever, but with a less entire dependence on his judgment than heretofore. Much as he had accomplished, she could not but observe that his most splendid successes were almost invariably failures, if compared with the ideal at which he aimed. His brightest diamonds were the merest pebbles, and felt to be so by himself, in comparison with the inestimable gems which lay hidden beyond his reach. The volume, rich with achievements that had won renown for its author, was yet as melancholy a record as ever mortal hand had penned. It was the sad confession and continual exemplification of the shortcomings of the composite man, the spirit burdened with clay and working in matter, and of the despair that assails the higher nature at finding itself so miserably thwarted by the earthly part. Perhaps every man of genius, in whatever sphere, might recognize the image of his own experience in Aylmer's journal.

So deeply did these reflections affect Georgiana that she laid her face upon the open volume and burst into tears. In this situation she was found by her husband.

"It is dangerous to read in a sorcerer's books," said he with a smile, though his countenance was uneasy and displeased. "Georgiana, there are pages in that volume which I can scarcely glance over and keep my senses. Take heed lest it prove detrimental to you."

"It has made me worship you more than ever," said she.

"Ah, wait for this one success," rejoined he, "then worship me if you will. I shall deem myself hardly unworthy of it. But come, I have sought you for the luxury of your voice. Sing to me, dearest."

So she poured out the liquid music of her voice to quench the thirst of his spirit. He then took his leave with a boyish exuberance of gayety, assuring her that her seclusion would endure but a little longer, and that the result was already certain. Scarcely had he departed when Georgiana felt irresistibly impelled to follow him. She had forgotten to inform Aylmer of a symptom which for two or three hours past had begun to excite her attention. It was a sensation in the fatal birthmark, not painful, but which induced a restlessness throughout her system. Hastening after her husband, she intruded for the first time into the laboratory.

The first thing that struck her eye was the furnace, that hot and feverish worker, with the intense glow of its fire, which by the quantities of soot clustered above it seemed to have been burning for ages. There was a distilling apparatus in full operation. Around the room were retorts, tubes, cylinders, crucibles, and other apparatus of chemical research. An electrical machine stood ready for immediate use. The atmosphere felt oppressively close, and was tainted with gaseous odors which had been tormented forth by the process of science. The severe and homely simplicity of the apartment, with its naked walls and brick pavement, looked strange, accustomed as Georgiana had become to the fantastic elegance of her boudoir. But what chiefly, indeed almost solely, drew her attention, was the aspect of Aylmer himself.

He was pale as death, anxious and absorbed, and hung over the furnace as if it depended upon his utmost watchfulness whether the liquid which it was distilling should be the draught of immortal happiness or misery. How different from the sanguine and joyous mien that he had assumed for Georgiana's encouragement!

"Carefully now, Aminadab; carefully, thou human machine; carefully, thou man of clay," muttered Aylmer, more to himself than his assistant. "Now, if there be a thought too much or too little, it is all over."

"Ho! ho!" mumbled Aminadab. "Look, master! look!"

Aylmer raised his eyes hastily, and at first reddened, then grew paler than ever, on beholding Georgiana. He rushed towards her and seized her arm with a gripe that left the print of his fingers upon it.

"Why do you come hither? Have you no trust in your husband?" cried he, impetuously. "Would you throw the blight of that fatal birthmark over my labors? It is not well done. Go, prying woman! go!"

"Nay, Aylmer," said Georgiana with the firmness of which she possessed no stinted endowment, "it is not you that have a right to complain. You mistrust your wife; you have concealed the anxiety with which you watch the development of this experiment. Think not so unworthily of me, my husband.

Tell me all the risk we run, and fear not that I shall shrink; for my share in it is far less than your own."

"No, no, Georgiana!" said Aylmer, impatiently; "it must not be."

"I submit," replied she, calmly. "And, Aylmer, I shall quaff whatever draught you bring me; but it will be on the same principle that would induce me to take a dose of poison if offered by your hand."

"My noble wife," said Aylmer, deeply moved, "I knew not the height and depth of your nature until now. Nothing shall be concealed. Know, then, that this crimson hand, superficial as it seems, has clutched its grasp into your being with a strength of which I had no previous conception. I have already administered agents powerful enough to do aught except to change your entire physical system. Only one thing remains to be tried. If that fail us we are ruined."

"Why did you hesitate to tell me this?" asked she.

"Because, Georgiana," said Aylmer, in a low voice, "there is danger."

"Danger? There is but one danger—that this horrible stigma shall be left upon my cheek!" cried Georgiana. "Remove it, remove it, whatever be the cost, or we shall both go mad!"

"Heaven knows your words are too true," said Aylmer, sadly. "And now, dearest, return to your boudoir. In a little while all will be tested."

He conducted her back and took leave of her with a solemn tenderness which spoke far more than his words how much was now at stake. After his departure Georgiana became rapt in musings. She considered the character of Aylmer and did it completer justice than at any previous moment. Her heart exulted, while it trembled, at his honorable love—so pure and lofty that it would accept nothing less than perfection nor miserably make itself contented with an earthlier nature than he had dreamed of. She felt how much more precious was such a sentiment than that meaner kind which would have borne with the imperfection for her sake, and have been guilty of treason to holy love by degrading its perfect idea to the level of the actual; and with her whole spirit she prayed that, for a single moment, she might satisfy his highest and deepest conception. Longer than one moment she well knew it could not be; for his spirit was ever on the march, ever ascending, and each instant required something that was beyond the scope of the instant before.

The sound of her husband's footsteps aroused her. He bore a crystal goblet containing a liquor colorless as water, but bright enough to be the draught of immortality. Aylmer was pale; but it seemed rather the consequence of a highly-wrought state of mind and tension of spirit than of fear or doubt.

"The concoction of the draught has been perfect," said he, in answer to Georgiana's look. "Unless all my science have deceived me, it cannot fail."

"Save on your account, my dearest Aylmer," observed his wife, "I might wish to put off this birthmark of mortality by relinquishing mortality itself in preference to any other mode. Life is but a sad possession to those who have attained precisely the degree of moral advancement at which I stand. Were I weaker and blinder, it might be happiness. Were I stronger, it might be endured hopefully. But, being what I find myself, methinks I am of all mortals the most fit to die."

"You are fit for heaven without tasting death!" replied her husband. "But why do we speak of dying? The draught cannot fail. Behold its effect upon this plant."

On the window seat there stood a geranium diseased with yellow blotches which had overspread all its leaves. Aylmer poured a small quantity of the liquid upon the soil in which it grew. In a little time, when the roots of the plant had taken up the moisture, the unsightly blotches began to be extinguished in a living verdure.

"There needed no proof," said Georgiana, quietly. "Give me the goblet. I joyfully stake all upon your word."

"Drink, then, thou lofty creature!" exclaimed Aylmer, with fervid admiration. "There is no taint of imperfection on thy spirit. Thy sensible frame, too, shall soon be all perfect."

She quaffed the liquid and returned the goblet to his hand.

"It is grateful," said she, with a placid smile. "Methinks it is like water from a heavenly fountain; for it contains I know not what of unobtrusive fragrance and deliciousness. It allays a feverish thirst that had parched me for many days. Now, dearest, let me sleep. My earthly senses are closing over my spirit like the leaves around the heart of a rose at sunset."

She spoke the last words with a gentle reluctance, as if it required almost more energy than she could command to pronounce the faint and lingering syllables. Scarcely had they loitered through her lips ere she was lost in slumber. Aylmer sat by her side, watching her aspect with the emotions proper to a man the whole value of whose existence was involved in the process now to be tested. Mingled with this mood, however, was the philosophic investigation characteristic of the man of science. Not the minutest symptom escaped him. A heightened flush of the cheek, a slight irregularity of breath, a quiver of the eyelid, a hardly perceptible tremor through the frame,—such were the details which, as the moments passed, he wrote down in his folio volume. Intense thought had set its stamp upon every previous page of that volume; but the thoughts of years were all concentrated upon the last.

While thus employed, he failed not to gaze often at the fatal hand, and not without a shudder. Yet once, by a strange and unaccountable impulse, he pressed it with his lips. His spirit recoiled, however, in the very act; and Georgiana, out of the midst of her deep sleep, moved uneasily and murmured as if in remonstrance. Again Aylmer resumed his watch. Nor was it without avail. The crimson hand, which at first had been strongly visible upon the marble paleness of Georgiana's cheek, now grew more faintly outlined. She remained not less pale than ever; but the birthmark, with every breath that came and went lost somewhat of its former distinctness. Its presence had been awful; its departure was more awful still. Watch the stain of the rainbow fading out of the sky, and you will know how that mysterious symbol passed away.

"By Heaven! it is well nigh gone!" said Aylmer to himself, in almost irrepressible ecstasy. "I can scarcely trace it now. Success! success! And now it is like the faintest rose color. The lightest flush of blood across her cheek would overcome it. But she is so pale!"

He drew aside the window curtain and suffered the light of natural day to fall into the room and rest upon her cheek. At the same time he heard a gross, hoarse chuckle, which he had long known as his servant Aminadab's expression of delight.

"Ah, clod! ah, earthly mass!" cried Aylmer, laughing in a sort of frenzy, "you have served me well! Matter and spirit—earth and heaven—have both

done their part in this! Laugh, thing of the senses! You have earned the right
to laugh."

These exclamations broke Georgiana's sleep. She slowly unclosed her eyes
and gazed into the mirror which her husband had arranged for that purpose.
A faint smile flitted over her lips when she recognized how barely perceptible
was now that crimson hand which had once blazed forth with such disastrous
brilliancy as to scare away all their happiness. But then her eyes sought Aylmer's face with a trouble and anxiety that he could by no means account for.

"My poor Aylmer!" murmured she.

"Poor? Nay, richest, happiest, most favored!" exclaimed he. "My peerless
bride, it is successful! You are perfect!"

"My poor Aylmer," she repeated, with a more than human tenderness,
"you have aimed loftily; you have done nobly. Do not repent that, with so
high and pure a feeling, you have rejected the best the earth could offer.
Aylmer, dearest Aylmer, I am dying!"

Alas! it was too true! The fatal hand had grappled with the mystery of life,
and was the bond by which an angelic spirit kept itself in union with a mortal
frame. As the last crimson tint of the birth-mark—that sole token of human
imperfection—faded from her cheek, the parting breath of the now perfect
woman passed into the atmosphere, and her soul, lingering a moment near
her husband, took its heavenward flight. Then a hoarse, chuckling laugh was
heard again! Thus ever does the gross fatality of earth exult in its invariable
triumph over the immortal essence which, in this dim sphere of half development, demands the completeness of a higher state. Yet, had Aylmer
reached a profounder wisdom, he need not thus have flung away the happiness which would have woven his mortal life of the selfsame texture with the
celestial. The momentary circumstance was too strong for him; he failed to
look beyond the shadowy scope of time, and, living once for all in eternity,
to find the perfect future in the present.

Suggestions for Discussion

1. What do you regard as the forces motivating Aylmer's attitude and behavior?

2. Discuss the multiple ways in which the dream advances the story's development.
   Justify or challenge the statement that Aylmer's dream marks the climax of the
   story.

3. Examine the language and imagery with special reference to the birthmark and the
   varied responses to it. How does the juxtaposition of religious and sexual imagery
   contribute to characterization, meaning, and tone? What is the function of the animistic detail? How does the contrasting imagery describing Georgiana's chambers
   and Aylmer's laboratory advance the action?

4. By what means are the polarities between the earthly and the spiritual developed?
   How are they reflected in the descriptions of Aylmer and Aminadab? What support
   can you find for the idea that Aminadab is presented as Aylmer's double, representing the submerged aspect of Aylmer's personality (note the significance of Aminadab spelled backward)? How would you define the opposing forces in Aylmer?
   At what point do they cease to contend? In responding to this question, identify
   the rising action, climax, falling action, and resolution.

5. What has been gained and lost by the use of the omniscient author point of view? How necessary are the author's interpolations to the reader's understanding of the story's latent meaning? Note especially the author's comments upon the dream; the expository first paragraph; the passage beginning, "It was the fatal flaw of humanity," and the later one on "the shortcomings of the composite man." (Cf. *Hamlet*, I, iv, 11. 23–38.)

6. Trace the changes that take place in Georgiana's consciousness in the course of the action. If her last words to Aylmer reflect a tragic recognition of what Aylmer has rejected, to what does she remain blind? Discuss the irony in her becoming the instrument of her own fate.

7. Find the examples of the skillful use of foreshadowing. How is suspense maintained? While the reader experiences a mounting sense of impending doom, does he completely surrender his disbelief in the possibility that a miracle might be wrought?

Suggestions for Writing

1. Define the relationship of Aylmer and Georgiana. To what extent is the story dated? Under what circumstances could the action of the story take place today?

2. Discuss "The Birthmark" as a story of moral flaw or of psychological determination. Bring to bear what evidence you can for either point of view by specific allusion to the imagery, setting, and characterizations.

Kate Chopin

A Respectable Woman

Kate Chopin (1851–1904) was an early feminist who did not begin to write until her late thirties. Her first novel, *At Fault* (1890), was followed by two volumes of short stories, *Bayou Folk* (1894) and *A Night in Acadie* (1897), and her masterpiece, the novel *The Awakening* (1899). The "respectable woman" undergoes a metamorphosis after her earlier indifference to her husband's friend.

Mrs. Baroda was a little provoked to learn that her husband expected his friend, Gouvernail, up to spend a week or two on the plantation.

They had entertained a good deal during the winter; much of the time had also been passed in New Orleans in various forms of mild dissipation. She was looking forward to a period of unbroken rest, now, and undisturbed tête-à-tête with her husband, when he informed her that Gouvernail was coming up to stay a week or two.

This was a man she had heard much of but never seen. He had been her husband's college friend; was now a journalist, and in no sense a society man or "a man about town," which were, perhaps, some of the reasons she had never met him. But she had unconsciously formed an image of him in her mind. She pictured him tall, slim, cynical; with eye-glasses, and his hands in his pockets; and she did not like him. Gouvernail was slim enough, but he wasn't very tall nor very cynical; neither did he wear eye-glasses nor carry his hands in his pockets. And she rather liked him when he first presented himself.

But why she liked him she could not explain satisfactorily to herself when she partly attempted to do so. She could discover in him none of those brilliant and promising traits which Gaston, her husband, had often assured her that he possessed. On the contrary, he sat rather mute and receptive before her chatty eagerness to make him feel at home and in face of Gaston's frank and wordy hospitality. His manner was as courteous toward her as the most exacting woman could require; but he made no direct appeal to her approval or even esteem.

Once settled at the plantation he seemed to like to sit upon the wide portico in the shade of one of the big Corinthian pillars, smoking his cigar lazily and listening attentively to Gaston's experience as a sugar planter.

"This is what I call living," he would utter with deep satisfaction, as the air that swept across the sugar field caressed him with its warm and scented velvety touch. It pleased him also to get on familiar terms with the big dogs that came about him, rubbing themselves sociably against his legs. He did not care to fish, and displayed no eagerness to go out and kill grosbecs when Gaston proposed doing so.

Gouvernail's personality puzzled Mrs. Baroda, but she liked him. Indeed, he was a lovable, inoffensive fellow. After a few days, when she could understand him no better than at first, she gave over being puzzled and remained piqued. In this mood she left her husband and her guest, for the most part, alone together. Then finding that Gouvernail took no manner of exception to her action, she imposed her society upon him, accompanying him in his idle strolls to the mill and walks along the batture. She persistently sought to penetrate the reserve in which he had unconsciously enveloped himself.

"When is he going—your friend?" she one day asked her husband. "For my part, he tires me frightfully."

"Not for a week yet, dear. I can't understand; he gives you no trouble."

"No. I should like him better if he did; if he were more like others, and I had to plan somewhat for his comfort and enjoyment."

Gaston took his wife's pretty face between his hands and looked tenderly and laughingly into her troubled eyes. They were making a bit of toilet sociably together in Mrs. Baroda's dressing-room.

"You are full of surprises, ma belle," he said to her. "Even I can never count upon how you are going to act under given conditions." He kissed her and turned to fasten his cravat before the mirror.

"Here you are," he went on, "taking poor Gouvernail seriously and making a commotion over him, the last thing he would desire or expect."

"Commotion!" she hotly resented. "Nonsense! How can you say such a thing? Commotion, indeed! But, you know, you said he was clever."

"So he is. But the poor fellow is run down by overwork now. That's why I asked him here to take a rest."

"You used to say he was a man of ideas," she retorted, unconciliated. "I expected him to be interesting, at least. I'm going to the city in the morning to have my spring gowns fitted. Let me know when Mr. Gouvernail is gone; I shall be at my Aunt Octavie's."

That night she went and sat alone upon a bench that stood beneath a live oak tree at the edge of the gravel walk.

She had never known her thoughts or her intentions to be so confused. She could gather nothing from them but the feeling of a distinct necessity to quit her home in the morning.

Mrs. Baroda heard footsteps crunching the gravel; but could discern in the darkness only the approaching red point of a lighted cigar. She knew it was Gouvernail, for her husband did not smoke. She hoped to remain unnoticed, but her white gown revealed her to him. He threw away his cigar and seated himself upon the bench beside her; without a suspicion that she might object to his presence.

"Your husband told me to bring this to you, Mrs. Baroda," he said, handing her a filmy, white scarf with which she sometimes enveloped her head and shoulders. She accepted the scarf from him with a murmur of thanks, and let it lie in her lap.

He made some commonplace observation upon the baneful effect of the night air at that season. Then as his gaze reached out into the darkness, he murmured, half to himself:

"'Night of south winds—night of the large few stars!
Still nodding night—'"

She made no reply to this apostrophe to the night, which indeed, was not addressed to her.

Gouvernail was in no sense a diffident man, for he was not a self-conscious one. His periods of reserve were not constitutional, but the result of moods. Sitting there beside Mrs. Baroda, his silence melted for the time.

He talked freely and intimately in a low, hesitating drawl that was not unpleasant to hear. He talked of the old college days when he and Gaston had been a good deal to each other; of the days of keen and blind ambitions and large intentions. Now there was left with him, at least, a philosophic acquiescence to the existing order—only a desire to be permitted to exist, with now and then a little whiff of genuine life, such as he was breathing now.

Her mind only vaguely grasped what he was saying. Her physical being was for the moment predominant. She was not thinking of his words, only drinking in the tones of his voice. She wanted to reach out her hand in the darkness and touch him with the sensitive tips of her fingers upon the face or the lips. She wanted to draw close to him and whisper against his cheek—she did not care what—as she might have done if she had not been a respectable woman.

The stronger the impulse grew to bring herself near him, the further, in fact, did she draw away from him. As soon as she could do so without an appearance of too great rudeness, she rose and left him there alone.

Before she reached the house, Gouvernail had lighted a fresh cigar and ended his apostrophe to the night.

Mrs. Baroda was greatly tempted that night to tell her husband—who was also her friend—of this folly that had seized her. But she did not yield to the temptation. Beside being a respectable woman she was a very sensible one; and she knew there are some battles in life which a human being must fight alone.

When Gaston arose in the morning, his wife had already departed. She had taken an early train to the city. She did not return till Gouvernail was gone from under her roof.

There was some talk of having him back during the summer that followed. That is, Gaston greatly desired it; but this desire yielded to his wife's strenuous opposition.

However, before the year ended, she proposed, wholly from herself, to have Gouvernail visit them again. Her husband was surprised and delighted with the suggestion coming from her.

"I am glad, chère amie, to know that you have finally overcome your dislike for him; truly he did not deserve it."

"Oh," she told him, laughingly, after pressing a long, tender kiss upon his lips, "I have overcome everything! you will see. This time I shall be very nice to him."

Suggestions for Discussion

1. How do you learn that Mrs. Baroda is ambivalent about Gouvernail?

2. Why do you think Mrs. Baroda left for the city? What precipitated the move?

3. What details suggest to you that this story was written in an earlier era?

4. What is the significance of the title? Relate it to the theme of the story. Is it used ironically?

5. What are you led to surmise is the relationship of Mrs. Baroda to her husband?

6. What do you think will happen on Gouvernail's next visit? How are you prepared for it?

Suggestions for Writing

Write an essay on questions 4 or 6 above.

James Thurber

The Unicorn in the Garden

James Thurber (1894–1961), American humorist and artist, began contributing in 1927 to *The New Yorker*, in which most of his work first appeared. His humorous essays and short stories are collected in such books as *The Owl in the Attic* (1931), *My Life and Hard Times* (1933), *The Thurber Carnival*, (1945), *The Beast in Me* (1948), and *Lanterns and Lances* (1961). He also wrote the short story "The Secret Life of Walter Mitty," several fantasies for children, and, with Elliot Nugent, a comedy called *The Male Animal* (1940). "The Unicorn in the Garden," a fable of hostile feelings between husband and wife, ends with a surprise twist.

Once upon a sunny morning a man who sat in a breakfast nook looked up from his scrambled eggs to see a white unicorn with a gold horn quietly cropping the roses in the garden. The man went up to the bedroom where his wife was still asleep and woke her. "There's a unicorn in the garden," he said. "Eating roses." She opened one unfriendly eye and looked at him. "The unicorn is a mythical beast," she said, and turned her back to him. The man walked slowly downstairs and out into the garden. The unicorn was still there; he was now browsing among the tulips. "Here, unicorn," said the man, and he pulled up a lily and gave it to him. The unicorn ate it gravely. With a high heart, because there was a unicorn in his garden, the man went upstairs and roused his wife again. "The unicorn," he said, "ate a lily." His wife sat up in bed and looked at him, coldly. "You are a booby," she said, "and I am going to have you put in the booby-hatch." The man, who had never liked the words "booby" and "booby-hatch," and who liked them even less on a shining morning when there was a unicorn in the garden, thought for a moment. "We'll see about that," he said. He walked over to the door. "He has a golden horn in the middle of his forehead," he told her. Then he went back to the garden to watch the unicorn; but the unicorn had gone away. The man sat down among the roses and went to sleep.

As soon as the husband had gone out of the house, the wife got up and dressed as fast as she could. She was very excited and there was a gloat in her eye. She telephoned the police and she telephoned a psychiatrist; she told them to hurry to her house and bring a strait-jacket. When the police and the psychiatrist arrived they sat down in chairs and looked at her, with great interest. "My husband," she said, "saw a unicorn this morning." The police looked at the psychiatrist and the psychiatrist looked at the police. "He told me it ate a lily," she said. The psychiatrist looked at the police and the police looked at the psychiatrist. "He told me it had a golden horn in the middle of its forehead," she said. At a solemn signal from the psychiatrist, the police leaped from their chairs and seized the wife. They had a hard time subduing her, for she put up a terrific struggle, but they finally subdued her. Just as they got her into the strait-jacket, the husband came back into the house.

"Did you tell your wife you saw a unicorn?" asked the police. "Of course not," said the husband. "The unicorn is a mythical beast." "That's all I wanted to know," said the psychiatrist. "Take her away. I'm sorry, sir, but your wife is as crazy as a jay bird." So they took her away, cursing and screaming, and shut her up in an institution. The husband lived happily ever after.

Moral: Don't count your boobies until they are hatched.

Suggestions for Discussion

1. From what details do you become aware of the hostile feelings between husband and wife?

2. What is Thurber's attitude toward his characters, including the psychiatrist? Refer to the diction, the role of the unicorn, the setting, the details of the action, the twist at the end, the moral, and the drawing.

3. What other "moral" might be appropriate to append to this fable?

4. What evidence can you find that the author is (or is not) detached from his subject?

Suggestions for Writing

1. Write an imaginary description of the events leading up to the situation at the beginning of the fable.

2. Read "The Secret Life of Walter Mitty" and compare situation, tone, and resolution with those of the fable of the unicorn.

3. Write a fable depicting a domestic relationship.

John Steinbeck

The Chrysanthemums

John Steinbeck (1902–1968) wrote novels, short stories, travel sketches, and essays. Born in Salinas, California, he studied at Stanford University. Before he achieved success as a writer, he worked as ranch hand, laborer, and newspaperman. Among his novels are *Tortilla Flat* (1935), *Of Mice and Men* (1937), *The Grapes of Wrath* (1939), which was awarded a Pulitzer Prize, and *East of Eden* (1952). In 1962 he was awarded the Nobel Prize for Literature. Although Elisa's encounter with the tinker in "The Chrysanthemums" leads to her awareness of herself as a woman and of formerly submerged feelings, nothing in her external world has been significantly altered. Her isolation, vitality, and creative energy leave her unfulfilled as a woman.

The high grey-flannel fog of winter closed off the Salinas Valley from the sky and from all the rest of the world. On every side it sat like a lid on the mountains and made of the great valley a closed pot. On the broad, level land floor the gang plows bit deep and left the black earth shining like metal where the shares had cut. On the foothill ranches across the Salinas River, the yellow stubble fields seemed to be bathed in pale cold sunshine, but there was no sunshine in the valley now in December. The thick willow scrub along the river flamed with sharp and positive yellow leaves.

It was a time of quiet and of waiting. The air was cold and tender. A light wind blew up from the southwest so that the farmers were mildly hopeful of a good rain before long; but fog and rain do not go together.

Across the river, on Henry Allen's foothill ranch there was little work to be done, for the hay was cut and stored and the orchards were plowed up to receive the rain deeply when it should come. The cattle on the higher slopes were becoming shaggy and rough-coated.

Elisa Allen, working in her flower garden, looked down across the yard and saw Henry, her husband, talking to two men in business suits. The three of them stood by the tractor shed, each man with one foot on the side of the little Fordson. They smoked cigarettes and studied the machine as they talked.

Elisa watched them for a moment and then went back to her work. She was thirty-five. Her face was lean and strong and her eyes were as clear as water. Her figure looked blocked and heavy in her gardening costume, a man's black hat pulled low down over her eyes, clodhopper shoes, a figured print dress almost completely covered by a big corduroy apron with four big pockets to hold the snips, the trowel and scratcher, the seeds and the knife she worked with. She wore heavy leather gloves to protect her hands while she worked.

She was cutting down the old year's chrysanthemum stalks with a pair of short and powerful scissors. She looked down toward the men by the tractor shed now and then. Her face was eager and mature and handsome; even her work with the scissors was over-eager, over-powerful. The chrysanthemum stems seemed too small and easy for her energy.

She brushed a cloud of hair out of her eyes with the back of her glove, and left a smudge of earth on the cheek in doing it. Behind her stood the neat white farm house with red geraniums close-banked around it as high as the windows. It was a hard-swept looking little house, with hard-polished windows, and a clean mud-mat on the front steps.

Elisa cast another glance toward the tractor shed. The strangers were getting into their Ford coupe. She took off a glove and put her strong fingers down into the forest of new green crysanthemum sprouts that were growing around the old roots. She spread the leaves and looked down among the close-growing stems. No aphids were there, no sowbugs or snails or cutworms. Her terrier fingers destroyed such pests before they could get started.

Elisa started at the sound of her husband's voice. He had come near quietly, and he leaned over the wire fence that protected her flower garden from cattle and dogs and chickens.

"At it again," he said. "You've got a strong new crop coming."

Elisa straightened her back and pulled on the gardening glove again. "Yes. They'll be strong this coming year." In her tone and on her face there was a little smugness.

"You've got a gift with things," Henry observed. "Some of those yellow chrysanthemums you had this year were ten inches across. I wish you'd work out in the orchard and raise some apples that big."

Her eyes sharpened. "Maybe I could do it, too. I've a gift with things, all right. My mother had it. She could stick anything in the ground and make it grow. She said it was having planters' hands that knew how to do it."

"Well, it sure works with flowers," he said.

"Henry, who were those men you were talking to?"

"Why, sure, that's what I came to tell you. They were from the Western Meat Company. I sold those thirty head of three-year-old steers. Got nearly my own price, too."

"Good," she said. "Good for you."

"And I thought," he continued, "I thought how it's Saturday afternoon, and we might go into Salinas for dinner at a restaurant, and then to a picture show—to celebrate, you see."

"Good," she repeated. "Oh, yes. That will be good."

Henry put on his joking tone. "There's fights tonight. How'd you like to go to the fights?"

"Oh, no," she said breathlessly. "No, I wouldn't like fights."

"Just fooling, Elisa. We'll go to a movie. Let's see. It's two now. I'm going to take Scotty and bring down those steers from the hill. It'll take us maybe two hours. We'll go in town about five and have dinner at the Cominos Hotel. Like that?"

"Of course I'll like it. It's good to eat away from home."

"All right, then. I'll go get up a couple of horses."

She said, "I'll have plenty of time to transplant some of these sets, I guess."

She heard her husband calling Scotty down by the barn. And a little later she saw the two men ride up the pale yellow hillside in search of the steers.

There was a little square sandy bed kept for rooting the chrysanthemums. With her trowel she turned the soil over and over, and smoothed it and patted it firm. Then she dug ten parallel trenches to receive the sets. Back at the chrysanthemum bed she pulled out the little crisp shoots, trimmed off the leaves of each one with her scissors and laid it on a small orderly pile.

A squeak of wheels and plod of hoofs came from the road. Elisa looked up. The country road ran along the dense bank of willows and cottonwoods that bordered the river, and up this road came a curious vehicle, curiously drawn. It was an old spring-wagon, with a round canvas top on it like the cover of a prairie schooner. It was drawn by an old bay horse and a little grey-and-white burro. A big stubble-bearded man sat between the cover flaps and drove the crawling team. Underneath the wagon, between the hind wheels, a lean and rangy mongrel dog walked sedately. Words were painted on the canvas in clumsy, crooked letters. "Pots, pans, knives, sisors, lawn mores. Fixed." Two rows of articles and the triumphantly definitive "Fixed" below. The black paint had run down in little sharp points beneath each letter.

Elisa, squatting on the ground, watched to see the crazy, loose-jointed wagon pass by. But it didn't pass. It turned into the farm road in front of her house, crooked old wheels skirling and squeaking. The rangy dog darted from between the wheels and ran ahead. Instantly the two ranch shepherds flew out at him. Then all three stopped, and with stiff and quivering tails, with taut straight legs, with ambassadorial dignity, they slowly circled, sniffing daintily. The caravan pulled up to Elisa's wire fence and stopped. Now the newcomer dog, feeling out-numbered, lowered his tail and retired under the wagon with raised hackles and bared teeth.

The man on the wagon seat called out. "That's a bad dog in a fight when he gets started."

Elisa laughed. "I see he is. How soon does he generally get started?"

The man caught up her laughter and echoed it heartily. "Sometimes not for weeks and weeks," he said. He climbed stiffly down, over the wheel. The horse and the donkey drooped like unwatered flowers.

Elisa saw that he was a very big man. Although his hair and beard were greying, he did not look old. His worn black suit was wrinkled and spotted with grease. The laughter had disappeared from his face and eyes the moment his laughing voice ceased. His eyes were dark, and they were full of the brooding that gets in the eyes of teamsters and of sailors. The calloused hands he rested on the wire fence were cracked, and every crack was a black line. He took off his battered hat.

"I'm off my general road, ma'am," he said. "Does this dirt road cut over across the river to the Los Angeles highway?"

Elisa stood up and shoved the thick scissors in her apron pocket. "Well, yes, it does, but it winds around and then fords the river. I don't think your team could pull through the sand."

He replied with some asperity, "It might surprise you what them beasts can pull through."

"When they get started?" she asked.

He smiled for a second. "Yes. When they get started."

"Well," said Elisa, "I think you'll save time if you go back to the Salinas road and pick up the highway there."

He drew a big finger down the chicken wire and made it sing. "I ain't in any hurry, ma'am. I go from Seattle to San Diego and back every year. Takes all my time. About six months each way. I aim to follow nice weather."

Elisa took off her gloves and stuffed them in the apron pocket with the scissors. She touched the under edge of her man's hat, searching for fugitive hairs. "That sounds like a nice kind of a way to live," she said.

He leaned confidentially over the fence. "Maybe you noticed the writing on my wagon. I mend pots and sharpen knives and scissors. You got any of them things to do?"

"Oh, no," she said quickly. "Nothing like that." Her eyes hardened with resistance.

"Scissors is the worst thing," he explained. "Most people just ruin scissors trying to sharpen 'em but I know how. I got a special tool. It's a little bobbit kind of thing, and patented. But is sure does the trick."

"No. My scissors are all sharp."

"All right, then. Take a pot," he continued earnestly, "a bent pot, or a pot with a hole. I can make it like new so you don't have to buy no new ones. That's a saving for you."

"No," she said shortly. "I tell you I have nothing like that for you to do."

His face fell to an exaggerated sadness. His voice took on a whining undertone. "I ain't had a thing to do today. Maybe I won't have no supper tonight. You see I'm off my regular road. I know folks on the highway clear from Seattle to San Diego. They save their things for me to sharpen up because they know I do it so good and save them money."

"I'm sorry," Elisa said irritably. "I haven't anything for you to do."

His eyes left her face and fell to searching the ground. They roamed about until they came to the chrysanthemum bed where she had been working. "What's them plants, ma'am?"

The irritation and resistance melted from Elisa's face. "Oh, those are chrysanthemums, giant whites and yellows. I raise them every year, bigger than anybody around here."

"Kind of a long-stemmed flower? Looks like a quick puff of colored smoke?" he asked.

"That's it. What a nice way to describe them."

"They smell kind of nasty till you get used to them," he said.

"It's a good bitter small," she retorted, "not nasty at all."

He changed his tone quickly. "I like the smell myself."

"I had ten-inch blooms this year," she said.

The man leaned farther over the fence. "Look. I know a lady down the road a piece, has got the nicest garden you ever seen. Got nearly every kind of flower but no chrysanthemums. Last time I was mending a copper-bottom washtub for her (that's a hard job but I do it good), she said to me, 'If you ever run acrost some nice chrysanthemums I wish you'd try to get me a few seeds.' That's what she told me."

Elisa's eyes grew alert and eager. "She couldn't have known much about chrysanthemums. You can raise them from seed, but it's much easier to root the little sprouts you see there."

"Oh," he said. "I s'pose I can't take none to her, then."

"Why yes you can," Elisa cried. "I can put some in damp sand, and you can carry them right along with you. They'll take root in the pot if you keep them damp. And then she can transplant them."

"She'd sure like to have some, ma'am. You say they're nice ones?"

"Beautiful," she said. "Oh, beautiful." Her eyes shone. She tore off the battered hat and shook out her dark pretty hair. "I'll put them in a flower pot, and you can take them right with you. Come into the yard."

While the man came through the picket gate Elisa ran excitedly along the geranium-bordered path to the back of the house. And she returned carrying a big red flower pot. The gloves were forgotten now. She kneeled on the ground by the starting bed and dug up the sandy soil with her fingers and scooped it into the bright new flower pot. Then she picked up the little pile of shoots she had prepared. With her strong fingers she pressed them into the sand and tamped around them with her knuckles. The man stood over her. "I'll tell you what to do," she said. "You remember so you can tell the lady."

"Yes, I'll try to remember."

"Well, look. These will take root in about a month. Then she must set them out, about a foot apart in good rich earth like this, see?" She lifted a handful of dark soil for him to look at. "They'll grow fast and tall. Now remember this. In July tell her to cut them down, about eight inches from the ground."

"Before they bloom?" he asked.

"Yes, before they bloom." Her face was tight with eagerness. "They'll come right up again. About the last of September the buds will start."

She stopped and seemed perplexed. "It's the budding that takes the most care," she said hesitantly. "I don't know how to tell you." She looked deep into his eyes, searchingly. Her mouth opened a little, and she seemed to be listening. "I'll try to tell you," she said. "Did you ever hear of planting hands?"

"Can't say I have, ma'am."

"Well, I can only tell you what it feels like. It's when you're picking off the buds you don't want. Everything goes right down into your fingertips. You watch your fingers work. They do it themselves. You can feel how it is. They pick and pick the buds. They never make a mistake. They're with the plant. Do you see? Your fingers and the plant. You can feel that, right up your arm. They know. They never make a mistake. You can feel it. When you're like that you can't do anything wrong. Do you see that? Can you understand that?"

She was kneeling on the ground looking up at him. Her breast swelled passionately.

The man's eyes narrowed. He looked away, self-consciously. "Maybe I know," he said. "Sometimes in the night in the wagon there—"

Elisa's voice grew husky. She broke in on him. "I've never lived as you do, but I know what you mean. When the night is dark—why, the stars are sharp-pointed, and there's quiet. Why, you rise up and up! Every pointed star gets driven into your body. It's like that. Hot and sharp and—lovely."

Kneeling there, her hand went out toward his legs in the greasy black trousers. Her hesitant fingers almost touched the cloth. Then her hand dropped to the ground. She crouched low like a fawning dog.

He said, "It's nice, just like you say. Only when you don't have no dinner, it ain't."

She stood up then, very straight, and her face was ashamed. She held the flower pot out to him and placed it gently in his arms. "Here. Put it in your wagon, on the seat, where you can watch it. Maybe I can find something for you to do."

At the back of the house she dug in the can pile and found two old and battered aluminum saucepans. She carried them back and gave them to him. "Here, maybe you can fix these."

His manner changed. He became professional. "Good as new I can fix them." At the back of his wagon he set a little anvil, and out of an oily tool box dug a small machine hammer. Elisa came through the gate to watch him while he pounded out the dents in the kettles. His mouth grew sure and knowing. At a difficult part of the work he sucked his under-lip.

"You sleep right in the wagon?" Elisa asked.

"Right in the wagon, ma'am. Rain or shine I'm dry as a cow in there."

"It must be nice," she said. "It must be very nice. I wish women could do such things."

"It ain't the right kind of a life for a woman."

Her upper lip raised a little, showing her teeth. "How do you know? How can you tell?" she said.

"I don't know ma'am," he protested. "Of course I don't know. Now here's your kettles, done. You don't have to buy no new ones."

"How much?"

"Oh, fifty cents'll do. I keep my prices down and my work good. That's why I have all them satisfied customers up and down the highway."

Elisa brought him a fifty-cent piece from the house and dropped it in his hand. "You might be surprised to have a rival some time. I can sharpen scissors, too. And I can beat the dents out of little pots. I could show you what a woman might do."

He put his hammer back in the oily box and shoved the little anvil out of sight. "It would be a lonely life for a woman, ma'am, and a scarey life, too, with animals creeping under the wagon all night." He climbed over the singletree, steadying himself with a hand on the burro's white rump. He settled himself in the seat, picked up the lines. "Thank you kindly, ma'am," he said. "I'll do like you told me; I'll go back and catch the Salinas road."

"Mind," she called, "if you're long in getting there, keep the sand damp."

"Sand, ma'am? . . . Sand? Oh, sure. You mean round the chrysanthemums. Sure I will." He clucked his tongue. The beasts leaned luxuriously into their collars. The mongrel dog took his place between the back wheels. The wagon turned and crawled out the entrance road and back the way it had come, along the river.

Elisa stood in front of her wire fence watching the slow progress of the caravan. Her shoulders were straight, her head thrown back, her eyes half-closed, so that the scene came vaguely into them. Her lips moved silently, forming the words "Good-bye—good-bye." Then she whispered. "That's a bright direction. There's a glowing there." The sound of her whisper startled her. She shook herself free and looked about to see whether anyone had been listening. Only the dogs had heard. They lifted their heads toward her from their sleeping in the dust, and then stretched out their chins and settled asleep again. Elisa turned and ran hurriedly into the house.

In the kitchen she reached behind the stove and felt the water tank. It was full of hot water from the noonday cooking. In the bathroom she tore off her soiled clothes and flung them into the corner. And then she scrubbed herself with a little block of pumice, legs and thighs, loins and chest and arms, until her skin was scratched and red. When she had dried herself she stood in front of a mirror in her bedroom and looked at her body. She tightened her stomach and threw out her chest. She turned and looked over her shoulder at her back.

After a while she began to dress, slowly. She put on her newest underclothing and her nicest stockings and the dress which was the symbol of her prettiness. She worked carefully on her hair, pencilled her eyebrows and rouged her lips.

Before she was finished she heard the little thunder of hoofs and the shouts of Henry and his helper as they drove the red steers into the corral. She heard the gate bang shut and set herself for Henry's arrival.

His step sounded on the porch. He entered the house calling "Elisa, where are you?"

"In my room, dressing. I'm not ready. There's hot water for your bath. Hurry up. It's getting late."

When she heard him splashing in the tub, Elisa laid his dark suit on the bed, and shirt and socks and tie beside it. She stood his polished shoes on the floor beside the bed. Then she went to the porch and sat primly and stiffly down. She looked toward the river road where the willow-line was still yellow with frosted leaves so that under the high grey fog they seemed a thin band of sunshine. This was the only color in the grey afternoon. She sat unmoving for a long time. Her eyes blinked rarely.

Henry came banging out of the door, shoving his tie inside his vest as he came. Elisa stiffened and her face grew tight. Henry stopped short and looked at her. "Why—why, Elisa. You look so nice!"

"Nice? You think I look nice? What do you mean by 'nice'?"

Henry blundered on. "I don't know. I mean you look different, strong and happy."

"I am strong? Yes, strong. What do you mean 'strong'?"

He looked bewildered. "You're playing some kind of a game," he said helplessly. "It's a kind of a play. You look strong enough to break a calf over your knee, happy enough to eat it like a watermelon."

For a second she lost her rigidity. "Henry! Don't talk like that. You didn't know what you said." She grew complete again. "I'm strong," she boasted. "I never knew before how strong."

Henry looked down toward the tractor shed, and when he brought his eyes back to her, they were his own again. "I'll get out the car. You can put on your coat while I'm starting."

Elisa went into the house. She heard him drive to the gate and idle down his motor, and then she took a long time to put on her hat. She pulled it here and pressed it there. When Henry turned the motor off she slipped into her coat and went out.

The little roadster bounced along on the dirt road by the river, raising the birds and driving the rabbits into the brush. Two cranes flapped heavily over the willow-line and dropped into the river-bed.

Far ahead on the road Elisa saw a dark speck. She knew.

She tried not to look as they passed it, but her eyes would not obey. She whispered to herself sadly. "He might have thrown them off the road. That wouldn't have been much trouble, not very much. But he kept the pot," she explained. "He had to keep the pot. That's why he couldn't get them off the road."

The roadster turned a bend and she saw the caravan ahead. She swung full around toward her husband so she could not see the little covered wagon and the mismatched team as the car passed them.

In a moment they had left behind them the man who had not known or needed to know what she said, the bargainer. She did not look back.

To Henry, she said loudly, to be heard above the motor, "It will be good, to-night, a good dinner."

"Now you're changed again," Henry complained. He took one hand from the wheel and patted her knee. "I ought to take you in to dinner oftener. It would be good for both of us. We get so heavy out on the ranch."

"Henry," she asked, "could we have wine at dinner?"

"Sure. Say! That will be fine."

She was silent for a while; then she said, "Henry, at those prize fights do the men hurt each other very much?"

"Sometimes a little, not often. Why?"

"Well, I've read how they break noses, and blood runs down their chests. I've read how the fighting gloves get heavy and soggy with blood."

He looked round at her. "What's the matter, Elisa? I didn't know you read things like that." He brought the car to a stop, then turned to the right over the Salinas River bridge.

"Do any women ever go to the fights?" she asked.

"Oh, sure, some. What's the matter, Elisa? Do you want to go? I don't think you'd like it, but I'll take you if you really want to go."

She relaxed limply in the seat. "Oh, no. I don't want to go. I'm sure I don't." Her face was turned away from him. "It will be enough if we can have wine. It will be plenty." She turned up her coat collar so he could not see that she was crying weakly—like an old woman.

Suggestions for Discussion

1. What descriptive details prepare you for Elisa's emotional isolation?

2. The action, rising in emotional intensity to its climax, is developed in four scenes. Describe Elisa's feelings in each scene and attempt to account for them.

3. Discuss the possible symbolic functions of the scissors, the chrysanthemum shoots, the wine, and the fights. How are they related to the complication and resolution of the action?

4. How is the tinker's deception foreshadowed?

5. By what means are we made aware of the change in Elisa's image of herself? How adequately does the story account for Elisa's frustration? Explain the fluctuations in her appearance and mood. By what means are we made aware that her relationship with Henry is not satisfying?

Suggestions for Writing

1. Relate the story to the essay by Greer.

2. Write a character study of Elisa.

3. Portray in narrative form a marital relationship in which there is a failure in communication.

James Thurber
The Catbird Seat

James Thurber (1894–1961), American humorist and artist, began contributing in 1927 to *The New Yorker,* in which most of his work first appeared. His humorous essays and short stories are collected in such books as *The Owl in the Attic* (1931), *My Life and Hard Times* (1933), *The Thurber Carnival* (1945), *The Beast in Me* (1948), and *Lanterns and Lances* (1961). He also wrote the short story "The Secret Life of Walter Mitty," several fantasies for children, and, with Elliot Nugent, a comedy called *The Male Animal* (1961). "The Catbird Seat" invites the reader to enter a world of fantasy in which the satiric commentary upon human frailty is subordinate to the spirit of fun and the ironic reversals of character and situation.

Mr. Martin bought the pack of Camels on Monday night in the most crowded cigar store on Broadway. It was theater time and seven or eight men were buying cigarettes. The clerk didn't even glance at Mr. Martin, who put the pack in his overcoat pocket and went out. If any of the staff at F & S had seen him buy the cigarettes, they would have been astonished, for it was generally known that Mr. Martin did not smoke, and never had. No one saw him.

It was just a week to the day since Mr. Martin had decided to rub out Mrs. Ulgine Barrows. The term "rub out" pleased him because it suggested nothing more than the correction of an error—in this case an error of Mr. Fitweiler. Mr. Martin had spent each night of the past week working out his plan and examining it. As he walked home now he went over it again. For the hundredth time he resented the element of imprecision, the margin of guesswork that entered into the business. The project as he had worked it out was casual and bold, the risks were considerable. Something might go wrong anywhere along the line. And therein lay the cunning of his scheme. No one would ever see in it the cautious, painstaking hand of Erwin Martin, head of the filing department at F & S of whom Mr. Fitweiler had once said, "Man is fallible but Martin isn't." No one would see his hand, that is, unless it were caught in the act.

Sitting in his apartment, drinking a glass of milk, Mr. Martin reviewed his case against Mrs. Ulgine Barrows, as he had every night for seven nights. He began at the beginning. Her quaking voice and braying laugh had first profaned the halls of F & S on March 7, 1941 (Mr. Martin had a head for dates). Old Roberts, the personnel chief, had introduced her as the newly appointed special adviser to the president of the firm, Mr. Fitweiler. The woman had appalled Mr. Martin instantly, but he hadn't shown it. He had given her his dry hand, a look of studious concentration, and a faint smile. "Well," she had said, looking at the papers on his desk, "are you lifting the oxcart out of the ditch?" As Mr. Martin recalled the moment, over his milk, he squirmed slightly. He must keep his mind on her crimes as a special adviser, not on her peccadillos as a personality. This he found difficult to do, in spite of entering an objection and sustaining it. The faults of the woman as a woman kept chattering on in his mind like an unruly witness. She had, for almost two years now, baited him. In the halls, in the elevator, even in his own office, into which she romped now and then like a circus horse, she was constantly shouting these silly questions at him. "Are you lifting the oxcart out of the ditch? Are you tearing up the pea patch? Are you hollering down the rain barrel? Are you scraping around the bottom of the pickle barrel? Are you sitting in the catbird seat?"

It was Joey Hart, one of Mr. Martin's two assistants, who had explained what the gibberish meant. "She must be a Dodger fan," he had said. "Red Barber announces the Dodger games over the radio and he uses those expressions—picked 'em up down South." Joey had gone on to explain one or two. "Tearing up the pea patch" meant going on a rampage; "sitting in the catbird seat" meant sitting pretty, like a batter with three balls and no strikes on him. Mr. Martin dismissed all this with an effort. It had been annoying, it had driven him near to distraction, but he was too solid a man to be moved to murder by anything so childish. It was fortunate, he reflected as he passed on to the important charges against Mrs. Barrows, that he had stood up under it so well. He had maintained always an outward appearance of polite tolerance. "Why, I even believe you like the woman," Miss Paird, his other assistant, had once said to him. He had simply smiled.

A gavel rapped in Mr. Martin's mind and the case was resumed. Mrs. Ulgine Barrows stood charged with willful, blatant, and persistent attempts to destroy the efficiency and system of F & S. It was competent, material, and relevant to review her advent and rise to power. Mr. Martin had got the story from Miss Paird, who seemed always able to find things out. According to her, Mrs. Barrows had met Mr. Fitweiler at a party, where she had rescued him from the embraces of a powerfully built drunken man who had mistaken the president of F & S for a famous retired Middle Western football coach. She had led him to a sofa and somehow worked upon him a monstrous magic.

The aging gentleman had jumped to the conclusion there and then that this was a woman of singular attainments, equipped to bring out the best in him and the firm. A week later he had introduced her into F & S as his special adviser. On that day confusion got its foot in the door. After Miss Tyson, Mr. Brundage, and Mr. Bartlett had been fired and Mr. Munson had taken his hat and stalked out, mailing in his resignation later, old Roberts had been emboldened to speak to Mr. Fitweiler. He mentioned that Mr. Munson's department had been "a little disrupted" and hadn't they perhaps better resume the old system there? Mr. Fitweiler had said certainly not. He had the greatest faith in Mrs. Barrows' ideas. "They require a little seasoning, a little seasoning, is all," he had added. Mr. Roberts had given it up. Mr. Martin reviewed in detail all the changes wrought by Mrs. Barrows. She had begun chipping at the cornices of the firm's edifice and now she was swinging at the foundation with a pickaxe.

Mr. Martin came now, in his summing up, to the afternoon of Monday, November 2, 1942—just one week ago. On that day, at 3 P.M., Mrs. Barrows had bounced into his office. "Boo!" she had yelled. "Are you scraping around the bottom of the pickle barrel?" Mr. Martin had looked at her from under his green eyeshade, saying nothing. She had begun to wander about the office, taking it in with her great, popping eyes. "Do you really need *all* these filing cabinets?" she had demanded suddenly. Mr. Martin's heart had jumped. "Each of these files," he had said, keeping his voice even, "plays an indispensable part in the system of F & S." She had brayed at him, "Well, don't tear up the pea patch!" and gone to the door. From there she had bawled, "But you sure have got a lot of fine scrap in here!" Mr. Martin could no longer doubt that the finger was on his beloved department. Her pickaxe was on the upswing, poised for the first blow. It had not come yet; he had received no blue memo from the enchanted Mr. Fitweiler bearing nonsensical instructions deriving from the obscene woman. But there was no doubt in Mr. Martin's mind that one would be forthcoming. He must act quickly. Already a precious week had gone by. Mr. Martin stood up in his living room, still holding his milk glass. "Gentlemen of the jury," he said to himself, "I demand the death penalty for this horrible person."

The next day Mr. Martin followed his routine, as usual. He polished his glasses more often and once sharpened an already sharp pencil, but not even Miss Paird noticed. Only once did he catch sight of his victim; she swept past him in the hall with a patronizing "Hi!" At five-thirty he walked home, as usual, and had a glass of milk, as usual. He had never drunk anything stronger in his life—unless you could count ginger ale. The late Sam Schlosser, the S of F & S, had praised Mr. Martin at a staff meeting several years before for his temperate habits. "Our most efficient worker neither drinks nor smokes," he had said. "The results speak for themselves." Mr. Fitweiler had sat by, nodding approval.

Mr. Martin was still thinking about that red-letter day as he walked over to the Schrafft's on Fifth Avenue near Forty-sixth Street. He got there, as he always did, at eight o'clock. He finished his dinner and the financial page of the *Sun* at a quarter to nine, as he always did. It was his custom after dinner to take a walk. This time he walked down Fifth Avenue at a casual pace. His gloved hands felt moist and warm, his forehead cold. He transferred the Camels from his overcoat to a jacket pocket. He wondered, as he did so, if they did not represent an unnecessary note of strain. Mrs. Barrows smoked only Luckies. It was his idea to puff a few puffs on a Camel (after the rubbing-out), stub it out in the ashtray holding her lipstick-stained Luckies, and thus drag a small red herring across the trail. Perhaps it was not a good idea. It would take time. He might even choke, too loudly.

Mr. Martin had never seen the house on West Twelfth Street where Mrs. Barrows lived, but he had a clear enough picture of it. Fortunately, she had bragged to everybody about her ducky first-floor apartment in the perfectly darling three-story red-brick. There would be no doorman or other attendants; just the tenants of the second and third floors. As he walked along, Mr. Martin realized that he would get there before nine-thirty. He had considered walking north on Fifth Avenue from Schrafft's to a point from which it would take him until ten o'clock to reach the house. At that hour people were less likely to be coming in or going out. But the procedure would have made an awkward loop in the straight thread of his casualness, and he had abandoned it. It was impossible to figure when people would be entering or leaving the house, anyway. There was a great risk at any hour. If he ran into anybody, he would simply have to place the rubbing-out of Ulgine Barrows in the inactive file forever. The same thing would hold true if there were someone in her apartment. In that case he would just say that he had been passing by, recognized her charming house, and thought to drop in.

It was eighteen minutes after nine when Mr. Martin turned into Twelfth Street. A man passed him, and a man and a woman, talking. There was no one within fifty paces when he came to the house, halfway down the block. He was up the steps and in the small vestibule in no time, pressing the bell under the card that said "Mrs. Ulgine Barrows." When the clicking in the lock started he jumped forward against the door. He got inside fast, closing the door behind him. A bulb in a lantern hung from the hall ceiling on a chain seemed to give a monstrously bright light. There was nobody on the stair, which went up ahead of him along the left wall. A door opened down the hall in the wall on the right. He went toward it swiftly, on tiptoe.

"Welll, for God's sake, look who's here!" bawled Mrs. Barrows, and her braying laugh rang out like the report of a shotgun. He rushed past her like a football tackle, bumping her. "Hey, quit shoving!" she said, closing the door behind them. They were in her living room, which seemed to Mr. Martin to be lighted by a hundred lamps. "What's after you?" she said. "You're as jumpy as a goat." He found he was unable to speak. His heart was wheezing in his throat. "I—yes," he finally brought out. She was jabbering and laughing as she started to help him off with his coat. "No, no," he said. "I'll put it here." He took it off and put it on a chair near the door. "Your hat and gloves, too," she said. "You're in a lady's house." He put his hat on top of the coat. Mrs. Barrows seemed larger than he had thought. He kept his gloves on. "I was passing by," he said. "I recognized—is there anyone here?" She laughed louder than ever. "No," she said, "we're all alone. You're as white as a sheet, you funny man. Whatever *has* come over you? I'll mix you a toddy." She started toward a door across the room. "Scotch-and-soda be all right? But say, you don't drink, do you?" She turned and gave him her amused look. Mr. Martin pulled himself together. "Scotch-and-soda will be all right," he heard himself say. He could hear her laughing in the kitchen.

Mr. Martin looked quickly around the living room for the weapon. He had counted on finding one there. There were andirons and a poker and something in a corner that looked like an Indian club. None of them would do. It couldn't be that way. He began to pace around. He came to a desk. On it lay a metal paper knife with an ornate handle. Would it be sharp enough? He reached for it and knocked over a small brass jar. Stamps spilled out of it and it fell to the floor with a clatter. "Hey," Mrs. Barrows yelled from the kitchen, "are you tearing up the pea patch?" Mr. Martin gave a strange laugh. Picking up the knife, he tried its point against his left wrist. It was blunt. It wouldn't do.

When Mrs. Barrows reappeared, carrying two highballs, Mr. Martin, standing there with his gloves on, became acutely conscious of the fantasy he had wrought. Cigarettes in his pocket, a drink prepared for him—it was all too grossly improbable. It was more than that; it was impossible. Somewhere in the back of his mind a vague idea stirred, sprouted. "For heaven's sake, take off those gloves," said Mrs. Barrows. "I always wear them in the house," said Mr. Martin. The idea began to bloom, strange and wonderful. She put the glasses on a coffee table in front of a sofa and sat on the sofa. "Come over here, you odd little man," she said. Mr. Martin went over and sat beside her. It was difficult getting a cigarette out of the pack of Camels, but he managed it. She held a match for him, laughing. "Well," she said, handing him his drink, "this is perfectly marvelous. You with a drink and a cigarette."

Mr. Martin puffed, not too awkwardly, and took of gulp of the highball. "I drink and smoke all the time," he said. He clinked his glass against hers. "Here's nuts to that old windbag, Fitweiler," he said, and gulped again. The stuff tasted awful, but he made no grimace. "Really, Mr. Martin," she said, her voice and posture changing, "you are insulting our employer." Mrs. Barrows was now all special adviser to the president. "I am preparing a bomb," said Mr. Martin, "which will blow the old goat higher than hell." He had only had a little of the drink, which was not strong. It couldn't be that. "Do you take dope or something?" Mrs. Barrows asked coldly. "Heroin," said Mr. Martin. "I'll be coked to the gills when I bump the old buzzard off." "Mr. Martin!" she shouted, getting to her feet. "That will be all of that. You must go at once." Mr. Martin took another swallow of his drink. He tapped his cigarette out in the ashtray and put the pack of Camels on the coffee table. Then he got up. She stood glaring at him. He walked over and put on his hat and coat. "Not a word about this," he said, and laid an index finger against his lips. All Mrs. Barrows could bring out was "Really!" Mr. Martin put his hand on the doorknob. "I'm sitting in the catbird seat," he said. He stuck his tongue out at her and left. Nobody saw him go.

Mr. Martin got to his apartment, walking, well before eleven. No one saw him go in. He had two glasses of milk after brushing his teeth, and he felt elated. It wasn't tipsiness, because he hadn't been tipsy. Anyway, the walk had worn off all effects of the whiskey. He got in bed and read a magazine for a while. He was asleep before midnight.

Mr. Martin got to the office at eight-thirty the next morning, as usual. At a quarter to nine, Ulgine Barrows, who had never before arrived at work before ten, swept into his office. "I'm reporting to Mr. Fitweiler now!" she shouted. "If he turns you over to the police, it's no more than you deserve!" Mr. Martin gave her a look of shocked surprise. "I beg your pardon?" he said. Mrs. Barrows snorted and bounced out of the room, leaving Miss Paird and

Joey Hart staring after her. "What's the matter with that old devil now?" asked Miss Paird. "I have no idea," said Mr. Martin, resuming his work. The other two looked at him and then at each other. Miss Paird got up and went out. She walked slowly past the closed door of Mr. Fitweiler's office. Mrs. Barrows was yelling inside, but she was not braying. Miss Paird could not hear what the woman was saying. She went back to her desk.

Forty-five minutes later, Mrs. Barrows left the president's office and went into her own, shutting the door. It wasn't until half an hour later that Mr. Fitweiler sent for Mr. Martin. The head of the filing department, neat, quiet, attentive, stood in front of the old man's desk. Mr. Fitweiler was pale and nervous. He took his glasses off and twiddled them. He made a small, bruffing sound in his throat. "Martin," he said, "you have been with us more than twenty years." "Twenty-two, sir," said Mr. Martin. "In that time," pursued the president, "your work and your—uh—manner have been exemplary." "I trust so, sir," said Mr. Martin. "I have understood, Martin," said Mr. Fitweiler, "that you have never taken a drink or smoked." "That is correct, sir," said Mr. Martin. "Ah, yes." Mr. Fitweiler polished his glasses. "You may describe what you did after leaving the office yesterday, Martin," he said. Mr. Martin allowed less than a second for his bewildered pause. "Certainly, sir," he said. "I walked home. Then I went to Schrafft's for dinner. Afterward I walked home again. I went to bed early, sir, and read a magazine for a while. I was asleep before eleven." "Ah, yes," said Mr. Fitweiler again. He was silent for a moment, searching for the proper words to say to the head of the filing department. "Mrs. Barrows," he said finally, "Mrs. Barrows has worked hard, Martin, very hard. It grieves me to report that she has suffered a severe breakdown. It has taken the form of a persecution complex accompanied by distressing hallucinations." "I am very sorry, sir," said Mr. Martin. "Mrs. Barrows is under the delusion," continued Mr. Fitweiler, "that you visited her last evening and behaved yourself in an—uh—unseemly manner." He raised his hand to silence Mr. Martin's little pained outcry. "It is the nature of these psychological diseases," Mr. Fitweiler said, "to fix upon the least likely and most innocent party as the—uh—source of persecution. These matters are not for the lay mind to grasp, Martin. I've just had my psychiatrist, Dr. Fitch, on the phone. He would not, of course, commit himself, but he made enough generalizations to substantiate my suspicions. I suggested to Mrs. Barrows, when she had completed her—uh—story to me this morning, that she visit Dr. Fitch, for I suspected a condition at once. She flew, I regret to say, into a rage, and demanded—uh—requested that I call you on the carpet. You may not know, Martin, but Mrs. Barrows had planned a reorganization of your department—subject to my approval, of course, subject to my approval. This brought you, rather than anyone else, to her mind—but again that is a phenomenon for Dr. Fitch and not for us. So, Martin, I am afraid Mrs. Barrows' usefulness here is at an end." "I am dreadfully sorry, sir," said Mr. Martin.

It was at this point that the door to the office blew open with the suddenness of a gas-main explosion and Mrs. Barrows catapulted through it. "Is the little rat denying it?" she screamed. "He can't get away with that!" Mr. Martin got up and moved discreetly to a point beside Mr. Fitweiler's chair. "You drank and smoked at my apartment," she bawled at Mr. Martin, "and you know it! You called Mr. Fitweiler an old windbag and said you were going to blow him up when you got coked to the gills on your heroin!" She stopped yelling to catch her breath and a new glint came into her popping eyes. "If you weren't such a drab, ordinary little man," she said, "I'd think you'd planned it all. Sticking your tongue out, saying you were sitting in the catbird seat, because you thought no one would believe me when I told it! My God, it's really too perfect!" She brayed loudly and hysterically, and the fury was on her again. She glared at Mr. Fitweiler. "Can't you see how he has tricked us, you old fool? Can't you see his little game?" But Mr. Fitweiler had been surreptitiously pressing all the buttons under the top of his desk and employees of F & S began pouring into the room. "Stockton," said Mr. Fitweiler, "you and Fishbein will take Mrs. Barrows to her home. Mrs. Powell, you will go with them." Stockton, who had played a little football in high school, blocked Mrs. Barrows as she made for Mr. Martin. It took him and Fishbein together to force her out of the door into the hall, crowded with stenographers and office boys. She was still screaming imprecations at Mr. Martin, tangled and contradictory imprecations. The hubbub finally died out down the corridor.

"I regret that this has happened," said Mr. Fitweiler. "I shall ask you to dismiss it from your mind, Martin." "Yes sir," said Mr. Martin, anticipating his chief's "That will be all" by moving to the door. "I will dismiss it." He went out and shut the door, and his step was light and quick in the hall. When he entered his department he had slowed down to his customary gait, and he walked quietly across the room to the W20 file, wearing a look of studious concentration.

Suggestions for Discussion

1. How does the point of view contribute to the comic effects? How are contrast and suspense used to develop the action? How does the simulation of a court case contribute to suspense and plot development? At what point can the reader predict the resolution of the action? How is tension maintained until the very end?

2. Explain the ironic reversals in character and situation. How are they prepared for? To what extent are Mr. Martin and Mrs. Barrows types? Caricatures? How are they individualized?

3. Bergson has said that a character is "generally comic in proportion to his ignorance of himself. The comic person is unconscious." Apply this theory to the two principal characters.

4. Why was Mrs. Barrows particularly repugnant to Mr. Martin? Cite examples from the mock trial to support your answer.

5. What is ironical in the final choice of weapon? What finally defeats Mrs. Barrows? Why does he call her obscene?

6. Study the diction in the retrospective exposition of the advent of Mrs. Barrows and in the scene in her apartment. What words are repeated? How do the verbs in the description of Mrs. Barrows and her own use of clichés contribute to characterization and tone? How else is repetition used to achieve comic effects? How do legal and psychiatric terminology and animal imagery contribute to tone?

7. Although the primary tone is one of burlesque, how does seriousness impinge upon the comic elements?

Suggestions for Writing

1. Create a portrait of an obsessive-compulsive character.

2. Invent a fantasy in which you are finally situated in the catbird seat.

Katherine Anne Porter

Rope

Katherine Anne Porter (1890–1980), American short-story writer, novelist, and critic, was born in Texas and educated in convent schools in Texas and New Orleans. She was a visiting lecturer at numerous colleges and universities and lived and traveled in Mexico, Germany, and France. Her books include *Flowering Judas* (1930), *Noon-Wine* (1937), *Pale Horse, Pale Rider* (1939), critical essays, *The Days Before* (1952), and a novel, *Ship of Fools* (1962). In "Rope," the frustration of husband and wife, expressed in displaced anger, is followed by an expression of the more enduring ties of a shared life.

On the third day after they moved to the country he came walking back from the village carrying a basket of groceries and a twenty-four-yard coil of rope. She came out to meet him, wiping her hands on her green smock. Her hair was tumbled, her nose was scarlet with sunburn; he told her that already she looked like a born country woman. His gray flannel shirt stuck to him, his heavy shoes were dusty. She assured him he looked like a rural character in a play.

Had he brought the coffee? She had been waiting all day long for coffee. They had forgot it when they ordered at the store the first day.

Gosh, no, he hadn't. Lord, now he'd have to go back. Yes, he would if it killed him. He thought, though, he had everything else. She reminded him it was only because he didn't drink coffee himself. If he did he would remember it quick enough. Suppose they ran out of cigarettes? Then she saw the rope. What was that for? Well, he thought it might do to hang clothes on, or something. Naturally, she asked him if he thought they were going to run a laundry. They already had a fifty-foot line hanging right before his eyes. Why, hadn't he noticed it, really? It was a blot on the landscape to her.

He thought there were a lot of things a rope might come in handy for. She wanted to know what, for instance. He thought a few seconds, but nothing occurred. They could wait and see, couldn't they? You need all sorts of strange odds and ends around a place in the country. She said, yes, that was so; but she thought just at that time when every penny counted, it seemed funny to buy more rope. That was all. She hadn't meant anything else. She hadn't just seen, not at first, why he felt it was necessary.

Well, thunder, he had bought it because he wanted to, and that was all there was to it. She thought that was reason enough, and couldn't understand why he hadn't said so, at first. Undoubtedly it would be useful, twenty-four yards of rope, there were hundreds of things, she couldn't think of any at the moment, but it would come in. Of course. As he had said, things always did in the country.

But she was a little disappointed about the coffee, and oh, look, look, look at the eggs! Oh, my, they're all running! What had he put on top of them? Hadn't he known eggs mustn't be squeezed? Squeezed, who had squeezed them, he wanted to know. What a silly thing to say. He had simply brought them along in the basket with the other things. If they got broke it was the grocer's fault. He should know better than to put heavy things on top of eggs.

She believed it was the rope. That was the heaviest thing in the pack, she saw him plainly when he came in from the road, the rope was a big package on top of everything. He desired the whole wide world to witness that this was not a fact. He had carried the rope in one hand and the basket in the other, and what was the use of her having eyes if that was the best they could do for her?

Well, anyhow, she could see one thing plain: no eggs for breakfast. They'd have to scramble them now, for supper. It was too damned bad. She had planned to have steak for supper. No ice, meat wouldn't keep. He wanted to know why she couldn't finish breaking the eggs in a bowl and set them in a cool place.

Cool place! if he could find one for her, she'd be glad to set them there. Well, then, it seemed to him they might very well cook the meat at the same time they cooked the eggs and then warm up the meat for tomorrow. The idea simply choked her. Warmed-over meat, when they might as well have had it fresh. Second best and scraps and makeshifts, even to the meat! He rubbed her shoulder a little. It doesn't really matter so much, does it, darling? Sometimes when they were playful, he would rub her shoulder and she would arch and purr. This time she hissed and almost clawed. He was getting ready to say that they could surely manage somehow when she turned on him and said, if he told her they could manage somehow she would certainly slap his face.

He swallowed the words red hot, his face burned. He picked up the rope and started to put it on the top shelf. She would not have it on the top shelf, the jars and tins belonged there; positively she would not have the top shelf cluttered up with a lot of rope. She had borne all the clutter she meant to bear in the flat in town, there was space here at least and she meant to keep things in order.

Well, in that case, he wanted to know what the hammer and nails were doing up there? And why had she put them there when she knew very well he needed that hammer and those nails upstairs to fix the window sashes? She simply slowed down everything and made double work on the place with her insane habit of changing things around and hiding them.

She was sure she begged his pardon, and if she had had any reason to believe he was going to fix the sashes this summer she would have left the hammer and nails right where he put them; in the middle of the bedroom floor where they could step on them in the dark. And now if he didn't clear the whole mess out of there she would throw them down the well.

Oh, all right, all right—could he put them in the closet? Naturally not, there were brooms and mops and dustpans in the closet, and why couldn't he find a place for his rope outside her kitchen? Had he stopped to consider there were seven God-forsaken rooms in the house, and only one kitchen?

He wanted to know what of it? And did she realize she was making a complete fool of herself? And what did she take him for, a three-year-old idiot? The whole trouble with her was she needed something weaker than she was to heckle and tyrannize over. He wished to God now they had a couple of children she could take it out on. Maybe he'd get some rest.

Her face changed at this, she reminded him he had forgot the coffee and had bought a worthless piece of rope. And when she thought of all the things they actually needed to make the place even decently fit to live in, well, she could cry, that was all. She looked so forlorn, so lost and despairing he couldn't believe it was only a piece of rope that was causing all the racket. What *was* the matter, for God's sake?

Oh, would he please hush and go away, and *stay* away, if he could, for five minutes? By all means, yes, he would. He'd stay away indefinitely if she wished. Lord, yes, there was nothing he'd like better than to clear out and never come back. She couldn't for the life of her see what was holding him, then. It was a swell time. Here she was, stuck, miles from a railroad, with a half-empty house on her hands, and not a penny in her pocket, and everything on earth to do; it seemed the God-sent moment for him to get out from under. She was surprised he hadn't stayed in town as it was until she had come out and done the work and got things straightened out. It was his usual trick.

It appeared to him that this was going a little far. Just a touch out of bounds, if she didn't mind his saying so. Why the hell had he stayed in town the summer before? To do a half-dozen extra jobs to get the money he had sent her. That was it. She knew perfectly well they couldn't have done it otherwise. She had agreed with him at the time. And that was the only time so help him he had ever left her to do anything by herself.

Oh, he could tell that to his great-grandmother. She had her notion of what had kept him in town. Considerably more than a notion, if he wanted to know. So, she was going to bring all that up again, was she? Well, she could just think what she pleased. He was tired of explaining. It may have looked funny but he had simply got hooked in, and what could he do? It was impossible to believe that she was going to take it seriously. Yes, yes, she knew how it was with a man: if he was left by himself a minute, some woman was certain to kidnap him. And naturally he couldn't hurt her feelings by refusing!

Well, what was she raving about? Did she forget she had told him those two weeks alone in the country were the happiest she had known for four years? And how long had they been married when she said that? All right, shut up! If she thought that hadn't stuck in his craw.

She hadn't meant she was happy because she was away from him. She meant she was happy getting the devilish house nice and ready for him. That was what she had meant, and now look! Bringing up something she had said a year ago simply to justify himself for forgetting her coffee and breaking the eggs and buying a wretched piece of rope they couldn't afford. She really thought it was time to drop the subject, and now she wanted only two things in the world. She wanted him to get that rope from underfoot, and go back to the village and get her coffee, and if he could remember it, he might bring a metal mitt for the skillets, and two more curtain rods, and if there were any rubber gloves in the village, her hands were simply raw, and a bottle of milk of magnesia from the drugstore.

He looked out at the dark blue afternoon sweltering on the slopes, and mopped his forehead and sighed heavily and said, if only she could wait a minute for *anything*, he was going back. He had said so, hadn't he, the very instant they found he had overlooked it?

Oh, yes, well . . . run along. She was going to wash windows. The country was so beautiful! She doubted they'd have a moment to enjoy it. He meant to go, but he could not until he had said that if she wasn't such a hopeless melancholiac she might see that this was only for a few days. Couldn't she remember anything pleasant about the other summers? Hadn't they ever had any fun? She hadn't time to talk about it, and now would he please not leave that rope lying around for her to trip on? He picked it up, somehow it had toppled off the table, and walked out with it under his arm.

Was he going this minute? He certainly was. She thought so. Sometimes it seemed to her he had second sight about the precisely perfect moment to leave her ditched. She had meant to put the mattresses out to sun, if they put them out this minute they would get at least three hours, he must have heard her say that morning she meant to put them out. So of course he would walk off and leave her to it. She supposed he thought the exercise would do her good.

Well, he was merely going to get her coffee. A four-mile walk for two pounds of coffee was ridiculous, but he was perfectly willing to do it. The habit was making a wreck of her, but if she wanted to wreck herself there was nothing he could do about it. If he thought it was coffee that was making a wreck of her, she congratulated him: he must have a damned easy conscience.

Conscience or no conscience, he didn't see why the mattresses couldn't very well wait until tomorrow. And anyhow, for God's sake, were they living in the house, or were they going to let the house ride them to death? She paled at this, her face grew livid about the mouth, she looked quite dangerous, and reminded him that housekeeping was no more her work than it was his: she had other work to do as well, and when did he think she was going to find time to do it at this rate?

Was she going to start on that again? She knew as well as he did that his work brought in the regular money, hers was only occasional, if they depended on what *she* made—and she might as well get straight on this question once for all!

That was positively not the point. The question was, when both of them were working on their own time, was there going to be a division of the housework, or wasn't there? She merely wanted to know, she had to make her plans. Why, he thought that was all arranged. It was understood that he was to help. Hadn't he always, in summers?

Hadn't he, though? Oh, just hadn't he? And when, and where, and doing what? Lord, what an uproarious joke!

It was such a very uproarious joke that her face turned slightly purple, and she screamed with laughter. She laughed so hard she had to sit down, and finally a rush of tears spurted from her eyes and poured down into the lifted corners of her mouth. He dashed towards her and dragged her up to her feet and tried to pour water on her head. The dipper hung by a string on a nail and he broke it loose. Then he tried to pump water with one hand while she struggled in the other. So he gave it up and shook her instead.

She wrenched away, crying for him to take his rope and go to hell, she had simply given him up: and ran. He heard her high-heeled bedroom slippers clattering and stumbling on the stairs.

He went out around the house into the lane; he suddenly realized he had a blister on his heel and his shirt felt as if it were on fire. Things broke so suddenly you didn't know where you were. She could work herself into a fury about simply nothing. She was terrible, damn it: not an ounce of reason. You might as well talk to a sieve as that woman when she got going. Damned if he'd spend his life humoring her! Well, what to do now? He would take back the rope and exchange it for something else. Things accumulated, things were mountainous, you couldn't move them or sort them out or get rid of them. They just lay around and rotted. He'd take it back. Hell, why should he? He wanted it. What was it anyhow? A piece of rope. Imagine anybody caring more about a piece of rope than about a man's feelings. What earthly right had she to say a word about it? He remembered all the useless, meaningless things she bought for herself: Why? because I wanted it; that's why! He stopped and selected a large stone by the road. He would put the rope behind it. He would put it in the tool-box when he got back. He'd heard enough about it to last him a life-time.

When he came back she was leaning against the post box beside the road waiting. It was pretty late, the smell of broiled steak floated nose high in the cooling air. Her face was young and smooth and fresh looking. Her unmanageable funny black hair was all on end. She waved to him from a distance, and he speeded up. She called out that supper was ready and waiting, was he starved?

You bet he was starved. Here was the coffee. He waved it at her. She looked at his other hand. What was that he had there?

Well, it was the rope again. He stopped short. He had meant to exchange it but forgot. She wanted to know why he should exchange it, if it was something he really wanted. Wasn't the air sweet now, and wasn't it fine to be here?

She walked beside him with one hand hooked into his leather belt. She pulled and jostled him a little as he walked, and leaned against him. He put his arm clear around her and patted her stomach. They exchanged wary smiles. Coffee, coffee for the Ootsum-Wootsums! He felt as if he were bringing her a beautiful present.

He was a love, she firmly believed, and if she had had her coffee in the morning, she wouldn't have behaved so funny . . . There was a whippoorwill still coming back, imagine, clear out of season, sitting in the crab-apple tree calling all by himself. Maybe his girl stood him up. Maybe she did. She hoped to hear him once more, she loved whippoorwills . . . He knew how she was, didn't he?

Sure, he knew how she was.

Suggestions for Discussion

1. Think of the multiple uses of rope and determine the ways in which the title serves as a metaphor for the quarrel and the bond between husband and wife. What does the phrase "enough rope" connote? How might it relate to the story?

2. What is the purpose of the indirect approach to the narrative through a third-person narrator? Is it more or less effective than if told from the point of view of husband or wife? Account for the frequent questions and their effect.

3. With what details are the character of husband and wife revealed?

4. What are the ostensible and real causes of the quarrel? Is the mechanism of displacement at work? Explain.

5. How do you learn of the husband and wife's economic situation?

6. How serious was the husband's threat to go away? How did the wife respond?

7. Account for the shift in tone on the husband's return. What other changes in tone do you find?

8. What does the introduction of the whippoorwill add to the resolution of the story?

9. Why was the wife particularly incensed at the time the husband asked if they were "going to let the house ride them to death"?

10. What effect is achieved by referring to the characters as husband and wife rather than as Dan and Mary or other proper names?

11. In what sense is this a story of affirmation?

Suggestions for Writing

1. Retell the story from the wife's or the husband's point of view.

2. Discuss the mechanism of displacement in human relationships. Account for it and illustrate it.

3. Argue for or against the idea that the title "Rope" is symbolic of the relationship. If you were to retitle the story what title would you give it and why?

Poetry

William Shakespeare

When in Disgrace with Fortune and Men's Eyes (Sonnet 29)
Let Me Not to the Marriage of True Minds (Sonnet 116)

William Shakespeare (1564–1616), is generally acknowledged to be the greatest playwright in the English language. He was born in Stratford-on-Avon, England. By 1592 he had become an actor and playwright in London, and in 1599 he helped establish the famous Globe Theater. In addition to the sonnets, his works include historical plays, comedies such as *A Midsummer Night's Dream* and tragedies such as *Macbeth, Hamlet, King Lear*, and *Othello*. The self-doubt in Sonnet 29 is resolved with the poet's thoughts of his love. In Sonnet 116 the poet attests to the inviolability and permanence of love.

SONNET 29

When, in disgrace with fortune and men's eyes,
I all alone beweep my outcast state,
And trouble deaf heaven with my bootless cries,
And look upon myself and curse my fate;
Wishing me like to one more rich in hope,
Featured like him, like him with friends possessed,
Desiring this man's art, and that man's scope,
With what I most enjoy contented least;
Yet in these thoughts myself almost despising,
Haply I think on thee, and then my state,
Like to the lark at break of day ,arising
From sullen earth, sings hymns at heaven's gate;
For thy sweet love remembered such wealth brings
That then I scorn to change my state with kings.

SONNET 116

Let me not to the marriage of true minds
Admit impediments. Love is not love
Which alters when it alteration finds,
Or bends with the remover to remove:
Oh, no! it is an ever-fixed mark,
That looks on tempests and is never shaken;
It is the star to every wandering bark,
Whose worth's unknown, although his height be taken.
Love's not Time's fool, though rosy lips and cheeks
Within his bending sickle's compass come;
Love alters not with his brief hours and weeks,
But bears it out even to the edge of doom.
If this be error and upon me proved,
I never writ, nor no man ever loved.

Suggestions for Discussion

1. How does the imagery in each of the sonnets contribute to its unity?

2. How does dramatic understatement at the end of the second of the two sonnets reinforce the theme?

William Blake

The Clod and the Pebble
The Garden of Love

William Blake (1757–1827), poet and artist, illustrated his poems with his own engravings. His works include *Songs of Innocence* (1789), *Songs of Experience* (1794), *The Marriage of Heaven and Hell* (1790), *The Gates of Paradise* (1793), and *Visions of the Daughters of Albion* (1793). The poems that follow suggest some of the contradictions inherent in concepts of love.

The Clod and the Pebble

"Love seeketh not Itself to please,
    Nor for itself hath any care,

But for another gives its ease,
  And builds a Heaven in Hell's despair."

So sung the Clod of Clay,
  Trodden with the cattle's feet,
But a Pebble in the brook
  Warbled out these metres meet:

"Love seeketh only Self to please,
  To bind another to its delight,
Joys in another's loss of ease,
  And builds a Hell in Heaven's Despite."

The Garden of Love

I went to the Garden of Love,
And I saw what I never had seen:
A Chapel was built in the midst,
Where I used to play on the green.

And the gates of this Chapel were shut,
And "Thou shalt not" writ over the door:
So I turned to the Garden of Love
That so many sweet flowers bore;

And I saw it was filled with graves,
And tomb-stones where flowers should be;
And Priests in black gowns were walking their rounds,
And binding with briars my joys and desires.

Suggestions for Discussion

Both of Blake's poems suggest some of the contradictions inherent in concepts of
"love." What are they and what seems to be the poet's conclusion?

W. H. Auden

Lay Your Sleeping Head, My Love

Wystan Hugh Auden (1907–1973), English poet educated at Oxford University, was early recognized as a leader of the poets of his generation. His poetry collections include *The Orators* (1932), *The Double Man* (1941), *The Shield of Achilles* (1955), *Homage to Clio* (1960), *About the House* (1965), and *The Age of Anxiety* (1947), which won a Pulitzer Prize in 1948. His autobiography, *Certain World: A Commonplace Book*, was published in 1970. Auden also experimented with drama, and his criticism was collected in *The Dyer's Hand* in 1963. In 1967 he was made a fellow of Christ College, Oxford. The writer speaks of the threats to love in this poem that weaves back and forth between the present and future, the concrete and abstract.

Lay your sleeping head, my love,
Human on my faithless arm;
Time and fevers burn away
Individual beauty from
Thoughtful children, and the grave
Proves the child ephemeral:
But in my arms till break of day
Let the living creature lie,
Mortal, guilty, but to me
The entirely beautiful.

Soul and body have no bounds:
To lovers as they lie upon
Her tolerant enchanted slope
In their ordinary swoon,
Grave the vision Venus sends
Of supernatural sympathy,
Universal love and hope;
While an abstract insight wakes
Among the glaciers and the rocks
The hermit's sensual ecstasy.

Certainty, fidelity
On the stroke of midnight pass
Like vibrations of a bell,
And fashionable madmen raise
Their pedantic boring cry:
Every farthing of the cost,
All the dreaded cards foretell,
Shall be paid, but from this night
Not a whisper, not a thought,
Not a kiss nor look be lost.

Beauty, midnight, vision dies:
Let the winds of dawn that blow
Softly round your dreaming head
Such a day of sweetness show
Eye and knocking heart may bless,
Find the mortal world enough;
Noons of dryness see you fed
By the involuntary powers,
Nights of insult let you pass
Watched by every human love.

Suggestions for Discussion

1. What images are employed by the speaker to suggest the hazards of love?
2. Account for the movement from present to future and from particular to general.

Edna St. Vincent Millay
Love Is Not All

Edna St. Vincent Millay (1892–1950), American poet, wrote "Renascence," her first major poem, while she was still in college. Her early works such as *A Few Figs from Thistles* (1920) exhibited a cynical flippancy that deepened into bitter disillusionment in later works such as *The Harp-Weaver and Other Poems* (1923), a Pulitzer Prize selection, and *The Buck in the Snow* (1928). In this sonnet the poet exalts the power of love.

Love is not all; it is not meat nor drink
Nor slumber nor a roof against the rain,
Nor yet a floating spar to men that sink
And rise and sink and rise and sink again;
Love can not fill the thickened lung with breath,
Nor clean the blood, nor set the fractured bone;
Yet many a man is making friends with death
Even as I speak, for lack of love alone.
It well may be that in a difficult hour,
Pinned down by pain and moaning for release,
Or nagged by want past resolution's power,

I might be driven to sell your love for peace,
To trade the memory of this night for food.
It well may be. I do not think I would.

Denise Levertov

The Third Dimension

Denise Levertov (b. 1923), English-born poet who became a United States citizen in 1956, has published many collections of poetry, including: *With Eyes at the Back of Our Heads* (1959), *O Taste and See* (1964), *The Sorrow Dance* (1966), *Relearning the Alphabet* (1970), and *Footprints* (1972). She has contributed to magazines and anthologies and has served as a visiting lecturer at several colleges. No words can express the depth and trauma of the speaker's love.

Who'd believe me if
I said, "They took and

split me open from
scalp to crotch, and

still I'm alive, and
walk around pleased with

the sun and all
the world's bounty." Honesty

isn't so simple:
a simple honesty is

nothing but a lie.
Don't the trees

hide the wind between
their leaves and

speak in whispers?
The third dimension

hides itself.
If the roadmen

crack stones, the
stones are stones:

but love
cracked me open

and I'm
alive to

tell the tale—but not
honestly:

the words
change it. Let it be—

here in the sweet sun
—a fiction, while I

breathe and
change pace.

Suggestions for Discussion

1. The poems by Millay and Levertov of a woman expressing her love are separated in time by approximately fifty years. What have they in common and how do they differ in mood, theme, style?

2. Millay's sonnet is Shakespearian in form. Compare her concluding couplet with that in "Let Me Not to the Marriage of True Minds".

3. How does Millay employ dramatic understatement? Compare her development of the love theme with that in the two sonnets by Shakespeare.

E. E. Cummings
I Like My Body When It Is with Your

E. E. Cummings (1894–1962) was an American whose book *The Enormous Room* (1922) and whose poetry *&* and *XLI Poems* (1925) established his reputation as an avant-garde writer interested in experimenting with stylistic techniques. Awarded several important prizes for poetry, he was also Charles Eliot Norton Lecturer at Harvard University in 1952 and published *i: six nonlectures* (1953). The repetitions and typography as well as the sensory detail contribute to Cummings's expression of joy in physical love.

I like my body when it is with your
body. It is so quite new a thing.

Muscles better and nerves more.
i like your body. i like what it does,
i like its hows. i like to feel the spine
of your body and its bones, and the trembling
-firm-smooth ness and which i will
again and again and again
kiss, i like kissing this and that of you,
i like, slowly stroking the, shocking fuzz
of your electric fur, and what-is-it comes
over parting flesh . . . . And eyes big love-crumbs,

and possibly i like the thrill

of under me you so quite new

Suggestions for Discussion

1. Account for the appeal of the poem.

2. How do the repetitions and the typography contribute to the poem's effectiveness?
   What distinguishes this poem from prose?

Adrienne Rich

Rape

Living in Sin

Adrienne Rich (b. 1929), contemporary American poet, is the author of *A Change of World* (1951), *The Diamond Cutters,* (1955), *Snapshots of a Daughter-in-Law* (1963), *Necessities of Life* (1966), and *Of Woman Born* (1976). She has contributed to such magazines as *Poetry, The Nation,* and *The New York Review of Books.* Her awards include a Guggenheim Fellowship and an Amy Lowell Traveling Scholarship. The graphic physical images in "Living in Sin" suggest that the lovers are emerging from an illusory world into a world of reality. "Rape," published in *Diving Into the Wreck* (1973), reflects the poet's anger in her ironic attribution of the crime and the portrait of the cop who is pleased by the hysteria of the speaker's voice.

Living in Sin

She had thought the studio would keep itself;
no dust upon the furniture of love.

Half heresy, to wish the taps less vocal,
the panes relieved of grime. A plate of pears,
a piano with a Persian shawl, a cat
stalking the picturesque amusing mouse
had risen at his urging.
Not that at five each separate stair would writhe
under the milkman's tramp; that morning light
so coldly would delineate the scraps
of last night's cheese and three sepulchral bottles;
that on the kitchen shelf among the saucers
a pair of beetle-eyes would fix her own—
envoy from some black village in the mouldings . . .
Meanwhile he, with a yawn,
sounded a dozen notes upon the keyboard,
declared it out of tune, shrugged at the mirror,
rubbed at his beard, went out for cigarettes;
while she, jeered by the minor demons,
pulled back the sheets and made the bed and found
a towel to dust the table-top,
and let the coffee-pot boil over on the stove.
By evening she was back in love again,
though not so wholly but throughout the night
she woke sometimes to feel the daylight coming
like a relentless milkman up the stairs.

Suggestions for Discussion

1. What physical images in the studio scene imply that the lovers are emerging from an illusory world into a world of reality?

2. Comment on the irony of the title. Do you perceive an end or a beginning to the relationship? Consider the clues in the final lines.

Rape

There is a cop who is both prowler and father:
he comes from your block, grew up with your brothers,
had certain ideals.
You hardly know him in his boots and silver badge,
on horseback, one hand touching his gun.

You hardly know him but you have to get to know him:
he has access to machinery that could kill you.
He and his stallion clop like warlords among the trash,
his ideals stand in the air, a frozen cloud
from between his unsmiling lips.

And so, when the time comes, you have to turn to him,
the maniac's sperm still greasing your thighs,
your mind whirling like crazy. You have to confess
to him, you are guilty of the crime
of having been forced.

And you see his blue eyes, the blue eyes of all the family
whom you used to know, grow narrow and glisten,
his hand types out the details
and he wants them all
but the hysteria in your voice pleases him best.

You hardly know him but now he thinks he knows you:
he has taken down your worst moment
on a machine and filed it in a file.
He knows, or thinks he knows, how much you imagined;
he knows, or thinks he knows, what you secretly wanted.

He has access to machinery that could get you put away;
and if, in the sickening light of the precinct,
and if, in the sickening light of the precinct,
your details sound like a portrait of your confessor,
will you swallow, will you deny them. will you lie your way home?

Suggestions for Discussion

1. How do the lines "you are guilty of the crime of having been forced" convey the author's point of view? How do you know she is being ironic?

2. With what details do you learn of the cop's pleasure in the narrator's report? How does the narrator view the cop?

3. What does the last series of questions signify?

Suggestions for Writing

1. Discuss the changing attitudes of society and the law toward the victims of rape.

Mae Swenson
Women Should Be Pedestals

Mae Swenson (b. 1919) is an American poet best known for *Another Animal* (1954), *A Cage of Spines* (1958), *To Mix with Time* (1963), *Poems to Solve* (1966), and *Half Sun Half Sleep* (1967). She has won numerous prizes and grants, including Guggenheim, Ford Foundation, and Rockefeller Foundation fellowships, the National Institute of Arts and Letters Award, and the Shelley Award. The poet's anger is reflected in the pedestal and rocking horse metaphors.

```
Women                          Or they
    should be                      should be
        pedestals                      little horses
            moving                         those wooden
                pedestals                      sweet
                    moving                         oldfashioned
                        to the                         painted
                            motions                        rocking
                                of men                         horses
            the gladdest things in the toyroom
                    The                            feelingly
                    pegs                           and then
                  of their                         unfeelingly
                    ears                              To be
                so familiar                        joyfully
                and dear                           ridden
            to the trusting                     rockingly
        fists                               ridden until
To be chafed                            the restored
egos dismount and the legs stride away
Immobile                       willing
    sweetlipped                    to bet set
        sturdy                         into motion
            and smiling                    Women
                women                          should be
                    should always                  pedestals
                        be waiting                     to men
```

Suggestions for Discussion

1. How does the central metaphor define the author's point of view? How does it contribute to tone?

2. How does the second extended metaphor contribute to purpose and tone?

3. How do alliteration and repetition function in the poem?

4. Comment on the function of the verbs and adjectives in creating mood and tone.

Suggestion for Writing

Using the same title, write an ironic sketch or poem.

The Cultural Tradition: Popular Culture

◆◆◆

I wince when I'm called a former beauty queen or Miss U.S.A.

—**Studs Terkel,** "Miss U.S.A."

"How can I go to work," I yelled, "when I've got so much leisure time on my hands?"

—**Art Buchwald,** "Leisure Will Kill You"

Baseball flows past us all through the summer—it is one of the reasons that summer exists.

—**Roger Angell,** "The Silence"

And so the American family muddles on, dimly aware that something is amiss but distracted from an understanding of its plight by an endless stream of television images.

—**Marie Winn,** "The Plug-In Drug: TV and the American Family"

"Kathie," I demanded, "why do you women in soap opera detest my sex?"

—**S. J. Perelman,** "Meanness Rising from the Suds"

For James Bond is the Renaissance man in mid-century guise, lover, warrior, connoisseur.

—**George Grella,** "James Bond: Culture Hero"

. . . what was happening at Minton's was a continuing symposium of jazz, a summation of all the styles, personal and traditional, of jazz.

—**Ralph Ellison,** "The Birth of Bebop"

"Oh, it's so horrible, it's so dreadful," Irene was sobbing. "I've been listening all day, and it's so depressing."

—**John Cheever,** "The Enormous Radio"

They was crying and crying and didn't even know what they was crying for. One day this is going to be a pitiful country, I thought.

—**Alice Walker,** "Nineteen Fifty-five"

Personal Reminiscence
◆◆◆

Studs Terkel
Miss U.S.A.

Studs Terkel (b. 1912) has been associated with radio station WFMT in Chicago for many years. He gained fame as an oral historian with the publication of *Division Street America* (1966), *Hard Times* (1970), *Working* (1974), and *American Dreams: Lost and Found* (1980), from which the following selection is taken.

Emma Knight, Miss U.S.A., 1973. She is twenty-nine.

I wince when I'm called a former beauty queen or Miss U.S.A. I keep thinking they're talking about someone else. There are certain images that come to mind when people talk about beauty queens. It's mostly what's known as t and a, tits and ass. No talent. For many girls who enter the contest, it's part of the American Dream. It was never mine.

You used to sit around the TV and watch Miss America and it was exciting, we thought, glamorous. Fun, we thought. But by the time I was eight or nine, I didn't feel comfortable. Soon I'm hitting my adolescence, like fourteen, but I'm not doing any dating and I'm feeling awkward and ugly. I'm much taller than most of the people in my class. I don't feel I can compete the way I see girls competing for guys. I was very much of a loner. I felt intimidated by the amount of competition females were supposed to go through with each other. I didn't like being told by *Seventeen* magazine: Subvert your interests if you have a crush on a guy, get interested in what he's interested in. If you play cards, be sure not to beat him. I was very bad at these social games.

After I went to the University of Colorado for three and a half years, I had it. This was 1968 through '71. I came home for the summer. An agent met me and wanted me to audition for commercials, modeling, acting jobs. Okay. I started auditioning and winning some.

I did things actors do when they're starting out. You pass out literature at conventions, you do print ads, you pound the pavements, you send out your resumés. I had come to a model agency one cold day, and an agent came out and said: "I want you to enter a beauty contest." I said: "No, uh-uh, never, never, never. I'll lose, how humiliating." She said: "I want some girls to represent the agency, might do you good." So I filled out the application blank: hobbies, measurements, blah, blah, blah. I got a letter: "Congratulations. You have been accepted as an entrant into the Miss Illinois-Universe contest." Now what do I do? I'm stuck.

You have to have a sponsor. Or you're gonna have to pay several hundred dollars. So I called up the lady who was running it. Terribly sorry, I can't do this. I don't have the money. She calls back a couple of days later: "We found you a sponsor, it's a lumber company."

It was in Decatur. There were sixty-some contestants from all over the place. I went as a lumberjack: blue jeans, hiking boots, a flannel shirt, a pair of suspenders, and carrying an axe. You come out first in your costume and you introduce yourself and say your astrological sign or whatever it is they want you to say. You're wearing a banner that has the sponsor's name on it. Then you come out and do your pirouettes in your one-piece bathing suit, and the judges look at you a lot. Then you come out in your evening gown and pirouette around for a while. That's the first night.

The second night, they're gonna pick fifteen people. In between, you had judges' interviews. For three minutes, they ask you anything they want. Can you answer questions? How do you handle yourself? Your pose, personality, blah, blah, blah. They're called personality judges.

I thought: This will soon be over, get on a plane tomorrow, and no one will be the wiser. Except that my name got called as one of the fifteen. You have to go through the whole thing all over again.

I'm thinking: I don't have a prayer. I'd come to feel a certain kind of distance, except that they called my name. I was the winner, Miss Illinois. All I could do was laugh. I'm twenty-two, standing up there in a borrowed evening gown, thinking: What am I doing here: This is like Tom Sawyer becomes an altar boy.

I was considered old for a beauty queen, which is a little horrifying when you're twenty-two. That's very much part of the beauty queen syndrome: the young, untouched, unthinking human being.

I had to go to this room and sign the Miss Illinois-Universe contract right away. Miss Universe, Incorporated, is the full name of the company. It's owned by Kayser-Roth, Incorporated, which was bought out by Gulf & Western. Big business.

I'm sitting there with my glass of champagne and I'm reading over this contract. They said: "Oh, you don't have to read it." And I said: "I never sign anything that I don't read." They're all waiting to take pictures, and I'm sitting there reading this long document. So I signed it and the phone rang and the guy was from a Chicago paper and said: "Tell me, is it Miss or Ms.?" I said: "It's Ms." He said: "You're kidding." I said: "No, I'm not." He wrote an article the next day saying something like it finally happened: a beauty queen, a feminist. I thought I was a feminist before I was a beauty queen, why should I stop now?

Then I got into the publicity and training and interviews. It was a throwback to another time where crossed ankles and white gloves and teacups were present. I was taught how to walk around with a book on my head, how to sit daintily, how to pose in a bathing suit, and how to frizz my hair. They wanted curly hair, which I hate.

One day the trainer asked me to shake hands. I shook hands. She said: "That's wrong. When you shake hands with a man, you always shake hands ring up." I said: "Like the pope? Where my hand is up, like he's gonna kiss it?" Right. I thought: Holy mackerel! It was a very long February and March and April and May.

I won the Miss U.S.A. pageant. I started to laugh. They tell me I'm the only beauty queen in history that didn't cry when she won. It was on network television. I said to myself: "You're kidding." Bob Barker, the host, said: "No, I'm not kidding." I didn't know what else to say at that moment. In the press releases, they call it the great American Dream. There she is, Miss America, your ideal. Well, not my ideal, kid.

The minute you're crowned, you become their property and subject to whatever they tell you. They wake you up at seven o'clock next morning and make you put on a negligee and serve you breakfast in bed, so that all the New York papers can come in and take your picture sitting in bed, while you're absolutely bleary-eyed from the night before. They put on the Kayser-Roth negligee, hand you the tray, you take three bites. The photographers leave, you whip off the negligee, they take the breakfast away, and that's it. I never did get any breakfast that day. (Laughs).

You immediately start making personal appearances. The Jaycees or the chamber of commerce says: "I want to book Miss U.S.A. for our Christmas Day parade." They pay, whatever it is, seven hundred fifty dollars a day, first-class air fare, round trip, expenses, so forth. If the United Fund calls and wants me to give a five-minute pitch on queens at a luncheon, they still have to pay a fee. Doesn't matter that it's a charity. It's one hundred percent to Miss Universe, Incorporated. You get your salary. That's your prize money for the year. I got fifteen thousand dollars, which is all taxed in New York. Maybe out of a check of three thousand dollars, I'd get fifteen hundred dollars.

From the day I won Miss U.S.A. to the day I left for Universe, almost two months, I got a day and a half off. I made about two hundred fifty appearances that year. Maybe three hundred. Parades, shopping centers, and things. Snip ribbons. What else do you do at a shopping center? Model clothes. The nice thing I got to do was public speaking. They said: "You want a ghost writer?" I said: "Hell, no, I know how to talk." I wrote my own speeches. They don't trust girls to go out and talk because most of them can't.

One of the big execs from General Motors asked me to do a speech in Washington, D.C., on the consumer and the energy crisis. It was the fiftieth anniversary of the National Management Association. The White House, for some reason, sent me some stuff on it. I read it over, it was nonsense. So I stood up and said: "The reason we have an energy crisis is because we are, industrially and personally, pigs. We have a short-term view of the resources available to us; and unless we wake up to what we're doing to our air and our water, we'll have a dearth, not just a crisis." Oh, they weren't real pleased. (Laughs.)

What I resent most is that a lot of people didn't expect me to live this version of the American Dream for myself. I was supposed to live it their way.

When it came out in a newspaper interview that I said Nixon should resign, that he was a crook, oh dear, the fur flew. They got very upset until I got an invitation to the White House. They wanted to shut me up. The Miss Universe corporation had been trying to establish some sort of liaison with the White House for several years. I make anti-Nixon speeches and get this invitation.

I figured they're either gonna take me down to the basement and beat me up with a rubber hose or they're gonna offer me a cabinet post. They had a list of fifteen or so people I was supposed to meet. I've never seen such a bunch of people with raw nerve endings. I was dying to bring a tape recorder but thought if you mention the word "Sony" in the Nixon White House, you're in trouble. They'd have cardiac arrest. But I'm gonna bring along a pad and paper. They were patronizing. And when one of 'em got me in his office and talked about all the journalists and television people being liberals, I brought up blacklisting, *Red Channels,* and the TV industry. He changed the subject.

Miss Universe took place in Athens, Greece. The junta was still in power. I saw a heck of a lot of jeeps and troops and machine guns. The Americans were supposed to keep a low profile. I had never been a great fan of the Greek junta, but I knew darn well I was gonna have to keep my mouth shut. I was still representing the United States, for better or for worse. Miss Philippines won. I ran second.

At the end of the year, you're run absolutely ragged. That final evening, they usually have several queens from past years come back. Before they crown the new Miss U.S.A., the current one is supposed to take what they call the farewell walk. They call over the PA: Time for the old queen's walk. I'm now twenty-three and I'm an old queen. And they have this idiot farewell speech playing over the airwaves as the old queen takes the walk. And you're sitting on the throne for about thirty seconds, then you come down and they announce the name of the new one and you put the crown on her head. And then you're old.

As the new one is crowned, the reporters and photographers rush on the stage. I've seen photographers shove the girl who has just given her reign up thirty seconds before, shove her physically. I was gone by that time. I had jumped off the stage in my evening gown. It is very difficult for girls who are terrified of this ending. All of a sudden (snaps fingers), you're out. Nobody gives a damn about the old one.

Miss U.S.A. and remnants thereof is the crown stored in the attic in my parents' home. I don't even know where the banners are. It wasn't me the fans of Miss U.S.A. thought was pretty. What they think is pretty is the banner and crown. If I could put the banner and crown on that lamp, I swear to God ten men would come in and ask it for a date. I'll think about committing an axe murder if I'm not called anything but a former beauty queen. I can't stand it any more.

Several times during my year as what's-her-face I had seen the movie *The Sting.* There's a gesture the characters use which means the con is on: they rub their nose. In my last fleeting moments as Miss U.S.A., as they were playing that silly farewell speech and I walked down the aisle and stood by the throne, I looked right into the camera and rubbed my finger across my nose. The next day, the pageant people spent all their time telling people that I hadn't done it. I spent the time telling them that, of course, I had. I simply meant: the con is on. (Laughs.)

Miss U.S.A. is in the same graveyard that Emma Knight the twelve-year-old is. Where the sixteen-year-old is. All the past selves. There comes a time when you have to bury those selves because you've grown into another one. You don't keep exhuming the corpses.

If I could sit down with every young girl in America for the next fifty years, I could tell them what I liked about the pageant. I could tell them what I hated. It wouldn't make any difference. There're always gonna be girls who want to enter the beauty pageant. That's the fantasy: the American Dream.

Suggestions for Discussion

1. What sequence of events led Emma Knight to win the title of Miss U.S.A.?

2. Describe her life as Miss U.S.A.

3. What evidence does she show of her interest in politics? in women's rights?

4. For what reasons does she signal "the con is on" at the end of her reign?

Suggestions for Writing

1. Explain why Emma Knight believes there will always be "girls who want to enter the beauty pageant." Do you agree?

2. Describe a contest in which you were a participant. Use details that the casual observer would not know.

Essays

Art Buchwald

Leisure Will Kill You

Art Buchwald (b. 1925), the nationally syndicated columnist, won the Pulitzer Prize for his humorous writings in 1982. Among his more than two dozen books are *Washington Is Looking* (1976), *The Buchwald Stops Here* (1978), *While Reagan Slept* (1983), and *Laid Back in Washington* (1981), from which the following selection is taken.

This country is producing so much leisure equipment for the home that nobody has any leisure time anymore to enjoy it. A few months ago I bought a television tape recorder to make copies of programs when I was out of the house.

Last week I recorded the Nebraska-Oklahoma football game. When I came home in the evening, I decided to play it back. But my son wanted to play "Baseball" on the TV screen with his Atari Computer. We finished four innings when my wife came in the room and asked me if I would like to listen to the Vienna Opera on our hi-fi stereo set. I told her I was waiting to finish the baseball match so I could watch the football game I had recorded.

She said if I watched the football game for three hours, I would miss *Love Boat*. I told her I would record *Love Boat* and we could watch it later in the evening. She protested that *Casablanca* was showing on Channel 5 at 11:30 and she wanted to see it again.

"Don't worry," I assured her, "we can watch *Love Boat* late Saturday and *Casablanca* on Sunday morning when we get up."

"But if we watch *Casablanca* tomorrow morning when can we see the instant Polaroid movies you took of Ben yesterday afternoon?"

"We'll see them after we play backgammon on the new table."

"If we do that," my daughter said, "we won't be able to see the Washington Redskins–New York Giants football game."

"I'll record the Redskins-Giants football game and we'll watch it while *60 Minutes* is on the air. We can see *60 Minutes* at 11 o'clock."

"But," my son said, "you promised to play the pinball machine with me at 11."

"Okay, we'll play pinball at 11 and watch *60 Minutes* at midnight."

My wife said, "Why don't we listen to the Vienna Opera while we're eating and then we can save an hour to play computer golf?"

"That's good thinking," I said. "The only problem is I've rented a TV tape for *Cleopatra* and that runs for three hours."

"You could show it on Monday night," she suggested.

"I can't do that. I have to return the tape Monday afternoon or be charged for it another week. I have an idea. I won't go to work Monday morning and we'll watch it then."

"I was hoping to use our Jacuzzi Monday morning," my wife said.

"Okay, then I'll tape *Cleopatra* and you can see it Monday afternoon."

"I'm using the set Monday afternoon," my son said, "to play digital hockey on the TV screen."

"You can't do that," I said. "I have to watch the *Today* show in the afternoon if I'm going to watch *Cleopatra* in the morning."

"Why can't you watch the *Today* show at dinnertime?" my wife asked.

"Because the Wolfingtons are coming over to hear me play 'Tea for Two' on the electric organ."

"I thought we might play computer bridge at dinner," my wife said.

"We'll play it after my encore," I assured her.

"Then when will we see *Monday Night Football?*" my son wanted to know.

"Tuesday," I said.

"Does that mean you're not going to work or Tuesday?" my wife asked.

"How can I go to work," I yelled, "when I've got so much leisure time on my hands?"

Suggestions for Discussion

1. Explain Buchwald's observation that our "country is producing so much leisure equipment for the home that nobody has any leisure time anymore to enjoy it." Do you agree? State your reasons.

2. Discuss whether or not the conflicts that Buchwald sets up in this short essay are realistic, believable, and resolvable.

3. Suggest solutions to the conflicts Buchwald identifies.

4. Discuss Buchwald's use of exaggeration and accumulated detail to give humour to his essay.

Suggestions for Writing

1. Identify and discuss dangers to the individual and to the family posed by excessive amounts of leisure.

2. Depict a busy scene in your own home.

Roger Angell
The Silence

Roger Angell (b.1920) is senior fiction editor for *The New Yorker.* He is the author of several books about baseball, including *The Summer Game* (1972), *Five Seasons* (1977), and *Late Innings* (1982), from which the following selection is taken.

July 1981

Last week, my wife and I came uptown late one night in a cab after having dinner with friends of ours in the Village. We wheeled through the warm and odorous light-strewn summer dark on the same northward route home we have followed hundreds of times over the years, I suppose: bumping and lurching up Sixth non-stop, with the successive gateways of staggered green lights magically opening before us, and the stately tall street lights (if you tipped your head back on the cab seat and watched them upside down through the back window of the cab: I had drunk a bit of wine) forming a narrowing golden archway astern; and then moving more quietly through the swerves and small hills of the Park, where the weight and silence of the black trees wrapped us in a special summer darkness. The cabdriver had his radio on, and the blurry sounds of the news—the midnight news, I suppose— passed over us there in the back seat, mixing with the sounds of the wind coming in through the open cab windows, and the motion of our ride, and the whole sense of city night. All was as always, I mean, except that now it came to me, unsurprisingly at first but then with a terrific jolt of unhappiness and mourning, that this radio news was altered for there was no baseball in it. Without knowing it, I had been waiting for those other particular sounds, for that other part of the summer night, but it was missing, or course—no line scores, no winning and losing pitchers, no homers and highlights, no records approached or streaks cut short, no "Meanwhile, over in the National League," no double-zip early innings from Anaheim or Chavez Ravine, no Valenzuela and no Rose, no Goose and no Tom, no Yaz, no Mazz, no nothing.

The strike by this time was more than a week old, and I had so far sustained the shock of it and the change of it with more fortitude and patience than I had expected of myself. The issues seemed far removed from me—too expensive or too complicated, for some reason, for me to hold them clearly in my mind for long, although I am an attentive and patient fan. I would wait, then, with whatever composure I could find, until it was settled, days or weeks from now, and in some fashion or other I would fill up the empty eveningtimes and morningtimes I had once spent (I did not say "wasted"; I would never say "wasted") before the tube and with the sports pages. It might even be better for me to do without baseball for a while, although I could not imagine why. All this brave nonsense was knocked out of me in an instant, there in the cab, and suddenly the loss of that murmurous little ribbon of baseball-by-radio, the ordinary news of the game, seemed to explain a lot of things about the much larger loss we fans are all experiencing because of the strike. The refrain of late-night baseball scores; the sounds of the televised game from the next room (the room empty, perhaps, for the moment, but the game running along in there just the same and quietly waiting for us to step in and rejoin it when we are of a mind to); the mid-game mid-event from some car or cab that pulls up beside us for a few seconds in traffic before the light changes; the baseball conversation in the elevator that goes away when two men get off together at the eleventh floor, taking the game with them; the flickery white fall of light on our hands and arms and the scary sounds of the crowd that suddenly wake us up, in bed or in the study armchair, where we have fallen asleep, with the set and the game still on—all these streams and continuities, it seems to me, are part of the greater, riverlike flow of baseball. No other sport, I think, conveys anything like this sense of cool depth and fluvial steadiness, and when you stop for a minute and think about the game it is easy to see why this should be so. The slow, inexorable progression of baseball events—balls and strikes, outs and innings, batters stepping up and batters being retired, pitchers and sides changing on the field, innings turning into games and games into series, and all these merging and continuing, in turn, in the box scores and the averages and the slowly fluctuous standings—are what make the game quietly and uniquely satisfying. Baseball flows past us all through the summer—it is one of the reasons that summer exists—and wherever we happen to stand on its green banks we can sense with only a glance across its shiny expanse that the long, unhurrying swirl and down-flowing have their own purpose and direction, that the river is headed, in its own sweet time, toward a downsummer broadening and debouchment and to its end in the estuary of October.

River people, it is said, count on the noises and movement of nearby water, even without knowing it, and feel uneasy and unaccountably diminished if they must move away for a while and stay among plains inhabitants. That is almost the way it is for us just now, but it is worse than that, really, because this time it is the river that has gone away—just stopped—and all of us who live along these banks feel a fretful sense of loss and a profound disquiet over the sudden cessation of our reliable old stream. The main issue of the baseball strike, I have read, concerns the matter of compensation for owners who have lost a player to free-agency, but when this difficulty is resolved and the two sides come to an agreement (as they will someday), what compensation can ever be made to us, the fans, who are the true owners and neighbors and keepers of the game, for this dry, soundless summer and for the loss of our joy?

Suggestions for Discussion

1. What event brings the baseball strike of 1981 to Angell's mind?

2. List the sights and sounds of baseball that he misses during the strike.

3. Explain Angell's reference to "river people." Do you find the allusion a good one? Explain.

4. In what sense are the fans "the true owners and neighbors and keepers of the game"?

Suggestions for Writing

1. Aside from playing, in what ways are you involved in a particular sport?

2. Remember in detail a pleasant event connected with sport.

Marie Winn

The Plug-In Drug: TV and the American Family

Marie Winn is the author of *The Playground Book, The Sick Book, The Baby Reader,* and other books for parents and children. The following selection is taken from *The Plug-In Drug,* published in 1977.

A quarter of a century after the introduction of television into American society, a period that has seen the medium become so deeply ingrained in American life that in at least one state the television set has attained the rank of a legal necessity, safe from repossession in case of debt along with clothes, cooking utensils, and the like, television viewing has become an inevitable and ordinary part of daily life. Only in the early years of television did writers and commentators have sufficient perspective to separate the activity of watching television from the actual content it offers the viewer. In those early days writers frequently discussed the effects of television on family life. However, a curious myopia afflicted those early observers: almost without exception they regarded television as a favorable, beneficial, indeed, wondrous influence upon the family.

"Television is going to be a real asset in every home where there are children," predicts a writer in 1949.

"Television will take over your way of living and change your children's habits, but this change can be a wonderful improvement," claims another commentator.

"No survey's needed, of course, to establish that television has brought the family together in one room," writes *The New York Times* television critic in 1949.

Each of the early articles about television is invariably accompanied by a photograph or illustration showing a family cozily sitting together before the television set, Sis on Mom's lap, Buddy perched on the arm of Dad's chair, Dad with his arm around Mom's shoulder. Who could have guessed that twenty or so years later Mom would be watching a drama in the kitchen, the kids would be looking at cartoons in their room, while Dad would be taking in the ball game in the living room?

Of course television sets were enormously expensive in those early days. The idea that by 1975 more than 60 percent of American families would own two or more sets was preposterous. The splintering of the multiple-set family was something the early writers could not foresee. Nor did anyone imagine the number of hours children would eventually devote to television, the common use of television by parents as a child pacifier, the changes television would effect upon child-rearing methods, the increasing domination of family schedules by children's viewing requirements—in short, the *power* of the new medium to dominate family life.

After the first years, as children's consumption of the new medium increased, together with parental concern about the possible effects of so much television viewing, a steady refrain helped to soothe and reassure anxious parents. "Television always enters a pattern of influences that already exist: the home, the peer group, the school, the church, and culture generally," write the authors of an early and influential study of television's effects on children. In other words, if the child's home life is all right, parents need not worry about the effects of all that television watching.

But television does not merely influence the child; it deeply influences that "pattern of influences" that is meant to ameliorate its effects. Home and family life has changed in important ways since the advent of television. The peer group has become television-oriented, and much of the time children spend together is occupied by television viewing. Culture generally has been transformed by television. Therefore it is improper to assign to television the subsidiary role its many apologists (too often members of the television industry) insist it plays. Television is not merely one of a number of important influences upon today's child. Through the changes it has made in family life, television emerges as *the* important influence in children's lives today.

Television's contribution to family life has been an equivocal one. For while it has, indeed, kept the members of the family from dispersing, it has not served to bring them *together*. By its domination of the time families spend together, it destroys the special quality that distinguishes one family from another, a quality that depends to a great extent on what a family *does*, what special rituals, games, recurrent jokes, familiar songs, and shared activities it accumulates.

"Like the sorcerer of old," writs Urie Bronfenbrenner, "the television set casts its magic spell, freezing speech and action, turning the living into silent statues so long as the enchantment lasts. The primary danger of the television screen lies not so much in the behavior it produces—although there is danger there—as in the behavior it prevents: the talks, the games, the family festivities and arguments through which much of the child's learning takes place and through which his character is formed. Turning on the television set can turn off the process that transforms children into people."

Yet parents have accepted a television-dominated family life so completely that they cannot see how the medium is involved in whatever problems they might be having. A first-grade teacher reports:

"I have one child in the group who's an only child. I wanted to find out more about her family life because this little girl was quite isolated from the group, didn't make friends, so I talked to her mother. Well, they don't have time to do anything in the evening, the mother said. The parents come home after picking up the child at the baby-sitter's. Then the mother fixes dinner while the child watches TV. Then they have dinner and the child goes to bed. I said to this mother, 'Well, couldn't she help you fix dinner? That would be a nice time for the two of you to talk,' and the mother said, 'Oh, but I'd hate to have her miss "Zoom." It's such a good program!' "

Even when families make efforts to control television, too often its very presence counterbalances the positive features of family life. A writer and mother of two boys aged 3 and 7 described her family's television schedule in an article in *The New York Times*:

> We were in the midst of a full-scale War. Every day was a new battle and every program was a major skirmish. We agreed it was a bad scene all around and were ready to enter diplomatic negotiations . . . . In principle we have agreed on 2½ hours of TV a day, "Sesame Street," "Electric Company" (with dinner gobbled up in between) and two half-hour shows between 7 and 8:30 which enables the grown-ups to eat in peace and prevents the two boys from destroying one another. Their pre-bedtime choice is dreadful, because, as Josh recently admitted, "There's nothing much on I really like." So . . . it's "What's My Line" or "To Tell the Truth." . . . Clearly there is a need for first-rate children's shows at this time. . . .

Consider the "family life" described here: Presumably the father comes home from work during the "Sesame Street"–"Electric Company" stint. The children are either watching television, gobbling their dinner, or both. While the parents eat their dinner in peaceful privacy, the children watch another hour of television. Then there is only a half-hour left before bedtime, just enough time for baths, getting pajamas on, brushing teeth, and so on. The children's evening is regimented with an almost military precision. They watch their favorite programs, and when there is "nothing much on I really like," they watch whatever else is on—because *watching* is the important thing. Their mother does not see anything amiss with watching programs just for the sake of watching; she only wishes there were some first-rate children's shows on at those times.

Without conjuring up memories of the Victorian era with family games and long, leisurely meals, and large families, the question arises: isn't there a better family life available than this dismal, mechanized arrangement of children watching television for however long is allowed them, evening after evening?

Of course, families today still do *special* things together at times: go camping in the summer, go to the zoo on a nice Sunday, take various trips and expeditions. But their *ordinary* daily life together is diminished—that sitting around at the dinner table, that spontaneous taking up of an activity, those little games invented by children on the spur of the moment when there is nothing else to do, the scribbling, the chatting, and even the quarreling, all the things that form the fabric of a family, that define a childhood. Instead, the children have their regular schedule of television programs and bedtime, and the parents have their peaceful dinner together.

The author of the article in the *Times* notes that "keeping a family sane means mediating between the needs of both children and adults." But surely the needs of adults are being better met than the needs of the children, who are effectively shunted away and rendered untroublesome, while their parents enjoy a life as undemanding as that of any childless couple. In reality, it is those very demands that young children make upon a family that lead to growth, and it is the way parents accede to those demands that builds the relationships upon which the future of the family depends. If the family does not accumulate its backlog of shared experiences, shared *everyday* experiences that occur and recur and change and develop, then it is not likely to survive as anything other than a caretaking institution.

Family Rituals

Ritual is defined by sociologists as "that part of family life that the family likes about itself, is proud of, and wants formally to continue." Another text notes that "the development of a ritual by a family is an index of the common interest of its members in the family as a group."

What has happened to family rituals, those regular, dependable, recurrent happenings that gave members of a family a feeling of *belonging* to a home rather than living in it merely for the sake of convenience, those experiences that act as the adhesive of family unity far more than any material advantages?

Mealtime rituals, going-to-bed rituals, illness rituals, holiday rituals, how many of these have survived the inroads of the television set?

A young woman who grew up near Chicago reminisces about her childhood and gives an idea of the effects of television upon family rituals:

"As a child I had millions of relatives around—my parents both come from relatively large families. My father had nine brothers and sisters. And so every holiday there was this great swoop-down of aunts, uncles, and millions of cousins. I just remember how wonderful it used to be. These thousands of cousins would come and everyone would play and ultimately, after dinner, all the women would be in the front of the house, drinking coffee and talking, all the men would be in the back of the house, drinking and smoking, and all the kids would be all over the place, playing hide and seek. Christmas time was particularly nice because everyone always brought all their toys and games. Our house had a couple of rooms with go-through closets, so there were always kids running in a great circle route. I remember it was just wonderful.

"And then all of a sudden one year I remember becoming suddenly aware of how different everything had become. The kids were no longer playing Monopoly or Clue or the other games we used to play together. It was because we had a television set which had been turned on for a football game. All of that socializing that had gone on previously had ended. Now everyone was sitting in front of the television set, on a holiday, at a family party! I remember being stunned by how awful that was. Somehow the television had become more attractive."

As families have come to spend more and more of their time together engaged in the single activity of television watching, those rituals and pastimes that once gave family life its special quality have become more and more uncommon. Not since prehistoric times when cave families hunted, gathered, ate, and slept, with little time remaining to accumulate a culture of any significance, have families been reduced to such a sameness.

Real People

It is not only the activities that a family might engage in together that are diminished by the powerful presence of television in the home. The relationships of the family members to each other are also affected, in both obvious and subtle ways. The hours that the young child spends in a one-way relationship with television people, an involvement that allows for no communication or interaction, surely affect his relationships with real-life people.

Studies show the importance of eye-to-eye contact, for instance, in real-life relationships, and indicate that the nature of a person's eye-contact patterns, whether he looks another squarely in the eye or looks to the side or shifts his gaze from side to side, may play a significant role in his success or failure in human relationships. But no eye contact is possible in the child-television relationship, although in certain children's programs people purport to speak directly to the child and the camera fosters this illusion by focusing directly upon the person being filmed. (Mr. Rogers is an example, telling the child "I like you, you're special," etc.) How might such a distortion of real-life relationships affect a child's development of trust, of openness, of an ability to relate well to other *real* people?

Bruno Bettelheim writes:

> Children who have been taught, or conditioned, to listen passively most of the day to the warm verbal communications coming from the TV screen, to the deep emotional appeal of the so-called TV personality, are often unable to respond to real persons because they arouse so much less feeling than the skilled actor. Worse, they lose the ability to learn from reality because life experiences are much more complicated than the ones they see on the screen. . . .

A teacher makes a similar observation about her personal viewing experiences:

"I have trouble mobilizing myself and dealing with real people after watching a few hours of television. It's just hard to make that transition from watching television to a real relationship. I suppose it's because there was no effort necessary while I was watching, and dealing with real people always requires a bit of effort. Imagine, then, how much harder it might be to do the same thing for a small child, particularly one who watches a lot of television every day."

But more obviously damaging to family relationships is the elimination of opportunities to talk, and perhaps more important, to argue, to air grievances, between parents and children and brothers and sisters. Families frequently use television to avoid confronting their problems, problems that will not go away if they are ignored but will only fester and become less easily resolvable as time goes on.

A mother reports:

"I find myself, with three children, wanting to turn on the TV set when they're fighting. I really have to struggle not to do it because I feel that's telling them this is the solution to the quarrel—but it's so tempting that I often do it."

A family therapist discusses the use of television as an avoidance mechanism:

"In a family I know the father comes home from work and turns on the television set. The children come and watch with him and the wife serves them their meal in front of the set. He then goes and takes a shower, or works on the car or something. She then goes and has her own dinner in front of the television set. It's a symptom of a deeper-rooted problem, sure. But it would help them all to get rid of the set. It would be far easier to work on what the symptom really means without the television. The television simply encourages a double avoidance of each other. They'd find out more quickly what was going on if they weren't able to hide behind the TV. Things wouldn't necessarily be better, of course, but they wouldn't be anesthetized."

The decreased opportunities for simple conversation between parents and children in the television-centered home may help explain an observation made by an emergency room nurse at a Boston hospital. She reports that parents just seem to sit there these days when they come in with a sick or seriously injured child, although talking to the child would distract and comfort him. "They don't seem to know *how* to talk to their own children at any length," the nurse observes. Similarly, a television critic writes in *The New York Times:* "I had just a day ago taken my son to the emergency ward of a hospital for stitches above his left eye, and the occasion seemed no more real to me than Maalot or 54th Street, south-central Los Angeles. There was distance and numbness and an inability to turn off the total institution. I didn't behave at all; I just watched. . . ."

A number of research studies substantiate the assumption that television interferes with family activities and the formation of family relationships. One survey shows that 78 percent of the respondents indicated no conversation taking place during viewing except at specified times such as commercials. The study notes: "The television atmosphere in most households is one of quiet absorption on the part of family members who are present. The nature of the family social life during a program could be described as 'parallel' rather than interactive, and the set does seem to dominate family life when it is on." Thirty-six percent of the respondents in another study indicated that television viewing was the only family activity participated in during the week.

In a summary of research findings on television's effect on family interactions James Gabardino states: "The early findings suggest that television had a dirsputive effect upon interaction and thus presumably human development. . . . It is not unreasonable to ask: 'Is the fact that the average American family during the 1950's came to include two parents, two children, and a television set somehow related to the psychosocial characteristics of the young adults of the 1970's?' "

Undermining the Family

In its effect on family relationships, in its facilitation of parental withdrawal from an active role in the socialization of their children, and in its replacement of family rituals and special events, television has played an important role in the disintegration of the American family. But of course it has not been the only contributing factor, perhaps not even the most important one. The steadily rising divorce rate, the increase in the number of working mothers, the decline of the extended family, the breakdown of neighborhoods and communities, the growing isolation of the nuclear family—all have seriously affected the family.

As Urie Bronfenbrenner suggests, the sources of family breakdown do not come from the family itself, but from the circumstances in which the family finds itself and the way of life imposed upon it by those circumstances. "When those circumstances and the way of life they generate undermine relationships of trust and emotional security between family members, when they make it difficult for parents to care for, educate and enjoy their children, when there is no support or recognition from the outside world for one's role as a parent and when time spent with one's family means frustration of career, personal fulfillment, and peace of mind, then the development of the child is adversely affected," he writes.

But while the roots of alienation go deep into the fabric of American social history, television's presence in the home fertilizes them, encourages their wild and unchecked growth. Perhaps it is true that America's commitment to the television experience masks a spiritual vacuum, an empty and barren way of life, a desert of materialism. But it is television's dominant role in the family that anesthetizes the family into accepting its unhappy state and prevents it from struggling to better its condition, to improve its relationships, and to regain some of the richness it once possessed.

Others have noted the role of mass media in perpetuating an unsatisfactory *status quo*. Leisure-time activity, writes Irving Howe, "must provide relief from work monotony without making the return to work too unbearable; it must provide amusement without insight and pleasure without disturbance— as distinct from art which gives pleasure through disturbance. Mass culture is thus oriented towards a central aspect of industrial society: the depersonalization of the individual." Similarly, Jacques Ellul rejects the idea that television is a legitimate means of educating the citizen: "Education . . . takes place only incidentally. The clouding of his consciousness is paramount. . . ."

And so the American family muddles on, dimly aware that something is amiss but distracted from an understanding of its plight by an endless stream of television images. As family ties grow weaker and vaguer, as children's lives become more separate from their parents', as parents' educational role in their children's lives is taken over by television and schools, family life becomes increasingly more unsatisfying for both parents and children. All that seems to be left is Love, an abstraction that family members *know* is necessary but find great difficulty giving each other because the traditional opportunities for expresssing love within the family have been reduced or destroyed.

For contemporary parents, love toward each other has increasingly come to mean successful sexual relations, as witnessed by the proliferation of sex manuals and sex therapists. The opportunities for manifesting other forms of love through mutual support, understanding, nurturing, even, to use an unpopular word, *serving* each other, are less and less available as mothers and fathers seek their independent destinies outisde the family.

As for love of children, this love is increasingly expressed through supplying material comforts, amusements, and educational opportunities. Parents show their love for their children by sending them to good schools and camps, by providing them with good food and good doctors, by buying them toys, books, games, and a television set of their very own. Parents will even go further and express their love by attending PTA meetings to improve their children's schools, or by joining groups that are acting to improve the quality of their children's television programs.

But this is love at a remove, and is rarely understood by children. The more direct forms of parental love require time and patience, steady, dependable, ungrudgingly given time actually spent *with* a child, reading to him, comforting him, playing, joking, and working with him. But even if a parent were eager and willing to demonstrate that sort of direct love to his children today, the opportunities are diminished. What with school and Little League and piano lessons and, of course, the inevitable television programs, a day seems to offer just enough time for a good-night kiss.

Suggestions for Discussion

1. Why did early critics regard television as a "favorable, beneficial, indeed, wondrous influence upon the family"?
2. Explain why television has not served to bring members of the family together.
3. Cite examples of the loss of social interaction in families described by Winn.
4. Explain Winn's belief that "television has played an important role in the disintegration of the American family." Do you agree? Explain.

Suggestions for Writing

1. Describe and comment on television viewing in your own home.
2. Compare and contrast Winn's depiction of family interaction with Art Buchwald's.

S. J. Perelman
Meanness Rising from the Suds

Sidney Joseph Perelman (1904–1979), distinguished American humorist, playwright, and screenwriter, is the author of many collections of essays and sketches, including *Crazy Like a Fox,* (1944), *The Swiss Family Perelman* (1950), and *The Last Laugh* (1981), from which the following selection is taken.

I used to pride myself on being impervious to the sentimentalities of soap opera, but when that loveliest of English actresses, Rachel Gurney, of *Upstairs, Downstairs,* perished on the *Titanic,* I wept so convulsively and developed such anorexia that I had to be force-fed. Hovering between life and death for weeks, I sat in a Bath chair on the great dappled lawns of my country house with my favorite collie at my feet and an alienist, until one of them—I can't recall which—recommended that I watch a few other soaps to palliate my anguish. So I did; I watched *Another World, Days of Our Lives, As the World Turns,* and *Somerset,* and in less time than you could say "Dr. Gregory Zilboorg" I was whole again. Compared to the torment their characters underwent, Rachel's fate was a piece of cake.

I usually avoid such personal revelations, reserving them for my diary and a few copies for friends, but not long ago a paragraph on this subject, in a periodical called *American Film,* horrified me anew. It said that *True* had examined the treatment of men in daytime soap opera and recoiled in shocked indignity. "Shows like 'Another World,' " it complained, "portrayed men as 'gutless and/or villainous boobs.' Moreover, [*True*] found that most male characters on daytime serials suffer from something, and listed the embarrassments that are visited on the stronger sex: 'sterility, stupidity, amnesia, alcoholism, impotence, night sweats, acne, acrophobia, senility, insecurity, and outright lunacy.' " The item continues, "An editor of a soap opera newsletter told *True* that some actors have quit in protest at the 'shambling fools' their characters were reduced to. Worse, some even found their characters so emasculated that their offscreen sex life was affected."

Hardly able to credit the evidence of my eyes, I swiftly dug up the relevant issue of *True* for confirmation. Every word was gospel. One actor, John Colenback, who has played Dr. Dan Stewart in *As the World Turns* for many years, charged, "The writers I worked with always managed to turn the men on the show into either evil or totally weak characters who were manipulated by women. . . . I was trapped in an extremely paranoid position. I was really vicious when I was working at the hospital, screaming at nurses and patients like a little Hitler. But at home I had to be the biggest of boobs, pushed around unmercifully by my wife and my mother." (And, judging from that adverb, Colenback's travail also fractured his English.) Furthermore, *True* pointed out, these shows were not alone in their castrating complex, and gave more examples of male *faiblesse* gleaned from *Days of Our Lives*: "A man turns out to be the father of his brother's child. A husband ruins his wife's career by refusing to let her sing in public. . . . A man shaves off his mustache because a girl tells him that she doesn't trust men with face hair." All of them, I was forced to acknowledge, were unspeakable bounders—the husband in particular. Rather than wicked, actually he was a dolt. The craftier way to ruin his wife's career would have been to *compel* her to sing in public.

The second dent of soap opera on my consciousness had barely faded to a purplish bruise when out of left field came another—this time, though, more in the nature of a soft nudge. A ravishing friend of mine who, by a coincidence, had won her acting spurs on *Another World* and was now starred in a network show called *Millionaire Pauper* rang me up one evening from the Coast. Not for nothing had Kathleen been called the Zuleika Dobson of Hofstra University; in addition to green eyes, honey-colored hair, and a figure that capsized the senses, she had a brain stored with more knowledge than Chamber's Encyclopedia and a gaiety unequalled since Carole Lombard's. But tonight she was in a sombre mood. "Look, baby, I've got to come up for air," she confided. "I'm skying into town for a couple of nights. Do you know a real person that a person could spend an evening with—not a chauvinist pig or a garter-snapper?"

I tried to think of one, and, failing, timidly nominated myself.

There was a curious pause, and a crackling akin to chuckling, as though we were disconnected. Then I heard her voice. "You?" she asked dubiously. "Yes, you're sweet. But, frankly, dear, I've always felt there was—how shall I say—something lacking in you."

I bristled. "You mean that I'm kind of weak? Gutless? A boob?"

"No, just ineffectual—sort of Pre-Raphaelite. A bush-league Dante Gabriel Rossetti, so to speak. You're not really *evil*, like the men on my show. The trouble with you, darling—"

"Listen, this call is costing you an arm and a leg," I broke in, forgetting that she had reversed the charges. "I'll meet you at '21' tomorrow at eight. No, wait—you don't want to be bothered signing autographs. Let's make the corner of Fifty-eighth and Fifth, and if I'm late you can look in Bergdorf's windows."

The realization that Kathleen conceived of me as a sheep rankled throughout the night, and by morning I decided to change my image. Fie on the funereal lounge suit from Brooks I had worn hitherto, the discreet neckwear, the bespoke shoes; I would transform myself into a swinger, one of those breezy, jovial loudmouths around the Americana Hotel, and sweep her off her feet. At a quarter to seven, I stood aghast regarding my alter ego in the bathroom mirror. The peacock-blue safari suit, the Tibetan prayer beads encircling my neck were disastrous. All I needed was a little tin can on my head to look like Happy Hooligan. Eyes aplenty popped at the Golden Noodle subsequently as the headwaiter ushered Kathleen and me to our table, but they were riveted on her Celtic beauty rather than on me. Understated my old Brooks number may have been; still, it didn't glow in the dark.

Our faces were greasy with egg rolls and spareribs before I mustered up courage to pose the question gnawing at my subconscious. "Kathie," I demanded, "why do you women in soap opera detest my sex?"

"Hate your sex?" The widened eyes turned on me were as lambent as a jaguar's. "My dear, you talk like a sausage. We don't at all."

"You do, you do!" I drummed my fists on the table. "We're always being portrayed as drunkards and eunuchs and fatheads—greedy, lascivious morons without one redeeming virtue."

"But you *are* swine, you can't deny," she said, palms outspread. "Look at Verdun, the Huguenot massacre, the annual statistics on rape."

"And women are angels, I suppose," I retorted. "What about Messalina knocking off her lovers? And Catherine of Russia, Madame Defarge, and Lizzie Borden?"

"Oh, we've had a few hotheads, sure, but if you dig into it, you'll find men were usually to blame. Remember the breakfast Andrew Borden had served up that blazing Fall River morning? Warmed-over mutton soup, leftover mutton, and bananas. No wonder the poor thing went berserk."

"Don't try to squirm out of it," I said roughly. "You and your ilk are helping to perpetrate a lie. How can you accept money for blackening the opposite gender?"

"Well, money is the only thing they give us. I guess it's better than nothing."

"Really. I'm surprised you can sleep nights with that on your conscience."

"I did have trouble at first, until I switched to Compoz. You should, too—it's great for the kind of indignation you're suffering from." She shovelled in a second helping of subgum chow mein with water chestnuts. Typical feminine behavior. They eat a spoonful of yogurt when they're alone, but when you're buying, man, it's like Thanksgiving. "Now, shape up, honey—you know better than to bad-mouth my profession. We just speak the words you writers give us."

"Then we're traitors to our sex," I snapped. "We ought to be horsewhipped for maligning ourselves."

"Hyperbole," Kathleen dismissed. "Those scribes out there are merely using soap opera as a confessional. Believe me, I speak from experience—I lived with one a couple of months last year. He was a gorgeous animal. Body by Mark Spitz, hair like the raven's wing, pearly teeth, Byronic profile; the man was a veritable collage. And clever, too—not a speck of talent, but he knew exactly whose work to plagiarize. So we're in paradise as envisioned nowadays by Erica Jong—though, between you and me, I was brought up on Andrew Lang's *Orange Fairy Book* and I like to do a little sewing betweentimes."

"What ever attracted you to a bullock like that?" I asked, repressing a shudder. "Sheer physical perfection is abhorrent to me. Lacking nobility of mind, love is a barrel without hoops."

"You don't say," she commented. "Would you mind disengaging your foot from mine? There, that's better. . . . Well, one day I was seated in front of my checkbook, as Sir Arthur Sullivan's song has it, weary and ill at ease. Not only did it not balance but, chancing to glance through the cancelled checks, I discovered that, unbeknownst to me, I was supporting a household in Redondo Beach. I taxed Wolf, my lover, with it, and learned the place was tenanted by an orphan—a wistful, flaxen-haired call girl to whom, out of compassion, he had also given a charge account at I. Magnin."

"Whereupon I imagine you sent him packing."

"Yes, in my white Mercedes 450–SEL, which, blinded by tears of remorse, he drove into a stanchion on the San Diego Freeway. The shock to his psyche might have been irreparable, except that he embodied our idyll in his soap opera and then wrote it off as a deductible business expense."

"Kathleen mavourneen." I reached over and took her hand—the one that was not busy spooning up water chestnuts. "How can you allow yourself to be endlessly exploited by such parasites, trapped in an environment so alien to you? Need I remind you that with each passing day you grow older?"

"Oh, remind me, do," she begged. "That's why I flew three thousand miles—to be warned I was becoming a raddled old crone."

"Well, it isn't too apparent yet," I comforted her. "And anyway there are lots of old-crone parts you'll be able to play. No, what I'm trying to convey is that however stupid or clumsy your past has been, I'm big enough to overlook it."

"Then nothing else matters," she said warmly. "As long as you think I'm straight and clean and fine—"

"I didn't say that," I interrupted. "Let me finish. Now, I'm not very rich in this world's goods, but I know where there's a tiny cabin in a bee-loud glade just large enough for two. Can you guess what I see there?"

Like so many of your Hibernian persuasion, Kathleen is more than a bit psychic, and, after a moment's reflection, she told me. She saw herself bent over a washtub humming contentedly as several chubby youngsters played around her knees and I sat indoors writing paperbacks that I hoped to sell for four hundred thousand each so as to put meat on the table.

"Yes, yes, go on," I encouraged. "Is there anything else you want to tell me?"

"Just one thing, lambie," she said, and patted my hand. "Fearing you might become sleepy after these Chinese dinners you consistently feed me, I availed myself of a backup date with a person staying at the Americana."

"Some loudmouth in a safari suit and prayer beads, no doubt," I said, stung to the quick.

She nodded. "Poor in spirit but not in this world's goods—he owns forty-one percent of the Texas Panhandle. Hence," she said, rising, "that's why I'm rushing off precipitately, because he can't bear to be kept waiting at '21.'" She imprinted a light kiss on my ear and was gone in a rustle of silk.

Temperamentally, I'm an easygoing, philosophical chap stimulated by rejection, as I've often noted in my diary and a few copies for friends, and within a month the entire episode had faded from memory. Then, one afternoon, as I was watching *Millionaire Pauper*, the soap Kathleen appears on, I was taken aback by a new character introduced as comic relief—a bespectacled writer hopelessly besotted with a glamorous young actress. Torn between satyriasis and parsimony, he insists on conducting her to substandard Chinese restaurants, where he fondles her over the less expensive choices on the á la carte menu—but why should I compound the humiliations? The whole thing is a cowardly slur on the masculine sex, and any male voluntarily tuning in on the show should be horsewhipped. Still, don't let me influence you. That's just one viewer's opinion.

Suggestions for Discussion

1. According to Perelman, how do daytime soap operas portray men?

2. Describe the responses of some men who have played roles in these shows.

3. Characterize Kathleen.

4. Summarize the conversation in the Golden Noodle restaurant.

5. Discuss Perelman's use of allusion as a source of humor in the essay.

Suggestions for Writing

1. Based on your observation of daytime soap opera, agree or disagree with Perelman's assertions about the depiction of men.

2. Write a humorous account of a date that went awry for you.

George Grella
James Bond: Culture Hero

George Grella (b. 1938), a member of the faculty at the University of Rochester, is the author of *Murders and Manners: The Formal Detective Novel* and of essays which have appeared in such journals as *Life,* the *New Republic,* and the *Kansas City Star.* The essay which follows (published in 1964) is a delightful exercise in ironic scholarship.

Ian Fleming's James Bond is the most famous spy since Mata Hari. The indomitable secret agent reaches every level of literacy: Presidents to popcorn chewers. Not only has the author become a kind of subliterary lion in *Time, The New Yorker,* and *The Saturday Review,* which have devoted interviews and articles to his work, but his opinion was solicited on a major network show about the U-2 affair, the producers seeming to consider Mr. Fleming something like the Walter Lippmann of espionage.

Yet there is no puzzle to solve, no criminal to discover, no brilliant method to reveal. Fleming has no view of a corrupt society in the manner of a Cain, a Hammett, or a Chandler; his style and outlook are facile and pedestrian. Unlike Mickey Spillane, he doesn't write pornographic thrillers. Unlike Graham Greene, he offers no metaphysical or psychological insight, no significant comment on the nature of good and evil. Eric Ambler, a genuine craftsman, gives us plausible incidents, people stumbling into affairs which are complex, ambiguous, and believable. Newer writers, such as John Le Carré in *The Spy Who Came in from the Cold* or Len Deighton in the largely unrecognized *Ipcress File,* portray the life of a professional spy as unglamorous, poverty-ridden, and full of odd danger—one never knows when his own organization may betray him, or how far a competing unit of his own government will go, or if he must kill someone on his side, or even what side he is on.

To put it plainly, James Bond, despite his lean good looks, his taste in food, wine, and women, his high standing in the British Secret Service, his license to kill, is stupid. He disobeys orders and blunders into situations he should have anticipated chapters in advance. He is almost always known to the enemy as soon as he arrives, undercover, on the scene of action. He usually flounders around long enough for his adversaries to disrupt his elaborate plans and capture him.

His only genius lies in an infinite capacity for taking pain. He has suffered (and survived) bombing, shooting, stabbing, poisoning, and automobile attack. He has managed to (barely) escape castration by carpet-beater; bisection by buzzsaw; rocket blast; shark, barracuda, and octopus attack; a near-fatal increase in height on a health farm stretching apparatus; and a dose of poison from the sex glands of a rare Eastern fish. Such bizarre punishment is oddly requited: Bond has enjoyed the charms of the expensive Tiffany Case; the Bahamian nature girl, Honeychile Rider; the mystic Solitaire; and the ineffable Pussy Galore.

No secret agent could behave with such incompetence and still achieve

such high renown, such titillating rewards. Fleming's characters are grotesques, the much-publicized sex is chrome-plated, not at all shocking, and
the plots are repetitive from book to book. The solution of the paradox of
James Bond's popularity may be, not in considering the novels as thrillers,
but as something very different, as historic epic and romance, based on the
stuff of myth and legend.

Thus, the affectionate fondling of brand names, which readers cite as an
example of authenticity, is a contemporary version of the conventional epic
catalog. It is important for the reader to know that Bond wears Sea Island
cotton shirts, smokes a Macedonian blend of cigarettes, tells time by a Rolex
Oyster watch, fires a Walther PPK 7.65 automatic in a Berns-Martin Triple
Draw holster, drives a Mark II Bentley Continental, and so on, just as it
important for the reader of the *Iliad* to be told the immense detail of Achilles'
shield. Instead of a catalog of ships, Fleming gives us a catalog of clothes,
toilet accessories, or background material about some exotic place or some
arcane field of knowledge. The catalogs reflect the culture: the long lists of
brand names suggest the affluence of a capitalist civilization, just as Bond
suggests the secure investment.

Bond fights epic battles, taking seriously what Pope used humorously in
his mock epic, *The Rape of the Lock*—the epic game of cards. James Bond
has won harrowing games of blackjack, baccarat, bridge, even canasta. Like
Ulysses, he travels far, from Turkey to Las Vegas, the Mediterranean, the
Caribbean, the Atlantic, even Miami Beach. He makes the obligatory trip to
the underworld when he skindives in the Bahamas, travels through the sew-
ers of Istanbul, visits the domain of Mr. Big in Harlem, negotiates Dr. No's
cruel tunnel of terror. His name indicates further facets of his character: he is
entrusted with the mammoth task of safeguarding an entire civilization; the
free world depends on his actions.

In *Moonraker* the situation parallels the Perseus–St. George myth, an appropriate one for Bond's rescue of London from the great rocket of Sir Hugo
Drax, the huge dragon menacing England. Drax has red hair, an ugly, burned
face which even plastic surgery cannot mask, splayed "ogre's teeth"; the great
burst of fire he hopes to turn on London is the modern equivalent of the
dragon's flames. Fleming employs an ironic reversal of one aspect of the Perseus myth: instead of rescuing Andromeda from the cliff where she is chained,
Bond and his Andromeda, Galatea Brand, are nearly killed when one of the
Dover cliffs, with some urging from Drax, falls on them. Of course Bond
survives and, after escaping steamhosing and the liftoff of the Moonraker
rocket (more fire from the dragon's nostrils), saves London. Alone among
Bond novels, the hero fails to get the girl at the end: as a modern St. George,
it would scarcely be appropriate for him to win the fair maiden.

In *Live and Let Die*, Bond travels to New York to confront Mr. Big, a giant
Negro who controls a black brotherhood of crime, gathering gold to aid the
Soviet Union. With his Negro network, his voodoo cult, his clairvoyant mistress, Mr. Big is almost omnipotent; his followers believe he is Baron Samedi,
the Devil himself. He even controls the fishes of the sea, summoning shark
and barracuda to defend his island. But Bond hurls the epic boast, which we
know will clinch his victory, "Big Man? Then let it be a giant, a homeric
slaying." His boast is fulfilled; just as he and Solitaire are to be dragged over
a coral reef and shredded, Bond's mine blows up Mr. Big's boat and Big is

devoured by the fish he tamed, his immense head bobbing bodyless in the sea. Bond again saves Civilization, this time from the powers of blackness.

Goldfinger is probably the most obvious reworking of early myth. Auric Goldfinger, who drives a gold car, carries his money in solid gold, dreams of robbing Fort Knox, and likes his women gold-plated all over, is a reincarnation of King Midas. Midas was tone deaf and earned a pair of ass's ears for misjudging a music contest between Pan and Apollo; Goldfinger, when Bond first meets him, is wearing a hearing aid and sunning himself with a set of tin wings resembling a pair of long, slightly pointed ears. Midas' barber, unable to contain the secret of his master's aural adornment, whispered his message into a hole. Later a reed grew and told the secret to all passersby. James Bond, in Goldfinger's captivity, must foil the planned robbery of Fort Knox; he tapes his message to an airplane toilet seat, the only hole available, and thus transmits it to the outside world.

Fleming's best-known book, *Dr. No* (there's a movie version too), is the most purely mythic of his works. Dr. No is the archetypal monster who casts a blight on the land and who must be conquered by the unquenchable spirit of life. He inhabits a lavish underground fortress in a guano island in the Caribbean, from which he misguides American missiles with intricate electronic apparatus. He has come to the British government's attention through complaints of the Audubon Society about the deaths of thousands of roseate spoonbills. Dr. No intimidates the natives and scares off the birds with a fire-breathing tractor made to resemble a dragon; his dragon is devastating the island of dung, killing the birds, the game wardens, all natural life. For his violation of nature, Dr. No must be punished by the grand spirit of affirmation, James Bond. Naturally Bond's mission fails at first; he is detected and captured by the evil doctor. After a rich meal and an opportunity to enumerate and use the deluxe living accommodations of the island fortress, Bond is subjected to an agonizing series of tortures in a tunnel of horrors, including an ordeal by fire and by water. He manages to crawl through the bowels of the island (anthropomorphically, the bowels of the monster as well), and kill Dr. No's pet giant octopus, displaying all the while superhuman strength and stamina. He buries Dr. No alive in a small mountain of guano. He has brought back the fertility of the land by ridding nature of the destroyer. As his reward, he spends a night with Honeychile Rider, the nymph of the Bahamas, who knows the secrets of snakes, spiders, and seashells. His heroic reward is the possession of the nature spirit herself; it is richly deserved. James Bond has redeemed the Waste Land.

The much-touted background which distinguishes the Bond novel, the close attention to real places and real names, the bits of esoteric information, are all products of an expensive research organization. Aside from their epic function, the lists of names lend only a spurious authenticity which is negated by other lapses from realism. Not only do people like Dr. No and Mr. Big inhabit an unreal world, but even their surface reality is questionable. Fleming's painstaking tour of Manhattan with Bond in *Live and Let Die* proves only that he can read a New York City map. Mr. Fleming is maladroit at transcribing American English; his Negro dialect echoes *Porgy and Bess*. His Americans, from cabdrivers to CIA agents, speak like graduates of non-U public schools. In *Diamonds Are Forever*, Bond thinks the tails attached to automobile antennas are beaver tails. No one in America hunts beaver for their tails or for anything else and not even teenagers fly squirrel tails (which don't look at all like beaver tails) from their cars any more. It's been thirty years since jaded Cafe Society types slummed in Harlem; Fleming seems to think it's still fashionable.

But no matter; we are dealing with myths. Vivienne Michel, the breathless French-Canadian girl who narrates *The Spy Who Loved Me,* may be intended as a representation of the typical James Bond fan. Most of the book concentrates on her rather unexciting sexual reminiscences in an odd fusion of *True Confessions* and *McCall's.* She is rescued from a pair of gangsters in an Adirondack motel by the coincidental appearance of our agent. After first fumbling the job (he can't kill in cold blood, he explains, forgetting that he's hired for that job and in another book he's detailed a couple of these jobs), Bond triumphs. He and Vivienne couple hygienically (in air-conditioned comfort, on Beautyrest mattresses, with Sanitized toilet facilities), and Vivienne comments of the action, "He had come from nowhere like the prince in the fairy tales, and he had saved me from the dragon . . . and then, when the dragon was dead, he had taken me as his reward." Vivienne doesn't have Bond's powerful Bentley, she drives a "cute little Vespa." She lists a variety of brand names, but hers consist of clothes and motel appliances. Her comments about the dragon indicate that she, at least, recognizes what's up.

In Fleming's most recent novel, *On Her Majesty's Secret Service,* Bond saves England from biological warfare waged by Ernst Blofeld, the elusive chief of SPECTRE. He narrowly escapes death and matrimony. Blofeld murders Bond's bride of a few hours and escapes, no doubt to reappear in a future novel. Bond, though hardly chaste, still must be unmarried, celibate in his fight against evil. Since there can be no Son of Bond, Blofeld does agent 007 a great service.

Mr. Anthony Boucher, an astute and prolific critic of thrillers, complained in a *New York Times* review of the book that only bad shooting enabled Bond to escape his enemies. Mr. Boucher is correct, but he criticizes the book as a poor thriller, neglecting the myth: since Bond leads a charmed life, no one can ever shoot him dead.

Perhaps centuries from now, scholars will trace assiduously those references to Yardley soap, Kent brushes, Lanvin perfume, Sanitized toilet seats. Perhaps there will be a variorum Fleming, and "Fleming men" as there are "Milton men." Theses may be written on the epicene role of M, clearly a father figure (yet why unmarried? and that maternal sounding initial is rather damning). For James Bond is the Renaissance man in mid-century guise, lover, warrior, connoisseur. He fights the forces of darkness, speaks for the sanitary achievements of the age, enjoys hugely the fruits of the free enterprise economy. He lives the dreams of countless drab people, his gun ready, his honor intact, his morals loose: the hero of our anxiety-ridden, mythless age: the savior of our culture.

Suggestions for Discussion

1. In what ways is James Bond "stupid"?

2. What is the importance of brand names in the Bond stories?

3. Explain the mythic qualities Grella ascribes to the Bond novels. Which of the allusions made by Grella seem most convincing to you?

4. Discuss Bond as "the hero of our anxiety-ridden, mythless age: the savior of our culture.

Suggestions for Writing

1. To what extent can any of Grella's observations apply to the James Bond films that you have seen?

2. Discuss the use of violence in a Bond novel or film.

Ralph Ellison
The Birth of Bebop

Ralph Ellison (b. 1914), the distinguished American novelist, is best known for *Invisible Man,* published in 1952. In "The Birth of Bebop" (1959), he describes the exciting music being played at Minton's Playhouse in Harlem in the 1940's.

When asked how it was back then, back in the Forties, they will smile, then, frowning with the puzzlement of one attempting to recall the details of a pleasant but elusive dream, they'll say: "Oh, man, it was a hell of a time! A wailing time! Things were jumping, you couldn't get in here for the people. The place was packed with celebrities. Park Avenue, man! Big people in show business, college professors along with the pimps and their women. And college boys and girls. Everybody came. You know how the old words to the *Basin Street Blues* used to go before Sinatra got hold of it? *Basin Street is the street where the dark and the light folks meet*—that's what I'm talking about. That was Minton's, man. It was a place where everybody could come to be entertained because it was a place that was jumping with good times."

Or some will tell you that it was here that Dizzy Gillespie found his own trumpet voice; that here Kenny Clarke worked out the patterns of his drumming style; where Charlie Christian played out the last creative and truly satisfying moments of his brief life, his New York home; where Charlie Parker built the monument of his art; where Thelonius Monk formulated his contribution to the chordal progressions and the hide-and-seek melodic methods of modern jazz. And they'll call such famous names as Lester Young and Ben Webster, Coleman Hawkins; or Fats Waller, who came here in the after-hour stillness of the early morning to compose. They'll tell you that Benny Good-man, Art Tatum, Count Basie, and Lena Horne would drop in to join in the fun; that it was here that George Shearing played on his first night in the U.S.; or Tony Scott's great love of the place; and they'll repeat all the stories of how, when, and by whom the word "bebop" was coined here. . . .

In 1941 [Henry] Minton handed over [the] management of Minton's Play-house to Teddy Hill, the saxophonist and former band leader, and Hill turned the Playhouse into a musical dueling ground. Not only did he continue Min-ton's policies, he expanded them. It was Hill who established the Monday Celebrity Nights, the house band which included such members from his own disbanded orchestra as Kenny Clarke, Dizzy Gillespie, along with Thelonius Monk, sometimes with Joe Guy, and later, Charlie Christian and Charlie Par-ker; and it was Hill who allowed the musicians free rein to play whatever they liked. Perhaps no other club except Clarke Monroe's Uptown House was so permissive, and with the hospitality extended to musicians of all schools the news spread swiftly. Minton's became the focal point for musicians all over the country.

Herman Pritchard, who presided over the bar in the old days, tells us that every time they came, "Lester Young and Ben Webster used to tie up in battle like dogs in the road. They'd fight on those saxophones until they were tired out, then they'd put in long distance calls to their mothers, both of whom lived in Kansas City, and tell them about it."

And most of the masters of jazz came either to observe or to participate and be influenced and listen to their own discoveries transformed; and the aspiring stars sought to win their approval, as the younger tenor men tried to win the esteem of Coleman Hawkins. Or they tried to vanquish them in jam-ming contests as Gillespie is said to have outblown his idol, Roy Eldridge. It was during this period that Eddie "Lockjaw" Davis underwent an ordeal of jeering rejection until finally he came through as an admired tenor man.

In the perspective of time we now see that what was happening at Minton's was a continuing symposium of jazz, a summation of all the styles, personal and traditional, of jazz. Here it was possible to hear its resources of tech-nique, ideas, harmonic structure, melodic phrasing, and rhythmical possibili-ties explored more thoroughly than was ever possible before. It was also pos-sible to hear the first attempts toward a conscious statement of the sensibility of the younger generation of musicians as they worked out the techniques, structures, and rhythmical patterns with which to express themselves. Part of this was arbitrary, a revolt of the younger against the established stylists; part of it was inevitable. For jazz had reached a crisis and new paths were certain to be searched for and found. An increasing number of the younger men were formally trained and the post-Depression developments in the country had made for quite a break between their experience and that of the older men. Many were even of a different physical build. Often they were quiet and of a reserve which contrasted sharply with the exuberant and outgoing lyricism of the older men, and they were intensely concerned that their identity as Negroes placed no restriction upon the music they played or the manner in which they used their talent. They were concerned, they said, with art, not entertain-ment. Especially were they resentful of Louis Armstrong whom (confusing the spirit of his music with his clowning) they considered an Uncle Tom.

But they too, some of them, had their own myths and misconceptions: That theirs was the only generation of Negro musicians who listened to or enjoyed the classics; that to be truly free they must act exactly the opposite of what white people might believe, rightly or wrongly, a Negro to be; that the performing artist can be completely and absolutely free of the obligations of the entertainer, and that they could play jazz with dignity only by frowning and treating the audience with aggressive contempt; and that to be in control, artistically and personally, one must be so cool as to quench one's own human fire.

Nor should we overlook the despair which must have swept Minton's before the technical mastery, the tonal authenticity, the authority, and the fecundity of imagination of such men as Hawkins, Young, Goodman, Tatum, Teagarden, Ellington, and Waller. Despair, after all, is ever an important force in revolutions.

They were also responding to the nonmusical pressures affecting jazz. It was a time of big bands and the greatest prestige and economic returns were falling outside the Negro community—often to leaders whose popularity grew from the compositions and arrangements of Negroes—to white instrumentalists whose only originality lay in the enterprise with which they rushed to market with some Negro musician's hard-won style. Still there was no policy of racial discrimination at Minton's. Indeed, it was very much like those Negro cabarets of the Twenties and Thirties in which a megaphone was placed on the piano so that anyone with the urge could sing a blues. Nevertheless, the inside-dopesters will tell you that the "changes" or chord progressions and the melodic inversions worked out by the creators of bop sprang partially from their desire to create a jazz which could not be so easily imitated and exploited by white musicians to whom the market was more open simply *because* of their whiteness. They wished to receive credit for what they created, and besides, it was easier to "get rid of the trash" who crowded the bandstand with inept playing and thus make room for the real musicians, whether white or black. Nevertheless, white musicians like Tony Scott, Remo Palmieri, and Al Haig who were part of the development at Minton's became so by passing a test of musicianship, sincerity, and temperament. Later, it is said, the boppers became engrossed in solving the musical problems which they set themselves. Except for a few sympathetic older musicians it was they who best knew the promise of the Minton moment, and it was they, caught like the rest in all the complex forces of American life which come to focus in jazz, who made the most of it. Now the tall tales told as history must feed on the results of their efforts.

Suggestions for Discussion

1. Why did Minton's become "the focal point for musicians all over the country" in the 1940's?

2. How were the younger stylists different from the older?

3. What goals did the boppers set for themselves?

4. Discuss the ways in which Ellison personalizes his characterizations of individual jazz musicians.

Suggestions for Writing

1. Discuss the music of any of the musicians mentioned by Ellison.

2. Describe a jazz club which you have visited.

◇◇◇◇

Fiction
— ◆◆◆ —

John Cheever
The Enormous Radio

John Cheever (1912–1982), distinguished American novelist and short-story writer, won many awards including the Pulitzer Prize and the American Book Award. His books include *The Enormous Radio and Other Stories* (1954), *The Wapshot Chronicle* (1957), *The Wapshot Scandal* (1964), *Bullet Park* (1969), *Falconer* (1977), and *The Stories of John Cheever* (1979).

Jim and Irene Westcott were the kind of people who seem to strike that satisfactory average of income, endeavor, and respectability that is reached by the statistical reports in college alumni bulletins. They were the parents of two young children, they had been married nine years, they lived on the twelfth floor of an apartment house near Sutton Place, they went to the theatre on an average of 10.3 times a year, and they hoped someday to live in Westchester. Irene Westcott was a pleasant, rather plain girl with soft brown hair and a wide, fine forehead upon which nothing at all had been written, and in the cold weather she wore a coat of fitch skins dyed to resemble mink. You could not say that Jim Westcott looked younger than he was, but you could at least say of him that he seemed to feel younger. He wore his graying hair cut very short, he dressed in the kind of clothes his class had worn at Andover, and his manner was earnest, vehement, and intentionally naïve. The Westcotts differed from their friends, their classmates, and their neighbors only in an interest they shared in serious music. They went to a great many concerts—although they seldom mentioned this to anyone—and they spent a good deal of time listening to music on the radio.

Their radio was an old instrument, sensitive, unpredictable, and beyond repair. Neither of them understood the mechanics of radio—or of any of the other appliances that surrounded them—and when the instrument faltered,

Jim would strike the side of the cabinet with his hand. This sometimes helped. One Sunday afternoon, in the middle of a Schubert quartet, the music faded away altogether. Jim struck the cabinet repeatedly, but there was no response; the Schubert was lost to them forever. He promised to buy Irene a new radio, and on Monday when he came home from work he told her that he had got one. He refused to describe it, and said it would be a surprise for her when it came.

The radio was delivered at the kitchen door the following afternoon, and with the assistance of her maid and the handyman Irene uncrated it and brought it into the living room. She was struck at once with the physical ugliness of the large gumwood cabinet. Irene was proud of her living room, she had chosen its furnishings and colors as carefully as she chose her clothes, and now it seemed to her that the new radio stood among her intimate possessions like an aggressive intruder. She was confounded by the number of dials and switches on the instrument panel, and she studied them thoroughly before she put the plug into a wall socket and turned the radio on. The dials flooded with a malevolent green light, and in the distance she heard the music of a piano quintet. The quintet was in the distance for only an instant; it bore down upon her with a speed greater than light and filled the apartment with the noise of music amplified so mightily that it knocked a china ornament from a table to the floor. She rushed to the instrument and reduced the volume. The violent forces that were snared in the ugly gumwood cabinet made her uneasy. Her children came home from school then, and she took them to the Park. It was not until later in the afternoon that she was able to return to the radio.

The maid had given the children their suppers and was supervising their baths when Irene turned on the radio, reduced the volume, and sat down to listen to a Mozart quintet that she knew and enjoyed. The music came through clearly. The new instrument had a much purer tone, she thought, than the old one. She decided that tone was most important and that she could conceal the cabinet behind a sofa. But as soon as she had made her peace with the radio, the interference began. A crackling sound like the noise of a burning powder fuse began to accompany the singing of the strings. Beyond the music, there was a rustling that reminded Irene unpleasantly of the sea, and as the quintet progressed, these noises were joined by many others. She tried all the dials and switches but nothing dimmed the interference, and she sat down, disappointed and bewildered, and tried to trace the flight of the melody. The elevator shaft in her building ran beside the living-room wall, and it was the noise of the elevator that gave her a clue to the character of the static. The rattling of the elevator cables and the opening and closing of the elevator doors were reproduced in her loudspeaker, and, realizing that the radio was sensitive to electrical currents of all sorts, she began to discern through the Mozart the ringing of telephone bells, the dialing of phones, and the lamentation of a vacuum cleaner. By listening more carefully, she was able to distinguish doorbells, elevator bells, electric razors, and Waring mixers, whose sounds had been picked up from the apartments that surrounded hers and transmitted through her loudspeaker. The powerful and ugly instrument, with its mistaken sensitivity to discord, was more than she could hope to master, so she turned the thing off and went into the nursery to see her children.

When Jim Westcott came home that night, he went to the radio confidently and worked the controls. He had the same sort of experience Irene had had. A man was speaking on the station Jim had chosen, and his voice swung instantly from the distance into a force so powerful that it shook the apartment. Jim turned the volume control and reduced the voice. Then, a minute or two later, the interference began. The ringing of telephones and doorbells set in, joined by the rasp of the elevator doors and the whir of cooking appliances. The character of the noise had changed since Irene had tried the radio earlier; the last of the electric razors was being unplugged, the vacuum cleaners had all been returned to their closets, and the static reflected that change in pace that overtakes the city after the sun goes down. He fiddled with the knobs but couldn't get rid of the noises, so he turned the radio off and told Irene that in the morning he'd call the people who had sold it to him and give them hell.

The following afternoon, when Irene returned to the apartment from a luncheon date, the maid told her that a man had come and fixed the radio. Irene went into the living room before she took off her hat or her furs and tried the instrument. From the loudspeaker came a recording of the "Missouri Waltz." It reminded her of the thin, scratchy music from an old-fashioned phonograph that she sometimes heard across the lake where she spent her summers. She waited until the waltz had finished, expecting an explanation of the recording, but there was none. The music was followed by silence, and then the plaintive and scratchy record was repeated. She turned the dial and got a satisfactory burst of Caucasian music—the thump of bare feet in the dust and the rattle of coin jewelry—but in the background she could hear the ringing of bells and a confusion of voices. Her children came home from school then, and she turned off the radio and went to the nursery.

When Jim came home that night, he was tired, and he took a bath and changed his clothes. Then he joined Irene in the living room. He had just turned on the radio when the maid announced dinner, so he left it on, and he and Irene went to the table.

Jim was too tired to make even a pretense of sociability, and there was nothing about the dinner to hold Irene's interest, so her attention wandered from the food to the deposits of silver polish on the candlesticks and from there to the music in the other room. She listened for a few moments to a Chopin prelude and then was surprised to hear a man's voice break in. "For Christ's sake, Kathy," he said, "do you always have to play the piano when I get home?" The music stopped abruptly. "It's the only chance I have," a woman said. "I'm at the office all day." "So am I," the man said. He added something obscene about an upright piano, and slammed a door. The passionate and melancholy music began again.

"Did you hear that?" Irene asked.

"What?" Jim was eating his dessert.

"The radio. A man said something while the music was still going on—something dirty."

"It's probably a play."

"I don't think it *is* a play," Irene said.

They left the table and took their coffee into the living room. Irene asked Jim to try another station. He turned the knob. "Have you seen my garters?" a man asked. "Button me up," a woman said. "Have you seen my garters?"

the man said again. "Just button me up and I'll find your garters," the woman said. Jim shifted to another station. "I wish you wouldn't leave apple cores in the ashtrays," a man said. "I hate the smell."

"This is strange," Jim said.

"Isn't it?" Irene said.

Jim turned the knob again. " 'On the coast of Coromandel where the early pumpkins blow,' " a woman with a pronounced English accent said, " 'in the middle of the woods lived the Yonghy-Bonghy-Bò. Two old chairs, and a candle, one old jug without a handle . . .' "

"My God!" Irene cried. "That's the Sweeneys' nurse."

" 'These were all his worldly goods,' " the British voice continued.

"Turn that thing off," Irene said. "Maybe they can hear *us*." Jim switched the radio off. "That was Miss Armstrong, the Sweeneys' nurse," Irene said. "She must be reading to the little girl. They live in 17-B. I've talked with Miss Armstrong in the Park. I know her voice very well. We must be getting other people's apartments."

"That's impossible," Jim said.

"Well, that was the Sweeneys' nurse," Irene said hotly. "I know her voice. I know it very well. I'm wondering if they can hear us."

Jim turned the switch. First from a distance and then nearer, nearer, as if borne on the wind, came the pure accents of the Sweeneys' nurse again: " *'Lady Jingly! Lady Jingly!'* " she said, " *'Sitting where the pumpkins blow, will you come and be my wife*, said the Yonghy-Bonghy-Bò . . .' "

Jim went over to the radio and said "Hello" loudly into the speaker.

" *'I am tired of living singly,'* " the nurse went on, " *'on this coast so wild and shingly, I'm a-weary of my life; if you'll come and be my wife, quite serene would be my life . . .'* "

"I guess she can't hear us," Irene said. "Try something else."

Jim turned to another station, and the living room was filled with the uproar of a cocktail party that had overshot its mark. Someone was playing the piano and singing the Whiffenpoof Song, and the voices that surrounded the piano were vehement and happy. "Eat some more sandwiches," a woman shrieked. There were screams of laughter and a dish of some sort crashed to the floor.

"Those must be the Fullers, in 11-E," Irene said. "I knew they were giving a party this afternoon. I saw her in the liquor store. Isn't this too divine? Try something else. See if you can get those people in 18-C."

The Westcotts overheard that evening a monologue on salmon fishing in Canada, a bridge game, running comments on home movies of what had apparently been a fortnight at Sea Island, and a bitter family quarrel about an overdraft at the bank. They turned off their radio at midnight and went to bed, weak with laughter. Sometime in the night, their son began to call for a glass of water and Irene got one and took it to his room. It was very early. All the lights in the neighborhood were extinguished, and from the boy's window she could see the empty street. She went into the living room and tried the radio. There was some faint coughing, a moan, and then a man spoke. "Are you all right, darling?" he asked. "Yes," a woman said wearily. "Yes, I'm all right, I guess," and then she added with great feeling, "but, you know, Charlie, I don't feel like myself any more. Sometimes there are about fifteen or twenty minutes in the week when I feel like myself. I don't like to go to another doctor, because the doctor's bills are so awful already, but I just don't feel like myself, Charlie. I just never fell like myself." They were not young, Irene thought. She guessed from the timbre of their voices that they were middle-aged. The restrained melancholy of the dialogue and the draft from the bedroom window made her shiver, and she went back to bed.

The following morning, Irene cooked breakfast for the family—the maid didn't come up from her room in the basement until ten—braided her daughters' hair, and waited at the door until her children and her husband had been carried away in the elevator. Then she went into the living room and tried the radio. "I don't want to go to school," a child screamed. "I hate school. I won't go to school. I hate school." "You will go to school," an enraged woman said. "We paid eight hundred dollars to get you into that school and you'll go if it kills you." The next number on the dial produced the worn record of the "Missouri Waltz." Irene shifted the control and invaded the privacy of several breakfast tables. She overheard demonstrations of indigestion, carnal love, abysmal vanity, faith, and despair. Irene's life was nearly as simple and sheltered as it appeared to be, and the forthright and sometimes brutal language that came from the loudspeaker that morning astonished and troubled her. She continued to listen until her maid came in. Then she turned off the radio quickly, since this insight, she realized, was a furtive one.

Irene had a luncheon date with a friend that day, and she left her apartment at a little after twelve. There were a number of women in the elevator when it stopped at her floor. She stared at their handsome and impassive faces, their furs, and the cloth flowers in their hats. Which one of them had been to Sea Island, she wondered. Which one had overdrawn her bank account? The elevator stopped at the tenth floor and a woman with a pair of Skye terriers joined them. Her hair was rigged high on her head and she wore a mink cape. She was humming the "Missouri Waltz."

Irene had two Martinis at lunch, and she looked searchingly at her friend and wondered what her secrets were. They had intended to go shopping after lunch, but Irene excused herself and went home. She told the maid that she was not to be disturbed; then she went into the living room, closed the doors, and switched on the radio. She heard, in the course of the afternoon, the halting conversation of a woman entertaining her aunt, the hysterical conclusion of a luncheon party, and a hostess briefing her maid about some cocktail guests. "Don't give the best Scotch to anyone who hasn't white hair," the hostess said. "See if you can get rid of that liver paste before you pass those hot things, and could you lend me five dollars? I want to tip the elevator man."

As the afternoon waned, the conversations increased in intensity. From where Irene sat, she could see the open sky above the East River. There were hundreds of clouds in the sky, as though the south wind had broken the winter into pieces and were blowing it north, and on her radio she could hear the arrival of cocktail guests and the return of children and businessmen from their schools and offices. "I found a good-sized diamond on the bathroom floor this morning," a woman said. "It must have fallen out of that bracelet Mrs. Dunston was wearing last night." "We'll sell it," a man said. "Take it down to the jeweller on Madison Avenue and sell it. Mrs. Dunston won't know the difference, and we could use a couple of hundred bucks . . ." " 'Oranges and lemons, say the bells of St. Clement's,' " the Sweeneys' nurse sang. " 'Halfpence and farthings, say the bells of St. Martin's. When will you pay me? say the bells at old Bailey . . .' " "It's not a hat," a woman cried, and at her back roared a cocktail party. "It's not a hat, it's a love affair. That's what Walter Florell said. He said it's not a hat, it's a love affair," and then, in a lower voice, the same woman added, "Talk to somebody, for Christ's sake, honey, talk to somebody. If she catches you standing here not talking to anybody, she'll take us off her invitation list, and I love these parties."

The Westcotts were going out for dinner that night, and when Jim came home, Irene was dressing. She seemed sad and vague, and he brought her a drink. They were dining with friends in the neighborhood, and they walked to where they were going. The sky was broad and filled with light. It was one of those splendid spring evenings that excite memory and desire, and the air that touched their hands and faces felt very soft. A Salvation Army band was on the corner playing "Jesus Is Sweeter." Irene drew on her husband's arm and held him there for a minute, to hear the music. "They're really such nice people, aren't they?" she said. "They have such nice faces. Actually, they're so much nicer than a lot of the people we know." She took a bill from her purse and walked over and dropped it into the tambourine. There was in her face, when she returned to her husband, a look of radiant melancholy that he was not familiar with. And her conduct at the dinner party that night seemed strange to him, too. She interrupted her hostess rudely and stared at the people across the table from her with an intensity for which she would have punished her children.

It was still mild when they walked home from the party, and Irene looked up at the spring stars. " 'How far that little candle throws its beams,' " she exclaimed. " 'So shines a good deed in a naughty world.' " She waited that night until Jim had fallen asleep, and then went into the living room and turned on the radio.

Jim came home at about six the next night. Emma, the maid, let him in, and he had taken off his hat and was taking off his coat when Irene ran into the hall. Her face was shining with tears and her hair was disordered. "Go up to 16-C, Jim!" she screamed. "Don't take off your coat. Go up to 16-C. Mr. Osborn's beating his wife. They've been quarrelling since four o'clock, and now he's hitting her. Go up there and stop him."

From the radio in the living room, Jim heard screams, obscenities, and thuds. "You know you don't have to listen to this sort of thing," he said. He strode into the living room and turned the switch. "It's indecent," he said. "It's iike looking in windows. You know you don't have to listen to this sort of thing. You can turn it off."

"Oh, it's so horrible, it's so dreadful," Irene was sobbing. "I've been listening all day, and it's so depressing."

"Well, if it's so depressing, why do you listen to it? I bought this damned radio to give you some pleasure," he said. "I paid a great deal of money for it. I thought it might make you happy. I wanted to make you happy."

"Don't, don't, don't, don't quarrel with me," she moaned, and laid her head on his shoulder. "All the others have been quarrelling all day. Everybody's been quarrelling. They're all worried about money. Mrs. Hutchinson's mother is dying of cancer in Florida and they don't have enough money to send her to the Mayo Clinic. At least, Mr. Hutchinson says they don't have enough money. And some woman in this building is having an affair with the handyman—with that hideous handyman. It's too disgusting. And Mrs. Melville has heart trouble and Mr. Hendricks is going to lose his job in April and Mrs. Hendricks is horrid about the whole thing and that girl who plays the 'Missouri Waltz' is a whore, a common whore, and the elevator man has tuberculosis and Mr. Osborn has been beating Mrs. Osborn." She wailed, she trembled with grief and checked the stream of tears down her face with the heel of her palm.

"Well, why do you have to listen?" Jim asked again. "Why do you have to listen to this stuff if it makes you so miserable?"

"Oh, don't, don't, don't," she cried. "Life is too terrible, too sordid and awful. But we've never been like that, have we, darling? Have we? I mean we've always been good and decent and loving to one another, haven't we? And we have two children, two beautiful children. Our lives aren't sordid, are they, darling? Are they?" She flung her arms around his neck and drew his face down to hers. "We're happy, aren't we, darling? We are happy, aren't we?"

"Of course we're happy," he said tiredly. He began to surrender his resentment. "Of course we're happy. I'll have that damned radio fixed or taken away tomorrow." He stroked her soft hair. "My poor girl," he said.

"You love me, don't you?" she asked. "And we're not hypercritical or worried about money or dishonest, are we?"

"No, darling," he said.

A man came in the morning and fixed the radio. Irene turned it on cautiously and was happy to hear a California-wine commerical and a recording of Beethoven's Ninth Symphony, including Schiller's "Ode to Joy." She kept the radio on all day and nothing untoward came from the speaker.

A Spanish suite was being played when Jim came home. "Is everything all right?" he asked. His face was pale, she thought. They had some cocktails and went in to dinner to the "Anvil Chorus" from "Il Trovatore." This was followed by Debussy's "La Mer."

"I paid the bill for the radio today," Jim said. "It cost four hundred dollars. I hope you'll get some enjoyment out of it."

"Oh, I'm sure I will," Irene said.

"Four hundred dollars is a good deal more than I can afford," he went on. "I wanted to get something that you'd enjoy. It's the last extravagance we'll be able to indulge in this year. I see that you haven't paid your clothing bills yet. I saw them on your dressing table." He looked directly at her. "Why did you tell me you'd paid them? Why did you lie to me?"

"I just didn't want you to worry, Jim," she said. She drank some water. "I'll be able to pay my bills out of this month's allowance. There were the slipcovers last month, and that party."

"You've got to learn to handle the money I give you a little more intelligently, Irene," he said. "You've got to understand the we won't have as much money this year as we had last. I had a very sobering talk with Mitchell today. No one is buying anything. We're spending all our time promoting new issues, and you know how long that takes. I'm not getting any younger, you know. I'm thirty-seven. My hair will be gray next year. I haven't done as well as I'd hoped to do. And I don't suppose things will get any better."

"Yes, dear," she said.

"We've got to start cutting down," Jim said. "We've got to think of the children. To be perfectly frank with you, I worry about money a great deal. I'm not at all sure of the future. No one is. If anything should happen to me, there's the insurance, but that wouldn't go very far today. I've worked awfully hard to give you and the children a comfortable life," he said bitterly. "I don't like to see all of my energies, all of my youth, wasted in fur coats and radios and slipcovers and—"

"Please, Jim," she said. "Please. They'll hear us."

"*Who'll hear us?* Emma can't hear us."

"The radio."

"Oh, I'm sick!" he shouted. "I'm sick to death of your apprehensiveness. The radio can't hear us. Nobody can hear us. And what if they can hear us? Who cares?"

Irene got up from the table and went into the living room. Jim went to the door and shouted at her from there. "Why are you so Christly all of a sudden? What's turned you overnight into a convent girl? You stole your mother's jewelry before they probated her will. You never gave your sister a cent of that money that was intended for her—not even when she needed it. You made Grace Howland's life miserable, and where was all your piety and your virtue when you went to that abortionist? I'll never forget how cool you were. You packed your bag and went off to have that child murdered as if you were going to Nassau. If you'd had any reasons, if you'd had any good reasons—"

Irene stood for a minute before the hideous cabinet, disgraced and sickened, but she held her hand on the switch before she extinguished the music and the voices, hoping that the instrument might speak to her kindly, that she might hear the Sweeneys' nurse. Jim continued to shout at her from the door. The voice on the radio was suave and noncommital. "An early-morning railroad disaster in Tokyo," the loudspeaker said, "killed twenty-nine people. A fire in a Catholic hospital near Buffalo for the care of blind children was extinguished early this morning by nuns. The temperature is forty-seven. The humidity is eighty-nine."

Suggestions for Discussion

1. Analyze the ways in which Cheever's characters deceive others and delude themselves.

2. Comment on the domestic life of the Westcotts and their neighbors. Discuss and evaluate their life styles and values.

3. What new insights do Jim or Irene gain during the story? Be specific.

4. Discuss the ways in which Cheever builds and maintains suspense.

Suggestions for Writing

1. Write a similar short story in which a television set plays the part of the radio. What differences might occur?

2. In what ways are the Westcotts typical of couples you know? In what ways do they differ? Compare and contrast them with a couple close to you.

Alice Walker
Nineteen Fifty-five

Alice Walker (b. 1944) has won the Pulitzer Prize and the American Book Award for her fiction. Her books include *Meridian* (1976), *The Color Purple* (1982), and *You Can't Keep a Good Woman Down* (1981), from which the following story is taken.

1955

The car is a brandnew red Thunderbird convertible, and it's passed the house more than once. It slows down real slow now, and stops at the curb. An older gentleman dressed like a Baptist deacon gets out on the side near the house, and a young fellow who looks about sixteen gets out on the driver's side. They are white, and I wonder what in the world they are doing in this neighborhood.

Well, I say to J. T., put your shirt on, anyway, and let me clean these glasses offa the table.

We had been watching the ballgame on TV. I wasn't actually watching, I was sort of daydreaming, with my foots up in J. T.'s lap.

I seen 'em coming on up the walk, brisk, like they coming to sell something, and then they rung the bell, and J. T. declined to put on a shirt but instead disappeared into the bedroom where the other television is. I turned down the one in the living room; I figured I'd be rid of these two double quick and J. T. could come back out again.

Are you Gracie Mae Still? asked the old guy, when I opened the door and put my hand on the lock inside the screen.

And I don't need to buy a thing, said I.

What makes you think we're sellin'? he asks, in that hearty Southern way that makes my eyeballs ache.

Well, one way or another and they're inside the house and the first thing the young fellow does is raise the TV a couple of decibels. He's about five feet nine, sort of womanish looking, with real dark white skin and a red pouting mouth. His hair is black and curly and he looks like a Loosianna creole.

About one of your songs, says the deacon. He is maybe sixty, with white hair and beard, white silk shirt, black linen suit, black tie, and black shoes. His cold gray eyes look like they're sweating.

One of my songs?

Traynor here just *loves* your songs. Don't you, Traynor? He nudges Traynor with his elbow. Traynor blinks, says something I can't catch in a pitch I don't register.

The boy learned to sing and dance livin' round you people out in the country. Practically cut his teeth on you.

Traynor looks up at me and bites his thumbnail.

I laugh.

Well, one way or another they leave with my agreement that they can record one of my songs. The deacon writes me a check for five hundred dollars, the boy grunts his awareness of the transaction, and I am laughing all over myself by the time I rejoin J. T.

Just as I am snuggling down beside him though I hear the front door bell going off again.

Forgit his hat? asks J. T.

I hope not, I say.

The deacon stands there leaning on the door frame and once again I'm thinking of those sweaty-looking eyeballs of his. I wonder if sweat makes your eyeballs pink because his are sure pink. Pink and gray and it strikes me that nobody I'd care to know is behind them.

I forgot one little thing, he says pleasantly. I forgot to tell you Traynor and I would like to buy up all of those records you made of the song. I tell you we sure do love it.

Well, love it or not, I'm not so stupid as to let them do that without making 'em pay. So I says, Well, that's gonna cost you. Because, really, that song never did sell all that good, so I was glad they was going to buy it up. But on the other hand, them two listening to my song by themselves, and nobody else getting to hear me sing it, give me a pause.

Well, one way or another the deacon showed me where I would come out ahead on any deal he had proposed so far. Didn't I give you five hundred dollars? he asked. What white man—and don't even mention colored—would give you more? We buy up all your records of that particular song: first, you git royalties. Let me ask you, how much you sell that song for in the first place? Fifty dollars? A hundred, I say. And no royalties from it yet, right? Right. Well, when we buy up all of them records you gonna git royalties. And that's gonna make all them race record shops sit up and take notice of Gracie Mae Still. And they gonna push all them other records of yourn they got. And you no doubt will become one of the big name colored recording artists. And then we can offer you another five hundred dollars for letting us do all this for you. And by God you'll be sittin' pretty! You can go out and buy you the kind of outfit a star should have. Plenty sequins and yards of red satin.

I had done unlocked the screen when I saw I could get some more money out of him. Now I held it wide open while he squeezed through the opening between me and the door. He whipped out another piece of paper and I signed it.

He sort of trotted out to the car and slid in beside Traynor, whose head was back against the seat. They swung around in a u-turn in front of the house and then they was gone.

J. T. was putting his shirt on when I got back to the bedroom. Yankees beat the Orioles 10–6, he said. I believe I'll drive out to Paschal's pond and go fishing. Wanta go?

While I was putting on my pants J. T. was holding the two checks.

I'm real proud of a woman that can make cash money without leavin' home, he said. And I said *Umph*. Because we met on the road with me singing in first one little low-life jook after another, making ten dollars a night for myself if I was lucky, and sometimes bringin' home nothing but my life. And J. T. just loved them times. The way I was fast and flashy and always on the go from one town to another. He loved the way my singin' made the dirt farmers cry like babies and the womens shout Honey, hush! But that's mens. They loves any style to which you can get 'em accustomed.

1956

My little grandbaby called me one night on the phone: Little Mama, Little Mama, there's a white man on the television singing one of your songs! Turn on channel 5.

Lord, if it wasn't Traynor. Still looking half asleep from the neck up, but kind of awake in a nasty way from the waist down. He wasn't doing too bad with my song either, but it wasn't just the song the people in the audience was screeching and screaming over, it was that nasty little jerk he was doing from the waist down.

Well, Lord have mercy, I said, listening to him. If I'da closed my eyes, it could have been me. He had followed every turning of my voice, side streets, avenues, red lights, train crossings and all. It give me a chill.

Everywhere I went I heard Traynor singing my song, and all the little white girls just eating it up. I never had so many ponytails switched across my line of vision in my life. They was so *proud*. He was a *genius*.

Well, all that year I was trying to lose weight anyway and that and high blood pressure and sugar kept me pretty well occupied. Traynor had made a smash from a song of mine, I still had seven hundred dollars of the original one thousand dollars in the bank, and I felt if I could just bring my weight down, life would be sweet.

1957

I lost ten pounds in 1956. That's what I give myself for Christmas. And J. T. and me and the children and their friends and grandkids of all description had just finished dinner—over which I had put on nine and a half of my lost ten—when who should appear at the front door but Traynor. Little Mama, Little Mama! It's that white man who sings ＿＿＿＿＿＿＿＿＿＿＿.
The children didn't call it my song anymore. Nobody did. It was funny how that happened. Traynor and the deacon had bought up all my records, true, but on his record he had put "written by Gracie Mae Still." But that was just another name on the label, like "produced by Apex Records."

On the TV he was inclined to dress like the deacon told him. But now he looked presentable.

Merry Christmas, said he.

And same to you, Son.

I don't know why I called him Son. Well, one way or another they're all our sons. The only requirement is that they be younger than us. But then again, Traynor seemed to be aging by the minute.

You looks tired, I said. Come on in and have a glass of Christmas cheer.

J. T. ain't never in his life been able to act decent to a white man he wasn't working for, but he poured Traynor a glass of bourbon and water, then he took all the children and grandkids and friends and whatnot out to the den. After while I heard Traynor's voice singing the song, coming from the stereo console. It was just the kind of Christmas present my kids would consider cute.

I looked at Traynor, complicit. But he looked like it was the last thing in the world he wanted to hear. His head was pitched forward over his lap, his hands holding his glass and his elbows on his knees.

I done sung that song seem like a million times this year, he said. I sung it on the Grand Ole Opry, I sung it on the Ed Sullivan show. I sung it on Mike Douglas, I sung it at the Cotton Bowl, the Orange Bowl. I sung it at Festivals. I sung it at Fairs. I sung it overseas in Rome, Italy, and once in a submarine *underseas*. I've sung it and sung it, and I'm making forty thousand dollars a day offa it, and you know what, I don't have the faintest notion what that song means.

Whatchumean, what do it mean? It mean what it says. All I could think was: These suckers is making forty thousand a *day* offa my song and now they gonna come back and try to swindle me out of the original thousand.

It's just a song, I said. Cagey. When you fool around with a lot of no count mens you sing a bunch of 'em. I shrugged.

Oh, he said. Well. He started brightening up. I just come by to tell you I think you are a great singer.

He didn't blush, saying that. Just said it straight out.

And I brought you a little Christmas present too. Now you take this little box and you hold it until I drive off. Then you take it outside under that first streetlight back up the street aways in front of that greenhouse. Then you open the box and see . . . Well, just *see*.

What had come over this boy, I wondered, holding the box. I looked out the window in time to see another white man come up and get in the car with him and then two more cars full of white mens start out behind him. They was all in long black cars that looked like a funeral procession.

Little Mama, Little Mama, what it is? One of my grandkids come running up and started pulling at the box. It was wrapped in gay Christmas paper—the thick, rich kind that's hard to picture folks making just to throw away.

J. T. and the rest of the crowd followed me out of the house, up the street to the streetlight and in front of the greenhouse. Nothing was there but somebody's gold-grilled white Cadillac. Brandnew and most distracting. We got to looking at it so till I almost forgot the little box in my hand. While the others were busy making 'miration I carefully took off the paper and ribbon and folded them up and put them in my pants pocket. What should I see but a pair of genuine solid gold caddy keys.

Dangling the keys in front of everybody's nose, I unlocked the caddy, motioned for J. T. to git in on the other side, and us didn't come back home for two days.

1960

Well, the boy was sure nuff famous by now. He was still a mite shy of twenty but already they was calling him the Emperor of Rock and Roll.

Then what should happen but the draft.

Well, says J. T. There goes all the Emperor of Rock and Roll business.

But even in the army the womens was on him like white on rice. We watched it on the News.

Dear Gracie Mae [he wrote from Germany],

How you? Fine I hope as this leaves me doing real well. Before I come in the army I was gaining a lot of weight and gitting jittery from making all them dumb movies. But now I exercise and eat right and get plenty of rest. I'm more awake than I been in ten years.

I wonder if you are writing any more songs?

Sincerely,
Traynor

I wrote him back:

Dear Son,

We is all fine in the Lord's good grace and hope this finds you the same. J. T. and me be out all times of the day and night in that car you give me— which you know you didn't have to do. Oh, and I do appreciate the mink and the new self-cleaning oven. But if you send anymore stuff to eat from Germany I'm going to have to open up a store in the neighborhood just to get rid of it. Really, we have more than enough of everything. The Lord is good to us and we don't know Want.

Glad to here you is well and gitting your right rest. There ain't nothing like exercising to help that along. J. T. and me work some part of every day that we don't go fishing in the garden.

Well, so long Soldier.

Sincerely,
Gracie Mae

He wrote:

Dear Gracie Mae,

I hope you and J. T. like that automatic power tiller I had one of the stores back home send you. I went through a mountain of catalogs looking for it—I wanted something that even a woman could use.

I've been thinking about writing some songs of my own but every time I finish one it don't seem to be about nothing I've actually lived myself. My agent keeps sending me other people's songs but they just sound mooney. I can hardly git through 'em without gagging.

Everybody still loves that song of yours. They ask me all the time what do I think it means, really. I mean, they want to know just what I want to know. Where out of your life did it come from?

Sincerely,
Traynor

1968

I didn't see the boy for seven years. No. Eight. Because just about everybody was dead when I saw him again. Malcolm X, King, the president and his brother, and even J. T. J. T. died of a head cold. It just settled in his head like a block of ice, he said, and nothing we did moved it until one day he just leaned out the bed and died.

His good friend Horace helped me put him away, and then about a year later Horace and me started going together. We was sitting out on the front porch swing one summer night, dusk-dark, and I saw this great procession of lights winding to a stop.

Holy Toledo! said Horace. (He's got a real sexy voice like Ray Charles.) Look *at* it. He meant the long line of flashy cars and the white men in white summer suits jumping out on the drivers' sides and standing at attention. With wings they could pass for angels, with hoods they could be the Klan.

Traynor comes waddling up the walk.

And suddenly I know what it is he could pass for. An Arab like the ones you see in storybooks. Plump and soft and with never a care about weight. Because with so much money, who cares? Traynor is almost dressed like someone from a storybook too. He has on, I swear, about ten necklaces. Two sets of bracelets on his arms, at least one ring on every finger, and some kind of shining buckles on his shoes, so that when he walks you get a quite a few twinkling lights.

Gracie Mae, he says, coming up to give me a hug. J. T.

I explain that J. T. passed. That this is Horace.

Horace, he says, puzzled but polite, sort of rocking back on his heels, Horace.

That's it for Horace. He goes in the house and don't come back.

Looks like you and me is gained a few, I say.

He laughs. The first time I ever heard him laugh. It don't sound much like a laugh and I can't swear that it's better than no laugh a'tall.

He's gitting fat for sure, but he's still slim compared to me. I'll never see three hundred pounds again and I've just about said (excuse me) fuck it. I got to thinking about it one day an' I thought: aside from the fact that they say it's unhealthy, my fat ain't never been no trouble. Mens always have loved me. My kids ain't never complained. Plus they's fat. And fat like I is I looks distinguished. You see me coming and know somebody's *there*.

Gracie Mae, he says, I've come with a personal invitation to you to my house tomorrow for dinner. He laughed. What did it sound like? I couldn't place it. See them men out there? he asked me. I'm sick and tired of eating with them. They don't never have nothing to talk about. That's why I eat so much. But if you come to dinner tomorrow we can talk about the old days. You can tell me about that farm I bought you.

I sold it, I said.

You did?

Yeah, I said, I did. Just cause I said I liked to exercise by working in a garden didn't mean I wanted five hundred acres! Anyhow, I'm a city girl now. Raised in the country it's true. Dirt poor—the whole bit—but that's all behind me now.

Oh well, he said, I didn't mean to offend you.

We sat a few minutes listening to the crickets.

Then he said: You wrote that song while you was still on the farm, didn't you, or was it right after you left?

You had somebody spying on me? I asked.

You and Bessie Smith got into a fight over it once, he said.

You *is* been spying on me!

But I don't know what the fight was about, he said. Just like I don't know what happened to your second husband. Your first one died in the Texas electric chair. Did you know that? Your third one beat you up, stole your touring costumes and your car and retired with a chorine to Tuskegee. He laughed. He's still there.

I had been mad, but suddenly I calmed down. Traynor was talking very dreamily. It was dark but seems like I could tell his eyes weren't right. It was like some*thing* was sitting there talking to me but not necessarily with a person behind it.

You gave up on marrying and seem happier for it. He laughed again. I married but it never went like it was supposed to. I never could squeeze any of my own life either into it or out of it. It was like singing somebody else's record. I copied the way it was sposed to be *exactly* but I never had a clue what marriage meant.

I bought her a diamond ring big as your fist. I bought her clothes. I built her a mansion. But right away she didn't want the boys to stay there. Said they smoked up the bottom floor. Hell, there were *five* floors.

No need to grieve, I said. No need to. Plenty more where she come from.

He perked up. That's part of what that song means, ain't it? No need to grieve. Whatever it is, there's plenty more down the line.

I never really believed that way back when I wrote that song, I said. It was all bluffing then. The trick is to live long enough to put your young bluffs to use. Now if I was to sing that song today I'd tear it up. 'Cause I done lived long enough to know it's *true*. Them words could hold me up.

I ain't lived that long, he said.

Look like you on your way, I said. I don't know why, but the boy seemed to need some encouraging. And I don't know, seem like one way or another you talk to rich white folks and you end up reassuring *them*. But what the hell, by now I feel something for the boy. I wouldn't be in his bed all alone in the middle of the night for nothing. Couldn't be nothing worse than being famous the world over for something you don't even understand. That's what I tried to tell Bessie. She wanted that same song. Overheard me practicing it one day, said, with her hands on her hips: Gracie Mae, I'ma sing your song tonight. I *likes* it.

Your lips be too swole to sing, I said. She was mean and she was strong, but I trounced her.

Ain't you famous enough with your own stuff? I said. Leave mine alone. Later on, she thanked me. By then she was Miss Bessie Smith to the World, and I was still Miss Gracie Mae Nobody from Notasulga.

The next day all these limousines arrived to pick me up. Five cars and twelve bodyguards. Horace picked that morning to start painting the kitchen.

Don't paint the kitchen, fool, I said. The only reason that dumb boy of ours is going to show me his mansion is because he intends to present us with a new house.

What you gonna do with it? he asked me, standing there in his shirtsleeves stirring the paint.

Sell it. Give it to the children. Live in it on weekends. It don't matter what I do. He sure don't care.

Horace just stood there shaking his head. Mama you sure looks *good*, he says. Wake me up when you git back.

Fool, I say, and pat my wig in front of the mirror.

The boy's house is something else. First you come to this mountain, and then you commence to drive and drive up this road that's lined with magnolias. Do magnolias grow on mountains? I was wondering. And you come to lakes and you come to ponds and you come to deer and you come up on some sheep. And I figure these two is sposed to represent England and Wales. Or something out of Europe. And you just keep on coming to stuff. And it's all pretty. Only the man driving my car don't look at nothing but the road. Fool. And then *finally*, after all this time, you begin to go up the driveway. And there's more magnolias—only they're not in such good shape. It's sort of cool up this high and I don't think they're gonna make it. And then I see this building that looks like if it had a name it would be The Tara Hotel. Columns and steps and outdoor chandeliers and rocking chairs. Rocking chairs? Well, and there's the boy on the steps dressed in a dark green satin jacket like you see folks wearing on TV late at night, and he looks sort of like a fat Dracula with all that house rising behind him, and standing beside him there's this little white vision of loveliness that he introduces as his wife.

He's nervous when he introduces us and he says to her: This is Gracie Mae Still, I want you to know me. I mean . . . and she gives him a look that would fry meat.

Won't you come in, Gracie Mae, she says, and that's the last I see of her.

He fishes around for something to say or do and decides to escort me to the kitchen. We go through the entry and the parlor and the breakfast room and the dining room and the servants' passage and finally get there. The first thing I notice is that, altogether, there are five stoves. He looks about to introduce me to one.

Wait a minute, I say. Kitchens don't do nothing for me. Let's go sit on the front porch.

Well, we hike back and we sit in the rocking chairs rocking until dinner.

Gracie Mae, he says down the table, taking a piece of fried chicken from the woman standing over him, I got a little surprise for you.

It's a house, ain't it? I ask, spearing a chitlin.

You're getting *spoiled*, he says. And the way he says *spoiled* sounds funny. He slurs it. It sounds like his tongue is too thick for his mouth. Just that quick he's finished the chicken and is now eating chitlins *and* a pork chop. *Me* spoiled, I'm thinking.

I already got a house. Horace is right this minute painting the kitchen. I bought that house. My kids feel comfortable in that house.

But this one I bought you is just like mine. Only a little smaller.

I still don't need no house. And anyway who would clean it?

He looks surprised.

Really, I think, some peoples advance *so* slowly.

I hadn't thought of that. But what the hell, I'll get you somebody to live in.

I don't want other folks living 'round me. Makes me nervous.

You *don't?* It *do?*

What I want to wake up and see folks I don't even know for?

He just sits there downtable staring at me. Some of that feeling is in the song, ain't it? Not the words, the *feeling*. What I want to wake up and see folks I don't even know for? But I see twenty folks a day I don't even know, including my wife.

This food wouldn't be bad to wake up to though, I said. The boy had found the genius of corn bread.

He looked at me real hard. He laughed. Short. They want what you got but they don't want you. They want what I got only it ain't mine. That's what makes 'em so hungry for me when I sing. They getting the flavor of something but they ain't getting the thing itself. They like a pack of hound dogs trying to gobble up a scent.

You talking 'bout your fans?

Right. Right. He says.

Don't worry 'bout your fans, I say. They don't know their asses from a hole in the ground. I doubt there's a honest one in the bunch.

That's the point. Dammit, that's the point! He hits the table with his fist. It's so solid it don't even quiver. You need a honest audience! You can't have folks that's just gonna lie right back to you.

Yeah, I say, it was small compared to yours, but I had one. It would have been worth my life to try to sing 'em somebody else's stuff that I didn't know nothing about.

He must have pressed a buzzer under the table. One of his flunkies zombies up.

Git Johnny Carson, he says.

On the phone? asks the zombie.

On the phone, says Traynor, what you think I mean, git him offa the front porch? Move your ass.

So two weeks later we's on the Johnny Carson show.

Traynor is all corseted down nice and looks a little bit fat but mostly good. And all the women that grew up on him and my song squeal and squeal. Traynor says: The lady who wrote my first hit record is here with us tonight, and she's agreed to sing it for all of us, just like she sung it forty-five years ago. Ladies and Gentlemen, the great Gracie Mae Still!

Well, I had tried to lose a couple of pounds my own self, but failing that I had me a very big dress made. So I sort of rolls over next to Traynor, who is dwarfted by me, so that when he puts his arm around back of me to try to hug me it looks funny to the audience and they laugh.

I can see this pisses him off. But I smile out there at 'em. Imagine squealing for twenty years and not knowing why you're squealing? No more sense of endings and beginnings than hogs.

It don't matter, Son, I say. Don't fret none over me.

I commence to sing. And I sound—wonderful. Being able to sing good ain't all about having a good singing voice a'tall. A good singing voice helps. But when you come up in the Hard Shell Baptist church like I did you understand early that the fellow that sings is the singer. Them that waits for programs and arrangements and letters from home is just good voices occupying body space.

So there I am singing my own song, my own way. And I give it all I got and enjoy every minute of it. When I finish Traynor is standing up clapping and clapping and beaming at first me and then the audience like I'm his mama for true. The audience claps politely for about two seconds.

Traynor looks disgusted.

He comes over and tries to hug me again. The audience laughs.

Johnny Carson looks at us like we both weird.

Traynor is mad as hell. He's supposed to sing something called a love ballad. But instead he takes the mike, turns to me and says: Now see if my imitation still holds up. He goes into the same song, *our song*, I think, looking out at his flaky audience. And he sings it just the way he always did. My voice, my tone, my inflection, everything. But he forgets a couple of lines. Even before he's finished the matronly squeals begin.

He sits down next to me looking whipped.

It don't matter, Son, I say, patting his hand. You don't even know those people. Try to make the people you know happy.

Is that in the song? he asks.

Maybe. I say.

1977

For a few years I hear from him, then nothing. But trying to lose weight takes all the attention I got to spare. I finally faced up to the fact that my fat is the hurt I don't admit, not even to myself, and that I been trying to bury it from the day I was born. But also when you git real old, to tell the truth, it ain't as pleasant. It gits lumpy and slack. Yuck. So one day I said to Horace, I'ma git this shit offa me.

And he fell in with the program like he always try to do and Lord such a procession of salads and cottage cheese and fruit juice!

One night I dreamed Traynor had split up with his fifteenth wife. He said: *You meet 'em for no reason. You date 'em for no reason. You marry 'em for no reason. I do it all but I swear it's just like somebody else doing it. I feel like I can't remember Life.*

The boy's in trouble, I said to Horace.

You've always said that, he said.

I have?

Yeah. You always said he looked asleep. You can't sleep through life if you wants to live it.

You not such a fool after all, I said, pushing myself up with my cane and hobbling over to where he was. Let me sit down on your lap, I said, while this salad I ate takes effect.

In the morning we heard Traynor was dead. Some said fat, some said heart, some said alcohol, some said drugs. One of the children called from Detroit. Them dumb fans of his is on a crying rampage, she said. You just ought to turn on the t.v.

But I didn't want to see 'em. They was crying and crying and didn't even know what they was crying for. One day this is going to be a pitiful country, I thought.

Suggestions for Discussion

1. What parallels with the career of Elvis Presley does Walker suggest?

2. Describe the relationship between Traynor and Gracie Mae Still.

3. Characterize Gracie Mae.

4. Why does Traynor shower Gracie Mae with gifts?

5. How does Gracie Mae respond to Traynor's death?

Suggestions for Writing

1. Discuss loneliness as a theme in "Nineteen Fifty-five."

2. Discuss Walker's use of dialect to add color and develop characterization.

The Cultural Tradition:
Art and Society
◆◆◆◆

I, too, dislike it: there are things that are important beyond
   all this fiddle,
  Reading it, however, with a perfect contempt for it, one
    discovers in
  it after all, a place for the genuine.
       —Marianne Moore, "Poetry"

The things of the poet are done to a man alone
As the things of love are done—or of death when he hears the
Step withdraw on the stair and the clock tick only.
       —Archibald MacLeish, "Invocation to the Social Muse"

Works of art, in my opinion, are the only objects in the material universe to possess internal order, and that is why,
though I don't believe that only art matters, I do believe in
Art for Art's sake.
       —E. M. Forster, "Art for Art's Sake"

Perhaps it will turn out that you are called to be an artist.
Then take that destiny upon yourself and bear it, its burdens and its greatness, without ever asking what recompense might come from outside.
       —Rainer Maria Rilke, "Letter to a Young Poet," 1903

But perhaps the voice of a great poet, the voice of the Bible, the eternal voice of humanity that speaks clearly to us
from art, would give you the power of true sight and hearing.
       —Hermann Hesse, "To a Cabinet Minister," August 1917

Letters and Personal Reminiscence

◆◆◆

Rainer Maria Rilke

Letter to a Young Poet
Translated by M. D. Herter Norton

Rainer Maria Rilke (1875–1926) was an Austrian writer born in Prague. He had an unhappy childhood, spent five years in a military academy, and attended the Universities of Prague, Munich, and Berlin. At the turn of the century he traveled to Russia where he met Tolstoi, who influenced him profoundly. For a time he was secretary to the sculptor Rodin. His early works reveal a deep association with mysticism and aestheticism. In *The Duino Elegies* (1930) and *Sonnets to Orpheus* (1936), both profound influences on all modern poetry, he saw the poet as mediator between God and man. In the following letter to a young poet, Rilke exhorts him to find his own voice and to base his writing on his own intimate experiences.

Paris, February 17th, 1903

My Dear Sir,

Your letter only reached me a few days ago. I want to thank you for its great and kind confidence. I can hardly do more. I cannot go into the nature of your verses; for all critical intention is too far from me. With nothing can one touch a work of art so little as with critical words: they always come down to more or less lucky misunderstandings. Things are not all so comprehensible and expressible as one would mostly have us believe; most events are inexpressible, take place in a realm which no word has ever entered, and more inexpressible than all else are works of art, mysterious existences, the life of which, while ours passes away, endures.

After these prefatory remarks, let me only tell you further that your verses have no individual style, although they do show a quiet and hidden incipience of the personal. I feel this most clearly in the last poem "My Soul." There something of your own wants to come through to expression. And in the lovely poem "To Leopardi" there does perhaps grow up a sort of kinship with that great solitary man. Nevertheless the poems are not yet anything on their own account, nothing independent, even the last and the one to Leopardi. Your kind letter, which accompanied them, does not fail to make clear to me various shortcomings which I felt in reading your verses without at the time being able particularly to name them.

You ask whether your verses are good. You ask me. You have asked others before. You send them to magazines. You compare them with other poems, and you are disturbed when certain editors reject your efforts. Now (since you have allowed me to advise you) I beg you to give up all that. You are looking outward, and that above all you should not now do. Nobody can counsel and help you, nobody. There is only one single way. Go into yourself. Investigate the reason that bids you write; find out whether it is spreading out its roots in the deepest places of your heart, acknowledge to yourself whether you would have to die if it were denied you to write. This above all: ask yourself in the stillest hour of your night: *must* I write? Delve into yourself for a deep answer. And if this should be affirmative, if you may meet this earnest question with a strong and simple "I must," then build your life according to this necessity; your life even into its most indifferent and slightest hour must be a sign of this urge and a testimony to it. Then draw near to Nature. Then try, as a first human being, to say what you see and experience and love and lose. Do not write love-poems; avoid at first those forms that are too hackneyed and commonplace: they are the most difficult, for it takes a great, fully matured power to give something of your own where good and even excellent traditions come to mind in quantity. Therefore save yourself from these general themes and seek those which your own everyday life offers you; describe your sorrows and desires, passing thoughts and the belief in some sort of beauty—describe all these with loving, quiet, humble sincerity and use, to express yourself, the things in your environment, the pictures from your dreams, and the subjects of your memory. If your daily life seems poor, do not blame it; blame yourself, tell yourself that you are not poet enough to call forth its riches; for to the creator there is no poverty and no poor indifferent place. And even if you were in some prison the walls of which let none of the sounds of the world come to your senses—would you not then still have your childhood, that precious, kingly possession, that treasure-house of memories? Turn your attention thither. Try to bring up the sunken sensations of that far past; your personality will grow more firm, your solitude will widen and will become a dusky dwelling by which the noise of others passes far away.—And if out of this turning inward, out of this sinking into your own world verses come, then it will not occur to you to ask any one whether they are good verses. Nor will you try to interest magazines in your poems: for you will see in them your fond natural possession, a fragment and a voice of your life. A work of art is good if it has sprung from necessity. In this nature of its origin lies its judgment: there is no other. Therefore, my dear sir, I have known no advice for you save this: to go into yourself and test the deeps in which your life takes rise; at its source you will find the answer to the question whether you *must* create. Accept it, just as it sounds, without trying to interpret it. Perhaps it will turn out that you are called to be an artist. Then take that destiny upon yourself and bear it, its burden and its greatness, without ever asking what recompense might come from outside. For the creator must be a world for himself and find everything in himself and in Nature with whom he has allied himself.

But perhaps after this descent into yourself and into your inner solitude you will have to give up becoming a poet (it is enough, as I have said, to feel that one could live without writing: then one should not be allowed to do it at all). But even then this inward searching which I ask of you will not have been in vain. Your life will in any case find its own ways thence, and that they may be good, rich and wide I wish you more than I can say.

What more shall I say to you? Everything seems to me to have its just emphasis; and after all I do only want to advise you to keep growing quietly and seriously throughout your development; you cannot disturb it more rudely than by looking outward and expecting from outside replies to questions that only your inmost feeling in your quietest hours can perhaps answer.

It was a pleasure to me to find in your letter the name of Professor Horaček; I keep for that lovable and learned man a great veneration and a gratitude that endures through the years. Will you, please, tell him how I feel; it is very good of him still to think of me, and I know how to appreciate it.

The verses which you kindly entrusted to me I am returning at the same time. And I thank you once more for your great and sincere confidence, of which I have tried, through this honest answer given to the best of my knowledge, to make myself a little worthier than, as a stranger, I really am.

Yours faithfully and with all sympathy:

RAINER MARIA RILKE

Suggestions for Discussion

1. What attitude toward art does Rilke express in the first paragraph of his letter?

2. What does Rilke seem to mean in the second paragraph by the term *individual style?* Is his use of the term a kind of criticism?

3. In the third paragraph Rilke analyzes the feelings that govern the life of a poet. How would you summarize his advice?

4. Explain Rilke's statement, "A work of art is good if it has sprung from necessity."

5. Rilke urges the young poet to "test the deeps in which your life takes rise." Is this advice pertinent to other aspects of life than the writing of poetry?

Suggestion for Writing

Read some of Rilke's poems in *Sonnets to Orpheus* or *Duino Elegies*. Write a paper in which you test some of his poems by the advice in this letter. Try to explain why Rilke's poems do have an individual voice.

Hermann Hesse

To a Cabinet Minister, August 1917

Translated by Ralph Manhelm

Hermann Hesse (1877–1962) received the Nobel Prize for Literature in 1946. He is ranked with Thomas Mann as one of the giants of modern German fiction. His best known works are *Magister Ludi* (1949), *Demian* (1919), *Siddhartha* (1923), and *Steppenwolf* (1927). The last three have achieved the status of cult novels for young readers throughout the world. This letter to a German cabinet minister, written during the First World War, states Hesse's belief in the power of art and thought to change people's lives, even in time of war.

This evening after a hard day's work I asked my wife to play me a Beethoven sonata. With its angelic voices the music recalled me from bustle and worry to the real world, to the one reality which we possess, which gives us joy and torment, the reality in which and for which we live.

Afterwards I read a few lines in the book containing the Sermon on the Mount and the sublime, age-old, and fundamental words: "Thou shalt not kill!"

But I found no peace, I could neither go to bed nor continue reading. I was filled with anxiety and unrest, and suddenly, Herr Minister, as I was searching my mind for their cause, I remembered a few sentences from one of your speeches that I read a few days ago.

Your speech was well constructed; otherwise, it was not particularly original, significant, or provocative. Reduced to the essentials, it said roughly what government officials have been saying in their speeches for a long time: that, generally speaking, "we" long for nothing so fervently as peace, as a new understanding among nations and fruitful collaboration in building the future, that we wish neither to enrich ourselves nor to satisfy homicidal lusts—but that the "time for negotiations" is not yet at hand and that for the present there is therefore no alternative but to go on bravely waging war. Just about every minister of any of the belligerent nations might have made such a speech, and probably will tomorrow or the day after.

If tonight your speech keeps me awake, although I have read many similar speeches with the same dreary conclusion and slept soundly afterwards, the fault, as I am now certain, lies with Beethoven's sonata and with that ancient book in which I afterwards read, that book which contains the wonderful commandments of Mount Sinai and the luminous words of the Savior.

Beethoven's music and the words of the Bible told me exactly the same thing; they were water from the same spring, the only spring from which man derives good. And then suddenly, Herr Minister, it came to me that your speech and the speeches of your governing colleagues in both camps do not flow from that spring, that they lack what can make human words important and valuable. They lack love, they lack humanity.

Your speech shows a profound feeling of concern and responsibility for your people, its army, and its honor. But it shows no feeling for mankind.

And, to put it bluntly, it implies hundreds of thousands more human sacrifices.

Perhaps you will call my reference to Beethoven sentimentality. I imagine, though, that you feel a certain respect for the Commandments and for the sayings of Jesus—at least in public. But if you believe in a single one of the ideals for which you are waging war, the freedom of nations, freedom of the seas, social progress, or the rights of small countries—if you truly, in your heart of hearts, believe in a single one of these generous ideals, you will have to recognize on rereading your speech that it does not serve that ideal or any other. It is not the expression and product of a faith, of any awareness of a human need, but, alas, the expression and product of a dilemma. An understandable dilemma, to be sure, for what could be more difficult at the present time than to acknowledge a certain disappointment with the course of the war and to start looking for the shortest way to peace?

But such a dilemma, even if it is shared by ten governments, cannot endure forever. Dilemmas are solved by necessities. One day it will become necessary for you and your enemy colleagues to face up to your dilemma and make decisions that will put an end to it.

The belligerents of both camps have long been disappointed with the course of the war. Regardless of who has won this battle or that battle, regardless of how much territory or how many prisoners have been taken or lost, the result has not been what one expects in a war. There has been no solution, no decision—and none is in sight.

You made your speech in order to hide this great dilemma from yourself and your people, in order to postpone vital decisions (which always call for sacrifices)—and other government officials make their speeches for the same reason. Which is understandable. It is easier for a revolutionary or even for a writer to see the human factor in a political situation and draw the proper inferences than for a responsible statesman. It is easier for one of us because he is under no obligation to feel personally responsible for the deep gloom that comes over a nation when it sees that it has not achieved its war aim and that many thousands of human lives and billions in wealth may well have been sacrificed in vain.

But that is not the only reason why it is harder for you to recognize the dilemma and make decisions that will put an end to the war. Another reason is that you hear too little music and read the Bible and the great authors too little.

You smile. Or perhaps you will say that you as a private citizen feel very close to Beethoven and to all that is noble and beautiful. And maybe you do. But my heartfelt wish is that one of these days, chancing to hear a piece of sublime music, you should suddenly recapture an awareness of those voices that well from a sacred spring. I wish that one of these days in a quiet moment you would read a parable of Jesus, a line of Goethe, or a saying of Lao-tzu.

That moment might be infinitely important to the world. You might find inner liberation. Your eyes and ears might suddenly be opened. For many years, Herr Minister, your eyes and ears have been attuned to theoretical aims rather than reality; they have long been accustomed—necessarily so!— to close themselves to much of what constitutes reality, to disregard it, to deny its existence. Do you know what I mean? Yes, you know. But perhaps the voice of a great poet, the voice of the Bible, the eternal voice of humanity that speaks clearly to us from art, would give you the power of true sight and hearing. What things you would see and hear! Nothing more about the labor shortage and the price of coal, nothing more about tonnages and alliances, loans, troop levies, and all the rest of what you have hitherto regarded as the sole reality. Instead, you would see the earth, our patient old earth, so littered with the dead and dying, so ravaged and shattered, so charred and desecrated. You would see soldiers lying for days in no-man's-land, unable with their mutilated hands to shoo the flies from their mortal wounds. You would hear the voices of the wounded, the screams of the mad, the accusing plaints of mothers and fathers, sweethearts and sisters, the people's cry of hunger.

If your ears should be opened once more to all these things that you have sedulously avoided hearing for months and years, then perhaps you would reexamine your aims, your ideals and theories, with a new mind and attempt to weigh their true worth against the misery of a single month, a single day, of war.

Oh, if this hour of music, this return to true reality, could somehow come your way! You would hear the voice of mankind, you would shut yourself up in your room and weep. And next day you would go out and do your duty toward mankind. You would sacrifice a few millions or billions in money, a trifling bit of prestige, and a thousand other things (all the things for which you are now prolonging the war), and, if need be, your minister's portfolio with them, and you would do what mankind, in untold fear and torment, is hoping and praying you will do. You would be the first among governing statesmen to condemn this wretched war, the first to tell his fellows what all feel secretly even now: that six months or even one month of war costs more than what anything it can achieve is worth.

If that were to happen, Herr Minister, your name would never be forgotten, your deed would stand higher in the eyes of mankind than the deeds of all those who have ever waged victorious wars.

Suggestions for Discussion

1. How does Hesse contrast Beethoven's music and Christ's Sermon on the Mount with the cabinet minister's speech?

2. How does this letter, written in 1917, speak to the world situation seventy years later?

3. What effect does Hesse believe the words of Christ or Goethe or Lao-tzu would have on the cabinet minister?

4. Discuss the tone of the letter writer. Is it respectful? How does he hope to persuade his reader?

Suggestion for Writing

The employment of the open letter as a vehicle of expressing opinion is an old custom. You may wish to write a paper comparing Hesse's letter with other statements in letter form by famous people. Or you may wish to write a paper analyzing the letters in your local newspaper that are written to express an opinion. How often are such letters carefully and calmly reasoned? What is the tone of most of these letters?

John Gardner

Learning from Disney and Dickens

John Champlin Gardner, Jr. (1933–1982) was a medieval and classical scholar, a professor of English Literature, head of the Creative Writing Program at the State University of New York at Binghamton, and author of novels, short stories, critical works, translations from Old and Middle English, and even opera librettos. In *On Moral Fiction* (1978), he calls upon the artist to act as a moral agent, saying, "I agree with Tolstoy. . . . The highest purpose of art is to make people good by choice." This essay from the *New York Times*, which he titled "Cartoons," is part of a book of essays by various writers, *In Praise of What Persists*, edited by Stephen Berg. Gardner wrote this memoir of his development as a writer shortly before his death in a motorcycle accident.

Trying to figure out the chief influences on my work as a writer turns out to be mainly a problem of deciding what not to include. I grew up in a family where literary influence was everywhere, including under the bridge on our dirt road, where I kept my comic books. My father is a memorizer of poetry and scripture, a magnificent performer in the old reciter tradition. (I once did a reading in Rochester, N.Y., near Batavia, where I grew up. After I'd finished several people remarked that I was a wonderful reader—"though not quite up to your father, of course.") He did readings of everything from Edgar Guest to Shakespeare and The Book of Job at the monthly Grange meetings, in schools, churches, hospitals. While he milked the cows, my mother (who'd once been his high school English teacher) would read Shakespeare's plays aloud to him from her three-legged stool behind the gutter, and he would take, yelling from the cow's flank, whatever part he'd decided on that night— Macbeth, King Lear, Hamlet, and so on.

My mother was a well-known performer too, except that she mainly sang. She had one of those honeysweet Welsh soprano voices and sang everything from anthems to the spirituals she'd learned from an old black woman who took care of her during her childhood in Missouri. Often my mother performed in blackface, with a red bandana, a practice that may sound distasteful unless you understand that she wasn't kidding; she was authentic, flatting, quarter-toning, belting it out: She was amazing. They frequently worked together, my mother and father, and were known all over western New York. Sometimes they were in plays—my mother often directed—and wherever they went, riding around in the beat-up farm truck or just sitting in the kitchen, they sang, always in harmony, like crazy people.

The house was full of books, very few of them books that would now be thought fashionable aside from the Shakespeare and Dickens. My parents read aloud a lot—the narrative poems of Scott, miles of Longfellow, spooky stories by Edgar Allan Poe, the poems of Tennyson and Browning, also rather goofy religious writers (I loved them; what did I know?) like Lloyd C. Douglas and some woman whose name escapes me now, who wrote Jesus-filled love stories with titles like "A Patch of Blue." My grandmother, who was bedridden through much of my childhood, was especially fond of this religious lady, and one of my more pleasant chores was to read her these tender little novels. The climax was always the moment the boy shyly touched the girl's hand. I've never found anything more sexually arousing than that Jesus-filled, long-delayed touch. I mean it was smut, it nearly made me a pervert, and not a court in the land could nail her.

My favorite authors, at least when I was between the ages of 8 and 18, were in what might be described as the nonrealistic tradition: God, Dickens, and Disney. One of my less pleasant chores when I was young was to read the Bible from one end to the other. Reading the Bible straight through is at least 70 percent discipline, like learning Latin. But the good parts are, of course, simply amazing. God is an extremely uneven writer, but when He's good, nobody can touch him. I learned to find the good parts easily (some very sexy stuff here too), and both the poetry and the storytelling had a powerful effect on what I think good fiction ought to be!

Dickens I ran into when I was in my early teens, when I began to find the Hardy boys tiresome and unconvincing. I never liked realism much, but the irrealism of two boys having long conversations while riding on motorcycles (I was big on motorcycles myself) was more than I could put up with. Running across Dickens was like finding a secret door. I read book after book, and when I'd finished the last one I remember feeling a kind of horror, as if suddenly the color had gone out of the world; then luckily I discovered that when you went back to one of the ones you had read first, you couldn't remember half of it, you could read it again and find it even better, so life wasn't quite as disappointing as for a moment I'd thought.

For me at that time Disney and Dickens were practically indistinguishable. Both created wonderful cartoon images, told stories as direct as fairy tales, knew the value of broad comedy spiced up with a little weeping. I have since learned that Dickens is occasionally profound, as Disney never deigns to be; but that was never why I valued Dickens or have, now, a bust of him in my study to keep me honest. Unconsciously—without ever hearing the term, in fact—I learned about symbolism from Dickens and Disney, with the result that I would never learn to appreciate, as I suppose one should, those realistic writers who give you life data without resonance, things merely as they are. Dickens's symbolism may never be very deep—the disguised witches and fairy princesses, Uriah Heep and his mother flapping around like buzzards, or all the self-conscious folderol of "A Tale of Two Cities"—but in my experience, anyway, it spoils you forever for books that never go *oo-boom*.

There were other important influences during this period of my life, probably the most important of which was opera. The Eastman School of Music presented operas fairly often (and of course played host to traveling opera companies, including the Met). From Dickens and Disney (not to mention God) it took no adjustment to become opera-addicted. The plots of most operas (not all, heaven knows) are gloriously simple-minded or, to put it more favorably, elemental; the stage is nothing if not a grand cartoon (Wagner's mountainscapes and gnomes, Mozart's crazies, Humperdinck's angels, the weirdness and clowning that show up everywhere from "La Bohème" to "The Tales of Hoffmann"). I was by this time playing French horn, and of course I'd always been around singing. So I got hooked at once—hence my special fondness now for writing librettos.

By the time I reached college my taste was, I'm afraid, hopelessly set. Predictably I was ravished by Melville—all those splendid cartoon images, for instance Ahab and the Chinese coolies he's kept hidden until the first time he needs to lower away after whale—and of course by Milton, who must be considered one of the all-time great cartoonists, as when Satan

> Puts on swift wings, and toward the Gates of Hell
> Explores his solitary flight; sometimes
> He scours the right hand coast, sometimes the left,
> Now shaves with level wing the Deep, then soars
> Up the fiery concave touring high.

(It's true, Milton's a little boring now and then, and Milton teachers often don't properly value the cartoonist in him and want to know things about "Paradise Lost" that only some kind of crazy could get seriously interested in; but never mind.) I'm afraid the embarrassing truth is that the whole literary tradition opened out, for me, from Disney and his kind. I got caught up in the mighty cartoons of Homer and Dante, (much later Virgil and Apollonius), the less realistic 18th-and 19th-century novelists (Fielding, Smollett, Collins, and the rest), the glorious mad Russians (Tolstoy, Dostoyevsky, Bely), and those kinds of poets who fill one's head with strange, intense visions, like Blake, Coleridge, and Keats.

For me the whole world of literature was at this time one of grand cartoons. I thought of myself mainly as a chemistry major and took courses in English just for fun. I guess I thought literature was unserious, like going to the movies or playing in a dance band, even an orchestra. It did not seem to me that one ought to spend one's life on mere pleasure, like a butterfly or cricket. Beethoven, Shakespeare, Richard Strauss, Conan Doyle might be a delight, but to fritter away one's life in the arts seemed, well, not quite honest. Then I came across the New Criticism.

At the first college I went to (for two years) I'd read nearly all of the Modern Library, partly for fun, partly because I felt ignorant around my fellow students, people who could talk with seeming wisdom about Camus and Proust, Nietzsche and Plato—I soon discovered they hadn't really read what they claimed to have read, they'd just come from the right part of town—but I'd never in any serious sense "studied" literature. (I took a couple of courses where one was examined on what Carlyle and Cardinal Newman said, without much emphasis on why or to whom). But when I moved to Washington University in St. Louis I got a whole new vision of what literature was for—that is, the vision of the New Criticism. Like the fanatic I've always been, I fell to analyzing fiction, digging out symbols and structural subtleties, learning about "levels" and so on.

I don't say this was a foolish activity—in fact I think the New Critics were basically right: It's much more interesting and rewarding to talk about how literature "works" than to read biographies of the writer, which is mainly what the New Criticism replaced. Working with the famous books by Cleanth Brooks and Robert Penn Warren, I began to love things in fiction and poetry that I'd never before noticed, things like meaning and design, and, like all my generation, I made the great discovery that literature is worthwhile, not a thing to be scorned by serious puritans but a thing to be embraced and turned cunningly to advantage. I learned that literature is Good for you, and that writers who are not deeply philosophical should be scorned. I began to read realists—two of whom, Jane Austen and James Joyce, I actually liked— and I began to write "serious" fiction; that is, instead of writing pleasant jingles or stories I desperately hoped would be published in *The Saturday Evening Post* or maybe *Manhunt*, I began shyly eyeing *The Kenyon Review*. With a sigh of relief (though I'd enjoyed them, in a way) I quit math and science and signed up, instead, for courses in philosophy and sociology and psychology, which I knew would make me a better person and perhaps a famous writer so brilliant and difficult that to get through my books you would need a teacher.

This period lasted longer than I care to admit. On the basis of my earnestness and a more or less astonishing misreading of Nietzsche (I was convinced that he was saying that only fiction can be truly philosophical) I won a Woodrow Wilson Fellowship to the University of Iowa, where I meant to study in the famous Writers' Workshop but soon ended up taking medieval language and literature, the literature God had been nudging me toward all along: "Beowulf," "The Divine Comedy," the Gawain poet, and Chaucer. The scales fell from my eyes. My New Critical compulsion to figure out exactly how everything works, how every nuance plays against every other, had suddenly an immense field to plow. I continued to read and think about other literature—I went through a Thomas Mann phase, a Henry James phase, and so on—but I found myself spending more and more time trying to figure out medieval works.

It seems to me that when I began working on medieval literature, in the late 50's and early 60's, scholars knew very little about even the greatest works in that literature. No one had really figured out the structure of the works of the Gawain poet, not to mention "Beowulf" or the poetry of Chaucer. People were still arguing about whether or not "Beowulf" is a Christian poem; people were still trying to shuffle around "The Canterbury Tales." The usual New Critical method, which is to stare and stare at the work until it becomes clear, was useless on this material, because again and again you found yourself staring at something that felt like a symbol or an allusion, or felt that maybe it ought to be some kind of joke but you couldn't see the humor. To figure out the poem you had to figure out the world it came from—read the books the poets knew, try to understand esthetic principles abandoned and forgotten centuries ago. One had no choice but to become a sort of scholar.

Literary detective work is always fun, for a certain kind of mind at least, but the work I did on medieval literature, then on later classical literature, was for me the most exciting detective work I've ever done or heard of. The thing was, not only did you solve interesting puzzles, but when you got them solved you found you'd restored something magnificent, a work of art—in the case of "Beowulf" or "The Canterbury Tales"—supremely beautiful and noble. One unearthed tricks of the craft that nobody'd known or used for a long, long time—tricks one could turn on one's own work, making it different from anybody else's and yet not crazy, not merely novel.

I think every writer wants to sound like him- or herself; that's the main reason one sees so many experimental novels. And of course the risk in the pursuit of newness is that, in refusing to do what the so-called tradition does, one ends up doing exactly the same thing everybody else trying to get outside the tradition does. For better or worse (I'm no longer much concerned about whether it's better or worse), I joined up with an alternative tradition, one with which I felt almost eerily comfortable. My church-filled childhood delighted in discovering a Christianity distant enough—in fact, for all practical purposes, *dead* enough—to satisfy nostalgia without stirring embarrassment and annoyance, as modern Christianity does. For instance, when one reads about "ensoulment" in a medieval book—that is, when one reads arguments on precisely when the soul enters the fetus, and the argument comes from someone of the 13th century—one can read with interest; but when one hears a living Christian hotly debating ensoulment, hoping to be able to support abortion without feelings of guilt, one shrinks away, tries to get lost in the crowd.

I found in medieval culture and art, in other words, exactly what I needed as an instrument for looking at my own time and place. I of course never became for a moment a medieval Christian believer, but medieval ideas and attitudes gave me a means of triangulating, a place to stand. And, needless to say, medieval literature had built into it everything I'd liked best from the beginning, back in the days of God, Dickens, and Disney, of grotesques (cartoon people and places), noble feeling, humor (God was perhaps a little short on humor), and real storytelling.

I said earlier that I'm no longer much concerned about whether the work I've done and am doing is for better or worse. That is not quite as true as I might wish. Egoistic ambition is the kind of weed that grows out of dragon's blood: The more you chop it away the more it flourishes. But it's true that at a certain point in one's career one begins to face up to one's limitations, and the way to stay sane at such a moment is to soften one's standards a little— find good reasons for approving lumpy but well-intentioned work, one's own and everybody else's.

To put all this another way, when I think back now over the influences which have helped to shape the way I write, I notice with a touch of dismay that they were as much bad influences as good ones. I won't criticize God (anyway, He's almost certainly been misquoted), but clearly the influence of Dickens and Disney was not all to the good. Both of them incline one toward stylized gestures. Instead of looking very closely at the world and writing it down, the way James Joyce does, brilliantly getting down, say, the way an old man moves his tongue over his gums, or the way a beautiful woman idly plays with her bracelets, a writer like me, seduced by cartoon vision, tends to go again and again for the same gestural gimmicks, a consistent pattern of caricature (compare the way doors in Dostoyevsky are forever flying open or slamming).

I look over my fiction of 20 years and see it as one long frenzy of tics—endlessly repeated words like *merely* and *grotesque,* a disproportionate number of people with wooden fingers and a dreary penchant for frowning thoughtfully or darting their eyes around like maniacs. I seem incapable of writing a story in which people do not babble philosophically, not really because they're saying things I want to get said but because earnest babbling is one of the ways I habitually give vitality to my short-legged, overweight, twitching cartoon creations. And needless to say, from artists like Dickens and Disney I get my morbid habit of trying to make the reader fall into tender weeping.

The whole New Critical period I went through, and the scholarly period that followed it, betrayed me, I think, into an excessive concern with significance. It's probably the case that novels and stories are more interesting if, in some sense or another, they mean something. But it has begun to dawn on me that—in fiction, as in all the arts—a little meaning goes a long way. I think what chiefly made me notice this is the work of my creative writing students. Until about five years ago, I never taught creative writing, only medieval literature and now and then a little Greek. When I began to look hard and often at student writing, I soon discovered that one of the main mistakes in their writing is that students think (probably because they've taken too many English literature courses) that fiction is supposed to tell us things—instruct us, improve us, show us.

In a sense of course they're right, but only in a subtle and mysterious sense. When one has analyzed every symbolically neat detail in a story like "Death in Venice" or "Disorder and Early Sorrow"—when one has accounted for every verbal repetition, every pattern and relationship, and set down in alphabetical order every thought to be lifted or wrenched from the story—one discovers that, when you come right down to it, Mann has told us nothing we didn't know already. More by my writing students' early bad examples (they later get better) than by all the good literary examples I ever read, I've come to see that fiction simply dramatizes. It gives importance to ideas, it seems to me, pretty much in the way the string on which a handful of pearls have been strung gives a kind of importance to the pearls. When I read my earliest, most ingeniously constructed fictions ("The Resurrection" and "Grendel") I find I can no longer figure the damn things out—would that I'd kept all my charts! Insofar as such books are interesting, for me at least, they're interesting because I like the characters and hope, as I reread, that life (the rest of the book) won't treat them too badly.

I don't mean, of course, that I intend never again to use symbols or to design my stories so that the reader has the kind of experience William James described with such delight: "There goes the same thing I saw before again." What I do mean is that when I was 3 or 4, or 12 or 13, I understood fiction more profoundly than I understood it through most of my writing years. I understood that a story, like a painting, or like a symphony, is one of the most wonderful, one of the most useless, things in the world. The magnificence of a work of art lies precisely in the fact that nobody made the artist make it, he just did, and—except when one's in school—nobody makes the receiver read it, or look at it, or listen to it; he just does. The influence of my writing students has been to lead me to understand (or imagine I understand) that art's value is not that it expresses life's meaning (though presumably it does, as do butterflies and crickets) but that it is, simply, splendidly, *there*.

I think of the performances my mother and father would sometimes do at, for instance, the monthly meetings of the Grange. The way the night would go is this: First everybody would crowd into one immense room with trestle-tables and white-paper tablecloths, the tables all loaded down with food, all the redfaced farmers and their plump wives and children finding folding chairs near friends, and somebody would tap a water glass with the side of his spoon and would say a quick, self-conscious prayer, and then everybody would eat.

It was a wonderfully pleasant social time, lots of jokes and stories and abundant country food; but it wasn't a time they chose solely for its pleasantness: If you wanted to get farmers to come from all over the county late at night, after chores, you had to feed them. Then they'd all go into another room and have their business meeting—how much or how little they should organize, how to keep the feed-mills, the truckers, and the United States Congress in line. Nobody much cared for the business meeting, though sometimes somebody would "get off a good one," as they used to say.

Then, when the work was done my mother and father would stand there in the middle of the big, bright room and say poems or sing. How strange it seemed to me that all these serious, hard-working people should sit there grinning for an hour or more, listening, for instance, to my father telling them an endless, pointless story of a ghost in armor, or a ship rescued by pigeons, or somebody called Dangerous Dan McGrew. It was absurd. I wasn't just imagining it. The whole thing was deeply, weirdly absurd. Clearly if one is to devote a lifetime to doing something as crazy as that, one had better do it well—not necessarily because there is any great virtue in doing it well but only because, if one does it badly, people may wake up and notice that what one's doing is crazy.

Suggestions for Discussion

1. John Gardner, like Anne Tyler, describes his family and their influence on him. How are the two families different and similar?

2. Why did Gardner learn so much from Dickens and Disney? To what kind of writers does he contrast them? Explain his statement that when he was young, God, Dickens, and Disney were his favorite authors.

3. Explain how Gardner became interested first in literature as a serious occupation and then in the study of medieval literature. Why did medieval literature become so important to him? How did literary study influence his own writing?

4. How similar in tone is the memoir to the one by Anne Tyler?

5. What does Gardner mean by "cartoons" in literature?

6. Why does Gardner both begin and end the essay with an account of his parents?

Suggestions for Writing

1. In an essay, compare and contrast the memoirs by Gardner and Tyler. Discuss the structure and tone of each.

2. Write an essay explaining why Gardner lists Disney in the same breath as God and Dickens. How are Disney's cartoons related to art?

Essays

Northrop Frye
The Keys to Dreamland

Northrop Frye (b. 1912), Distinguished Professor of English at the University of Toronto, is a leading literary critic. His essays have influenced generations of university English professors. Among his works are *Fearful Symmetry: A Study of William Blake* (1947), *Anatomy of Criticism* (1957), *The Well-Tempered Critic* (1963), and two collections of lectures, *A Natural Perspective* (1965) and *The Modern Century* (1967). In "The Keys to Dreamland" from *The Educated Imagination* (1964), Frye asserts that literature, which plays a significant role in our lives, is autonomous and must be judged on its own terms.

I have been trying to explain literature by putting you in a primitive situation on an uninhabited island, where you could see the imagination working in the most direct and simple way. Now let's start with our own society, and see where literature belongs in that, if it does. Suppose you're walking down the street of a North American city. All around you is a highly artificial society, but you don't think of it as artificial: you're so accustomed to it that you think of it as natural. But suppose your imagination plays a little trick on you of a kind that it often does play, and you suddenly feel like a complete outsider, someone who's just blown in from Mars on a flying saucer. Instantly you see how conventionalized everything is: the clothes, the shop windows, the movement of the cars in traffic, the cropped hair and shaved faces of the men, the red lips and blue eyelids that women put on because they want to conventionalize their faces, or "look nice," as they say, which means the same thing. All this convention is pressing toward uniformity or likeness. To be outside the convention makes a person look queer, or, if he's driving a car, a menace to life and limb. The only exceptions are people who have decided to conform to different conventions, like nuns or beatniks. There's clearly a strong force making toward conformity in society, so strong that it seems to have something to do with the stability of society itself. In ordinary life even the most splendid things we can think of, like goodness and truth and beauty, all mean essentially what we're accustomed to. As I hinted just now in speaking of female make-up, most of our ideas of beauty are pure convention, and even truth has been defined as whatever doesn't disturb the pattern of what we already know.

When we move on to literature, we again find conventions, but this time we notice that they are conventions, because we're not so used to them. These conventions seem to have something to do with making literature as unlike life as possible. Chaucer represents people as making up stories in ten-syllable couplets. Shakespeare uses dramatic conventions, which means, for instance, that Iago has to smash Othello's marriage and dreams of future happiness and get him ready to murder his wife in a few minutes. Milton has two nudes in a garden haranguing each other in set speeches beginning with such lines as "Daughter of God and Man, immortal Eve"—Eve being Adam's daughter because she's just been extracted from his ribcase. Almost every story we read demands that we accept as fact something that we know to be nonsense: that good people always win, especially in love; that murders are complicated and ingenious puzzles to be solved by logic, and so on. It isn't only popular literature that demands this: more highbrow stories are apt to be more ironic, but irony has its conventions too. If we go further back into literature, we run into such conventions as the king's rash promise, the enraged cuckold, the cruel mistress of love poetry—never anything that we or any other time would recognize as the normal behavior of adult people, only the maddened ethics of fairyland.

Even the details of literature are equally perverse. Literature is a world where phoenixes and unicorns are quite as important as horses and dogs—and in literature some of the horses talk, like the ones in *Gulliver's Travels*. A random example is calling Shakespeare the "swan of Avon"—he was called that by Ben Jonson. The town of Stratford, Ontario, keeps swans in its river partly as a literary allusion. Poets of Shakespeare's day hated to admit that they were writing words on a page: they always insisted that they were producing music. In pastoral poetry they might be playing a flute (or more accurately an oboe), but every other kind of poetic effort was called song, with a harp, a lyre, or a lute in the background, depending on how highbrow the song was. Singing suggests birds, and so for their typical songbird and emblem of themselves, the poets chose the swan, a bird that can't sing. Because it can't sing, they made up a legend that it sang once before death, when nobody was listening. But Shakespeare didn't burst into song before his death: he wrote two plays a year until he'd made enough money to retire, and spend the last five years of his life counting his take.

So however useful literature may be in improving one's imagination or vocabulary, it would be the wildest kind of pedantry to use it directly as a guide to life. Perhaps here we see one reason why the poet is not only very seldom a person one would turn to for insight into the state of the world, but often seems even more gullible and simple-minded than the rest of us. For the poet, the particular literary conventions he adopts are likely to become, for him, facts of life. If he finds that the kind of writing he's best at has a good deal to do with fairies, like Yeats, or a white goddess, like Graves, or a life-force, like Bernard Shaw, or episcopal sermons, like T. S. Eliot, or bullfights, like Hemingway, or exasperation at social hypocrisies, as with the so-called angry school, these things are apt to take on a reality for him that seems badly out of proportion to his contemporaries. His life may imitate literature in a way that may warp or even destroy his social personality, as Byron wore himself out at thirty-four with the strain of being Byronic. Life and literature, then, are both conventionalized, and of the conventions of literature about all we can say is that they don't much resemble the conditions of life. It's when the two sets of conventions collide that we realize how different they are.

In fact, whenever literature gets too probable, too much like life, some self-defeating process, some mysterious law of diminishing returns, seems to set in. There's a vivid and expertly written novel by H. G. Wells called *Kipps*, about a lower-middle-class, inarticulate, very likeable Cockney, the kind of character we often find in Dickens. Kipps is carefully studied: he never sounds the "h" in home or head; nothing he does is out of line with what we expect such a person to be like. It's an admirable novel, well worth reading, and yet I have a nagging feeling that there's some inner secret in bringing him completely to life that Dickens would have and that Wells doesn't have. All right, then, what would Dickens have done? Well, one of the things that Dickens often does do is write *badly*. He might have given Kipps sentimental speeches and false heroics and all sorts of inappropriate verbiage to say; and some readers would have clucked and tut-tutted over these passages and explained to each other how bad Dickens's taste was and how uncertain his hold on character could be. Perhaps they'd be right to. But we'd have had Kipps a few times the way he'd look to himself or the way he'd sometimes wish he could be: that's part of his reality, and the effect would remain with us however much we disapproved of it. Whether I'm right about this book or not, and I'm not at all sure I am, I think my general principle is right. What we'd never see except in a book is often what we go to books to find. Whatever is completely lifelike in literature is a bit of a laboratory specimen there. To bring anything really to life in literature we can't be lifelike: we have to be literaturelike.

The same thing is true even of the use of language. We're often taught that prose is the language of ordinary speech, which is usually true in literature. But in ordinary life prose is no more the language of ordinary speech than one's Sunday suit is a bathing suit. The people who actually speak prose are highly cultivated and articulate people, who've read a good many books, and even they can speak prose only to each other. If you read the beautiful sentences of Elizabeth Bennett's conversation in *Pride and Prejudice*, you can see how in that book they give a powerfully convincing impression of a sensible and intelligent girl. But any girl who talked as coherently as that on a street car would be stared at as though she had green hair. It isn't only the difference between 1813 and 1962 that's involved either, as you'll see if you compare her speech with her mother's. The poet Emily Dickinson complained that everybody said "What?" to her, until finally she practically gave up trying to talk altogether, and confined herself to writing notes.

All this is involved with the principle I've touched on before: the difference between literary and other kinds of writing. If we're writing to convey information, or for any practical reason, our writing is an act of will and intention: we mean what we say, and the words we use represent that meaning directly. It's different in literature, not because the poet doesn't mean what he says too, but because his real effort is one of putting words together. What's important is not what he may have meant to say, but what the words themselves say when they get fitted together. With a novelist it's rather the incidents in the story he tells that get fitted together—as D. H. Lawrence says, don't trust the novelist; trust his story. That's why so much of a writer's best writing is or seems to be involuntary. It's involuntary because the forms of literature itself are taking control of it, and these forms are what are embodied in the conventions of literature. Conventions, we see, have the same role in literature that they have in life: they impose certain patterns of order and stability on the writer. Only, if they're such different conventions, it seems clear that the order of words, or the structure of literature, is different from the social order.

The absence of any clear line of connection between literature and life comes out in the issues involved in censorship. Because of the large involuntary element in writing, works of literature can't be treated as embodiments of conscious will or intention, like people, and so no laws can be framed to control their behavior which assume a tendency to do this or an intention of doing that. Works of literature get into legal trouble because they offend some powerful religious or political interest, and this interest in its turn usually acquires or exploits the kind of social hysteria that's always revolving around sex. But it's impossible to give legal definitions of such terms as obscenity in relation to works of literature. What happens to the book depends mainly on the intelligence of the judge. It he's a sensible man we get a sensible decision; if he's an ass we get that sort of decision, but what we don't get is a legal decision, because the basis for one doesn't exist. The best we get is a precedent tending to discourage cranks and pressure groups from attacking serious books. If you read the casebook on the trial of *Lady Chatterley's Lover,* you may remember how bewildered the critics were when they were asked what the moral effect of the book would be. They weren't putting on an act: they didn't know. Novels can only be good or bad in their own categories. There's no such thing as a morally bad novel: its moral effect depends entirely on the moral quality of its reader, and nobody can predict what that will be. And if literature isn't morally bad it isn't morally good either. I suppose one reason why *Lady Chatterley's Lover* dramatized this question so vividly was that it's a rather preachy and self-conscious book: like the Sunday-school novels of my childhood, it bores me a little because it tries so hard to do me good.

So literature has no consistent connection with ordinary life, positive or negative. Here we touch on another important difference between structures of the imagination and structures of practical sense, which include the applied sciences. Imagination is certainly essential to science, applied or pure. Without a constructive power in the mind to make models of experience, get hunches and follow them out, play freely around with hypotheses, and so forth, no scientist could get anywhere. But all imaginative effort in practical fields has to meet the test of practicability, otherwise it's discarded. The imagination in literature has no such test to meet. You don't relate it directly to life or reality: you relate works of literature, as we've said earlier, to each other. Whatever value there is in studying literature, cultural or practical, comes from the total body of our reading, the castle of words we've built, and keep adding new wings to all the time.

So it's natural to swing to the opposite extreme and say that literature is really a refuge or escape from life, a self-contained world like the world of the dream, a world of play or make-believe to balance the world of work. Some literature is like that, and many people tell us that they only read to get away from reality for a bit. And I've suggested myself that the sense of escape, or at least detachment, does come into everybody's literary experience. But the real point of literature can hardly be that. Think of such writers as William Faulkner or François Mauriac, their great moral dignity, the intensity and compassion that they've studied the life around them with. Or think of James Joyce, spending seven years on one book and seventeen on another, and having them ridiculed or abused or banned by the customs when they did get published. Or of the poets Rilke and Valéry, waiting patiently for years in silence until what they had to say was ready to be said. There's a deadly seriousness in all this that even the most refined theories of fantasy or make-believe won't quite cover. Still, let's go along with the idea for a bit, because we're not getting on very fast with the relation of literature to life, or what we could call the horizontal perspective of literature. That seems to block us off on all sides.

The world of literature is a world where there is no reality except that of the human imagination. We see a great deal in it that reminds us vividly of the life we know. But in that very vividness there's something unreal. We can understand this more clearly with pictures, perhaps. There are trick-pictures—*trompe l'oeil*, the French call them—where the resemblance to life is very strong. An American painter of this school played a joke on his bitchy wife by painting one of her best napkins so expertly that she grabbed at the canvas trying to pull it off. But a painting as realistic as that isn't a reality but an illusion: it has the glittering unnatural clarity of a hallucination. The real realities, so to speak, are things that don't remind us directly of our own experience, but are such things as the wrath of Achilles or the jealousy of Othello, which are bigger and more intense experiences than anything we can reach—except in our imagination, which is what we're reaching with. Sometimes, as in the happy endings of comedies, or in the ideal world of romances, we seem to be looking at a pleasanter world than we ordinarily know. Sometimes, as in tragedy and satire, we seem to be looking at a world more devoted to suffering or absurdity than we ordinarily know. In literature we always seem to be looking either up or down. It's the vertical perspective that's important, not the horizontal one that looks out to life. Of course, in the greatest works of literature we get both the up and down views, often at the same time as different aspects of one event.

There are two halves to the literary experience, then. Imagination gives us both a better and a worse world than the one we usually live with, and demands that we keep looking steadily at them both. I said in my first talk that the arts follow the path of the emotions, and of the tendency of the emotions to separate the world into a half that we like and a half that we don't like. Literature is not a world of dreams, but it would be if we had only one half without the other. If we had nothing but romances and comedies with happy endings, literature would express only a wish-fulfillment dream. Some people ask why poets want to write tragedies when the world's so full of them anyway, and suggest that enjoying such things has something morbid or gloating about it. It doesn't, but it might if there were nothing else in literature.

This point is worth spending another minute on. You recall that terrible scene in *King Lear* where Gloucester's eyes are put out on the stage. That's part of a play, and a play is supposed to be entertaining. Now in what sense can a scene like that be entertaining? The fact that it's not really happening is certainly important. It would be degrading to watch a real blinding scene, and far more so to get any pleasure out of watching it. Consequently, the entertainment doesn't consist of its reminding us of a real blinding scene. If it did, one of the great scenes of drama would turn into a piece of repulsive pornography. We couldn't stop anyone from reading in this way, and it certainly wouldn't cure him, much less help the public, to start blaming or censoring Shakespeare for putting sadistic ideas in his head. But a reaction of that kind has nothing to do with drama. In a dramatic scene of cruelty and hatred we're seeing cruelty and hatred, which we know are permanently real things in human life, from the point of view of the imagination. What the imagination suggests is horror, not the paralyzing sickening horror of a real blinding scene, but an exuberant horror, full of the energy of repudiation. This is as powerful a rendering as we can ever get of life as we don't want it.

So we see that there are moral standards in literature after all, even though they have nothing to do with calling the police when we see a word in a book that's more familiar in sound than in print. One of the things Gloucester says in that scene is: "I am tied to the stake, and I must stand the course." In Shakespeare's day it was a favourite sport to tie a bear to a stake and set dogs on it until they killed it. The Puritans suppressed this sport, according to Macaulay, not because it gave pain to the bear but because it gave pleasure to the spectators. Macaulay may have intended his remark to be a sneer at the Puritans, but surely if the Puritans did feel this way they were one hundred percent right. What other reason is there for abolishing public hangings? Whatever their motives, the Puritans and Shakespeare were operating in the same direction. Literature keeps presenting the most vicious things to us as entertainment, but what it appeals to is not any pleasure in these things, but the exhilaration of standing apart from them and being able to see them for what they are because they aren't really happening. The more exposed we are to this, the less likely we are to find an unthinking pleasure in cruel or evil things. As the eighteenth century said in a fine mouth-filling phrase, literature refines our sensibilities.

The top half of literature is the world expressed by such words as sublime, inspiring, and the like, where what we feel is not detachment but absorption. This is the world of heroes and gods and titans and Rabelaisian giants, a world of powers and passions and moments of ecstasy far greater than anything we meet outside the imagination. Such forces would not only absorb but annihilate us if they entered ordinary life, but luckily the protecting wall of the imagination is here too. As the German poet Rilke says, we adore them because they disdain to destroy us. We seem to have got quite a long way from our emotions with their division of things into "I like this" and "I don't like this." Literature gives us an experience that stretches us vertically to the heights and depths of what the human mind can conceive, to what corresponds to the conceptions of heaven and hell in religion. In this perspective what I like or don't like disappears, because there's nothing left of me as a separate person: as a reader of literature I exist only as a representative of humanity as a whole. We'll see in the last talk how important this is.

No matter how much experience we may gather in life, we can never in life get the dimension of experience that the imagination gives us. Only the arts and sciences can do that, and of these, only literature gives us the whole sweep and range of human imagination as it sees itself. It seems to be very difficult for many people to understand the reality and intensity of literary experience. To give an example that you may think a bit irrelevant: why have so many people managed to convince themselves that Shakespeare did not write Shakespeare's plays, when there is not an atom of evidence that any-body else did? Apparently because they feel that poetry must be written out of personal experience, and that Shakespeare didn't have enough experience of the right kind. But Shakespeare's plays weren't produced by his experi-ence: they were produced by his imagination, and the way to develop the imagination is to read a good book or two. As for us, we can't speak or think or comprehend even our own experience except within the limits of our own power over words, and those limits have been established for us by our great writers.

Literature, then, is not a dream-world: it's two dreams, a wish-fulfillment dream and an anxiety dream, that are focused together, like a pair of glasses, and become a fully conscious vision. Art, according to Plato, is a dream for awakened minds, a work of imagination withdrawn from ordinary life, domi-nated by the same forces that dominate the dream, and yet giving us a per-spective and dimension on reality that we don't get from any other approach to reality. So the poet and the dreamer are distinct, as Keats says. Ordinary life forms a community, and literature is among other things an art of com-munication, so it forms a community too. In ordinary life we fall into a private and separate subconscious every night, where we reshape the world according to a private and separate imagination. Underneath literature there's another kind of subconscious, which is social and not private, a need for forming a community around certain symbols, like the Queen and the flag, or around certain gods that represent order and stability, or becoming and change, or death and rebirth to a new life. This is the mythmaking power of the human mind, which throws up and dissolves one civilization after another.

I've taken my title for this talk, "The Keys to Dreamland," from what is possibly the greatest single effort of the literary imagination in the twentieth century, Joyce's *Finnegans Wake*. In this book a man goes to sleep and falls, not into the Freudian separate or private subconscious, but into the deeper dream of man that creates and destroys his own societies. The entire book is written in the language of this dream. It's a subconscious language, mainly English, but connected by associations and puns with the eighteen or so other languages that Joyce knew. *Finnegans Wake* is not a book to read, but a book to decipher: as Joyce says, it's about a dreamer, but it's addressed to an ideal reader suffering from an ideal insomnia. The reader or critic, then, has a role complementing the poet's role. We need two powers in literature, a power to create and a power to understand.

In all our literary experience there are two kinds of response. There is the direct experience of the work itself, while we're reading a book or seeing a play, especially for the first time. This experience is uncritical, or rather pre-critical, so it's not infallible. If our experience is limited, we can be roused to enthusiasm or carried away by something that we can later see to have been second-rate or even phony. Then there is the conscious, critical response we make after we've finished reading or left the theatre, when we compare what we've experienced with other things of the same kind, and form a judgment of value and proportion on it. This critical response, with practice, gradually makes our pre-critical responses more sensitive and accurate, or improves our taste, as we say. But behind our responses to individual works, there's a bigger response to our literary experience as a whole, as a total possession.

The critic has always been called a judge of literature, which means, not that he's in a superior position to the poet, but that he ought to know something about literature, just as a judge's right to be on a bench depends on his knowledge of law. If he's up against something the size of Shakespeare, he's the one being judged. The critic's function is to interpret every work of literature in the light of all the literature he knows, to keep constantly struggling to understand what literature as a whole is about. Literature as a whole is not an aggregate of exhibits with red and blue ribbons attached to them, like a cat-show, but the range of articulate human imagination as it extends from the height of imaginative heaven to the depth of imaginative hell. Literature is a human apocalypse, man's revelation to man, and criticism is not a body of adjudications, but the awareness of that revelation, the last judgment of mankind.

Suggestions for Discussion

1. Explain Frye's belief in the power of conformity in society. What role does conformity play in the very life of society? How does it affect our habits and our ideas about beauty?

2. How does conformity, or convention, work in art? Frye says, "Almost every story we read demands that we accept as fact something that we know to be nonsense. . . ." What examples does Fry use to illustrate? Why is it important for Frye to establish the use of conventions in art?

3. What are Frye's objections to literature that is too much like real life? Are his objections valid? How does he relate Jane Austen and Emily Dickinson to his argument?

4. How does the use of imagination work differently in science and in literature?

5. Why is it important for the audience watching the scene in *King Lear* in which Gloucester's eyes are put out to know that the action is not real? What would happen to the audience if the action were really taking place?

6. What dimension of experience does the imagination (through art) give us that is unattainable in real life?

7. Frye says paradoxically that art is "dreamland" at the same time that it represents the greatest reality. Discuss the meaning of this paradox.

8. What is the style of this essay? What methods does Frye use to achieve it?

Suggestions for Writing

1. Investigate some of Shakespeare's plays with which you are familiar for additional examples of painful scenes that are, as we read or watch them, pleasurable. Write a paper in which you deal with the causes of this curious situation. A research project might explore literary critics, beginning with Aristotle, who have attempted to explain the relation of art to life.

2. Write a paper comparing Forster's "Art for Art's Sake" with Frye's essay. On what points do they seem to agree?

Mike Royko

The Virtue of Prurience

Mike Royko (b. 1932) is thoroughly a Chicagoan, having been born there and having worked on Chicago newspapers most of his life. He was for many years a columnist for the *Chicago Sun-Times*, is now a columnist for the *Chicago Tribune*, winner of a Pulitzer Prize for commentary, and author of four books. His essay on censorship provides a good example of how to treat a serious subject with wit.

My first right-wing endeavor—helping get a book banned—has failed miserably. I now can appreciate how frustrating life in our permissive society must be for such grim-lipped groups as the Moral Majority.

Normally, I don't favor censorship and have never before tried to get anything banned. But several months ago, I joined in a crusade that was being led by Bill and Barbara Younis of Hannibal, N.Y.

Bill and Barbara are parents of an 18-year-old high school senior, and they became alarmed when they discovered that their daughter was being required to read a book they considered vulgar.

They went to the school superintendent and demanded that the book be removed from the reading list. He refused.

So they asked friends and neighbors to sign petitions supporting them, and they demanded that the school board ban the book.

That's when I found out about it. A reporter from that part of New York called to ask me what I thought of the censorship efforts.

I responded by dropping the phone, shouting, "Hot damn, yowee!" and dancing gleefully around my office.

I reacted that way because it is a book that I wrote about 12 years ago. It is called "Boss" and is about Mayor Richard J. Daley, power, and Chicago politics.

Before long, there were news stories about the censorship efforts of the Younises, and my phone started ringing with calls from other writers.

One of them said:

"You slick devil, how did you ever pull that off?"

I'm just lucky, I guess.

"Well, I don't get it. My last book was so torrid and lurid that I blushed while writing it. And there hasn't even been a hint from anybody about banning it."

You're just unlucky, I guess.

Another writer called and said: "This is so unfair. In my last book, George did it with Lucy, Lucy did it with Wally, Wally did it with Evelyn, Evelyn did it with George, George did it with Wally, Lucy did it with Sally, and then they all did it together."

Sounds exhausting.

"What I don't understand, is why you, but not me. I mean, I could really use a break like that."

Maybe I just live right.

What they were talking about was the tremendous commercial value of being banned. By anyone, anywhere, just as long as you are banned. It works this way:

If you can get a book banned in, say, Minneapolis, and there is a great furor about it, the book will suddenly become a best-seller next door in St. Paul. Sure, you won't sell any books in Minneapolis. But for every book you don't sell in Minneapolis, you'll sell 10 in St. Paul.

That's all part of the forbidden-fruit syndrome. Tell people they can't have or do something, and they immediately want to do it.

With this in mind, I called my publisher and said: "Get those presses rolling. We're going to sell a ton."

He said: "Not yet. You haven't been banned yet. And just being threatened with censorship isn't enough. You've got to be tossed off the shelves."

So I got on the phone and called Mr. and Mrs. Younis.

"Your book is vulgar," they said. "It is filled with swear words."

I know. That's the way Chicago politicians talk, so I quoted them. But you're right. It's vulgar. Shocking.

"You agree?"

Hell . . . I mean, heck, yes. And I'm behind you 100 percent.

"You are?"

Of course I am. I think what you're doing is terrific. And if I were there, I'd sign your petition.

"You would?"

Darn right. I don't want 18-year-olds reading words like (bleep) and (censored) and (deleted). Who ever heard of 18-year-olds being exposed to such language?

"Would you send us a letter expressing your support?"

Of course. I'll do more than that. I'll write a column urging that my book be banned.

And I did.

Since then, I've been thumbing through travel folders, real-estate brochures for tropical hideaways, yachting magazines, and girlie magazines, anticipating life as a rich and censored author.

Nothing ever works out.

The school board set up a three-member committee to review the book and the Younises' complaint.

Then a hearing was held. Mr. and Mrs. Younis, bless them, came to the hearing and said things like: "It's got the kind of language you see painted on bridges. Books like this encourage young ladies to become prostitutes."

That's dynamite stuff. Would you want your daughter to read a book that would encourage her to enter the employ of a brothel? I should hope not.

Despite this, the committee ruled that the book would remain on the reading list.

Mr. and Mrs. Younis have now removed three of their four children from the school system and say they will send them to private schools.

A noble effort, but it doesn't do me much good. As the school superintendent said:

"We made our decision, and it was a good one. There is nothing wrong with that book."

Doggone busybody.

Suggestions for Discussion

1. What is the tone of Royko's essay? How does he achieve the right tone? Is it appropriate to the subject of the essay? Explain its title.

2. Why are fellow authors jealous of Royko? What examples of their works does he use? How are those works different from his? Should the book about George and Lucy and the others be banned? Explain.

3. What is "the forbidden-fruit syndrome"?

4. What serious issue does Royko suggest in his description of the Younis couple?

5. Why is censorship a danger to human freedom? Are there instances in which censorship might safely be imposed?

Suggestions for Writing

1. Royko says, "Tell people they can't have or do something, and they immediately want to do it." Write an essay illustrating this comment. Explain why you think Royko's observation about people may be accurate.

2. Write an essay in which you discuss a play, movie, poem, painting, or novel which you think should be banned. Explain your reasons. If you don't believe in banning anything, explain why, giving your reasons carefully.

E. M. Forster

Art for Art's Sake

Edward Morgan Forster (1879–1970) was a British novelist educated at King's College, Cambridge. He lived for a time in Italy, was a member of the Bloomsbury Group of writers and artists in London, and spent the major part of his life in Cambridge. His works include *Where Angels Fear to Tread* (1905), *A Room With a View* (1908), and *A Passage to India* (1924). In this essay from *Two Cheers for Democracy* (1951), Forster explains the importance of art as a source of comfort and order in a troubled society.

I believe in art for art's sake. It is an unfashionable belief, and some of my statements must be of the nature of an apology. Sixty years ago I should have faced you with more confidence. A writer or a speaker who chose "Art for Art's Sake" for his theme sixty years ago could be sure of being in the swim, and could feel so confident of success that he sometimes dressed himself in aesthetic costumes suitable to the occasion—in an embroidered dressing-gown, perhaps, or a blue velvet suit with a Lord Fauntleroy collar; or a toga, or a kimono, and carried a poppy or a lily or a long peacock's feather in his mediaeval hand. Times have changed. Not thus can I present either myself or my theme to-day. My aim rather is to ask you quietly to reconsider for a few minutes a phrase which has been much misused and much abused, but which has, I believe, great importance for us—has, indeed, eternal importance.

Now we can easily dismiss those peacock's feathers and other affectations—they are but trifles—but I want also to dismiss a more dangerous heresy, namely the silly idea that only art matters, an idea which has somehow got mixed up with the idea of art for art's sake, and has helped to discredit it. Many things besides art, matter. It is merely one of the things that matter, and high though the claims are that I make for it, I want to keep them in proportion. No one can spend his or her life entirely in the creation or the appreciation of masterpieces. Man lives, and ought to live, in a complex world, full of conflicting claims, and if we simplified them down into the aesthetic he would be sterilised. Art for art's sake does not mean that only art matters and I would also like to rule out such phrases as, "The Life of Art," "Living for Art," and "Art's High Mission." They confuse and mislead.

What does the phrase mean? Instead of generalising, let us take a specific instance—Shakespeare's *Macbeth*, for example, and pronounce the words, *"Macbeth for Macbeth's sake."* What does that mean? Well, the play has several aspects—it is educational, it teaches us something about legendary Scotland, something about Jacobean England, and a good deal about human nature and its perils. We can study its origins, and study and enjoy its dramatic technique and the music of its diction. All that is true. But *Macbeth* is furthermore a world of its own, created by Shakespeare and existing in virtue of its own poetry. It is in this aspect *Macbeth* for *Macbeth*'s sake, and that is what I intend by the phrase "art for art's sake." A work of art—whatever else it may be—is a self-contained entity, with a life of its own imposed on it by its creator. It has internal order. It may have external form. That is how we recognise it.

Take for another example that picture of Seurat's which I saw two years ago in Chicago—*"La Grande Jatte."* Here again there is much to study and to enjoy: the pointillism, the charming face of the seated girl, the nineteenth-century Parisian Sunday sunlight, the sense of motion in immobility. But here again there is something more; *"La Grande Jatte"* forms a world of its own, created by Seurat and existing by virtue of its own poetry: *"La Grande Jatte" pour "La Grande Jatte": l'art pour l'art.* Like *Macbeth* it has internal order and internal life.

It is to the conception of order that I would now turn. This is important to my argument, and I want to make a digression, and glance at order in daily life, before I come to order in art.

In the world of daily life, the world which we perforce inhabit, there is much talk about order, particularly from statesmen and politicians. They tend, however, to confuse order with orders, just as they confuse creation with regulations. Order, I suggest, is something evolved from within, not something imposed from without; it is an internal stability, a vital harmony, and in the social and political category, it has never existed except for the convenience of historians. Viewed realistically, the past is really a series of *dis*orders, succeeding one another by discoverable laws, no doubt, and certainly marked by an increasing growth of human interference, but disorders all the same. So that, speaking as a writer, what I hope for today is a disorder which will be more favourable to artists than is the present one, and which will provide them with fuller inspirations and better material conditions. It will not last—nothing lasts—but there have been some advantageous disorders in the past—for instance, in ancient Athens, in Renaissance Italy, eighteenth-century France, periods in China and Persia—and we may do something to accelerate the next one. But let us not again fix our hearts where true joys are not to be found. We were promised a new order after the first world war through the League of Nations. It did not come, nor have I faith in present promises, by whomsoever endorsed. The implacable offensive of Science forbids. We cannot reach social and political stability for the reason that we continue to make scientific discoveries and to apply them, and thus to destroy the arrangements which were based on more elementary discoveries. If Science would discover rather than apply—if, in other words, men were more interested in knowledge than in power—mankind would be in a far safer position, the stability statesmen talk about would be a possibility, there could be a new order based on vital harmony, and the earthly millennium might approach. But Science shows no signs of doing this: she gave us the internal combustion engine, and before we had digested and assimilated it with terrible pains into our social system, she harnessed the atom, and destroyed any new order that seemed to be evolving. How can man get into harmony with his surroundings when he is constantly altering them? The future of our race is, in this direction, more unpleasant than we care to admit, and it has sometimes seemed to me that its best chance lies through apathy, uninventiveness, and inertia. Universal exhaustion might promote that Change of Heart which is at present so briskly recommended from a thousand pulpits. Universal exhaustion would certainly be a new experience. The human race has never undergone it, and is still too perky to admit that it may be coming and might result in a sprouting of new growth through the decay.

I must not pursue these speculations any further—they lead me too far from my terms of reference and maybe from yours. But I do want to emphasize that order in daily life and in history, order in the social and political category, is unattainable under our present psychology.

Where is it attainable? Not in the astronomical category, where it was for many years enthroned. The heavens and the earth have become terribly alike since Einstein. No longer can we find a reassuring contrast to chaos in the night sky and look up with George Meredith to the stars, the army of unalterable law, or listen for the music of the spheres. Order is not there. In the entire universe there seem to be only two possibilities for it. The first of them—which again lies outside my terms of reference—is the divine order, the mystic harmony, which according to all religions is available for those who can contemplate it. We much admit its possibility, on the evidence of the adepts, and we must believe them when they say that it is attained, if attainable, by prayer. "O thou who changest not, abide with me," said one of its poets. "*Ordina questo amor, o tu che m'ami,*" said another: "Set love in order thou who lovest me." The existence of a divine order, though it cannot be tested, has never been disproved.

The second possibility for order lies in the aesthetic category, which is my subject here: the order which an artist can create in his own work, and to that we must now return. A work of art, we are all agreed, is a unique product. But why? It is unique not because it is clever or noble or beautiful or enlightened or original or sincere or idealistic or useful or educational—it may embody any of those qualities—but because it is the only material object in the universe which may possess internal harmony. All the others have been pressed into shape from outside, and when their mold is removed they collapse. The work of art stands up by itself, and nothing else does. It achieves something which has often been promised by society, but always delusively. Ancient Athens made a mess—but the *Antigone* stands up. Renaissance Rome made a mess—but the ceiling of the Sistine got painted. James I made a mess—but there was *Macbeth*. Louis XIV—but there was *Phedre*. Art for art's sake? I should just think so, and more so than ever at the present time. It is the one orderly product which our muddling race has produced. It is the cry of a thousand sentinels, the echo from a thousand labyrinths; it is the lighthouse which cannot be hidden: *c'est le meilleur témoignage que nous puissions donner de notre dignité. Antigone* for *Antigone's* sake, *Macbeth* for *Macbeth's*, "*La Grande Jatte*" *pour* "*La Grande Jatte.*"

If this line of argument is correct, it follows that the artist will tend to be an outsider in the society to which he has been born, and that the nineteenth century conception of him as a Bohemian was not inaccurate. The conception erred in three particulars: it postulated an economic system where art could be a full-time job, it introduced the fallacy that only art matters, and it overstressed idiosyncrasy and waywardness—the peacock-feather aspect—rather than order. But it is a truer conception than the one which prevails in official circles on my side of the Atlantic—I don't know about yours: the conception which treats the artist as if he were a particularly bright government advertiser and encourages him to be friendly and matey with his fellow citizens, and not to give himself airs.

Estimable is mateyness, and the man who achieves it gives many a pleasant little drink to himself and to others. But it has no traceable connection with the creative impulse, and probably acts as an inhibition on it. The artist who is seduced by mateyness may stop himself from doing the one thing which he, and he alone, can do—the making of something out of words or sounds or paint or clay or marble or steel or film which has internal harmony and presents order to a permanently disarranged planet. This seems worth doing, even at the risk of being called uppish by journalists. I have in mind an article which was published some years ago in the London *Times*, an article called "The Eclipse of the Highbrow," in which the "Average Man" was exalted, and all contemporary literature was censured if it did not toe the line, the precise position of the line being naturally known to the writer of the article. Sir Kenneth Clark, who was at that time director of our National Gallery, commented on this pernicious doctrine in a letter which cannot be too often quoted. "The poet and the artist," wrote Clark, "are important precisely because they are not average men; because in sensibility, intelligence, and power of invention they far exceed the average." These memorable words, and particularly the words "power of invention," are the Bohemian's passport. Furnished with it, he slinks about society, saluted now by a brickbat and now by a penny, and accepting either of them with equanimity. He does not consider too anxiously what his relations with society may be, for he is aware of something more important than that—namely the invitation to invent, to create order, and he believes he will be better placed for doing this if he attempts detachment. So round and round he slouches, with his hat pulled over his eyes, and maybe with a louse in his beard, and—if he really wants one—a peacock's feather in his hand.

If our present society should disintegrate—and who dare prophesy that it won't?—this old-fashioned and démodé figure will become clearer: the Bohemian, the outsider, the parasite, the rat—one of those figures which have at present no function either in a warring or a peaceful world. It may not be dignified to be a rat, but many of the ships are sinking, which is not dignified either—the officials did not build them properly. Myself, I would sooner be a swimming rat than a sinking ship—at all events I can look around me for a little longer—and I remember how one of us, a rat with particularly bright eyes called Shelley, squeaked out, "Poets are the unacknowledged legislators of the world," before he vanished into the waters of the Mediterranean.

What laws did Shelley propose to pass? None. The legislation of the artist is never formulated at the time, though it is sometimes discerned by future generations. He legislates through creating. And he creates through his sensitiveness and power to impose form. Without form the sensitiveness vanishes. And form is as important today, when the human race is trying to ride the whirlwind, as it ever was in those less agitating days of the past, when the earth seemed solid and the stars fixed, and the discoveries of science were made slowly, slowly. Form is not tradition. It alters from generation to generation. Artists always seek a new technique, and will continue to do so as long as their work excites them. But form of some kind is imperative. It is the surface crust of the internal harmony, it is the outward evidence of order.

My remarks about society may have seemed too pessimistic, but I believe that society can only represent a fragment of the human spirit, and that another fragment can only get expressed through art. And I wanted to take this opportunity, this vantage ground, to assert not only the existence of art, but its pertinacity. Looking back into the past, it seems to me that that is all there has ever been: vantage grounds for discussion and creation, little vantage grounds in the changing chaos, where bubbles have been blown and webs spun, and the desire to create order has found temporary gratification, and the sentinels have managed to utter their challenges, and the huntsmen, though lost individually, have heard each other's calls through the impenetrable wood, and the lighthouses have never ceased sweeping the thankless seas. In this pertinacity there seems to me, as I grow older, something more and more profound, something which does in fact concern people who do not care about art at all.

In conclusion, let me summarise the various categories that have laid claim to the possession of Order.

(1) The social and political category. Claim disallowed on the evidence of history and of our own experience. If man altered psychologically, order here might be attainable: not otherwise.

(2) The astronomical category. Claim allowed up to the present century, but now disallowed on the evidence of the physicists.

(3) The religious category. Claim allowed on the evidence of the mystics.

(4) The aesthetic category. Claim allowed on the evidence of various works of art, and on the evidence of our own creative impulses, however weak these may be or however imperfectly they may function. Works of art, in my opinion, are the only objects in the material universe to possess internal order, and that is why, though I don't believe that only art matters, I do believe in Art for Art's Sake.

Suggestions for Discussion

1. Why does Forster make clear that the belief in art for art's sake does not mean a belief that only art matters?

2. Where does art stand, for Forster, in the list of things that matter?

3. Explain Forster's phrase, *"Macbeth* for *Macbeth's* sake." How does he use it to explain his main argument?

4. Explain Forster's comparison of the order of art with order in life. How does this comparison function in his argument?

5. What does Forster mean by claiming that a work of art is a unique product?

6. Examine Forster's categories that have laid claim to the possession of order. Why does he reject all but the religious and aesthetic categories?

Suggestions for Writing

1. Write a paper explaining Forster's defense of art.

2. Obviously, many people feel differently from Forster about the autonomy of art. In Marxist countries, for example, art is often considered to be a servant of the state. Write a paper in which you argue for or against Forster's position.

Oscar Mandel

Dissonant Music Sixty Years After

Oscar Mandel (b. 1926) is a professor in the Division of Humanities and Social Sciences at the California Institute of Technology. He is the author of numerous books and articles about drama, fiction, poetry, and literary criticism. He is also a playwright, poet, and fiction writer. In this extended essay, published in 1973, Mandel makes a strong argument against atonal music while defending experimentation in visual art and literature. Throughout, he shows his concern for the relation of art to society.

> *What will "vanguardism" leave to posterity? Nothing*
> *but smoldering cinders which its propagandists, shout-*
> *ing from the housetops, are trying to make us believe*
> *are a living forest.*
> **—Dmitri Shostakovitch**

> *Taking the "average" audience for major symphony*
> *concerts, and speaking personally, I can say that I*
> *care no more about them and their reactions than I do*
> *about the audience for jukeboxes in bars.*
> **—Charles Wuorinen**

I

There is no single musical term that neatly covers the multiple experiments and adventures in music launched in our century. We all know that the music of our epoch is impossible to confuse with that of the century before, whether it is composed by a moderate respectful of tradition or by an extremist sick of all precedent, and whether it is scored for a string quartet or issues from a formidable piece of electronic equipment. Yet how can one place a composer like Hindemith (for instance) in the company of the beep/blop magnetic-tape sound producers? Only by asserting that every age is endowed with a loose yet essential "philosophical" coherence which gives it identity. Thus, set off from a Beethoven or a Tchaikovsky, the most disparate and mutually hostile schools and individuals of our time keep company after all in the same cultural basket. In the following pages I will use the term "dissonant" as my unifying cultural concept for the simple reason that every layman recognizes it and himself applies it with a rough justice of his own to pretty nearly all serious music that has been composed since Schönberg. I might have preferred a term like "malsonant," because it has the merit of clearly including the break-down of "beautiful melody" and cadence along with the collapse of traditional codes regarding harmony and tonality. But there are too many word-coins in circulation already. I merely ask that the reader accept the term "dissonant" for the purposes of this paper in an untechnically comprehensive sense.

Is it still possible, in the declining half of the twentieth century, to raise a sensible argument against dissonant music? Or is the question dead? In a recent issue of the *Columbia Forum* there appeared an article by a music critic, Joan Peyser, in praise of the "annihilation of tonality" which was carried out in the days of Schönberg and Alban Berg. That such an article should be printed in a serious journal suggests that the liquidation of *beauty* in music—because beauty is what it is finally all about—still needs defending. If so, all hope is not lost. Those of us who have sometimes felt like pitiable fossils because the experts and the professionals have been treating us like pitiable fossils for sixty or seventy years might try our voices again, take heart, and discover that we are still alive. Let us see therefore whether we can speak to our atonalists so sensibly that even if their very nursery ditties were dodecaphonic snatches, they might be willing to reconsider the foundations of their musical lives.

II

To begin at the beginning, we must come to an understanding about the aim of music. Why does music exist at all in an "advanced civilization"? Professionals are unlikely to trouble their minds with a "silly question" of this sort, but this is precisely where the appearance of an innocent outsider is important—someone who asks the unblushing primary questions. Leaving aside the practical uses of music—the bugle that wakes soldiers up, the band to which people dance, the organ helping a religious service along—we ask what is the purpose of music for the sake of which people sit down in large rooms and to which they listen for an hour, two hours, or three hours, with evident attention and satisfaction.

What if I propose that the aim of music (the aim, that is, of most music most of the time for most people in our civilization today) is to "refresh our spirits"? I take this modest phrase from the title page of Bach's *Clavier-Übung* of 1735. The idea of refreshing our spirits can be stated in many ways. Some ways will seem useless merely because the phrasing is archaic, or because certain words have been appropriated by groups of people we do not like to be associated with. Other ways will seem pertinent because the idioms are "in" with the experts. Furthermore, there is always a moderate "classical" approach and a titanic "romantic" attitude toward life and art: one person will say "Music must make me happy for a moment," another will say "Music must arouse my profoundest feelings," and neither may realize that the difference between them lies not in their feelings, but in their feelings about their feelings. I propose "refreshing our spirits," but I am willing to offer "a delight that goes to the roots of our being." Whichever phrase I choose, I am talking about pleasure.

Search as I will among all manner of possibilities, I cannot find another purpose to challenge that of refreshing our spirits. If we still believed in God, and especially in a Lutheran God, we might well make it an axiom that music exists to celebrate His glory. But even then, how would we know whether He felt celebrated or insulted, except by consulting our own delight first?

In the absence of God, what else can reasonably be proposed? That the purpose of music is to create knowledge about the world in the listener's or the composer's mind? I think it would be difficult to make this stick. This is a claim which we men of letters often assert for our poems, our novels, and our plays. Because literature uses words in common with philosophy, theology, history, journalism, and most sciences, a reasonable case can be made for the instructive value of literature. For many centuries now, literary critics and writers themselves have insisted that literature does, or at least ought to, inculcate. Inculcate what? Knowledge or Morality or both. Literature, the saying goes, is Interpretation of Life.

Even those of us who emphasize the primacy of pleasure in literature no less than in music would have to agree that if a child were brought up on nothing but poems, novels, and plays, he would acquire a tolerable view of life, not to mention an impressive battery of plain facts. A child brought up on nothing but music would grow up an idiot. If he were given a great deal of vocal music—songs, motets, masses, operas—the knowledge of life he would gain would come overwhelmingly from the separable texts. To say this is not to deny that instrumental music can accomplish *something* in the world of concepts and views of life. Ideas and images (along with feelings) of devotion, misery, enthusiasm, mockery, and the like can be induced by music, but they occur as random bobs on the surface, without logical integrations, and they cannot be marshaled into organized insights into the world. Music reminds us of ideas, while literature asserts them. Then again, when music carries a text, the composer occasionally uses his instruments to throw an idea, as it were, at the text. If a group of twittering flutes is brought in at the moment the text is expressing a "noble" thought, the music is being ironical: it flings a denial at the words. This is undoubtedly a thought. But how far does all this carry us? A few steps, and then we are back with "emotional power." Music creates emotion; and to say emotion (in this case) is to say pleasure.

If, however, I am told that my view is wrong, that atonal music, for example, is a commentary upon modern life, a way of grasping and understanding the quality of modern civilization, then I am forced to remove myself with my own axioms and to leave my dissenter with his. He will tell me, "Of course you reject atonal music; you insist on *enjoying* it, while I am showing you that it must interpret contemporary life for you." Our conversation founders on incompatible axioms for which there is no court of appeal.

It founders too when the professional musician claims that music exists primarily in order to further music—that music is an exploration of the endless possibilities of producing sounds, and as such is sufficient unto itself. This person considers the end of music achieved if he hears a new electronic sound-producer or if he creates a timbre never before heard by human ears. He might classify one of his products as irritating and another as gentle, but the two are equally successful in his mind. More: he strives as hard to obtain "intolerable" sounds as any other kind. The pleasure he creates in his listeners is defined most properly as a sense of satisfaction in invention: invention of sounds, combinations of sounds, and organizing principles for sounds. It is, in short, a professional's pleasure in the tools of his profession.

Two other avenues are open: Morality and Hygiene. Here discourse becomes easier. Music can be thought of as an aid to fervor in battle or success in love; its mission might be to assuage hatred and promote sympathy, to further digestion, or to tranquilize workers in a business office. Its therapeutic usefulness to the nervous may be stressed. Platonic warnings against seductive musical modes can be countered with case histories of recuperation under the influence of melody.

Those who subscribe to any of the moral or hygienic possibilities of music will agree that music "stirs our emotions," but for them stirring our emotions is never the end of the road. What is the good, they ask, of having our emotions stirred? Does the stirring make us better men, saner men, healthier men, or happier men? This is the real question.

The answer is yes: perhaps all of these together. And perhaps the expression "refreshing our spirits" amiably includes them all. If so, I would suggest that music cannot make us better, saner, or healthier unless it has first given us pleasure. Neither my digestion nor my humanity will be helped if I am actively hating what I hear. The pathway runs from the sounds of the instruments to our ears, thence to the stirring of emotions on the pleasurable side of the cerebral fence, and then finally, if at all, to moral or physical "refreshment." My own inclination is to call moral or physical amelioration an optional end (that is to say, music *can* do these things) and to insist that the only obligatory end is to give pleasure. For I can easily conceive of music that gives intense pleasure to a cheat, a terminal patient, or a psychotic, without mending any of them. Yet they will unhesitatingly call such music good. Fortunately, this particular doctrinal difference does not mean a parting of the ways. I do not care whether giving pleasure is the rigorously necessary means or the end itself. It is understood that if music fails to give sensuous delight, it will also fail to make us better, saner, or healthier.

III

The thorns become sharper as soon as we ask, Sensuous delight for whom? Artists are often irrational creatures. We hear them over and over again complaining about the lack of communication in our society; but the next moment they blithely recommend self-expression as the only genuine purpose of art. "I write to please myself." "I paint what I need to paint." "I compose in order to express my inner needs." Alas, there are as many platitudes for intellectuals in every age as there are saws for simple-minded burghers, and a young person can rise from the ranks of the average and take his place in the herd of the intellectual elite by means of a sincere exchange of commonplaces. From saying "I write in order to make lots of money," he ascends to "I write in order to obey an inner necessity."

Composers are not behindhand with these claims. "I do but sing because I must" is a favorite among them. And, like artists everywhere today, they leap easily from the idea that artistic creation arises from an inner need to express oneself to the notion that once the self has been expressed, the work of art is a success. This is in its way a fine notion. It admits no rebuttal. If the primary aim of a musical composition is to give satisfaction to its composer, all is well: thousands upon thousands of musical scores succeed every year; the world is rolling in masterpieces.

I take polite leave of the school of self-expression and turn to those who affirm as an axiomatic point that a piece of music must please "the public." But what public is "the public"? Let me cautiously accept the traditional distinction among three possible audiences. I know the drawbacks of these divisions and categories; reality keeps refuting them; reality insists on its own ambiguities. Yet reality does come in clusters, and I think we catch certain genuine clusters if we speak of (i) an audience of specialists (composers, performers, teachers, students, scholars, critics, and a few highly trained amateurs), (ii) a general educated audience with a taste for the arts, and (iii) the mass uneducated public whose aesthetic needs are satisfied by the jukebox.

Now if the aim of music is to satisfy the musicians themselves and a small band of believers at their side, we are almost as well off as under the axiom that music exists so that artists can express themselves, and we roundly declare this age of ours a great age of music. Dissonant music pleases not only each sound-maker by himself, it is also applauded by friends and allies. This music thrives especially in academic circles, where dissidence from intellectual commonplaces is quickly tamed by means of the well-placed snicker. Programs devoted exclusively to dissonant music are presented to small audiences of followers at infrequent intervals. Then again these refractory pieces are literally forced upon the general public by performers and conductors who feel that in good conscience they ought to promote the music of contemporary composers. Carefully cushioned by Mozart on one side of the program and Beethoven on the other, a grim little noise computed by Webern can dare scratch at the audience before retreating again to the academic nest. As Joan Peyser herself bluntly states: "The composer is alienated from his audience." But not from his audience of fellow technicians.

This is where I become uneasy. I cannot think of another period in history in which the primary aim of music—the music composed by nearly all the serious artists of a given time—was to please the musical group itself. Is this aim satisfactory? To whom? And why? Or is this one more instance of the "fragmentation" of our civilization? I am tempted to speak of sickness, of deterioration—somehow it would be better, I feel, if we all addressed each other, if a poet understood a physicist, if a chemist knew the secrets of convertible debentures, if a plumber could tell what makes his light bulb give light, and if a serious composer made music for himself, you and me, and congressmen from Indiana, all in one piece.

But these are axioms again. Once more the argument closes its doors. If Mr. Stockhausen were to tell me that he is perfectly satisfied with the audience he has—"let Puccini get the rest"—what could I say? Nothing. These considerations of "the health of civilization" are too distant. Who knows whether it is not a good thing that we should all be specialists in corners? Those of us who feel that dissonant music is an aberration must fall back on another axiom.

This axiom, of course, is that the primary aim of music is to delight a large audience of nonspecialists. There is nothing sacred about this axiom; nothing intrinsically superior to the axioms I have left behind. It is simply another yardstick. According to one yardstick, music is a success. According to another, it is a failure. Who decides which yardstick is the better one? Obviously the man who is doing the measuring. This leads me to the possibility of turning my axiom around. Instead of saying that the primary aim of music is to delight a large audience of nonspecialists, I can say, a little more humanely, that a great number of people who are not themselves musicians or critics *need* the pleasure of music, and *search* for it.

At this stage I dismiss the third audience I have mentioned: the mass audience. This audience is well served by contemporary music. It has the sweet violin music it needs for candlelight situations, it has trombone bands to dance by, it has crooners delivering simple love songs, it has the frenzies of acid rock for its orgiastic needs—in short, there is a vast supply of twentieth-century sound to delight the mass twentieth-century ear. One music in our time has satisfied the specialists, and another has satisfied the uneducated. There remains, in the vast middle, that class to which millions of us belong: the educated nonspecialists, to whom, *for sixty years*, fresh music has been denied.

I launch the exaggeration and then retreat from it—in order to recapture my ground and hold it. Stravinsky is practically a popular composer—through half a dozen of his works. Benjamin Britten, another moderate, has created intense beauty without lapsing into Victorian romanticism. Certain highly expressive works, like Bartók's quartets, which still play off discord against concord, attract the sophisticated wing of my second public. Besides, my argument concerns the Western world; it does not touch Soviet composers, who are not at liberty to manufacture any sounds they please and to express their "alienation." I could hedge, border, and clip in this vein for several pages. But when all the qualifying is done, the large truths stand unaltered: thoroughgoing dissonance dominates the field of "serious" music; all other styles are on the defensive; and thoroughgoing dissonance, according to the confession or the boast of our composers themselves, has been repelling the general public for the entire sixty-odd years of its existence.

IV

The claim that the future will love cacophony (or will no longer call it that) is beginning to sound as funny as the warnings of hopeful Christians, these two thousand years, that the end of the world is at hand. "In a few decades," Schönberg wrote a few decades ago, "audiences will recognize the *tonality* of this music today called atonal. . . . Atonal is what will be understood in the future." For Miss Peyser, this stale prophecy still has charm. "In time," she writes, "the strangeness will fade and men will embrace the great works that will appear." But in what time, may we ask? In the twentieth century sixty years is an epoch. Time is becoming more and more compressed; that is to say, more and more events are occurring in any given time span. Therefore, when we are told again and again that eventually dissonant music will seem normal, beautiful, inspiring, or what have you, we may be excused, we denizens of the twentieth century, for turning our backs at last.

Beethoven was a revolutionary composer; Wagner was a revolutionary composer; Debussy was a revolutionary composer. But did it take these men sixty years to persuade the educated thousands or millions? By no means. In their much slower times, they converted their thousands and millions in a decade or less. Dissonant composers clearly staged a revolution of a different order. They demolished the socioaesthetic foundations of art. From the revolutionary summons of a new music for society—which had given society Beethoven, Wagner, Debussy—they proceeded to organize a music *outside* of society. I do not assert that they intended this exit. But depart from society they did. And I add: any composer who dislikes the huddle of composers outdoors in exile must be ready as a rational being to declare the experiment of dissonance bankrupt.

This bankruptcy is clearest in the realm of vocal music. Since Puccini died in 1924, not a single opera has imposed itself as a permanent and reliable piece in the world's repertory. In agony are the mass, the oratorio, and the serious song. Instrumental music may hobble forward on its crutches without beauty, but the human voice clambering cheerlessly from sound to sound, forbidden on pain of death by ridicule to utter a melody, has absolutely nowhere to go. It seems never to occur to our experts and professionals that history offers no precedent for an entire epoch unable or unwilling to furnish singable music to the educated public. Nor that this fact is astounding. Nor that it proves that music is sick.

For the specialist it is not sick at all, I repeat. He and his friends in the trade congratulate themselves and one another in journals, congresses, at concerts, and in their correspondence on the unbelievable technical prowesses that have eliminated vulgar melodic expressiveness, that is to say, beauty. It is not sick for the masses, who go to their own sources; it is sick only for the millions who are the equivalent today of the audience in Prague that Mozart intoxicated with *Don Giovanni*. An entire age without serious music for itself! An entire age that must choose between the primitive structures of proletarian music and the utterly joyless constructions of specialists.

V

Music is the only bankrupt art. In the days when composers began killing beauty in music, painters and sculptors were scrapping the art of imitating beautiful nature. Everyone is agreed that this simultaneity was not a coincidence. A universal renovation of the arts was taking place, itself a portion of an even vaster movement of civilization into new areas of knowing, feeling, and judging. But when the same yardstick I have proposed for music is applied to the visual arts, the results are brutally different. In the visual arts, the time lag was no more and no less than what is to be expected. Nonrepresentational art, cubism, surrealism—the various modalities of the new age— all produced shock and outrage, and then were promptly integrated into the general sensibility. Today the same crowds that flock to their Philharmonic Halls to hear Beethoven's Seventh are interested and even avid supporters of contemporary artists, beginning of course with Picasso: not, I insist, five or six works by Picasso (as they will listen to five or six works by Stravinsky) but all of Picasso, down to his napkin doodles. Moreover, the same people who would not dream of buying a Boulez recording decorate their rooms with nonfigurative pictures. Very simply, the visual artists have succeeded, the composers have failed. If the composers assert, and many of them do, that the general public is benighted, they had better explain why this same public accepts modern painting.

But there is more. Another sign of success for the visual arts is that they have percolated down to the masses. I do not mean that in their popular forms they are at their best; this is not the point. The point is that an idiom meaningful to the large educated public of any given generation will inevitably influence the taste of the masses as well. Modern visualization is everywhere: the advertiser uses it; it appears in the work of church, bank, office, or restaurant decorators; it dominates the design of useful objects like airplanes, coffeepots, and chairs. Visual art lives; it speaks to the educated and the uneducated; it flows gracefully and normally from sophisticated specialist to naive layman. We do not have to say that "in time the strangeness will fade and men will embrace the great works that will appear." Let the future take care of itself. The visual artists and designers of our time have won their own time.

The failure of dissonant music to reach the popular consciousness, even in a debased and vulgarized form, is a remarkable symptom. One would expect that something of Alban Berg would have penetrated at least the music of the Beatles and their innumerable successors, whose appeal is to the supposedly sophisticated young. But not only is atonal music inaudible in the advertising jingle, in piped elevator music, and in dance music, it has not touched the folksingers who perform for undergraduates at Berkeley, or hairy quartets that pummel masses of young listeners into states of frenzy. They make odd sounds on odd instruments, to be sure; they use electronic equipment side by side with the academic composers; but their music is as lusciously harmonic and melodic as music can be; their effects are expressive and gorgeous. Are they forming the audience of the future that will applaud great atonal works? Far from it.

If we could raise a few hundred newborn infants in isolation from traditional classical music and contemporary popular music, and expose them to nothing but dissonant works, we would discover whether our revulsion is a judgment we make as prisoners of our culture or a result of basic physiological "lesions." But this we cannot do. Inevitably, our children hear the latest pop tune or Mozart. Obstinately, they grow up preferring either or both to dissonant music. I see no indication that the children of our grandchildren will make a different choice.

VI

Why has music failed, when the other arts have succeeded? Why have three generations of music lovers been compelled to turn for nearly all their musical experience to works of the past? It is hard to believe that the public has taken a mysterious plunge from the level of taste at which it operated in the days when, after certain difficulties, it managed to follow Beethoven or Wagner. Public taste has not degenerated with respect to the visual arts, and no one can show that it has collapsed vis-á-vis music. Music is "out in the cold" not because the house fell down on it, but because it vacated the house.

But why? The question is still unanswered. It is not enough to accuse modern composers of having deliberately declared war on humanity—of having invented poisonous sound combinations and sound sequences for the express purpose of pestering society. To be sure, in part they joined with other artists in the ever-enjoyable game of baiting-the-babbitt. But mostly they stumbled into a way by accident.

One explanation for this accident is to be found in the unequal vulnerability of our sight and hearing. Let me offer a simple example. We are more easily offended and hurt by a bawled or strident radio commercial than by a stupid advertising display in a newspaper. "At least the picture doesn't make noise!" Our hearing is more readily irritated than our sight, just as our sense of smell is more easily offended than either. It takes an extreme explosion of light to hurt us, whereas sound disturbs us all the time. There is no visual counterpart, for example, to the physical misery we feel when a knife is scraped against a plate. In sum, our sensory territory seems to have areas of tolerance of varying magnitudes. Because the area of tolerable sound experiences is relatively small, experiments in music reached and then crossed the boundary far more rapidly than parallel experiments in the visual arts.

I do not doubt that training or exposure can affect the extent and the precise contour of these areas of tolerance. But can they be stretched indefinitely? Partisans of dissonant music like Miss Peyser believe that time, training, and exposure will colonize new ground. A new generation will respond to Stockhausen and Boulez as we, laggards, adore Bach. However, two new generations have refused to budge, and Webern is still performed—sixty years later!—as "avant-garde music." I submit that our composers strayed into an area of aesthetic intolerance that will never be colonized—either, as I firmly believe, because this music inflicts physiological lesions on the human brain, or because it is kept at bay by the unavoidable presence and damaging otherness of traditional "beautiful sounds."

Those who like to speak of "the wonderful capacity of the human ear to adapt to new conditions"—I am quoting Professor Joseph Machlis—overestimate this capacity. The areas of tolerance do expand, contract, or simply alter in individuals and societies; and it is true that sounds which scraped at our nerves at one time may appear beautiful a year or a decade later. But to turn this limited flexibility and adaptability into a principle of infinite plasticity is mere recklessness.

How then is it that the first audience I have described—the audience of disciples and specialists—does exist, and does renew itself year after year? Are we dealing with special beings endowed by heredity with areas of tolerance distinct from our own? And if not, why can we not join this audience where it lives?

In the first place, we must keep in mind that an impassable gulf exists between this first audience and ourselves with regard to the aim of music itself. Much of this audience has lost interest in sensuous delight, in "refreshing the spirit," in beauty. Much of this audience, as I have noted earlier, is interested chiefly in refining the tools of the musical profession. Hence the complacency of this group, and its undeniable success. Success, that is, on the basis of an axiom which does not interest the second audience. Still, a few members of this audience will firmly state that atonal music, for example, is "beautiful." *They* experience none of the lesions I so mysteriously allude to; *they* feel the sensuous rapture that others feel in the presence of Bach. To those in this group whose training and exposure are no different in their essentials from ours, I reply that strong variations in the areas of tolerance—or, in other words, the physiology of beauty—do exist; that in sensing beauty in dissonant music they happen to lie at the far end of the curve; and that sixty years of dissonance have failed to move the center of that curve in any perceptible way.

To those in this group who claim that only extremes of training and discipline can reveal the beauty of dissonance and its ability to "refresh our spirits," I reply that life is short, we can all be trained in but a few disciplines, and the artist, like the engineer or the doctor, must take us as we are. Anyone who writes music that can be considered beautiful only by an audience which has, in effect, duplicated the composer's training, condemns himself to solitude. Less than anyone else can he hope that dissonant music will some day seem beautiful to the general intelligentsia.

Those who genuinely sense beauty in dissonant music, whether by natural endowment or through rigorous training, resemble nothing so much as the Hindu fakir lying on a bed of nails. Whether by nature or nurture, he too has a special area of tolerance. He despises us, perhaps, for feeling that sharp nails are unpleasant. To him they are kind. He argues that we are fusty conservatives. He believes the future is with beds of nails. He invites us to train ourselves to enjoy them. "In a few decades," he says, "men will recognize the softness of nails that today are called sharp." But we refuse to credit him. We say that beds of nails will be unpleasant to most people forever; we doubt that even of those who did train themselves like the fakir, more than a few would get to enjoy a bed of nails; we say that even if the effort succeeded, it would not be worth the time and energy expended: for is he happier on his bed of nails than we are on our spring mattresses? And finally we admire in and through him the curious diversity of human powers and sensibilities.

All in all, therefore, I maintain that dissonant music has taken us outside the general area of human tolerance. Most of those who "appreciate" this music do so without regard to tolerance or intolerance (I mean beauty or ugliness) because they are interested in sound organization—in the tools of their profession. The others are the fakirs of music; they are not harbingers of a new sensibility, but eccentrics of perception.

VII

The line of reasoning that tries to integrate dissonant music, now or in the future, for the untrained or the trained, into a system of "beautiful sounds" is better abandoned altogether. Theory is on much firmer ground if it proposes instead that music joined the other arts at the beginning of this century in a vast and exhaustive exploitation of ugliness (in the sensuous arts) and evil (in literature). This is the mainstream of twentieth-century art as a whole. By this double exploitation more than anything else it is marked off from the art that preceded it. As late as the 1890's, when the art-for-art's-sake movement was breaking with so much of the past and announcing so much of the future, the cult of beauty was still intact. A first liberation from bourgeois morality had yet to be followed by a second liberation from the cult of beauty. All the arts joined hands to carry out this revolution.

It so happens that music could not afford to make this revolution succeed. For literature and representational art, the exploitation of ugliness and evil left intact their moral, psychological, and philosophical interests—interests upon which writers and representational artists draw heavily for the aesthetic pleasure they create in their audience. But music, we have seen, is not Interpretation of Life. Music does not know the world, it surpasses the world. A string quartet does not tell us whether God is alive or dead, or what to do about the generation gap. For music, giving up beauty means rashly stripping itself naked. It had nothing else to fall back on.

At this point the arguments I have offered combine. As we glance at contemporary painting and sculpture, whether abstract or figurative, we discover that the dismissal of Renaissance standards of beauty did not lead instantly to ugliness. It turned out, instead, that the entire tradition of Western art, long and glorious though it was, had failed to occupy all the areas of possible beauty. The beauty of streamlining—to take one simple example—had yet to be exploited when the twentieth century opened. It became clear that the area of visual tolerance (to use the minimal term) was far larger than expected. Virgin land was available—room for exploration in effects of beauty.

This room for exploration did not exist for music because here the area of tolerance was and is much smaller. Music fell out of traditional areas of beauty and immediately lapsed into ugliness. But painters and sculptors did more than explore new areas of beauty: they also explored ugliness and evil as never before. However, the *figurative* painters and sculptors who did so retained their grasp on the worlds of moral, psychological, historical, and metaphysical interest. These worlds were closed to music. Music flung itself into ugliness, but found nothing outside the sensuous experience to relieve it. The artistic revolution of the twentieth century, so fruitful to the other arts, had spun music out of its proper orbit.[1] Composers who thought they would educate society to a new sense of beauty failed because they required either an aberrant physiological toleration or a peculiar discipline. Only those who aspired to confine their music to a minute public of professionals and disciples achieved the goal they had set for themselves and must therefore be called successful on their own axiomatic terms.

We who work from another axiom do not dismiss the ideals of these hermetic artists laboring for the few, or for themselves alone. Happy is the culture that can offer itself the luxury of art for all classes, including a class that savors esoterica. But here we see hermeticism excluding all else; dissonance monopolizing the field of serious music; an avant-garde, in short, without a main body in sight.

Every scientist knows that a hypothesis which refuses to work ought to be replaced by another one. The hypothesis of dissonance—it is fair to call it that—has refused to work for sixty years. It has refused to work, that is, for composers who have wanted to be, like Mozart and Beethoven, members of the general elite. If they are rational beings able to make fresh choices when old ones prove fruitless, they must now strike out in new directions. For let me assert as strongly as possible that I believe in change and in experiment, and that an arrest at the point reached by Brahms or Debussy or anyone else would simply have been another kind of death for music. But this does not mean that invention is good because it is invention, or that experiment is successful because it is experiment. In 1900 it was time for music, like the other arts, to move. By taking the same direction as the other arts, music happened to move into a climate refreshing for these others, but suffocating for itself.

What would have been the true direction, or what the true direction will be in the future, I do not even dream of knowing. If a composer eager to rejoin civilization were to ask my advice, I would underscore two points I have made: the first, that the sense of beauty is not quite as flexible a faculty as many think; and the second, that ugliness, like pepper, is an excellent condiment, but a wretched meal. I will not change history if I declare that for

---

[1] Along with nonrepresentational painting that confined itself to the exploitation of ugliness. I discussed the catastrophe of ugly abstract visual art in the *Columbia Forum* in 1965. Ugly abstract art and ugly music are the two cripples of our culture.

me, works like Benjamin Britten's *Rape of Lucrece* and *Les Illuminations* seem not only masterpieces in themselves but also sufficient explorations beyond Romantic territory. Perhaps this is the destined avenue; perhaps Britten is a dead end. Perhaps the solution will come from the world of electronics; perhaps from entirely unsuspected quarters. Perhaps there will be no solution at all. Every civilization has its obsessive failures.

For us, the large audience of men and women who are not, when all is said, hopeless cretins, a few contemporary works remain to be cherished, and the past keeps our spirits refreshed. Thank God for the past! For imagine the horror if all the sounds created before Schönberg suddenly disappeared and we were reduced to nothing but "avant-garde" music. Strong men would begin to rave in the streets. And yet every age but our own seems to have been cozy with its own music. Nineteenth-century music lovers felt little need to hear eighteenth-century scores; eighteenth-century music lovers lived peacefully with a minimum of Renaissance music; and so on down to the remotest past. Any generation of the past could have survived exclusively on its own music. Only for us is the past a life-need of the present.

Bereft of all that beauty, who would find comfort in the idea, even if he were simple enough to believe it, that sometime in the future the melodic fragments, the strident polychords, the atonalities that make his flesh crawl today will appear canorous? Even the Stockhausens and the Boulezes might take fright at their own noises. Perhaps it would occur to us that the cacophonists could afford to "realize musical structures" in their laboratories because they had the old masters to cover for them. They could say, "Beauty? That was taken care of long ago. Listen to Vivaldi. We have moved on to something else."

But there is nothing else.

Suggestions for Discussion

1. Why does Mandel settle on the term *dissonant?* Why is he unwilling to employ a coined word like *malsonant?*

2. What does Mandel consider the aim of music? How does this aim (or other aims he mentions) relate to his attack on dissonant music?

3. What important distinction does Mandel make between music on the one hand and visual art on the other? Is this a distinction with which you can agree?

4. What is Mandel's response to the assertion that music exists to interpret contemporary life, or to further music itself, or for moral or hygienic purposes? How does he dispose of such arguments?

5. Why does Mandel believe that music must please the public? How does he define *public?* Why does he confine his argument to the second group which makes up the term?

6. Mandel declares "the experiment of dissonance bankrupt." Explain. Why does he believe that music has failed?

7. Mandel says that "every age but our own seems to have been cozy with its own music." Relate this statement to his argument.

8. This essay is divided into seven parts. Explain the relation of the argument to each part.

Suggestions for Writing

1. People in the *second public* Mandel refers to don't seem to care for the music of either the *first* or the *third public*. Write an essay in which you explain the value or assert the worthlessness of "pop" music.

2. Assume that Mandel is wrong in his argument against atonal music. Write an essay defending atonal music as an important part of modern life. You should refer to specific composers and their work.

3. Write an essay in which you develop Mandel's statements about the success of modern painting. Do you agree with him? If not explain your position. Whether you agree or not, use specific examples of modern art to make your point. Are there examples of modern art which you might compare to atonal music—that is, bankrupt?

Anne Tyler

Still Just Writing

Anne Tyler (b. 1941) won creative writing awards while majoring in Russian at Duke, where she received her degree at 19. She went on to graduate study in Russian, worked as a librarian, and published her first novel at 22. She has published forty short stories situated in the contemporary South and seven novels, including *Searching for Caleb* (1975), *Earthly Possessions* (1977), and *The Dinner at Homesick Restaurant* (1982). This essay, published in 1980 in *The Writer and Her Work,* explains with understated wit how she has managed at the same time to be a successful writer, wife, and mother of two daughters.

While I was painting the downstairs hall I thought of a novel to write. Really I just thought of a character; he more or less wandered into my mind, wearing a beard and a broad-brimmed leather hat. I figured that if I sat down and organized this character on paper, a novel would grow up around him. But it was March and the children's spring vacation began the next day, so I waited.

After spring vacation the children went back to school, but the dog got worms. It was a little complicated at the vet's and I lost a day. By then it was Thursday; Friday is the only day I can buy the groceries, pick up new cedar chips for the gerbils, scrub the bathrooms. I waited till Monday. Still, that left me four good weeks in April to block out the novel.

By May I was ready to start actually writing, but I had to do it in patches. There was the follow-up treatment at the vet, and then a half-day spent trailing the dog with a specimen tin so the lab could be sure the treatment had really worked. There were visits from the washing machine repairman and the Davey tree man, not to mention briefer interruptions by the meter reader, five Jehovah's Witnesses, and two Mormons. People telephoned wanting to sell me permanent light bulbs and waterproof basements. An Iranian cousin of my husband's had a baby; the cousin's uncle died; then the cousin's mother decided to go home to Iran and needed to know where to buy a black American coat before she left. There *are* no black American coats; don't Americans wear mourning? I told her no, but I checked around at all the department stores anyway because she didn't speak English. Then I wrote chapters one and two. I had planned to work till 3:30 every day, but it was a month of early quittings: once for the children's dental appointment, once for the cat's rabies shot, once for our older daughter's orthopedist, and twice for her gymnastic meets. Sitting on the bleachers in the school gymnasium, I told myself I could always use this in a novel someplace, but I couldn't really picture writing a novel about 20 little girls in leotards trying to walk the length of a wooden beam without falling off. By the time I'd written chapter three, it was Memorial Day and the children were home again.

Characters on Hold

I knew I shouldn't expect anything from June. School was finished then and camp hadn't yet begun. I put the novel away. I closed down my mind and planted some herbs and played cribbage with the children. Then on the 25th, we drove one child to a sleepaway camp in Virginia and entered the other in a day camp, and I was ready to start work again. First I had to take my car in for repairs and the mechanics lost it, but I didn't get diverted. I sat in the garage on a folding chair while they hunted my car all one afternoon, and I hummed a calming tune and tried to remember what I'd planned to do next in my novel. Or even what the novel was about, for that matter. My character wandered in again in his beard and his broad-brimmed hat. He looked a little pale and knuckly, like someone scrabbling at a cliff edge so as not to fall away entirely.

I had high hopes for July, but it began with a four-day weekend, and on Monday night we had a long-distance call from our daughter's camp in Virginia. She was seriously ill in a Charlottesville hospital. We left our youngest with friends and drove three hours in a torrent of rain. We found our daughter frightened and crying, and another child (the only other child I knew in all of Virginia) equally frightened and crying down in the emergency room with possible appendicitis, so I spent that night alternating between a chair in the pediatraic wing and a chair in the emergency room. By morning, it had begun to seem that our daughter's illness was typhoid fever. We loaded her into the car and took her back to Baltimore, where her doctor put her on drugs and prescribed a long bed-rest. She lay in bed six days, looking wretched and calling for fluids and cold cloths. On the seventh day she got up her same old healthy self, and the illness was declared to be not typhoid fever after all but a simple virus, and we shipped her back to Virginia on the evening train. The next day I was free to start writing again but sat, instead, on the couch in my study, staring blankly at the wall.

Part-time Creativity

I could draw some conclusions here about the effect that being a woman/wife/mother has upon my writing, except that I am married to a writer who is also a man/husband/father. He published his first novel while he was a medical student in Iran; then he came to America to finish his training. His writing fell by the wayside, for a long while. You can't be on call in the emergency room for 20 hours and write a novel during the other four. Now he's a child psychiatrist, fulltime, and he writes his novels in the odd moments here and there—when he's not preparing a lecture, when he's not on the phone with a patient, when he's not attending classes at the psychoanalytic institute. He writes in Persian, still, in those black-and-white speckled composition books. Sometimes one of the children will interrupt him in English and he will answer in Persian, and they'll say, "What?" and he'll look up blankly, and it seems a sheet has to fall from in front of his eyes before he remembers where he is and switches to English. Often, I wonder what he would be doing now if he didn't have a family to support. He cares deeply about his writing and he's very good at it, but every morning at 5:30 he gets up and puts on a suit and tie and drives in the dark to the hospital. Both of us, in different ways, seem to be hewing our creative time in small, hard chips from our living time.

Drained and Drawn

Occasionally, I take a day off. I go to a friend's house for lunch, or weed the garden, or rearrange the linen closet. I notice that at the end of one of these days, when my husband asks me what I've been doing, I tend to exaggerate any hardships I may have encountered. ("A pickup nearly sideswiped me on Greenspring Avenue. I stood in line an hour just trying to buy the children some flip-flops.") It seems sinful to have lounged around so. Also, it seems sinful that I have more choice than my husband as to whether or not to undertake any given piece of work. I can refuse to do an article if it doesn't appeal to me, refuse to change a short story, refuse to hurry a book any faster than it wants to go—all luxuries. My husband, on the other hand, is forced to rise and go off to that hospital every blessed weekday of his life. *His* luxury is that no one expects him to drop all else for two weeks when a child has chicken pox. The only person who has no luxuries at all, it seems to me, is the woman writer who is the sole support of her children. I often think about how she must manage. I think that if I were in that position, I'd have to find a job involving manual labor. I have spent so long erecting partitions around the part of me that writes—learning how to close the door on it when ordinary life intervenes, how to close the door on ordinary life when it's time to start writing again—that I'm not sure I could fit the two parts of me back together now.

Before we had children I worked in a library. It was a boring job, but I tend to like doing boring things. I would sit on a stool alphabetizing Russian catalogue cards and listening to the other librarians talking around me. It made me think of my adolescence, which was spent listening to the tobacco stringers while I handled tobacco. At night I'd go home from the library and write. I never wrote what the librarians said, exactly, but having those voices in my ears all day helped me summon up my own characters' voices. Then our first baby came along—an insomniac. I quit work and stayed home all day with her and walked her all night. Even if I had found the time to write, I wouldn't have had the insides. I felt drained; too much care and feeling were being drawn out of me. And the only voices I heard now were by appointment—people who came to dinner, or invited us to dinner, and who therefore felt they had to make deliberate conversation. That's one thing writers never have, and I still miss it: the easy-going, on-again-off-again, gossipy murmurs of people working alongside each other all day.

Free and Useful

I enjoyed tending infants (though I've much preferred the later ages), but it was hard to be solely, continually in their company and not to be able to write. And I couldn't think of any alternative. I know it must be possible to have a child raised beautifully by a housekeeper, but every such child I've run into has seemed dulled and doesn't use words well. So I figured I'd better stick it out. As it happened, it wasn't that long—five years, from the time our first daughter was born till our second started nursery school and left me with my mornings free. But while I was going through it I thought it would be a lot longer. I couldn't imagine any end to it. I felt that everything I wanted to write was somehow coagulating in my veins and making me fidgety and slow. Then after a while I didn't have anything to write anyhow, but I still had the fidgets. I felt useless, no matter how many diapers I washed or strollers I pushed. The only way I could explain my life to myself was to imagine that I was living in a very small commune. I had spent my childhood in a commune, or what would nowadays be called a commune, and I was used to the idea of division of labor. What we had here, I told myself, was a perfectly sensible arrangement: One member was the liaison with the outside world, bringing in money; another was the caretaker, reading the Little Bear books to the children and repairing the electrical switches. This second member might have less physical freedom, but she had much more freedom to arrange her own work schedule. I must have sat down a dozen times a week and very carefully, consciously thought it all through. Often, I was merely trying to convince myself that I really did pull my own weight.

Strung Up

This Iranian cousin who just had the baby: She sits home now and cries a lot. She was working on her master's degree and is used to being out in the world more. "Never mind," I tell her, "you'll soon be out again. This stage doesn't last long."

"How long?" she asks.

"Oh . . . three years, if you just have the one."

"Three years!"

I can see she's appalled. Her baby is beautiful, very dark and Persian; and what's more, he sleeps—something I've rarely seen a baby do. What I'm trying to say to her (but of course, she'll agree without really hearing me) is that he's worth it. It seems to me that since I've had children, I've grown richer and deeper. They may have slowed down my writing for a while, but when I did write, I had more of a self to speak from. After all, who else in the world do you *have* to love, no matter what? Who else can you absolutely not give up on? My life seems more intricate. Also more dangerous.

After the children started school, I put up the partitions in my mind. I would rush around in the morning braiding their hair, packing their lunches; then the second they were gone I would grow quiet and climb the stairs to my study. Sometimes a child would come home early and I would feel a little tug between the two parts of me; I'd be absent-minded and short-tempered. Then gradually I learned to make the transition more easily. It feels like a sort of string that I tell myself to loosen. When the children come home, I drop the string and close the study door and that's the end of it. It doesn't always work perfectly, of course. There are times when it doesn't work at all: If a child is sick, for instance, I can't possibly drop the children's end of the string, and I've learned not to try. It's easier just to stop writing for a while. Or if they're home but otherwise occupied, I no longer attempt to sneak off to my study to finish that one last page; I know that instantly, as if by magic, assorted little people will be pounding on my door requiring Band-Aids, tetanus shots, and a complete summation of the facts of life.

Last spring, I bought a midget tape recorder to make notes on. I'd noticed that my best ideas came while I was running the vacuum cleaner, but I was always losing them. I thought this little recorder would help. I carried it around in my shirt pocket. But I was ignoring the partitions, is what it was; I was letting one half of my life intrude upon the other. A child would be talking about her day at school and suddenly I'd whip out the tape recorder and tell it, "Get Morgan out of that cocktail party; he's not the type to drink." "Huh?" the child would say. Both halves began to seem ludicrous, unsynchronized. I took the recorder back to Radio Shack.

Faith and Adaptation

A few years ago, my parents went to the Gaza Strip to work for the American Friends Service Committee. It was a lifelong dream of my father's to do something with the AFSC as soon as all his children were grown, and he'd been actively preparing for it for years. But almost as soon as they got there, my mother fell ill with a mysterious fever that neither the Arab nor the Israeli hospitals could diagnose. My parents had to come home for her treatment, and since they'd sublet their house in North Carolina, they had to live with us. For four months, they stayed here—but only on a week-to-week basis, not knowing when they were going back, or whether they were going back at all, or how serious my mother's illness was. It was hard for her, of course, but it should have been especially hard in another way for my father, who had simply to hang in suspended animation for four months while my mother was whisked in and out of hospitals. However, I believe he was as pleased with life as he always is. He whistled Mozart and puttered around insulating our windows. He went on long walks collecting firewood. He strolled over to the meetinghouse and gave a talk on the plight of the Arab refugees. "Now that we seem to have a little time," he told my mother, "why not visit the boys?" and during one of her outpatient periods he took her on a gigantic cross-country trip to see all my brothers and any other relatives they happened upon. Then my mother decided she ought to go to a faith healer. (She wouldn't usually do such a thing, but she was desperate.) "Oh. Okay," my father said, and he took her to a faith healer, whistling all the way. And when the faith healer didn't work, my mother said, "I think this is psychosomatic. Let's go back to Gaza." My father said, "Okay," and reserved two seats on the next plane over. The children and I went to see them the following summer: My mother's fever was utterly gone, and my father drove us down the Strip, weaving a little Renault among the tents and camels, cheerfully whistling Mozart.

I hold this entire, rambling set of events in my head at all times, and remind myself of it almost daily. It seems to me that the way my father lives (infinitely adapting, and looking around him with a smile to say, "Oh! So *this* is where I am!") is also the way to slip gracefully through a choppy life of writing novels, plastering the dining room ceiling, and presiding at slumber parties. I have learned, bit by bit, to accept a school snow-closing as an unexpected holiday, an excuse to play 17 rounds of Parcheesi instead of typing up a short story. When there's a midweek visitation of uncles from Iran (hordes of great, bald, yellow men calling for their glasses of tea, sleeping on guest beds, couches, two armchairs pushed together, and discarded crib mattresses), I have decided that I might as well listen to what they have to say, and work on my novel tomorrow instead. I smile at the uncles out of a kind of clear, swept space inside me. What this takes, of course, is a sense of limitless time, but I'm getting that. My life is beginning to seem unusually long. And there's a danger to it: I could wind up as passive as a piece of wood on a wave. But I try to walk a middle line.

Wait for Heaven

I was standing in the schoolyard waiting for a child when another mother came up to me. "Have you found work yet?" she asked. "Or are you still just writing?"

Now, how am I supposed to answer that?

I could take offense, come to think of it. Maybe the reason I didn't is that I halfway share her attitude. They're *paying* me for this? For just writing down untruthful stories? I'd better look around for more permanent employment. For I do consider writing to be a finite job. I expect that any day now, I will have said all I have to say; I'll have used up all my characters, and then I'll be free to get on with my real life. When I make a note of new ideas on index cards, I imagine I'm clearing out my head, and that soon it will be empty and spacious. I file the cards in a little blue box, and I can picture myself using the final card one day—ah! through at last!—and throwing the blue box away. I'm like a dentist who continually fights tooth decay, working toward the time when he's conquered it altogether and done himself out of a job. But my head keeps loading up again; the little blue box stays crowded and messy. Even when I feel I have no ideas at all, and can't possibly start the next chapter, I have a sense of something still bottled in me, trying to get out.

People have always seemed funny and strange to me, and touching in unexpected ways. I can't shake off a sort of mist of irony that hangs over whatever I see. Probably that's what I'm trying to put across when I write; I may believe that I'm the one person who holds this view of things. And I'm always hurt when a reader says that I choose only bizarre or eccentric people to write about. It's not a matter of choice; it just seems to me that even the most ordinary person, in real life, will turn out to have something unusual at his center. I like to think that I might meet up with one of my past characters at the very next street corner. The odd thing is, sometimes I have. And if I were remotely religious, I'd believe that a little gathering of my characters would be waiting for me in heaven when I died. "*Then* what happened?" I'd ask them. "How have things worked out, since the last time I saw you?"

Eudora's Legacy

I think I was born with the impression that what happened in books was much more reasonable, and interesting, and *real,* in some ways, than what happened in life. I hated childhood, and spent it sitting behind a book waiting for adulthood to arrive. When I ran out of books I made up my own. At night, when I couldn't sleep, I made up stories in the dark. Most of my plots involved girls going west in covered wagons. I was truly furious that I'd been born too late to go west in a covered wagon.

I know a poet who says that in order to be a writer, you have to have had rheumatic fever in your childhood. I've never had rheumatic fever, but I believe that any kind of setting-apart situation will do as well. In my case, it was emerging from that commune—really an experimental Quaker community in the wilderness—and trying to fit into the outside world. I was eleven. I had never used a telephone and could strike a match on the soles of my bare feet. All the children in my new school looked very peculiar to me, and I certainly must have looked peculiar to them. I am still surprised, to this day, to find myself where I am. My life is so streamlined and full of modern conveniences. How did I get here? I have given up hope, by now, of ever losing my sense of distance; in fact, I seem to have come to cherish it. Neither I nor any of my brothers can stand being out among a crowd of people for any length of time at all.

I spent my adolescence planning to be an artist, not a writer. After all, books had to be about major events, and none had ever happened to me. All I knew were tobacco workers, stringing the leaves I handed them and talking up a storm. Then I found a book of Eudora Welty's short stories in the high school library. She was writing about Edna Earle, who was so slow-witted she could sit all day just pondering how the tail of the *C* got through the loop of the *L* on the Coca-Cola sign. Why, I knew Edna Earle. You mean you could *write* about such people? I have always meant to send Eudora Welty a thank-you note, but I imagine she would find it a little strange.

The Write of Passage

I wanted to go to Swarthmore College, but my parents suggested Duke instead, where I had a full scholarship, because my three brothers were coming along right behind me and it was more important for boys to get a good education than for girls. That was the first and last time that my being female was ever a serious issue. I still don't think it was just, but I can't say it ruined my life. After all, Duke had Reynolds Price, who turned out to be the only person I ever knew who could actually teach writing. It all worked out, in the end.

I believe that for many writers, the hardest time is that dead spot after college (where they're wonder-children, made much of) and before their first published work. Luckily, I didn't notice that part; I was so vague about what I wanted to do that I could hardly chafe at not yet doing it. I went to graduate school in Russian studies; I scrubbed decks on a boat in Maine; I got a job ordering books from the Soviet Union. Writing was something that crept in around the edges. For a while I lived in New York, where I became addicted to riding any kind of train or subway, and while I rode I often felt I was nothing but an enormous eye, taking things in and turning them over and sorting them out. But who would I tell them to, once I'd sorted them? I have never had more than three or four close friends, at any period of my life; and anyway, I don't talk well. I am the kind of person who wakes up at four in the morning and suddenly thinks of what she should have said yesterday at lunch. For me, writing something down was the only road out.

Rewarding Routines and Rituals

You would think, since I waited so long and so hopefully for adulthood, that it would prove to be a disappointment. Actually, I figure it was worth the wait. I like everything about it but the paperwork—the income tax and pro-testing the Sears bill and renewing the Triple-A membership. I always did count on having a husband and children, and here they are. I'm surprised to find myself a writer but have fitted it in fairly well, I think. The only real trouble that writing has ever brought me is an occasional sense of being invaded by the outside world. Why do people imagine that writers, having chosen the most private of professions, should be any good at performing in public, or should have the slightest desire to tell their secrets to interviewers from ladies' magazines? I feel I am only holding myself together by being extremely firm and decisive about what I will do and what I will not do. I will write my books and raise the children. Anything else just fritters me away. I know this makes me seem narrow, but in fact, I *am* narrow. I like routine and rituals and I hate leaving home; I have a sense of digging my heels in. I refuse to drive on freeways. I dread our annual vacation. Yet I'm continually prepared for travel: It is physically impossible for me to buy any necessity without buying a travel-sized version as well. I have a little toilet kit, with soap and a nightgown, forever packed and ready to go. How do you explain that?

As the outside world grows less dependable, I keep buttressing my inside world, where people go on meaning well and surprising other people with little touches of grace. There are days when I sink into my novel like a pool and emerge feeling blank and bemused and used up. Then I drift over to the schoolyard, and there's this mother wondering if I'm doing anything halfway useful yet. Am I working? Have I found a job? No, I tell her.

I'm still just writing.

Suggestions for Discussion

1. This essay is about a writer who is a woman, wife, and mother. Would a male writer have written a much different essay?

2. In what ways does the author keep her life compartmentalized? What advantages are there for her in doing so?

3. Anne Tyler writes about her difficulties objectively and without self-pity. What impact does this style of writing have?

4. Is this a formal or an informal essay? Explain your answer.

5. Explain the relevance of two incidents to the theme of the essay: her daughter's illness while at camp and her mother's illness which began on the Gaza strip.

6. Why does Tyler say she is not a good talker? In what way is the writer's job different from most others?

Suggestions for Writing

1. This essay explains a professional writer's methods of coping with the details of life from a woman's point of view. Write an essay showing how your gender shapes the way you meet your daily duties and imposes restraints on you.

2. Tyler presents her family as both loving and cohesive. Write an essay in which you explain how the love in this family is expressed. Is it supportive of the parents' lives?

Fiction
—◆◆◆◆—

Willa Cather
The Sculptor's Funeral

Willa Cather (1873–1947) was born in Virginia and grew up in Nebraska. On leaving the University of Nebraska, where as an undergraduate she had written for a Lincoln newspaper, she worked in Pittsburgh as a reporter and then as a teacher, and published her first collection of stories, *The Troll Garden* (1905). Her works include *My Antonia* (1918), *A Lost Lady* (1923), *The Professor's House* (1925), *Death Comes for the Archbishop* (1927), and *Sapphira and the Slave Girl* (1940), which dealt with her native Virginia. She celebrated the frontier spirit, whether of art or of action. However, in this story, she shows how small-town intolerance and demands for conformity are inimical to artistic impulses and creativity.

A group of the townspeople stood on the station siding of a little Kansas town, awaiting the coming of the night train, which was already twenty minutes overdue. The snow had fallen thick over everything; in the pale starlight the line of bluffs across the wide, white meadows south of the town made soft, smoke-coloured curves against the clear sky. The men on the siding stood first on one foot and then on the other, their hands thrust deep into their trousers pockets, their overcoats open, their shoulders screwed up with the cold; and they glanced from time to time toward the southeast, where the railroad track wound along the river shore. They conversed in low tones and moved about restlessly, seeming uncertain as to what was expected of them. There was but one of the company who looked as though he knew exactly why he was there; and he kept conspicuously apart; walking to the far end of the platform, returning to the station door, then pacing up the track again, his chin sunk in the high collar of his overcoat, his burly shoulders drooping forward, his gait heavy and dogged. Presently he was approached by a tall, spare, grizzled man clad in a faded Grand Army suit, who shuffled out from the group and advanced with a certain deference, craning his neck forward until his back made the angle of a jackknife three-quarters open.

"I reckon she's a-goin' to be pretty late agin tonight, Jim," he remarked in a squeaky falsetto. "S'pose it's the snow?"

"I don't know," responded the other man with a shade of annoyance, speaking from out an astonishing cataract of red beard that grew fiercely and thickly in all directions.

The spare man shifted the quill toothpick he was chewing to the other side of his mouth. "It ain't likely that anybody from the East will come with the corpse, I s'pose," he went on reflectively.

"I don't know," responded the other, more curtly than before.

"It's too bad he didn't belong to some lodge or other. I like an order funeral myself. They seem more appropriate for people of some repytation," the spare man continued, with an ingratiating concession in his shrill voice, as he carefully placed his toothpick in his vest pocket. He always carried the flag at the G.A.R. funerals in the town.

The heavy man turned on his heel, without replying, and walked up the siding. The spare man shuffled back to the uneasy group. "Jim's ez full ez a tick, ez ushel," he commented commiseratingly.

Just then a distant whistle sounded, and there was a shuffling of feet on the platform. A number of lanky boys of all ages appeared as suddenly and slimily as eels wakened by the crack of thunder; some came from the waiting-room, where they had been warming themselves by the red stove, or half asleep on the slat benches; others uncoiled themselves from baggage trucks or slid out of express wagons. Two clambered down from the driver's seat of a hearse that stood backed up against the siding. They straightened their stooping shoulders and lifted their heads, and a flash of momentary animation kindled their dull eyes at that cold, vibrant scream, the worldwide call for men. It stirred them like the note of a trumpet; just as it had often stirred the man who was coming home to-night, in his boyhood.

The night express shot, red as a rocket, from out the eastward marsh lands and wound along the river shore under the long lines of shivering poplars that sentineled the meadows, the escaping steam hanging in grey masses against the pale sky and blotting out the Milky Way. In a moment the red glare from the headlight streamed up the snow-covered track before the siding and glittered on the wet, black rails. The burly man with the dishevelled red beard walked swiftly up the platform toward the approaching train, uncovering his head as he went. The group of men behind him hesitated, glanced questioningly at one another, and awkwardly followed his example. The train stopped, and the crowd shuffled up to the express car just as the door was thrown open, the spare man in the G.A.R. suit thrusting his head forward with curiosity. The express messenger appeared in the doorway, accompanied by a young man in a long ulster and traveling cap.

"Are Mr. Merrick's friends here?" inquired the young man.

The group of the platform swayed and shuffled uneasily. Philip Phelps, the banker, responded with dignity: "We have come to take charge of the body. Mr. Merrick's father is very feeble and can't be about."

"Send the agent out here," growled the express messenger, "and tell the operator to lend a hand."

The coffin was got out of its rough box and down on the snowy platform. The townspeople drew back enough to make room for it and then formed a close semicircle about it, looking curiously at the palm leaf which lay across the black cover. No one said anything. The baggage man stood by his truck, waiting to get at the trunks. The engine panted heavily, and the fireman dodged in and out among the wheels with his yellow torch and long oilcan, snapping the spindle boxes. The young Bostonian, one of the dead sculptor's pupils who had come with the body, looked about him helplessly. He turned to the banker, the only one of that black, uneasy, stoop-shouldered group who seemed enough of an individual to be addressed.

"None of Mr. Merrick's brothers are here?" he asked uncertainly.

The man with the red beard for the first time stepped up and joined the group. "No, they have not come yet: the family is scattered. The body will be taken directly to the house." He stooped and took hold of one of the handles of the coffin.

"Take the long hill road up, Thompson, it will be easier on the horses," called the liveryman as the undertaker snapped the door of the hearse and prepared to mount to the driver's seat.

Laird, the red-bearded lawyer, turned again to the stranger: "We didn't know whether there would be any one with him or not," he explained. "It's a long walk, so you'd better go up in the hack." He pointed to a single battered conveyance, but the young man replied stiffly: "Thank you, but I think I will go up with the hearse. If you don't object," turning to the undertaker, "I'll ride with you."

They clambered up over the wheels and drove off in the starlight up the long, white hill toward the town. The lamps in the still village were shining from under the low, snow-burdened roofs; and beyond, on every side, the plains reached out into emptiness, peaceful and wide as the soft sky itself, and wrapped in a tangible, white silence.

When the hearse backed up to a wooden sidewalk before a naked, weather-beaten frame house, the same composite, ill-defined group that had stood upon the station siding was huddled about the gate. The front yard was an icy swamp, and a couple of warped planks, extending from the sidewalk to the door, made a sort of rickety footbridge. The gate hung on one hinge, and was opened wide with difficulty. Steavens, the young stranger, noticed that something black was tied to the knob of the front door.

The grating sound made by the casket, as it was drawn from the hearse, was answered by a scream from the house; the front door was wrenched open, and a tall, corpulent woman rushed out bareheaded into the snow and flung herself upon the coffin, shrieking: "My boy, my boy! And this is how you've come home to me!"

As Steavens turned away and closed his eyes with a shudder of unutterable repulsion, another woman, also tall, but flat and angular, dressed entirely in black, darted out of the house and caught Mrs. Merrick by the shoulders, crying sharply: "Come, come, mother; you mustn't go on like this!" Her tone changed to one of obsequious solemnity as she turned to the banker: "The parlour is ready, Mr. Phelps."

The bearers carried the coffin along the narrow boards, while the undertaker ran ahead with the coffin rests. They bore it into a large, unheated room that smelled of dampness and disuse and furniture polish, and set it down under a hanging lamp ornamented with jingling glass prisms and before a "Rogers group" of John Alden and Priscilla, wreathed with smilax. Henry Steavens stared about him with the sickening conviction that there had been

some horrible mistake, and that he had somehow arrived at the wrong destination. He looked painfully about over the clover-green Brussels, the fat
plush upholstery; among the hand-painted china plaques and panels, and
vases, for some mark of identification, for something that might once conceivably have belonged to Harvey Merrick. It was not until he recognized his
friend in the crayon portrait of a little boy in kilts and curls hanging above
the piano, that he felt willing to let any of these people approach the coffin.

"Take the lid off, Mr. Thompson; let me see my boy's face," wailed the
elderly woman between her sobs. This time Steavens looked fearfully, almost
beseechingly into her face, red and swollen under its masses of strong, black,
shiny hair. He flushed, dropped his eyes, and then, almost incredulously,
looked again. There was a kind of power about her face—a kind of brutal
handsomeness, even, but it was scarred and furrowed by violence, and so
coloured and coarsened by fiercer passions that grief seemed never to have
laid a gentle finger there. The long nose was distended and knobbed at the
end, and there were deep lines on either side of it; her heavy, black brows
almost met across her forehead, her teeth were large and square, and set far
apart—teeth that could tear. She filled the room; the men were obliterated,
seemed tossed about like twigs in an angry water, and even Steavens felt
himself being drawn into the whirlpool.

The daughter—the tall, raw-boned woman in crêpe, with a mourning comb
in her hair which curiously lengthened her long face—sat stiffly upon the sofa,
her hands, conspicuous for their large knuckles, folded in her lap, her mouth
and eyes drawn down, solemnly awaiting the opening of the coffin. Near the
door stood a mulatto woman, evidently a servant in the house, with a timid
bearing and an emaciated face pitifully sad and gentle. She was weeping silently, the corner of her calico apron lifted to her eyes, occasionally suppressing a long, quivering sob. Steavens walked over and stood beside her.

Feeble steps were heard on the stairs, and an old man, tall and frail, odorous of pipe smoke, with shaggy, unkempt grey hair and a dingy beard, tobacco stained about the mouth, entered uncertainly. He went slowly up to
the coffin and stood rolling a blue cotton handkerchief between his hands,
seeming so pained and embarrassed by his wife's orgy of grief that he had no
consciousness of anything else.

"There, there, Annie, dear, don't take on so," he quavered timidly, putting
out a shaking hand and awkwardly patting her elbow. She turned with a cry,
and sank upon his shoulder with such violence that he tottered a little. He
did not even glance toward the coffin, but continued to look at her with a
dull, frightened, appealing expression, as a spaniel looks at the whip. His
sunken cheeks slowly reddened and burned with miserable shame. When his
wife rushed from the room, her daughter strode after her with set lips. The
servant stole up to the coffin, bent over it for a moment, and then slipped
away to the kitchen, leaving Steavens, the lawyer, and the father to themselves. The old man stood trembling and looking down at his dead son's face.
The sculptor's splendid head seemed even more noble in its rigid stillness
than in life. The dark hair had crept down upon the wide forehead; the face
seemed strangely long, but in it there was not that beautiful and chaste repose
which we expect to find in the faces of the dead. The brows were so drawn
that there were two deep lines above the beaked nose, and the chin was
thrust forward defiantly. It was as though the strain of life had been so sharp

and bitter that death could not at once wholly relax the tension and smooth the countenance into perfect peace—as though he were still guarding something precious and holy, which might even yet be wrested from him.

The old man's lips were working under his stained beard. He turned to the lawyer with timid deference: "Phelps and the rest are comin' back to set up with Harve, ain't they?" he asked. "Thank 'ee, Jim, thank 'ee." He brushed the hair back gently from his son's forehead. "He was a good boy, Jim; always a good boy. He was ez gentle ez a child and the kindest of 'em all—only we didn't none of us ever onderstand him." The tears trickled slowly down his beard and dropped upon the sculptor's coat.

"Martin, Martin. Oh, Martin! come here," his wife wailed from the top of the stairs. The old man started timorously: "Yes, Annie, I'm coming." He turned away, hesitated, stood for a moment in miserable indecision; then reached back and patted the dead man's hair softly, and stumbled from the room.

"Poor old man, I didn't think he had any tears left. Seems as if his eyes would have gone dry long ago. At his age nothing cuts very deep," remarked the lawyer.

Something in his tone made Steavens glance up. While the mother had been in the room, the young man had scarcely seen any one else; but now, from the moment he first glanced into Jim Laird's florid face and blood-shot eyes, he knew that he had found what he had been heartsick at not finding before—the feeling, the understanding that must exist in some one, even here.

The man was red as his beard, with features swollen and blurred by dissipation, and a hot, blazing blue eye. His face was strained—that of a man who is controlling himself with difficulty—and he kept plucking at his beard with a sort of fierce resentment. Steavens, sitting by the window, watched him turn down the glaring lamp, still its jangling pendants with an angry gesture, and then stand with his hands locked behind him, staring down into the master's face. He could not help wondering what link there could have been between the porcelain vessel and so sooty a lump of potter's clay.

From the kitchen an uproar was sounding; when the dining-room door opened, the import of it was clear. The mother was abusing the maid for having forgotten to make the dressing for the chicken salad which had been prepared for the watchers. Steavens had never heard anything in the least like it; it was injured, emotional, dramatic abuse, unique and masterly in its excruciating cruelty, as violent and unrestrained as had been her grief of twenty minutes before. With a shudder of disgust the lawyer went into the dining room and closed the door into the kitchen.

"Poor Roxy's getting it now," he remarked when he came back. "The Merricks took her out of the poorhouse years ago; and if her loyalty would let her, I guess the poor old thing could tell tales that would curdle your blood. She's the mulatto woman who was standing in here a while ago, with her apron to her eyes. The old woman is a fury; there never was anybody like her for demonstrative piety and ingenious cruelty. She made Harvey's life a hell for him when he lived at home; he was so sick ashamed of it. I never could see how he kept himself so sweet."

"He was wonderful," said Steavens slowly, "wonderful; but until tonight I have never known how wonderful."

"That is the true and eternal wonder of it, anyway; that it can come even from such a dung heap as this," the lawyer cried, with a sweeping gesture which seemed to indicate much more than the four walls within which they stood.

"I think I'll see whether I can get a little air. The room is so close I am beginning to feel rather faint," murmured Steavens, struggling with one of the windows. The sash was stuck, however, and would not yield, so he sat down dejectedly and began pulling at his collar. The lawyer came over, loosened the sash with one blow of his red fist and sent the window up a few inches. Steavens thanked him, but the nausea which had been gradually climbing into his throat for the last half hour left him with but one desire—a desperate feeling that he must get away from this place with what was left of Harvey Merrick. Oh, he comprehended well enough now the quiet bitterness of the smile that he had seen so often on his master's lips!

He remembered that once, when Merrick returned from a visit home, he brought with him a singularly feeling and suggestive bas-relief of a thin, faded old woman, sitting and sewing something pinned to her knee; while a full-lipped, full-blooded little urchin, his trousers held up by a single gallus, stood beside her, impatiently twitching her gown to call her attention to a butterfly he had caught. Steavens, impressed by the tender and delicate modelling of the thin, tired face, had asked him if it were his mother. He remembered the dull flush that had burned up in the sculptor's face.

The lawyer was sitting in a rocking-chair beside the coffin, his head thrown back and his eyes closed. Steavens looked at him earnestly, puzzled at the line of the chin, and wondering why a man should conceal a feature of such distinction under that disfiguring shock of beard. Suddenly, as though he felt the young sculptor's keen glance, he opened his eyes.

"Was he always a good deal of an oyster?" he asked abruptly. "He was terribly shy as a boy."

"Yes, he was an oyster, since you put it so," rejoined Steavens. "Although he could be very fond of people, he always gave one the impression of being detached. He disliked violent emotion; he was reflective, and rather distrustful of himself—except, of course, as regarded his work. He was surefooted enough there. He distrusted men pretty thoroughly and women even more, yet somehow without believing ill of them. He was determined, indeed, to believe the best, but he seemed afraid to investigate."

"A burnt dog dreads the fire," said the lawyer grimly, and closed his eyes.

Steavens went on and on, reconstructing that whole miserable boyhood. All this raw, biting ugliness had been the portion of the man whose tastes were refined beyond the limits of the reasonable—whose mind was an exhaustless gallery of beautiful impressions, and so sensitive that the mere shadow of a poplar leaf flickering against a sunny wall would be etched and held there forever. Surely, if ever a man had the magic word in his fingertips, it was Merrick. Whatever he touched, he revealed its holiest secret; liberated it from enchantment and restored to it its pristine loveliness, like the Arabian prince who fought the enchantress spell for spell. Upon whatever he had come in contact with, he had left a beautiful record of the experience—a sort of ethereal signature; a scent, a sound, a colour that was his own.

Steavens understood now the real tragedy of his master's life; neither love nor wine, as many had conjectured; but a blow which had fallen earlier and cut deeper than these could have done—a shame not his, and yet so unescapably his, to hide in his heart from his very boyhood. And without—the frontier warfare; the yearning of a boy, cast ashore upon a desert of newness and ugliness and sordidness, for all that is chastened and old, and noble with traditions.

At eleven o'clock the tall, flat woman in black crêpe entered and announced that the watchers were arriving, and asked them "to step into the dining-room." As Steavens rose, the lawyer said dryly: "You go on—it'll be a good experience for you, doubtless; as for me, I'm not equal to that crowd tonight; I've had twenty years of them."

As Steavens closed the door after him he glanced back at the lawyer, sitting by the coffin in the dim light, with his chin resting on his hand.

The same misty group that had stood before the door of the express car shuffled into the dining room. In the light of the kerosene lamp they separated and became individuals. The minister, a pale, feeble-looking man with white hair and blond chin-whiskers, took his seat beside a small side table and placed his Bible upon it. The Grand Army man sat down behind the stove and tilted his chair back comfortably against the wall, fishing his quill toothpick from his waistcoat pocket. The two bankers, Phelps and Elder, sat off in a corner behind the dinner table, where they could finish their discussion of the new usury law and its effect on chattel security loans. The real estate agent, an old man with a smiling, hypocritical face, soon joined them. The coal and lumber dealer and the cattle shipper sat on opposite sides of the hard coal-burner, their feet on the nickelwork. Steavens took a book from his pocket and began to read. The talk around him ranged through various topics of local interest while the house was quieting down. When it was clear that the members of the family were in bed, the Grand Army man hitched his shoulders and, untangling his long legs, caught his heels on the rounds of his chair.

"S'pose there'll be a will, Phelps?" he queried in his weak falsetto.

The banker laughed disagreeably, and began trimming his nails with a pearl-handled pocketknife.

"There'll scarcely be any need for one, will there?" he queried in his turn.

The restless Grand Army man shifted his position again, getting his knees still nearer his chin. "Why, the ole man says Harve's done right well lately," he chirped.

The other banker spoke up. "I reckon he means by that Harve ain't asked him to mortgage any more farms lately, so as he could go on with his education."

"Seems like my mind don't reach back to a time when Harve wasn't bein' edycated," tittered the Grand Army man.

There was a general chuckle. The minister took out his handkerchief and blew his nose sonorously. Banker Phelps closed his knife with a snap. "It's too bad the old man's sons didn't turn out better," he remarked with reflective authority. "They never hung together. He spent money enough on Harve to stock a dozen cattle farms and he might as well have poured it into Sand Creek. If Harve had stayed at home and helped nurse what little they had, and gone into stock on the old man's bottom farm, they might all have been well fixed. But the old man had to trust everything to tenants and was cheated right and left."

"Harve never could have handled stock none," interposed the cattleman. "He hadn't it in him to be sharp. Do you remember when he bought Sander's mules for eight-year olds, when everybody in town knew that Sander's father-in-law give 'em to his wife for a wedding present eighteen years before, an' they was full-grown mules then."

Every one chuckled, and the Grand Army man rubbed his knees with a spasm of childish delight.

"Harve never was much account for anything practical, and he shore was never fond of work," began the coal and lumber dealer. "I mind the last time he was home; the day he left, when the old man was out to the barn helpin' his hand hitch up to take Harve to the train, and Cal Moots was patchin' up the fence, Harve, he come out on the step and sings out, in his ladylike voice: 'Cal Moots, Cal Moots! please come cord my trunk.'"

"That's Harve for you," approved the Grand Army man gleefully. "I kin hear him howlin' yet when he was a big feller in long pants and his mother used to whale him with a rawhide in the barn for lettin' the cows get foundered in the cornfield when he was drivin' 'em home from pasture. He killed a cow of mine that-a-way onct—a pure Jersey and the best milker I had, an' the ole man had to put up for her. Harve, he was watchin' the sun set acrost the marshes when the anamile got away; he argued that sunset was oncommon fine."

"Where the old man made his mistake was in sending the boy East to school," said Phelps, stroking his goatee and speaking in a deliberate, judicial tone. "There was where he got his head full of trapesing to Paris and all such folly. What Harve needed, of all people, was a course in some first-class Kansas City business college."

The letters were swimming before Steavens's eyes. Was it possible that these men did not understand, that the palm of the coffin meant nothing to them? The very name of their town would have remained forever buried in the postal guide had it not been now and again mentioned in the world in connection with Harvey Merrick's. He remembered what his master had said to him on the day of his death, after the congestion of both lungs had shut off any probability of recovery, and the sculptor had asked his pupil to send his body home. "It's not a pleasant place to be lying while the world is moving and doing and bettering," he had said with a feeble smile, "but it rather seems as though we ought to go back to the place we came from in the end. The townspeople will come in for a look at me; and after they have had their say I shan't have much to fear from the judgment of God. The wings of the Victory, in there"—with a weak gesture toward his studio—"will not shelter me."

The cattleman took up the comment. "Forty's young for a Merrick to cash in; they usually hang on pretty well. Probably he helped it along with whisky."

"His mother's people were not long-lived, and Harvey never had a robust constitution," said the minister mildly. He would have liked to say more. He had been the boy's Sunday-school teacher, and had been fond of him; but he felt that he was not in a position to speak. His own sons had turned out badly, and it was not a year since one of them had made his last trip home in the express car, shot in a gambling house in the Black Hills.

"Nevertheless, there is no disputin' that Harvey frequently looked upon the wine when it was red, also variegated, and it shore made an oncommon fool of him," moralized the cattleman.

Just then the door leading into the parlor rattled loudly and everyone started involuntarily, looking relieved when only Jim Laird came out. His red face was convulsed with anger, and the Grand Army man ducked his head when he saw the spark in his blue, bloodshot eye. They were all afraid of Jim; he was a drunkard, but he could twist the law to suit his client's needs as no other man in all western Kansas could do; and there were many who tried. The lawyer closed the door gently behind him, leaned back against it and folded his arms, cocking his head a little to one side. When he assumed this attitude in the courtroom, ears were always pricked up, as it usually foretold a flood of withering sarcasm.

"I've been with you gentlemen before," he began in a dry, even tone, "when you've sat by the coffins of boys born and raised in this town; and, if I remember rightly, you were never any too well satisfied when you checked them up. What's the matter, anyhow? Why is it that reputable young men are as scarce as millionaires in Sand City? It might almost seem to a stranger that there was some way something the matter with your progressive town. Why did Ruben Sayer, the brightest young lawyer you ever turned out, after he had come home from the university as straight as a die, take to drinking and forge a check and shoot himself? Why did Bill Merrit's son die of the shakes in a saloon in Omaha? Why was Mr. Thomas's son, here, shot in a gambling-house? Why did young Adams burn his mill to beat the insurance companies and go to the pen?"

The lawyer paused and unfolded his arms, laying one clenched fist quietly on the table. "I'll tell you why. Because you drummed nothing but money and knavery into their ears from the time they wore knickerbockers; because you carped away at them as you've been carping here tonight, holding our friends Phelps and Elder up to them for their models, as our grandfathers held up George Washington and John Adams. But the boys, worse luck, were young and raw at the business you put them to; and how could they match coppers with such artists as Phelps and Elder? You wanted them to be successful rascals; they were only unsuccessful ones—that's all the difference. There was only one boy ever raised in this borderland between ruffianism and civilization, who didn't come to grief, and you hated Harvey Merrick more for winning out than you hated all the other boys who got under the wheels. Lord, Lord, how you did hate him! Phelps, here, is fond of saying that he could buy and sell us all out any time he's a mind to; but he knew Harve wouldn't have given a tinker's damn for his bank and all his cattle farms put together; and a lack of appreciation, that way, goes hard with Phelps.

"Old Nimrod, here, thinks Harve drank too much; and this from such as Nimrod and me!

"Brother Elder says Harve was too free with the old man's money—fell short in filial consideration, maybe. Well, we can all remember the very tone in which brother Elder swore his own father was a liar, in the county court; and we all know that the old man came out of that partnership with his son as bare as a sheared lamb. But maybe I'm getting personal, and I'd better be driving ahead at what I want to say."

The lawyer paused a moment, squared his heavy shoulders, and went on: "Harvey Merrick and I went to school together, back East. We were dead in earnest, and we wanted you all to be proud of us some day. We meant to be great men. Even I, and I haven't lost my sense of humour, gentlemen, I meant to be a great man. I came back here to practise, and I found you didn't in the least want me to be a great man. You wanted me to be a shrewd lawyer—oh, yes! Our veteran here wanted me to get him an increase of pension, because he had dyspepsia; Phelps wanted a new country survey that would put the widow Wilson's little bottom farm inside his south line; Elder wanted to lend money at 5 percent a month, and get it collected; old Stark here wanted to wheedle old women up in Vermont into investing their annuities in real-estate mortgages that are not worth the paper they are written on. Oh, you needed me hard enough, and you'll go on needing me; and that's why I'm not afraid to plug the truth home to you this once.

"Well, I came back here and became the damned shyster you wanted me to be. You pretend to have some sort of respect for me; and yet you'll stand up and throw mud at Harvey Merrick, whose soul you couldn't dirty and whose hands you couldn't tie. Oh, you're a discriminating lot of Christians! There have been times when the sight of Harvey's name in some Eastern paper has made me hang my head like a whipped dog; and, again, times when I liked to think of him off there in the world, away from all this hogwallow, doing his great work and climbing the big, clean up-grade he'd set for himself.

"And we? Now that we've fought and lied and sweated and stolen, and hated as only the disappointed strugglers in a bitter, dead little Western town know how to do, what have we got to show for it? Harvey Merrick wouldn't have given one sunset over your marshes for all you've got put together, and you know it. It's not for me to say why, in the inscrutable wisdom of God, a genius should ever have been called from his place of hatred and bitter waters; but I want this Boston man to know that the drivel he's been hearing here tonight is the only tribute any truly great man could ever have from such a lot of sick, side-tracked, burnt-dog, land-poor sharks as the here-present financiers of Sand City—upon which town may God have mercy!"

The lawyer thrust out his hand to Steavens as he passed him, caught up his overcoat in the hall, and had left the house before the Grand Army man had had time to lift his ducked head and crane his long neck about at his fellows.

Next day Jim Laird was drunk and unable to attend the funeral services. Steavens called twice at his office, but was compelled to start East without seeing him. He had a presentiment that he would hear from him again, and left his address on the lawyer's table; but if Laird found it, he never acknowledged it. The thing in him that Harvey Merrick had loved must have gone underground with Harvey Merrick's coffin; for it never spoke again, and Jim got the cold he died of driving across the Colorado mountains to defend one of Phelps's sons who had got into trouble out there by cutting government timber.

Suggestions for Discussion

1. Discuss the details Cather uses to characterize the small Kansas town to which the dead sculptor's body is brought for burial. Why is Steavens repelled by the furnishings in the house of Merrick's mother?

2. The sculptor's mother is overcome by grief. Steavens is repelled by her outburst of emotion. Why? How does Cather arrange details so that we will agree with Steavens?

3. How does Cather contrast Mrs. Merrick with her daughter? What function do both characters have in the story?

4. Why does Cather portray Jim Laird as a heavy drinker? What is his function in the story?

5. What was the real tragedy of the dead sculptor's life? How had it affected his work?

6. What is the theme of Cather's story? Why does she use the long speech by Laird to express it?

7. Contrast "The Sculptor's Funeral" with "Is He Living or Is He Dead?"

Suggestion for Writing

Cather's view of the artist as somehow alienated from his society is illustrated in this story. Write a paper dealing with the issue, using examples of well-known artists. You might make this a research project by investigating the life of Beethoven, Mozart, Baudelaire, or Poe. What about the relation of the artists to society in other cultures; for example, China, India, or Bali?

Poetry

William Blake

London

William Blake (1757–1827), one of the most innovative of English poets, was also a painter. A printer by trade, he printed and illustrated his own books of poetry, and also illustrated the Book of Job and Dante's *Divine Comedy.* He achieved some recognition for his painting, but none for his poetry, and lived in London an industrious and personally happy life of poverty. His *Songs of Innocence* and *Songs of Experience* are now viewed as significant events in the development of romanticism in English poetry. "London," which portrays the degradation of life in the great city, states with ironic power the gulf which lies between innocence and experience.

> I wander thro' each charter'd street,
> Near where the charter'd Thames does flow,
> And mark in every face I meet
> Marks of weakness, marks of woe.
>
> In every cry of every Man,
> In every Infant's cry of fear,
> In every voice, in every ban,
> The mind-forg'd manacles I hear.
>
> How the Chimney-sweeper's cry
> Every black'ning Church appalls;
> And the hapless Soldier's sigh
> Runs in blood down Palace walls.
>
> But most thro' midnight streets I hear
> How the youthful Harlot's curse
> Blasts the new born Infant's tear,
> And blights with plagues the Marriage hearse.

Suggestions for Discussion

1. What statement is Blake making about London?

2. Why does the poet use the word "charter'd" for both the streets of the city and the river that flows through it?

3. Why does the Chimney-sweeper's cry appall the "black'ning Church"?

4. Why does the "Harlot's curse" blast the "Infant's tear" and blight the "Marriage hearse"?

5. Is *hearse* the usual word associated with marriage? Why does Blake use it here?

6. The poem is filled with the poet's indignation. What is the cause of his feeling?

7. Is this a typical poem addressed to a city?

8. Does the social comment interfere in any way with the "art" of the poem? How are the two related?

Suggestion for Writing

Write an essay in which you relate "London" to several other poems of social protest.

Muriel Rukeyser

The Backside of the Academy

Muriel Rukeyser (b. 1913) is a member of the National Institute of Arts and Letters and an American poet whose works often center on social themes. She was educated at Vassar and received a Guggenheim Fellowship in 1943 and the Levinson Prize for Poetry in 1947. Her books include *Elegies* (1949), *The Green Wave* (1948), *Mazes* (1970), *The Gates* (1976), and *The Speed of Darkness* (1968), from which the following poem is taken. The speaker in the poem balances the "truths" printed over the doors of the Academy (for example, "Art Remains the One Way Possible of Speaking Truth") with the graffiti on the back of the building to create an ironic effect.

Five brick panels, three small windows, six lions' heads with rings in their
    mouths, five pairs of closed bronze doors—
the shut wall with the words carved across its head

ART REMAINS THE ONE WAY POSSIBLE OF SPEAKING TRUTH.—
On this May morning, light swimming in this street, the children running,
on the church beside the Academy the lines are flying
of little yellow-and-white plastic flags flapping in the light;
and on the great shut wall, the words are carved across:
WE ARE YOUNG AND WE ARE FRIENDS OF TIME.—
Below that, a light blue asterisk in chalk
and in white chalk, Hector, Joey, Lynn, Rudolfo.
A little up the street, a woman shakes a small dark boy,
she shouts What's wrong with you, ringing that bell!
In the street of rape and singing, poems, small robberies,
carved in an oblong panel of the stone:
CONSCIOUS UTTERANCE OF THOUGHT BY SPEECH OR ACTION
TO ANY END IS ART.—
On the lowest reach of the walls are chalked the words: Jack is a object,
Walter and Trina, Goo Goo, I love Trina,
and further along Viva Fidel now altered to Muera Fidel.
A deep blue marble is lodged against the curb.
A phone booth on one corner; on the other, the big mesh basket for trash.
Beyond them, the little park is always locked. For the two soldier brothers.
and past that goes on an eternal football game
which sometimes, as on this day in May, transforms to stickball
as, for one day in May,
five pairs of closed bronze doors will open
and the Academy of writers, sculptors, painters, composers, their guests and
    publishers will all roll in and
the wave of organ music come rolling out into
The street where light now blows and papers and little children and words,
    some breezes of Spanish blow and many colors of people.
A watch cap lies fallen against a cellophane which used to hold pistachio nuts
and here before me, on my street,
five brick panels, three small windows, six lions' heads with rings in their
    mouths, five pairs of closed bronze doors,
light flooding the street I live and write in; and across the river the one word
    FREE against the ferris wheel and the roller coaster,
and here, painted upon the stones, Chino, Bobby, Joey, Fatmoma, Willy,
    Holy of God
and also Margaret is a shit and also fuck and shit;
far up, invisible at the side of the building:
WITHOUT VISION THE PEO
and on the other side, the church side,
where shadows of trees and branches, this day in May, are printed balanced
    on the church wall,
in-focus trunks and softened-focus branches
below the roof where the two structures stand,
bell and cross, antenna and weathervane,
I can see past the church the words of an ending line:
IVE BY BREAD ALONE.

Suggestions for Discussion

1. Explain the ironic meaning of the title. What does the word *backside* mean? Does it point to an ironic attitude in the poem?

2. Where is the Academy? Is its location important?

3. What is suggested by the change in the slogan "Viva Fidel" to "Muera Fidel"?

4. The speaker in the poem suggests that the Academy is comprised of writers, painters, sculptors, and composers. With what group are the members of the Academy contrasted? What is the point of the contrast?

5. Some of the capitalized phrases are fragmentary. Explain the fragmentary last line. How does it serve as a comment on the rest of the poem?

6. How would you summarize the poet's position in the debate over the commitment of the artist to a cause?

Suggestions for Writing

1. Write a paper comparing this poem to MacLeish's poem about the role of the poet. How do the two poets disagree?

2. *Theory of Flight* was Rukeyser's first collection. Many of its poems relate to social themes. You may wish to read them and compare them with the poem in this text. How much historical annotation do such poems require? Is such annotation, in your opinion, a negative aspect of the poetry? Write a paper carefully explaining your opinions.

Archibald MacLeish

Invocation to the Social Muse

Archibald MacLeish (1892–1982) was born in Glencoe, Illinois, and educated at Yale and Harvard. He practiced law briefly and lived most of the decade of the 1920's in France. He won the Pulitzer Prize for *Conquistador* in 1932. His volume *Frescoes for Mr. Rockefeller's City* (1933), his play in verse, *Panic* (1935), and the play written for radio, *The Fall of the City* (1937), all reveal his concern over the rise of fascism and his own move toward liberal politics. He was Librarian of Congress from 1939 to 1944 and Undersecretary of State during the Roosevelt administration. From 1949 to 1962 he was Boyleston Professor of Rhetoric at Harvard and won another Pulitzer Prize in 1958 for his verse drama *J. B.* "Invocation to the Social Muse" predates his poetry of social commitment and like his brief "Ars Poetica" expresses belief in art for art's sake.

Señora, it is true the Greeks are dead.

It is true also that we here are Americans:
That we use the machines: that a sight of the god is unusual:
That more people have more thoughts: that there are

Progress and science and tractors and revolutions and
Marx and the wars more antiseptic and murderous
And music in every home: there is also Hoover.

Does the lady suggest we should write it out in The Word?
Does Madame recall our responsibilities? We are
Whores, Fräulein: poets, Fräulein, are persons of

Known vocation following troops: they must sleep with
Stragglers from either prince and of both views.
The rules permit them to further the business of neither.

It is also strictly forbidden to mix in maneuvers.
Those that infringe are inflated with praise on the plazas—
Their bones are resultantly afterwards found under newspapers.

Preferring life with the sons to death with the fathers,
We also doubt on the record whether the sons
Will still be shouting around with the same huzzas—

For we hope Lady to live to lie with the youngest.
There are only a handful of things a man likes,
Generation to generation, hungry or

Well fed: the earth's one: life's
One: Mister Morgan is not one.
There is nothing worse for our trade than to be in style.

He that goes naked goes further at last than another.
Wrap the bard in a flag or a school and they'll jimmy his
Door down and be thick in his bed—for a month:

(Who recalls the address now of the Imagists?)
But the naked man has always his own nakedness.
People remember forever his live limbs.

They may drive him out of the camps but one will take him.
They may stop his tongue on his teeth with a rope's argument—
He will lie in a house and be warm when they are shaking.

Besides, Tovarishch, how to embrace an army?
How to take to one's chamber a million souls?
How to conceive in the name of a column of marchers?

The things of the poet are done to a man alone
As the things of love are done—or of death when he hears the
Step withdraw on the stair and the clock tick only.

Neither his class nor his kind nor his trade may come near him
There where he lies on his left arm and will die,
Nor his class nor his kind nor his trade when the blood is jeering

And his knee's in the soft of the bed where his love lies.
I remind you, Barinya, the life of the poet is hard—
A hardy life with a boot as quick as a fiver:

Is it just to demand of us also to bear arms?

Suggestions for Discussion

1. Whom does the poet address at various times in the poem? Explain his use of "Señora," "Lady," "Barinya."

2. Why does MacLeish say, "There is nothing worse for our trade than to be in style"? What "style" does he refer to in the context of the poem?

3. The invocation to the muse is a device of epic poetry. Why does MacLeish make use of the device in his title?

4. In the third from the last line, MacLeish asserts that "the life of the poet is hard." In what ways does he seem to argue that this is true?

5. Summarize the position in the poem about role of the poet.

Suggestion for Writing

Write an analysis of this poem in which you discuss MacLeish's concept of the poet and his role in society. In your paper explain whom the poet is addressing. What is the meaning of the four lines that begin, "There are only a handful of things a man likes"?

Marianne Moore

Poetry

Marianne Moore (1877–1972) was born in Missouri, graduated from Bryn Mawr college, taught at an Indian school, worked in the New York Public Library, edited *The Dial* between 1925 and 1929, and was a distinguished resident of Brooklyn Heights. Her first collection of poems was published in 1921, her *Collected Poems* in 1951. Among her works are *Predilection* (1955), a volume of critical essays, a poetic translation of La Fontaine's *Fables* (1954), and the volume of poetry *Tell Me, Tell Me* (1967). In the following poem, as she appears to put poetry in its place and dismisses high-flown theories about art, she affirms the power of the genuine article and the real significance of poetry.

I, too, dislike it: there are things that are important beyond all this fiddle,
Reading it, however, with a perfect contempt for it, one discovers in
it after all, a place for the genuine.
Hands that can grasp, eyes
that can dilate, hair that can rise
if it must, these things are important not because a

high-sounding interpretation can be put upon them but because they are
useful. When they become so derivative as to become unintelligible,
the same thing may be said for all of us, that we
do not admire what
we cannot understand: the bat
holding on upside down or in quest of something to

eat, elephants pushing, a wild horse taking a roll, a tireless wolf under
a tree, the immovable critic twitching his skin like a horse that feels a flea,
the base-
ball fan, the statistician—
nor is it valid
to discriminate against "business documents and

school-books"; all these phenomena are important. One must make a
distinction
however: when dragged into prominence by half poets, the result is not
poetry,
nor till the poets among us can be
"literalists of
the imagination"—above
insolence and triviality and can present

for inspection, "imaginary gardens with real toads in them," shall we have
it. In the meantime, if you demand on the one hand,
the raw material of poetry in
all its rawness and
that which is on the other hand
genuine, you are interested in poetry.

Suggestions for Discussion

1. Why does the poet, on one hand, refer to poetry as "all this fiddle" and, on the other, find in it "a place for the genuine"?

2. What does the poet list as the important parts of poetry? Why does she dismiss the unintelligible in poetry?

3. Moore wants poets to become "'literalists of the imagination.'" Relate this phrase to her belief that the poets must create "'imaginary gardens with real toads in them.'"

Suggestions for Writing

1. Write a paper in which you compare the view of poetry in this poem with the view that poetry is a romantic outburst of pure emotion. What arguments would you use in defense of either position?

2. Rewrite the poem in prose sentences in a paragraph. Write a comment on what you have done with the poem. How have you changed it? Does your change effect a change in defining the piece as a poem?

Science, Technology, and the Future

◆◆◆

Science . . . is neither human nor inhuman. So far as the well-being of humanity is concerned, science needs guidance from other sources. Science in itself is not enough—or should not be.

—**Karl Jaspers,** "Is Science Evil?"

The universe is vast and men are but tiny specks on an insignificant planet. But the more we realize our minuteness and our impotence in the face of cosmic forces, the more astonishing becomes what human beings have achieved.

—**Bertrand Russell,** "If We are to Survive This Dark Time"

The power that man has over nature and himself, and that a dog lacks, lies in his command of imaginary experience. He alone has the symbols which fix the past and play with the future.

—**Jacob Bronowski,** "The Reach of Imagination"

Nature's oddities are more than good stories. They are material for probing the limits of interesting theories about life's history and meaning.

—**Stephen Jay Gould,** "Death Before Birth, or a Mite's *Nunc Dimittis*"

The direct societal effects of any pervasive technology are as nothing compared to its much more subtle and ultimately much more important side effects.

—**Joseph Weizenbaum,** "On the Impact of the Computer on Society"

Essays

Francis Bacon

Idols of the Mind

Sir Francis Bacon (1561–1626) was a lawyer, essayist, philosopher, and statesman. Among his best known works are *The Advancement of Learning* (1605),
The New Organum (1620), and *The New Atlantis* (1627). He is considered the
originator of modern scientific induction because of his insistence on observation and experimentation as a means to knowledge. In "Idols of the Mind,"
from *The New Organum,* Bacon illustrates those habits of thought which inhibit
human understanding and the spirit of scientific inquiry.

XXIII

There is a great difference between the Idols of the human mind and the
Ideals of the divine. That is to say, between certain empty dogmas, and the
true signatures and marks set upon the works of creation as they are found in
nature.

XXXVIII

The idols and false notions which are now in possession of the human understanding, and have taken deep root therein, not only so beset men's minds
that truth can hardly find entrance, but even after entrance obtained, they
will again in the very instauration of the sciences meet and trouble us, unless
men being forewarned of the danger fortify themselves as far as may be
against their assaults.

XXXIX

There are four classes of Idols which beset men's minds. To these for distinction's sake I have assigned names,—calling the first class *Idols of the Tribe;*
the second, *Idols of the Cave;* the third, *Idols of the Market place;* the fourth,
Idols of the Theater.

XL

The formation of ideas and axioms by true induction is no doubt the proper remedy to be applied for the keeping off and clearing away of idols. To point them out, however, is of great use; for the doctrine of Idols is to the Interpretation of Nature what the doctrine of the refutation of Sophisms is to common Logic.

XLI

The Idols of the Tribe have their foundation in human nature itself, and in the tribe or race of men. For it is a false assertion that the sense of man is the measure of things. On the contrary, all perceptions as well of the sense as of the mind are according to the measure of the individual and not according to the measure of the universe. And the human understanding is like a false mirror, which, receiving rays irregularly, distorts and discolors the nature of things by mingling its own nature with it.

XLII

The Idols of the Cave are the idols of the individual man. For everyone (besides the errors common to human nature in general) has a cave or den of his own, which refracts and discolours the light of nature; owing either to his own proper and peculiar nature; or to his education and conversation with others; or to the reading of books, and the authority of those whom he esteems and admires; or to the differences of impressions, accordingly as they take place in a mind preoccupied and predisposed or in a mind indifferent and settled; or the like. So that the spirit of man (according as it is meted out to different individuals) is in fact a thing variable and full of perturbation, and governed as it were by chance. Whence it was well observed by Heraclitus that men look for sciences in their own lesser worlds, and not in the greater or common world.

XLIII

There are also Idols formed by the intercourse and association of men with each other, which I call Idols of the Market Place, on account of the commerce and consort of men there. For it is by discourse that men associate; and words are imposed according to the apprehension of the vulgar. And therefore the ill and unfit choice of words wonderfully obstructs the understanding. Nor do the definitions or explanations wherewith in some things learned men are wont to guard and defend themselves, by any means set the matter right. But words plainly force and overrule the understanding, and throw all into confusion, and lead men away into numberless empty controversies and idle fancies.

XLIV

Lastly, there are Idols which have immigrated into men's minds from the various dogmas of philosophies, and also from wrong laws of demonstration.

These I call Idols of the Theater; because in my judgment all the received systems are but so many stage-plays, representing worlds of their own creation after an unreal and scenic fashion. Nor is it only of the systems now in vogue, or only of the ancient sects and philosophies, that I speak; for many more plays of the same kind may yet be composed and in like artificial manner set forth; seeing that errors the most widely different have nevertheless causes for the most part alike. Neither again do I mean this only of entire systems, but also of many principles and axioms in science, which by tradition, credulity, and negligence have come to be received.

But of these several kinds of Idols I must speak more largely and exactly, that the understanding may be duly cautioned.

XLV

The human understanding is of its own nature prone to suppose the existence of more order and regularity in the world than it finds. And though there be many things in nature which are singular and unmatched, yet it devises for them parallels and conjugates and relatives which do not exist. Hence the fiction that all celestial bodies move in perfect circles; spirals and dragons being (except in name) utterly rejected. Hence too the element of Fire with its orb is brought in, to make up the square with the other three which the sense perceives. Hence also the ratio of density of the so-called elements is arbitrarily fixed at ten to one. And so on of other dreams. And these fancies affect not dogmas only, but simple notions also.

XLVI

The human understanding when it has once adopted an opinion (either as being the received opinion or as being agreeable to itself) draws all things else to support and agree with it. And though there be a greater number and weight of instances to be found on the other side, yet these it either neglects and despises, or else by some distinction sets aside and rejects; in order that by this great and pernicious predetermination the authority of its former conclusions may remain inviolate. And therefore it was a good answer that was made by one who when they showed him hanging in a temple a picture of those who had paid their vows as having escaped shipwreck, and would have him say whether he did not now acknowledge the power of the gods,—"Aye," asked he again, "but where are they painted that were drowned after their vows?" And such is the way of all superstition, whether in astrology, dreams, omens, divine judgments, or the like; wherein men, having a delight in such vanities, mark the events where they are fulfilled, but where they fail, though this happen much oftener, neglect and pass them by. But with far more subtlety does this mischief insinuate itself into philosophy and the sciences; in which the first conclusion colors and brings into conformity with itself all that come after, though far sounder and better. Besides, independently of that delight and vanity which I have described, it is the peculiar and perpetual error of the human intellect to be more moved and excited by affirmatives than by negatives; whereas it ought properly to hold itself indifferently disposed towards both alike. Indeed in the establishment of any true axiom, the negative instance is the more forcible of the two.

XLVII

The human understanding is moved by those things most which strike and enter the mind simultaneously and suddenly, and so fill the imagination; and then it feigns and supposes all other things to be somehow, though it cannot see how, similar to those few things by which it is surrounded. But for that going to and fro to remote and heterogeneous instances, by which axioms are tried as in the fire, the intellect is altogether slow and unfit, unless it be forced thereto by severe laws and overruling authority.

XLVIII

The human understanding is unquiet; it cannot stop or rest, and still presses onward, but in vain. Therefore it is that we cannot conceive of any end or limit to the world; but always as of necessity it occurs to us that there is something beyond. Neither again can it be conceived how eternity has flowed down to the present day; for that distinction which is commonly received of infinity in time past and in time to come can by no means hold; for it would thence follow that one infinity is greater than another, and that infinity is wasting away and tending to become finite. The like subtlety arises touching the infinite divisibility of lines, from the same inability of thought to stop. But this inability interferes more mischievously in the discovery of causes: for although the most general principles in nature ought to be held merely positive, as they are discovered, and cannot with truth be referred to a cause; nevertheless the human understanding being unable to rest still seeks something prior in the order of nature. And then it is that in struggling toward that which is further off it falls back upon that which is more nigh at hand; namely, on final causes: which have relation clearly to the nature of man rather than to the nature of the universe; and from this source have strangely defiled philosophy. But he is no less an unskilled and shallow philosopher who seeks causes of that which is most general, than he who in things subordinate and subaltern omits to do so.

XLIX

The human understanding is no dry light, but receives an infusion from the will and affections; whence proceed sciences which may be called "sciences as one would." For what a man had rather were true he more readily believes. Therefore he rejects difficult things from impatience of research; sober things, because they narrow hope; the deeper things of nature, from superstition; the light of experience, from arrogance and pride, lest his mind should seem to be occupied with things mean and transitory; things not commonly believed, out of deference to the opinion of the vulgar. Numberless in short are the ways, and sometimes imperceptible, in which the affections color and infect the understanding.

L

But by far the greatest hindrance and aberration of the human understanding proceeds from the dullness, incompetency, and deceptions of the senses; in that things which strike the sense outweigh things which do not immediately strike it, though they be more important. Hence it is that speculation commonly ceases where sight ceases; insomuch that of things invisible there is little or no observation. Hence all the working of the spirits enclosed in tangible bodies lies hid and unobserved by men. So also all the more subtle changes of form in the parts of coarser substances (which they commonly call alteration, though it is in truth local motion through exceedingly small spaces) is in like manner unobserved. And yet unless these two things just mentioned be searched out and brought to light, nothing great can be achieved in nature, as far as the production of works is concerned. So again the essential nature of our common air, and of all bodies less dense than air (which are very many), is almost unknown. For the sense by itself is a thing infirm and erring; neither can instruments for enlarging or sharpening the senses do much; but all the truer kind of interpretation of nature is effected by instances and experiments fit and apposite; wherein the sense decides touching the experiment only, and the experiment touching the point in nature and the thing itself.

LI

The human understanding is of its own nature prone to abstractions and gives a substance and reality to things which are fleeting. But to resolve nature into abstractions is less to our purpose than to dissect her into parts; as did the school of Democritus, which went further into nature than the rest. Matter rather than forms should be the object of our attention, its configurations and changes of configuration, and simple action, and law of action or motion; for forms are figments of the human mind, unless you will call those laws of action forms.

LII

Such then are the idols which I call *Idols of the Tribe;* and which take their rise either from the homogeneity of the substance of the human spirit, or from its preoccupation, or from its narrowness, or from its restless motion, or from an infusion of the affections, or from the incompetency of the senses, or from the mode of impression.

LIII

The *Idols of the Cave* take their rise in the peculiar constitution, mental or bodily, of each individual; and also in education, habit, and accident. Of this kind there is a great number and variety; but I will instance those the pointing out of which contains the most important caution, and which have most effect in disturbing the clearness of the understanding.

LIV

Men become attached to certain particular sciences and speculations, either because they fancy themselves the authors and inventors thereof, or because they have bestowed the greatest pains upon them and become most habituated to them. But men of this kind, if they betake themselves to philosophy and contemplations of a general character, distort and color them in obedience to their former fancies; a thing especially to be noticed in Aristotle, who made his natural philosophy a mere bond-servant to his logic, thereby rendering it contentious and well nigh useless. The race of chemists again out of a few experiments of the furnace have built up a fantastic philosophy, framed with reference to a few things; and Gilbert also, after he had employed himself most laboriously in the study and observation of the lodestone, proceeded at once to construct an entire system in accordance with his favourite subject.

LVI

There are found some minds given to an extreme admiration of antiquity, others to an extreme love and appetite for novelty; but few so duly tempered that they can hold the mean, neither carping at what has been well laid down by the ancients, nor despising what is well introduced by the moderns. This however turns to the great injury of the sciences and philosophy; since these affectations of antiquity and novelty are the humors of partisans rather than judgments; and truth is to be sought for not in the felicity of any age, which is an unstable thing, but in the light of nature and experience, which is eternal. These factions therefore must be abjured, and care must be taken that the intellect be not hurried by them into assent.

LVIII

Let such then be our provision and contemplative prudence for keeping off and dislodging the *Idols of the Cave*, which grow for the most part either out of the predominance of a favourite subject, or out of an excessive tendency to compare or to distinguish, or out of partiality for particular ages, or out of the largeness of minuteness of the objects contemplated. And generally let every student of nature take this as a rule—that whatever his mind seizes and dwells upon with peculiar satisfaction is to be held in suspicion, and that so much the more care is to be taken in dealing with such questions to keep the understanding even and clear.

LIX

But the *Idols of the Market Place* are the most troublesome of all: idols which have crept into the understanding through the alliances of words and names. For men believe that their reason governs words; but it is also true that words react on the understanding; and this it is that had rendered philosophy and the sciences sophistical and inactive. Now words, being commonly framed and applied according to the capacity of the vulgar, follow those lines of division which are most obvious to the vulgar understanding. And whenever an understanding of greater acuteness or a more diligent observation would alter those lines to suit the true divisions of nature, words stand in the way and resist the change. Whence it comes to pass that the high and formal discussions of learned men end oftentimes in disputes about words and names; with which (according to the use and wisdom of the mathematicians) it would be more prudent to begin, and so by means of definitions reduce them to order. Yet even definitions cannot cure this evil in dealing with natural and material things; since the definitions themselves consist of words, and those words beget others: so that it is necessary to recur to individual instances, and those in due series and order; as I shall say presently when I come to the method and scheme for the formation of notions and axioms.

LX

The idols imposed by words on the understanding are of two kinds. They are either names of things which do not exist (for as there are things left unnamed through lack of observation, so likewise are there names which result from fantastic suppositions and to which nothing in reality corresponds), or they are names of things which exist, but yet confused and illdefined, and hastily and irregularly derived from realities. Of the former kind are Fortune, the Prime Mover, Planetary Orbits, Element of Fire, and like fictions which owe their origin to false and idle theories. And this class of idols is more easily expelled, because to get rid of them it is only necessary that all theories should be steadily rejected and dismissed as obsolete.

But the other class, which springs out of a faulty and unskillful abstraction, is intricate and deeply rooted. Let us take for example such a word as *humid;* and see how far the several things which the word is used to signify agree with each other; and we shall find the word *humid* to be nothing else than a mark loosely and confusedly applied to denote a variety of actions which will not bear to be reduced to any constant meaning. For it both signifies that which easily spreads itself round any other body; and that which in itself is indeterminate and cannot solidify; and that which readily yields in every direction; and that which easily divides and scatters itself; and that which easily unites and collects itself; and that which readily flows and is put in motion; and that which readily clings to another body and wets it; and that which is easily reduced to a liquid, or being solid easily melts. Accordingly when you come to apply the word—if you take it in one sense, flame is humid; if in another, air is not humid; if in another, fine dust is humid; if in another, glass is humid. So that it is easy to see that the notion is taken by abstraction only from water and common and ordinary liquids, without any due verification.

There are however in words certain degrees of distortion and error. One of the least faulty kinds is that of names of substances, especially of lowest species and well-deduced (for the notion of *chalk* and of *mud* is good, of *earth* bad); a more faulty kind is that of actions, as *to generate, to corrupt, to alter;* the most faulty is of qualities (except such as are the immediate objects of the sense) as *heavy, light, rare, dense,* and the like. Yet in all these cases some notions are of necessity a little better than others, in proportion to the greater variety of subjects that fall within the range of the human sense.

LXI

But the *Idols of the Theater* are not innate, nor do they steal into the understanding secretly, but are plainly impressed and received into the mind from the play-books of philosophical systems and the perverted rules of demonstration. To attempt refutations in this case would be merely inconsistent with what I have already said: for since we agree neither upon principles nor upon demonstrations there is no place for argument. And this is so far well, inasmuch as it leaves the honor of the ancients untouched. For they are no wise disparaged—the question between them and me being only as to the way. For as the saying is, the lame man who keeps the right road outstrips the runner who takes a wrong one. Nay it is obvious that when a man runs the wrong way, the more active and swift he is the further he will go astray.

But the course I propose for the discovery of sciences is such as leaves but little to the acuteness and strength of wits, but places all wits and understandings nearly on a level. For as in the drawing of a straight line or a perfect circle, much depends on the steadiness and practice of the hand, if it be done by aim of hand only, but if with the aid of rule or compass, little or nothing; so is it exactly with my plan. But though particular confutations would be of no avail, yet touching the sects and general divisions of such systems I must say something; something also touching the external signs which show that they are unsound; and finally something touching the causes of such great infelicity and of such lasting and general agreement in error; that so the access to truth may be made less difficult, and the human understanding may the more willingly submit to its purgation and dismiss its idols.

LXII

Idols of the Theater, or of Systems, are many, and there can be and perhaps will be yet many more. For were it not that now for many ages men's minds have been busied with religion and theology; and were it not that civil governments, especially monarchies, have been averse to such novelties, even in matters speculative; so that men labor therein to the peril and harming of their fortunes—not only unrewarded, but exposed also to contempt and envy; doubtless there would have arisen many other philosophical sects like to those which in great variety flourished once among the Greeks. For as on the phenomena of the heavens many hypotheses may be constructed, so likewise (and more also) many various dogmas may be set up and established on the phenomena of philosophy. And in the plays of this philosophical theater you may observe the same thing which is found in the theater of the poets, that stories invented for the stage are more compact and elegant, and more as one would wish them to be, than true stories out of history.

LXVII

A caution must also be given to the understanding against the intemperance which systems of philosophy manifest in giving or withholding assent; because intemperance of this kind seems to establish Idols and in some sort to perpetuate them, leaving no way open to reach and dislodge them.

This excess is of two kinds: the first being manifest in those who are ready in deciding, and render sciences dogmatic and magisterial: the other in those who deny that we can know anything, and so introduce a wandering kind of inquiry that leads to nothing: of which kinds the former subdues, the latter weakens the understanding. For the philosophy of Aristotle, after having by hostile confutations destroyed all the rest (as the Ottomans serve their brothers), has laid down the law on all points; which done, he proceeds himself to raise new questions of his own suggestion, and dispose of them likewise; so that nothing may remain that is not certain and decided: a practice which holds and is in use among his successors.

LXVIII

So much concerning the several classes of Idols, and their equipage: all of which must be renounced and put away with a fixed and solemn determination, and the understanding thoroughly freed and cleansed; the entrance into the kingdom of man, founded on the sciences, being not much other than the entrance into the kingdom of heaven, whereinto none may enter except as a little child.

Suggestions for Discussion

1. Bacon names the four idols he is going to discuss. They can be represented diagrammatically as follows:

of Tribe	of Cave	of Market Place	of Theater

 Relate each aphorism to one of the idols Bacon has named. How does each aphorism apply to or illustrate an idol?

2. In discussing the idols of the market place Bacon deals with nonexistent and ill-defined things. Why does he separate the two? He rapidly disposes of the first category with a number of short examples. The second he divides into three degrees of distortion. What are the degrees? Why does Bacon deal with ill-defined things more precisely than with nonexistent things?

3. For almost every division or subdivision Bacon provides an example or illustration. List at least one example for each. Which are the most important examples? Which divisions have no examples? Why?

4. The language of the aphorisms often has an archaic flavor. Examples: *instauration, whence*. What elements other than archaic words contribute to this flavor? What examples are no longer meaningful to a modern reader?

5. Bacon frequently uses vivid imagery. The concept of "idols of the mind" is imagistic. Discuss some of the images and show how they function to support his arguments in the aphorisms.

Suggestions for Writing

1. Select one of the idols and define it in your own words. Using contemporary illustrations, write an essay (approximately 500 words) to apply the idol to your own world.

2. You may wish to write a paper on some idols of the American mind. Follow Bacon's idols as a guide and try to classify your categories as Bacon does.

◇◇◇

Bertrand Russell

If We Are to Survive This Dark Time

Bertram Arthur William Russell (1872–1970), third Earl Russell, studied at Trinity College, Cambridge, where he later was lecturer and fellow. He lost his post because of his opposition to World War I. With Alfred North Whitehead he wrote *Principia Mathematica*, (1910–1913), a major contribution to symbolic logic which helped determine much of the course of modern philosophy. Among his many other works are *The Analysis of Mind* (1921), *Human Knowledge, Its Scope and Limits* (1948), and *The Impact of Science on Society* (1952). He was also an educator and a spokesman for many causes, popular and unpopular, all his life. He won the Nobel Prize for Literature in 1950. This essay (1961) clearly distinguishes between democratic and totalitarian concepts of man and society and projects hope for the future.

There is only too much reason to fear that Western civilization, if not the whole world, is likely in the near future to go through a period of immense sorrow and suffering and pain—a period during which, if we are not careful to remember them, the things that we are attempting to preserve may be forgotten in bitterness and poverty and disorder. Courage, hope, and unshakable conviction will be necessary if we are to emerge from the dark time spiritually undamaged. It is worth while, before the actual danger is upon us, to collect our thoughts, to marshal our hopes, and to plant in our hearts a firm belief in our ideals.

It is not the first time that such disasters have threatened the Western World. The fall of Rome was another such time, and in that time, as now, varying moods of despair, escape, and robust faith were exemplified in the writings of leading men. What emerged and became the kernel of the new civilization was the Christian Church. Many pagans were noble in their thoughts and admirable in their aspirations, but they lacked dynamic force.

Plotinus, the founder of neo-Platonism, was the most remarkable of the pagans of that time. In his youth he hoped to play some part in world affairs and accompanied the emperor in a campaign against Persia, but the Roman soldiers murdered the emperor and decided to go home. Plotinus found his way home as best he could, and decided to have done with practical affairs.

He then retired into meditation and wrote books full of beauty, extolling the eternal world and the inactive contemplation of it. Such philosophy, however admirable in itself, offered no cure for the ills from which the empire was suffering.

I think Plotinus was right in urging contemplation of eternal things, but he was wrong in thinking of this as enough to constitute a good life. Contemplation, if it is to be wholesome and valuable, must be married to practice; it must inspire action and ennoble the aims of practical statesmanship. While it remains secluded in the cloister it is only a means of escape.

Boethius, who represents the very last blossoming of Roman civilization, was a figure of more use to our age. After a lifetime spent in public administration and in trying to civilize a Gothic king, he fell into disfavour and was condemned to death. In prison he composed his great book, *The Consolations of Philosophy,* in which, with a combination of majestic calm and sweet reasonableness, he sets forth, as imperturbably as though he were still a powerful minister, the joys of contemplation, the delight in the beauty of the world and the hopes for mankind, which, even in that situation, did not desert him. Throughout the Dark Ages his book was studied and it transmitted to happier times the last purified legacy of the ancient world.

The sages of our times have a similar duty to perform. It is their duty to posterity to crystallize the achievements, the hopes, and the ideals which have made our time great—to study them with monumental simplicity, so they may shine like a beacon light through the coming darkness.

Two very different conceptions of human life are struggling for mastery of the world. In the West we see man's greatness in the individual life. A great society for us is one which is composed of individuals who, as far as is humanly possible, are happy, free, and creative. We do not think that individuals should be alike. We conceive society as like an orchestra, in which the different performers have different parts to play and different instruments upon which to perform, and in which cooperation results from a conscious common purpose. We believe that each individual should have his proper pride. He should have his personal conscience and his personal aims, which he should be free to develop except where they can be shown to cause injury to others. We attach importance to the diminution of suffering and poverty, to the increase of knowledge, and the production of beauty and art. The State for us is a convenience, not an object of worship.

The Russian Government has a different conception of the ends of life. The individual is thought of no importance: he is expendable. What is important is the State, which is regarded as something almost divine and having a welfare of its own not consisting in the welfare of citizens. This view, which Marx took over from Hegel, is fundamentally opposed to the Christian ethic, which in the West is accepted by free-thinkers as much as by Christians. In the Soviet world human dignity counts for nothing.

It is thought right and proper that men should be groveling slaves, bowing down before the semidivine beings who embody the greatness of the State. When a man betrays his dearest friend and causes him, as a penalty for a moment's peevish indiscretion, to vanish into the mysterious horror of a Siberian labor camp; when a schoolchild, as a result of indoctrination by his teacher, causes his parents to be condemned to death; when a man of exceptional courage, after struggling against evils, is tried, convicted, and abjectly confesses that he has sinned in opposing the Moloch power of the authorities, neither the betrayal nor the confession brings any sense of shame to the perpetrator, for has he not been engaged in the service of his divinity?

It is this conception that we have to fight, a conception which, to my mind and to that of most men who appreciate what the Western world stands for, would, if it prevailed, take everything out of life that gives it value, leaving nothing but a regimented collection of grovelling animals. I cannot imagine a greater or more profound cause for which to fight. But if we are to win a victory—not only on the battlefield but in the hearts of men and in the institutions that they support—we must be clear in our own minds as to what it is that we value, and we must, like Boethius, fortify our courage against the threat of adversity.

While Russia underestimates the individual, there are those in the West who unduly magnify the separateness of separate persons. No man's ego should be enclosed in granite walls; its boundaries should be translucent. The first step in wisdom, as well as in morality, is to open the windows of the ego as wide as possible. Most people find little difficulty in including their children within the compass of their desires. In slightly lesser degree they include their friends, and in time of danger their country. Very many men feel that what hurts their country hurts them. In 1940 I knew Frenchmen living prosperously in America who suffered from the fall of France almost as they would have suffered from the loss of a leg. But it is not enough to enlarge our sympathies to embrace our own country. If the world is ever to have peace it will be necessary to learn to embrace the whole human race in the same kind of sympathy which we now feel toward our compatriots. And if we are to retain calm and sanity in difficult times, it is a great help if the furniture of our minds contains past and future ages.

Few things are more purifying to our conception of values than to contemplate the gradual rise of man from his obscure and difficult beginnings to his present eminence. Man, when he first emerged, was a rare and hunted species, not so fleet as the deer, not so nimble as the monkey, unable to defend himself against wild beasts, without the protection of warm fur against rain and cold, living precariously upon the food that he could gather, without weapons, without domestic animals, without agriculture.

The one advantage that he possessed—intelligence—gave him security. He learned the use of fire, of bows and arrows, of language, of domestic animals and, at last, of agriculture. He learned to co-operate in communities, to build great palaces and pyramids, to explore the world in all directions and, at last, to cope with disease and poverty. He studied the stars, he invented geometry, and he learned to substitute machines for muscles in necessary labour. Some of the most important of these advances are very recent and are as yet confined to Western nations.

In the former days most children died in infancy, mortality in adult life was very high, and in every country the great majority of the population endured abject poverty. Now certain nations have succeeded in preserving the lives of the overwhelming majority of infants, in lowering enormously the adult death rate, and in nearly eliminating abject poverty. Other nations, where disease and abject poverty are still the rule, could achieve the same level of wellbeing by adopting the same methods. There is, therefore, a new hope for mankind.

The hope cannot be realized unless the causes of present evils are understood. But it is the hope that needs to be emphasized. Modern man is master of his fate. What he suffers he suffers because he is stupid or wicked, not because it is nature's decree. Happiness is his if he will adopt the means that lie ready to his hands.

We of the Western world, faced with Communisms's hostile criticism, have been too modest and too defensive in our attitude. Throughout the long ages since life began the mechanism of evolution has involved cruel suffering, endless struggle for bare subsistence, and in the end, in most cases, death by starvation. This is the law in the animal kingdom, and it remained, until the present century, the law among human beings also. Now, at last, certain nations have discovered how to prevent abject poverty, how to prevent the pain and sorrow and waste of useless births condemned to premature death, and how to substitute intelligence and care for the blind ruthlessness of nature.

The nations that have made this discovery are trustees for the future of mankind. They must have the courage of their new way of life and not allow themselves to be bemused or bewildered by the slogans of the semicivilized. We have a right to hopes that are rational, that can be itemized and set forth in statistics. If we allow ourselves to be robbed of these hopes for the sake of irrational dreams, we shall be traitors to the human race.

If bad times lie ahead of us, we should remember while they last the slow march of man, chequered in the past by devastations and retrogressions, but always resuming the movement toward progress. Spinoza, who was one of the wisest of men and who lived consistently in accordance with his own wisdom, advised men to view passing events "under the aspect of eternity." Those who can learn to do this will find a painful present much more bearable than it would otherwise be. They can see it as a passing moment—a discord to be resolved, a tunnel to be traversed. The small child who has hurt himself weeps as if the world contained nothing but sorrow, because his mind is confined to the present. A man who has learned wisdom from Spinoza can see even a lifetime of suffering as a passing moment in the life of humanity. And the human race itself, from its obscure beginning to its unknown end, is only a minute episode in the life of the universe.

What may be happening elsewhere we do not know, but it is improbable that the universe contains nothing better than ourselves. With increase of wisdom our thoughts acquire a wider scope both in space and in time. The child lives in the minute, the boy in the day, the instinctive man in the year. The man imbued with history lives in the epoch. Spinoza would have us live not in the minute, the day, the year or the epoch but in eternity. Those who learn to do this will find that it takes away the frantic quality of misfortune and prevents the trend towards madness that comes with overwhelming disaster. He spent the last day of his life telling cheerful anecdotes to his host. He had written: "The wise man thinks less about death than about anything else," and he carried out this precept when it came to his own death.

I do not mean that the wise man will be destitute of emotion—on the contrary, he will feel friendship, benevolence, and compassion in a higher degree than the man who has not emancipated himself from personal anxieties. His ego will not be a wall between him and the rest of mankind. He will feel, like Buddha, that he cannot be completely happy while anybody is miserable. He will feel pain—a wider and more diffused pain than that of the egoist—but he will not find the pain unendurable. He will not be driven by it to invent comfortable fairy-tales which assure him that the sufferings of others are illusory. He will not lose poise and self-control. Like Milton's Satan, he will say:

> The mind is its own place, and in itself
> Can make a Heav'n of Hell, a Hell of Heav'n.

Above all, he will remember that each generation is trustee to future generations of the mental and moral treasure that man has accumulated through the ages. It is easy to forget the glory of man. When King Lear is going mad he meets Edgar, who pretends to be mad and wears only a blanket. King Lear moralizes: "Unaccommodated, man is no more but such a poor, bare, forked animal as thou art."

This is half of the truth. The other half is uttered by Hamlet:

"What a piece of work is a man! how noble in reason; how infinite in faculty! In form and moving how express and admirable; in action how like an angel! in apprehension how like a god!"

Soviet man, crawling on his knees to betray his friends and family to slow butchery, is hardly worthy of Hamlet's words, but it is possible to be worthy of them. It is possible for every one of us. Every one of us can enlarge his mind, release his imagination, and spread wide his affection and benevolence. And it is those who do this whom ultimately mankind reveres. The East reveres Buddha, the West reveres Christ. Both taught love as the secret of wisdom. The earthly life of Christ was contemporary with that of the Emperor Tiberius, who spent his life in cruelty and disgusting debauchery. Tiberius had pomp and power; in his day millions trembled at his nod. But he is forgotten by historians.

Those who live nobly, even if in their day they live obscurely, need not fear that they will have lived in vain. Something radiates from their lives, some light that shows the way to their friends, their neighbours—perhaps to long future ages. I find many men nowadays oppressed with a sense of impotence, with the feeling that in the vastness of modern societies there is nothing of importance that the individual can do. This is a mistake. The individual, if he is filled with love of mankind, with breadth of vision, with courage and with endurance, can do a great deal.

As geological time goes, it is but a moment since the human race began and only the twinkling of an eye since the arts of civilization were first invented. In spite of some alarmists, it is hardly likely that our species will completely exterminate itself. And so long as man continues to exist, we may be pretty sure that, whatever he may suffer for a time, and whatever brightness may be eclipsed, he will emerge sooner or later, perhaps strengthened and reinvigorated by a period of mental sleep. The universe is vast and men are but tiny specks on an insignificant planet. But the more we realize our minuteness and our impotence in the face of cosmic forces, the more astonishing becomes what human beings have achieved.

It is to the possible achievements of man that our ultimate loyalty is due, and in that thought the brief troubles of our unquiet epoch become endurable. Much wisdom remains to be learned, and if it is only to be learned through adversity, we must endeavour to endure adversity with what fortitude we can command. But if we can acquire wisdom soon enough, adversity may not be necessary and the future of man may be happier than any part of his past.

Suggestions for Discussion

1. How does the first paragraph summarize the concerns that Russell treats in the rest of the essay?

2. What is the function of Russell's references to Plotinus and Boethius?

3. Russell distinguishes between totalitarian and democratic governments in their attitude toward individual freedom. Explain his argument.

4. What is the tone of this essay? Why does Russell hold out promise of hope in "this dark time"?

Suggestion for Writing

Write an essay in which you define Russell's "dark time." Your essay should attempt to evaluate his optimism in face of the difficulties that he considers to lie ahead.

Karl Jaspers

Is Science Evil?

Karl Jaspers (1883–1969) was a German philosopher who deeply influenced the modern existentialist movement in philosophy and literature. His works include *Reason and Anti-Reason in Our Time* (1952), *Tragedy is Not Enough* (1952), and *The Future of Man* (1961). In "Is Science Evil?" published in *Commentary* in 1950, Jaspers answers the accusation that modern science is responsible for the perverted experiments of Nazi doctors. Pointing out that crimes against humanity appeared long before science appeared, Jaspers defines the limits of science, but asserts its commitment to reason and truth.

No one questions the immense significance of modern science. Through industrial technology it has transformed our existence, and its insights have transformed our consciousness, all this to an extent hitherto unheard of. The human condition throughout the millennia appears relatively stable in comparison with the impetuous movement that has now caught up mankind as a result of science and technology, and is driving it no one knows where. Science has destroyed the substance of many old beliefs and has made others questionable. Its powerful authority has brought more and more men to the point where they wish to know and not believe, where they expect to be helped by science and only by science. The present faith is that scientific understanding can solve all problems and do away with all difficulties.

Such excessive expectations result inevitably in equally excessive disillusionment. Science has still given no answer to man's doubts and despair. Instead, it has created weapons able to destroy in a few moments that which science itself helped build up slowly over the years. Accordingly, there are today two conflicting viewpoints: first, the superstition of science, which holds scientific results to be as absolute as religious myths used to be, so that even religious movements are now dressed in the garments of pseudoscience. Second, the hatred of science, which sees it as a diabolical evil of mysterious origin that has befallen mankind.

These two attitudes—both nonscientific—are so closely linked that they are usually found together, either in alternation or in an amazing compound.

A very recent example of this situation can be found in the attack against science provoked by the trial in Nuremberg of those doctors who, under Nazi orders, performed deadly experiments on human beings. One of the most esteemed medical men among German university professors has accepted the verdict on these crimes as a verdict on science itself, as a stick with which to beat "purely scientific and biological" medicine, and even the modern science of man in general: "this invisible spirit sitting on the prisoner's bench in Nuremberg, this spirit that regards men merely as objects, is not present in Nuremberg alone—it pervades the entire world." And he adds, if this generalization may be viewed as an extenuation of the crime of the accused doctors, that is only a further indictment of purely scientific medicine.

Anyone convinced that true scientific knowledge is possible only of things that *can* be regarded as objects, and that knowledge of the subject is possible only when the subject attains a form of objectivity; anyone who sees science as the one great landmark on the road to truth, and sees the real achievements of modern physicians as derived exclusively from biological and scientific medicine—such a person will see in the above statements an attack on what he feels to be fundamental to human existence. And he may perhaps have a word to say in rebuttal.

In the special case of the crimes against humanity commited by Nazi doctors and now laid at the door of modern science, there is a simple enough argument. Science was not needed at all, but only a certain bent of mind for the perpetration of such outrages. Such crimes were already possible millennia ago. In the Buddhist Pali canon, there is the report of an Indian prince who had experiments performed on criminals in order to determine whether they had an immortal soul that survived their corpses: "You shall—it was ordered—put the living man in a tub, close the lid, cover it with a damp hide. lay on a thick layer of clay, put it in the oven, and make a fire. This was done. When we knew the man was dead, the tub was drawn forth, uncovered, the lid removed, and we looked carefully inside to see if we could perceive the escaping soul. But we saw no escaping soul." Similarly, criminals were slowly skinned alive to see if their souls could be observed leaving their bodies. Thus there were experiments on human beings before modern science.

Better than such a defense, however, would be a consideration of what modern science really genuinely is, and what its limits are.

Science, both ancient and modern, has, in the first place, three indispensable characteristics:

First, it is *methodical* knowledge. I know something scientifically only when I also know the method by which I have this knowledge, and am thus able to ground it and mark its limits.

Second, it is *compellingly certain*. Even the uncertain—i.e., the probable or improbable—I know scientifically only insofar as I know it clearly and compellingly as such, and know the degree of its uncertainly.

Third, it is *universally valid*. I know scientifically only what is identically valid for every inquirer. Thus scientific knowledge spreads over the world and remains the same. Unanimity is a sign of universal validity. When unanimity is not attained, when there is a conflict of schools, sects, and trends of fashion, then universal validity becomes problematic.

This notion of science as methodical knowledge, compellingly certain, and universally valid, was long ago possessed by the Greeks. Modern science has not only purified this notion; it has also transformed it: a transformation that can be described by saying that modern science is *indifferent to nothing*. Everything—the smallest and meanest, the furthest and strangest—that is in any way and at any time *actual*, is relevant to modern science, simply because it *is*. Modern science wants to be thoroughly universal, allowing nothing to escape it. Nothing shall be hidden, nothing shall be silent, nothing shall be a secret.

In contrast to the science of classical antiquity, modern science is *basically unfinished*. Whereas ancient science had the appearance of something completed, to which the notion of progress was not essential, modern science progresses into the infinite. Modern science has realized that a finished and total world-view is scientifically impossible. Only when scientific criticism is crippled by making particulars absolute can a closed view of the world pretend to scientific validity—and then it is a false validity. Those great new unified systems of knowledge—such as modern physics—that have grown up in the scientific era, deal only with single aspects of reality. And reality as a whole has been fragmented as never before; whence the openness of the modern world in contrast to the closed Greek cosmos.

However, while a total and finished world-view is no longer possible to modern science, the idea of a unity of the sciences has now come to replace it. Instead of the cosmos of the world, we have the cosmos of the sciences. Out of dissatisfaction with all the separate bits of knowledge is born the desire to unite all knowledge. The ancient sciences remained dispersed and without mutual relations. There was lacking to them the notion of a concrete totality of science. The modern sciences, however, seek to relate themselves to each other in every possible way.

At the same time the modern sciences have increased their claims. They put a low value on the possibilities of speculative thinking, they hold thought to be valid only as part of definite and concrete knowledge, only when it has stood the test of verification and thereby become infinitely modified. Only superficially do the modern and the ancient atomic theories seem to fit into the same theoretical mold. Ancient atomic theory was applied as a plausible interpretation of common experience; it was a statement complete in itself of what might possibly be the case. Modern atomic theory has developed through experiment, verification, refutation: that is, through an incessant transformation of itself in which theory is used not as an end in itself but as a tool of inquiry. Modern science, in its questioning, pushes to extremes. For example: the rational critique of appearance (as against reality) was begun in antiquity, as in the concept of perspective and its application to astronomy, but it still had some connection with immediate human experiences; today, however, this same critique, as in modern physics for instance, ventures to the very extremes of paradox, attaining a knowledge of the real that shatters any and every view of the world as a closed and complete whole.

So it is that in our day a scientific attitude has become possible that addresses itself inquisitively to everything it comes across, that is able to know what it knows in a clear and positive way, that can distinguish between the known and the unknown, and that has acquired an incredible mass of knowledge. How helpless was the Greek doctor or the Greek engineer! The ethos of modern science is the desire for reliable knowledge based on dispassionate investigation and criticism. When we enter its domain we feel as though we were breathing pure air, and seeing the dissolution of all vague talk, plausible opinions, haughty omniscience, blind faith.

But the greatness and the limitations of science are inseparable. It is a characteristic of the greatness of modern science that it comprehends its own limits:

(1) Scientific, objective knowledge is not a knowledge of Being. This means that scientific knowledge is particular, not general, that it is directed toward specific objects, and not toward Being itself. Through knowledge itself, science arrives at the most positive recognition of what it does *not* know.

(2) Scientific knowledge or understanding cannot supply us with the aims of life. It cannot lead us. By virtue of its very clarity it directs us elsewhere for the sources of our life, our decisions, our love.

(3) Human freedom is not an object of science, but is the field of philosophy. Within the purview of science there is no such thing as liberty.

These are clear limits, and the person who is scientifically minded will not expect from science what it cannot give. Yet science has become, nevertheless, the indispensable element of all striving for truth, it has become the premise of philosophy and the basis in general for whatever clarity and candor are today possible. To the extent that it succeeds in penetrating all obscurities and unveiling all secrets, science directs to the most profound, the most genuine secret.

The unique phenomenon of modern science, so fundamentally different from anything in the past, including the science of the Greeks, owes its character to the many sources that were its origin; and these had to meet together in Western history in order to produce it.

One of these sources was Biblical religion. The rise of modern science is scarcely conceivable without its impetus. Three of the motives that have spurred research and inquiry seem to have come from it:

(1) The ethos of Biblical religion demanded truthfulness at all costs. As a result, truthfulness became a supreme value and at the same time was pushed to the point where it became a serious problem. The truthfulness demanded by God forbade making the search for knowledge a game or amusement, an aristocratic leisure activity. It was a serious affair, a calling in which everything was at stake.

(2) The world is the creation of God. The Greeks knew the cosmos as that which was complete and ordered, rational and regular, eternally subsisting. All else was nothing, merely material, not knowable and not worth knowing. But if the world is the creation of God, then everything that exists is worth knowing, just because it is God's creation; there is nothing that ought not to

be known and comprehended. To know is to reflect upon God's thought. And God as creator is—in Luther's words—present even in the bowels of a louse.

The Greeks remained imprisoned in their closed world-view, in the beauty of their rational cosmos, in the logical transparency of the rational whole. Not only Aristotle and Democritus, but Thomas Aquinas and Descartes, too, obey this Greek urge, so paralyzing to the spirit of science, toward a closed universe. Entirely different is the new impulse to unveil the totality of creation. Out of this there arises the pursuit through knowledge of that reality which is not in accord with previously established laws. In the Logos itself [the Word, Reason] there is born the drive toward repeated self-destruction—not as self-immolation, but in order to arise again and ever again in a process that is to be continued infinitely. This science springs from a Logos that does not remain closed within itself, but is open to an anti-Logos which it permeates by the very act of subordinating itself to it. The continuous, unceasing reciprocal action of theory and experiment is the simple and great example and symbol of the universal process that is the dialectic between Logos and anti-Logos.

This new urge for knowledge sees the world no longer as simply beautiful. This knowledge ignores the beautiful and the ugly, the good and the wicked. It is true that in the end, *omne ens est bonum* [all Being is good], that is, as a creation of God. This goodness, however, is no longer the transparent and self-sufficient beauty of the Greeks. It is present only in the love of all existent things as created by God, and it is present therefore in our confidence in the significance of inquiry. The knowledge of the createdness of all worldly things replaces indifference in the face of the flux of reality with limitless questioning, an insatiable spirit of inquiry.

But the world that is known and knowable is, as created Being, Being of the second rank. For the world is unfathomable, it has its ground in another, a Creator, it is not self-contained and it is not containable by knowledge. The Being of the world cannot be comprehended as definitive, absolute reality but points always to another.

The idea of creation makes worthy of love whatever is, for it is God's creation; and it makes possible, by this, an intimacy with reality never before attained. But at the same time it gives evidence of the incalculable distance from that Being which is not merely created Being but Being itself, God.

(3) The reality of this world is full of cruelty and horror for men. "That's the way things are," is what man must truthfully say. If, however, God is the world's creator, then he is responsible for his creation. The question of justifying God's way becomes with Job a struggle with the divine for the knowledge of reality. It is a struggle against God, for God. God's existence is undisputed and just because of this the struggle arises. It would cease if faith were extinguished.

This God, with his unconditional demand for truthfulness, refuses to be grasped through illusions. In the Bible, he condemns the theologians who wish to console and comfort Job with dogmas and sophisms. This God insists upon science, whose content always seems to bring forth an indictment of him. Thus we have the adventure of knowledge, the furtherance of unrestricted knowledge—and at the same time, a timidity, an awe in the face of it. There was an inner tension to be observed in many scientists of the past century, as if they heard: God's will is unconfined inquiry, inquiry is in the service of God—and at the same time: it is an encroachment on God's domain, all shall not be revealed.

This struggle goes hand in hand with the struggle of the man of science against all that he holds most dear, his ideals, his beliefs; they must be proven, newly verified, or else transformed. Since God could not be believed in if he were not able to withstand all the questions arising from the facts of reality, and since the seeking of God involves the painful sacrifice of all illusions, so true inquiry is the struggle against all personal desires and expectations.

This struggle finds its final test in the struggle of the scientist with his own theses. It is the determining characteristic of the modern scientist that he seeks out the strongest points in the criticism of his opponents and exposes himself to them. What in appearance is self-destructiveness becomes, in this case, productive. And it is evidence of a degradation of science when discussion is shunned or condemned, when men imprison themselves and their ideas in a milieu of like-minded savants and become fanatically aggressive to all outside it.

That modern science, like all things, contains its own share of corruption, that men of science only too often fail to live up to its standards, that science can be used for violent and criminal ends, that man will steal, plunder, abuse, and kill to gain knowledge—all this is no argument against science.

To be sure, science as such sets up no barriers. As science, it is neither human nor inhuman. So far as the well-being of humanity is concerned, science needs guidance from other sources. Science in itself is not enough—or should not be. Even medicine is only a scientific means, serving an eternal ideal, the aid of the sick and the protection of the healthy.

When the spirit of a faithless age can become the cause of atrocities all over the world, then it can also influence the conduct of the scientist and the behavior of the physician, especially in those areas of activity where science itself is confused and unguided. It is not the spirit of science but the spirit of its vessels that is depraved. Count Keyserling's dictum—"The roots of truth-seeking lie in primitive aggression"—is as little valid for science as it is for any genuine truth seeking. The spirit of science is in no way primarily aggressive, but becomes so only when truth is prohibited; for men rebel against the glossing over of truth or its suppression.

In our present situation the task is to attain to that true science which knows what it knows at the same time that it knows what it cannot know. This science shows us the ways to the truth that are the indispensable precondition of every other truth. We know what Mephistopheles knew when he thought he had outwitted Faust:

> *Verachte nur Vernunft und Wissenschaft*
> *Des Menschen allerhöchste Kraft*
> *So habe ich Dich schon unbedingt.*

> (Do but scorn Reason and Science
> Man's supreme strength
> Then I'll have you for sure.)

Suggestions for Discussion

1. What is the function of the first two paragraphs of the essay? How is the third paragraph linked to the first two?

2. How does Jaspers use the Nuremberg trail to develop his ideas? Discuss Jasper's statement that there were experiments on human beings before science.

3. What role do the three characteristics of science play in Jaspers's defense of science?

4. Explain Jaspers's statement that "modern science is *basically unfinished.*" Is this statement part of his defense of science? How does it also serve as a definition of the limits of scientific knowledge? What are the limits?

5. How does Jaspers relate the limits of science to the area of what is unknowable scientifically? What is Jaspers' attitude toward this area?

Suggestions for Writing

1. Although Jaspers's essay is complex, is it difficult to read? If you think not, explain how the language and the organization of the essay contribute to its clarity.

2. Why does Jaspers close his essay with a quotation from Goethe's *Faust?* Write a paper in which you relate the quotation to the essay.

Jacob Bronowski
The Reach of the Imagination

Jacob Bronowski (1908–1974) was a Polish-born American scientist who has played a significant role in the scientific and cultural life of America. He has been particularly active in attempting to explain scientific concepts to humanists. He wrote *The Common Sense of Science* (1951), *Science and Human Values* (1959), and *William Blake, A Man with a Mask* (1965). His *Ascent of Man* (1974), a series of television essays which combined art, philosophy, and science, was a major effort to bridge the gap between the worlds of science and humanism. "The Reach of Imagination" argues that imagination is common to literature and science, and inspires creativity in both.

For three thousand years, poets have been enchanted and moved and perplexed by the power of their own imagination. In a short and summary essay I can hope at most to lift one small corner of that mystery; and yet it is a critical corner. I shall ask, What goes on in the mind when we imagine? You will hear from me that one answer to this question is fairly specific: which is to say, that we can describe the working of the imagination. And when we describe it as I shall do, it becomes plain that imagination is a specifically *human* gift. To imagine is the characteristic act, not of the poet's mind, or the painter's, or the scientist's, but of the mind of man.

My stress here on the word *human* implies that there is a clear difference in this between the actions of men and those of other animals. Let me then start with a classical experiment with animals and children which Walter Hunter thought out in Chicago about 1910. That was the time when scientists were agog with the success of Ivan Pavlov in forming and changing the reflex actions of dogs, which Pavlov had first announced in 1903. Pavlov had been given a Nobel Prize the next year, in 1904; although in fairness I should say that the award did not cite his work on the conditioned reflex, but on the digestive gland.

Hunter duly trained some dogs and other animals on Pavlov's lines. They were taught that when a light came on over one of three tunnels out of their cage, that tunnel would be open; they could escape down it, and were rewarded with food if they did. But once he had fixed that conditioned reflex, Hunter added to it a deeper idea: he gave the mechanical experiment a new dimension, literally—the dimension of time. Now he no longer let the dog go to the lighted tunnel at once; instead, he put out the light, and then kept the dog waiting a little while before he let him go. In this way Hunter timed how long an animal can remember where he has last seen the signal light to his escape route.

The results were and are staggering. A dog or a rat forgets which one of three tunnels has been lit up within a matter of seconds—in Hunter's experiment, ten seconds at most. If you want such an animal to do much better than this, you must make the task much simpler: you must face him with only two tunnels to choose from. Even so, the best that Hunter could do was to have a dog remember for five minutes which one of two tunnels had been lit up.

I am not quoting these times as if they were exact and universal: they surely are not. Hunter's experiment, more than fifty years old now, had many faults of detail. For example, there were too few animals, they were oddly picked, and they did not all behave consistently. It may be unfair to test a dog for what he *saw*, when he commonly follows his nose rather than his eyes. It may be unfair to test any animal in the unnatural setting of a laboratory cage. And there are higher animals, such as chimpanzees and other primates, which certainly have longer memories than the animals that Hunter tried.

Yet when all these provisos have been made (and met, by more modern experiments) the facts are still startling and characteristic. An animal cannot recall a signal from the past for even a short fraction of the time that a man can—for even a short fraction of the time that a child can. Hunter made comparable tests with six-year-old children, and found, of course, that they were incomparably better than the best of his animals. There is a striking and basic difference between a man's ability to imagine something that he saw or experienced, and an animal's failure.

Animals make up for this by other and extraordinary gifts. The salmon and the carrier pigeon can find their way home as we cannot: they have, as it were, a practical memory that man cannot match. But their actions always depend on some form of habit: on instinct or on learning, which reproduce by rote a train of known responses. They do not depend, as human memory does, on calling to mind the recollection of absent things.

Where is it that the animal falls short? We get a clue to the answer, I think, when Hunter tells us how the animals in his experiment tried to fix their recollection. They most often pointed themselves at the light before it went out, as some gun dogs point rigidly at the game they scent—and get the name *pointer* from the posture. The animal makes ready to act by building the signal into its action. There is a primitive imagery in its stance, it seems to me; it is as if the animal were trying to fix the light on its mind by fixing it in its body. And indeed, how else can a dog mark and (as it were) name one of the three tunnels, when he has no such words as *left* and *right,* and no such numbers as *one, two, three?* The directed gesture of attention and readiness is perhaps the only symbolic device that the dog commands to hold on to the past, and thereby to guide himself into the future.

I used the verb *to imagine* a moment ago, and now I have some ground for giving it a meaning. *To imagine* means to make images and to move them about inside one's head in new arrangements. When you and I recall the past, we imagine it in this direct and homely sense. The tool that puts the human mind ahead of the animal is imagery. For us, memory does not demand the preoccupation that it demands in animals, and it lasts immensely longer, because we fix it in images or other substitute symbols. With the same symbolic vocabulary we spell out the future—not one but many futures, which we weigh one against another.

I am using the word *image* in a wide meaning, which does not restrict it to the mind's eye as a visual organ. An image in my usage is what Charles Peirce called a *sign,* without regard for its sensory quality. Peirce distinguished between different forms of signs, but there is no reason to make his distinction here, for the imagination works equally with them all, and that is why I call them all images.

Indeed, the most important images for human beings are simply words, which are abstract symbols. Animals do not have words, in our sense: there is no specific center for language in the brain of any animal, as there is in the human being. In this respect at least we know that the human imagination depends on a configuration in the brain that has only evolved in the last one or two million years. In the same period, evolution has greatly enlarged the front lobes in the human brain, which govern the sense of the past and the future; and it is a fair guess that they are probably the seat of our other images. (Part of the evidence for this guess is that damage to the front lobes in primates reduces them to the state of Hunter's animals.) If the guess turns out to be right, we shall know why man has come to look like a highbrow or an egghead: because otherwise there would not be room in his head for his imagination.

The images play out for us events which are not present to our senses, and thereby guard the past and create the future—a future that does not yet exist, and may never come to exist in that form. By contrast, the lack of symbolic ideas, or their rudimentary poverty, cuts off an animal from the past and the future alike, and imprisons him in the present. Of all the distinctions between man and animal, the characteristic gift which makes us human is the power to work with symbolic images: the gift of imagination.

This is really a remarkable finding. When Philip Sidney in 1580 defended poets (and all unconventional thinkers) from the Puritan charge that they were liars, he said that a maker must imagine things that are not. Halfway between Sidney and us, William Blake said, "What is now proved was once only imagined." About the same time, in 1796, Samuel Taylor Coleridge for the first time distinguished between the passive fancy and the active imagination, "the living Power and prime Agent of all human Perception." Now we see that they were right, and precisely right: the human gift is the gift of imagination—and that is not just a literary phrase.

Nor is it just a literary gift; it is, I repeat, characteristically human. Almost everything that we do that is worth doing is done in the first place in the mind's eye. The richness of human life is that we have many lives; we live the events that do not happen (and some that cannot) as vividly as those that do; and if thereby we die a thousand deaths, that is the price we pay for living a thousand lives. (A cat, of course, has only nine.) Literature is alive to us because we live its images, but so is any play of the mind—so is chess: the lines of play that we foresee and try in out heads and dismiss are as much a part of the game as the moves that we make. John Keats said that the unheard melodies are sweeter, and all chess players sadly recall that the combinations that they planned and which never came to be played were the best.

I make this point to remind you, insistently, that imagination is the manipulation of images in one's head; and that the rational manipulation belongs to that, as well as the literary and artistic manipulation. When a child begins to play games with things that stand for other things, with chairs or chessmen, he enters the gateway to reason and imagination together. For the human reason discovers new relations between things not by deduction, but by that unpredictable blend of speculation and insight that scientists call induction, which—like other forms of imagination—cannot be formalized. We see it at work when Walter Hunter inquires into a child's memory, as much as when Blake and Coleridge do. Only a restless and original mind would have asked Hunter's questions and could have conceived his experiments, in a science that was dominated by Pavlov's reflex arcs and was heading toward the behaviorism of John Watson.

Let me find a spectacular example for you from history. What is the most famous experiment that you had described to you as a child? I will hazard that it is the experiment that Galileo is said to have made in Sidney's age, in Pisa about 1590, by dropping two unequal balls from the Leaning Tower. There, we say, is a man in the modern mold, a man after our own hearts: he insisted on questioning the authority of Aristotle and St. Thomas Aquinas, and seeing with his own eyes whether (as they said) the heavy ball would reach the ground before the light one. Seeing is believing.

Yet seeing is also imagining. Galileo did challenge the authority of Aristotle, and he did look at his mechanics. But the eye that Galileo used was the minds's eye. He did not drop balls from the Leaning Tower of Pisa—and if he had, he would have got a very doubtful answer. Instead, Galileo made an imaginary experiment in his head, which I will describe as he did years later in the book he wrote after the Holy Office silenced him: *Discorsi . . . intorno a due nuove scienze,* which was smuggled out to be printed in the Netherlands in 1638.

Suppose, said Galileo, that you drop two unequal balls from the tower at the same time. And suppose that Aristotle is right—suppose that the heavy ball falls faster, so that it steadily gains on the light ball, and hits the ground first. Very well. Now imagine the same experiment done again, with only one difference: this time the two unequal balls are joined by a string between them. The heavy ball will again move ahead, but now the light ball holds it back and acts as a drag or brake. So the light ball will be speeded up and the heavy ball will be slowed down; they must reach the ground together because they are tied together, but they cannot reach the ground as quickly as the heavy ball alone. Yet the string between them has turned the two balls into a single mass which is heavier than either ball—and surely (according to Aristotle) this mass should therefore move faster than either ball? Galileo's imaginary experiment has uncovered a contradiction; he says trenchantly, "You see how, from your assumption that a heavier body falls more rapidly than a lighter one, I infer that a (still) heavier body falls more slowly." There is only one way out of the contradiction: the heavy ball and the light ball must fall at the same rate, so that they go on falling at the same rate when they are tied together.

This argument is not conclusive, for nature might be more subtle (when the two balls are joined) than Galileo has allowed. And yet it is something more important: it is suggestive, it is stimulating, it opens a new view—in a work, it is imaginative. It cannot be settled without an actual experiment, because nothing that we imagine can become knowledge until we have translated it into, and backed it by, real experience. The test of imagination is experience. But then, that is as true of literature and the arts as it is of science. In science, the imaginary experiment is tested by confronting it with physical experience; and in literature, the imaginative conception is tested by confronting it with human experience. The superficial speculation in science is dismissed because it is found to falsify nature; and the shallow work of art is discarded because it is found to be untrue to our own nature. So when Ella Wheeler Wilcox died in 1919, more people were reading her verses than Shakespeare's; yet in a few years her work was dead. It had been buried by its poverty of emotion and its trivialness of thought: which is to say that it had been proved to be as false to the nature of man as, say, Jean Baptiste Lamarck and Trofim Lysenko were false to the nature of inheritance. The strength of the imagination, its enriching power and excitement, lies in its interplay with reality—physical and emotional.

I doubt if there is much to choose here between science and the arts: the imagination is not much more free, and not much less free, in one than in the other. All great scientists have used their imagination freely, and let it ride them to outrageous conclusions without crying "Halt!" Albert Einstein fiddled with imaginary experiments from boyhood, and was wonderfully ignorant of the facts that they were supposed to bear on. When he wrote the first of his beautiful papers on the random movement of atoms, he did not know that the Brownian motion which it predicted could be seen in any laboratory. He was sixteen when he invented the paradox that he resolved ten years later, in 1905, in the theory of relativity, and it bulked much larger in his mind than the experiment of Albert Michelson and Edward Morley which had upset every other physicist since 1881. All his life Einstein loved to make up teasing puzzles like Galileo's, about falling lifts and the detection of gravity; and they carry the nub of the problems of general relativity on which he was working.

Indeed, it could not be otherwise. The power that man has over nature and himself, and that a dog lacks, lies in his command of imaginary experience. He alone has the symbols which fix the past and play with the future, possible and impossible. In the Renaissance, the symbolism of memory was thought to be mystical, and devices that were invented as mnemonics (by Giordano Bruno, for example, and by Robert Fludd) were interpreted as magic signs. The symbol is the tool which gives man his power, and it is the same tool whether the symbols are images or words, mathematical signs or mesons. And the symbols have a reach and a roundness that goes beyond their literal and practical meaning. They are the rich concepts under which the mind gathers many particulars into one name, and many instances into one general induction. When a man says *left* and *right*, he is outdistancing the dog not only in looking for a light; he is setting in train all the shifts of meaning, the overtones and the ambiguities, between *gauche* and *adroit* and *dexterous*, between *sinister* and the sense of right. When a man counts *one, two, three*, he is not only doing mathematics; he is on the path to the mysticism of numbers in Pythagoras and Vitruvius and Kepler, to the Trinity and the signs of the Zodiac.

I have described imagination as the ability to make images and to move them about inside one's head in new arrangements. This is the faculty that is specifically human, and it is the common root from which science and literature both spring and grow and flourish together. For they do flourish (and languish) together; the great ages of science are the great ages of all the arts, because in them powerful minds have taken fire from one another breathless and higgledy-piggledy, without asking too nicely whether they ought to tie their imagination to falling balls or a haunted island. Galileo and Shakespeare, who were born in the same year, grew into greatness in the same age; when Galileo was looking through his telescope at the moon, Shakespeare was writing *The Tempest* and all Europe was in ferment, from Johannes Kepler to Peter Paul Rubens, and from the first table of logarithms by John Napier to the Authorized Version of the Bible.

Let me end with a last and spirited example of the common inspiration of literature and science, because it is as much alive today as it was three hundred years ago. What I have in mind is man's ageless fantasy, to fly to the moon. I do not display this to you as a high scientific enterprise; on the contrary, I think we have more important discoveries to make here on earth than wait for us, beckoning, at the horned surface of the moon. Yet I cannot belittle the fascination which that ice-blue journey has had for the imagination of men, long before it drew us to our television screens to watch the tumbling astronauts. Plutarch and Lucian, Ariosto and Ben Jonson wrote about it, before the days of Jules Verne and H. G. Wells and science fiction. The seventeenth century was heady with new dreams and fables about voyages to the moon. Kepler wrote one full of deep scientific ideas, which (alas) simply got his mother accused of witchcraft. In England, Francis Godwin wrote a wild and splendid work, *The Man in the Moone*, and the astronomer John Wilkins wrote a wild and learned one, *The Discovery of a New World*. They did not draw a line between science and fancy; for example, they all tried to guess just where in the journey the earth's gravity would stop. Only Kepler understood that gravity has no boundary, and put a law to it—which happened to be the wrong law.

All this was a few years before Isaac Newton was born, and it was all in his head that day in 1666 when he sat in his mother's garden, a young man of twenty-three, and thought about the reach of gravity. This was how he came to conceive his brilliant image, that the moon is like a ball which has been thrown so hard that it falls exactly as fast as the horizon, all the way round the earth. The image will do for any satellite, and Newton modestly calculated how long therefore an astronaut would take to fall round the earth once. He made it ninety minutes, and we have all seen now that he was right; but Newton had no way to check that. Instead he went on to calculate how long in that case the distant moon would take to round the earth, if indeed it behaves like a thrown ball that falls in the earth's gravity, and if gravity obeyed a law of inverse squares. He found that the answer would be twenty-eight days.

In that telling figure, the imagination that day chimed with nature, and made a harmony. We shall hear an echo of that harmony on the day when we land on the moon, because it will be not a technical but an imaginative triumph, that reaches back to the beginning of modern science and literature both. All great acts of imagination are like this, in the arts and in science, and convince us because they fill out reality with a deeper sense of rightness. We start with the simplest vocabulary of images, with *left* and *right* and *one, two, three,* and before we know how it happened the words and the numbers have conspired to make a match with nature: we catch in them the pattern of mind and matter as one.

Suggestions for Discussion

1. Although Bronowski proposes to discuss the imagination of man, he begins his essay by describing an experiment conducted on animals. How does Bronowski use the experiment to explore or define man's imagination?

2. Bronowski uses the metaphor of "reaching" in the essay. What objects does the imagination reach for? What is the function of the metaphor in the argument?

3. Explain how Bronowski uses Galileo and Newton in his argument.

Suggestion for Writing

Write a paper in which you compare Bronowski the scientist with Whitman the poet, based entirely on this essay and the poem by Whitman "When I Heard the Learn'd Astronomer." Might Whitman have been surprised at the poetic nature of Bronowski the scientist?

Joseph Weizenbaum
The Compulsive Programmer

Joseph Weizenbaum (b. 1923) was born in Berlin but educated at Wayne State University. A professor of Computer Science and Engineering at MIT since 1970, he has done research in artificial intelligence and the structure of computer languages. He is concerned with the social impact of computers and cybernetics. His program "ELIZA" simulated the words of a nondirective psychological therapist. In this essay from *Computer Powers and Human Reason* (1976), Weizenbaum distinguishes between the compulsive programmer and the merely hard-working programmer. The former suffers from a neurotic disorder that incapacitates him from making a serious contribution since he is too emotionally involved with the machine to think clearly about the problems which face the ordinary, dedicated programmer.

Wherever computer centers have become established, that is to say, in countless places in the United States, as well as in virtually all other industrial regions of the world, bright young men of disheveled appearance, often with sunken glowing eyes, can be seen sitting at computer consoles, their arms tensed and waiting to fire their fingers, already poised to strike, at the buttons and keys on which their attention seems to be as riveted as a gambler's on the rolling dice. When not so transfixed, they often sit at tables strewn with computer printouts over which they pore like possessed students of a cabalistic text. They work until they nearly drop, twenty, thirty hours at a time. Their food, if they arrange it, is brought to them: coffee, Cokes, sandwiches. If possible, they sleep on cots near the computer. But only for a few hours— then back to the console or the printouts. Their rumpled clothes, their unwashed and unshaven faces, and their uncombed hair all testify that they are oblivious to their bodies and to the world in which they move. They exist, at least when so engaged, only through and for the computers. These are computer bums, compulsive programmers. They are an international phenomenon.

How may the compulsive programmer be distinguished from a merely dedicated, hard-working professional programmer? First, by the fact that the ordinary professional programmer addresses himself to the problem to be solved, whereas the compulsive programmer sees the problem mainly as an opportunity to interact with the computer. The ordinary computer programmer will usually discuss both his substantive and his technical programming problem with others. He will generally do lengthy preparatory work, such as writing and flow diagramming, before beginning work with the computer itself. His sessions with the computer may be comparatively short. He may even let others do the actual console work. He develops his program slowly and systematically. When something doesn't work, he may spend considerable time away from the computer, framing careful hypotheses to account for the malfunction and designing crucial experiments to test them. Again, he may leave the actual running of the computer to others. He is able, while waiting for results from the computer, to attend to other aspects of his work, such as documenting what he has already done. When he has finally composed the program he set out to produce, he is able to complete a sensible description of it and to turn his attention to other things. The professional regards programming as a means toward an end, not as an end in itself. His satisfaction comes from having solved a substantive problem, not from having bent a computer to his will.

The compulsive programmer is usually a superb technician, moreover, one who knows every detail of the computer he works on, its peripheral equipment, the computer's operating system, etc. He is often tolerated around computer centers because of his knowledge of the system and because he can write small subsystem programs quickly, that is, in one or two sessions of, say, twenty hours each. After a time, the center may in fact be using a number of his programs. But because the compulsive programmer can hardly be motivated to do anything but program, he will almost never document his programs once he stops working on them. A center may therefore come to depend on him to teach the use of, and to maintain, the programs that he wrote and whose structure only he, if anyone, understands. His position is rather like that of a bank employee who doesn't do much for the bank, but who is kept on because only he knows the combination to the safe. His main interest is, in any case, not in small programs, but in very large, very ambitious systems of programs. Usually the systems he undertakes to build, and on which he works feverishly for perhaps a month or two or three, have very grandiose but extremely imprecisely stated goals. Some examples of these ambitions are new computer languages to facilitate man-machine communication; a general system that can be taught to play any board game; a system to make it easier for computer experts to write supersystems (this last is a favorite). It is characteristic of many such projects that the programmer can long continue in the conviction that they demand knowledge about nothing but computers, programming, etc. And that knowledge he, of course, commands in abundance. Indeed, the point at which such work is often abandoned is precisely when it ceases to be purely incestuous, i.e., when programming would have to be interrupted in order that knowledge from outside the computer world may be acquired.

Unlike the professional, the compulsive programmer cannot attend to other tasks, not even to tasks closely related to his program, during periods when he is not actually operating the computer. He can barely tolerate being away from the machine. But when he is nevertheless forced by circumstances to be separated from it, at least he has his computer printouts with him. He studies them, he talks about them to anyone who will listen—though, of course, no one else can understand them. Indeed, while in the grip of his compulsion, he can talk of nothing but his program. But the only time he is, so to say, happy is when he is at the computer console. Then he will not converse with anyone but the computer. We will soon see what they converse about.

The compulsive programmer spends all the time he can working on one of his big projects. "Working" is not the word he uses; he calls what he does "hacking." To hack is, according to the dictionary, "to cut irregularly, without skill or definite purpose; to mangle by or as if by repeated strokes of a cutting instrument." I have already said that the compulsive programmer, or hacker as he calls himself, is usually a superb technician. It seems therefore that he is not "without skill" as the definition would have it. But the definition fits in the deeper sense that the hacker is "without definite purpose": he cannot set before himself a clearly defined long-term goal and a plan for achieving it, for he has only technique, not knowledge. He has nothing he can analyze or synthesize; in short, he has nothing to form theories about. His skill is therefore aimless, even disembodied. It is simply not connected with anything other than the instrument on which it may be exercised. His skill is like that of a monastic copyist, who though illiterate, is a first-rate calligrapher. His grandiose projects must therefore necessarily have the quality of illusions, indeed, of illusions of grandeur. He will construct the one grand system in which all other experts will soon write their systems.

(It has to be said that not all hackers are pathologically compulsive programmers. Indeed, were it not for the often, in its own terms, highly creative labor of people who proudly claim the title "hacker," few of today's sophisticated computer time-sharing systems, computer language translators, computer graphics systems, etc., would exist.)

Programming systems can, of course, be built without plan and without knowledge, let alone understanding, of the deep structural issues involved, just as houses, cities, systems of dams, and national economic policies can be similarly hacked together. As a system so constructed begins to get large, however, it also becomes increasingly unstable. When one of its subfunctions fails in an unanticipated way, it may be patched until the manifest trouble disappears. But since there is no general theory of the whole system, the system itself can be only a more or less chaotic aggregate of subsystems whose influence on one another's behavior is discoverable only piecemeal and by experiment. The hacker spends part of his time at the console piling new subsystems onto the structure he has already built—he calls them "new features"—and the rest of his time in attempts to account for the way in which substructures already in place misbehave. That is what he and the computer converse about.

The psychological situation the compulsive programmer finds himself in while so engaged is strongly determined by two apparently opposing facts: first, he knows that he can make the computer do anything he wants it to do; and second, the computer constantly displays undeniable evidence of his failures to him. It reproaches him. There is no escaping this bind. The engineer can resign himself to the truth that there are some things he doesn't know. But the programmer moves in a world entirely of his own making. The computer challenges his power, not his knowledge.

Indeed, the compulsive programmer's excitement rises to its highest, most feverish pitch when he is on the trail of a most recalcitrant error, when everything ought to work but the computer nevertheless reproaches him by misbehaving in a number of mysterious, apparently unrelated ways. It is then that the system the programmer has himself created gives every evidence of having taken on a life of its own and, certainly, of having slipped from his control. This too is the point at which the idea that the computer can be "made to do anything" becomes most relevant and most soundly based in reality. For, under such circumstances, the misbehaving artifact is, in fact, the programmer's own creation. Its very misbehavior can, as we have already said, be the consequence only of what the programmer himself has done. And what he has done he can presumably come to understand, to undo, and to redo to better serve his purpose. Accordingly his mood and his activity become frenzied when he believes he has finally discovered the source of the trouble. Should his time at the console be nearly up at that moment, he will take enormous risks with his program, making substantial changes, one after another, in minutes or even seconds without so much as recording what he is doing, always pleading for just another minute. He can, under such circumstances, rapidly and virtually irretrievably destroy weeks and weeks of his own work. Should he, however, find a deeply embedded error, one that actually does account for much of the program's misbehaviour, his joy is unbounded. It *is* a thrill to see a hitherto moribund program suddenly come back to life; there is no other way to say it. When some deep error has been found and repaired, many different portions of the program, which until then had given nothing but incomprehensible outputs, suddenly behave smoothly and deliver precisely the intended results. There is reason for the diagnostician to be pleased and, if the error was really deep inside the system, even proud.

But the compulsive programmer's pride and elation are very brief. His success consists of his having shown the computer who its master is. And having demonstrated that he can make it do this much, he immediately sets out to make it do even more. Thus the entire cycle begins again. He begins to "improve" his system, say, by making it run faster, or by adding "new features" to it, or by improving the ease with which data can be entered into it and gotten out of it. The act of modifying the then-existing program invariably causes some of its substructures to collapse; they constitute, after all, an amorphous collection of processes whose interactions with one another are virtually fortuitous. His apparently devoted efforts to improve and promote his own creation are really an assault on it, an assault whose only consequence can be to renew his struggle with the computer. Should he be prevented from so sabotaging his own work, say, by administrative decision, he will become visibly depressed, begin to sulk, display no interest in anything around him, etc. Only a new opportunity to compute can restore his spirit.

It must be emphasized that the portrait I have drawn is instantly recognizable at computing installations all over the world. It represents a psychopathology that is far less ambiguous than, say, the milder forms of schizophrenia or paranoia. At the same time, it represents an extremely developed form of a disorder that afflicts much of our society.

Suggestions for Discussion

1. Discuss Weizenbaum's description of the compulsive programmer. How prevalent is the compulsive programmer in society?

2. How does the author distinguish the compulsive programmer from the merely dedicated programmer? Which of the two is the more valuable worker? Why?

3. What are the weaknesses of the compulsive programmer?

4. How does the author compare computer programming to other programming systems such as city planning or planning economic policy? What qualities must exist in all such planning? In what ways does the compulsive programmer lack these qualities?

5. Explain the terms "hacking" and "hacker." Why does the author introduce them in the middle of his essay?

6. Why and how does the compulsive programmer inevitably sabotage his own work? What virtues do such programmers possess?

Suggestion for Writing

Weizenbaum describes the compulsive programmer as having a pathological character. Write an essay, using the author's evidence or evidence from your own observation in which you either support or refute his position.

A. M. Turing

The Imitation Game

Alan Mathison Turing (1912–1954) was made a fellow of Kings College, Cambridge, at twenty-three for his thesis "On the Gaussian Error Function." At twenty-five he made a significant contribution to mathematical logic with his paper "On Computable Numbers," proving that there are classes of mathematical problems which cannot be solved by an automatic machine. His theoretical "universal" thinking machine incorporated ideas later found in all computing machines. He designed the Automatic Computing Engine while senior principal officer in mathematics at the National Physical Laboratory and from 1948 until his death was the director of the Manchester Automatic Digital Machine at the University of Manchester. Shy, eccentric, an advocate of long distance running in lieu of public transportation, he states in "Computing Machinery and Intelligence" (in *Mind*, October 1950) that machines may eventually "compete with men in all purely intellectual fields." "The Imitation Game," from "Computing Machinery and Intelligence" (1950), considers the question of whether machines can think. To impose real meaning to the question, Turing devises a question and answer game for three players as well as a variant which assigns to a machine the part of one of the players. He suggests that, if a machine can think, the best answers it would make are those that resemble most closely those made by man. Turing draws back, however, from positively answering the question with which he begins.

I propose to consider the question, "Can machines think?" This should begin with definitions of the meaning of the terms "machine" and "think".

The definitions might be framed so as to reflect so far as possible the normal use of the words, but this attitude is dangerous. If the meaning of the words "machine" and "think" are to be found by examining how they are commonly used it is difficult to escape the conclusion that the meaning and the answer to the question "Can machines think?" is to be sought in a statistical survey such as a Gallup poll. But this is absurd. Instead of attempting such a definition I shall replace the question by another, which is closely related to it and is expressed in relatively unambiguous words.

The new form of the problem can be described in terms of a game which we call the "imitation game". It is played with three people, a man (A), a woman (B), and an interrogator (C) who may be of either sex. The interrogator stays in a room apart from the other two. The object of the game for the interrogator is to determine which of the other two is the man and which is the woman. He knows them by labels X and Y, and at the end of the game he says either "X is A and Y is B" or "X is B and Y is A". The interrogator is allowed to put questions to A and B thus:

C: Will X please tell me the length of his or her hair? Now suppose X is actually A, then A must answer. It is A's object in the game to try and cause C to make the wrong identification. His answer might therefore be

"My hair is shingled, and the longest strands are about nine inches long."

In order that tones of voice may not help the interrogator the answers should be written, or better still, typewritten. The ideal arrangement is to have a teleprinter communicating between the two rooms. Alternatively the question and answers can be repeated by an intermediary. The object of the game for the third player (B) is to help the interrogator. The best strategy for her is probably to give truthful answers. She can add such things as "I am the woman, don't listen to him!" to her answers, but it will avail nothing as the man can make similar remarks.

We now ask the question, "What will happen when a machine takes the part of A in this game?" Will the interrogator decide wrongly as often when the game is played like this as he does when the game is played between a man and a woman? These questions replace our original, "Can machines think?"

Critique of the New Problem

As well as asking, "What is the answer to this new form of the question," one may ask, "Is this new question a worthy one to investigate?" This latter question we investigate without further ado, thereby cutting short an infinite regress.

The new problem has the advantage of drawing a fairly sharp line between the physical and the intellectual capacities of a man. No engineer or chemist claims to be able to produce a material which is indistinguishable from the human skin. It is possible that at some time this might be done, but even supposing this invention available we should feel there was little point in trying to make a "thinking machine" more human by dressing it up in such artificial flesh. The form in which we have set the problem reflects this fact in the condition which prevents the interrogator from seeing or touching the other competitors, or hearing their voices. Some other advantages of the proposed criterion may be shown up by specimen questions and answers. Thus:

Q: *Please write me a sonnet on the subject of the Forth Bridge.*
A: Count me out on this one. I never could write poetry.
Q: *Add 34957 to 70764*
A: (Pause about 30 seconds and then give as answer) 105621.
Q: *Do you play chess?*
A: Yes.
Q: *I have K at my K1, and no other pieces. You have only K at K6 and R at R1. It is your move. What do you play?*
A: (After a pause of 15 seconds) R-R8 mate.

The question and answer method seems to be suitable for introducing almost any one of the fields of human endeavour that we wish to include. We do not wish to penalize the machine for its inability to shine in beauty competitions, nor to penalize a man for losing in a race against an airplane. The conditions of our game make these disabilities irrelevant. The "witnesses" can brag, if they consider it advisable, as much as they please about their charms, strength, or heroism, but the interrogator cannot demand practical demonstrations.

The game may perhaps be criticised on the ground that the odds are weighted too heavily against the machine. If the man were to try and pretend to be the machine he would clearly make a very poor showing. He would be given away at once by slowness and inaccuracy in arithmetic. May not machines carry out something which ought to be described as thinking but which is very different from what a man does? This objection is a very strong one, but at least we can say that if, nevertheless, a machine can be constructed to play the imitation game satisfactorily, we need not be troubled by this objection.

It might be urged that when playing the "imitation game" the best strategy for the machine may possibly be something other than imitation of the behaviour of a man. This may be, but I think it is unlikely that there is any great effect of this kind. In any case there is no intention to investigate here the theory of the game, and it will be assumed that the best strategy is to try to provide answers that would naturally be given by a man.

Suggestions for Discussion

1. To answer the question "Can machines think?" Turing proposed to define the terms *machine* and *think*. Why does he abandon the traditional attempt to define in favor of describing the problem in what he calls "the imitation game"?

2. Describe the "imitation game." What is its purpose? How is it related to his original question of whether machines can think? Turing raises the issue of whether the question is worth an answer. Explain his reasons for doing so.

3. How is the question related to the physical and intellectual capacities of man? Explain the dialogue which begins, "Q. Please write me a sonnet on the subject of the Forth Bridge."

4. How does Turing's imitation game explore the problem of artificial intelligence?

Suggestion for Writing

Turing's essay is a comment on the probable development of artificial intelligence—the ability of computers to think. What would be some consequences of such a development? Write an essay presenting your opinion. Consult other writers who have explored the issue. You could make this paper a thousand-word research essay with appropriate library research.

Joseph Weizenbaum

On the Impact of the Computer on Society

Joseph Weizenbaum (b. 1923) was born in Berlin but educated at Wayne State University. A professor of Computer Science and Engineering at MIT since 1979, he has done research in artificial intelligence and the structure of computer languages. He is concerned with the social impact of computers and cybernetics. His program "ELIZA" simulated the words of a nondirective psychological therapist. "On the Impact of the Computer of Society" (1972) asserts that if technology is a nightmare it is one of man's making, and that it is possible for man to formulate his own questions and find humane answers.

The direct societal effects of any pervasive new technology are as nothing compared to its much more subtle and ultimately much more important side effects. In that sense, the societal impact of the computer has not yet been felt.

To help firmly fix the idea of the importance of subtle indirect effects of technology, consider the impact on society of the invention of the microscope. When it was invented in the middle of the 17th century, the dominant commonsense theory of disease was fundamentally that disease was a punishment visited upon an individual by God. The sinner's body was thought to be inhabited by various so-called humors brought into disequilibrium in accordance with divine justice. The cure for disease was therefore to be found first in penance and second in the balancing of humors as, for example, by bleeding. Bleeding was, after all, both painful, hence punishment and penance, and potentially balancing in that it actually removed substance from the body. The microscope enabled man to see microorganisms and thus paved the way for the germ theory of disease. The enormously surprising discovery of extremely small living organisms also induced the idea of a continuous chain of life which, in turn, was a necessary intellectual precondition for the emergence of Darwinism. Both the germ theory of disease and the theory of evolution profoundly altered man's conception of his contract with God and consequently his self-image. Politically these ideas served to help diminish the power of the Church and, more generally, to legitimize the questioning of the basis of hitherto unchallenged authority. I do not say that the microscope alone was responsible for the enormous social changes that followed its invention. Only that it made possible the kind of paradigm shift, even on the commonsense level, without which these changes might have been impossible.

Is it reasonable to ask whether the computer will induce similar changes in man's image of himself and whether that influence will prove to be its most important effect on society? I think so, although I hasten to add that I don't believe the computer has yet told us much about man and his nature. To come to grips with the question, we must first ask in what way the computer is different from man's many other machines. Man has built two fundamentally different kinds of machines, nonautonomous and autonomous. An autonomous machine is one that operates for long periods of time, not on the basis of inputs from the real world, for example from sensors or from human drivers, but on the basis of internalized models of some aspects of the real world. Clocks are examples of autonomous machines in that they operate on the basis of an internalized model of the planetary system. The computer is, of course, the example par excellence. It is able to internalize models of essentially unlimited complexity and of a fidelity limited only by the genius of man.

It is the autonomy of the computer we value. When, for example, we speak of the power of computers as increasing with each new hardware and software development, we mean that, because of their increasing speed and storage capacity, and possibly thanks to new programming tricks, the new computers can internalize ever more complex and ever more faithful models of ever larger slices of reality. It seems strange then that, just when we exhibit virtually an idolatry of autonomy with respect to machines, serious thinkers in respected academies [I have in mind B. F. Skinner of Harvard University] can rise to question autonomy as a fact for man. I do not think that the appearance of this paradox at this time is accidental. To understand it, we must realize that man's commitment to science has always had a masochistic component.

Time after time science has led us to insights that, at least when seen superficially, diminish man. Thus Galileo removed man from the center of the universe, Darwin removed him from his place separate from the animals, and Freud showed his rationality to be an illusion. Yet man pushes his inquiries further and deeper. I cannot help but think that there is an analogy between man's pursuit of scientific knowledge and an individual's commitment to psychoanalytic therapy. Both are undertaken in the full realization that what the inquirer may find may well damage his self-esteem. Both may reflect his determination to find meaning in his existence through struggle in truth, however painful that may be, rather than to live without meaning in a world of ill-disguised illusion. However, I am also aware that sometimes people enter psychoanalysis unwilling to put their illusions at risk, not searching for a deeper reality but in order to convert the insights they hope to gain to personal power. The analogy to man's pursuit of science does not break down with that observation.

Each time a scientific discovery shatters a hitherto fundamental cornerstone of the edifice on which man's self-esteem is built, there is an enormous reaction, just as is the case under similar circumstances in psychoanalytic therapy. Powerful defense mechanisms, beginning with denial and usually terminating in rationalization, are brought to bear. Indeed, the psychoanalyst suspects that, when a patient appears to accept a soul-shattering insight without resistance, his very casualness may well mask his refusal to allow that insight truly operational status in his self-image. But what is the psychoanalyst to think about the patient who positively embraces tentatively proffered, profoundly humiliating self-knowledge, when he embraces it and instantly converts it to a new foundation of his life? Surely such an event is symptomatic of a major crisis in the mental life of the patient.

I believe we are now at the beginning of just such a crisis in the mental life of our civilization. The microscope, I have argued, brought in its train a revision of man's image of himself. But no one in the mid-17th century could have foreseen that. The possibility that the computer will, one way or another, demonstrate that, in the inimitable phrase of one of my esteemed colleagues, "the brain is merely a meat machine" is one that engages academicians, industrialists, and journalists in the here and now. How has the computer contributed to bringing about this very sad state of affairs? It must be said right away that the computer alone is not the chief causative agent. It is merely an extreme extrapolation of technology. When seen as an inducer of philosophical dogma, it is merely the reductio ad absurdum of a technological ideology. But how does it come to be regarded as a source of philosophic dogma?

I have suggested that the computer revolution need not and ought not to call man's dignity and autonomy into question, that it is a kind of pathology that moves men to wring from it unwarranted, enormously damaging interpretations. Is then the computer less threatening than we might have thought? Once we realize that our visions, possibly nightmarish visions, determine the effect of our own creations on us and on our society, their threat to us is surely diminished. But that is not to say that this realization alone will wipe out all danger. For example, apart from the erosive effect of a technological mentality on man's self-image, there are practical attacks on the freedom and dignity of man in which computer technology plays a critical role.

I mentioned earlier that computer science has come to recognize the importance of building knowledge into machines. We already have a machine—Dendral—that commands more chemistry than do many Ph.D. chemists, and another—Mathlab—that commands more applied mathematics than do many applied mathematicians. Both Dendral and Mathlab contain knowledge that can be evaluated in terms of the explicit theories from which it was derived. If the user believes that a result Mathlab delivers is wrong, then apart from possible program errors, he must be in disagreement, not with the machine or its programmer, but with a specific mathematical theory. But what about the many programs on which management, most particularly the government and the military, rely, programs which can in no sense be said to rest on explicable theories but are instead enormous patchworks of programming techniques strung together to make them work?

Incomprehensible Systems

In our eagerness to exploit every advance in technique we quickly incorporate the lessons learned from machine manipulation of knowledge in theory-based systems into such patchworks. They then "work" better. I have in mind systems like target selection systems used in Vietnam and war games used in the Pentagon, and so on. These often gigantic systems are put together by teams of programmers, often working over a time span of many years. But by the time the systems come into use, most of the original programmers have left or turned their attention to other pursuits. It is precisely when gigantic systems begin to be used that their inner workings can no longer be understood by any single person or by a small team of individuals. Norbert Wiener, the father of cybernetics, foretold of this phenomenon in a remarkably prescient article published more than a decade ago. He said there:

> It may well be that in principle we cannot make any machine the elements of whose behavior we cannot comprehend sooner or later. This does not mean in any way that we shall be able to comprehend these elements in substantially less time than the time required for operation of the machine, or even within any given number of years or generations.

> An intelligent understanding of [machines'] mode of performance may be delayed until long after the task which they have been set has been completed. This means that though machines are theoretically subject to human criticism, such criticism may be ineffective until long after it is relevant.

This situation, which is now upon us, has two consequences: first that decisions are made on the basis of rules and criteria no one knows explicitly, and second that the system of rules and criteria becomes immune to change. This is so because, in the absence of detailed understanding of the inner workings of a system, any substantial modification is very likely to render the system altogether inoperable. The threshold of complexity beyond which this phenomenon occurs has already been crossed by many existing systems, including some compiling and computer operating systems. For example, no one likes the operating systems for certain large computers, but they cannot be substantially changed nor can they be done away with. Too many people have become dependent on them.

An awkward operating system is inconvenient. That is not too bad. But the growing reliance on supersystems that were perhaps designed to help people make analyses and decisions, but which have since surpassed the understanding of their users while at the same time becoming indispensable to them is another matter. In modern war it is common for the soldier, say the bomber pilot, to operate at an enormous psychological distance from his victims. He is not responsible for burned children because he never sees their village, his bombs, and certainly not the flaming children themselves. Modern technological rationalizations of war, diplomacy, politics, and commerce such as computer games have an even more insidious effect on the making of policy. Not only have policy makers abdicated their decision-making responsibility to a technology they don't understand, all the while maintaining the illusion that they, the policy makers, are formulating policy questions and answering them, but responsibility has altogether evaporated. No human is any longer responsible for "what the machine says." Thus there can be neither right nor wrong, no question of justice, no theory with which one can agree or disagree, and finally no basis on which one can challenge "what the machine says." My father used to invoke the ultimate authority by saying to me, "it is written." But then I could read what was written, imagine a human author, infer his values, and finally agree or disagree. The systems in the Pentagon, and their counterparts elsewhere in our culture, have in a very real sense no authors. They therefore do not admit of exercises of imagination that may ultimately lead to human judgment. No wonder that men who live day in and out with such machines and become dependent on them begin to believe that men are merely machines. They are reflecting what they themselves have become.

The potentially tragic impact on society that may ensue from the use of systems such as I have just discussed is greater than might at first be imagined. Again it is side effects, not direct effects, that matter most. First, of course, there is the psychological impact on individuals living in a society in which anonymous, hence irresponsible, forces formulate the large questions of the day and circumscribe the range of possible answers. It cannot be surprising that large numbers of perceptive individuals living in such a society experience a kind of impotence and fall victim to the mindless rage that often accompanies such experiences. But even worse, since computer-based knowledge systems become essentially unmodifiable except in that they can grow, and since they induce dependence and cannot, after a certain threshold is crossed, be abandoned, there is an enormous risk that they will be passed from one generation to another, always growing. Man too passes knowledge from one generation to another. But because man is mortal, his transmission of knowledge over the generations is at once a process of filtering and accrual. Man doesn't merely pass knowledge, he rather regenerates it continuously. Much as we may mourn the crumbling of ancient civilizations, we know nevertheless that the glory of man resides as much in the evolution of his cultures as in that of his brain. The unwise use of ever larger and ever more complex computer systems may well bring this process to a halt. It could well replace the ebb and flow of culture with a world without values, a world in which what counts for a fact has long ago been determined and forever fixed.

Positive Effects

I've spoken of some potentially dangerous effects of present computing trends. Is there nothing positive to be said? Yes, but it must be said with caution. Again, side effects are more important than direct effects. In particular, the idea of computation and of programming languages is beginning to become an important metaphor which, in the long run, may well prove to be responsible for paradigm shifts in many fields. Most of the common-sense paradigms in terms of which much of mankind interprets the phenomena of the everyday world, both physical and social, are still deeply rooted in fundamentally mechanistic metaphors. Marx's dynamics as well as those of Freud are, for example, basically equilibrium systems. Any hydrodynamicist could come to understand them without leaving the jargon of his field. Languages capable of describing ongoing processes, particularly in terms of modular subprocesses, have already had an enormous effect on the way computer people think of every aspect of their worlds, not merely those directly related to their work. The information-processing view of the world so engendered qualifies as a genuine metaphor. This is attested to by the fact that it (i) constitutes an intellectual framework that permits new questions to be asked about a wide-ranging set of phenomena, and (ii) that it itself provides criteria for the adequacy of proffered answers. A new metaphor is important not in that it may be better than existing ones, but rather in that it may enlarge man's vision by giving him yet another perspective on his world. Indeed, the very effectiveness of a new metaphor may seduce lazy minds to adopt it as a basis for universal explanations and as a source of panaceas. Computer simulation of social processes has already been advanced by single-minded generalists as leading to general solutions of all of mankind's problems.

The metaphors given us by religion, the poets, and by thinkers like Darwin, Newton, Freud, and Einstein have rather quickly penetrated to the language of ordinary people. These metaphors have thus been instrumental in shaping our entire civilization's imaginative reconstruction of our world. The computing metaphor is as yet available to only an extremely small set of people. Its acquisition and internalization, hopefully as only one of many ways to see the world, seems to require experience in program composition, a kind of computing literacy. Perhaps such literacy will become very widespread in the advanced societal sectors of the advanced countries. But, should it become a dominant mode of thinking and be restricted to certain social classes, it will prove not merely repressive in the ordinary sense, but an enormously divisive societal force. For then classes which do and do not have access to the metaphor will, in an important sense, lose their ability to communicate with one another. We know already how difficult it is for the poor and the oppressed to communicate with the rest of the society in which they are embedded. We know how difficult it is for the world of science to communicate with that of the arts and of the humanities. In both instances the communication difficulties, which have grave consequences, are very largely due to the fact that the respective communities have unsharable experiences out of which unsharable metaphors have grown.

Responsibility

Given these dismal possibilities, what is the responsibility of the computer scientist? First I should say that most of the harm computers can potentially entrain is much more a function of properties people attribute to computers than of what a computer can or cannot actually be made to do. The nonprofessional has little choice but to make his attributions of properties to computers on the basis of the propaganda emanating from the computer community and amplified by the press. The computer professional therefore has an enormously important responsibility to be modest in his claims. This advice would not even have to be voiced if computer science had a tradition of scholarship and of self-criticism such as that which characterizes the established sciences. The mature scientist stands in awe before the depth of his subject matter. His very humility is the wellspring of his strength. I regard the instilling of just this kind of humility, chiefly by the example set by teachers, to be one of the most important missions of every university department of computer science.

The computer scientist must be aware constantly that his instruments are capable of having gigantic direct and indirect amplifying effects. An error in a program, for example, could have grievous direct results, including most certainly the loss of much human life. On 11 September 1971, to cite just one example, a computer programming error caused the simultaneous destruction of 117 high-altitude weather balloons whose instruments were being monitored by an earth satellite. A similar error in a military command and control system could launch a fleet of nuclear-tipped missiles. Only censorship prevents us from knowing how many such events involving nonnuclear weapons have already occurred. Clearly then, the computer scientist has a heavy responsibility to make the fallibility and limitations of the systems he is capable of designing brilliantly clear. The very power of his systems should serve to inhibit the advice he is ready to give and to constrain the range of work he is willing to undertake.

Of course, the computer scientist, like everyone else, is responsible for his actions and their consequences. Sometimes that responsibility is hard to accept because the corresponding authority to decide what is and what is not to be done appears to rest with distant and anonymous forces. That technology itself determines what is to be done by a process of extrapolation and that individuals are powerless to intervene in that determination is precisely the kind of self-fulfilling dream from which we must awaken.

Consider gigantic computer systems. They are, of course, natural extrapolations of the large systems we already have. Computer networks are another point on the same curve extrapolated once more. One may ask whether such systems can be used by anybody except by governments and very large corporations and whether such organizations will not use them mainly for antihuman purposes. Or consider speech recognition systems. Will they not be used primarily to spy on private communications? To answer such questions by saying that big computer systems, computer networks, and speech recognition systems are inevitable is to surrender one's humanity. For such an answer must be based either on one's profound conviction that society has already lost control over its technology or on the thoroughly immoral position that "if I don't do it, someone else will."

I don't say that systems such as I have mentioned are necessarily evil—only that they may be and, what is most important, that their inevitability cannot be accepted by individuals claiming autonomy, freedom, and dignity. The individual computer scientist can and must decide. The determination of what the impact of computers on society is to be is, at least in part, in his hands.

Finally, the fundamental question the computer scientist must ask himself is the one that every scientist, indeed every human, must ask. It is not "what shall I do?" but rather "what shall I be?" I cannot answer that for anyone save myself. But I will say again that if technology is a nightmare that appears to have its own inevitable logic, it is our nightmare. It is possible, given courage and insight, for man to deny technology the prerogative to formulate man's questions. It is possible to ask human questions and to find humane answers.

References

1. B. F. Skinner, *Beyond Freedom and Dignity* (Knopf, New York, 1971).
2. K. M. Colby, S. Weber, F. D. Hilf, *Artif. Intell.* 1, 1 (1971).
3. N. Chomsky, *Aspects of the Theory of Syntax* (M.I.T. Press, Cambridge, Mass., 1965);—and M. Halle, *The Sound Pattern of English* (Harper & Row, New York, 1968).
4. L. Mumford, *The Pentagon of Power* (Harcourt Brace Jovanovich, New York, 1970).

5. H. A. Simon, *The Sciences of the Artificial* (M.I.T. Press, Cambridge, Mass., 1969), pp. 22–25.
6. B. Buchanan, G. Sutherland, E. A. Feigenbaum, in *Machine Intelligence*, B. Meltzer, Ed. (American Elsevier, New York, 1969).
7. W. A. Martin and R. J. Fateman, "The Macsyma system," in *Proceedings of the 2nd Symposium on Symbolic and Algebraic Manipulation* (Association for Computer Machines, New York, 1971); J. Moses, *Commun. Assoc. Computer March.* **14** (No. 8), 548 (1971).
8. N. Wiener, *Science* **131**, 1355 (1960).
9. R. Gillette, **174**, 477 (1971).

Suggestions for Discussion

1. Explain the meaning of the brief opening paragraph of this essay. How does Weizenbaum develop the ideas presented in this paragraph?

2. Why does Weizenbaum place so much importance on the invention of the microscope in the 17th century? What new developments in science did that invention make possible? What have been some consequences of those developments?

3. How does Weizenbaum define nonautonomous and autonomous machines? In what category does the computer fall? What does Weizenbaum mean when he speaks of the power of the computer?

4. Weizenbaum refers to B.F. Skinner's theories which question the autonomy of man. What is his reaction to Skinner's ideas?

5. Weizenbaum mentions the theories of Galileo, Darwin, and Freud. What do they have in common? Why, according to Weizenbaum, do men continue to be attracted to the theories of all three?

6. What positive effects on man and society does the author envision for the computer?

7. What are the responsibilities of the computer scientist in the future development of the computer?

8. How do we help determine the impact of the computer on society?

Suggestions for Writing

1. Weizenbaum is optimistic about the positive impact of computers on society. On what grounds does he base his optimism? Write an essay in which you agree or disagree with his conclusions. You might find it useful to compare this essay with those by Bronowski and Jaspers.

2. If you are able to use a computer or a word processor, write an essay in which you explain how you are positively aided by this ability. Have you found any negative results of your skill?

Lewis Thomas

A Trip Abroad

Lewis Thomas (b. 1913) is a physician whose medical career has centered on the Sloan Kettering Cancer Center in New York, the city of his birth. He has written for medical journals at the same time that he has written popular essays to present science and the scientist's view of the world to the lay public. He won the National Book Award in 1974 for *The Lives of a Cell: Notes of a Biology Watcher*. Other collections include *The Medusa and the Snail* (1979), *More Notes of a Biology Watcher* (1979) and *The Youngest Science: Notes of a Medicine-Watcher* (1983). "A Trip Abroad," from *The Medusa and the Snail*, glances irreverently at the accomplishments of science and longs for a simpler, less plastic life which, Lewis imagines, may soon be easier to find in space than here on earth.

I do not believe for a minute that we are nearing the end of human surprise, despite resonantly put arguments by wonderfully informed scientists who tell us that after molecular biology and astrophysics there is really very little more to learn of substance. Except, they always add, for the nature of human consciousness, and that, they always add, is placed beyond our reach by the principle of indeterminacy; that is, our thought is so much at the center of life that it cannot sit still while we examine it.

But there may be a way out of this; it may turn out that consciousness is a much more generalized mechanism, shared round not only among ourselves but with all the other conjoined things of the biosphere. Thus, since we are not, perhaps, so absolutely central, we may be able to get a look at it, but we will need a new technology for this kind of neurobiology; in which case we will likely find that we have a whole eternity of astonishment stretching out ahead of us. Always assuming, of course, that we're still here.

We must rely on our scientists to help us find the way through the near distance, but for the longer stretch of the future we are dependent on the poets. We should learn to question them more closely, and listen more carefully. A poet is, after all, a sort of scientist, but engaged in a qualitative science in which nothing is measurable. He lives with data that cannot be numbered, and his experiments can be done only once. The information in a poem is, by definition, not reproducible. His pilot runs involve a recognition of things that pop into his head. The skill consists in his capacity to decide quickly which things to retain, which to eject. He becomes an equivalent of scientist, in the act of examining and sorting the things popping in, finding the marks of remote similarity, points of distant relationship, tiny irregularities that indicate that this one is really the same as that one over there only more important. Gauging the fit, he can meticulously place pieces of the universe together, in geometric configurations that are as beautiful and balanced as crystals. Musicians and painters listen, and copy down what they hear.

I wish that poets were able to give straight answers to straight questions, but that is like asking astrophysicists to make their calculations on their fingers, where we can watch the process. What I would like to know is: how should I feel about the earth, these days? Where has all the old nature gone? What became of the wild, writhing, unapproachable mass of the life of the world, and what happened to our old, panicky excitement about it? Just in fifty years, since I was a small boy in a suburban town, the world has become a structure of steel and plastic, intelligible and diminished. Mine was a puzzling maple grove of a village on the outskirts of New York City, and it vanished entirely, trees and all. It is now a syncytium of apartment houses, sprouting out of a matrix of cement flooded and jelled over an area that once contained 25,000 people who walked on grass. Now I live in another, more distant town, on a street with trees and lawns, and at night I can hear the soft sound of cement, moving like incoming tide, down the Sunrise Highway from New York.

If you fly around the earth and keep looking down, you will see that we have inserted ourselves everywhere. All fields are tilled. All mountains have been climbed and are being covered with concrete and plastic; some mountains, like the Appalachians, are simply cut down like trees. The fish are all trapped and domesticated, farmed in zoned undersea pastures. As for the animals, we will never have enough plastic bags for the bodies; soon the only survivors will be the cattle and sheep for the feeding of us, and the dogs and cats in our houses, fed while it lasts on the flesh of whales. And the rats and roaches, and a few reptiles.

The winged insects are vanishing, the calcium in the shells of eggs, and the birds.

We have dominated and overruled nature, and from now on the earth is ours, a kitchen garden until we learn to make our own chlorophyll and float it out in the sun inside plastic membranes. We will build Scarsdale on Mount Everest.

We will have everything under control, managed. Then what do we do? On long Sunday afternoons, what do we do, when there is nobody to talk to but ourselves?

It is because of these problems that we are now engaged in scrutinizing with such intensity the dark, bare flanks of Mars, hideous with lifelessness as it seems to be. We are like a family looking through travel brochures.

There is such a thing as too much of this. Because of our vast numbers and the rapidity with which we have developed prosthetic devices enabling us to hear and see each other, in person, all around the earth, we have become obsessed with ourselves. You'd think, to hear us think, that there was nothing else of significance on the earth except us.

Perhaps we should try to get away, for a while anyway. A change of scene might do us a world of good.

The trouble is, the barrenness of all the local planets. Perhaps we will be unlucky with our green thumbs, unable to create or maintain the faintest gasp of life on Mars or Titan. What's to stop us from looking elsewhere, farther on? If we can learn to navigate before the solar wind, we could, out there, hoist sail and tack our way out to where the wind fades off, practicing freefalls all the while, probing for gravity, trusting to luck, taking our chances. It would be like old times.

Suggestions for Discussion

1. Why does Lewis suggest that poets rather than scientists may be our source of comfort in the long run? Why are scientists good enough for the present? What limits does he see for science? for poets?

2. What are the differences between poets and scientists?

3. Summarize Lewis's dissatisfaction with modern suburbia. Why does he use the term "syncitium" to describe it?

4. What is the tone of this essay? What role does the last paragraph play in establishing that tone? the title of the essay?

5. What are the questions about life which, according to Lewis, need answering? Where will we get answers?

Suggestion for Writing

Write an essay describing the area in which you live. Is it different from Lewis's home? In what way? How is it similar? What is your attitude toward your hometown? Does it resemble Lewis's?

Stephen Jay Gould

Death Before Birth, or a Mite's *Nunc Dimittis*

Stephen Jay Gould (b. 1941), a New Yorker by birth, teaches geology, biology, and the history of science at Harvard and writes a column, "This View of Life," for *Natural History*. His books include *Ever Since Darwin* (1977), *Ontogeny and Phylogeny* (1977), and *Hen's Teeth and Horse's Toes* (1983). This selection from *The Panda's Thumb* (1980) explains how seemingly simple questions in science have amazingly complex answers. Exploring an answer to the question of why males and females are produced in approximately equal numbers in most familiar species, he leads us to consider the dramatic life of the male mite in the genus *Adactylidium*.

Can anything be more demoralizing than parental incompetence before the most obvious and innocent of children's questions: why is the sky blue, the grass green? Why does the moon have phases? Our embarrassment is all the more acute because we thought we knew the answer perfectly well, but hadn't rehearsed it since we ourselves had received a bumbled response in similar circumstances a generation earlier. It is the things we think we know—because they are so elementary, or because they surround us—that often present the greatest difficulties when we are actually challenged to explain them.

One such question, with an obvious and incorrect answer, lies close to our biological lives: why, in humans (and in most species familiar to us), are males and females produced in approximately equal numbers? (Actually, males are more common than females at birth in humans, but differential mortality of males leads to a female majority in later life. Still, the departures from a one to one ratio are never great.) At first glance, the answer seems to be, as in Rabelais's motto, "plain as the nose on a man's face." After all, sexual reproduction requires a mate; equal numbers imply universal mating—the happy Darwinian status of maximal reproductive capacity. At second glance, it isn't so clear at all, and we are drawn in confusion to Shakespeare's recasting of the simile: "A jest unseen, inscrutable, invisible, as a nose on a man's face." If maximal reproductive capacity is the optimal state for a species, then why make equal numbers of males and females? Females, after all, set the limit upon numbers of offspring, since eggs are invariably so much larger and less abundant than sperm in species familiar to us—that is, each egg can make an offspring, each sperm cannot. A male can impregnate several females. If a male can mate with nine females and the population contains a hundred individuals, why not make ten males and ninety females? Reproductive capacity will certainly exceed that of a population composed of fifty males and fifty females. Populations made predominantly of females should, by their more rapid rates of reproduction, win any evolutionary race with populations that maintain equality in numbers between the sexes.

What appeared obvious is therefore rendered problematical and the question remains: why do most sexual species contain approximately equal numbers of males and females? The answer, according to most evolutionary biologists, lies in a recognition that Darwin's theory of natural selection speaks only of struggle among *individuals* for reproductive success. It contains no statement about the good of populations, species, or ecosystems. The argument for ninety females and ten males was framed in terms of advantages for populations as a whole—the usual, congenial, and dead wrong, way in which most people think of evolution. If evolution worked for the good of populations as a whole, then sexual species would contain relatively few males.

The observed equality of males and females, in the face of obvious advantages for female predominance if evolution worked upon groups, stands as one of our most elegant demonstrations that Darwin was right—natural selection works by the struggle of individuals to maximize their own reproductive success. The Darwinian argument was first framed by the great British mathematical biologist R.A. Fisher. Suppose, Fisher argued, that either sex began to predominate. Let us say, for example, that fewer males than females are born. Males now begin to leave more offspring than females since their opportunities for mating increase as they become rarer—that is, they impregnate more than one female on average. Thus, if any genetic factors influence the relative proportion of males born to a parent (and such factors do exist), then parents with a genetic inclination to produce males will gain a Darwinian advantage—they will produce more than an average number of grandchildren thanks to the superior reproductive success of their predominantly male offspring. Thus, genes that favor the production of males will spread and male births will rise in frequency. But, this advantage for males fades out as male births increase and it disappears entirely when males equal females in number. Since the same argument works in reverse to favor female births when females are rare, the sex ratio is driven by Darwinian processes to its equilibrium value of one to one.

But how would a biologist go about testing Fisher's theory of sex ratio? Ironically, the species that confirm its predictions are no great help beyond the initial observation. Once we frame the basic argument and determine that the species we know best have approximately equal numbers of males and females, what do we achieve by finding that the next thousand species are similarly ordered? Sure, it all fits, but we do not gain an equal amount of confidence each time we add a new species. Perhaps the one to one ratio exists for another reason.

To test Fisher's theory, we must look for exceptions. We must seek unusual situations in which the premises of Fisher's theory are not met—situations that lead to a specific prediction about how sex ratio should depart from one to one. If change of premises leads to a definite and successful prediction of altered outcome, then we have an independent test that strongly boosts our confidence. This method is embodied in the old proverb that "the exception proves the rule," although many people misunderstand the proverb because it embodies the less common meaning of "prove." Prove comes from the Latin *probare*—to test or to try. Its usual, modern meaning refers to final and convincing demonstration and the motto would seem to say that exceptions establish indubitable validity. But in another sense, closer to its root, "prove" (as in "proving ground" or printer's "proof") is more like its cognate "probe"—a test or an exploration. It is the exception that probes the rule by testing and exploring its consequences in altered situations.

Here nature's rich diversity comes to our aid. The sterotyped image of a birder assiduously adding the rufous-crowned, peg-legged, speckle-backed, cross-billed, and cross-eyed towhee to his life list gives, in unwarranted ridicule, a perverted twist to the actual use made by naturalists of life's diversity. It is nature's richness that permits us to establish a science of natural history in the first place—for the variety virtually guarantees that appropriate exceptions can be found to probe any rule. Oddities and weirdnesses are tests of generality, not mere peculiarities to describe and greet with awe or a chuckle.

Fortunately, nature has been profligate in providing species and modes of life that violate the premises of Fisher's argument. In 1967, British biologist W.D. Hamilton (now at the University of Michigan) gathered the cases and arguments into an article entitled "Extraordinary sex ratios." I will discuss in this essay only the clearest and most important of these probing violations.

Nature rarely heeds our homilies in all cases. We are told, and with good reason, that mating of brothers and sisters should be avoided, lest too many unfavorable recessive genes gain an opportunity to express themselves in double dose. (Such genes tend to be rare, and chances are small that two unrelated parents will both carry them. But the probability that two sibs carry the same gene is usually fifty percent.) Nonetheless, some animals never heard the rule and indulge, perhaps exclusively, in sib mating.

Exclusive sib mating destroys the major premise of Fisher's argument for one to one sex ratios. If females are always fertilized by their brothers, then the same parents manufacture both partners of any mating. Fisher assumed that the males had different parents and that an undersupply of males awarded genetic advantages to those parents that could produce males preferentially. But if the same parents produce *both* the mothers and fathers of their grandchildren, then they have an equal genetic investment in each grandchild, no matter what percentage of males and females they produce among their children. In this case, the reason for an equal balance of males and females disappears and the previous argument for female predominance reasserts itself. If each pair of grandparents has a limited store of energy to invest in offspring, and if grandparents producing more offspring gain a Darwinian edge, then grandparents should make as many daughters as possible, and produce only enough sons to ensure that all their daughters will be fertilized. In fact, if their sons can muster sufficient sexual prowess, then parents should make just one son and use every bit of remaining energy to produce as many daughters as they can. As usual, bountiful nature comes to our aid with numerous exceptions to probe Fisher's rule: indeed, species with sib mating also tend to produce a minimal number of males.

Consider the curious life of a male mite in the genus *Adactylidium*, as described by E. A. Albadry and M. S. F. Tawfik in 1966. It emerges from its mother's body and promptly dies within a few hours, having done apparently nothing during its brief life. It attempts, while outside its mother, neither to feed nor to mate. We know about creatures with short adult lives—the mayfly's single day after a much lengthier larval life, for example. But the mayfly mates and insures the continuity of its kind during these few precious hours. The males of *Adactylidium* seem to do nothing at all but emerge and die.

To solve the mystery, we must study the entire life cycle and look inside the mother's body. The impregnated female of *Adactylidium* attaches to the egg of a thrips. That single egg provides the only source of nutrition for rearing all her offspring—for she will feed on nothing else before her death. This mite, so far as we know, engages exclusively in sib mating; thus, it should produce a minimal number of males. Moreover, since total reproductive energy is so strongly constrained by the nutritional resources of a single thrips' egg, progeny are strictly limited, and the more females the better. Indeed, *Adactylidium* matches our prediction by raising a brood of five to eight sisters accompanied by a single male who will serve as both brother and husband to them all. But producing a single male is chancy; if it dies, all sisters will remain virgins and their mother's evolutionary life is over.

If the mite takes a chance on producing but a single male, thus maximizing its potential brood of fertile females, two other adaptations might lessen the risk—providing both protection for the male and guaranteed proximity to his sisters. What better than to rear the brood entirely within a mother's body, feeding both larvae and adults within her, and even allowing copulation to occur inside her protective shell. Indeed, about forty-eight hours after she attaches to the thrips' egg, six to nine eggs hatch within the body of a female *Adactylidium*. The larvae feed on their mother's body, literally devouring her from inside. Two days later, the offspring reach maturity, and the single male copulates with all his sisters. By this time, the mother's tissues have disintegrated, and her body space is a mass of adult mites, their feces, and their discarded larval and nymphal skeletons. The offspring then cut holes through their mother's body wall and emerge. The females must now find a thrips' egg and begin the process again, but the males have already fulfilled their evolutionary role before "birth." They emerge, react however a mite does to the glories of the outside world, and promptly die.

But why not carry the process one stage further? Why should the male be born at all? After copulating with its sisters, its work is done, it is ready to chant the acarine version of Simeon's prayer, *Nunc dimittis*—Oh Lord, now lettest thou thy servant depart in peace. Indeed, since everything that is possible tends to occur at least once in the multifarious world of life, a close relative of *Adactylidium* does just this. *Acarophenax tribolii* also indulges exclusively in sib mating. Fifteen eggs, including but a single male, develop within the mother's body. The male emerges within his mother's shell, copulates with all his sisters, and dies before birth. It may not sound like much of a life, but the male *Acarophenax* does as much for its evolutionary continuity as Abraham did in fathering children into his tenth decade.

Nature's oddities are more than good stories. They are material for probing the limits of interesting theories about life's history and meaning.

Suggestions for Discussion

1. Gould begins his essay with children's questions which, while seemingly simple, are very difficult to answer. Explain why this is an effective introduction to his topic.

2. How does he answer the biological question of why in familiar species known to man, including our own, males and females are produced in approximately equal numbers? How does he show that an attempt to answer this question is much more complex than it first appears? How does he relate the question to Darwin's theory of natural selection?

3. Summarize R. A. Fisher's restatement of Darwin's theory that "natural selection works by the struggle of individuals to maximize their own reproductive success." How does Gould propose to test Fisher's theory?

4. How does Gould treat the history of the male mite of the genus *Adactylidium*? How does he make its history interesting and dramatic?

5. What is the role of the mite as chanted in Simeon's prayer, "*Nunc dimittis*—Oh Lord, now lettest thou thy servant depart in peace"?

Suggestion for Writing

Using Gould as a model, attempt to explore the implications of a scientific principle you have studied in one of your science courses. This attempt may lead you into further reading on the subject. Your purpose in this paper is to make clear, understandable—and interesting—to a common reader the complexities of scientific thought.

◇ ◇ ◇ ◇

Aldous Huxley

Brave New World Revisited

Aldous Huxley (1894–1963) was born in England and educated at Oxford. He is the author of many novels including *Point Counter Pount* (1928) and the anti-Utopian *Brave New World* (1932). He also wrote essays, short stories, poetry, and plays. After he moved to Southern California, he became increasingly interested in Hindu philosophy and mysticism. *The Doors of Perception* (1954) describes his experience with hallucenogenic drugs. In "Brave New World Revisited" he examined in 1956 the accuracy of his predictions. He admits that, in *1984*, Orwell (see Irving Howe's "The Enigmas of Power") foresaw political developments more preceptively than he. The essay concludes with a serious reflection on the difference between present-day attitudes toward drugs and those attitudes explored in *Brave New World*.

The most distressing thing that can happen to a prophet is to be proved wrong; the next most distressing thing is to be proved right. In the twenty-five years that have elapsed since *Brave New World* was written, I have undergone both these experiences. Events have proved me distressingly wrong; and events have proved me distressingly right.

Here are some of the points on which I was wrong. By the early Thirties Einstein had equated mass and energy, and there was already talk of chain reactions; but the Brave New Worlders knew nothing of nuclear fission. In the early Thirties, too, we knew all about conservation and irreplaceable resources; but their supply of metals and mineral fuel was just as copious in the seventh century After Ford as ours is today. In actual fact the raw-material situation will already be subcritical by A.F. 600 and the atom will be the principal source of industrial power. Again, the Brave New Worlders had solved the population problem and knew how to maintain a permanently favorable relationship between human numbers and natural resources. In actual fact, will our descendants achieve this happy consummation within the next six centuries? And if they *do* achieve it, will it be by dint of rational planning, or through the immemorial agencies of pestilence, famine, and internecine warfare? It is, of course, impossible to say. The only thing we can predict with a fair measure of certainty is that humanity (if its rulers decide to refrain from collective suicide) will be traveling at vertiginous speed along one of the most dangerous and congested stretches of its history.

The Brave New Worlders produced their children in biochemical factories. But though bottled babies are not completely out of the question, it is virtually certain that our descendants will in fact remain viviparous. Mother's Day is in no danger of being replaced by Bottle Day. My prediction was made for strictly literary purposes, and not as a reasoned forecast of future history. In this matter I knew in advance that I should be proved wrong.

From biology we now pass to politics. The dictatorship described in *Brave New World* was global and in its own peculiar way, benevolent. In the light of current events and developing tendencies, I sadly suspect that in this forecast, too, I may have been wrong. True, the seventh century After Ford is still a long way off, and it is possible that, by then, hard economic necessity, or the social chaos resulting from nuclear warfare, or military conquest by one Great Power, or some grisly combination of all three will have bludgeoned our descendants into doing what we ought to be doing now, from motives of enlightened self-interest and common humanity—namely, to collaborate for the common good. In time of peace, and when things are going tolerably well, people cannot be expected to vote for measures which, though ultimately beneficial, may be expected to have certain disagreeable consequences in the short run. Divisive forces are more powerful than those which make for union. Vested interests in languages, philosophies of life, table manners, sexual habits, political, ecclesiastical, and economic organizations are sufficiently powerful to block all attempts, by rational and peaceful methods, to unite mankind for its own good. And then there is nationalism. With its Fifty-Seven Varieties of tribal gods, nationalism is the religion of the twentieth century. We may be Christians, Jews, Moslems, Hindus, Buddhists, Confucians, or Atheists; but the fact remains that there is only one faith for which large masses of us are prepared to die and kill, and that faith is nationalism. That nationalism will remain the dominant religion of the human race for the next two or three centuries at the very least seems all too probable. If total nuclear war should be avoided, we may expect to see not the rise of a single world state but the continuance, in worsening conditions, of the present system, under which national states compete for markets and raw materials and prepare for partial wars. Most of these states will probably be dictatorships. Inevitably so; for the increasing pressure of population upon resources will make domestic conditions more difficult and international competition more intense. To prevent economic breakdown and to repress popular discontent, the governments of hungry countries will be tempted to enforce ever-stricter controls. Furthermore, chronic undernourishment reduces physical energy and disturbs the mind. Hunger and self-government are incompatible. Even where the average diet provides three thousand calories a day, it is hard enough to make democracy work. In a society in which most members are living on seventeen hundred to two thousand calories a day, it is simply impossible. The undernourished majority will always be ruled, from above, by the well-fed few. As population increases (twenty-seven hundred millions of us are now adding to our numbers at the rate of forty millions a year, and this increase is increasing according to the rules of compound interest); as geometrically increasing demands press more and more heavily on static or, at best, arithmetically increasing supplies; as standards of living are forced down and popular discontent is forced up; as the general scramble for diminishing resources becomes ever fiercer, these national dictatorships will tend to become more oppressive at home, more ruthlessly competitive abroad. "Government," says one of the Brave New Worlders, "is an affair of sitting, not hitting. You rule with the brains and the buttocks, not the fists." But where there are many competing national dictatorships, each in trouble at home and each preparing for total or partial war against its neighbors, hitting tends to be preferred to sitting, fists, as an instrument of policy, to brains, and the "masterly inactivity" (to cite Lord Salisbury's immortal phrase) of the hindquarters. In politics, the near future is likely to be closer to George Orwell's *1984* than to *Brave New World*.

Let me now consider a few of the points on which, I fear, I may have been right. The Brave New Worlders were the heirs and exploiters of a new kind of revolution, and this revolution was, in effect, the theme of my fable. Past revolutions have all been in fields external to the individual as a psycho-physical organism—in the field, for example, of ecclesiastical organization and religious dogma, in the field of economics, in the field of political organization, in the field of technology. The coming revolution—the revolution whose consequences are described in *Brave New World*—will affect men and women, not peripherally, but at the very core of their organic being. The older revolutionaries sought to change the social environment in the hope (if they were idealists and not mere power seekers) of changing human nature. The coming revolutionaries will make their assult directly on human nature as they find it, in the minds and bodies of their victims or, if you prefer, their beneficiaries.

Among the Brave New Worlders, the control of human nature was achieved by eugenic and dysgenic breeding, by systematic conditioning during infancy and, later on, by "hypnopaedia," or instruction during sleep. Infant conditioning is as old as Pavlov and hypnopaedia, though rudimentary, is already a well-established technique. Phonographs with built-in clocks, which turn them on and off at regular intervals during the night, are already on the market and are being used by students of foreign languages, by actors in a hurry to memorize their parts, by parents desirous of curing their children of bed-wetting and other troublesome habits, by self-helpers seeking moral and physical improvement through autosuggestion and "affirmations of positive thought." That the principles of selective breeding, infant conditioning, and hypnopaedia have not yet been applied by governments is due, in the democratic countries, to the lingering, liberal conviction that persons do not exist for the state, but that the state exists for the good of persons; and in the totalitarian countries to what may be called revolutionary conservatism—attachment to yesterday's revolution instead of the revolution of tomorrow. There is, however, no reason for complacently believing that this revolutionary conservatism will persist indefinitely. In totalitarian hands, applied psychology is already achieving notable results. One third of all the American prisoners captured in Korea succumbed, at least partially, to Chinese brainwashing, which broke down the convictions, installed by their education and childhood conditioning, and replaced these comforting axioms by doubt, anxiety, and a chronic sense of guilt. This was achieved by thoroughly old-fashioned procedures, which combined straight-forward instruction with what may be called conventional psychotherapy in reverse, and made no use of hypnosis, hypnopaedia, or mind-modifying drugs. If all or even some of these more powerful methods had been employed, brainwashing would probably have been successful with all the prisoners, and not with a mere thirty percent of them. In their vague, rhetorical way, speech-making politicians and sermon-preaching clergymen like to say that the current struggle is not material, but spiritual—an affair not of machines, but of ideas. They forget to add that the effectiveness of ideas depends very largely on the way in which they are inculcated. A true and beneficent idea may be so ineptly taught as to be without effect on the lives of individuals and societies. Conversely, grotesque and harmful notions may be so skillfully drummed into people's heads that, filled with faith, they will rush out and move mountains—to the glory of the devil and their own destruction. At the present time the dynamism of totalitarian ideas is greater than the dynamism of liberal, democratic ideas. This is not due, of course, to the intrinsic superiority of totalitarian ideas. It is due partly to the fact that, in a world where population is fast outrunning resources, ever larger measures of governmental control become necessary—and it is easier to exercise centralized control by totalitarian than by democratic methods. Partly, too, it is due to the fact that the means employed for the dissemination of totalitarian ideas are more effective, and are used more systematically, than the means employed for disseminating democratic and liberal ideas. These more effective methods of totalitarian propaganda, education, and brainwashing are, as we have seen, pretty old-fashioned. Sooner or later, however, the dictators will abandon their revolutionary conservatism and, along with it, the old-world procedures inherited from the prepsychological and palaeopharmacological past. After which, heaven help us all!

Among the legacies of the protopharmacological past must be numbered our habit, when we feel in need of a lift, a release from tension, a mental vacation from unpleasant reality, of drinking alcohol or, if we happen to belong to a non-Western culture, of smoking hashish or opium, of chewing coca leaves or betel or any one of scores of intoxicants. The Brave New Worlders did none of these things; they merely swallowed a tablet or two of a substance called Soma. This, needless to say, was not the same as the Soma mentioned in the ancient Hindu scriptures—a rather dangerous drug derived from some as yet unidentified plant native to South Central Asia—but a synthetic, possessing "all the virtues of alcohol and Christianity, none of their defects." In small doses the Soma of the Brave New Worlders was a relaxant, an inducer of euphoria, a fosterer of friendliness and social solidarity. In medium doses it transfigured the external world and acted as a mild hallucinant; and in large doses it was a narcotic. Virtually all the Brave New Worlders thought themselves happy. This was due in part to the fact that they had been bred and conditioned to take the place assigned to them in the social hierarchy, in part to the sleep-teaching which had made them content with their lot and in part to Soma and their ability, by its means, to take holidays from unpleasant circumstances and their unpleasant selves.

All the natural narcotics, stimulants, relaxants, and hallucinants known to the modern botanist and pharmacologist were discovered by primitive man and have been in use from time immemorial. One of the first things that Homo sapiens did with his newly devoloped rationality and self-consciousness was to set them to work finding out ways to bypass analytical thinking and to transcend or, in extreme cases, temporarily obliterate the isolating awareness of the self. Trying all things that grew in field or forest, they held fast to that which, in this context, seemed good—everything, that is to say, that would change the quality of consciousness, would make it different, no matter how, from everyday feeling, perceiving, and thinking. Among the Hindus, rhythmic breathing and mental concentration have, to some extent, taken the place of the mind-transforming drugs used elsewhere. But even in the land of yoga, even among the religious and even for specifically religious purposes, cannabis indica has been freely used to supplement the effects of spiritual exercises. The habit of taking vacations from the more-or-less purgatorial world, which we have created for ourselves, is universal. Moralists may denounce it; but, in the teeth of disapproving talk and repressive legislation, the habit persists, and mind-transforming drugs are everywhere available. The Marxian formula, "Religion is the opium of the people," is reversible, and one can say, with even more truth, that "Opium is the religion of the people." In other words, mind-transformation, however induced (whether by devotional or ascetic or psychogymnastic or chemical means), has always been felt to be one of the highest, perhaps the very highest, of all attainable goods. Up to the present, governments have thought about the problem of mind-transforming chemicals only in terms of prohibition or, a little more realistically, of control and taxation. None, so far, has considered it in its relation to individual well-being and social stability; and very few (thank heaven!) have considered it in terms of Machiavellian statecraft. Because of vested interests and mental inertia, we persist in using alcohol as our main mind-transformer—just as our neolithic ancestors did. We know that alcohol is responsible for a high proportion of our traffic accidents, our crimes of violence, our domestic miseries; and yet we make no effort to replace this old-fashioned and extremely unsatisfactory drug by some new, less harmful, and more enlightening mind-transformer. Among the Brave New Worlders, Noah's prehistoric invention of fermented liquor has been made obsolete by a modern synthetic, specifically designed to contribute to social order and the happiness of the individual, and to do so at the minimum physiological cost.

In the society described in my fable, Soma was used as an instrument of statecraft. The tyrants were benevolent, but they were still tyrants. Their subjects were not bludgeoned into obedience; they were chemically coerced to love their servitude, to cooperate willingly and even enthusiastically in the preservation of the social hierarchy. By the malignant or the ignorant, anything and everything can be used badly. Alcohol, for example, has been used, in small doses, to facilitate the exchange of thought in a symposium (literally, a drinking party) of philosophers. It has also been used, as the slave traders used it, to facilitate kidnapping. Scopolamine may be used to induce "twilight sleep"; it may also be used to increase suggestibility and soften up political prisoners. Heroin may be used to control pain; it may also be used (as it is said to have been used by the Japanese during their occupation of China) to produce an incapacitating addiction in a dangerous adversary. Directed by the wrong people, the coming revolution could be as disastrous, in its own way, as a nuclear and bacteriological war. By systematically using the psychological, chemical, and electronic instruments already in existence (not to mention those new and better devices which the future holds in store), a tyrannical oligarchy could keep the majority in permanent and willing subjection. This is the prophecy I made in *Brave New World*. I hope I may be proved wrong, but am sorely afraid that I may be proved right.

Meanwhile it should be pointed out that Soma is not intrinsically evil. On the contrary, a harmless but effective mind-transforming drug might prove a major blessing. And anyhow (as history makes abundantly clear) there will never be any question of getting rid of chemical mind-transformers altogether. The choice confronting us is not a choice between Soma and nothing; it is a choice between Soma and alcohol, Soma and opium, Soma and hashish, ololiuqui, peyote, datura, agaric, and all the rest of the natural mind-transformers; between Soma and such products of scientific chemistry and pharmacology as ether, chloral, veronal, benzedrine, and the barbiturates. In a word, we have to choose between a more-or-less harmless all-around drug and a wide variety of more-or-less harmful and only partially effective drugs. And this choice will not be delayed until the seventh century After Ford. Pharmacology is on the march. The Soma of *Brave New World* is no longer a distant dream. Indeed, something possessing many of the characteristics of Soma is already with us. I refer to the most recent of the tranquilizing agents—the Happiness Pill, as its users affectionately call it, known in America under the trade names of Miltown and Equinel. These Happiness Pills exert a double action; they relax the tension in striped muscle and so relax the associated tensions in the mind. At the same time they act on the enzyme system of the brain in such a way as to prevent disturbances arising in the hypothalamus from interfering with the workings of the cortex. On the mental level, the effect is a blessed release from anxiety and self-regarding emotivity.

In my fable the savage expresses his belief that the advantages of Soma must be paid for by losses on the highest human levels. Perhaps he was right. The universe is not in the habit of giving us something for nothing. And yet there is a great deal to be said for a pill which enables us to assume an attitude toward circumstances of detachment, ataraxia, "holy indifference." The moral worth of an action cannot be measured exclusively in terms of intention. Hell is paved with good intentions, and we have to take some account of results. Rational and kindly behavior tends to produce good results, and these results remain good even when the behavior which produced them was itself produced by a pill. On the other hand, can we with impunity replace systematic self-discipline by a chemical? It remains to be seen.

Of all the consciousness-transforming drugs the most interesting, if not the most immediately useful, are those which, like lysergic acid and mescaline, open the door to what may be called the Other World of the mind. Many workers are already exploring the effects of these drugs, and we may be sure that other mind-transformers, with even more remarkable properties, will be produced in the near future. What man will ultimately do with these extraordinary elixirs, it is impossible to say. My own guess is that they are destined to play a part in human life at least as great as the part played, up till now, by alcohol, and incomparably more beneficent.

Suggestions for Discussion

1. Huxley reviews the predictions in his novel after twenty-five years. How does he regard his record of prediction?

2. How does Huxley use the occasion of "revisiting" his novel to discuss world problems in 1973? In what ways is Huxley pessimistic about the future of the world?

3. What reasons does Huxley give for his belief that Orwell's predictions were politically more accurate than his own?

4. What revolution does Huxley believe he has accurately predicted in his novel? Explain.

5. Huxley contends that the history of mankind involves various ways of bypassing thought, transcendence, or obliteration of self-awareness. Relate this contention to his discussion of historical problems.

6. What is Huxley's attitude toward "Soma" in the essay? What role does he think drugs will continue to play in society?

7. Explain the subtitle of the essay, "Proleptic meditations on Mother's Day."

Suggestions for Writing

1. Write an essay comparing the ideas in this piece with the selection from *Brave New World* in this anthology. How does the selection from the novel emphasize or explain Huxley's ideas in the essay?

2. Huxley analyzes the political role that nationalism now plays and may play in the future. Is his analysis correct? Write a paper which reflects your own ideas about nationalism. How would you define it? How is it related to patriotism?

Arthur C. Clarke

Broadway and the Satellites

Arthur C. Clarke (b. 1917) was born in England and served in the Royal Air Force during World War II. The originator of the idea of communications satellites, he has written about aeronautics, astronauts, astronomy, and underwater exploration. Among his best-known science fiction works are *Going into Space* (1954), *The Exploration of the Moon* (1954), and *The Lost Worlds of 2001* (1971). The following essay, taken from his *Voices from the Sky* (1965), discusses the emergence of a global communications network.

Sometime before the end of this century, a billion people will attend the same first night. They will do it, of course, not in person, but via the worldwide TV network foreshadowed by the Telstar satellite.

Before we consider the impact of communications satellites on the performing arts, let us see what technical developments may be expected. In a very few years, intercontinental TV will be commonplace. Viewers will think no more of being taken, live, from New York to New Delhi than they do today of being switched from one town to the next.

At first, however, ordinary viewers will still remain tuned to the local stations: unlike the short-wave ham, the TV viewer will not be able to roam at will over the world. The antennas needed to catch the feeble voices of today's satellites are so enormous, and must be backed by such elaborate receiving and tracking gear, that direct domestic reception is out of the question. We will be able to see only the foreign programs that our local networks decide to relay to us.

But this will not always be the case. Perhaps ten years from now, really high-powered TV transmitters will be put into orbit—and into the very special orbit that allows them to remain fixed in the sky (the so-called synchronous or stationary orbit). When that time comes, you will be able to tune in *directly* to European, Russian, or Chinese programs coming straight down from the sky; and there will be weeping and wailing on Madison Avenue.

And on Broadway? Not necessarily, though there will undoubtedly be profound changes, some for the better, some for the worse. Recently I had the interesting experience of seeing, while sitting in one midtown theater, a play being staged in another. The large-screen projection, the presence of the audience, and the usual intervals, gave a sense of immediacy and participation which home TV lacks. One can see a whole new art form springing up, with production techniques similar to those employed in studio TV and the movies, but quite different in other respects. Perhaps we may call it Teletheater.

TT, if it develops, will presumably move into the large number of surplus cinemas now threatened with conversion into bowling alleys or (as in England) legalized gambling dens. Every town or community of any size will have such a theater, and everyone from Alaska to Florida will be able to enjoy an identical performance. The show will be the same; only the audiences will be different. And the expression "Off Broadway" will start to look a little sick.

Now TT can obviously flourish without the use of communications satellites, but they will give it a tremendous boost. When the whole world can tune into the Comédie Française, Drury Lane, the Bolshoi, all the Stratfords, Lincoln Center, La Scala, the incentive to build teletheaters will be very great. And such theaters could, at least in principle, be independent of their own national networks: they could present foreign programs by direct pickup.

It is obvious that home TV, with its own widening frontiers, will compete to some extent with the new theaters; and the recent contest between cinema and TV may be repeated in a slightly different arena. The outcome may be much the same as before; the theaters will provide high definition, color, wide-screen, and stereo sound of a quality which home viewers will be unable to match. The aesthetic effect of all these gimmicks will doubtless be deplorable, at least until the producers learn to handle their new powers with moderation.

Any form of instantaneous, worldwide entertainment raises a whole host of problems—technical, cultural, and economic—only a few of which can be mentioned here. The first that comes to mind is the question of language.

This is not as important as might be thought, for it does not affect the majority of the performing arts. Ballet means as much (or as little) to an Eskimo as to a Basque. Even when there are words, the example of opera proves that the audience doesn't have to understand them; only for the play are they vital.

Time, I think, will take care of this difficulty. The development of truly global communications will accelerate, as nothing else has done, the adoption of a world language (almost certainly English) which will be spoken as a second tongue by all educated men. And the revolution in transport which is just getting underway may succeed in making even the English and the Americans bilingual. (I would like to think that the Peace Corps is the first step toward a world in which *all* men and women spend a couple of their formative years in a foreign country, which they will come to regard as their second home.)

Time zones present more fundamental difficulties. The Late, Late Show is already bad enough, but how many of us would get up in the middle of the night to watch anything short of a world heavyweight fight or the first landing on the Moon? Certainly, few people would enjoy "Hamlet" at 4 A.M.

I suspect (and fear) that this problem will also bring its own solutions. When everyone in the world is plugged into the same telephone exchange, and all calls are local ones, sleep is going to become impossible anyway. Physiologists and electronics experts are already at work on a "sleep compressor" which will allow two hours of artificial rest to be as effective as eight of the old-fashioned variety. When this dubious blessing is perfected, well in advance of 1984, the twenty-two-hour day will be upon us. We will need those pre-dawn premieres to occupy our copious leisure time.

And there is the intriguing problem of censorship. For the first time in history, no country will have any control over the entertainment sampled by its citizens. (At least in their own homes; the teletheaters will presumably have to watch their licenses.) Just what may happen if some really uninhibited client gets hold of a channel, I've described in *Tales of Ten Worlds*.

However, I must not raise false hopes. The global communications network will operate according to strict international rules, as all telecommunications have done for the last century. (A big UN-sponsored conference to lay down these regulations took place in 1963.) Nevertheless, there will be a lot of fun when the French beam raw Genet to the United States, and the U.S. aims the riper offerings of T. Williams at the U.S.S.R.

More seriously, it will be of great interest to watch the effects upon standards of performance when productions of all types can be exchanged freely over the whole Earth. Will there be a leveling down, or a leveling up? When I think that half the globe may soon be receiving instant soap opera from communications satellites, I sometimes feel more than a distant kinship to the late Dr. Frankenstein.

Before you get back for the second act, let me chill your blood a little further. Sooner or later, we are going to learn how to transmit electronically not only sights and sounds, but actual sensations, which will be fed directly into the nervous system. Then you will no longer look at pictures on an illuminated screen: the images will bypass your eyes and you will "experience" them inside your brain. The same thing would be true for sound, touch, smell, and all the other senses.

Many years ago, the "Feelies" of Aldous Huxley's *Brave New World* barely hinted at these possibilities, and for a much juicier treatment I refer you to Shepherd ("How To Succeed In Business . . .") Mead's novel *The Big Ball of Wax*. The ultimate development would be a world of dreamers, packed by their millions in the stately pleasure domes of Electro-sensory Entertainment, Inc. Here they would live vicarious lives that might be so much more vivid and exciting than mere reality that they would awake only with the utmost reluctance.

The French aristocrat who remarked haughtily "Life? I leave *that* to my servants," may have spoken for the future. Our descendants a hundred years hence may hand over the running of the world to their robots, while they themselves retire into a realm of electronically induced fantasies. And so they will pass away their lives, wired not merely for sound, but for everything.

I do hope you enjoy the rest of the performance.

Suggestions for Discussion

1. What technical developments does Clarke outline?

2. Explain what he means by Teletheater.

3. Discuss problems with any form of instantaneous worldwide entertainment.

4. Comment on his assertion that the ultimate development will be "a world of dreamers" living "vicarious lives."

Suggestions for Writing

1. To what extent does global Teletheater already exist? Explain and give examples.

2. Write a short story about a time when our descendants have retired "into a realm of electronically induced fantasies."

Fiction
—◆◆◆—

Aldous Huxley
Conditioning the Children

Aldous Huxley (1894–1963) was born in England and educated at Oxford. He is the author of many novels including *Point Counter Point* (1928) and the anti-utopian *Brave New World* (1932). He also wrote essays, short stories, poetry, and plays. After he moved to Southern California, he became increasingly interested in Hindu philosophy and mysticism. *The Doors of Perception* (1954) describes his experience with hallucenogenic drugs. This brief selection from *Brave New World* describes without comment painful experiments to condition the minds of new-born infants.

The D.H.C.[1] and his students stepped into the nearest lift and were carried up to the fifth floor.

INFANT NURSERIES. NEO-PAVLOVIAN CONDITIONING ROOMS, announced the notice board.

The Director opened a door. They were in a large bare room, very bright and sunny; for the whole of the southern wall was a single window. Half a dozen nurses, trousered and jacketed in the regulation white viscose-linen uniform, their hair aseptically hidden under white caps, were engaged in setting out bowls of roses in a long row across the floor. Big bowls, packed tight with blossom. Thousands of petals, ripeblown and silkily smooth, like the cheeks of innumerable little cherubs, but of cherubs, in that bright light, not exclusively pink and Aryan, but also luminously Chinese, also Mexican, also apoplectic with too much blowing of celestial trumpets, also pale as death, pale with the posthumous whiteness of marble.

The nurses stiffened to attention as the D.H.C. came in.

"Set out the books," he said curtly.

In silence the nurses obeyed his command. Between the rose bowls the

[1]Director of Hatcheries and Conditioning.

491

books were duly set out—a row of nursery quartos opened invitingly each at some gaily coloured image of beast or fish or bird.

"Now bring in the children."

They hurried out of the room and returned in a minute or two, each pushing a kind of tall dumb-waiter laden, on all its four wire-netted shelves with eight-month-old babies, all exactly alike (a Bokanovsky Group, it was evident) and all (since their caste was Delta) dressed in khaki.

"Put them down on the floor."

The infants were unloaded.

"Now turn them so that they can see the flowers and books."

Turned, the babies at once fell silent, then began to crawl towards those clusters of sleek colors, those shapes so gay and brilliant on the white pages. As they approached, the sun came out of a momentary eclipse behind a cloud. The roses flamed up as though with a sudden passion from within; a new and profound significance seemed to suffuse the shining pages of the books. From the ranks of the crawling babies came little squeals of excitement, gurgles and twitterings of pleasure.

The Director rubbed his hands. "Excellent!" he said. "It might almost have been done on purpose."

The swiftest crawlers were already at their goal. Small hands reached out uncertainly, touched, grasped, unpetaling the transfigured roses, crumpling the illuminated pages of the books. The Director waited until all were happily busy. Then, "Watch carefully," he said. And, lifting his hand, he gave the signal.

The Head Nurse, who was standing by a switchboard at the other end of the room, pressed down a little lever.

There was a violent explosion. Shriller and ever shriller, a siren shrieked. Alarm bells maddeningly sounded.

The children started, screamed; their faces were distorted with terror.

"And now," the Director shouted (for the noise was deafening), "now we proceed to rub in the lesson with a mild electric shock."

He waved his hand again, and the Head Nurse pressed a second lever. The screaming of the babies suddenly changed its tone. There was something desperate, almost insane, about the sharp spasmodic yelps to which they now gave utterance. Their little bodies twitched and stiffened; their limbs moved jerkily as if to the tug of unseen wires.

"We can electrify that whole strip of floor," bawled the Director in explanation. "But that's enough," he signalled to the nurse.

The explosions ceased, the bells stopped ringing, the shriek of the siren died down from tone to tone into silence. The stiffly twitching bodies relaxed, and what had become the sob and yelp of infant maniacs broadened out once more into a normal howl of ordinary terror.

"Offer them the flowers and the books again."

The nurses obeyed; but at the approach of the roses, at the mere sight of those gaily-coloured images of pussy and cock-a-doodle-doo and baa-baa black sheep, the infants shrank away in horror; the volume of their howling suddenly increased.

"Observe," said the Director triumphantly, "observe."

Books and loud noises, flowers and electric shocks—already in the infant mind the couples were compromisingly linked; and after two hundred repetitions of the same or a similar lesson would be wedded indissolubly. What man has joined, nature is powerless to put asunder.

"They'll grow up with what the psychologists used to call an 'instinctive' hatred of books and flowers. Reflexes unalterably conditioned. They'll be safe from books and botany all their lives." The Director turned to his nurses. "Take them away again."

Still yelling, the khaki babies were loaded on to their dumb-waiters and wheeled out, leaving behind them the smell of sour milk and a most welcome silence.

Suggestions for Discussion

1. Summarize the Pavlovian experiment demonstrated on the children. Do the doctor and the student observers regard the experiment as cruel? Explain their attitude.

2. What details in the selection would you regard as contributing to the anti-utopian atmosphere? How does Huxley employ imagery in the details?

Suggestion for Writing

Write a story that describes a method of controlling human behavior. You may wish to place the events in a utopian, anti-utopian, or in a completely ordinary setting.

Poetry

Walt Whitman

When I Heard the Learn'd Astronomer

Walt Whitman (1819–1892), regarded by many as the greatest American poet, was born on Long Island, New York. He was a printer, a journalist, and a nurse during the Civil War. Strongly influenced by Ralph Waldo Emerson, he published *Leaves of Grass* in 1855 at his own expense. He added sections to new editions over the years. By the time of his death, he had become a major influence on younger poets who were moved by his experiments in free verse and by his transcendental ideas. In "When I Heard the Learn'd Astronomer," impatient with explanations of abstract science, he turns instead to silent contemplation of nature which, he implies, provides a profounder insight than do the "charts and diagrams" of science.

When I heard the learn'd astronomer,
When the proofs, the figures, were ranged in columns before me,
When I was shown the charts and diagrams, to add, divide, and measure them,
When I sitting heard the astronomer where he lectured with much applause
    in the lecture-room,
How soon unaccountable I became tired and sick,
Till rising and gliding out I wander'd off by myself,
In the mystical moist night-air, and from time to time,
Look'd up in perfect silence at the stars.

Suggestions for Discussion

1. Notice that this poem is contained in one sentence. How does Whitman organize the sentence to lead to the climax of the last line?

2. What is the poet's attitude toward the scientist? Why does he reject the scientific method of looking at nature? Why is his response "unaccountable"?

3. What is the significance of the phrase "perfect silence" in the last line?

Suggestion for Writing

Write an essay in which you explain not only the idea in the poem but how the idea is developed. Your essay should consider how a prose statement of the idea would differ.

Freedom and Human Dignity

◆◆◆

The bureaucratization of life brings about its absolute decay in all orders. Wealth diminishes, births are few. Then the State, in order to attend to its own needs, forces on still more the bureaucratization of human existence. . . . The State's most urgent need is its apparatus of war, its army.

— **José Ortega y Gasset,** "The Greatest Danger, the State"

"Liberty consists in being able to do anything which is not harmful to another or to others. . . ."

— **"Declaration of the Rights of Man,"** Paris, August 27, 1789

I have a dream that my four little children will one day live in a nation where they will not be judged by the color of their skin but by the content of their character.

— **Martin Luther King, Jr.,** "I Have a Dream", August 23, 1963

I believe that man will not merely endure: he will prevail. He is immortal, not because he alone among creatures has an inexhaustible voice but because he has a soul, a spirit capable of compassion and sacrifice and endurance."

— **William Faulkner,** Nobel Prize Award Speech, 1949

Was he free? Was he happy? The question is absurd:
Had anything been wrong, we should certainly have heard.

— **W. H. Auden,** "The Unknown Citizen"

Personal Reminiscence

◆◆◆

W. E. B. Du Bois

On Being Crazy

William Edward Burghardt Du Bois (1868–1963) was born in Massachusetts. In the course of his life he became a major influence on American blacks. By 1903 he had written *The Souls of Black Folk* which stated his major objections to the attitudes found in the writings of Booker T. Washington, the most influential black figure in the early twentieth century. In 1909 he helped found the National Association for the Advancement of Colored People. He edited *Crisis*, the magazine of the NAACP, and also founded the influential quarterly *Phylon* at Atlanta University. In this brief sketch (1907), Du Bois, in a series of conversations, touches ironically on the insanity of the relations between blacks and whites in the early days of the twentieth century. It might be instructive to consider just how different the relations between the races are today.

It was one o'clock and I was hungry. I walked into a restaurant, seated myself, and reached for the bill of fare. My table companion rose.

"Sir," said he, "do you wish to force your company on those who do not want you?"

No, said I, I wish to eat.

"Are you aware, sir, that this is social equality?"

Nothing of the sort, sir, it is hunger—and I ate.

The day's work done, I sought the theatre. As I sank into my seat, the lady shrank and squirmed.

I beg pardon, I said.

"Do you enjoy being where you are not wanted?" she asked coldly.

Oh no, I said.

"Well you are not wanted here."

I was surprised. I fear you are mistaken, I said, I certainly want the music, and I like to think the music wants me to listen to it.

"Usher," said the lady, "this is social equality."

"No, madame," said the usher, "it is the second movement of Beethoven's Fifth Symphony."

After the theatre, I sought the hotel where I had sent my baggage. The clerk scowled.

"What do you want?"

Rest, I said.

"This is a white hotel," he said.

I looked around. Such a color scheme requires a great deal of cleaning, I said, but I don't know that I object.

"We object," said he.

Then why, I began, but he interrupted.

"We don't keep niggers," he said, "we don't want social equality."

Neither do I, I replied gently, I want a bed.

I walked thoughtfully to the train. I'll take a sleeper through Texas. I'm a little bit dissatisfied with this town.

"Can't sell you one."

I only want to hire it, said I, for a couple of nights.

"Can't sell you a sleeper in Texas," he maintained. "They consider that social equality."

I consider it barbarism, I said, and I think I'll walk.

Walking, I met another wayfarer, who immediately walked to the other side of the road, where it was muddy. I asked his reason.

"Niggers is dirty," he said.

So is mud, said I. Moreover, I am not as dirty as you—yet.

"But you're a nigger, ain't you?" he asked.

My grandfather was so called.

"Well then!" he answered triumphantly.

Do you live in the South?' I persisted, pleasantly.

"Sure," he growled, "and starve there."

I should think you and the Negroes should get together and vote out starvation.

"We don't let them vote."

We? Why not? I said in surprise.

"Niggers is too ignorant to vote."

But, I said, I am not so ignorant as you.

"But you're a nigger."

Yes, I'm certainly what you mean by that.

"Well then!" he returned, with that curiously inconsequential note of triumph. "Moreover," he said, "I don't want my sister to marry a nigger."

I had not seen his sister, so I merely murmured, let her say no.

"By God, you shan't marry her, even if she said yes."

But—but I don't want to marry her, I answered, a little perturbed at the personal turn.

"Why not!" he yelled, angrier than ever.

Because I'm already married and I rather like my wife.

"Is she a nigger?" he asked suspiciously.

Well, I said again, her grandmother was called that.

"Well then!" he shouted in that oddly illogical way.

I gave up.

Go on, I said, either you are crazy or I am.

"We both are," he said as he trotted along in the mud.

Suggestions for Discussion

1. Why has Du Bois chosen these specific scenes for his conversations with white people?

2. In what way is the final conversation different from those preceding it?

3. Discuss some of the examples of Du Bois' use of irony.

Suggestion for Writing

Write an essay in which you examine the areas of racism dealt with in this selection from today's perspective. What significant differences would you find? What similarities? In what way is "On Being Crazy" relevant for our time?

Richard Wright

The Ethics of Living Jim Crow

A major American black writer, Richard Wright (1908–1960) published stories, novels, an autobiography, and other books about America's racial problems. His best known works are *Native Son* (1940), *Black Boy* (1945), and *White Man, Listen* (1957). The following autobiographical account of his education in race relations in a totally segregated South is from *Uncle Tom's Children* (1938).

I

My first lesson in how to live as a Negro came when I was quite small. We were living in Arkansas. Our house stood behind the railroad tracks. Its skimpy yard was paved with black cinders. Nothing green ever grew in that yard. The only touch of green we could see was far away, beyond the tracks, over where the white folks lived. But cinders were good enough for me and I never missed the green growing things. And anyhow cinders were fine weapons. You could always have a nice hot war with huge black cinders. All you had to do was crouch behind the brick pillars of a house with your hands full of gritty ammunition. And the first woolly black head you saw pop out from behind another row of pillars was your target. You tried your very best to knock it off. It was great fun.

I never fully realized the appalling disadvantages of a cinder environment till one day the gang to which I belonged found itself engaged in a war with the white boys who lived beyond the tracks. As usual we laid down our cinder barrage, thinking that this would wipe the white boys out. But they replied with a steady bombardment of broken bottles. We doubled our cinder barrage, but they hid behind trees, hedges, and the sloping embankments of their lawns. Having no such fortifications, we retreated to the brick pillars of our homes. During the retreat a broken milk bottle caught me behind the ear, opening a deep gash which bled profusely. The sight of blood pouring over my face completely demoralized our ranks. My fellow-combatants left me standing paralyzed in the center of the yard, and scurried for their homes. A kind neighbor saw me and rushed me to a doctor, who took three stitches in my neck.

I sat brooding on my front steps, nursing my wound and waiting for my mother to come from work. I felt that a grave injustice had been done me. It was all right to throw cinders. The greatest harm a cinder could do was leave a bruise. But broken bottles were dangerous; they left you cut, bleeding, and helpless.

When night fell, my mother came from the white folks' kitchen. I raced down the street to meet her. I could just feel in my bones that she would understand. I knew she would tell me exactly what to do next time. I grabbed her hand and babbled out the whole story. She examined my wound, then slapped me.

"How come yuh didn't hide?" she asked me. "How come yuh awways fightin'?"

I was outraged, and bawled. Between sobs I told her that I didn't have any trees or hedges to hide behind. There wasn't a thing I could have used as a trench. And you couldn't throw very far when you were hiding behind the brick pillars of a house. She grabbed a barrel stave, dragged me home, stripped me naked, and beat me till I had a fever of one hundred and two. She would smack my rump with the stave, and, while the skin was still smarting, impart to me gems of Jim Crow wisdom. I was never to throw cinders any more. I was never to fight any more wars. I was never, never, under any conditions, to fight *white* folks again. And they were absolutely right in clouting me with the broken milk bottle. Didn't I know she was working hard every day in the hot kitchens of the white folks to make money to take care of me? When was I ever going to learn to be a good boy? She couldn't be bothered with my fights. She finished by telling me that I ought to be thankful to God as long as I lived that they didn't kill me.

All that night I was delirious and could not sleep. Each time I closed my eyes I saw monstrous white faces suspended from the ceiling, leering at me.

From that time on, the charm of my cinder yard was gone. The green trees, the trimmed hedges, the cropped lawns grew very meaningful, became a symbol. Even today when I think of white folks, the hard, sharp outlines of white houses surrounded by trees, lawns, and hedges are present somewhere in the background of my mind. Through the years they grew into an over-reaching symbol of fear.

It was a long time before I came in close contact with white folks again. We moved from Arkansas to Mississippi. Here we had the good fortune not to live behind the railroad tracks, or close to white neighborhoods. We lived in the very heart of the local Black belt. There were black churches and black preachers; there were black schools and black teachers; black groceries and black clerks. In fact, everything was so solidly black that for a long time I did not even think of white folks, save in remote and vague terms. But this could not last forever. As one grows older one eats more. One's clothing costs more. When I finished grammar school I had to go to work. My mother could no longer feed and clothe me on her cooking job.

There is but one place where a black boy who knows no trade can get a job, and that's where the houses and faces are white, where the trees, lawns, and hedges are green. My first job was with an optical company in Jackson, Mississippi. The morning I applied I stood straight and neat before the boss, answering all his questions with sharp yessirs and nosirs. I was very careful to pronounce my *sirs* distinctly, in order that he might know that I was polite, that I knew where I was, and that I knew he was a *white* man. I wanted that job badly.

He looked me over as though he were examining a prize poodle. He questioned me closely about my schooling, being particularly insistent about how much mathematics I had had. He seemed very pleased when I told him I had had two years of algebra.

"Boy, how would you like to try to learn something around here?" he asked me.

"I'd like it fine, sir," I said, happy. I had visions of "working my way up." Even Negroes have those visions.

"All right," he said. "Come on."

I followed him to the small factory.

"Pease," he said to a white man of about thirty-five, "this is Richard. He's going to work for us."

Pease looked at me and nodded.

I was then taken to a white boy of about seventeen.

"Morrie, this is Richard, who's going to work for us."

"Whut yuh sayin' there, boy!" Morrie boomed at me.

"Fine!" I answered.

The boss instructed these two to help me, teach me, give me jobs to do, and let me learn what I could in my spare time.

My wages were five dollars a week.

I worked hard, trying to please. For the first month I got along O.K. Both Pease and Morrie seemed to like me. But one thing was missing. And I kept thinking about it. I was not learning anything and nobody was volunteering to help me. Thinking they had forgotten that I was to learn something about the mechanics of grinding lenses, I asked Morrie one day to tell me about the work. He grew red.

"Whut yuh tryin' t' do, nigger, get smart?" he asked.

"Naw; I ain't tryin' t' git smart," I said.

"Well, don't, if yuh know whut's good for yuh!"

I was puzzled. Maybe he just doesn't want to help me, I thought. I went to Pease.

"Say, are yuh crazy, you black bastard?" Pease asked me, his gray eyes growing hard.

I spoke out, reminding him that the boss had said I was to be given a chance to learn something.

"Nigger, you think you're *white*, don't you?"

"Naw, sir!"

"Well, you're acting mighty like it!"

"But, Mr. Pease, the boss said . . ."

Pease shook his fist in my face.

"This is a *white* man's work around here, and you better watch yourself!"

From then on they changed toward me. They said good-morning no more. When I was just a bit slow in performing some duty, I was called a lazy black son-of-a-bitch.

Once I thought of reporting all this to the boss. But the mere idea of what would happen to me if Pease and Morrie should learn that I had "snitched" stopped me. And after all the boss was a white man, too. What was the use?

The climax came at noon one summer day. Pease called me to his work-bench. To get to him I had to go between two narrow benches and stand with my back against a wall.

"Yes, sir," I said.

"Richard, I want to ask you something," Pease began pleasantly, not look-ing up from his work.

"Yes, sir," I said again.

Morrie came over, blocking the narrow passage between the benches. He folded his arms, staring at me solemnly.

I looked from one to the other, sensing that something was coming.

"Yes, sir," I said for the third time.

Pease looked up and spoke very slowly.

"Richard, *Mr.* Morrie here tells me you called me *Pease.*"

I stiffened. A void seemed to open up in me. I knew this was the show-down.

He meant that I had failed to call him Mr. Pease. I looked at Morrie. He was gripping a steel bar in his hands. I opened my mouth to speak, to protest, to assure Pease that I had never called him simply *Pease*, and that I had never had any intentions of doing so, when Morrie grabbed me by the collar, ram-ming my head against the wall.

"Now, be careful, nigger!" snarled Morrie, baring his teeth. "*I* heard yuh call 'im *Pease!* 'N' if yuh say yuh didn't yuh're callin' me a *lie*, see?" He waved the steel bar threateningly.

If I had said: No, sir, Mr. Pease, I never called you *Pease*, I would have been automatically calling Morrie a liar. And if I had said: Yes, sir, Mr. Pease, I called you *Pease*, I would have been pleading guilty to having uttered the worst insult that a Negro can utter to a southern white man. I stood hesitat-ing, trying to frame a neutral reply.

"Richard, I asked you a question!" said Pease. Anger was creeping into his voice.

"I don't remember calling you *Pease*, Mr. Pease," I said cautiously. "And if I did, I sure didn't mean . . ."

"You black son-of-a-bitch! You called me *Pease*, then!" he spat, slapping me till I bent sideways over a bench. Morrie was on top of me, demanding:

"Didn't yuh call 'im *Pease?* If yuh say yuh didn't, I'll rip yo' gut string loose with this bar, yuh black granny dodger! Yuh can't call a white man a liar 'n' git erway with it, you black son-of-a-bitch!"

I wilted. I begged them not to bother me. I knew what they wanted. They wanted me to leave.

"I'll leave," I promised. "I'll leave right *now.*"

They gave me a minute to get out of the factory. I was warned not to show up again, or tell the boss.

I went.

When I told the folks at home what had happened, they called me a fool. They told me that I must never again attempt to exceed my boundaries. When you are working for white folks, they said, you got to "stay in your place" if you want to keep working.

II

My Jim Crow education continued on my next job, which was portering in a clothing store. One morning, while polishing brass out front, the boss and his twenty-year-old son got out of their car and half dragged and half kicked a Negro woman into the store. A policeman standing at the corner looked on, twirling his night-stick. I watched out of the corner of my eye, never slackening the strokes of my chamois upon the brass. After a few minutes, I heard shrill screams coming from the rear of the store. Later the woman stumbled out, bleeding, crying, and holding her stomach. When she reached the end of the block, the policeman grabbed her and accused her of being drunk. Silently, I watched him throw her into a patrol wagon.

When I went to the rear of the store, the boss and his son were washing their hands at the sink. They were chuckling. The floor was bloody and strewn with wisps of hair and clothing. No doubt I must have appeared pretty shocked, for the boss slapped me reassuringly on the back.

"Boy, that's what we do to niggers when they don't want to pay their bills," he said, laughing.

His son looked at me and grinned.

"Here, hava cigarette," he said.

Not knowing what to do, I took it. He lit his and held the match for me. This was a gesture of kindness, indicating that even if they had beaten the poor old woman, they would not beat me if I knew enough to keep my mouth shut.

"Yes, sir," I said, and asked no questions.

After they had gone, I sat on the edge of a packing box and stared at the bloody floor till the cigarette went out.

That day at noon, while eating in a hamburger joint, I told my fellow Negro porters what had happened. No one seemed surprised. One fellow, after swallowing a huge bite, turned to me and asked:

"Huh! Is tha' all they did t' her?"

"Yeah. Wasn't tha' enough?" I asked.

"Shucks! Man, she's a lucky bitch!" he said, burying his lips deep into a juicy hamburger. "Hell, it's a wonder they didn't lay her when they got through."

III

I was learning fast, but not quite fast enough. One day, while I was delivering packages in the suburbs, my bicycle tire was punctured. I walked along the hot, dusty road, sweating and leading my bicycle by the handlebars.

A car slowed at my side.

"What's the matter, boy?" a white man called.

I told him my bicycle was broken and I was walking back to town.

"That's too bad," he said. "Hop on the running board."

He stopped the car. I clutched hard at my bicycle with one hand and clung to the side of the car with the other.

"All set?"

"Yes, sir," I answered. The car started.

It was full of young white men. They were drinking. I watched the flask pass from mouth to mouth.

"Wanna drink, boy?" one asked.

I laughed as the wind whipped my face. Instinctively obeying the freshly planted precepts of my mother, I said:

"Oh, no!"

The words were hardly out of my mouth before I felt something hard and cold smash me between the eyes. It was an empty whisky bottle. I saw stars, and fell backwards from the speeding car into the dust of the road, my feet becoming entangled in the steel spokes of my bicycle. The white men piled out and stood over me.

"Nigger, ain' yuh learned no better sense'n tha' yet?" asked the man who hit me. "Ain' yuh learned t' say *sir* t' a white man yet?"

Dazed, I pulled to my feet. My elbows and legs were bleeding. Fists doubled, the white man advanced, kicking my bicycle out of the way.

"Aw, leave the bastard alone. He's got enough," said one.

They stood looking at me. I rubbed my shins, trying to stop the flow of blood. No doubt they felt a sort of contemptuous pity, for one asked:

"Yuh wanna ride t' town now, nigger? Yuh reckon yuh know enough t' ride now?"

"I wanna walk," I said, simply.

Maybe it sounded funny. They laughed.

"Well, walk, yuh black son-of-a-bitch!"

When they left they comforted me with:

"Nigger, yuh sho better be damn glad it wuz us yuh talked t' tha' way. Yuh're a lucky bastard, 'cause if yuh'd said tha' t' somebody else, yuh might've been a dead nigger now."

IV

Negroes who had lived South know the dread of being caught alone upon the streets in white neighborhoods after the sun has set. In such a simple situation as this the plight of the Negro in America is graphically symbolized. While white strangers may be in these neighborhoods trying to get home, they can pass unmolested. But the color of a Negro's skin makes him easily recognizable, makes him suspect, converts him into a defenseless target.

Late one Saturday night I made some deliveries in a white neighborhood. I was pedaling my bicycle back to the store as fast as I could, when a police car, swerving toward me, jammed me into the curbing.

"Get down and put up your hands!" the policemen ordered.

I did. They climbed out of the car, guns drawn, faces set, and advanced slowly.

"Keep still!" they ordered.

I reached my hands higher. They searched my pockets and packages. They seemed dissatisfied when they could find nothing incriminating. Finally, one of them said:

"Boy, tell your boss not to send you out in white neighborhoods after sundown."

As usual, I said:

"Yes, sir."

V

My next job was a hall-boy in a hotel. Here my Jim Crow education broadened and deepened. When the bell-boys were busy, I was often called to assist them. As many of the rooms in the hotel were occupied by prostitutes, I was constantly called to carry them liquor and cigarettes. These women were nude most of the time. They did not bother about clothing, even for bell-boys. When you went into their rooms, you were supposed to take their nakedness for granted, as though it startled you no more than a blue vase or a red rug. Your presence awoke in them no sense of shame, for you were not regarded as human. If they were alone, you could steal sidelong glimpses at them. But if they were receiving men, not a flicker of your eyelids could show. I remember one incident vividly. A new woman, a huge, snowy-skinned blonde, took a room on my floor. I was sent to wait upon her. She was in bed with a thick-set man; both were nude and uncovered. She said she wanted some liquor and slid out of bed and waddled across the floor to get her money from a dresser drawer. I watched her.

"Nigger, what in hell you looking at?" the white man asked me, raising himself upon his elbows.

"Nothing," I answered, looking miles deep into the blank wall of the room.

"Keep your eyes where they belong, if you want to be healthy!" he said.

"Yes, sir."

VI

One of the bell-boys I knew in this hotel was keeping steady company with one of the Negro maids. Out of a clear sky the police descended upon his home and arrested him, accusing him of bastardy. The poor boy swore he had had no intimate relations with the girl. Nevertheless, they forced him to marry her. When the child arrived, it was found to be much lighter in complexion than either of the two supposedly legal parents. The white men around the hotel made a great joke of it. They spread the rumor that some white cow must have scared the poor girl while she was carrying the baby. If you were in their presence when this explanation was offered, you were supposed to laugh.

VII

One of the bell-boys was caught in bed with a white prostitute. He was castrated and run out of town. Immediately after this all the bell-boys and hall-boys were called together and warned. We were given to understand that the boy who had been castrated was a "mighty, mighty lucky bastard." We were impressed with the fact that next time the management of the hotel would not be responsible for the lives of "trouble-makin' niggers." We were silent.

VIII

One night, just as I was about to go home, I met one of the Negro maids. She lived in my direction, and we fell in to walk part of the way home together. As we passed the white night-watchman, he slapped the maid on her buttock. I turned around, amazed. The watchman looked at me with a long, hard, fixed-under stare. Suddenly he pulled his gun and asked:

"Nigger, don't yuh like it?"

I hesitated.

"I asked yuh don't yuh like it?" he asked again, stepping forward.

"Yes, sir." I mumbled.

"Talk like it, then!"

"Oh, yes, sir!" I said with as much heartiness as I could muster.

Outside, I walked ahead of the girl, ashamed to face her. She caught up with me and said:

"Don't be a fool! Yuh couldn't help it!"

This watchman boasted of having killed two Negroes in self-defense.

Yet, in spite of all this, the life of the hotel ran with an amazing smoothness. It would have been impossible for a stranger to detect anything. The maids, the hall-boys, and the bell-boys were all smiles. They had to be.

IX

I had learned my Jim Crow lessons so thoroughly that I kept the hotel job till I left Jackson for Memphis. It so happened that while in Memphis I applied for a job at a branch of the optical company. I was hired. And for some reason, as long as I worked there, they never brought my past against me.

Here my Jim Crow education assumed quite a different form. It was no longer brutally cruel, but subtly cruel. Here I learned to lie, to steal, to dissemble. I learned to play that dual role which every Negro must play if he wants to eat and live.

For example, it was almost impossible to get a book to read. It was assumed that after a Negro had imbibed what scanty schooling the state furnished he had no further need for books. I was always borrowing books from men on the job. One day I mustered enough courage to ask one of the men to let me get books from the library in his name. Surprisingly, he consented. I cannot help but think that he consented because he was a Roman Catholic and felt a vague sympathy for Negroes, being himself an object of hatred. Armed with a library card, I obtained books in the following manner: I would write a note to the librarian, saying: "Please let this nigger boy have the following books." I would then sign it with the white man's name.

When I went to the library, I would stand at the desk, hat in hand, looking as unbookish as possible. When I received the books desired I would take them home. If the books listed in the note happened to be out, I would sneak into the lobby and forge a new one. I never took any chances guessing with the white librarian about what the fictitious white man would want to read. No doubt if any of the white patrons had suspected that some of the volumes they enjoyed had been in the home of a Negro, they would not have tolerated it for an instant.

The factory force of the optical company in Memphis was much larger than that in Jackson, and more urbanized. At least they liked to talk, and would engage the Negro help in conversation whenever possible. By this means I found that many subjects were taboo from the white man's point of view. Among the topics they did not like to discuss with Negroes were the following: American white women; the Ku Klux Klan; France, and how Negro soldiers fared while there; French women; Jack Johnson; the entire northern part of the United States; the Civil War; Abraham Lincoln; U. S. Grant; General Sherman; Catholics; the Pope; Jews; the Republican Party; slavery; social equality; Communism; Socialism; the 13th and 14th Amendments to the Constitution; or any topic calling for positive knowledge or manly self-assertion on the part of the Negro. The most accepted topics were sex and religion.

There were many times when I had to exercise a great deal of ingenuity to keep out of trouble. It is a southern custom that all men must take off their hats when they enter an elevator. And especially did this apply to us blacks with rigid force. One day I stepped into an elevator with my arms full of packages. I was forced to ride with my hat on. Two white men stared at me coldly. Then one of them very kindly lifted my hat and placed it upon my armful of packages. Now the most accepted response for a Negro to make under such circumstances is to look at the white man out of the corner of his eye and grin. To have said: "Thank you!" would have made the white man *think* that you *thought* you were receiving from him a personal service. For such an act I have seen Negroes take a blow in the mouth. Finding the first alternative distasteful, and the second dangerous, I hit upon an acceptable course of action which fell safely between these two poles. I immediately— no sooner than my hat was lifted—pretended that my packages were about to spill, and appeared deeply distressed with keeping them in my arms. In this fashion I evaded having to acknowledge his service, and, in spite of adverse circumstances, salvaged a slender shred of personal pride.

How do Negroes feel about the way they have to live? How do they discuss it when alone among themselves? I think this question can be answered in a single sentence. A friend of mine who ran an elevator once told me:

"Lawd, man! Ef it wuzn't fer them polices 'n' them ol' lynch-mobs, there wouldn't be nothin' but uproar down here!"

Suggestions for Discussion

1. Analyze Wright's sketch in terms of (a) structure, (b) progression and unity in nine segments, (c) expository-narrative style, and/or (d) themes.

2. How does Wright's title contribute to the development of the major themes of the sketch? Why does he use *ethics* and *living?*

3. Discuss his use of personal experiences to illustrate his themes.

4. Discuss his use of violence in the sketch. Is it believable? significant? Explain.

Suggestions for Writing

1. Analyze the motivation behind an incident of discrimination that you have observed or experienced.

2. Analyze the dramatic irony in the last line and its climactic effect as the final comment on the whole sketch.

Andrew Hill
Visible Man

Andrew Hill, who attended Manhattan College in New York, was given his first job in radio because a station in his hometown of Atlanta needed to hire a black reporter to avoid an affirmative action suit. He was later, as he says, hired as a television reporter and anchorman in San Francisco "because [he] didn't scare white people." After a brief period as a television celebrity, he resigned to live in an upper middle class town on the West Coast. "Visible Man," which appeared in the San Francisco *Sunday Examiner and Chronicle* in May 1983, illustrates the racism that infects American life. Hill wonders bleakly how uneducated blacks who do scare white people survive in a world where racism persists.

A few years ago, when I was still working as a television news anchorman in San Francisco, I used to wonder what life would be like for me, a black man, without the immunity that is a by-product of celebrity. Today, six years after my last newscast, I no longer have to wonder about such things because the limited fame I used to enjoy is gone. My life is a lot different, but the discoveries I have made in the interim suggest that the evolution of consciousness with respect to race may not be as promising as it appears.

First, a little background. For several years I was a reporter and anchor at a network-affiliated station. When I was hired I was told pointblank by the station manager that the reason I was placed out front as an anchor was "because you don't scare white people." The newscasts I anchored had the numbers (ratings) to prove it. During those days I looked like a tweedy member of the Jackson Five. I made lots of money, lived in elegant, Bayview splendor at the top of Russian Hill, attended the symphony and ballet, hosted celebrity auctions, signed autographs, and, in general, played the role to the hilt.

Television made my life easy, but the creature comforts I reaped were not altogether unearned. It is true that the only reason I was hired at all at the very beginning of my broadcasting career—way back in 1971, in Atlanta, after I had just returned home from college in New York—was because the radio station that signed me on had been threatened with a lawsuit for not having a full-time black reporter. And although I was not fully conscious of this at the time, I had been raised to take advantage of just such a situation.

The civil rights movement was taking place all round me while I was growing up in Atlanta. The cousin of a classmate of mine was killed when a church in Alabama was bombed. A cross was burned on the lawn of the school I attended. The parents of children I knew were arrested for sitting down at a restaurant counter and requesting service.

My neighbors, Charlayne Hunter—now a correspondent for "The MacNeil-Lehrer Report" on PBS—and Hamilton Holmes, a prominent Atlanta physician, were the first blacks to enroll at the University of Georgia. Maynard Jackson, Atlanta's first black mayor, helped me get my first summer job at the National Labor Relations Board. Martin Luther King Jr. once shook my hand.

Although I was not out there on the front lines getting arrested, sprayed with water hoses, or beaten with clubs, I was very much a part of that younger group waiting in the wings who would be expected to walk through the doors that were going to be opened for blacks sooner or later, one way or another. Somehow my father, who was a waiter on the railroads, and my mother, a high school graduate who earned extra money by running a day-care service in our home, raised the tuition year in and year out to send me, my two brothers, and a sister to private schools. Their efforts paid off somewhat when I became a National Merit semifinalist and received the financial assistance that made it possible to go to Manhattan College, a Catholic college for men in New York. As one of the educated chosen, I was expected to return one day to the South and take my place in the second, more politically conventional wave of the movement, as a member, at some level, of a governmental structure that would not only be more responsive to blacks in general but would include black members as well.

It was the kind of upbringing that made sense in the days before Stokely and Rap and black separatism. Before that pop poster of Huey Newton sitting like a chic, black Caesar on a fanbacked rattan throne. Before Afro hairdos and the FBI's CoIntel Program. Before Martin's death in April of 1968 and Bobby Kennedy's later that year. Before the race riots and the Kerner Commission, which announced that America was becoming two separate and unequal states, one black, the other white.

In any case, I grew up presuming that I was one of those who would be sent out to the larger culture as an example of how really wonderful black people could be. After the Jim Crow laws were abolished, I ate in downtown restaurants as often as possible. Once forced to sit in the balcony at downtown movie houses ("nigger heaven" is what it used to be called), I began to take comfortable rocking-chair seats in the orchestra section of those same theaters.

Whenever emissaries from our neighborhood, church, or school were chosen for some kind of cultural exchange program, I was among them, whether as a page at the state legislature or a member of the Governor's Youth Council. While enrolled in a college that was 99.1 percent white, I was elected student body president.

This, then, was my real training for television. Yes, it was programming, but I was certainly a willing victim. So when a San Francisco tv station manager said to me, "We're putting you out front because you don't scare white people," I knew he was right. It was what I had been trained to do, one of the three "dont's" of my upbringing: Don't make them feel guilty, don't make them feel afraid; don't ever let them think that you are interested in a white woman.

My rise was somewhat meteoric partly because pressure from the Federal Communications Commission was pretty constant in those days. One tv executive told Mike Wallace on "60 Minutes" that if the FCC told him to put dogs and cats on the anchor desk, that's exactly what he'd do.

Also, I had a knack for being in exactly the right place at precisely the right time. A year of radio was followed by a year in Atlanta television at a station that brought in a host of network professionals—who literally had been bought away from a respected, network-owned and -operated station from the North—to change its image. The network people trained me from the ground up in all the little tricks of the trade. It was the kind of opportunity that comes around about as often as Halley's comet.

A year later, I moved to San Francisco, and was hired by a big station only a few months before Patricia Hearst was kidnapped by the Symbionese Liberation Army. I did a live-shot every night from the Hearst mansion in Hillsborough. The station offered to make me an anchor, a star.

At the same time, network executives in New York, who keep an eye on the national airwaves the way the CIA keeps tabs on Cuba, also became aware of my "presence" and began making offers, too. Just to prove they were serious, they flew me to New York to meet with the president of the network news operation. This, I believe, is what is known as a good bargaining position. But to give up San Francisco, the most beautiful city in the United States, for New York or Washington, which is what the network had in mind, was no bargain, so I took a chance. I asked the local station for $20,000 more than their highest offer, knowing that at the very worst I would wind up as a network correspondent. (I know. Correspondents are glamorous and have lots of prestige, but they live out of suitcases and the divorce rate is phenomenal.) The local station said no at first, but three days later changed its response to yes. All because I didn't scare white people.

With a poker hand like that, you'd think I would be sitting pretty a long time. Right? Wrong. My resolve to learn everything I could about media showed me much more than I ever wanted to know. Without going into a long diatribe against television news and its limitations, let me say simply that I felt as if I had sold out. The ideals I had been raised with, however naive, had been subverted in a scheme to market my race, and the knowledge that I had participated in this made me feel worthless. In any case, to the surprise of everyone, I submitted a letter of resignation one day and never returned.

Why? That is always the most important question in every story. Why, indeed? To live quietly and in peace with myself. To find out who I really was behind the persona I had constructed. To get beyond the superego, the thou-shalts of family, society, and religion. You don't take your identity—an identity that is producing ratings—and call it into question while on the air. The stakes are too high. So I quit. If all that money wasn't going to help me find out who I really was, what good was it?

But there was another reason, too. It was this: The economics of television news often produced an appalling blindness that was very much like racism. It became clear to me that I could not retain a seat of prominence, as a kind of spokesman for this particular system of information processing, without lending tacit support to its values through my very presence on the air.

News people often think of themselves as liberal, and many of them are right out there with old Lou Grant. In the name of the First Amendment they helped make civil rights the movement that it was. Many of them championed the impeachment of Richard Nixon and have advocated the causes of the elderly and of gays and of women's rights. But in television this liberalism stands always in the shadow of the bottom line. If a story doesn't sell toothpaste, it's not important.

Okay, that makes sense enough. But when your information about what really happened at the city council meeting is limited to a 30-second reader because it cost too much to send a minicam to city hall—or worse, because the assignment editor elected to send the camera crew to do a story on topless dancers instead—then the buck has interfered with your right to know. Liberal is only as liberal as the bottom line will allow.

So much for background.

A funny thing happened to me while I was walking along the ocean promenade the other day. A police officer came up to me and asked to see my I.D. "We've had some reports from a couple of ladies in town who say that you have approached them, and we want to make sure you're not weird or anything." What could I say? Something, perhaps, like, "You got me all wrong, officer. I used to be on television. There must be some mistake"?

Only there was no mistake. I really had approached two ladies to ask if I could rent vacant apartments that were on the premises, and they reported me to the police as someone who might have been casing the respective establishments for a possible burglary. Two separate inquiries about a place to stay. Two separate calls to the police. While I do not look like an anchorman anymore, I know enough to wear a tie and have a shave, which I did, before trying to find a place to live. So I was dumbfounded by this incident. I kept asking myself why this thing had happened to me until the police officer, who was soon joined by a back-up officer (two squad cars parked in the street with those blue and red lights flashing on top ever so discreetly) said somewhat apologetically but not very, "Well, you have to understand, sir, that we don't have many blacks around here. The only blacks who show up are from across the freeway, and they come over here to victimize our people. I really hope you can find a place to live in our town, but it is expensive to live here."

Later, after I had found a nice place to live, I got a flat tire one night while leaving a dinner party. It was just after 9:30 p.m., and I pulled into a closed service station to change the tire instead of jacking up the car on Main Street. You guessed it. Two more police cars. Two officers, different from the previous two policemen, pulled into the station behind me and ran up to me while beaming flashlights into my eyes. "Can we help you with something?" they asked. "Speak up, buddy. Can we help you with something?" They were quite hostile, which generated a similar feeling in me. But by now I have been influenced enough by the likes of Sidney Poitier that I managed somehow, without effort, to utter a few statements that said College, Job, and Flat Tire. Want to help? So once again I was left alone, although it really would have been nice if they could have helped me with that tire.

These experiences are not entirely new to me. In New York I had difficulty renting in places like Kew Gardens and Riverdale. It is an old story that goes something like this: "Well, it's not you. You're obviously very nice, but you might have friends who aren't so nice, and it's not me either, you know, it's my neighbors who just would not understand." But things have changed enough on the surface in the dozen or so years since I lived in New York that even I began to be fooled. Besides, by the time I had moved to San Francisco (and I grant you that San Francisco is unusual in America for more than one reason), landlords welcomed me and my famous face with open arms.

Now I live in a coastal town that is like Cheever Country on the West Coast. Most of my neighbors are rich. Many of them look right past me as if I were not even present (shades of Ralph Ellison's *Invisible Man*) but many others have kind, open faces and greet me with a smile. It is not a racist town. However, the people who live here have possessions that need to be protected from burglars and other thieves. And that is why the police department, I finally understood, watches me and follows me and stops me sometimes to make sure I am not weird. If I were white, however, there would be no question of weirdness. But, well, er, after all. Right. I understand. I understand now what I never could have been made to understand as long as I had a well-known face and an identity that was immune to the kinds of things ordinary people experience.

In those days the police officers who came up to me wanted only to say hello or to give me a tip on a story or invite me to a party. Now, when I go out at night I am watched as closely as a parolee by the police in this small town, this place where I thought I might find a peaceful life. I do not drink, smuggle drugs, gamble or engage in acts of prostitution. But I have been seen hanging out in some pretty wild places since I moved here—the public library, the art center, the museum.

In the town where I live today, which I do not name because I do not wish to draw unnecessary attention to it or to myself, the police have demonstrated that they regard me as a potential threat to the money and property of the white citizens who live here. There is an automatic assumption that blackness is related to crime. Their overreactions say that if you are black and in this town you must be doing something wrong. It is an unspoken acknowledgment that blacks are still largely a deprived people in this country and that whites are still enormously afraid of blacks, especially black men, either because of some guilt left over from slavery or because those who accumulate riches, as Lao-tse points out, have a tendency to fear those who have not been able to do so. That fear, as it is manifested in the police I have had the misfortune to encounter, is really the important issue, for the police represent the values of a community, what the civilian members of the community expect and tolerate and believe. So, if the police in a town like this are afraid, imagine what that suggests about the people whom those police are hired to protect, people who run corporations and make movies and give guidance counseling.

There are those who would say that I should move if it is so clear to me that I am not wanted. But why should I move from a beautiful environment because of fear? Do the rich have a monopoly on places with fresh air that overlook the ocean? I am black, but I am also American enough to know that it's not supposed to be that way.

I have been learning all sorts of things about myself and my country in the years since I left television, and now that I am not insulated anymore, I understand something else. If the kind of thing I have described is happening to me—a man who does not scare white people, someone who was trained to be accepted by them—what on earth is happening to my poor brothers who have not had that opportunity, especially now when the economy and our incredible loyalty to it are making cowards of us all?

Suggestions for Discussion

1. The TV station manager who hired Hill as a news anchorman told him frankly that he was hired because he didn't "scare white people." What characteristics in Hill does the remark refer to? What is Hill's initial response to it?

2. Hill explains carefully who he is. What function does his description play in the essay?

3. Why does Hill turn in his resignation? Do you agree with his reasons?

4. What are the consequences to Hill of his resignation? How does he deal with these consequences?

5. Is Hill optimistic about race relations in the U.S.?

Suggestions for Writing

1. Hill refers to Ellison's *Invisible Man*. Read essays on Ellison or read the novel itself and discuss the relation between Ellison's thesis and the one Hill develops here.

2. Write an essay in which you explore some examples of racist action. Is racism prevalent in your community? If so, how would you go about illustrating it?

Essays

Thomas Jefferson
The Declaration of Independence

The Continental Congress assembled in Philadelphia in 1776 delegated to
Thomas Jefferson the task of writing a declaration of independence from Great
Britain which the Congress amended and adopted on July 4. After the Revolution, Jefferson (1743–1826) became Governor of Virginia and in 1801 the third
President of the United States. He was the father of what is called "Jeffersonian
democracy," which exceeded the democracy then advocated by either Washington or Jefferson's rival, Alexander Hamilton. After leaving the presidency,
he founded the University of Virginia as a place where truth could assert itself
in free competition with other ideas. In its theory as well as in its style, the
Declaration is a typical eighteenth-century view of man's place in society which
included the right to overthrow a tyrannical ruler.

When in the course of human events, it becomes necessary for one people
to dissolve the political bands which have connected them with another, and
to assume among the powers of the earth, the separate and equal station to
which the Laws of Nature and of Nature's God entitle them, a decent respect
to the opinions of mankind requires that they should declare the causes which
impel them to the separation.

We hold these truths to be self-evident, that all men are created equal,
that they are endowed by their Creator with certain unalienable rights, that
among these are life, liberty, and the pursuit of happiness. That to secure
these rights, governments are instituted among men, deriving their just powers from the consent of the governed. That whenever any form of government
becomes destructive of these ends, it is the right of the people to alter or to
abolish it, and to institute new government, laying its foundation on such
principles and organizing its powers in such form, as to them shall seem most
likely to effect their safety and happiness. Prudence, indeed, will dictate that

governments long established should not be changed for light and transient causes; and accordingly all experience hath shown, that mankind are more disposed to suffer, while evils are sufferable, than to right themselves by abolishing the forms to which they are accustomed. But when a long train of abuses and usurpations, pursuing invariably the same object, evinces a design to reduce them under absolute despotism, it is their right, it is their duty, to throw off such government, and to provide new guards for their future security. Such has been the patient sufferance of these Colonies; and such is now the necessity which constrains them to alter their former systems of government. The history of the present King of Great Britain is a history of repeated injuries and usurpations, all having in direct object the establishment of an absolute tyranny over these States. To prove this, let facts be submitted to a candid world.

He has refused his assent to laws, the most wholesome and necessary for the public good.

He has forbidden his Governors to pass laws of immediate and pressing importance, unless suspended in their operation till his assent should be obtained; and when so suspended, he has utterly neglected to attend to them.

He has refused to pass other laws for the accommodation of large districts of people, unless those people would relinquish the right of representation in the legislature, a right inestimable to them and formidable to tyrants only.

He has called together legislative bodies at places unusual, uncomfortable, and distant from the depository of their public records, for the sole purpose of fatiguing them into compliance with his measures.

He has dissolved representative houses repeatedly, for opposing with manly firmness his invasions on the rights of the people.

He has refused for a long time, after such dissolutions, to cause others to be elected; whereby the legislative powers, incapable of annihilation, have returned to the people at large for their exercise; the State remaining in the meantime exposed to all the dangers of invasion from without and convulsions within.

He has endeavoured to prevent the population of these states; for that purpose obstructing the laws for naturalization of foreigners; refusing to pass others to encourage their migration hither, and raising the conditions of new appropriations of lands.

He has obstructed the administration of justice, by refusing his assent to laws for establishing judiciary powers.

He has made judges dependent on his will alone, for the tenure of their offices, and the amount and payment of their salaries.

He has erected a multitude of new offices, and sent hither swarms of officers to harass our people, and eat out their substance.

He has kept among us, in times of peace, standing armies without the consent of our legislatures.

He has affected to render the military independent of and superior to the civil power.

He has combined with others to subject us to a jurisdiction foreign of our constitution, and unacknowledged by our laws; giving his assent to their acts of pretended legislation:

For quartering large bodies of armed troops among us:

For protecting them, by a mock trial, from punishment for any murders which they should commit on the inhabitants of these States:

For cutting off our trade with all parts of the world:

For imposing taxes on us without our consent:

For depriving us in many cases of the benefits of trial by jury:

For transporting us beyond seas to be tried for pretended offences:

For abolishing the free system of English laws in a neighbouring Province, establishing therein an arbitrary government, and enlarging its boundaries so as to render it at once an example and fit instrument for introducing the same absolute rule into these Colonies:

For taking away our Charters, abolishing our most valuable laws, and altering fundamentally the forms of our governments:

For suspending our own legislatures, and declaring themselves invested with power to legislate for us in all cases whatsoever.

He has abdicated government here, by declaring us out of his protection and waging war against us.

He has plundered our seas, ravaged our coasts, burnt our towns, and destroyed the lives of our people.

He is at this time transporting large armies of foreign mercenaries to complete the works of death, desolation, and tyranny, already begun with circumstances of cruelty and perfidy scarcely paralleled in the most barbarous ages, and totally unworthy the head of a civilized nation.

He has contrained our fellow citizens taken captive on the high seas to bear arms against their country, to become the executioners of their friends and brethren, or to fall themselves by their hands.

He has excited domestic insurrections amongst us, and has endeavored to bring on the inhabitants of our frontiers, the merciless Indian savages, whose known rule of warfare, is an undistinguished destruction of all ages, sexes, and conditions.

In every stage of these oppressions we have petitioned for redress in the most humble terms: our repeated petitions have been answered only by repeated injury. A prince whose character is thus marked by every act which may define a tyrant is unfit to be the ruler of a free people.

Nor have we been wanting in attention to our British brethren. We have warned them from time to time of attempts by their legislature to extend an unwarrantable jurisdiction over us. We have reminded them of the circumstances of our emigration and settlement here. We have appealed to their native justice and magnanimity, and we have conjured them by the ties of our common kindred to disavow these usurpations, which would inevitably interrupt our connections and correspondence. They too have been deaf to the voice of justice and of consanguinity. We must, therefore, acquiesce in the necessity, which denounces our separation, and hold them, as we hold the rest of mankind, enemies in war, in peace friends.

We, therefore, the Representatives of the United States of America, in General Congress assembled, appealing to the Supreme Judge of the world for the rectitude of our intentions, do, in the name, and by authority of the good people of these Colonies, solemnly publish and declare, That these United Colonies are, and of right ought to be, Free and Independent States; that they are absolved from all allegiance to the British Crown, and that all political connection between them and the state of Great Britain, is and ought to be totally dissolved; and that as Free and Independent States, they have full power to levy war, conclude peace, contract alliances, establish commerce, and to do all other acts and things which Independent States may of right do. And for the support of this declaration, with a firm reliance on the protection of Divine Providence, we mutually pledge to each other our lives, our fortunes, and our sacred honor.

Suggestions for Discussion

1. What is the basis for Jefferson's belief that "all men are created equal"?

2. In the eighteenth century, the notion of the "divine right" of kings was still popular. How does Jefferson refute that notion?

3. Discuss the list of tyrannical actions which Jefferson attributes to the King of Great Britain. Account for the order in which he lists them.

4. This essay has been called a "model of clarity and precision." Explain your agreement with this statement. How does Jefferson balance strong feeling with logical argument?

Suggestion for Writing

Jefferson asserts that "all men are created equal," and yet he does not include black slaves as equals. In Jefferson's *Autobiography*, he wrote that a clause "reprobating the enslaving the inhabitants of Africa" was omitted in the final draft "in complaisance to South Carolina and Georgia." Was Jefferson merely opportunistic in agreeing to strike this clause? Write an essay in which you relate the ideas of the Declaration to the ideas in Lincoln's Gettysburg Address. Show how one set of ideas leads to the other.

The Declaration of the Rights of Man

Soon after the fall of the Bastille on July 14, 1789, a day celebrated in France as July 4th is celebrated in the United States, the National Assembly was asked to provide a declaration which would correspond to the American Declaration of Independence. The Assembly appointed a committee of five to draft the document. After several weeks of debate and compromise, the completed declaration was approved and proclaimed on August 27, 1789. An analysis of the Declaration shows that while a number of phrases resemble the American model, it derived more particularly from the English Bill of Rights of 1689. Ironically, the basis for democratic government embodied in this document was to be subverted by a leader of the new republic who would declare himself Emperor.

The representatives of the French people, gathered in the National Assembly, believing that ignorance, neglect, and disdain of the rights of men are the sole causes of public misfortunes and of the corruption of governments, have resolved to set forth, in solemn declaration, the natural, inalienable, and sacred rights of men, in order that this Declaration, held always before the members of the body social, will forever remind them of their rights and duties; that the acts of legislative and executive power, always identifiable with the ends and purposes of the whole body politic, may be more fully respected; that the complaints of citizens, founded henceforth on simple and incontrovertible principles, may be turned always to the maintaining of the Constitution and to the happiness of all.

The National assembly therefore recognizes and declares, in the presence and under the auspices of the Supreme Being, the following rights of Man and of citizen:

1. Men are born and will remain free and endowed with equal rights. Social distinctions can be based only upon usefulness to the common weal.

2. The end and purpose of all political groups is the preservation of the natural and inalienable rights of Man. These rights are Liberty, the Possession of Property, Safety, and Resistance to Oppression.

3. The principle of all sovereignty will remain fundamentally in the State. No group and no individual can exercise authority which does not arise expressly from the State.

4. Liberty consists in being able to do anything which is not harmful to another or to others; therefore, the exercise of the natural rights of each individual has only such limits as will assure to other members of society the enjoyment of the same rights. These limits can be determined only by the Law.

5. The Law has the right to forbid only such actions as are harmful to society. Anything not forbidden by the Law can never be forbidden; and none can be forced to do what the Law does not prescribe.

6. The Law is the expression of the will of the people. All citizens have the right and the duty to concur in the formation of the Law, either in person or through their representatives. Whether it punishes or whether it protects, the Law must be the same for all. All citizens, being equal in the eyes of the Law, are to be admitted equally to all distinctions, ranks, and public employment, according to their capacities, and without any other discrimination than that established by their individual abilities and virtues.

7. No individual can be accused, arrested, or detained except in cases determined by the Law, and according to the forms which the Law has prescribed. Those who instigate, expedite, execute, or cause to be executed any arbitrary or extralegal prescriptions must be punished; but every citizen called or seized through the power of the Law must instantly obey. He will render himself culpable by resisting.

8. The Law should establish only those penalties which are absolutely and evidently necessary, and none can be punished except through the power of the Law, as already established and proclaimed for the public good and legally applied.

9. Every individual being presumed innocent until he has been proved guilty, if it is considered necessary to arrest him, the Law must repress with severity any force which is not required to secure his person.

10. None is to be persecuted for his opinions, even his religious beliefs,

provided that his expression of them does not interfere with the order established by the Law.

11. Free communication of thought and opinion is one of the most precious rights of Man; therefore, every citizen can speak, write, or publish freely, except that he will be required to answer for the abuse of such freedom in cases determined by the Law.

12. The guarantee of the rights of man and of the citizen makes necessary a Public Force and Administration; this Force and Administration has therefore been established for the good of all, and not for the particular benefit of those to whom it has been entrusted.

13. For the maintaining of this Public Force and Administration, and for the expense of administering it, a common tax is required; it must be distributed equally among the people, in accordance with their ability to pay.

14. All citizens have the right and duty to establish, by themselves or by their representatives, the requirements of a common tax, to consent to it freely, to indicate its use, and to determine its quota, its assessment, its collection, and its duration.

15. Society has the right and duty to demand from every public servant an accounting of his administration.

16. No society in which the guarantee of rights is not assured nor the distinction of legal powers determined can be said to have a constitution.

17. The possession of property being an inviolable and sacred right, none can be deprived of it, unless public necessity, legally proved, clearly requires the deprivation, and then only on the necessary condition of a previously established just reparation.

Suggestions for Discussion

1. What is the major purpose of setting forth the principles enunciated in this declaration?

2. The declaration refers to a Supreme Being. Why did not the writers of the declaration refer simply to God?

3. How do the seventeen "rights of the Man and of the citizen" define the relationship between the individual person and the State?

4. How does the declaration define the function of the Law and of the State?

5. How does the declaration propose to guarantee freedom of speech?

6. Can you explain why the declaration says that the possession of property is an "inviolable and sacred right"? How does this statement basically differ from modern revolutionary thought?

7. On what principles is this declaration based?

Suggestions for Writing

1. Write an essay about the similarities to and differences from this declaration with the American Declaration of Independence and with the Bill of Rights of the American Constitution.

2. Examine the English Bill of Rights of 1689 and write an essay in which you explain the close relationship between the French and English declarations.

Abraham Lincoln
The Gettysburg Address

Abraham Lincoln (1809–1865), the sixteenth President of the United States, is generally regarded, along with Thomas Jefferson, as one of the greatest American prose stylists. On November 19, 1863, he traveled to Gettysburg in southern Pennsylvania to dedicate the cemetery for the soldiers killed there the previous July. The simple words he composed form the most famous speech ever delivered in America. A close reading reveals why it continues to live for Americans today.

Four score and seven years ago our fathers brought forth on this continent, a new nation, conceived in Liberty, and dedicated to the proposition that all men are created equal.

Now we are engaged in a great civil war, testing whether that nation, or any nation so conceived and so dedicated, can long endure. We are met on a great battlefield of that war. We have come to dedicate a portion of that field, as a final resting place for those who here gave their lives that that nation might live. It is altogether fitting and proper that we should do this.

But, in a larger sense, we can not dedicate—we can not consecrate—we can not hallow—this ground. The brave men, living and dead, who struggled here, have consecrated it, far above our poor power to add or detract. The world will little note nor long remember what we say here, but it can never forget what they did here. It is for us the living, rather, to be dedicated here to the unfinished work which they who fought here have thus far so nobly advanced. It is rather for us to be here dedicated to the great task remaining before us—that from these honored dead we take increased devotion to that cause for which they gave the last full measure of devotion—that we here highly resolve that these dead shall not have died in vain—that this nation, under God, shall have a new birth of freedom—and that government of the people, by the people, for the people, shall not perish from the earth.

Suggestions for Discussion

1. How is the proposition "that all men are created equal" related to the issues of the Civil War?

2. Why does Lincoln not simply begin his essay "Eighty-seven years ago"? What would he lose in tone if he had done so?

3. In paragraph three, Lincoln says "The world will little note, nor long remember what we say here. . . ." How do you account for the fact that he was wrong? Why did he make this statement? What function does it serve?

4. How does Lincoln use the verbs "dedicate," "consecrate," "hallow"? Could one easily change the order of these words?

5. How does Lincoln connect the first paragraph of his speech to the last?

6. What was the "unfinished work" of the soldiers who died at the Battle of Gettysburg?

Suggestion for Writing

Write an essay in which you relate the power of this speech to the simplicity of its language.

Niccolò Machiavelli

Of Cruelty and Clemency, and Whether It Is Better to Be Loved or Feared

Niccolò Machiavelli (1469–1527) was a Florentine statesman. His best-known work, *The Prince,* written in 1513, is an astute analysis of the contemporary political scene. The work was first translated into English in 1640. This selection from *The Prince,* translated by Luigi Ricci and revised by E. R. P. Vincent, explains by examples from history why the prince must rely on the fear he creates rather than the love he might generate. Machiavelli explains also why the prince, though causing fear, must avoid incurring hatred.

Proceeding to the other qualities before named, I say that every prince must desire to be considered merciful and not cruel. He must, however, take care not to misuse this mercifulness. Cesare Borgia was considered cruel, but his cruelty had brought order to the Romagna, united it, and reduced it to peace and fealty. If this is considered well, it will be seen that he was really much more merciful than the Florentine people, who, to avoid the name of cruelty, allowed Pistoia to be destroyed. A prince, therefore, must not mind incurring the charge of cruelty for the purpose of keeping his subjects united and faithful; for, with a very few examples, he will be more merciful than those who, from excess of tenderness, allow disorders to arise, from whence spring bloodshed and rapine; for these as a rule injure the whole community, while the executions carried out by the prince injure only individuals. And of all princes, it is impossible for a new prince to escape the reputation of cruelty, new states being always full of dangers. Wherefore Virgil through the mouth of Dido says:

> Res dura, et regni novitas me talia cogunt
> Moliri, et late fines custode tueri.[1]

Nevertheless, he must be cautious in believing and acting, and must not be afraid of his own shadow, and must proceed in a temperate manner with prudence and humanity, so that too much confidence does not render him incautious, and too much diffidence does not render him intolerant.

From this arises the question whether it is better to be loved more than feared, or feared more than loved. The reply is, that one ought to be both feared and loved, but as it is difficult for the two to go together, it is much safer to be feared than loved, if one of the two has to be wanting. For it may be said of men in general that they are ungrateful, voluble dissemblers, anxious to avoid danger, and covetous of gain; as long as you benefit them, they are entirely yours; they offer you their blood, their goods, their life, and their children, as I have before said, when the necessity is remote; but when it approaches, they revolt. And the prince who has relied solely on their words, without making other preparations, is ruined; for the friendship which is gained by purchase and not through grandeur and nobility of spirit is bought but not secured, and at a pinch is not to be expended in your service. And men have less scruple in offending one who makes himself loved than one who makes himself feared; for love is held by a chain of obligation which, men being selfish, is broken whenever it serves their purpose; but fear is maintained by a dread of punishment which never fails.

Still, a prince should make himself feared in such a way that if he does not gain love, he at any rate avoids hatred; for fear and the absence of hatred may well go together, and will be always attained by one who abstains from interfering with the property of his citizens and subjects or with their women. And when he is obliged to take the life of anyone, let him do so when there is proper justification and manifest reason for it; but above all he must abstain from taking the property of others, for men forget more easily the death of their father than the loss of their patrimony. Then also pretexts for seizing property are never wanting, and one who begins to live by rapine will always find some reason for taking the goods of others, whereas causes for taking life are rarer and more fleeting.

But when the prince is with his army and has a large number of soldiers under his control, then it is extremely necessary that he should not mind being thought cruel; for without this reputation he could not keep an army united or disposed to any duty. Among the noteworthy actions of Hannibal is numbered this, that although he had an enormous army, composed of men of all nations and fighting in foreign countries, there never arose any dissension

---

[1] Our harsh situation and the newness of our kingdom compel me to contrive such measures and to guard our territory far and wide. (Dido offers this explanation to the newly landed Trojans of why her guards received them with hostile and suspicious measures.)

either among them or against the prince, either in good fortune or in bad. This could not be due to anything but his inhuman cruelty, which together with his infinite other virtues, made him always venerated and terrible in the sight of his soldiers, and without it his other virtues would not have sufficed to produce that effect. Thoughtless writers admire on the one hand his actions, and on the other blame the principal cause of them.

And that it is true that his other virtues would not have sufficed may be seen from the case of Scipio (famous not only in regard to his own times, but all times of which memory remains), whose armies rebelled against him in Spain, which arose from nothing but his excessive kindness, which allowed more licence to the soldiers than was consonant with military discipline. He was reproached with this in the senate by Fabius Maximus, who called him a corrupter of the Roman militia. Locri having been destroyed by one of Scipio's officers was not revenged by him, nor was the insolence of that officer punished, simply by reason of his easy nature; so much so, that some one wishing to excuse him in the senate, said that there were many men who knew rather how not to err, than how to correct the errors of others. This disposition would in time have tarnished the fame and glory of Scipio had he persevered in it under the empire, but living under the rule of the senate this harmful quality was not only concealed but became a glory to him.

I conclude, therefore, with regard to being feared and loved, that men love at their own free will, but fear at the will of the prince, and that a wise prince must rely on what is in his power and not on what is in the power of others, and he must only contrive to avoid incurring hatred, as has been explained.

Suggestions for Discussion

1. How does Machiavelli show that Cesare Borgia, known for his cruelty, was more merciful than the people of Florence?

2. Explain the use of the quotation from Virgil.

3. Explain Machiavelli's argument that the prince cannot rely on the love of his subjects.

4. What attitudes does Machiavelli express when he says that "men forget more easily the death of their father than the loss of their patrimony"?

5. Compare and contrast the actions of Scipio and Hannibal. How does Machiavelli explain their actions to prove his point about the need of the prince to inspire fear?

Suggestion for Writing

Write an essay in which you comment on the ideas in this selection which may be brilliant but not admirable. What aspects of life does the author ignore? Why? Why does this selection not express the concern for freedom and human dignity which characterizes most of the selections in this section?

◇◇◇◇

José Ortega y Gassett

The Greatest Danger, the State

Anonymous Translation

José Ortega y Gasset (1883–1955) was a Spanish philosopher who wrote in opposition to authoritarianism in the late 1930's. His most accessible works are *The Revolt of the Masses* (1932) and *The Dehumanization of Art* (1948). This selection from *The Revolt of the Masses* clearly expresses his fear of the dangers of statism exemplified in fascist Italy and foreshadows the rise of fascism in Spain.

In a right ordering of public affairs, the mass is that part which does not act of itself. Such is its mission. It has come into the world in order to be directed, influenced, represented, organised—even in order to cease being mass, or at least to aspire to this. But it has not come into the world to do all this by itself. It needs to submit its life to a higher court, formed of the superior minorities. The question as to who are these superior individuals may be discussed *ad libitum*, but that without them, whoever they be, humanity would cease to preserve its essentials is something about which there can be no possible doubt, though Europe spend a century with its head under its wing, ostrich-fashion, trying if she can to avoid seeing such a plain truth. For we are not dealing with an opinion based on facts more or less frequent and probable, but on a law of social "physics," much more immovable than the laws of Newton's physics. The day when a genuine philosophy[1] once more holds sway in Europe—it is the one thing that can save her—that day she will once again realise that man, whether he like it or no, is a being forced by his nature to seek some higher authority. If he succeeds in finding it of himself, he is a superior man; if not, he is a mass-man and must receive it from his superiors.

For the mass to claim the right to act of itself is then a rebellion against its own destiny, and because that is what it is doing at present, I speak of the rebellion of the masses. For, after all, the one thing that can substantially and truthfully be called rebellion is that which consists in not accepting one's own destiny, in rebelling against one's self. The rebellion of the archangel Lucifer would not have been less if, instead of striving to be God—which was not his destiny—he had striven to be the lowest of the angels—equally not his destiny. (If Lucifer had been a Russian, like Tolstoi, he would perhaps have preferred this latter form of rebellion, none the less against God than the other more famous one.)

When the mass acts on its own, it does so only in one way, for it has no other: it lynches. It is not altogether by chance that lynch law comes from

[1]For philosophy to rule, it is not necessary that philosophers be the rulers—as Plato at first wished—nor even for rulers to be philosophers—as was his later, more modest wish. Both these things are, strictly speaking, most fatal. For philosophy to rule, it is sufficient for it to exist; that is to say, for the philosophers to be philosophers. For nearly a century past, philosophers have been everything but that—politicians, pedagogues, men of letters, and men of science.

America, for America is, in a fashion, the paradise of the masses. And it will cause less surprise, nowadays, when the masses triumph; that violence should triumph and be made the one *ratio*, the one doctrine. It is now some time since I called attention to this advance of violence as a normal condition.[2] Today it has reached its full development, and this is a good symptom, because it means that automatically the descent is about to begin. Today violence is the rhetoric of the period, the empty rhetorician has made it his own. When a reality of human existence has completed its historic course, has been shipwrecked and lies dead, the waves throw it up on the shores of rhetoric, where the corpse remains for a long time. Rhetoric is the cemetery of human realities, or at any rate a Home for the Aged. The reality itself is survived by its name, which, though only a word, is after all at least a word and preserves something of its magic power.

But though it is not impossible that the prestige of violence as a cynically established rule has entered on its decline, we shall still continue under that rule, though in another form. I refer to the gravest danger now threatening European civilization. Like all other dangers that threaten it, this one is born of civilization itself. More than that, it constitutes one of its glories: it is the State as we know it today. We are confronted with a replica of what we said in the previous chapter about science: the fertility of its principles brings about a fabulous progress, but this inevitably imposes specialization, and specialization threatens to strangle science.

The same thing is happening with the State. Call to mind what the State was at the end of the XVIIIth Century in all European nations. Quite a small affair! Early capitalism and its industrial organizations, in which the new, rationalised technique triumphs for the first time, had brought a commencement of increase in society. A new social class appeared, greater in numbers and power than the pre-existing: the middle class. This astute middle class possessed one thing, above and before all: talent, practical talent. It knew how to organize and discipline, how to give continuity and consistency to its efforts. In the midst of it, as in an ocean, the "ship of State" sailed its hazardous course. The ship of State is a metaphor reinvented by the bourgeoisie, which felt itself oceanic, omnipotent, pregnant with storms. That ship was, as we said, a very small affair: it had hardly any soldiers, bureaucrats, or money. It had been built in the Middle Ages by a class of men very different from the bourgeois—the nobles, a class admirable for their courage, their gifts of leadership, their sense of responsibility. Without them the nations of Europe would not now be in existence. But with all those virtues of the heart, the nobles were, and always have been, lacking in virtues of the head. Of limited intelligence, sentimental, instinctive, intuitive—in a word, "irrational." Hence they were unable to develop any technique, a thing which demands rationalization. They did not invent gunpowder. Incapable of inventing new arms, they allowed the bourgeois, who got it from the East or somewhere else, to utilize gunpowder and automatically to win the battle against the warrior noble, the "caballero," stupidly covered in iron so that he could hardly move in the fight, and who had never imagined that the eternal secret

---

[2]Vide *España Invertebrada*, 1912.

of warfare consists not so much in the methods of defense as in those of attack, a secret which was to be rediscovered by Napoleon.[3]

As the State is a matter of technique—of public order and administration— the "ancien régime" reaches the end of the XVIIIth Century with a very weak State, harassed on all sides by a widespread social revolt. The disproportion between State power and social power at this time is such that, comparing the situation then with that of the time of Charlemagne, the XVIIIth-Century State appears degenerate. The Carolingian State was of course much less powerful than the State of Louis XVI, but, on the other hand, the society surrounding it was entirely lacking in strength.[4] The enormous disproportion between social strength and the strength of public power made possible the Revolution, the revolutions—up to 1848.

But with the Revolution the middle class took possession of public power and applied their undeniable qualities to the State, and in little more than a generation created a powerful State, which brought revolution to an end. Since 1848, that is to say, since the beginning of the second generation of bourgeois governments, there have been no genuine revolutions in Europe. Not assuredly because there were not motives for them, but because there were no means. Public power was brought to the level of social power. *Goodbye forever to Revolutions!* The only thing now possible in Europe is their opposite: the *coup d'état.* Everything which in following years tried to look like a revolution was only a *coup d'état* in disguise.

In our days the State has come to be a formidable machine which works in marvelous fashion; of wonderful efficiency by reason of the quantity and precision of its means. Once it is set up in the midst of society, it is enough to touch a button for its enormous levers to start working and exercise their overwhelming power on any portion whatever of the social framework.

The contemporary State is the easiest seen and best-known product of civilization. And it is an interesting revelation when one takes note of the attitude that mass-man adopts before it. He sees it, admires it, knows that *there it is,* safeguarding his existence; but he is not conscious of the fact that it is a human creation invented by certain men and upheld by certain virtues and

---

[3]We owe to Ranke this simple picture of the great historic change by which for the supremacy of the nobles is substituted the predominance of the bourgeois; but of course its symbolic geometric outlines require no little filling-in in order to be completely true. Gunpowder was known from time immemorial. The invention by which a tube was charged with it was due to someone in Lombardy. Even then it was not efficacious until the invention of the cast cannonball. The "nobles" used firearms to a small extent, but they were too dear for them. It was only the bourgeois armies, with their better economic organisation, that could employ them on a large scale. It remains, however, literally true that the nobles, represented by the medieval type of army of the Burgundians, were definitely defeated by the new army, not professional but bourgeois, formed by the Swiss. Their primary force lay in the new discipline and the new rationalism of tactics.

[4]It would be worth while insisting on this point and making clear that the epoch of absolute monarchies in Europe has coincided with very weak States. How is this to be explained? Why, if the State was all-powerful, "absolute," did it not make itself stronger? One of the causes is that indicated, the incapacity—technical, organizing, bureaucratic—of the aristocracies of blood. But this is not enough. Besides that, it also happened that the absolute State and those aristocracies *did not want to aggrandize the State at the expense of society in general.* Contrary to the common belief, the absolute State instinctively respects society much more than our democratic State, which is more intelligent but has less sense of historic responsibility.

fundamental qualities which the men of yesterday had and which may vanish into air tomorrow. Furthermore, the mass-man sees in the State an anonymous power, and feeling himself, like it, anonymous, he believes that the State is something of his own. Suppose that in the public life of a country some difficulty, conflict, or problem presents itself, the mass-man will tend to demand that the State intervene immediately and undertake a solution directly with its immense and unassailable resources.

This is the gravest danger that today threatens civilization: State intervention; the absorption of all spontaneous social effort by the State, that is to say, of spontaneous historical action, which in the long run sustains, nourishes, and impels human destinies. When the mass suffers any ill-fortune or simply feels some strong appetite, its great temptation is that permanent, sure possibility of obtaining everything—without effort, struggle, doubt, or risk— merely by touching a button and setting the mighty machine in motion. The mass says to itself, "*L'Etat, c'est moi,*" which is a complete mistake. The state is the mass only in the sense in which it can be said of two men that they are identical because neither of them is named John. The contemporary State and the mass coincide only in being anonymous. But the mass-man does in fact believe that he is the State, and he will tend more and more to set its machinery working on whatsoever pretext, to crush beneath it any creative minority which disturbs it—disturbs it in any order of things: in politics, in ideas, in industry.

The result of this tendency will be fatal. Spontaneous social action will be broken up over and over again by State intervention; no new seed will be able to fructify. Society will have to live *for* the State, man *for* the governmental machine. And as, after all, it is only a machine whose existence and maintenance depend on the vital supports around it, the State, after sucking out the very marrow of society, will be left bloodless, a skeleton, dead with that rusty death of machinery, more gruesome than the death of a living organism.

Such was the lamentable fate of ancient civilization. No doubt the imperial State created by the Julii and the Claudii was an admirable machine, incomparably superior as a mere structure to the old republican State of the patrician families. But, by a curious coincidence, hardly had it reached full development when the social body began to decay.

Already in the times of the Antonines (IInd Century), the State overbears society with its anti-vital supremacy. Society begins to be enslaved, to be unable to live except *in the service of the State*. The whole of life is bureaucratized. What results? The bureaucratization of life brings about its absolute decay in all orders. Wealth diminishes, births are few. Then the State, in order to attend to its own needs, forces on still more the bureaucratization of human existence. This bureaucratization to the second power is the militarization of society. The State's most urgent need is its apparatus of war, its army. Before all the State is the producer of security (that security, be it remembered, of which the mass-man is born). Hence, above all, an army. The Severi, of African origin, militarize the world. Vain task! Misery increases, women are every day less fruitful, even soldiers are lacking. After the time of the Severi, the army had to be recruited from foreigners.

Is the paradoxical, tragic process of Statism now realized? Society, that it may live better, creates the State as an instrument. Then the State gets the upper hand and society has to begin to live for the State.[5] But for all that the State is still composed of the members of that society. But soon these do not suffice to support it, and it has to call in foreigners: first Dalmatians, then Germans. These foreigners take possession of the State, and the rest of society, the former populace, has to live as their slaves—slaves of people with whom they have nothing in common. That is what State intervention leads to: the people are converted into fuel to feed the mere machine which is the State. The skeleton eats up the flesh around it. The scaffolding becomes the owner and tenant of the house.

When this is realized, it rather confounds one to hear Mussolini heralding as an astounding discovery just made in Italy, the formula: "All for the State; nothing outside the State; nothing against the State." This alone would suffice to reveal in Fascism a typical movement of mass-men. Mussolini found a State admirably built up—not by him, but precisely by the ideas and the forces he is combating: by liberal democracy. He confines himself to using it ruthlessly, and, without entering now into a detailed examination of his work, it is indisputable that the results obtained up the present cannot be compared with those obtained in political and administrative working by the liberal State. If he has succeeded in anything it is so minute, so little visible, so lacking in substance as with difficulty to compensate for the accumulation of the abnormal powers which enable him to make use of that machine to its full extent.

Statism is the higher form taken by violence and direct action when these are set up as standards. Through and by means of the State, the anonymous machine, the masses act for themselves. The nations of Europe have before them a period of great difficulties in their internal life, supremely arduous problems of law, economics, and public order. Can we help feeling that under the rule of the masses the State will endeavor to crush the independence of the individual and the group, and thus definitely spoil the harvest of the future?

A concrete example of this mechanism is found in one of the most alarming phenomena of the last thirty years: the enormous increase in the police force of all countries. The increase of population has inevitably rendered it necessary. However accustomed we may be to it, the terrible paradox should not escape our minds that the population of a great modern city, in order to move about peaceably and attend to its business, necessarily requires a police force to regulate the circulation. But it is foolishness for the party of "law and order" to imagine that these "forces of public authority" created to preserve order are always going to be content to preserve the order that that party desires. Inevitably they will end by themselves defining and deciding on the order they are going to impose—which, naturally, will be that which suits them best.

It might be well to take advantage of our touching on this matter to observe the different reaction to a public need manifested by different types of society. When, about 1800, the new industry began to create a type of man—the industrial worker—more criminally inclined than traditional types, France hastened to create a numerous police force. Towards 1810 there occurs in England, for the same reasons, an increase in criminality, and the English

---

[5]Recall the last words of Septimus Severus to his sons: "Remain united, pay the soldiers, and take no heed of the rest."

suddenly realise that they have no police. The Conservatives are in power. What will they do? Will they establish a police force? Nothing of the kind. They prefer to put up with crime, as well as they can. "People are content to let disorder alone, considering it the price they pay for liberty." "In Paris," writes John William Ward, "they have an admirable police force, but they pay dear for its advantages. I prefer to see, every three or four years, half a dozen people getting their throats cut in the Ratcliffe Road, than to have to submit to domiciliary visits, to spying, and to all the machinations of Fouché."[6] Here we have two opposite ideas of the State. The Englishman demands that the State should have limits set to it.

[6]*Vide* Elie Halevy, *Historie du peuple anglais au XIX siècle,* Vol. I, p. 40 (1912).

Suggestions for Discussion

1. Why does a strong state emerge? What dangers does it pose for individual rights? Cite arguments from the text.

2. Explain why the state is so efficient a mechanism.

3. The author contrasts the attitudes of the British toward the rise of crime with those of the French. With whom does he sympathize? Why?

Suggestions for Writing

1. From your personal experience or from your reading or viewing demonstrate that the state can threaten individual freedoms.

2. Compare and contrast the ideas in this essay with those in Auden's poem, "The Unknown Citizen".

H. L. Mencken

The Nature of Liberty

Henry Louis Mencken (1880–1956), journalist, critic, and philologist, edited the magazines *The Smart Set* and *The American Mercury.* In addition to his auto-biography, he published six volumes of *Prejudices,* (1919–1927) containing his often irascible comments on American life and art, and the three-volume *The American Language,* (1918). The Sage of Baltimore was no admirer of democ-racy, and in this selection from *Prejudices* he wryly and outrageously pokes fun at police power and the invasion of the rights of the citizen in the United States.

Every time an officer of the constabulary, in the execution of his just and awful powers under American law, produces a compound fracture of the occiput of some citizen in his custody, with hemorrhage, shock, coma, and death, there comes a feeble, falsetto protest from specialists in human liberty. Is it a fact without significance that this protest is never supported by the great body of American freemen, setting aside the actual heirs and creditors of the victim? I think not. Here, as usual, public opinion is very realistic. It does not rise against the policeman for the plain and simple reason that it does not question his right to do what he has done. Policemen are not given nightsticks for ornament. They are given them for the purpose of cracking the skulls of the recalcitrant plain people, Democrats and Republicans alike. When they execute that high duty they are palpably within their rights.

The specialists aforesaid are the same fanatics who shake the air with sobs every time the Postmaster General of the United States bars a periodical from the mails because its ideas do not please him, and every time some poor Russian is deported for reading Karl Marx, and every time a Prohibition enforcement officer murders a bootlegger who resists his levies, and every time agents of the Department of Justice throw an Italian out of the window, and every time the Ku Klux Klan or the American Legion tars and feathers a Socialist evangelist. In brief, they are Radicals, and to scratch one with a pitchfork is to expose a Bolshevik. They are men standing in contempt of American institutions and in enmity to American idealism. And their evil principles are no less offensive to right-thinking and red-blooded Americans when they are United States Senators or editors of wealthy newspapers than when they are degraded I. W. W.'s throwing dead cats and infernal machines into meetings of the Rotary Club.

What ails them primarily is the ignorant and uncritical monomania that afflicts every sort of fanatic, at all times and everywhere. Having mastered with their limited faculties the theoretical principles set forth in the Bill of Rights, they work themselves into a passionate conviction that those principles are identical with the rules of law and justice, and ought to be enforced literally, and without the slightest regard for circumstance and expediency. It is precisely as if a High Church rector, accidentally looking into the Book of Chronicles and especially Chapter II, should suddenly issue a mandate from his pulpit ordering his parishioners, on penalty of excommunication and the fires of hell, to follow exactly the example set forth, to wit: "And Jesse begat his first born Eliab, and Abinadab the second, and Shimma the third, Netheneel the fourth, Raddai the fifth, Ozen the sixth, David the seventh," and so on. It might be very sound theoretical theology, but it would surely be out of harmony with modern ideas, and the rev. gentleman would be extremely lucky if the bishop did not give him 10 days in the diocesan hoosegow.

So with the Bill of Rights. As adopted by the Fathers of the Republic, it was gross, crude, inelastic, a bit fanciful and transcendental. It specified the rights of a citizen, but it said nothing whatever about his duties. Since then, by the orderly processes of legislative science and by the even more subtle and beautiful devices of juridic art, it has been kneaded and mellowed into a far greater pliability and reasonableness. On the one hand, the citizen still retains the great privilege of membership in the most superb free nation ever witnessed on this earth. On the other hand, as a result of countless shrewd enactments and sagacious decisions, his natural lusts and appetites are held in laudable check, and he is thus kept in order and decorum. No artificial impediment stands in the way of his highest aspiration. He may become anything, including even a policeman. But once a policeman, he is protected by the legislative and judicial arms in the peculiar rights and prerogatives that go with his high office, including especially the right to jug the laity at his will, to sweat and mug them, to subject them to the third degree, and to subdue their resistance by beating out their brains. Those who are unaware of this are simply ignorant of the basic principles of American jurisprudence, as they have been exposed times without number by the courts of first instance and ratified in lofty terms by the Supreme Court of the United States. The one aim of the controlling decisions, magnificently attained, is to safeguard public order and the public security, and to substitute a judicial process for the inchoate and dangerous interaction of discordant egos.

Let us imagine an example. You are, say, a peaceable citizen on your way home from your place of employment. A police sergeant, detecting you in the crowd, approaches you, lays his hand on your collar, and informs you that you are under arrest for killing a trolley conductor in Altoona, Pa., in 1917. Amazed by the accusation, you decide hastily that the officer has lost his wits, and take to your heels. He pursues you. You continue to run. He draws his revolver and fires at you. He misses you. He fires again and fetches you in the leg. You fall and he is upon you. You prepare to resist his apparently maniacal assault. He beats you into insensibility with his espantoon, and drags you to the patrol box.

Arrived at the watch house you are locked in a room with five detectives, and for six hours they question you with subtle art. You grow angry—perhaps robbed of your customary politeness by the throbbing in your head and leg—and answer tartly. They knock you down. Having failed to wring a confession from you, they lock you in a cell, and leave you there all night. The next day you are taken to police headquarters, your photograph is made for the Rogues' Gallery, and a 'print is duly deposited in the section labeled "Murderers." You are then carted to jail and locked up again. There you remain until the trolley conductor's wife comes down from Altoona to identify you. She astonishes the police by saying that you are not the man. The actual murderer, it appears, was an Italian. After holding you a day or two longer, to search your house for stills, audit your income tax returns, and investigate the premarital chastity of your wife, they let you go.

You are naturally somewhat irritated by your experience and perhaps your wife urges you to seek redress. Well, what are your remedies? If you are a firebrand, you reach out absurdly for those of a preposterous nature: the instant jailing of the sergeant, the dismissal of the Police Commissioner, the release of Mooney, a fair trial for Sacco and Vanzetti, free trade with Russia, One Big Union. But if you are a 100 per cent American and respect the laws and institutions of your country, you send for your solicitor—and at once he shows you just how far your rights go, and where they end. You cannot cause the arrest of the sergeant, for you resisted him when he attempted to arrest you, and when you resisted him he acquired an instant right to take you by force. You cannot proceed against him for accusing you falsely, for he has a right to make summary arrests for felony, and the courts have many times decided that a public officer, so long as he cannot be charged with corruption or malice, is not liable for errors of judgment made in the execution of his sworn duty. You cannot get the detectives on the mat, for when they questioned you you were a prisoner accused of murder, and it was their duty and their right to do so. You cannot sue the turnkey at the watch house or the warden at the jail for locking you up, for they received your body, as the law says, in a lawful and regular manner, and would have been liable to penalty if they had turned you loose.

But have you no redress whatever, no rights at all? Certainly you have a right, and the courts have jealously guarded it. You have a clear right, guaranteed to you under the Constitution, to go into a court of equity and apply for a mandamus requiring the *Polizei* to cease forthwith to expose your portrait in the Rogues' Gallery among the murderers. This is your inalienable right, and no man or men on earth can take it away from you. You cannot prevent them cherishing your portrait in their secret files, but you can get an order commanding them to refrain forever from exposing it to the gaze of idle visitors, and if you can introduce yourself unseen into their studio and prove that they disregard that order, you can have them haled into court for contempt and fined by the learned judge.

Thus the law, statute, common and case, protects the free American against injustice. It is ignorance of that subtle and perfect process and not any special love of liberty *per se* that causes radicals of anti-American kidney to rage every time an officer of the *gendarmerie*, in the simple execution of his duty, knocks a citizen in the head. The *gendarme* plainly has an inherent and inalienable right to knock him in the head: it is an essential part of his general prerogative as a sworn officer of the public peace and a representative of the sovereign power of the state. He may, true enough, exercise that prerogative in a manner liable to challenge on the ground that it is imprudent and lacking in sound judgment. On such questions reasonable men may differ. But it must be obvious that the sane and decorous way to settle differences of opinion of that sort is not by public outcry and florid appeals to sentimentality, not by ill-disguised playing to class consciousness and antisocial prejudice, but by an orderly resort to the checks and remedies superimposed upon the Bill of Rights by the calm deliberation and austere logic of the courts of equity.

The law protects the citizen. But to get its protection he must show due respect for its wise and delicate processes.

Suggestions for Discussion

1. Discuss the serious points about liberty that Mencken tries to make in this wry and ironic essay.

2. Analyze Mencken's use of irony. Identify specific examples.

3. Does Mencken choose his examples because they are true, amusing, or outrageous? Examine his motivation.

Suggestion for Writing

Write an ironic sketch about a local or national political situation.

William Faulkner

Nobel Prize Award Speech

William Faulkner (1897–1962) lived most of his life in Oxford, Mississippi. After a year at the university of his native state, he joined the Royal Canadian Air Force, eager to participate in World War I. His novels set in his imaginary Yoknapatawpha County include *The Sound and the Fury* (1929), *Light in August* (1932), *Absalom, Absalom!* (1936), and *The Hamlet* (1940). In his speech accepting the Nobel Prize for Literature in 1949, he states his belief in the significance and dignity of humankind and the need for the writer to reassert the universal truths of "love and honor and pity and pride and compassion and sacrifice."

I feel that this award was not made to me as a man but to my work—a life's work in the agony and sweat of the human spirit, not for glory and least of all for profit, but to create out of the materials of the human spirit something which did not exist before. So this award is only mine in trust. It will not be difficult to find a dedication for the money part of it commensurate with the purpose and significance of its origin. But I would like to do the same with the acclaim too, by using this moment as a pinnacle from which I might be listened to by the young men and women already dedicated to the same anguish and travail, among whom is already that one who will some day stand here where I am standing.

Our tragedy today is a general and universal physical fear so long sustained by now that we can even bear it. There are no longer problems of the spirit. There is only the question: When will I be blown up? Because of this, the young man or woman writing today has forgotten the problems of the human heart in conflict with itself which alone can make good writing because only that is worth writing about, worth the agony and the sweat.

He must learn them again. He must teach himself that the basest of all things is to be afraid; and, teaching himself that, forget it forever, leaving no room in his workshop for anything but the old verities and truths of the heart, the old universal truths lacking which any story is ephemeral and doomed— love and honor and pity and pride and compassion and sacrifice. Until he does so, he labors under a curse. He writes not of love but of lust, of defeats in which nobody loses anything of value, of victories without hope and, worst of all, without pity or compassion. His griefs grieve on no universal bones, leaving no scars. He writes not of the heart but of the glands.

Until he relearns these things, he will write as though he stood alone and watched the end of man. I decline to accept the end of man. It is easy enough to say that man is immortal simply because he will endure; that when the last ding-dong of doom has clanged and faded from the last worthless rock hanging tideless in the last red and dying evening, that even then there will still be one more sound: that of his puny inexhaustible voice, still talking. I refuse to accept this. I believe that man will not merely endure: he will prevail. He is immortal, not because he alone among creatures has an inexhaustible voice but because he has a soul, a spirit capable of compassion and sacrifice and endurance. The poet's, the writer's, duty is to write about these things. It is his privilege to help man endure by lifting his heart, by reminding him of the courage and honor and hope and pride and compassion and pity and sacrifice which have been the glory of his past. The poet's voice need not merely be the record of man, it can be one of the props, the pillars to help him endure and prevail.

Suggestions for Discussion

1. Do you agree with Faulkner's optimistic statement about man's ability to "endure and prevail"? Explain.

2. Do you think Faulkner's speech too brief for a major occasion such as the Nobel Prize Awards? Explain your answer.

3. Discuss whether or not man still lives in that state of general and universal physical fear to which Faulkner refers.

Suggestions for Writing

1. Summarize your own opinions about man's ability to survive the challenges of the next hundred years.

2. Prepare a formal speech in which you accept an international prize for literature or some other accomplishment.

Harriet Jacobs

The Women

Harriet Jacobs (1818–1896) describes the effects of Nat Turner's Rebellion in *Incidents in the Life of a Slave Girl* (1861). This selection from *Black Slave Narratives* pinpoints with simple clarity the moral dilemmas which face a young female slave caught between her owner's desires and his wife's jealousy.

I would ten thousand times rather that my children should be the half-starved paupers of Ireland than to be the most pampered among the slaves of America. I would rather drudge out my life on a cotton plantation, till the grave opened to give me rest, than to live with an unprincipled master and a jealous mistress. The felon's home in a penitentiary is preferable. He may repent, and turn from the error of his ways, and so find peace, but it is not so with a favorite slave. She is not allowed to have any pride of character. It is deemed a crime in her to wish to be virtuous.

Mrs. Flint possessed the key to her husband's character before I was born. She might have used this knowledge to counsel and to screen the young and the innocent among her slaves; but for them she had no sympathy. They were the objects of her constant suspicion and malevolence. She watched her husband with unceasing vigilance; but he was well practiced in means to evade it. What he could not find opportunity to say in words he manifested in signs. He invented more than were ever thought of in a deaf and dumb asylum. I let them pass, as if I did not understand what he meant; and many were the curses and threats bestowed on me for my stupidity. One day he caught me teaching myself to write. He frowned, as if he was not well pleased; but I suppose he came to the conclusion that such an accomplishment might help to advance his favorite scheme. Before long, notes were often slipped into my hand. I would return them, saying, "I can't read them, sir." "Can't you?" he replied; "then I must read them to you." He always finished the reading by asking, "Do you understand?" Sometimes he would complain of the heat of the tea room, and order his supper to be placed on a small table in the piazza. He would seat himself there with a well-satisfied smile, and tell me to stand by and brush away the flies. He would eat very slowly, pausing between the mouthfuls. These intervals were employed in describing the happiness I was so foolishly throwing away, and in threatening me with the penalty that finally awaited my stubborn disobedience. He boasted much of the forbearance he had exercised toward me, and reminded me that there was a limit to his patience. When I succeeded in avoiding opportunities for him to talk to me at home, I was ordered to come to his office, to do some errand. When there, I was obliged to stand and listen to such language as he saw fit to address to me. Sometimes I so openly expressed my contempt for him that he would become violently enraged, and I wondered why he did not strike me. Circumstanced as he was, he probably thought it was better policy to be forebearing. But the state of things grew worse and worse daily. In desperation I told him that I must and would apply to my grandmother for protection. He threatened me with death, and worse than death, if I made my complaint to her. Strange to say, I did not despair. I was naturally of a buoyant disposition, and always I had a hope of somehow getting out of his clutches. Like many a poor, simple slave before me, I trusted that some threads of joy would yet be woven into my dark destiny.

I had entered my sixteenth year, and every day it became more apparent that my presence was intolerable to Mrs. Flint. Angry words frequently passed between her and her husband. He had never punished me himself, and he would not allow anybody else to punish me. In that respect, she was never satisfied; but, in her angry moods, no terms were too vile for her to bestow upon me. Yet I, whom she detested so bitterly, had far more pity for her than he had, whose duty it was to make her life happy. I never wronged her, or wished to wrong her; and one word of kindness from her would have brought me to her feet.

After repeated quarrels between the doctor and his wife, he announced his intention to take his youngest daughter, then four years old, to sleep in his apartment. It was necessary that a servant should sleep in the same room, to be on hand if the child stirred. I was selected for that office, and informed for what purpose that arrangement had been made. By managing to keep within sight of people, as much as possible, during the daytime, I had hitherto succeeded in eluding my master, though a razor was often held to my throat to force me to change this line of policy. At night I slept by the side of my great aunt, where I felt safe. He was too prudent to come into her room. She was an old woman, and had been in the family many years. Moreover, as a married man, and a professional man, he deemed it necessary to save appearances in some degree. But he resolved to remove the obstacle in the way of his scheme; and he thought he had planned it so that he should evade suspicion. He was well aware how much I prized my refuge by the side of my old aunt, and he determined to dispossess me of it. The first night the doctor had the little child in his room alone. The next morning, I was ordered to take my station as nurse the following night. A kind Providence interposed in my favor. During the day Mrs. Flint heard of this new arrangement, and a storm followed. I rejoiced to hear it rage.

After a while my mistress sent for me to come to her room. Her first question was, "Did you know you were to sleep in the doctor's room?"

"Yes, ma'am."

"Who told you?"

"My master."

"Will you answer truly all the questions I ask?"

"Yes, ma'am."

"Tell me, then, as you hope to be forgiven, are you innocent of what I have accused you?"

"I am."

She handed me a Bible, and said, "Lay your hand on your heart, kiss this holy book, and swear before God that you tell me the truth."

I took the oath she required, and I did it with a clear conscience.

"You have taken God's holy word to testify your innocence," said she. "If you have deceived me, beware! Now take this stool, sit down, look me directly in the face, and tell me all that has passed between your master and you."

I did as she ordered. As I went on with my account her color changed frequently, she wept, and sometimes groaned. She spoke in tones so sad, that I was touched by her grief. The tears came to my eyes; but I was soon convinced that her emotions arose from anger and wounded pride. She felt that her marriage vows were desecrated, her dignity insulted; but she had no compassion for the poor victim of her husband's perfidy. She pitied herself as a martyr; but she was incapable of feeling for the condition of shame and misery in which her unfortunate, helpless slave was placed.

Yet perhaps she had some touch of feeling for me; for when the conference was ended, she spoke kindly, and promised to protect me. I should have been much comforted by this assurance if I could have had confidence in it; but my experiences in slavery had filled me with distrust. She was not a very refined woman, and had not much control over her passions. I was an object of her jealousy, and, consequently, of her hatred; and I knew I could not expect kindness or confidence from her under the circumstances in which I was placed. I could not blame her. Slaveholders' wives feel as other women would under similar circumstances. The fire of her temper kindled from small sparks, and now the flame became so intense that the doctor was obliged to give up his intended arrangement.

I knew I had ignited the torch, and I expected to suffer for it afterward; but I felt too thankful to my mistress for the timely aid she rendered me to care much about that. She now took me to sleep in a room adjoining her own. There I was an object of her especial care, though not of her especial comfort, for she spent many a sleepless night to watch over me. Sometimes I woke up, and found her bending over me. At other times she whispered in my ear, as though it was her husband who was speaking to me, and listened to hear what I would answer. If she startled me, on such occasions, she would glide stealthily away; and the next morning she would tell me I had been talking in my sleep, and ask who I was talking to. At last I began to be fearful for my life. It had been often threatened; and you can imagine, better than I can describe, what an unpleasant sensation it must produce to wake up in the dead of night and find a jealous woman bending over you. Terrible as this experience was, I had fears that it would give place to one more terrible.

My mistress grew weary of her vigils; they did not prove satisfactory. She changed her tactics. She now tried the trick of accusing my master of crime, in my presence, and gave my name as the author of the accusation. To my utter astonishment, he replied, "I don't believe it; but if she did acknowledge it, you tortured her into exposing me." Tortured into exposing him! Truly, Satan had no difficulty in distinguishing the color of his soul! I understood his object in making this false representation. It was to show me that I gained nothing by seeking the protection of my mistress; that the power was still all in his own hands. I pitied Mrs. Flint. She was a second wife, many years the junior of her husband; and the hoary-headed miscreant was enough to try the patience of a wiser and better woman. She was completely foiled, and knew not how to proceed. She would gladly have had me flogged for my supposed false oath; but, as I have already stated, the doctor never allowed anyone to whip me. The old sinner was politic. The application of the lash might have led to remarks that would have exposed him in the eyes of his children and grandchildren. How often did I rejoice that I lived in a town where all the inhabitants knew each other! If I had been on a remote plantation, or lost among the multitude of a crowded city, I should not be a living woman at this day.

The secrets of slavery are concealed like those of the Inquisition. My master was, to my knowledge, the father of eleven slaves. But did the mothers dare to tell who was the father of their children? Did the other slaves dare to allude to it, except in whispers among themselves? No, indeed! They knew too well the terrible consequences.

My grandmother could not avoid seeing things which excited her suspicions. She was uneasy about me, and tried various ways to buy me; but the never-changing answer was always repeated: "Linda does not belong to *me*. She is my daughter's property, and I have no legal right to sell her." The conscientious man! He was too scrupulous to *sell* me; but he had no scruples whatever about committing a much greater wrong against the helpless young girl placed under his guardianship, as his daughter's property. Sometimes my persecutor would ask me whether I would like to be sold. I told him I would rather be sold to anybody than to lead such a life as I did. On such occasions he would assume the air of a very injured individual, and reproach me for my ingratitude. "Did I not take you into the house, and make you the companion of my own children?" he would say. "Have I ever treated you like a Negro? I have never allowed you to be punished, not even to please your mistress. And this is the recompense I get, you ungrateful girl!" I answered that he had reasons of his own for screening me from punishment, and that the course he pursued made my mistress hate me and persecute me. If I wept, he would say, "Poor child! Don't cry! don't cry! I will make peace for you with your mistress. Only let me arrange matters in my own way. Poor, foolish girl! you don't know what is for your own good. I would cherish you. I would make a lady of you. Now go, and think of all I have promised you."

I did think of it.

Reader, I draw no imaginary pictures of southern homes. I am telling you the plain truth. Yet when victims make their escape from this wild beast of Slavery, northerners consent to act the part of bloodhounds, and hunt the poor fugitive back into his den, "full of dead men's bones, and all uncleanness." Nay, more, they are not only willing, but proud, to give their daughters in marriage to slaveholders. The poor girls have romantic notions of a sunny clime, and of the flowering vines that all the year round shade a happy home. To what disappointments are they destined! The young wife soon learns that the husband in whose hands she has placed her happiness pays no regard to his marriage vows. Children of every shade of complexion play with her own fair babies, and too well she knows that they are born unto him of his own household. Jealousy and hatred enter the flowery home, and it is ravaged of its loveliness.

Southern women often marry a man knowing that he is the father of many little slaves. They do not trouble themselves about it. They regard such children as property, as marketable as the pigs on the plantation; and it is seldom that they do not make them aware of this by passing them into the slave-trader's hands as soon as possible, and thus getting them out of their sight. I am glad to say there are some honorable exceptions.

I have myself known two southern wives who exhorted their husbands to free those slaves toward whom they stood in a "parental relation"; and their request was granted. These husbands blushed before the superior nobleness of their wives' natures. Though they had only counseled them to do that which it was their duty to do, it commanded their respect, and rendered their conduct more exemplary. Concealment was at an end, and confidence took the place of distrust.

Though this bad institution deadens the moral sense, even in white women, to a fearful extent, it is not altogether extinct. I have heard southern ladies say of Mr. Such-a-one, "He not only thinks it no disgrace to be the father of those little niggers, but he is not ashamed to call himself their master. I declare, such things ought not to be tolerated in any decent society!"

Suggestions for Discussion

1. Discuss the effectiveness of the author's narrative method. Compare it with that used by Richard Wright.

2. How successfully does she communicate her desperation? How does she do so?

Suggestion for Writing

Write a newspaper editorial commenting on the events reported by Harriet Jacobs.

Martin Luther King Jr.

I Have a Dream

Martin Luther King Jr. (1929–1968) was the most charismatic leader of the civil rights movement of the 1950's and 1960's until his assassination in 1968 in Memphis, Tennessee. He led sit-ins and demonstrations throughout the South and was president of the Southern Christian Leadership Conference as well as pastor of a large congregation in Atlanta. He followed the principles of Ghandi and Thoreau in all of his public actions and utterances. This speech, delivered in front of the Lincoln Memorial at a centennial celebration of the Emancipation Proclamation, moves us as deeply on paper today as it did when it was delivered with Martin Luther King's powerful skills of oratory. It points the way to a world free from the burden of racism.

Five score years ago, a great American, in whose symbolic shadow we stand, signed the Emancipation Proclamation. This momentous decree came as a great beacon light of hope to millions of Negro slaves who had been seared in the flames of withering injustice. It came as a joyous daybreak to end the long night of captivity.

But one hundred years later, we must face the tragic fact that the Negro is still not free. One hundred years later, the life of the Negro is still sadly crippled by the manacles of segregation and the chains of discrimination. One hundred years later, the Negro lives on a lonely island of poverty in the midst of a vast ocean of material prosperity. One hundred years later, the Negro is still languished in the corners of American society and finds himself an exile in his own land. So we have come here today to dramatize an appalling condition.

In a sense we have come to our nation's Capital to cash a check. When the architects of our republic wrote the magnificent words of the Constitution and the Declaration of Independence, they were signing a promissory note to which every American was to fall heir. This note was a promise that all men would be guaranteed the unalienable rights of life, liberty, and the pursuit of happiness.

It is obvious today that America has defaulted on this promissory note insofar as her citizens of color are concerned. Instead of honoring this sacred obligation, America has given the Negro people a bad check; a check which has come back marked "insufficient funds." But we refuse to believe that the bank of justice is bankrupt. We refuse to believe that there are insufficient funds in the great vaults of opportunity of this nation. So we have come to cash this check—a check that will give us upon demand the riches of freedom and the security of justice. We have also come to this hallowed spot to remind America of the fierce urgency of *now*. This is no time to engage in the luxury of cooling off or to take the tranquilizing drug of gradualism. *Now* is the time to make real the promises of Democracy. *Now* is the time to rise from the dark and desolate valley of segregation to the sunlit path of racial justice. *Now* is the time to open the doors of opportunity to all of God's children. *Now* is the time to lift our nation from the quicksands of racial injustice to the solid rock of brotherhood.

It would be fatal for the nation to overlook the urgency of the moment and to underestimate the determination of the Negro. This sweltering summer of the Negro's legitimate discontent will not pass until there is an invigorating autumn of freedom and equality. 1963 is not an end, but a beginning. Those who hope that the Negro needed to blow off steam and will now be content will have a rude awakening if the nation returns to business as usual. There will be neither rest nor tranquillity in America until the Negro is granted his citizenship rights. The whirlwinds of revolt will continue to shake the foundations of our nation until the bright day of justice emerges.

But there is something that I must say to my people who stand on the warm threshold which leads into the palace of justice. In the process of gaining our rightful place we must not be guilty of wrongful deeds. Let us not seek to satisfy our thirst for freedom by drinking from the cup of bitterness and hatred. We must forever conduct our struggle on the high plane of dignity and discipline. We must not allow our creative protest to degenerate into physical violence. Again and again we must rise to the majestic heights of meeting physical force with soul force. The marvelous new militancy which has engulfed the Negro community must not lead us to a distrust of all white people, for many of our white brothers, as evidenced by their presence here today, have come to realize that their destiny is tied up with our destiny and their freedom is inextricably bound to our freedom. We cannot walk alone.

And as we walk, we must make the pledge that we shall march ahead. We cannot turn back. There are those who are asking the devotees of civil rights, "When will you be satisfied?" We can never be satisfied as long as the Negro is the victim of the unspeakable horrors of police brutality. We can never be satisfied as long as our bodies, heavy with fatigue of travel, cannot gain lodging in the motels of the highways and the hotels of the cities. We cannot be satisfied as long as the Negro's basic mobility is from a smaller ghetto to a larger one. We can never be satisfied as long as a Negro in Mississippi cannot vote and a Negro in New York believes he has nothing for which to vote. No, no, we are not satisfied, and we will not be satisfied until justice rolls down like waters and righteousness like a mighty stream.

I am not unmindful that some of you have come here out of great trials and tribulations. Some of you have come fresh from narrow jail cells. Some of you have come from areas where your quest for freedom left you battered by the storms of persecution and staggered by the winds of police brutality. You have been the veterans of creative suffering. Continue to work with the faith that unearned suffering is redemptive.

Go back to Mississippi, go back to Alabama, go back to South Carolina, go back to Georgia, go back to Louisiana, go back to the slums and ghettos of our northern cities, knowing that somehow this situation can and will be changed. Let us not wallow in the valley of despair.

I say to you today, my friends, that in spite of the difficulties and frustrations of the moment I still have a dream. It is a dream deeply rooted in the American dream.

I have a dream that one day this nation will rise up and live out the true meaning of its creed: "We hold these truths to be self-evident; that all men are created equal."

I have a dream that one day on the red hills of Georgia the sons of former slaves and the sons of former slaveowners will be able to sit down together at the table of brotherhood.

I have a dream that one day even the state of Mississippi, a desert state sweltering with the heat of injustice and oppression, will be transformed into an oasis of freedom and justice.

I have a dream that my four little children will one day live in a nation where they will not be judged by the color of their skin but by the content of their character.

I have a dream today.

I have a dream that one day the state of Alabama, whose governor's lips are presently dripping with the words of interposition and nullification, will be transformed into a situation where little black boys and black girls will be able to join hands with little white boys and white girls and walk together as sisters and brothers.

I have a dream today.

I have a dream that one day every valley shall be exalted, every hill and mountain shall be made low, the rough places will be made plains, and the crooked places will be made straight, and the glory of the Lord shall be revealed, and all flesh shall see it together.

This is our hope. This is the faith with which I return to the South. With this faith we will be able to hew out of the mountain of despair a stone of hope. With this faith we will be able to transform the jangling discords of our nation into a beautiful symphony of brotherhood. With this faith we will be able to work together, to pray together, to struggle together, to go to jail together, to stand up for freedom together, knowing that we will be free one day.

This will be the day when all of God's children will be able to sing with new meaning

> My country, 'tis of thee,
> Sweet land of liberty,
> Of thee I sing:
> Land where my fathers died,
> Land of the pilgrims' pride,
> From every mountainside
> Let freedom ring.

And if America is to be a great nation this must become true. So let freedom ring from the prodigious hilltops of New Hampshire. Let freedom ring from the mighty mountains of New York. Let freedom ring from the heightening Alleghenies of Pennsylvania!

Let freedom ring from the snowcapped Rockies of Colorado!

Let freedom ring from the curvacious peaks of California!

But not only that; let freedom ring from Stone Mountain of Georgia.

Let freedom ring from Lookout Mountain of Tennessee!

Let freedom ring from every hill and molehill of Mississippi. From every mountainside, let freedom ring.

When we let freedom ring, when we let it ring from every village and every hamlet, from every state and every city, we will be able to speed up that day when all of God's children, black men and white men, Jews and Gentiles, Protestants and Catholics, will be able to join hands and sing in the words of the old Negro spiritual, "Free at last! free at last! thank God almighty, we are free at last!"

Suggestions for Discussion

1. What role does repetition play in this speech?

2. Discuss Reverend King's use of the Bible, the spiritual song, and the Declaration of Independence in this speech. How is each source dependent upon the other?

3. It is clear that this selection was designed as an oration. What are its oratorical qualities? Compare it with "Visible Man" by Andrew Hill as a statement on civil rights.

4. Why does King stress pacifism as a means in the struggle for civil rights?

Suggestions for Writing

1. What do you think has been the outcome of King's dream? Write an essay in which you discuss where the dream has been fulfilled and where it has remained unfulfilled.

2. Write a paragraph about the effective use of repetition in King's oration.

E. M. Forster

Jew-Consciousness

Edward Morgan Forster (1879–1970) was a British novelist educated at King's College, Cambridge. He lived for a time in Italy, was a member of the Bloomsbury Group of writers and artists in London, and spent the major part of his life in Cambridge. His works include *Where Angels Fear to Tread* (1905), *A Room With a View* (1908), *Howard's End* (1910), and *A Passage to India* (1924). In this selection (written in 1939) from *Two Cheers for Democracy* (1951) he tends to equate anti-Semitism with the nonsensical ideas which he says were prevalent in his public school days in the nineteenth century. His ironic stance was suitable for the English temperament of 1939. One wonders what he might have said had he known of the Holocaust which was soon to descend on European Jewry.

Long, long ago, while Queen Victoria reigned, I attended two preparatory schools. At the first of these, it was held to be a disgrace to have a sister. Any little boy who possessed one was liable to get teased. The word would go round: "Oh, you men, have you seen the Picktoes' sister?" The men would then reel about with sideway motions, uttering cries of "sucks" and pretending to faint with horror, while the Picktoes, who had hitherto held their own socially in spite of their name, found themselves banished into the wilderness, where they mourned. Major with Minor, in common shame. Naturally anyone who had a sister hid her as far as possible, and forbade her to sit with him at a Prizegiving or to speak to him except in passing and in a very formal manner. Public opinion was not bitter on the point, but it was quite definite. Sisters were disgraceful. I got through all right myself, because my conscience was clear, and though charges were brought against me from time to time they always fell through.

It was a very different story at my second school. Here, sisters were negligible, but it was a disgrace to have a mother. Crabbe's mother, Gob's mother, eeugh! No words were too strong, no sounds too shrill. And since mothers at that time of life are commoner than sisters, and also less biddable, the atmosphere of this school was less pleasant, and the sense of guilt stronger. Nearly every little boy had a mother in a cupboard, and dreadful revelations occurred. A boy would fall ill and a mother would swoop and drive him away in a cab. A parcel would arrive with "From Mummy for her darling" branded upon it. Many tried to divert suspicion by being aggressive and fastening female parents upon the weak. One or two, who were good at games and had a large popularity-surplus, took up a really heroic line, acknowledged their mother brazenly, and would even be seen walking with her across the playing-field, like King Carol with Madame Lupescu. We admired such boys and envied them, but durst not imitate them. The margin of safety was too narrow. The convention was established that a mother spelt disgrace, and no individual triumph could reverse this.

Those preparatory schools prepared me for life better than I realised, for having passed through two imbecile societies, a sister-conscious and a mother-conscious, I am now invited to enter a third. I am asked to consider whether the people I meet and talk about are or are not Jews, and to form no opinion on them until this fundamental point has been settled. What revolting tosh! Neither science nor religion nor common sense has one word to say in its favour. All the same, Jew-consciousness is in the air, and it remains to be seen how far it will succeed in poisoning it. I don't think we shall ever reintroduce ghettos in England; I wouldn't say for certain, since no one knows what wickedness may not develop in his country or in himself if circumstances change. I don't think we shall go savage. But I do think we shall go silly. Many people have gone so already. Today, the average man suspects the people he dislikes of being Jews, and is surprised when the people he likes are Jews. Having been a Gentile at my first preparatory school and a Jew at my second, I know what I am talking about. I know how the poison works, and I know too that if the average man is anyone in particular he is a preparatory school boy. On the surface, things do not look too bad. Labour and Liberalism behave with their expected decency and denounce persecution, and respectability generally follows suit. But beneath the surface things are not so good, and anyone who keeps his ears open in railway carriages or pubs or country lanes can hear a very different story. A nasty side of our nation's character has been scratched up—the sniggering side. People who would not ill-treat Jews themselves, or even be rude to them, enjoy tittering over their misfortunes; they giggle when pogroms are instituted by someone else and synagogues defiled vicariously. "Serve them right really, Jews." This makes unpleasant reading, but anyone who cares to move out of his own enlightened little corner will discover that it is true. The grand Nordic argument, "He's a bloody capitalist so he must be a Jew, and as he's a Jew he must be a Red," has already taken root in our filling-stations and farms. Men employ it more frequently than women, and young men more frequently than old ones. The best way of confuting it is to say sneeringly, "That's propaganda." When "That's propaganda" has been repeated several times, the sniggering stops, for no goose likes to think that he has been got at. There is another reply which is more intellectual but which requires more courage. It is to say, "Are you sure you're not a Jew yourself? Do you know who your eight great-grandparents were? Can you swear that all the eight are Aryan?" Cool reasonableness would be best of all, of course, but it does not work in the world of today any better than in my preparatory schools. The only effective check to silliness is silliness of a cleverer type.

Jew-mania was the one evil which no one foretold at the close of the last war. All sorts of troubles were discerned and discernible—nationalism, class-warfare, the split between the haves and the have-nots, the general lowering of cultural values. But no prophet, so far as I know, had foreseen this anti-Jew horror, whereas today no one can see the end of it. There had been warnings, of course, but they seemed no more ominous than a poem by Hilaire Belloc. Back in India, in 1921, a Colonel lent me the Protocols of the Elders of Zion, and it was such an obvious fake that I did not worry. I had forgotten my preparatory schools, and did not see that they were about to come into their own. To me, anti-Semitism is now the most shocking of all things. It is destroying much more than the Jews; it is assailing the human mind at its source, and inviting it to create false categories before exercising judgment. I am sure we shall win through. But it will take a long time. Perhaps a hundred years must pass before men can think back to the mentality of 1918, or can say with the Prophet Malachi, "Have we not all one father? Hath not one God created us?" For the moment, all that we can do is to dig in our heels, and prevent silliness from sliding into insanity.

Suggestions for Discussion

1. Discuss the pictures of life in preparatory schools with which Forster opens his essay. What do his comments on "sister-consciousness' and "mother-consciousness" have to do with the rest of the essay?

2. Define what he calls the "grand Nordic argument" against the Jews. What does he mean by "Jew-mania"?

3. In this chapter from *Two Cheers for Democracy* (copyrighted in 1951), Forster refers to "the mentality of 1918." Define that mentality and discuss whether or not it still exists.

Suggestion for Writing

Write an essay discussing how widespread and how serious, in your experience, anti-Semitism is today.

Jonathan Schell
The Choice

Jonathan Schell was born in New York in 1943. His writings for *The New Yorker* have been expanded into books on international and domestic politics. In 1967 he published *The Village of Ben Suc* and in 1976 *The Time of Illusion*. In this excerpt from the concluding section of *The Fate of the Earth* (1982), Schell says that our present inaction in the face of possible annihilation is intolerable, and he proposes that we act now if we are to survive.

Four and a half billion years ago, the earth was formed. Perhaps a half billion years after that, life arose on the planet. For the next four billion years, life became steadily more complex, more varied, and more ingenious, until, around a million years ago, it produced mankind—the most complex and ingenious species of them all. Only six or seven thousand years ago—a period that is to the history of the earth as less than a minute is to a year—civilization emerged, enabling us to build up a human world, and to add to the marvels of evolution marvels of our own: marvels of art, of science, of social organization, of spiritual attainment. But, as we built higher and higher, the evolutionary foundation beneath our feet became more and more shaky, and now, in spite of all we have learned and achieved—or, rather, because of it—we hold this entire terrestrial creation hostage to nuclear destruction, threatening to hurl it back into the inanimate darkness from which it came. And this threat of self-destruction and planetary destruction is not something that we will pose one day in the future, if we fail to take certain precautions; it is here now, hanging over the heads of all of us at every moment. The machinery of destruction is complete, poised on a hair trigger, waiting for the "button" to be "pushed" by some misguided or deranged human being or for some faulty computer chip to send out the instruction to fire. That so much should be balanced on so fine a point—that the fruit of four and a half billion years can be undone in a careless moment—is a fact against which belief rebels. And there is another, even vaster measure of the loss, for stretching ahead from our present are more billions of years of life on earth, all of which can be filled not only with human life but with human civilization. The procession of generations that extends onward from our present leads far, far beyond the line of our sight, and, compared with these stretches of human time, which exceed the whole history of the earth up to now, our brief civilized moment is almost infinitesimal. And yet we threaten, in the name of our transient aims and fallible convictions, to foreclose it all. If our species does destroy itself, it will be a death in the cradle—a case of infant mortality. The disparity between the cause and the effect of our peril is so great that our minds seem all but powerless to encompass it. In addition, we are so fully enveloped by that which is menaced, and so deeply and passionately immersed in its events, which are the events of our lives, that we hardly know how to get far enough away from it to see it in its entirety. It is as though life itself were one huge distraction, diverting our attention from the peril to life. In its apparent durability, a world menaced with imminent doom is in a way deceptive: It is almost an illusion. Now we are sitting at the breakfast table drinking our coffee and reading the newspaper, but in a moment we may be inside a fireball whose temperature is tens of thousands of degrees. Now we are on our way to work, walking through the city streets, but in a moment we may be standing on an empty plain under a darkened sky looking for the charred remnants of our children. Now we are alive, but in a moment we may be dead. Now there is human life on earth, but in a moment it may be gone.

Once, there was time to reflect in a more leisurely way on our predicament. In August, 1945, when the invention of the bomb was made known through its first use on a human population, the people of Hiroshima, there lay ahead an interval of decades which might have been used to fashion a world that would be safe from extinction by nuclear arms, and some voices were in fact heard counseling deep reflection on the looming peril and calling for action to head it off. On November 28, 1945, less than four months after the bombing of Hiroshima, the English philosopher Bertrand Russell rose in the House of Lords and said:

> We do not want to look at this thing simply from the point of view of the
> next few years; we want to look at it from the point of view of the future of

mankind. The question is a simple one: Is it possible for a scientific society to continue to exist, or must such a society inevitably bring itself to destruction? It is a simple question but a very vital one. I do not think it is possible to exaggerate the gravity of the possibilities of evil that lie in the utilization of atomic energy. As I go about the streets and see St. Paul's, the British Museum, the Houses of Parliament, and the other monuments of our civilization, in my mind's eye I see a nightmare vision of those buildings as heaps of rubble with corpses all round them. That is a thing we have got to face, not only in our own country and cities, but throughout the civilized world.

Russell and others, including Albert Einstein, urged full, global disarmament, but the advice was disregarded. Instead, the world set about building the arsenals that we possess today. The period of grace we had in which to ward off the nuclear peril before it became a reality—the time between the moment of the invention of the weapons and the construction of the full-scale machinery for extinction—was squandered, and now the peril that Russell foresaw is upon us. Indeed, if we are honest with ourselves we have to admit that unless we rid ourselves of our nuclear arsenals a holocaust not only *might* occur but *will* occur—if not today, then tomorrow; if not this year, then the next. We have come to live on borrowed time: every year of continued human life on earth is a borrowed year, every day a borrowed day.

In the face of this unprecedented global emergency, we have so far had no better idea than to heap up more and more warheads, apparently in the hope of so thoroughly paralyzing ourselves with terror that we will hold back from taking the final, absurd step. Considering the wealth of our achievement as a species, this response is unworthy of us. Only by a process of gradual debasement of our self-esteem can we have lowered our expectations to this point. For, of all the "modest hopes of human beings," the hope that mankind will survive is the most modest, since it only brings us to the threshold of all the other hopes. In entertaining it, we do not yet ask for justice, or for freedom, or for happiness, or for any of the other things that we may want in life. We do not even necessarily ask for our personal survival; we ask only that we *be survived*. We ask for assurance that when we die as individuals, as we know we must, mankind will live on. Yet once the peril of extinction is present, as it is for us now, the hope for human survival becomes the most tremendous hope, just because it is the foundation for all the other hopes, and in its absence every other hope will gradually wither and die. Life without the hope for human survival is a life of despair.

The death of our species resembles the death of an individual in its boundlessness, its blankness, its removal beyond experience, and its tendency to baffle human thought and feeling, yet as soon as one mentions the hope of survival the similarities are clearly at an end. For while individual death is inevitable, extinction can be avoided; while every person must die, mankind can be saved. Therefore, while reflection on death may lead to resignation and acceptance, reflection on extinction must lead to exactly the opposite response: to arousal, rejection, indignation, and action. Extinction is not something to contemplate, it is something to rebel against. To point this out might seem like stating the obvious if it were not that on the whole the world's reaction to the peril of extinction has been one of numbness and inertia, much as though extinction were as inescapable as death is. Even today, the official response to the sickening reality before us is conditioned by a grim fatalism,

in which the hope of ridding the world of nuclear weapons, and thus of surviving as a species, is all but ruled out of consideration as "utopian" or "extreme"—as though it were "radical" merely to want to go on living and to
want one's descendants to be born. And yet if one gives up these aspirations
one has given up on everything. As a species, we have as yet done nothing to
save ourselves. The slate of action is blank. We have organizations for the
preservation of almost everything in life that we want but no organization for
the preservation of mankind. People seem to have decided that our collective
will is too weak or flawed to rise to this occasion. They see the violence that
has saturated human history, and conclude that to practice violence is innate
in our species. They find the perennial hope that peace can be brought to the
earth once and for all a delusion of the well-meaning who have refused to face
the "harsh realities" of international life—the realities of self-interest, fear,
hatred, and aggression. They have concluded that these realities are eternal
ones, and this conclusion defeats at the outset any hope of taking the actions
necessary for survival. Looking at the historical record, they ask what has
changed to give anyone confidence that humanity can break with its violent
past and act with greater restraint. The answer, of course, is that everything
has changed. To the old "harsh realities" of international life has been added
the immeasurably harsher new reality of the peril of extinction. To the old
truth that all men are brothers has been added the inescapable new truth that
not only on the moral but also on the physical plane the nation that practices
aggression will itself die. This is the law of the doctrine of nuclear deterrence—the doctrine of "mutual assured destruction"—which "assures" the destruction of the society of the attacker. And it is also the law of the natural
world, which, in its own version of deterrence, supplements the oneness of
mankind with a oneness of nature, and guarantees that when the attack rises
above a certain level the attacker will be engulfed in the general ruin of the
global ecosphere. To the obligation to honor life is now added the sanction
that if we fail in our obligation life will actually be taken away from us, individually and collectively. Each of us will die, and as we die we will see the
world around us dying. Such imponderables as the sum of human life, the
integrity of the terrestrial creation, and the meaning of time, of history, and
of the development of life on earth, which were once left to contemplation
and spiritual understanding, are now at stake in the political realm and demand a political response from every person. As political actors, we must, like
the contemplatives before us, delve to the bottom of the world, and, Atlas-
like, we must take the world on our shoulders.

The self-extinction of our species is not an act that anyone describes as sane
or sensible; nevertheless, it is an act that, without quite admitting it to ourselves, we plan in certain circumstances to commit. Being impossible as a
fully intentional act, unless the perpetrator has lost his mind, it can come
about only through a kind of inadvertence—as a "side effect" of some action
that we do intend, such as the defense of our nation, or the defense of liberty,
or the defense of socialism, or the defense of whatever else we happen to
believe in. To that extent, our failure to acknowledge the magnitude and significance of the peril is a necessary condition for doing the deed. We can do
it only if we don't quite know what we're doing. If we did acknowledge the
full dimensions of the peril, admitting clearly and without reservation that

any use of nuclear arms is likely to touch off a holocaust in which the continuance of all human life would be put at risk, extinction would at that moment become not only "unthinkable" but also undoable. What is needed to make extinction possible, therefore, is some way of thinking about it that at least partly deflects our attention from what it is. And this way of thinking is supplied to us, unfortunately, by our political and military traditions, which, with the weight of almost all historical experience behind them, teach us that it is the way of the world for the earth to be divided up into independent, sovereign states, and for these states to employ war as the final arbiter for settling the disputes that arise among them. This arrangement of the political affairs of the world was not intentional. No one wrote a book proposing it; no parliament sat down to debate its merits and then voted it into existence. It was simply there, at the beginning of recorded history; and until the invention of nuclear weapons it remained there, with virtually no fundamental changes. Unplanned though this arrangement was, it had many remarkably durable features, and certain describable advantages and disadvantages; therefore, I shall refer to it as a "system"—the system of sovereignty. Perhaps the leading feature of this system, and certainly the most important one in the context of the nuclear predicament, was the apparently indissoluble connection between sovereignty and war. For without sovereignty, it appeared, peoples were not able to organize and launch wars against other peoples, and without war they were unable to preserve their sovereignty from destruction by armed enemies. (By "war" I here mean only international war, not revolutionary war, which I shall not discuss.) Indeed, the connection between sovereignty and war is almost a definitional one—a sovereign state being a state that enjoys the right and the power to go to war in defense or pursuit of its interests.

It was into the sovereignty system that nuclear bombs were born, as "weapons" for "war." As the years have passed, it has seemed less and less plausible that they have anything to do with war; they seem to break through its bounds. Nevertheless, they have gone on being fitted into military categories of thinking. One might say that they appeared in the world in a military disguise, for it has been traditional military thinking, itself an inseparable part of the traditional political thinking that belonged to the system of sovereignty, that has provided those intentional goals—namely, national interests—in the pursuit of which extinction may now be brought about unintentionally, or semi-intentionally, as a "side effect." The system of sovereignty is now to the earth and mankind what a polluting factory is to its local environment. The machine produces certain things that its users want—in this case, national sovereignty—and as unhappy side effect extinguishes the species.

The ambivalence resulting from the attempt to force nuclear weapons into the pre-existing military and political system has led to a situation in which, in the words of Einstein—who was farseeing in his political as well as in his scientific thought—"the unleashed power of the atom has changed everything save our modes of thinking, and we thus drift toward unparalleled catastrophes." As Einstein's observation suggests, the nuclear revolution has gone quite far but has not been completed. The question we have to answer is whether the completion will be extinction or a global political revolution—whether the "babies" that the scientists at Alamogordo brought forth will put an end to us or we will put an end to them. For it is not only our thoughts but also our actions and our institutions—our global political arrangements in their entirety—that we have failed to change. We live with one foot in each of two worlds. As scientists and technicians, we live in the nuclear world, in which whether we choose to acknowledge the fact or not, we possess instruments of violence that make it possible for us to extinguish ourselves as a species. But as citizens and statesmen we go on living in the prenuclear world, as though extinction were not possible and sovereign nations could still employ the instruments of violence as instruments of policy—as "a continuation of politics by other means," in the famous phrase of Karl von Clausewitz, the great philosopher of war. In effect, we try to make do with a Newtonian politics in an Einsteinian world. The combination is the source of our immediate peril. For governments, still acting within a system of independent nation-states, and formally representing no one but the people of their separate, sovereign nations, are driven to try to defend merely national interests with means of destruction that threaten not only international but intergenerational and planetary doom. In our present-day world, in the councils where the decisions are made there is no one to speak for man and for the earth, although both are threatened with annihilation.

The dilemma of the nation that in order to protect its national sovereignty finds that it must put the survival of mankind at risk is a trap from which there is no escape as long as nations possess arsenals of nuclear weapons. The deterrence doctrine seeks to rationalize this state of affairs, but it fails, because at the crucial moment it requires nations to sacrifice mankind for their own interests—an absurdity as well as a crime beyond reckoning. Indeed, the deterrence doctrine actually almost *compels* the world to live perpetually on the brink of doom, for any nation that took a step or two back would put its interests and, ultimately, its independence at the mercy of the military forces of its adversaries. And although, for any number of reasons, an adversary might not press its advantage (as, for example, the United States did not right after the Second World War, when it possessed a monopoly of nuclear weapons), no nation has yet volunteered to put itself at this competitive disadvantage. It appears that the only way to escape from the trap is to change the system, and take away from nuclear weapons the responsibility for defending nations. But unless one supposes that, in a global spread of quietism, nations and people in general are going to give up the pursuit of their interests and their ideals and become wholly inactive, this separation can be achieved only if a new way—a nonviolent way—of making and guaranteeing these decisions is found.

In the decades since nuclear arms first appeared in the world, the doctrine of nuclear deterrence has commanded the sincere respect and adherence of many people of good will—especially when they found themselves arguing, as they so often did, with the adherents of traditional military doctrine, who even today, in the face of extinction itself, go on arguing for "military superiority" and the like. And if one once accepts the existence of the doomsday machine, then deterrence theory, however flawed, does offer the hope of certain benefits, the main one being a degree of "stability." Therefore, the perpetual struggle of its adherents against the sheer lunacy of "fighting a nuclear war" is a creditable one. But the fundamental truth about the doctrine and about its role in the wider political—and, it must be added, biological—scheme of things also has to be recognized. For the doctrine's central claim—

that it deploys nuclear weapons only in order to prevent their use—is simply not true. Actually, it deploys them to protect national sovereignty, and if this aim were not present they could be quickly dismantled. The doctrine, then, has been the intellectual screen behind which the doomsday machine was built. And its deceptive claim that only by building nuclear weapons can we save ourselves from nuclear weapons lent the doomsday machine a veneer of reason and of respectability—almost of benevolence—that it should never have been given. For to build this machine at all was a mistake of the hugest proportions ever known—without question the greatest ever made by our species. The only conceivable worse mistake would be to put the machine to use. Now deterrence, having rationalized the construction of the machine, weds us to it, and, at best, offers us, if we are lucky, a slightly extended term of residence on earth before the inevitable human or mechanical mistake occurs and we are annihilated.

Yet the deterrence policy in itself is clearly not the deepest source of our difficulty. Rather, as we have seen, it is only a piece of repair work on the immeasurably more deeply entrenched system of national sovereignty. People do not want deterrence for its own sake; indeed, they hardly know what it is, and tend to shun the whole subject. They want the national sovereignty that deterrence promises to preserve. National sovereignty lies at the very core of the political issues that the peril of extinction forces upon us. Sovereignty is the "reality" that the "realists" counsel us to accept as inevitable, referring to any alternative as "unrealistic" or "utopian." If the argument about nuclear weapons is to be conducted in good faith, then just as those who favor the deterrence policy (not to speak of traditional military doctrine) must in all honesty admit that their scheme contemplates the extinction of man in the name of protecting national sovereignty, so must those who favor complete nuclear and conventional disarmament, as I do, admit that their recommendation is inconsistent with national sovereignty; to pretend otherwise would be to evade the political question that is central to the nuclear predicament. The terms of the deal that the world has now struck with itself must be made clear. On the one side stand human life and the terrestrial creation. On the other side stands a particular organization of human life—the system of independent, sovereign nation-states. Our choice so far has been to preserve that political organization of human life at the cost of risking all human life. We are told that "realism" compels us to preserve the system of sovereignty. But that political realism is not biological realism; it is biological nihilism—and for that reason is, of course, political nihilism, too. Indeed, it is nihilism in every conceivable sense of that word. We are told that it is human fate—perhaps even "a law of human nature"—that, in obedience, perhaps, to some "territorial imperative," or to some dark and ineluctable truth in the bottom of our souls, we must preserve sovereignty and always settle our differences with violence. If this is our fate, then it is our fate to die. But must we embrace nihilism? Must we die? Is self-extermination a law of our nature? Is there nothing we can do? I do not believe so. Indeed, if we admit the reality of the basic terms of the nuclear predicament—that present levels of global armament are great enough to possibly extinguish the species if a holocaust should occur; that in extinction every human purpose would be lost; that because once the species has been extinguished there will be no second chance, and the game will be over for all time; that therefore this possibility must be dealt with morally and politically as though it were a certainty; and that either by accident or by design a holocaust can occur at any second—then, whatever political views we may hold on other matters, we are driven almost inescapably to take action to rid the world of nuclear arms. Just as we have chosen to make nuclear weapons, we can choose to unmake them. Just as we have chosen to live in the system of sovereign states, we can choose to live in some other system. To do so would, of course, be unprecedented, and in many ways frightening, even truly perilous, but it is by no means impossible. Our present system and the institutions that make it up are the debris of history. They have become inimical to life, and must be swept away. They constitute a noose around the neck of mankind, threatening to choke off the human future, but we can cut the noose and break free. To suppose otherwise would be to set up a false, fictitious fate, molded out of our own weaknesses and our own alterable decisions. We are indeed fated by our acquisition of the basic knowledge of physics to live for the rest of time with the knowledge of how to destroy ourselves. But we are not for that reason fated to destroy ourselves. We can choose to live.

Suggestions for Discussion

1. In the first paragraph, Schell says "that the fruit of four and a half billion years can be undone in a careless moment . . . is a fact against which belief rebels." How does this comment prepare us for what follows in the rest of the paragraph? in the rest of the essay?

2. Why, according to Schell, did Russell and Einstein urge full global disarmament? Why was their advice not followed? What have governments done instead?

3. Why does Schell say that merely wanting "to go on living" is regarded as "radical" or "extreme"?

4. Compare the point Schell makes about the dangers of sovereignty with the point made by Milton Mayer's essay, "A World Without Government."

5. What are the inherent difficulties and self-contradictions of trying to live in the prenuclear and the nuclear world at the same time?

6. Schell ends with the sentence, "We can choose to live." Is this an effective ending? What does choosing to live imply as a course of action?

Suggestions for Writing

1. Write an essay in which you discuss Schell's statement, "Life without hope for human survival is a life of despair." Relate the force of this statement to the alternatives which Schell offers.

2. Schell states that nuclear weapons are actually not military weapons. Write an essay agreeing or disagreeing with his position. You should entertain the notion of a limited nuclear war.

Milton Mayer

A World Without Government

Milton Mayer was born in Chicago in 1908 and attended the University of Chicago. A writer on national and international politics and on education, he is a consultant to the Center for the Study of Democratic Institutions now housed on the campus of the University of California at Santa Barbara. He was a pioneer in the Great Books program initiated by Robert Maynard Hutchins and Mortimer Adler and has frequently been a visiting lecturer at universities in this country and abroad. His books include *They Thought They Were Free: The Germans, 1933–1945* (1955), *What Can a Man Do?* (1964), and *The Nature of the Beast* (1975), a collection of his essays. He lives in Carmel, California, where he is writing a biography of Hutchins. This essay, printed in *The Center Magazine* (1983), outlines a dilemma: is it impossible to realize a world government at a time when it alone can save us from destruction?

The morning of April 18, 1861, President Lincoln offered the command of the Union forces in the field to a cavalry officer named Lee, with the rank of major general. Lee was a Virginian, but he was a staunch Unionist and an opponent of both slavery and secession. He didn't hesitate: he declined the offer and resigned his commission in the U.S. Army.

That same afternoon, Virginia seceded and Robert E. Lee took command of its military and naval forces—and, ultimately, of the forces of the Confederate States of America.

Lee was a Virginian first; he believed that the nation had its authority from the several sovereign states. Four years and six hundred thousand lives later he accepted the authority of the nation at the point of the sword and became, outwardly, an American first; inwardly he never regretted his decision to "go with Virginia."

The idea of the separate sovereign state was crushed at Appomattox, but the archaic sovereignties lived on—fifty of them now, every day losing more of their reason for being. For the past year or so, the country has been subjected to a collapsing crusade by President Ronald Reagan to pump new life into these obsolete organs of public administration under the alias of the New Federalism. The New Federalism is neither new nor federal. It is a scheme not to distribute the powers of government but to do away with them by saddling the onetime sovereign states with them. But the states are (as we say in Virginia) too po' to tote them.

In the age of high-speed technology the states have no proper function left. Banking and finance, commerce and industry, law enforcement (corporate, criminal, and investment), basic taxation, civil rights and civil liberties, welfare, employment, job training, Social Security, conservation, pollution, drug and liquor control, pornography, public health, and, of course, long-distance transportation and communication are all self-evidently interstate (or, more precisely, trans-state). The truck with a half-dozen license plates is just another only-in-America phenomenon.

The state no longer has a viable existence except as an obstacle to local government on the one hand and national government on the other. It locks town and country into an utterly misbegotten union. New York City and "up-state" have no more in common than Chicago and "downstate" or Atlanta and pineywoods Georgia. Both physiographically and demographically the United States does provide the occasion for regional associations with real but limited sovereignty within the national union where such areas have common problems, such as the ecology of the Great Lakes basin or the transportation needs of the Boston-Washington corridor. But the state regulatory bodies are as often as not regulated by the private enterprises they are supposed to regulate—notoriously in the case of the public utilities and transportation commissions.

The Virginia of today is not only a political nullity but an economic racket, as James Madison of Virginia warned that it would be. Madison argued on behalf of the new Constitution that the larger the geographical unit of government, the less susceptible it would be to all the evils of what he called faction (i.e., special interest), the less anarchical, and the less readily corrupted. The loss of the representatives' familiarity with local situations would be compensated by the greater likelihood of the selection of good men to govern from the ranks of the larger electorate. Having never dreamed of the railroad and the airplane, the telephone and the telegraph, the corporation and the trade union, Madison could not foresee the total obliteration of the state's usefulness.

The great lobbyist for a strong central government had before him the reduction of the thirteen ex-colonies to a condition of national anarchy after the Revolution. Already two centuries ago the state made little sense; already the new Americans were wandering all over the land, transferring their geographical allegiances as they went. They would soon be interrupting their sentimental rendition of "Carry Me Back to Old Virginny," to shout, "Eureka! I've found it!" when they crossed the mythical state line from the western territories into California.

Where is the Virginian today whose heart, like Lee's, bleeds for Virginia as he curses the morning traffic across the Potomac or shows his badge at the intercontinental spooks' entrance to the Central Intelligence Agency in Langley, "VA."? Where is the Idahoan (or Idahan) who knows the state motto (unless it's on his license plates), the Iowan (or Iowayan) who doesn't gag when the band at the national convention strikes up for the fiftieth time with "That's where the tall corn grows," the crazy California delegate who doesn't whoop when the band plays "California, Here I Come" (which he mistakes for the state song)?

These people are Americans first and last except, possibly, for Lone Star Texans (but never was heard a discouraging word like "secession" when, last spring, the U.S. Supreme Court compelled the outraged heirs of the Alamo to provide public education for the children of Mexican wetbacks, much to the dismay of Justice Sandra Day O'Connor, who said in her dissent, "Each state is sovereign within its own domain, governing its citizens and providing for their general welfare. While the Constitution and federal statutes define the boundaries of that domain, they do not harness state power for national purposes").

The eighteenth-century role of the federal government, apart from the national defense, was to arbitrate the disputes between or among the states. It was soon extended to jurisdiction over any interest which affected more than one state directly. By the middle of the next century—when Lee went with Virginia—the Great Emancipator was holding that it was proper business of the nation as such to do the things for people that people could not do for themselves. Steadily, at first, and then cornucopic with the development of the steam engine and the telegraph, fewer and fewer public functions could be contained within the state. One by one almost every human action and reaction leaped across the union—VD, the gypsy moth, the fugitive criminal, the cigarette taxed high here and low there (and "imported" illegally).

Die-hard tradition alone reserved education to the states, and that began to crumble, but only after the Second World War when the illiteracy of the poor states was finally recognized as a threat to the survival of the Republic. (Forty per cent of the draftees in the three most deprived states of the South were rejected, in contrast with less than two per cent from Minnesota and Iowa.) The state was the bastion of public-school segregation until 1954, when the judicial arm of the nation held it unconstitutional. And it was only a year ago that the federal denial of tax exemption to segregated private schools was finally settled over the joint objection of the states *and* the national administration. After Pearl Harbor, the federal government (which had merely sponsored the Reserve Officers Training Corps before) as good as took over the state universities, along with the private ones, for research and training; and when the Soviet Union lofted Sputnik in 1957, President Dwight Eisenhower called for and got a stupendous appropriation for scientific and technological programs to be disbursed to the nation's high schools and colleges without regard to state lines.

The once sovereign state today provides the kind of pervasive corruption that enables Madison's "factions" to control the generality of state governments. The control is pervasive because there is so little glamour in state office, so little in the way of pay and perquisites, and, above all, so little noonday exposure to public assessment of either the candidate or the officeholder. (Local officials have much greater exposure.) However brutally it is boodled in Congress or in the agencies like the Pentagon, integrity is urged in Washington by the national spotlight; the state capital simply isn't newsworthy. Rare the congressman whose every constituent feels that he doesn't know at least a little something about the man; rare the state legislator whose every constituent feels that he does. Progressive legislation nearly all originates at the federal level, opposition to it at the state.

The motivation of Mr. Reagan's new Federalism, or Old Statism, was obvious as soon as it surfaced; it was obviously part and parcel of Reaganism. Our President—and his California friends, including Vice-President George Bush of Connecticut, Texas, and Connecticut again—has no consuming interest in maintaining government powers at any level, except, of course, defense so-called. They have every interest in eliminating them in favor of the trickle doctrine. The transfer of powers to the states is a transfer of costs. Those functions which cannot be got rid of altogether, when they have been dumped on the states will to that extent have got, not government, but Washington "off the people's backs." Less will be spent by the visible spender, Washington, and less will be taken (except for defense) by the visible taker, Washington. But the states will have to exercise in an ever-increasing degree the one real power remaining to them—the power of the kinds of levy, like the property, gasoline, and sales taxes, which fall most heavily on the poor because of the classic corruption of the legislatures by the special interests. Mr. Reagan's friends are content to see *that* power quietly expanded while the power of Washington (that is, the responsibility) is loudly reduced.

The worm in the vermiform apple is, of course, the Reagan depression, which has busted the states. Under the current welfare arrangement the federal government puts up ninety-three dollars and the state twenty-seven dollars for a total of one-seventh of poverty-level income for a family of four in Mississippi. "Simple logic and history," says Carl Rowan, "tell us that if the federal government walks away from welfare, through a programs 'swap' or any other means, Mississippi is not going to make up the lost ninety-three dollars." As the federal government walks away, the states have had to cut services to the counties, the counties to the municipalities. A recent survey by the National League of Cities reports that ninety per cent of the seventy-nine municipalities queried say they will not be able to make up with local funds the cuts in community and urban development grants planned by the Reagan Administration for fiscal 1984. The survey showed that seventy-one percent of the cities raised municipal fees last year while thirty-eight per cent introduced fees for services formerly provided free. Courtesy of Reagan & Co. public services are going through the wringer the country over. The New Federalism is dead in the womb. The powers—that is, the costs—laid on the states are fast falling into desuetude.

But the stillborn New Federalism has had a certainly unintended effect that may be of some ultimate use to the nation, and, indeed, to the world. It has thrown additional light on the hopelessness of the federal arrangement at the end of the twentieth century. With fifty sets of conflicting and overlapping statutes civil and criminal, and with fifty appellate courts handing down a tumultuous succession of conflicting and overlapping decisions, it has long been impossible to reach a national determination on crucial issues like desegregation or abortion or capital punishment. Fifty sets of lawyers have got richer and richer. The country swarms with large and small offenders against the general welfare scurrying from state to state to get the best deal they can—be it tax exemption in Connecticut, murder in Oregon, or incorporation in Delaware. With the ascension and bursting of the New Federalism balloon, the case against states' rights mounts.

So far has technology carried us beyond the reduction of the states to absurdities that the justification of the sovereign *nation*-state—except in the romantic terms advanced for Lee's Virginia in 1861—comes into critical question as the red button awaits pressing to launch the intercontinental ballistic missiles with thermonuclear warheads and a ten-to-twenty-minute around-the-world delivery time. The transmission of missiles, and missives, people, and goods, is almost as instantaneous across national borders as it is across states—and in the case of electronic transmission exactly as instantaneous.

True, the manners of the Andaman Islanders, if they are still eating their grandparents, are still measurably different from those of the Parisians or the Peorians—but not as different as they were a century, or even a half-century, ago. It is only a matter of time—another century?—before the Andamanders and the Peorians are as interchangeable as the Wyominganders and the Connecticutters are today. With the ever-faster proliferation of non-political institutions, commercial, industrial, financial, cultural, the ancient dictum of Marx that the workingmen have no country can be much more accurately applied to Coca-Cola, Sony, Volkswagen, and IBM (and McDonald's). The great cartels, growing always greater, huckster everybody everywhere (including the Andaman Islands).

The imminent question is insistent: as the United States is to Virginia, so the world is to the United States. What is, or soon will be, left to perpetuate the nation-state is a millennium or two of custom and one people's fanatical hatred of another (or of all others). But the Swiss confederation accommodates three sets of different—even inimical—customs and three and a half different languages. The American melting pot has accommodated a stupendous variety of ethnic usages, large and small, in the process absorbing provincial consciousness into emotional attachment to the nation. In the sixty-five years since the Great War of the old nations this national attachment has, on balance, subsided very considerably and, as technology proceeds apace, seems destined to go on subsiding, without, however, a corresponding transfer to a larger conceptual unit than the nation-state. (No "national" of any of the contracting parties seems greatly disposed to attach himself to, say, the North Atlantic Treaty Organization or the Warsaw Pact.) Provincial chauvinism was intractable in the case of Robert E. Lee. It seems to be equally intractable today on the national level, when it is aroused against a national enemy. With rare exceptions—France and Germany come to mind, but not Poland and Russia—nationalist hatreds flourish today as fiercely as they ever did.

Thirty-five years ago, the atomic bomb appeared to have illuminated the human political condition almost as brilliantly as it had Hiroshima. Not only was no man an island; no island was an island. Previously sedate people were crying, "One world or none." Was President Harry Truman sounding the death knell of the nation-state when he said, after Hiroshima and Nagasaki, "There must never be another war"? (Five years later he decided to have one more for the road.) But if there was to be no more war, what would generate or regenerate the chauvinist passion? What would hold the nation-state together?

Before the year 1945 was out, everyone everywhere in the literate world was familiar, however vaguely, with the idea of world federalism or world government. In the United States the United World Federalists spread rapidly in intellectual circles and for a couple of seasons became the "in" thing socially. The lecturers were all lecturing for it except for the handful of world-government "maximalists" who rejected the federalists' minimal surrender of sovereignty; along with the minuscule Socialist Party, doughty little organizations like the Campaign for World Government maintained that a federated world which did not disturb the world-wide economic balance between rich and poor would collapse in civil war—or, likelier, never come to be. The UWF, or minimalist, position was presented as the only realism: since the rich Americans (and a few others similarly situated) would never join a world which taxed them to feed its starving hundreds of millions, federalism would have to freeze the world's stupendous economic imbalance. A world organization without the power to levy near-confiscatory income or capital taxes on the people of the rich nations was an impossibility, with it a hallucination.

Within five years, the world organizationalists—minimalist and maximalist alike—were succumbing to the joint pressures of the cold war abroad and McCarthyism at home. Within a decade of its birth, the world government movement was somewhere between dormant and dead, and a radically shrunken UWF had given up lobbying and undertaken long-term education instead. The toothless United Nations was early made a laughingstock by the successive Security Council vetos—first of the Soviet Union, then of the United States—and fast lost its hold on the public imagination. Naked cynicism characterized the unilateral moves of the several great powers in hot spots all over the world. When Mr. Reagan rejected the International Law of the Sea treaty he said blandly that "the 120"—the correct figure is 130— "nations who voted for the pact represent only about 12.5 per cent of the global gross national product."

Appomattox was the formal prelude to the conversion into one nation, indivisible, of the separate sovereign states dwelling together in more or less amiable anarchy until a crucial interest split them down the middle. But the substantive conversion had to wait until the adoption of the federal income tax recognized, at last, that it is not the states that constitute the nation but the people. State residence restrictions on welfare, employment, and electoral eligibility gave way, gradually, and with Lyndon Johnson's civil- and voting-rights legislation throwing the whole mantle of national protection over the politically disadvantaged blacks, it was tacitly conceded that the folly of the fifty states had to be ended.

The dismantlement (without a prior mantlement) of Mr. Reagan's New Federalism underscores the greatest single fact of the nation's political history and generates a faint spark of life in the moribund One World movement. As the anarchy of the New Federalism is intolerable in the nation, so the anarchy of the nations is intolerable in the world, intolerable among the hapless dwellers in the roofless house under the awful sky of the nuclear age. By now we ought to know what the ancients knew: that nations with no judge between them, no parliament to write the law that binds them both, and no executive to enforce that law, must fight when they cannot negotiate their differences. People talk about accidental war, but it is peace that is accidental. And there is only a modicum of hope that the accident of peace will long continue.

The swelling struggle in the European and American streets against the nuclear arms race betokens one of three alternative outcomes—the end of the world in nuclear war; a truce or cease-fire (or "freeze") doomed to go the way of every unenforceable truce before it; or the abdication of the classic and unexceptional device for rallying chauvinist passion, the sovereign national power to make war for the sole purpose of preserving the nation-state. That state, like Lee's Virginia, is indefensible theoretically, indefensible historically, and in 1983 mortally indefensible in fact.

Robert M. Hutchins used to say that what is necessary must be possible. Not necessarily. World government seems now to be urgently necessary to save the world. But it would not appear urgently possible to achieve. Most of the people of the world—the great preponderance of them—live as tribes ruled by chieftains or chieftainly apparatus. (Some of the tribes are vast, and many are anciently established as nation-states.) The members of these tribes have had little or no political experience or political responsibility. Their comprehension of government is limited, of self-government still more limited. A "democratic" world government would be dominated by those tribes or their chieftains and, if it did not succumb to civil war (which would leave us all where we are today), would certainly be a world tyranny. The best of the nation-states has both oppressive potentialities and oppressive tendencies. It is painful to make an argument for a still greater state than the one we know; the oppressive potentialities and tendencies of any and all states would be mightily magnified in the tribally dominated world state.

Not only would the rich members of that state be rabidly disinclined to support the poor, the civil liberties and civil rights inhering, by and large, in the rich nation-states would fall instantly in those same nation-states as the world political process supervened. As between tyranny and anarchy, on any scale, anarchy, when there is no third alternative, is the more palatable choice. But the likely tyranny of the world government, with the likely secessionist revolution against it by the one-time libertarian nation-states does not promise much more relief from the nuclear threat than the present anarchy and imposes, while it lasts, the additional inconveniences of tyranny.

The civil and political liberties of the libertarian nations are insecure. Liberty is always and everywhere insecure. But the few nations which have had the good fortune—it is nothing but fortune—to be schooled in it are much more surely attached to it than those that have not had the schooling. These latter that are long established have to go through that schooling before world government is thinkable, while the others, the newly established nations, are just beginning to have the national experience and are still delirious in their virginal chauvinism. Like our own thirteen colonies, the new nations are rebellious, not revolutionary.

Historian William H. McNeill says that "when and whether a transition will be made from a system of states to an empire of the earth is the gravest question humanity confronts." It will be a quantum leap, but some such analogous leap has been made before, long, slow, tortuous, from the tribal city to the tribal state. The race has pretty well rid itself of chattel slavery, and a fair part of it has pretty well rid itself of the profit system; these too are quantum leaps. War abides, war and the plurality of sovereign states which causes war. In five hundred years the peoples of the earth may be able to think of themselves as the people of the earth and of one world, indivisible, with liberty and justice for all. Five hundred years. Say a hundred. Say fifty. But war does not seem likely to wait five hundred years, or a hundred, or fifty (or five?). We are between the urgent necessity and the historical impossibility of world government right now; between the devil and the deep.

Suggestions for Discussion

1. The essay begins with a discussion of Robert E. Lee and the American Civil War. Is this an effective opening? Explain.

2. What is Mayer's estimate of the limitations as well as the usefulness of state government in contemporary America? How does he use the ideas of James Madison of Virginia to support his position? Why is Madison an effective person to refer to?

3. Why does Mayer single out Texans as different from other Americans? On the other hand, how does he find them like other Americans?

4. Mayer argues that it is easier for integrity to survive in national government than in state government. Explain his position.

5. Discuss Mayer's attitude toward the New Federalism. What does he mean by the term "Reaganism"? What larger use, however, does Mayer see for the New Federalism?

6. Explain how Mayer equates states' rights with national rights. What is the equation he establishes?

7. Why, according to Mayer, did the movement for World Federalism fail after 1945? What conditions make the idea of One World possible today?

8. What positive advantages does Mayer foresee from World Federalism? Why does he believe that we must move toward it sooner than later?

9. How does Mayer use language to establish the tone of this essay? What is its tone? Is this a hopeful essay?

Suggestion for Writing

Write an essay describing the strong nationalist feelings which stand in the way of united world government. Use several countries as examples. Does world government seem an unrealistic dream?

George Orwell

The Principles of Newspeak

George Orwell (1903–1950), pseudonym of Eric Arthur Blair, a British writer with socialist sympathies, wrote essays and novels based on his experiences as a British imperial policeman in Burma, as an impoverished writer in Paris and London, and as a volunteer in the republican army in the Spanish Civil War. He was for a few years the editor of the magazine of the British Labour Party. Although his essays and letters are considered masterpieces of prose style, he is probably best known for the satirical anticommunist fable *Animal Farm* (1945) and for the novel *1984* published in 1949. Orwell conceived a terrifying vision of a future where mechanized language and thought have become the tools of a totalitarian society. This essay, written as an appendix to *1984,* presents "Newspeak," the official language of Oceania, as the logical outcome and instrument of a repressive government. It also suggests the Newspeak has its basis in what Orwell considered our degradation of the English language.

Newspeak was the official language of Oceania and had been devised to meet the ideological needs of Ingsoc, or English Socialism. In the year 1984 there was not as yet anyone who used Newspeak as his sole means of communication, either in speech or writing. The leading articles in the *Times* were written in it, but this was a tour de force which could only be carried out by a specialist. It was expected that Newspeak would have finally superseded Oldspeak (or Standard English, as we should call it) by about the year 2050. Meanwhile it gained ground steadily, all Party members tending to use Newspeak words and grammatical constructions more and more in their everyday speech. The version in use in 1984, and embodied in the Ninth and Tenth Editions of the Newspeak dictionary, was a provisional one, and contained many superfluous words and archaic formations which were due to be suppressed later. It is with the final, perfected version, as embodied in the Eleventh Edition of the dictionary, that we are concerned here.

The purpose of Newspeak was not only to provide a medium of expression for the world-view and mental habits proper to the devotees of Ingsoc, but to make all other modes of thought impossible. It was intended that when Newspeak had been adopted once and for all and Oldspeak forgotten, a heretical thought—that is, a thought diverging from the principles of Ingsoc—should be literally unthinkable, at least so far as thought is dependent on words. Its vocabulary was so constructed as to give exact and often very subtle expression to every meaning that a Party member could properly wish to express, while excluding all other meanings and also the possibility of arriving at them by indirect methods. This was done partly by the invention of new words, but chiefly by eliminating undesirable words and by stripping such words as remained of unorthodox meanings, and so far as possible of all secondary meanings whatever. To give a single example. The word *free* still existed in Newspeak, but it could only be used in such statements as "This dog is free from lice" or "This field is free from weeds." It could not be used in its old sense of "politically free" or "intellectually free," since political and intellectual freedom no longer existed even as concepts, and were therefore of necessity nameless. Quite apart from the suppression of definitely heretical works, reduction of vocabulary was regarded as an end in itself, and no word that could be dispensed with was allowed to survive. Newspeak was designed not to extend but to *diminish* the range of thought, and this purpose was indirectly assisted by cutting the choice of words down to a minimum.

Newspeak was founded on the English language as we now know it, though many Newspeak sentences, even when not containing newly created words, would be barely intelligible to an English-speaker of our own day. Newspeak words were divided into three distinct classes, known as the A vocabulary, the B vocabulary (also called compound words), and the C vocabulary. It will be simpler to discuss each class separately, but the grammatical peculiarities of the language can be dealt with in the section devoted to the A vocabulary, since the same rules held good for all three categories.

The A vocabulary. The A vocabulary consisted of the words needed for the business of everyday life—for such things as eating, drinking, working, putting on one's clothes, going up and down stairs, riding in vehicles, gardening, cooking, and the like. It was composed almost entirely of words that we already possess—words like *hit, run, dog, tree, sugar, house, field*—but in comparison with the present-day English vocabulary, their number was extremely small, while their meanings were far more rigidly defined. All ambiguities and shades of meaning had been purged out of them. So far as it could be achieved, a Newspeak word of this class was simply a staccato sound expressing *one* clearly understood concept. It would have been quite impossible to use the A vocabulary for literary purposes or for political or philosophical discussion. It was intended only to express simple, purposive thoughts, usually involving concrete objects or physical actions.

The grammar of Newspeak had two outstanding peculiarities. The first of these was an almost complete interchangeability between different parts of speech. Any word in the language (in principle this applied even to very abstract words such as *if* or *when*) could be used either as verb, noun, adjective, or adverb. Between the verb and the noun form, when they were of the same root, there was never any variation, this rule of itself involving the destruction of many archaic forms. The word *thought,* for example, did not exist in Newspeak. Its place was taken by *think,* which did duty for both noun and verb. No etymological principle was involved here; in some cases it was the original noun that was chosen for retention, in other cases the verb. Even where a noun and a verb of kindred meaning were not etymologically connected, one or other of them was frequently suppressed. There was, for example, no such word as *cut,* its meaning being sufficiently covered by the noun-verb *knife.* Adjectives were formed by adding the suffix *-ful* to the noun-verb, and adverbs by adding *-wise.* Thus, for example, *speedful* meant "rapid" and *speedwise* meant "quickly." Certain of our present-day adjectives, such as *good, strong, big, black, soft,* were retained, but their total number was very small. There was little need for them, since almost any adjectival meaning could be arrived at by adding *-ful* to a noun-verb. None of the now-existing adverbs was retained, except for a very few already ending in *-wise;* the *-wise* termination was invariable. The word *well,* for example, was replaced by *goodwise.*

In addition, any word—this again applied in principle to every word in the language—could be negatived by adding the affix *un-,* or could be strengthened by the affix *plus-,* or, for still greater emphasis, *doubleplus-.* Thus, for example, *uncold* meant "warm," while *pluscold* and *doublepluscold* meant, respectively, "very cold" and "superlatively cold." It was also possible, as in present-day English, to modify the meaning of almost any word by prepositional affixes such as *ante-, post-, up-, down-,* etc. By such methods it was found possible to bring about an enormous diminution of vocabulary. Given, for instance, the word *good,* there was no need for such a word as bad, since the required meaning was equally well—indeed, better—expressed by *ungood.* All that was necessary, in any case where two words formed a natural pair of opposites, was to decide which of them to suppress. *Dark,* for example, could be replaced by *unlight,* or *light* by *undark,* according to preference.

The second distinguishing mark of Newspeak grammar was its regularity. Subject to a few exceptions which are mentioned below, all inflections followed the same rules. Thus, in all verbs the preterite and the past participle were the same and ended in *-ed.* The preterite of *steal* was *stealed,* the preterite of *think* was *thinked,* and so on throughout the language, all such forms as *swam, gave, brought, spoke, taken,* etc., being abolished. All plurals were made by adding *-s* or *-es* as the case might be. The plurals of *man, ox, life* were *mans, oxes, lifes.* Comparison of adjectives was invariably made by adding -er, -est (good, gooder, goodest), irregular forms and the *more, most* formation being suppressed.

The only classes of words that were still allowed to inflect irregularly were the pronouns, the relatives, the demonstrative adjectives, and the auxiliary verbs. All of these followed their ancient usage, except that *whom* had been scrapped as unnecessary, and the *shall, should* tenses had been dropped, all their uses being covered by *will* and *would*. There were also certain irregularities in word-formation arising out of the need for rapid and easy speech. A word which was difficult to utter, or was liable to be incorrectly heard, was held to be ipso facto a bad word; occasionally therefore, for the sake of euphony, extra letters were inserted into a word or an archaic formation was retained. But this need made itself felt chiefly in connection with the B vocabulary. *Why* so great an importance was attached to ease of pronunciation will be made clear later in this essay.

The B vocabulary. The B vocabulary consisted of words which had been deliberately constructed for political purposes: words, that is to say, which not only had in every case a political implication, but were intended to impose a desirable mental attitude upon the person using them. Without a full understanding of the principles of Ingsoc it was difficult to use these words correctly. In some cases they could be translated into Oldspeak, or even into words taken from the A vocabulary, but this usually demanded a long paraphrase and always involved the loss of certain overtones. The B words were a sort of verbal shorthand, often packing whole ranges of ideas into a few syllables, and at the same time more accurate and forcible than ordinary language.

The B words were in all cases compound words.* They consisted of two or more words, or portions of words, welded together in an easily pronounceable form. The resulting amalgam was always a noun-verb, and inflected according to the ordinary rules. To take a single example: the word *goodthink*, meaning, very roughly, "orthodoxy," or, if one chose to regard it as a verb, "to think in an orthodox manner." This inflected as follows: noun-verb, *goodthink;* past tense and past participle, *goodthinked;* present participle, *goodthinking;* adjective, *goodthinkful;* adverb, *goodthinkwise;* verbal noun, *goodthinker.*

The B words were not constructed on any etymological plan. The words of which they were made up could be any parts of speech, and could be placed in any order and mutilated in any way which made them easy to pronounce while indicating their derivation. In the word *crimethink* (thoughtcrime), for instance, the *think* came second, whereas in *thinkpol* (Thought Police) it came first, and in the latter word police had lost its second syllable. Because of the greater difficulty in securing euphony, irregular formations were commoner in the B vocabulary than in the A vocabulary. For example, the adjectival forms of *Minitrue, Minipax,* and *Miniluv* were, respectively, *Minitruthful, Minipeaceful,* and *Minilovely,* simply because *-trueful, paxful, and loveful* were slightly awkward to pronounce. In principle, however, all B words could inflect, and all inflected in exactly the same way.

Some of the B words had highly subtilized meanings, barely intellibile to anyone who had not mastered the language as a whole. Consider, for exam-

---

*Compound words, such as *speakwrite,* were of course to be found in the A vocabulary, but these were merely convenient abbreviations and had no special ideological color.

ple, such a typical sentence from a *Times* leading article as *Oldthinkers un-bellyfeel Ingsoc*. The shortest rendering that one could make of this in Old-speak would be: "Those whose ideas were formed before the Revolution can-not have a full emotional understanding of the principles of English Social-ism." But this is not an adequate translation. To begin with, in order to grasp the full meaning of the Newspeak sentence quoted above, one would have to have a clear idea of what is meant by *Ingsoc*. And, in addition, only a person thoroughly grounded in Ingsoc could appreciate the full force of the word *bellyfeel*, which implied a blind, enthusiastic acceptance difficult to imagine today; or of the word *oldthink*, which was inextricably mixed up with the idea of wickedness and decadence. But the special function of certain Newspeak words, of which *oldthink* was one, was not so much to express meanings as to destroy them. These words, necessarily few in number, had had their meanings extended until they contained within themselves whole batteries of words which, as they were sufficiently covered by a single com-prehensive term, could now be scrapped and forgotten. The greatest difficulty facing the compilers of the Newspeak dictionary was not to invent new words, but, having invented them, to make sure what they meant: to make sure, that is to say, what ranges of words they canceled by their existence.

As we have already seen in the case of the word *free*, words which had once borne a heretical meaning were sometimes retained for the sake of con-venience, but only with the undesirable meanings purged out of them. Countless other words such as *honor, justice, morality, internationalism, de-mocracy, science*, and *religion* had simply ceased to exist. A few blanket words covered them, and, in covering them, abolished them. All words grouping themselves round the concepts of liberty and equality, for instance, were contained in the single word *crimethink*, while all words grouping them-selves round the concepts of objectivity and rationalism were contained in the single word *oldthink*. Greater precision would have been dangerous. What was required in a Party member was an outlook similar to that of the ancient Hebrew who knew, without knowing much else, that all nations other than his own worshipped "false gods." He did not need to know that these gods were called Baal, Osiris, Moloch, Ashtaroth, and the like; probably the less he knew about them the better for his orthodoxy. He knew Jehovah and the commandments of Jehovah; he knew, therefore, that all gods with other names or other attributes were false gods. In somewhat the same way, the Party member knew what constituted right conduct, and in exceedingly vague, generalized terms he knew what kinds of departure from it were pos-sible. His sexual life, for example, was entirely regulated by the two New-speak words *sexcrime* (sexual immorality) and *goodsex* (chastity). *Sexcrime* covered all sexual misdeeds whatever. It covered fornication, adultery, ho-mosexuality, and other perversions, and in addition, normal intercourse prac-ticed for its own sake. There was no need to enumerate them separately, since they were all equally culpable, and, in principle, all punishable by death. In the C vocabulary, which consisted of scientific and technical words, it might be necessary to give specialized names to certain sexual aberrations, but the ordinary citizen had no need of them. He knew what was meant by *goodsex*—that is to say, normal intercourse between man and wife, for the sole purpose of begetting children, and without physical pleasure on the part of the woman; all else was *sexcrime*. In Newspeak it was seldom possible to follow a heretical thought further than the perception that it *was* heretical; beyond that point the necessary words were nonexistent.

No word in the B vocabulary was ideologically neutral. A great many were euphemisms. Such words, for instance, as *joycamp* (forced-labor camp) or *Minipax* (Ministry of Peace, i. e., Ministry of War) meant almost the exact opposite of what they appeared to mean. Some words, on the other hand, displayed a frank and contemptuous understanding of the real nature of Oceanic society. An example was *prolefeed*, meaning the rubbishy entertainment and spurious news which the Party handed out to the masses. Other words, again, were ambivalent, having the connotation "good" when applied to the Party and "bad" when applied to its enemies. But in addition there were great numbers of words which at first sight appeared to be mere abbreviations and which derived their ideological color not from their meaning but from their structure.

So far as it could be contrived, everything that had or might have political significance of any kind was fitted into the B vocabulary. The name of every organization, or body of people, or doctrine, or country, or institution, or public building, was invariably cut down into the familiar shape; that is, a single easily pronounced word with the smallest number of syllables that would preserve the original derivation. In the Ministry of Truth, for example, the Records Department, in which Winston Smith worked, was called *Recdep*, the Fiction Department was called *Ficdep*, the Teleprograms Department was called *Teledep*, and so on. This was not done solely with the object of saving time. Even in the early decades of the twentieth century, telescoped words and phrases had been one of the characteristic features of political language; and it had been noticed that the tendency to use abbreviations of this kind was most marked in totalitarian countries and totalitarian organizations. Examples were such words as *Nazi, Gestapo, Comintern, Inprecorr, Agitprop*. In the beginning the practice had been adopted as it were instinctively, but in Newspeak it was used with a conscious purpose. It was perceived that in thus abbreviating a name one narrowed and subtly altered its meaning, by cutting out most of the associations that would otherwise cling to it. The words *Communist International*, for instance, call up a composite picture of universal human brotherhood, red flags, barricades, Karl Marx, and the Paris Commune. The word Comintern, on the other hand, suggests merely a tightly knit organization and a well-defined body of doctrine. It refers to something almost as easily recognized, and as limited in purpose, as a chair or a table. *Comintern* is a word that can be uttered almost without taking thought, whereas *Comminust International* is a phrase over which one is obliged to linger at least momentarily. In the same way, the associations called up by a word like *Minitrue* are fewer and more controllable that those called up by *Ministry of Truth*. This accounted not only for the habit of abbreviating whenever possible, but also for the almost exaggerated care that was taken to make every word easily pronounceable.

In Newspeak, euphony outweighed every consideration other than exactitude of meaning. Regularity of grammar was always sacrificed to it when it seemed necessary. And rightly so, since what was required, above all for political purposes, were short clipped words of unmistakable meaning which could be uttered rapidly and which roused the minimum of echoes in the speaker's mind. The words of the B vocabulary even gained in force from the fact that nearly all of them were very much alike. Almost invariably these words—*good-think, Minipax, prolefeed, sexcrime, joycamp, Ingsoc, bellyfeel, thinkpol,* and countless others—were words of two or three syllables, with the stress distributed equally between the first syllable and the last. The use of them encouraged a gabbling style of speech, at once staccato and monotonous. And this was exactly what was aimed at. The intention was to make speech, and especially speech on any subject not ideologically neutral, as nearly as possible independent of consciousness. For that purpose of everyday life it was no doubt necessary, or sometimes necessary, to reflect before speaking, but a Party member called upon to make a political or ethical judgment should be able to spray forth the correct opinions as automatically as a machine gun spraying forth bullets. His training fitted him to do this, the language gave him an almost foolproof instrument, and the texture of the words, with their harsh sound and a certain willful ugliness which was in accord with the spirit of Ingsoc, assisted the process still further.

So did the fact of having very few words to choose from. Relative to our own, the Newspeak vocabulary was tiny, and new ways of reducing it were constantly being devised. Newspeak, indeed, differed from almost all other languages in that its vocabulary grew smaller instead of larger every year. Each reduction was a gain, since the smaller the area of choice, the smaller the temptation to take thought. Ultimately it was hoped to make articulate speech issue from the larynx without involving the higher brain centers at all. This aim was frankly admitted in the Newspeak word *duckspeak,* meaning "to quack like a duck." Like various other words in the B vocabulary, *duckspeak* was ambivalent in meaning. Provided that the opinions which were quacked out were orthodox ones, it implied nothing but praise, and when the *Times* referred to one of the orators of the Party as a *double-plusgood duckspeaker* it was paying a warm and valued compliment.

The C vocabulary. The C vocabulary was supplementary to the others and consisted entirely of scientific and technical terms. These resembled the scientific terms in use today, and were constructed from the same roots, but the usual care was taken to define them rigidly and strip them of undesirable meanings. They followed the same grammatical rules as the words in the other two vocabularies. Very few of the C words had any currency either in everyday speech or in political speech. Any scientific worker or technician could find all the words he needed in the list devoted to his own speciality, but he seldom had more than a smattering of the words occurring in the other lists. Only a very few words were common to all lists, and there was no vocabulary expressing the function of Science as a habit of mind, or a method of thought, irrespective of its particular branches. There was, indeed, no word for "Science," any meaning that it could possibly bear being already sufficiently covered by the word *Ingsoc.*

From the foregoing account it will be seen that in Newspeak the expression of unorthodox opinions, above a very low level, was well-nigh impossible. It was of course possible to utter heresies of a very crude kind, a species of blasphemy. It would have been possible, for example, to say *Big Brother is ungood.* But this statement, which to an orthodox ear merely conveyed a self-evident absurdity, could not have been sustained by reasoned argument, because the necessary words were not available. Ideas inimical to Ingsoc could only be entertained in a vague wordless form, and could only be named in very broad terms which lumped together and condemned whole groups of heresies without defining them in doing so. One could, in fact, only use Newspeak for unorthodox purposes by illegitimately translating some of the words back into Oldspeak. For example, *All mans are equal* was a possible Newspeak sentence, but only in the same sense in which *All men are red-haired* is a possible Oldspeak sentence. It did not contain a grammatical error, but it expressed a palpable untruth, i.e., that all men are of equal size, weight, or strength. The concept of political equality no longer existed, and the secondary meaning had accordingly been purged out of the word *equal*. In 1984, when Oldspeak was still the normal means of communication, the danger theoretically existed that in using Newspeak words one might remember their original meanings. In practice it was not difficult for any person well grounded in *doublethink* to avoid doing this, but within a couple of generations even the possibility of such a lapse would have vanished. A person growing up with Newspeak as his sole language would no more know that *equal* had once had the secondary meaning of "politically equal," or that *free* had once meant "intellectually free," than, for instance, a person who had never heard of chess would be aware of the secondary meanings attaching to *queen* and *rook*. There would be many crimes and errors which it would be beyond his power to commit, simply because they were nameless and therefore unimaginable. And it was to be foreseen that with the passage of time the distinguishing characteristics of Newspeak would become more and more pronounced—its words growing fewer and fewer, their meanings more and more rigid, and the chance of putting them to improper uses always diminishing.

When Oldspeak had been once and for all superseded, the last link with the past would have been severed. History had already been rewritten, but fragments of the literature of the past survived here and there, imperfectly censored, and so long as one retained one's knowledge of Oldspeak it was possible to read them. In the future such fragments, even if they chanced to survive, would be unintelligible and untranslatable. It was impossible to translate any passage of Oldspeak into Newspeak unless it either referred to some techincal process or some very simple everyday action, or was already orthodox (*goodthinkful* would be the Newspeak expression) in tendency. In practice this meant that no book written before approximately 1960 could be translated as a whole. Prerevolutionary literature could only be subjected to ideological translation—that is, alteration in sense as well as language. Take for example the well-known passage from the Declaration of Independence:

> We hold these truths to be self-evident, that all men are created equal, that they are endowed by their Creator with certain inalienable rights, that among these are life, liberty and the pursuit of happiness. That to secure these rights, Governments are instituted among men, deriving their powers from the consent of the governed. That whenever any form of Government becomes destructive of those ends, it is the right of the People to alter or abolish it, and to institute new Government . . .

It would have been quite impossible to render this into Newspeak while keeping to the sense of the original. The nearest one could come to doing so would be to swallow the whole passage up in the single word *crimethink*. A full translation could only be an ideological translation, whereby Jefferson's words would be changed into a panegyric on absolute government.

A good deal of the literature of the past was, indeed, already being transformed in this way. Considerations of prestige made it desirable to preserve the memory of certain historical figures, while at the same time bringing their achievements into line with the philosophy of Ingsoc. Various writers, such as Shakespeare, Milton, Swift, Byron, Dickens, and some others were therefore in process of translation; when the task had been completed, their original writings, with all else that survived of the literature of the past, would be destroyed. These translations were a slow and difficult business, and it was not expected that they would be finished before the first or second decade of the twenty-first century. There were also large quantities of merely utilitarian literature—indispensable technical manuals and the like—that had to be treated in the same way. It was chiefly in order to allow time for the preliminary work of translation that the final adoption of Newspeak had been fixed for so late a date as 2050.

Suggestions for Discussion

1. Explain Orwell's statement that Newspeak was designed to "diminish the range of thought." How does he demonstrate this statement by the use of the word *free?*

2. Summarize the uses of the A Vocabulary. Contrast it with present-day English and discuss the former's use of the parts of speech. Why are verbs usually suppressed? Why were most existing adverbs abolished? Why were all noun plurals formed by adding -s or -es?

3. Define the B Vocabulary. What were its uses? Discuss the examples given, particularly the sentence, "Oldthinkers unbellyfeel Ingsoc."

4. What difficulties faced the compilers of the Newspeak dictionary?

5. What are the precedents for Newspeak word combinations such as *Recdep* and *Ficdep?* What comment on current standard English does Orwell make here?

6. How does the word *duckspeak* symbolize the purpose of Newspeak?

7. What are the uses of the C Vocabulary? Why did the word *science* cease to exist?

8. Discuss the sentences, "Big Brother is ungood" and "All mans are equal" as examples of Newspeak.

9. What is the Newspeak equivalent of the opening passage of the Declaration of Independence? Discuss Orwell's reasons for inventing this translation. Relate the translation to the entire essay.

Suggestions for Writing

1. Examine your local newspaper for examples of words that resemble Newspeak and write an essay discussing the reasons for your choice.

2. Write an essay explaining how Newspeak is an instrument of power. Why is it a necessary ideal of Oceania? Discuss some words or sentences from contemporary political speeches or essays which come close to Newspeak.

Irving Howe

Enigmas of Power: George Orwell's *1984* Reconsidered

Irving Howe (b. 1920) is a Distinguished Professor in the Graduate Center of the City University of New York. He is an important literary critic as well as an analyst of American life and politics. An editor of the magazine *Dissent,* he has written many books including *William Faulkner: A Critical Study* (1952), *Politics and the Novel* (1957), *The Critical Point* (1973), and *A Margin of Hope: An Intellectual Biography* (1982). This essay, originally published in *The New Republic* and reprinted in *1984 Revisited,* edited by Howe, offers a brilliant reevaluation of Orwell's novel based on Howe's observations of modern political history.

It is a common experience to fear that the admirations of one's youth will wear thin, and precisely because *1984* had so enormous an impact on me when it first came out more than thirty years ago, I hesitated for a long time before returning to it. I can still remember the turbulent feelings—the bottomless dismay, the sense of being undone—with which many people first read Orwell's book. My fear now was that it would seem a passing sensation of its moment or even, as some leftist critics have charged, a mere reflex of the cold war. But these fears were groundless. Having reread *1984,* I am convinced, more than ever, that it is a classic of our age.

Whether it is also a classic for the ages is another question. What people of the future will think about Orwell's book we cannot know, nor can we say what it might mean to those who will remember so little about the time of totalitarianism they will need an editor's gloss if they chance upon a copy. But for us, children of this century, the relation to *1984* must be intimate, troubled, nerve-wracking. In 1938 or 1939 the idea of a world divided among a few totalitarian superpowers, which Orwell made into the premise of his book, had not seemed at all farfetched. I remember hushed conversations about the possible shape of a world dominated by Hitler and Stalin, with perhaps a shrinking enclave of democracy in North America. Such nightmare visions seemed entirely real during the years just before the war, and with sufficient reason. When Orwell published his book a decade later, in 1949, one felt that, despite his obvious wish to unnerve us with an extreme version of the total state, he was presenting something all too familiar, even commonplace.

Also familiar, though in a somewhat different sense, was a body of detail about daily life in Oceania that Orwell built up. Many of the descriptive passages in *1984* were simply taken over, with a degree of stretching here and there, from Orwell's earlier books or from his life-long caustic observations of twentieth-century England. In a review for the London *Times Literary Supplement* Julian Symons keenly remarked that

> In some ways life [in the Oceania of *1984*] does not differ very much from the life we live now. The pannikin of pinkish-grey stew, the hunk of bread and cube of cheese, the mug of milkless Victory coffee with its saccharine tablet—that is the kind of meal we may very well remember; and the pleasures of recognition

are roused, too, by the description of Victory gin (reserved for the privileged—the "proles" drink beer), which has "a sickly oily smell, as of Chinese rice-spirit," and gives to those who drink it "the sensation of being hit on the back of the head with a rubber club." We can generally view projections of the future with detachment because they seem to refer to people altogether unlike ourselves. By creating a world in which the "proles" still have their sentimental songs and their beer, and the privileged consume their Victory gin, Orwell involves us most skilfully and uncomfortably in his story. . . .

Symons might have added that in Orwell's earlier writing he had already focused almost obsessively on the gritty discomforts of urban life, the bad smells, the sour tastes, the grimy streets, the filthy rooms, the sweat-stained bodies. As it turned out, the unfuture of Oceania had some pretty keen resemblances to the immediate past of England.

Resemblances, also, to the years of Stalinist terror in Russia. The grilling of Winston Smith by the Oceania authorities, the alternation between physical beatings and sympathetic conversations, the final terrifying appearance of O'Brien, master of power—all these recall or parallel Arthur Koestler's account in *Darkness at Noon* of how the N.K.V.D interrogated its victims. Koestler's description, in turn, anticipated closely what we have since learned about the methods of the Soviet secret police. It was to Orwell's credit that he understood how the imagination flourishes when it is grounded in common reality.

He knew, as well, that to make credible the part of his book that would spiral into the extraordinary, he had first to provide it with a strong foundation of the ordinary. Or to put it another way, he knew that his main problem was to make plausible—which, one might remember, is not the same as probable—his vision of how certain destructive tendencies of modern society could drive insanely forward, unbraked by sentiments of humaneness or prudence.

Yet while rereading *1984* I have come to recognize still another way in which it all seems decidedly familiar—but *this* familiarity causes shock.

The very idea of a totally controlled society in which a self-perpetuating elite rules through terror and ideology no longer strikes us as either a dim horror or a projection of the paranoid mind. In the few decades since Orwell wrote, we have gone a long way toward domesticating the idea of the total state, indeed, to the point where it now seems just one among a number of options concerning the way men live. The thought that totalitarianism is a constant, even commonplace possibility in the history of our time—this may prove to be as terrifying as the prospect that we might sooner or later be living under an Orwellian regime. No sensible person could have taken *1984* as an actual prediction; even those who read the book with malice or loathing knew it had to be taken as a warning, no doubt a fearful warning. That in its fundamental conception it should now seem so familiar, so plausible, is—when you come to think of it—a deeply unnerving fact about the time in which we live. But a fact it is.

To ask what kind of book *1984* is may seem a strange, even pedantic question. After all, you might say, millions of people have read the book and appreciated it well enough without troubling their heads about fine points of genre. Yet the question is neither strange nor pedantic, since in my experience there remains among Orwell's readers a good portion of uncertainty and confusion about what he was trying to do. People will often say, "Look, we're getting close to the year 1984 and we aren't living in the kind of society Orwell summoned—doesn't that mean he was exaggerating or even perhaps that he was morbid?" To this kind of complaint there is a simple enough answer: it's in the very nature of anti-utopian fiction to project a degree of exaggeration, since without exaggeration the work would be no more than still another realistic portrait of totalitarian society.

Other complaints, being more sophisticated, take on a "literary" edge. One of them, still often heard, is that the book contains no "real characters," or that there isn't enough of a credible social setting, or that the psychological vision of the story is somewhat rudimentary. Such complaints have really to do with genres or misunderstandings of genres; they reflect a failure to grasp the kind of fiction Orwell was writing and what could legitimately be expected from it. When a critic like Raymond Williams says that *1984* lacks "a substantial society and correspondingly substantial persons," he is (almost willfully, one suspects) missing the point. For the very premise of anti-utopian fiction is that it sketch an "inconceivable" world in such a way as to force us, provisionally, to credit its conceivability; that it project a world in which categories like "substantial society . . . substantial persons" have largely been suppressed or rendered obsolete. In actuality a society like that of Oceania may be impossible to realize, but that is not at issue here. A writer may, in the kind of fiction Orwell was composing, draw the shadows of "the impossible" as if they were real possibilities—if only in order to persuade us that finally these are not possible. As it happens, we have come close enough during the last half-century to a society like Oceania for the prospect of its realization to be within reach of the imagination. And that is all a writer of fiction needs.

There are kinds of fictions that should not really be called novels at all: think of Voltaire's *Candide*, Swift's *Gulliver's Travels*, Peacock's *Crotchet Castle*. Northrop Frye, hoping, probably in vain, to check the modern tendency to lump all fictions as novels, describes a kind of fiction he calls Menippean satire, "allegedly invented by a Greek cynic named Menippus." This fiction "deals less with people as such than with mental attitudes . . . and differs from the novel in its characterization, which is stylized rather than naturalistic. . . ."

A quarter of a century ago, when first writing about *1984*, I thought this a satisfactory description of the kind of book Orwell had composed; but now I would like to modify that opinion. Almost everyone has recognized how brilliant Orwell was in finding symbolic vehicles and dramatic instances through which to render the "mental attitudes" about which Frye speaks. Think only of Newspeak and Big Brother, Hate Week and Memory Hole, all of which have entered our speech and consciousness as vivid figures. (A few years ago I visited a Canadian university where the wicked students had baptized a new campus building—vast, windowless, cement-ugly—as the Ministry of Love; and so, I am certain, it will be called for decades to come.) There remains, then, good reason to see *1984* as an instance of "Menippean satire"—but only in part.

For in going back to the book I have learned to appreciate parts that now strike me as novelistic in the usual sense. Especially those parts in which Winston Smith and Julia try to find for themselves a patch, a corner where they can be alone and make love. Here bits of individuality begin to make themselves felt: Julia's boldness, for instance, in arranging their escapade to the country, where they can be free of the hated telescreen, or her charming indifference to all ideologies, as when she falls asleep during Winston's excited reading from the forbidden book, Emanuel Goldstein's *Theory and Practise of Oligarchical Collectivism.*

I now think that *1984* ought to be read as a mixture of genres, mostly Menippean satire and conventional novel, but also bits of tract and a few touches of transposed romance. Such a description may be helpful, though not because anyone is foolish enough to want exact categories; it may train us, at the least, to avoid false expectations when we read.

An anti-utopian fiction must have a touch or two of excess. There has to be a story that takes the familiar conventions of the once-fashionable utopian novel and stands them on their heads. Elsewhere I've described that touch of excess as

> the dramatic strategy and narrative psychology of "one more step" . . . one step beyond our known reality—not so much a picture of modern totalitarianism as an extension, by just one and no more than one step, of the essential pattern of the total state.

But this excess can of course consist of more than one step, it might be two or three—yet not many more than two or three, since then the link of credence between writer and reader might be broken by a piling-on of improbabilities.

What has especially struck me in rereading *1984* is that, yes, it's true that in an anti-utopian fiction the writer can afford at most a few steps beyond our known reality, but he is likely to achieve his strongest effects precisely at the moment when the balance teeters between minimal credence and plummeting disbelief. For at such a moment, we ask ourselves, can things *really* go this far?, and it is then that our deepest anxieties are aroused. Is it conceivable that the total state could be so "total," could break and transform human beings so far beyond what "human nature" may be expected to endure? We think and hope not, but we cannot be certain. We know that the total state has already done things earlier generations would have supposed to be impossible.

One such moment occurs in *1984* when Orwell turns to sexuality in Oceania. Members of the Outer Party—we remain in the dark about the Inner Party—are shown to be trained systematically to minimize and deny the sexual instinct, certainly to separate the act of intercourse from sensual pleasure or imaginative play. There can be no "free space" in the lives of the Outer Party faithful, nothing that remains beyond the command of the state. Sexual energy is to be transformed into political violence and personal hysteria. The proles are permitted to drift into promiscuity, their very sloth and sleaziness a seeming guarantee against rebellion, but members of the Outer Party caught in promiscuous relations with one another face the most stringent penalties.

About all this Orwell is very careful: "The aim of the Party was not merely to prevent men and women from forming loyalties which it might not be able to control. Its real, undeclared purpose was to remove all pleasure from the sexual act. Not love so much as eroticism was the enemy, inside marriage as well as outside. . . . Sexual intercourse was to be looked upon as a slightly disgusting minor operation. . . . The Party was trying to kill the sex instinct or, if it could not be killed, then to distort and dirty it. . . ."

It remains a fascinating question whether Orwell had captured here an essential part of the totalitarian outlook or had gone too far beyond "one more step." We know that in the years of Stalinism the Soviet Union favored, at least publicly, a prudish, sometimes a repressive antisexuality. But there is no evidence that during those years—and this is the period upon which Orwell drew for his book—Communist Party members were forced to suffer greater sexual repressiveness than the rest of the population. If the evidence is skimpy, Orwell was nonetheless touching on something very important; he was taking an imaginative leap from totalitarian "first principles" concerning, not so much sex, certainly not sex in its own right but the threat of "free space," that margin of personal autonomy that even in the worst moments of Stalinism and Hitlerism some people still wanted to protect. And it was this margin that Orwell took to be the single great "flaw" of all previous efforts to realize the totalitarian vision. Whether a complete or "total" totalitarianism is possible, or possible for any length of time, is not, I want to repeat, the question. All that matters, for our purposes, is that it be plausible enough to allow a fictional representation.

Winston Smith's journey from rebellion to breakdown is a doomed effort to recover the idea, perhaps even more than the experience, of a personal self; to regain the possibility of individual psychology and the memory of free introspection. And this occurs in *1984*—I think it is one of Orwell's greatest strokes!—not so much through ratiocination as through an encounter between two bodies. When Winston Smith and Julia make their first escapade out of London, carefully finding a patch in the woods where they can make love, they are not "in love," at least not yet. What happens between them is only— only!—the meeting of two eager bodies, animal-like if you must, but wonderfully urgent, alive, and good. They are free from the grip of the Party: this moment is theirs.

In this and a few other sections Orwell writes with a kind of grieving, muted lyricism, a hoarse lyricism that is about as much as, under the circumstances, he can allow himself. I have found myself moved, far more than when I first read the book, by these brief and abashed celebrations of the body. A little freer in our language than in 1949, we would now say that Julia is a woman who likes to fuck, and it seems important to put it exactly that way, since in the wretched precincts of Oceania just about the best that anyone can do is fucking.

Bolder still than Orwell's strategy of "one more step" in treating sexuality is his treatment of power. He tends to see the lust for power as a root experience, something that need not or cannot be explained in terms other than itself, and here too, I think, the passage of time has largely confirmed his intuitions. Let me draw upon your patience for a minute as I recall certain criticisms made by admiring critics of Orwell soon after *1984* came out. Philip Rahv, in a fine essay-review of the book, said that in one respect Orwell may have surpassed even Dostoevsky in grasping "the dialectic of power." *The Brothers Karamazov* shows the Grand Inquisitor as a tyrant ruling from benevolent intent: he believes man to be a weak creature who needs the lash for his own good and can be happy only when the burden of freedom is lifted from his back. During the interrogation conducted by O'Brien, Winston Smith, hoping to appease his tormentor, repeats the Grand Inquisitor's rationale for the holding of power:

> That the Party did not seek power for its own ends, but only for the good of the majority. That it sought power because men in the mass were frail, cowardly creatures who could not endure liberty or face the truth. . . . That the choice for mankind lay between freedom and happiness, and that, for the great bulk of mankind, happiness was better. That the Party was the eternal guardian of the weak, a dedicated sect doing evil that good might come, sacrificing its own happiness to that of others.

All of this strikes O'Brien as mere cant, he scorns it as "stupid." Turning up the dial of the machine that regulates Winston Smith's pain, he chastizes him in these memorable words:

> The Party seeks power for its own sake. We are not interested in the good of others; we are interested solely in power. . . . One does not establish a dictatorship in order to safeguard a revolution; one makes a revolution in order to establish a dictatorship. The object of persecution is persecution. The object of torture is torture. The object of power is power. . . . Power is in inflicting pain and humiliation. Power is in tearing human minds to pieces and putting them together again in new shapes of your own choosing.

This exchange forms a key passage in *1984*, perhaps in the entirety of modern political discourse. Commenting on it, Philip Rahv offered a criticism in 1949 that seemed to me at the time both shrewd and valid:

> There is one aspect of the psychology of power in which Dostoevsky's insight strikes me as being more viable than Orwell's strict realism. It seems to me that Orwell fails to distinguish, in the behavior of O'Brien, between psychological and objective truth. Undoubtedly it is O'Brien, rather than Dostoevsky's Grand Inquisitor, who reveals the real nature of total power; yet that does not settle the question of O'Brien's personal psychology, that is, of his ability to live with this naked truth as his sole support; nor is it conceivable that the party elite to which he belongs could live with this truth for very long. Evil, far more than good, is in need of the pseudoreligious justifications so readily provided by the ideologies of world-salvation and compulsory happiness. . . . Power is its own end, to be sure, but even the Grand Inquisitors are compelled . . . to believe in the fiction that their power is a means to some other end, gratifyingly noble and supernal.

Several decades have passed since Rahv wrote these trenchant lines and most of what has since happened gives one reason to doubt that he was entirely correct. Orwell was writing at a time when Stalin was alive and Hitler only recently dead: totalitarianism seemed an overpowering force, perhaps on the verge of taking Europe. The ideological fanaticism that a few years later would strike Hannah Arendt as one of the two underpinnings of the total state, was still strong. For while it is true that Hitler and Stalin ruled through terror, it is also true that there were millions of people who took the Nazi and Communist ideologies, myths, and slogans with the utmost seriousness, yielding to them a devotion far more intense than traditonal religions have been able to elicit in this century. Power may indeed be the beginning and the end of Party rule in Oceania, but at least in 1949 and for some years afterward it seemed hard to believe that an O'Brien would or could speak as openly as Orwell had him do, even to a victim he was soon to break.

Can we now be so certain that Orwell was wrong in giving O'Brien that speech about power? I think not. For we have lived to witness a remarkable development of the Communist state: its ideology has decayed, far fewer people give credence to its claims than in the past, yet its power remains virtually unchecked. True, there is a less open use of terror, but the power of the state—a sort of terror-in-reserve—remains a total power. As lethargy and sloth overtake the Communist societies, it begins to seem that ideology will become among them a kind of fossilized body of tiresome and half-forgotten slogans. Not many educated Russians, including those highly placed within the Party, can be supposed still to "believe" they are building the Communist society first expounded by Marx and Lenin. But the Party remains.

What then do the apparatchiks believe in? They believe in their apparatus. They believe in the Party. They believe in the power these enable. That a high Soviet bureaucrat might now talk to an imprisoned dissident in the bluntly cynical style that O'Brien employs in talking to Winston Smith does not therefore seem inconceivable. It does not even seem farfetched. The bureaucrat, especially if he is intelligent and has some pretensions to being sophisticated, might like to show his victim that he knows perfectly well that the totalitarian ethos has begun to decay, indeed, has entered a phase of transparency in which its cloak of the ideal has been stripped away. Now, this bureaucrat might not be as lucid as O'Brien, but he could easily speak to his victim as if to say,

> Look here, my good fellow, I don't want to make a fool of myself with all that big talk about the "classless society," I simply want you to recognize, for your own good, who has the power and who intends to keep it.

I take it as a sign of Orwell' intuitive gifts that he should have foreseen this historical moment when belief in the total state is crumbling yet its power survives. Whether such a condition signifies an explosive crisis or a period of low-keyed stability, we do not yet know. But there is now at least some ground for lending credence to Orwell's admittedly extreme notion that the rulers of the total state no longer need trouble to delude themselves, perhaps because they no longer can, about their motives and claims. The grim possibility is that they now have a realistic view of themselves as creatures holding power simply for the sake of power, and that they find this quite sufficient.

The most problematic, but also interesting, aspect of *1984* is Orwell's treatment of the proles.

> They were governed by private loyalties which they did not question. What mattered were individual relationships, and a completely helpless gesture, an embrace, a tear, a word spoken to a dying man, could have value in itself. The proles, it suddenly occurred to [Winston Smith] . . . were not loyal to a party or a country or an idea, they were loyal to one another.

With its echo of E. M. Forster, this is very touching, and it becomes more than touching when Winston Smith looks for some agency or lever of rebellion that might threaten the power of the Party. *"If there is hope,"* he writes in his notebook, *"it lies in the proles. . . ."* If . . . and then the paradox that even in the half-forgotten era of capitalism used to bedevil socialists: *"Until [the proles] become conscious they will never rebel, and until after they have rebelled they cannot become conscious."* Orwell knew of course that traditionally Marxists had offered a "dialectical" resolution of this dilemma: the imperatives of action stir people into consciousness, and the stimulants of consciousness enable further action. A powerful formula, and millions of people have repeated it; but like other left-wing intellectuals of his day, he had come to feel dubious about its accuracy or usefulness. In writing *1984*, however, Orwell was wise enough to leave slightly open the question of whether the proles could exert a decisive power in modern society.

Here, if anywhere, Orwell made his one major error. The proles are allowed more privacy than Party members, the telescreen does not bawl instructions at them, and the secret police seldom trouble them, except occasionally to wipe out a talented or independent prole. What this must mean is that the Inner Party judges the proles to be completely crushed and tamed, no threat to its power either now or in the future, quite demoralized as individuals and helpless as a social class.

But the evidence of history—which ought, after all, to be crucial for a writer of an anti-utopian fiction—comes down strongly against Orwell's vision of the future. Europe this past half-century has been convulsed by repeated, if unsuccessful, rebellions in which the workers (or proles) have played a major role, from East Berlin in 1956 to France in 1968, from the Hungarian Revolution to the rise of Solidarity in Poland.

But let us agree, for the sake of the argument, to move past the historical actuality or probability, since, after all, it's always possible to read the evidence in conflicting ways. Suppose, instead, we focus only on the criterion of imaginative plausibility in forming a judgment about Orwell's treatment of the proles. Even then, I think, our sense of credence must be strained excessively. Let me take the liberty of quoting a few sentences I wrote soon after *1984* came out, because I think they are still pertinent:

> Orwell's treatment of the proles can be questioned on . . . fundamental grounds. The totalitarian state can afford no luxury, allow no exception; it cannot tolerate the existence of any group beyond the perimeter of its control; it can never become so secure as to lapse into indifference. Scouring every corner of society for rebels it knows do not exist [yet they might, they could!], the totalitarian state cannot come to rest for any prolonged period of time. To do so would be to risk disintegration. It must always tend toward a condition of self-agitation, shaking and reshaking its members. . . . And since, as Winston Smith concludes, the proles remain one of the few possible sources of revolt, it can hardly seem plausible that Oceania would permit them even the relative freedom Orwell describes.

If the "ruling circles" of Poland, Czechoslovakia, and Hungary could talk in private to O'Brien, they would tell him that, lucid as he may be on the subject of power, he may well be making a mistake in his view of the proles.

An aura of gloom hangs over *1984*: the book ends with a broken Winston Smith drinking Victory Gin and blubbering his drunken love for Big Brother. He has made his "adjustment." *"If there is any hope, it lies with the proles,"* Winston Smith had said; but is there any hope? That is not a question Orwell is obliged to answer; he need only ask it, with sufficient honesty and the despair that shows him to be a man of his century. The gloom that hovers over the book has been "explained" by some critics as a symptom of the grave illness Orwell was suffering at the end of his life, at the very time he wrote his book. Perhaps there is a small measure of truth in this, but basically it seems to me a rather stupid idea. A merely sick or depressed man could not have written with the surging inventiveness that shapes 1984—and, in any case, where have these critics kept themselves this past half-century? Haven't they heard the bad news? No, the gloom of 1984 is real and justified; but it is an energizing and passionate gloom.

If the extremism of Orwell's vision derives from a close responsiveness to the idea of a world in which human life is shorn of dynamic possibilities, it also reflects his growing distaste for politics itself, at least a politics that leaves no margin for anything but itself. And this may also account for the streak of conservatism in Orwell's outlook—a conservatism less of politics than of sensibility: that is, an appreciation for the way people actually live, the strengths of received ties and feelings. One of the most affecting bits in 1984 is Winston Smith's recurrent effort to recall fragments of the past, the days before the Party took power. He tries to remember how his mother caressed him as a child, simply because he was her child; he tries to summon the appearance of a destroyed church; he tries to put together an old rhyme, trivial in itself but rich with associations:

> Oranges and lemons, say the bells of St. Clement's,
> You owe me three farthings, say the bells of St. Martin's,
> When will you pay me? say the bells of old Bailey,
> When I grow rich, say the bells of Shoreditch.

This conservatism of feeling, already present in Orwell's earlier books, is taken by some readers to conflict with his democratic socialist convictions. That would be true only if socialism were seen—so indeed both authoritarian left and reactionary right see it—as a total expurgation of the past, an attempt by a bureaucratic elite to impose "utopia" through terror. Orwell understood, however, that democratic socialism is an effort to extend what is valid in the past, to enlarge our freedoms and deepen our culture. The conservative sentiments Orwell reveals in 1984 not only aren't in conflict with his socialist opinions, they can be seen as sustaining them. Or so, at least, one hopes.

While writing this essay I have been asked several times by an editor of an American magazine eager for a quick word: "If Orwell were still alive, would he have remained a socialist?" The question is absurd, on the face of it, since no one can possibly know. But this much can be said: within his generation of left-wing writers and intellectuals, some have turned to the right, some have tried to refine their socialist values toward a greater stress on democracy, and others have abandoned their interest in politics entirely. Which of these directions Orwell might have taken it would be foolish to say, except that it's hard to imagine him dropping his interest in politics entirely.

We do know that Orwell publicly repudiated efforts to use 1984 as a piece of anti-socialist propaganda. A letter he wrote to an American correspondent puts his opinion with characteristic bluntness and lucidity:

My recent novel [*1984*] is NOT intended as an attack on socialism or on the British Labour Party (of which I am a supporter) but as a show-up of the perversions to which a centralized economy is liable and which have already been realized in Communism and Fascism. I do not believe that the kind of society I describe *necessarily* will arrive, but I believe (allowing of course for the fact that the book is a satire) that something resembling it *could* arrive. . . .

This is simply Orwell's opinion, and we know that writers often don't grasp the full implications of their work. It is quite possible, therefore, for some readers to say that while Orwell did not intend his book to be an attack on the socialist idea, it can be read that way.

And so it can. The vision of things Orwell presents need not necessarily lead to any one political conclusion, except a stress upon the urgency of democratic norms. Liberals, conservatives, and socialists can all argue from Orwell's text in behalf of their views, though the more sophisticated among them will recognize that a political position must be justified in its own terms, independently of any literary text.

Orwell understood that there is a profound tendency within modern society toward economic collectivism; that this tendency can take on a wide range of political colorations, from authoritarian to democratic; and that it can be deflected or modulated but probably cannot simply be annulled. The interpenetration of state and society, government and economy is simply a fact of modern life, quite as industrialization and urbanization have been. In 1940 Orwell wrote, "There is [little] question of avoiding collectivism. The only question is whether it is to be founded on willing cooperation or on the machine gun"—that is, whether it will be democratic or authoritarian. This puts the matter with admirable precision. *1984* shows us what might happen if "the machine gun" triumphs, but the other choice remains to us.

Suggestions for Discussion

1. Howe makes clear how Orwell's picture of 1984 was grounded in the sights and smells of contemporary England. Why does he regard this fact as important to Orwell's view of the future?

2. Howe says that totalitarianism, enforced by terror, has become a commonplace of our time. Do you believe that this erosion of democratic government will lead us to our own "1984"?

3. What distinction does Howe make between mere portrayal of the totalitarian state and the anti-Utopian view? What, according to Howe, are the basic premises of anti-Utopian fiction?

4. Explain Howe's use of the term "Menippian satire". How, according to Howe, is *1984* unlike Voltaire's *Candide* or Swift's *Gulliver's Travels*?

5. How does Orwell, according to this essay, arouse our deepest anxieties about the future? Explain what Howe means by "free space."

6. Howe believes that Winston Smith's search for a personal self—doomed to failure— is one of the most brilliant strokes of *1984*. How does the essay relate this search to the love affair between Smith and Julia?

7. Explain Howe's examination of the treatment of power in the novel and why this treatment is so important to contemporary readers. Compare O'Brien's statement about power with Machiavelli's statement on the uses of fear.

8. Howe says that history has demonstrated Orwell to be in error in his portrait of the "proles." Explain his position in light of historical events since 1949.

9. What is Howe's view of the relationship between democracy and collectivization?

Suggestions for Writing

1. Write an essay comparing Machiavelli's comments on the uses of fear with Howe's observations on the totalitarian uses of terror.

2. Write a research paper on *1984*. For your paper use Howe's estimate of the novel as well as his quotations from other critics (you will need to look up their essays). Try to narrow your paper to a consideration of one of the major points Irving Howe has made.

Rebecca West
The Meaning of Treason

Rebecca West (1892–1983) was born in Ireland. She was briefly an actress until she began to write on politics for the London press. She was the author of several novels, but her two most successful works were *Black Lamb and Gray Falcon*, a study of Jugoslavia published in 1941, and her penetrating account of the treason trials after the defeat of Germany in the second World War. The following essay from *Harper's Magazine*, October 1947, became the epilogue to her book *The Meaning of Treason* (1947). In it she explains how easy the descent was into treason when patriotism was undermined by prevailing attitudes of internationalism, and when commitment to one's own land became subservient to commitment to an idea or an ideal.

From time to time during my career as a journalist I have reported notable law cases, and I know that it is not only morbidity which makes the public enjoy following the trial of a serious crime. It is very difficult for those who study life to find a story that comes to its end under their eyes. When we select an individual whose course we want to trace, it is as likely as not that he covers his tracks with secrecy, or moves to a field outside our view, or delays his end until we ourselves have ended. That is why classical history is a valuable study; we can see the whole story, the beginning, the middle, and the end of Greece and Rome, Egypt and Persia. That is why the lives of great men in the past teach us more than knowledge of great men in the present; we know their remoter consequences. The dock brings a like illumination.

Here an individual story comes to its end in a collision with the community. Every case has its unique intellectual and spiritual significance. The appearance of the accused person, the changes in his face and voice, his agreement with society as disclosed by the witnesses who approve of him, his conflict with society as disclosed by the witnesses who disapprove of him, his relation to the crime of which he is truly or falsely accused, always reveal a special case. But the crime which he committed, if he was justly accused, or the other crime which was committed by the representatives of society if he was falsely accused, has always the same cause: refusal to respect the individuality of another or others. A world in which each man respected the soul of all other men, no matter how little they seemed to merit respect, would be crimeless.

There is an obvious political implication to be drawn from this. The authoritarian state is *ipso facto* criminal. When I covered the trial of William Joyce ("Lord Haw-Haw") for the *New Yorker* I saw a man in the dock who was doubly criminal. He had committed crimes against the law out of his desire to substitute a criminal state for a state which, if not completely innocent, aimed at the innocence of freedom. It was obviously doubtful if he would ever have been guilty of any offense had he not been tainted by this political guilt. But when his actual offense against the law was examined it was seen that he had acted in a manner which had long been extolled by many who were in theory pure of that guilt and firmly opposed to the authoritarian state.

Almost all contemporary left-wing writers of this generation and the last attacked the idea of nationalism. It was true that many of these attacks were made under the delusion that the words nationalism and imperialism mean the same thing, whereas nationalism—which means simply a special devotion of a people to its own material and spiritual achievements—implies no desire for the annexation of other territories and enslavement of other peoples. But a great many of these attacks were made under no such apprehension. It was genuinely felt that it was pure superstition which required a man to feel any warmer emotion about his own land, race, and people than about any other. Why then should any man feel a lump in his throat when he saw his flag or the statue at the harbor gate of his native land, or feel that in a dispute between his people and another he must obey the will of his kin and not aid their enemy?

I watched the trial of William Joyce, and of all traitors who were charged in courts which I could conveniently attend. They had all cleared their throats of that lump, they had all made that transit of frontiers recommended by the nationalists; and this had landed them in the service of the persecutors of reason, the fanatical believers in frontiers as the demarcation lines between the saved and the damned. But as their lives were unfolded it appeared that none of them had cast off their nationalist prejudice because of their strength, but had been divested of it by maladjusted ambition, by madness, by cowardice, by weakness. It seemed as if contemporary rationalists had been wrong, and I remembered that the trouble about man is twofold. He cannot learn truths which are too complicated; he forgets truths which are too simple. After I had seen twenty traitors tried it seemed to me that the reason why they were in the dock, why intellectuals preach against nationalism, is that we have forgotten certain simple truths.

We have forgotten that we live outward from the center of a circle and that what is nearest to the center is most real to us. If a man cut his hand, it hurts him more than if he cut some other man's hand; therefore he is more careful to guard his own. Even if he spend his whole life in teaching himself that we are all of one body, and that therefore his neighbor's pain is his also, he will still suffer more when his own hand is hurt, for the message then runs straight from his palm and fingers to his brain, traveling at a speed faster than light or sound, which bear the news of others' accidents. Throughout his life it remains true that what is nearest to his body is of greatest interest to his mind. When a baby is given food and held warmly by a certain woman, he grows up to feel a closer concern for her than for other women of her generation, and at her death will feel greatly disturbed. Should he be institution-bred and have no woman as his particular slave and tyrant, grievance will sour him till his last day.

If in his maturity he should live with a woman for any considerable period of time, he and she are apt, unless they are overtaken by certain obviously disagreeable circumstances, to behave as though there were a complete community of interest between them. There must have been some instinctive liking between them or they would never have been drawn together in the first place; they became involved in each other's prosperity; experience has taught each how the other will behave in most eventualities. Therefore they do better by one another than strangers would. Should he have children by this or any other woman, they will have great power over him, while other children will have little or none. He will know so much more about them. The veiled moment of their conception is his secret, and resemblances to him, to a familiar woman, or to his kin enable him to trace their inner lives, disguised though they be first by their inarticulateness and then by their articulateness. He can read them by the light of his own nature, and read his own nature by their light, and will have a sense of fusion between himself and those who are so inextricably tangled with that self.

If that man live in a house during the days of his childhood, he will know it better than any house he lives in later, though it shelter him forty years longer; and though the staircase wind as deviously as any in the world he will find his way down it in the darkness as surely as if it were straight. All his life long, when he hears talk of woods, he shall see beechwoods, if he come from a Buckinghamshire village, and a castle to him shall stand on Castle Rock, if Edinburgh was his home; and in the one case he shall know Southern English country folk, and in the other Lowland Scottish townsfolk, better than other Britons. Born and bred in England, he will find it easier to understand the English than the rest of men, not for any mystical reason, but because their language is his, because he is fully acquainted with their customs, and because he is the product of their common history. So also each continent enjoys a vague unity of self-comprehension, and is divided from the others by a sharp disunity; and even those who profess the closest familiarity with the next world speak with more robust certainty of this world and seem not to want to leave it.

This is not to say that a man loves what is nearest to him. He may hate his parents, his wife, and his children. Millions have done so. On the tables of the Law it was written "Honor thy father and thy mother, as the Lord God hath commanded thee; that thy days may be prolonged, and that it may go well with thee in the land which the Lord thy God giveth thee," and it is advice of almost gross practicality aimed at preventing the faithful from abandoning themselves to their natural impulses and wasting all their force on family rows. St. Paul, that great artist who perpetually betrayed his art because he was also a great man of action, and constantly abandoned the search for truth to seek instead a myth to inspire vigorous action, tried to gild the bondage of man to the familiar. "So ought men to love their own wives as their own body," he says. "He that loveth his wife loveth himself. For no man ever yet hated his own flesh, but nourisheth it and cherisheth it, even as the Lord the Church." But countless men have hated their own flesh. Everywhere and at all times men have carried such hatred to the point of slaying it, and still more have persecuted it by abstinence and mortification and debauchery. It has a value to them far above their loathing or their liking. It is their own flesh and they can have no direct experience of any other. Not with all the gold in the world or by incessant prayer can we obtain another instrument-case, packed with these our only instruments, the five senses, by which alone we can irradiate the universe that is a black void around us, and build a small irradiated platform in that darkness. A wife is someone who has stood on that irradiated platform long enough to be fully examined and to add the testimony of her own senses as to the nature of that encircling mystery. She may be loved or hated, or loved and hated, and serve in that research.

A child knows that what is near is easier for him to handle than what is far. All men took it for granted till recent times, when it was challenged, together with some other traditional assumptions, not because they had proved unsound, but because a number of urbanized populations from which the intellectual classes were largely drawn had lost their sense of spiritual as well as material process. They had lost their sense of material process owing to the development of the machine; goods which had formerly been produced by simple and comprehensible processes, often carried on where they could be witnessed by the consumer, were now produced by elaborate processes, not to be grasped by people without mechanical training, and carried on in the privacy of the large factories.

The reason for their ignorance of spiritual process was the urban lack of the long memory and the omniscient gossip enjoyed by the village. The townsman is surrounded by people whose circumstances he does not know and whose heredities are the secrets of other districts; and he is apt to take their dissimulating faces and their clothed bodies as the sum of them. People began to think of each other in a new way; as simple with a simplicity in fact unknown in organic life. They ignored the metabolism of human nature, by which experiences are absorbed into the mind and magically converted into personality, which rejects much of the material life brings to it and handles the rest to serve the interests of love or hate, good or evil, life or death, according to an inhabiting daemon, whose reasons are never given. Man conceived himself as living reasonably under the instruction of the five senses, which tell him to seek pleasure and avoid pain.

The first effect of this rational conception of life was cheerful vulgarity; and there are worse things than that. Man might well have felt this view of his destiny as a relief after the Christian philosophy, which abased his origin to criminality, and started him so low only to elevate him to the height, most disagreeable to most people, of company with godhead, after dragging him through all sorts of unpalatable experiences, including participation in a violent and apparently unnecessary death. In so far as a man adopted the new and rationalist philosophy he could be compared to an actor who, after spending a lifetime playing Hamlet and Othello and King Lear, retires to keep a country pub. All was thenceforward to go at a peaceable jog-trot. Children were to grow up straight striplings of light, undeformed by repression, unscarred by conflicts, because their parents would hand them over in their earliest years to the care of pedagogic experts. Divorce was not to be reckoned as a disgrace nor as a tragedy nor even as a failure, but as a pleasurable extension of experience, like travel. Furthermore—and this was considered as the sanest adjustment of all—the ardors of patriotism were to be abandoned, and replaced by a cool resolution to place one's country on a level with all others in one's affections, and to hand it over without concern to the dominion of any other power which could offer it greater material benefits. It was not out of cynicism that the benefits demanded were material: it was believed that the material automatically produced the intellectual and the spiritual. These reasonable steps having been taken, there was to follow harmony. The only peril was that it might become too sweet.

But the five senses had evidently not been rightly understood. Such children as were surrendered by their parents to expert treatment, complained against that surrender as if it had been any other kind of abandonment. They quarreled with the pedagogues as much as they would have quarreled with their parents; but, the bond of the flesh being absent, there was something sapless in their quarrels, and there was less energy engendered. Sexual life was not noticeably smoother than it had been. The epic love of marriage and the lyric love-song of the encounter both lost much by the pretense that they were the same. Nor, as patriotism was discredited, did peace come nearer. Indeed, the certainty of war now arched over the earth like a second sky, inimical to the first. If harmony had been our peril, we were preserved from it, both within and without. For it was plain that, as Christian philosophy had so harshly averred, the world was a stage on which an extraordinary drama, not yet fully comprehended by the intellect, was being performed; and its action was now an agony. But, owing to the adoption of the rationalist philosophy, some of the actors filling the most important parts were now incapable of speaking their lines. It appeared that *Hamlet* and *Othello* and *King Lear* would be no longer cathartic tragedies but repellent and distressing farces if the leading characters had, in the climactic scenes, been overtaken by the delusion that they had retired and were keeping country pubs.

So the evil moment came and was clear: not surpassed in evil since the days of the barbarian invasions. The devil of nationalism had been driven out of man, but he had not become the headquarters of the dove. Instead there had entered into him the seven devils of internationalism, and he was torn by their frenzies. Then what is against all devils came to his aid. The achievement (which, as yet, is unfinished, since peace does not reign) was accomplished by a continuance of the drama in spite of the difficulties created by the rationalist philosophy. Since 'the actors cast to play the leading parts would not speak, the action was carried on by the peoples who used to walk to and fro at the back of the scene, softly laughing or softly weeping, or simply quietly being. Now these people streamed across the continents, inscribing their beliefs on the surface of the earth by the course of their flights, and on the sites of their martyrdoms. They defeated fascism by not being fascist.

They showed the contrast between fascism and nonfascism so clearly that the world, wishing to live, defended their side because it could be seen that they were the representatives of life. As they exorcised the devils from the body of Europe they seemed to affirm certain values. It was perhaps true that the origin of man was in criminality, for once a community refused to make the effort of seeking the company of godhead it certainly became criminal. It was perhaps true that hedonism is an impotent gospel, for now it could be seen that pleasure means nothing to many men. As fast as those who ran to save their lives ran those who ran to slay them, even if their pursuit, pressed too hard, might change them into fugitives, whose own lives were in danger. Now the scorned bonds of the flesh asserted their validity. It was the final and unbearable misery of these flights that husbands were separated from their wives, and parents lost sight of their children. The men who performed the cruelest surgery on these families, who threw the husband and wife into the gas chamber while the children traveled by train to an unknown destination, had themselves been brought up to condemn their own ties of blood. The anguish of the divided was obviously holy. The contentment of those who felt no reluctance to divide was plainly damned.

In this day of exposition those who made the other sacrifice of the near for the far, and preferred other countries to their own, proved also to be unholy. The relationship between a man and a fatherland is always disturbed by conflict, if either man or fatherland is highly developed. A man's demands for liberty must at some point challenge the limitations the state imposes on the individual for the sake of the mass. If he is to carry on the national tradition he must wrestle with those who, speaking in its name, desire to crystallize it at the point reached by the previous generation. In any case national life itself must frequently exasperate him, because it is the medium in which he is expressing himself, and every craftsman or artist is repelled by the resistance of his medium to his will. All men should have a drop or two of treason in their veins, if the nations are not to go soft like so many sleepy bears.

Yet to be a traitor is most miserable. All the men I saw in the prisoner's dock were sad as they stood their trials, not only because they were going to be punished. They would have been sad even if they had never been brought to justice. They had forsaken the familiar medium; they had trusted themselves to the mercies of those who had no reason to care for them; knowing their custodians' indifference they had lived for long in fear; and they were aware that they had thrown away their claim on those who might naturally have felt affection for them. Strangers, as King Solomon put it, were filled with their wealth, and their labors were in the house of a stranger, and they mourned at the last when their flesh and body were consumed. As a divorce sharply recalls what a happy marriage should be, so the treachery of these men recalled what a nation should be; a shelter where all talents are generously recognized, all forgivable oddities forgiven, all viciousness quietly frustrated, and those who lack talent honored for equivalent contributions of graciousness. Each of these men was as dependent on the good opinion of others as one is oneself; they needed a nation which was also a hearth, and their capacity for suffering made it tragic that they had gone out from their own hearth to suffer among strangers, because the intellectual leaders of their time had professed a philosophy which was scarcely more than a lapse of memory, and had forgotten, that a hearth gives out warmth.

Suggestions for Discussion

1. According to Rebecca West, how is the observation of a courtroom trial similar to the study of the history of the past?

2. How does West relate the act of treason to the life of crime? How is this relationship connected to the totalitarian state?

3. What does West see as the major dangerous consequences of the decline in nationalism before World War II? What led to the decline of nationalist feeling?

4. How does West connect feeling for home, parents, children, one's neighborhood, or one's town with nationalist feelings?

5. As you read the essay, does West's position seem blindly or narrowly patriotic? How does she achieve an objective and detached tone in her writing?

6. Explain the use of biblical references in the essay. What value do they have in establishing tone?

7. What does West see as an antidote or corrective to the attitudes which led to the treasonous acts of the people whose trials she observed?

Suggestions for Writing

1. Look up facts about "Lord Haw-Haw" and, based on what you discover, write an essay in which you show how his life illustrates the ideas advanced by Rebecca West in this essay.

2. Third World nationalism since World War II is very different from the nationalism examined in this essay. Try to discover through research some of the major differences and contrast the two. What have been some consequences of contemporary nationalism? What might be the consequences of a loss of such nationalist feeling?

Carol Tavris

Anger in an Unjust World

Carol Tavris is a social psychologist and magazine writer. She is author of *The Redbook Report on Female Sexuality* (1977) and of *Anger: The Misunderstood Emotion* (1982). This essay, excerpted from that book for *Ms. Magazine*, examines the reasons why most of us, in one way or another, contrive to tolerate injustice by suppressing our anger.

St. Thomas Aquinas imagined that people feel angry only when they are offended by their inferiors: "Thus a nobleman is angry if he be insulted by a peasant; a wise man, if by a fool; a master, if by a servant." If the nobleman insults the peasant, on the other hand, "anger does not ensue, but only sorrow." The irritating habit of modern peasants to react to insult with anger instead of sorrow, is, of course, the story of revolution.

Yet Aquinas was making an important point about the power of authority to establish legitimacy, and legitimacy is death to anger. For, in fact, most peasants, fools, and servants have not protested the injustices done them, nor even regarded them as injustices. The sense of injustice is made, not born, and although we think of anger as the handmaiden of justice, it is not its inevitable companion. Anger depends on our perceptions of a situation, perceptions of injustice included.

Many people believe that if they feel angry now about something, they must always have felt that way, although the anger may previously have been repressed, distorted, or displaced. A woman who, in 1975, feels angry with herself for having dropped out of medical school for marriage in 1955 wonders what she did with the anger she assumes she felt at the time. A man who, as an adult, feels angry with his parents for making him eat all the food on his plate when he was young thinks he felt as angry when he *was* young. The ex-medical student and the little boy may truly have felt angry in the past, but it's more likely that they were just going along with the times, following the rules, with perhaps a squawk or two of protest. Not only do people attribute their emotions backward to what they felt years ago, but they attribute them sideways, to what they think others should be feeling. Some attribute anger to women or minorities of previous generations and even centuries. When they wonder why a battered woman stays with a vicious husband, blaming herself instead of him for her abuse; or why a slave does not rebel; or why the Untouchables accept their caste of degradation; they are assuming that these sufferers interpret the situation as they do—and see a way out of it, as well.

The forces that keep people in their places, if not entirely contented then at least not angry, are not always as irrational as they seem. The decision that a particular situation is unjust must overcome a few psychological and practical hurdles, and so must the next decision: that the injustice merits anger instead of apathy. The question, therefore, is not simply "Why do people become angry?" but why they do not.

The Rationalizing Species

Golfer Tom Watson seemed to be cruising to an easy victory in the $300,000 Bryon Nelson Classic a few years ago when the weather and his luck turned suddenly against him. From a comfortable score of eight under par he dropped to four over par. "It doesn't upset me," Watson told a reporter. "Golf is not a fair game."

Life is not a fair game, either, but people have a curious capacity to behave as if it were. We tend to equate what is with what ought to be, and react with outrage to attacks on our way of doing things. We accept injustices more readily when they are built into the system, because the roles we play seem so normal and inevitable. For example, we take it for granted that it is within a boss's right to set working hours; but Eskimo workers in factories in Alaska found it hilarious that the white workers responded so obediently to the whistles summoning them to stop work or start it. To the Eskimo, the only authority that determines when people shall work is the tide. Yet American workers would find it just as hilarious, to say nothing of an infringement on their liberty, if they had to sing the company song in unison every morning, as many Japanese workers do, without question or anger.

What happens when people's faith in the legitimacy of the system is put to the test? Usually, it is the test that fails. The very organization of our mental faculties seems designed to screen out information we don't want to hear, information that is at odds with our basic beliefs. Psychologist Anthony G. Greenwald calls the self "The Totalitarian Ego," arguing that the ego organizes its knowledge, perceptions, and memory in predictably biased ways that are designed (like totalitarian governments) primarily to protect its organization.

The ego, says Greenwald, is a "self justifying historian," which seeks only that information that agrees with it, rewrites history when it needs to, and does not even see the evidence that threatens it. The organization of knowledge in the mind is like a library system: our built-in biases allow us to retrieve any specific information that we need rapidly; once we make a commitment to a particular cataloging system (say, a conservative ideology or a religious framework of belief), we spend more time maintaining the system than revising it. The biases of the mind persist because they work: they preserve self-confidence, they keep our mental organization in order, and they keep us persevering toward our goals, whatever those may be. The mind's cautiousness about accepting new ideas may seem foolhardy in a world bursting with innovation and discovery, but (at least until recently) it has been an adaptive success for our species. The flash of anger that people may feel when they are threatened with conflicting information is the mind's way of protecting its organization. "My mind's made up—don't confuse me with the facts" seems to have been an oddly successful strategy in the evolution of the brain. After all, if we kept "changing our minds" with each new bit of experience and observation, we would never know how to behave, what to think, or why we were working so hard for a future reward.

Many psychologists have by now posed theories of cognitive consistency to predict how people handle information that conflicts with their beliefs: we shall shift the belief slightly, or more likely the new information, to make the two coexist harmoniously.

Consistency theories all assume that human beings have a fundamental need to find meaning and order in life's experiences. Psychologist Melvin J. Lerner adds that we need to believe in a just world, one in which people get what they deserve, good is rewarded, the sinful punished. The Belief in a Just World, he argues, is "a fundamental delusion" that is central to the way we organize experience, making sense out of confusion, justice out of cruelty and unfairness, and orderliness out of random events. And it protects the legitimacy of the established order. Researchers have by now conducted dozens of experiments that show what happens when the belief in a just world clashes with an obvious fact of injustice. If you cannot do anything about the injustice, you will tend to denigrate the victim, deny the evidence, or reinterpret the event entirely. You will go to great lengths to protect the basic faith.

Denigrate the Victim

In a just world, innocent women are not raped. Women who are raped, therefore, must have "invited it"—by being seductive, or perhaps by merely being. In one experiment that simulated a jury trial, a defendant was depicted as having raped a married woman, a virgin, or a divorcee. The subjects in the study gave longer sentences to rapists of virgins than to rapists of divorcees, as you might expect, but, more interesting, they attributed more responsibility for the rape to the virgins and wives than to the divorcees. Apparently the knowledge that innocent, "respectable" women can be raped was too threatening to the jurors' belief in a just world, and so they found fault with the victims' behavior.

Similarly, many vehement antiabortionists cannot accept the statistics of rape, incest, poverty, contraceptive ignorance, and woman battering, preferring to believe that it is only immoral women who have abortions. Women are blamed for "getting themselves pregnant," as one Congressman put it, in that bizarre, anachronistic phrasing that exonerates the role of the male in conception. (The same Congressmen who advise that "the best contraceptive is the word no" would not take it kindly, I bet, if their women applied that word to them.)

Women are not the only objects of rationalizing denigration. The poor bring their suffering on themselves (say many of the well-to-do) because they are lazy, conniving, drunk, and violent. A man who is fired for trying to improve working conditions must have deserved it; he should have kept his mouth shut. Neoconservative Jews such as Norman Podhoretz and Irving Kristol must, to preserve their commitment to fascist but anticommunist nations such as Argentina, denigrate victims of Argentine anti-Semitism, most notably Jacobo Timerman; accepting his testimony threatens their political philosophy and their sense of religious security. Fighter pilots, on hearing that a buddy has been killed in a plane crash, will blame the buddy for having made a stupid error; if it was the plane that failed or the Air Force's error, the survivors are in danger too. All of these rationalizations help people avoid the panicky thought that poverty, job loss, anti-Semitism, or death could strike *them*.

Denial

Here's a familiar term for the psychoanalytic archives, this time referring not to an unconscious process but often a perfectly conscious one: screening out unpleasant information that might threaten one's convictions. Fundamentalist parents are fighting to have their children taught absolute values of right and wrong: they worry that schools are subjecting their children to information that might jeopardize their religious certainty. When writer Frances Fitz-Gerald asked one such mother whether she would consider sending her children to a nonfundamentalist school, the mother said, "No, because our eternal destiny is all-important, so you can't take a chance. College so often throws kids into confusion." To avoid confusion, many people prefer ignorance.

Denial seems to be at the heart of political philosophies. As a particularly depressing (if extreme) case, there are people who will tell you that the Holocaust never happened. But you can see garden-variety denial in the way individuals respond to the news that innocent people have been imprisoned or murdered by the Soviet Union, the United States, China, Vietnam, Argentina, Chile, France, Japan, South Africa, Haiti, Cuba . . . (fill in your choice for infamy). Depending on your politics, you will tend to deny the crimes committed by your favorite nations (for such crimes jeopardize your desire to believe in you allies' basic integrity and justice, and possibly jeopardize your economic interests as well), and emphasize those committed by your enemies (it is perfectly consistent to believe in the sins of your opponents). If you believe in the basic corruptibility of most political systems, however, you won't find it inconsistent evidence to be denied when one of them does something criminal or stupid.

Reinterpretation of the Injustice and Its Outcome

This mechanism to preserve faith in a world requires some flights of imagination: people "rewrite" the injustice they hear about so that it simply disappears, taking with it the need to be emotionally disturbed. For example, you might reinterpret the result of injustice, deciding that the victim wasn't such a victim after all; suffering is a good thing that builds moral character and makes the sufferer a better person. Or you might decide that the cause of the injustice was, let's say, not the government's decision to release Agent Orange on Vietnam, but a result of something the victim did or failed to do; perhaps those servicemen who now complain they were poisoned just forgot to take adequate precautions. Or might extend the time frame of the whole event to maintain your belief in ultimate justice: eventually, heroes and bastards will get their just deserts, but it may take a few years. Maybe a lifetime. Maybe in the afterlife . . .

So great is the need to believe in justice and order, says Lerner, that many people will even assume a large burden of anguish, blaming themselves, rather than yield the belief. Parents of terminally ill children, the most poignantly undeserving of victims, frequently berate themselves for their children's fate: "If I had only done this . . . " "If we'd never done that . . ." This self-blame, paradoxically, allays the anxiety of the intolerable conclusion that no one is responsible.

In the laboratory, psychologists have watched before their very eyes as the belief in a just world "cools out" anger. Young adults observed a videotape of what they thought was a real experiment in learning (in fact, it was staged), in which another young woman suffered a series of severe shocks whenever she made "errors." At first the observers would flinch empathetically with each televised shock, and many expressed fury and indignation at the treatment they were watching: "I was really mad." "I felt like getting up and walking out." "I thought it was disgusting." In spite of these strong affirmations of anger, *not one* of the thousand people who have by now participated in this experiment have actually complained. Instead, most of them decided that the victim was a fool or a weakling for sitting still and allowing herself to be shocked. "I would never let anyone do that to me!" they asserted. Unable as they were to do anything about the injustice they observed, they condemned the victim and evaluated her critically. The more strongly the experimenters portrayed the innocent victim as a martyr, the more vehemently the observers condemned her.

Religion, of course, offers the ultimate just world, if not in this life then in the next. Religion and political ideology organize our angers as they legitimize our social systems. Indeed all the great religions have made the management of anger a central concern, with prescriptions designed to protect the social order and to generate anger, if at all, only on its behalf.

For instance, although the Old Testament itself is a veritable catalog of family squabbles, internecine wars, and the smiting of heathens, it continually reminds its readers that "He that is slow to anger is better than the mighty"— surely a sermon that would reassure the mighty. Jehovah of the Old Testament and Allah of Islam are angry gods, who require anger to be used freely in their service against enemies, infidels, and the wicked; but anger *within* the community is to be suppressed. This was a smart and successful philosophy for small nations surrounded by competing groups, the situation then and now in the Middle East.

In contrast, the religions of Taoism, Vishnuism, and Buddhism advocate the complete eradication of anger and any other emotion that serves a this-worldly desire (such as lust and greed). Because everything that happens in this world is predestined, according to these theologies, there is no point in getting riled up about evil, war, and sin. There is certainly no point in protesting one's caste; obedient behavior in this life will be rewarded with caste advancement in the next incarnation. (War and anger may be an occasional necessity, but they are not to be sought after or celebrated.)

Christianity stands between the martial religions and the pacifist ones: anger may be used to combat evil and injustice; anger is good or bad depending on its use, not its nature. Although in the New Testament divine vengeance has subsided in favor of divine forgiveness, human beings are still supposed to wait for forgiveness in heaven and not raise their voices too loudly for justice on earth. If we consider the secular results of Christianity, however, we see that those who turned the other cheek usually got a slap in return; and that the meek did indeed inherit the earth—to plow, to plant, and to harvest for their masters.

Ideas about justice are not all in the mind. Realistic, practical motives hold people in roles as victims of manipulation or injustice without their perceiving either. Sociologist Barrington Moore, Jr., calls their condition one of "exploitative reciprocity," and if revolutionaries emphasize the "exploitative," the people involved tend to emphasize the "reciprocity." Every social system, from the family to a nation, is based on a social contract of the rights and duties of its participants. The contract may be written or implicit, but the rules are usually clear to all, or become clear once they are broken.

Some feminists, for example, who feel angry about genital mutilation, such as circumcision or even excision of the clitoris that women in many Third World cultures endure, cannot understand why the women tolerate these practices and continue them. Yet these horrendous, painful customs are as essential to the women's security and survival—because they guarantee that the woman will continue to be protected by men—as a job contract is to a union worker here. (Many Third World feminists themselves put food, education and work at the top of their list of reforms for this reason.) In any relationship between authority and subordinate, the subordinate gives up something to get something: the benefits of the authority's protection, expertise, talent, access to the rain god, earnings.

The anger that fuels revolt does not arise, therefore, from objective conditions of deprivation or misery; as long as people regard those conditions as natural and inevitable, as God's law or man's way, they do not feel angry about them. So sociologists speak instead of "relative deprivation," the subjective comparisons that people make when they compare their actual lives to *what might be possible.* Alexis de Tocqueville observed that "evils which are patiently endured when they seem inevitable become intolerable when once the idea of escape from them is suggested," and the freed slave Frederick Douglass put the same idea more passionately: "Beat and cuff your slave," he wrote, "keep him hungry and spiritless, and he will follow the chain of his master like a dog, but feed and clothe him well, work him moderately, surround him with physical comfort, and dreams of freedom intrude."

In this country, the civil rights, women's rights, and human rights movements have been organized and sustained primarily by those who already had more education, opportunities, and success in the system than the less-fortunate members of their race, sex, or class.

Margaret Mead once said of liberals that they are "the yeast within the body politic upon which American society relies to keep its dream worth following. Without them, we should be lost. Yet with them, we are uncomfortable. For they draw their strength from the discrepancies in the very heart of American life." Rebels and dissidents challenge the complacent belief in a just world, and, as the theory would predict, they are usually denigrated for their efforts. While they are alive, they may be called "cantankerous," "crazy," "hysterical," "uppity," or "duped." Dead, some of them become saints and heroes, the sterling characters of history. It's a matter of proportion. One angry rebel is crazy, three is a conspiracy, 50 is a movement.

Suggestions for Discussion

1. Why does Tavris begin her discussion of anger with a reference to St. Thomas Aquinas? What important point did Aquinas make about the legitimacy of authority?

2. The author is concerned with the behavior of those who tolerate injustice by suppressing their anger. Does she believe this act is difficult? Natural? What does Tom Watson's statement, "Golf is not a fair game" mean in the context of this essay?

3. How does Tavris use the example of American, Eskimo, and Japanese workers to illustrate the way in which we learn to tolerate certain rules?

4. Tavris lists three categories of behavior which we use to protect our basic faith in existing order. Discuss these categories. How do they relate to each other to form a coherent system of acceptance?

5. What role does religion play in helping us suppress anger in an unjust world?

6. Tavris quotes from Frederick Douglass and Margaret Mead. Show how she uses their remarks.

Suggestions for Writing

1. Choose an example of your own tolerance of injustice. Examine the reasons for your tolerance. Can you explain them? Write an essay in which you analyze this example and either defend your actions or reject them.

2. This essay makes a significant statement about the modern feminist movement. Write an essay explaining the relation of the argument of the essay to the feminist position. Use some of Tavris's examples of how we tolerate injustice to illustrate your point. Relate the last two sentences of her essay to your discussion.

Fiction

Franz Kafka

A Report to an Academy
Translated by Willa and Edwin Muir

Franz Kafka (1883–1924) portrayed alienated characters in an absurd world. He made little mark during his life, but is now considered a major modern writer. Many of his novels were published posthumously, including *The Trial, The Castle,* and *Amerika.* In his well-known story "Metamorphosis" he described the fate of an ordinary young man who awakens one morning to discover he has become a large bug. In the story before the reader, Kafka ironically describes how the need for freedom leads a captured ape to assume the characteristics of man.

Honored members of the Academy!

You have done me the honor of inviting me to give your Academy an account of the life I formerly led as an ape.

I regret that I cannot comply with your request to the extent you desire. It is now nearly five years since I was an ape, a short space of time, perhaps, according to the calendar, but an infinitely long time to gallop through at full speed, as I have done, more or less accompanied by excellent mentors, good advice, applause, and orchestral music, and yet essentially alone, since all my escorters, to keep the image, kept well off the course. I could never have achieved what I have done had I been stubbornly set on clinging to my origins, to the remembrances of my youth. In fact, to give up being stubborn was the supreme commandment I laid upon myself; free ape as I was, I submitted myself to that yoke. In revenge, however, my memory of the past has closed the door against me more and more. I could have returned at first, had human beings allowed it, through an archway as wide as the span of heaven over the earth, but as I spurred myself on in my forced career, the opening narrowed and shrank behind me; I felt more comfortable in the world of men and fitted it better; the strong wind that blew after me out of my past began to slacken; today it is only a gentle puff of air that plays around my heels; and the opening in the distance, through which it comes and through which I once came myself, has grown so small that, even if my strength and my will power sufficed to get me back to it, I should have to scrape the very skin from my body to crawl through. To put it plainly, much as I like expressing myself in images, to put it plainly: your life as apes, gentlemen, insofar as something of that kind lies behind you, cannot be farther removed from you than mine is from me. Yet everyone on earth feels a tickling at the heels; the small chimpanzee and the great Achilles alike.

But to a lesser extent I can perhaps meet your demand, and indeed I do so with the greatest pleasure. The first thing I learned was to give a hand-shake; a handshake betokens frankness; well, today, now that I stand at the very peak of my career, I hope to add frankness in words to the frankness of that first handshake. What I have to tell the Academy will contribute nothing essentially new, and will fall far behind what you have asked of me and what with the best will in the world I cannot communicate—nonetheless, it should indicate the line an erstwhile ape has had to follow in entering and establishing himself in the world of men. Yet I could not risk putting into words even such insignificant information as I am going to give you if I were not quite sure of myself and if my position on all the great variety stages of the civilized world had not become quite unassailable.

I belong to the Gold Coast. For the story of my capture I must depend on the evidence of others. A hunting expedition sent out by the firm of Hagen-beck—by the way, I have drunk many a bottle of good red wine since then with the leader of that expedition—had taken up its position in the bushes by the shore when I came down for a drink at evening among a troop of apes. They shot at us; I was the only one that was hit; I was hit in two places.

Once in the cheek; a slight wound; but it left a large, naked, red scar which earned me the name of Red Peter, a horrible name, utterly inappropriate, which only some ape could have thought of, as if the only difference between me and the performing ape Peter, who died not so long ago and had some small local reputation, were the red mark on my cheek. This by the way.

The second shot hit me below the hip. It was a severe wound, it is the cause of my limping a little to this day. I read an article recently by one of the ten thousand windbags who vent themselves concerning me in the newspapers, saying: my ape nature is not yet quite under control; the proof being that when visitors come to see me, I have a predilection for taking down my trousers to show them where the shot went in. The hand which wrote that should have its fingers shot away one by one. As for me, I can take my trousers down before anyone if I like; you would find nothing but a well-groomed fur and the scar made—let me be particular in the choice of a word for this particular purpose, to avoid misunderstanding—the scar made by a wanton shot. Everything is open and aboveboard; there is nothing to conceal; when the plain truth is in question, great minds discard the niceties of refinement. But if the writer of the article were to take down his trousers before a visitor, that would be quite another story, and I will let it stand to his credit that he does not do it. In return, let him leave me alone with his delicacy!

After these two shots I came to myself—and this is where my own memories gradually begin—between decks in the Hagenbeck steamer, inside a cage. It was not a four-sided barred cage; it was only a three-sided cage nailed to a locker; the locker made the fourth side of it. The whole construction was too low for me to stand up in and too narrow to sit down in. So I had to squat with my knees bent and trembling all the time, and also, since probably for a time I wished to see no one, and to stay in the dark, my face was turned toward the locker while the bars of the cage cut into my flesh behind. Such a method of confining wild beasts is supposed to have its advantages during the first days of captivity, and out of my own experiences I cannot deny that from the human point of view this is really the case.

But that did not occur to me then. For the first time in my life I could see no way out; at least no direct way out; directly in front of me was the locker, board fitted close to board. True, there was a gap running right through the boards which I greeted with the blissful howl of ignorance when I first discovered it, but the hole was not even wide enough to stick one's tail through and not all the strength of an ape could enlarge it.

I am supposed to have made uncommonly little noise, as I was later informed, from which the conclusion was drawn that I would either soon die or if I managed to survive the first critical period would be very amenable to training. I did survive this period. Hopelessly sobbing, painfully hunting for fleas, apathetically licking a cocoanut, beating my skull against the locker, sticking out my tongue at anyone who came near me—that was how I filled in time at first in my new life. But over and above it all only the one feeling: no way out. Of course what I felt then as an ape I can represent now only in human terms, and therefore I misrepresent it, but although I cannot reach back to the truth of the old ape life, there is no doubt that it lies somewhere in the direction I have indicated.

Until then I had had so many ways out of everything, and now I had none. I was pinned down. Had I been nailed down, my right to free movement would not have been lessened. Why so? Scratch your flesh raw between your toes, but you won't find the answer. Press yourself against the bar behind you till it nearly cuts you in two, you won't find the answer. I had no way out but I had to devise one, for without it I could not live. All the time facing that locker—I should certainly have perished. Yet as far as Hagenbeck was concerned, the place for apes was in front of a locker—well then, I had to stop being an ape. A fine, clear train of thought, which I must have constructed somehow with my belly, since apes think with their bellies.

I fear that perhaps you do not quite understand what I mean by "way out." I use the expression in its fullest and most popular sense. I deliberately do not use the word "freedom." I do not mean the spacious feeling of freedom on all sides. As an ape, perhaps, I knew that, and I have met men who yearn for it. But for my part I desired such freedom neither then nor now. In passing: may I say that all too often men are betrayed by the word freedom. And as freedom is counted among the most sublime feelings, so the corresponding disillusionment can be also sublime. In variety theaters I have often watched, before my turn came on, a couple of acrobats performing on trapezes high in the roof. They swung themselves, they rocked to and fro, they sprang into the air, they floated into each other's arms, one hung by the hair from the teeth of the other. "And that too is human freedom," I thought, "self-controlled movement." What a mockery of holy Mother Nature! Were the apes to see such a spectacle, no theater walls could stand the shock of their laughter.

No, freedom was not what I wanted. Only a way out; right or left, or in any direction; I made no other demand; even should the way out prove to be an illusion; the demand was a small one, the disappointment could be no bigger. To get out somewhere, to get out! Only not to stay motionless with raised arms, crushed against a wooden wall.

Today I can see it clearly; without the most profound inward calm I could never have found my way out. And indeed perhaps I owe all that I have become to the calm that settled within me after my first few days in the ship. And again for that calmness it was the ship's crew I had to thank.

They were good creatures, in spite of everything. I find it still pleasant to remember the sound of their heavy footfalls which used to echo through my half-dreaming head. They had a habit of doing everything as slowly as possible. If one of them wanted to rub his eyes, he lifted a hand as if it were a drooping weight. Their jests were coarse, but hearty. Their laughter had always a gruff bark in it that sounded dangerous but meant nothing. They always had something in their mouths to spit out and did not care where they spat it. They always grumbled that they got fleas from me; yet they were not seriously angry about it; they knew that my fur fostered fleas, and that fleas jump; it was a simple matter of fact to them. When they were off duty some of them often used to sit down in a semicircle around me; they hardly spoke but only grunted to each other; smoked their pipes, stretched out on lockers; smacked their knees as soon as I made the slightest movement; and now and then one of them would take a stick and tickle me where I liked being tickled. If I were to be invited today to take a cruise on that ship I should certainly refuse the invitation, but just as certainly the memories I could recall between its decks would not all be hateful.

The calmness I acquired among these people kept me above all from trying to escape. As I looked back now, it seems to me I must have had at least an inkling that I had to find a way out or die, but that my way out could not be reached through flight. I cannot tell now whether escape was possible, but I believe it must have been; for an ape it must always be possible. With my teeth as they are today I have to be careful even in simply cracking nuts, but at that time I could certainly have managed by degrees to bite through the lock of my cage. I did not do it. What good would it have done me? As soon as I had poked out my head I should have been caught again and put in a worse cage; or I might have slipped among the other animals without being noticed, among the pythons, say, who were opposite me, and so breathed out my life in their embrace; or supposing I had actually succeeded in sneaking out as far as the deck and leaping overboard, I should have rocked for a little on the deep sea and then been drowned. Desperate remedies. I did not think it out in this human way, but under the influence of my surroundings I acted as if I had thought it out.

I did not think things out; but I observed everything quietly. I watched these men go to and fro, always the same faces, the same movements, often it seemed to me there was only the same man. So this man or these men walked about unimpeded. A lofty goal faintly dawned before me. No one promised me that if I became like them the bars of my cage would be taken away. Such promises for apparently impossible contingencies are not given. But if one achieves the impossible, the promises appear later retrospectively precisely where one had looked in vain for them before. Now, these men in

themselves had no great attraction for me. Had I been devoted to the aforementioned idea of freedom, I should certainly have preferred the deep sea to
the way out that suggested itself in the heavy faces of these men. At any rate,
I watched them for a long time before I even thought of such things, indeed,
it was only the mass weight of my observations that impelled me in the right
direction.

It was so easy to imitate these people. I learned to spit in the very first
days. We used to spit in each other's faces; the only difference was that I
licked my face clean afterwards and they did not. I could soon smoke a pipe
like an old hand; and if I also pressed my thumb into the bowl of the pipe, a
roar of appreciation went up between decks; only it took me a very long time
to understand the difference between a full pipe and an empty one.

My worst trouble came from the schnapps bottle. The smell of it revolted
me; I forced myself to it as best I could; but it took weeks for me to master
my repulsion. This inward conflict, strangely enough, was taken more seriously by the crew than anything else about me. I cannot distinguish the men
from each other in my recollection, but there was one of them who came
again and again, alone or with friends, by day, by night, at all kinds of hours;
he would post himself before me with the bottle and give me instructions. He
could not understand me, he wanted to solve the enigma of my being. He
would slowly uncork the bottle and then look at me to see if I had followed
him; I admit that I always watched him with wildly eager, too eager attention;
such a student of humankind no human teacher ever found on earth. After
the bottle was uncorked he lifted it to his mouth; I followed it with my eyes
right up to his jaws; he would nod, pleased with me, and set the bottle to his
lips; I, enchanted with my gradual enlightenment, squealed and scratched
myself comprehensively wherever scratching was called for; he rejoiced, tilted
the bottle, and took a drink; I, impatient and desperate to emulate him, be-
fouled myself in my cage, which again gave him great satisfaction; and then,
holding the bottle at arm's length and bringing it up with a swing, he would
empty it at one draught, leaning back at an exaggerated angle for my better
instruction. I, exhausted by too much effort, could follow him no farther and
hung limply to the bars, while he ended his theoretical exposition by rubbing
his belly and grinning.

After theory came practice. Was I not already quite exhausted by my theoretical instruction? Indeed I was; utterly exhausted. That was part of my
destiny. And yet I would take hold of the proffered bottle as well as I was
able; uncork it, trembling; this successful action would gradually inspire me
with new energy; I would lift the bottle, already following my original model
almost exactly; put it to my lips and—and then throw it down in disgust, utter
disgust, although it was empty and filled only with the smell of the spirit,
throw it down on the floor in disgust. To the sorrow of my teacher, to the
greater sorrow of myself, neither of us being really comforted by the fact that
I did not forget, even though I had thrown away the bottle, to rub my belly
most admirably and to grin.

Far too often my lesson ended in that way. And to the credit of my teacher,
he was not angry; sometimes indeed he would hold his burning pipe against
my fur, until it began to smolder in some place I could not easily reach, but
then he would himself extinguish it with his own kind, enormous hand; he

was not angry with me, he perceived that we were both fighting on the same side against the nature of apes and that I had the more difficult task.

What a triumph it was then both for him and for me, when one evening before a large circle of spectators—perhaps there was a celebration of some kind, a gramophone was playing, an officer was circulating among the crew—when on this evening, just as no one was looking, I took hold of a schnapps bottle that had been carelessly left standing before my cage, uncorked it in the best style, while the company began to watch me with mounting attention, set it to my lips without hesitation, with no grimace, like a professional drinker, with rolling eyes and full throat, actually and truly drank it empty; then threw the bottle away, not this time in despair but as an artistic performer; forgot, indeed, to rub my belly; but instead of that, because I could not help it, because my senses were reeling, called a brief and unmistakable "Hallo!" breaking into human speech, and with this outburst broke into the human community, and felt its echo: "Listen, he's talking!" like a caress over the whole of my sweat-drenched body.

I repeat: there was no attraction for me in imitating human beings; I imitated them because I needed a way out, and for no other reason. And even that triumph of mine did not achieve much. I lost my human voice again at once; it did not come back for months; my aversion for the schnapps bottle returned again with even greater force. But the line I was to follow had in any case been decided, once for all.

When I was handed over to my first trainer in Hamburg I soon realized that there were two alternatives before me: the Zoological Gardens or the variety stage. I did not hesitate. I said to myself: do your utmost to get onto the variety stage; the Zoological Gardens means only a new cage; once there, you are done for.

And so I learned things, gentlemen. Ah, one learns when one has to; one learns when one needs a way out; one learns at all costs. One stands over oneself with a whip; one flays oneself at the slightest opposition. My ape nature fled out of me, head over heels and away, so that my first teacher was almost himself turned into an ape by it, had soon to give up teaching and was taken away to a mental hospital. Fortunately he was soon let out again.

But I used up many teachers, indeed, several teachers at once. As I became more confident of my abilities, as the public took an interest in my progress and my future began to look bright, I engaged teachers for myself, established them in five communicating rooms, and took lessons from them all at once by dint of leaping from one room to the other.

That progress of mine! How the rays of knowledge penetrated from all sides into my awakening brain! I do not deny it: I found it exhilarating. But I must also confess: I did not overestimate it, not even then, much less now. With an effort which up till now has never been repeated I managed to reach the cultural level of an average European. In itself that might be nothing to speak of, but it is something insofar as it has helped me out of my cage and opened a special way out for me, the way of humanity. There is an excellent idiom: to fight one's way through the thick of things; that is what I have done, I have fought through the thick of things. There was nothing else for me to do, provided always that freedom was not to be my choice.

As I look back over my development and survey what I have achieved so far, I do not complain, but I am not complacent either. With my hands in my trouser pockets, my bottle of wine on the table, I half lie and half sit in my rocking chair and gaze out of the window: if a visitor arrives, I receive him with propriety. My manager sits in the anteroom; when I ring, he comes and listens to what I have to say. Nearly every evening I give a performance, and I have a success that could hardly be increased. When I come home late at night from banquets, from scientific receptions, from social gatherings, there sits waiting for me a half-trained little chimpanzee and I take comfort from her as apes do. By day I cannot bear to see her; for she has the insane look of the bewildered half-broken animal in her eye; no one else sees it, but I do, and I cannot bear it. On the whole, at any rate, I have achieved what I set out to achieve. But do not tell me that it was not worth the trouble. In any case, I am not appealing for any man's verdict, I am only imparting knowledge, I am only making a report. To you also, honored Members of the Academy, I have only made a report.

Suggestions for Discussion

1. Why is the speaker, an ape, addressing an academy? What tone does he use in his address?

2. How does Kafka contrast the life of the ape in Africa with the life of the human being in Europe? Who suffers from the contrast?

3. Kafka presents the story matter-of-factly and also ironically. Explain his use of irony in the story, referring to specific details during the ape's time of capture and after.

4. Why did the ape choose the variety stage over the Zoological Gardens as a way of life?

Suggestion for Writing

Write an essay in which you explain how the history of this ape is related to mankind's struggle for freedom. What is the ape's attitude toward freedom? How does it differ from man's?

William Faulkner
Dry September

William Faulkner (1897–1962) lived most of his life in Oxford, Mississippi. After a year at the university of his native state, he joined the Royal Canadian Air Force, eager to participate in World War I. His novels set in his imaginary Yoknapatawpha County include *The Sound and the Fury* (1929), *Light in August* (1932), *Absalom, Absalom!* (1936), and *The Hamlet* (1940). This story, taken from the section of Faulkner's *Collected Stories* (1950) called "The Village," offers an acute social and psychological analysis of life in a small Southern town after World War I. Notice how Faulkner focuses on the gentle barber, the hysterical spinster, and the brutal ex-soldier to provide social commentary.

I

Through the bloody September twilight, aftermath of sixty-two rainless days, it had gone like a fire in dry grass—the rumor, the story, whatever it was. Something about Miss Minnie Cooper and a Negro. Attacked, insulted, frightened: none of them, gathered in the barber shop on that Saturday evening where the ceiling fan stirred, without freshening it, the vitiated air, sending back upon them, in recurrent surges of stale pomade and lotion, their own stale breath and odors, knew exactly what had happened.

"Except it wasn't Will Mayes," a barber said. He was a man of middle age; a thin, sand-colored man with a mild face, who was shaving a client. "I know Will Mayes. He's a good nigger. And I know Minnie Cooper, too."

"What do you know about her?" a second barber said.

"Who is she?" the client said. "A young girl?"

"No," the barber said. "She's about forty, I reckon. She ain't married. That's why I dont believe—"

"Believe, hell!" a hulking youth in a sweat-stained silk shirt said. "Wont you take a white woman's word before a nigger's?"

"I dont believe Will Mayes did it," the barber said. "I know Will Mayes."

"Maybe you know who did it, then. Maybe you already got him out of town, you damn niggerlover."

"I dont believe anybody did anything. I dont believe anything happened. I leave it to you fellows if them ladies that get old without getting married dont have notions that a man cant—"

"Then you are a hell of a white man," the client said. He moved under the cloth. The youth had sprung to his feet.

"You dont?" he said. "Do you accuse a white woman of lying?"

The barber held the razor poised above the half-risen client. He did not look around.

"It's this durn weather," another said. "It's enough to make a man do anything. Even to her."

Nobody laughed. The barber said in his mild, stubborn tone: "I ain't accusing nobody of nothing. I just know and you fellows know how a woman that never—"

"You damn niggerlover!" the youth said.

"Shut up, Butch," another said. "We'll get the facts in plenty of time to act."

"Who is? Who's getting them?" the youth said. "Facts, hell! I—".

"You're a fine white man," the client said. "Aint you?" In his frothy beard he looked like a desert rat in the moving pictures. "You tell them, Jack," he said to the youth. "If there aint any white men in this town, you can count on me, even if I aint only a drummer and a stranger."

"That's right, boys," the barber said. "Find out the truth first. I know Will Mayes."

"Well, by God!" the youth shouted. "To think that a white man in this town—"

"Shut up, Butch," the second speaker said. "We got plenty of time."

The client sat up. He looked at the speaker. "Do you claim that anything excuses a nigger attacking a white woman? Do you mean to tell me you are a white man and you'll stand for it? You better go back North where you came from. The South dont want your kind here."

"North what?" the second said. "I was born and raised in this town."

"Well, by God!" the youth said. He looked about with a strained, baffled gaze, as if he was trying to remember what it was he wanted to say or to do. He drew his sleeve across his sweating face. "Damn if I'm going to let a white woman—"

"You tell them, Jack," the drummer said. "By God, if they—"

The screen door crashed open. A man stood in the floor, his feet apart and his heavy-set body poised easily. His white shirt was open at the throat; he wore a felt hat. His hot, bold glance swept the group. His name was Mc-Lendon. He had commanded troops at the front in France and had been decorated for valor.

"Well," he said, "are you going to sit there and let a black son rape a white woman on the streets of Jefferson?"

Butch sprang up again. The silk of his shirt clung flat to his heavy shoulders. At each armpit was a dark halfmoon. "That's what I been telling them! That's what I—"

"Did it really happen?" a third said. "This aint the first man scare she ever had, like Hawkshaw says. Wasn't there something about a man on the kitchen roof, watching her undress, about a year ago?"

"What?" the client said. "What's that?" The barber had been slowly forcing him back into the chair; he arrested himself reclining, his head lifted, the barber still pressing him down.

McLendon whirled on the third speaker. "Happen? What the hell difference does it make? Are you going to let the black sons get away with it until one really does it?"

"That's what I'm telling them!" Butch shouted. He cursed, long and steady, pointless.

"Here, here," a fourth said. "Not so loud. Dont talk so loud."

"Sure," McLendon said; "no talking necessary at all. I've done my talking. Who's with me?" He poised on the balls of his feet, roving his gaze.

The barber held the drummer's face down, the razor poised. "Find out the facts first, boys. I know Willy Mayes. It wasn't him. Let's get the sheriff and do this thing right."

McLendon whirled upon him his furious, rigid face. The barber did not look away. They looked like men of different races. The other barbers had ceased also above their prone clients. "You mean to tell me," McLendon said, "that you'd take a nigger's word before a white woman's? Why, you damn niggerloving—"

The third speaker rose and grasped McLendon's arm; he too had been a soldier. "Now, now. Let's figure this thing out. Who knows anything about what really happened?"

"Figure out hell!" McLendon jerked his arm free. "All that're with me get up from there. The ones that aint—" He roved his gaze, dragging his sleeve across his face.

Three men rose. The drummer in the chair sat up. "Here," he said, jerking at the cloth about his neck; "get this rag off me. I'm with him. I dont live here, but by God, if our mothers and wives and sisters—" He smeared the cloth over his face and flung it to the floor. McLendon stood in the floor and cursed the others. Another rose and moved toward him. The remainder sat uncomfortable, not looking at one another, then one by one they rose and joined him.

The barber picked the cloth from the floor. He began to fold it neatly. "Boys, dont do that. Will Mayes never done it. I know."

"Come on," McLendon said. He whirled. From his hip pocket protruded the butt of a heavy automatic pistol. They went out. The screen door crashed behind them reverberant in the dead air.

The barber wiped the razor carefully and swiftly, and put it away, and ran to the rear, and took his hat from the wall. "I'll be back as soon as I can," he said to the other barbers. "I cant let—" He went out, running, The two other barbers followed him to the door and caught it on the rebound, leaning out and looking up the street after him. The air was flat and dead. It had a metallic taste at the base of the tongue.

"What can he do?" the first said. The second one was saying "Jees Christ, Jees Christ" under his breath. "I'd just as lief be Will Mayes as Hawk, if he gets McLendon riled."

"Jees Christ, Jees Christ," the second whispered

"You reckon he really done it to her?" the first said.

II

She was thirty-eight or thirty-nine. She lived in a small frame house with her invalid mother and a thin, sallow, unflagging aunt, where each morning between ten and eleven she would appear on the porch in a lace-trimmed boudoir cap, to sit swinging in the porch swing until noon. After dinner she lay down for a while, until the afternoon began to cool. Then, in one of the three or four new voile dresses which she had each summer, she would go downtown to spend the afternoon in the stores with the other ladies, where they would handle the goods and haggle over the prices in cold, immediate voices, without any intention of buying.

She was of comfortable people—not the best in Jefferson, but good people enough—and she was still on the slender side of ordinary looking, with a bright, faintly haggard manner and dress. When she was young she had had a slender, nervous body and a sort of hard vivacity which had enabled her for a time to ride upon the crest of the town's social life as exemplified by the high school party and church social period of her contemporaries while still children enough to be unclassconscious.

She was the last to realize that she was losing ground; that those among whom she had been a little brighter and louder flame than any other were beginning to learn the pleasure of snobbery—male—and retaliation—female. That was when her face began to wear that bright, haggard look. She still carried it to parties on shadowy porticoes and summer lawns, like a mask or a flag, with that bafflement of furious repudiation of truth in her eyes. One evening at a party she heard a boy and two girls, all schoolmates, talking. She never accepted another invitation.

She watched the girls with whom she had grown up as they married and got homes and children, but no man ever called on her steadily until the children of the other girls had been calling her "aunty" for several years, the while their mothers told them in bright voices about how popular Aunt Minnie had been as a girl. Then the town began to see her driving on Sunday afternoons with the cashier in the bank. He was a widower of about forty—a high-colored man, smelling always faintly of the barber shop or of whisky. He owned the first automobile in town, a red runabout; Minnie had the first motoring bonnet and veil the town ever saw. Then the town began to say: "Poor Minnie." "But she is old enough to take care of herself," others said. That was when she began to ask her old schoolmates that their children call her "cousin" instead of "aunty."

It was twelve years now since she had been relegated into adultery by public opinion, and eight years since the cashier had gone to a Memphis bank, returning for one day each Christmas, which he spent at an annual bachelors' party at a hunting club on the river. From behind their curtains the neighbors would see the party pass, and during the over-the-way Christmas day visiting they would tell her about him, about how well he looked, and how they heard that he was prospering in the city, watching with bright, secret eyes her haggard, bright face. Usually by that hour there would be the scent of whisky on her breath. It was supplied her by a youth, a clerk at the soda fountain: "Sure; I buy it for the old gal. I reckon she's entitled to a little fun."

Her mother kept to her room altogether now; the gaunt aunt ran the house. Against that background Minnie's bright dresses, her idle and empty days, had a quality of furious unreality. She went out in the evenings only with women now, neighbors, to the moving pictures. Each afternoon she dressed in one of the new dresses and went downtown alone, where her young "cousins" were already strolling in the late afternoons with their delicate, silken heads and thin, awkward arms and conscious hips, clinging to one another or shrieking and giggling with paired boys in the soda fountain when she passed and went on along the serried store fronts, in the doors of which the sitting and lounging men did not even follow her with their eyes any more.

III

The barber went swiftly up the street where the sparse lights, insect-swirled, glared in rigid and violent suspension in the lifeless air. The day had died in a pall of dust; above the darkened square, shrouded by the spent dust, the sky was as clear as the inside of a brass bell. Below the east was a rumor of the twice-waxed moon.

When he overtook them McLendon and three others were getting into a car parked in an alley. McLendon stooped his thick head, peering out beneath the top. "Changed your mind, did you?" he said. "Damn good thing; by God, tomorrow when this town hears about how you talked tonight—"

"Now, now," the other ex-soldier said. "Hawkshaw's all right. Come on, Hawk; jump in."

"Will Mayes never done it, boys," the barber said. "If anybody done it. Why, you all know well as I do there ain't any town where they got better niggers than us. And you know how a lady will kind of think things about men when there aint any reason to, and Miss Minnie anyway—"

"Sure, sure," the soldier said. "We're just going to talk to him a little; that's all."

"Talk hell!" Butch said. "When we're through with the—"

"Shut up, for God's sake!" the soldier said. "Do you want everybody in town—"

"Tell them, by God!" McLendon said. "Tell every one of the sons that'll let a white woman—"

"Let's go; let's go: here's the other car." The second car slid squealing out of a cloud of dust at the alley mouth. McLendon started his car and took the lead. Dust lay like fog in the street. The street lights hung nimbused as in water. They drove on out of town.

A rutted lane turned at right angles. Dust hung above it too, and above all the land. The dark bulk of the ice plant, where the Negro Mayes was night watchman, rose against the sky. "Better stop here, hadn't we?" the soldier said. McLendon did not reply. He hurled the car up and slammed to a stop, the headlights glaring on the blank wall.

"Listen here, boys," the barber said, "if he's here, don't that prove he never done it? Don't it? If it was him, he would run. Don't you see he would?" The second car came up and stopped. McLendon got down; Butch sprang down beside him. "Listen, boys," the barber said.

"Cut the lights off!" McLendon said. The breathless dark rushed down. There was no sound in it save their lungs as they sought air in the parched dust in which for two months they had lived; then the diminishing crunch of McLendon's and Butch's feet, and a moment later McLendon's voice:

"Will! . . . Will!"

Below the east the wan hemorrhage of the moon increased. It heaved above the ridge, silvering the air, the dust, so that they seemed to breathe, live, in a bowl of molten lead. There was no sound of nightbird nor insect, no sound save their breathing and a faint ticking of contracting metal about the cars. Where their bodies touched one another they seemed to sweat dryly, for no more moisture came. "Christ!" a voice said; "let's get out of here."

But they didn't move until vague noises began to grow out of the darkness ahead; then they got out and waited tensely in the breathless dark. There was another sound: a blow, a hissing expulsion of breath and McLendon cursing in undertone. They stood a moment longer, then they ran forward. They ran in a stumbling clump, as though they were fleeing something. "Kill him, kill the son," a voice whispered. McLendon flung them back.

"Not here," he said. "Get him into the car." "Kill him, kill the black son!"

the voice murmured. They dragged the Negro to the car. The barber had waited beside the car. He could feel himself sweating and he knew he was going to be sick at the stomach.

"What is it, captains?" the Negro said. "I ain't done nothing. 'Fore God, Mr. John." Someone produced handcuffs. They worked busily about the Negro as though he were a post, quiet, intent, getting in one another's way. He submitted to the handcuffs, looking swiftly and constantly from dim face to dim face. "Who's here, captains?" he said, leaning to peer into the faces until they could feel his breath and smell his sweaty reek. He spoke a name or two. "What you all say I done, Mr. John?"

McLendon jerked the car door open. "Get in!" he said.

The Negro did not move. "What you all going to do with me, Mr. John? I aint done nothing. White folks, captains, I aint done nothing: I swear 'fore God." He called another name.

"Get in!" McLendon said. He struck the Negro. The others expelled their breath in a dry hissing and struck him with random blows and he whirled and cursed them, and swept his manacled hands across their faces and slashed the barber upon the mouth, and the barber struck him also. "Get him in there," McLendon said. They pushed at him. He ceased struggling and got in and sat quietly as the others took their places. He sat between the barber and the soldier, drawing his limbs in so as not to touch them, his eyes going swiftly and constantly from face to face. Butch clung to the running board. The car moved on. The barber nursed his mouth with his handkerchief.

"What's the matter, Hawk?" the soldier said.

"Nothing," the barber said. They regained the highroad and turned away from town. The second car dropped back out of the dust. They went on, gaining speed; the final fringe of houses dropped behind.

"Goddamn, he stinks!" the soldier said.

"We'll fix that", the drummer in front beside McLendon said. On the running board Butch cursed into the hot rush of air. The barber leaned suddenly forward and touched McLendon's arm.

"Let me out, John," he said.

"Jump out, niggerlover," McLendon said without turning his head. He drove swiftly. Behind them the sourceless lights of the second car glared in the dust. Presently McLendon turned into a narrow road. It was rutted with disuse. It led back to an abandoned brick kiln—a series of reddish mounds and weed- and vine-choked vats without bottom. It had been used for pasture once, until one day the owner missed one of his mules. Although he prodded carefully in the vats with a long pole, he could not even find the bottom of them.

"John," the barber said.

"Jump out, then," McLendon said, hurling the car along the ruts. Beside the barber the Negro spoke:

"Mr. Henry."

The barber sat forward. The narrow tunnel of the road rushed up and past. Their motion was like an extinct furnace blast: cooler, but utterly dead. The car bounded from rut to rut.

"Mr. Henry," the Negro said.

The barber began to tug furiously at the door. "Look out, there!" the soldier said, but the barber had already kicked the door open and swung onto the running board. The soldier leaned across the Negro and grasped at him, but he had already jumped. The car went on without checking speed.

The impetus hurled him crashing through dust-sheathed weeds, into the ditch. Dust puffed about him, and in a thin, vicious crackling of sapless stems he lay choking and retching until the second car passed and died away. Then he rose and limped on until he reached the highroad and turned toward town, brushing at his clothes with his hands. The moon was higher, riding high and clear of the dust at last, and after a while the town began to glare beneath the dust. He went on, limping. Presently he heard cars and the glow of them grew in the dust behind him and he left the road and crouched again in the weeds until they passed. McLendon's car came last now. There were four people in it and Butch was not on the running board.

They went on; the dust swallowed them; the glare and the sound died away. The dust of them hung for a while, but soon the eternal dust absorbed it again. The barber climbed back onto the road and limped on toward town.

IV

As she dressed for supper on that Saturday evening, her own flesh felt like fever. Her hands trembled among the hooks and eyes, and her eyes had a feverish look, and her hair swirled crisp and crackling under the comb. While she was still dressing the friends called for her and sat while she donned her sheerest underthings and stockings and a new voile dress. "Do you feel strong enough to go out?" they said, their eyes bright too, with a dark glitter. "When you have had time to get over the shock, you must tell us what happened. What he said and did; everything."

In the leafed darkness, as they walked toward the square, she began to breathe deeply, something like a swimmer preparing to dive, until she ceased trembling, the four of them walking slowly because of the terrible heat and out of solicitude for her. But as they neared the square she began to tremble again, walking with her head up, her hands clenched at her sides, their voices about her murmurous, also with that feverish, glittering quality of their eyes.

They entered the square, she in the center of the group, fragile in her fresh dress. She was trembling worse. She walked slower and slower, as children eat ice cream, her head up and her eyes bright in the haggard banner of her face, passing the hotel and the coatless drummers in chairs along the curb looking around at her: "That's the one: see? The one in pink in the middle." "Is that her? What did they do with the nigger? Did they—?" "Sure. He's all right." "All right, is he?" "Sure. He went on a little trip." Then the drug store, where even the young men lounging in the doorway tipped their hats and followed with their eyes the motions of her hips and legs when she passed.

They went on, passing the lifted hats of the gentlemen, the suddenly ceased voices, deferent, protective. "Do you see?" the friends said. Their voices sounded like long, hovering sighs of hissing exultation. "There's not a Negro on the square. Not one."

They reached the picture show. It was like a miniature fairyland with its lighted lobby and colored lithographs of life caught in its terrible and beautiful mutations. Her lips began to tingle. In the dark, when the picture began, it would be all right; she could hold back the laughing so it would not waste away so fast and so soon. So she hurried on before the turning faces, the undertones of low astonishment, and they took their accustomed places where she could see the aisle against the silver glare and the young men and girls coming in two and two against it.

The lights flicked away; the screen glowed silver, and soon life began to unfold, beautiful and passionate and sad, while still the young men and girls entered, scented and sibilant in the half dark, their paired backs in silhouette delicate and sleek, their slim, quick bodies awkward, divinely young, while beyond them the silver dream accumulated, inevitably on and on. She began to laugh. In trying to suppress it, it made more noise than ever; heads began to turn. Still laughing, her friends raised her and led her out, and she stood at the curb, laughing on a high, sustained note, until the taxi came up and they helped her in.

They removed the pink voile and the sheer underthings and the stockings, and put her to bed, and cracked ice for her temples, and sent for the doctor. He was hard to locate, so they ministered to her with hushed ejaculations, renewing the ice and fanning her. While the ice was fresh and cold she stopped laughing and lay still for a time, moaning only a little. But soon the laughing welled again and her voice rose screaming.

"Shhhhhhhhhh! Shhhhhhhhhhhhh!" they said, freshening the icepack, smoothing her hair, examining it for gray; "poor girl!" Then to one another: "Do you suppose anything really happened?" their eyes darkly aglitter, secret and passionate. "Shhhhhhhhhh! Poor girl! Poor Minnie!"

V

It was midnight when McLendon drove up to his neat new house. It was trim and fresh as a birdcage and almost as small, with its clean, green-and-white paint. He locked the car and mounted the porch and entered. His wife rose from a chair beside the reading lamp. McLendon stopped in the floor and stared at her until she looked down.

"Look at that clock," he said, lifting his arm, pointing. She stood before him, her face lowered, a magazine in her hands. Her face was pale, strained, and weary-looking. "Haven't I told you about sitting up like this, waiting to see when I come in?"

"John," she said. She laid the magazine down. Poised on the balls of his feet, he glared at her with his hot eyes, his sweating face.

"Didn't I tell you?" He went toward her. She looked up then. He caught her shoulder. She stood passive, looking at him.

"Don't, John. I couldn't sleep . . . The heat; something. Please, John. You're hurting me."

"Didn't I tell you?" He released her and half struck, half flung her across the chair, and she lay there and watched him quietly as he left the room.

He went on through the house, ripping off his shirt, and on the dark, screened porch at the rear he stood and mopped his head and shoulders with the shirt and flung it away. He took the pistol from his hip and laid it on the table beside the bed, and sat on the bed and removed his shoes, and rose and slipped his trousers off. He was sweating again already, and he stooped and hunted furiously for the shirt. At last he found it and wiped his body again, and, with his body pressed against the dusty screen, he stood panting. There was no movement, no sound, not even an insect. The dark world seemed to lie stricken beneath the cold moon and the lidless stars.

Suggestions for Discussion

1. Faulkner tells this story of a lynching in five parts. Discuss the relation of the parts to each other.

2. What is the function of Hawkshaw? Why is it appropriate for the story to open in a barber shop? Explain the discussion between the barbers and the customers.

3. In what ways is John McLendon different from the other men? What explains his power over them?

4. Explain the significance of the scene in which Will Mayes hits Hawkshaw in the mouth.

5. How do you know that nothing has happened to Miss Minnie Cooper? What aspects of her character make clear that she has invented an affront?

6. Explain the title of the story. How does Faulkner use weather as a force in the story? What has weather to do with the lynching?

Suggestions for Writing

1. Write an essay in which you explain how this story is an eloquent attack on lynching. Does the author permit himself to comment on what has occurred?

2. Write an essay in which you explain how the characters in this story provide a comment on the relation between the races.

Ray Bradbury

Perhaps We Are Going Away

Ray Bradbury (b. 1920), who lives in Southern California, is among the most popular and prolific of science fiction writers. He is particularly well-known for *The Martian Chronicles* (1950), *The Illustrated Man* (1951), and *Dandelion Wine* (1957). In this brief and powerful story from *The Machineries of Joy* (1963), Bradbury imagines the sense of danger and of coming disaster which a young Indian boy feels as he gets his first glimpse of European soldiers in America.

It was a strange thing that could not be told. It touched along the hairs on his neck as he lay wakening. Eyes shut, he pressed his hands to the dirt.

Was the earth, snaking old fires under its crust, turning over in its sleep?

Were buffalo on the dust prairies, in the whistling grass, drumming the sod, moving this way like a dark weather?

No.

What? What, then?

He opened his eyes and was the boy Ho-Awi, of a tribe named for a bird, by the hills named for the shadows of owls, near the great ocean itself, on a day that was evil for no reason.

Ho-Awi stared at the tent flaps, which shivered like a great beast remembering winter.

Tell me, he thought, the terrible thing, where does it come from? Whom will it kill?

He lifted the flap and stepped out into his village.

He turned slowly, a boy with bones in his dark cheeks like the keels of small birds flying. His brown eyes saw god-filled, cloud-filled sky, his cupped ear heard thistles ticking the war drums, but still the greater mystery drew him to the edge of the village.

Here, legend said, the land went on like a tide to another sea. Between here and there was as much earth as there were stars across the night sky. Somewhere in all that land, storms of black buffalo harvested the grass. And here stood Ho-Awi, his stomach a fist, wondering, searching, waiting, afraid.

You too? said the shadow of a hawk.

Ho-Awi turned.

It was the shadow of his grandfather's hand that wrote on the wind.

No. The grandfather made the sign for silence. His tongue moved soft in a toothless mouth. His eyes were small creeks running behind the sunken flesh beds, the cracked sand washes of his face.

Now they stood on the edge of the day, drawn close by the unknown.

And Old Man did as the boy had done. His mummified ear turned, his nostril twitched. Old Man too ached for some answering growl from any direction that would tell them only a great timberfall of weather had dropped from a distant sky. But the wind gave no answer, spoke only to itself.

The Old Man made the sign which said they must go on the Great hunt. This, said his hands like mouths, was a day for the rabbit young and the featherless old. Let no warrior come with them. The hare and the dying vulture must track together. For only the very young saw life ahead, and only the very old saw life behind; the others between were so busy with life they saw nothing.

The Old Man wheeled slowly in all directions.

Yes! He knew, he was certain, he was sure! To find this thing of darkness would take the innocence of the newborn and the innocence of the blind to see very clear.

Come! said the trembling fingers.

And snuffing rabbit and earthbound hawk shadowed out of the village into changing weather.

They searched the high hills to see if the stones lay atop each other, and they were so arranged. They scanned the prairies, but found only the winds which played there like tribal children all day. And found arrowheads from old wars.

No, the Old Man's hand drew on the sky, the men of this nation and that beyond smoke by the summer fires while the squaws cut wood. It is not arrows flying that we almost hear.

At last, when the sun sank into the nation of buffalo hunters, the Old Man looked up.

The birds, his hands cried suddenly, are flying south! Summer is over!

No, the boy's hands said, summer has just begun! I see no birds!

They are so high, said the Old Man's fingers, that only the blind can feel their passage. They shadow the heart more than the earth. I feel them pass south in my blood. Summer goes. We may go with it. Perhaps we are going away.

No! cried the boy aloud, suddenly afraid. Go where? Why? For what?

Who knows? said the Old Man, and perhaps we will not move. Still, even without moving, perhaps we are going away.

No! Go back! cried the boy, to the empty sky, the birds unseen, the un-shadowed air. Summer, stay!

No use, said the Old One's single hand, moving by itself. Not you or me or our people can stay this weather. It is a season changed, come to live on the land for all time.

But from where does it come?

This way, said the Old Man at last.

And in the dusk they looked down at the great waters of the east that went over the edge of the world, where no one had ever gone.

There. The Old Man's hand clenched and thrust out. There *it* is.

Far ahead, a single light burned on the shore.

With the moon rising, the Old Man and the rabbit boy padded on the sands, heard strange voices in the sea, smelled wild burnings from the now suddenly close fire.

They crawled on their bellies. They lay looking in at the light.

And the more he looked, the colder Ho-Awi became, and he knew that all the Old Man had said was true.

For drawn to this fire built of sticks and moss, which flickered brightly in the soft evening wind which was cooler now, at the heart of summer, were such creatures as he had never seen.

These were men with faces like white-hot coals, with some eyes in these faces as blue as sky. All these men had glossy hair on their cheeks and chins, which grew to a point. One man stood with raised lightning in his hand and a great moon of sharp stuff on his head like the face of a fish. The others had bright round tinkling crusts of material cleaved to their chests which gonged slightly when they moved. As Ho-Awi watched, some men lifted the gonging bright things from their heads, unskinned the eye-blinding crab shells, the turtle casings from their chests, their arms, their legs, and tossed these discarded sheaths to the sand. Doing this, the creatures laughed, while out in the bay stood a black shape on the waters, a great dark canoe with things like torn clouds hung on poles over it.

After a long while of holding their breath, the Old Man and the boy went away.

From a hill, they watched the fire that was no bigger than a star now. You could wink it out with an eyelash. If you closed your eyes, it was destroyed.

Still, it remained.

Is this, asked the boy, the great happening?

The Old One's face was that of a fallen eagle, filled with dreadful years and unwanted wisdom. The eyes were resplendently bright, as if they welled with a rise of cold clear water in which all could be seen, like a river that drank the sky and earth and knew it, accepted silently and would not deny the accumulation of dust, time, shape, sound and destiny.

The Old Man nodded, once.

This was the terrible weather. This was how summer would end. This made the birds wheel south, shadowless, through a grieving land.

The worn hands stopped moving. The time of questions was done.

Far away, the fire leaped. One of the creatures moved. The bright stuff on his tortoise-shell body flashed. It was like an arrow cutting a wound in the night.

Then the boy vanished in darkness, following the eagle and the hawk that lived in the stone body of his grandfather.

Below, the sea reared up and poured another great salt wave in billions of pieces which crashed and hissed like knives swarming along the continental shores.

Suggestions for Discussion

1. Explain the power of this account of the advent of Western man in America.

2. Discuss Bradbury's characterizations. Are they as important to the story as the events that occur or the descriptions of the setting? Explain.

3. This story is extremely brief. Would you want it any longer? Explain.

Suggestions for Writing

1. Describe the first encounter between the Indians and the Europeans.

2. Write an essay in which you try to warn the Indians to be wary of the Europeans. Be as convincing as possible.

Poetry

Wilfred Owen

Dulce et Decorum Est

Wilfred Owen (1893–1918) was born in Shropshire, England, and educated at Birkenhead Institute. Among the most celebrated of the English war poets, he was killed in action in World War I. Another war poet, Siegfried Sassoon, collected Owen's poems which were first published in 1920. Other collections followed as did critical studies and memoirs. "Dulce et Decorum Est" (taken from Horace's statement, "It is sweet and fitting to die for one's country") opposes vivid and devastating images of the casualties of war with statements of sentimental patriotism. It shows war as the ultimate insult to human dignity.

Bent double, like old beggars under sacks,
Knock-kneed, coughing like hags, we cursed through sludge,
Till on the haunting flares we turned our backs,
And towards our distant rest began to trudge.
Men marched asleep. Many had lost their boots,
But limped on, blood-shod. All went lame, all blind;
Drunk with fatigue; deaf even to the hoots
Of gas-shells dropping softly behind.

Gas!GAS! Quick, boys!—An ecstasy of fumbling,
Fitting the clumsy helmets just in time,
But someone still was yelling out and stumbling
And flound'ring like a man in fire or lime.—
Dim through the misty panes and thick green light,
As under a green sea, I saw him drowning.
In all my dreams before my helpless sight
He plunges at me, guttering, choking, drowning.

If in some smothering dreams, you too could pace
Behind the wagon that we flung him in,

And watch the white eyes writhing in his face,
His hanging face, like a devil's sick of sin,
If you could hear, at every jolt, the blood
Come gargling from the froth-corrupted lungs
Bitter as the cud
Of vile, incurable sores on innocent tongues,—
My friend, you would not tell with such high zest
To children ardent for some desperate glory,
The old lie: *Dulce et decorum est*
Pro patria mori.

Suggestions for Discussion

1. In the first two stanzas, Owen presents two connected scenes of war. How are these two stanzas related to the final one?

2. Discuss the use of irony in the poem. Show why Owen uses the quotation from Horace.

3. Examine the series of images which Owen uses to describe war. Do they progress through the poem? Show why one cannot interchange the first two stanzas.

Suggestion for Writing

Owen's picture of the destruction of lives constitutes a poetic statement against war. Does this poem lead you to a belief in pacifism? Are there "just" and "unjust" wars? Try to sort out your attitudes and write an essay explaining under what conditions, if any, you might be willing to fight for your country. Support your statements with detailed arguments.

William Stafford
Freedom

William Edgar Stafford (b. 1914) was for many years a professor of English and humanities. He has published poetry in such journals as *The Atlantic, Harper's,* and *The New Yorker.* His collections of poetry include *Traveling Through the Dark* (1963) and *The Rescued Years* (1966). In this brief reflection he shows how society limits our freedom and how ingenious we must be to enjoy it.

Freedom is not following a river.
Freedom is following a river,
   though, if you want to.
It is deciding now by what happens now.
It is knowing that luck makes a difference.

No leader is free; no follower is free—
   the rest of us can often be free.
Most of the world are living by
creeds too odd, chancey, and habit-forming
   to be worth arguing about by reason.

If you are oppressed, wake up about
four in the morning: most places,
you can usually be free some of the time
   if you wake up before other people.

Suggestions for Discussion

1. How would you characterize this poem: powerful, moving, provocative, disturbing, trivial? Explain your answer.

2: Discuss the significance of Stafford's title.

Suggestion for Writing

Compare and contrast this poem with "The Unknown Citizen" by Auden.

W. H. Auden

The Unknown Citizen

Wystan Hugh Auden (1907–1973), educated at Oxford University, was early recognized as a leader of the poets of his generation. His volumes of poetry include *The Orators* (1932), *The Double Man* (1941), and *The Age of Anxiety* (1947), which won a Pulitzer Prize in 1948. Born in England, he came to the United States at the outbreak of World War II. His autobiography, *Certain World: A Commonplace Book,* published in 1970, traces his return from leftist agnostic to the Church of England. In 1967 he was made a fellow of Christ Church, Oxford. In the following poem, published in 1940, Auden comments satirically on the behavior of a good citizen in a totalitarian state which resembles not only fascist Italy and Nazi Germany but democratic America and Britain as well.

The Unknown Citizen
(To JS/07/M/378
This Marble Monument
Is Erected by the State)

He was found by the Bureau of Statistics to be
One against whom there was no official complaint,
And all the reports on his conduct agree
That, in the modern sense of an old-fashioned word, he was a saint,
For in everything he did he served the Greater Community.
Except for the War till the day he retired
He worked in a factory and never got fired,
But satisfied his employers, Fudge Motors Inc.
Yet he wasn't a scab or odd in his views,
For his Union reports that he paid his dues,
(Our report on his Union shows it was sound)
And our Social Psychology workers found
That he was popular with his mates and liked to drink.
The Press are convinced that he bought a paper every day
And that his reactions to advertisements were normal in every way.
Policies taken out in his name prove that he was fully insured,
And his Health-card shows he was once in a hospital but left it cured,
Both Producers Research and High-Grade Living declare
He was fully sensible to the advantages of the Installment Plan
And had everything necessary to the Modern Man,
A phonograph, a radio, a car and a frigidaire.
Our researchers into Public Opinion are content
That he held the proper opinions for the time of year;
When there was peace, he was for peace; when there was war, he went.
He was married and added five children to the population,
Which our Eugenist says was the right number for a parent of his generation,
And our teachers report that he never interfered with their education.
Was he free? Was he Happy? The question is absurd:
Had anything been wrong, we should certainly have heard.

Suggestions for Discussion

1. Discuss reasons for the state to bother erecting such a monument.

2. Analyze the strengths and weaknesses of the society described by Auden.

3. Discuss Auden's use of irony in the poem. Find specific examples.

Suggestions for Writing

1. Write a sketch describing and evaluating a typical day in the life of the unknown citizen.

2. Provide an alternative inscription for the monument.

◇◇◇◇

Robert Frost
Departmental

Robert Frost (1874–1963) was born in San Francisco, but of New England stock. At his father's death when Frost was eleven, he and his mother settled in Massachusetts. He studied for only seven weeks at Dartmouth and married two years later. After Frost's second unsuccessful attempt at college, this time at Harvard, his grandfather gave him a farm in Derry, New Hampshire, on the condition that he live there for ten years. When the ten years were up he left with his family for England where his first two books of poetry, *A Boy's Will* (1913) and *North of Boston* (1914) were published. He returned to America in 1915 to discover that he had a reputation as a poet. Eventually settling in Vermont, he traveled throughout America for many years giving lectures and public readings. He wrote many volumes of poetry and won four Pulitzer Prizes, many honorary degrees, and membership in distinguished academies. The United States Senate extended him greetings on his seventy-fifth and eighty-fifth birthdays, and he read one of his poems at the inauguration of President John F. Kennedy. "Departmental", from *A Further Range* (1936), reveals, with great irony, his commitment to a society which values human feelings and nourishes human dignity.

An ant on the tablecloth
Ran into a dormant moth
Of many times his size.
He showed not the least surprise.
His business wasn't with such.
He gave it scarcely a touch,
And was off on his duty run.
Yet if he encountered one
Of the hive's enquiry squad
Whose work is to find out God
And the nature of time and space,
He would put him onto the case.
Ants are a curious race;
One crossing with hurried tread
The body of one of their dead
Isn't given a moment's arrest—
Seems not even impressed.
But he no doubt reports to any
With whom he crosses antennae,
And they no doubt report
To the higher up at court.
Then word goes forth in Formic:
'Death's come to Jerry McCormic,
Our selfless forager Jerry.
Will the special Janizary
Whose office it is to bury

The dead of the commissary
Go bring him home to his people.
Lay him in state on a sepal.
Wrap him for shroud in a petal.
Embalm him with ichor of nettle.
This is the word of your Queen.'
And presently on the scene
Appears a solemn mortician;
And taking formal position
With feelers calmly atwiddle,
Seizes the dead by the middle,
And heaving him high in air,
Carries him out of there.
No one stands round to stare.
It is nobody else's affair.

It couldn't be called ungentle.
But how thoroughly departmental.

Suggestions for Discussion

1. What is the nature of the society of ants described in this poem?

2. Do the actions of the society of ants have relevance for human society?

3. What is the tone of the poem? Relate the line "Then word goes forth in Formic:" to the tone. What is "formic"?

4. What is the attitude of the speaker toward the "departmental" natures of the society of ants? How do we learn of his attitude?

5. How does the poet use meter to help establish the tone of the poem?

Suggestion for Writing

Compare the society depicted in "Departmental" with that of Auden's "The Unknown Citizen." How do both poets make use of irony in commenting on their world?

The Examined Life: Education

◆◆◆◆

We survived. The depths had been icy and dark, but now a bright sun spoke to our souls. I was no longer simply a member of the proud graduating class of 1940; I was a proud member of the wonderful, beautiful Negro race.

   —Maya Angelou, "Graduation"

More than any other time in history, mankind faces a crossroads. One path leads to despair and utter hopelessness. The other to total extinction. Let us hope that we have the wisdom to choose correctly.

   —Woody Allen, "My Speech to the Graduates"

In no other century of our brief existence have human beings learned so deeply, and so painfully, the extent and depth of their ignorance about nature. We are beginning to confront this, and trying to do something about it with science. . . . But we are starting almost from scratch, and we have a long, long way to go.

   —Lewis Thomas, "The Youngest and Brightest Thing Around"

That man, I think, has had a liberal education, . . . who, no stunted ascetic, is full of life and fire, but whose passions are trained to come to heel by a vigorous will, the servant of a tender conscience; who has learned to love all beauty, whether of Nature or of art, to hate all vileness, and to respect others as himself.

   —T. H. Huxley, "A Liberal Education"

The meaning of life is unclear, but that is why we must spend our lives clarifying it rather than letting the question go. The university's function is to remind students of the importance and urgency of the question and give them the means to pursue it.

—**Allan Bloom,** "Our Listless Universities"

Personal Reminiscence

◆◆◆◆

Lincoln Steffens

I Go to College

Joseph Lincoln Steffens (1866–1936) was born in San Francisco and graduated from the University of California at Berkeley. After his return from three years of study in Europe, he became a well-known muckraker and journalist. As editor of *McClures, The American,* and *Everybody's* magazines he exposed corruption in business and government. His collections of essays include *The Shame of the Cities* (1904) and *The Struggle for Self-government* (1906). His *Autobiography* (1931) is a very personal account of the history not only of journalism in the United States but of the leftist movement as well. This selection from it recalls his carefree days as an undergraduate and the beginnings of his serious interest in learning, while it questions the connection between the search for knowledge and the baccalaureate degree.

Going to college is, to a boy, an adventure into a new world, and a very strange and complete world too. Part of his preparation for it is the stories he hears from those that have gone before; these feed his imagination, which cannot help trying to picture the college life. And the stories and the life are pretty much the same for any college. The University of California was a young, comparatively small institution when I was entered there in 1885 as a freshman. Berkeley, the beautiful, was not the developed villa community it is now; I used to shoot quail in the brush under the oaks along the edges of the college grounds. The quail and the brush are gone now, but the oaks are there and the same prospect down the hill over San Francisco Bay out through the Golden Gate between the low hills of the city and the high hills of Marin County. My class numbered about one hundred boys and girls, mostly boys, who came from all parts of the State and represented all sorts of people and occupations. There was, however, a significant uniformity of opinion and spirit among us, as there was, and still is, in other, older colleges. The American is molded to type early. And so are our college ways. We found already formed at Berkeley the typical undergraduate customs, rights, and privileged vices which we had to respect ourselves and defend against the faculty, regents, and the State government.

One evening, before I had matriculated, I was taken out by some upper classmen to teach the president a lesson. He had been the head of a private preparatory school and was trying to govern the private lives and the public morals of university "men" as he had those of his schoolboys. Fetching a long ladder, the upper classmen thrust it through a front window of Prexy's house and, to the chant of obscene songs, swung it back and forth, up and down, round and round, till everything breakable within sounded broken and the drunken indignation outside was satisfied or tired.

This turned out to be one of the last battles in the war for liberty against that president. He was allowed to resign soon thereafter and I noticed that not only the students but many of the faculty and regents rejoiced in his downfall and turned with us to face and fight the new president when, after a lot of politics, he was appointed and presented. We learned somehow a good deal about the considerations that governed our college government. They were not only academic. The government of a university was—like the State government and horse-racing and so many other things—not what I had been led to expect. And a college education wasn't, either, nor the student mind.

Years later, when I was a magazine editor, I proposed a series of articles to raise and answer the question: Is there any intellectual life in our colleges? My idea sprang from my remembered disappointment at what I found at Berkeley and some experiences I was having at the time with the faculties and undergraduates of the other colleges in the east. Berkeley, in my day, was an Athens compared with New Haven, for example, when I came to know Yale undergraduates.

My expectations of college life were raised too high by Nixon's Saturday nights. I thought, and he assumed, that at Berkeley I would be breathing in an atmosphere of thought, discussion, and some scholarship; working, reading, and studying for the answers to questions which would be threshed out in debate and conversation. There was nothing of the sort. I was primed with questions. My English friends never could agree on the answers to any of the many and various questions they disputed. They did not care; they enjoyed their talks and did not expect to settle anything. I was more earnest. I was not content to leave things all up in the air. Some of those questions were very present and personal to me, as some of those Englishmen meant them to be. William Owen was trying to convert me to the anarchistic communism in which he believed with all his sincere and beautiful being. I was considering his arguments. Another earnest man, who presented the case for the Roman Catholic Church, sent old Father Burchard and other Jesuits after me. Every conversation at Mr. Nixon's pointed some question, academic or scientific, and pointed them so sharp that they drove me to college with an intense desire to know. And as for communism or the Catholic Church, I was so torn that I could not answer myself. The Jesuits dropped me and so did Owen, in disgust, when I said I was going to wait for my answer till I had heard what the professors had to say and had learned what my university had to teach me upon the questions underlying the questions Oxford and Cambridge and Rome quarreled over and could not agree on. Berkeley would know.

There were no moot questions in Berkeley. There was work to do, knowledge and training to get, but not to answer questions. I found myself engaged, as my classmates were, in choosing courses. The choice was limited and, within the limits, had to be determined by the degree we were candidates for. My questions were philosophical, but I could not take philosophy, which fascinated me, till I had gone through a lot of higher mathematics which did not interest me at all. If I had been allowed to take philosophy, and so discovered the need and the relation of mathematics, I would have got the philosophy and I might have got the mathematics which I miss now more than I do the Hegelian metaphysics taught at Berkeley. Or, if the professor who put me off had taken the pains to show me the bearing of mathematical thought on theoretical logic, I would have undertaken the preparation intelligently. But no one ever developed for me the relation of any of my required subjects to those that attracted me; no one brought out for me the relation of anything I was studying to anything else, except, of course, to that wretched degree. Knowledge was absolute, not relative, and it was stored in compartments, categorical and independent. The relation of knowledge to life, even to student life, was ignored, and as for questions, the professors asked them, not the students; and the students, not the teachers, answered them—in examinations.

The unknown is the province of the student; it is the field for his life's adventure, and it is a wide field full of beckonings. Curiosity about it would drive a boy as well as a child to work through the known to get at the unknown. But it was not assumed that we had any curiosity or the potential love of skill, scholarship, and achievement or research. And so far as I can remember now, the professors' attitude was right for most of the students who had no intellectual curiosity. They wanted to be told not only what they had to learn, but what they had to want to learn—for the purpose of passing. That came out in the considerations which decided the choice among optional courses. Students selected subjects or teachers for a balance of easy and hard, to fit into their time and yet "get through." I was the only rebel of my kind, I think. The nearest to me in sympathy were the fellows who knew what they wanted to be: engineers, chemists, professional men, or statesmen. They grunted at some of the work required of them, studies that seemed useless to their future careers. They did not understand me very well, nor I them, because I preferred those very subjects which they called useless, highbrow, cultural. I did not tell them so; I did not realize it myself definitely; but I think now that I had had as a boy an exhausting experience of *being* something great. I did not want now to be but rather to know things.

And what I wanted to know was buried deep under all this "college stuff" which was called "shop." It had nothing to do with what really interested us in common. Having chosen our work and begun to do it as a duty, we turned to the socially important question: which fraternity to join. The upper classmen tried to force our answers. They laid aside their superiority to "rush" those of us whose antecedents were known and creditable. It was all snobbish, secret, and exclusive. I joined a fraternity out of curiosity: What were the secrets and the mystic rites? I went blindfold through the silly initiation to find that there were no secrets and no mysteries, only pretensions and bunk, which so disgusted me that I would not live at the clubhouse, preferring for a year the open doors of a boarding-house. The next great university question was as to athletics. My ex-athletes from Oxford and Cambridge, with their lung and other troubles, warned me; but it was a mistake that saved me. I went with the other freshmen to the campus to be tried out for football, baseball, running, jumping, etc. Caught by the college and class spirit, I hoped to give promise of some excellence. Baseball was impossible for me; I had been riding horses when the other boys were preparing for college on the diamond. I had learned to run at the military academy and in the first freshman tests I did one hundred yards enough under eleven seconds to be turned over to an athletic upper classman for instruction. Pointing up to Grizzly Peak, a high hill back of the college, he said: "All you need is wind and muscle. Climb that mountain every day for a year; then come back and we'll see."

I did not climb Grizzly Peak every day, but I went up so often that I was soon able to run up and back without a halt. At the end of the year I ran around the cinder track so long that my student instructor wearied of watching me, but, of course, I could not do a hundred yards much under twelve seconds. Muscle and wind I had, but all my physical reactions were so slow that I was of no social use in college athletics. I was out of the crowd as I had been as a boy.

I shone only in the military department. The commandant, a U.S. Army officer, seeing that I had had previous training, told me off to drill the awkward squad of my class, and when I had made of them the best-drilled company in college, he gave me the next freshman class to drill. In the following years I was always drillmaster of the freshmen and finally commanded the whole cadet corps. Thus I led my class in the most unpopular and meaningless of undergraduate activities. I despised it myself, prizing it only for the chances it gave me to swank and, once a week, to lord it over my fellow students, who nicknamed me the "D. S."—damn stinker.

My nickname was won not only as a disciplinarian, however; I rarely punished any one; I never abused my command. I could persuade the freshmen to drill by arguing that, since it was compulsory, they could have more fun doing it well than badly; and that it was the one exercise in which they could beat and shame the upper classmen whose carelessness was as affected as their superiority. That is to say, I engaged their enthusiasm. All other student enthusiasms, athletics, class and college politics, fashions, and traditions I laughed at and damned. I was a spoilsport. I was mean, as a horse is mean, because I was unhappy myself. I could be enthusiastic in a conversation about something we were learning, if it wasn't too cut and dried; we had such talks now and then at the clubhouse in my later years. But generally speaking we were discussing the news or some prank of our own.

One night, for example, we sallied forth to steal some chickens from Dr. Bonte, the popular treasurer of the university. I crawled into the coop and selected the chickens, wrung their necks, and passed them out with comments to the other fellows who held the bag.

"Here," I said, "is the rooster, Dr. Bonte himself; he's tough, but good enough for the freshmen. Next is a nice fat hen, old Mrs. Bonte. This one's a pullet, Miss Bonte," and so on, naming each of the Bonte girls, till we were interrupted.

There was a sound from the house, the lights flashed in the windows, and—some one was coming. The other fellows ran, and I—when I tore myself out—I ran too. Which was all right enough. But when I caught up with the other thieves I learned that they had left the sack of chickens behind! Our Sunday dinner was spoiled, we thought, but no: the next day the whole fraternity was invited to dinner at Dr. Bonte's on Sunday. We accepted with some suspicion, we went in some embarrassment, but we were well received and soon put at our ease by Dr. Bonte, who explained that some thieves had been frightened while robbing his roost. "They were not students, I take it," he said. "Students are not so easily frightened; they might have run away, but students would have taken the bag of chickens with them. I think they were niggers or Chinamen."

So seated hospitably at table we watched with deep interest the great platter of roasted chickens borne in and set down before Dr. Bonte, who rose, whetted his carving-knife, and turning first to me, said: "Well, Steffens, what will you have, a piece of this old cock, Dr. Bonte? Or is he too tough for any but a freshman? Perhaps you would prefer the old hen, Mrs. Bonte, or, say, one of the Bonte girls."

I couldn't speak. No one could; and no one laughed, least of all Dr. Bonte, who stood there, his knife and fork in the air, looking at me, at the others, and back at me. He wanted an answer; I must make my choice, but I saw a gleam of malicious humor in his eye; so I recovered and I chose the prettiest of the girls, pointing to the tenderest of the pullets. Dr. Bonte laughed, gave me my choice, and we had a jolly, ample dinner.

We talked about that, we and the students generally and the faculty—we discussed that incident long enough and hard enough to have solved it, if it had been a metaphysical problem. We might have threshed out the psychology of thieves, or gamblers, but no. We liked to steal, but we didn't care to think about it, not as stealing. And some of us gambled. We had to get money for theaters, operas, and other expenses in the city. I had only my board, lodging, and clothes paid for by my father, and others had not even that. We played cards, therefore, among ourselves, poker and whist, so that a lucky few got each month about all the money all of the other hard-ups had, and so had all the fun. We played long, late, and hard, and for money, not sport. The strain was too great.

One night my roommate, sunk low in his chair, felt a light kick on one of his extended legs; a second later there were two kicks against his other leg. Keeping still and watching the hands shown down, he soon had the signal system of two men playing partners, the better hand staying in the game. We said nothing but, watching, saw that others cheated, too. We knew well an old professional gambler from the mining-camps who was then in San Francisco. We told him all about it.

"Sure," he said, "cheating will sneak into any game that's played long enough. That's why you boys oughtn't to gamble. But if you do, play the game that's played. Cards is like horse-racing. I never bet a cent except I know, and know how, the game is crooked."

Having advised against it, he took us around to the gambling-houses and the race course and showed us many of the tricks of his trade, how to spot and profit by them—if we must play. "Now you won't need never to be suckers," he said. "And ye needn't be crooks either," he added after a pause. But we had it in for our opponents. We learned several ways to cheat; we practiced them till we were cool and sure. After that our "luck" was phenomenal. We had money, more than we needed. In my last two years at the university

I had a salary as military instructor at a preparatory school in the town, and my roommate, the adopted son of a rich goldminer, had a generous allowance. But we went on playing and cheating at cards for the excitement of it, we said, but really it was for the money. And afterward, when I was a student in Germany, I played on, fair but hard—and for money I did not need, till one night at the Café Bauer in Berlin, sitting in a poker game that had been running all night, an American who had long been playing in hard luck, lost a large amount, of which I carried away more than my share. The next day we read in the papers that when he got home he had shot himself. I have never gambled since—at cards.

I Become a Student

It is possible to get an education at a university. It has been done; not often, but the fact that a proportion, however small, of college students do get a start in interested, methodical study, proves my thesis, and the two personal experiences I have to offer illustrate it and show how to circumvent the faculty, the other students, and the whole college system of mind-fixing. My method might lose a boy his degree, but a degree is not worth so much as the capacity and the drive to learn, and the undergraduate desire for an empty baccalaureate is one of the holds the educational system has on students. Wise students some day will refuse to take degrees, as the best men (in England, for instance) give, but do not themselves accept, titles.

My method was hit on by accident and some instinct. I specialized. With several courses prescribed, I concentrated on the one or two that interested me most, and letting the others go, I worked intensively on my favorites. In my first two years, for example, I worked at English and political economy and read philosophy. At the beginning of my junior year I had several cinches in history. Now I liked history; I had neglected it partly because I rebelled at the way it was taught, as positive knowledge unrelated to politics, art, life, or anything else. The professors gave us chapters out of a few books to read, con, and be quizzed on. Blessed as I was with a "bad memory," I could not commit to it anything that I did not understand and intellectually need. The bare record of the story of man, with names, dates, and irrelative events, bored me. But I had discovered in my readings of literature, philosophy, and political economy that history had light to throw upon unhistorical questions. So I proposed in my junior and senior years to specialize in history, taking all the courses required and those also that I had flunked in. With this in mind I listened attentively to the first introductory talk of Professor William Cary Jones on American constitutional history. He was a dull lecturer, but I noticed that, after telling us what pages of what books we must be prepared in, he mumbled off some other references "for those that may care to dig deeper."

When the rest of the class rushed out into the sunshine, I went up to the professor and, to his surprise, asked for this memorandum. He gave it to me. Up in the library I ran through the required chapters in the two different books, and they differed on several points. Turning to the other authorities, I saw that they disagreed on the same facts and also on others. The librarian, appealed to, helped me search the book-shelves till the library closed, and then I called on Professor Jones for more references. He was astonished, invited me in, and began to approve my industry, which astonished me. I was not trying to be a good boy; I was better than that: I was a curious boy. He lent me a couple of his books, and I went off to my club to read them. They only deepened the mystery, clearing up the historical question, but leaving the answer to be dug for and written.

The historians did not know! History was not a science, but a field for research, a field for me, for any young man, to explore, to make discoveries in and write a scientific report about. I was fascinated. As I went on from chapter to chapter, day after day, finding frequently essential differences of opinion and of fact, I saw more and more work to do. In this course, American constitutional history, I hunted far enough to suspect that the Fathers of the Republic who wrote our sacred Constitution of the United States not only did not, but did not want to, establish a democratic government, and I dreamed for a while—as I used as a child to play I was Napoleon or a trapper—I promised myself to write a true history of the making of the American Constitution. I did not do it; that chapter has been done or well begun since by two men: Smith of the University of Washington and Beard (then) of Columbia (afterward forced out, perhaps for this very work). I found other events, men, and epochs waiting for students. In all my other courses, in ancient, in European, and in modern history, the disagreeing authorities carried me back to the need of a fresh search for (or of) the original documents or other clinching testimony. Of course I did well in my classes. The history professors soon knew me as a student and seldom put a question to me except when the class had flunked it. Then Professor Jones would say, "Well, Steffens, tell them about it."

Fine. But vanity wasn't my ruling passion then. What I had was a quickening sense that I was learning a method of studying history and that every chapter of it, from the beginning of the world to the end, is crying out to be rewritten. There was something for Youth to do; these superior old men had not done anything, finally.

Years afterward I came out of the graft prosecution office in San Francisco with Rudolph Spreckels, the banker and backer of the investigation. We were to go somewhere, quick, in his car, and we couldn't. The chauffeur was trying to repair something wrong. Mr. Spreckels smiled; he looked closely at the defective part, and to my silent, wondering inquiry he answered: "Always, when I see something badly done or not done at all, I see an opportunity to make a fortune. I never kick at bad work by my class: there's lots of it and we suffer from it. But our failures and neglects are chances for the young fellows coming along and looking for work."

Nothing is done. Everything in the world remains to be done or done over. "The greatest picture is not yet painted, the greatest play isn't written (not even by Shakespeare), the greatest poem is unsung. There isn't in all the world a perfect railroad, nor a good government, nor a sound law." Physics, mathematics, and especially the most advanced and exact of the sciences, are being fundamentally revised. Chemistry is just becoming a science; psychology, economics, and sociology are awaiting a Darwin, whose work in turn is awaiting an Einstein. If the rah-rah boys in our colleges could be told this, they might not all be such specialists in football, petting parties, and unearned degrees. They are not told it, however; they are told to learn what is known. This is nothing, philosophically speaking.

Somehow or other in my later years at Berkeley, two professors, Moses and Howison, representing opposite schools of thought, got into a controversy, probably about their classes. They brought together in the house of one of them a few of their picked students, with the evident intention of letting us show in conversation how much or how little we had understood of their respective teachings. I don't remember just what the subject was that they threw into the ring, but we wrestled with it till the professors could stand it no longer. Then they broke in, and while we sat silent and highly entertained, they went at each other hard and fast and long. It was after midnight when, the debate over, we went home. I asked the other fellows what they had got out of it, and their answers showed that they had seen nothing but a fine, fair fight. When I laughed, they asked me what I, the D.S., had seen that was so much more profound.

I said that I had seen two highly trained, well-educated Masters of Arts and Doctors of Philosophy disagreeing upon every essential point of thought and knowledge. They had all there was of the sciences; and yet they could not find any knowledge upon which they could base an acceptable conclusion. They had no test of knowledge; they didn't know what is and what is not. And they have no test of right and wrong; they have no basis for even an ethics.

Well, and what of it? They asked me that, and that I did not answer. I was stunned by the discovery that it was philosophically true, in a most literal sense, that nothing is known; that it is precisely the foundation that is lacking for science; that all we call knowledge rested upon assumptions which the scientists did not all accept; and that, likewise, there is no scientific reason for saying, for example, that stealing is wrong. In brief: there was no scientific basis for an ethics. No wonder men said one thing and did another; no wonder they could settle nothing either in life or in the academies.

I could hardly believe this. Maybe these professors, whom I greatly respected, did not know it all. I read the books over again with a fresh eye, with a real interest, and I could see that, as in history, so in other branches of knowledge, everything was in the air. And I was glad of it. Rebel though I was, I had got the religion of scholarship and science; I was in awe of the authorities in the academic world. It was a release to feel my worship cool and pass. But I could not be sure. I must go elsewhere, see and hear other professors, men these California professors quoted and looked up to as their high priests. I decided to go as a student to Europe when I was through Berkeley, and I would start with the German universities.

My father listened to my plan, and he was disappointed. He had hoped I would succeed him in his business; it was for that that he was staying in it. When I said that, whatever I might do, I would never go into business, he said, rather sadly, that he would sell out his interest and retire. And he did soon after our talk. But he wanted me to stay home and, to keep me, offered to buy an interest in a certain San Francisco daily paper. He had evidently had this in mind for some time. I had always done some writing, verse at the poetical age of puberty, then a novel which my mother alone treasured. Journalism was the business for a boy who liked to write, he thought, and he said I had often spoken of a newspaper as my ambition. No doubt I had in the intervals between my campaigns as Napoleon. But no more. I was now going to be a scientist, a philosopher. He sighed; he thought it over, and with the approval of my mother, who was for every sort of education, he gave his consent.

Suggestions for Discussion

1. The first part of this reminiscence tells us about Steffens' carefree days as a student at Berkeley in the late 19th century. How does he describe student life? What was the main interest of most students at the university?

2. Why did Steffens fail to get ahead in athletics while achieving great success as a drillmaster? Why did military drill appeal to him?

3. What was Steffens' attitude toward money while he was a student? Why did he gamble? Explain how he learned to be a successful gambler. Explain why he gave up gambling.

4. Why was Steffens disappointed in his fraternity?

5. Explain the significance of the incident of the stealing of Dr. Bonte's chickens. Why is it included in this section?

6. What is the major difference between the first and second parts of the reminiscence?

7. How does Steffens get interested in the study of history? What determines his decision to continue his education in Germany?

8. Why were most of the students whom Steffens knew attending Berkeley? Does he respect their reasons? What does he think is the real reason for education?

9. How would you describe Steffens during his student days? Was he likeable? Explain your answer.

Suggestions for Writing

1. Using Steffens as a model, write an essay in which you attempt to summarize most of your classmates' reasons for going to college. Try to develop a questionnaire in which you sample opinion so that you have information to summarize. Write an opinion of the reasons you discover.

2. College life differs greatly from one institution to another. Write an essay in which you compare college life at your own college or university with that of another. You may wish to ask someone much older than yourself how his or her college life differed from yours. You may wish to contrast your own experiences with those of Steffens.

Maya Angelou
Graduation

Maya Angelou (b. 1928) was born in Stamps, Arkansas, to a childhood of poverty and pain. She has been a dancer and an actress, a coordinator of the Southern Christian Leadership Conference , a television writer and producer, and a poet. She is best known for her autobiographical works, *I Know Why the Caged Bird Sings* (1970), from which "Graduation" is taken, and *The Heart of a Woman* (1981). In "Graduation" the entire black community has prepared for graduation only to have its excitement destroyed by the white speaker who patronizingly offers them the prospect of servile jobs or, perhaps, athletic fame. While Angelou captures the pain of racial discrimination, she reaffirms finally the power of the blacks to survive.

The children in Stamps trembled visibly with anticipation. Some adults were excited too, but to be certain the whole young population had come down with graduation epidemic. Large classes were graduating from both the grammar school and the high school. Even those who were years removed from their own day of glorious release were anxious to help with preparations as a kind of dry run. The junior students who were moving into the vacating classes' chairs were tradition-bound to show their talents for leadership and management. They strutted through the school and around the campus exerting pressure on the lower grades. Their authority was so new that occasionally if they pressed a little too hard it had to be overlooked. After all, next term was coming, and it never hurt a sixth-grader to have a play sister in the eighth grade, or a tenth-year student to be able to call a twelfth-grader Bubba. So all was endured in a spirit of shared understanding. But the graduating classes themselves were the nobility. Like travelers with exotic destinations on their minds, the graduates were remarkably forgetful. They came to school without their books, or tablets or even pencils. Volunteers fell over themselves to secure replacements for the missing equipment. When accepted, the willing workers might or might not be thanked, and it was of no importance to the pregraduation rites. Even teachers were respectful of the now quiet and aging seniors, and tended to speak to them, if not as equals, as beings only slightly lower than themselves. After tests were returned and grades given, the student body, which acted like an extended family, knew who did well, who excelled, and what piteous ones had failed.

Unlike the white high school, Lafayette County Training School distinguished itself by having neither lawn, nor hedges, nor tennis court, nor climbing ivy. Its two buildings (main classrooms, the grade school and home economics) were set on a dirt hill with no fence to limit either its boundaries or those of bordering farms. There was a large expanse to the left of the school which was used alternately as a baseball diamond or a basketball court. Rusty hoops on the swaying poles represented the permanent recreational equipment, although bats and balls could be borrowed from the P.E. teacher if the borrower was qualified and if the diamond wasn't occupied.

Over this rocky area relieved by a few shady tall persimmon trees the graduating class walked. The girls often held hands and no longer bothered to speak to the lower students. There was a sadness about them, as if this old world was not their home and they were bound for higher ground. The boys, on the other hand, had become more friendly, more outgoing. A decided change from the closed attitude they projected while studying for finals. Now they seemed not ready to give up the old school, the familiar paths and class-rooms. Only a small percentage would be continuing on to college—one of the South's A & M (agricultural and mechanical) schools, which trained Negro youths to be carpenters, farmers, handymen, masons, maids, cooks and baby nurses. Their future rode heavily on their shoulders, and blinded them to the collective joy that had pervaded the lives of the boys and girls in the grammar school graduating class.

Parents who could afford it had ordered new shoes and ready-made clothes for themselves from Sears, Roebuck or Montgomery Ward. They also engaged the best seamstresses to make the floating graduating dresses and to cut down secondhand pants which would be pressed to a military slickness for the im-portant event.

Oh, it was important, all right. Whitefolks would attend the ceremony, and two or three would speak of God and home, and the Southern way of life, and Mrs. Parsons, the principal's wife, would play the graduation march while the lower-grade graduates paraded down the aisles and took their seats below the platform. The high school seniors would wait in empty classrooms to make their dramatic entrance.

In the Store I was the person of the moment. The birthday girl. The cen-ter. Bailey had graduated the year before, although to do so he had had to forfeit all pleasures to make up for his time lost in Baton Rouge.

My class was wearing butter-yellow piqué dresses, and Momma launched out on mine. She smocked the yoke into tiny crisscrossing puckers, then shirred the rest of the bodice. Her dark fingers ducked in and out of the lemony cloth as she embroidered raised daisies around the hem. Before she considered herself finished she had added a crocheted cuff on the puff sleeves, and a pointy crocheted collar.

I was going to be lovely. A walking model of all the various styles of fine hand sewing and it didn't worry me that I was only twelve years old and merely graduating from the eighth grade. Besides, many teachers in Arkansas Negro schools had only that diploma and were licensed to impart wisdom.

The days had become longer and more noticeable. The faded beige of for-mer times had been replaced with strong and sure colors. I began to see my classmates' clothes, their skin tones, and the dust that waved off pussy wil-lows. Clouds that lazed across the sky were objects of great concern to me. Their shiftier shapes might have held a message that in my new happiness and with a little bit of time I'd soon decipher. During that period I looked at the arch of heaven so religiously my neck kept a steady ache. I had taken to smiling more often, and my jaws hurt from the unaccustomed activity. Be-tween the two physical sore spots, I suppose I could have been uncomforta-ble, but that was not the case. As a member of the winning team (the gradu-ating class of 1940) I had outdistanced unpleasant sensations by miles. I was headed for the freedom of open fields.

Youth and social approval allied themselves with me and we trammeled memories of slights and insults. The wind of our swift passage remodeled my features. Lost tears were pounded to mud and then to dust. Years of withdrawal were brushed aside and left behind, as hanging ropes of parasitic moss.

My work alone had awarded me a top place and I was going to be one of the first called in the graduating ceremonies. On the classroom blackboard, as well as on the bulletin board in the auditorium, there were blue stars and white stars and red stars. No absences, no tardinesses, and my academic work was among the best of the year. I could say the preamble to the Constitution even faster than Bailey. We timed ourselves often: "Wethepeopleofthe-UnitedStatesinordertoformamoreperfectunion . . ." I had memorized the Presidents of the United States from Washington to Roosevelt in chronological as well as alphabetical order.

My hair pleased me too. Gradually the black mass had lengthened and thickened, so that it kept at last to its braided pattern, and I didn't have to yank my scalp off when I tried to comb it.

Louise and I had rehearsed the exercises until we tired out ourselves. Henry Reed was class valedictorian. He was a small, very black boy with hooded eyes, a long, broad nose and an oddly shaped head. I had admired him for years because each term he and I vied for the best grades in our class. Most often he bested me, but instead of being disappointed I was pleased that we shared top places between us. Like many Southern Black children, he lived with his grandmother, who was as strict as Momma and as kind as she knew how to be. He was courteous, respectful, and soft-spoken to elders, but on the playground he chose to play the roughest games. I admired him. Anyone, I reckoned, sufficiently afraid or sufficiently dull could be polite. But to be able to operate at a top level with both adults and children was admirable.

His valedictory speech was entitled "To Be or Not to Be." The rigid tenth-grade teacher had helped him write it. He'd been working on the dramatic stresses for months.

The weeks until graduation were filled with heady activities. A group of small children were to be presented in a play about buttercups and daisies and bunny rabbits. They could be heard throughout the building practicing their hops and their little songs that sounded like silver bells. The older girls (nongraduates, of course) were assigned the task of making refreshments for the night's festivities. A tangy scent of ginger, cinnamon, nutmeg and chocolate wafted around the home economics building as the budding cooks made samples for themselves and their teachers.

In every corner of the workshop, axes and saws split fresh timber as the woodshop boys made sets and stage scenery. Only the graduates were left out of the general bustle. We were free to sit in the library at the back of the building or look in quite detachedly, naturally, on the measures being taken for our event.

Even the minister preached on graduation the Sunday before. His subject was, "Let your light so shine that men will see your good works and praise your Father, Who is in Heaven." Although the sermon was purported to be addressed to us, he used the occasion to speak to backsliders, gamblers, and general ne'er-do-wells. But since he had called our names at the beginning of the service we were mollified.

Among Negroes the tradition was to give presents to children going only from one grade to another. How much more important this was when the person was graduating at the top of the class. Uncle Willie and Momma had sent away for a Mickey Mouse watch like Bailey's. Louise gave me four embroidered handkerchiefs. (I gave her three crocheted doilies.) Mrs. Sneed, the minister's wife, made me an underskirt to wear for graduation, and nearly every customer gave me a nickel or maybe even a dime with the instruction "Keep on moving to higher ground," or some such encouragement.

Amazingly the great day finally dawned and I was out of bed before I knew it. I threw open the back door to see it more clearly, but Momma said, "Sister, come away from that door and put your robe on."

I hoped the memory of that morning would never leave me. Sunlight was itself still young, and the day had none of the insistence maturity would bring it in a few hours. In my robe and barefoot in the backyard, under cover of going to see about my new beans, I gave myself up to the gentle warmth and thanked God that no matter what evil I had done in my life He had allowed me to live to see this day. Somewhere in my fatalism I had expected to die, accidentally, and never have the chance to walk up the stairs in the auditorium and gracefully receive my hard-earned diploma. Out of God's merciful bosom I had won reprieve.

Bailey came out in his robe and gave me a box wrapped in Christmas paper. He said he had saved his money for months to pay for it. It felt like a box of chocolates, but I knew Bailey wouldn't save money to buy candy when we had all we could want under our noses.

He was as proud of the gift as I. It was a soft-leatherbound copy of a collection of poems by Edgar Allan Poe, or, as Bailey and I called him, "Eap." I turned to "Annabel Lee" and we walked up and down the garden rows, the cool dirt between our toes, reciting the beautifully sad lines.

Momma made a Sunday breakfast although it was only Friday. After we finished the blessing, I opened my eyes to find the watch on my plate. It was a dream of a day. Everything went smoothly and to my credit. I didn't have to be reminded or scolded for anything. Near evening I was too jittery to attend to chores, so Bailey volunteered to do all before his bath.

Days before, we had made a sign for the Store, and as we turned out the lights Momma hung the cardboard over the doorknob. It read clearly: CLOSED. GRADUATION.

My dress fitted perfectly and everyone said that I looked like a sunbeam in it. On the hill, going toward the school, Bailey walked behind with Uncle Willie, who muttered, "Go on, Ju." He wanted him to walk ahead with us because it embarrassed him to have to walk so slowly. Bailey said he'd let the ladies walk together, and the men would bring up the rear. We all laughed, nicely.

Little children dashed by out of the dark like fireflies. Their crepe-paper dresses and butterfly wings were not made for running and we heard more than one rip, dryly, and the regretful "uh uh" that followed.

The school blazed without gaiety. The windows seemed cold and unfriendly from the lower hill. A sense of ill-fated timing crept over me, and if Momma hadn't reached for my hand I would have drifted back to Bailey and Uncle Willie, and possibly beyond. She made a few slow jokes about my feet getting cold, and tugged me along to the now-strange building.

Around the front steps, assurance came back. There were my fellow "greats," the graduating class. Hair brushed back, legs oiled, new dresses and pressed pleats, fresh pocket handkerchiefs and little handbags, all homesewn. Oh, we were up to snuff, all right. I joined my comrades and didn't even see my family go in to find seats in the crowded auditorium.

The school band struck up a march and all classes filed in as had been rehearsed. We stood in front of our seats, as assigned, and on a signal from the choir director, we sat. No sooner had this been accomplished than the band started to play the national anthem. We rose again and sang the song, after which we recited the pledge of allegiance. We remained standing for a brief minute before the choir director and the principal signaled to us, rather desperately I thought, to take our seats. The command was so unusual that our carefully rehearsed and smooth-running machine was thrown off. For a full minute we fumbled for our chairs and bumped into each other awkwardly. Habits change or solidify under pressure, so in our state of nervous tension we had been ready to follow our usual assembly pattern: the American national anthem, then the pledge of allegiance, then the song every Black person I knew called the Negro National Anthem. All done in the same key, with the same passion and most often standing on the same foot.

Finding my seat at last, I was overcome with a presentiment of worse things to come. Something unrehearsed, unplanned, was going to happen, and we were going to be made to look bad. I distinctly remember being explicit in the choice of pronoun. It was "we," the graduating class, the unit, that concerned me then.

The principal welcomed "parents and friends" and asked the Baptist minister to lead us in prayer. His invocation was brief and punchy, and for a second I thought we were getting back on the high road to right action. When the principal came back to the dais, however, his voice had changed. Sounds always affected me profoundly and the principal's voice was one of my favorites. During assembly it melted and lowed weakly into the audience. It had not been in my plan to listen to him, but my curiosity was piqued and I straightened up to give him my attention.

He was talking about Booker T. Washington, our "late great leader," who said we can be as close as the fingers on the hand, etc. . . . Then he said a few vague things about friendship and the friendship of kindly people to those less fortunate than themselves. With that his voice nearly faded, thin, away. Like a river diminishing to a stream and then to a trickle. But he cleared his throat and said, "Our speaker tonight, who is also our friend, came from Texarkana to deliver the commencement address, but due to the irregularity of the train schedule, he's going to, as they say, 'speak and run.'" He said that we understood and wanted the man to know that we were most grateful for the time he was able to give us and then something about how we were willing always to adjust to another's program, and without more ado—"I give you Mr. Edward Donleavy."

Not one but two white men came through the door offstage. The shorter one walked to the speaker's platform, and the tall one moved over to the center seat and sat down. But that was our principal's seat, and already occupied. The dislodged gentleman bounced around for a long breath or two before the Baptist minister gave him his chair, then with more dignity than the situation deserved, the minister walked off the stage.

Donleavy looked at the audience once (on reflection, I'm sure that he wanted only to reassure himself that we were really there), adjusted his glasses and began to read from a sheaf of papers.

He was glad "to be here and to see the work going on just as it was in the other schools."

At the first "Amen" from the audience I willed the offender to immediate death by choking on the word. But Amens and Yes, sir's began to fall around the room like rain through a ragged umbrella.

He told us of the wonderful changes we children in Stamps had in store. The Central School (naturally, the white school was Central) had already been granted improvements that would be in use in the fall. A well-known artist was coming from Little Rock to teach art to them. They were going to have the newest microscopes and chemistry equipment for their laboratory. Mr. Donleavy didn't leave us long in the dark over who made these improvements available to Central High. Nor were we to be ignored in the general betterment scheme he had in mind.

He said that he had pointed out to people at a very high level that one of the first-line football tacklers at Arkansas Agricultural and Mechanical College had graduated from good old Lafayette County Training School. Here fewer Amen's were heard. Those few that did break through lay dully in the air with the heaviness of habit.

He went on to praise us. He went on to say how he had bragged that "one of the best basketball players at Fisk sank his first ball right here at Lafayette County Training School."

The white kids were going to have a chance to become Galileos and Madame Curies and Edisons and Gauguins, and our boys (the girls weren't even in on it) would try to be Jesse Owenses and Joe Louises.

Owens and the Brown Bomber were great heroes in our world, but what school official in the white-goddom of Little Rock had the right to decide that those two men must be our only heroes? Who decided that for Henry Reed to become a scientist he had to work like George Washington Carver, as a bootblack, to buy a lousy microscope? Bailey was obviously always going to be too small to be an athlete, so which concrete angel glued to what country seat had decided that if my brother wanted to become a lawyer he had to first pay penance for his skin by picking cotton and hoeing corn and studying correspondence books at night for twenty years?

The man's dead words fell like bricks around the auditorium and too many settled in my belly. Constrained by hard-learned manners I couldn't look behind me, but to my left and right the proud graduating class of 1940 had dropped their heads. Every girl in my row had found something new to do with her handkerchief. Some folded the tiny squares into love knots, some into triangles, but most were wadding them, then pressing them flat on their yellow laps.

On the dais, the ancient tragedy was being replayed. Professor Parsons sat, a sculptor's reject, rigid. His large, heavy body seemed devoid of will or willingness, and his eyes said he was no longer with us. The other teachers examined the flag (which was draped stage right) or their notes, or the windows which opened on our now-famous playing diamond.

Graduation, the hush-hush magic time of frills and gifts and congratulations and diplomas, was finished for me before my name was called. The accomplishment was nothing. The meticulous maps, drawn in three colors of ink, learning and spelling decasyllabic words, memorizing the whole of *The Rape of Lucrece*—it was for nothing. Donleavy had exposed us.

We were maids and farmers, handymen and washerwomen, and anything higher that we aspired to was farcical and presumptuous.

Then I wished that Gabriel Prosser and Nat Turner had killed all whitefolks in their beds and that Abraham Lincoln had been assassinated before the signing of the Emancipation Proclamation, and that Harriet Tubman had been killed by that blow on her head and Christopher Columbus had drowned in the *Santa María*.

It was awful to be Negro and have no control over my life. It was brutal to be young and already trained to sit quietly and listen to charges brought against my color with no chance of defense. We should all be dead. I thought I should like to see us all dead, one on top of the other. A pyramid of flesh with the whitefolks on the bottom, as the broad base, then the Indians with their silly tomahawks and teepees and wigwams and treaties, the Negroes with their mops and recipes and cotton sacks and spirituals sticking out of their mouths. The Dutch children should all stumble in their wooden shoes and break their necks. The French should choke to death on the Louisiana Purchase (1803) while silkworms ate all the Chinese with their stupid pigtails. As a species, we were an abomination. All of us.

Donleavy was running for election, and assured our parents that if he won we could count on having the only colored paved playing field in that part of Arkansas. Also—he never looked up to acknowledge the grunts of acceptance—also, we were bound to get some new equipment for the home economics building and the workshop.

He finished, and since there was no need to give any more than the most perfunctory thank-you's, he nodded to the men on the stage, and the tall white man who was never introduced joined him at the door. They left with the attitude that now they were off to something really important. (The graduation ceremonies at Lafayette Country Training School had been a mere preliminary.)

The ugliness they left was palpable. An uninvited guest who wouldn't leave. The choir was summoned and sang a modern arrangement of "Onward, Christian Soldiers," with new words pertaining to graduates seeking their place in the world. But it didn't work. Elouise, the daughter of the Baptist minister, recited "Invictus," and I could have cried at the impertinence of "I am the master of my fate, I am the captain of my soul."

My name had lost its ring of familiarity and I had to be nudged to go and receive my diploma. All my preparations had fled. I neither marched up to the stage like a conquering Amazon, nor did I look in the audience for Bailey's nod of approval. Marguerite Johnson, I heard the name again, my honors were read, there were noises in the audience of appreciation, and I took my place on the stage as rehearsed.

I thought about colors I hated: ecru, puce, lavender, beige and black.

There was shuffling and rustling around me, then Henry Reed was giving his valedictory address, "To Be or Not to Be." Hadn't he heard the whitefolks? We couldn't *be,* so the question was a waste of time. Henry's voice came out clear and strong. I feared to look at him. Hadn't he got the message? There was no "nobler in the mind" for Negroes because the world didn't think we had minds, and they let us know it. "Outrageous fortune"? Now, that was a joke. When the ceremony was over I had to tell Henry Reed some things. That is, if I still cared. Not "rub," Henry, "erase." "Ah, there's the erase." Us.

Henry had been a good student in elocution. His voice rose on tides of promise and fell on waves of warnings. The English teacher had helped him to create a sermon winging through Hamlet's soliloquy. To be a man, a doer, a builder, a leader, or to be a tool, an unfunny joke, a crusher of funky toadstools. I marveled that Henry could go through with the speech as if we had a choice.

I had been listening and silently rebutting each sentence with my eyes closed; then there was a hush, which in an audience warns that something unplanned is happening. I looked up and saw Henry Reed, the conservative, the proper, the A student, turn his back to the audience and turn to us (the proud graduating class of 1940) and sing, nearly speaking,

> "Lift ev'ry voice and sing[1]
> Till earth and heaven ring
> Ring with the harmonies of Liberty . . ."

It was the poem written by James Weldon Johnson. It was the music composed by J. Rosamond Johnson. It was the Negro national anthem. Out of habit we were singing it.

Our mothers and fathers stood in the dark hall and joined the hymn of encouragement. A kindergarten teacher led the small children onto the stage and the buttercups and daisies and bunny rabbits marked time and tried to follow:

> "Stony the road we trod
> Bitter the chastening rod
> Felt in the days when hope, unborn, had died.
> 'Yet with a steady beat
> Have not our weary feet
> Come to the place for which our fathers sighed?"

Every child I knew had learned that song with his ABC's and along with "Jesus Loves Me This I Know." But I personally had never heard it before. Never heard the words, despite the thousands of times I had sung them. Never thought they had anything to do with me.

On the other hand, the words of Patrick Henry had made such an impression on me that I had been able to stretch myself tall and trembling and say, 'I know not what course others may take, but as for me, give me liberty or give me death."

And now I heard, really for the first time:

> "We have come over a way that with tears
> has been watered,
> We have come, treading our path through
> the blood of the slaughtered."

[1]"Lift Ev'ry Voice and Sing"—words by James Weldon Johnson and music by J. Rosamond Johnson. Copyright by Edward B. Marks Music Corporation. Used by permission.

While echoes of the song shivered in the air, Henry Reed bowed his head, said "Thank you," and returned to his place in the line. The tears that slipped down many faces were not wiped away in shame.

We were on top again. As always, again. We survived. The depths had been icy and dark, but now a bright sun spoke to our souls. I was no longer simply a member of the proud graduating class of 1940; I was a proud member of the wonderful, beautiful Negro race.

Oh, Black known and unknown poets, how often have your auctioned pains sustained us? Who will compute the lonely nights made less lonely by your songs, or the empty pots made less tragic by your tales?

If we were a people much given to revealing secrets, we might raise monuments and sacrifice to the memories of our poets, but slavery cured us of that weakness. It may be enough, however, to have it said that we survive in exact relationship to the dedication of our poets (include preachers, musicians and blues singers).

Suggestions for Discussion

1. Describe the feeling that comes over the students and teachers at school at the prospect of graduation.

2. How does Angelou describe the feelings in her own family? How is she treated by her brother? her grandmother?

3. How does the black community become involved in the graduation? What special meaning does it have for them?

4. When do you begin to understand that something will go wrong? What details help you to understand? How do you know that the disappointment will come about from racial causes?

5. Summarize Donleavy's speech. How does Angelou make us feel its condescension and contempt?

6. How does the black community respond? What is the meaning of this response to Angelou? Explain.

Suggestions for Writing

1. Write an essay in which you contrast Angelou and Charles in the story "Expelled." Your paper should include an explanation of why school has such different significance for the two of them.

2. Angelou describes a situation once common in segregated Southern schools which were separate but "unequal." Since the 1960s that situation has presumably changed. Write a research paper of 1,000 words in which you report your findings about schools in the South since desegregation. What new problems may have replaced those which Angelou describes?

◇◇◇◇

Essays

—◆◆◆—

Lewis Thomas

The Youngest and Brightest Thing Around

Lewis Thomas (b. 1913) is a physician whose medical career has centered on the Sloan Kettering Cancer Center in New York, the city of his birth. He has written for medical journals at the same time that he has written popular essays to present science and the scientist's view of the world to the lay public. He won the National Book Award in 1974 for *The Lives of a Cell: Notes of a Biology Watcher*. Other collections include *The Medusa and the Snail* (1979), in which "The Youngest and the Brightest Thing Around" appears, and *The Youngest Science: Notes of a Medicine-Watcher* (1983). In this essay Thomas explains to a graduating class of medical doctors why life on earth is worthy of their concern.

Doctors:

Somewhere, on some remote planet set at precisely the right distance from a star of just the right magnitude and the right temperature, on the other side of our galaxy, there is at this moment a committee nearing the end of a year-long study of our own tiny, provincial solar system. The intelligent beings of that place are putting their signatures (numbers of some sort, no doubt) to a paper which asserts, with finality, that life is out of the question here and the place is not worth an expedition. Their instruments have detected the presence of that most lethal of all gases, oxygen, and that is the end of that. They had planned to come, bringing along mobile factories for manufacturing life-giving ammonia, but what's the use of risking strangulation?

The only part of this scenario that I really believe is that committee. I take it as an article of faith that this is the most fundamental aspect of nature that we know about. If you are going to go looking for evidences of life on other celestial bodies, you need special instruments with delicate sensors for detecting the presence of committees. If there is life there, you will find consortia, collaborating groups, working parties, all over the place.

At least this is true for our kind of life.

Mars, from the look we've had at it thus far, is a horrifying place. It is, by all appearances, stone dead, surely the deadest place any of us has ever seen, hard to look at without flinching. Come to think of it, it is probably the only really dead place of any size we've ever caught a close glimpse of, and the near view is incredibly sad.

Or maybe there is life on Mars, and we've simply missed it so far. The innumerable consultants orbiting around NASA are confounded, just now, by intense arguments, highly technical, over this point. Could there be an island of life at the bottom of one of the Martian ravines? Shouldn't we set down fleets of wheeled vehicles on various parts of the surface, deployed to nose about from place to place, in and out of deep crevices, turning over rocks, sniffing for life? Maybe there is a single spot, just one, where living organisms are holed up.

Maybe so, but if so it would be the strangest thing of all, absolutely incomprehensible. For we are not familiar with this kind of living. We do not have solitary, isolated creatures. It is beyond our imagination to conceive of a single form of life that exists alone and independent, unattached to other forms.

If you dropped a vehicle, or a billion vehicles, for that matter, on our planet you might be able to find one or two lifeless spots, but only if you took very small samples. There are living cells in our hottest deserts and at the tops of our coldest mountains. Even in the ancient frozen rocks recently dug out in Antarctica there are endolithic organisms tucked up comfortably in porous spaces beneath the rock face, as much alive as the petunia in the florist's window.

If you did find a single form of life on Mars, in a single place, how would you go about explaining it? The technical term for this arrangement is a "closed ecosystem," and there is the puzzle. We do not have closed ecosystems here, at all. The only closed ecosystem we know about is the earth itself, and even here the term has to be expanded to include the sun as part of the system, and lord knows what sorts of essential minerals that have drifted onto our surface from outside, at one time or another long ago.

Everything here is alive thanks to the living of everything else. All the forms of life are connected. This is what I meant in proposing the committee as the basis of terrestrial life. The most centrally placed committee, carrying the greatest responsibility, more deeply involved in keeping the whole system running than any other body, or any other working part of the earth's whole body, is the vast community of prokaryotic, unnucleated, microbes. Without bacteria for starters, we would never have had enough oxygen to go around, nor could we have found and fixed the nitrogen for making enzymes, nor could we recycle the solid matter of life for new generations.

One technical definition of a system is as follows: a system is a structure of interacting, intercommunicating components that, as a group, act or operate individually and jointly to achieve a common goal through the concerted activity of the individual parts. This is, of course, a completely satisfactory definition of the earth, except maybe for that last part about a common goal. What on earth is *our* common goal? How did we ever get mixed up in a place like this?

This is the greatest discomfort for our species. Some of us simply write it off by announcing that our situation is ridiculous, that the whole place is ungovernable, and that our responsibilities are therefore to ourselves alone. And yet, there it is: we are components in a dense, fantastically complicated system of life, we are enmeshed in the interliving, and we really don't know what we're up to.

The earth holds together, its tissues cohere, and it has the look of a structure that really would make comprehensible sense if only we knew enough about it. From a little way off, photographed from the moon, it seems to be a kind of organism. Looked at over its whole time, it is plainly in the process of developing, like an enormous embryo. It is, for all its stupendous size and the numberless units and infinite variety of its life forms, coherent. Every tissue is linked for its viability to every other tissue; it gets along by symbiosis, and the invention of new modes of symbiotic coupling is a fundamental process in its embryogenesis. We have no rules for the evolution of this kind of life. We have learned a lot, and in some biomathematical detail, about the laws governing the evolution of individual species on the earth, but no Darwin has yet emerged to take account of the orderly, coordinated growth and differentiation of the whole astonishing system, much less its seemingly permanent survival. It makes an interesting problem: how do mechanisms that seem to be governed entirely by chance and randomness bring into existence new species which fit so neatly and precisely, and usefully, as though they were the cells of an organism? This is a wonder puzzle.

And now human beings have swarmed like bees over the whole surface, changing everything, meddling with all the other parts, making believe we are in charge, risking the survival of the entire magnificent creature.

You could forgive us, or excuse us anyway, on grounds of ignorance, and at least it can be said for us that we are, at long last, becoming aware of that. In no other century of our brief existence have human beings learned so deeply, and so painfully, the extent and depth of their ignorance about nature. We are beginning to confront this, and trying to do something about it with science, and this may save us all if we are clever enough, and lucky enough. But we are starting almost from scratch, and we have a long, long way to go.

Mind you, I do not wish to downgrade us; I believe fervently in our species and have no patience with the current fashion of running down the human being as a useful part of nature. On the contrary, we are a spectacular, splendid manifestation of life. We have language and can build metaphors as skillfully and precisely as ribosomes make proteins. We have affection. We have genes for usefulness, and usefulness is about as close to a "common goal" for all of nature as I can guess at. And finally, and perhaps best of all, we have music. Any species capable of producing, at this earliest, juvenile stage of its development—almost instantly after emerging on the earth by any evolutionary standard—the music of Johann Sebastian Bach, cannot be all bad. We ought to be able to feel more secure for our future, with Julian of Norwich at our elbow: "But all shall be well and all shall be well and all manner of thing shall be well." For our times of guilt we have Montaigne to turn to: "If it did not seem crazy to talk to oneself, there is not a day when I would not be heard growling at myself, 'Confounded fool.'"

But security is the last thing we feel entitled to feel. We are, perhaps uniquely among the earth's creatures, the worrying animal. We worry away our lives, fearing the future, discontent with the present, unable to take in the idea of dying, unable to sit still. We deserve a better press, in my view. We have always had a strong hunch about our origin, which does us credit; from the oldest language we know, the Indo-European tongue, we took the word for earth—*Dhghem*—and turned it into "humus" and "human"; "humble" too, which does us more credit. We are by all odds the most persistently and obsessively social of all species, more dependent on each other than the famous social insects, and really, when you look at us, infinitely more imaginative and deft at social living. We are good at this; it is the way we have built all our cultures and the literature of our civilizations. We have high expectations and set high standards for our social behavior, and when we fail at it and endanger the species—as we have done several times in this century—the strongest words we can find to condemn ourselves and our behavior are the telling words "inhuman" and "inhumane."

There is nothing at all absurd about the human condition. We matter. It seems to me a good guess, hazarded by a good many people who have thought about it, that we may be engaged in the formation of something like a mind for the life of this planet. If this is so, we are still at the most primitive stage, still fumbling with language and thinking, but infinitely capacitated for the future. Looked at this way, it is remarkable that we've come as far as we have in so short a period, really no time at all as geologists measure time. We are the newest, the youngest, and the brightest thing around.

Suggestions for Discussion

1. This essay is designed as a commencement address to new medical school graduates. Is the subject of the address appropriate for such an occasion? Explain.

2. Why does Thomas call the "near view" of the planet Mars "incredibly sad"? Does he believe there is life on Mars? How does he contrast Mars with the earth?

3. Explain the effect of Thomas's opening paragraph. How does it prepare us for the rest of the essay?

4. Summarize the thesis of Thomas's essay. Contrast it with Matthew Arnold's poem "Dover Beach". How are their attitudes toward the meaning of life essentially different?

5. Explain Thomas's definition of an ecosystem. How does it apply to the earth?

6. Why does Thomas consider the human being as important? Why does he use Johann Sebastian Bach in his evaluation?

7. Relate the thesis of this essay to medical education. What part of a doctor's education would have prepared him or her to sympathize with Thomas's remarks?

8. What part of the education in your university or college has prepared you to sympathize with his remarks?

9. Explain the last sentence of the essay.

Suggestion for Writing

Write an essay contrasting Woody Allen's commencement address with this one. Can you find implied in Allen's comically confused remarks the kernel of a serious comment?

◇◇◇◇

Woody Allen
My Speech to the Graduates

Woody Allen (b. 1935) is an American actor, film maker, and writer, best known for such outstanding films as *Annie Hall* (1977), *Interiors* (1978), *Manhattan* (1979), and *Zelig* (1983). His humorous essays have appeared in *The New Yorker* and in the collections *Getting Even* (1971), *Without Feathers* (1975), and *The Floating Lightbulb.* (1981). In the following parody of a commencement address, Allen faces a world of gloom and chaos with humorous platitudes and endless good will as he displays his mastery of the anticlimax and the nonsequitur.

More than any other time in history, mankind faces a crossroads. One path leads to despair and utter hopelessness. The other, to total extinction. Let us pray we have the wisdom to choose correctly. I speak, by the way, not with any sense of futility but with a panicky conviction of the absolute meaninglessness of existence which could easily be misinterpreted as pessimism. It is not. It is merely a healthy concern for the predicament of modern man. (Modern man is here defined as any person born after Nietzche's edict that "God is dead," but before the hit recording "I Wanna Hold Your Hand.") This "predicament" can be stated one of two ways, though certain linguistic philosophers prefer to reduce it to a mathematical equation where it can be easily solved and even carried around in the wallet.

Put in its simplest form, the problem is: How is it possible to find meaning in a finite world given my waist and shirt size? This is a very difficult question when we realize that science has failed us. True, it has conquered many diseases, broken the genetic code, and even placed human beings on the moon, and yet when a man of 80 is left in a room with two 18-year-old cocktail waitresses nothing happens. Because the real problems never change. After all, can the human soul be glimpsed through a microscope? Maybe—but you'd definitely need one of those very good ones with two eyepieces. We know that the most advanced computer in the world does not have a brain as sophisticated as that of an ant. True, we could say that of many of our relatives but we only have to put up with them at weddings or special occasions. Science is something we depend on all the time. If I develop a pain in the chest I must take an X-ray. But what if the radiation from the X-ray causes me deeper problems? Before I know it, I'm going in for surgery. Naturally, while they're giving me oxygen an intern decides to light up a cigarette. The next thing you know I'm rocketing over the World Trade Center in bed clothes. Is this science? True, science has taught us how to pasteurize cheese. And true, this can be fun in mixed company—but what of the H-bomb? Have you ever seen what happens when one of those things falls off a desk accidentally? And where is science when one ponders the eternal riddles? How did the cosmos originate? How long has it been around? Did matter begin with an explosion or by the word of God? And if by the latter, could He not have begun it just two weeks earlier to take advantage of some of the warmer weather? Exactly what do we mean when we say, man is mortal? Obviously it's not a compliment.

Religion too has unfortunately let us down. Miguel de Unamuno writes blithely of the "eternal persistence of consciousness," but this is no easy feat. Particularly when reading Thackeray. I often think how comforting life must have been for early man because he believed in a powerful, benevolent Creator who looked after all things. Imagine his disappointment when he saw his wife putting on weight. Contemporary man, of course, has no such peace of mind. He finds himself in the midst of a crisis of faith. He is what we fashionably call "alienated." He has seen the ravages of war, he has known natural catastrophes, he has been to singles bars. My good friend Jacques Monod spoke often of the randomness of the cosmos. He believed everything in existence occurred by pure chance with the possible exception of his breakfast, which he felt certain was made by his housekeeper. Naturally belief in a divine intelligence inspires tranquility. But this does not free us from our human responsibilities. Am I my brother's keeper? Yes. Interestingly, in my case I share that honor with the Prospect Park Zoo. Feeling godless then, what we have done is made technology God. And yet can technology really be the answer when a brand new Buick, driven by my close associate, Nat Persky, winds up in the window of Chicken Delight causing hundreds of customers to scatter? My toaster has never once worked properly in four years. I follow the instructions and push two slices of bread down in the slots and seconds later they rifle upward. Once they broke the nose of a woman I loved very dearly. Are we counting on nuts and bolts and electricity to solve our problems? Yes, the telephone is a good thing—and the refrigerator—and the air conditioner. But not every air conditioner. Not my sister Henny's, for instance. Hers makes a loud noise and still doesn't cool. When the man comes over to fix it, it gets worse. Either that or he tells her she needs a new one. When she complains, he says not to bother him. This man is truly alienated. Not only is he alienated but he can't stop smiling.

The trouble is, our leaders have not adequately prepared us for a mechanized society. Unfortunately our politicians are either incompetent or corrupt. Sometimes both on the same day. The Government is unresponsive to the needs of the little man. Under five-seven, it is impossible to get your Congressman on the phone. I am not denying that democracy is still the finest form of government. In a democracy at least, civil liberties are upheld. No citizen can be wantonly tortured, imprisoned, or made to sit through certain Broadway shows. And yet this is a far cry from what goes on in the Soviet Union. Under their form of totalitarianism, a person merely caught whistling is sentenced to 30 years in a labor camp. If, after 15 years, he still will not stop whistling they shoot him. Along with this brutal fascism we find its handmaiden, terrorism. At no other time in history has man been so afraid to cut his veal chop for fear that it will explode. Violence breeds more violence and it is predicted that by 1990 kidnapping will be the dominant mode of social interaction. Overpopulation will exacerbate problems to the breaking point. Figures tell us there are already more people on earth than we need to move even the heaviest piano. If we do not call a halt to breeding, by the year 2000 there will be no room to serve dinner unless one is willing to set the table on the heads of strangers. Then they must not move for an hour while we eat. Of course energy will be in short supply and each car owner will be allowed only enough gasoline to back up a few inches.

Instead of facing these challenges we turn instead to distractions like drugs and sex. We live in far too permissive a society. Never before has pornography been this rampant. And those films are lit so badly! We are a people who lack defined goals. We have never learned to love. We lack leaders and coherent programs. We have no spiritual center. We are adrift alone in the cosmos wreaking monstrous violence on one another out of frustration and pain. Fortunately, we have not lost our sense of proportion. Summing up, it is clear the future holds great opportunities. It also holds pitfalls. The trick will be to avoid the pitfalls, seize the opportunities, and get back home by six o'clock.

Suggestions for Discussion

1. Discuss Allen's use of exaggeration and understatement as sources of humor.
2. What real social problems does Allen address?
3. How does Allen's choice of allusion and vocabulary contribute to the effectiveness of his parody?

Suggestion for Writing

Write an essay in which, without diminishing Allen's skill as a comic writer, you consider why it is easy to parody a commencement address. Is it possible to compose an address which does not invite parody? What might be the content and tone of an effective address?

Anna Tuttle Villegas

The Teacher as Dragon

Anna Tuttle Villegas teaches English at the University of the Pacific in Stockton, California. "The Teacher as Dragon," which appeared in the San Francisco *Sunday Examiner and Chronicle* in 1983, describes the difficult task which faces the teacher of writing. It shows how easily students perceive the writing teacher as monster and how easily teachers assume that shape if they lose their optimism.

A few semesters ago, in fulfillment of a descriptive paper assignment, I received a student essay describing a high school English teacher. To this day I vividly recall the image it created. It was of a stout, ham-like body perched atop two trunkish legs that ended in toes having not toenails but yellow, calcified claws (which were always, the student noted, causing damage to hosiery). On top of this lumbering figure was planted a savage, baleful countenance fringed with sparse, kinky, red hair. Behind the inevitable thick-lensed spectacles glared beady porcine eyes whose sole purpose, it seems, was to seek out ne'er-do-wells and inflict on them stinging lashes of shame and guilt.

The indelible impression I have of the essay (and the woman) is the intricately painted relationship between appearance and character. True, I had emphasized to my students that they describe their subjects along thematic lines, but there was something supernaturally real and uncannily familiar to me about this fire-breathing dragon of an English teacher. I caught, in the reflections of her horn-rims, an image of myself.

In appearance I am nothing like her. Where she is short and stout, I am tall and leaning to the skinny side. Where she wears gaudy and sackish dresses, I wear informal pants and shirts, not unlike those of my students. The closest my hair comes to red are the few rusty strands left over from the chlorine bleach of last summer's daily swimming. I am blind as a bat, and my prescription is strong—but I don't wear horn-rimmed glasses. And my eyes are blue, not beady black.

Why, then, in the midst of midnight insomnia or the predawn stirrings of the soul, do I see myself in this red-haired vixen?

The teaching of writing, of good writing, is the teaching of thinking—not thinking presented in a general, abstracted, grandiose way, but thinking applied to the individual mind. When, as a writing teacher, I ask for an argumentative essay that springs from a student's interest in a subject, I am not asking for a legislative document or a psychological treatise. I am asking for reasonable thought on a limited topic conveyed from a unique perspective, the student's own.

To ask for reasonable thought—to ask for any individual thought—is a very risky business. It means that what will finally be evaluated by the teacher is a projection of the student's self, and, unless the student is that rare one who enters a writing class articulate, skilled and independently thoughtful, that part of the self tends to be particularly vulnerable.

No matter how often a writing teacher chants that "receiving a D grade doesn't mean you are a D person," students interpret a grade as a grade on their characters, and they react much like a calf whose flank is singed with a hot iron: bawling and kicking and protesting throatily against convention and authority, in their pained rage mistaking blue eyes for black ones.

No one likes to be told, or even have hinted at, that his mind is cluttered, untidy, disordered, lacking purpose. Yet when I comment that an essay fails to meet the objectives the writer has set for it, that it dawdles from point to point without developing any one idea, I have the unpleasant task of pointing a finger at the clutter.

I believe myself to be an expert at supportive tact, but it is in this aspect of my job and my relationship to my students that I find my kinship with the red-haired dragon. We are both concerned with the nurturing of creative thought, and in our attempts to bribe and cajole thought from our students we sometimes have to point out where it is wilting from the neglect of haste or lack of commitment. Then we become sisters: dragon ladies who bleed red ink instead of blood.

Our genealogy follows a long engagement in the profession. Although I don't yet resemble the red-haired teacher in person, in spirit I am beginning to. In her youth she, like me, must have entertained the belief that in teaching her students to write she was endowing them with an enduring tool for discovering themselves and their relationship to their world. She must have felt the thrill of discovery herself when she received papers that rewarded her with the richness of shared experience.

Unfortunately, long before I stood nervously before my first expository class, she must have encountered the disappointment of failed expectations. Subconsciously perhaps, she rallied by convincing herself that with gentle and persistent prodding of her students' minds she could extract from them substance for good essays and sustenance for her belief in their capacity to think. This, I speculate, may have delayed her eventual disenchantment with the human imagination for a few years. But as time and students passed by her, she was forced to accept the decay of her initial illusion about the rational animal's ability to communicate. It was at this time that her eyes got bad, her prescription thicker and her hair unruly. She was transforming herself into a person who was impervious to disappointment. She began to shield herself in her scales.

One doesn't have to count the dragon ladies one has known to realize that the constant failure of expectations creates bitterness, sours the appeal of meeting new minds, and physically transforms a person. The dragon teacher is an understandable product of many years of a gradual lowering of standards. Ultimately she found it easier to torment than to teach. With tormenting she could see at least an emotional response, while with teaching she despaired of ever finding an intellectual one.

I remember reading amid cheers that essay to my class. After reviewing the descriptive techniques the writer had used, we turned to a discussion of the relationship between thesis and descriptive detail. In a class of twenty students from widely varying geographic backgrounds, I found that fifteen of them had been taught high school English, if not by the dragon lady herself, by her identical sister. Her attitude and her appearance, even down to the fine detail of the calcified toenails, were those of an entire nation of English schoolmarms. And I am of the same breed.

I admit that I read the essay to my class with the intention of milking from it every ounce of humor that it had. In retrospect I see that what I was really doing, in a sneaky and lowdown way, was saying to my students: Look, here is what you might have had for a writing teacher. But you didn't. You have me—and aren't I different? Aren't I breaking the mold? Won't you write your hearts out for me?

I don't like the image of myself that I caught reflected in that essay. I don't like the image of my profession that appeared there, either. Writing well is the most powerful intellectual tool that a person—student or teacher or layman—can develop. I go to school every day, talk about conventions and rhetorical modes and ideas, drag home stacks of student essays, comment on conventions and modes and ideas and return to school the next day to begin again because I believe in the written word's power. And I refuse to succumb to the stereotype the outside world has of me.

I have great sympathy for the red-haired woman whom I have used so badly. I understand how she has evolved into her present state. But I am sorry she gave up. Our job is too important, our students' minds too precious, for me to give up too. My hair will not turn red.

Suggestions for Discussion

1. How does the student essay describe a high school English teacher? Why does the author begin her essay with this description? What use does she make of this description in the rest of the essay?

2. Why does the author believe it is difficult to teach writing? Do you agree with her analysis of student reaction to receiving a poor grade?

3. What does Villegas consider her primary function as a teacher of writing? Is she subject to frustration? Do you imagine that frustration will cause her to give up?

4. How does the author begin to identify with the high school teacher described in the student paper?

Suggestion for Writing

Have you had an English teacher who resembles the author of this essay or the high school teacher described by her student? Write an essay in which you discuss those qualities in your teacher which resemble those of either. Could you see qualities below the surface? Your essay should enable the reader to understand something about the character of your teacher as well as see him or her plainly.

T. H. Huxley

A Liberal Education

Thomas Henry Huxley (1825–1895), a biologist, was first of a line of important English scientists and writers bearing his name. He gave up his career in science to publicize Darwinism and to influence and change education in England. He was an agnostic and a believer in progress controlled by evolution. His works include *Evolution and Ethics* (1893) and nine volumes of collected essays and four volumes of memoirs. The following selection from *A Liberal Education* (1868) defines the goals of a liberal education and relates it to our need to learn the laws of nature.

Suppose it were perfectly certain that the life and fortune of every one of us would, one day or other, depend upon his winning or losing a game of chess. Don't you think that we should all consider it to be a primary duty to learn at least the names and the moves of the pieces; to have a notion of a gambit, and a keen eye for all the means of giving and getting out of check? Do you not think that we should look with a disapprobation amounting to scorn, upon the father who allowed his son, or the state which allowed its members, to grow up without knowing a pawn from a knight?

Yet it is a very plain and elementary truth, that the life, the fortune, and the happiness of every one of us, and, more or less, of those who are connected with us, do depend upon our knowing something of the rules of a game infinitely more difficult and complicated than chess. It is a game which has been played for untold ages, every man and woman of us being one of the two players in a game of his or her own. The chessboard is the world, the pieces are the phenomena of the universe, the rules of the game are what we call the laws of Nature. The player on the other side is hidden from us. We know that his play is always fair, just, and patient. But also we know, to our cost, that he never overlooks a mistake, or makes the smallest allowance for ignorance. To the man who plays well, the highest stakes are paid, with that sort of overflowing generosity with which the strong shows delight in strength. And one who plays ill is checkmated—without haste, but without remorse.

My metaphor will remind some of you of the famous picture in which Retzsch has depicted Satan playing at chess with man for his soul. Substitute for the mocking fiend in that picture, a calm, strong angel who is playing for love, as we say, and would rather lose than win—and I should accept it as an image of human life.

Well, what I mean by Education is learning the rules of this mighty game. In other words, education is the instruction of the intellect in the laws of Nature, under which name I include not merely things and their forces, but men and their ways; and the fashioning of the affections and of the will into an earnest and loving desire to move in harmony with those laws. For me education means neither more nor less than this. Anything which professes to call itself education must be tried by this standard, and if it fails to stand the test, I will not call it education, whatever may be the force of authority, or of numbers, upon the other side.

It is important to remember that, in strictness, there is no such thing as an uneducated man. Take an extreme case. Suppose that an adult man, in the full vigor of his faculties, could be suddenly placed in the world, as Adam is said to have been, and then left to do as he best might. How long would he be left uneducated? Not five minutes. Nature would begin to teach him, through the eye, the ear, the touch, the properties of objects. Pain and pleasure would be at his elbow telling him to do this and avoid that; and by slow degrees the man would receive an education, which, if narrow, would be thorough, real, and adequate to his circumstances, though there would be no extras and very few accomplishments.

And if to this solitary man entered a second Adam, or better still, an Eve, a new and greater world, that of social and moral phenomena, would be revealed. Joys and woes, compared with which all others might seem but faint shadows, would spring from the new relations. Happiness and sorrow would take the place of the coarser monitors, pleasure and pain; but conduct would still be shaped by the observation of the natural consequences of actions; or, in other words, by the laws of the nature of man.

To everyone of us the world was once as fresh and new as to Adam. And then, long before we were susceptible of any other mode of instruction, Nature took us in hand, and every minute of waking life brought its educational influence, shaping our actions into rough accordance with Nature's laws, so that we might not be ended untimely by too gross disobedience. Nor should

I speak of this process of education as past for any one, be he as old as he may. For every man the world is as fresh as it was at the first day, and as full of untold novelties for him who has the eyes to see them. And Nature is still continuing her patient education of us in that great university, the universe, of which we are all members—Nature having no Test-Acts.

Those who take honors in Nature's university, who learn the laws which govern men and things and obey them, are the really great and successful men in this world. The great mass of mankind are the "Poll," who pick up just enough to get through without much discredit. Those who won't learn at all are plucked; and then you can't come up again. Nature's pluck means extermination.

Thus the question of compulsory education is settled so far as Nature is concerned. Her bill on that question was framed and passed long ago. But, like all compulsory legislation, that of Nature is harsh and wasteful in its operation. Ignorance is visited as sharply as willful disobedience—incapacity meets with the same punishment as crime. Nature's discipline is not even a word and a blow, and the blow first; but the blow without the word. It is left to you to find out why your ears are boxed.

The object of what we commonly call education—that education in which man intervenes and which I shall distinguish as artificial education—is to make good these defects in Nature's methods; to prepare the child to receive Nature's education, neither incapably nor ignorantly, nor with willful disobedience; and to understand the preliminary symptoms of her displeasure, without waiting for the box on the ear. In short, all artificial education ought to be an anticipation of natural education. And a liberal education is an artificial education, which has not only prepared a man to escape the great evils of disobedience to natural laws, but has trained him to appreciate and to seize upon the rewards, which Nature scatters with as free a hand as her penalties.

That man, I think, has had a liberal education, who has been so trained in youth that his body is the ready servant of his will, and does with ease and pleasure all the work that, as a mechanism, it is capable of; whose intellect is a clear, cold, logic engine, with all its parts of equal strength, and in smooth working order; ready, like a steam engine, to be turned to any kind of work, and spin the gossamers as well as forge the anchors of the mind; whose mind is stored with a knowledge of the great and fundamental truths of Nature and of the laws of her operations; one who, no stunted ascetic, is full of life and fire, but whose passions are trained to come to heel by a vigorous will, the servant of a tender conscience; who has learned to love all beauty, whether of Nature or of art, to hate all vileness, and to respect others as himself.

Such an one and no other, I conceive, has had a liberal education; for he is, as completely as a man can be, in harmony with Nature. He will make the best of her, and she of him. They will get on together rarely; she as his ever beneficent mother, he as her mouth-piece, her conscious self, her minister and interpreter.

Suggestions for Discussion

1. What is the function of the analogy of the rules of the game of chess and the laws of nature introduced in the first two paragraphs?

2. How does nature repay those who learn its rules? those who do not? What is Huxley's attitude toward nature?

3. How does Huxley define education? What does he regard as its major function? How is education related to the teachings of nature?

4. How does Huxley define liberal education? What qualities of life does a liberal education bestow on its recipients?

Suggestions for Writing

1. This essay dates from the mid-nineteenth century. What details in the writing reveal this fact to you? Write an essay in which you attempt to restate Huxley's major ideas in your own language.

2. Write an essay in which you comment on Huxley's ideas about the value of liberal education. Are they similar to your own? Do you believe that his ideas are necessarily dated? Explain.

Allan Bloom

Our Listless Universities

Allan Bloom (b. 1930), born in Indianapolis, holds all of his degrees from the University of Chicago where he is now professor of the Committee on Social Thought and the College. He has taught government and political science at the Universities of Yale, Cornell, Tel Aviv, and Toronto. A winner of a distinguished teaching award, he is also the author of *Shakespeare's Politics* and a translator and commentator of Plato and Rousseau. "Our Listless Universities," printed in *Change Magazine* in April 1983, describes the nihilism in American universities which has stultified their intellectual life and undermined teaching in the humanities and the social sciences.

I begin with my conclusions: students in our best universities do not believe in anything, and those universities are doing nothing about it, nor can they. An easy-going American kind of nihilism has descended upon us, a nihilism without terror of the abyss. The great questions—God, freedom, and immortality, according to Kant—hardly touch the young. And the universities, which should encourage the quest for the clarification of such questions, are the very source of the doctrine which makes that quest appear futile.

The heads of the young are stuffed with a jargon derived from the despair of European thinkers, gaily repackaged for American consumption and presented as the foundation for a pluralistic society. That jargon becomes a substitute for real experiences and instinct; one suspects that modern thought has produced an artificial soul to replace the old one supplied by nature, which was full of dangerous longings, loves, hates, and awes. The new soul's language consists of terms like *value, ideology, self, commitment, identity*—every word derived from recent German philosophy, and each carrying a heavy baggage of dubious theoretical interpretation of which its users are blissfully unaware. They take such language to be as unproblematic and immediate as night and day. It now constitutes our peculiar common sense.

The new language subtly injects into our system the perspective of "do your own thing" as the only plausible way of life. I know that sounds vaguely passé, a remnant leftover from the Sixties. But it is precisely the routinization of the passions of the Sixties that is the core of what is going on now, just as the Sixties were merely a radicalization of earlier tendencies.

The American regime has always attempted to palliate extreme beliefs that lead to civil strife, particularly religious beliefs. The members of sects had to obey the laws and be loyal to the Constitution; if they did so, others had to leave them alone. To make things work, it was thought helpful that men's beliefs be moderated. There was a conscious, if covert, effort to weaken religious fervor by assigning religion to the realm of opinion as opposed to knowledge. But everyone had to have an intense belief in the right of freedom of religion; the existence of that natural right was not to be treated as a matter of opinion.

The insatiable appetite for freedom to live as one pleases thrives on this aspect of modern democratic thought. The expansion of the area exempt from legitimate regulation is effected by contracting the claims to moral and political knowledge. It appears that full freedom can be attained only when there is no such knowledge. The effective way to defang oppressors is to persuade them that they are ignorant of the good. There are no absolutes: freedom is absolute.

A doctrine that gives equal rights to any way of life whatsoever has the double advantage of licensing one's own way of life and of giving one a democratic good conscience. The very lack of morality is a morality and permits what Saul Bellow has called "easy virtue," a mixture of egotism and high-mindedness. Now, in feeling as well as in speech, a large segment of our young are open, open to every "lifestyle." But the fatal consequence of this openness has been the withering of their belief in their own way of life and of their capacity to generate goals. The palliation of beliefs culminates in pallid belief. A soul which esteems indiscriminately must be an artificial soul, and that, to repeat, is what we are coming near to constituting, not by some inevitable historical process but by a conscious education project. This project masquerades as the essential democratic theory without which we would collapse into tyranny or the war of all prejudices against all. Its premise is that truth itself must be prejudice or at least treated as such.

The tendency toward indiscriminateness—the currently negative connotation of the word *discrimination* tells us much—is apparently perennial in democracy. The need to subordinate the more refined sensibilities to a common denominator and the unwillingness to order the soul's desires according to their rank conduce to easygoingness. The democratic ethos obscures the reason for the desirability of such self-mastery. This is the moral problem of democracy and why fortuitous external necessities like war or poverty seem to bring out the best in us. Plato describes the natural bent of the democratic man thus:

> He . . . also lives along day by day, gratifying the desire that occurs to him, at one time drinking and listening to the flute, at another downing water and reducing; now practicing gymnastics, and again idling and neglecting everything; and sometimes spending his time as though he were occupied with philosophy. Often he engages in politics and, jumping up, says and does whatever chances to come to him; and if he ever admires any soldiers, he turns in that direction; and if it's moneymakers, in that one. And there is neither order nor necessity in his life, but calling this life sweet, free, and blessed he follows it throughout.

This account is easily recognizable when applied to the middle-class youth who attend America's top colleges and universities. But Plato's description omits a more sinister element in our situation. Plato's young man believes that each of the lives he follows is really good, at least when he follows it. His problem is that he cannot keep his mind made up. Our young person, by contrast, is always plagued by a gnawing doubt as to whether the activity he undertakes is worth anything, whether this end is not just another "value," an illusion that men once believed in but which our "historical consciousness" reveals as only a cultural phenomenon. There are a thousand and one such goals; they are not believed in because they exist, they exist because one believes in them. Since we now know this, we can no longer believe. The veil of illusion has been torn away forever. The trendy language for this alleged experience is *demystification* or *demythologization*. This teaching now has the status of dogma. It leads to a loss of immediacy in all experience and a suspicion that every way of life is a "role." The substitution of the expression "lifestyle," which we can change at will, for the good life, the rational quest for which is the origin of philosophy, tells the story. That is what I mean by nihilism, and this nihilism has resulted from a questionable doctrine that we seem no longer to question.

All of us who are under sixty know something about this doctrine and its transmission, for since the Thirties it is what the schools have been teaching. For fifty years the only spiritual substance they have been trying to convey is openness, the disdain for the ethnocentric. Of course, they have also been teaching the three Rs, but their moral and intellectual energy has been turned almost exclusively in this direction. Schools once produced citizens, or gentlemen, or believers; now they produce the unprejudiced. A university professor confronting entering freshmen can be almost certain that most of them will know that there are no absolutes and that one cannot say that one culture is superior to another. They can scarcely believe that someone might seriously argue the contrary; the attempt to do so meets either self-satisfied smiles at something so old-fashioned or outbursts of anger at a threat to decent respect for other human beings. In the Thirties this teaching was actually warring against some real prejudices of race, religion, or nation; but what remains now is mostly the means for weakening conviction when convictions have disappeared.

The doctrine of cultural relativism did not emerge from the study of cultures. It was a philosophic doctrine that gave a special interpretation of the meaning of culture and had a special political attractiveness. It could appeal to the taste for diversity as opposed to our principled homogeneity. All kinds of people climbed aboard—disaffected Southern snobs who had never accepted the Declaration and the Constitution anyhow, Stalinists who wanted us to love Soviet tyranny without being too explicit about it, and similar types. No choices would have to be made. We could have the charms of old cultures, of what one now calls roots, along with democratic liberties. All that was required was an education making other ways attractive and disenchanting one's own. It is not so much the knowledge of other cultures that is important, but the consciousness that one loves one's own way because it is one's own, not because it is good. People must understand that they are what they are and what they believe only because of accidents of time and place.

The equality of values seemed to be a decisive step in the march of equality. So sure were our social scientists of the truth and vigor of democracy that they did not even dimly perceive what Weber knew, that this view undermined democracy, which stands or falls with reason. Only democracy traces all its authority to reason; other kinds of regimes can more or less explicitly appeal to other sources. When we talk about the West's lack of conviction or lack of will, we show that we are beginning to recognize what has happened to us. Exhortations to believe, however, are useless. It is only by thinking ideas through again that we can determine whether our reason can any longer give assent to our principles.

But this serious reconsideration is not taking place in the universities.

II

Today a young person does not generally go off to the university with the expectation of having an intellectual adventure, of discovering strange new worlds, of finding out what the comprehensive truth about man is. This is partly because he thinks he already knows, partly because he thinks such truth unavailable. And the university does not try to persuade him that he is coming to it for the purpose of being liberally educated, at least in any meaningful sense of the term—to study how to be free, to be able to think for himself. The university has no vision, no view of what a human being must know in order to be considered educated. Its general purpose is lost amid the incoherent variety of special purposes that have accreted within it. Such a general purpose may be vague and undemonstrable, but for just this reason it requires the most study. The meaning of life is unclear, but that is why we must spend our lives clarifying it rather than letting the question go. The university's function is to remind students of the importance and urgency of the question and give them the means to pursue it. Universities do have other responsibilities, but this should be their highest priority.

They have, however, been so battered by modern doctrines, social demands, the requirements of the emancipated specialties, that they have tacitly agreed not to open Pandora's box and start a civil war. They provide a general framework that keeps the peace but they lack a goal of their own.

When the arriving student surveys the scene, he sees a bewildering variety of choices. The professional schools beckon him by providing him with an immediate motive: a lucrative and prestigious livelihood guaranteed by simply staying in the university to the conclusion of training. Medicine and law were always such possibilities; with the recent addition of the MBA, the temptation has radically increased. If the student decides to take this route, liberal education is practically over for him.

If he first turns his eye to what was traditionally thought to be the center of the university, he will confront—aside from a few hot programs like black studies, native studies, women's studies, which are largely exercises in consciousness-raising—the natural sciences, the social sciences, and the humanities.

The natural sciences thrive, full of good conscience and good works. But they are ever more specialized and ever more separate from the rest of the university; they have no need of it. They don't object to liberal education, if it doesn't get in the way of their research and training. And they have nothing to say, even about themselves or their role in the whole human picture, let alone about the kinds of questions that agitated Descartes, Newton, and Leibniz. Their results speak for themselves, but they do not say quite enough.

The social sciences are the source of much useful research and information, but they are long past the first effervescence of their Marxist-Freudian-Weberian period. Then they expected to find a new and more scientific way to answer the old questions of philosophy. Such hopes and claims quietly disappeared from the scene during the past 15 years. Their solid reasons for existence are in specialized study of interest rates, Iranian politics, or urban trends. Practically no economist conceives of doing what Adam Smith did, and the few who try produce petty and trivial stuff. The case is pretty much the same for the other social sciences. They are theoretically barren, and the literature read and used by them is mostly ephemera of the last fifty years.

The remainder is to be found in the humanities, the smallest, least funded, most dispirited part of the university. The humanities are the repository of the books that are at the foundation of our religion, our philosophy, our politics, our science, as well as our art. Here, if anywhere, one ought to find the means to doubt what seems most certain. Only here are the questions about knowledge, about the good life, about God and love and death, at home in the university. If, however, one looks at the humanistic side of the campus, one finds a hodgepodge of disciplines, not integrally related with one another and without much sense of common purpose. The books are divided up among language departments, according to the largely accidental fact of the language in which they were written. Such departments have as their primary responsibility the teaching of the language in question (a very depressing responsibility now that languages have fallen into particular disfavor with students).

Humanists in general are the guardians of great books, but rarely take seriously the naive notion that these books might contain the truth which has escaped us. Yet without the belief that from Plato one might learn how to live or that from Shakespeare one might get the deepest insight into the passions and the virtues, no one who is not professionally obligated will take them seriously. Try as they may, the humanities will fail to interest if they do not teach *the truth* even as natural and social science are supposed to do. To present the great writers and artists as representatives of cultures or examples of the way thought is related to society, or in any of the other modes common today, is to render them uninteresting to the healthy intellect. The comprehensive questions have their natural home in the humanities, but it is there that the historical-cultural doubt about the possibility of answering them is most acute. Professors of humanities more than any others wonder whether they have a truth to tell.

Philosophy should, of course, provide the focus for the most needful study. But it is just one department among many and, in the democracy of the specialties, it no longer has the will to insist that it is the queen of the sciences. Moreover, in most philosophy departments the study of the classic texts is not central. Professors "do" their own philosophy and do not try to pose the questions as they were posed by the old writers. This is especially the case for the dominant school of thought in the United States, the Oxford school.

Of all university members, humanists have the least self-confidence. The students are abandoning them, and they have difficulty speaking to the concerns of the age. They fear they may have to huckster—if they are not already doing so—in order to keep afloat. In their heart of hearts many doubt that they have much to say. After all, most of the writers they promote can be convicted of elitism and sexism, the paramount sins of the day.

There are, to be sure, many dedicated individuals in the humanities who know what needs to be done and can draw students' attention to the impoverished state of their experience and show them that great texts address their concerns. But the endeavor of these professors is a lonely one with little corporate resonance. The students are not reading the same books and addressing the same questions, so that their common social life cannot be affected by a common intellectual life.

It should be added that the humanities are also the center of some of the fastest selling intellectual items of the day—structuralism, deconstructionism, and Marxist humanism. The members of these schools—particularly rampant in comparative literature—do read books and talk big ideas. In that sense they are the closest thing to what the university should be about. The problem with them, and all of them are alike in this respect, is that the books are not taken seriously on their own grounds but are used as vile bodies for the sake of demonstrating theses brought to them by the interpreters. They know what they are looking for before they begin. Their approaches are ultimately derived from Marx or Nietzsche, whose teachings are tacitly taken to be true.

It is small wonder that the student is bewildered about what it means to be educated. The new liberal education requirements some universities are instituting are little more than tours of what is being done in the various workshops. To be sure, they always add on a course requirement, in a non-Western civilization or culture, but that is just another bit of demagogy serving the indoctrination of openness. Serious physicists would never require a course in non-Western physics. Culture and civilization are irrelevant to the truth. One finds it where one can. Only if truth is relative to culture does this make sense. But, once again, this is our dogma, accepted for covert political reasons. This dogma is the greatest enemy of liberal education. It undermines the unity of man, our common humanity in the intellect, which makes the university possible and permits it to treat man as simply without distinction.

III

Three conclusions have forced themselves on me about students, their characters and ways, conclusions that have to do with their education and their educability. They are not scientific generalizations based on survey research, but they are the result of long observation of, and careful listening to, young people in our better universities by one who is intensely interested in their real openness, their openness to higher learning.

1. *Books*. They are no longer an important part of the lives of students. "Information" is important, but profound and beautiful books are not where they go for it. They have no books that are companions and friends to which they look for counsel, companionship, inspiration, or pleasure. They do not expect to find in them sympathy for, or clarification of, their inmost desires and experiences. The link between the classic books and the young, which persisted for so long and in so many circumstances, and is the only means of connecting the here and the now with the always, this link has been broken. The Bible and Plutarch have ceased to be a part of the soul's furniture, an incalculable loss of fullness and awareness of which the victims are unaware.

The loss of the taste for reading has been blamed on television, the universal villain of social critics. But lack of reverence for antiquity and contempt for tradition are democratic tendencies. It should be the university's business to provide a corrective to these tendencies; however, I believe that the universities are most to blame for them. After all, they taught the schoolteachers. For a very long time now the universities have been preoccupied with abstract modern schools of thought that were understood to have surpassed all earlier thought and rendered it obsolete. And their primary concern has been to indoctrinate social attitudes, to "socialize," rather than to educate. The old books are still around, but one "knows" that they contain mere opinions, no better than any others. The result is true philistinism, a withering of taste and a conformity to what is prevalent in the present. It means the young have no heroes, no objects of aspiration. It is all both relaxing and boring, a soft imprisonment.

2. *Music*. While I am not certain about the effects of television, I am quite certain about those of music. Many students do not watch much television while in college, but they do listen to music. From the time of puberty, and earlier, music has been the food of their souls. This is the audio generation. And classical music is dead, at least as a common taste. Rock is all there is.

There is now one culture for everyone, in music as in language. It is a music that moves the young powerfully and immediately. Its beat goes to the depth of their souls and inarticulately expresses their inarticulate longings. Those longings are sexual, and the beat appeals almost exclusively to that. It caters to kiddy sexuality, at best to puppy love. The first untutored feelings of adolescents are taken over by this music and given a form and a satisfaction. The words make little difference; they may be explicitly sexual, or sermons in favor of nuclear disarmament, or even religious—the motor of it all is eroticism. The youngsters know this perfectly well, even if their parents do not.

Rock music caused a great evolution in the relations between parents and children. Its success was the result of an amazing cooperation among lust, art, and commercial shrewdness. Without parents realizing it, their children were liberated from them. The children had money to spend. The record companies recognized as much and sold them music appealing to their secret desires. Never before was a form of art (however unquestionable) directed to so young an audience. This art gave children's feelings public respectability. The education of children had escaped their parents, no matter how hard they tried to prevent it. The most powerful formative influence on children between 12 and 18 is not the school, not the church, not the home, but rock music and all that goes with it. It is not an elevating but a leveling influence. The children have as their heroes banal, drug-, and sex-ridden guttersnipes who foment rebellion not only against parents but against all noble sentiments. This is the emotional nourishment they ingest in these precious years. It is the real junk food.

One thing I have no difficulty teaching students today is the passage in the *Republic* where Socrates explains that control over music is control over character and that the rhythm and the melody are more powerful than the words. They do not especially like Socrates's views on music, but they understand perfectly what he is about and the importance of the issue.

3. *Sex*. No change has been so rapid, so great, and so surprising as the change in the last twenty years concerning sex and the relations between the sexes. Young people of college age are very much affected by the sexual passion and preoccupied with love, marriage, and the family (to use an old formula that is now painfully inadequate to what is really meant). It is an age of excitement and uncertainty, and much of the motivation for study and reflection of a broader sort comes from the will to adorn and clarify erotic longings.

It is, however, in this domain that the listless, nihilistic mood has its practical expression and most affects the life of the students. The prevailing atmosphere deprives sex of seriousness as well as of charm. And, what is more, it makes it very difficult to think about sex. In a permissive era, when it is almost respectable to think and even do the deeds of Oedipus, shame and guilt have taken refuge in a new redoubt and made certain things unthinkable. Terror grips man at the thought he might be sexist. For all other tastes there is sympathy and support in universities. Sexism, whatever it may mean, is unpardonable.

The great change in sexual behavior has taken place in two stages. The first is what was called the sexual revolution. This meant simply that pre- and extra-marital sex became much more common, and the various penalties for promiscuity were either much reduced or disappeared. In the middle Sixties I noticed that very nice students who previously would have hidden their affairs abandoned all pretense. They would invite their professors to dine in apartments where they lived together and not hesitate to give expression to physical intimacy in a way that even married couples would rarely do before their peers.

This kind of change, of course, implied a very different way of thinking about things. Desire always existed, but it used to war with conscience, shame, and modesty. These now had to be deprecated as prejudices, as pointing to nothing beyond themselves. Religious and philosophic moral teachings that supported such sentiments became old hat, and a certain materialism which justified bodily satisfaction seemed more plausible.

The world looks very different than it once did to young people entering college. The kinds of questions they ask, and the sensitivities they bring to these fresh circumstances, are vastly altered. The tension of high expectation has been relaxed; there is much they no longer have to find out. A significant minority of students couple off very early and live together throughout college with full awareness that they intend to go their separate ways afterward. They are just taking care of certain needs in a sensible way. There is, for a member of an older generation, an incomprehensible slackness of soul in all this. Certainly the adventurousness of such people, who are half-married but without the moral benefits of responsibility, is lamed. There is nothing wild, Dionysian, searching, in our promiscuity. It has a dull, sterilized, scientific character.

One must add that an increasing number of students come from divorced families and include in their calculation the possibility or the likelihood of divorce in their own future. The possibility of separation is not a neutral fact, allowing people to stay or go; it encourages separation because it establishes a psychology of separateness.

The result is inevitably egotism, not because the individuals are evil or naturally more prone to selfishness than those of another era. If there is no other thing to be attached to, the desires concerning ourselves are ever present. This tendency is particularly pronounced in an age when political ties are weak. People can hardly be blamed for not being attached when there is nothing that calls forth attachment. There can be no doubt that the sexual revolution plays a great role in dissolving the bonds founded on sexual relationships. What is not sufficiently understood is that in modern society there is little else that can be the basis for moral association. There is a repulsive lack of self-knowledge in those who attack the "nuclear family" and are rhapsodic about the "extended family" and real "community." Looseness is thus made into an ethical critique of our society. The "extended family" is no more possible in our time or consonant with our principles than is feudalism, while the "nuclear family" is still a viable alternative, but one that needs support in theory and practice. It provides a natural basis for connectedness. One can give it up, but one has to know the price. There is simply nothing else that is generally operative in society at large.

But even more powerful than all of the above changes are the effects of feminism, which is still early in its career of reform and is the second stage of the great change of which I am speaking. The theme is too vast to treat properly, but one can say that it, much more than the sexual revolution, takes place on the level of thought rather than that of instinct. Consciousness must be altered. Women have been exploited and misused throughout the entire past, and only now can one find out their real potential. We are on the threshold of a whole new world and a whole new understanding. And Right and Left are in large measure united on the issue. There is an almost universal agreement, among those who count for university students, that feminism is simply justified as is.

The degree of common agreement comes home to me when I teach the Socrates fantasy in the *Republic* about the abolition of the difference between the sexes. Twenty years ago it was an occasion of laughter, and my problem was to get students to take it seriously. Today it seems perfectly commonplace, and students take it all too seriously, failing to catch the irony. They do not note the degree to which Socrates acts as though men and women have no bodies and lightly give up all the things that are one's own, particularly those one loves—parents, spouses, children. All of them are connected with the bisexuality of the species. In doing this, Socrates shows the ambiguity of our nature and the degree of tension between our common humanity and our sexual separateness. The balance between the two is always fraught with difficulties. One must decide which has primacy; and this decision must be made in full awareness of the loss entailed by it. Our students no longer understand this.

It is here that a great difference between the situation of women and that of men comes to light. Women today have, to use our new talk, an agenda. They want to have the opportunity to pursue careers, and they want to find ways to reconcile this goal with having families. Also, it is their movement, so they are involved and excited, have much to talk about. The men, on the other hand, are waiting to be told what is on the agenda and ready to conform to its demands. There is little inclination to resist. All the principles have been accepted; it only remains to see how to live by them. Women are to have careers just as do men and, if there is to be marriage, the wife's career is not to be sacrificed to the man's; home and children are a shared responsibility; when and if there are to be children is up to the woman, and the decision to terminate or complete a pregnancy is a woman's right. Above all, women are not to have a "role" imposed on them. They have a right of self-definition. The women were the victims and must be the leaders in their recovery from victimization. The men, as they themselves see it, have to be understanding and flexible. There are no guidelines; each case is individual. One can't know what to expect. Openness, again, is the virtue.

The result is a desexualization of life, all the while that a lot of sexual activity is going on, and a reduction of the differences between the sexes. Anger and spiritedness are definitely out. Men and women in universities frequently share common dwellings and common facilities. Sex is all right, but it creates a problem. There are no forms in which it is to express itself, and it is a reminder of differentiation where there is supposed to be none. It is difficult to shift from the mode of sameness into that of romance. Therefore advances are tentative, nobody is quite sure where they are to begin, and men's fear of stereotyping women is ever-present. It is love that is being sacrificed, for it makes woman into an object to be possessed. Dating is almost a thing of the past. Men and women are together in what is supposed to be an easy camaraderie. If coupling takes place, it must not disturb the smooth surface of common human endeavor. Above all: no courtship or courtliness. Now there is friendship, mutual respect, communication; realism without foolish fabulation or hopes. One wonders what primal feelings and desires are pushed down beneath the pat uniformity of the speech they almost all use, a self-congratulatory speech which affirms that they are the first to have discovered how to relate to other people.

This conviction has as its first consequence that all old books are no longer relevant, because their authors were sexists (if they happened to be women, they were maimed by living in sexist society). There is little need of the commissars who are popping up all over the place to make the point that Eve, Cleopatra, Emma Bovary, and Anna Karenina are parts of male chauvinist propaganda. The students have gotten the point. These figures can't move their imaginations because their situations have nothing to do with situations in which students expect to find themselves. They need no inquisition to root out sexist heresies—although they will get one. And in the absence (temporary, of course) of a literature produced by feminism to rival the literature of Sophocles, Shakespeare, Racine, and Stendhal, students are without literary inspiration. Teaching romantic novels to university students (in spite of a healthy perseverance of this genre, as indicated by the success of the Harlequin romances—I find one free in every box of Hefty garbage bags I buy these days) is a quasi-impossibility. Students are either not interested or use it as grist for their ideological mill. Such books do not cause them to wonder whether they are missing something. All that passion seems pointless.

Notwithstanding all our relativism, there are certain things we know and which cannot be doubted. These are the tenets of the egalitarian creed, and today its primary tenet is that the past was sexist. This means that all the doubts which tradition should inspire in us in order to liberate us from the prejudices of our time are in principle closed to us. This is the source of the countless certainty that is the hallmark of the young. This is what a teacher faces today. I do not say that the situation is impossible or worse than it ever was. The human condition is always beset by problems. But these are *our* problems, and we must face them clearly. They constitute a crisis for humane learning but also reaffirm the need for it. The bleak picture is often relieved by the rays of natural curiosity about a better way; it can happen any time a student confronts a great book.

Suggestions for Discussion

1. What is the advantage for Bloom of beginning his essay with his conclusion?

2. Describe the nihilism which, according to Bloom, governs our lives both within and without the universities.

3. What language from German philosophy does Bloom regard as antithetical to education? Why does he call that language *jargon*?

4. Explain his quotation from Saul Bellow that describes a mixture of egotism and high-mindedness as "easy virtue." How does he relate "easy virtue" to what is wrong in American life? in its universities?

5. What is Bloom's objection to the word "lifestyle"? How does he connect this term to what he calls "openness" or "the disdain for the ethnocentric" or "cultural relativism"? Why does he believe that "openness" has undermined our schools?

6. Why do students who attend the university fail to regard this experience as an intellectual adventure?

7. In part II of his essay, Bloom discusses the failure of the sciences, the social sciences, and the humanities to provide substance to a university education. Explain his position. Why does he say that "of all university members, humanists have the least self-confidence"?

8. What are his three conclusions, developed in part III, about changes which have taken place among students? Explain his observations about rock music. What does he describe as the effect of feminism on students?

9. What does Bloom believe to be the true function of liberal education?

Suggestions for Writing

1. Write an essay in which you comment on Bloom's opinions on the role of books, music, and sex in the lives of students. Your essay should come not only from your own immediate experience but from your observation of others.

2. Write an essay in which you agree or disagree with his comments on the effects of feminism on university life and on life outside the universities.

3. Examine the General Education portion of your university's curriculum. Does it meet the requirements Bloom sets for such study? Is it subject to Bloom's criticism? Write an essay in which you report your experiences with your university's general education requirement and explain why they have been positive or negative.

◇ ◇ ◇ ◇

Otto Friedrich

Five Ways to Wisdom

Otto Friedrich (b. 1929) was born in Boston. A journalist and writer, he now writes for *Time*. His books on history and biography include *Before the Deluge: A Portrait of Berlin in the 1920s* (1972) and *Clover: The Tragic Love of Clover and Henry Adams* (1979). In this feature article on education from *Time* written in the fall of 1982, Friedrich (with assistance from *Time* reporters Dorothy Ferenbaugh and J. Madeline Nash) examines the problems facing higher education in the United States and reports on differing philosophies of education.

Opening day! In front of the brick dormitory, the dust-streaked family car lurches to a halt with its load of indispensable college supplies: one Sony stereo with headphones, two gooseneck lamps, five pairs of blue jeans, two down parkas (one old, one new) one pair of Rossignol skis . . . and one nervous freshman wondering whether anybody will like him. The older students have an easier time of it, needing only to unpack what they left in storage over the summer: more lamps, more blue jeans, boots, bicycles, one unused thesaurus donated by an out-of-date uncle . . . And now, from any reopening dormitory window on any campus from Chapel Hill to Santa Cruz, can be heard the thrumming, insistent sound of the contemporary campus: *Tattoo You . . . Vacation . . . Hold Me . . .*

These are the rites of initiation. Orientation meetings on subjects like time management. Tryouts for the glee club or the football team. Beer bashes. Join the struggle to save Lebanon; join the struggle to save Israel. At Princeton the freshmen and sophomores meet each other in a traditional series of games and rope pulls known as Cane Spree, which custom decrees that the freshmen lose. At Gettysburg College, the rituals of getting acquainted are even more folksy: a "shoe scramble" determines who will dance with whom. At Carleton, there is a fried-chicken picnic and square dancing on the grassy area known as the Bald Spot.

Along with the social games, though, a lot of intellectual choices have to be made, courses picked, books bought. Will it be the class known as "Slums and Bums" (Urban Government) or "Nuts and Sluts" (Abnormal Psychology)? The students joke about these things because they know the choices are serious; their future lives depend on them, and so does much else besides. It has been said that every nation has only a few years in which to civilize an onrushing horde of barbarians, its own children.

The barbarian hordes beginning their classes this month may be the largest in U.S. history, a tribute to both parental prodigality and the ideal of universal education. Though the crest of the 1950s baby boom has passed the college years, a larger percentage of high school graduates now goes to college (61%, *vs* 40% a generation ago), and the number of older and part-time students keeps increasing (34% of students are over 25). All in all, the number of Americans who are signing up for some form of higher education this fall totals a mind-boggling 12.5 million. Mind-boggling not only because of the quantity, but because there is very little agreement on what they are learning or should be learning.

Under the dappling elms of Harvard, which likes to think that is sets the national tone in such matters, President Derek Bok traditionally welcomes each graduating class into "the company of educated men and women." The phrase goes trippingly on the tongue, but what does it mean? Does any such community exist? Are the millions of people now engaged in earning diplomas really being educated?

The statistics of growth, unfortunately, are also the statistics of glut. When the 2.4 million college students of 1949 swelled into today's 12.5 million, the educational system was all but overwhelmed. The most prestigious institutions took easy pride in the numbers they turned away, but the states, somewhat idealistically committed to a policy of open admissions, had to double the number of public colleges, from some 600 to more than 1,250. Most of the new schools were two-year community colleges that featured remedial and vocational classes.

The overall quality of education almost inevitably sank. "Every generation since Roman days has decried the weakening of educational standards," sighs one Midwestern university dean, but the statistics provide sad evidence that there has been a genuine decline. Average scores in reading on the Scholastic Aptitude Tests (SATs) have dropped from 466 out of a possible 800 in 1968 to 424 in 1981, when the decline leveled out; mathematics scores over the same period sank from 492 to 466. A study conducted at the University of Wisconsin reported that at least 20% of last year's entering freshmen "lack the skill to write [acceptably] and 50% are not ready to succeed in college algebra."

"They don't know how to write, they don't read, they have little contact with culture," says Professor Norman Land, who teaches art history at the University of Missouri, in a typical complaint. "Every so often I give them a list of names, and they can identify Timothy Leary or the Who but not Dante or Vivaldi. They haven't received an education: they've just had baby sitting." Nor are the criticisms entirely about intellectual shortcomings. "I think students are becoming less reflective, less concerned about fellow human beings, more greedy, more materialistic," says Alexander Astin, professor of higher education at U.C.L.A. "They're interested in making money and in finding a job that gives them a lot of power and a lot of status."

College officials tend to blame student shortcomings on the high schools, which undeniably need reform and renewal, but the high schools can blame the elementary schools, the elementary schools the family at home, and everybody blames TV. Wisconsin's President Robert O'Neil, however, argues that the colleges are "in part to blame." Says he: "Having diluted the requirements and expectations, they indicated that students could succeed in college with less rigorous preparation." Mark H. Curtis, president of the Association of American Colleges, is more caustic: "We might begin to define the educated person as one who can overcome the deficiencies in our educational system."

The traditional curriculum, such as it was, virtually disintegrated during the campus upheavals of the 1960s, when millions of students demanded and won the right to get academic credit for studying whatever they pleased. There were courses in soap opera and witchcraft. Even more fundamental, and even more damaging, was the spread of the "egalitarian" notion that everybody was entitled to a college degree, and that it was undemocratic to base that degree on any differentiations of intellect or learning. "The idea that cosmetology is just as important as physics is still with us but is being challenged," says Curtis.

"Quality," argues Chester E. Finn Jr., professor of education and public policy at Vanderbilt, "is almost certainly going to turn out to be the foremost national education concern of the 1980s, much as equity was the premier issue of the 1960s and 1970s." The counterrevolution has actually been well under way for some time. In 1978 Harvard announced with great fanfare a controversial new core curriculum, and in 1980 Stanford inaugurated an elaborate system of seven tracks that would carry every student through the basics of Western civilization. "A miracle has happened among Stanford undergraduates," Charles Lyons, director of the Western-culture program, proudly told the faculty senate last spring. "They do talk about Plato at dinner and about Shakespeare on the lawns."

Other colleges followed suit. Amherst now requires all freshmen to take an interdisciplinary program called Introduction to Liberal Studies. At Washington University in St. Louis, the science and math requirements, which were cut in half during the heady days of student power, have been restored to the old levels (four semester-long courses). "The students were evading the real purpose of their education," says Associate Dean Harold Levin, adding, in the language of deans everywhere, "The product we were turning out was not what we wanted." All told, according to a survey of 272 universities and colleges last spring, 88% are engaged in revising their curriculums, and 59% of these are increasing their programs of required courses in general education. That, presumably, will improve the "product."

While the educators reorganize their methods, the fundamental goals of the process—truth, knowledge, the understanding of the world—remain somewhere just beyond the horizon. It was said of Goethe, after his death in 1832, that he was the last man to know everything worth knowing. Today's cliché is that 90% of all scientists in the history of the world are alive now. Yet their knowledge has become hopelessly fragmented; the specialist in recombinant DNA feels no more obligation to understand laser surgery than to hear the latest composition by Pierre Boulez.

As scientific specialties spawn subspecialties, the rapidly growing mass of information has confused the arts and humanities as well. Historical research now presupposes a mastery of old tax records and population movements, and anyone who ventures into such popular fields as American literature or impressionist art must wade into a rising tide of studies, analyses, psychographic portraits and sheer verbiage. In addition, all the political trends of the past two decades have tended to multiply the demands for studies in fields once ignored: Chinese history, the languages of Africa, the traffic in slaves, the thwarted ambitions of women.

Not everyone is overawed by the so-called knowledge explosion. "What happens," says Computer Scientist Joseph Weizenbaum of M.I.T., "is that educators, all of us, are deluged by a flood of messages disguised as valuable information, most of which is trivial and irrelevant to any substantive concern. This is the elite's equivalent of junk mail, but many educators can't see through it because they are not sufficiently educated to deal with such random complexity." To many experts, the computer seems a symbol of both the problem and its solution. "What the computer has done," according to Stephen White of the Alfred P. Sloan Foundation, "is to provide scope for analytical skills that never before existed, and in so doing it has altered the world in which the student will live as well as the manner in which he will think about the world . . . No adult is truly civilized unless he is acquainted with the civilization of which he is a member, and the liberal arts curriculum of 50 years ago no longer provides that acquaintance."

Acquaintance seems a bare minimum, and even that is difficult enough to attain in a world where millions cannot read and millions more read mainly falsehoods or formulas. Yet the basic questions of education still reach deep into every aspect of life: What is it essential to learn—to know—and why? Everyone seems to have his own answer, but there are interesting patterns among those answers. They can be organized into five main ideas:

I: Education Means Careers

Today's most popular answer is the practical one, on which students are most likely to agree with parents virtually impoverished by tuition bills: an education should enable a student to get a better job than he would otherwise be able to find or fill. In a Carnegie Council poll, 67% of students cited this as an "essential" purpose of their education. A 9.8% unemployment rate makes this purpose seem all the more essential. Michael Adelson, 23, who studied psychology at U.C.L.A., has been unable to find a job in his field for a year and a half, and he now wishes he had chosen engineering. He calls his bachelor of arts degree "completely useless."

The idea that education has a basically social purpose derives more or less from Plato. In his *Republic*, the philosopher portrayed a utopia governed by an intellectual elite specially trained for that purpose. This form of education was both stern and profoundly conservative. Children who attempt innovations, warned Socrates, acting as Plato's narrator, will desire a different sort of life when they grow up to be men, with other institutions and laws. And this "is full of danger to the whole state." To prevent any innovations, Socrates forthrightly demanded censorship so that students could not "hear any casual tales which may be devised by casual persons." When asked whose works he would ban, Socrates specifically named Homer. The poet's crime, he said, was to provide "an erroneous representation of the nature of gods and heroes."

Political pressure of this kind has never been far from the campus, but the overwhelming influence of U.S. education has been not politics but economics: the need for a technologically trained managerial caste. The very first Land Grant Act, in 1862, handed out 30,000 acres per Congressman for the building of state colleges at which "the leading object shall be . . . to teach such branches of learning as are related to agriculture and the mechanic arts." These needs keep changing, of course, and over the decades the U.S. economy demanded of its universities not only chemists and engineers but lawyers and accountants and personnel analysts, and then, after Sputnik's shocking revelation of the Soviet lead in space, yet more engineers.

Students naturally respond to the economy's needs. The Rev. Theodore Hesburgh, president of Notre Dame, complained last year that "the most popular course on the American college campus is not literature or history but accounting." This criticism reflects the fact that less than half the nation's swarm of college students go to liberal arts colleges; the rest are seeking not just jobs but entry into the middle class.

There are now thousands of Ph.D.s unable to find anyone willing to pay them for the hard-earned knowledge of Renaissance painting or the history of French monasticism, but any Sunday newspaper overflows with ads appealing for experts in electromagnetic capability, integrated logistics support, or laser electro-optics. Says George W. Valsa, supervisor of the college-recruiting section at Ford: "We are not ready to sign a petition to burn down liberal arts colleges, but don't expect us to go out and hire many liberal arts graduates." Ford does hire nearly 1,000 graduates a year, and most of them are engineers or M.B.A.s.

This is not the old argument between the "two cultures" of science and the humanities, for science too is often forced to defer to technical and vocational training. In 1979, according to one Carnegie study, 58% of all undergraduates pursued "professional" majors (up from 38% a decade earlier), in contrast to 11% in social sciences, 7% in biological sciences, 6% in the arts and 4% in physical sciences. Rich and prestigious private universities can resist this rush toward vocational training, but public and smaller private colleges are more vulnerable. "The bulk of the institutions will have to give in to a form of consumerism" says U.C.L.A.'s Astin, "in that they need applicants and will therefore have to offer students what they want."

Says Paul Ginsberg, dean of students at Wisconsin: "It's becoming increasingly difficult to persuade a student to take courses that will contribute to his intellectual development in addition to those that will make him a good accountant." Quite apart from the pros and cons of professional training, the idea of educating oneself in order to rise in the world is a perfectly legitimate goal. But Ginsberg has been receiving letters from high school freshmen asking about the prospects for professional schools and job opportunities when they graduate from college seven years hence. Says he: "I don't know at what point foresight ends and panic sets in."

II: Education Transmits Civilization

Jill Ker Conway, president of Smith, echoes the prevailing view of contemporary technology when she says that "anyone in today's world who doesn't understand data processing is not educated." But she insists that the increasing emphasis on these matters leaves certain gaps. Says she: "The very strongly utilitarian emphasis in education, which is an effect of Sputnik and the cold war, has really removed from this culture something that was very profound in its 18th and 19th century roots, which was a sense that literacy and learning were ends in themselves for a democratic republic."

In contrast to Plato's claim for the social value of education, a quite different idea of intellectual purposes was propounded by the Renaissance humanists. Intoxicated with their rediscovery of the classical learning that was thought to have disappeared during the Dark Ages, they argued that the imparting of knowledge needs no justification—religious, social, economic, or political. Its purpose, to the extent that it has one, is to pass on from generation to generation the corpus of knowledge that constitutes civilization. "What could man acquire, by virtuous striving, that is more valuable than knowledge?" asked Erasmus, perhaps the greatest scholar of the early 16th century. That idea has acquired a tradition of its own. "The educational process has no end beyond itself," said John Dewey. "It is its own end."

But what exactly is the corpus of knowledge to be passed on? In simpler times, it was all included in the medieval universities' *quadrivium* (arithmetic, geometry, astronomy, music) and *trivium* (grammar, rhetoric, logic). As recently as the last century, when less than 5% of Americans went to college at all, students in New England establishments were compelled mainly to memorize and recite various Latin texts, and crusty professors angrily opposed the introduction of any new scientific discoveries or modern European languages. "They felt," said Charles Francis Adams Jr., the Union Pacific Railroad president who devoted his later years to writing history, "that a classical education was the important distinction between a man who had been to college and a man who had not been to college, and that anything that diminished the importance of this distinction was essentially revolutionary and tended to anarchy."

Such a view was eventually overcome by the practical demands of both students and society, yet it does not die. In academia, where every professor is accustomed to drawing up lists of required reading, it can even be played as a game. Must an educated man have head Dostoyevsky, Rimbaud, Tacitus, Kafka? (Yes.) Must he know both Bach's *Goldberg Variations* and Schoenberg's *Gurrelieder*? (Perhaps.) Must he know the Carnot Cycle and Boole's Inequality? (Well . . .) And then languages—can someone who reads only Constance Garnett's rather wooden version of *Anna Karenina* really know Tolstoy's masterpiece any better than some Frenchman can know Shakespeare by reading André Gide's translation of *Hamlet*? Every scholar likes to defend his own specialty as a cornerstone of Western civilization, and any restraints can seem philistine. George Steiner approvingly quotes, in *Language and Silence*, a suggestion that "an acqaintance with a Chinese novel or a Persian lyric is almost indispensable to contemporary literacy." On a slightly more practical level, intellectual codifiers like to draw up lists of masterworks that will educate any reader who is strong enough to survive them—thus Charles Eliot's famous five-foot shelf of Harvard Classics and all its weighty sequels.

It was the immensely influential Eliot, deeply impressed with the specialized scholarly and scientific research performed at German universities, who proclaimed in 1869, upon becoming president of Harvard, the abolition of its rigid traditional curriculum. Basic education should be performed by the high schools, Eliot declared; anyone who went on to college should be free to make his own choice among myriad elective courses. The students chose the practical. "In the end, it was the sciences that triumphed, guided by the hidden hand of capitalism and legitimated by the binding ideology of positivism," Ernest Boyer and Martin Kaplan observe in *Educating for Survival*. Before long, however, the inevitable counterrevolution against the elective system began; there was a "core" of certain things that every student must learn. Columbia established required courses in contemporary civilization; the University of Chicago and St. John's College duly followed with programs solidly based on required readings of classic texts.

St. John's, which is based in Annapolis, Md., and has a smaller campus in Santa Fe, N. Mex., is a remarkable example of an institution resolutely taking this approach. Ever since 1937, all of St. John's students (683 this fall on both campuses) have been required to read and discuss a list of 130 great books, drawn heavily from the classics and philosophy but also from the ranks of modern novelists like Faulkner and Conrad. The students must take four years of math, three of a laboratory science, two of music and two years each of Greek and French. That is just about it. This modern liberal arts version of the *trivium* and *quadrivium* includes no such novelties as psychology (except what can be learned in the works of Freud and William James) and no sociology (except perhaps Jane Austen).

St. John's is aware of the obvious criticism that its approach is "elitist" and even "irrelevant" to the real world. But President Edwin DeLattre's mild voice turns a bit sharp when he retorts, "If knowing the foundations of one's country—the foundations of one's civilization—if understanding and learning how to gain access to the engines of political and economic power in the world—if knowing how to learn in mathematics and the sciences, the languages, the humanities—if having access to the methods that have advanced civilizations since the dawn of human intelligence . . . if all those things are irrelevant, then boy, are we irrelevant!" De Lattre is a philosopher by training, and he offers one definition that has an ominous but compelling reverberation in the thermonuclear age: "Don't forget the notion of an educated person as someone who would understand how to refound his or her own civilization."

III: Education Teaches How to Think

Aristotle was one of those who could found a civilization, and while he thought of education as both a social value and an end in itself, he ascribed its chief importance to what might be considered a third basic concept of education: to train the mind to think, regardless of what it is thinking about. The key is not what it knows but how it evaluates any new fact or argument. "An educated man," Aristotle wrote in *On the Parts of Animals*, "should be able to form a fair offhand judgment as to the goodness or badness of the method used by a professor in his exposition. To be educated is in fact to be able to do this."

The Aristotelian view of education as a process has become the conventionally worthy answer today whenever college presidents and other academic leaders are asked what an education should be. An educated man, says Harvard President Bok, taking a deep breath, must have a "curiosity in exploring the unfamiliar and unexpected, an open-mindedness in entertaining opposing points of view, tolerance for the ambiguity that surrounds so many important issues, and a willingness to make the best decisions he can in the face of uncertainty and doubt . . ."

"The educated person," says University of Chicago President Hanna Holborn Gray, taking an equally deep breath, "is a person who has a respect for rationality, and who understands some of the limits of rationality as well, who has acquired independent critical intelligence, and a sense not only for the complexity of the world and different points of view but of the standards he or she would thoughtfully want to be pursuing in making judgments."

This is an approach that appears to attach more importance to the process of learning than to the substance of what is learned, but it does provide a way of coping with the vast increase of knowledge. "The old notion of the generalist who could comprehend all subjects is an impossibility, and it was even in past ages," says Chicago's Gray. "Renaissance humanism concentrated on social living and aesthetic engagement but left out most of science. To know all about today's physics, biology and mathematics, or even the general principles of all these fields, would be impossible." To make matters still more difficult, the fields of knowledge keep changing. Says Harvard's Henry Rosovsky, dean of the faculty of arts and sciences: "We can't prepare students for an explosion of knowledge because we don't know what is going to explode next. The best we can do is to make students capable of gaining new knowledge."

The old Aristotelian idea, combined with a contemporary sense of desperation about coping with the knowledge explosion, helped inspire a complete reorganization—yet again—of Harvard's curriculum. At the end of World War II, Harvard had curtailed Eliot's electives and launched a series of general education courses that were supposed to teach everyone the rudiments of science and the humanities. But by the 1960s, when rebellious students seized an administration building, that whole system had broken down. "At the moment," a saddened Dean Rosovsky later wrote to his colleagues, "to be an educated man or woman doesn't mean anything . . . The world has become a Tower of Babel."

Out of Rosovsky's unhappiness came what Harvard somewhat misleadingly calls its core curriculum. Inaugurated in 1979, after much faculty debate and amid considerable press attention, this core turned out to be a rather sprawling collection of 122 different courses, ranging from Abstraction in Modern Art to Microbial and Molecular Biology. Students are required to select eight of their 32 courses from five general areas of knowledge (science, history, the arts, ethics and foreign cultures).

Harvard's eminence exerts a wide influence, but other first-rate institutions, like Columbia, Chicago, and Princeton, point out that they have taught a more concentrated core and steadfastly continued doing so throughout the 1960s. "It makes me unhappy when people think that Harvard has done some innovative curriculum work," says Columbia College Associate Dean Michael Rosenthal (a Harvard graduate). "They have millions of courses, none of which, you could argue, represents any fundamental effort to introduce people to a kind of thinking or to a discipline."

But that is exactly what Harvard does claim to be doing. "The student should have an understanding of the major ways mankind organizes knowledge," says Rosovsky. "That is done in identifiable ways: in sciences by experiment, conducted essentially in mathematics; in social science through quantitative and historical analysis; in the humanities by studying the great traditions. We are not ignoring content but simply recognizing that because of the knowledge explosion, it makes sense to emphasize the gaining of knowledge."

If anyone objects that it is still perfectly possible to graduate from Harvard without having read a word of Shakespeare, Rosovsky is totally unfazed. Says he: "That's not necessary."

IV: Education Liberates the Individual

The current trend toward required subjects—a kind of intellectual law-and-order—reflects contemporary political conservatism. It implies not only that there is a basic body of knowledge to be learned but also that there is a right way to think. It implies that a certain amount of uniformity is both socially and intellectually desirable.

Perhaps, but the excesses of the 1960s should not be used to besmirch reforms that were valuable. They too derived from a distinguished intellectual tradition. Its founding father was Jean-Jacques Rousseau, who argued in his novel *Emile* that children are not miniature adults and should not be drilled into becoming full-grown robots. "Everything is good as it comes from the hand of the Creator," said Rousseau; "everything degenerates in the hands of man."

Isolated from the corrupting world, Rousseau's young Emile was given no books but encouraged to educate himself by observing the workings of nature. Not until the age of twelve, the age of reason, was he provided with explanations in the form of astronomy or chemistry, and not until the social age of 15 was he introduced to aesthetics, religion, and, eventually, female company. That was how Emile met Sophie and lived happily ever after. It is a silly tale, and yet there is considerable power to the idea that a student should be primarily educated not to hold a job or to memorize literary monuments or even to think like Aristotle, but simply to develop the potentialities of his own self—and that everyone's self is different.

While there is probably not a single university that has not retreated somewhat from the experimentation of the 1960s, and while the rhetoric of that decade is now wildly out of fashion, a few small institutions have tried to keep the faith. For them, education is, in a sense, liberation, personal liberation. At Evergreen State College in Washington, which has no course requirements of any kind and no letter grades, a college spokesman describes a class on democracy and tyranny by saying, "We will try to find out who we are, and what kind of human beings we should become." At Hampshire College, founded in Massachusetts in 1970 as a resolutely experimental school, students still design their own curriculums, take no exams and talk of changing the world. "I don't see myself as giving a body of knowledge or even 'a way of learning,' " says Physics Professor Herbert Bernstein, "but as involved in something beyond that—to help people find their own path and the fullness of who they are."

The times have not been easy for such colleges. Not only do costs keep rising, but many students now prefer conventional courses and grades that will look impressive on job applications. Antioch, which expanded into an unmanageable national network of 32 experimental institutions, stumbled to the verge of bankruptcy in the 1970s, and is drastically cutting costs to survive. But the spirit of Rousseau flickers on. Rollins, which has sometimes been dismissed as a Florida tennis school, is trying to organize a conference for such like-minded colleges as Bard, Bennington, Sarah Lawrence, and Scripps on how best to pursue the goal of "making higher education more personal and developmental rather than formalistic."

Even when these enthusiasts do bend to the current pressures for law-and-order, they tend to do it in their own dreamy way. At Bard, where President Leon Botstein decided last year that all students should attend an intensive three-week workshop on how to think and write, the students pondered such questions as the nature of justice. What color is justice? What shape is it? What sound does it make? What does it eat? "I can't think of anything," one student protested at the first such writing class. "Don't worry about it," the teacher soothingly answered. Among the students' offerings: "Justice is navy blue, it's square. It weaves in and out and backs up . . . Justice is black and white, round . . . It has the sound of the cracked Liberty Bell ringing." Workshop Director Peter Elbow's conclusion: "We're trying an experiment here, and we're not pretending that we have it under control or that we know how it works."

V: Education Teaches Morals

The U.S. Supreme Court has forbidden prayers in public schools, but many Americans cling to the idea that their educational system has a moral purpose. It is an idea common to both the Greeks and the medieval church ("O Lord my King," St. Augustine wrote in his *Confessions*, "whatsoever I speak or write, or read, or number, let all serve Thee"). In a secular age, the moral purpose of education takes secular forms: racial integration, sex education, good citizenship. At the college level, the ambiguities become more complex. Should a morally objectionable person be allowed to teach? (Not Timothy Leary, said Harvard.) Should a morally objectionable doctrine be permitted? (Not Arthur Jensen's claims of racial differences in intelligence, said student protesters at Berkeley.)

Many people are understandably dismayed by such censorship. But would they prefer ethical neutrality? Should engineers be trained to build highways without being taught any concern for the homes they displace? Should prospective corporate managers learn how to increase profits regardless of pollution or unemployment? Just the opposite, according to *Beyond the Ivory Tower*, a new book by Harvard's Bok, which calls for increased emphasis on "applied ethics." (Writes Bok: "A university that refuses to take ethical dilemmas seriously violates its basic obligations to society.")

Religious colleges have always practiced a similar preaching. But some 500 schools now offer courses in the field. The Government supports such studies with a program known as EVIST, which stands for Ethics and Values in Science and Technology (and which sounds as though a computer had already taken charge of the matter). "The modern university is rooted in the scientific method, having essentially turned its back on religion," says Steven Muller, president of Johns Hopkins. "The scientific method is a marvelous means of inquiry, but it really doesn't provide a value system. The biggest failing in higher education today is that we fall short in exposing students to values."

Charles Muscatine, a professor of English at Berkeley and member of a committee that is analyzing liberal arts curriculums for the Association of American Colleges, is even harsher. He calls today's educational programs "a marvelous convenience for a mediocre society." The key goal of education, says Muscatine, should be "informed decision making that recognizes there is a moral and ethical component to life." Instead, he says, most universities are "propagating the dangerous myth that technical skills are more important than ethical reasoning."

Psychiatrist Robert Coles, who teaches at both Harvard and Duke, is still more emphatic in summing up the need: "Reading, writing, and arithmetic. That's what we've got to start with, and all that implies, at every level. If people can't use good, strong language, they can't think clearly, and if they haven't been trained to use good, strong language, they become vulnerable to all the junk that comes their way. They should be taught philosophy, moral philosophy and theology. They ought to be asked to think about moral issues, especially about what use is going to be made of knowledge, and why—a kind of moral reflection that I think has been supplanted by a more technological education. Replacing moral philosophy with psychology has been a disaster, an absolute disaster!"

Each of these five ways to wisdom has its strengths and weaknesses, of course. The idea that education provides better jobs promises practical rewards for both the student and the society that trains him, but it can leave him undernourished in the possibilities of life away from work. The idea that education means the acquisition of a cultural heritage does give the student some grasp of that heritage, but it can also turn into glib superficialities or sterile erudition. The idea that education consists mainly of training the mind does provide a method for further education, but it can also make method seem more important than knowledge. So can the idea that education is a form of self-development. And the teaching of ethics can unfortunately become a teaching of conventional pieties.

To define is to limit, as we all learned in school, and to categorize is to oversimplify. To some extent, the five ways to wisdom all overlap and blend, and though every educator has his own sense of priorities, none would admit that he does not aspire to all five goals. Thus the student who has mastered the riches of Western civilization has probably also learned to think for himself and to see the moral purposes of life. And surely such a paragon can find a good job even in the recession of 1982.

Are there specific ways to come nearer to achieving these goals? The most obvious is money. Good teachers cost money; libraries cost money; so do remedial classes for those who were short-changed in earlier years. Only mediocrity comes cheap. Those who groan at the rising price of college tuition (up as much as $7,000 since 1972) may not realize that overall, taking enrollment growth into account, college budgets have just barely kept up with inflation. Indeed, adjusted for inflation, four years of college today costs less than a decade ago, and faculty salaries in real dollars declined about 20% during the 1970s. Crocodile tears over the cost of higher education come in waves from the federal government, which has so far held spending to roughly 1981 levels, and proposes deep cuts (e.g., nearly 40% in basic grants) by 1985. This is an economy comparable to skimping on the maintenance of an expensive machine.

But money alone will not solve all problems, as is often said, and this is particularly true in the field of education. If improving the quality of American education is a matter of urgent national concern—and it should be—then what is required besides more dollars is more sense: a widespread rededication to a number of obvious but somewhat neglected principles. That probing research and hard thinking be demanded of students (and of teachers too). That academic results be tested and measured. That intellectual excellence be not just acknowledged but rewarded.

These principles admittedly did serve the system that educated primarily those few who were born into the governing classes, but the fact that elitist education once supported elitist politics does not mean that egalitarian politics requires egalitarian education. Neither minds nor ideas are all the same.

All that the schools can be asked to promise is that everyone will be educated to the limit of his capacities. Exactly what this means, everyone must discover for himself. At the community college minimum, it may have to mean teaching basic skills, at least until the weakened high schools begin doing their job properly, as Philosopher Mortimer Adler urges in his new *Paideia Proposal*. This calls for a standardized high school curriculum in three categories: fundamental knowledge such as history, science, and arts; basic skills such as reading and mathematical computation; and critical understanding of ideas and values. These essentials must really be taught, not just certified with a passing grade. Beyond such practical benefits, though, and beyond the benefits that come from exercising the muscles of the mind, higher education must ultimately serve the higher purpose of perpetuating whatever it is in civilization that is worth perpetuating. Or as Ezra Pound once said of the craft that he later betrayed, "The function of literature is precisely that it does incite humanity to continue living."

This is the core of the core idea, and surely it is by now indisputable that every college student improves by learning the fundamentals of science, literature, art, history. Harvard's Rosovsky may be right in suggesting that it is "not necessary" to have read Shakespeare as part of the process of learning how to think, but he is probably wrong. Not because anyone really *needs* to have shared in Lear's howling rage or because anyone can earn a better salary from having heard Macbeth declaim "Tomorrow and tomorrow and tomorrow . . ." But he is enriched by knowing these things, impoverished by not knowing them. And *The Marriage of Figaro* enriches. *The Cherry Orchard* enriches. *The City of God* enriches. So does a mastery of Greek, or of subnuclear particles, or of Gödel's theorem.

In a sense, there really is no core, except as a series of arbitrary choices, for there is no limit to the possibilities of learning. There are times when these possibilities seem overwhelming, and one hears echoes of Socrates' confession, "All I know is that I know nothing." Yet that too is a challenge. "We shall not cease from exploration," as T.S. Eliot put it, "and the end of all our exploring/Will be to arrive where we started/And know the place for the first time." The seemingly momentous years of schooling, then, are only the beginning.

Henry Adams, who said in *The Education of Henry Adams* that Harvard "taught little and that little ill," was 37 when he took up the study of Saxon legal codes and 42 when he first turned to writing the history of the Jefferson and Madison Administrations, and 49 when he laboriously began on Chinese. In his 50s, a tiny, wiry figure with a graying beard, the future master of Gothic architecture solemnly learned to ride a bicycle.

Suggestions for Discussion

1. This essay begins with a list of rites typical of the opening of the college year. How would you characterize the details? What do they say about college life? Compare this description with the beginning of Lincoln Steffen's reminiscence of his early days at Berkeley.

2. Why does the article raise the issue of whether the large numbers of students attending college are receiving an education? How does this question relate to the *growth* and *glut* in college enrollments? What evidence is there of some real decline in the quality of education?

3. What happened to education in American universities during the 1960's? How does the author relate what happened then to the quality of education today? Compare Allan Bloom's remarks on the problems facing the liberal arts with the point made here.

4. What are colleges and universities doing to change the existing curriculum? Why does the author refer to these changes as a counterrevolution?

5. What are the consequences of overspecialization in education?

6. What are the five concepts of education which the author describes? How does he define each of them? What does the author conclude about their strengths and weaknesses?

7. Summarize the author's account of the use of electives in college education. Why did certain colleges object and move toward abolishing electives?

8. The article quotes a number of people who define what it means to be educated. Compare these definitions with that of T. H. Huxley.

9. What colleges have tried to maintain the attitude toward education prevalent in the 1960's? Why have they persisted? What does their persistence tell us about their basic attitude toward education? Why at the end of the essay does the author quote from T. S. Eliot and describe the activities of Henry Adams? Do these details provide a good way to close the essay?

Suggestions for Writing

1. Throughout the essay, Friedrich quotes from a number of educators. Choose several of these quotations and write an essay in which you explain how they complement or contradict each other. Why has Friedrich used so many quotations? What function do they serve in the essay? From the quotations you use for your essay, choose one that makes the most sense to you and explain why.

2. Summarize briefly and then comment on the five patterns of education which Friedrich describes. Where do the patterns intersect? Which,pattern most clearly matches your purpose in getting an education?

Fiction
—◆◆◆—

John Cheever
Expelled

John Cheever (1912–1982) was born in Massachusetts where he was expelled from a prep school, and thereby propelled into a literary career. He devoted himself primarily to writing novels and stories, and published often in *The New Yorker*. He won the Pulitzer Prize in 1979 for the collection *The Stories of John Cheever*. His best known novels of suburban life are *The Wapshot Chronicle* (1957) and *The Wapshot Scandal* (1964). The prep school in "Expelled", which Cheever wrote at seventeen, exists to prepare the sons of the middle class for admission into acceptable Eastern colleges with little concern for aesthetic, moral, or intellectual values.

It didn't come all at once. It took a very long time. First I had a skirmish with the English department and then all the other departments. Pretty soon something had to be done. The first signs were cordialities on the part of the headmaster. He was never nice to anybody unless he was a football star, or hadn't paid his tuition, or was going to be expelled. That's how I knew.

He called me down to his office with the carved chairs arranged in a semi-circle and the brocade curtains resting against the vacant windows. All about him were pictures of people who had got scholarships at Harvard. He asked me to sit down.

"Well, Charles," he said, "some of the teachers say you aren't getting very good marks."

"Yes," I said, "that's true." I didn't care about the marks.

"But Charles," he said, "you know the scholastic standard of this school is very high and we have to drop people when their work becomes unsatisfactory." I told him I knew that also. Then he said a lot of things about the traditions, and the elms, and the magnificent military heritage from our West Point founder.

It was very nice outside of his room. He had his window pushed open halfway and one could see the lawns pulling down to the road behind the

675

trees and the bushes. The gravy-colored curtains were too heavy to move about in the wind, but some papers shifted around on his desk. In a little while I got up and walked out. He turned and started to work again. I went back to my next class.

The next day was very brilliant and the peach branches were full against the dry sky. I could hear people talking and a phonograph playing. The sounds came through the peach blossoms and crossed the room. I lay in bed and thought about a great many things. My dreams had been thick. I remembered two converging hills, some dry apple trees, and a broken blue egg cup. That is all I could remember.

I put on knickers and a soft sweater and headed toward school. My hands shook on the wheel. I was like that all over.

Through the cloudy trees I could see the protrusion of the new tower. It was going to be a beautiful new tower and it was going to cost a great deal of money. Some thought of buying new books for the library instead of putting up a tower, but no one would see the books. People would be able to see the tower five miles off when the leaves were off the trees. It would be done by fall.

When I went into the building the headmaster's secretary was standing in the corridor. She was a nice sort of person with brown funnels of hair furrowed about a round head. She smiled. I guess she must have known.

The Colonel

Every morning we went up into the black chapel. The brisk headmaster was there. Sometimes he had a member of the faculty with him. Sometimes it was a stranger.

He introduced the stranger, whose speech was always the same. In the spring life is like a baseball game. In the fall it is like football. That is what the speaker always said.

The hall is damp and ugly with skylights that rattle in the rain. The seats are hard and you have to hold a hymnbook in your lap. The hymnbook often slips off and that is embarrassing.

On Memorial Day they have the best speaker. They have a mayor or a Governor. Sometimes they have a Governor's second. There is very little preference.

The Governor will tell us what a magnificent country we have. He will tell us to beware of the Red menace. He will want to tell us that the goddam foreigners should have gone home a hell of a long time ago. That they should have stayed in their own goddam countries if they didn't like ours. He will not dare say this though.

If they have a mayor the speech will be longer. He will tell us that our country is beautiful and young and strong. That the War is over, but that if there is another war we must fight. He will tell us that war is a masculine trait that has brought present civilization to its fine condition. Then he will leave us and help stout women place lilacs on graves. He will tell them the same thing.

One Memorial Day they could not get a Governor or a mayor. There was a colonel in the same village who had been to war and who had a chest thick with medals. They asked him to speak. Of course he said he would like to speak.

He was a thin colonel with a soft nose that rested quietly on his face. He was nervous and pushed his wedding ring about his thin finger. When he was introduced he looked at the audience sitting in the uncomfortable chairs. There was silence and the dropping of hymnbooks like the water spouts in the aftermath of a heavy rain.

He spoke softly and quickly. He spoke of war and what he had seen. Then he had to stop. He stopped and looked at the boys. They were staring at their boots. He thought of the empty rooms in the other buildings. He thought of the rectangles of empty desks. He thought of the curtains on the stage and the four Windsor chairs behind him. Then he started to speak again.

He spoke as quickly as he could. He said war was bad. He said that there would never be another war. That he himself should stop it if he could. He swore. He looked at the young faces. They were all very clean. The boys' knees were crossed and their soft pants hung loosely. He thought of the empty desks and began to whimper.

The people sat very still. Some of them felt tight as though they wanted to giggle. Everybody looked serious as the clock struck. It was time for another class.

People began to talk about the colonel after lunch. They looked behind them. They were afraid he might hear them.

It took the school several weeks to get over all this. Nobody said anything, but the colonel was never asked again. If they could not get a Governor or a mayor they could get someone besides a colonel. They made sure of that.

Margaret Courtwright

Margaret Courtwright was very nice. She was slightly bald and pulled her pressed hair down across her forehead. People said that she was the best English teacher in this part of the country, and when boys came back from Harvard they thanked her for the preparation she had given them. She did not like Edgar Guest, but she did like Carl Sandburg. She couldn't seem to understand the similarity. When I told her people laughed at Galsworthy she said that people used to laugh at Wordsworth. She did not believe people were still laughing at Wordsworth. That was what made her so nice.

She came from the West a long time ago. She taught school for so long that people ceased to consider her age. After having seen twenty-seven performances of "Hamlet" and after having taught it for sixteen years, she became a sort of immortal. Her interpretation was the one accepted on college-board papers. That helped everyone a great deal. No one had to get a new interpretation.

When she asked me for tea I sat in a walnut armchair with grapes carved on the head and traced and retraced the arms on the tea caddy. One time I read her one of my plays. She thought it was wonderful. She thought it was wonderful because she did not understand it and because it took two hours to read. When I had finished, she said, "You know that thing just took right hold of me. Really it just swept me right along. I think it's fine that you like to write. I once had a Japanese pupil who liked to write. He was an awfully nice chap until one summer he went down to Provincetown. When he came back he was saying that he could express a complete abstraction. Fancy . . . a complete abstraction. Well, I wouldn't hear of it and told him how absurd it all was and tried to start him off with Galsworthy again, but I guess he had gone just too far. In a little while he left for New York and then Paris. It was really too bad. One summer in Provincetown just ruined him. His marks fell down . . . he cut classes to go to symphony. . . ." She went into the kitchen and got a tray of tarts.

The pastries were flaky and covered with a white coating that made them shine in the dead sunlight. I watched the red filling burst the thin shells and stain the triangles of bright damask. The tarts were good. I ate most of them.

She was afraid I would go the way of her Japanese pupil. She doubted anyone who disagreed with Heine on Shakespeare and Croce on expression.

One day she called me into her antiseptic office and spoke to me of reading Joyce. "You know, Charles," she said, "this sex reality can be quite as absurd as a hypercritical regard for such subjects. You know that, don't you? Of course, you do." Then she went out of the room. She had straight ankles and wore a gold band peppered with diamond chips on her ring finger. She seemed incapable of carrying the weight of the folds in her clothing. Her skirt was askew, either too long in front or hitching up on the side. Always one thing or the other.

When I left school she did not like it. She was afraid I might go too near Provincetown. She wished me good luck and moved the blotter back and forth on her desk. Then she returned to teaching "Hamlet."

Late in February Laura Driscoll got fired for telling her history pupils that Sacco and Vanzetti were innocent. In her farewell appearance the headmaster told everyone how sorry he was that she was going and made it all quite convincing. Then Laura stood up, told the headmaster that he was a damned liar, and waving her fan-spread fingers called the school a hell of a dump where everyone got into a rut.

Miss Courtwright sat closely in her chair and knew it was true. She didn't mind much. Professor Rogers with his anti-feminization movement bothered her a little, too. But she knew that she had been teaching school for a long time now and no movement was going to put her out of a job overnight— what with all the boys she had smuggled into Harvard and sixteen years of "Hamlet."

Laura Driscoll

History classes are always dead. This follows quite logically, for history is a dead subject. It has not the death of dead fruit or dead textiles or dead light. It has a different death. There is not the timeless quality of death about it. It is dead like scenery in the opera. It is on cracked canvas and the paint has faded and peeled and the lights are too bright. It is dead like old water in a zinc bathtub.

"We are going to study ancient history this year," the teacher will tell the pupils. "Yes, ancient history will be our field.

"Now of course, this class is not a class of children any longer. I expect the discipline to be the discipline of well-bred young people. We shall not have to waste any time on the scolding of younger children. No. We shall just be able to spend all our time on ancient history.

"Now about questions. I shall answer questions if they are important. If I do not think them important I shall not answer them, for the year is short, and we must cover a lot of ground in a short time. That is, if we all cooperate and behave and not ask too many questions we shall cover the subject and have enough time at the end of the year for review.

"You may be interested in the fact that a large percentage of this class was certified last year. I should like to have a larger number this year. Just think, boys: wouldn't it be fine if a very large number—a number larger than last year—was certified? Wouldn't that be fine? Well, there's no reason why we can't do it if we all cooperate and behave and don't ask too many questions.

"You must remember that I have twelve people to worry about and that you have only one. If each person will take care of his own work and pass in his notebook on time it will save me a lot of trouble. Time and trouble mean whether you get into college or not, and I want you all to get into college.

"If you will take care of your own little duties, doing what is assigned to you and doing it well, we shall all get along fine. You are a brilliant-looking group of young people, and I want to have you all certified. I want to get you into college with as little trouble as possible.

"Now about the books. . . ."

I do not know how long history classes have been like this. One time or another I suppose history was alive. That was before it died its horrible fly-dappled unquivering death.

Everyone seems to know that history is dead. No one is alarmed. The pupils and the teachers love dead history. They do not like it when it is alive. When Laura Driscoll dragged history into the classroom, squirming and smelling of something bitter, they fired Laura and strangled the history. It was too tumultuous. Too turbulent.

In history one's intellect is used for mechanical speculation on a probable century or background. One's memory is applied to a list of dead dates and names. When one begins to apply one's intellect to the mental scope of the period, to the emotional development of its inhabitants, one becomes dangerous. Laura Driscoll was terribly dangerous. That's why Laura was never a good history teacher.

She was not the first history teacher I had ever had. She is not the last I will have. But she is the only teacher I have ever had who could feel history with an emotional vibrance—or, if the person was too oblique, with a poetic understanding. She was five feet four inches tall, brown-haired, and bent-legged from horseback riding. All the boys thought Laura Driscoll was a swell teacher.

She was the only history teacher I have ever seen who was often ecstatical. She would stand by the boards and shout out her discoveries on the Egyptian cultures. She made the gargoylic churnings of Chartres in a heavy rain present an applicable meaning. She taught history as an interminable flood of events viewed through the distortion of our own immediacy. She taught history in the broad-handed rhythms of Hauptmann's drama, in the static melacholy of Egypt moving before its own shadow down the long sand, in the fluted symmetry of the Doric culture. She taught history as a hypothesis from which we could extract the evaluation of our own lives.

She was the only teacher who realized that, coming from the West, she had little business to be teaching these children of New England.

"I do not know what your reaction to the sea is," she would say. "For I have come from a land where there is no sea. My elements are the fields, the sun, the plastic cadence of the clouds and the cloudlessness. You have been brought up by the sea. You have been coached in the cadence of the breakers and the strength of the wind.

"My emotional viewpoints will differ from yours. Do not let me impose my perceptions upon you."

However, the college-board people didn't care about Chartres as long as you knew the date. They didn't care whether history was looked at from the mountains or the sea. Laura spent too much time on such trivia and all of her pupils didn't get into Harvard. In fact, very few of her pupils got into Harvard, and this didn't speak well for her.

While the other members of the faculty chattered over Hepplewhite legs and Duncan Phyfe embellishments, Laura was before five-handed Siva or the sexless compassion glorious in its faded polychrome. Laura didn't think much of America. Laura made this obvious and the faculty heard about it. The faculty all thought America was beautiful. They didn't like people to disagree.

However, the consummation did not occur until late in February. It was cold and clear and the snow was deep. Outside the windows there was the enormous roaring of broken ice. It was late in February that Laura Driscoll said Sacco and Vanzetti were undeserving of their treatment.

This got everyone all up in the air. Even the headmaster was disconcerted.

The faculty met.

The parents wrote letters.

Laura Driscoll was fired.

"Miss Driscoll," said the headmaster during her last chapel at the school, "has found it necessary to return to the West. In the few months that we have had her with us, she has been a staunch friend of the academy, a woman whom we all admire and love and who, we are sure, loves and admires the academy and its elms as we do. We are all sorry Miss Driscoll is leaving us. . . ."

Then Laura got up, called him a damned liar, swore down the length of the platform and walked out of the building.

No one ever saw Laura Driscoll again. By the way everyone talked, no one wanted to. That was all late in February. By March the school was quiet again. The new history teacher taught dates. Everyone carefully forgot about Laura Driscoll.

"She was a nice girl," said the headmaster, "but she really wasn't made for teaching history. . . . No, she really wasn't a born history teacher."

Five Months Later

The spring of five months ago was the most beautiful spring I have ever lived in. The year before I had not known all about the trees and the heavy peach blossoms and the tea-colored brooks that shook down over the brown rocks. Five months ago it was spring and I was in school.

In school the white limbs beyond the study hall shook out a greenness, and the tennis courts became white and scalding. The air was empty and hard, and the vacant wind dragged shadows over the road. I knew all this only from the classrooms.

I knew about the trees from the window frames. I knew the rain only from the sounds on the roof. I was tired of seeing spring with walls and awnings to intercept the sweet sun and the hard fruit. I wanted to go outdoors and see the spring. I wanted to feel and taste the air and be among the shadows. That is perhaps why I left school.

In the spring I was glad to leave school. Everything outside was elegant and savage and fleshy. Everything inside was slow and cool and vacant. It seemed a shame to stay inside.

But in a little while the spring went. I was left outside and there was no spring. I did not want to go in again. I would not have gone in again for anything. I was sorry, but I was not sorry over the fact that I had gone out. I was sorry that the outside and the inside could not have been open to one another. I was sorry that there were roofs on the classrooms and trousers on the legs of the instructors to insulate their contacts. I was not sorry that I had left school. I was sorry that I left for the reasons that I did.

If I had left because I had to go to work or because I was sick it would not have been so bad. Leaving because you are angry and frustrated is different. It is not a good thing to do. It is bad for everyone.

Of course it was not the fault of the school. The headmaster and faculty were doing what they were supposed to do. It was just a preparatory school trying to please the colleges. A school that was doing everything the colleges asked it to do.

It was not the fault of the school at all. It was the fault of the system—the noneducational system, the college-preparatory system. That was what made the school so useless.

As a college-preparatory school it was a fine school. In five years they could make raw material look like college material. They could clothe it and breed it and make it say the right things when the colleges asked it to talk. That was its duty.

They weren't prepared to educate anybody. They were members of a college-preparatory system. No one around there wanted to be educated. No sir.

They presented the subjects the colleges required. They had math, English, history, languages, and music. They once had had an art department but it had been dropped. "We have enough to do," said the headmaster, "just to get all these people into college without trying to teach them art. Yes sir, we have quite enough to do as it is."

Of course there were literary appreciation and art appreciation and musical appreciation, but they didn't count for much. If you are young, there is very little in Thackeray that is parallel to your own world. Van Dyke's "Abbé Scaglia" and the fretwork of Mozart quartets are not for the focus of your ears and eyes. All the literature and art that holds a similarity to your life is forgotten. Some of it is even forbidden.

Our country is the best country in the world. We are swimming in prosperity and our President is the best president in the world. We have larger apples and better cotton and faster and more beautiful machines. This makes us the greatest country in the world. Unemployment is a myth. Dissatisfaction is a fable. In preparatory school America is beautiful. It is the gem of the ocean and it is too bad. It is bad because people believe it all. Because they become indifferent. Because they marry and reproduce and vote and they know nothing. Because the tempered newspaper keeps its eyes ceilingwards and does not see the dirty floor. Because all they know is the tempered newspaper.

But I will not say any more. I do not stand in a place where I can talk.

And now it is August. The orchards are stinking ripe. The tea-colored brooks run beneath the rocks. There is sediment on the stone and no wind in the willows. Everyone is preparing to go back to school. I have no school to go back to.

I am not sorry. I am not at all glad.

It is strange to be so very young and to have no place to report to at nine o'clock. That is what education has always been. It has been laced curtseys and perfumed punctualities.

But now it is nothing. It is symmetric with my life. I am lost in it. That is why I am not standing in a place where I can talk.

The school windows are being washed. The floors are thick with fresh oil.

Soon it will be time for the snow and the symphonies. It will be time for Brahms and the great dry winds.

Suggestions for Discussion

1. Why is Charles expelled from his school? How does he respond to his expulsion?

2. Explain the form the story takes as a series of short portraits. How do these portraits serve to express Charles's view of the school?

3. Compare Margaret Courtwright with Laura Driscoll. Which was the better teacher? Why?

4. How did the Colonel embarrass the school on Memorial Day? What is Charles's reaction to him? What does his reaction reveal about Charles?

5. Explain the function of the last section of the story.

Suggestion for Writing

What do you believe to be the primary purpose of education? Is it different from that described in the story? What do you expect from an education? Write an essay in which you explain your ideas.

Poetry
—◆◆◆—

Langston Hughes
Theme for English B

Langston Hughes (1902–1962), a prominent black poet, was born in Missouri and educated at Lincoln University in Pennsylvania. Often using dialect and jazz rhythms, his work expresses the concerns and feelings of American blacks. His collections of poetry include *The Weary Blues* (1926) and *Shakespeare in Harlem* (1940); his novels include *Not Without Laughter* (1930) and *The Best of Simple* (1950). In "Theme for English B" he clearly expresses the chasm between the races which exists even in the college classroom.

> The instructor said,
>> *Go home and write*
>> *a page tonight.*
>> *And let that page come out of you—*
>> *Then, it will be true.*
>
> I wonder if it's that simple?
> I am twenty-two, colored, born in Winston-Salem.
> I went to school there, then Durham, then here
> to this college on the hill above Harlem.
> I am the only colored student in my class.
> The steps from the hill lead down into Harlem,
> through a park, then I cross St. Nicholas,
> Eighth Avenue, Seventh, and I come to the Y,
> the Harlem Branch Y, where I take the elevator
> up to my room, sit down, and write this page:
>
> It's not easy to know what is true for you or me
> at twenty-two, my age. But I guess I'm what
> I feel and see and hear, Harlem, I hear you:
> hear you, hear me—we two—you, me, talk on this page.
> (I hear New York, too.) Me—who?

Well, I like to eat, sleep, drink, and be in love.
I like to work, read, learn, and understand life.
I like a pipe for a Christmas present,
or records—Bessie, bop, or Bach.
I guess being colored doesn't make me *not* like
the same things others folks like who are other races.
So will my page be colored that I write?

Being me, it will not be white.
But it will be
a part of you, instructor.
You are white—
yet a part of me, as I am a part of you.
That's American.
Sometimes perhaps you don't want to be a part of me.
Nor do I often want to be a part of you.
But we are, that's true!
As I learn from you,
I guess you learn from me—
Although you're older—and white—
and somewhat more free.

This is my page for English B.

Suggestions for Discussion

1. With what details does Hughes convey a strong sense of identity?

2. How does he reveal his feelings about composition, learning, Harlem, his racial background, and his instructor?

Suggestion for Writing

Write an essay in which you attempt to convey some of your feelings about your own background, your likes and dislikes. Try to focus on details as Hughes has done in his poem.

Theodore Roethke
Elegy for Jane: My Student, Thrown by a Horse

Theodore Roethke (1908–1963) was born in Michigan and educated at the universities of Michigan and Harvard. His poetry celebrated human relationships, the land and all growing things with wit, an inventive verse form and, at times, an almost surrealist language. He taught poetry writing for many years at the University of Washington in Seattle, and won the Pulitzer Prize for *The Waking* (1953). His other collections include *The Lost Son and Other Poems* (1949) and *The Far Field* (1964). Essays and lectures are collected in *The Poet and His Craft* (1965). "Elegy for Jane" is a tender poem expressing grief at the death of one of his students. Like many other modern poems on death, it achieves its force through wit and understatement.

Elegy for Jane
My Student, Thrown by a Horse

I remember the neckcurls, limp and damp as tendrils;
And her quick look, a sidelong pickerel smile;
And how, once startled into talk, the light syllables leaped for her,
And she balanced in the delight of her thought,
A wren, happy, tail into the wind,
Her song trembling the twigs and small branches.
The shade sang with her;
The leaves, their whispers turned to kissing;
And the mold sang in the bleached valleys under the rose.

Oh, when she was sad, she cast herself down into such a pure depth,
Even a father could not find her:
Scraping her cheek against straw;
Stirring the clearest water.

My sparrow, you are not here,
Waiting like a fern, making a spiny shadow.
The sides of wet stones cannot console me,
Nor the moss, wound with the last light.

If only I could nudge you from this sleep,
My maimed darling, my skittery pigeon.
Over this damp grave I speak the words of my love:
I, with no rights in this matter,
Neither father nor lover.

Suggestions for Discussion

1. What is the relation of the first two stanzas to the rest of the poem?

2. How does the poet remember his dead student? What is the effect of the details he recalls?

3. Why does he call his dead student "my maimed darling" or "my skittery pigeon"? How would you describe this language?

4. Discuss the feelings which the poem expresses. How do you relate these feelings to the poet's language?

5. Explain the last two lines of the poem.

Suggestion for Writing

This poem expresses the feelings of a teacher for a dead student. Does this expression of feeling come as a surprise to you? Write an essay in which you discuss, from your experience, the kinds of relationships which exist between teachers and students. Relate your comments to the feelings expressed in this poem.

The Examined Life: Personal Values

◆◆◆

The secret of seeing, then, is the pearl of great price. If I thought he could teach me to find it and keep it forever, I would stagger barefoot across a hundred deserts after any lunatic at all. But although the pearl may be found, it may not be sought. The literature of illumination reveals this above all: although it comes to those who wait for it, it is always even to the most practiced and adept, a gift and a total surprise.

　　—**Annie Dillard,** "Sight into Insight"

. . . I cannot give up the idea that out of democracy will be born the new world—richer, braver, freer, more beautiful. As for me, I don't know what I can do to help—I don't know yet. All I know is that my happiness is built on the misery of other people, that I eat because others go hungry, that I am clothed when other people go almost naked through the frozen cities in winter; and that fact poisons me, disturbs my serenity, makes me write propaganda when I would rather play. . . .

　　—**John Reed,** "Almost Thirty"

Four hundred years ago a young poet and potential rival of Shakespeare had written of the knowledge-hungry Faust of legend:

　　Thou are still but Faustus and a man.

In that phrase Christopher Marlowe had epitomized the human tragedy: We were world eaters and knowledge seekers but we were also men. It was a well-nigh fatal flaw. Whether we, like the makers of stone spearpoints in Wyoming, are a fleeting illusion of the autumn light depends upon whether any remain to decipher Marlowe's words one thousand years in the future.

The events of my century had placed the next millennium as far off as a star. All the elaborate mechanisms of communication we have devised have not ennobled, nor brought closer, individual men to men. The means exist. It is Faustus who remains a man. Beyond this dark, I, who was also a man, could not penetrate.

—**Loren Eiseley,** "Man in the Autumn Light"

Ever playful with words, but at the same time, dead serious in such fun, Williams once told me: "There are those who bear, and those who overbear," and if such sexually connected, large-scale distinctions now seem outdated or naive (over thirty years have passed!), then his way of connecting those two categories of "being" to the matter of happiness may still offer us reason for appreciative pause: "Those who bear, who give life and nourish life, and you can do so, if you're a bachelor or a spinster, in the way you care for others—those are the people who find happiness only gradually, in the long run; the others, who are overbearing, grab what they can, pronto, and call it happiness, but they're always grabbing, so there's a discontent there, lots of it!"

—**Robert Coles,** "Happiness"

Our humanity is at risk. It's too powerful a thing to just lie down and give up the ghost. But we have to face the fact it is in danger. It is at risk because the feeling that life is sacred has died away in this century.

—**Saul Bellow,** "Lives of Organized Terror"

I went to the woods because I wished to live deliberately, to confront only the essential facts of life, and see if I could not learn what it had to teach, and not, when I came to die, discover that I had not lived. I did not wish to live what was not life, living is so dear; nor did I wish to practise resignation, unless it was quite necessary. I wanted to live deep and suck out all the marrow of life, to live so sturdily and Spartan-like as to put to rout all that was not life, to cut a broad swath and shave close, to drive life into a corner, and reduce it to its lowest terms, and, if it proved to be mean, why then to get the whole and genuine meanness of it, and publish its meanness to the world; or if it were sublime, to know it by experience, and be able to give a true account of it in my next excursion.

—**Henry David Thoreau,** "Why I Went to the Woods"

Personal Reminiscence

◆◆◆

Annie Dillard

Sight into Insight

Annie Dillard (b. 1945), a contributing editor to *Harper's*, won a Pulitzer Prize in 1974 for *Pilgrim at Tinker Creek*. Her more recent books are *Living by Fiction* and *Teaching a Stone to Talk: Expeditions and Encounters* both published in 1982. There are people of dull vision who don't really see and those like the writer for whom the effort truly to see is "a discipline requiring a lifetime of dedicated struggle."

When I was six or seven years old, growing up Pittsburgh, I used to take a precious penny of my own and hide it for someone else to find. It was a curious compulsion; sadly, I've never been seized by it since. For some reason I always "hid" the penny along the same stretch of sidewalk up the street. I'd cradle it at the roots of a maple, say, or in a hole left by a chipped-off piece of sidewalk. Then I'd take a piece of chalk and, starting at either end of the block, draw hugh arrows leading up to the penny from both directions. After I learned to write I labeled the arrows "SURPRISE AHEAD" or "MONEY THIS WAY." I was greatly excited, during all this arrow-drawing, at the thought of the first lucky passerby who would receive in this way, regardless of merit, a free gift from the universe. But I never lurked about. I'd go straight home and not give the matter another thought, until, some months later, I would be gripped by the impulse to hide another penny.

There are lots of things to see, unwrapped gifts and free surprises. The world is fairly studded and strewn with pennies cast broadside from a generous hand. But—and this is the point—who gets excited by a mere penny? If you follow one arrow, if you crouch motionless on a bank to watch a tremulous ripple thrill on the water, and are rewarded by the sight of a muskrat kit paddling from its den, will you count that sight a chip of copper only, and go your rueful way? It is a very dire poverty indeed for a man to be so malnourished and fatigued that he won't stoop to pick up a penny. But if you cultivate a healthy poverty and simplicity, so that finding a penny will make your day, then, since the world is in fact planted in pennies, you have with your poverty bought a lifetime of days. What you see is what you get.

Unfortunately, nature is very much a now-you-see-it, now-you-don't affair. A fish flashes, then dissolves in the water before my eyes like so much salt. Deer apparently ascend bodily into heaven; the brightest oriole fades into leaves. These disappearances stun me into stillness and concentration; they say of nature that it conceals with a grand nonchalance, and they say of vision that it is a deliberate gift, the revelation of a dancer who for my eyes only flings away her seven veils.

For nature does reveal as well as conceal: now-you-don't-see-it, now-you-do. For a week this September migrating red-winged blackbirds were feeding heavily down by Tinker Creek at the back of the house. One day I went out to investigate the racket; I walked up to a tree, an Osage orange, and a hundred birds flew away. They simply materialized out of the tree. I saw a tree, then a whisk of color, then a tree again. I walked closer and another hundred blackbirds took flight. Not a branch, not a twig budged: the birds were apparently weightless as well as invisible. Or, it was as if the leaves of the Osage orange had been freed from a spell in the form of red-winged blackbirds; they flew from the tree, caught my eye in the sky, and vanished. When I looked again at the tree, the leaves had reassembled as if nothing had happened. Finally I walked directly to the trunk of the tree and a final hundred, the real diehards, appeared, spread, and vanished. How could so many hide in the tree without my seeing them? The Osage orange, unruffled, looked just as it had looked from the house, when three hundred red-winged blackbirds cried from its crown. I looked upstream where they flew, and they were gone. Searching, I couldn't spot one. I wandered upstream to force them to play their hand, but they'd crossed the creek and scattered. One show to a customer. These appearances catch at my throat: they are the free gifts, the bright coppers at the roots of trees.

It's all a matter of keeping my eyes open. Nature is like one of those line drawings that are puzzles for children: Can you find hidden in the tree a duck, a house, a boy, a bucket, a giraffe, and a boot? Specialists can find the most incredibly hidden things. A book I read when I was young recommended an easy way to find caterpillars: you simply find some fresh caterpillar droppings, look up, and there's your caterpillar. More recently an author advised me to set my mind at ease about those piles of cut stems on the ground in grassy fields. Field mice make them; they cut the grass down by degrees to reach the seeds at the head. It seems that when the grass is tightly packed, as in a field of ripe grain, the blade won't topple at a single cut through the stem; instead, the cut stem simply drops vertically, held in the crush of grain. The mouse severs the bottom again and again, the stem keeps dropping an inch at a time, and finally the head is low enough for the mouse to reach the seeds. Meanwhile the mouse is positively littering the field with its little piles of cut stems into which, presumably, the author is constantly stumbling.

If I can't see this minutiae, I still try to keep my eyes open. I'm always on the lookout for ant lion traps in sandy soil, monarch pupae near milkweed, skipper larvae in locust leaves. These things are utterly common, and I've not seen one. I bang on hollow trees near water, but so far no flying squirrels have appeared. In flat country I watch every sunset in hopes of seeing the green ray. The green ray is a seldom-seen streak of light that rises from the sun like a spurting fountain at the moment of sunset; it throbs into the sky for two seconds and disappears. One more reason to keep my eyes open. A photography professor at the University of Florida just happened to see a bird die in midflight; it jerked, died, dropped, and smashed on the ground.

I squint at the wind because I read Stewart Edward White: "I have always maintained that if you looked closely enough you could *see* the wind—the dim, hardly-made-out, fine débris fleeing high in the air." White was an excellent observer, and devoted an entire chapter of *The Mountains* to the subject of seeing deer: "As soon as you can forget the naturally obvious and construct an artificial obvious, then you too will see deer."

But the artificial obvious is hard to see. My eyes account for less than 1 percent of the weight of my head; I'm bony and dense; I see what I expect. I just don't know what the lover knows; I can't see the artificial obvious that those in the know construct. The herpetologist asks the native, "Are there snakes in that ravine?" "No, sir." And the herpetologist comes home with, yessir, three bags full. Are there butterflies on that mountain? Are the bluets in bloom? Are there arrowheads here, or fossil ferns in the shale?

Peeping through my keyhole I see within the range of only about 30 percent of the light that comes from the sun; the rest is infrared and some little ultraviolet, perfectly apparent to many animals, but invisible to me. A nightmare network of ganglia, charged and firing without my knowledge, cuts and splices what I do see, editing it for my brain. Donald E. Carr points out that the sense impressions of one-celled animals are *not* edited for the brain: "This is philosophically interesting in a rather mournful way, since it means that only the simplest animals perceive the universe as it is."

A fog that won't burn away drifts and flows across my field of vision. When you see fog move against a backdrop of deep pines, you don't see the fog itself, but streaks of clearness floating across the air in dark shreds. So I see only tatters of clearness through a pervading obscurity. I can't distinguish the fog from the overcast sky; I can't be sure if the light is direct or reflected. Everywhere darkness and the presence of the unseen appalls. We estimate now that only one atom dances alone in every cubic meter of intergalactic space. I blink and squint. What planet or power yanks Halley's Comet out of orbit? We haven't seen it yet; it's a question of distance, density, and the pallor of reflected light. We rock, cradled in the swaddling band of darkness. Even the simple darkness of night whispers suggestions to the mind. This summer, in August, I stayed at the creek too late.

Strangers to Darkness

Where Tinker Creek flows under the sycamore log bridge to the tear-shaped island, it is slow and shallow, fringed thinly in cattail marsh. At this spot an astonishing bloom of life supports vast breeding populations of insects, fish, reptiles, birds, and mammals. On windless summer evenings I stalk along the creek bank or straddle the sycamore log in absolute stillness, watching for muskrats. The night I stayed too late I was hunched on the lawn staring spellbound at spreading, reflected stains of lilac on the water. A cloud in the sky suddenly lighted as if turned on by a switch; its reflection just as suddenly materialized on the water upstream, flat and floating, so that I couldn't see the creek bottom, or life in the water under the cloud. Downstream, away from the cloud on the water, water turtles smooth as beans were gliding down with the current in a series of easy, weightless push-offs, as men bound on the moon. I didn't know whether to trace the progress of one turtle I was sure of, risking sticking my face in one of the bridge's spider webs made invisible by the gathering dark, or take a chance on seeing the carp, or scan the mudbank in hope of seeing a muskrat, or follow the last of the swallows who caught at my heart and trailed it after them like streamers as they appeared from directly below, under the log, flying upstream with their tails forked, so fast.

But shadows spread and deepened and stayed. After thousands of years we're still strangers to darkness, fearful aliens in an enemy camp with our arms crossed over our chests. I stirred. A land turtle on the bank, startled, hissed the air from its lungs and withdrew to its shell. An uneasy pink here, an unfathomable blue there, gave great suggestion of lurking beings. Things were going on. I couldn't see whether that rustle I heard was a distant rattlesnake, slit-eyed, or a nearby sparrow kicking in the dry flood debris slung at the foot of a willow. Tremendous action roiled the water everywhere I looked, big action, inexplicable. A tremor welled up beside a gaping muskrat burrow in the bank and I caught my breath, but no muskrat appeared. The ripples continued to fan upstream with a steady, powerful thrust. Night was knitting an eyeless mask over my face, and I still sat transfixed. A distant airplane, a delta wing out of a nightmare, made a gliding shadow on the creek's bottom that looked like a stingray cruising upstream. At once a black fin slit the pink cloud on the water, shearing it in two. The two halves merged together and seemed to dissolve before my eyes. Darkness pooled in the cleft of the creek and rose, as water collects in a well. Untamed, dreaming lights flickered over the sky. I saw hints of hulking underwater shadows, two pale splashes out of the water, and round ripples rolling close together from a blackened center.

At last I stared upstream where only the deepest violet remained of the cloud, a cloud so high its underbelly still glowed, its feeble color reflected from a hidden sky lighted in turn by a sun halfway to China. And out of that violet, a sudden enormous black body arched over the water. Head and tail, if there was a head and tail, were both submerged in cloud. I saw only one ebony fling, a headlong dive to darkness; then the waters closed, and the lights went out.

I walked home in a shivering daze, up hill and down. Later I lay open-mouthed in bed, my arms flung wide at my sides to steady the whirling darkness. At this latitude I'm spinning 836 miles an hour round the earth's axis; I feel my sweeping fall as a breakneck arch like the dive of dolphins, and the hollow rushing of wind raises the hairs on my neck and the side of my face. In orbit around the sun I'm moving 64,800 miles an hour. The solar system as a whole, like a merry-go-round unhinged, spins, bobs, and blinks at the speed of 43,200 miles an hour along a course set east of Hercules. Someone has piped, and we are dancing a tarantella until the sweat pours. I open my eyes and I see dark, muscled forms curl out of water, with flapping gills and flattened eyes. I close my eyes and I see stars, deep stars giving way to deeper stars, deeper stars bowing to deepest stars at the crown of an infinite cone.

"Still," wrote Van Gogh in a letter, "a great deal of light falls on everything." If we were blinded by darkness, we are also blinded by light. Sometimes here in Virginia at sunset low clouds on the southern or northern horizon are completely invisible in the lighted sky. I only know one is there because I can see its reflection in still water. The first time I discovered this mystery I looked from cloud to no-cloud in bewilderment, checking my bearings over and over, thinking maybe the ark of the covenant was just passing by south of Dead Man Mountain. Only much later did I learn the explanation: polarized light from the sky is very much weakened by reflection, but the light in clouds isn't polarized. So invisible clouds pass among visible clouds, till all slide over the mountains; so a greater light extinguishes a lesser as though it didn't exist.

In the great meteor shower of August, the Perseid, I wail all day for the shooting stars I miss. They're out there showering down, committing hara-kiri in a flame of fatal attraction, and hissing perhaps at last into the ocean. But at dawn what looks like a blue dome clamps down over me like a lid on a pot. The stars and planets could smash and I'd never know. Only a piece of ashen moon occasionally climbs up or down the inside of the dome, and our local star without surcease explodes on our heads. We have really only that one light, one source for all power, and yet we must turn away from it by universal decree. Nobody here on the planet seems aware of this strange, powerful taboo, that we all walk about carefully averting our faces, this way and that, lest our eyes be blasted forever.

Darkness appalls and light dazzles; the scrap of visible light that doesn't hurt my eyes hurts my brain. What I see sets me swaying. Size and distance and the sudden swelling of meanings confuse me, bowl me over. I straddle the sycamore log bridge over Tinker Creek in the summer. I look at the lighted creek bottom: snail tracks tunnel the mud in quavering curves. A crayfish jerks, but by the time I absorb what has happened, he's gone in a billowing smoke screen of silt. I look at the water: minnows and shiners. If I'm thinking minnows, a carp will fill my brain till I scream. I look at the water's surface: skaters, bubbles, and leaves sliding down. Suddenly, my own face, reflected, startles me witless. Those snails have been tracking my face! Finally, with a shuddering wrench of the will, I see clouds, cirrus clouds. I'm dizzy, I fall in.

This looking business is risky. Once I stood on a humped rock on nearby Purgatory Mountain, watching through binoculars the great autumn hawk migration below, until I discovered that I was in danger of joining the hawks on a vertical migration of my own. I was used to binoculars, but not, apparently, to balancing on humped rocks while looking through them. I reeled. Everything advanced and receded by turns; the world was full of unexplained foreshortenings and depths. A distant huge object, a hawk the size of an elephant, turned out to be the browned bough of a nearby loblolly pine. I followed a sharp-skinned hawk against a featureless sky, rotating my head unawares as it flew, and when I lowered the glass a glimpse of my own looming shoulder sent me staggering. What prevents the men on Palomar from falling, voiceless and blinded, from their tiny, vaulted chairs?

I reel in confusion; I don't understand what I see. With the naked eye I can see two million light-years to the Andromeda galaxy. Often I slop some creek water in a jar, and when I get home I dump it in a white china bowl.

After the silt settles I return and see tracings of minute snails on the bottom, a planarian or two winding round the rim of water, roundworms shimmying frantically, and finally, when my eyes have adjusted to these dimensions, amoebae. At first the amoebae look like *muscae volitantes*, those curled moving spots you seem to see in your eyes when you stare at a distant wall. Then I see the amoebae as drops of water congealed, bluish, translucent, like chips of sky in the bowl. At length I choose one individual and give myself over to its idea of an evening. I see it dribble a grainy foot before it on its wet, unfathomable way. Do its unedited sense impressions include the fierce focus of my eyes? Shall I take it outside and show it Andromeda, and blow its little endoplasm? I stir the water with a finger, in case it's running out of oxygen. Maybe I should get a tropical aquarium with motorized bubblers and lights, and keep this one for a pet. Yes, it would tell its fissioned descendants, the universe is two feet by five, and if you listen closely you can hear the buzzing music of the spheres.

Oh, it's mysterious, lamplit evenings here in the galaxy, one after the other. It's one of those nights when I wander from window to window, looking for a sign. But I can't see. Terror and a beauty insoluble are a riband of blue woven into the fringes of garments of things both great and small. No culture explains, no bivouac offers real haven or rest. But it could be that we are not seeing something. Galileo thought comets were an optical illusion. This is fertile ground: since we are certain that they're not, we can look at what our scientists have been saying with fresh hope. What if there are *really* gleaming, castellated cities hung upside-down over the desert sand? What limpid lakes and cool date palms have our caravans always passed untried? Until, one by one, by the blindest of leaps, we light on the road to these places, we must stumble in darkness and hunger. I turn from the window. I'm blind as a bat, sensing only from every direction the echo of my own thin cries.

Learning to See

I chanced on a wonderful book called *Space and Sight,* by Marius Von Senden. When Western surgeons discovered how to perform safe cataract operations, they ranged across Europe and America operating on dozens of men and women of all ages who had been blinded by cataracts since birth. Von Senden collected accounts of such cases; the histories are fascinating. Many doctors had tested their patients' sense perceptions and ideas of space both before and after the operations. The vast majority of patients, of both sexes and all ages, had, in Von Senden's opinion, no idea of space whatsoever. Form, distance, and size were so many meaningless syllables. A patient "had no idea of depth, confusing it with roundness." Before the operation a doctor would give a blind patient a cube and a sphere; the patient would tongue it or feel it with his hands, and name it correctly. After the operation the doctor would show the same objects to the patient without letting him touch them; now he had no clue whatsoever to what he was seeing. One patient called lemonade "square" because it pricked on his tongue as a square shape pricked on the touch of his hands. Of another postoperative patient the doctor writes, "I have found in her no notion of size, for example, not even within the narrow limits which she might have encompassed with the aid of touch. Thus when I asked her to show me how big her mother was, she did not stretch out her hands, but set her two index fingers a few inches apart."

For the newly sighted, vision is pure sensation unencumbered by meaning. When a newly sighted girl saw photographs and paintings, she asked, "'Why do they put those dark marks all over them?' 'Those aren't dark marks,' her mother explained, 'those are shadows. That is one of the ways the eye knows that things have shape. If it were not for shadows, many things would look flat.' 'Well, that's how things do look,' Joan answered. 'Everything looks flat with dark patches.'"

In general the newly sighted see the world as a dazzle of "color-patches." They are pleased by the sensation of color, and learn quickly to name the colors, but the rest of seeing is tormentingly difficult. Soon after his operation, a patient "generally bumps into one of these color-patches and observes them to be substantial, since they resist him as tactual objects do. In walking about it also strikes him—or can if he pays attention—that he is continually passing in between the colors he sees, that he can go past a visual object, that a part of it then steadily disappears from view; and that in spite of this, however he twists and turns—whether entering the room from the door, for example, or returning back to it—he always has a visual space in front of him. Thus he gradually comes to realize that there is also space behind him, which he does not see."

The mental effort involved in these reasonings proves overwhelming for many patients. It oppresses them to realize, if they ever do at all, the tremendous size of the world, which they had previously conceived of as something touchingly manageable. It oppresses them to realize that they have been visible to people all along, perhaps unattractively so, without their knowledge or consent. A disheartening number of them refuse to use their new vision, continuing to go over objects with their tongues, and lapsing into apathy and despair.

On the other hand, many newly sighted people speak well of the world, and teach us how dull our own vision is. To one patient, a human hand, unrecognized, is "something bright and then holes." Shown a bunch of grapes, a boy calls out, "It is dark, blue and shiny. . . . It isn't smooth, it has bumps and hollows." A little girl visits a garden. "She is greatly astonished, and can scarcely be persuaded to answer, stands speechless in front of the tree, which she only names on taking hold of it, and then as 'the tree with the lights in it.'" Another patient, a twenty-two-year-old girl, was dazzled by the world's brightness and kept her eyes shut for two weeks. When at the end of that time she opened her eyes again, she did not recognize any objects, but "the more she now directed her gaze upon everything about her, the more it could be seen how an expression of gratification and astonishment overspread her features; she repeatedly exclaimed: 'Oh God! How beautiful!'"

I saw color-patches for weeks after I read this wonderful book. It was summer; the peaches were ripe in the valley orchards. When I woke in the morning, color-patches wrapped round my eyes, intricately, leaving not one unfilled spot. All day long I walked among shifting color-patches that parted before me like the Red Sea and closed again in silence, transfigured, wherever I looked back. Some patches swelled and loomed, while others vanished utterly, and dark marks flitted at random over the whole dazzling sweep. But I couldn't sustain the illusion of flatness. I've been around for too long. Form is condemned to an eternal danse macabre with meaning: I couldn't unpeach the peaches. Nor can I remember ever having seen without understanding; the color-patches of infancy are lost. My brain then must have been smooth as any balloon. I'm told I reached for the moon; many babies do. But the color-patches of infancy swelled as meaning filled them; they arrayed themselves in solemn ranks down distance which unrolled and stretched before me like a plain. The moon rocketed away. I live now in a world of shadows that shape and distance color, a world where space makes a kind of terrible sense. What Gnosticism is this, and what physics? The fluttering patch I saw in my nursery window—silver and green and shape-shifting blue—is gone; a row of Lombardy poplars takes its place, mute, across the distant lawn. That humming oblong creature pale as light that stole along the walls of my room at night, stretching exhilaratingly around the corners, is gone, too, gone the night I ate of the bittersweet fruit, put two and two together, and puckered forever my brain. Martin Buber tells this tale: "Rabbi Mendel once boasted to his teacher Rabbi Elimelekh that evenings he saw the angel who rolls away the light before the darkness, and mornings the angel who rolls away the darkness before the light. 'Yes,' said Rabbi Elimelekh, 'in my youth I saw that too. Later on you don't see these things anymore.'"

Why didn't someone hand these newly sighted people paints and brushes from the start, when they still didn't know what anything was? Then maybe we all could see color-patches too, the world unraveled from reason, Eden before Adam gave names. The scales would drop from my eyes; I'd see trees like men walking; I'd run down the road against all orders, hallooing and leaping.

Silver Flashes

Seeing is of course very much a matter of verbalization. Unless I call my attention to what passes before my eyes, I simply won't see it. If Tinker Mountain erupted, I'd be likely to notice. But if I want to notice the lesser cataclysms of valley life, I have to maintain in my head a running description of the present. It's not that I'm observant; it's just that I talk too much. Otherwise, especially in a strange place, I'll never know what's happening. Like a blind man at the ball game, I need a radio.

When I see this way I analyze and pry. I hurl over logs and roll away stones; I study the bank a square foot at a time, probing and tilting my head. Some days when a mist covers the mountains, when the muskrats won't show and the microscope's mirror shatters, I want to climb up the blank blue dome as a man would storm the inside of a circus tent, wildly, dangling, and with a steel knife claw a rent in the top, peep, and, if I must, fall.

But there is another kind of seeing that involves a letting go. When I see this way I sway transfixed and emptied. The difference between the two ways of seeing is the difference between walking with and without a camera. When I walk with a camera I walk from shot to shot, reading the light on a calibrated meter. When I walk without a camera, my own shutter opens, and the moment's light prints on my own silver gut. When I see this second way I am above all an unscrupulous observer.

It was sunny one evening last summer at Tinker Creek; the sun was low in the sky, upstream. I was sitting on the sycamore log bridge with the sunset at my back, watching the shiners the size of minnows who were feeding over the muddy sand in skittery schools. Again and again, one fish, then another, turned for a split second across the current and flash! the sun shot out from its silver side. I couldn't watch for it. It was always just happening somewhere else, and it drew my vision just as it disappeared: flash! like a sudden dazzle of the thinnest blade, a sparking over a dun and olive ground at chance intervals from every direction. Then I noticed white specks, some sort of pale petals, small, floating from under my feet on the creek's surface, very slow and steady. So I blurred my eyes and gazed toward the brim of my hat and saw a new world. I saw the pale white circles roll up, roll up, like the world's turning, mute and perfect, and I saw the linear flashes, gleaming silver, like stars being born at random down a rolling scroll of time. Something broke and something opened. I filled up like a new wineskin. I breathed an air like light; I saw a light like water. I was the lip of a fountain the creek filled forever; I was ether, the leaf in the zephyr; I was flesh-flake, feather, bone.

When I see this way I see truly. As Thoreau says, I return to my senses. I am the man who watches the baseball game in silence in an empty stadium. I see the game purely; I'm abstracted and dazed. When it's all over and the white-suited players lope off the green field to their shadowed dugouts, I leap to my feet, I cheer and cheer.

But I can't go out and try to see this way. I'll fail, I'll go mad. All I can do is try to gag the commentator, to hush the noise of useless interior babble that keeps me from seeing just as surely as a newspaper dangled before my eyes. The effort is really a discipline requiring a lifetime of dedicated struggle; it marks the literature of saints and monks of every order east and west, under every rule and no rule, discalced and shod. The world's spiritual geniuses seem to discover universally that the mind's muddy river, this ceaseless flow of trivia and trash, cannot be dammed, and that trying to dam it is a waste of effect that might lead to madness. Instead you must allow the muddy river to flow unheeded in the dim channels of consciousness; you raise your sights; you look along it, mildly, acknowledging its presence without interest and gazing beyond it into the realm of the real where subjects and objects act and rest purely, without utterance. "Launch into the deep," says Jacques Ellul, "and you shall see."

The secret of seeing, then, is the pearl of great price. If I thought he could teach me to find it and keep it forever I would stagger barefoot across a hundred deserts after any lunatic at all. But although the pearl may be found, it may not be sought. The literature of illumination reveals this above all: although it comes to those who wait for it, it is always, even to the most practiced and adept, a gift and a total surprise. I return from one walk knowing where the killdeer nests in the field by the creek and the hour the laurel blooms. I return from the same walk a day later scarcely knowing my own name. Litanies hum in my ears; my tongue flaps in my mouth, *Alimonon*, alleluia! I cannot cause light; the most I can do is try to put myself in the path of its beam. It is possible, in deep space, to sail on solar wind. Light, be it particle or wave, has force: you rig a giant sail and go. The secret of seeing is to sail on solar wind. Hone and spread your spirit till you yourself are a sail, whetted, translucent, broadside to the merest puff.

When her doctor took her bandages off and led her into the garden, the girl who was no longer blind saw "the tree with the lights in it." It was for this tree I searched through the peach orchards of summer, in the forests of fall and down winter and spring for years. Then one day I was walking along Tinker Creek thinking of nothing at all and I saw the tree with the lights in it. I saw the backyard cedar where the mourning doves roost charged and transfigured, each cell buzzing with flame. I stood on the grass with the lights in it, grass that was wholly fire, utterly focused and utterly dreamed. It was less like seeing than like being for the first time seen, knocked breathless by a powerful glance. The flood of fire abated, but I'm still spending the power. Gradually the lights went out in the cedar, the colors died, the cells unflamed and disappeared. I was still ringing. I had been my whole life a bell, and never knew it until at that moment I was lifted and struck. I have since only very rarely seen the tree with the lights in it. The vision comes and goes, mostly goes, but I live for it, for the moment when the mountains open and a new light roars in spate through the crack, and the mountains slam.

Suggestions for Discussion

1. What is the central point of this essay?

2. How does the author's story about hiding pennies as a child relate to the thesis of the piece?

3. Discuss the tone of Dillard's description of observations of nature. How honest do you feel her reactions to nature are? Compare her reaction to nature with those of other naturalists you have read.

Suggestions for Writing

1. Recall a scene, either natural or social, to which you reacted strongly. Write about it.

2. Write a piece in which you analyze your attitude toward the natural world.

3. With wax crayons, magic markers, or water colors, attempt to represent a sight common to you as "patches of color." Then write a paper in which you describe the difficulties or pleasures you found in your attempt.

John Reed
Almost Thirty

John Reed (1887–1920), born in Portland, Oregon, was called by Upton Sinclair "the playboy of the social revolution." He worked on the *American Magazine,* became managing editor of *the Masses,* and when Villa's revolt broke out in Mexico, he reported for the *World* and sent graphic sketches to *Metropolitan.* After the Russian revolution he wrote his most famed book, *Ten Days That Shook the World* (1919). In these reflections, Reed reviews significant events in his past and his failure to discover any final answers to sustain him.

In 1906 I went up to Harvard almost alone, knowing hardly a soul in the university. My college class entered over seven hundred strong, and, for the three months it seemed to me, going around to lectures and meetings, as if every one of the seven hundred had friends but me. I was thrilled with the immensity of Harvard, its infinite opportunities, its august history and traditions—but desperately lonely. I didn't know which way to turn, how to meet people. Fellows passed me in the Yard, shouting gaily to one another; I saw parties off to Boston Saturday night, whooping and yelling on the back platform of the street car, and they passed hilariously singing under my window in the early dawn. Athletes and musicians and writers and statesmen were emerging from the ranks of the class. The freshman clubs were forming.

And I was out of it all. I "went out" for the college papers, and tried to make the freshman crew, even staying in Cambridge vacations to go down to the empty boat-house and plug away at the machines—and was the last man kicked off the squad before they went to New London. I got to know many fellows to nod to, and a very few intimately; but most of my friends were whirled off and up into prominence, and came to see me no more. One of them said he'd room with me sophomore year—but he was tipped off that I wasn't "the right sort" and openly drew away from me. And I, too, hurt a boy who was my friend. He was a Jew, a shy, rather melancholy person. We were always together, we two outsiders. I became irritated and morbid about it— it seemed I would never be part of the rich splendor of college life with him around—so I drew away from him. . . . It hurt him very much, and it taught me better. Since then he has forgiven it, and done wonderful things for me, and we are friends.

My second year was better. I was elected an editor of two of the papers, and knew more fellows. The fortunate and splendid youths, the aristocrats who filled the clubs and dominated college society, didn't seem so attractive. In two open contests, the trial for editor of the college daily paper and that for assistant manager of the varsity crew, I qualified easily for election; but the aristocrats blackballed me. However, that mattered less. During my freshman year I used to *pray* to be liked, to have friends, to be popular with the crowd. Now I had friends, plenty of them; and I have found that when I am working hard at something I love, friends come without my trying, and stay; and fear goes, and that sense of being lost which is so horrible.

From that time on I never felt out of it. I was never popular with the aristocrats; I was never elected to any clubs but one, and that one largely because of a dearth of members who could write lyrics for the annual show. But I was on the papers, was elected president of the Cosmopolitan Club, where forty-three nationalities met, became manager of the Musical Clubs, captain of the water-polo team, and an officer in many undergraduate activities. As song-leader of the cheering section, I had the supreme blissful sensation of swaying two thousand voices in great crashing choruses during the big football games. The more I met the college aristocrats, the more their cold, cruel stupidity repelled me. I began to pity them for their lack of imagination, and the narrowness of their glittering lives—clubs, athletics, society. College is like the world; outside there is the same class of people, dull and sated and blind.

Harvard University under President Eliot was unique. Individualism was carried to the point where a man who came for a good time could get through and graduate without having learned anything; but on the other hand, anyone could find there anything he wanted from all the world's store of learning. The undergraduates were practically free from control; they could live pretty much where they pleased, and do as they pleased—so long as they attended lectures. There was no attempt made by the authorities to weld the student body together, or to enforce any kind of uniformity. Some men came with allowances of fifteen thousand dollars a year pocket money, with automobiles and servants, living in gorgeous suites in palatial apartment houses; others in the same class starved in attic bedrooms.

All sorts of strange characters, of every race and mind, poets, philosophers, cranks of every twist, were in our class. The very hugeness of it prevented any one man from knowing more than a few of his classmates, though I managed to make the acquaintance of about five hundred of them. The aristocrats controlled the places of pride and power, except when a democratic revolution, such as occurred in my senior year, swept them off their feet; but they were so exclusive that most of the real life went on outside their ranks—and all the intellectual life of the student body. So many fine men were outside the charmed circle that, unlike most colleges, there was no disgrace in not being a "club man." What is known as "college spirit" was not very powerful; no odium attached to those who didn't go to football games and cheer. There was talk of the world, and daring thought, and intellectual insurgency; heresy has always been a Harvard and a New England tradition. Students themselves criticized the faculty for not educating them, attacked the sacred institution of intercollegiate athletics, sneered at undergraduate clubs so holy that no one dared mention their names. No matter what you were or what you did—at Harvard you could find your kind. It wasn't a breeder for masses of mediocrely educated young men equipped with "business" psychology; out of each class came a few creative minds, a few scholars, a few "gentlemen" with insolent manners, and a ruck of nobodies. . . . Things have changed now. I liked Harvard better then.

Toward the end of my college course two influences came into my life, which had a good deal to do with shaping me. One was contact with Professor Copeland, who, under the pretense of teaching English composition, has stimulated generations of men to find color and strength and beauty in books and in the world, and to express it again. The other was what I call, for lack of a better name, the manifestation of the modern spirit. Some men, notably Walter Lippmann, had been reading and thinking and talking about politics and economics, not as dry theoretical studies, but as live forces acting on the world, on the University even. They formed the Socialist Club, to study and discuss all modern social and economic theories, and began to experiment with the community in which they lived.

Under their stimulus the college political clubs, which had formerly been quadrennial mushroom growths for the purpose of drinking beer, parading and burning red fire, took on a new significance. The Club drew up a platform for the Socialist Party in the city elections. It had social legislation introduced into the Massachusetts Legislature. Its members wrote articles in the college papers challenging undergraduate ideals, and muckraked the University for not paying its servants living wages, and so forth. Out of the agitation sprang the Harvard Men's League for Women's Suffrage, the Single Tax Club, an Anarchist group. The faculty was petitioned for a course in socialism. Prominent radicals were invited to Cambridge to lecture. An open forum was started, to debate college matters and the issues of the day. The result of this movement upon the undergraduate world was potent. All over the place radicals sprang up, in music, painting, poetry, the theatre. The more serious college papers took a socialistic or at least progressive tinge. Of course all this made no ostensible difference in the look of Harvard society, and probably the clubmen and the athletes, who represented us to the world, never even heard of it. But it made me, and many others, realize that there was something going on in the dull outside world more thrilling than college activities, and turned our attention to the writings of men like H. G. Wells and Graham Wallas, wrenching us away from the Oscar Wildean dilettantism that had possessed undergraduate littérateurs for generations.

After college Waldo Peirce and I went abroad as "bull-pushers" on a cattle-boat, for a year's happy-go-lucky wandering. Waldo rebelled at the smells and the ship's company, and jumped overboard off Boston Light, swimming back to shore and later taking the *Lusitania* to Liverpool; meanwhile, I was arrested for his murder, clapped in irons and brought before an Admiralty court at Manchester, where Waldo turned up in the nick of time. I tramped down across England alone, working on farms and sleeping in haymows, meeting Peirce in London again. Then we hoofed it to Dover and tried to stow away on a Channel steamer for France—and got arrested in Calais, of course. Separating, we went through northern France on foot, to Rouen and Paris, and started on a wild automobile trip through Touraine to the Spanish border, and across; and I proceeded into Spain alone, having adventures. I spent the winter in Paris, with excursions around the country, letting it soak in. Then I came home to America to settle down and make my living.

Lincoln Steffens recommended me for a job on *The American Magazine*, where I stayed three years, reading manuscripts and writing stories and verses. More than any other man Lincoln Steffens has influenced my mind. I met him first while I was at Harvard, where he came loving youth, full of understanding, with the breath of the world clinging to him. I was afraid of him then—afraid of his wisdom, his seriousness, and we didn't talk. But when

I came back from France I told him what I had seen and done, and he asked me what I wanted to do. I said I didn't know, except that I wanted to write. Steffens looked at me with that lovely smile: "You can do anything you want to," he said; and I believed him. Since then I have gone to him with my difficulties and troubles, and he has always listened while I solved them myself in the warmth of his understanding. Being with Steffens is to me like flashes of clear light; it is as if I see him, and myself, and the world, with new eyes. I tell him what I see and think, and it comes back to me beautiful, full of meaning. He does not judge or advise—he simply makes everything clear. There are two men who give me confidence in myself, who make me want to work, and to do nothing unworthy—Copeland and Steffens.

New York was an enchanted city to me. It was on an infinitely grander scale than Harvard. Everything was to be found there—it satisfied me utterly. I wandered about the streets, from the soaring imperial towers of down-town, along the East River docks, smelling of spices and the clipper ships of the past, through the swarming East Side—alien towns within towns—where the smoky flare of miles of clamorous pushcarts made a splendor of shabby streets; coming upon sudden shrill markets, dripping blood and fish-scales in the light of torches, the big Jewish women bawling their wares under the roaring great bridges; thrilling to the ebb and flow of human tides sweeping to work and back, west and east, south and north. I knew Chinatown, and Little Italy, and the quarter of the Syrians; the marionette theatre, Sharkey's and McSorley's saloons, the Bowery lodging houses and the places where the tramps gathered in winter; the Haymarket, the German Village, and all the dives of the Tenderloin. I spent all one summer night on top of a pier of the Williamsburg Bridge; I slept another night in a basket of squid in the Fulton Market, where the red and green and gold sea things glisten in the blue light of the sputtering arcs. The girls that walk the streets were friends of mine, and the drunken sailors off ships new-come from the world's end, and the Spanish longshoremen down on West Street.

I found wonderful obscure restaurants, where the foods of the whole world could be found. I knew how to get dope; where to go to hire a man to kill an enemy; what to do to get into gambling rooms, and secret dance halls. I knew well the parks, and streets of palaces, the theatres and hotels; the ugly growth of the city spreading like a disease, the decrepit places whence life was ebbing, and the squares and streets where an old, beautiful leisurely existence was drowned in the mounting roar of the slums. I knew Washington Square, and the artists and writers, the near-Bohemians, the radicals. I went to gangsters' balls at Tammany Hall, on excursions of the Tim Sullivan Association, to Coney Island on hot summer nights. . . . Within a block of my house was all the adventure of the world; within a mile was every foreign country.

In New York I first loved, and I first wrote of the things I saw, with a fierce joy of creation—and knew at last that I could write. There I got my first perceptions of the life of my time. The city and its people were an open book to me; everything had its story, dramatic, full of ironic tragedy and terrible humor. There I first saw that reality transcended all the fine poetic inventions of fastidiousness and medievalism. I was not happy or well long away from New York . . . I am not now, for that matter; but I cannot live continually in its heart any more. In the city I have no time for much but sensation and experience; but now I want some time of quiet, and leisure for thought, so I can extract from the richness of my life something beautiful and strong. I am living now in the country, within an hour of town, so I can go down occasionally and plunge into the sea of people, the roaring and the lights—and then come back here to write of it, in the quiet hills, in sunshine and clean wind.

During this time I read a good deal of radical literature, attended meetings of all sorts, met socialists, anarchists, single-taxers, labor-leaders, and besides, all the hair-splitting Utopians and petty doctrine-mongers who cling to skirts of Change. They interested me, so many different human types; and the livingness of theories which could dominate men and women captivated my imagination. On the whole, ideas alone didn't mean much to me. I had to see. In my rambles about the city I couldn't help but observe the ugliness of poverty and all its train of evil, the cruel inequality between rich people who had too many motor cars and poor people who didn't have enough to eat. It didn't come to me from books that the workers produced all the wealth of the world, which went to those who did not earn it.

The Lawrence strike of the textile workers had just ended, and the I.W.W. dominated the social and industrial horizon like a portent of the rising of the oppressed. That strike brought home to me hard the knowledge that the manufacturers get all they can out of labor, pay as little as they must, and permit the existence of great masses of the miserable unemployed in order to keep wages down; that the forces of the State are on the side of property against the propertyless. Our Socialist Party seemed to me duller than religion, and almost as little in touch with labor. The Paterson strike broke out. I met Bill Haywood, Elizabeth Gurley Flynn, Tresca, and the other leaders; they attracted me. I liked their understanding of the workers, their revolutionary thought, the boldness of their dream, the way immense crowds of people took fire and came alive under their leadership. Here was drama, change, democracy on the march and visible—a war of the people. I went to Paterson to watch it, was mistaken for a striker while walking the public street, beaten by the police, and jailed without any charge. In the jail I talked with exultant men who had blithely defied the lawless brutality of the city government and gone to prison laughing and singing. There were horrors in that jail too; men and boys shut up for months without trial, men going mad and dying, bestial cruelty and disease and filth—and all for the poor. When I came out I helped to organize the Pageant of the Paterson Strike, in Madison Square Garden, New York, drilling a thousand men and women in Paterson and bringing them across New Jersey to act out, before an immensely moved audience of twenty thousand people, the wretchedness of their lives and the glory of their revolt.

Since then I have seen and reported many strikes, most of them desperate struggles for the bare necessities of life; and all I have witnessed only confirms my first idea of the class struggle and its inevitability. I wish with all my heart that the proletariat would rise and take their rights—I don't see how else they will get them. Political relief is so slow to come, and year by year the opportunities of peaceful protest and lawful action are curtailed. But I am not sure any more that the working class is capable of revolution, peaceful or otherwise; the workers are so divided and bitterly hostile to each other, so badly led, so blind to their class interest. The War has been a terrible shatterer of faith in economic and political idealism. And yet I cannot give up the idea that out of democracy will be born the new world—richer, braver, freer, more beautiful. As for me, I don't know what I can do to help—I don't know yet. All I know is that my happiness is built on the misery of other people, that I eat because others go hungry, that I am clothed when other people go almost naked through the frozen cities in winter; and that fact poisons me, disturbs my serenity, makes me write propaganda when I would rather play— through not so much as it once did.

I quit my job to work on the Pageant, and when it was all over I went to pieces nervously, and friends took me abroad for the summer. The strike was starved and lost, the men went back to work dispirited and disillusioned, and the leaders, too, broke down under the long strain of the fight. The I.W.W. itself seemed smashed—indeed it has never recovered its old prestige. I got diphtheria in Italy, and came back to New York weak and despondent. For six months I did almost nothing. And then, through the interest of Lincoln Steffens, *The Metropolitan Magazine* asked me to go to Mexico as a war cor- respondent, and I knew that I must do it.

Villa had just captured Chihuahua when I got to the border, and was get- ting ready to move on Torreón. I made straight for Chihuahua, and there got a chance to accompany an American mining man down into the mountains of Durango. Hearing that an old half-bandit, half-general was moving to the front, I cut loose and joined him, riding with a wild troop of Mexican cavalry two weeks across the desert, seeing battle at close range, in which my com- panions were defeated and killed, and fleeing for my life across the desert. I joined Villa then in his march on Torreón, and was in at the fall of that strong- hold.

Altogether I was four months with the Constitutionalist armies in Mexico. When I first crossed the border deadliest fear gripped me. I was afraid of death, of mutilation, of a strange land and strange people whose speech and thought I did not know. But a terrible curiosity urged me on; I felt I *had to know* how I would act under fire, how I would get along with these primitive folks at war. And I discovered that bullets are not very terrifying, that the fear of death is not such a great thing, and that the Mexicans are wonderfully congenial. That four months of riding hundreds of miles across the blazing plains, sleeping on the ground with the *hombres*, dancing and carousing in looted haciendas all night after an all-day ride, being with them intimately in play, in battle, was perhaps the most satisfactory period of my life. I made good with these wild fighting men, and with myself. I loved them and I loved the life. I found myself again. I wrote better than I have ever written.

Then came the European War, to which I went as correspondent, spending a year and a half traveling in all the belligerent countries and on the front of five nations in battle. In Europe I found none of the spontaneity, none of the idealism of the Mexican revolution. It was a war of the workshops, and the trenches were factories turning out ruin—ruin of the spirit as well as of the body, the real and only death. Everything had halted but the engines of hate and destruction. European life, that flashed so many vital facets, ran in one channel, and runs in it now. There seems to me little to choose between the sides; both are horrible to me. The whole Great War is to me just a stoppage of the life and ferment of human evolution. I am waiting, waiting for it all to end, for life to resume so I can find my work.

In thinking it over, I find little in my thirty years that I can hold to. I haven't any God and don't want one; faith is only another word for finding oneself. In my life as in most lives, I guess, love plays a tremendous part. I've had love affairs, passionate happiness, wretched maladjustments; hurt deeply and been deeply hurt. But at last I have found my friend and lover, thrilling and satisfying, closer to me than anyone has ever been. And now I don't care what comes.

Suggestions for Discussion

1. What were Reed's most significant experiences at Harvard? How does he contrast the dominant groups of students?

2. What was the nature of Steffens's influence on Reed?

3. How would you sum up what living in New York meant to him?

4. What are the sources of Reed's pessimism? Of his affirmation?

Suggestions for Writing

1. "The end of a part of my life . . . the beginning of a new phase of life". What are some of your thoughts as you review your high school years and begin your work in college?

2. Have you had any great teacher or any subject at school so far that caught your imagination?

3. Describe your life at college or university, commenting upon its traditions, student body, activities, educational ideals, and faculty or focusing on a single aspect of college life.

4. Describe a mentor or teacher who has influenced your life.

Essays

Rollo May

The Man Who Was Put in a Cage

Rollo May (b. 1909) is a practicing psychotherapist in New York. He is a member of the William Alanson White Institute of Psychiatry, Psychoanalysis, and Psychology. In addition to *Man's Search for Himself* (1953), he is author of *The Meaning of Anxiety* (1950), *Love and Will* (1969), and *Power and Innocence* (1972). In this parable from *Psychology and the Human Dilemma* (1966) the psychologist is impelled to act on the man's impassioned cry in the dream: when any man's freedom is taken away, the freedom of everyone is also taken away.

> *What a piece of work is man! how noble in reason!*
> *how infinite in faculty! in form and moving how ex-*
> *press and admirable! . . . The paragon of animals!*
> —*Shakespeare,* Hamlet

We have quite a few discrete pieces of information these days about what happens to a person when he is deprived of this or that element of freedom. We have our studies of sensory deprivation and of how a person reacts when put in different kinds of authoritarian atmosphere, and so on. But recently I have been wondering what pattern would emerge if we put these various pieces of knowledge together. In short, what would happen to a living, whole person if his total freedom—or as nearly total as we can imagine—were taken away? In the course of these reflections, a parable took form in my mind.

The story begins with a king who, while standing in reverie at the window of his palace one evening, happened to notice a man in the town square below. He was apparently an average man, walking home at night, who had taken the same route five nights a week for many years. The king followed this man in his imagination—pictured him arriving home, perfunctorily kissing his wife, eating his late meal, inquiring whether everything was all right with the children, reading the paper, going to bed, perhaps engaging in the sex relation with his wife or perhaps not, sleeping, and getting up and going off to work again the next day.

And a sudden curiosity seized the king, which for a moment banished his fatigue: "I wonder what would happen if a man were kept in a cage, like the animals at the zoo?" His curiosity was perhaps in some ways not unlike that of the first surgeons who wondered what it would be like to perform a lobotomy on the human brain.

So the next day the king called in a psychologist, told him of his idea, and invited him to observe the experiment. When the psychologist demurred saying, "It's an unthinkable thing to keep a man in a cage," the monarch replied that many rulers had in effect, if not literally, done so, from the time of the Romans through Genghis Khan down to Hitler and the totalitarian leaders; so why not find out scientifically what would happen? Furthermore, added the king, he had made up his mind to do it whether the psychologist took part or not; he had already gotten the Greater Social Research Foundation to give a large sum of money for the experiment, and why let that money go to waste? By this time the psychologist also was feeling within himself a great curiosity about what would happen if a man were kept in a cage.

And so the next day the king caused a cage to be brought from the zoo—a large cage that had been occupied by a lion when it was new, then later by a tiger; just recently it had been the home of a hyena who died the previous week. The cage was put in an inner private court in the palace grounds, and the average man whom the king had seen from the window was brought and placed therein. The psychologist, with his Rorschach and Wechsler-Bellevue tests in his brief case to administer at some appropriate moment, sat down outside the cage.

At first the man was simply bewildered, and he kept saying to the psychologist, I have to catch the tram, I have to get to work, look what time it is, I'll be late for work!" but later on in the afternoon the man began soberly to realize what was up, and then he protested vehemently, "The king can't do this to me! It is unjust! It's against the law." His voice was strong, and his eyes full of anger. The psychologist liked the man for his anger, and he became vaguely aware that this was a mood he had encountered often in people he worked with in his clinic. "Yes," he realized, "this anger is the attitude of people who—like the healthy adolescents of any era—want to fight what's wrong, who protest directly against it. When people come to the clinic in this mood, it is good—they can be helped."

During the rest of the week the man continued his vehement protests. When the king walked by the cage, as he did every day, the man made his protests directly to the monarch.

But the king answered, "Look here, you are getting plenty of food, you have a good bed, and you don't have to work. We take good care of you; so why are you objecting?"

After some days had passed, the man's protests lessened and then ceased. He was silent in his cage, generally refusing to talk. But the psychologist could see hatred glowing in his eyes. When he did exchange a few words, they were short, definite words uttered in the strong, vibrant, but calm voice of the person who hates and knows whom he hates.

Whenever the king walked into the courtyard, there was a deep fire in the man's eyes. The psychologist thought, "This must be the way people act when they are first conquered." He remembered that he had also seen that expression of the eyes and heard that tone of voice in many patients at his clinic: the adolescent who had been unjustly accused at home or in school and could do nothing about it; the college student who was required by public and campus opinion to be a star on the gridiron, but was required by his professors to pass courses he could not prepare for if he were to be successful in football—and who was then expelled from college for the cheating that resulted. And the psychologist, looking at the active hatred in the man's eyes, thought, "It is still good; a person who has this fight in him can be helped."

Every day the king, as he walked through the courtyard, kept reminding the man in the cage that he was given food and shelter and taken good care of, so why did he not like it? And the psychologist noticed that, whereas at first the man had been entirely impervious to the king's statements, it now seemed more and more that he was pausing for a moment after the king's speech—for a second the hatred was postponed from returning to his eyes— as though he were asking himself if what the king said were possibly true.

And after a few weeks more, the man began to discuss with the psychologist how it was a useful thing that a man is given food and shelter; and how man had to live by his fate in any case, and the part of wisdom was to accept fate. He soon was developing an extensive theory about security and the acceptance of fate, which sounded to the psychologist very much like the philosophical theories that Rosenberg and others worked out for the fascists in Germany. He was very voluble during this period, talking at length, although the talk was mostly a monologue. The psychologist noticed that his voice was flat and hollow as he talked, like the voice of people in TV previews who make an effort to look you in the eye and try hard to sound sincere as they tell you that you should see the program they are advertising, or the announcers on the radio who are paid to persuade you that you should like high-brow music.

And the psychologist also noticed that now the corners of the man's mouth always turned down, as though he were in some gigantic pout. Then the psychologist suddenly remembered: this was like the middle-aged, middle-class people who came to his clinic, the respectable bourgeois people who went to church and lived morally but were always full of resentment, as though everything they did was conceived, born, and nursed in resentment. It reminded the psychologist of Nietzsche's saying that the middle class was consumed with resentment. He then for the first time began to be seriously worried about the man in the cage, for he knew that once resentment gets a firm start and becomes well rationalized and structuralized, it may become like cancer. When the person no longer knows whom he hates, he is much harder to help.

During this period the Greater Social Research Foundation had a board of trustees meeting, and they decided that since they were expending a fund to keep a man supported in a cage, it would look better if representatives of the Foundation at least visited the experiment. So a group of people, consisting of two professors and a few graduate students, came in one day to look at the man in the cage. One of the professors then proceeded to lecture to the group about the relation of the autonomic nervous system and the secretions of the ductless glands to human existence in a cage. But it occurred to the other professor that the verbal communications of the victim himself might just possibly be interesting, so he asked the man how he felt about living in a cage. The man was friendly toward the professors and students and explained to them that he had chosen this way of life, that there were great values in security and in being taken care of, that they would of course see how sensible this course was, and so on.

"How strange!" thought the psychologist, "and how pathetic; why is it he struggles so hard to get them to approve his way of life?"

In the succeeding days when the king walked through the courtyard, the man fawned upon him from behind the bars in his cage and thanked him for the food and shelter. But when the king was not in the yard and the man was not aware that the psychologist was present, his expression was quite different—sullen and morose. When his food was handed to him through the bars by the keeper, the man would often drop the dishes or dump over the water and then would be embarrassed because of his stupidity and clumsiness. His conversation became increasingly one-tracked; and instead of the involved philosophical theories about the value of being taken care of, he had gotten down to simple sentences such as "It is fate," which he would say over and over again, or he would just mumble to himself, "It is." The psychologist was surprised to find that the man should now be so clumsy as to drop his food, or so stupid as to talk in those barren sentences, for he knew from his tests that the man had originally been of good average intelligence. Then it dawned upon the psychologist that this was the kind of behavior he had observed in some anthropological studies among the Negroes in the South—people who had been forced to kiss the hand that fed and enslaved them, who could no longer either hate or rebel. The man in the cage took more and more to simply sitting all day long in the sun as it came through the bars, his only movement being to shift his position from time to time from morning through the afternoon.

It was hard to say just when the last phase set in. But the psychologist became aware that the man's face now seemed to have no particular expression; his smile was no longer fawning, but simply empty and meaningless, like the grimace a baby makes when there is gas on its stomach. The man ate his food and exchanged a few sentences with the psychologist from time to time; but his eyes were distant and vague, and though he looked at the psychologist, it seemed that he never really *saw* him.

And now the man, in his desultory conversations, never used the word "I" any more. He had accepted the cage. He had no anger, no hate, no rationalizations. But he was now insane.

The night the psychologist realized this, he sat in his apartment trying to write a concluding report. But it was very difficult for him to summon up words, for he felt within himself a great emptiness. He kept trying to reassure himself with the words, "They say that nothing is ever lost, that matter is merely changed to energy and back again." But he could not help feeling that something *had* been lost, that something had gone out of the universe in this experiment.

He finally went to bed with his report unfinished. But he could not sleep; there was a gnawing within him which, in less rational and scientific ages, would have been called a conscience. Why didn't I tell the king that this is the one experiment that no man can do—or at least why didn't I shout that I would have nothing to do with the whole bloody business? Of course, the king would have dismissed me, the foundations would never have granted me any more money, and at the clinic they would have said that I was not a real scientist. But maybe one could farm in the mountains and make a living, and maybe one could paint or write something that would make future men happier and more free. . . .

But he realized that these musings were, at least at the moment, unrealistic, and he tried to pull himself back to reality. All he could get, however, was this feeling of emptiness within himself, and the words, "Something has been taken out of the universe, and there is left only a void."

Finally he dropped off to sleep. Some time later, in the small hours of the morning, he was awakened by a startling dream. A crowd of people had gathered, in the dream, in front of the cage in the courtyard, and the man in the cage—no longer inert and vacuous—was shouting through the bars of the cage in impassioned oratory. "It is not only I whose freedom is taken away!" he was crying. "When the king puts me or any man in a cage, the freedom of each of you is taken away also. The king must go!" The people began to chant, "The king must go!" and they seized and broke out the iron bars of the cage, and wielded them for weapons as they charged the palace.

The psychologist awoke, filled by the dream with a great feeling of hope and joy—an experience of hope and joy probably not unlike that experienced by the free men of England when they forced King John to sign the Magna Charta. But not for nothing had the psychologist had an orthodox analysis in the course of his training, and as he lay surrounded by this aura of happiness, a voice spoke within him: "Aha, you had this dream to make yourself feel better; it's just a wish fulfillment."

"The hell it is!" said the psychologist as he climbed out of bed. "Maybe some dreams are to be acted on."

Suggestions for Discussion

1. What possible implicit judgment of the average man is evident in the king's imaginative recreation of his life? What is the significance of the king's selection of an average man for his experiment?

2. Formulate a plausible explanation of the fact that the anger and subsequent hate manifested by the man in the cage signified that he could be helped.

3. Define the various phases of the victim's response to his imprisonment and account for each of them. Include an analysis of the changes in his conversations with the several observers. How did the analogies cited contribute to your understanding of his metamorphosis?

4. Account for the reactions of the psychologist after his realization that the man was no longer sane, especially his feeling of emptiness within himself, the sense that "there is left only a void." Account for his final postdream resolution.

Suggestions for Writing

1. What does the form of the parable contribute to May's thesis? Write a paragraph elaborating on May's thesis. What is lost when you state it directly?

2. Using a vital subject like freedom of choice or love or the dignity of man, write a parable of your own in which you place it in fresh perspective.

3. Read one of the works that depicts man as prisoner and victim by Robert Lifton, Bruno Bettleheim, Charles Frankl, or Hannah Arendt. Write an analysis of the effects of incarceration on the human spirit, paying special attention to what qualities and activities of the mind distinguish one man from another under such adverse circumstances.

4. Relate the opening lines from *Hamlet* to the parable. Or develop an essay on the most difficult or the most crucial choices you have ever made, or are currently contemplating, and the factors you regard as central in arriving at a resolution.

5. May attributes the man's capitulation largely to the fact of his security. Defend or criticize this thesis. What if the victim were not an average man but a bright member of a youth commune, a poet, or a mystic? Rewrite the parable using one of the latter or any other victim as your protagonist.

Loren Eiseley

Man in the Autumn Light

Loren Eiseley (1907–1977) was an anthropologist and an academic administrator at the University of Pennsylvania. His publications include *Darwin's Century* (1958), which won the National Phi Beta Kappa Science Award and the Atheneum of Philadelphia Literature Award, *The Mind as Nature* (1962), *Francis Bacon and the Modern Dilemma* (1962), and *The Unexpected Universe* (1969). His last book *All the Strange Hours: The Excavation of a Life* (1975) was an autobiography. In the essay that follows, from *The Invisible Pyramid* (1970), Eiseley reflects his concern for preserving the natural environment as well as his deep respect for the poets whose power in his view exceeds that of molecular biologists.

The French dramatist Jean Cocteau has argued persuasively about the magic light of the theatre. People must remember, he contended, that "the theatre is a trick factory where the truth has no currency, where anything natural has no value, where the only things that convince us are card tricks and sleights of hand of a difficulty unsuspected by the audience."

The cosmos itself gives evidence, on an infinitely greater scale, of being just such a trick factory, a set of lights forever changing, and the actors themselves shape shifters, elongated shadows of something above or without. Perhaps in the sense men use the word natural, there is really nothing at all natural in the universe or, at best, that the world is natural only in being unnatural, like some variegated, color-shifting chameleon.

In Brazilian rivers there exists a fish, one of the cyprinodonts, which sees with a two-lensed eye, a kind of bifocal adjustment that permits the creature to examine the upper world of sunlight and air, while with the lower half of the lens he can survey the watery depths in which he lives. In this quality the fish resembles Blake, the English poet who asserted he saw with a double vision into a farther world than the natural. Now the fish, we might say, looks simultaneously into two worlds of reality, though what he makes of this divided knowledge we do not know. In the case of man, although there are degrees of seeing, we can observe that the individual has always possessed the ability to escape beyond naked reality into some other dimension, some place outside the realm of what might be called "facts."

Man is no more natural than the world. In reality he is, as we have seen, the creator of a phantom universe, the universe we call culture—a formidable realm of cloud shapes, ideas, potentialities, gods, and cities, which with man's death will collapse into dust and vanish back into "expected" nature.

Some landscapes, one learns, refuse history; some efface it so completely it is never found; in others the thronging memories of the past subdue the living. In my time I have experienced all these regions, but only in one place has the looming future overwhelmed my sense of the present. This happened in a man-made crater on the planet earth, but to reach that point it is necessary to take the long way round and to begin where time had lost its meaning. As near as I can pinpoint the place, it was somewhere at the edge of the Absaroka range along the headwaters of the Bighorn years ago in Wyoming. I had come down across a fierce land of crags and upland short-grass meadows, past aspens shivering in the mountain autumn. It was the season of the golden light. I was younger then and a hardened foot traveler. But youth had little to do with what I felt. In that country time did not exist. There was only the sound of water hurrying over pebbles to an unknown destination—water that made a tumult drowning the sound of human voices.

Somewhere along a creek bank I stumbled on an old archaeological site whose beautifully flaked spearpoints of jasper represented a time level remote from me by something like ten thousand years. Yet, I repeat, this was a country in which time had no power because the sky did not know it, the aspens had not heard it passing, the river had been talking to itself since before man arose, and in that country it would talk on after man had departed.

I was alone with the silvery aspens in the mountain light, looking upon time thousands of years remote, yet so meaningless that at any moment flame might spurt from the ash of a dead campfire and the hunters come slipping through the trees. My own race had no role in these mountains and would never have.

I felt the light again, the light that was falling across the void on other worlds. No bird sang, no beast stirred. To the west the high ranges with their snows rose pure and cold. It was a place to meet the future quite as readily as the past. The fluttering aspens expressed no choice, and I, a youngster with but few memories, chose to leave them there. The place was of no true season, any more than the indifferent torrent that poured among the boulders through summer and deep snow alike.

I camped in a little grove as though waiting, filled with a sense of incompleteness, alert for some intangible message that was never uttered. The philosopher Jacques Maritain once remarked that there is no future thing for

God. I had come upon what seemed to be a hidden fragment of the days before creation. Because I was mortal and not an omniscient creature, I lingered beside the stream with a growing restlessness. I had brought time in my perishable body into a place where, to all intents, it could not exist. I was moving in a realm outside of time and yet dragging time with me in an increasingly excruciating effort. If man was a creature obliged to choose, then choice was here denied me. I was forced to wait because a message from the future could not enter this domain. Here was pure, timeless nature—sequences as incomprehensible as pebbles—dropped like the shaped stones of the red men who had no history. The world eaters, by contrast, with their insatiable hunger for energy, quickly ran through nature; they felt it was exhaustible. They had, like all the spore-bearing organisms, an instinctive hunger for flight. They wanted more from the dark storehouse of a single planet than a panther's skin or a buffalo robe could offer. They wanted a greater novelty, only to be found far off in the orchard of the worlds.

Eventually, because the message never came, I went on. I could, I suppose, have been safe there. I could have continued to hesitate among the stones and been forgotten, or, because one came to know it was possible, I could simply have dissolved in the light that was of no season but eternity. In the end, I pursued my way downstream and out into the sagebrush of ordinary lands. Time reasserted its hold upon me but not quite in the usual way. Sometimes I could almost hear the thing for which I had waited in vain, or almost remember it. It was as though I carried the scar of some unusual psychical encounter.

A physician once described to me in detail the body's need to rectify its injuries, to restore, insofar as possible, mangled bones and tissues. A precisely arranged veil of skin is drawn over ancient wounds. Similarly the injured mind struggles, even in a delusory way, to reassemble and make sense of its shattered world. Whatever I had been exposed to among the snow crests and the autumn light still penetrated my being. Mine was the wound of a finite creature seeking to establish its own reality against eternity.

I am all that I have striven to describe of the strangest organism on the planet. I am one of the world eaters in the time when that species has despoiled the earth and is about to loose its spores into space. As an archaeologist I also know that our planet-effacing qualities extend to time itself. When the swarming phase of our existence commences, we struggle both against the remembered enchantment of childhood and the desire to extinguish it under layers of concrete and giant stones. Like some few persons in the days of the final urban concentrations, I am an anachronism, a child of the dying light. By those destined to create the future, my voice may not, perhaps, be trusted. I know only that I speak from the timeless country revisited, from the cold of vast tundras and the original dispersals, not from the indrawings of men.

II

The nineteenth-century novelist Thomas Love Peacock once remarked critically that "a poet in our times is a semibarbarian in a civilized community. . . . The march of his intellect is like that of a crab, backward." It is my suspicion that though many moderns would applaud what Peacock probably meant only ironically, there is a certain virtue in the sidelong retreat of the crab. He never runs, he never ceases to face what menaces him, and he always keeps his pincers well to the fore. He is a creature adapted by nature for rearguard action and withdrawal, but never rout.

The true poet is just such a fortunate creation as the elusive crab. He is born wary and is frequently in retreat because he is a protector of the human spirit. In the fruition time of the world eaters he is threatened, not with obsolescence, but with being hunted to extinction. I rather fancy such creatures—poets, I mean—as lurking about the the edge of all our activities, testing with a probing eye, if not claw, our thoughts as well as our machines. Blake was right about the double vision of poets. There is no substitute, in a future-oriented society, for eyes on stalks, or the ability to move suddenly at right angles from some dimly imminent catastrophe. The spore bearers, once they have reached the departure stage, are impatient of any but acceptable prophets—prophets, that is, of the swarming time. These are the men who uncritically proclaim our powers over the cosmic prison and who dangle before us ill-assorted keys to the gate.

By contrast, one of the most perceptive minds in American literature, Ralph Waldo Emerson, once maintained stubbornly: "The soul is no traveler." Emerson spoke in an era when it was a passion with American writers to go abroad, just as today many people yearn for the experience of space. He was not engaged in deriding the benefits of travel. The wary poet merely persisted in the recognition that the soul in its creative expression is genuinely *not* a traveler, that the great writer is peculiarly a product of his native environment. As an untraveled traveler, he picks up selectively from his surroundings a fiery train of dissimilar memory particles—"unlike things" which are woven at last into the likeness of truth.

Man's urge toward transcendence manifests itself even in his outward inventions. However, crudely conceived, his rockets, his cyborgs, are intended to leap some void, some recently discovered chasm before him, even as long ago he cunningly devised language to reach across the light-year distances between individual minds. The spore bearers of thought have a longer flight history than today's astronauts. They found, fantastic though it now seems, the keys to what originally appeared to be the impregnable prison of selfhood.

But these ancient word-flight specialists the poets have another skill that enhances their power beyond even the contemporary ability they have always had to sway minds. They have, in addition, a preternatural sensitivity to the backward and forward reaches of time. They probe into life as far as, if not farther than, the molecular biologist does, because they touch life itself and not its particulate structure. The latter is a recent scientific disclosure, and hence we acclaim the individual discoverers. The poets, on the other hand, have been talking across the ages until we have come to take their art for granted. It is useless to characterize them as dealers in the obsolete, because this venerable, word-loving trait in man is what enables him to transmit his eternal hunger—his yearning for the country of the unchanging autumn light. Words are man's domain, from his beginning to his fall.

Many years ago I chanced to read a story by Don Stuart entitled "Twilight." It is an account of the further history of humanity many millions of years in the future. The story is told by a man a few centuries beyond our time, who in the course of an experiment had been accidentally projected forward into the evening of the race. He had then escaped through his own powers, but in doing so had overleaped his own era and reached our particular century. The time voyager sings an unbearably sad song learned in that remote future—a song that called and sought and searched in hopelessness. It was the song of man in his own twilight, a song of the final autumn when hope had gone and man's fertility with it, though he continued to linger on in the shadow of the perfect machines which he had created and which would long outlast him.

What lifts this story beyond ordinary science fiction is its compassionate insight into the basic nature of the race—the hunger that had accompanied man to his final intellectual triumph in earth's garden cities. There he had lost the will and curiosity to seek any further to transcend himself. Instead, that passion had been lavished upon his great machines. But the songs wept and searched for something that had been forgotten—something that could never be found again. The man from the open noonday of the human triumph, the scientist of the thirty-first century, before seeking his own return down the time channel, carries out one final act that is symbolic of man's yearning and sense of inadequacy before the universe, even though he had wished, like Emerson, "to climb the steps of paradise." Man had failed in the end to sanctify his own being.

The indomitable time voyager standing before the deathless machines performs the last great act of the human twilight. He programs the instruments to work toward the creation of a machine which would incorporate what man by then had lost: curiosity and hope. In dying, man had transmitted his hunger to the devices which had contributed to his death. Is this act to be labeled triumph or defeat? We do not learn; we are too far down in time's dim morning. The poet speaks with man's own Delphic ambiguity. We are left wondering whether the time voyager had produced the only possible solution to the final decay of humanity—that is, the transference of human values to the world of imperishable machines—or, on the other hand, whether less reliance upon the machine might have prevented the decay of the race. These are questions that only the long future will answer, but "Twilight" is a magnificent evocation of man's ending that only a poet of this century could have adequately foreseen—that man in the end forgets the message that started him upon his journey.

III

On a planet where snow falls, the light changes, and when the light changes all is changed, including life. I am not speaking now of daytime things but of the first snows of winter that always leave an intimation in each drifting flake of a thousand-year turn toward a world in which summer may sometime forget to come back. The world has known such episodes: it has not always been the world it is. Ice like a vast white amoeba has descended at intervals from the mountains and crept over the hills and valleys of the continents, ingesting forests and spewing forth boulders.

Something still touches me from that vanished world as remote from us in years as an earth rocket would be from Alpha Centauri. Certainly Cocteau spoke the truth: to add to all the cosmic prisons that surround us there is the prison of the golden light that changes in the head of man—the light that cries to memory out of vanished worlds, the leaf-fall light of the earth's eternally changing theatre. And then comes the night snow that in some late hour transports us into that other, that vanished but unvanquished, world of the frost.

Near my house in the suburbs is a remaining fragment of woodland. It once formed part of a wealthy man's estate, and in one corner of the wood a huge castle created by imported workmen still looms among the trees that have long outlasted their original owner. A path runs through these woods and the people of multiplying suburbia hurry past upon it. For a long time I had feared for the trees.

One night it snowed and then a drop in temperature brought on the clear night sky. Dressed in a heavy sheepskin coat and galoshes, I had ventured out toward midnight upon the path through the wood. Out of old habit I studied the tracks upon the snow. People had crunched by on their way to the train station, but no human trace ran into the woods. Many little animals had ventured about the margin of the trees, perhaps timidly watching; none had descended to the path. On impulse, for I had never done so before in this spot, I swung aside into the world of no human tracks. At first it pleased me that the domain of the wood had remained so far untouched and undesecrated. Did man, still, after all his ravages, possess some fear of the midnight forest or some unconscious reverence toward the source of his origins? It seemed hardly likely in so accessible a spot, but I trudged on, watching the pole star through the naked branches. Here, I tried to convince myself, was a fragment of the older world, something that had momently escaped the eye of the world eaters.

After a time I came to a snow-shrouded clearing, and because my blood is, after all, that of the spore bearers, I sheltered my back against an enormous oak and continued to watch for a long time the circling of remote constellations above my head. Perhaps somewhere across the void another plotting eye on a similar midnight errand might be searching this arm of the galaxy. Would our eyes meet? I smiled a little uncomfortably and let my eyes drop, still unseeing and lost in contemplation, to the snow about me. The cold continued to deepen.

We were a very young race, I meditated, and of civilizations that had yet reached the swarming stage there had been but few. They had all been lacking in some aspect of the necessary technology, and their doom had come swift upon them before they had grasped the nature of the cosmos toward which they unconsciously yearned.

Egypt, which had planted in the pyramids man's mightiest challenge to effacing time, had conceived long millennia ago the dream of a sky-traveling boat that might reach the pole star. The Maya of the New World rain forests had also watched the drift of the constellations from their temples situated above the crawling vegetational sea about them. But of what their dreamers thought, the remaining hieroglyphs tell us little. We know only that the Maya were able to grope with mathematical accuracy through unlimited millions of years of which Christian Europe had no contemporary comprehension. The lost culture had remarkably accurate eclipse tables and precise time-commemorating monuments.

Ironically the fragments of those great stelae with all their learned calculations were, in the end, to be dragged about and worshiped upside down by a surviving peasantry who had forgotten their true significance. I, in this wintry clime under the shifting of the Bear, would no more be able to enter the mythology of that world of vertical time than to confront whatever eye might roam the dust clouds at this obscure corner of the galaxy. So it was, in turning, that I gazed in full consciousness at last upon the starlit clearing that surrounded me.

Except for the snow, I might as well have been standing upon the ruins that had thronged my mind. The clearing was artificial, a swath slashed by instruments of war through the center of the wood. Shorn trees toppled by bulldozers lay beneath the snow. Piles of rusted machinery were cast indiscriminately among the fallen trees. I came forward, groping like the last man out of a shell hole in some giant, unseen conflict. Iron, rust, timbers—the place was like the graveyard of an unseen, incessant war.

In the starlight my eye caught a last glimpse of living green. I waded toward the object but it lay upon its side. I rolled it over. It was a still-living Christmas tree hurled out with everything dispensable from an apartment house at the corner of the wood. I stroked it in wordless apology. Like others, I had taken the thin screen remaining from the original wood for reality. Only the snow, only the tiny footprints of the last surviving wood creatures, had led me to this unmasking. Behind this little stand of trees the world eaters had all the time been assiduously at work.

Well, and why not, countered my deviant slime-mold mind? The sooner men finished the planet, the sooner the spores would have to fly. I kicked vaguely at some geared piece of mechanism under its cover of snow. I thought of the last Mayan peasants worshiping the upended mathematical tablets of their forerunners. The supposition persisted in the best scientific circles that the astronomer priests had in the end proved too great a burden, they and their temples and observatories too expensive a luxury for their society to maintain—that revolt had cut them down.

But what if, a voice whispered at the back of my mind, as though the indistinct cosmic figure I had earlier conjured up had just spoken, what if during all that thousand years of computing among heavy unnatural numbers they had found a way to clamber through some hidden galactic doorway? Would it not have been necessary to abandon these monumental cities and leave their illiterate worshipers behind?

I turned over a snow-covered cogwheel. Who, after all, among such ruins could be sure that we were the first of the planet viruses to depart? Perhaps in the numbers and the hieroglyphs of long ago there had been hidden some other formula than that based upon the mathematics of rocket travel—some key to a doorway of air, leaving behind only the empty seedpods of the fallen cities. Slowly my mind continued to circle that dead crater under the winter sky.

Suppose, my thought persisted, there is still another answer to the ruins in the rain forests of Yucatan, or to the incised brick tablets baking under the Mesopotamian sun. Suppose that greater than all these, vaster and more impressive, an invisible pyramid lies at the heart of every civilization man has created, that for every visible brick or corbeled vault or upthrust skyscraper or giant rocket we bear a burden in the mind to excess, that we have a biological urge to complete what is actually uncompletable.

Every civilization, born like an animal body, has just so much energy to expend. In its birth throes it chooses a path, the pathway perhaps of a great religion as in the time when Christianity arose. Or an empire of thought is built among the Greeks, or a great power extends its roads, and governs as did the Romans. Or again, its wealth is poured out upon science, and science endows the culture with great energy, so that far goals seem attainable and yet grow illusory. Space and time widen to weariness. In the midst of triumph disenchantment sets in among the young. It is as though with the growth of cities an implosion took place, a final unseen structure, a spore-bearing structure, towering upward toward its final release.

Men talked much of progress and enlightenment on the path behind the thin screen of trees. I myself had walked there in the cool mornings awaiting my train to the city. All the time this concealed gash in the naked earth had been growing. I was wrong in just one thing in my estimate of civilization. I have said it is born like an animal and so, in a sense, it is. But an animal is whole. The secret tides of its body balance and sustain it until death. They draw it to its destiny. The great cultures, by contrast, have no final homeostatic feedback like that of the organism. They appear to have no destiny unless it is that of the slime mold's destiny to spore and depart. Too often they grow like a malignancy, in one direction only. The Maya had calculated the drifting eons like gods but they did not devise a single wheeled vehicle. So distinguished an authority as Eric Thompson has compared them to an overspecialized Jurassic monster.

A monster? My eyes swept slowly over the midnight clearing and its hidden refuse of fallen trunks and cogwheels. This was the pyramid that our particular culture was in the process of creating. It represented energy beyond anything the world of man had previously known. Our first spore flight had burst against the moon and reached, even now, toward Mars, but its base was a slime-mold base—the spore base of the world eaters. They fed upon the world, and the resources they consumed would never be duplicable again because their base was finite. Neither would the planet long sustain this tottering pyramid thrust upward from what had once been the soil of a consumed forest.

A rising wind began to volley snow across the clearing, burying deeper the rusted wheels and shrieking over the cast-off tree of Christmas. There was a hint in the chill air of a growing implacable winter, like that which finally descends upon an outworn planet—a planet from which life and oxygen are long since gone.

I returned to the shelter of the oak, my gaze sweeping as I did so the night sky of earth, now dark and overcast. It came to me then, in a lonely surge of feeling, that I was childless and my destiny not bound to my kind. With the tough oak at my back I remembered the feel of my father's face against my own on the night I had seen Halley's star. The comet had marked me. I was a citizen and a scientist of that nation which had first reached the moon. There in the ruined wood, remembering the shrunken seedpods of dead cities, I yearned silently toward those who would come after me if the race survived.

Four hundred years ago a young poet and potential rival of Shakespeare had written of the knowledge-hungry Faust of legend:

Thou art still but Faustus and a man.

In that phrase Christopher Marlowe had epitomized the human tragedy; We were world eaters and knowledge seekers but we were also men. It was a well-nigh fatal flaw. Whether we, like the makers of stone spearpoints in Wyoming, are a fleeting illusion of the autumn light depends upon whether any remain to decipher Marlowe's words one thousand years in the future.

The events of my century had placed the next millennium as far off as a star. All the elaborate mechanisms of communication we have devised have not ennobled, nor brought closer, individual men to men. The means exist. It is Faustus who remains a man. Beyond this dark, I, who was also a man, could not penetrate.

In the deepening snow I made a final obeisance to the living world. I took the still green, everlasting tree home to my living room for Christmas rites that had not been properly accorded it. I suppose the act was blindly compulsive. It was the sort of thing that Peacock in his time would have termed the barbarism of poets.

Suggestions for Discussion

1. How does the theater analogy pertain to the cosmos?

2. In what sense is man "the creator of a phantom universe"?

3. How does Eiseley contrast what he calls "the world eaters" and "pure, timeless nature"?

4. How does the simile of the crab relate to Eiseley's thesis? Why is there virtue in the retreat of the crab?

5. Why does the author admire the poets? Why does he feel their power exceeds that of the molecular biologist?

6. How does Eiseley interpret Emerson's belief that the great writer is peculiarly a product of his native environment?

7. How is the story *"Twilight"* invoked to advance Eiseley's philosophy? What is its theme? Its resolution or irresolution?

8. How does the metaphor of the autumn light relate to Eiseley's thesis?

9. What does the use of the words "world eaters" convey of Eiseley's tone and attitudes? Select other figures of speech and relate them to substance and tone.

10. When Eiseley ventured out on his midnight walk, what were his thoughts of past and present? What do his rhetorical questions signify?

11. On what historical basis does Eiseley suggest that the great cultures appear to have no destiny "unless it is that of the slime mold's destiny to spore and depart. Too often they grow like a malignancy, in one direction only"?

12. What is the meaning of the Marlowe quotation and its relationship to Eiseley's thesis?

13. Discuss the irony in Eiseley's gesture of providing Christmas rites for the tree.

Suggestions for Writing

1. What "degrees of seeing" have you observed among your acquaintances?

2. What steps do you feel should be taken to protect our environment?

3. Speculate on whether man's machines rob life of its human values, or whether they are capable of enhancing them.

Robert Coles

Happiness

Robert Coles (b. 1929) is a research psychiatrist at Harvard University. His work has focused on problems of poverty and discrimination. Among his publications are *Children of Crisis: A Study of Courage and Fear* (1967), *Migrants, Sharecroppers, Mountaineers* (1971), *The South Goes North* (1971), and *Privileged Ones: The Well-off and the Rich in America* (1978). In this essay Coles reviews the varied sources of happiness and suggests that happiness has a moral dimension.

No other country in the world has worked the notion of happiness into its Constitution, the very source of its national authority, the way the founding fathers of the United States of America chose to do when they linked the pursuit of happiness with life and with liberty as a trio of utterly inalienable rights. Not that happiness was, thereupon, defined. Anyway, a "pursuit" was specified—perhaps a rather knowing decision, in the tradition of Don Quixote, that the journey or way is better than the inn. "Happiness," a psychoanalytic supervisor of mine used to tell me, again and again, as I presented information to him about my patients, "is something people *yearn* for." He'd stop, and after a while I'd know the next sentence: "When they have it, they've redefined it, so they can keep searching." Again, one thinks of Cervantes' hero—not to mention any number of restless heroes and heroines in the novels of, say, George Eliot or Hardy or D. H. Lawrence.

What *is* happiness? The word itself only appeared in our English language during the sixteenth century, and is etymologically and, yes, spiritually connected to the word "happen"—which, of course, has to do with the occurrence of an event. Happiness in Shakespeare's time, and later as well, referred to good fortune, good luck, to favorable circumstances visited, somehow, on a particular person who registered such a state of affairs subjectively with a condition of good cheer, pleasurable feeling. One was satisfied with one's situation, glad to be in one's given place and time by virtue of how one's life has gone. The emphasis is, put differently, upon fate—an almost external force. To be sure, individuals craved pleasure, money, power, territory, a certain woman, a certain man—but "happiness" was not in itself sought. Rather, a person's personal and workaday success was noted by that person, and thankfully acknowledged—his or hers by virtue of divine grace, or the stars and their mysterious doings, or, quite simply, a series of fortuitous events.

Without question there were different interpretations of what prompts happiness, and what constitutes it. For many devoutly religious people (to this day), a stroke of business success, a marriage that works, the emergence over time of strong, intelligent, well-behaved children who seem able and content with their lot in life are all signs of sorts, evidence of God's favor. For those who don't know what to believe (about this life, and our place or purpose on earth), happiness seems something accidental, contingent, or, at best, a feeling for which one has worked hard indeed. But now we are a bit ahead of ourselves, historically: four hundred years ago, there was a sense of awe about happiness—as if it were visited upon some in accordance with the unfathomable workings of an inscrutable universe. It was only in more recent times, as men and women became more the center of this world (in their own minds, more the makers, the doers, the ones who wield and see the consequences), that happiness became, with everything else, a goal, a purpose, or, as those hard working, ambitious rationalists who framed our Constitution put it, something for which a "pursuit" is waged. No longer does *happ*iness *happen*; happiness is obtained.

But again the question has to be asked: what *was* this "happiness" which increasingly became mentioned by people in England and America from, say, 1600 or so onward? The English poet Alexander Pope, always one to render a quotable statement, once exclaimed "Oh Happiness!" Then he tried his hand at spelling the matter out: "Our being's end and aim! Good, Pleasure, Ease, Content! Whate'er thy name." An interesting way of regarding an elusive quality of mind and heart. First, the avowal that the possession of happiness is connected to our very purpose in life, to the central thrust of our human striving, to our aspirations as the peculiar creature which—well, has just that, the capacity to have aspirations. Then, a kind of bafflement: the poet, handy with words as he was, surrenders to the puzzling variety of hope and direction and orientation among us mortals. He makes a list, a various one at that; and yes, the list still works as we consider "happiness."

For some, "Good" is yet what counts: happiness as the inner feeling that corresponds to a moral perception on the part of a person. "I have done my duty to God and country; I have lived as I was taught it is right to live, and I'm ready to die happy"—the words of an ordinary twentieth-century American working woman, a nurse of fifty, actually, who'd raised her two children well, lived out a solid, satisfying marriage with her optometrist husband, and now was struggling with the effects of a breast cancer that had defied the surgeons, the oncologists, and, she would sometimes add, her minister. "He prays for my recovery," she once told me, and then added, "but I don't believe you can bargain with God that way. I'll be dying soon, and I know it. I don't pray to God that He give me *more* life; I pray to God that the life I've already lived not be judged too bad and too sinful when I meet Him. I think I've been a fairly decent person, and so I'm not afraid. To tell the truth, except when I'm in pain, I'm quite happy."

She is? The skeptical doctor wonders whether she *really* is happy; whether she is, in fact, fooling herself and her listener—denying all too vigorously the *un*happiness of an ordeal with a fatal disease. She is quick, however, to spot a visitor's doubt. "Oh, I'm sure you think I'm talking a big line, but underneath I'm scared. I know what they say in the "Living" section of the paper— that people say funny things when they're seriously ill. I'm no expert, but I've been out there, on the front lines, day after day, talking with sick people on the wards, hearing them sum up their lives; and I'll tell you, that's just what they do—they take stock of what it's been like, living, and they're plenty happy, some of them, and plenty others are sad."

The doctor has been given good pause—made to realize that happiness does indeed possess, at least for some, a longitudinal and evaluative, if not moral, dimension. Put differently, for a significant number of men and women happiness has to do with how a life has been lived, as determined by the one who has done the living—encouraged, perhaps, in his or her judgment, by particular moments, stresses, or simply, events. That same nurse, for instance, a little later, remembered a previous time when she'd thus taken stock of herself: "My daughter was graduating from college, and I was *so* happy—not just because she'd got a degree, but because she'd turned out to be the kind of person she is: kind, considerate, loving, a real fine person, everything she should be, if I say so myself—and I know I'm not the best judge of my own child, but I've heard her teachers talk, and her friends, and our minister—and that day, as she came toward us with her academic robe on, and the big smile on her face, I was just plain proud, and as happy as I'll ever be."

Pope's next category is "Pleasure," and in years of medical and psychiatric work, I find that second line of response ever on the minds of today's men and women, especially the young. I happen to give a course at Harvard College (and another, similar one, at Harvard Medical School) titled "Moral and Social Inquiry." We read poets, documentary essayists, and novelists who have, in their own ways, tried to figure out what men and women want out of life, and why. After exposure to the likes of James Agee and George Orwell, Tillie Olsen and Flannery O'Connor, Walker Percy and Ralph Ellison, Dorothy Day and Simone Weil, and, not least, those three marvelous Victorian storytellers, Dickens, George Eliot, and Hardy, the students write their papers; and often enough, the papers are deeply personal: an effort to connect what they've read to what the students are struggling to do, to be. Not rarely, the question of "happiness" comes up.

Here is one young woman saying a few things about a college, a culture, a class of people, and, not least, herself: "I guess I expected to come to school here. I know I sound spoiled, but I was brought up to think I'd go to a good college, an Ivy League school, and that I'd have most of the good things in life, as 'a matter of course.' I put quotation marks around that phrase, because it's my mother's. She would tell us that she expected us to behave, and work hard, but there'd be lots of fun, and if we would just be patient, we'd get all we'd ever want, as 'a matter of course.' And mostly, I just assumed she was right, and we'd get all the joy life has to offer. And that's how it's turned out: I've had just about every opportunity there is, every luxury I've ever wanted. Sometimes, I wonder what's left in life! Is there any enjoyment I *haven't* had? And I get the impression it'll go on and on, until I die: comforts galore!"

I have, in my study of well-to-do children (*Privileged Ones*, the fifth volume of *Children of Crisis*), remarked upon an "entitlement" one sees in such young people, a sense that the world is, indeed, their oyster. Again and again, as I have asked such youths about their hopes or expectations, I end up hearing what they *have*, what they *own*, what they know they will *get*: possessions, sights and sounds, experiences here, there, everywhere, and not least, distractions, entertainment, sex (often called "satisfying relationships").

Pleasure, then, is for many of us happiness: pleasure in possessions, and pleasure in the capital we've accumulated, and pleasure in the authority we wield over others, and pleasure in the involvements we are taught we must have with others. As a Harvard sophomore, an intelligent, good-looking young man let me know once: "For me, a happy life is a life of love! I don't want to get married until I really know what love is; until I've experienced it often enough, so it's unmistakable to me. And I don't want to stay married, if there's no longer love between me and my wife!" Asked what "love" is by a doctor a bit astonished that a nineteen-year-old student should be so emphatic and sure of himself, he replied: "Love is good sex, and it's really caring for the person, and she cares for you. Love is intimacy of body and of mind. You both have to be on the same wavelength. Your vibes are the same as hers, and you feel hers and she feels yours, they're good for each other—the vibes."

So it goes, in the higher realms of our academic life, among many other places. I must say, I don't think that young man completely irregular or atypical. He is a product of a given background, a given era in our country's history: Both parents have had "therapy"; an upper-middle-class home in the Northeast; "sophisticated" in everything—where to eat and what to eat, musical preferences, when to dress this way, when to dress that way, where to stay in which cities, an endless amount of savvy, all of it "extracurricular." As for school, here is how that fits into a life's destiny: "I can't say I *like* school; but it has to be part of my life—just a few years. In the long run, I'll be happy I've stuck it out." When the listener asks him why, the answer is forthcoming: "It'll help with my career. You meet people who are friends for life. You feel more secure, with an education behind you: people look up to you, and that's always a trip!"

Yes, a "trip," a contemporary way of describing happiness: the pleasure of sex, drugs, drink, music, dancing, travel, food, one's appearance, one's social status, one's mailing address, one's college "background"—many "trips." Clearly, this life of the senses, of the "self" that is affirmed endlessly, of me, me, me, addressed in encounter groups and advertising slogans and an entire culture's preferences (be good to yourself, take care of yourself) turns out to be, for many of us, what happiness means: pleasure found, experienced, multiplied. And Pope's next variable, "Ease," is for us much connected to that "pleasure." Such was not, of course, always the case.

Years ago pleasure was not so readily obtained, had to be sought long and hard, and was by no means the mark of an entire "life style." William Carlos Williams, in a letter to a young friend (1950), pointed out that pleasure had to do with time—and not the extent of it some of us might think desirable: "I'm up early, and to bed late, working with my patients all day, and working at my poems or stories at night. It's the long haul that counts! Every once in a while, I'll stop and realize that I'm happy with my doctoring and happy with what I've been writing and happy at home, with my family; but hell, you don't live your life thinking that way. Happiness is an after-thought; it comes after years of putting out the energy, making the commitments, standing by them, through thick and thin."

An American modernist writer, an American physician of this century, Williams was hardly a stoic or a puritan. On the contrary, he was a passionate person whose poetry reveals a constant delight in the everyday things (and people!) of this life. His eye took great pleasure in the natural landscape, and in the human one as well. His ears caught with joy the music of this world—sounds, accents, whispers, outbursts, sheer noise. He could celebrate the sensual. He loved, especially, the feminine side of this earthly existence—women as our bearers, providers, and for him, the incarnation of so very much that is civilized, as opposed to crude and truculent and demanding.

Ever playful with words, but at the same time, dead serious in such fun, Williams once told me: "There are those who bear, and those who overbear," and if such sexually connected, large-scale distinctions now seem outdated or naïve (over thirty years have passed!), then his way of connecting those two categories of "being" to the matter of happiness may still offer us reason for appreciative pause: "Those who bear, who give life and nourish life, and you can do so, if you're a bachelor or a spinster, in the way you care for others—those are the people who find happiness only gradually, in the long run; the others, who are overbearing, grab what they can, pronto, and call it happiness, but they're always grabbing, so there's a discontent there, lots of it!"

The word "discontent" connects, of course, with Pope's last, categorical effort to provide a synonym for happiness: Content. He meant, one assumes, not the dubious contentment of smugness, of pride, of self-importance, but rather a state of mind characterized by a restfulness of sorts with respect to oneself: a self-respect that lasts, and prompts, yes, happiness. Nor is such a "content" feeling only the property of old age. The college students and medical students I teach have come to see me during my office hours and they have told me of decisions they've made (serious ones, indeed) and the subsequent (and consequent!) contentment they've experienced, often to their surprise. One young woman wanted me to know this: "I've struggled for two years about what I'm going to do with myself—my future, my career. I've struggled with my personal life, too: what kind of man will I get *really* serious with, and end up marrying. I don't have the answers for others, not even for my good friends; but I've thought of others, as well as me. And the result is I feel a little better about things—a little peace within myself!"

She was, in her own fashion, indicating that there is a moral side to this life—that happiness has to do, finally, with a leap toward others. To be tactful, considerate, kind-hearted—such old-fashioned virtues bring in their own reward, a kind of self-transcendence that can, indeed, be liberating. No wonder William Carlos Williams, in the Second Book of his long, lyrical poem about American life, "Paterson," exhorted himself and the rest of us: "Outside/outside myself/there is a world . . ." Pure common sense, one says—yet, how often we forget such ordinary wisdom in favor of the latest faddish, egoistic mandate.

"Sometimes I think I'm happiest when I've forgotten myself for a long, long time," a mere eight-year-old black child told me, two decades ago, as she struggled in the face of a hostile mob to enter an all-white Southern school. At the time, I worried hard about what was happening to her psychologically: the fear, the tension, the threats, the evident persisting danger. But she persisted, she endured, and she always and thereafter called that time her "big chance." She had stumbled the hard way upon wisdom, upon grace, upon a kind of release based upon moral purpose; and maybe many of us, so much better off in our lives, may still be waiting for *our* "big chance."

Suggestions for Discussion

1. What qualification of happiness is expressed in the constitution?

2. What was the historical meaning of happiness? How does it differ in more recent times?

3. With what details does the author suggest that happiness has a moral dimension?

4. How does Coles illustrate the relationship of pleasure to happiness?

5. How do the following relate to happiness: possessions, love, education, a "trip," an afterthought, good, contentment.

6. What was Williams's view of happiness?

7. How does Coles use Pope's lines to develop his essay on happiness?

8. Coles's own view of happiness is implicit in his discussion of others' attitudes. What is it?

Suggestions for Writing

1. How valid is the psychoanalyst's belief that when people obtain happiness, they redefine it so they can keep searching?

2. Analyze: "No longer does happiness *happen*; happiness is obtained."

3. What is your definition of happiness? Draw upon comparison and contrast as well as illustrations in developing it.

4. What do you want out of life and what steps are you taking to achieve it?

Tom Wolfe

Mauve Gloves & Madmen, Clutter & Vine

Tom Wolfe (b. 1931) has been called "supercontemporary," "parajournalistic," and the "poet laureate of pop." Probably the most famous of the "new journalists," he is the author of *The Kandy-Kolored Tangerine-Flake Streamline Baby* (1965), *The Electric Kool-Aid Acid Test* (1968), *The Pump House Gang* (1968), *Radical Chic and Mau-Mauing the Flak Catchers* (1970), and *The Right Stuff* (1979). Wolfe's portrait of a writer, *Mauve Gloves & Madmen, Clutter & Vine* (1976), is a satiric commentary on superficial and materialistic values as well as those of the culture.

The well-known American writer . . . but perhaps it's best not to say exactly which well-known American writer . . . they're a sensitive breed! The most ordinary comments they take personally! And why would the gentleman we're about to surprise be any exception? He's in his apartment, a seven-room apartment on Riverside Drive, on the West Side of Manhattan, in his study, seated at his desk. As we approach from the rear, we notice a bald spot on the crown of his head. It's about the size of a Sunshine Chip-a-Roo cookie, this bald spot, freckled and toasty brown. Gloriously suntanned, in fact. Around this bald spot swirls a corona of dark-brown hair that becomes quite thick by the time it completes its mad Byronic rush down the back over his turtleneck and out to the side in great bushes over his ears. He knows the days of covered ears are numbered, because this particular book has become somewhat *Low Rent.* When he was coming back from his father's funeral, half the salesmen lined up at O'Hare for the commuter flights, in their pajama-striped shirts and diamond-print double-knit suits, had groovy hair much like his. And to think that just six years ago such a hairdo seemed . . . so defiant!

Meeting his sideburns at mid-jowl is the neck of his turtleneck sweater, an authentic Navy turtleneck, and the sweater tucks into his Levi's, which are the authentic Original XX Levi's, the original straight stovepipes made for wearing over boots. He got them in a bona fide cowhand's store in La Porte, Texas, during his trip to Houston to be the keynote speaker in a lecture series on "The American Dream: Myth and Reality." No small part of the latter was a fee of two thousand dollars plus expenses. This outfit, the Navy turtleneck and the double-X Levi's, means work & discipline. *Discipline!* as he says to himself every day. When he puts on these clothes, it means that he intends to write, and do nothing else, for at least four hours. *Discipline,* Mr. Wonderful!

But on the desk in front of him—that's not a manuscript or even the beginnings of one . . . that's *last month's bank statement,* which just arrived in the mail. And those are his canceled checks in a pile on top of it. In that big ledger-style checkbook there (the old-fashioned kind, serious-looking, with no crazy Peter Max designs on the checks) are his check stubs. And those slips of paper in the promiscuous heap are all unpaid bills, and he's taking the nylon cover off his Texas Instruments desk calculator, and he is about to measure the flow, the tide, the mad sluice, the crazy current of the money that pours through his fingers every month and which is now running against him in the most catastrophic manner, like an undertow, a riptide, pulling him under—

—him and this apartment, which cost him $75,000 in 1972; $20,000 cash, which came out of the $25,000 he got as a paperback advance for his fourth book, *Under Uncle's Thumb,* and $536.36 a month in bank-loan payments (on the $55,000 he borrowed) ever since, plus another $390 a month in so-called maintenance, which has steadily increased until it is now $460 a month . . . and although he already knows the answer, the round number, he begins punching the figures into the calculator . . . 536.36 plus . . . 460 . . . times 12 . . . and the calculator keys go *chuck chuck chuck chuck* and the curious little orange numbers, broken up like stencil figures, go trucking across the black path of the display panel at the top of the machine, giving a little orange shudder every time he hits the *plus* button, until there it is, stretching out seven digits long—11956.32—$12,000 a year! One thousand dollars a month—this is what he spends on his apartment alone! and by May he will have to come up with another $6,000 so he can rent the house on Martha's Vineyard again *chuck chuck chuck chuck* and by September another $6,750— $3,750 to send his daughter, Amy, to Dalton and $3,000 to send his son, Jonathan, to Collegiate (on those marvelous frog-and-cricket evenings up on the Vineyard he and Bill and Julie and Scott and Henry and Herman and Leon and Shelly and the rest, all Media & Lit. people from New York, have discussed why they send their children to private schools, and they have pretty well decided that it is the educational turmoil in the New York public schools that is the problem—the kids just wouldn't be educated!—plus some considerations of their children's personal safety—but—needless to say!—it has nothing to do with the matter of . . . well, *race*) and he punches that in . . . 6750 . . . *chuck chuck chuck chuck* . . . and hits the *plus* button . . . an orange shimmer . . . and beautiful! there's the figure—the three items, the apartment in town, the summer place, and the children's schooling— $24,706.32!—almost $25,000 a year in fixed costs, just for a starter! for lodging and schooling! nothing else included! A grim nut!

It's appalling, and he's drowning, and this is only the beginning of it, just the basic grim nut—and yet in his secret heart he loves these little sessions with the calculator and the checks and the stubs and the bills and the marching orange numbers that stretch on and on . . . into such magnificently huge figures. It's like an electric diagram of his infinitely expanding life, a score-board showing the big league he's now in. Far from throwing him into a panic, as they well might, these tote sessions are one of the most satisfying habits he has. A regular vice! Like barbiturates! Calming the heart and slowing the respiration! Because it seems *practical,* going over expenses, his conscience sanctions it as a permissible way to avoid the only thing that can possibly keep him afloat: namely, more writing . . . He's deep into his calculator trance now . . . The orange has him enthralled. Think of it! He has now reached a stage in his life when not only a $1,000-a-month apartment but also a summer house on an island in the Atlantic is an absolute necessity—precisely that, absolute necessity . . . It's appalling!—and yet it's the most inexplicable bliss!—nothing less.

As for the apartment, even at $1,000 a month it is not elegant. Elegance would cost at least twice that. No, his is an apartment of a sort known as West Side Married Intellectual. The rooms are big, the layout is good, but the moldings, cornices, covings, and chair rails seem to be corroding. Actually, they are merely lumpy from too many coats of paint over the decades, and the parquet sections in the floor have dried out and are sprung loose from one another. It has been a long time since this apartment has had an owner who could both meet the down-payment nut *and* have the woodwork stripped and the flooring replaced. The building has a doorman but no elevator man, and on Sundays the door is manned by a janitor in gray khaki work clothes. But what's he supposed to do? He needs seven rooms. His son and daughter now require separate bedrooms. He and his wife require a third one (a third and fourth if the truth be known, but he has had to settle for three). He now needs, not just likes, this study he's in, a workroom that is his exclusively. He now *needs* the dining room, which is a real dining room, not a dogleg off the living room. Even if he is giving only a cocktail party, it is . . . *necessary* that they (one & all) note—however unconsciously—that he *does* have a dining room!

Right here on his desk are the canceled checks that have come in hung over from the cocktail party he gave six weeks ago. They're right in front of him now . . . $209.60 to the florists, Clutter & Vine, for flowers for the hallway, the living room, the dining room, and the study, although part of that, $100, was for a bowl of tightly clustered silk poppies that will become a permanent part of the living-room decor . . . $138.18 to the liquor store (quite a bit was left over however, meaning that the bar will be stocked for a while) . . . $257.50 to Mauve Gloves & Madmen, the caterers, even though he had chosen some of the cheaper hors d'oeuvres. He also tipped the two butlers $10 each, which made him feel a little foolish later when he learned that one of them was co-owner of Mauve Gloves & Madmen . . . $23.91 to the grocery store for he couldn't remember what . . . $173.95 to the Russian Tea Room for dinner afterward with Henry and Mavis (the guests of honor) and six other stragglers . . . $12.84 for a serving bowl from Bloomingdale's . . . $20 extra to the maid for staying on late . . . and he's chucking all these figures into the calculator *chuck chuck chuck chuck* blink blink blink blink *truck truck truck truck* the slanted orange numbers go trucking and winking across the panel . . . 855.98 . . . $855.98 for a cocktail party!—not even a dinner party!—appalling!—and how slyly sweet . . .

Should he throw in the library stairs as a party expense, too? Perhaps, he thought, if he were honest, he would. The checks were right here: $420 to Lum B. Lee Ltd. for the stairs themselves, and another $95 to the customs broker to get the thing through customs and $45 to the trucker to deliver it making a total of $560! In any event, they're terrific . . . Mayfair heaven . . . the classic English type, stairs to nowhere, going up in a spiral around a central column, carved in the ancient bamboo style, rising up almost seven feet, so he can reach books on his highest shelf . . . He had had it made extra high by a cabinetmaking firm in Hong Kong, the aforementioned Lum B. Lee . . . Now, if the truth be known, the stairs are the result of a habit he has: he goes around the apartment after giving a party and stands where he saw particular guests standing, people who stuck in his mind, and tries to see what they saw from that position; in other words, how the apartment looked in their eyes. About a year ago he has seen Lenny Johns of the *Times* standing in the doorway of his study and looking in, so afterward, after Lenny and everyone else had gone, he took up the same position and looked in . . . and what he saw did not please him. In fact, it looked sad. Through Lenny Johns's eyes it must have looked like the basic writer's workroom out of *Writer's Digest:* a plain Danish-style desk (The Door Store) with dowel legs (dowel legs!), a modernistic (modernistic!) metal-and-upholstery office swivel chair, a low-slung (more Modernismus!) couch, a bank of undistinguished-looking file cabinets, a bookcase covering one entire wall but made of plain white-painted boards and using the wall itself as its back. The solution, as he saw it—without going into huge costs—was the library stairs—the stairs to nowhere!—an object indisputably useful and yet with an air of elegant folly!

It was after that same party that his wife had said to him: "Who was that weepy-looking little man you were talking to so much?"

"I don't know who you're talking about."

"The one with the three strands of hair pulled up from the side and draped over his scalp."

He knew she was talking about Johns. And he knew *she* knew Johns's name. She had met him before, on the Vineyard.

Meeting Lenny Johns socially was one of the many dividends of Martha's Vineyard. They have been going there for three summers now, renting a house on a hill on Chilmark . . . until it has become, well a *necessity!* It's no longer possible to stay in New York over the summer. It's not fair to the children. They shouldn't have to grow up that way. As for himself, he's gotten to know Lenny and Bill and Scott and Julie and Bob and Dick and Jody and Gillian and Frank and Shelly and the rest in a way that wouldn't be possible in New York. But quite aside from all that . . . just that clear sparkling late-August solitude, when you can smell the pine and the sea . . . heading down the piney path from the house on the hill . . . walking two hundred yards across the marshes on the pedestrian dock, just one plank wide, so that you have to keep staring down at it . . . it's hypnotic . . . the board, the marsh grass, your own tread, the sound of the frogs and the crickets . . . and then getting into the rowboat and rowing across the inlet to . . . the *dune* . . . the great swelling dune, with the dune grass waving against the sky on top . . . and then over the lip of it—to the beach! the most pristine white beach in the world! and the open sea . . . all spread out before you—yours! Just that! the sand, the sea, the sky—and solitude! No gates, no lifeguard stands, no concessions, no sprawling multitudes of transistor radios and plaid plastic beach chairs . . .

It is chiefly for these summers on the Vineyard that he has bought a car, a BMW sedan—$7,200—but very lively! It costs him $76 a month to keep it in a garage in the city for nine months of the year, another $674 in all, so that the hard nut for Martha's Vineyard is really $6,684—but it's a necessity, and one sacrifices for necessities. After three years on the Vineyard he feels very possessive about the place, even though he's a renter, and he immediately joined in with the move to publish a protest against "that little Albanian with a pickup truck," as he was (wrongly) called, some character named Zarno or something who had assembled a block of fifty acres on the Vineyard and was going to develop it into 150 building lots—one third of an acre each! (Only dimly did he recall that the house he grew up in, in Chicago, had been on about one fifth of an acre and hadn't seemed terribly hemmed in.) Bill T— wrote a terrific manifesto in which he talked about "these Snopes-like little men with their pickup trucks"—Snopes-like!—and all sorts of people signed it.

This campaign against the developers also brought the New York Media & Lit. people into contact for the first time with the Boston people. Until the Media & Lit. people began going there about ten years before, Martha's Vineyard had always been a Boston resort, "Boston" in the most proper social sense of the word. There wasn't much the Boston people could do about the New York people except not associate with them. When they said "New York people," they no doubt meant "Jews & Others," he figured. So when he was first invited to a Boston party, thanks to his interest in the antidevelopers campaign, he went with some trepidation and with his resentment tucked into his waistband like a .38. His mood darkened still more when he arrived in white ducks and an embroidered white cotton shirt, yoke-shouldered and open to the sternum—a little eccentric (actually a harmless sort of shirt known in Arizona as Fruit Western) but perfectly in the mood of standard New York People Seaside Funk—and found that the Boston men, to a man, had on jackets and ties. Not only that, they had on their own tribal colors. The jackets were mostly navy blazers, and the ties were mostly striped ties or ties with little jacquard emblems on them, but the pants had a go-to-hell air: checks and plaids of the loudest possible sort, madras plaids, yellow-on-orange windowpane checks, crazy-quilt plaids, giant houndstooth checks, or else they were a solid airmail red or taxi yellow or some other implausible go-to-hell color. They finished that off with loafers and white crew socks or no socks at all. The pants were their note of Haitian abandon . . . weekends by the sea. At the same time the jackets and ties showed they had not forgotten for a moment where the power came from. He felt desolate. He slipped the loaded resentment out of his waistband and cocked it. And then the most amazing thing happened—

His hostess came up and made a fuss over him! Exactly! She had read *Under Uncle's Thumb!* So had quite a few of the men, infernal pants and all! Lawyers and investment counselors! They were all interested in him! Quite a stream—he hardly had to move from the one spot all evening! And as the sun went down over the ocean, and the alcohol rose, and all of their basted teeth glistened—he could almost see something . . . *presque vu!* . . . a glimmer of the future . . . something he could barely make out . . . a vision in which America's best minds, her intellectuals, found a common ground, a natural unity, with the enlightened segments of her old aristocracy, her old money . . . the two groups bound together by . . . but by what? . . . he could *almost* see it, but not quite . . . it was *presque vu* . . . it was somehow a matter of taste . . . of sensibility . . . of grace, natural grace . . . just as he himself had a natural feel for the best British styles, which were after all the source of the Boston manners . . . What were the library stairs, if they weren't that? What were the Lobb shoes?

For here, now, surfacing to the top of the pile, is the check for $248 to John Lobb & Sons Ltd. Boot Makers—that was the way he wrote it out, Boot Makers, two words, the way it was on their bosky florid London letterhead—$248!—for one pair of shoes!—from England!—handmade! And now, all at once, even as *chuck chuck chuck* he punches it into the calculator, he is swept by a wave of sentiment, of sadness, sweet misery—guilt! Two hundred and forty-eight dollars for a pair of handmade shoes from England . . . He thinks of his father. He wore his first pair of Lobb shoes to his father's funeral. Black cap toes they were, the most formal daytime shoes made, and it was pouring that day in Chicago and his incomparable new shoes from England were caked with mud when he got back to his father's house. He took the shoes off, but then he froze—he couldn't bring himself to remove the mud. His father had come to the United States from Russia as a young man in 1922. He had to go to work at once, and in no time, it seemed, came the Depression, and he struggled through it as a tailor, although in the forties he acquired a dry-cleaning establishment and, later, a second one, plus a diaper-service business and a hotel-linen service. But this brilliant man—oh, how many times had his mother assured him of that!—had had to spend all those years as a tailor. This cultivated man!—more assurances—oh, how many yards of Goethe and Dante had he heard him quote in an accent that gripped the English language like a full nelson! And now his son, the son of this brilliant, cultivated but uneducated and thwarted man—now his son, his son with his education and his literary career, his son who had never had to work with his hands more than half an hour at a stretch in his life—his son had turned up at his funeral in a pair of handmade shoes from England! . . . Well, he let the mud dry on them. He didn't touch them for six months. He didn't even put the shoe trees (another $47) in. Perhaps the goddamned boots would curl up and die.

The number . . . 248 . . . is sitting right up there in slanted orange digits on the face of the calculator. That seems to end the reverie. He doesn't want to continue it just now. He doesn't want to see the 6684 for Martha's Vineyard up there again for a while. He doesn't want to see the seven digits of his debts (counting the ones after the decimal point) glowing in their full, magnificent, intoxicating length. It's time to get serious! *Discipline!* Only one thing will pull him out of all this: work . . . writing . . . and there's no way to put it off any longer. *Discipline*, Mr. Wonderful! This is the most difficult day of all, the day when it falls to his lot to put a piece of paper in the typewriter and start on page 1 of a new book, with that horrible arthritic siege—writing a book!—stretching out ahead of him (a tubercular blue glow, as his mind comprehends it) . . . although it lifts his spirits a bit to know that both *The Atlantic* and *Playboy* have expressed an interest in running chapters as he goes along, and *Penthouse* would pay even more, although he doesn't want it to appear in a one-hand magazine, a household aid, as literary penicillin to help quell the spirochetes oozing from all the virulent vulvas . . . Nevertheless! help is on the way! Hell!—there's not a magazine in America that wouldn't publish something from this book!

So he feeds a sheet of paper into his typewriter, and in the center, one third of the way down from the top, he takes care of the easy part first—the working title, in capital letters:

RECESSION AND REPRESSION
POLICE STATE AMERICA
AND THE SPIRIT OF '76

Suggestions for Discussion

1. How do the details of the writer's hair and clothes give you a sense of his personality? What do they tell you of Wolfe's view of him?

2. What is the tone conveyed in the paragraphs on the writer's finances?

3. How do you explain the writer's sense that his expenses are appalling and at the same time provide "inexplicable bliss"?

4. With what details do you learn that what others think is important to the writer?

5. What purpose is served by the repetition of the phrase "needs, not just likes"?

6. What does the importing of the library stairs contribute to your understanding of the writer's character?

7. With what details do you learn why Martha's Vineyard was "a necessity"?

8. How does Wolfe regard the Boston people? How does the writer view them?

9. Identify ironical and satiric elements in the essay.

10. Discuss the ways in which Wolfe's figurative language affects the tone and substance of the essay.

11. How does the sentence structure reflect the writer's state of mind?

12. What is the significance of the title?

13. What are the writer's values?

14. Why is the writer never named?

Suggestions for Writing

1. Discuss the shifts in your purchases from mere *likes* to *needs*.

2. Analyze the values of the writer as portrayed in this essay. What is your attitude toward them?

Norman Cousins
Beyond Invalidism

Norman Cousins (b. 1912) served as editor of *The Saturday Review* for over thirty-five years and wrote weekly editorials on the most significant issues of our times. In response to our use of the atomic bomb on Hiroshima he wrote *Modern Man Is Obsolete* (1945). More recently he wrote *Anatomy of an Illness* (1982) and *The Healing Heart* (1983). He is currently serving as Adjunct Professor in the School of Medicine at the University of California at Los Angeles. In this excerpt from *The Healing Heart* Cousins places responsibility upon individuals to put all of their powers to work in their own behalf.

The sense of being locked into a body that is inadequate for its needs, the sense of living under a lowering ceiling, the sense of having to separate oneself from vital prospects, the sense of coming to terms with bleakness—all these are the stuff of invalidism. The person who is put on notice by the physician that he or she has a "bad heart" tends to live a life of reduced expectations, to take slower and fewer steps, and to move more tentatively in the outside world.

How does one avoid the feeling of being an invalid when underlying conditions create and indeed seem to dictate it? When a physician tells you that your heart is weak and must be spared the strains that other people routinely and joyously bear, how do you go through life without flinching when you approach stairs or hilly streets or children reaching out to be lifted?

Perhaps the best way to answer these questions is to begin by reflecting on the way the human body works. A weak body becomes weaker in a mood of total surrender. The mechanisms of repair and rehabilitation that are built into the human system have a natural drive to assert themselves under conditions of illness, but that natural tendency is deferred or deflected by an erosion of the will to live, or by the absence of confidence in one's physician or in one's own ability to play a vital part in the attack on disease.

Obviously, it is absurd to suppose that there is no illness or somber circumstance that can't be reversed. But it is also true that under conditions of extreme illness we need all the help we can get. For the same reason it is necessary to put all our own powers to work in our own behalf. We want to get the most out of whatever is possible. An integral part of this process is respect for the human body—an organism of astounding tenacity, resiliency, and recuperative capability. And, since the human body tends to move in the direction of its expectations—plus or minus—it is important to know that attitudes of confidence and determination are no less a part of the treatment program than medical science and technology.

The day after I came home from the hospital, I arranged with a building contractor to construct a new study and storage facility for all the *Saturday Review* files and other books and records that had been moved out from the East. The only place available for the new construction was above a steep hill in back of the house. This meant I would have to climb the equivalent of four flights of stairs every time I wanted to go to the study.

The building was completed in about three months. I have never felt the slightest hesitation in making the ascent, which I have done at least twice daily. The sense of pleasurable anticipation is enough to allow me to endure any strain.

I do know this, however: if I had any distasteful expectations or reactions, my body would supply all the signs of chest pressure to accommodate that distaste. More and more, I am inclined to accept the notion that the body produces its own poisons under circumstances of apprehension or emotional strain and that this factor is intimately involved in serious illness, whether it takes the form of cardiac disease, joint disabilities, or even cancer. The title of Kenneth Pelletier's book *Mind as Healer, Mind as Slayer* may say it all.

Nothing is more amazing or heartening to me than to see the way in which many persons with severe afflictions or handicaps nonetheless manage to affirm life. Just in the act of mobilizing their emotional resources they help to potentiate themselves physically. I am not saying here that no one ever need feel disadvantaged; all I am doing is making a distinction between being an invalid and thinking and acting like one.

I know that I am still at risk. I know that, without warning, my heart could suddenly fail. If that should happen, I will have no complaints. As I told Dr. Shine, I have nothing but gratitude for a heart that has seen me through an eventful life and several medical ordeals, beginning in childhood.

Death is not the enemy; living in constant fear of it is. I have no intention of swathing myself in cotton to soften a possibly fatal episode. I will continue to live and think as actively and creatively as it is physically possible for me to do, knowing that longevity by itself can be sterile but that vital feelings and thoughts give meaning and depth to life and provide a true sense of the possibilities of human existence.

I have already lived more than an average lifetime, but I want to continue to live long enough to see the establishment of a world under law and a planet made safe and fit for human habitation. I hope, too, to live long enough to see the conquest of human squalor. What stands in the way is not insufficiency of natural resources but the way people choose to think about their problems and opportunities. In any event, I am grateful that I am able to continue working for those causes that seek to free our age from gross indignities and the fear of nuclear devastation.

What seems especially important to me in retrospect is that I am the beneficiary of the best that modern medical science has to offer. For many years, deaths from heart attacks have outnumbered fatalities from all other diseases. That number is now on the decline and will, I believe, decline further still with the full recognition, not just by the profession but by the general public, that a comprehensive program of treatment involves both the full utilization of medical science and the full development of the human healing system. The fact that the belief system can be a vital activator of the healing system may open the door to an auspicious future in medical research and practice.

I look up at the calendar as I put down these final notes and see that it is two years and five months since the heart attack of December 22, 1980. Dr. Shine has gone out of his way to congratulate me, using the word "magnificent" to describe my progress, even though he feels I may still be at substantial risk. Dr. Cannom does not refute the fact of ongoing risk but sees no evidence that my heart is not getting all the blood and oxygen my life style requires. The portion of the heart muscle that was destroyed during the heart attack will not regenerate, but the rest of the heart muscle has been strengthened and has adapted itself to my needs. Dr. Cannom says it is difficult to believe that bypass surgery could have achieved a better functional result than has been achieved without it. The original treadmill results that produced the finding of severe coronary insufficiency have been reversed.

I manage to set aside time each week for the sports I enjoy—doubles or singles in tennis, and golf with old friends. Golf does not really qualify as exercise, but it is a game that offers tangible and tantalizing possibilities for measurable improvement of one's skill. Besides, it provides an arena for banter and the rewards of companionship in an outdoor setting. I maintain a full working schedule, and I pay visits to the hospital at the request of physicians to see ill persons in need of a morale boost. The difference between what I did before the heart attack and what I am doing now is that I now maintain some semblance of control. I try to run my schedule instead of letting the schedule run me.

What is to me most fascinating of all in retrospect about the entire episode is the evidence that it is possible for the heart to create its own bypass. A surgical bypass would have removed portions of veins from my leg and substituted them for the clogged portions of arteries going into the heart. The way nature accomplishes the same purpose is twofold. In response to the systematic regimen of careful diet, regular exercise, control of stress, and a philosophy of life that provides ample nourishment for the generous appetite of the spirit, the body slowly creates a rich network of new blood vessels across the heart, bypassing the deficient arteries with new conduits of its own, carrying the life-giving blood and oxygen.

The second way the damaged heart tries to meet its needs is through increased arterial flow. Not all medical opinion holds that arteries, once clogged, can never become unclogged. Scientific research has not yet established beyond question that the clogging substances will dissolve naturally. But what has been established is that even a little widening or clearing will accommodate a disproportionately larger blood flow. Some cardiologists believe that a course of action that does not add to the clogging will produce some shrinkage—enough, at least to make possible such enhanced circulation.

Neither of those two processes is automatic. The ability of the heart to function in these ways does not become manifest under ordinary circumstances. Sometimes, indeed, the effects of blockage are so pervasive that surgical bypass is absolutely required to save a life. But a stern and unyielding regimen combining diet, exercise, and positive attitudes with the natural drive of the body to heal and regenerate can sometimes produce amazing results. So long as progress in this direction is discernible, it is reasonable to try to extend it as far as it will go. It is like the case of the stalled car that needs a push to give it enough momentum so that the gears, when engaged, can start the engine.

As I said earlier, I was extremely reluctant to undergo heart surgery; I wanted to see whether significant improvement was possible without it. If such improvement had not taken place, I would have accepted the option of surgery. The course I pursued was not an easy one; it should not be adopted by anyone who is not prepared to accept its highly disciplined requirements. Nor does my experience mean that what I did would necessarily work just as well for others.

The belief that illness is something that comes into us from the outside—a sort of hostile organism or substance that gains entry—is so firmly ingrained in us that we naturally look to available outside forces to do battle with it and evict it. Since we are attacked from without we tend to believe we can be rescued only from without. We have little knowledge of, and therefore little confidence in, the numberless ways the human body goes about righting itself. The absence of such knowledge leads not only to excessive dependence on external agencies but also to undue fears and even panic, which interfere with the proper functioning of the restorative mechanisms.

The role of the physician needs to be properly understood. The physician is best qualified to determine what is wrong and to intervene to whatever extent is necessary. In doing so, however, he combines his resources with the resources of the patient.

Dr. Ingelfinger, the late editor of the *New England Journal of Medicine*, wrote that about 85 percent of the patients the physician is called upon to treat have self-limiting illnesses. That is, the human body is equipped to meet most of its own health problems. The doctor's job is to distinguish between the 85 percent that don't really need his ministrations and the 15 percent that do. The physician must then decide exactly what is required to reassure the 85 percent and to mobilize his knowledge and skills in dealing with the 15 percent.

In any case, a distinction must be made between the treating process and the healing process. The treating process seeks to do that which the body itself may be incapable of doing, but at the same time attempts, to the fullest possible extent, to restore the body's own healing capabilities. The notion that the center of the healing process is lodged with the physician is incorrect. It is lodged within the individual, and the wise physician knows how to summon and release it. The individual cannot expect to be relieved of all responsibility in the recovery effort. If he looks completely outside himself for help, he places an unreasonably large part of the burden on the physician and may retard his own recovery to that extent.

What can the individual do? First of all, it is important to be aware of the body's natural drive to heal itself, once freed of the provocations that played a part in bringing on the illness. If a person has a heart attack, for example, the first order of business is to attempt to perceive possible connections between that heart attack and the precipitating causes. If, as in my case, I was engaged in a losing war against congested highways, airport mazes, delayed check-ins, overbooked planes, lost luggage, and late lecture arrivals, it was up to me to tame the schedule and make the necessary adjustments. Also, if my body craved exercise it was not receiving, only I was in a position to satisfy that want. And if my physical nourishment had to be augmented with nutrients for the mind, including joyous thoughts and experiences, I could not expect others to meet those needs for me.

Each individual presides over the totality of himself or herself. Assuming life is worth living—and the act of reaching out for medical help is proof positive that we think it is—it is imperative that we take on that part of the battle that is uniquely ours. It is a serious error to think of medical treatment as a total answer to all the problems of illness. In the end, the war against serious illness calls not only for expert medical attention but also for a summoning of values. Victory may not always be possible—if it were, we would all live forever—but it is sometimes within reach even in cases when the conventional wisdom holds the opposite.

It is in this sense that we retain control—recognizing the existence of resources represented by the healing system and the belief system that activates it. And the belief system is not just a collection of mechanical parts but a confluence of values and attitudes—hope, faith, confidence, purpose, will to live, and a capacity for joyous living.

Few of us will pass through this lifetime without the challenge of one or more serious illnesses. We need not feel angry or guilty when that illness occurs, nor is it reasonable to expect that recovery is always within easy reach. But we have the obligation to ourselves and those we love not to invite defeat by being defeatist.

If it is true that nothing is more striking about how the human body functions than its regenerative drive, it is also true that the regenerative drive works better under some circumstances than others. What we think, what we believe, what we eat, and what we do with our bodies are all involved in the circumstances of regeneration.

If it is important to avoid a sense of defeat, it is equally important to avoid a sense of guilt when progress or recovery may not be possible. Although we want to be able to mobilize all the resources inside us and make the fullest use of the resources outside us, there are times when disease cannot be reversed. We need not feel, at such times, that we have somehow failed, or that our faith and hope were insufficient to our requirements. Nor need we feel that personal adequacy or character is measured only by the ability to prevail.

The ultimate truth about life is that it is transient. We have a certain margin for the pursuit of our aims; we have powerful natural assets in the form of the will to live and a joyous response to life. These assets serve us well and help us to make the most out of ourselves; but they are not eternal elixirs. To feel despair or guilt because we may not always be successful in overcoming illness is to put ourselves above the basic laws of life.

We are not capable of banishing death. The final triumph is beyond us. But we are entitled to the fullest measure of help the world has to offer, just as those who are close to us are entitled to feel that we ourselves have offered the best within us. Death becomes tragic only when we have allowed things to die inside us that give meaning to life.

Even when the verdict is certain, we are not barred from the exercise of powers that rarely come into play at other times. I think of Hans Zinsser, the physician-philosopher, stricken with incurable illness, writing about the wide range of new perceptions that enabled him to sense and see things he had never sensed or seen before. His book *As I Remember Him* is a tribute not just to the man but to the uniqueness of human life.

"My mind is more alive and vivid than ever before," he wrote during his illness in a passage remarkably similar to L. E. Trombley's observations quoted earlier in this book. "My sensitivities are keener; my affections stronger. I seem for the first time to see the world in clear perspective. I love people more deeply and comprehensively. I seem to be just beginning to learn my business and see my work in its proper relationship to science as a whole. I seem to myself to have entered into a period of stronger feelings and saner understanding."

Zinsser made an important discovery about life—the way time can be transformed into energy. Time is the most important capital we own. We can lose great fortunes, and, if we are lucky, we may be able to regain them. But time is the only source of wealth which, once spent, can never be regained. There is only a finite amount of it for every person. "Ask me for anything," Napoleon is supposed to have said at the height of his power, "and I will be able to give it to you. Anything, that is, except time."

The way we choose to live and the depth of our feelings, our ability to love and be loved and to take in all the colors of the world around us—these determine the worth and true extent of whatever time we have. The clock keeps ticking away. Our job is to put as much meaning as possible into the intervals between the ticks. A minute can open out into a vast realm in which all our senses, finely attuned, can come into full and splendid play—or those same senses can be shut down, imparting nothing to our years except numbers.

What makes time so valuable is that it is convertible into nourishing memory. Memory is where the proof of life is stored. It offers material for stocktaking and provides clues about where our lives are going. Serious illness can be redemptive if it opens the sluices of vital memory, sharpens the focus, transforms the improbable into the possible, and imparts a quality of high art to the gift of time.

Suggestions for Discussion

1. How does one avoid invalidism?

2. How would you describe Cousins's method of persuasion?

3. What arguments does Cousins offer for moving in the direction of one's expectations? What does he mean by such movement?

4. With what details does the author describe his resolve to forestall the fear of death?

5. What values in life does Cousins affirm?

6. On what basis does he warn the reader against dependence upon external agencies?

7. How does Cousins distinguish between the healing process and the treating process?

8. How does Cousins relate the war against serious illness to a summoning of values?

9. Sum up Cousins's thesis in a single statement.

Suggestions for Writing

1. By drawing upon your own experience or your observation of others, evaluate one or more of Cousins's conclusions.

2. In his last paragraph Cousins attests to the importance of memory. Reread the paragraph and develop its theme by referring to your own experience.

3. What pleasures that Cousins cherishes do you share and why?

4. Describe a physician you know and his approach to the "soft" side of medicine.

5. Discuss the components of an ideal patient–physician relationship.

Saul Bellow

Lives of Organized Terror

Saul Bellow (b. 1915) is a professor in the Department of Social Thought at the University of Chicago. Among his novels are *The Adventures of Augie Marsh,* (1953), *Seize the Day* (1956), *Herzog,* (1964), and *The Dean's December* (1982). He won the Nobel Prize for literature in 1976. In his response to an interview (published 1982) the author expresses his belief that only through literature, philosophy, and religion are we able to think about brutality and savagery.

Hundreds of millions of people in the 20th century have been murdered—in the Chinese revolution, in Stalin's terror, in Cambodia, in the Horn of Africa, in Latin America, and on and on. We are all highly conscious creatures, and we know that this is what goes on. Yet we are inclined to cancel out horror after horror. We say: "What are the sufferings of x compared with those of *y*? What are the sufferings of the Gulag inmates compared with those of Auschwitz?" An immense mass of suffering is eliminated in this way. Total-itarianism has taught us this.

We have become used to brutality and savagery. Human life has been described in those terms ever since Machiavelli and Hobbes. Then, in the 19th century, Marx promised that it would be OK after the victory of the proletariat. Finally, there was the actual application of those principles in cold blood by Lenin and the advent of Hitler, who described himself as a socialist.

As a writer, I struggle with these facts. I'm preoccupied with the way in which value is—or is not—assigned to human life. A writer comes to feel that there is a way of grasping these horrors that is peculiar to poetry, drama and fiction. I don't admit the defeat of the humane tradition.

How are we going to think about these events and facts without literature, philosophy and religion? Without these, we have no way to think about them.

Yet in America we persist in turning over these problems to experts. We had Great Society programs that raised money and turned it over to the peo-ple who *knew* how to solve human problems—the experts.

I remember former Senator Jacob Javits of New York saying to a confer-ence of so-called intellectuals: "You guys have a duty, a solemn obligation, to give us the answers." Well, *those* guys have no answers. They were trained in departments of education or social-service adminstration or psychology, but they didn't know how to deal with the big human questions.

Today there's shock and disillusionment at the failure of the experts, but the experts failed in part because *they were experts.* They were devoid of the humanistic knowledge that comes from literature, philosophy, and the classics of history. It's not that writers of novels have the answers, but to pose the questions significantly—*that* writers can do.

People today in the cities feel isolation and powerlessness. They can feel their weakness, their impotency, and their entrapment. They don't know what to do.

A woman comes up to me in my neighborhood on the North Side of Chi-cago and says: "My husband and I worked very hard to bring up the children. We bought this condominium, and now look what's happening right across the way. I can't even go across the street to shop. My neighbor's arm was broken by a purse snatcher because she had the strap wound around her arm. I can't have my grown daughters come here from the suburbs to see us, because I am afraid for them. We thought we were providing for our old age, and we are trapped here now."

Now, I ask: Who discusses these questions? Who has the answers? People sit at home in terror and read horror stories for diversion or watch violent TV programs. But what to do? Really, matters have gotten out of hand.

I'm not saying that cities are doomed places, but I will say that the hard core of the welfare society is doomed. There are no prospects for these peo-ple. Nobody ever took the trouble to teach them anything. They live in a kind of perpetual chaos, in a great noise. And, you know, they really are startled souls. They cannot be reasoned with or talked to about anything.

Isn't it time for us to admit this? For a long time, the subject lay under a taboo. Nobody was going to talk about it. Now people are beginning to do so. Though I consider myself a kind of liberal, I have to admit that the taboos were partly of liberal origin. It was supposed to be wrong to speak with candor. But lying in a good cause only aggravates disorder.

There's a scheme of evasion that has gotten into everybody. It's as though people were to say: "I get home dog tired after a terrible day out in that jungle, and then I don't want to think about it. Enough! I want to be brainwashed. I'm going to have my dinner and drink some beer, and I'm going to sit watching TV until I pass out—because that's how I feel." That means people are not putting up a struggle for the human part of themselves.

People have organized the terror in such a way as to expel it from their lives with doormen, security precautions, alarm systems. They don't go out at night. They avoid walking in certain streets. Many are only half aware that they have done this; it's only half conscious, not fully real. What's real is the daily grind, hardships, and ailments, tax questions, the traffic, how long you have to wait for the elevator—all these little things. Those are real.

In spite of all this, when we think of what human beings really are, the sublimity of their greatest powers, the capacities of the least of them, even the most criminal—human powers in an inverted form—we can't fail to be impressed.

In the United States, freedom became corrupted through its abuses. In the 1960s, the individual was told: "You have a life, and now you have autonomy to regulate it. Now, go ahead." Very few people were able to do it. Everything was happening so fast.

A guy came to New York from Butte, Mont., and found himself an executive in an industry that didn't exist when he was at school. Now he has to live up to his position. He has to learn to be an executive. He has to find out how to dress and what car to buy and how to entertain his colleagues or seduce their wives. So he starts to read certain magazines and join this club and that to get advice.

You call that self-regulation? I call it chaos.

We've lost the penumbra of private inviolability and mystery that used to surround people. We are sort of ciphers under a 200-watt bulb.

I was reading Tolstoy the other night. There you have a sense of the gradualness that is natural to human beings—of the way in which they think or feel things through. When you read about people in Tolstoy, you're aware that you approach them through a territory of their own. There is a private sphere that surrounds them.

In modern times, all that has been wiped out. Everything has been done brutally and in haste and processed quickly. We are divested of the deeper human meaning that has traditionally been attached to human life. So it becomes possible to send people to extermination camps because their lives don't have any meaning.

There's no sacred space around human beings anymore. It's not necessary to approach them with the tentativeness and respect that civilization always accorded them. People now are out there in the open. They're fair game. This is true in many spheres, including our sexual life and the education of our children. We are turning the kids over to the computers to be taught. This is proof that the teacher, with his or her penumbra, doesn't matter anymore. You learn everything you need to know from a box.

Our humanity is at risk. It's too powerful a thing to just lie down and give up the ghost. But we have to face the fact it is in danger. It is at risk because the feeling that life is sacred has died away in this century.

Suggestions for Discussion

1. Why does the author believe that only through literature, philosophy, and religion are we able to think about brutality and savagery?

2. Account for Bellow's attitude toward the experts. What is the meaning of the statement: ". . . the experts failed in part because *they were experts*"?

3. How does the author support his belief that "People have organized the terror in such a way as to expel it from their lives"?

4. What evidences are there in this article that Bellow was responding to an interview rather than writing a formal essay?

5. Find examples of both cynicism and optimism about the human race.

6. How does Bellow distinguish between self-regulation and chaos?

7. What does Bellow mean by his metaphor: "we are sort of ciphers under a 200-watt bulb"?

8. How does Bellow's allusion to Tolstoy support his thesis?

Suggestions for Writing

1. How do you assign value to human life?

2. Discuss a novel in which significant questions are posed and illuminated.

3. Discuss the relative merits of teaching by computer versus "by the teacher, with his or her penumbra."

Henry David Thoreau
Why I Went to the Woods

Henry David Thoreau (1817–1862) was a philosopher and poet-naturalist whose independent spirit led him to the famous experiment recorded in *Walden, or Life in the Woods* (1854). Thoreau's passion for freedom and his lifetime resistance to conformity in thought and manners are forcefully present in his famous essay, "On the Duty of Civil Disobedience." Thoreau states that he went to the woods in order to encounter only the essential facts of life and avoid all that is petty, trivial, and unnecessary.

I went to the woods because I wished to live deliberately, to front only the essential facts of life, and see if I could not learn what it had to teach, and not, when I came to die, discover that I had not lived. I did not wish to live what was not life, living is so dear; nor did I wish to practise resignation, unless it was quite necessary. I wanted to live deep and suck out all the marrow of life, to live so sturdily and Spartan-like as to put to rout all that was not life, to cut a broad swath and shave close, to drive life into a corner, and reduce it to its lowest terms, and, if it proved to be mean, why then to get the whole and genuine meanness of it, and publish its meanness to the world; or if it were sublime, to know it by experience, and be able to give a true account of it in my next excursion. For most men, it appears to me, are in a strange uncertainty about it, whether it is of the devil or of God, and have *somewhat hastily* concluded that it is the chief end of man here to "glorify God and enjoy him forever."

Still we live meanly, like ants; though the fable tells us that we were long ago changed into men; like pygmies we fight with cranes; it is error upon error, and clout upon clout, and our best virtue has for its occasion a superfluous and evitable wretchedness. Our life is frittered away by detail. An honest man has hardly need to count more than his ten fingers, or in extreme cases he may add his ten toes, and lump the rest. Simplicity, simplicity, simplicity! I say, let your affairs be as two or three, and not a hundred or a thousand; instead of a million count half a dozen, and keep your accounts on your thumb-nail. In the midst of this chopping sea of civilized life, such are the clouds and storms and quicksands and thousand-and-one items to be allowed for, that a man has to live, if he would not founder and go to the bottom and not make his port at all, by dead reckoning, and he must be a great calculator indeed who succeeds. Simplify, simplify. Instead of three meals a day, if it be necessary eat but one; instead of a hundred dishes, five; and reduce other things in proportion. Our life is like a German Confederacy, made of up petty states, with its boundary forever fluctuating, so that even a German cannot tell you how it is bounded at any moment. The nation itself, with all its so-called internal improvements, which, by the way are all external and superficial, is just such an unwieldy and overgrown establishment, cluttered with furniture and tripped up by its own traps, ruined by luxury and heedless expense, by want of calculation and a worthy aim, as the million households in the lands; and the only cure for it, as for them, is in a rigid economy, a stern and more than Spartan simplicity of life and elevation of purpose. It lives too fast. Men think that it is essential that the *Nation* have commerce, and export ice, and talk through a telegraph, and ride thirty miles an hour, without a doubt, whether *they* do or not; but whether we should live like baboons or like men, is a little uncertain. If we do not get our sleepers, and forge rails, and devote days and nights to the work, but go to tinkering upon our *lives* to improve *them*, who will build railroads? And if railroads are not built, how shall we get to heaven in season? But if we stay at home and mind our business, who will want railroads? We do not ride on the railroad; it rides upon us. Did you ever think what those sleepers are that underlie the railroad? Each one is a man, an Irishman, or a Yankee man. The rails are laid on them, and they are covered with sand, and the cars run smoothly over them. They are sound sleepers, I assure you. And every few years a new lot is laid down and run over; so that, if some have the pleasure of riding on a rail, others have the misfortune to be ridden upon. And when they run over a man that is walking in his sleep, a supernumerary sleeper in the wrong position, and wake him up, they suddenly stop the cars, and make a hue and cry about it, as if this were an exception. I am glad to know that it takes a gang of men for every five miles to keep the sleepers down and level in their beds as it is, for this is a sign that they may sometimes get up again.

Why should we live with such hurry and waste of life? We are determined to be starved before we are hungry. Men say that a stitch in time saves nine, and so they take a thousand stitches to-day to save nine tomorrow. As for *work*, we haven't any of any consequence. We have the Saint Vitus' dance, and cannot possibly keep our heads still. If I should only give a few pulls at the parish bell-rope, as for a fire, that is, without setting the bell, there is hardly a man on his farm in the outskirts of Concord, notwithstanding that press of engagements which was his excuse so many times this morning, nor a boy, nor a woman, I might almost say, but would foresake all and follow that sound, not mainly to save property from the flames, but, if we will confess the truth, much more to see it burn, since burn it must, and we, be it known, did not set it on fire—or to see it put out, and have a hand in it, if that is done as handsomely; yes, even if it were the parish church itself. Hardly a man takes a half-hour's nap after dinner, but when he wakes he holds up his head and asks, "What's the news?" as if the rest of mankind had stood his sentinels. Some give directions to be waked every half-hour, doubtless for no other purpose; and then, to pay for it, they tell what they have dreamed. After a night's sleep the news is as indispensable as the breakfast. "Pray tell me anything new that has happened to a man anywhere on this globe"—and he reads it over his coffee and rolls, that a man has had his eyes gouged out this morning on the Wachito River; never dreaming the while that he lives in the dark unfathomed mammoth cave of this world, and has but the rudiment of an eye himself.

For my part, I could easily do without the post-office. I think that there are very few important communications made through it. To speak critically, I never received more than one or two letters in my life—I wrote this some years ago—that were worth the postage. The penny-post is, commonly, an institution through which you seriously offer a man that penny for his thoughts which is so often safely offered in jest. And I am sure that I never read any memorable news in a newspaper. If we read of one man robbed, or murdered, or killed by accident, or one house burned, or one vessel wrecked, or one steamboat blown up, or one cow run over on the Western Railroad, or one mad dog killed, or one lot of grasshoppers in the winter—we never need read of another. One is enough. If you are acquainted with the principle, what do you care for a myriad instances and applications? To a philosopher all *news*, as it is called, is gossip, and they who edit and read it are old women over their tea. Yet not a few are greedy after this gossip. There was such a rush, as I hear, the other day at one of the offices to learn the foreign news by the last arrival, that several large squares of plate glass belonging to the establishment were broken by the pressure—news which I seriously think a ready wit might write a twelvemonth, or twelve years, beforehand with sufficient accuracy. As for Spain, for instance, if you know how to throw in Don Carlos and the Infanta, and Don Pedro and Seville and Granada, from time to time in the right proportions—they may have changed the names a little since I saw the papers—and serve up a bullfight when other entertainments fail, it will be true to the letter, and give us as good an idea of the exact state or ruin of things in Spain as the most succinct and lucid reports under this head in the newspapers; and as for England, almost the last significant scrap of news from that quarter was the revolution of 1649; and if you have learned the history of her crops for an average year, you never need attend to that thing again, unless your speculations are of a merely pecuniary character. If one may judge who rarely looks into the newspapers, nothing new does ever happen in foreign parts, a French revolution not excepted.

What news! how much more important to know what that is which was never old! "Kieou-he-yu (great dignitary of the state of Wei) sent a man to Khoung-tseu to know his news. Khoung-tseu caused the messenger to be seated near him, and questioned him in these terms: What is your master doing? The messenger answered with respect: My master desires to diminish the number of his faults, but he cannot come to the end of them. The messenger being gone, the philosopher remarked: What a worthy messenger! What a worthy messenger!" The preacher, instead of vexing the ears of drowsy farmers on their day of rest at the end of the week—for Sunday is the fit conclusion of an ill-spent week, and not the fresh and brave beginning of a new one—with this one other draggle-tail of a sermon, should shout with thundering voice, "Pause! Avast! Why so seeming fast, but deadly slow?"

Shams and delusions are esteemed for soundless truths, while reality is fabulous. If men would steadily observe realities only, and not allow themselves to be deluded, life, to compare it with such things as we know, would be like a fairy tale and the Arabian Nights' Entertainments. If we respected only what is inevitable and has a right to be, music and poetry would resound along the streets. When we are unhurried and wise, we perceive that only great and worthy things have any permanent and absolute existence, that petty fears and petty pleasures are but the shadow of the reality. This is always exhilarating and sublime. By closing the eyes and slumbering, and consenting to be deceived by shows, men establish and confirm their daily life of routine and habit everywhere, which still is built on purely illusory foundations. Children, who play life, discern its true law and relations more clearly than men, who fail to live it worthily, but who think that they are wiser by experience. that is, by failure. I have read in a Hindoo book, that "there was a king's son, who, being expelled in infancy from his native city, was brought up by a forester, and, growing up to maturity in that state, imagined himself to belong to the barbarous race with which he lived. One of his father's ministers having discovered him, revealed to him what he was, and the misconception of his character was removed, and he knew himself to be a prince. So soul," continues the Hindoo philosopher, "from the circumstances in which it is placed, mistakes its own character, until the truth is revealed to it by some holy teacher and then it knows itself to be *Brahme*." I perceive that we inhabitants of New England live this mean life that we do because our vision does not penetrate the surface of things. We think that that *is* which *appears* to be. If a man should walk through this town and see only the reality, where, think you, would the "Milldam" go to? If he should give us an account of the realities he beheld there, we should not recognize the place in his description. Look at the meetinghouse, or a courthouse, or a jail, or a shop, or a dwelling-house, and say what that thing really is before a true gaze, and they would all go to pieces in your account of them. Men esteem truth remote, in the outskirts of the system, behind the farthest star, before Adam and after the last man. In eternity there is indeed something true and sublime. But all these times and places and occasions are now and here. God himself culminates in the present moment, and will never be more divine in the lapse of all the ages. And we are enabled to apprehend at all what is sublime and noble only by the perpetual instilling and drenching of the reality that surrounds us. The universe constantly and obediently answers to our conceptions; whether we travel fast or slow, the track is laid for us. Let us spend our lives in conceiving then. The poet or the artist never yet had so fair and noble a design but some of his posterity at least could accomplish it.

Let us spend one day as deliberately as Nature, and not be thrown off the track by every nutshell and mosquito's wing that falls on the rails. Let us rise early and fast, or breakfast, gently and without perturbation; let company come and let company go, let the bells ring and the children cry—determined to make a day of it. Why should we knock under and go with the stream? Let us not be upset and overwhelmed in that terrible rapid and whirlpool called a dinner, situated in the meridian shallows. Weather this danger and you are safe, for the rest of the way is downhill. With unrelaxed nerves, with morning vigor, sail by it, looking another way, tied to the mast like Ulysses. If the engine whistles, let it whistle till it is hoarse for its pains. If the bell rings, why should we run? We will consider what kind of music they are like. Let us settle ourselves and work and wedge our feet downward through the mud and slush of opinion, and prejudice, and tradition, and delusion, and appearance, that alluvion which covers the globe, through Paris and London, through New York and Boston and Concord, through Church and State, through poetry and philosophy and religion, till we come to a hard bottom and rocks in place, which we can call *reality*, and say, This is, and no mistake; and then begin, having a *point d'appui*, below freshet and frost and fire, a place where you might found a wall or a state, or set a lamppost safely, or perhaps a gauge, not a Nilometer, but a Realometer, that future ages might know how deep a freshet of shams and appearances had gathered from time to time. If you stand right fronting and face to face to a fact, you will see the sun glimmer on both its surfaces, as if it were a cimeter, and feel its sweet edge dividing you through the heart and marrow, and so you will happily conclude your mortal career. Be it life or death, we crave only reality. If we are really dying, let us hear the rattle in our throats and feel cold in the extremities; if we are alive, let us go about our business.

Time is but the stream I go afishing in. I drink at it; but while I drink I see the sandy bottom and detect how shallow it is. Its thin current slides away but eternity remains. I would drink deeper; fish in the sky, whose bottom is pebbly with stars. I cannot count one. I know not the first letter of the alphabet. I have always been regretting that I was not as wise as the day I was born. The intellect is a cleaver; it discerns and rifts its way into the secret of things. I do not wish to be any more busy with my hands than is necessary. My head is hands and feet. I feel all my best faculties concentrated in it. My instinct tells me that my head is an organ for burrowing, as some creatures use their snout and fore paws, and with it I would mine and burrow my way through these hills. I think that the richest vein is somewhere hereabouts; so by the divining-rod and thin rising vapors, I judge; and here I will begin to mine.

Suggestions for Discussion

1. Why did Thoreau go to the woods?

2. With what details does Thoreau support his statement that "we live meanly like ants"?

3. Interpret Thoreau's rhetorical question in the context of his philosophy: "If you are acquainted with the principle, what do you care for a myriad instances and applications"?

4. With what details does Thoreau illustrate his impatience with man's proclivity for being deluded?

5. How do Thoreau's rhetorical questions, metaphors, and allusions contribute to substance and tone?

6. What aspects of American life does Thoreau repudiate and why?

7. What does he affirm? Paraphrase his last two paragraphs.

Suggestions for Writing

1. Discuss what you have learned from your observations of nature.

2. "Our life is frittered away by detail".

3. "Shams and delusions are esteemed for soundless truths, while reality is fabulous."

4. What would Thoreau's impressions be of our current preoccupations?

Jeffrey H. Goldstein
The Healing Power of Laughter

Jeffrey H. Goldstein (b. 1942) received his Ph.D. from Ohio State University and teaches psychology at Temple University. He has been a consultant to the National Science Foundation and the U.S. Department of Labor. He has co-edited *The Psychology of Humor* (1972) and written *Aggression and Crimes of Violence* (1975). He has contributed to a number of psychology, sociology, and anthropology journals. He traces the historical roots of the theory that laughter is conducive to healing and concludes that a sense of humor at least improves the quality of life.

There are fads in medicine and psychiatry just as surely as there are in art, literature, and styles of dress. Today it is fashionable to attribute healing and restorative powers to laughter, a claim that only 30 or 40 years ago would itself have been laughable.

Only since the end of the Second World War have Westerners come to think that stress and anxiety might lead to disease. To suggest the opposite—that laughter, relaxation, and joy could be therapeutic—was nearly unthinkable.

The notion that laughter is healthy owes much of its current popularity to Norman Cousins's "Anatomy of an Illness," published in the *New England Journal of Medicine* in 1976 and expanded into a best-selling book in 1979.

Cousins, then editor of the *Saturday Review,* described his bout with ankylosing spondylitis, a chronic, progressive disease inflaming the joints of the spine; and he attributed his rather remarkable recovery to self-treatment with vitamin C and laughter. The vitamin C, he believed, could combat inflammation, and the laughter could have positive effects on the body—since negative emotions, he had read, could produce negative effects.

Cousins's account was praised by many in the medical community, but others were skeptical. The late Sidney Kahn, of Mount Sinai School of Medicine, for instance, noted in the *Mount Sinai Journal of Medicine* that Cousins drew some arbitrary conclusions from the medical literature, and that spontaneous remissions of ankylosing spondylitis do occur. In other words, Cousins may have recovered naturally; he did not necessarily laugh his way back to health.

But despite some criticism, Cousins's influence has remained strong (indeed, after leaving *Saturday Review,* he became a senior lecturer in medical humanities at the University of California at Los Angeles School of Medicine). Partly as a result of his book, physicians are more likely than ever to think of humor and other sources of emotional comfort as part of treatment.

A worrisome consequence of this is that the patient may be held responsible for his or her failure to recover; that by not having the will to live, the proper outlook on life, or a sufficient sense of humor, the patient will be seen to suffer willfully.

Though Cousins's suggestions will require serious scientific investigation, the idea that laughter is therapeutic does have a long history. From the time of Aristotle, a few scholars have recommended laughter as a means of strengthening the lungs and of furthering the health of the organism as a whole.

In the 13th century, Henri de Mondeville, a surgeon, proposed that laughter be used as an aid to recovery from surgery. Foreshadowing Cousins, de Mondeville also noted that negative emotions might interfere with recovery: "The surgeon must forbid anger, hatred, and sadness in the patient, and remind him that the body grows fat from joy and thin from sadness."

And Richard Mulcaster, a 16th-century physician, believed that laughter was a physical exercise and, as such, was healthy. He wrote that laughter could help those who have cold hands and cold chests and are troubled with melancholia, since "it moveth much aire in the breast, and sendeth the warmer spirites outward."

In one of the most thoughtful and complete analyses of laughter ever written, the 16th-century physician Laurent Joubert presented several views on its origin and function that are still accepted, though in slightly different form.

Like Aristotle, Joubert saw laughter as arising from "a defect or ugliness that is not painful or destructive." In this view, the ugliness incited sadness while its relative painlessness incited joy. These contrary emotions were said to stir the heart in alternating contractions and expansions, sadness causing the contractions and joy the expansions. The to-and-fro movement was transferred to the diaphragm, leading to the rapid breathing we call "hearty laughter." To Joubert, the consequences of laughter were manifestly beneficial, and could be seen in the face and eyes. He wrote:

> Is it not in the face, and especially in the eyes which [laughter] moves so freely that nothing surpasses it? . . . Certainly there is nothing that gives more pleasure and recreation than a laughing face, with its wide, shining, clear, and serene forehead, eyes shining, resplendent from any vantage point, and casting fire as do diamonds; cheeks vermillion and incarnate, mouth flush with the face, lips handsomely drawn back . . . chin drawn in, widened, and a bit recessed.

References to laughter's healthful effects are scattered through the philosophical and medical literature of the 18th and 19th centuries as well. Laughter was thought to be good exercise and more. Gottlieb Huçeland, a 19th-century German professor, said, "Laughter is one of the most important helps to digestion with which we are acquainted; the custom in vogue among our ancestors, of exciting it by jesters and buffoons, was founded on true medical principles. Cheerful and joyous companions are invaluable at meals."

Herbert Spencer proposed, in 1860, that laughter was a way of releasing excess tension, and, therefore, is an important restorative mechanism—a view of laughter influential even today.

Spencer's idea was taken up and elaborated, in 1928, by James Walsh, an American physician, who wrote that the beneficial physical effects of laughter are mediated by psychological effects:

> The best formula for the health of the individual is contained in the mathematical expression: health varies as the amount of laughter. The effect of laughter upon the mind not only brings relaxation with it, so far as mental tension is concerned, but makes it also less prone to dreads and less solicitous about the future. This favorable effect on the mind influences various functions of the body and makes them healthier than would otherwise be the case.

Despite these statements extolling laughter's medical benefits, the moral view of laughter has usually been negative—decidedly so. It is only within the last hundred years or so that laughter in public has even been socially acceptable.

For much of Western history, laughter was considered impolite at best, satanic at worst. Medieval physicians tended to locate each emotion in some organ of the body. The seat of love, for instance, was the heart (and a good thing, too, or who knows what shapes we'd be sending on Valentine's Day). The seat of laughter was the spleen—an assignment apparently meant to assure that laughter was viewed as a "low" form of behavior.

In 1676, Robert Barclay wrote in "Apology for the True Christian Divinity":

> It is not lawful to use games, sports, plays, nor among other things comedies among Christians, under the notion of recreations, since they do not agree with Christian silence, gravity, and sobriety; for laughing, sporting, gaming, mocking, jesting, vain talking, etc., is not Christian liberty, nor harmless mirth.

The pilgrim settlers to America likewise looked upon laughter with disdain and permitted it only when it would serve to illustrate a moral lesson.

Victorian England, not surprisingly, frowned on laughter as well. While girls and women were permitted to smile in deference or to giggle at the slightest suggestion of impropriety, they were not to laugh with glee. They could be embarrassed but not happy. (Today, of course, they may be happy, but not embarrassed.) George Vasey, a philosopher of that era, argued in "The Philosophy of Laughter and Smiling" that children laugh, not out of any sense of joy or humor, but because they were tickled as infants.

In our century, the negative view of laughter received some support from the new field of psychology. Once Sigmund Freud had written on humor and laughter, in 1905, it was increasingly credible that humor reflected bitterness, underlying anxiety, or unspoken hostility. In "Jokes and Their Relation to the Unconscious," he discussed the functions and techniques of "tendentious wit," humor with an underlying motive, or tendency. Joking, he argued, can provide an outlet—though not a conscious one—for underlying sexual and aggressive impulses.

But Freud was careful to distinguish between hostile wit and benign humor, and recognized that some laughter, at least, might indicate the absence of underlying pathology. He wrote, in 1928:

> Humor . . . has also something fine and elevating . . . the triumph of narcissism, the ego's victorious assertion of its own vulnerability. It refuses to be hurt by the arrows of reality or be compelled to suffer. It insists that it is impervious to wounds dealt by the outside world, in fact, that these are merely occasions for affording it pleasure.

That is, a person in an unfortunate or unpleasant situation can become its master (at least temporarily) by turning it around and making a joke of it.

When opinions vacillate from one extreme to another—between the belief that laughter is evil and symptomatic of disease, and the belief that it is health giving and beneficial—there is likely to be some validity in each position.

It is true that laughter can indicate underlying, and perhaps unconscious, hostility and conflict. It is also true that laughter can express self-acceptance, joy, inner strength, and adjustment. There is considerable evidence on both sides, but we do not yet know enough about laughter and humor to evaluate its meaning with confidence. Nor do we know how to distinguish reliably between "healthy" and "malevolent" laughter. In short, laughter cannot be treated as a single, undifferentiated phenomenon.

Current evidence, more psychological than physiological suggests that laughter does not always reflect a state of adjustment or physical well-being. Psychologically, it may indicate self-deprecation, hostility toward others—as in racist joking—defensiveness, closed mindedness, or a preoccupation with scatology or sex. Socially, humor may be used to break the ice; but it may also be used defensively as a barrier to communication. Filling a conversation with jokes and witty remarks can be a way to avoid participation, to close oneself off from the proceedings.

Laughter and humor also may drive a wedge between people, as when a hostile or pointed remark makes another person or group the butt of a joke. Or humor may serve as a tactic of ingratiation, a way to manipulate others.

Physically, we now know that there are any number of conditions in which laughter indicates underlying pathology. In three neurological disorders—pseudobulbar palsy, amyotrophic lateral sclerosis (Lou Gehrig's disease), and multiple sclerosis—there is a distinctive type of "aberrant" laughter. Sudden outbursts occur often, but the laughter is beyond the control of the patient and does not reflect any sense of elation.

Similarly, a form of epilepsy, called gelastic epilepsy, involves dull, hollow, and clearly inappropriate laughter.

A change in the sense of humor often accompanies Alzheimer's disease and Pick's disease, also known as presenile dementias (early senility). Sufferers of these disorders tend to crack silly jokes, and cannot take serious matters seriously. There are also acute conditions, such as ethyl alcohol poisoning, that can result in inappropriate, excessive, or uncontrollable laughter.

It is clear that pathological laughter generally does not reflect an underlying sense of joy or elation, is not under the patient's conscious control, and is inappropriate to the social situation in which it occurs. But this suggests that the converse is also true: that healthy or normal laughter does reflect a sense of mirth, is to some degree under conscious control, and is appropriate to the situation.

The best-documented studies of healthy laughter examine those of its correlates that can be measured most readily: variations in heart rate, respiration, and the skin's electrical conductance, just prior to, during, and after laughter. In most of these studies, tension or arousal is found to increase during the telling of a joke, to increase further during laughter, and then to decrease following laughter.

Studies that combine psychological and physiological measures typically find that, over the short term, laughter may reduce arousal from whatever source, supporting the theory that laughter is sometimes effective for reducing stress. It is conceivable, too, that laughter or spontaneous joking can be used to indicate a person's general level of stress or anxiety, though the content and social nature of joking in these cases needs to be taken into account. For instance, if a person chronically jokes about a particular subject such as sex, it may indicate an area of conflict that the person cannot express in any other way. And the failure to laugh about certain subjects may convey as much information as laughter itself.

In these studies, laughter was examined only in experimental settings, and only for brief periods. To my knowledge, no one has ever studied the long-term consequences of chronic and repeated laughter. Though it has been argued for centuries that laughter is good exercise, and we do know that laughter does not deplete the amount of oxygen in peripheral blood, we still do not know whether those who laugh regularly—many times a day, for example—are really healthier and better adjusted than those who do not.

It is not too farfetched to speculate, however, that laughter is related in several ways to longevity. Of the major heart attack risks that have been identified (cigaret smoking, obesity, diabetes, hypertension, high blood levels of cholesterol, stress, and lack of exercise), laughter is clearly related to the reduction of stress and to physical exercise, and may be related to hypertension. We know that someone with a "Type A" personality, characterized by seriousness, stress, concern with time, impatience, and hostility, has a greater risk of heart attack than the "Type B" person, in whom a sense of humor may displace anger, anxiety, and hostility. We know, too, that people who are in a good mood, stimulated by epinephrine, are more apt to experience laughter and mirth than those who are unaroused or depressed, as by a tranquilizer such as chlorpromazine.

Cousins, and the late Rene Dubos, in his introduction to Cousins's book, have speculated that the newly discovered pituitary secretions called endorphins are related to laughter and its beneficial effects.

Endorphins are chemically related to opiates, such as heroin and morphine, and act to reduce pain and instill feelings of elation. Many long-distance runners, for instance, experience a state of euphoria that is related to the amount of betaendorphin in their bloodstreams. Laughter may act on the endocrine system, the pituitary gland in particular, to produce not only a reduction in physical stress and pain, but a sense of euphoria as well.

Of course, from reading some of the recent popular books on humor and health, one might think that all the research needed to support these speculations had already been conducted—that laughter has already been categorically proven to promote a long and healthy life. Cousins, for example, notes approvingly the sense of humor, love of baroque music, and longevity of Albert Schweitzer and Pablo Casals. But it is well to remember that the connections between laughter and long life, if any, have yet to be demonstrated. Indeed, as far as I can determine from a cursory reading of biographies and recent necrologies, comedians and comic writers do not live any longer than other people—they do not dramatically survive those of their contemporaries who have chosen the graver specialties of law, medicine, and investment banking.

It would be surprising if they did. At this point, one can say with confidence only that a sense of humor enhances the quality of life—but not necessarily its duration.

Suggestions for Discussion

1. What are the historical roots of Cousins's theory that laughter is conducive to healing?

2. What is one unfortunate consequence of Cousins's theory?

3. How do you explain the fact that the moral view of laughter has usually been negative in the light of the medical benefits that have been extolled?

4. How did Freud distinguish between hostile and benign humor and the sources of each? Explain his statement that humor represents "the triumph of narcissism, the ego's victorious assertion of its own vulnerability."

5. How does Goldstein's essay support his view that "laughter cannot be treated as a single, undifferentiated phenomenon"? Cite examples of the several rhetorical devises he uses to develop his thesis.

6. What evidence is brought to bear to suggest that laughter does not always reflect a state of adjustment or physical well being?

7. What studies give support to the view that laughter can be healing?

8. On what evidence does the author speculate that laughter may be related to longevity? What is the role of endorphins?

Suggestions for Writing

1. Analyze the nature of the humor in a favorite comedian or in a humorous writer.

2. Think of the demeanor and conversations of one or more of your friends or acquaintances. What role does humor or laughter seem to play in their lives? To what do you attribute its source?

3. Characterize a person whose humor seems pathological or one whose humor appears to be an outlet for aggressive impulses.

Malcolm Cowley

Vices and Pleasures: The View from 80

Malcolm Cowley (b. 1898) is a distinguished critic, poet, editor, and literary historian. He was literary editor of *The New Republic* in the nineteen-thirties and has served as a visiting professor at many universities. Among his publications are *Exiles Return* (1934), *The Literary Situation* (1954), *Blue Juanita: Collected Poems* (1964), and *The View from Eighty* (1981), which opens with this essay. Although some aging persons suffer from an identity crisis, it is clear that Cowley finds pleasure in his late years.

Even before he or she is 80, the aging person may undergo another identity crisis like that of adolescence. Perhaps there had also been a middle-aged crisis, the male or the female menopause, but for the rest of adult life he had taken himself for granted, with his capabilities and failings. Now, when he looks in the mirror, he asks himself, "Is this really me?"—or he avoids the mirror out of distress at what it reveals, those bags and wrinkles. In his new makeup he is called upon to play a new role in a play that must be improvised. André Gide, that long-lived man of letters, wrote in his journal, "My heart has remained so young that I have continual feeling of playing a part, the part of the 70-year-old that I certainly am; and the infirmities and weaknesses that remind me of my age act like a prompter, reminding me of my lines when I tend to stray. Then, like the good actor I want to be, I go back into my role, and I pride myself on playing it well."

In his new role the old person will find that he is tempted by new vices, that he receives new compensations (not so widely known), and that he may possibly achieve new virtues. Chief among these is the heroic or merely obstinate refusal to surrender in the face of time. One admires the ships that go down with all flags flying and the captain on the bridge.

Among the vices of age are avarice, untidiness, and vanity, which last takes the form of a craving to be loved or simply admired. Avarice is the worst of those three. Why do so many old persons, men and women alike, insist on hoarding money when they have no prospect of using it and even when they have no heirs? They eat the cheapest food, buy no clothes, and live in a single room when they could afford better lodging. It may be that they regard money as a form of power; there is a comfort in watching it accumulate while other powers are dwindling away. How often we read of an old person found dead in a hovel, on a mattress partly stuffed with bankbooks and stock certificates! The bankbook syndrome, we call it in our family, which has never succumbed.

Untidiness we call the Langley Collyer syndrome. To explain, Langley Collyer was a former concert pianist who lived alone with his 70-year-old brother in a brownstone house on upper Fifth Avenue. The once fashionable neighborhood had become part of Harlem. Homer, the brother, had been an admiralty lawyer, but was now blind and partly paralyzed; Langley played for him and fed him on buns and oranges, which he thought would restore Homer's sight. He never threw away a daily paper because Homer, he said, might want to read them all. He saved other things as well and the house became filled with rubbish from roof to basement. The halls were lined on both sides with bundled newspapers, leaving narrow passageways in which Langley had devised booby traps to catch intruders.

On March 21, 1947, some unnamed person telephoned the police to report that there was a dead body in the Collyer house. The police broke down the front door and found the hall impassable, then they hoisted a ladder to a second-story window. Behind it Homer was lying on the floor in a bathrobe; he had starved to death. Langley had disappeared. After some delay, the police broke into the basement, chopped a hole in the roof, and began throwing junk out of the house, top and bottom. It was 18 days before they found Langley's body, gnawed by rats. Caught in one of his own booby traps, he had died in a hallway just outside Homer's door. By that time the police had collected, and the Department of Sanitation had hauled away, 120 tons of rubbish, including besides the newspapers, 14 grand pianos and the parts of a dismantled Model T Ford.

Why do so many old people accumulate junk, not on the scale of Langley Collyer, but still in a dismaying fashion? Their tables are piled high with it, their bureau drawers are stuffed with it, their closet rods bend with the weight of clothes not worn for years. I suppose that the piling up is partly from lethargy and partly from the feeling that everything once useful, including their own bodies, should be preserved. Others, though not so many, have such a fear of becoming Langley Collyers that they strive to be painfully neat. Every tool they own is in its place, though it will never be used again; every scrap of paper is filed away in alphabetical order. At last their immoderate neatness becomes another vice of age, if a milder one.

The vanity of older people is an easier weakness to explain, and to condone. With less to look forward to, they yearn for recognition of what they have been: the reigning beauty, the athlete, the soldier, the scholar. It is the beauties who have the hardest time. A portrait of themselves at twenty hangs on the wall, and they try to resemble it by making an extravagant use of creams, powders, and dyes. Being young at heart, they think they are merely revealing their essential persons. The athletes find shelves for their silver trophies, which are polished once a year. Perhaps a letter sweater lies wrapped in a bureau drawer. I remember one evening when a no-longer ath-lete had guests for dinner and tried to find his sweater, "Oh, that old thing," his wife said. "The moths got into it and I threw it away." The athlete sulked and his guests went home early.

Often the yearning to be recognized appears in conversation as an innocent boast. Thus, a distinguished physician, retired at 94, remarks casually that a disease was named after him. A former judge bursts into chuckles as he re-peats bright things that he said on the bench. Aging scholars complain in letters (or one of them does), "As I approach 70 I'm becoming avid of honors, and such things—medals, honorary degrees, etc.—are only passed around among academics on a *quid pro quo* basis (one hood capping another)." Or they say querulously, "Bill Underwood has ten honorary doctorates and I have only three. Why didn't they elect me to. . . ?" and they mention the name of some learned society. That search for honors is a harmless passion, though it may lead to jealousies and deformations of character, as with Robert Frost in his later years. Still, honors cost little. Why shouldn't the very old have more than their share of them?

To be admired and praised, especially by the young, is an autumnal plea-sure enjoyed by the lucky ones (who are not always the most deserving). "What is more charming," Cicero observes in his famous essay *De Senectute,* "than an old age surrounded by the enthusiasm of youth! . . . Attentions which seem trivial and conventional are marks of honor—the morning call, being sought after, precedence, having people rise for you, being escorted to and from the forum. . . . What pleasures of the body can be compared to the prerogatives of influence?" But there are also pleasures of the body, or the mind, that are enjoyed by a greater number of older persons.

Those pleasures include some that younger people find hard to appreciate. One of them is simply sitting still, like a snake on a sun-warmed stone, with a delicious feeling of indolence that was seldom attained in earlier years. A leaf flutters down; a cloud moves by inches across the horizon. At such mo-ments the older person, completely relaxed, has become a part of nature—and a living part, with blood coursing through his veins. The future does not exist for him. He thinks, if he thinks at all, that life for younger persons is still a battle royal of each against each, but that now he has nothing more to win or lose. He is not so much above as outside the battle, as if he had assumed the uniform of some small neutral country, perhaps Liechtenstein or Andorra. From a distance he notes that some of the combatants, men or women, are jostling ahead—but why do they fight so hard when the most they can hope for is a longer obituary? He can watch the scrounging and gouging, he can hear the shouts of exultation, the moans of the gravely wounded, and meanwhile he feels secure; nobody will attack him from am-bush.

Age has other physical compensations besides the nirvana of dozing in the sun. A few of the simplest needs become a pleasure to satisfy. When an old woman in a nursing home was asked what she really liked to do, she answered in one word: "Eat." She might have been speaking for many of her fellows. Meals in a nursing home, however badly cooked, serve as climactic moments of the day. The physical essence of the pensioners is being renewed at an appointed hour; now they can go back to meditating or to watching TV while looking forward to the next meal. They can also look forward to sleep, which has become a definite pleasure, not the mere interruption it once had been.

Here I am thinking of old persons under nursing care. Others ferociously guard their independence, and some of them suffer less than one might expect from being lonely and impoverished. They can be rejoiced by visits and meetings, but they also have company inside their heads. Some of them are busiest when their hands are still. What passes through the minds of many is a stream of persons, images, phrases, and familiar tunes. For some that stream has continued since childhood, but now it is deeper; it is their present and their past combined. At times they conduct silent dialogues with a vanished friend, and these are less tiring—often more rewarding—than spoken conversations. If inner resources are lacking, old persons living alone may seek comfort and a kind of companionship in the bottle. I should judge from the gossip of various neighborhoods that the outer suburbs from Boston to San Diego are full of secretly alcoholic widows. One of those widows, an old friend, was moved from her apartment into a retirement home. She left behind her a closet in which the floor was covered wall to wall with whiskey bottles. "Oh, those empty bottles!" she explained. "They were left by a former tenant."

Not whiskey or cooking sherry but simply giving up is the greatest temptation of age. It is something different from a stoical acceptance of infirmities, which is something to be admired. At 63, when he first recognized that his powers were failing, Emerson wrote one of his best poems, "Terminus":

> It is time to be old,
> To take in sail:—
> The god of bounds,
> Who sets to seas a shore,
> Came to me in his fatal rounds,
> And said: "No more!
> No farther shoot
> Thy broad ambitious branches, and thy root.
> Fancy departs: no more invent;
> Contract thy firmament
> To compass of a tent."

Emerson lived in good health to the age of 79. Within his narrowed firmament, he continued working until his memory failed; then he consented to having younger editors and collaborators. The givers-up see no reason for working. Sometimes they lie in bed all day when moving about would still be possible, if difficult. I had a friend, a distinguished poet, who surrendered in that fashion. The doctors tried to stir him to action, but he refused to leave his room. Another friend, once a successful artist, stopped painting when his eyes began to fail. His doctor made the mistake of telling him that he suffered from a fatal disease. He then lost interest in everything except the splendid Rolls-Royce, acquired in his prosperous days, that stood in the garage. Daily he wiped the dust from its hood. He couldn't drive it on the road any longer, but he used to sit in the driver's seat, start the motor, then back the Rolls out of the garage and drive it in again, back twenty feet and forward twenty feet; that was his only distraction.

I haven't the right to blame those who surrender, not being able to put myself inside their minds or bodies. Often they must have compelling reasons, physical or moral. Not only do they suffer from a variety of ailments, but also they are made to feel that they no longer have a function in the community. Their families and neighbors don't ask them for advice, don't really listen when they speak, don't call on them for efforts. One notes that there are not a few recoveries from apparent senility when that situation changes. If it doesn't change, old persons may decide that efforts are useless. I sympathize with their problems, but the men and women I envy are those who accept old age as a series of challenges.

For such persons, every new infirmity is an enemy to be outwitted, an obstacle to be overcome by force of will. They enjoy each little victory over themselves, and sometimes they win a major success. Renoir was one of them. He continued painting, and magnificently, for years after he was crippled by arthritis; the brush had to be strapped to his arm. "You don't need your hand to paint," he said. Goya was another of the unvanquished. At 72 he retired as an official painter of the Spanish court and decided to work only for himself. His later years were those of the famous "black paintings" in which he let his imagination run (and also of the lithographs, then a new technique). At 78 he escaped a reign of terror in Spain by fleeing to Bordeaux. He was deaf and his eyes were failing; in order to work he had to wear several pairs of spectacles, one over another, and then use a magnifying glass; but he was producing splendid work in a totally new style. At 80 he drew an ancient man propped on two sticks, with a mass of white hair and beard hiding his face and with the inscription "I am still learning."

Giovanni Papini said when he was nearly blind, "I prefer martyrdom to imbecility." After writing sixty books, including his famous *Life of Christ,* he was at work on two huge projects when he was stricken with a form of muscular atrophy. He lost the use of his left leg, then of his fingers, so that he couldn't hold a pen. The two big books, though never to be finished, moved forward slowly by dictation; that in itself was a triumph. Toward the end, when his voice had become incomprehensible, he spelled out a word, tapping on the table to indicate letters of the alphabet. One hopes never to be faced with the need for such heroic measures.

"Eighty years old!" the great Catholic poet Paul Claudel wrote in his journal. "No eyes left, no ears, no teeth, no legs, no wind! And when all is said and done, how astonishingly well one does without them!"

Suggestions for Discussion

1. How does Cowley illustrate the possible identity crisis of the aging person?

2. How does he explain and illustrate "the vices of age"?

3. Show how language, tone, and analogy in his discussion of "sitting still" convey the author's feeling of pleasure.

4. How does Cowley distinguish between those who stoically accept their infirmities and those who surrender? What are some of the causes of the latter?

5. How does Cowley explain his envy of those who accept old age as a series of challenges?

Suggestions for Writing

1. How do you interpret the words *identity crisis?* Develop your essay by using concrete illustrations.

2. What are your observations of the vices and/or pleasures of age? Make specific references to acquaintances in the course of your discussion.

3. Apart from your academic studies, what lessons are you still learning?

Stuart Chase

A Very Private Utopia

Stuart Chase (b. 1888) has been a lifelong critic of social conditions in the United States. Among his published works are *The Tragedy of Waste* (1925), *Men and Machines* (1931), *The Economy of Abundance* (1934), and *Rich Land, Poor Land* (1936). Although Chase mentions very personal attributes of the good life, his essay transcends the personal; the ultimate goal is not what would make one happy but rather what would make one more alive.

Lewis Mumford in the *Golden Day* has given us a brilliant review of American culture as reflected in American literature from Jonathan Edwards to John Dewey. It is on the whole an exceedingly critical review. He tells us frequently, passionately, and beautifully what he is against, but only rarely does he let it be known what he is for. Modern industrial civilization has nourished a great array of critics. Few of them are as competent or as penetrating as Mr. Mumford, but all of them—save possibly the Utopians—follow his general method. They are indefatigable in pointing out the shortcomings of society, but they are vague as to the precise nature of available substitutes. They seldom define their standards. Yet standards they must have; otherwise it would be impossible to criticize. They either take it for granted that the reader shares their inward knowledge, or else, and more probably, the standards have never been formulated in the critic's conscious processes at all. They have grown in the back of his mind, darkly.

From the artists, the dramatists, the socialists, the poets, the uplifters of all varieties, has poured forth in never-ending flood the challenge that *homo sapiens* is only half alive.

What does he look like when he is alive?

The question would seem to be a fair one, but it is seldom answered. The writers of Utopia have struggled with it, but their canvases are usually so great that we are seldom able to see ourselves or our neighbors living or behaving in that world. There is a strange chill about all Utopias; they are inhabited by gods, not men. Even when a critical play of modern manners, the "Beggar on Horseback," forsook its role of satire for a moment and gave us a picture of happiness about a sun-drenched breakfast table, we stared unconvinced at such very yellow bliss. The negatives stretch to the horizon, but the positives are either lacking entirely or, when focused before us, appear cold or a little absurd. Indeed to seek to describe with clearness and precision the specific target at which programs for ushering in the good life should aim can only be an adventure tinged with absurdity. But a possible approach may be to delimit the kind of life one personally would like to live. Will this remove the Utopian chill and at the same time furnish the beginnings of a standard? We can but test it.

I have thrown my arrows with the rest at the sweating corpus of the world as it is. I have called it ugly, machine-minded, dull, ignorant, and cruel. I have said that the few live, and they precariously, while the many exist, half-dead in their frustrations and blind alleys. Before hurling another quiver it would seem only fair—however dubious the result—to define rather specifically what I mean, or think I mean, when I mark off the quick from the dead.

The hours roll into days, the days into years. Down this funnel of time one drifts, now easily, now painfully. One is happy, one is miserable. There are days of the most intense blue; days of a terrible black; with perhaps the majority of days an all-pervading mauve-gray. The causes for the color of these days are far from clear; one takes life as it comes. Modern psychology is groping for causes, but it has not as yet brought much that is genuinely helpful into the light. It cannot tell you where the good life has been competently analyzed or even adequately described. Science has perhaps even less to report than the poets and the critics. And so about all the data is oneself.

I note that the following things or conditions do, by and large, kill the juices of zestful living, and reduce me to mere existing, I state the negative first, the positive to follow shortly:

Ill health.

Monotonous work with no discernible goal—such as auditing, indexing, dishwashing.

Eating poor food; eating in ugly places.

The sensation of living in ugly or uncomfortable houses.

All transit, whether by foot or on wheels, about New York City.

Being looked down upon, or laughed at (save for very minor foibles).

The bulk of all business interviews, conferences, talks—the juicelessness of the personal contact.

The defacement of natural beauty with billboards, pop stands, suburban lots, gas tanks, shacks, factories. (A factory can be made to respond to architecture as well as a skyscraper.)

Reading newspapers—save for perhaps one one-hundredth of the surface of not more than three of them.

Going to formal entertainments—particularly dinners devoted to the raising of funds for worthy causes.

Treating relatives as preferred creditors.

Wearing ugly or uncomfortable clothes as decreed by the *mores*, e.g., coats and hats for men in summer.

Shopping—with rare exceptions.

Worrying about money.

> Being bored with bad plays, concerts, lectures, radios, meetings, conversations—especially the last.
> Being everlastingly hustled around.
> Seeing other people bored, unhappy, or in pain. Looking down mean streets and into frowsy windows.

My notebooks show scores of other conditions which take the joy out of life, but the above are the chief ones in the daily run of my activity. They consume, on the basis of a rough estimate, upwards of two thirds of my waking hours, though the ratio shifts with the seasons, being noticeably worse in winter. The average annual ratio, furthermore, is better when living in the country the year around than in the city. I am dead, I conclude, about two thirds of the time. I am alive, by and large, under the following conditions:

> On encountering a vivid awareness of health.
> In pursuing creative work, intellectual or manual. There are definite time limits to both.
> Eating good food, drinking good wine, in comfortable places.
> The sensation of living in well-designed and sunny houses.
> Being looked up to and praised—but the butter must not be spread too thick.
> Being with my friends.
> Looking at beautiful scenery, beautiful pictures, beautiful things.
> Reading great books; reading of new and stimulating ideas.
> Looking at Charlie Chaplin's feet.
> Swimming, diving, playing tennis, dancing, skiing, mountain climbing. Watching good sport at not too frequent intervals.
> Daydreaming.
> Going on spontaneous and amusing parties.
> Making love spontaneously.
> Wearing beautiful—not fashionable—clothes.
> Collecting things. For me, certain sorts of information.
> Listening to good music—especially Russian gypsy songs.
> The sensation of being some paces in front of the wolf.
> Home life—in fits and starts.
> Kindly casual contacts with strangers.
> Travel, other than for business reasons.
> Keen discussion.
> A good fight, not necessarily sanguinary, in what seems to be a decent cause.
> The sense of being in bodily danger.

So runs the major classification of what seem to constitute the good life for me. To hold that the list is applicable to all is, of course, ridiculous. Yet it must serve as a starting-point for the thing we have set ourselves to define. I do not know how other people feel. Logic declares that, conditioned by the same forces that have conditioned me, other people would feel much the same, but logic is not an infallible guide in human affairs.

What kind of a community would I build to increase the count of the hours that live as against the count of the hours that die? God knows. The difficulty is that the pluses and the minuses are never clean-cut emotional states, registering faithfully at every exposure to a given condition. When one is in abounding health, even filling-station architecture is tolerable if not positively enjoyable. When one sits, like Mr. Polly, athwart a stile, with civil war in his interior, the sunset itself becomes a flat and overestimated spectacle. There are times when the best of friends becomes a bore, when one wishes all printing presses would stop forever. Indeed, the whole concept is in the curved grip of relativity.

Nevertheless, I think that I would be appreciably more alive in a community that deliberately fostered the sorts of things enumerated on the second list, of which good health is probably the most important single factor. If it be objected that the animals are mostly healthy, I would reply that they appear to get more out of life than the majority of human beings. Fortunately the laws underlying the promotion of health are beginning to be understood. We already have the technical knowledge available to increase immeasurably bodily well-being. Here and there it is being applied, as the declining death-rate and the lengthening age span show.

Secondly, I would like to live in a community where beauty abounded; where cities were nobly planned, industrial areas segregated; where great stretches of forest, lake, and mountain were left wild and free and close at hand; where houses and their furnishings were spare and fine and colorful, and there was not a single billboard in a day's march. Cities and houses have been so built; nature over great (but distant) areas is still free; advertising is only a century old, despite the pious historical labors of Bruce Barton. Surely a community rich in natural beauty, rich in architecture, is no Utopia. It has been repeatedly achieved, and without the vast potential assistance of mechanical power.

Thirdly, I would like to live, and to have my neighbors live, free from the fear of want. Such communities there have been, but not many of them. Peru under the Incas is said to have achieved this goal; Denmark is not far from it today. Not only is it the release of the individual which is desirable, but, vastly more important, the release of the whole group. As things are in America today I never know how far my own actions are ignoble by economic considerations, nor how far my neighbors and associates regard me on my own merits or as a means to a hopefully profitable end. All human relationships are poisoned with this suspicion; or cut and bruised with the frank brutality of elbowing one's way above the line of economic insecurity. This is the more lamentable in that the industrial arts have already demonstrated how utterly to abolish poverty, double—aye treble—the standard of living, produce more than enough to go around.

Fourthly, I would like to live in a community where I could do the kind of work that is the most fun. Fun for me is economic research and writing about it. If there should prove a plethora of better men in this field, I would have a lot of fun as an anthropologist, a psychologist, or a biologist. Or I might go back to my boyhood dreams of architecture. In exchange for the fun, the giving of an hour or two on the average day to the necessary manual work of the world would seem, in anticipation at least, the merest justice. Furthermore, digging ditches, painting walls, simple carpentry would both preserve the sense of reality and serve by contrast to heighten the fun of the chosen occupation.

I would like to be able to dress as I pleased, or indeed not to dress at all when the sun was high and the water blue. I should like to experiment with colors and combinations now rigidly proscribed for males by the folkways—save at fancy-dress balls. I should like to be able to dance more, sing more, let myself go more. Here New England dogs me like an iron shroud. I should like ampler and less hurried opportunities to play the games I enjoy. I should like to travel more; to visit the lost cities of which I dream; to climb in the Andes and the Himalayas. It does not do to turn one's back for long on the bright face of danger.

I should like to be a more compelling and less self-conscious lover, but just how a community would proceed to organize great lovers escapes me. (Here we hover at once on absurdity and on what, following health, is probably the most important factor in the good life—a balanced sexual rhythm.)

I would like to live is a world where many good books were being published—fiction, poetry, science, history, philosophy; where good plays and good music were just around the corner—without too much standing in line and too little ventilation; where good pictures were being hung; where the arts and crafts were flourishing on indigenous rather than imitative material; and particularly and especially, where good conversation abounded, together with the leisure to pursue it. Of all the joys which life has to offer none, for me, can exceed that of keen stimulating talk; and nothing is rarer in America today.

Finally, I would like to live in a community that held a genuine sense of its uniqueness; where one could take pride in community achievements, match one's art and craftsmanship and sport against a neighbor group; where one could contribute in person to the local theater, the local schools; help to plan a beautiful region, and see that plan grow before one's eyes—and so take root in one's own soil, a part of the earth, earthy, as well as a dreamer in the clouds. So the Greeks must have looked back to the plains and hills and cedar trees of Attica and Laconia. Here one might have the leisure to play with children as they should be played with; here one might bring the carnival and the pageant—with color and wine and flowers—back to meaning and to life.

Above all, leisure, leisure, a break in the remorseless and meaningless urgencies of the twentieth-century pace.

This—if you will—Utopia may be cold to you, but it is not cold to me. I can see it, feel it, aye, long for it. How would you change it to include the things for which you long? Anthropologists, you say, have yet to find a people without a well-marked religion; that need is indigenous, cardinal, and necessary to you. Good. Let us have a church with a great nave and a great organ and the sound of vespers across the evening fields. You dislike my games and want other games. Again good. The more games the better so long as we play them ourselves. You want to paint or design or build bridges. Each to his own desire, so long as the necessary work is done. You do not want to do anything. There will be a nice, forest-circled, psychopathic hospital until sanity returns. You do not want roots, you want to keep on the move. Would you object to moving through communities which had abolished squalor and striven to individualize and beautify themselves?

Add what you please, so long as it does not make for ugliness or drabness or cruelty; so long as it does not quench life that the lives of a few may burn with a spurious brightness. I do not know what your desires may be, but if they make you happy and others not too unhappy they are welcome. The question is not what is good for other people but good for you.

The preliminary definition of the good life which I have tried to outline is crude enough, but it can be used. Swing it as a searchlight where you will—on Mr. Calvin Coolidge or on Mr. Bernard Shaw; on Miss Jane Addams or on Mrs. Peaches Browning; on a soap factory, a department store, an iron mine, an advertising campaign, a prize fight, a laboratory, a best seller; swing it upon Wall Street or Main Street or Downing Street; on Denmark or on Pittsburgh—it can give basis for judgment. Would this person, or thing, or area, be out of place in such a community? Would it clash, jar, disintegrate; or would it be welcomed and at home? The architecture of Beacon Hill would, the architecture of South Chicago would not; the Lincoln Memorial would, Park Avenue would not; Mr. Chaliapin would, Mr. Shubert would not; the Olympic games would, professional baseball would not; Mr. H. G. Wells would (very much at home he would be), Dr. Frank Crane would not. Mark for yourself the quick from the dead.

The question is not primarily what would make you happy, but rather what would make you more alive. Perhaps complete Nirvana is the happiest conceivable state, but it remains at the opposite pole from vivid life. Pain, heartache, failure in achievement, failure in love, the shock of physical danger, even envy, must remain so long as we behave like human beings. Only the surplus of pain and confusion induced by stupidity would tend to disappear.

It would seem that the end of human effort upon this planet should be to give a maximum of living and a minimum of existing—the life more abundant. Against such an end, those who regard life as a gateway of mortification to a Utopia beyond the grave make their sincere protest. But it is doubtful how far that protest can continue effective in an era of wide knowledge and unlimited possibilities for technical control over nature.

Even if we can win to life ourselves, the contemplation of the existing of those over the brink about us takes, in a sensitive heart, most of the joy out of personal salvation here below. Even if democracy is not sound doctrine, and biological inferiority can be definitely established, there is no particular reason why those handicapped from the germ plasm—and who will perforce have to do most of the dirty work of the world—should not be given surroundings from which they can take the maximum of what life holds for them. Lafcadio Hearn can tell you about the ancient Japanese communities and how extraordinarily high in the sense of beauty and appreciation it has been proved possible for the mass to go.

Granting for the time being—until coal is gone, and the Ice Cap moves south again—granting that a beautiful life here and now should be the major goal of human effort, of what strands shall it be woven? How shall Mr. Mumford and his fellow-critics be appeased? The above is, if you will, a feeble and absurd beginning. But perhaps it will serve as a point of departure for the speculations of wise men and women.

Suggestions for Discussion

1. Although Chase entitles his essay *A Very Private Utopia,* his vision transcends the personal. Cite evidence to support this view.

2. Chase equates the good life with being fully alive. With what illustrations does he establish this definition? Under what general categories do they fall?

3. How does Chase distinguish being fully alive from being happy?

4. How does Chase indirectly define the self? Relate his concept to that of other writers in this book.

Suggestions for Writing

1. What is your personal conception of Utopia? Define its elements by means of a generalization and particulars to support it.

2. Describe your community as it fosters and/or impedes living the good life.

Joyce Carol Oates

New Heaven and Earth

Joyce Carol Oates (b. 1938) is an American novelist, who was awarded a Guggenheim Fellowship in 1967, and a professor of English at Princeton University. Her novels include the prize-winning *Them* (1969), and *With Shuddering Fall* (1964), *Upon the Sweeping Flood* (1966), *Garden of Earthly Delights* (1967), and *Expensive People* (1968). She was also the O'Henry Prize Story winner in 1967–1968 and contributes fiction to national magazines. In this essay she affirms that our old "objective, valueless philosophies" that have always worked to preserve the status quo will be replaced by a new, higher humanism or pantheism.

In spite of current free-roaming terrors in this country, it is really not the case that we are approaching some apocalyptic close. Both those who seem to be awaiting it with excitement and dread and those who are trying heroically to comprehend it in terms of recent American history are mistaking a crisis of transition for a violent end. Even Charles Reich's much maligned and much misinterpreted *The Greening of America*, which was the first systematic attempt to indicate the direction we are surely moving in, focuses much too narrowly upon a single decade in a single nation and, in spite of its occasional stunning accuracy, is a curiously American product—that is, it imagines all of history as running up into and somehow culminating in the United States. Consider Reich's last two sentences:

> . . . For one almost convinced that it was necessary to accept ugliness and evil, that it was necessary to be a miser of dreams, it is an invitation to cry or laugh. For one who thought the world was irretrievably encased in metal and plastic and sterile stone, it seems a veritable greening of America.

Compare that with the following passage from Teilhard de Chardin's *The Phenomenon of Man*, a less historical-nationalistic vision:

> In every domain, when anything exceeds a certain measurement, it suddenly changes its aspect, condition, or nature. The curve doubles back, the surface contracts to a point, the solid disintegrates, the liquid boils, the germ cell divides, intuition suddenly bursts on the piled up facts. . . . Critical points have been reached, rungs on the ladder, involving a change of state—jumps of all sorts *in the course* of development.

Or consider these lines from D. H. Lawrence's poem "Nullus," in which he is speaking of the private "self" that is Lawrence but also of the epoch in which this self exists:

> There are said to be creative pauses,
> pauses that are as good as death, empty and dead as death itself.
> And in these awful pauses the evolutionary change takes place.

What appears to be a breaking-down of civilization may well be simply the breaking-up of old forms by life itself (not an eruption of madness or self-destruction), a process that is entirely natural and inevitable. Perhaps we are in the tumultuous but exciting close of a centuries-old kind of consciousness— a few of us like theologians of the medieval church encountering the unstoppable energy of the Renaissance. What we must avoid is the paranoia of history's "true believers," who have always misinterpreted a natural, evolutionary transformation of consciousness as being the violent conclusion of all of history.

The God-centered, God-directed world of the Middle Ages was transformed into the complex era we call the Renaissance, but the transition was as terrifying as it was inevitable, if the innumerable prophecies of doom that were made at the time are any accurate indication. Shakespeare's most disturbing tragedies—*King Lear* and *Troilus and Cressida*—reflect that communal anxiety, as do the various expressions of anxiety over the "New Science" later in the seventeenth century. When we look back into history, we are amazed, not at the distance that separates one century from another, but at their closeness, the almost poetic intimacy.

As I see it, the United States is the first nation—though so complex and unclassifiable an entity almost resists definition as a single unit—to suffer/ enjoy the death throes of the Renaissance. How could it be otherwise, since our nation is sensitive, energetic, swarming with life, and, beyond any other developed nation in the world, the most obsessed with its own history and its own destiny? Approaching a kind of manic stage, in which suppressed voices are at last being heard, in which *no extreme viewpoint is any longer "extreme,"* the United States is preparing itself for a transformation of "being" similar to that experienced by individuals as they approach the end of one segment of their lives and must rapidly, and perhaps desperately, sum up everything that has gone before.

It is easy to misread the immediate crises, to be frightened by the spontaneous eruptions into consciousness of disparate groups (blacks, women, youth, "the backlash of the middle class"); it is possible to overlook how the collective voices of many of our best poets and writers serve to dramatize and exorcise current American nightmares. Though some of our most brilliant creative artists are obsessed with disintegration and with the isolated ego, it is clear by now that they are all, with varying degrees of terror, saying the same thing—that we are helpless, unconnected with any social or cultural unit, unable to direct the flow of history, that we cannot effectively communicate. The effect is almost that of a single voice, as if a communal psychoanalytic process were taking place. But there does come a time in an individual writer's experience when he realizes, perhaps against his will, that his voice is one of many, his fiction one of many fictions, and that all serious fictions are half-conscious dramatizations of what is going on in the world.

Here is a simple test to indicate whether you are ready for the new vision of man or whether you will fear and resist it: Imagine you are high in the air, looking down on a crowded street scene from a height so great that you cannot make out individual faces but can see only shapes, scurrying figures rather like insects. Your imagination projects you suddenly down into that mass. You respond with what emotion—dread or joy?

In many of us the Renaissance ideal is still powerful, its voice tyrannical. It declares: *I will, I want, I demand, I think, I am.* This voice tells us that we are not quite omnipotent but must act as if we were, pushing out into a world of other people or of nature that will necessarily resist us, that will try to destroy us, and that we must conquer. *I will exist* has meant only *I will impose my will on others.* To that end man has developed his intellect and has extended his physical strength by any means possible because, indeed, at one time the world did have to be conquered. The Renaissance leapt ahead into its own necessary future, into the development and near perfection of machines. Machines are not evil, or even "unnatural," but simply extensions of the human brain. The designs for our machines are no less the product of our creative imaginations than are works of art, though it might be difficult for most people—especially artists—to acknowledge this. But a great deal that is difficult, even outrageous, will have to be acknowledged.

If technology appears to have dehumanized civilization, that is a temporary failing or error—for the purpose of technology is the furthering of the "human," the bringing to perfection of all the staggering potentialities in each individual, which are nearly always lost, layered over with biological or social or cultural crusts. Anyone who imagines that a glorious pastoral world has been lost, through machines, identifies himself as a child of the city, perhaps a second- or third-generation child of the city. An individual who has lived close to nature, on a farm, for instance, knows that "natural" man was never *in* nature; he had to fight nature, at the cost of his own spontaneity and, indeed, his humanity. It is only through the conscious control of the "machine" (i.e., through man's brain) that man can transcend the miserable struggle with nature, whether in the form of sudden devastating hailstorms that annihilate an entire crop, or minute deadly bacteria in the bloodstream, or simply the commonplace (but potentially tragic) condition of poor eyesight. It is only through the machine that man can become more human, more spiritual. Understandably, only a handful of Americans have realized this obvious fact, since technology seems at present to be villainous. Had our earliest ancestors been gifted with a box of matches, their first actions would probably have been destructive—or self-destructive. But we know how beneficial fire has been to civilization.

The Renaissance man invented and brought to near perfection the civilization of the machine. In doing this, he was simply acting out the conscious and unconscious demand of his time—the demand that man (whether man-in-the-world or man supposedly superior to worldly interests) master everything about him, including his own private nature, his own "ego," redefining himself in terms of a conqueror whose territory should be as vast as his own desire to conquer. The man who "masters" every aspect of his own being, subduing or obliterating his own natural instincts, leaving nothing to be unknown, uninvestigated, is the ideal of our culture, whether he is an industrialist or a "disinterested" scientist or a literary man. In other words, I see no difference between the maniacal acquisitiveness of traditional American capitalists and the meticulous, joyless, ironic manner of many scholars and writers.

It is certainly time to stop accusing "industry" or "science" or the "Corporate State" or "Amerika" of being inhuman or antihuman. The exaggerated and suprahuman potency attributed to machines, investing them with the power of the long-vanquished Devil himself, is amazing. It is also rather disheartening, if we observe the example of one of our most brilliant writers, Norman Mailer, who argues—with all the doomed, manic intensity of a late-medieval churchman resisting the future even when it is upon him—that the universe can still sensibly be divided into God and Devil, that there can be an "inorganic" product of the obviously organic mind of man. Mailer (and many others) exemplifies the old, losing, pitiful Last Stand of the Ego, the Self-Against-All-Others, the Conqueror, the Highest of all Protoplasms, Namer and Begetter of all Fictions.

What will the next phase of human experience be? A simple evolution into a higher humanism, perhaps a kind of intelligent pantheism, in which all substance in the universe (including the substance fortunate enough to perceive it) is there by equal right.

We have come to the end of, we are satiated with, the "objective," valueless philosophies that have always worked to preserve a status quo, however archaic. We are tired of the old dichotomies: Sane/Insane, Normal/Sick, Black/White, Man/Nature, Victor/Vanquished, and—above all this Cartesian dualism—I/It. Although once absolutely necessary to get us through the exploratory, analytical phase of our development as human beings, they are no longer useful or pragmatic. They are no longer *true*. Far from being locked inside our own skins, inside the "dungeons" of ourselves, we are now able to recognize that our minds belong, quite naturally, to a collective "mind," a mind in which we share everything that is mental, most obviously language itself, and that the old boundary of the skin is no boundary at all but a membrane connecting the inner and outer experiences of existence. Our intelligence, our wit, our cleverness, our unique personalities—all are simultaneously "our own" possessions and the world's. This has always been a mystical vision, but more and more in our time it is becoming a rational truth. It is no longer the private possession of a Blake, a Whitman, or a Lawrence, but the public, articulate offering of a Claude Lévi-Strauss, to whom anthropology is "part of a cosmology" and whose humanism is one that sees everything in the universe, including man, in its own place. It is the lifelong accumulative statement of Abraham Maslow, the humanist psychologist who extended the study of psychology from the realm of the disordered into that of the normal and the "more-than-normal," including people who would once have been termed mystics and been dismissed as irrational. It is the unique, fascinating voice of Buckminster Fuller, who believes that "human minds and brains may be essential in the total design" of the universe. And it is the abrasive argument of R. D. Laing, the Freudian/post-Freudian mystic, who has denied the medical and legal distinctions between "normal" and "abnormal" and has set out not only to experience but to articulate a metaphysical "illumination" whereby self and other become joined. All these are men of genius, whose training has been rigorously scientific. That they are expressing views once considered the exclusive property of mystics proves that the old dichotomy of Reason/Intuition has vanished or is vanishing.

As with all dichotomies, it will be transcended—not argued away, not battered into silence. The energies wasted on the old debates—Are we rational? Are we 90 percent Unconscious Impulses?—will be utilized for higher and more worthy human pursuits. Instead of hiding our most amazing, mysterious, and inexplicable experiences, we will learn to articulate and share them; instead of insisting upon rigid academic or intellectual categories (for instance, that "science fiction" is different from other fiction, or less traditional than the very recent "realistic novel"), we will see how naturally they flow into one another, supporting and explaining each other. Yesterday's wildly ornate, obscure, poetic prophecies evolve into today's calm statements of fact.

The vision of a new, higher humanism or pantheism is not irrational but is a logical extension of what we now know. It may frighten some of us because it challenges the unquestioned assumptions that we have always held. But these assumptions were never *ours*. We never figured them out, never discovered them for ourselves; we inherited them from the body of knowledge created by our men of genius. Now men of genius, such as British physicist/philosopher Sir James Jeans, are saying newer, deeper things:

> Today there is a wide measure of agreement, which on the physical side of science approaches almost to unanimity, that the stream of knowledge is heading toward a nonmechanical reality; the universe begins to look more like a great thought than like a great machine. Mind no longer appears as an accidental intruder into the realm of matter; we are beginning to suspect that we ought rather to hail it as the creator and governor of the realm of matter. . . .

Everywhere, suddenly, we hear the prophetic voice of Nietzsche once again, saying that man must overcome himself, that he must interpret and create the universe. (Nietzsche was never understood until now, until the world caught up with him, or approached him.) In such a world, which belongs to consciousness, there can be no distracting of energies from the need to push forward, to synthesize, to converge, to make a unity out of ostensible diversity. But too facile optimism is as ultimately distracting as the repetitive nihilism and despair we have inherited from the early part of this century. An absolutely honest literature, whether fiction or nonfiction, must dramatize for us the complexities of this epoch, showing us how deeply related we are to one another, how deeply we act out, even in our apparently secret dreams, the communal crises of our world. If demons are reawakened and allowed to run loose across the landscape of suburban shopping malls and parks, it is only so that their symbolic values—wasteful terror, despair, entropy—can be recognized. If all other dichotomies are ultimately transcended, there must still be the tension between a healthy acceptance of change and a frightened, morbid resistance to change.

The death throes of the old values are everywhere around us, but they are not at all the same thing as the death throes of particular human beings. We can transform ourselves, overleap ourselves beyond even our most flamboyant estimations. A conversion is always imminent; one cannot revert back to a lower level of consciousness. The "conversion" of the I-centered personality into a higher, or transcendental, personality cannot be an artifically, externally enforced event; it must be a natural event. It is surely as natural as the upward growth of a plant—if the plant's growth is not impeded. It has nothing to do with drugs, with the occult, with a fashionable cultivation of Eastern mysticism (not at all suitable for us in the West—far too passive, too life-denying, too ascetic); it has nothing to do with political beliefs. It is not Marxist, not Communist, not Socialist, not willing to align itself with any particular ideology. If anything, it is a flowering of the democratic ideal, a community of equals, but not a community mobilized against the rest of the world, not a unity arising out of primitive paranoia.

In the Sixties and at present we hear a very discordant music. We have got to stop screaming at one another. We have got to bring into harmony the various discordant demands, voices, stages of personality. Those more advanced must work to transform the rest, by being, themselves, models of sanity and integrity. The angriest of the ecologists must stop blaming industry for having brought to near perfection the implicit demands of society, as if anyone in our society—especially at the top—has ever behaved autonomously, unshaped by that society and its history. The optimism of *The Greening of America* seems to me a bit excessive or at least premature. There is no doubt that the future—the new consciousness—is imminent, but it may take generations to achieve it. The rapidly condensed vision, the demand for immediate gratification, is, once again, typically (and sadly) American. But, though the achievement of Reich's vision is much farther off than he seems to think, it is an inevitable one, and those of us who will probably not share personally in a transformed world can, in a way, anticipate it now, almost as if experiencing it now. If we are reasonably certain of the conclusion of a novel (especially one we have ourselves imagined), we can endure and even enjoy the intermediary chapters that move us toward that conclusion.

One of the unfortunate aspects of American intellectual life has been the nearly total divorce of academic philosophy from the issues of a fluid, psychic social reality. There are obvious reasons for this phenomenon, too complex to consider at the moment. But the book that needs to be written about the transformation of America cannot really be written by anyone lacking a thorough knowledge of where we have been and where we are right now, in terms of an intellectual development that begins and ends with the faculties of the mind. We require the meticulous genius of a Kant, a man of humility who is awakened from some epoch-induced "slumber" to synthesize vast exploratory fields of knowledge, to write the book that is the way into the future for us.

This essay, totally nonacademic in its lyric disorganization, in its bringing together of voices that, for all their differences, seem to be saying one thing, is intended only to suggest—no, really, to make a plea for—the awakening of that someone's slumber, the rejection of the positivist-linguist-"naming" asceticism that has made American philosophy so disappointing. We need a tradition similar to that in France, where the role of "philosopher" is taken naturally by men of genius who can address themselves to varied groups of people—scientists, writers, artists, and the public itself. Our highly educated and highly cultivated reading public is starved for books like *The Greening of America*. We have an amazingly fertile but somehow separate nation of writers and poets, living dreamily inside a culture but no more than symbiotically related to it. Yet these writers and poets are attempting to define that culture, to "act it out," to somehow make sense of it. The novel is the most human of all art forms—there are truths we can get nowhere else but in the novel— but now our crucial need is for something else. We need a large, generous, meticulous work that will synthesize our separate but deeply similar voices, one that will climb up out of the categories of "rational" and "irrational" to show why the consciousness of the future will feel joy, not dread, at the total rejection of the Renaissance ideal, the absorption into the psychic stream of the universe.

Lawrence asks in his strange poem "New Heaven and Earth" a question that seems to me parallel with Yeats's famous question in the sonnet "Leda and the Swan." In the Yeats poem mortal woman is raped by an immortal force, and, yes, this will and must happen; this cannot be escaped. But the point is: Did she put on his knowledge *with* his power, before the terrifying contact was broken? Lawrence speaks of mysterious "green streams" that flow from the new world (our everyday world—seen with new eyes) and asks, ". . . what are they?" What are the conversions that await us?

Suggestions for Discussion

1. Comment on Oates's observation that "Perhaps we are in the tumultuous but exciting close of a centuries-old kind of consciousness—a few of us like theologians of the medieval church encountering the unstoppable energy of the Renaissance."

2. Do you agree that contemporary crises often cause unwarranted fears because they are misread? Explain. Cite examples.

3. What does she believe to be the next phase of human experience? Do you agree? Explain.

4. Discuss her opinions about technology and industry.

5. Upon what assumptions about man and the universe is her optimism based? What personal values does she affirm?

Suggestions for Writing

1. Describe, in a speech or essay, your vision of man's future.

2. Examine Oates's use of literary references. How do they help to support her thesis?

Fiction

Anton Chekhov

The Bet

Translated by Constance Garnett

Anton Chekhov (1860–1904), Russian story writer and playwright, practiced medicine briefly before devoting himself to literature. Among his plays are *The Sea Gull* (1896), *Uncle Vanya* (1900), *The Three Sisters* (1901), and *The Cherry Orchard* (1904). His stories, translated by Constance Garnett, were published as *The Tales of Chekhov* (1916–1923). The drama of the lawyer's solitary existence constitutes the central action of the story; it culminates in his walking out of the lodge a few hours before fulfilling the conditions of the bet; and it reaches its highest point of intensity, and its resolution, in the letter which passionately expresses his nihilism and supreme contempt for his fellow men.

I

It was a dark autumn night. The old banker was pacing from corner to corner of his study, recalling to his mind the party he gave in the autumn fifteen years before. There were many clever people at the party and much interesting conversation. They talked among other things of capital punishment. The guests, among them not a few scholars and journalists, for the most part disapproved of capital punishment. They found it obsolete as a means of punishment, unfitted to a Christian State and immoral. Some of them thought that capital punishment should be replaced universally by life imprisonment.

"I don't agree with you," said the host. "I myself have experienced neither capital punishment nor life imprisonment, but if one may judge *a priori*, then in my opinion capital punishment is more moral and more humane than imprisonment. Execution kills instantly, life imprisonment kills by degrees. Who is the more humane executioner, one who kills you in a few seconds or one who draws the life out of you incessantly, for years?"

"They're both equally immoral," remarked one of the guests, "because their purpose is the same, to take away life. The State is not God. It has no right to take away that which it cannot give back, if it should so desire."

Among the company was a lawyer, a young man of about twenty-five. On being asked his opinion, he said:

"Capital punishment and life imprisonment are equally immoral; but if I were offered the choice between them, I would certainly choose the second. It's better to live somehow than not to live at all."

There ensued a lively discussion. The banker who was then younger and more nervous suddenly lost his temper, banged his fist on the table, and turning to the young lawyer, cried out:

"It's a lie. I bet you two millions you wouldn't stick in a cell even for five years."

"If you mean it seriously," replied the lawyer, "then I bet I'll stay not five but fifteen."

"Fifteen! Done!" cried the banker. "Gentlemen, I stake two millions."

"Agreed. You stake two millions, I my freedom," said the lawyer.

So this wild, ridiculous bet came to pass. The banker, who at that time had too many millions to count, spoiled and capricious, was beside himself with rapture. During supper he said to the lawyer jokingly:

"Come to your senses, young man, before it's too late. Two millions are nothing to me, but you stand to lose three or four of the best years of your life. I say three or four, because you'll never stick it out any longer. Don't forget either, you unhappy man, that voluntary is much heavier than enforced imprisonment. The idea that you have the right to free yourself at any moment will poison the whole of your life in the cell. I pity you."

And now the banker, pacing from corner to corner, recalled all this and asked himself:

"Why did I make this bet? What's the good? The lawyer loses fifteen years of his life and I throw away two millions. Will it convince people that capital punishment is worse or better than imprisonment for life? No, no! all stuff and rubbish. On my part, it was the caprice of a well-fed man; on the lawyer's, pure greed of gold."

He recollected further what happened after the evening party. It was decided that the lawyer must undergo his imprisonment under the strictest observation, in a garden wing of the banker's house. It was agreed that during the period he would be deprived of the right to cross the threshold, to see living people, to hear human voices, and to receive letters and newspapers. He was permitted to have a musical instrument, to read books, to write letters, to drink wine, and smoke tobacco. By the agreement he could communicate, but only in silence, with the outside world through a little window specially constructed for this purpose. Everything necessary, books, music, wine, he could receive in any quantity by sending a note through the window. The agreement provided for all the minutest details, which made the confinement strictly solitary, and it obliged the lawyer to remain exactly fifteen years from twelve o'clock of November 14th, 1870 to twelve o'clock of November 14th, 1885. The least attempt on his part to violate the conditions, to escape if only for two minutes before the time freed the banker from the obligation to pay him the two millions.

During the first year of imprisonment, the lawyer, as far as it was possible to judge from his short notes, suffered terribly from loneliness and boredom.

From his wing day and night came the sound of the piano. He rejected wine and tobacco. "Wine," he wrote, "excites desires, and desires are the chief foes of a prisoner; besides, nothing is more boring than to drink good wine alone, and tobacco spoils the air in his room." During the first year the lawyer was sent books of a light character; novels with a complicated love interest, stories of crime and fantasy, comedies, and so on.

In the second year the piano was heard no longer and the lawyer asked only for classics. In the fifth year, music was heard again, and the prisoner asked for wine. Those who watched him said that during the whole of that year he was only eating, drinking, and lying on his bed. He yawned often and talked angrily to himself. Books he did not read. Sometimes at nights he would sit down to write. He would write for a long time and tear it all up in the morning. More than once he was heard to weep.

In the second half of the sixth year, the prisoner began zealously to study languages, philosophy, and history. He fell on these subjects so hungrily that the banker hardly had time to get books enough for him. In the space of four years about six hundred volumes were brought at his request. It was while that passion lasted that the banker received the following letter from the prisoner: "My dear gaoler, I am writing these lines in six languages. Show them to experts. Let them read them. If they do not find one single mistake, I beg you to give orders to have a gun fired off in the garden. By the noise I shall know that my efforts have not been in vain. The geniuses of all ages and countries speak in different languages; but in them all burns the same flame. Oh, if you knew my heavenly happiness now that I can understand them!" The prisoner's desire was fulfilled. Two shots were fired in the garden by the banker's order.

Later on, after the tenth year, the lawyer sat immovable before his table and read only the New Testament. The banker found it strange that a man who in four years had mastered six hundred erudite volumes, should have spent nearly a year in reading one book, easy to understand and by no means thick. The New Testament was then replaced by the history of religions and theology.

During the last two years of his confinement the prisoner read an extraordinary amount, quite haphazard. Now he would apply himself to the natural sciences, then he would read Byron or Shakespeare. Notes used to come from him in which he asked to be sent at the same time a book on chemistry, a text-book of medicine, a novel, and some treatise on philosophy or theology. He read as though he were swimming in the sea among broken pieces of wreckage, and in his desire to save his life was eagerly grasping one piece after another.

II

The banker recalled all this, and thought:

"To-morrow at twelve o'clock he receives his freedom. Under the agreement, I shall have to pay him two millions. If I pay, it's all over with me. I am ruined for ever. . . ."

Fifteen years before he had too many millions to count, but now he was afraid to ask himself which he had more of, money or debts. Gambling on the

Stock-Exchange, risky speculation, and the recklessness of which he could not rid himself even in old age, had gradually brought his business to decay; and the fearless, self-confident, proud man of business had become an ordinary banker, trembling at every rise and fall in the market.

"That cursed bet," murmured the old man clutching his head in despair. . . . "Why didn't the man die? He's only forty years old. He will take away my last farthing, marry, enjoy life, gamble on the Exchange, and I will look on like an envious beggar and hear the same words from him every day: 'I'm obliged to you for the happiness of my life. Let me help you.' No, it's too much! The only escape from bankruptcy and disgrace—is that the man should die."

The clock had just struck three. The banker was listening. In the house every one was asleep, and one could hear only the frozen trees whining outside the windows. Trying to make no sound, he took out of his safe the key of the door which had not been opened for fifteen years, put on his overcoat, and went out of the house. The garden was dark and cold. It was raining. A damp, penetrating wind howled in the garden and gave the trees no rest. Though he strained his eyes, the banker could see neither the ground, nor the white statues, nor the garden wing, nor the trees. Approaching the garden wing, he called the watchman twice. There was no answer. Evidently the watchman had taken shelter from the bad weather and was now asleep somewhere in the kitchen or the greenhouse.

"If I have the courage to fulfill my intention," thought the old man, "the suspicion will fall on the watchman first of all."

In the darkness he groped for the steps and the door and entered the hall of the garden-wing, then poked his way into a narrow passage and struck a match. Not a soul was there. Some one's bed, with no bedclothes on it, stood there, and an iron stove loomed dark in the corner. The seals on the door that led into the prisoner's room were unbroken.

When the match went out, the old man, trembling from agitation, peeped into the little window.

In the prisoner's room a candle was burning dimly. The prisoner himself sat by the table. Only his back, the hair on his head and his hands were visible. Open books were strewn about on the table, the two chairs, and on the carpet near the table.

Five minutes passed and the prisoner never once stirred. Fifteen years' confinement had taught him to sit motionless. The banker tapped on the window with his finger, but the prisoner made no movement in reply. Then the banker cautiously tore the seals from the door and put the key into the lock. The rusty lock gave a hoarse groan and the door creaked. The banker expected instantly to hear a cry of surprise and the sound of steps. Three minutes passed and it was as quiet inside as it had been before. He made up his mind to enter.

Before the table sat a man, unlike an ordinary human being. It was a skeleton, with tight-drawn skin, with long curly hair like a woman's, and a shaggy beard. The colour of his face was yellow, of an earthy shade; the cheeks were sunken, the back long and narrow, and the hand upon which he leaned his hairy head was so lean and skinny that it was painful to look upon. His hair was already silvering with grey, and no one who glanced at the senile emaciation of the face would have believed that he was only forty years old. On the table, before his bended head, lay a sheet of paper on which something was written in a tiny hand.

"Poor devil," thought the banker, "he's asleep and probably seeing millions in his dreams. I have only to take and throw this half-dead thing on the bed, smother him a moment with the pillow, and the most careful examination will find no trace of unnatural death. But, first, let us read what he has written here."

The banker took the sheet from the table and read:

"Tomorrow at twelve o'clock midnight, I shall obtain my freedom and the right to mix with people. But before I leave this room and see the sun I think it necessary to say a few words to you. On my own clear conscience and before God who sees me I declare to you that I despise freedom, life, health, and all that your books call the blessings of the world.

"For fifteen years I have diligently studied earthly life. True, I saw neither the earth nor the people, but in your books I drank fragrant wine, sang songs, hunted deer and wild boar in the forests, loved women. . . . And beautiful women, like clouds ethereal, created by the magic of your poets' genius, visited me by night, and whispered to me wonderful tales, which made my head drunken. In your books I climbed the summits of Elbruz and Mont Blanc and saw from there how the sun rose in the morning, and in the evening suffused the sky, the ocean and the mountain ridges with a purple gold. I saw from there how above me lightnings glimmered cleaving the clouds; I saw green forests, fields, rivers, lakes, cities; I heard sirens singing, and the playing of the pipes of Pan; I touched the wings of beautiful devils who came flying to me to speak of God. . . . In your books I cast myself into bottomless abysses, worked miracles, burned cities to the ground, preached new religions, conquered whole countries. . . .

"Your books gave me wisdom. All that unwearying human thought created in the centuries is compressed to a little lump in my skull. I know that I am cleverer than you all.

"And I despise your books, despise all worldly blessings and wisdom. Everything is void, frail, visionary and delusive as a mirage. Though you be proud and wise and beautiful, yet will death wipe you from the face of the earth like the mice underground; and your posterity, your history, and the immorality of your men of genius will be as frozen slag, burnt down together with the terrestrial globe.

"You are mad, and gone the wrong way. You take falsehood for truth and ugliness for beauty. You would marvel if suddenly apple and orange trees should bear frogs and lizards instead of fruit, and if roses should begin to breathe the odour of a sweating horse. So do I marvel at you, who have bartered heaven for earth. I do not want to understand you.

"That I may show you in deed my contempt for that by which you live, I waive the two millions of which I once dreamed as of paradise, and which I now despise. That I may deprive myself of my right to them, I shall come out from here five minutes before the stipulated term, and thus shall violate the agreement."

When he had read, the banker put the sheet on the table, kissed the head of the strange man, and began to weep. He went out of the wing. Never at any other time, not even after his terrible losses on the Exchange, had he felt such contempt for himself as now. Coming home, he lay down on his bed, but agitation and tears kept him a long time from sleeping. . . .

The next morning the poor watchman came running to him and told him that they had seen the man who lived in the wing climb through the window into the garden. He had gone to the gate and disappeared. The banker instantly went with his servants to the wing and established the escape of his prisoner. To avoid unnecessary rumours he took the paper with the renunciation from the table and, on his return, locked it in his safe.

Suggestions for Discussion

1. If you agree that "The Bet" is primarily the lawyer's story, why is our view of the lawyer filtered through the reminiscences and observations of the banker? Why are we permitted to see the lawyer directly only twice? What artistic purposes are served by the use of hearsay and notes and letters, and by the sparseness and flatness of the account of the lawyer's years of confinement?

2. Trace the changes in the lawyer's activities as they mark the development and resolution of the action. What are the implications as to his ultimate fate?

3. How do the shifts in time contribute to suspense and tone?

4. Find examples of irony and paradox.

5. How do you reconcile the lawyer's nihilism with his lyrical assertion that he has known the beauty of earth and love, has seen nature in her glory and tempestousness, and has achieved wisdom—"all that the unresting thought of man has created"? What evidence can you find that Chekhov's vision of life extends beyond negation of all values?

Suggestions for Writing

1. Chekhov has said, "When you depict sad or unlucky people and want to touch the reader's heart, try to be colder—it gives their grief, as it were, a background against which it stands out in greater relief. . . . You must be unconcerned when you write pathetic stories, . . . the more objective, the stronger will be the effect." Write an evaluation of Chekhov's theories in relation to the characters of the banker and the lawyer, the tone of the story, and its denouement.

2. Write a position paper on the lawyer's (banker's) "examined life."

3. Write your own preferred conclusion to "The Bet"; or describe the lawyer's next fifteen years; or recount a conversation in which the banker tells his story the next morning.

Walter Van Tilburg Clark

The Portable Phonograph

Walter Van Tilburg Clark (1909–1972) was an American short-story writer and novelist, many of whose works reflect his intense awareness of nature and of the relation between man and nature. His novels include *The Ox-Bow Incident* (1942), *The City of Trembling Leaves* (1945), and *The Track of the Cat* (1949). His collected stories have been published under the title *The Watchful Gods and Other Stories* (1950). In "The Portable Phonograph," survivors of war find momentary relief from their grim and threatened existence in the words of *The Tempest* and the music of Debussy.

The red sunset with narrow, black cloud strips like threads across it, lay on the curved horizon of the prairie. The air was still and cold, and in it settled the mute darkness and greater cold of night. High in the air there was wind, for through the veil of the dusk the clouds could be seen gliding rapidly south and changing shapes. A queer sensation of torment, of two-sided, unpredictable nature, arose from the stillness of the earth air beneath the violence of the upper air. Out of the sunset, through the dead, matted grass and isolated weed stalks of the prairie, crept the narrow and deeply rutted remains of a road. In the road, in places, there were crusts of shallow, brittle ice. There were little islands of an old oiled pavement in the road too, but most of it was mud, now frozen rigid. The frozen mud still bore the toothed impress of great tanks, and a wanderer on the neighboring undulations might have stumbled, in this light, into large, partially filled-in and weed-grown cavities, their banks channeled and beginning to spread into badlands. These pits were such as might have been made by falling meteors, but they were not. They were the scars of gigantic bombs, their rawness already made a little natural by rain, seed, and time. Along the road, there were rakish remnants of fence. There was also, just visible, one portion of tangled and multiple barbed wire still erect, behind which was a shelving ditch with small caves, now very quiet and empty, at intervals in its back wall. Otherwise there was no structure or remnant of a structure visible over the dome of the darkling earth, but only, in sheltered hollows, the darker shadows of young trees trying again.

Under the withering arch of the high wind a V of wild geese fled south. The rush of their pinions sounded briefly, and the faint, plaintive notes of their expeditionary talk. Then they left a still greater vacancy. There was the smell and expectation of snow, as there is likely to be when the wild geese fly south. From the remote distance, towards the red sky, came faintly the protracted howl and quick yap-yap of a prairie wolf.

North of the road, perhaps a hundred yards, lay the parallel and deeply intrenched course of a small creek, lined with leafless alders and willows. The creek was already silent under ice. Into the bank above it was dug a sort of cell, with a single opening, like the mouth of a mine tunnel. Within the cell there was a little red of fire, which showed dully through the opening, like a reflection or a deception of the imagination. The light came from the chary burning of four blocks of poorly aged peat, which gave off a petty warmth and much acrid smoke. But the precious remnants of wood, old fence posts and timbers from the long-deserted dugouts, had to be saved for the real cold, for the time when a man's breath blew white, the moisture in his nostrils stiffened at once when he stepped out, and the expansive blizzards paraded for days over the vast open, swirling and settling and thickening, till the dawn of the cleared day when the sky was thin blue-green and the terrible cold, in which a man could not live for three hours unwarmed, lay over the uniformly drifted swell of the plain.

Around the smoldering peat, four men were seated cross-legged. Behind them, traversed by their shadows, was the earth bench, with two old and dirty army blankets, where the owner of the cell slept. In a niche in the opposite wall were a few tin utensils which caught the glint of the coals. The host was rewrapping in a piece of daubed burlap four fine, leather-bound books. He worked slowly and very carefully, and at last tied the bundle securely with a piece of grass-woven cord. The other three looked intently upon the process, as if a great significance lay in it. As the host tied the cord, he spoke. He was an old man, his long, matted beard and hair gray to nearly white. The shadows made his brows and cheekbones appear gnarled, his eyes and cheeks deeply sunken. His big hands, rough with frost and swollen by rheumatism, were awkward but gentle at their task. He was like a prehistoric priest performing a fateful ceremonial rite. Also his voice had in it a suitable quality of deep, reverent despair, yet perhaps at the moment, a sharpness of selfish satisfaction.

"When I perceived what was happening," he said, "I told myself, 'It is the end. I cannot take much; I will take these.'"

"Perhaps I was impractical," he continued. "But for myself, I do not regret, and what do we know of those who will come after us? We are the doddering remnant of a race of mechanical fools. I have saved what I love; the soul of what was good in us is here; perhaps the new ones will make a strong enough beginning not to fall behind when they become clever."

He rose with slow pain and placed the wrapped volumes in the niche with his utensils. The others watched him with the same ritualistic gaze.

"Shakespeare, the Bible, *Moby Dick*, the *Divine Comedy*," one of them said softly. "You might have done worse, much worse."

"You will have a little soul left until you die," said another harshly. "That is more than is true of us. My brain becomes thick, like my hands." He held the big, battered hands, with their black nails, in the glow to be seen.

"I want paper to write on," he said. "And there is none."

The fourth man said nothing. He sat in the shadow farthest from the fire, and sometimes his body jerked in its rags from the cold. Although he was still young, he was sick and coughed often. Writing implied a greater future than he now felt able to consider.

The old man seated himself laboriously, and reached out, groaning at the movement, to put another block of peat on the fire. With bowed heads and averted eyes, his three guests acknowledged his magnanimity.

"We thank you, Doctor Jenkins, for the reading," said the man who had named the books.

They seemed then to be waiting for something. Doctor Jenkins understood, but was loath to comply. In an ordinary moment he would have said nothing. But the words of *The Tempest,* which he had been reading, and the religious attention of the three made this an unusual occasion.

"You wish to hear the phonograph," he said grudgingly.

The two middle-aged men stared into the fire, unable to formulate and expose the enormity of their desire.

The young man, however, said anxiously, between suppressed coughs, "Oh, please," like an excited child.

The old man rose again in his difficult way, and went to the back of the cell. He returned and placed tenderly upon the packed floor, where the fire-light might fall upon it, an old portable phonograph in a black case. He smoothed the top with his hand, and then opened it. The lovely green-felt-covered disk became visible.

"I have been using thorns as needles," he said. "But tonight, because we have a musician among us"—he bent his head to the young man, almost invisible in the shadow—"I will use a steel needle. There are only three left."

The two middle-aged men stared at him in speechless adoration. The one with the big hands, who wanted to write, moved his lips, but the whisper was not audible.

"Oh, don't!" cried the young man, as if he were hurt. "The thorns will do beautifully."

"No," the old man said. "I have become accustomed to the thorns, but they are not really good. For you, my young friend, we will have good music tonight."

"After all," he added generously, and beginning to wind the phonograph, which creaked, "they can't last forever."

"No, nor we," the man who needed to write said harshly. "The needle, by all means."

"Oh, thanks," said the young man. "Thanks," he said again in a low, excited voice, and then stifled his coughing with a bowed head.

"The records, though," said the old man when he had finished winding, "are a different matter. Already they are very worn. I do not play them more than once a week. One, once a week, that is what I allow myself."

"More than a week I cannot stand it; not to hear them," he apologized.

"No, how could you?" cried the young man. "And with them here like this."

"A man can stand anything," said the man who wanted to write, in his harsh, antagonistic voice.

"Please, the music," said the young man.

"Only the one," said the old man. "In the long run, we will remember more that way."

He had a dozen records with luxuriant gold and red seals. Even in that light the others could see that the threads of the records were becoming worn. Slowly he read out the titles and the tremendous, dead names of the composers and the artists and the orchestras. The three worked upon the names in their minds, carefully. It was difficult to select from such a wealth what they would at once most like to remember. Finally, the man who wanted to write named Gershwin's "New York."

"Oh, no," cried the sick young man, and then could say nothing more because he had to cough. The others understood him, and the harsh man withdrew his selection and waited for the musician to choose.

The musician begged Doctor Jenkins to read the titles again, very slowly, so that he could remember the sounds. While they were read, he lay back against the wall, his eyes closed, his thin, horny hand pulling at his light beard, and listened to the voices and the orchestras and the single instruments in his mind.

When the reading was done he spoke despairingly. "I have forgotten," he complained; "I cannot hear them clearly."

"There are things missing," he explained.

"I know," said Doctor Jenkins. "I thought that I knew all of Shelley by heart. I should have brought Shelley."

"That's more soul than we can use," said the harsh man. "*Moby Dick* is better."

"By God, we can understand that," he emphasized.

The Doctor nodded.

"Still," said the man who had admired the books, "we need the absolute if we are to keep a grasp on anything."

"Anything but these sticks and peat clods and rabbit snares," he said bitterly.

"Shelley desired an ultimate absolute," said the harsh man. "It's too much," he said. "It's no good; no earthly good."

The musician selected a Debussy nocturne. The others considered and approved. They rose to their knees to watch the Doctor prepare for the playing, so that they appeared to be actually in an attitude of worship. The peat glow showed the thinness of their bearded faces, and the deep lines in them, and revealed the condition of their garments. The other two continued to kneel as the old man carefully lowered the needle onto the spinning disk, but the musician suddenly drew back against the wall again, with his knees up, and buried his face in his hands.

At the first notes of the piano the listeners were startled. They stared at each other. Even the musician lifted his head in amazement, but then quickly bowed it again, strainingly, as if he were suffering from a pain he might not be able to endure. They were all listening deeply, without movement. The wet, blue-green notes tinkled forth from the old machine, and were individual, delectable presences in the cell. The individual, delectable presences swept into a sudden tide of unbearably beautiful dissonance, and then continued fully the swelling and ebbing of that tide, the dissonant inpourings, and the resolutions, and the diminishments, and the little, quiet wavelets of interlude lapping between. Every sound was piercing and singularly sweet. In all the men except the musician, there occurred rapid sequences of tragically heightened recollection. He heard nothing but what was there. At the final, whispering disappearance, but moving quietly so that the others would not hear him and look at him, he let his head fall back in agony, as if it were drawn there by the hair, and clenched the fingers of one hand over his teeth. He sat that way while the others were silent, and until they began to breathe again normally. His drawn-up legs were trembling violently.

Quickly Doctor Jenkins lifted the needle off, to save it and not to spoil the recollection with scraping. When he had stopped the whirling of the sacred disk, he courteously left the phonograph open and by the fire, in sight.

The others, however, understood. The musician rose last, but then abruptly, and went quickly out at the door without saying anything. The others stopped at the door and gave their thanks in low voices. The Doctor nodded magnificently.

"Come again," he invited, "in a week. We will have the 'New York.'"

When the two had gone together, out towards the rimed road, he stood in the entrance, peering and listening. At first, there was only the resonant boom of the wind overhead, and then far over the dome of the dead, dark plain, the wolf cry lamenting. In the rifts of clouds the Doctor saw four stars flying. It impressed the Doctor that one of them had just been obscured by the beginning of a flying cloud at the very moment he heard what he had been listening for, a sound of suppressed coughing. It was not nearby, however. He believed that down against the pale alders he could see the moving shadow.

With nervous hands he lowered the piece of canvas which served as his door, and pegged it at the bottom. Then quickly and quietly, looking at the piece of canvas frequently, he slipped the records into the case, snapped the lid shut, and carried the phonograph to his couch. There, pausing often to stare at the canvas and listen, he dug earth from the wall and disclosed a piece of board. Behind this there was a deep hole in the wall, into which he put the phonograph. After a moment's consideration, he went over and reached down his bundle of books and inserted it also. Then, guardedly, he once more sealed up the hole with the board and the earth. He also changed his blankets, and the grass-stuffed sack which served as a pillow, so that he could lie facing the entrance. After carefully placing two more blocks of peat upon the fire, he stood for a long time watching the stretched canvas, but it seemed to billow naturally with the first gusts of a lowering wind. At last he prayed, and got in under his blankets, and closed his smoke-smarting eyes. On the inside of the bed, next the wall, he could feel with his hand the comfortable piece of lead pipe.

Suggestions for Discussion

1. What does the setting contribute to the tone of the story? What details prepare you for what follows? Describe the situation in which the four men find themselves.

2. The description of each man is restrained and sparse. With what details do you learn of the inner life and character of each? of what they have in common? of their differences?

3. Account for the old man's choice of books. Why would he take *The Tempest?* Explain the "harsh" man's allusion to Shelley with reference to the man's situation.

4. How does repetition contribute to tone and characterization?

5. How does the last sentence illuminate the action?

Suggestions for Writing

1. Compare "The Bet" and "The Portable Phonograph" as they portray their authors' respective structures of the world.

2. Place yourself in the host's position. What books or records would you have selected? Why?

◇◇◇◇

E. B. White

The Second Tree from the Corner

E. B. White (b. 1899), perhaps America's best personal essayist, was a contributor of a monthly department to *Harper's* magazine (1938–1943), and has been
a contributing editor of *The New Yorker* magazine since 1926. His lightly satirical essays show great depth of feeling. They have been published under the
titles *One Man's Meat* (1942), *The Second Tree from the Corner* (1947), and *The
Points of My Compass* (1962). Among his other books are *Stuart Little* (1945),
The Wild Flag (1946), *Charlotte's Web* (1952), and his revision, with additions,
of William Strunk's *The Elements of Style* (1959, 1972, 1979). The second tree
from the corner is a metaphor for what all men wanted, and Trexler was glad
that "what he wanted, and what, in general, all men wanted . . . was both
inexpressible and unattainable, and that it wasn't a wing".

"Ever had any bizarre thoughts?" asked the doctor.

Mr. Trexler failed to catch the word. "What kind?" he said.

"Bizarre," repeated the doctor, his voice steady. He watched his patient
for any slight change of expression, any wince. It seemed to Trexler that the
doctor was not only watching him closely but was creeping slowly toward him,
like a lizard toward a bug. Trexler shoved his chair back an inch and gathered
himself for a reply. He was about to say "Yes" when he realized that if he said
yes the next question would be unanswerable. Bizarre thoughts, bizarre
thoughts? Ever have any bizarre thoughts? What kind of thoughts *except* bizarre had he had since the age of two?

Trexler felt the time passing, the necessity for an answer. These psychiatrists were busy men, overloaded, not to be kept waiting. The next patient
was probably already perched out there in the waiting room, lonely, worried,
shifting around on the sofa, his mind stuffed with bizarre thoughts and amorphous fears. Poor bastard, thought Trexler. Out there all alone in that misshapen antechamber, staring at the filing cabinet and wondering whether to
tell the doctor about that day on the Madison Avenue bus.

Let's see, bizarre thoughts. Trexler dodged back along the dreadful corridor of the years to see what he could find. He felt the doctor's eyes upon him
and knew that time was running out. Don't be so conscientious, he said to
himself. If a bizarre thought is indicated here, just reach into the bag and pick
anything at all. A man as well supplied with bizarre thoughts as you are
should have no difficulty producing one for the record. Trexler darted into
the bag, hung for a moment before one of his thoughts, as a hummingbird
pauses in the delphinium. No, he said, not that one. He darted to another
(the one about the rhesus monkey), paused, considered. No, he said, not that.

Trexler knew he must hurry. He had already used up pretty nearly four
seconds since the question had been put. But it was an impossible situation—
just one more lousy, impossible situation such as he was always getting himself into. When, he asked himself, are you going to quit maneuvering yourself
into a pocket? He made one more effort. This time he stopped at the asylum,
only the bars were lucite—fluted, retractable. Not here, he said. Not
this one.

He looked straight at the doctor. "No," he said quietly. "I never have any bizarre thoughts."

The doctor sucked in on his pipe, blew a plume of smoke toward the rows of medical books. Trexler's gaze followed the smoke. He managed to make out one of the titles, "The Genito-Urinary System." A bright wave of fear swept cleanly over him, and he winced under the first pain of kidney stones. He remembered when he was a child, the first time he ever entered a doctor's office, sneaking a look at the titles of the books—and the flush of fear, the shirt wet under the arms, the book on t.b., the sudden knowledge that he was in the advanced stages of consumption, the quick vision of the hemorrhage. Trexler sighed wearily. Forty years, he thought, and I still get thrown by the title of a medical book. Forty years and I still can't stay on life's little bucky horse. No wonder I'm sitting here in this dreary joint at the end of this woebegone afternoon, lying about my bizarre thoughts to a doctor who looks, come to think of it, rather tired.

The session dragged on. After about twenty minutes, the doctor rose and knocked his pipe out. Trexler got up, knocked the ashes out of his brain, and waited. The doctor smiled warmly and stuck out his hand. "There's nothing the matter with you—you're just scared. Want to know how I know you're scared?"

"How?" asked Trexler.

"Look at the chair you've been sitting in! See how it has moved back away from the desk? You kept inching away from me while I asked you questions. That means you're scared."

"Does it?" said Trexler, faking a grin. "Yeah, I suppose it does."

They finished shaking hands. Trexler turned and walked out uncertainly along the passage, then into the waiting room and out past the next patient, a ruddy pin-striped man who was seated on the sofa twirling his hat nervously and staring straight ahead at the files. Poor, frightened guy, thought Trexler, he's probably read in the *Times* that one American male out of every two is going to die of heart disease by twelve o'clock next Thursday. It says that in the paper almost every morning. And he's also probably thinking about that day on the Madison Avenue bus.

A week later, Trexler was back in the patient's chair. And for several weeks thereafter he continued to visit the doctor, always toward the end of the afternoon, when the vapors hung thick above the pool of the mind and darkened the whole region of the East Seventies. He felt no better as time went on, and he found it impossible to work. He discovered that the visits were becoming routine and that although the routine was one to which he certainly did not look forward, at least he could accept it with cool resignation, as once, years ago, he had accepted a long spell with a dentist who had settled down to a steady fooling with a couple of dead teeth. The visits, moreover, were now assuming a pattern recognizable to the patient.

Each session would begin with a résumé of symptoms—the dizziness in the streets, the constricting pain in the back of the neck, the apprehensions, the tightness of the scalp, the inability to concentrate, the despondency and the melancholy times, the feeling of pressure and tension, the anger at not being able to work, the anxiety over work not done, the gas on the stomach. Dullest set of neurotic symptoms in the world, Trexler would think, as he obediently trudged back over them for the doctor's benefit. And then, having listened attentively to the recital, the doctor would spring his question: "Have you ever found anything that gives you relief?" And Trexler would answer, "Yes. A drink." And the doctor would nod his head knowingly.

As he became familiar with the pattern Trexler found that he increasingly tended to identify himself with the doctor, transferring himself into the doctor's seat—probably (he thought) some rather slick form of escapism. At any rate, it was nothing new for Trexler to identify himself with other people. Whenever he got into a cab, he instantly became the driver, saw everything from the hackman's angle (and the reaching over with the right hand, the nudging of the flag, the pushing it down, all the way down along the side of the meter), saw everything—traffic, fare, everything—through the eyes of Anthony Rocco, or Isidore Freedman, or Matthew Scott. In a barbershop, Trexler was the barber, his fingers curled around the comb, his hand on the tonic. Perfectly natural, then, that Trexler should soon be occupying the doctor's chair, asking the questions, waiting for the answers. He got quite interested in the doctor, in this way. He liked him, and he found him a not too difficult patient.

It was on the fifth visit, about halfway through, that the doctor turned to Trexler and said, suddenly, "What do you want?" He gave the word "want" special emphasis.

"I d'know," replied Trexler uneasily. "I guess nobody knows the answer to that one."

"Sure they do," replied the doctor.

"Do you know what you want?" asked Trexler narrowly.

"Certainly," said the doctor. Trexler noticed that at this point the doctor's chair slid slightly backward, away from him. Trexler stifled a small, internal smile. Scared as a rabbit, he said to himself. Look at him scoot!

"What *do* you want?" continued Trexler, pressing his advantage, pressing it hard.

The doctor glided back another inch away from his inquisitor. "I want a wing on the small house I own in Westport. I want more money, and more leisure to do the things I want to do."

Trexler was just about to say, "And what are those things you want to do, Doctor?" when he caught himself. Better not go too far, he mused. Better not lose possession of the ball. And besides, he thought, what the hell goes on here, anyway—me paying fifteen bucks a throw for these séances and then doing the work myself, asking the questions, weighing the answers. So he wants a new wing! There's a fine piece of theatrical gauze for you! A new wing.

Trexler settled down again and resumed the role of patient for the rest of the visit. It ended on a kindly, friendly note. The doctor reassured him that his fears were the cause of his sickness, and that his fears were unsubstantial. They shook hands, smiling.

Trexler walked dizzily through the empty waiting room and the doctor followed along to let him out. It was late; the secretary had shut up shop and gone home. Another day over the dam. "Goodbye," said Trexler. He stepped into the street, turned west toward Madison, and thought of the doctor all alone there, after hours, in that desolate hole—a man who worked longer hours than his secretary. Poor, scared, overworked bastard, thought Trexler. And that new wing!

It was an evening of clearing weather, the Park showing green and desirable in the distance, the last daylight applying a high lacquer to the brick and brownstone walls and giving the street scene a luminous and intoxicating splendor. Trexler meditated, as he walked, on what he wanted. "What do you want?" he heard again. Trexler knew what he wanted, and what, in general, all men wanted; and he was glad, in a way, that it was both inexpressible and unattainable, and that it wasn't a wing. He was satisfied to remember that it was deep, formless, enduring, and impossible of fulfillment, and that it made men sick, and that when you sauntered along Third Avenue and looked through the doorways into the dim saloon, you could sometimes pick out from the unregenerate ranks the ones who had not forgotten, gazing steadily into the bottoms of the glasses on the long chance that they could get another little peek at it. Trexler found himself renewed by the rememberance that what he wanted was at once great and microscopic, and that although it borrowed from the nature of large deeds and of youthful love and of old songs and early intimations, it was not any one of these things, and that it had not been isolated or pinned down, and that a man who attempted to define it in the privacy of a doctor's office would fall flat on his face.

Trexler felt invigorated. Suddenly his sickness seemed health, his dizziness stability. A small tree, rising between him and the light, stood there saturated with the evening, each gilt-edged leaf perfectly drunk with excellence and delicacy. Trexler's spine registered an ever so slight tremor as it picked up this natural disturbance in the lovely scene. "I want the second tree from the corner, just as it stands," he said, answering an imaginary question from an imaginary physician. And he felt a slow pride in realizing that what he wanted none could bestow, and that what he had none could take away. He felt content to be sick, unembarrassed at being afraid; and in the jungle of his fear he glimpsed (as he had so often glimpsed them before) the flashy tail feathers of the bird courage.

Then he thought once again of the doctor, and of his being left there all alone, tired, frightened. (The poor, scared guy, thought Trexler.) Trexler began humming "Moonshine Lullaby," his spirit reacting instantly to the hypodermic of Merman's healthy voice. He crossed Madison, boarded a downtown bus, and rode all the way to Fifty-second Street before he had a thought that could rightly have been called bizarre.

Suggestions for Discussion

1. Each paragraph describes Mr. Trexler's sessions in the psychiatrist's office or his subsequent reflections about them. How does each sequence contribute to the resolution of the narrative? Describe the changes in Trexler's behavior and attitudes toward the psychiatrist. State in your own words what Trexler wanted. What is he satirizing? What values is he affirming?

2. Discuss the appropriateness and effectiveness of the following images in relation to purpose and tone: "Trexler darted into the bag, hung for a moment before one of his thoughts, as a hummingbird pauses in the delphinium"; "he stopped at the asylum, only the bars were lucite—fluted, retractable"; "life's little bucky horse"; "the vapors hung thick above the pool of the mind"; "So he wants a new wing! There's a fine piece of theatrical gauze for you!"; "the flashy tail feathers of the bird

courage"; "the hypodermic of Merman's healthy voice." In your analysis, generalize on the kinds of language represented by these quotations. What other contexts might you expect to contain such words as *hummingbird, bucky horse, theatrical gauze, tail feathers, hypodermic?* Why are the bars made of lucite and fluted and retractable? What is the effect on the reader of comparing Merman's voice to a hypodermic?

3. How does the use of specific details contribute to the illusion of reality? What sensory images do you find most vivid?

4. Characterize the humor. How does the diction, particularly the use of metaphor, contribute to the purpose and tone? Cite specific illustrations. How does the contrast between Trexler's unvoiced free associations and his actual statements in the psychiatrist's office contribute to the ironic tone?

5. From what point of view is the story written? What relationship does the narrator establish with the reader?

Suggestions for Writing

1. Write a narrative presenting your view of some aspect of our culture. Your feelings and attitudes should become apparent to the reader by implication rather than by explicit statement.

2. Write your own answer to the question "What do you want?" in the manner of the next to the last two paragraphs.

3. Recreate an imaginary session with one of your parents, your psychiatrist, your boss, your teacher, or your Congressman in which your feelings and attitudes are implicitly expressed.

Poetry
—◆◆◆—

Mattthew Arnold
Dover Beach

Matthew Arnold (1822–1888), son of the famous Headmaster of Rugby, Thomas Arnold, was first a poet but later abandoned poetry to become a lecturer, a critic of life and literature, and an inspector of schools. His *Collected Poems* appeared in 1869, *Essays in Criticism* in 1865 and 1888, *Culture and Anarchy* in 1869, *Friendship's Garland* in 1879, and *Mixed Essays* in 1879. In "Dover Beach," the speaker at a moment of emotional crisis, speaking to one he loves, raises the question of whether man can find any peace or joy or release from pain in a world of conflict.

The sea is calm tonight.
The tide is full, the moon lies fair
Upon the straits; on the French coast the light
Gleams and is gone; the cliffs of England stand,
Glimmering and vast, out in the tranquil bay.
Come to the window, sweet is the night-air!
Only, from the long line of spray
Where the sea meets the moon-blanched land,
Listen! you hear the grating roar
Of pebbles which the waves draw back, and fling,
At their return, up the high strand,
Begin, and cease, and then again begin,
With tremulous cadence slow, and bring
The eternal note of sadness in.

Sophocles long ago
Heard it on the Aegean, and it brought
Into his mind the turbid ebb and flow
Of human misery; we

Find also in the sound a thought,
Hearing it by this distant northern sea.
The Sea of Faith
Was once, too, at the full, and round earth's shore
Lay like the folds of a bright girdle furled.
But now I only hear
Its melancholy, long, withdrawing roar,
Retreating, to the breath
Of the night-wind, down the vast edges drear
And naked shingles ·of the world.

Ah, love, let us be true
To one another! for the world, which seems
To lie before us like a land of dreams,
So various, so beautiful, so new,
Hath really neither joy, nor love, nor light,
Nor certitude, nor peace, nor help for pain;
And we are here as on a darkling plain
Swept with confused alarms of struggle and flight,
Where ignorant armies clash by night.

Suggestions for Discussion

1. How does the sea symbolize modern life?

2. What is the speaker seeking and what values does he affirm?

Marianne Moore

The Mind Is an Enchanting Thing

Marianne Moore (1887–1972) was born in Missouri, was graduated from Bryn Mawr College, taught at an Indian school, worked in the New York Public Library, and edited *The Dial* (1925–1929). Her early poems were published in 1921, her *Collected Poems* in 1951. She is also the author of *Predilections* (1955), a volume of critical essays, a poetic translation of La Fontaine's *Fables* (1954), and a collection of poetry, *Tell Me, Tell Me* (1967). The symbols of enchantment are drawn from nature, science, and art.

is an enchanted thing
   like the glaze on a
katydid-wing
      subdivided by sun
       till the nettings are legion.
Like Gieseking playing Scarlatti;

like the apteryx-awl
   as a beak, or the
kiwi's rain-shawl
      of haired feathers, the mind
       feeling its way as though blind,
walks along with its eyes on the ground.

It has memory's ear
   that can hear without
having to hear.
      Like the gyroscope's fall,
       truly unequivocal
because trued by regnant certainty,

it is a power of
   strong enchantment. It
is like the dove-
      neck animated by
       sun; it is memory's eye;
it's conscientious inconsistency.

It tears off the veil; tears
   the temptation, the
mist the heart wears,
      from its eyes,—if the heart
       has a face; it takes apart
dejection. It's fire in the dove-neck's

iridescence; in the
   inconsistencies
of Scarlatti.
      Unconfusion submits
       its confusion to proof; it's
not a Herod's oath that cannot change.

Suggestions for Discussion

1. The symbols of the poem derive from nature, art, and science. Identify them.

2. How do the similes contribute to the theme of enchantment? What paradoxes do
you find, and how do they underscore the central theme?

◇◇◇◇

Theodore Roethke

The Waking

Theodore Roethke (1908–1963), American poet, taught during the last years of his life at the University of Washington. *The Waking: Poems, 1933–1953* was the winner of the Pulitzer Prize for Poetry in 1953. He received the Bollingen Award for Poetry in 1958. A collected volume, *Words for the Wind*, appeared in 1958, and *The Far Field* was published posthumously in 1964. Among the many modes of learning, the poet learns "by going where I have to go".

I wake to sleep, and take my waking slow.
I feel my fate in what I cannot fear.
I learn by going where I have to go.

We think by feeling. What is there to know?
I hear my being dance from ear to ear.
I wake to sleep, and take my waking slow.

Of those so close beside me, which are you?
God bless the Ground! I shall walk softly there,
And learn by going where I have to go.

Light takes the Tree; but who can tell us how?
The lowly worm climbs up a winding stair;
I wake to sleep, and take my waking slow.

Great Nature has another thing to do
To you and me; so take the lively air,
And, lovely, learn by going where to go.

This shaking keeps me steady. I should know.
What falls away is always. And is near.
I wake to sleep, and take my waking slow.
I learn by going where I have to go.

Suggestions for Discussion

1. Relate the title to the substance of the poem.

2. What are the modes of learning? Cite specific passages.

3. How does the use of paradox contribute to tone and substance? Comment on the rhythm, rhyme scheme, repetition of refrain, imagery, and diction.

Suggestion for Writing

Examine your own processes of learning and comment on their relative effectiveness. Relate the mode of learning to the nature of what is to be learned.

Glossary

◆◆◆◆

Abstraction, levels of   Distinguished in two ways: in the range between the general and the specific and in the range between the abstract and the concrete.

A general word refers to a class, genus, or group; a specific word refers to a member of that group. *Ship* is a general word, but *ketch, schooner, liner,* and *tugboat* are specific. It must be remembered, however, that the terms *general* and *specific* are relative, not absolute. *Ketch,* for example, is more specific than *ship,* for a ketch is a kind of ship. But *ketch,* on the other hand, is more general than *Tahiti ketch,* for a Tahiti ketch is a kind of ketch.

The distinction between the abstract and the concrete also is relative. Ideas, qualities, and characteristics which do not exist by themselves may be called abstract; physical things such as *house, shoes,* and *horse* are concrete. Notice, however, that concrete words not only can range further into the specific (*bungalow, moccasin,* and *stallion*), but they also can range back toward the general (*domicile, clothing,* and *cattle*). In making these distinctions between the abstract and the concrete and between the general and the specific, there is no implication that good writing should be specific and concrete and that poor writing is general and abstract. Certainly most good writing is concrete and specific, but it is also general and abstract, constantly moving from the general to the specific and from the abstract to the concrete.

Allusion   Reference to a familiar person, place, or thing, whether real or imaginary: Woodrow Wilson or Zeus, Siam or Atlantis, kangaroo or phoenix. The allusion is an economical way to evoke an atmosphere, a historical era, or an emotion.

Analogy   In exposition, usually a comparison of some length in which the unknown is explained in terms of the known, the unfamiliar in terms of the familiar, the remote in terms of the immediate.

In argument, an analogy consists of a series of likenesses between two or more dissimilar things, demonstrating that they are either similar or identical in other respects also. The use of analogy in argument is open to criticism, for two things alike in many respects are not necessarily alike in all (for example, lamp-black and diamonds are both pure carbon; they differ only in their crystal structure). Although analogy never *proves* anything, its dramatic quality, its assistance in establishing tone, its vividness make it one of the most valuable techniques of the writer.

791

Analysis   A method of exposition by logical division, applicable to anything that can be divided into component parts: an object, such as an automobile or a watch; an institution, such as a college; or a process, such as mining coal or writing a poem. Parts or processes may be described technically and factually or impressionistically and selectively. In the latter method the parts are organized in relation to a single governing idea so that the mutually supporting function of each of the components in the total structure becomes clear to the reader. Parts may be explained in terms of their characteristic function. Analysis may also be concerned with the connection of events; given this condition or series of conditions, what effects will follow?

Argument   Often contains the following parts: the *proposition,* that is, an assertion that leads to the issue; the *issue,* that is, the precise phase of the proposition which the writer is attempting to prove and the question on which the whole argument rests; the *evidence,* the facts and opinions which the author offers as testimony. He may order the evidence deductively by proceeding from certain premises to a *conclusion;* or *inductively* by generalizing from a number of instances and drawing a *conclusion.* Informal arguments frequently make greater use of the methods of exposition than they do of formal logic. See Deduction, Induction, Logic, and Analogy.

   The attempt to distinguish between argument and persuasion is sometimes made by reference to means (Argument makes appeals to reason: persuasion, to emotions); sometimes to ends (Argument causes someone to change his mind; persuasion moves him to action). These distinctions, however, are more academic than functional, for in practice argument and persuasion are not discrete entities. Yet the proof in argument rests largely upon the objectivity of evidence; the proof in persuasion, upon the heightened use of language.

Assumption   That part of an argument which is unstated because it is either taken for granted by the reader and writer or undetected by them. When the reader consciously disagrees with an assumption, the writer has misjudged his audience by assuming what the reader refuses to concede.

Attitude   Toward subject, see Tone. Toward audience, see Audience.

Audience   For the writer, his expected readers. When the audience is a general, unknown one, and the subject matter is closely related to the writer's opinions, preferences, attitudes, and tastes, then the writer's relationship to his audience is in a very real sense his relationship to himself. The writer who distrusts the intelligence of his audience or who adapts his material to what he assumes are the tastes and interests of his readers compromises his integrity.

   On the other hand, if the audience is generally known (a college class, for example), and the subject matter is factual information, then the beginning writer may well consider the education, interests, and tastes of his audience. Unless he keeps a definite audience in mind, the beginner is apt to shift levels of usage, use inappropriate diction, and lose the reader by appealing to none of his interests.

   "It is now necessary to warn the writer that his concern for the reader must be pure; he must sympathize with the reader's plight (most readers are in trouble about half the time) but never seek to know his wants. The whole duty of a writer is to please and satisfy himself, and the true writer always plays to an audience of one. Let him start sniffing the air, or glancing at the Trend Machine, and he is as good as dead although he may make a nice living." Strunk and White, *The Elements of Style* (Macmillan).

Cause and Effect   A seemingly simple method of development in which either the cause of a particular effect or the effects of a particular cause are investigated.

However, because of the philosophical difficulties surrounding causality, the writer should be cautious in ascribing causes. For the explanation of most processes, it is probably safer to proceed in a sequential order, using transitional words to indicate the order of the process.

Classification The division of a whole into the classes that comprise it; or the placement of a subject into the whole of which it is a part. See Definition and Analysis.

Coherence Literally, a sticking together, therefore, the joining or linking of one point to another. It is the writer's obligation to make clear to the reader the relationship of sentence to sentence and paragraph to paragraph. Sometimes coherence is simply a matter of putting the parts in a sequence which is meaningful and relevant—logical sequence, chronological order, order of importance. Other times it is helpful to underscore the relationship. An elementary but highly useful method of underscoring relationships is the use of transitional words; *but, however, yet* inform the reader that what is to follow contrasts with what went before; *furthermore, moreover, in addition to* continue or expand what went before.

Another elementary way of achieving coherence is the enumeration of ideas—"first," "second," "third"—so as to remind the reader of the development. A more subtle transition can be gained by repeating at the beginning of a paragraph a key word or idea from the end of the preceding paragraph. Such a transition reminds the reader of what has gone before and simultaneously prepares him for what is to come.

Comparison and Contrast The presentation of a subject by indicating similarities between two or more things (comparison); by indicating differences (contrast). The basic elements in a comparative process, then, are (1) the terms of the comparison, or the various objects compared, and (2) the points of likeness or difference between the objects compared. Often comparison and contrast are used in definition and other methods of exposition.

Concreteness See Abstraction, Levels of.

Connotation All that the word suggests or implies in addition to its literal meaning. However, this definition is arbitrary and, from the standpoint of the writer, artificial, because the meaning of a word includes *all* that it suggests and implies.

Contrast See Comparison.

Coordination Elements of like importance in like grammatical construction. Less important elements should be placed in grammatically subordinate positions. See Parallelism and Subordination.

Deductive Reasoning In logic, the application of a generalization to a particular; by analogy, in rhetoric, that development which moves from the general to the specific.

Definition In logic, the placing of the word to be defined in a general class and then showing how it differs from other members of the class; in rhetoric, the meaningful extension (usually enriched by the use of detail, concrete illustration, anecdote, metaphor) of a logical definition in order to answer fully, clearly, and often implicitly the question, "What is——?"

Denotation The literal meaning of a word. See Connotation.

Description That form of discourse whose primary purpose is to present factual information about an object or experience (objective description); or to report the impression or evaluation of an object or experience (subjective description). Most description combines the two purposes. *It was a frightening night.* (An evalua-tion with which others might disagree.) *The wind blew the shingles off the north side of the house and drove the rain under the door.* (Two facts about which there can be little disagreement.)

Diction   Style as determined by choice of words. Good diction is characterized by accuracy and appropriateness to subject matter; weak diction, by the use of inappropriate, vague, or trite words. The relationship between the kinds of words a writer selects and his subject matter in large part determines tone. The deliberate use of inappropriate diction is a frequent device of satire.

Discourse, forms of   Traditionally, exposition, argument, description, and narration. See entries under each. These four kinds of traditional discourse are rarely found in a pure form. Argument and exposition may be interfused in the most complex fashion. Exposition often employs narration and description for purposes of illus-tration. It is important to remember, however, that in an effective piece of writ-ing the use of more than one form of discourse is never accidental. It always serves the author's central purpose.

Emphasis   The arrangement of the elements of a composition so that the important meanings occur in structurally important parts of the composition. Repetition, order of increasing importance, exclamation points, rhetorical questions, and fig-ures of speech are all devices to achieve emphasis.

Evidence   That part of argument or persuasion that involves proof. It usually takes the form of facts, particulars deduced from general principles, or opinions of authorities.

Exposition   That form of discourse which explains or informs. Most papers required of college students are expository. The *methods* of exposition presented in this text are identification, definition, classification, illustration, comparison and con-trast, and analysis. See separate entries in glossary.

Figure of Speech   A form of expression in which the meanings of words are ex-tended beyond the literal. The common figures of speech are metaphor, simile, analogy.

Generalization   A broad conception or principle derived from particulars. Often, sim-ply a broad statement. See Abstraction.

Identification   A process preliminary to definition of a subject. For the writer it is that vastly important period preliminary to writing when, wrestling with inchoate glimmerings, he begins to select and shape his materials. As a method of expo-sition, it brings the subject into focus by describing it.

Illustration   A particular member of a class used to explain or dramatize a class, a type, a thing, a person, a method, an idea, or a condition. The idea explained may be either stated or implied. For purposes of illustration, the individual mem-ber of a class must be a fair representation of the distinctive qualities of the class. The use of illustrations, examples, and specific instances adds to the con-creteness and vividness of writing. See Narration.

Image   A word or statement which makes an appeal to the senses. Thus, there are visual images, auditory images, *etc.* As the most direct experience of the world is through the senses, writing which makes use of sense impressions (images) can be unusually effective.

Inductive Reasoning   In logic, the formulation of a generalization after the obser-vation of an adequate number of particular instances; by analogy, in rhetoric, that development which moves from the particular to the general.

Intention For the particular purpose or function of a single piece of writing see Purpose. Intention determines the four forms of discourse. See Exposition, Argument, Description, Narration. These intentions may be explicitly or implicitly set forth by the writer.

Irony At its simplest, involves a discrepancy between literal and intended meaning; at its most complex, it involves an utterance more meaningful (and usually meaningful in a different way) to the listener than to the speaker. For example, Oedipus's remarks about discovering the murderer of the king are understood by the audience in a way Oedipus himself cannot understand them. The inability to grasp the full implications of his own remark is frequently feigned by the satirist.

Issue The limitation of a general proposition to the precise point on which the argument rests. Defeating the issue defeats the argument. Typically the main proposition of an argument will raise at least one issue for discussion and controversy.

Limitation of Subject Restriction of the subject to one that can be adequately developed with reference to audience and purpose.

Metaphor An implied comparison between two things that are seemingly different; a compressed analogy. Effectively used, metaphors increase clarity, interest, vividness, and concreteness.

Narration A form of discourse the purpose of which is to tell a story. If a story is significant in itself, the particulars appealing to the imagination, it is *narration*. If a story illustrates a point in exposition or argument, it may be called *illustrative narration*. If a story outlines a process step by step, the particulars appealing to the understanding, it is designated as *expository narration*.

Organization, methods of Vary with the form of discourse. Exposition uses in part, in whole, or in combination identification, definition, classification, illustration, comparison and contrast, and analysis. Argument and persuasion often use the method of organization of inductive or deductive reasoning, or analogy. Description is often organized either around a dominant impression or by means of a spatial arrangement. Narration, to give two examples, may be organized chronologically or in terms of point of view.

Paradox An assertion or sentiment seemingly self-contradictory, or opposed to common sense, which may yet be true.

Paragraph A division of writing that serves to discuss one topic or one aspect of a topic. The central thought is either implied or expressed in a topic sentence. Paragraphs have such a great variety of organization and function that it is almost impossible to generalize about them.

Parallelism Elements of similar rhetorical importance in similar grammatical patterns. See Coordination.

Parody Mimicking the language and style of another.

Perspective The vantage point chosen by the writer to achieve his purpose, his strategy. It is reflected in his close scrutiny of, or distance from, his subject; his objective representation or subjective interpretation of it. See *Diction, Purpose, Tone*.

Persuasion See Argument.

Point of View In description, the position from which the observer looks at the object described; in narration, the person who sees the action, who tells the story; in exposition, the grammatical person of the composition. First person or the more impersonal third person is commonly used.

Proposition   See Argument.

Purpose   What the writer wants to accomplish with a particular piece of writing.

Rhetoric   The art of using language effectively.

Rhetorical Question   A question asked in order to induce thought and to provide emphasis rather than to evoke an answer.

Rhythm   In poetry and prose, patterned emphasis. Good prose is less regular in its rhythm than poetry.

Satire   The attempt to effect reform by exposing an object to laughter. Satire makes frequent recourse to irony, wit, ridicule, parody. It is usually classified under such categories as the following: social satire, personal satire, literary satire.

Style   "The essence of a sound style is that it cannot be reduced to rules—that it is a living and breathing thing, with something of the demoniacal in it—that it fits its proprietor tightly and yet ever so loosely, as his skin fits him. It is, in fact, quite as securely an integral part of him as that skin is . . . In brief, a style is always the outward and visible symbol of a man, and it cannot be anything else." H. L. Mencken, *On Style,* used with permission of Alfred A. Knopf, Inc.

"Young writers often suppose that style is a garnish for the meat of prose, a sauce by which a dull dish is made palatable. Style has no such separate entity; it is nondetachable, unfilterable. The beginner should approach style warily, realizing that it is himself he is approaching, no other; and he should begin by turning resolutely away from all devices that are popularly believed to indicate style—all mannerisms, tricks, adornments. The approach to style is by way of plainness, simplicity, orderliness, sincerity." E. B. White from *The Elements of Style* (Macmillan).

Subordination   Less important rhetorical elements in gramatically subordinate positions. See Parallelism and Coordination.

Syllogism   In formal logic, a deductive argument in three steps: a major premise, a minor premise, a conclusion. The major premise states a quality of a class (All men are mortal); the minor premise states that X is a member of the class (Socrates is a man); the conclusion states that the quality of a class is also a quality of a member of the class (Socrates is mortal). In rhetoric, the full syllogism is rarely used; instead, one of the premises is usually omitted. "You can rely on him; he is independent," is an abbreviated syllogism. Major premise: Independent people are reliable; minor premise: He is independent; conclusion: He is reliable. Constructing the full syllogism frequently reveals flaws in reasoning, such as the above, which has an error in the major premise.

Symbol   A concrete image which suggests a meaning beyond itself.

Tone   The manner in which the writer communicates his attitude toward the materials he is presenting. Diction is the most obvious means of establishing tone. See Diction.

Topic Sentence   The thesis which the paragraph as a whole develops. Some paragraphs do not have topic sentences, but the thesis is implied.

Transition   The linking together of sentences, paragraphs, and larger parts of the composition to achieve coherence. See Coherence.

Unity   The relevance of selected material to the central theme of an essay. See Coherence.

Acknowledgments,
Continued

this story appears in *Go Down Moses*, by William Faulkner.

Ernest Hemingway, "Indian Camp." "Indian Camp" is reprinted by permission of Charles Scribner's Sons from *In Our Time* by Ernest Hemingway. Copyright 1925 Charles Scribner's Sons; renewal copyright 1953 Ernest Hemingway.

Elizabeth Taylor, "Girl Reading," from *A Dedicated Man and Other Stories*. Copyright © by Elizabeth Taylor. Reprinted by permission of the estate of Elizabeth Taylor. This material was first published in *The New Yorker*.

T. S. Eliot, "The Love Song of J. Alfred Prufrock." From *Collected Poems 1909–1962* by T. S. Eliot, copyright 1936, by Harcourt Brace Jovanovich, Inc. Copyright © 1963, 1964, by T. S. Eliot. Reprinted by permission of the publishers. Reprinted by permission of Faber and Faber Ltd. from *Collected Peoms 1909-1962* by T.S. Eliot.

Dylan Thomas, "The Force That Through the Green Fuse Drives the Flower." From *The Poems of Dylan Thomas*. Copyright 1939 by New Directions Publishing Corporation. Reprinted by permission of New Directions Publishing Corporation.

Sherwood Anderson, "Discovery of a Father." From *Sherwood Anderson's Memoirs: A Critical Edition*, edited by Ray Lewis White. Copyright 1939 by Eleanor Anderson. Reprinted with the permission of the University of North Carolina Press.

Franz Kafka, "Letter to His Father." Reprinted by permission of Schocken Books Inc. from *Letter to His Father* by Franz Kafka. Copyright © 1953, 1954, 1966 by Schocken Books Inc.

Adrienne Rich, "The Anger of a Child." "The Anger of a Child" is reprinted from *Of Woman Born* by Adrienne Rich, by permission of W. W. Norton & Company, Inc. Copyright © 1976 by W. W. Norton.

John Gregory Dunne, "Quintana." From the book *Quintana and Friends*. Copyright © 1978 by John Gregory Dunne. Published by E. P. Dutton & Co., Inc. and used with their permission.

Richard Rodriguez, "Mr. Secrets." From *Hunger of Memory* by Richard Rodriguez. Copyright © 1981 by Richard Rodriguez. Reprinted by permission of David R. Godine, Publisher, Boston.

William Carlos Williams, "The Use of Force." From William Carlos Williams, *The Farmer's Daughters*. Copyright 1938 by William Carlos Williams. Reprinted by permission of New Directions Publishing Corporation.

Flannery O'Connor, "Everything That Rises Must Converge," from *Everything That Rises Must Converge* by Flannery O'Connor. Copyright © 1961, 1965 by the Estate of Mary Flannery O'Connor. Reprinted by permission of Farrar, Straus & Giroux, Inc.

Delmore Schwartz, "In Dreams Begin Responsibilities." From *The World Is a Wedding*. Copyright © 1948 by Delmore Schwartz. Reprinted by permission of New Directions Publishing Corporation.

E. E. Cummings, "My Father Moved Through Dooms of Love." Copyright 1940, by E. E. Cummings; renewed 1968 by Marion Morehouse Cummings. From *Complete Poems 1913–1962*. By permission of Harcourt Brace Jovanovich, Inc.

Sylvia Plath, "Daddy." From *Ariel* by Sylvia Plath. Copyright © 1963 by Ted Hughes. By permission of Harper & Row, Publishers, Inc.

Theodore Roethke, "My Papa's Waltz." Copyright 1942 by Hearst Magazines, Inc. Reprinted by permission of Doubleday & Company, Inc.

William Butler Yeats, "A Prayer for My Daughter." Reprinted with permission of Macmillan Publishing Co., Inc., from *Collected Poems* by William Butler Yeats. Copyright 1924 by Macmillan Publishing Co., Inc., renewed 1952 by Bertha Georgie Yeats.

Gwendolyn Brooks, "Life for My Child Is Simple, and Is Good." From *The World of Gwendolyn Brooks* by Gwendolyn Brooks. Copyright 1949 by Gwendolyn Brooks Blakely. By permission of Harper & Row, Publishers, Inc.

Randall Jarrell, "The Player Piano." Reprinted with the permission of Farrar, Straus & Giroux, Inc., from *The Complete Poems* by Randall Jarrell, copyright © 1967 by Mrs. Randall Jarrell.

James Wright, "Mutterings Over

the Crib of a Deaf Child." Copyright © 1971 by James Wright. Reprinted from *Collected Poems* by permission of Wesleyan University Press.

Nancy Willard, "Questions My Son Asked Me, Answers I Never Gave Him," from *The Longman Anthology of Contemporary American Poetry 1950–1980*, edited by Friebert and Young. Copyright by Nancy Willard. Reprinted by permission of Nancy Willard.

D. H. Lawrence, "Give Her a Pattern." From *Phoenix II: Uncollected Papers of D. H. Lawrence*, ed. by Warren Roberts and Harry T. Moore. All rights reserved. Reprinted by permission of The Viking Press, Inc.

Virginia Woolf, "The Angel in the House." From *The Death of the Moth* by Virginia Woolf, copyright, 1942, by Harcourt Brace Jovanovich, Inc.; renewed, 1970, by Marjorie T. Parsons, Executrix. Reprinted by permission of the publishers.

Germaine Greer, "The Stereotype." From *The Female Eunuch* by Germaine Greer. Copyright © 1970, 1971 by Germaine Greer. Used with permission of McGraw-Hill Book Company.

Norman Mailer, "Who Would Finally Do the Dishes?" an excerpt from *The Prisoner of Sex*. Copyright 1971 by Norman Mailer. Reprinted by permission of the author and the author's agents, Scott Meredith Literary Agency, Inc., 845 Third Avenue, New York, NY 10022.

Calvin Trillin, "Incompatible, with One L," from *Uncivil Liberties*. Copyright © 1982 by Calvin Trillin. Reprinted by permission of Lescher & Lescher, Ltd.

Carolyn Heilbrun, "Androgyny," from *Toward a Recognition of Androgyny*, Alfred A. Knopf Publishers, 1973. Reprinted by permission of Curtis Brown Associates, Ltd. Copyright © 1964, 1965, 1968, 1971, 1972, 1973 by Carolyn Heilbrun.

Betty Friedan, "Why Feminism Must Keep Moving," from *The San Francisco Chronicle*, March 7, 1984. Reprinted by permission of Curtis Brown, Ltd. Copyright © 1983 by Betty Friedan.

Benjamin R. Barber, "Beyond the Feminist Mystique," from *The New Republic*, July 11, 1983. Reprinted by permission of *The New Republic*, © 1983 The New Republic, Inc.

Lillian B. Rubin, "Love, Work, and Identity," from *Intimate Strangers*. Copyright © 1983 by Lillian B. Rubin. Reprinted by permission of Harper & Row, Publishers, Inc.

James Thurber, "The Unicorn in the Garden." Copyright © 1940 James Thurber. Copyright © 1968 Helen Thurber. From *Fables for Our Time* published by Harper & Row. Originally printed in *The New Yorker*.

John Steinbeck, "The Chrysanthemums." From *The Long Valley* by John Steinbeck. Copyright 1938 by John Steinbeck. Copyright renewed © 1966 by John Steinbeck. Reprinted by permission of Viking Penguin Inc.

James Thurber, "The Catbird Seat." Copyright © 1945 James Thurber. Copyright © 1973 Helen W. Thurber and Rosemary T. Sauers. From *The Thurber Carnival*, published by Harper & Row, Publishers.

Katherine Anne Porter, "Rope," from *Flowering Judas and Other Stories*. Copyright © 1958 by Katherine Anne Porter. Reprinted by permission of Harcourt Brace Jovanovich, Inc.

W. H. Auden, "Lay Your Sleeping Head, My Love." Copyright 1940 and renewed 1968 by W. H. Auden. Reprinted from *Collected Shorter Poems 1927–1957*, by W. H. Auden, by permission of Random House, Inc.

Edna St. Vincent Millay, "Love Is Not All." From *Collected Poems*, Harper & Row. Copyright 1931, 1958 by Edna St. Vincent Millay and Norma Millay Ellis. Reprinted by permission of Norma Millay Ellis.

Denise Levertov, "The Third Dimension." Copyright © 1957 by Denise Levertov. Reprinted by permission of the author.

E. E. Cummings, "I Like My Body When It Is with Your." Copyright 1925, by E. E. Cummings. From *Complete Poems 1913–1962*. By permission of Harcourt Brace Jovanovich, Inc.

Adrienne Rich, "Rape." "Rape" is reprinted from *Poems, Selected and New, 1950–1974* by Adrienne Rich, by permission of W. W. Norton & Company, Inc. Copyright © 1975, 1973, 1971, 1969, 1966 by W. W. Norton & Company, Inc. Copyright © 1967, 1963, 1962, 1961, 1960, 1959, 1958, 1957, 1956, 1955, 1954, 1953, 1952, 1951 by Adrienne Rich.

Adrienne Rich, "Living in Sin." From *The Diamond Cutters*, published by Harper & Row, New York, 1955. Reprinted by permission of Adrienne Rich.

May Swenson, "Women Should Be Pedestals." "Women" by May Swenson (copyright © 1968 May Swenson), which first appeared in the *New American Review #3*, is reprinted by permission of Charles Scribner's Sons from *Iconographs*.

Studs Terkel, "Miss U. S. A.," from *American Dreams: Lost and Found*. Copyright © 1980 by Studs Terkel. Reprinted by permission of Random House, Inc.

Art Buchwald, "Leisure Will Kill You." Reprinted by permission of G. P. Putnam's Sons from *Laid Back in Washington* by Art Buchwald. Copyright © 1978, 1979, 1980, 1981 by Art Buchwald.

Roger Angell, "The Silence," from *Late Innings*. Copyright © 1982 by Roger Angell. Reprinted by permission of Simon & Schuster, Inc.

Marie Winn, "TV and the American Family." Originally titled "Family Life." From *The Plug-In Drug* by Marie Winn. Copyright © 1977 by Marie Winn Miller. Reprinted by permission of Viking Penguin Inc.

S. J. Perelman, "Meanness Rising from the Suds," from *The Last Laugh*. Copyright © 1981 by James H. Mathias as Executor of the Estate of S. J. Perelman. Reprinted by permission of Simon & Schuster, Inc. This material was first published in *The New Yorker*.

George Grella, "James Bond: Culture Hero," from *The New Republic*, 1964. Copyright 1964 by George Grella. Reprinted by permission of George Grella.

Ralph Ellison, "The Birth of Bebop." Reprinted by permission of William Morris Agency, Inc. on behalf of author. Copyright © 1959 by Ralph Ellison.

John Cheever, "The Enormous Radio," from *The Enormous Radio and Other Stories*. Reprinted by permission of International Creative Management. Copyright © 1953 by John Cheever. Copyright renewed 1981 by John Cheever.

Alice Walker, "Nineteen Fifty-Five," from *You Can't Keep a Good Woman Down*. Copyright © 1955 by Alice Walker. Reprinted by permission of Harcourt Brace Jovanovich, Inc.

Rainer Maria Rilke, "Letter to a Young Poet." Reprinted from *Letters to a Young Poet* by Rainer Maria Rilke, translated by M. D. Herter Norton, by permission of W. W. Norton & Company, Inc. Copyright 1934 by W. W. Norton & Company, Inc. Copyright renewed 1962 by M. D. Herter Norton. Revised Edition copyright 1954 by W. W. Norton & Company, Inc. Copyright renewed 1982 by M. D. Herter Norton.

Hermann Hesse, "To A Cabinet Minister, August 1917." From *If the War Goes On* by Hermann Hesse, translation copyright © 1970, 1971 by Farrar, Straus & Giroux, Inc.

John Gardner, "Learning from Disney and Dickens," from *The New York Times*, January 30, 1983, Book Review. © 1983 by the New York Times Company. Reprinted by permission.

Northrop Frye, "The Keys to Dreamland," from *The Educated Imagination*. Reprinted by permission of Indiana University Press and CBC Enterprises/Les Entreprises Radio-Canada.

Mike Royko, "The Virtue of Prurience," from the *Chicago Sun-Times*, April 17, 1983. © Chicago Sun-Times, 1983. Column by Mike Royko. Reprinted with permission.

E. M. Forster, "Art for Art's Sake." Copyright, 1949, by E. M. Forster. From *Two Cheers for Democracy*, by permission of Harcourt Brace Jovanovich, Inc.

Oscar Mandel, "Dissonant Music Sixty Years After," from *South Atlantic Quarterly*, 72(1), Winter, 1973.

Anne Tyler, "Still Just Writing." Reprinted from *The Writer on Her Work*, Edited by Janet Sternburg, by permission of W. W. Norton & Company, Inc. Copyright © 1980 by Janet Sternburg.

Muriel Rukeyser, "The Backside of the Academy," from *The Speed of Darkness*. Reprinted by permission of International Creative Management. Copyright © 1968 by Muriel Rukeyser.

Archibald MacLeish, "Invocation to the Social Muse." From *Collected Poems 1917–1952*. Copyright © 1962 by Archibald MacLeish. Reprinted by permission of Houghton Mifflin Company.

Marianne Moore, "Poetry." Reprinted with permission of Macmillan Publishing Co., Inc., from *Collected Poems* by Marianne Moore. Copyright 1935 by Marianne Moore, renewed 1963 by Marianne Moore and T. S. Eliot.

Bertrand Russell, "If We Are to Survive this Dark Time —," from *The Basic Writings of Bertrand Russell*, edited by Robert E. Egner and Lester E. Denonn. Copyright © 1961 by Allen & Unwin, Ltd. Reprinted by permission of Simon & Schuster, Inc.

Karl Jaspers, "Is Science Evil?" Reprinted from *Commentary*, by permission; copyright © 1950 by the American Jewish Committee. Reprinted by permission of the publisher.

Jacob Bronowski, "The Reach of Imagination." *American Scholar*, Spring 1967. Reprinted by permission of the author.

Joseph Weizenbaum, "The Compulsive Programmer," from *Computer Power and Human Reason* by Joseph Weizenbaum. W. H. Freeman and Company. Copyright © 1976. Reprinted by permission of W. H. Freeman and Company.

A. M. Turing, "The Imitation Game," from "Computing Machinery and Intelligence," *Mind*, 59:236, 1950. Reprinted by permission of Basil Blackwell publisher.

Joseph Weizenbaum, "On the Impact of the Computer on Society," from *Science, 176*:609–614, May 1972. © 1972 by The American Association for the Advancement of Science. Reprinted by permission of the American Association for the Advancement of Science and by permission of Joseph Weizenbaum.

Lewis Thomas, "A Trip Abroad," from *The Medusa and the Snail* by Lewis Thomas. Copyright © 1974, 1979 by Lewis Thomas. Reprinted by permission of Viking Penguin Inc.

Stephen Jay Gould, "Death Before Birth, or a Mite's *Nunc Dimittis*." Reprinted from *The Panda's Thumb, More Reflections in Natural History*, by Stephen Jay Gould, by permission of W. W. Norton & Company, Inc. Copyright © 1980 by Stephen Jay Gould.

Aldous Huxley, "*Brave New World* Revisited," from *Esquire*, July 1956. Reprinted by permission of Laura Huxley.

Arthur C. Clarke, "Broadway and the Satellites," from *Voices from the Sky*. Reprinted by permission of the author and the author's agents, Scott Meredith Literary Agency, Inc., 845 Third Avenue, New York, NY 10022.

Aldous Huxley, "Conditioning the Children." From pp. 20–24 ("The D.H.C. and his students . . . sour milk and a most welcome silence.") in *Brave New World* by Aldous Huxley. Copyright 1932, 1960 by Aldous Huxley. By permission of Harper & Row, Publishers, Inc.

W. E. B. DuBois, "On Being Crazy," from *From These Roots*, edited by Charles L. James, Dodd, Mead & Company, Inc., 1970. Copyright 1907 by W. E. B. DuBois. Reprinted by permission of Shirley Graham Dubois.

Richard Wright, "The Ethics of Living Jim Crow," From *Uncle Tom's Children* by Richard Wright. Copyright 1937 by Richard Wright; renewed 1965 by Ellen Wright. By permission of Harper & Row, Publishers, Inc.

Andrew Hill, "Visible Man," from *California Living Magazine*, May 15, 1983. Reprinted with permission from California Living Magazine of the San Francisco Sunday Examiner and Chronicle. Copyright © 1983, San Francisco Examiner.

Niccolò Machiavelli, "Of Cruelty and Clemency, and Whether It is Better to Be Loved or Feared." From *The Prince* by Niccolò Machiavelli translated by Luigi Ricci revised by E. R. P. Vincent (1935). Reprinted by permission of Oxford University Press.

José Ortega y Gasset, "The Greatest Danger, the State." Reprinted from *The Revolt of the Masses* by José Ortega y Gasset, by permission of W. W. Norton & Company, Inc. Copyright 1932 by W. W. Norton & Company, Inc. Copyright renewed 1960 by Teresa Carey.

H. L. Mencken, "The Nature of Liberty." From *Prejudices: A Selection*, by H. L. Mencken, James T. Farrell, editor. Copyright © 1958 by Alfred A. Knopf, Inc. Reprinted by permission of the publisher.

William Faulkner, "Nobel Prize Award Speech." Reprinted from *The Faulkner Reader.* Copyright 1954 by William Faulkner (Random House, Inc.). By permission of the Publisher.

Harriet Jacobs, "The Women," from *Black Slave Narratives,* edited and with an introduction by John F. Bayliss. Copyright © 1970 by John F. Bayliss. Reprinted with permission from Macmillan Publishing Company.

Martin Luther King, "I Have a Dream." Reprinted by permission of Joan Daves. Copyright © 1963 by Martin Luther King, Jr.

E. M. Forster, "Jew-Consciousness." Copyright, 1939, renewed, 1967, by E. M. Forster. From *Two Cheers for Democracy* by permission of Harcourt Brace Jovanovich, Inc.

Jonathan Schell, "The Choice," from *The Fate of the Earth,* Alfred A. Knopf, Inc. Copyright © 1982 by Jonathan Schell. Reprinted by permission of Random House, Inc. This excerpt appeared in *Lifestudies,* by David Cavitch, under the title, "The Choice."

Milton Mayer, "A World Without Government," from *The Center Magazine* 16(2), May/April 1983. Reprinted by permission of Milton Mayer.

George Orwell, "The Principles of Newspeak," from *Nineteen Eighty-Four.* Copyright © 1949 by Harcourt Brace Jovanovich, Inc. Reprinted by permission of Harcourt Brace Jovanovich, Inc.

Irving Howe, "Enigmas of Power: George Orwell's *1984* Reconsidered," from *The New Republic,* Year End Issue, 1982. Reprinted by permission of *The New Republic,* © 1982 The New Republic, Inc.

Rebecca West, "The Meaning of Treason," from *Harper's,* October 1947. Reprinted by permission of A D Peters & Co Ltd.

Carol Tavris, Anger in an Unjust World," from *Anger: The Misunderstood Emotion.* Copyright © 1983 by Carol Tavris. Reprinted by permission of Simon & Schuster, Inc.

Franz Kafka, "A Report to an Academy." Reprinted by permission of Schocken Books Inc. from *The Penal Colony* by Franz Kafka. Copyright © 1948, 1976 by Schocken Books, Inc.

William Faulkner, "Dry September," from *Collected Stories of William Faulkner.* Reprinted by permission of Random House.

Ray Bradbury, "Perhaps We Are Going Away," from *The Machineries of Joy.* Copyright 1963 by Ray Bradbury. Reprinted by permission of Harold Matson Co., Inc.

Wilfred Owen, *"Dulce et Decorum Est."* Wilfred Owen, *Collected Poems of Wilfred Owen.* Copyright © Chatto & Windus, Ltd., 1963. Reprinted by permission of New Directions Publishing Corporation.

William Stafford, "Freedom." *New American Review 2,* 1968. Copyright © 1968. Reprinted by permission of the author.

W. H. Auden, "The Unknown Citizen." Copyright 1940 and renewed 1968 by W. H. Auden. Reprinted from *Collected Shorter Poems 1927–1957,* by W. H. Auden, by permission of Random House. Inc.

Robert Frost, "Departmental," from *The Poetry of Robert Frost* edited by Edward Connery Lathem. Copyright 1936 by Robert Frost. Copyright © 1964 by Lesley Frost Ballantine. Copyright © 1969 by Holt, Rinehart and Winston. Reprinted by permission of Holt, Rinehart and Winston, Publishers.

Lincoln Steffens, "I Go to College," Parts I and II from *The Autobiography of Lincoln Steffens.* Copyright © 1959 by Peter Steffens. Reprinted by permission of Harcourt Brace Jovanovich, Inc.

Maya Angelou, "Graduation," from *I Know Why the Caged Birds Sing* by Maya Angelou. Reprinted by permission of Random House, Inc.

Lewis Thomas, "The Youngest and Brightest Thing Around," from *The Medusa and the Snail* by Lewis Thomas. Copyright © 1974, 1979 by Lewis Thomas. Reprinted by permission of Viking Penguin Inc.

Woody Allen, "My Speech to the Graduates," from *The New York Times,* August 10, 1979 (Op-Ed). © 1979 by The

ACKNOWLEDGMENTS 803

New York Times Company. Reprinted by permission.

Anna Tuttle Villegas, "The Teacher as Dragon," from *California Living Magazine*, January 23, 1983. Reprinted with permission from California Living Magazine of the San Francisco Sunday Examiner and Chronicle, copyright © 1984, San Francisco Examiner.

Alan Bloom, "Our Listless Universities," from *Change*, *15*(3), April 1983, a publication of the Helen Dwight Reid Educational Foundation. Reprinted by permission of the Helen Dwight Reid Educational Foundation.

Otto Friedrich, "Five Ways to Wisdom," from *Time Magazine*. Copyright 1982 Time Inc. All rights reserved. Reprinted by permission from *Time*.

John Cheever, "Expelled." Reprinted by permission of International Creative Management. Copyright 1930 by John Cheever. This story first appeared in *The New Republic*, October 1, 1930 and again in July 19 & 26, 1982.

Langston Hughes, "Theme for English B." Reprinted by permission of Harold Ober Associates Incorporated. Copyright 1951 by Langston Hughes.

Theodore Roethke, "Elegy for Jane: My Student Thrown by a Horse," copyright © 1950 by Theodore Roethke from the book *The Collected Poems of Theodore Roethke* by Theodore Roethke. Reprinted by permission of Doubleday & Company, Inc.

Annie Dillard, "Sight into Insight," from *Harper's Magazine*, February, 1974. Reprinted by permission of the author and her agent Blanche C. Gregory, Inc. Copyright © 1974 by Annie Dillard.

John Reed, "Almost Thirty," from *The New Republic*, April 15, 1936. Reprinted by permission of *The New Republic*.

Rollo May, "The Man Who Was Put in a Cage," from *Psychology and the Human Dilemma*. Reprinted by permission of Van Nostrand Reinhold Co.

Lauren Eiseley, "Man in the Autumn Light," in *The Invisible Pyramid*, Copyright © 1970 Loren Eiseley. Reprinted with the permission of Charles Scribner's Sons.

Robert Coles, "Happiness," from *Vogue*, January 1983. Courtesy *Vogue*.

Copyright © 1982 the Condé Nast Publications Inc.

Tom Wolfe, "Mauve Gloves and Madmen, Clutter and Vine." Reprinted by permission of Farrar, Straus and Giroux, Inc. "Mauve Gloves and Madmen, Clutter and Vine" from *Mauve Gloves and Madmen, Clutter and Vine* by Tom Wolfe. Copyright © 1975, 1976 by Tom Wolfe.

Norman Cousins, "Beyond Invalidism." "Beyond Invalidism" is reprinted from *The Healing Heart, Antidotes to Panic and Helplessness*, by Norman Cousins, by permission of W. W. Norton & Company, Inc. Copyright © 1983 by Norman Cousins.

Saul Bellow, "Lives of Organized Terror." This material was published under the title " 'Matters Have Gotten Out of Hand' in a Violent Society," *U.S.News & World Report*, June 28, 1982. Reprinted from *U.S.News & World Report*. Copyright, 1982, U.S.News & World Report, Inc.

Jeffrey H. Goldstein, "The Healing Power of Laughter," from *The Sciences*, Aug./Sept. 1982. 1982 © by The New York Academy of Sciences. Reprinted by permission of The New York Academy of Sciences.

Malcolm Cowley, "Vices and Pleasures," from *The View from 80* by Malcolm Cowley. Copyright © 1976, 1979, and 1980 by Malcolm Cowley. Reprinted by permission of Viking Penguin Inc.

Stuart Chase, "A Very Private Utopia," from *The Nation*, *126*, May 16, 1928. Reprinted by permission of the publisher.

Joyce Carol Oates, "New Heaven and Earth." Reprinted by permission of the author and her agent, Blanche C. Gregory, Inc. Copyright © 1972 by Joyce Carol Oates.

Anton Chekhov, "The Bet," from *The Schoolmistress and Other Stories* by Anton Chekhov, translated from the Russian by Constance Garnett. Reprinted with permission of Macmillan Publishing Company. Copyright © 1979 by Macmillan Publishing Co., Inc.

Walter Van Tilburg Clark, "The Portable Phonograph." Reprinted by permission of International Famous Agency.

Index

—◆◆◆—